The BP Book of Industrial Archaeology

The BP Book of Industrial Archaeology

NEIL COSSONS

David & Charles
Newton Abbot . London
North Pomfret (Vt) . Vancouver

ISBN 0 7153 6250 X

Library of Congress Catalog Card Number 74-20468

Set in 11 on 13-pt Bembo and printed in Great Britain
at the Alden Press, Oxford

for David & Charles (Holdings) Limited
South Devon House Newton Abbot Devon

Published in the United States of America
by David & Charles Inc North Pomfret
Vermont 05053 USA

Published in Canada by Douglas David & Charles Limited
3645 McKechnie Drive West Vancouver BC

Contents

List of Illustrations

PLATES

6

LINE ILLUSTRATIONS

Preface

To indulge oneself in reminiscences is something which occurs all too infrequently, so this preface affords one of those rare opportunities for which I make no excuses. In looking back on the development of my own interest in industrial archaeology there are several quite specific events which I remember with vivid clarity as well as others which were no doubt equally significant but which by their nature are hazy and diffuse. The germ of the infection was without doubt caught from my father whose interest in turnpike roads led him and later both of us to seek out bridges and tollhouses, and those remaining milestones which had not been buried or destroyed in the war. A journey by Barton's bus (were Barton's buses *really* all different?) from Beeston near Nottingham to Shardlow to see the flood-damaged remains of Cavendish Bridge brought me into contact, for the first time consciously, with a place which breathed the atmosphere of the Industrial Revolution and of past prosperity and activity, the inland port on the Trent and Mersey Canal with its superb warehouses and basins. There was a magic about deserted Shardlow. Here was a *place* where things had happened but where nothing happened now. On the line of the Ashby and Ticknall Tramway or the Charnwood Forest Canal, at King's Mills on the edge of Donington Park, beside the remains of the Morley Park blast furnaces at Heage or the great mills at Cromford, this sensation of place became overwhelming, the essential ingredient which stimulated the imagination and brought alive for me the men and horses, the boats, wagons, flames and smoke of a period which was otherwise as distant and unreal as that of ancient Egypt or Rome. There were also from time to time interminable Sunday afternoons which then passed me by completely, when my father's smoke-filled study was full too of J. D. Chambers or W. E. Tate or on occasion both. They were decrying the desecration of Nottingham in a period before a conservation movement existed — and so the threatened extinction of the Collins almshouses in Friar Lane inexorably became a reality. Who could stand in the way of progress?

Much later, with Michael Rix at Preston Montford in Shropshire, I realised there were lots of other people with broadly the same sort of interest and that it was gaining a corporate identity under the name 'industrial archaeology'. But by then I was already in the business myself and the opportunities to practise were broadening rapidly. The diversity of the interest in industrial archaeology was, and still is, astonishing and has undoubtedly been one of the great aids to its rapid evolution over the last couple of decades, to the growth of a broad base of popular interest and to the awakening of an active appreciation that the remains of industrialisation in Britain are the tangible marks of the beginnings of a new civilisation which a thousand years hence the archaeologist and historian will identify, categorise and possibly revere in the same way as we do the ancient cultures of the Mediterranean. With the Industrial Revolution period, however, we have the opportunity to keep the surviving remains alive because we are close enough to identify with the people who were involved. This book is largely concerned with the physical remains as such, with sketching in their historical and technological background and with guiding the visitor to the *place* where his imagination may be stimulated.

In compiling this work I owe thanks to many people who have offered encouragement and given me active help and advice. My wife and children have entered very much into the spirit of industrial archaeology; at the age of four my daughter Elisabeth could recognise a tower mill at half a mile, model blast furnaces clutter the bedroom of her elder brother Nigel, while Malcolm, who was born during Chapter 4, is already showing signs of becoming infected too. My colleagues at Ironbridge have made many useful suggestions and brought to my notice innumerable sites of interest. To Brian Bowers, Ivor Brown, Keith Gale, Charles Hadfield, John Iredale, Kenneth Major and George Watkins I am particularly grateful, for their kindness in reading sections of the draft text and giving invaluable comment and criticism. I am deeply indebted to Peter Stoddart, who prepared the line drawings, for his painstaking attention to detail and his sensitivity to the problems of interpreting mechanisms in what we both hope will be a comprehensible manner. Brian Bracegirdle was also of very great assistance with the visual aspects of the book in making available to me photographs from his wide-ranging collection. Angus Buchanan, whose friendship I have enjoyed over many years, has been of great help and encouragement to me and to Kenneth Hudson I have been continually indebted for jerking me out of those inadvertent lapses into antiquarianism into which anybody involved in archaeology is so easily inveigled. Gordon Payne deserves my special thanks for his numerous and helpful suggestions and his comments on the draft manuscript.

Many other people have supplied me with information, verified facts and offered suggestions and without their help this book could not have been written. In recording their names here I am expressing my gratitude but at the same time in no way wish them to be associated with any errors of fact or of emphasis, for which I am wholly responsible: David Anderson, Frank Atkinson, Kenneth Barton, John Butt, John Cockcroft, Arthur Corney, Joan and Roy Day, Paul Elkin, Keith Falconer, Bill Gilmour, Douglas Hague, Bob Hawkins, Kenneth Hawley, Dan Hogan, John Hume, Derek Janes, Michael Lewis, Jeremy Lowe, Morgan Rees, Michael Rix, John Robinson, John Sawtell, Michael Stammers, John Stengelhofen, Donald Storer, Michael Thomas, Barrie Trinder, Rex Wailes, Margaret Weston and Peter White.

Ironbridge N. C.

1 A Perspective on the Nature of Industrial Archaeology

In the history of mankind the Industrial Revolution in Britain was a unique phenomenon whose repercussions have spread throughout the world. We live today in a society whose economy is essentially industrial, our prosperity is based on the fruits of industrial activity and our surroundings, both urban and rural, are largely the result of over two centuries of progressive industrialisation. Industrial archaeology is concerned largely with those surroundings. In simple terms it is the examination and analysis of the physical remains of the Industrial Revolution period.

The traditionally accepted archaeologist is one who investigates past cultures by delving into their surviving remains, and his primary investigative technique is often excavation. The results of excavation as a means of acquiring evidence have enabled archaeologists over the years to establish the chronological and geographical divides in man's evolution and to classify particular periods by specific characteristics, often based on a type of technology. Thus we have periods identified by man's use of stone, bronze or iron implements, by the dominance of an imperialist culture like that of the Romans, or by a more straightforward chronological division of convenience, as with medieval archaeology. It might appear logical that the period of industrialisation should receive similar treatment, but until relatively recently this has not been done. Firstly there was a failure, perhaps because of the closeness in time, to recognise the full implications of the Industrial Revolution in cultural terms, coupled with an all too clear appreciation of the damage and suffering which it had caused. On the other hand historians had been looking at aspects of the industrial period using documentary sources for their evidence for many years; in other words the accepted investigative technique was one based on archival research rather than excavation. The historian, interpreting his evidence to shed light on the nature of a period, was fulfilling the same role as that of the archaeologist whose only source of information might be what he found by digging for it.

However, in the last 20 years or so there has been a growing appreciation that the physical remains of the Industrial Revolution period might also have some significance as sources of evidence. The growth of a widespread interest in those remains, on the other hand, has been motivated by much more deep-seated and emotionally based feelings than the purely academic recognition that they were a source of potentially valuable information. The interest is more than simply 'archaeological', a fact which has led to much questioning of the validity of the term 'industrial archaeology' and to an almost obsessive desire to define it and justify its existence. It is essential, therefore, in reaching our own definition of the subject not to resort to excessive pontification or the setting of strict and rigid boundaries around something which is so new, so dynamic in character and in such a fluid stage of development. Industrial archaeology will define its own boundaries, techniques and disciplines, given time.

We have suggested that industrial archaeology is, in essence, a period or cultural archaeology as Neolithic archaeology, Roman archaeology or medieval archaeology are. It is the archaeology of an era, which in Britain is reasonably well defined, called the Industrial Revolution. As a term, therefore, industrial archaeology has its greatest relevance when seen in the context of more traditional archaeological period divisions. One of its short-comings has been the word 'industrial', which has created problems of definition. Some interpretations suggest that industrial archaeology is concerned specifically with buildings and machines directly associated with industrialisation in the last $2\frac{1}{2}$ centuries. Others deny the period division and regard the subject as covering any industrial activity of whatever date from flint axe factories and Roman bread ovens to the Industrial Revolution and even later. If we accept the traditional archaeological approach, however, industrial archaeology might be defined as embracing an epoch in man's evolution, an epoch which in this case has been characterised by industrialisation. Perhaps 'modern archaeology' would be more appropriate.

The Industrial Revolution period provides then the core area, the mainspring of industrial archaeology. But there is a diffuse penumbra too, into which the industrial archaeologist, like the archaeologist of any other period, must go to provide a perspective and context for his main area of interest. Industrial archaeology spreads out chronologically, in terms of subject area and in terms of technique well beyond its obvious centre—hence the need for flexible boundaries. Like any other archaeologist (or historian), the industrial archaeologist must have an understanding of the antecedents of his particular area of study. Thus the evolution of wind and water power in the eighteenth and nineteenth centuries can only be fully appreciated in the context of much earlier developments. But to regard industrial archaeology as being concerned with only *industrial* activity within the last 2 centuries or so is also to reject the cultural definition. The industrial archaeologist, if he is to have any real understanding of the sites and artefacts of the Industrial Revolution, must look at the landscape in its entirety. Industrial archaeology is in part a landscape study, and the industrial archaeologist cannot restrict himself wholly to the thematic approach. The Industrial Revolution created a new economy, a new landscape, a new way of life. In terms of the lives of all of us, as inhabitants of an industrial nation— the first industrial nation—it is the most relevant period of our past, not only because it is the most recent but because the specific changes wrought during the last 2½ centuries provide the foundations of our present society and of all other industrial societies throughout the world.

This one word 'relevance' provides the key to the phenomenal growth of interest in industrial archaeology in recent years—a widespread realisation that this particular period of our past was in world terms unique and that amongst its physical remains are monuments of outstanding and exceptional significance. There had been no Industrial Revolution before in the world, and no other nation's subsequent progress towards industrialisation had the same spontaneity, generated the same range of technological innovations or produced the same landscape changes. Industrial archaeology was thus born not out of a detached or academic interest but on a wave of emotional involvement and a deep-seated feeling that a vital part of our past was being destroyed. The ambient conditions of the mid-1950s were exactly right for the growth of this new interest. The postwar years were dominated by a preoccupation with growth in an obsessive, almost nineteenth-century, way – with the creation of new industry, new towns, a new foundation for future prosperity—but at the same time coupled quite specifically with the destruction of much which was old. For once the occurrences of the past provided the lessons for the future and the new period of exploitation of resources created a backlash—a vital and dynamic feeling for the environment based on an appreciation, for the first time, that it was delicate and sensitive to uninformed meddling. The Industrial Revolution had provided the awful example, and while most people recognised that the worst excesses of industrialisation had to go, they recognised too that society was not in a sufficient state of moral responsibility to prevent the same sort of thing from happening again. The growth of industrial archaeology is just one facet of this widespread interest in the landscape and its future.

Other factors contributed to the growth of industrial archaeology. Not only did the destruction of huge areas of eighteenth- and nineteenth-century Britain create a reaction and an awareness of their significance but the preoccupation with the stimulation of new economic activity resulted in past periods of growth and their achievements taking on a new fascination. The physical monuments of those who had so spectacularly generated growth in the Industrial Revolution were appreciated in a way which would have been impossible in the 1930s, when industry was associated in the minds of everybody with unemployment, decay, desperately miserable towns, and landscapes of destruction. The mid-1950s, therefore, saw for the first time the growth of a national pride in past industrial achievement which began to counterbalance those adverse social consequences that had formerly been so wholeheartedly associated with it. There was thus the curious phenomenon of a new and widespread environmental awareness arising in response to the depredations of postwar development and the fear that 'history might repeat itself' coupled with the beginnings of an appreciation that the Industrial Revolution period, so long held in disregard, was of very special significance and that some of its physical remains formed, in effect, the real and tangible evidence of the origins of our present culture. This paradox has caused the industrial archaeologist some difficulty in establishing his credibility, particularly when it comes to the preservation of sites and areas which are historically significant but are outside the currently accepted and relatively narrow areas of contemporary aesthetic appreciation. Nevertheless, within this new climate of environmental and historical awareness, industrial archaeology was able to grow from a seed into a sturdy sapling.

The factors providing the essential motivation for the widespread interest in industrial archaeology were therefore numerous, embracing not only the recording of the archaeological evidence which sites might hold but the desire to preserve a vital part of the national heritage. In addition came new interest, in the aesthetic aspects of industrial artefacts, a further stimulation to the enthusiasm for things mechanical which had always had a large following, and more recently the appreciation of some of the possible social benefits which the conservation of, for example, industrial residential areas might have. Industrial archaeology has thus grown to be a broad-based study encompassing more than the words 'industrial' and 'archaeology' would seem to imply. It is already inconceivable that another, more appropriate, term will ever emerge to supplant it. 'Industrial Archaeology' is obscure in origin but was probably coined in Manchester in the early 1950s. Its first appearance in print occurred in 1955, when Michael Rix published an article in *The Amateur Historian* emphasising the need to record and preserve the remains of industrialisation before they disappeared.

The dynamism which has characterised the growth of industrial archaeology over the past few years has resulted from the fact that large numbers of people with differing backgrounds of work and education can make a real contribution to its advancement. As a study it draws its life-blood from a wide variety of disciplines, demanding an appreciation on the one hand of economic or social history or geography and on the other of a knowledge of mechanical or civil engineering, of metallurgy or architecture. But because it is so all-embracing, almost anybody, regardless of any specialist knowledge or skill, can make a contribution in one way or another. Industrial archaeology, like the other archaeologies, has attracted a wide variety of people from many different walks of life, and numerous local societies have been formed. Unlike traditional archaeology, however, industrial archaeology has not developed a caucus of trained professionals— there is as yet no way of becoming a qualified industrial archaeologist.

This broad base of awareness which enabled industrial archaeology to gain ground so rapidly has been both its strength and its weakness. Lacking respectable academic origins, industrial archaeology has been the subject of considerable criticism, its inter-disciplinary nature and absence of accepted technical standards making it unpalatable to many traditionally based academics. Nevertheless the problems of industrial archaeology have caught the imagination of large numbers of people, who as amateurs or professionals are rapidly gaining the skills necessary to achieve the right sort of standards. Industrial archaeology has developed, generally speaking, outside the orbit of traditional archaeological activity, and only very recently have industrial archaeologists begun to pick up the well established techniques of the traditional archaeologist and apply them to this new study. There are few practical techniques peculiar to industrial archaeology, although some, such as the recording of machinery and various aspects of conservation, pose specific problems which will undoubtedly provide the foundation for considerable industrial archaeological research in the future.

It is becoming increasingly clear that the industrial archaeologist by working in the field, analysing sites, can make a real contribution to our sum total of knowledge. In other words there is a truly 'archaeological' element of the study, the potential of which has hardly been developed. Not only is the industrial archaeologist, in his role as a fieldworker and interpreter of the landscape, in a position to provide an extra dimension to the existing findings of historians who have used only documentary sources but there are a number of areas of investigation where field evidence is itself the primary source. For example, no documentary information exists to provide a detailed explanation of the development of iron railways, or plateways, from the mid-eighteenth century onwards. Archaeological evidence alone exists to reveal the regional differences between various types of primitive plateway, the technology of their track systems, rail and sleeper design and earthworks. Documentary evidence fails to provide information on the philosophy applied to their capitalisation but the industrial archaeologist in the field, using the simplest techniques of observation and surveying, can readily appreciate the fact that some early railways were literally laid on the existing ground surface while others, designed to fulfil the same function, needed massive earthworks with major embankments, cuttings and bridges.

Similarly, industrial archaeological investigation has provided conclusive evidence of the evolutionary stages in the transition from timber to iron framing in factory buildings. Again, no extraordinary techniques have been used, merely those already developed by historians of architecture; but without the availability of the physical remains of the buildings themselves our understanding of this fundamental advance in structural engineering would be incomplete. Metallurgical analysis applied to the slags of early blast furnaces provides yet another example of physical remains yielding evidence of value. Although by no means restricted to Industrial Revolution sites, slag analysis enables the historian of metallurgy to gain a good idea of the raw materials used and their sources, the temperatures at which the furnace operated and the nature of the finished product. As yet in its infancy, laboratory analysis of slags, and indeed of the metal products themselves, may provide a relative dating technique of great importance.

A completely different approach to site evidence is the area surveying and mapping of types of industrial installation, workers' housing, watermills or mine shafts as a means of establishing distributional patterns. Here the techniques of the geographer and statistician are required, coupled, as always, with an understanding of the general picture of economic activity. Relations can be established between types of waterwheel and the gradient profile and consistency of flow of streams, between blast furnace design and the qualities of the raw materials charge, between topography and the flue arrangements of lead smelters and between surface geology and road turnpiking. These are all simple examples of the role field evidence can play in the assembly of information. The industrial archaeologist then is a correlator of evidence, synthesising data from documents, maps and field remains to gain a general picture.

The artefacts of industrialisation can in other ways also provide an appreciation of the evolution of technology which would be quite impossible from documentary sources. Many of the innovations which formed the basis for progress in the eighteenth and early nineteenth centuries were brought about by craftsmen whose contribution was rarely, if ever, documented. Frequently the situation arises of a company with substantially complete commercial records being able to give no information at all on the manufacturing processes which provided the foundation of its existence. The key to the understanding of these processes is in the surviving artefacts, which may take the form of the manufacturing equipment or the products that were made with it. They often also provide an insight into the lives and intellects of the people who made and worked with them far more potent than any written evidence could do, even supposing it existed. The craftsman as an innovator as well as a producer, personally and physically involved in the manufacturing process, using the craft skills he had acquired through an apprenticeship and which he applied intuitively in his everyday work, was fundamental to the progress of industrial technology. James Nasmyth, himself an inventor of some stature, wrote of that great craftsman, entrepreneur and innovator Henry Maudslay, with whom he worked for a time as an assistant: 'To be permitted to stand by and watch the systematic way in which Mr. Maudslay would first mark or line out his work, and the masterly manner in which he would deal with his materials and cause them to assume the desired forms, was a treat beyond all expression. Every stroke of the hammer, chisel or file, told as an effective step towards the intended result. It was a never-to-be-forgotten lesson in workmanship in the most exalted sense of the term.' Herein lies what much of industrial archaeology is all about: appreciation and understanding of the genius for innovation and the skill in making things combined with recognition of the practical and aesthetic qualities of workmanship, for which the original object is essential.

The physical remains of industrialisation thus far transcend in importance their role as pure historical evidence, which fact has provided the primary motivating spirit behind the widespread interest in industrial archaeology. To an increasing number of people the engines and machines, factories, mills and warehouses, canals and railways which came to dominate the landscape in the last 2 centuries have become significant as part of our cultural heritage; they are implanted in the subconscious of innumerable ordinary people who, with no background of scholarship or training in artistic or architectural appreciation, find themselves responding aesthetically to the sweep of a railway curving through a wooded valley, to the triumphant striding of a viaduct, to the sound and smells of a perfectly running mill engine or the rhythm and symmetry of an eighteenth-century textile mill. Not only do these monuments to industrialisation represent a functional perfection of design but their heroic scale, often so perfectly assimilated into the landscape, excites the imagination and stimulates the senses. They represent the skill and inventiveness, adventurousness and suffering of the first Industrial Revolution. Their study and preservation is the justification for industrial archaeology.

THE GROWTH OF INDUSTRIAL ARCHAEOLOGY

As we have seen, industrial archaeology is relatively new, but some people had been concerned with it very early on. As early as the Great Exhibition of 1851 it was appreciated that there were technologically important machines dating from the early years of the Industrial Revolution that were worthy of presentation to the public. The beginnings of what is now called the Science Museum, in London, were a tangible expression of this appreciation, and items such as early stationary steam engines and railway locomotives

were collected and preserved. Indeed the importance of preserving locomotives was recognised at a remarkably early date, with the result that
Britain, the birthplace of the steam railway, possesses a very complete series
of early examples, including, in the Science Museum alone, *Puffing Billy* of
1813, and *Rocket, Sans Pareil* and *Novelty* of 1829, all three of which were
competitors at the Rainhill trials. Museums in Edinburgh, Newcastle and
York also contain pre-1830 locomotives. The York Railway Museum,
opened in 1928 by the London & North Eastern Railway in the aftermath of
the Stockton & Darlington Railway centenary celebrations of 1925, was the
first large museum of its type, and another exhibition, in Newcastle-upon-
Tyne, provided the initial collections and led to the opening there of the
Museum of Science & Engineering in 1934. These are all museums of the
traditional type in which exhibits are collected and brought into a building
where they are, space permitting, exhibited to the public, and the justification
for most of these early collections was that the items in them represented
outstanding contributions to the development of engineering and technology;
in many cases they were 'firsts'. Little if any recognition was given to the
social or economic context of the material collected.

Active study of at least the technological aspects of industrialisation is
also much older than industrial archaeology and centres largely around the
work of the Newcomen Society, which was formed as a result of the James
Watt centenary celebrations held in Birmingham in 1919. Its object is to
support and encourage study and research in the history of engineering and
technology, and the preservation of records, both technical and biographical.
Although the society takes its name from Thomas Newcomen (1663-1729),
the father of the steam engine, its interests cover all aspects of industrial, and
in some cases pre-industrial, technology. The *Transactions* form an invaluable
source of information, and to these and the dedication and enthusiasm of
Newcomen members over more than 50 years, industrial archaeology owes
a great debt. There were, of course, individuals working in the field and
publishing the results of their work in the transactions of local archaeological,
historical and philosophical societies. An early and unusual example deserves
note because of its title, 'The Archaeology of the West Cumberland Coal
Trade' by Isaac Fletcher, published in the *Transactions of the Cumberland and
Westmorland Antiquarian and Archaeological Society* in 1878, but there is no
evidence that this use of the term 'archaeology' in the context of industrial

remains had any influence on the development of the modern term 80 years later.

The spontaneous growth of industrial archaeology in the late 1950s and early 1960s manifested itself in a variety of ways. Workers' Educational Association and University Extra-Mural Department classes were some of the first 'formal' gatherings of people interested in the subject, together with a number of regional conferences from which grew the first local industrial archaeological societies. Almost invariably the driving force behind these newly formed groups was the need to record industrial monuments before they were destroyed, and the early lead given by the Council for British Archaeology (CBA) in establishing a basic recording system provided a focal point and stimulus of considerable importance.

In 1959 the CBA established an Industrial Archaeological Research Committee as a means of extending into this new field its existing role, which it had played since its inception in 1945, of coordinating the work of regional archaeological societies. Subsequently an Advisory Panel was set up as a sub-committee of the Research Committee in order to develop policies for the recording of industrial monuments and, in the event more important, procedures for ensuring that they received the right sort of legislative protection. The then Ministry of Public Buildings &Works, the government department responsible for scheduling ancient monuments, also recognised at least the theoretical need for an active policy towards the recording and preservation of industrial sites and, in conjunction with the CBA, launched the Industrial Monuments Survey (IMS). Rex Wailes, a pillar of the Newcomen Society and an authority on windmills, was appointed full-time consultant to the Survey, and he undoubtedly played an important role in his travels throughout the country in stimulating industrial archaeological work at a local level. Later the Survey was transferred to the care of the CBA, to whom the Ministry, now part of the Department of the Environment, makes a cost-covering contribution. On the retirement of Mr Wailes, Keith Falconer was appointed Survey Officer, reporting to the Advisory Panel and the Research Committee. His work, carried out on a region-by-region basis and in consultation with innumerable local fieldworkers, enables the CBA to recommend industrial monuments for Scheduling, under the Ancient Monuments Acts, and Listing, under planning legislation, thus bringing industrial archaeological sites into line in law with those of other periods.

As part of its policy to embrace industrial archaeology, the CBA also initiated a record card system with the object of establishing a 'national record' of industrial monuments and provide the Survey with a basis for defining its priorities for listing and scheduling. This system was based on a record card designed to be filled in by fieldworkers and, despite its well recognised inadequacies, this National Record of Industrial Monuments (NRIM) has provided the only theoretically comprehensive and all-embracing record of industrial sites for over 10 years. In its early years the NRIM suffered from lack of a tight definition of how the cards should be used and, with their compilers ranging from groups of schoolchildren to trained engineers, architects and museum curators, the results have inevitably been uneven. Not only is there a wide variation in the quality of the entries but their spread nationally reflects the distribution of active fieldworkers rather than of industrial sites. Very few local societies have systematically used the CBA card as the basic recording instrument to work over an area, although individuals with specialist interests have made attempts to cover specific subjects comprehensively. Despite these failings and the fact that the NRIM has not provided its originally intended service to the Industrial Monuments Survey, it is the only existing record with anything like a national coverage, and although it does not generally offer much information on specific sites, it could form the basis for a national inventory.

An important contribution to the administration of the NRIM came in 1965, when it had become increasingly clear that the CBA and its Survey Officer could not offer the secretarial facilities necessary to operate the system properly. As a result the Director of the Centre for the Study of the History of Technology at the University of Bath, Dr R. A. Buchanan, offered to provide a base for the Record, and it has been operated from there ever since. Cards are filled in and returned to the Centre for copying. The original is returned to the fieldworker concerned and the three copies made are filed for reference, one with the CBA, one with the National Monuments Record and one at the University of Bath.

Industrial archaeology, however, has now outgrown the sort of record represented by the NRIM, and important decisions about its future must be made before long. Most important perhaps is the need to make clear to local societies and individual fieldworkers what the needs are, particularly in relation to sites which are threatened with destruction. Here the continued existence of the NRIM, unless supported by other mechanisms for more sophisticated recording, could form a positive drawback to industrial archaeology, as many people, having filled in a card, feel that they have fulfilled the necessary archaeological obligation towards a site about to be destroyed.

The situation today then comprises a basic national record in the form of the NRIM, the CBA Survey Officer in close touch with appropriate inspectors and investigators in the Department of the Environment, and a wide variety of regional recording systems ranging from the superb work of the Royal Commission on Ancient and Historical Monuments of Scotland (unfortunately not paralleled in England and Wales), to building surveys by schools of architecture, photographic and drawing surveys by some local authorities and, very selectively, by the National Monuments Record, and various record data assembled by some museums. The assembled information compiled over the years by the CBA Survey Officer provides a surprisingly comprehensive basic record of sites, while there are certain specialist records such as that of wind and watermill sites put together by the Wind and Watermill Section of the Society for the Protection of Ancient Buildings. As if this is not enough to bewilder the newcomer anxious to make his contribution to industrial archaeology, he is also faced with an increasing number of local or regional gazetteers of sites covering, for example, Devon, the Bristol area, Bath, Greater London, Hertfordshire, Bedfordshire, Sussex, Wiltshire and Lancaster.

How then can the uninitiated amateur make contact with what is going on in his region? Firstly, there are the numerous local societies (listed in Appendix 3) which cover much of the country. If there is no local society, contact with the Council for British Archaeology may result in a link being established with one of the fourteen regional CBA groups, some of which have industrial archaeology sections. If nothing comes of this approach, try the local museum, which may afford one an opportunity to be involved in survey work and/or a practical contribution to preservation. Lastly, but perhaps most important, there are WEA and university extra-mural courses, which teach the techniques and at the same time allow one to participate in what work is going on. Although only the two universities of Newcastle-upon-Tyne and Hull have staff tutors concerned specifically with industrial archaeology, almost all run courses of some sort, usually with outside lecturers.

One of the curious aspects of the development of industrial archaeology over the last 20 years has been the absence of any central society or co-ordinating body concerned specifically with its needs. The nearest approach has been the CBA's Industrial Archaeological Research Committee. In other branches of archaeological activity the situation is quite different; there are a number of national organisations representing all aspects and periods of traditional archaeology, together with specific societies covering, for example, prehistoric, medieval and nautical archaeology. In addition there are organisations such as the Victorian Society or the Georgian Group, concerned primarily with architecture but impinging on industrial structures to some extent. The Newcomen Society, though already well established and respected in the field of engineering history, does not fill the apparent gap, as its concern is by no means primarily 'archaeological'.

This central 'vacuum' within industrial archaeology was partially filled until quite recently by two things. One was the journal *Industrial Archaeology*, inaugurated in 1964 and still the only national periodical for the subject in Britain or, for that matter, anywhere in the world. Initially edited by Kenneth Hudson, whose book of the same title published in the previous year was the first general text on the subject, it is now published in Scotland under the editorship of Dr John Butt of the University of Strathclyde. The other focal point for industrial archaeology in Britain was the annual conference held initially in the University of Bath, which from 1966 onwards provided a yearly opportunity for industrial archaeologists to assemble, exchange views and discuss mutual problems. Before long it uprooted itself and moved to Bradford, Glasgow and, in 1973, the Isle of Man. By now the need for a national organisation was becoming imperative, and it was this annual conference which provided the obvious opportunity for its conception. Inaugurated in March 1974, the new Association for Industrial Archaeology has been set up to represent the interests of industrial archaeology at a national level, to assist and coordinate the work of existing regional groups and to continue the well established pattern of annual conferences. A *Bulletin* is produced six times a year. The AIA has not been formed to compete with or replace the CBA, or to challenge its relation with government departments, but to strengthen its hand, press for more support for industrial recording and conservation and improve the 'watchdog' surveillance so necessary to prevent important structures being demolished willy-nilly.

CONSERVATION

The dynamic growth of industrial archaeology throughout the 1960s was instigated by an awareness that Britain's industrial heritage was vanishing and the new 'movement', if such an all-embracing term is appropriate, manifested itself in two quite separate bodies of activity—those who recorded and those who conserved. Naturally enough there was some overlap between the two but distinct areas can nevertheless be identified, with local industrial archaeological societies engaged primarily in recording, an increasing number of established museums expanding to embrace industrial archaeology and, perhaps most important, a wave of trusts being set up to preserve industrial monuments *in situ*.

We have already touched on the involvement of museums, both nationally and locally financed, in industrial preservation well before industrial archaeology was born. The Science Museum in London needs no introduction as the national museum of science and technology, while the three other national museums, in Cardiff, Edinburgh and Belfast, all have well established departments of industry or technology with trained curatorial and technical staff. From the point of view of conserving industrial artefacts, however, all have reached that situation in which the museum as a building, as opposed to the museum as an institutional organisation, is now markedly unsuited for what it has always traditionally been supposed to do. The reaction has been curious and not altogether satisfactory. Some museums have bent over backwards to continue their traditional role, so that one has the remarkable sight in Edinburgh of an immense industrial waterwheel incorporated, without the machinery it drove, in a new museum building, while in the National Maritime Museum at Greenwich the dismembered remains of a paddle-tug have been similarly treated. Conservation is a function of all museums, and their basic philosophy must therefore stem from the most satisfactory means of achieving this end. All these national museums have large items of industrial material in store, which at least means that they have saved equipment from destruction; it is important now to ensure that the museums themselves do not destroy primary exhibits in order to 'make them fit'. Clearly there are opportunities, where several items of the same type survive, to dismantle or section in order to explain and interpret their method of operation (indeed not enough of this sort of thing is done with, for example, locomotives), but, as with all other types of museum collection, the integrity of the primary material must be maintained intact. The National Museum of Wales has realised its conservation responsibilities admirably with the retention *in situ* of the Dinorwic slate quarry workshops, and with its plans to develop site museums for coal-mining in Glamorgan.

Provincial museums have also responded to the demands of industrial conservation by setting up departments to collect machinery, although few have yet had the opportunity to present it to their public. Several have been able to acquire a suitable site, with its own intrinsic importance, and develop that as a museum. Thus Leicester Corporation has taken over the disused Abbey Lane sewage pumping station in the city to preserve the four beam engines and develop the site as a museum of technology for the East Midlands. Generally speaking, however, the established local authority museum has not responded, either through lack of money or lack of interest, to the conservation demands posed by obsolete industrial buildings and the machinery they contain. The net result has been the formation of numerous private bodies, most of which are registered with the Charity Commissioners as trusts, in order to conserve, usually on site, important industrial monuments. It would be wrong to imagine that all these have developed as a result of the recent growth of interest in industrial archaeology, although by far the majority have done so. Several wind and watermill preservation schemes have been going for many years: the Cornish Engines Preservation Society, formed as early as 1935 and now incorporated into the Trevithick Society, preserved several Cornish mine engines before handing them over to the National Trust, while in Sheffield the Council for the Conservation of Sheffield Antiquities was instrumental in restoring the cutlers' grinding shop known as Shepherd Wheel.

The boom in industrial archaeological conservation, however, is much more recent, reflecting the general growth of the study but more particularly perhaps the higher degree of general concern about demolition of historically important structures and areas of towns. For the first time conservation has had to become a positive and dynamic force in its own right in order to counter the effects of widespread area redevelopment. In the past an urban area tended to regenerate on a piecemeal basis, a building going here and there and being replaced by another with the same plan and building line. Massive redevelopment, stimulated by the blitz but more particularly the motor car, resulted, virtually for the first time, in huge urban areas being replaced by a totally new landscape bearing no relation whatsoever to what was there before. Few people would argue for the retention of most of what has gone but the great pressures which built up, particularly as the result of road building, have affected much more of our surroundings than just the parts that needed replacement. A sudden state of appalled realisation of the irreplaceable monuments which have been lost, often unwittingly, has generated a widespread reaction, and large numbers of people have become personally involved in conservation projects. The change in the climate of awareness and susceptibility has been quite remarkable, with terms such as 'conservation', 'environment' and 'pollution' receiving such unprecedented exposure that they have become almost hackneyed. In an era during which the word 'Victorian' changed from being a derogatory term of abuse to a mark of approval, industrial archaeological conservation became well established.

Undoubtedly the greatest stimulus to this movement was the destruction of the Euston arch, Philip Hardwick's triumphal entrance to the London & Birmingham Railway. Looking back now on its demolition and the controversy which surrounded it, the Euston arch clearly marked the turning point; it was the initial sacrificial offering necessary to save succeeding generations of structures threatened by redevelopment proposals. What is also particularly pertinent about the Euston disaster is the subsequent realisation that the arch would have had even more relevance, significance and monumentality had it been allowed to perform its original function for the new station. There have been numerous other losses too, including the demolition of the world's first shot tower, in Bristol, for road widening and that of a slightly later but quite different type in Newcastle-upon-Tyne. In Glasgow the magnificent Randolph & Elder engineering building has gone, as has the spectacular group of six Cornish beam engines at Sudbrook, Gloucestershire, which drained the Severn Tunnel. Other losses, as the result of fire, have pinpointed the need for vigilance, where empty buildings are concerned in the case of the great Telford warehouses burned down at

Ellesmere Port, Cheshire, and over structures which are still in regular everyday use as demonstrated by the loss of the Britannia tubular bridge across the Menai Straits.

The requirements of industrial archaeological conservation are multifarious, ranging from the site taken over for its historic significance and preserved as a monument or museum to the need to ensure that important industrial structures which are still in use, such as bridges and tunnels, are not treated unsympathetically by their owners. In addition there is a growing appreciation of the possibilities which obsolete industrial buildings offer for adaptation to new uses. Thus maltings have become concert halls or colour-processing laboratories, warehouses have been converted into flats, granaries into offices and mills into hotels. In Liverpool the city council is considering plans for siting the local polytechnic institute in the empty and long-threatened warehouses of Albert Dock, Jesse Hartley's monumental quadrangle of iron, brick and granite dating from the mid-1840s. This latter type of industrial archaeological conservation is in many ways the most encouraging, as it demonstrates the enormous potential which existing structures have for adaptation and affords excellent opportunities not only to keep buildings and dying areas alive but also to retain the essential architectural, technological or landscape value. The industrial archaeologist has a real and constructive role to play here in the identification of significant buildings and in ensuring that the specific features which make them important are not compromised.

Far and away the most active sector of industrial archaeological conservation activity is represented by private trusts or museum societies of enthusiastic part-time industrial archaeologists whose initiative, ingenuity and prodigious energies have resulted in large numbers of new projects being undertaken in recent years. Many have the support of local authorities and an increasing number receive grants from the Department of the Environment and, if they are in Development Areas, from the national tourist boards. Most are concerned with a specific site, such as a watermill or a pumping station, but others cover substantial areas within which individual monuments are maintained. There are an increasing number of open-air museums which include industrial archaeological material within the scope of their collecting. These are the successors of the continental open-air folk museums in which an area of land is designated and buildings and machines are reconstructed on it.

About eighty bodies now administer individual sites, and the number is increasing almost weekly. A few examples will give some idea of the general pattern. At Cheddleton in Staffordshire a trust has restored to working condition a water-powered flint mill used originally in the preparation of flint for the pottery industry. Beam pumping engines have attracted particular attention, and private groups have restored to steaming condition the Ryhope water-pumping station in Sunderland, and the Crofton engines on the Kennet & Avon Canal, Wiltshire, which were used to lift water into the summit level. Preserved manufacturing sites are less common, but at Ruddington in Nottinghamshire a local society intends to buy and restore a complex consisting of two framework knitters' shops, together with the hosier's cottage and store. Metalworking projects include Finch Foundry, an early nineteenth-century scythe works at Sticklepath near Okehampton in Devon, and Top Forge, Wortley, in Yorkshire, where wrought-iron railway axles were made. One of the largest organisations with nationwide involvement in industrial archaeological conservation is the National Trust which, besides administering the Cornish engines already mentioned, is responsible for Conway suspension bridge, Nether Alderley corn mill in Cheshire and several watermills in the Eastern Counties, and windmills such as Pitstone Green in Buckinghamshire and High Ham in Somerset.

Local authority involvement in conservation is very varied, illustrating clearly the way in which industrial archaeology 'falls between the stools' of responsibility. In a recent survey on the role of local authorities in industrial archaeological conservation carried out for the Royal Town Planning Institute, the replies to questionnaires revealed that responsibility for industrial monuments rested with departments as diverse as town clerks, libraries, education, records office, archives, engineers and landscape architects. Of the 126 respondents, seventeen said their museums were responsible, while the greatest majority, forty, said that responsibility rested primarily or solely with the planning department or with a joint architects' and planning department. Even within planning departments a variety of sections held responsibility; historic buildings was most common, but urban renewal, conservation and environment were also named. It is clear that industrial archaeology, where it comes into contact with the established order of things, be this represented by an archaeological body, a university, a government department or a local authority, has not been able to find a logical and obvious niche in which it can happily be accommodated.

In Sheffield the museum has taken responsibility for Abbeydale industrial hamlet, with its crucible steelworks and water-powered hammers, and the same applies in Portsmouth with Eastney pumping station, in Birmingham with Sarehole Mill and in Shrewsbury with Coleham pumping station. In Derbyshire, however, the planning department has taken the iniative over the preservation of Middleton Top winding engine and sections of the Cromford & High Peak Railway, and there are innumerable other examples up and down the country. It is important to appreciate, however, that conservation of the industrial archaeological assets of a site is not always, or indeed usually, the primary motivation behind a planning department's involvement; the main reason is usually derelict land reclamation, with the provision of scenic walkways, picnic sites and nature trails. It is essential, therefore, for the industrial archaeological viewpoint to be built into the decision-making processes when environmental conservation schemes of this type are mooted to ensure that the archaeological integrity of sites is not destroyed. A similar problem arises, although not quite so acutely, with the application of tourist board capital to conservation projects, as here again it is not primarily the archaeological significance of a site which gains it the grant but its potential as a tourist attraction. The problem, then, is to ensure that the fundamental industrial archaeological conservation principles and priorities are soundly worked out before sites come under the various competing pressures of demolition and redevelopment.

Another area of growth recently has been in the establishment of open-air museums of various types. At Beamish in County Durham a consortium of local authorities supports the North of England Open Air Museum, set up formally in 1970 to establish 'an open air museum for the purpose of studying, collecting, preserving and exhibiting buildings, machinery, objects and information illustrating the development of industry and way of life in the north of England.' Work is now actively in hand on developing the 200 acre site, and the first stage of an electric tramway system to transport visitors around the museum came into operation in the Spring of 1973.

A rather different type of project is the Ironbridge Gorge Museum in Shropshire, set up under the auspices of a Trust formed in 1968. Here the object is to establish a 'network museum' in which the buildings, furnaces, forges and machinery of this centre of the early Industrial Revolution will be preserved *in situ*. Centred on the Iron Bridge is an area containing many other remains of early ironworking, together with coalmining, brick and tile making and porcelain manufacture. The Coalbrookdale furnace where Abraham Darby perfected his coke-smelting technique in 1709 was originally cleared, and a small museum established nearby, in 1959 by the then owners, Allied Ironfounders, and both are now administered by the Ironbridge Gorge Museum Trust. Three miles away at the other end of the Gorge is the Blists Hill Open Air Museum, also run by the Trust, which is being developed as a site on to which buildings and machines can be moved when they cannot be preserved *in situ*. Here are colliery winding engines, a re-excavated section of canal, blast furnace blowing engines, a printing shop, a pottery, brick and tile works and numerous other exhibits. Ultimately the area will become a landscape of the past designed to re-create in operational form various industries which contributed to making East Shropshire so important in the eighteenth and nineteenth centuries. Most of the capital for this project, which is estimated to cost something over £1 million, has been raised by appeal to industry, but the Department of the Environment has also made a substantial contribution, notably to the restoration of the bridge itself.

The role of the Department of the Environment is fundamental in the development of industrial archaeological conservation policy and practice. Not only is the Department responsible for the listing and scheduling of industrial monuments but it also makes available capital grants towards conservation work and occasionally maintains sites itself. Numerous projects, both local authority and private, have received grants from the Ancient Monuments Directorate, while money for buildings usually comes through the Historic Buildings Council. It is unlikely that large numbers of industrial monuments will come wholly under the guardianship of the state, as many traditional archaeological sites do; and perhaps only relatively small-scale industrial conservation projects need to. Government assistance to private projects, however, is generally money well spent and a highly effective method of conservation. It is to the largely unrecognised credit of the Department of the Environment that it has made special provisions for industrial archaeology; as early as 1965 the Report of the Ancient Monuments Board recognised that the time had come for a set policy for dealing with industrial monuments and that this should as far as possible be assimilated, within the framework of existing legislation, into the policy for more traditional monuments.

The legislative protection for industrial monuments, like government sources of money, is diverse in nature, again reflecting the inter-disciplinary nature of industrial archaeology and the difficulty of fitting it neatly into existing compartments. The most important protection is scheduling under the Ancient Monuments Acts, which is designed to register the fact that the preservation of a monument is in the national interest, thereby enlisting the support of owners and others in the protection of the monument and minimising the danger of interference with its essential features. There are now well over 100 scheduled industrial monuments in Britain. Listing is carried out under the Planning Acts and is designed to identify and protect buildings of architectural and historical importance either individually or in groups, as well as buildings which make an important contribution to a townscape. Statutory lists grade buildings into three categories: Grade I covers those of 'outstanding importance', totalling some 4 per cent of the total or about 4,500 in England and 150 in Wales; Grade II covers buildings of 'special interest', with particularly important examples being classified as Grade II*, the so-called 'Grade II star'; and Grade III covers buildings that do not normally qualify for the statutory lists but are important enough to be drawn to the attention of local authorities and others so that the case for preserving them may be fully considered. Another important piece of legislation of increasing importance to industrial monuments is the Civic Amenities Act 1967, under which conservation areas are designated. Of the 3,000 conservation areas in Britain, about one-third are estimated to contain industrial buildings and in some, such as the Ironbridge and Coalbrookdale Conservation Area in Shropshire, the industrial archaeological features provide the *raison d'etre* for designation.

In its short life to date industrial archaeology has evolved at a startling pace, providing a focal point for the interests of many people and affording a new outlook on a vital period of our past. The haphazard nature of some of its techniques is perhaps almost inevitable, but the opportunities exist and are rapidly being grasped for improving the situation and systematising without stultifying the further pursuit of information and evidence. Already industrial archaeology can command large television audiences, is making a contribution to the growth of tourism and has a rapidly growing range of literature, all developments which would have been inconceivable 20 years ago. Its growth is likely to continue, with a better organised approach to recording, particularly in the field of what might be called 'rescue industrial archaeology', the systematic recording of structures before they are demolished. In the conservation field there may well be a more positive involvement of the Department of the Environment in the running and financing of private trusts, and a recognition, hopefully, by the Department of Education and Science that the conservation and interpretation of industrial monuments, even where it is outside the scope of the traditional local authority museum structure, is a vital part of the national picture. The concept of industrial archaeology as a fully fledged academic discipline in its own right is a long way from realisation, but it may well eventually come. There are already the beginnings of an appreciation that the physical remains of the Industrial Revolution contain a body of information whose isolation and interpretation require a formalised and disciplined approach. Certainly the role of the amateur, or rather part-time, industrial archaeologist—distinctions between amateur and professional are to a great extent irrelevant—will expand greatly, although again based on the evolution of accepted standards of technique, such as those traditional archaeology has established for itself over the last half-century or more. Industrial archaeology is in a way at a turning point, having come through the early stages of youth to adolescence and the verge of manhood. In its progress towards maturity industrial archaeology will be seen in a new perspective, and the viewpoint of the industrial archaeologist will become appreciated as an essential element in the understanding of the society, the economy, the technology and the landscape of the Industrial Revolution. The aim of this book is to point out the remains of the Industrial Revolution that survive and to sketch in something of their context.

2 The Industrialisation of Britain

THE industrial archaeologist, as we have seen, is primarily concerned with the examination and analysis of the physical remains of the age of industrialisation, accepting, as would the archaeologist of any other major epoch, that there are specialist antecedents, within various branches of technology, for example, which must be understood before a full appreciation of the events of the period itself can be gained. Before considering the areas of specific interest to the industrial archaeologist industry by industry, it is important to consider the historical, social, economic and technological framework within which something as complex as an industrial revolution could occur. The term 'Industrial Revolution' itself has been in common usage now for nearly a century and was coined at least as early as the 1830s. What was the Industrial Revolution? Why did it happen in Britain first?

Historians have been arguing for three generations over the causes behind the Industrial Revolution, but the accumulated literature is largely the literature of disagreement. What *is* certain is that at some point, probably in the second half of the eighteenth century—although some would put it slightly earlier—Britain reached the point of 'take-off' into self-sustained growth' based on radical changes in methods of production. These changes, occurring over a relatively short time, had widespread repercussions throughout society, the national economy and the landscape. The changes were rapid and their results were there for everyone to see. The rate of change was indeed 'revolutionary'.

The beginning of the Industrial Revolution, therefore, is marked by the start of a rapid rate of change in the economy from one of a backward or underdeveloped country to one of a modern industrial nation. In quantitative terms it might be possible to pinpoint the start of the Industrial Revolution by identifying the date when the gross national product, representing the national income or the total value of goods and services produced in the economy, first began to increase by about 2 per cent per annum, for any pre-industrial economy would be growing at less than 1 per cent per annum. This take-off point occurred in Britain somewhere between 1740 and 1780.

One of the problems of using the term 'revolution', and it was taken from what started in France in 1789, is that it implies instant upheaval, an over-turning of old values and their immediate substitution by new, a dramatic change whose beginning can be precisely dated. It appears that this apoca-lyptic element of comparison is unreal, and this has led many to criticise the use or relevance of the term at all. But if one looks, from the standpoint of the second half of the twentieth century, at the changes wrought by the French Revolution and by the British Industrial Revolution, the com-parison again becomes valid. The eighteenth century in Britain saw changes which produced similar long-term political effects to those created by the bloody revolution in France. There was as much, if not more, of a difference between pre- and post-industrial Britain as between pre- and post-revolutionary France. The watershed between the essentially medieval and the essentially modern economy, if not marked by a sharp ridge, was nevertheless a real one.

Britain was the first country in the world to undergo an industrial trans-formation of its national economy. This transformation occurred spon-taneously, without any outside direction, without any conscious policy of stimulating industrial growth, without any momentum being directly imparted through taxation or through capital being made available. Indeed the state showed no interest whatsoever in promoting industrial activity or encouraging new skills. The revolution just happened, and we can only surmise at the reasons why.

It is unlikely that any *single* factor brought the economy to this point of take-off. A whole complex of interrelated movements, some with their origins as far back as the Middle Ages, reacted with each other to produce a situation in which the economy 'went critical' in the second half of the eighteenth century. Once the chain reaction had begun, growth became more or less automatic. What factors were involved? There were the direct economic forces of population growth, of agricultural improvement, of increasing trade and the growth of markets, of capital accumulation and the development of a flexible banking system, of the breakdown of medieval conditions of control and regulation and their supersession by those of competition, of business enterprise, of improvements in communication and of technological innovation. There must also have been many subtler in-fluences resulting from deep-seated stirrings within society—changes ·in religion and conditions of religious tolerance, scientific advances and a political situation in which government, if not giving active support to industrial enterprise, was at least acquiescent. Conditions of relative stability in Britain must also have been important. The country became a haven for political and religious refugees, many of whom brought with them manufacturing techniques and the enterprise necessary to put those techniques into practice. There were also natural advantages in the availability and, in some cases more importantly, the close proximity to each other of raw materials such as good quality sheep pasture, iron ore and coking coal and consistently flowing streams for power. Also to be considered must be those entirely fortuitous occurrences such as the succession of good harvests in the 1730s, which contributed to general prosperity and the creation of surpluses, and thus helped to generate a climate within which the other components of change could interact more satisfactorily.

We are not here primarily concerned with the causes of the Industrial Revolution but more with the fact of its occurrence and its physical effects on society and the landscape. Nevertheless it is worthwhile looking a little deeper into causes in order to gain some understanding of the enormous changes brought about by industrialisation, and to follow them through into the period of the Industrial Revolution itself. Firstly, population. This was increasing at the end of the seventeenth century in parallel with a gradual increase in food supplies. The population of England in 1700 was probably slightly more than 6 millions; it had increased to 6½ millions by about 1750 and then started climbing rapidly to reach just over 9 millions by 1801, the date of the first census. Economic expansion in the first half of the eighteenth century was facilitated by two decades of good harvests after 1730. The increase of real incomes provided a market incentive, a stimulus to producers of goods and imported commodities. The increase in foreign trade, in addition to the new home demand, was opening up colonial markets to home manufacturers. Population growth, therefore, was only one of the features of this first phase of industrial growth. But was it in fact a cause or a consequence of the economic changes? The dramatic growth rate after 1770 may have been a result of the rise in birth rate, itself resulting from the demand for labour leading to earlier marriage and therefore earlier parenthood. On the other hand social and economic factors such as improved food supply and better clothing and housing substantially reduced the death rate, a trend accentuated by the beginnings of smallpox inoculation and improved medical knowledge applied to the feeding of children. In the middle of the eighteenth century, however, the initial growth took place before the period of rapid economic expansion and must therefore be regarded as one of its causes. What is also certain is that once the balance had been tipped in favour of self-sustained growth, an increased number of consumers and workers became a necessary condition of further industrially based economic advance.

Population growth was by no means evenly distributed and, once industrialisation had got under way, the effects of a reorientation of the population axis were, in terms of landscape changes, of very great importance. Fig 1 shows population distributions at the beginning and end of the eighteenth century. In 1700 the population was thickest along a line running south-west to north-east through the fat agricultural lands of lowland England. By 1800 that axis had been turned through 90 degrees and there it still lies today. The areas in which industry was centred saw a more rapid population growth than predominantly rural counties, which, although in a few small areas suffering a decline, continued to grow but at a less rapid rate. The growth in the new industrial areas was not generated entirely from within, there being massive migrations from the countryside.

By 1831 about one-third of England's population was engaged in industry, a proportion, but not of course a total number, which remained more or less stable throughout the rest of the century. The 'new population' was predominantly concentrated in towns and cities in the Midlands and North. Previously towns, particularly in lowland England, had been evenly spread nodal points with primarily market functions. (The area of densest population on the 1700 map, Fig 1, still has this essential character today.) After the axis had shifted, enormous urban concentrations grew up. London had always been much larger than all other towns. In 1800 it had nearly 900,000 inhabitants but there were only fourteen other towns with populations of over 20,000. By 1851 London had a population of over 2¼ millions; by then, however, there were fifty-four towns and cities with a population between 20,000 and 100,000, and seven (Birmingham, Bradford, Bristol, Leeds, Liverpool, Manchester and Sheffield) with over 100,000 inhabitants. Of these only Bristol lay outside the new axial belt of economic and population growth.

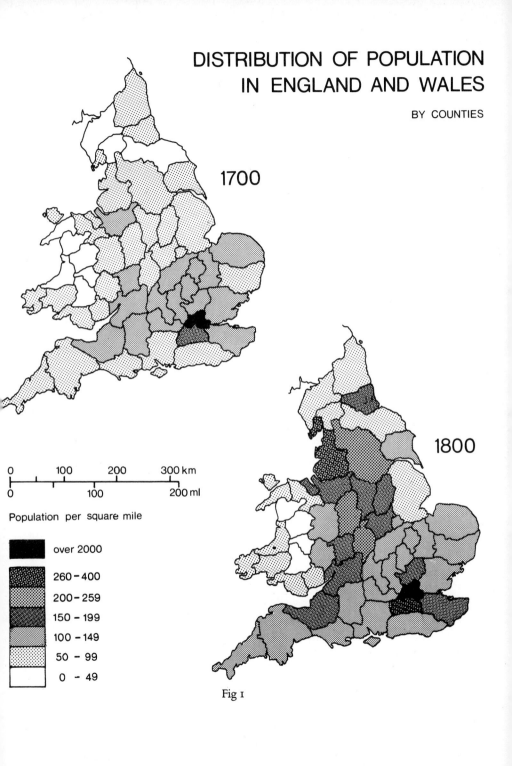

DISTRIBUTION OF POPULATION
IN ENGLAND AND WALES

BY COUNTIES

1700

1800

0   100   200   300 km

0   100   200 ml

Population per square mile

over 2000

260 – 400

200 – 259

150 – 199

100 – 149

50 – 99

0 – 49

Fig I

There were two major factors in the increased agricultural output which went hand in hand with population growth throughout the eighteenth century. The first was enclosure, the second the superior methods of husbandry and of farming technology introduced by the great improvers. Both were closely interlocked, enclosure being the essential prerequisite for the introduction of new techniques. Much of the new equipment introduced after 1750 would have been useless on the old strips of the open-field system. Similarly, introduction of new crops or rotations and methods of animal breeding was out of the question in an essentially feudal agricultural system where custom, tradition and the standards of the poorest quality cultivator were dominant. In other European countries, where enclosure lagged behind Britain, the introduction of new methods was slower and confined to large estate farms. Enclosure then was the largest single movement affecting land use, and therefore output, because it made possible all other innovations. Enclosure increased the cultivable area by eliminating the commons and wastelands which had been essential rough grazing areas under the old system, and bringing them into active agricultural use on the regular sequential basis of the new rotation farming.

By 1750 perhaps half of England (and the open-field system was confined almost entirely to lowland England) was enclosed. In some areas open fields had never existed and in others they had been long outmoded. These areas lay around the edges of a core of unenclosed land with counties such as Northamptonshire at its centre. The south-west and the grass counties of the Welsh marches, the north-west and the south-eastern counties of Suffolk, Essex, Sussex and Kent were all substantially or completely enclosed by the middle of the century. For the remainder of England the major period of the enclosure movement was 1760–1815, when most enclosures, in contrast to the earlier period, were made as the result of Parliamentary awards. Over 1,000 Acts covering 7 million acres were passed between 1760 and 1800, with a further 800 by 1815. The first batch related generally to areas where grazing and cattle-fattening were the dominant forms of husbandry, and the latter mainly to arable land, whose enclosure was stimulated mainly by the rise of grain prices during the Napoleonic wars. These enclosures took in most of the remaining open fields. Today one or two areas still survive— Laxton in Nottinghamshire and Portland in Dorset, for example—where traditional practices are continued.

The sequence of events, therefore, was firstly the introduction of new theories and new crops in the seventeenth century, such as Townshend's turnip-fed stock, followed by the first stages of mechanisation promulgated by men like Jethro Tull. Diffusion of these ideas on a wide scale came later with enclosure and with the increased demand resulting from a growing population, particularly in towns.

Capital availability was significant to this 'agricultural revolution', but it was much more important to the new industrial entrepreneurs. The early growth of banks, not only in London but in country areas too, made short-term credit available for agriculture, industry and transport. By 1780, when there were 100 banks outside London, a network of credit extended throughout the country, facilitating the transfer of funds, the settling of debts and the obtaining of cash. By the late 1820s there were 554 country banks, after which numbers declined as they were absorbed into the big joint-stock banks with their networks of branches.

The banks did not, however, provide the key to the much larger quantities of capital required by industrialists to launch their enterprises. Most manu-facturing industry was in the hands of family businesses or partnerships in the middle of the eighteenth century. This was to some extent inevitable, as without the protection of Limited Liabilities Acts (which did not come in until 1855–62) each partner in an unincorporated business was totally liable for its debts, however little he had invested in it. The 'South Sea Bubble' Act of 1720 had limited the number of shareholders to eight, so unless the company was set up by Act of Parliament, as a few large enterprises like canals and later railways were, the corporate responsibilities carried by those in industry were considerable. Partners tended, therefore, to be found within the framework of a family or a church where the ties of trust were strongest. With some sectors of the community, such as the Quakers, family and faith were often inextricably interwoven, and the fact that they were debarred from political positions made them turn to those avenues which were open to them—industry and commerce.

Most of the capital that financed the early phase of the Industrial Revolu-tion came from two main sources. Firstly, there was accumulated capital, the result of the more or less continuous expansion in the economy in the middle years of the eighteenth century before industrialisation really got under way. Accumulation of capital in the hands of landowners and merchants, for example, was considerable, and much of this found its way into industry, often industry within the family network. 'Outside' capital was the other source, the investment by many sectors of the community of relatively small sums in an industrial enterprise. The landed aristocracy, traditional holders of wealth, were frequently energetic investors and in many cases financed new industries directly themselves, but the savings of the professional classes, craftsmen and working men, often through their friendly societies, found its way into industry also. One of the great strengths of industry in Britain, and conversely one of the greatest heartaches when a company failed, was the broad base of industrial investment, seen at its extreme in the capitalisation of the railways.

Another important factor was that, for many industrial enterprises, the cost of the initial fixed assets was relatively low, so it was possible to start on a small scale and expand almost entirely on the reinvestment of profits. Technology was relatively simple and the cost of buildings and equipment not inordinately large. Given technical expertise in the process, perhaps the most valuable single asset in setting up a new manufacturing firm, it was not too difficult to make a start. The number of skilled craftsmen who left established organisations to set up on their own with no more than the traditional 'life's savings' was considerable, and an almost typical feature of some sections of industry.

We have mentioned population increase as an important factor, representing both a new source of labour and also a new market for manufactured goods. Of increasing significance throughout the eighteenth century also was the development of Britain's overseas trading connections. In the 1570s England had one major export commodity in woollen cloth, which accounted for some 80 per cent of the value of her trade, nearly all of which was with North Sea ports or the Atlantic seaboard of Europe. By the 1770s she had a wide range of manufactured exports, of which wool still constituted the largest, and a big re-export trade in colonial and export goods. Her trade extended not only throughout Europe but to America, Africa, India and China. Indeed the century after about 1660 has been titled the period of the 'Commercial Revolution', so important was it to the development of merchant organisation, to capital accumulation and investment and to the market opportunities which were provided to the new industries.

Firstly, the collapse of Antwerp in the late sixteenth century as the entrepot for Europe led, after a period of initial uncertainty, to English merchants having to seek their own connections, by sea, with their European markets. Because the system of money transfer by bills of exchange was not developed in these new markets, merchants were bringing back materials for which there was initially no immediate home sale, including coarse linens, sugar, drugs, cotton, silk, flax, hemp and timber. In consequence, a thriving re-export business developed at the beginning of the seventeenth century, but it gradually declined as the home market became more sophisticated and as new, often port-located, industries grew up; these industries sometimes used immigrant labour, as with silk weaving, to absorb these readily available raw materials. London began to assume the position once held by Antwerp, becoming the base for merchants and, as the eighteenth century progressed, for financiers, bankers, insurance companies and shipping underwriters.

Before 1640 there was little home demand for the products resulting from Britain's small but increasing long-distance trade with Asia and America, which was beginning to thrive on the re-export business. Indeed Europe, by far the largest single market until well into the nineteenth century, had great attractions to Britain, whose direct access to distant ports enabled her to re-export directly or process and then re-export the imports resulting from this trade. The notorious triangular trade with West Africa and the Americas developed in this way, with weapons and 'toys' from Britain being exchanged for slaves in West Africa, and those slaves exchanged for sugar, tobacco, dyestuffs or hardwood in the West Indies. These imports were frequently processed in London, Bristol or Glasgow and then re-exported to Europe. As home demand grew, however, the need to re-export died away, and completely new imports provided the basis for industrial growth. The Lancashire fustian industry and the Nottinghamshire cotton hosiery trade were both based initially on imported Indian cotton. In a city like Bristol a high proportion of the considerable industrial activity became based on imported raw materials for eventual home consumption. Sugar refining, sherry blending and wine bottling, chocolate making, tobacco processing, logwood dye manufacture, even cotton spinning and weaving for a short time, all grew up in or around Bristol because it was the place of import and thus the logical break-of-bulk point at which to carry out processing.

By the latter part of the eighteenth century the 'Commercial Revolution' of the previous 100 years had provided Britain with trading connections throughout the world, had made London the financial and mercantile centre of Europe and was producing an accumulation of capital much of which was finding its way into industrial investment. Much of the profit from trade went into mining and manufacturing industry. Bristol and London merchants helped finance coalmining and ironmaking in South Wales, and Glasgow and Liverpool merchants put capital into the cotton industries of Scotland and Lancashire respectively.

We have now looked at a number of the major factors which combined to trigger off the Industrial Revolution. One classic prerequisite, however, of the British Industrial Revolution, although not necessarily of others that have come since, remains to be examined—the role of technological innovation. The development of new technologies was such a remarkable and obvious feature of the Industrial Revolution that many people have regarded it as the primary cause. To them the Industrial Revolution was a technological revolution in which new manufacturing machines were driven by new sources of power in new large-scale units called factories. So enthusiastic was Samuel Smiles about this thesis that he wrote in his *Lives of the Engineers*, 'Our engineers may be regarded in some measure as the makers of modern civilization . . .', and then went on to pose the question, 'Are not the men who made the motive power of the country, and immensely increased its productive strength, the men above all others who have tended to make the country what it is?' To some extent Smiles was right, but for new inventions in technology to be relevant a whole range of other factors, such as those we have already considered, had to be there too.

Given these favourable base conditions, there also had to be a will to generate new ideas and a climate in which new ideas, if not universally acceptable, could find currency amongst other enthusiasts, who would implement, multiply and perhaps improve upon them. That climate was growing in Britain throughout the latter part of the seventeenth century and the whole of the eighteenth in the form of a new class of bourgeoisie, intelligent but not always educated, well-to-do but not always wealthy, articulate but not always cultured, who owned property, manipulated money or followed one of the growing professions. These were not often the people who created the new ideas, but they were the ones who were prepared to listen, who were capable of understanding and who were prepared to offer backing.

Another requirement of technological innovation, although not necessarily of the invention which might precede it, was need. 'Necessity is the mother of invention' is one of those catchphrases which provides a surprising amount of food for thought. The steam engines of Savery and then of Newcomen were developed because of the specific problem of draining mines and, at a much later date, Watt was almost forcibly directed into developing a *rotative* steam engine capable of driving rotating machinery because Boulton appreciated that the need was there. In the United States a different sort of necessity in the middle of the nineteenth century resulted in the development of sophisticated production machinery as a means of maintaining and increasing output in the face of an acute shortage of skilled manpower. The finished product was not necessarily any better, but the technique of making it certainly was.

Some inventions relied on intellectual genius, others on the systematic investigation of possible alternatives until the right answer came up, and others still required some almost fortuitous outside factor to intervene. Abraham Darby I was undoubtedly aware of the social and economic need for an alternative fuel to charcoal for iron smelting, although how far that need was being directly felt in Coalbrookdale in 1709 is difficult to assess. The geological accident of the eminent suitability of the Coalbrookdale 'Clod' coal for making coke for smelting purposes must be borne in mind when measuring the significance of the coke smelting technique which he perfected. Over a century and a half later another attempt to find an alternative fuel, in this case the substitution of coal for coke in locomotive fireboxes, was tortuously pursued for years, with innumerable patents and experimental designs, before the perfection of the brick arch in 1859 allowed coal to be burnt successfully. Successful invention and innovation demand a number of prerequisites — a climate of acceptability, perhaps the one feature unique in Britain in the eighteenth century; an obvious need; and an element of genius, perseverance or opportunism, or possibly all three.

Undoubtedly the cumulative effect of innovation in technology was beginning to be felt on a large scale by the end of the eighteenth century. Using the simple indicator of patents, of the 2,600 for the whole of the century, more than half were registered after 1780. We must, however, allow innovation in technology no more than its proper importance, for although the products of many of the great inventive engineers provide much of the inspiration for the study of industrial archaeology, they had relevance only when combined with entrepreneurial ability and the effective organisation of capital, the market and the methods of production. Thomas Telford was arguably an organiser of men first and foremost and an engineer second. The canal network owed little or nothing to advanced technology but much more to the organisation of large numbers of men and the mobilisation of capital. In the textile industry a whole range of closely interlinked inventions provided the baseline from which the industry could free itself from its medieval shackles, though it was in the factory, which was primarily a symbol of organisation rather than technology, that the potential of these inventions was realised. The factory system was being exploited for its organisational advantages by people like Benjamin Gott in Leeds, for example, before the advantages of power applied to a multiplicity of machines were fully realised.

It we accept that the Industrial Revolution had its beginning in the eighteenth century, when, if at all, did it end? Application of the self-sustaining growth theory has suggested that 1830 was the terminal date, the point by which the chain reaction had got going and the economy was in a state of more or less automatic and continuous growth. Certainly some industries had undergone a complete technological change by that date: the textile industry was largely mechanised and power-driven; and the iron industry, where both cast iron and wrought iron were available in quantity, was using coal instead of charcoal and the puddling furnace instead of the finery and chafery. Canals networked the country and, although not representing any major technological breakthrough, they were an essential ingredient of industrial growth both as an internal transport system and as a means of getting commodities to and from the ports. If 'revolution' in this context only means the period of change from one style of economy to another, the period when growth rate in the economy accelerated, then the choice of 1830 has some validity; but if continuity of growth, particularly growth based on new technologies and new industries, is included, that date is clearly of no significance at all. Indeed, if we assume continued growth based on technology and industry, we must seriously ask ourselves whether we are not still in the period of the Industrial Revolution.

The industrial archaeologist needs to take a much broader approach. He is looking primarily at the period of industrialisation beginning in the eighteenth century, but he has to look back beyond that date to find the antecedents, to explain the evolution of the waterwheel, to understand the transfer from charcoal smelting to coke smelting, to discover the scientific ground rules which had been established in the sixteenth century and were implicit in the development of the atmospheric steam engine. Having accepted that industrialisation is under way he must apply archaeological rather than historical criteria when trying to settle how far he goes chronologically. The period of take-off as seen by the economic historian is quite unsatisfactory for the industrial archaeologist, who is looking at the remains of industrial activity over a much longer period. To him the obsolescence of a process or of a social or economic demand for an industry must form the terminal criteria; absolute date is almost irrelevant.

Let us consider 1830 as a terminal date in relation to the whole period of industrialisation. Railways were only just beginning to be accepted, the Liverpool & Manchester Railway opening in that year. The shipping industry was still largely traditional and pre-industrial in character, although steam power was beginning to be applied. There were no iron ships, let alone steel ones. Cheap steel was still more than a quarter of a century away, with Henry Bessemer and the converter. Michael Faraday, in 1831, produced a continuous electric current, the beginnings of one of the most fundamental developments in power for industry of the latter part of the century. These events and many that have come since are the valid concern of the industrial archaeologist.

Let us examine the magnitude of the effects of industrialisation on Britain. The economic consequences are measurable and staggering in their scale. National income in England and Wales was £130m in 1770; in Great Britain as a whole in 1800 it was £230m, in 1830 £350m and in 1850 £525m. This shows a doubling of average income per head. By the end of the nineteenth century the national income had increased by a factor of about fourteen and real income per head had roughly quadrupled. Despite the traditionally pessimistic view of the horrors of industrialisation seen in terms of poverty, of appalling living conditions and of periodic heavy unemployment, the real wages of the majority of workers in British industry were rising and their living and working conditions, *on average*, were improving.

The statistics of growth for individual industries provide some of the most startling indicators of the effects of industrial activity. There were less than twenty blast furnaces in 1760. By 1790 this figure had increased to over eighty and in 1797 England became for the first time an exporter of iron and iron goods. There were 177 blast furnaces in 1805, 372 in 1830 and 655 in 1852. The majority were coke-fired after 1800. Pig iron output increased from 30,000 tons in 1700 to 250,000 tons by 1805, 650,000 by 1830 and 2 million tons by mid-century. In the cotton industry growth was still more spectacular, largely as the result of the improvements made in machine spinning by James Hargreaves, Richard Arkwright and Samuel Crompton with the introduction of the jenny, the water frame and the mule respectively. Import of raw cotton, which was less than 8 million lb per year in 1780 had risen to over 25 million lb by 1790, 37·5 million lb by 1800 and nearly 60 million lb in 1805. The 100 million lb point was reached in 1815, 250 million lb in 1830 and 620 million in 1850. The number of cotton spindles increased similarly from less than 2 million in 1780 to 21 million by the middle of the nineteenth century. Mechanisation in weaving of cloth developed slightly later but, once under way, the results in terms of production were no less remarkable. With hardly any power looms in 1820 the industry grew to have 50,000 in 1830 and 250,000 in 1850. The cotton industry as a whole employed about half a million people in 1830, of whom about half were working in factories. Over 50 per cent of total production was exported, representing in value about 40 per cent of all British exports.

'Good roads, canals and navigable rivers, by diminishing the expense of carriage, put the remote parts of the country nearly on a level with those in the neighbourhood of the town; they are, upon that account, the greatest of all improvements.' So wrote Adam Smith (1723–90) in the late eighteenth century and, without doubt, good communications provided the basis for the factory growth of the iron, the cotton, and many other industries. In 1750 there were about 1,000 miles of navigable river in England. In the following century over 4,000 miles of canals had been built, linking the main industrial areas with the rivers, ports and coalfields. What is more significant, however, is that nearly three-quarters of that canal mileage had been completed by 1800, thus providing, at the beginning of the Industrial Revolution period, the consolidation and unification of the English market that was so essential for growth. The significance of railways was still greater, and between 1840 and 1850 5,000 route miles were built, more than the whole of the country's total canal mileage. The effects of railways were felt in many fields beyond those connected directly with the transport of goods. Besides reducing the time and cost of travel and extending the communications system over a wider area than that covered by the canal network, the railways increased the mobility of labour and further encouraged concentrations of population, gave an enormous boost to the iron and engineering industries with their demand for rails and locomotives and were largely responsible for the new and widespread habit of investment in industry. By 1850, for the first time ever, a nation was devoting at least 10 per cent of its total income to capital accumulation in one form or another.

In addition to communications, coal was essential to the development of industry, and the discovery of ways of using coal where once wood had been essential was a decisive technological factor in allowing many industries to 'take off'. The use of coal to generate steam removed industry still further from its reliance on nature by reducing dependence on water power. As early as the beginning of the eighteenth century England had been unique in Europe for its large consumption of coal, probably then about 3 million tons per year. By 1800 it had grown to 10 million tons, almost entirely as the result of increased industrial activity. Coal (in the form of coke) began to replace charcoal for iron smelting and later for puddling of wrought iron, it was the primary fuel of the rapidly expanding brick industry and, of ever-increasing importance, it powered the new steam engines. By 1800 there were perhaps 1,000 steam engines in use in England, the large majority pumping water from rivers. About 250, however, were driving machines in the cotton industry and, as the nineteenth century progressed, steam engines increasingly replaced human, animal, wind and water power. Thus, by 1838 the cotton industry was using 46,000 steam hp and the woollen industry 17,000. By 1850 the textile industry as a whole was using nearly 100,000 steam-generated hp. All of this was provided by coal, the first raw material in history to be measured in millions of tons. From 10 million tons produced in 1800 output grew to 25 million tons in 1830 and 50 million tons in 1850.

These statistical indices of growth tell only a small part of the story of industrial development in Britain during the eighteenth and nineteenth centuries, covering up at a single sweep the subtleties of social change and enormities of social cost which can never be fully documented. The remains of the landscape changes wrought by industry are still there to be seen and studied by the industrial archaeologist, but the effects on ordinary people of those changes, the most radical changes of environment which any society had ever experienced, can only be pieced together from fragmentary evidence. Much of this evidence results from the observations of outsiders not directly involved themselves in industrial activity—in the diaries of travellers, the reports of commissions of enquiry, and the essays of political writers, all of which reflect to a greater or lesser extent the particular axe which their authors had to grind. Moreover, those artists who did not regard it as beneath their dignity to portray industrial subjects, provide a startling and perhaps slightly less biased insight into the nature of Industrial Revolution Britain. But despite these conscious attempts at documentation, objective or not, the real magnitude of the change in the way of life of the ordinary man as industrialisation gathered momentum and eventually became a tide carrying all before it can never be assessed. He rarely documented himself or his doings, although his songs have sometimes survived, and his artefacts— few at the time—are almost non-existent today. Only the houses in which he lived and the factories in which he worked provide today a widespread, tangible and emotive source of evidence which can be analysed, in association with oral and documentary sources, to gain some insight into his way of life, his attitudes and aspirations. The industrial landscape is the *place* where it all happened and as such represents one of the closest contacts we have with the people who made it happen.

3 Wind and Water Power

THE twentieth century has witnessed the virtual extinction in Britain of the use of wind and water power for commercial purposes. Man's earliest engines, the first mechanisms to release him from the slow and tedious labour of grinding corn by hand, have almost ceased working. The crafts of milling and millwrighting, passed on without interruption through many centuries, have also now almost disappeared, and only our nostalgia and the respect in which we hold these reminders of the beginnings of civilisation have led us to preserve both windmills and watermills in considerable numbers. A few of them are still working, and in this way we can keep alive their techniques of operation.

The earliest application of the power of water was perhaps in the first century BC, probably in Greece. The earliest known record of a watermill in England is much later, in a charter granted in AD 762 by King Ethelbert of Kent to the owners of a monastic mill east of Dover. Wind power on the other hand is of more recent usage, and although early windmills were known in Persia and Asia Minor well before the tenth century AD, they do not seem to have been used in north-west Europe until the twelfth century. The earliest known in England appears in a documentary reference of AD 1158 recording a corn mill in the village of Weedley in Yorkshire. It is just conceivable that such early English mills, which are recognisable from illustrations as post mills, were the first of their type, for there was a noticeable spread of them eastward through Europe during the thirteenth century, suggesting that they may have developed quite independently of the primitive windmills of Persia. If this is so, it represents a significant reversal of the prevailing flow of ideas from the East, and may be the first example of West European technology to find widespread use.

Wind power had nothing like the impact water had on the growth of industrialisation, for while the waterwheel developed into a reliable, controllable and powerful prime mover for driving a wide variety of machinery, often in very large factories, the windmill kept very much to its traditional role of grinding corn and draining low-lying land. Considerable efforts were

made to improve its efficiency, but the inherent unreliability of the wind
prevented it being used to drive manufacturing equipment where regular
hours of work and continuity of output were essential. It is worthwhile
therefore considering the windmill first, as the story of its evolution and
decline is outside the mainstream of events that led up to and carried forward
the large-scale industrialisation of Britain during the eighteenth and nineteenth centuries. Indeed the improvements made to the windmill, all of
which came after the waterwheel and steam engine were well established,
may be regarded as products of the new technology, used to increase the
efficiency and reliability of existing capital equipment in an area where
investment potential was low.

The question of availability of capital was an important one, as a major
obstacle to the use of power during the sixteenth and seventeenth centuries
had been cost, a factor which remained relevant in some agricultural areas
almost to the end of the nineteenth century. The capital involved in a windmill or watermill relative to the power generated was fairly high, so there
was a tendency to perpetuate man- or, more frequently, animal-powered
equipment. At a later date the same factors militated in favour of the waterwheel when it came to the question of its replacement by steam power. A
number of disused horse-powered mechanisms still survive, mainly those
employed for driving farm machinery, but also a few used to raise coal or
water. More often the building alone remains. In a county like Durham,
where horse gins were exceptionally numerous, a typical feature of many of
the farms is an octagonal building with a pointed roof; such buildings once
housed a horse walking endlessly around a central spindle coupled by drive
shafts to machinery.

WINDMILLS

The earliest type of windmill in England was the post mill (Plate 1);
its body, which contained the machinery and on which the sails were
mounted, stood on a central post about which it could be rotated to bring
the sails into the wind. The absence of a dominant wind in Britain meant
that the simpler type of uni-directional mill which originated in east and
south Europe could not be adopted. None of these medieval mills survive,
but illustrations are profuse, all showing the post mill in a form almost
identical to those existing today. St Margaret's Church, King's Lynn,

1 A post mill: Drinkstone,
Suffolk

Norfolk (124/TF 617197), has a mid-fourteenth century memorial brass
depicting a post mill, and representations carved in wood can be seen on a
fifteenth-century misericord in Bristol Cathedral (156/ST 584726) and on a
sixteenth-century bench end in the parish church of Bishops Lydeard,
Somerset (164/ST 168298). This last example clearly shows the sails in their
earliest form, symmetrically mounted on the stocks.

The post mill, even today, is remarkable for its technical ingenuity,
representing one of the medieval carpenter's greatest achievements in design
and construction. It consisted of a small timber-framed building designed to
balance and pivot on a single vertical post. The post was held in position by
diagonal quarter bars resting on a pair of oak crosstrees that were arranged

at right-angles to each other and provided the base for the whole structure. The weight of the body or 'buck' of the mill was borne by a transverse beam, the 'crown tree', which rested across the top of the post and was free to rotate on it. Originally an oak pintle would have provided the centre, but later an iron gudgeon was usually fitted. The end of the crown tree carried the frame of the mill, mortice and tenon jointed and dowelled together, with timber diagonal braces providing rigidity. Very little iron was used. From the back of the buck projected a tail pole that was used like a tiller to orient the mill towards the wind. The pole was moored to wooden posts arranged around the circumference of the circle described by its tip. In some cases, such as in Chillenden Mill, Kent (173/TR 268543), a wheel on the end of the tail pole helped support some of the weight of the tail ladder.

Early post mills, like Bourn Mill, Cambridgeshire (134/TL 312580), had a simple pitched roof but most have the familiar curved shape, providing greater clearance for the brake wheel, and are generally clad in horizontal weatherboarding. From the eighteenth century it became common to enclose the underframe in a roundhouse, usually built of brick, with a conical roof. This provided useful storage and protected the frame timbers from the weather. Holton Mill, Suffolk (137/TM 402776), has a very typical roundhouse.

The earliest surviving post mills in England probably date from the beginning of the seventeenth century, when the first dated inscriptions occur; the date 1627 carved on a timber of Pitstone Mill, Bucks (159/SP 945157), is perhaps the oldest. By this time a new type of mill had been introduced from Europe—the tower mill, which possibly had its origins in the fifteenth century. In this type of mill the grinding machinery was mounted in a fixed stone or masonry tower, circular in plan and usually conical in elevation. On top of the tower was a movable cap on which the windshaft and sails were mounted. Only the cap had to be turned to bring the sails into the wind, and the drive from the windshaft was transmitted to the millstones mounted in the tower by a central vertical spindle, the main shaft. The early towers were squat and cylindrical, like those still to be seen in Spain. In Britain the type has only survived in Somerset where Ashton Mill, Chapel Allerton (165/ST 414504), is the last complete example. It is maintained by Bristol City Museum and is open to the public. The cap was usually conical and covered with thatch or tiles. A thatched cap survives, also in Somerset, at High Ham Mill (165/ST 433305).

The first tower mills had tail poles for rotating the cap and this effectively limited their height. Similarly the cylindrical shape of the tower was dictated by the angle of the windshaft, which was initially horizontal. Later the windshaft was inclined, balancing the weight of the sails and reducing the likelihood of them being lifted out of the mill by a freak wind catching them from behind. Mill towers could then be conical in shape, and much more satisfying structurally (Fig 2). Not all were circular in plan: the tower of Wheatley Mill, Oxfordshire (158/SP 589052), is octagonal and that at West Wittering, Sussex (181/SZ 797972), is circular, though standing on an octagonal base.

The third basic type of windmill in England was the smock mill (Plate 2), its name allegedly derived from its similarity in appearance to a man wearing a smock. It was basically a tower mill, the tower being built of timber, usually on an octagonal plan. At each corner a 'cant post' extended the full height of the mill, its foot resting on a timber cill, its top providing support for the circular curb on which the cap rotated. The sides between the cant posts had horizontal and diagonal framing and the whole was clad in weatherboards, often painted white. The cill was normally set on a brickwork plinth to provide a firm foundation, but in the nineteenth century brick bases as high as one or even two storeys became common and the height of the mill was no longer restricted by the availability of long timbers for the cant posts. The Willingham smock mill in Cambridgeshire (135/TL 404697) and the very fine Cranbrook Mill, Kent (172/TQ 779359), the tallest mill in England, are both of this type. The oldest English smock mill is at Lacey Green, Buckinghamshire (159/SP 819009). It was originally erected at Chesham about 1650 and moved to its present site in 1821, and although substantially complete, it is now in poor condition. The last mill to be built in England was also a smock mill, in 1929 at St Margaret's Bay, Kent (173/TR 363435).

Both tower and smock mills were surmounted by timber-framed caps of a wide variety of shapes. The cap was carried on horizontal beams that supported the weight of the sails and windshaft. It revolved on a circular curb of timber forming the top of the tower. In early mills this was greased and the cap simply slid on the smooth surface—a 'dead curb'—but later hardwood or iron rollers were fitted to form a 'live curb'. At the front of the

TOWER MILL

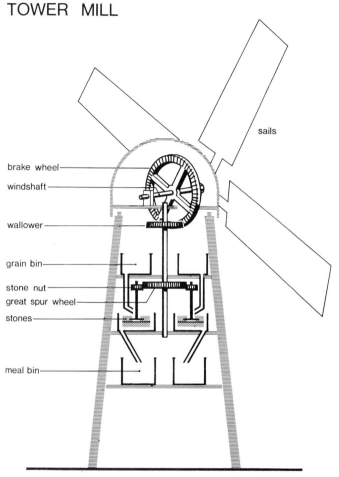

sails

brake wheel
windshaft

wallower

grain bin

stone nut
great spur wheel
stones

meal bin

Fig 2

cap the 'weather' or 'breast' beam carried the neck journal of the windshaft, the other end of which was mounted in a thrust bearing on the tail beam. The distinctive shapes of windmill caps seem to have some regional variation, although how far these are significant is difficult to assess. The simplest form is a triangular gable, as at Bembridge, Isle of Wight (180/SZ 640875), an eighteenth-century stone tower mill, cement-rendered on its weather side.

2 A smock mill: Great Thur-
low, Suffolk

In Kent, Essex, Surrey and Sussex caps are shaped like small post mills with
curved gables. Notable examples are at Herne (173/TR 184665) and Cranbrook in Kent. A variation of this type but curved in both planes to conform
more to the plan of the top of the tower is the boat-shaped cap found in the
eastern counties and exemplified by Gibraltar Mill, Great Bardfield, Essex
(148/TL 681308). Simple cones do not occur in England, as they do on the
continent, but domes have a wide distribution, ranging from Polegate
(183/TQ 581041) and Selsey (181/SZ 843933) in Sussex to West Wratting
Cambridgeshire (148/TL 604510), and Wilton (167/SU 276617) in Wiltshire.
Far and away the most exotic are the ogee mill caps of Lincolnshire, which
are made all the more prominent by the tall brick towers they usually

surmount. They occur throughout eastern England, however, with subtle variations in shape from one area to another. Some have slightly flared bases, as at Burwell, Cambridgeshire (135/TL 590665), while others achieve an almost onion shape. Some are boarded and covered in painted canvas, and others have sheet copper cladding that has often weathered green. Almost all have finials, usually in the form of a ball, though occasionally an acorn style is used.

Early windmills had simple wooden frames on which the canvas sails were spread. These frames were mounted symmetrically on stout tapering beams known as stocks, which were crossed at right-angles and morticed through the end of the windshaft. Lateral support was provided by short 'sail bars', rather like the rungs of a ladder, which were connected at their outer ends by light longitudinal 'hemlaths'. By the eighteenth century the symmetrical sail had given way to the 'common sail' seen on many mills today, in which the whole surface area was on the trailing side of the stock. A narrow windboard along the leading edge directed the air flow on to the cloth which was arranged on the front of the sail frame. 'Pointing lines' secured the canvas and were used by the miller in reefing the sails to suit the speed of the wind. As mills grew larger, it became common to construct the sails as separate units on long tapered 'whips' which were strapped and bolted to the stocks. A major point of weakness on early mills was the joint where the stocks were morticed through the windshaft, but the introduction of cast iron provided something of a solution to the problem, the end of the shaft being replaced by a massive casting known as a 'canister' or poll end into which the stocks were secured by wedges.

The common sail was light, simple and aerodynamically fairly efficient but it suffered a major disadvantage in that a change in wind speed necessitated stopping the mill and re-arranging the canvas a sail at a time. In 1772 a Scottish millwright, Andrew Meikle of East Lothian, invented a sail composed of shutters arranged like a Venetian blind and linked by a connecting rod or shutter bar which ran the length of the sail. An adjustable spring at the windshaft end maintained the shutters in the closed position under normal wind pressure but allowed them to open and spill air during gusts. Spring sails controlled by elliptic leaf springs can be seen on Outwood Mill, Surrey (170/TQ 327456), and Chillenden Mill, Kent (173/TR 268543). The miller still had to stop the mill to make adjustments to the spring tension but the automatic regulation was a valuable benefit. In 1789 a Captain Stephen Hooper introduced a roller reefing gear similar to that used on sailing craft but it found little favour.

The most significant step forward in sail design came in 1807 when William Cubitt's patent sail appeared. For the first time in nearly 1,000 years the windmill had become a controllable machine in which the sails could be matched to the wind speed while they rotated. Patent sails retained Meikle's shutters and shutter bars but at the centre the springs were replaced by bell-cranks connected to an iron 'spider'. The spider was mounted on an iron 'striking rod' which passed through the hollow windshaft and emerged at the back of the mill where it terminated in a rack-and-pinion drive controlled by an endless chain hanging down to the ground. Moving the striking rod backwards and forwards operated the shutters. A fully automatic control was achieved by hanging weights on the chain which held the shutters closed against the air pressure but still allowed spillage if wind speed increased or conditions were gusty. Patent sails are found on, for example, Cranbrook Mill and Herne Mill, Kent (173/TR 184665), and at West Wratting in Cambridgeshire (148/TL 604510) the mill combines two patent with two common sails.

Although most mills had four sails, some were built with five, six and even eight in an attempt to increase sail area and efficiency. Five sails were least common, as the loss of a sail resulted in imbalance and stoppage until a replacement could be fitted. Three five-sail mills still exist, all in Lincolnshire: Maud Foster Mill, Boston (Plate 3, 114/TF 333447), Burgh-le-Marsh (114/TF 504650) and Alford (105/TF 457766) in which the sails are mounted on an iron cross instead of the conventional poll end. Six sails were more satisfactory and a six-sail mill could still operate in balance with only four if necessary. Sibsey Mill, Lincolnshire (114/TF 344510), is an example. Of the seven eight-sail mills built in England, only one still survives, the spectacular Heckington Mill in Lincolnshire (113/TF 145436), originally built in the early nineteenth century but fitted with its present cap and sails in 1892. Bought by Kesteven County Council in 1953 and subsequently restored, the mill is accessible to the public on enquiry at the adjacent mill house.

As we have seen, it was necessary to keep the mill's sails facing into the wind, and with the medieval post mill, the miller hauled the tail pole around and moored it in a suitable position. He had to keep a constant eye on the

3 A tower mill: detail of the cap of the five-sail Maud Foster Mill, Boston, Lincolnshire

wind direction and strength to ensure efficient operation and to avoid possible disaster if the mill was 'tail winded' in a storm. Although some of the Dutch tower mills also have complex tail pole arrangements for moving their caps, in England it became general practice to rotate the cap by continuous chain operating a worm driving on to wooden cogs projecting from the curb. A good example, and one that may easily be seen, is on Bembridge Mill, Isle of Wight, but numerous variations exist, frequently with cast-iron gears and a toothed iron curb cast in segments. Fully automatic luffing of the sails came in the eighteenth century after Edmund Lee's 1745 patent for the 'fantail' or 'fly'. This early example of a servo-mechanism is very simple in principle and heralded the large number of improvements which were to culminate in the highly efficient nineteenth-century tower mills of the eastern counties. The fantail was a small wooden vaned wind-wheel fitted to the back of the mill at right-angles to the sails and coupled through gears and shafts to a winding mechanism. As the wind veered or backed, the fantail rotated and turned the sails into the wind. With the high gearing ratios used there was great sensitivity to minor variations in wind direction, so typical in England, and the fantail became a characteristic feature in other European countries as well. Generally speaking the fantail drove on to the curb of a tower or smock mill to rotate the cap but a few post mills had them also and in these cases the drive was transmitted to wheels at the foot of the 'tail pole', which ran on a circular track. Post mills with fantails include Saxtead Green, Suffolk (137/TM 254644), maintained by the Department of the Environment and open to the public, Great Chishill Mill, Cambridgeshire (148/TL 413388), Holton Mill, Suffolk (137/TM 402776), and Cross-in-Hand Mill, Sussex (183/TQ 558218).

Transmission of power from the sails to the grinding stones was modelled initially on the medieval watermill and the design of gearing passed through similar stages of development in both types. Most early waterwheels, particularly in corn mills, had 'compass arms', that is spokes morticed into the wooden shaft, which was thereby not only weakened but made liable to rotting. An initial improvement was to provide 'clasp arms', whereby the spokes embraced rather than penetrated the shaft, and in the late eighteenth century cast-iron bevel wheels superseded the traditional combination of wooden face wheel and lantern pinion. Timber gears were never entirely displaced, however, and many can still be seen in both windmills and watermills. So too can morticed gears in which wooden teeth, usually of hornbeam or apple, are wedged into a cast-iron wheel which runs against the teeth of an all iron gear. This arrangement runs quietly with the minimum of wear.

In the windmill the general arrangement of the drive was from the great face wheel or 'brake-wheel' mounted on the windshaft to the 'wallower' on the top of the vertical main shaft running down the centre of the mill body or tower. A 'great spur wheel' on the main shaft drove a small 'stone nut' on top of the 'stone spindle', which in turn rotated the upper runner stone. Early mills had one pair of stones, but as post mills increased in size, a second pair were usually included.

Grain was fed to the millstones by gravity. Corn was initially taken by sack hoist, which was usually powered by the sails, to the top of the mill where it was put in the grain bin. A chute took it to a hopper above the millstones and the grain trickled from the bottom of the hopper into a 'feed shoe' which was vibrated by the 'damsel', an extension of the stone spindle in the form of a cam. As the upper or runner stone revolved, grain was fed into the eye to be ground and expelled at the outer circumference of the stones. Only the upper stone revolved, and it did not come into contact with the stationary bedstone below. The space between the surfaces of the stones was carefully controlled to produce the best results. Nevertheless the meal falling away from the rim of the stones into the meal spout and finally into the bin on the floor below is surprisingly warm to the touch, an indication of the considerable power absorbed in the grinding process. Keeping the stones in correct relation to each other is known as 'tentering' and taxed the ingenuity of both millwright and miller to find a means of carrying out the operation automatically. The distance apart of the stones must relate to the speed of the mill, so a number of factors had to be related. As we have seen, the fantail and various automatic patent sails were in effect regulators or servo-mechanisms. Another type, which probably originated in mills, was the centrifugal ball governor in which two bob weights when rotated at speed moved outwards from the drive spindle. This movement could be coupled to brake the speed of the sails or, more commonly, to regulate the distance apart of the millstones. The use of these governors in windmills and watermills almost certainly predates their introduction and patenting by James Watt for regulating the supply of steam to steam engines.

Many mills operated two types of stone and both can frequently be seen today, in mills or standing decoratively in the open, often an indication that a windmill or watermill nearby has gone out of use or been demolished. Derbyshire Peak stones of grey millstone grit were used for barley, but flour was usually processed on the harder French burr stones which were more suitable for finer grinding. These latter stones were not cut from a single piece, as were the Derbyshire ones, but built up out of sections of quartz cemented together and bound with iron bands. The surfaces of the stones had a series of radial grooves in them which facilitated the grinding of the grain and encouraged the resultant meal outwards towards the rim.

The stones would be dressed from time to time by recutting the grooves using hardened steel mill bits wedged into a mason's maul. Not all stones revolved in the same direction, although millstones which revolved clockwise were easier to dress. This usually implied an anti-clockwise rotation of the sails in the normal post mill. It is always possible to work out which way the sails rotated on a derelict or disused mill by examining the sailstock or whip, which was always at the leading edge of the sails, or by observing the wear on the gear teeth.

Not all windmills were for grinding corn, their other major use being for drainage of low-lying areas such as the Fens. Wind power was used extensively from the sixteenth century onwards in the numerous Fenland drainage schemes and a number of windmills still survive, although no longer working. Naturally enough they derive some of their design features from Holland and many had a distinctly Dutch look, with squat towers, common sails and tail poles. Most early drainage mills were of the smock type but later examples were brick, often tarred. The machinery inside was much simpler than that in a corn mill. A conventional brake wheel on the windshaft drove the wallower on the vertical shaft, which at ground level had a bevel gear that drove in its turn a pit wheel on a horizontal shaft. On the other end of this shaft, usually on the outside of the windmill structure, was a scoop wheel which lifted water up and discharged it at a higher level. Sometimes, as at Horsey, a turbine pump was used.

Today few drainage mills survive intact, their decline beginning quite early in the nineteenth century when large capacity steam pumps were installed, each one capable of replacing a number of windmills. Fine examples of mills can still be seen, however, at Wicken Fen, Cambridgeshire (135/TL 562706), belonging to the National Trust; Horsey Mill (126/TG 457223) and Berney Arms Mill (126/TG 465051), both in Norfolk. This last mill, said to be the tallest in East Anglia, has a 70 ft tower and is preserved by the Department of the Environment. A curious features is that the scoop wheel is separate from the mill itself and connected to it by a rotating drive shaft. It is also unusual in being used for grinding cement clinker and having access only by rail or water.

Although the traditional mill is now completely obsolete, a much more recent counterpart, which enjoyed considerable popularity down to the 1930s, can still be found fairly commonly. Wind pumps, used for raising water for farm use, are automatic in operation. Most types have a steel wire-braced tower, with a multi-bladed wind vane and driving a reciprocating lift pump by means of a crankshaft geared down from the windshaft. Although relatively modern, operating examples are becoming surprisingly scarce, their role usually having been usurped by electric or internal combustion engine pumps.

There are still some 300 windmills in Britain of which reasonably complete remains survive and many more in the form of derelict towers or conversions into houses. Most are in the Eastern Counties, with notable concentrations in Essex, Kent, Lincolnshire, Norfolk, Suffolk and Sussex. Many of them are preserved. There were isolated pockets of wind power in the west, however, usually in areas where surface water was unavailable or not easily utilised. In England the Somerset levels, Wirral peninsula of Cheshire and Fylde of Lancashire all once had numerous windmills, although little evidence of them now survives. Ashton Mill, Chapel Allerton (165/ST 414504), is the best Somerset example; Bidston Mill (100/ST 287894) near Birkenhead still has sails but no internal machinery, while on the Fylde, Marsh Mill, Thornton Cleveleys (94/SD 335426), is being preserved by the local District Council.On Anglesey, the single area of Wales where windmills were common, only derelict towers survive.

WATER POWER

The first watermills in Britain were for grinding corn and this purpose remained by far the most widespread use of water power. Unlike the windmill, however, water was employed to drive a wide variety of industrial equipment, beginning with the water-powered textile fulling mill that was probably developed during the twelfth century. The earliest types of waterwheel used in Britain, of which examples still survive, were called Norse mills. They had vertical shafts and inclined wooden blades rather like scoops and developed at the most about $\frac{1}{2}$hp. One Norse mill preserved in Britain is Click Mill in Orkney (HY 290200), which is maintained by the Department of the Environment as an Ancient Monument. The wheel powers directly a single pair of millstones, the drive being taken through the eye of the bottom stone, which remains stationary, the top stone rotating above it.

It is known that the Romans used water power in Britain—three water-mill sites have been excavated along Hadrian's Wall, for example—but no detailed evidence survives. These Roman mills were probably very like the waterwheels used extensively in Britain from the eighth century onwards. Known generally as Vitruvian mills after Vitruvius, the engineer and architect who first described them, they had horizontal shafts with flat buckets that dipped into fast running water of a stream or river. Besides these primitive stream wheels the Romans also used overshot wheels at least as early as the fourth century AD and possibly earlier.

Little is known of the development of water power during the Dark Ages but by the *Domesday Survey*, begun in 1080 and completed in 1086, there were over 5,000 corn mills in England, most of them south and east of the Rivers Trent and Severn. These were probably of both Norse and Vitruvian types, but the latter eventually predominated. A watermill is shown in Fig 3.

By the sixteenth century water was by far the most important source of motive power throughout Europe, and Britain was no exception. Although primarily used for corn milling, water also drove fulling mills, and hammers and bellows necessary for the manufacture of wrought and cast iron, wire drawing equipment, drills for gun barrels and machinery used to hoist, crush and stamp metalliferous ores. The availability of water for driving wheels became an important factor in the location of industry, and in the manufacture of wool textiles, for instance, where manual spinning, carding and weaving were carried out as a cottage industry in East Anglia and the East Midlands, the new water-powered fulling mills set up on streams in the Cotswolds, Yorkshire, the Lake District and the West of England drew the other processes to them. Similarly the iron industry, although primarily located near raw materials such as iron ore and charcoal, took advantage where possible of streams to power hammers and bellows. In Kent, Sussex and Surrey where the industry was centred this was not always easy, as streams were inconsistent in flow. In summer men might have to work the wheels like treadmills to keep things going. In the Lake District and Shropshire, however, two other areas where blast furnaces in particular became established, the streams had a more consistent flow, and it is interesting to speculate on how influential this factor was in encouraging the industry to these areas.

WATERMILL

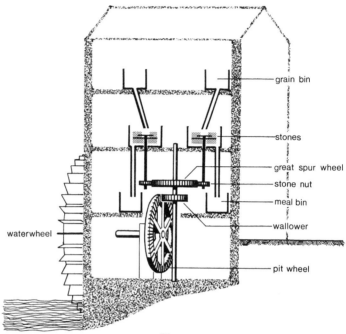

Fig 3

By the sixteenth century too a corpus of knowledge on waterwheel technology was being established. John Fitzherbert's *Boke of Surveyinge and Improvements*, published posthumously in 1539, notes that it was common to build corn mills not on large rivers but on a more convenient site served by a man-made millstream to a weir. Fitzherbert also refers to the need for an adequate fall in tailrace to minimise the disadvantages of back-watering, which in time of flood might cause the wheel to slow down through water building up below it. He also confirms that breastshot and overshot wheels produced more power than undershot wheels if their buckets were well filled, and that water should, as far as possible, be prevented from leaving the buckets before they reached their lowest point by the building of a close fitting breast of brick or stone shaped to the profile of about a quarter of the wheel and only an inch or so from it. Types of waterwheel are shown in Fig 4.

TYPES OF WATERWHEEL

Stream

Horizontal
or
Norse mill

Undershot

Breastshot

High
breastshot

Low
breastshot

Overshot

Pitchback

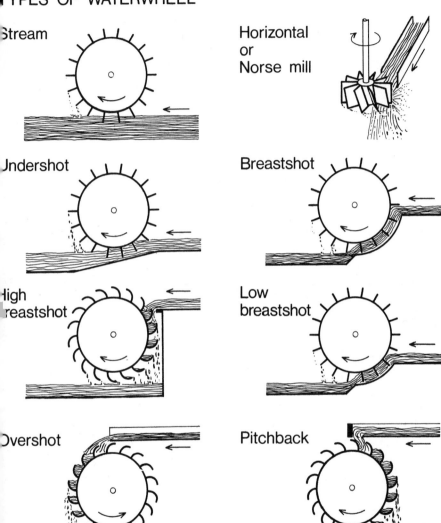

Fig 4

As industrialisation got under way in the early years of the eighteenth century, the simple undershot wheel was then the most numerous in Britain. It was cheap and easy to install, needed a minimum of groundworks to arrange its water supply and did the job for which it was required effectively if not efficiently. Mechanical inefficiency was of little importance if there was adequate water in the stream all the year round to drive a low hp wheel reliably. Only when greater power was demanded from limited supplies of water did other types of waterwheel become necessary. Thus in the eighteenth century eminent engineers such as John Rennie (1761–1821) and Sir Marc Isambard Brunel (1769–1849) used large undershot wheels to drive saw mills at Dartford and Chatham. One important modification in the design of the undershot wheel was made in the early years of the nineteenth century by J. V. Poncelet (1788–1867), and became widely adopted where maximum efficiency was required from a small head of water. By curving the paddles or blades of the wheel, as shown in Fig 4, he provided for the entry of water into the compartments without shock, the idea being that water would run up the surface of the vanes, come to rest at the inner diameter and then fall away from the wheel with practically no velocity. This design raised the efficiency of the undershot wheel from about 22 per cent to about 65 per cent.

Between 1750 and 1850 the waterwheel came into its own for industrial purposes, well after the steam engine had become firmly established. Water had been the primary source of power in the early years of the Industrial Revolution and the steam engine was at first as much a product of industrial growth as a contributor to its development. Waterwheels were cheap and easy to install and could drive machinery which the early non-rotative steam engines could not. Indeed the steam engine was used in the middle of the eighteenth century to pump back the tail water of the waterwheel and even to supply water to wheels which had no stream supply of their own. For example, Bedlam furnaces, built on the bank of the Severn at Ironbridge in 1757, relied on a Newcomen type steam engine to lift water from the river to drive an overshot and undershot wheel on each of the two sets of bellows. It is significant too that almost all the really high hp waterwheel installations, developing more than about 100 hp, were built between 1820 and 1850, long after the rotative steam engine had become well established.

4 Rossett Mill, Denbighshire. A seventeenth-century watermill with a nineteenth-century wheel

A major contribution to the improvement of waterwheel design resulted from the experiments of John Smeaton (1724–92), who built and tested models to determine the most efficient type of wheel. He established the principle that there must be considerable losses when a jet of water strikes the flat blade of an undershot wheel, and that it was clearly much better to develop power by filling the buckets of an overshot or breast wheel with water and doing the work by gravity rather than by impulse. Smeaton also introduced the first cast-iron shaft in 1769, which was fitted to the waterwheel of a furnace blowing engine at the Carron Ironworks in Scotland. This in itself was an important step forward as one of the major problems with developing a large output waterwheel was designing a shaft capable of transmitting the power. Smeaton's iron shafts were strong, and although they did not solve all the difficulties—they were subject to fracture in the region of the flanges—they provided some sort of answer to the problem until better designs were evolved. Plates 4 and 5, Rossett Mill, show a cast-iron shaft with wooden arms.

5 Rossett Mill. Detail of wheel showing cast-iron shaft and wooden arms

Metal construction throughout followed in the early years of the nineteenth century with cast iron replacing wood. Buckets were made of curved sheet iron, with the inlet angle carefully designed to reduce the shock loss of water entering the wheel and the bucket shaped to retain as much water as possible during the descent. As the size of waterwheels increased, both in diameter and width, trouble was experienced with air locks as the water entered the buckets and also, when water in the tailrace was high and the bottom of the wheel submerged, with water leaving. The remedy was found by Sir William Fairbairn (1789–1874) who described it thus:

It was observed that when the wheel was loaded in flood waters, each of the buckets acted as a water blast, and forced the water and spray to a height of 6 or 8 feet above the orifice at which it entered . . . in order to remedy it openings were cut in the sole plates, and small interior buckets attached, inside the sole . . . The air in the bucket made its escape through the opening and passed upwards . . . permitting the free reception of the water . . . The buckets were thus effectively cleared of air as they were filling . . .

Fairbairn claimed an increase of power resulting from this modification of some 25 per cent.

From the end of the eighteenth century the use of high hp waterwheels for driving factories posed new transmission design problems. Wheels developing as much as 100 hp were becoming common, and contemporary wheel shafts, even those made of iron, could not transmit this power at the low speeds then employed. The difficulty was overcome by taking the power from the wheel at its periphery where a segmental gear wheel, usually of cast-iron sections attached to the rim or spokes of the waterwheel, drove a smaller pinion wheel. Thus the secondary shaft rotated at a much higher speed and the wheel shaft had only to be strong enough to support the weight of the waterwheel itself. Spokes too could be of lighter section as they no longer transmitted power, the ultimate result of this trend being the suspension wheel in which the spokes, like the spokes of a bicycle wheel, were of thin section and in tension rather than compression. Generally speaking the position of the power take-off on waterwheels with a rim drive was as close as possible to where the power was being generated—immediately below the sluice through which water entered the wheel.

The suspension wheel was developed by Thomas Cheek Hewes (1768–1832), an engineer and textile machine manufacturer of Manchester, in association with William Strutt (1756–1830) of Derby. Hewes was an early pioneer in the application of cast and wrought iron and for a short but crucial period in 1816–17 employed William Fairbairn (later Sir William), who later achieved much greater renown. Thwaite Mill, Hunslet, Leeds (96/SE 318312), rebuilt in 1823 by Hewes and Wren, still uses water power in the manufacture of putty. Perhaps the finest suspension wheel still in existence was made by the same firm in 1826 for Woodside Mills, Aberdeen, and is now preserved in the Royal Scottish Museum, Edinburgh. The wheel is 25ft in diameter and 21ft wide. It generated over 200 hp with an 18ft head of water, transmitting power by a rim gear of twelve cast-iron segments. There are forty-eight wooden ventilated buckets, twelve wrought-iron spokes of 2½in diameter on each side of the wheel and a similar number of diagonal wrought-iron braces. The shaft, of cast iron with a cruciform section, is of a type known as a feathered shaft. Similar ones can be seen at Thwaite Mill, Leeds, and Styal Mill, Cheshire (101/SJ 834830), although the latter no longer has the wheel itself. Another large suspension wheel is at

Hartlington Mill, Burnsall, Wharfedale (90/SE 042609). Unfortunately these most sophisticated of waterwheels, nearly all of which were installed to drive factories, have largely disappeared as the result of the competition from steam engines during the latter part of the nineteenth century. Thus, while many hundreds of relatively primitive wheels in rural corn mills survive, very few high hp industrial waterwheels still remain *in situ*.

Not all large wheels were of the pure suspension type although a number had lightweight spokes. An example is the 33 ft diameter overshot wheel at Killhope lead mill in Weardale, County Durham (84/NY 827429). Here the spokes are of flat section wrought iron and rigidity is maintained by cross bracing. The wheel once drove lead crushers which, like the wooden launder that supplied its water, have now gone. The site is preserved as part of a Durham County Council picnic area. Another large diameter wheel is at Lothersdale Mill, Keighley, Yorkshire (95/SD 959459). Built in 1861 it is 44ft in diameter, 5ft 1in wide and has an unusual arrangement of alternating wooden spokes and wrought-iron tension rods. It is a high breast wheel with U-shaped floats of sheet iron and there is an outside rim drive. It powered cotton spinning and weaving machinery until the 1930s. At Foster Beck Mill, Pateley Bridge, Yorkshire (91/SD 148664), is a fine external breast wheel 35ft in diameter. It has wooden spokes and rim drive but no bracing, and the 'penstock' from which the water was fed to the wheel through a sliding hatch or 'shuttle' is particularly conspicuous. The wheel drove a hemp mill which has now closed and the machinery has been removed.

The largest waterwheel ever built in Britain is the celebrated *Lady Isabella* installed in 1854 by the Great Laxey Mining Company of the Isle of Man (87/SC 432852). It is 72ft in diameter and 6ft 1in wide and was built to pump water from a lead and zinc mine 1,480ft deep. The drive was by means of a crank on the shaft and 600ft of timber connecting rods. The wheel, which has wooden spokes and wrought-iron diagonal bracing rods, is of the pitchback type (see Fig 4) in which the water is reversed in direction at the point of access, in contrast to the conventional overshot wheel where the direction of flow is continuous. This somewhat unusual feature was probably adopted as a means of securing efficient entry of water into the buckets and to avoid the constructional problems of carrying the high-level leat beyond the wheel centre as in a normal overshot wheel. Another possible advantage was that the water leaving the wheel flowed away down the tailrace in the same direction as the wheel was rotating. The *Lady Isabella* last worked the mine pumps in 1926, was restored in the late 1920s, and in 1965 was bought by the Manx Government whose Tourist Board now maintains it. During recent renovations the spokes have been replaced by steel girders, clad in timber to retain the original appearance.

In coastal areas tide mills took advantage of the fact that water could be ponded up in a small estuary or creek at high tide and used to drive a water-wheel—usually of the low breast or undershot type—over the period of low tide. There were two working shifts in each 24 hr period and, because of the successional movement of the tides, the tide miller worked somewhat unusual hours. The last operating tide mill (Plate 6) in Britain, on the River Deben at Woodbridge in Suffolk (150/TM 276847), is the subject of a preservation scheme. The mill ran until 1956 when the 22in square oak shaft of the waterwheel broke, but since then a trust has been established to raise the money necessary to restore the machinery and timber-framed building. A much less common use of water power was to drive beam pumps used in mine drainage and one incomplete example survives at

6 Woodbridge tide mill, Suffolk. The waterwheel before restoration

Straitsteps lead mine, Wanlockhead, Dumfriesshire (68/NS 855144). At one end of the beam is a broken pump rod which once went down the mine shaft. At the other end a bucket rod is connected to the beam via a crosshead moving in guides and a connecting rod. The method of operation was for the the bucket to be filled from a nearby stream supply until the weight of water caused the beam to fall, raising the other end and the column of water in the pump barrel in the shaft. When the full bucket reached the end of its travel, a valve in the bottom was triggered open, the water flowed out, and the pump end of the beam, appropriately weighted, fell, filling the pump barrel again. The Wanlockhead water-bucket engine, which is thought to date from the 1880s, is being preserved by the Leadhills and Wanlockhead Mines Research Group. It is scheduled as an Ancient Monument. A recently restored waterwheel-powered beam pump is situated at Wheal Martyn in Cornwall (185/SX 004555).

The use of water for power provides a fruitful and worthwhile area of study for the industrial archaeologist, as surviving evidence in the form of wheels and the watercourses associated with them is plentiful. There are thousands of sites, in England particularly, where a small weir, a rotting sluice-gate or a dried-up leat provide the clue to a once thriving water-powered mill or factory. Investigation of these remains is in many cases truly archaeological in nature, as although documentary or map evidence is often available to locate a watermill site, most details of its technology— what type of wheel and transmission gear was used, for example—can only be discovered by fieldwork.

A number of basic principles can be applied to help with these on-site investigations. The basic requirements of a waterwheel were a head of water to drive it, a consistent and controllable flow of water and avoidance, if possible, of the effects of mild flooding. On a large slow-flowing stream or river with a relatively low gradient the easiest and cheapest mill to build would have a short leat taking water to the wheel which, because only a low head would be available, would have to be of the undershot type. The mill might be susceptible to flooding and a more reliable siting might involve a longer leat and tailrace (to avoid water backing up on the wheel) and per-haps a low weir in the river. By using a long leat a greater head of water would be made available, and a breastshot or overshot wheel might be installed to provide greater power for a given size of wheel. If the stream or river was particularly susceptible to minor changes in level, a long weir placed diagonally across the stream could minimise these effects, combining the merits of a long leat in creating a good head of water and an efficient governor for the wheel. The longer the weir, the less variation is there in water level during spates.

If the stream supply was small or the flow inconsistent, water would have to be collected in a millpond and, in certain cases, a type of wheel that would derive maximum power from a limited supply would have to be devised. There are two ways of gaining more power from a waterwheel—increasing its width or increasing its diameter. A good example of a wide wheel is to be found at Claverton (166/ST 791644) on the River Avon near Bath, where a waterwheel provided power for a beam pump designed to lift water from the river into the Kennet & Avon Canal. Here the head is low but the supply plentiful, so to obtain the necessary power, this low breastshot wheel was built some 24ft wide. The present installation contains an interesting design modification, as the shaft of the original c 1810 wheel was not stiff enough, and a cast-iron A frame and bearing had to be fitted to provide intermediate support to the shaft, which now carries two wheels in parallel, each one 11ft 6in wide.

In situations where the volume of water was low and water storage impracticable or too expensive the only way to obtain high power outputs was by building large-diameter wheels. In some cases the supply of the waterwheel would be by a pipe, as at Pateley Bridge (91/SD 148664) and the *Lady Isabella*; with the latter the pipe approaches at ground level and rises vertically inside a stone tower to feed the top of the wheel. Another large diameter wheel where water supply has always been a problem is at Priston Mill in Somerset (166/ST 695615) where an iron overshot wheel is fed from a pond.

The factors which led to the decline of water power are more complex than might at first be imagined. The popular notion that the steam engine was immediately responsible for the elimination of the waterwheel is far from true, and many large and successful waterwheels were being installed throughout the first half of the nineteenth century. Indeed it was not until the 1840s that steam engines were being built to exceed the hp of the largest waterwheels. As late as 1834 estimates by the first four factory inspectors indicate that approximately one-third of the power used in cotton mills in Britain was from water. A further factor in the decline of water power during the latter part of the nineteenth century was the steadily increasing diversion of water from higher districts to supply the domestic needs of the new towns, while Fairbairn, writing in 1864, claimed that land drainage schemes had altered river regimes drastically, resulting in rapid run-off, a higher incidence of flooding and subsequent low water conditions, all of which were detrimental to water power users.

By the latter part of the nineteenth century, however, steam engines began to replace waterwheels, particularly in large-scale industrial locations where technology was evolving rapidly and power requirements were increasing. The rurally based industry on the other hand often continued to use the waterwheel as its main source of power, perhaps adding a small steam engine or later an oil engine as a supplementary source. There was little incentive to change from water if it did the job. Maintenance costs were low and nothing went on fuel. The major factor in bringing about the closure of the large majority of watermills (those grinding corn) was not directly related to the power source. During the latter years of the nineteenth century the increasing importation of foreign grains and the introduction of roller mills led to very large flour milling complexes being set up at the major ports. The small miller, whether he was using wind or water power, could rarely compete and almost all flour production soon passed into the hands of big companies. Today a few small corn mills are still working, mainly for the production of animal feed.

Nevertheless a surprising number of waterwheels can still be seen in operation, in most cases preserved, but indicating the very wide variety of applications in which water power has been used in very recent years. At Sticklepath in Devon (175/SX 643940) is Finch Foundry, a water-powered scythe and edge tool works with hammers and grinding wheels. Abbeydale (111/SK 325820) and Shepherd Wheel (111/SK 317854) in Sheffield also have preserved and operational waterwheels driving basically the same types of equipment, while in Cornwall the Tolgus Tin Company (189/SW 690438) uses water to drive ore-crushing stamps. At Redditch, Worcestershire (131/SP 046686), a needle mill is water-driven; and at Cheddleton in North Staffordshire (110/SJ 973526) flint grinding mills are water-powered. Working preserved corn mills include High Mill, Skipton (95/SD 989518), Nether Alderley, Cheshire (101/SJ 844763), and Preston Mill, East Linton, East Lothian (63/NT 595779).

4 Steam and Internal Combustion Engines

It is perhaps not generally realised that a high proportion of the total requirements of energy in Britain today is satisfied by steam power in the form of steam turbines, which are amongst the largest and most efficient prime movers employing heat energy, and generate most of the electricity we use. At one time the reciprocating steam engine, that is one employing a piston moving backwards and forwards in a cylinder, held this pre-eminent position, but although it has not been entirely displaced, still finding specialist applications in a number of fields, its use has declined considerably. Steam turbines, diesel engines and gas turbines have superseded it after over 250 years, during which period the steam engine was unchallenged for almost two centuries. In those 200 years Britain and many other countries were transformed into highly industrialised, technology-based societies; the significance of the steam engine in bringing about this transformation is inestimable. As a means of draining mines, of powering textile machinery, of driving railway locomotives and ships, and now of generating electricity, the power of steam, harnessed successfully in the early years of the eighteenth century, is without doubt the greatest single technological factor in the huge social and economic changes which we have called the Industrial Revolution. The significance of the steam engine far transcends its purely technical aspects; its evolution was the first major step in the liberation of mankind from toil and the development of our complex society.

THE STEAM ENGINE

In the late seventeenth century mines had become sufficiently deep to create serious problems of drainage, a difficulty overcome in some instances by the use of water-powered pumps but more often by men and horses. Severe limitations were imposed on further deep mining by the capacity and expense of mine-pumping equipment. It was into this field of outstanding need that the steam engine came as a result of the discovery that the pressure of the atmosphere could be applied to do useful work.

Before examining the evolution of the steam engine proper it will be worthwhile to consider the state of experimental science at the end of the seventeenth century and the extent of the knowledge about the atmosphere and the properties of gases at that time. As early as the first century AD Hero of Alexandria had demonstrated that gases expanded and contracted when heated and cooled respectively, but it was not until 1606 that an experiment, carried out by Giovanni Battista della Porta of Naples, used the pressure of steam generated in a flask to force the water out of an enclosed tank. He also described how a flask full of steam and with its neck in a vessel of water would draw up water as the steam condensed, the principle being that 'nature abhorred a vacuum'. The fundamental breakthrough, the realisation that the atmosphere has weight, was made in 1643 by Evangelista Torricelli (1608–47), a pupil of Galileo, when attempting to explain why a suction pump would not draw water from a depth greater than about 28 ft. After experiments with mercury he stated that the atmosphere exerted a pressure because of its weight and that this would support a column of water 28 ft high or, in the case of the much denser mercury, some 30 in in height. It was this discovery that established one of the basic principles on which the first generation of steam engines depended and also, of course, resulted in the invention of the mercurial barometer.

The power of atmospheric pressure was further demonstrated in the 1650s by Otto von Guericke (1602–66), of Magdeburg, who succeeded in evacuating a copper sphere, which resulted in its collapse. Later he evacuated the air from a cylinder having an accurately fitting piston and utilised the atmospheric pressure to raise a weight of over a ton. It was the Dutch scientist Christiaan Huygens (1629–95), and his assistant Denis Papin (1647–1712?), however, who in 1690 used the condensation of steam beneath a piston in a cylinder as a means of creating the vacuum, a great improvement on the air pump used by von Guericke. Although Papin never developed his ideas to a larger scale than an experimental model with a $2\frac{1}{2}$in diameter cylinder, he had in his grasp all the fundamentals that were to be applied in practical terms by Thomas Newcomen 20 years later.

The first practical application of steam power and a steam-generated vacuum for mine drainage was, however, not evolved from Papin's work with pistons in cylinders but derived its principles from della Porta's steam pressure and vacuum experiments of 1606. In 1698 Thomas Savery (c 1650–

1717), a Cornish engineer, patented a machine for the 'Raiseing of Water . . . by the Impellant Force of Fire'. Steam from a boiler was admitted into a closed vessel and condensed by pouring water on its outside. The resultant vacuum caused water to rise up a suction pipe through a non-return valve into the bottom of the vessel. Steam was then admitted again and the pressure drove the water in the vessel through a second non-return valve and up the delivery pipe. The major difficulties encountered with the Savery engine, the so-called 'Miners' Friend' which probably never actually operated in service at a mine, was that boilers capable of withstanding pressures of several atmospheres could not be easily made at that time and that the length of the suction pipe was limited to about 25ft, making the engine unsuitable for deep drainage work. Certainly Savery's engine never entered widespread use and there are no surviving remains. Savery's work was not completely a dead end, however, as in the late-nineteenth century the portable Pulsometer steam pump was developed on very similar principles. The main working part was an oscillating valve admitting steam alternately to two water chambers. The steam pressure acted directly on the surface of the water in the chamber and ejected it through a flexible hose. Pulsometer pumps can still be seen occasionally, their main use being for draining excavations and flooded mines, and ship salvage. Lightweight internal-combustion engine pumps are supplanting them.

To return to the early development of the steam engine, it was in Papin's piston and cylinder experiments that the germ of the commercially successful machine lay. Papin did not pursue his experiments but Thomas Newcomen (1663–1729), an ironmonger of Dartmouth working on similar principles but almost certainly without knowledge of the Dutch scientist's work, was actively pushing towards a practical application. Newcomen was well aware of the critical drainage problems in the Cornish tin mines, and after pursuing experiments for some 15 years in an attempt to find a solution, he erected his first engine in 1712 (Fig 5). Curiously this was not in Cornwall but at a colliery near Dudley Castle, Worcestershire. It had a cylinder of 19in diameter, a stroke of 6ft and developed some 5½ hp.

The principle of operation was both simple and extremely reliable and, at least as important, no advanced technology was involved in the engine's manufacture or erection. An open-topped vertical cylinder contained a piston connected through a piston rod and chain to the arch head of a

NEWCOMEN'S ATMOSPHERIC ENGINE, 1712

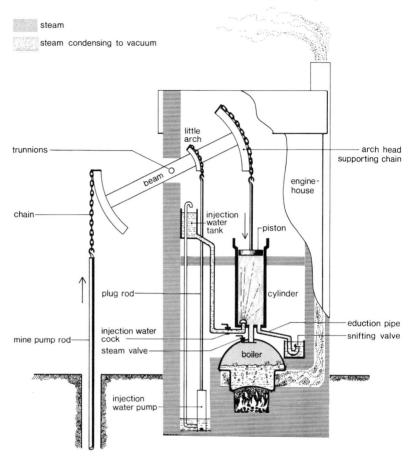

steam

steam condensing to vacuum

little arch

trunnions

arch head supporting chain

beam

engine-house

chain

injection water tank

piston

plug rod

cylinder

injection water cock

eduction pipe

snifting valve

mine pump rod

steam valve

boiler

injection water pump

Fig 5

rocking beam. The 'piston ring' consisted of a disc of leather cupped upwards and kept pressed against the bore of the cylinder by a layer of water
on top. From the end of the beam distant from the steam cylinder the pump
rods were suspended. Below the cylinder was mounted a boiler which was
little more than a tank of water with a fire beneath it and rather like a
brewer's copper in appearance. When steam at slightly above atmospheric
pressure was admitted into the cylinder, the piston was drawn upwards by

the weight of the pump rods on the other end of the beam. At the same time any air in the cylinder was ejected through non-return valves. Closure of the steam inlet valve was followed by condensation of the steam in the cylinder by a jet of cold water which created a partial vacuum and allowed the unbalanced atmospheric pressure on the top of the piston to push it down, raise the pump rods and thus make a working stroke. The cycle was then repeated, the steam valve and injection cock being opened and closed by a plug rod also hung from the beam.

Newcomen's initial design was thoroughly practical and was little altered for more than half a century. At first royalty payments had to be made to Savery, whose original patent covered all methods of raising water by fire, but after 1715, when Savery died, a group of speculators, including Newcomen himself until his death in 1729, acquired the rights and administered them until they expired in 1733. By the time of Newcomen's death his engine was in use throughout Britain and in Hungary, France, Belgium and possibly Germany and Spain. It is doubtful if Newcomen gained much, if any, financial benefit from his invention, which with the possible exception of Abraham Darby's perfection of coke smelting of iron ore, perhaps constituted the most important single technological factor in bringing man into the modern world.

One of the most important surviving memorials to Thomas Newcomen is the Hawkesbury engine, re-erected in the Royal Avenue Gardens, Dartmouth (188/SX 879515), and opened to the public in July 1964 to commemorate the 300th anniversary of its inventor's birth. The engine probably dates from the mid-1720s and is the oldest steam engine in existence. It was originally installed at Griff Colliery, Warwickshire, later moved to Measham, and in 1821 was installed on the bank of the Coventry Canal at Hawkesbury Junction (132/SP 363846), where it was used to raise water from a sump into the canal itself. The engine was occasionally worked until 1913 and in 1963 was presented to the Newcomen Society by its owners, the then British Transport Commission. Incidentally the canal-side site at Hawkesbury is in itself still well worth a visit as a relatively unspoilt junction with cast-iron bridges and boatmen's pub.

A number of modifications may be seen on the Hawkesbury engine, the most significant of which is the 'pickle-pot' condenser below the cylinder, an improvement in design to increase thermal efficiency and at the same time avoid an infringement of Watt's separate condenser patent, discussed below. Another surviving engine of Newcomen type stands at Elsecar (102/SE 390003) in the West Riding of Yorkshire, where it was used for colliery drainage from 1787 until 1923. Again numerous modifications have been made from the original, including replacement of the wooden beam by a cast-iron one. Condensation of the steam, however, was effected within the working cylinder by the use of a jet of cold water in almost exactly the same manner which Newcomen had applied in his first 1712 engine. The Elsecar engine (Plates 7–10) is now preserved on its original site by the National Coal Board and may be visited by arrangement with the South Yorkshire Area office at Wath-upon-Dearne, Rotherham.

Before leaving the Newcomen type of atmospheric engine it is worthwhile considering some of its constructional details and the improvements which were made in its efficiency. The atmospheric engine was a thoroughly practical machine and the techniques necessary for its manufacture were all well known to the millwrights and similar men who were responsible for its erection. Only the cylinders caused any serious problem. Initially these were cast in brass and, as no means of accurately machining the bore existed, they were rubbed smooth on the inside with abrasives. Small wonder,

7 Atmospheric beam pumping engine, Elsecar, near Rotherham, Yorkshire, preserved by the National Coal Board

8 Elsecar beam engine. Detail of beam and parallel motion

therefore, that the cylinder was the most expensive single component of the engine, exceeding even the engine-house in cost. A 1733 estimate for a Newcomen-type engine near Newcastle-upon-Tyne totalled £849, of which £150 was accounted for by the cylinder alone. By the 1740s cast-iron cylinders were becoming common and, although less efficient thermally because of their greater wall thickness, they were significantly cheaper in first cost.

John Smeaton (1724–92) was responsible for bringing about the greatest improvements in efficiency of the Newcomen engine, and a machine which he erected at Long Benton Colliery, Northumberland, in 1772 achieved a duty of 9·45 million foot-pounds of useful work per bushel (84 lb) of coal. The average Newcomen engine only achieved 6 million foot-pounds. Despite his improvements, which were largely the result of careful design and manufacture, particularly of the cylinder, Smeaton's engine had a

9 Elsecar beam engine. Detail of cast-iron beam

thermal efficiency of less than 1 per cent.

It was James Watt (1736–1819) who solved the problem of the fundamental inefficiency of Newcomen's steam engine. Watt, a first-class craftsman, was employed as an instrument maker in Glasgow University where in the winter of 1763–4 he was responsible for the repair of a model Newcomen engine which was faulty in operation. His investigations led to the realisation that enormous thermal losses resulted from having to raise and lower the temperature of the cylinder at each stroke, as steam was admitted

10 Elsecar beam engine. Open top of steam cylinder showing piston

and subsequently condensed. As he wrote later: 'I perceived that, in order
to make the best use of steam, it was necessary—first, that the cylinder
should be maintained always as hot as the steam which entered it; and,
secondly, that when the steam was condensed, the water of which it was
composed, and the injection itself, should be cooled down to 100° (F), or
lower, where that was possible.' His solution was to connect a closed vessel,
exhausted of air, to the steam cylinder by a pipe. Steam rushed into this
vessel, which was kept cool by cold water injection, and continued to do so
until all had condensed. This was the basis of Watt's separate condenser
(Fig 6), perhaps the greatest single improvement ever made in the efficiency
of the steam engine. In order to keep the condenser free of air and the
water resulting from injection and condensation, he used a pump connected

NEWCOMEN & WATT ENGINES
Showing method of condensing steam

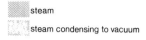

steam

steam condensing to vacuum

NEWCOMEN
condenses in cylinder

WATT
has separate condenser

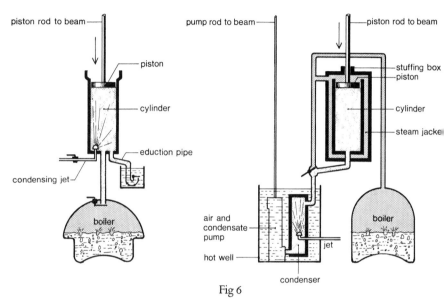

Fig 6

to the beam, while the working cylinder was kept permanently hot by means of a steam jacket. To improve efficiency still further, steam instead of atmospheric air was used to press the piston down, the piston rod passing through a steam-tight gland or stuffing box in the cover of the cylinder.

Watt patented his separate condenser in 1769 and in 1773 entered into partnership with the Birmingham entrepreneur and industrialist Matthew Boulton (1728–1809), whose works he had once visited when on a journey to London. There were only 8 years to run on the condenser patent but Watt successfully petitioned Parliament for an extension to 1800 and in 1776 completed his first two full-size engines, one for colliery drainage at Tipton, Staffordshire, and the other for blast furnace blowing at John Wilkinson's ironworks near Broseley in Shropshire. At his Broseley works

2 years earlier Wilkinson (1728–1808) had developed and patented a boring mill, initially for guns and then for steam engine cylinders. The significance of the boring mill in the success of the Watt engine cannot be overstimated as, for the first time, a large diameter bore could be cut so accurately that 'a 72 inch cylinder would not be further from absolute truth than the thickness of a thin sixpence in the worst part'. A model of a water-powered multiple-spindle cylinder boring mill can be seen in the Science Museum, South Kensington. There too are some of the most important relics of Watt's early career, including the cylinder and condenser which he probably used in his original experiments and the contents of his garret workshop from Heathfield, Birmingham. The workshop, containing some 6,000 separate items, was left undisturbed from 1819, when Watt died, until its removal in 1924 to the museum, where it has been set up in a replica room. The model Newcomen engine on which Watt carried out his earliest work on steam power is preserved in the Hunterian Museum at Glasgow University.

The first Boulton & Watt engines were an immediate success, consuming less than one-third of the coal used by the Newcomen types commonly in use, and as a result bringing enquiries from all over the country. The demand was greatest in Cornwall, where coal was expensive, so that within a few years all the atmospheric engines there had been replaced. The basis for installation of a Boulton & Watt engine was to charge a royalty equal to one-third of the saving in the cost of fuel as compared with that of a 'common' or atmospheric engine. Two engines at Poldice Mine, Cornwall, were tested and used as the standard. To register the number of strokes of the engine, from which the premium payments were calculated, a pendulum-operated counter in a locked box was attached to the beam.

Further improvements were devised by Watt, with the active encouragement of Matthew Boulton, who fully appreciated the potential market for efficient and reliable steam engines. In 1782, three important advances in design were patented by Watt. The first was to make the engine double-acting, that is to apply steam alternately on each face of the piston instead of only to the top as had been the previous practice. Thus twice the power could be developed from the same cylinder volume. The second used the steam expansively and, when perfected, resulted in considerable savings of fuel. The principle was that by closing the inlet valve to the cylinder when the piston had completed only a part of its stroke the steam already in the cylinder would still do useful work by expanding and pushing the piston through the remainder of the stroke, but with diminishing force. Although less work would be done, still less steam would be used, hence the fuel saving. At first the economies resulting were very small, but as steam pressures increased, the practice of expansive working became all-important, forming the basis for the highly efficient compound engines of the late nineteenth century.

Watt's third 1782 patent was a second best, an attempt to circumvent another idea patented 2 years earlier and possibly stolen from him by one of his own workmen. The idea of developing the steam engine to provide rotary power and thus drive machinery was exercising the minds of several engineers in the 1770s and early 1780s. The far-seeing Boulton was well aware of the huge new market that the 'rotative' steam engine could tap and pressed Watt hard to produce a satisfactory design. It is characteristic of the two that Boulton, the enthusiastic businessman, should write in 1781 '. . . the people in London, Manchester, and Birmingham are *Steam mill mad* . . .' and that the dour Watt should grumble in the following year '. . . surely the devils of rotations is afoot'. The problem was to adapt the simple reciprocating movements of the beam engine to produce rotary power. Nowadays one would imagine nothing could be simpler than the use of the common crank to connect the end of the beam to a rotating shaft, and even in Watt's time the crank was a well known mechanism in everyday use on the foot lathe and spinning wheel. What was not appreciated, however, was the fact that the variable stroke of the beam engine, which Watt at first feared would wreck any attempt to adapt it to rotary motion, would be controlled and regulated by using a connecting rod, crank and flywheel. Unfortunately for Watt another engineer, James Pickard of Birmingham, patented the crank first in 1780 after using it to replace an unsatisfactory rack-and-pinion drive to a rotating shaft. Watt held numerous patents himself and suffered throughout his life from others infringing them. Instead of contesting Pickard's patent, he thought it politic to devise a substitute. The result was the sun-and-planet or epicyclic gear in which the 'planet' wheel, fixed rigidly to the end of the connecting rod, is made to move round the perimeter of a 'sun' wheel keyed to the driven shaft. A property of this gear is that the flywheel will revolve twice for every double stroke of the piston, something of an advantage with the early and slow-moving engines. The gear was used until 1802 although Boulton & Watt built engines with cranks before and after the expiry of Pickard's patent in 1794.

Two further Watt inventions are worthy of note, particularly as they cover features familiar on almost all the beam engines surviving today. In 1784 Watt solved the problem of a satisfactory connection to transmit the simple up-and-down movement of the piston rod to the end of the beam, which described a segment of an arc. The 'parallel motion' devised by Watt combined the three-bar motion and the pantograph in a most elegant way and Watt himself stated that he was more proud of this invention than any of his others.

To ensure steady motion of the engine under variable load conditions, Watt introduced, in 1787, the conical pendulum centrifugal governor, consisting of two balls which flew outwards as speed increased to move a sleeve which by linkage controlled a butterfly valve in the steam pipe. Watt neither claimed this invention as his own nor attempted to patent it, as it had already been used in flour mills to regulate the speed and distance apart of millstones.

With the advent of rotary power generated by steam, industry was on the verge of a major technological breakthrough. By 1800, when Watt's partnership with Boulton ended and the patent on the separate condenser expired, 496 engines had been built, of which 308 were rotative. A few of these were rated at 40 hp but most had an output of between 15 and 20 hp, well within the capacities of the major prime mover in use at that time, the waterwheel. The main advantages of the steam engine, however, were its freedom from siting problems and unreliability of water flow, which restricted the widespread application of water power. Indeed Matthew Boulton's first interest in the steam engine was aroused by the lack of water for driving waterwheels in summer, the 'thirsty season'.

The distribution of Boulton & Watt engines, drawn up from the very full records of the firm's trading now housed in the Birmingham Reference Library, provides an indication of the impact of steam power on industry in the last quarter of the eighteenth century. It shows a wide dispersion both geographically and in terms of the variety of industries in which the engines were used. The poor representation of Watt engines at collieries is to some extent misleading, however, as the coal industry had actively taken up the Newcomen engine for pumping purposes and, as fuel costs were not an important factor, there was little incentive to change. Thus in the Northumberland-Durham coalfield, which had fifty-seven Newcomen type engines in 1769, only six Boulton & Watt engines were in use by 1800.

Those industries able to take greatest advantage of the rotative engine did so enthusiastically. Cotton mills, woollen and worsted mills, flax mills, textile finishing works, forges and foundries, metal workshops, pot banks and glassworks, corn mills, breweries and distilleries, canals and waterworks were all using steam to some extent by 1800. Over one-third, 114 engines, were in use in the textile industry and cotton alone accounted for ninety-two of these. Next were ironworks, with a total of thirty-seven engines, followed by collieries with thirty-three mainly for pumping, while corn mills, breweries and distilleries together employed thirty-nine engines. As Watt had a virtual monopoly of steam power until 1800, these figures represent fairly accurately the relative degree of penetration of steam power into industrial activity in Britain. The geographical distribution, shown in Fig 7, is just as interesting, illustrating the early establishment and relative importance of the industrial areas we know today. Only Shropshire and Cornwall, where the iron and tin industries respectively have declined, are over-represented in terms of today's pattern of industrial distribution. A total of fifty-five engines were in use in Lancashire, largely in the cotton industry. The next highest total, of forty-one, was in Middlesex, demonstrating the enormous, and often overlooked, significance of London as an industrial centre.

The beam engine enjoyed greatest popularity for driving machinery between 1800 and 1860, but in both its rotative and non-rotative forms it was in vogue for water and sewage pumping until the early 1900s. Few non-pumping engines are still in active use, although a number are preserved. An early example of a Watt engine, dating from 1788 and complete with sun-and-planet gear, wooden beam and centrifugal governor, may be seen in the Science Museum, South Kensington. A pair of beam engines still in regular use drive mashing and milling machinery in the Ram Brewery, Wandsworth (170/TQ 256747). Built by Wentworth & Sons in 1835 and 1867 these compound engines exhibit all the classic features, including slide valves, lattice eccentric rods (introduced by Murdock in 1799), cast-iron beams, timber-lagged cylinders and the immaculate cleanliness so typical of steam engine maintenance.

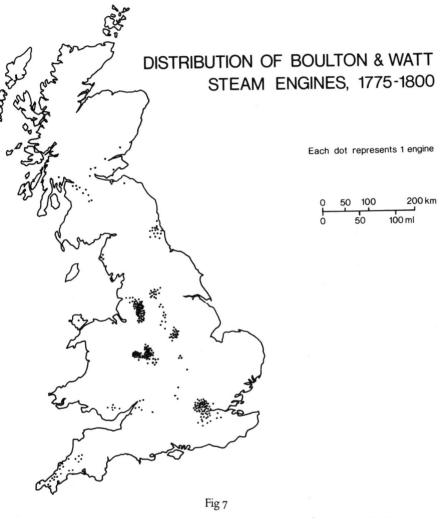

DISTRIBUTION OF BOULTON & WATT
STEAM ENGINES, 1775-1800

Each dot represents 1 engine

Fig 7

The mechanical fascination and tremendous visual impact of the large beam engine has led to numerous examples being preserved *in situ*, although all too few are in steam. At Stretham in Cambridgeshire (135/TL 517730) one survives for fen drainage. Installed in 1831 by the Butterley Company of Derbyshire, it has a single cylinder of 39in diameter and 8ft stroke and developed 105 hp at 13 to 16 rpm. A scoopwheel (Plate 11) acting, in effect,

Newcomen atmospheric beam engine

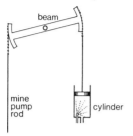

Fig 8 A Developed for mine pumping, the Newcomen engine used the pressure of the atmosphere for its power stroke. A partial vacuum was created in the cylinder beneath the piston by condensing the steam with a cold water jet.

Watt single-acting beam engine

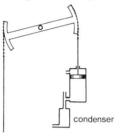

B In Watt's engine the efficiency was improved by condensing the steam in a separate vessel — the separate condenser — thus avoiding the alternate heating and cooling of the cylinder. The engine was still only for pumping

Watt double-acting rotative beam engine

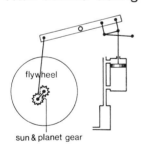

C In the rotative engine — the first heat engine to drive machinery — a number of new features were introduced. The piston had steam pressure applied to both top and bottom, making the engine double-acting. A linkage — the parallel motion — connected piston rod to beam. The other end of the beam drove a flywheel through a connecting rod and sun-and-planet gear

94

Single-cylinder rotative beam engine

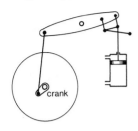

D After about 1800 the Common crank was almost universally used for the drive from the beam and connecting rod. Beam engines of this type were built in large numbers for driving all types of factory machinery down to the 1880s

Woolf compound beam engine

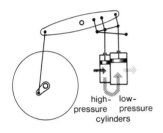

high- low-
pressure pressure
cylinders

E Efficiency was still further improved by compound expansion using a high- and low-pressure cylinder both at the same end of the beam. Woolf compound engines were widely used in water pumping stations and to a lesser extent in small factories

Cornish beam engine

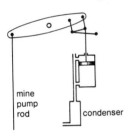

mine
pump
rod   condenser

F The Cornish engine was a highly efficient single-acting development of the non-rotative beam pumping engine, and was used extensively in tin mines. Developed by Richard Trevithick it used high-pressure steam, expansive working and condensation to obtain maximum economy

McNaught compound beam engine

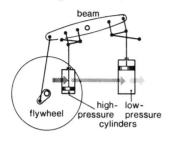

beam

high- low-
flywheel pressure pressure
cylinders

Fig 9 A Patented in 1845, the McNaught principle consisted initially of the addition of a high-pressure cylinder to the flywheel end of an existing beam engine, thus deriving compound expansion and reducing stress. Later many large beam engines were built in this form

Grasshopper engine

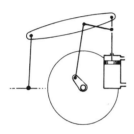

B The grasshopper engine was usually small and compact, based on a single bedplate, allowing easy instalation. The beam was pivoted at one end instead of at the centre, and the drive to the connecting rod was taken off at an intermediate point near the piston rod end

Maudslay table engine

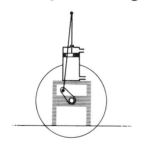

C Maudslay's table engine also had the advantage of compactness and ease of installation. The beam was dispensed with altogether and a direct connection made between the vertical piston rod and the crankshaft mounted at a low level below the cylinder. It was widely used as a small factory power unit

Single-cylinder vertical engine

D In the single-cylinder vertical engine the drive was similar but the crankshaft was mounted vertically above the cylinder. The type was used in factories and mills and for colliery winding particularly in the North East

Single-cylinder inverted vertical engine

E The inverted vertical single-cylinder engine, introduced in the 1840s, was rarely large. The type was particularly common for small factories and, with reverse gear, for marine applications. Later versions had enclosed crankcases and forced lubrication

Single-cylinder horizontal engine

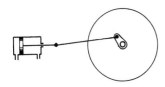

F Perhaps the most common simple type of steam engine, the single-cylinder horizontal was built in large numbers in the second half of the nineteenth century. Most had slide valves, were non-condensing and the compact cast-iron bed made them easy to install

Horizontal tandem-compound engine

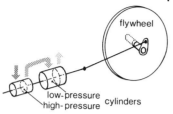

flywheel

low-pressure
high-pressure cylinders

Fig 10 A A logical development from the single-cylinder horizontal was the tandem-compound in which high- and low-pressure cylinders were mounted one behind the other on the same piston rod. Highly sophisticated, tandem compounds of medium power output were built for textile mills

Horizontal cross-compound engine

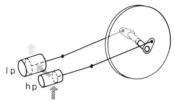

l p
h p

B Another means of compounding the horizontal engine was to have high- and low-pressure cylinders side by side driving each end of the crankshaft. Many mill engines were of this type, the drive being taken off the flywheel rim between the two cranks

Horizontal triple-expansion engine

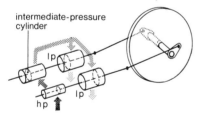

intermediate-pressure
cylinder

l p
l p
h p

C A development of the compound principle involved three stages of expansion. Steam passed from a high-pressure to an intermediate-pressure cylinder on the other piston rod and thence to a pair of equal diameter low-pressure cylinders, one on each side of the engine

Horizontal twin tandem-compound engine

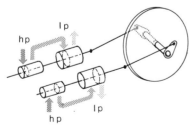

l p
h p
l p
h p

D The twin-tandem compound consisted simply of two tandem compounds driving a single crankshaft. Like the other compound and multiple expansion engines, this type became highly developed for powering textile mills

Vertical compound engine

Vertical triple-expansion engine

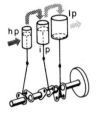

Twin-cylinder oscillating engine

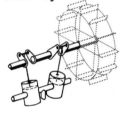

Side-lever engine

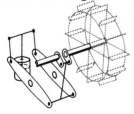

E In its simplest form the vertical compound was used mainly in ships, but a small enclosed-crankcase high-speed type, developed from the end of the nineteenth century, became popular for generating electricity

F Vertical triple-expansion engines were almost universally used in large ships before the introduction of steam turbines. On land they became the generally accepted successors to beam engines for water and sewage pumping

G The oscillating engine, in which rocking cylinders were mounted on trunnions formed from the steam inlet and exhaust pipes, had no connecting rods, the piston rod being attached directly to the crank. Their compactness made them particularly suited for use in paddle steamers

H The side-lever engine with its low centre of gravity was designed for marine application and was used extensively in paddle steamers before 1850. It was basically a beam engine with the beam pivoted at a low level,

12 Papplewick pumping station, Notts. Detail of beam trunnion with engine stroke counter

like a waterwheel in reverse lifted some 30 tons of water at each revolution. The original wheel was 28ft in diameter but this was increased to 33ft in 1848. The engine last operated in 1941 and is now under the care of the Stretham Engine Preservation Trust.

The robust reliability of the beam engine made it popular with water supply companies and for sewage pumping, and in these roles it reached a high degree of development by the latter years of the nineteenth century. Two late engines of this type are preserved at Papplewick, Nottinghamshire (112/SK 583522). Built by James Watt & Co in 1884, these rotative engines (Plate 12), with their 46in diameter cylinders and 7ft 6in stroke, each raised 1,500,000 gallons of water per day from the Bunter sandstone to supply the city of Nottingham. The iron pillars supporting the engine are covered in intricate decoration, which recurs throughout the interior of the engine house in tilework and stained glass windows. The whole effect is heightened by the landscaped setting and ornamental pool beloved of water-works companies at this period. Also preserved in the East Midlands are four sewage pumping engines at Abbey Lane, Leicester (121/SK 589066),

11 Stretham pumping station, Cambridgeshire. Detail of scoop wheel

13 Cromford pumping
station, Derbyshire

built in 1891 by Messrs Gimson, a local firm. They form the centrepiece for
a museum of technology of the East Midlands, currently under active
development. In County Durham, Ryhope pumping station near Sunderland
(78/NZ 403523), with its two 1868 rotative compound engines by Hawthorns
of Newcastle, is under the care of the Ryhope Pumping Engines Preservation
Fund, while in Hampshire, Portsmouth City Museums are restoring two
sewage pumping engines of 1887 at Eastney (181/SZ 675989).

A specialised, and in many cases very large, type of beam engine was the
Cornish pump (Fig 8) developed by Richard Trevithick (1771–1833) from
an engine erected in 1812 at Wheal Prosper tin mine at Gwithian in Cornwall.
The Cornish engine operated at a much higher pressure than contemporary

Watt engines, usually about 50 lb per sq in, and used expansive working to gain high efficiency. It was a single-acting, usually non-rotative beam engine in which steam applied above the piston lifted, through the beam, pump rods in the mine shaft. The sequence of operation was then as follows:

With the piston at the bottom of the cylinder the equilibrium valve was opened, allowing steam to be transferred from the upper to the lower side of the piston as the unbalanced weight of the pump rods caused the piston to ascend.

When the piston was at the top of the stroke the equilibrium valve was closed and steam admitted above the piston.

At the same time the eduction valve at the bottom of the cylinder opened to the condenser.

Thus the power stroke was effected using steam pressure on top of the piston and a partial vacuum below caused by condensation of steam in the condenser.

Cornish engines were extensively used for draining mines and also found widespread favour for water supply pumping and other drainage applications, as in the Severn railway tunnel. The increase in thermal efficiency over Watt engines was enormous with 125 million foot/pounds per bushel claimed in 1834 from an engine with an 80 in diameter cylinder as compared with the 20 millions normally attained by the low pressure engines.

As their name suggests, they were most numerous in Cornwall, where five engines were preserved by the Cornish Engines Preservation Society and are now in the care of the National Trust. These include one of the largest, built in 1892, with a 90in diameter cylinder, at Taylor's shaft, East Pool (189/SW 674416), and an early rotative winding engine of 1840 at Levant Mine (189/SW 375346), 6 miles from Land's End. In Scotland the Cornish engine at Prestongrange Colliery, East Lothian (62/NT 374737), built by Harvey & Co of Hayle, Cornwall, in 1874, is being restored to form the centre of a historical site devoted to the Scottish coal industry. Last worked in 1954, this pumping engine has a steam cylinder 70 in in diameter with a stroke of 12ft.

Crofton on the Kennet & Avon Canal in Wiltshire (167/SU 262623) has the oldest engine in the world still to operate on steam. The pumping

steam from boiler exhaust

STEAM ENGINE VALVES

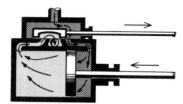

Slide valve

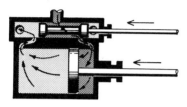

Piston valve

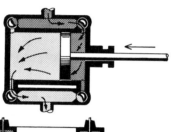

Corliss valve

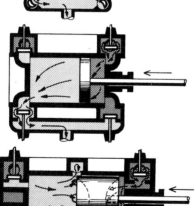

Drop valve

Uniflow engine

Fig 11 Steam Engine Valves

Slide valve

The slide valve, invented in 1799 by William Murdock (1754-1839), consisted of a metal box sliding on a flat face in which were cut the steam inlet and exhaust ports. Steam was usually admitted at the ends and exhausted through a central port under the hollow box valve, as shown in the example illustrated. Steam pressure thus helped retain the valve in contact with the face.

Piston valve

Like the slide valve, the piston valve was a single unit controlling steam inlet and exhaust. It consisted of a pair of pistons on a single spindle moving in a cylindrical bore that had inlet and exhaust ports in its sides. As the valve spindle moved backwards and forwards in the steam chest, the appropriate ports were uncovered to admit and exhaust steam. Both slide and piston valves had the disadvantage of steam being admitted and exhausted through the same channels, with consequent loss of efficiency resulting from alternate heating and cooling.

Corliss valve

The Corliss valve had none of these disadvantages, as a separate inlet and exhaust valve was provided at each end of the cylinder. Developed by the American George H. Corliss (1817-88) and patented in 1849, this type of valve became widely used on large mill engines. Each valve consisted of a barrel that partially rotated in a bored chamber to uncover the steam port. The inlet valves were opened by the valve rods against a dashpot. At the cut-off point the valve was released by trip gear to be closed rapidly by the dashpot.

Drop valve

Drop valves had turned circular faces fitting into valve seats in the steam chests. Valve and seat were ground together to ensure that they were steamtight. There were four valves per cylinder, the inlet valves being raised to admit steam and dropped by a trip gear to provide instantaneous admission cut off. Both Corliss and drop valves gave very economical steam consumption and steady governing, essential in driving textile machinery.

Uniflow engine

In the uniflow engine only admission valves were provided, as exhausting the steam was achieved by the piston at the end of its stroke uncovering a ring of ports in the wall of the cylinder. Although there were manufacturing difficulties with the uniflow type, it was highly efficient because there was no alternate heating and cooling of the cylinder ends by steam being admitted and exhausted through them.

TYPES OF BOILER

CUT OPEN TO SHOW INTERIORS

Haystack

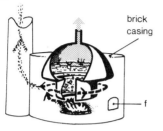

brick
casing

 steam

 water

 flow of hot combustion gases through boiler

 flow of hot combustion gases in brick flues alo
outer surface of boiler, giving extra heating

 smoke to chimney

f   firehole door(s)

Wagon

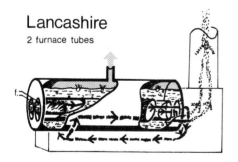

Cornish

1 furnace tube

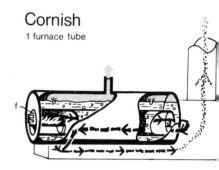

Lancashire

2 furnace tubes

Fire-tube

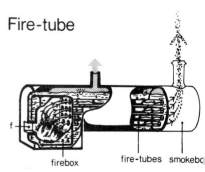

firebox   fire-tubes smokebc

Fig 12

14 Haystack boiler, Blists Hill Open Air Museum, Ironbridge, Shropshire

station was begun in 1803 and designed to supply the 35 mile section of the canal between Bedwyn and Seend with water lifted some 40 ft out of Wilton Water. The first engine began pumping in November 1809. It was built by Boulton & Watt in 1801 for the West India Dock, London, but was diverted to the canal company in 1802. On the initiative of John Rennie, the engineer for the canal, a more powerful engine was ordered from Boulton & Watt and began work in 1812. Originally both engines were of the single-acting atmospheric type operating at about 5 lb per sq in steam pressure and using Watt patented separate condensers, but in 1844, in an effort to increase efficiency, they were converted to the Cornish cycle of operation by Messrs Harvey of Hayle, Cornwall, with new boilers providing steam at 20 lb per

Fig 13 Lancashire boiler for 3,000 ihp triple-expansion engines

sq in. Later, in 1844, a Sims Combined Engine was installed to replace the 1801 machine, but this gave considerable trouble and was rebuilt in 1905 as a simple condensing engine, with a new 42 in cylinder. The 1812 Boulton & Watt engine has been restored to working order and is doing the work for which it was originally installed. It can be seen every Sunday and is in steam on selected weekends throughout the year. Restoration of the second engine is in progress.

The higher steam pressures at which the Cornish engine operated demanded stronger boilers (Fig 12) than the 'haystack' (Plate 14) or 'wagon' types which were used with Newcomen and Watt engines. The earliest haystack boilers were made of copper with a lead top, but after about 1725 hammered wrought-iron plates were used. The wagon boiler used by Watt had a similar cross-section to the haystack but was elongated to give more heating surface. Its rectangular shape was also easier to make. Neither was suitable for pressures in excess of 10 lb per sq in, so about 1812 Trevithick developed a cylindrical boiler with a grate set at one end of an internal tube running through its length. At the rear the hot gases divided and passed forward in brick flues along each side before returning beneath the bottom to the chimney. These Cornish boilers, as they came to be called, generated steam at some 50 lb per sq in and were widely adopted as high-pressure steam engines spread. They remained popular until the introduction of the Lancashire boiler (Fig 13) after 1844. In that year William (later Sir William) Fairbairn (1789–1874) and John Hetherington of Manchester patented a cylindrical boiler with two flues, devised, as Fairbairn stated, 'with a view to alternate firing in the two furnaces in order to prevent the formation of smoke', but also, of course, providing a substantially increased heating surface. Lancashire boilers are still in common use and examples may be seen in association with most of the preserved engines already mentioned. The Cornish boiler has almost completely disappeared, but Trevithick's 1812 original is preserved at the Science Museum, South Kensington. Many boiler shells of both Cornish and Lancashire types may be seen converted for use as oil storage tanks.

The opening years of the nineteenth century saw several alternatives to the beam engine introduced to achieve greater thermal and mechanical efficiency, higher speeds and simplicity of erection. This last factor was of some importance as the cumbersome beam engine required skilled engineers to assemble it on site, was not easily adaptable to the often rapid rate of development of factories, could not easily by resited and took up a lot of space. Thus relatively portable self-contained direct-acting engines, dispensing with the heavy rocking beam between connecting rod and crankshaft, began to appear in increasing numbers. An early form was the table engine (Fig 9) introduced in 1807 by Henry Maudslay (1771–1831) and this was followed after about 1825 by numerous designs of the soon to be popular horizontal engine having a single cylinder, slide bars and crankshaft bearings on a cast-iron bedplate of box-girder section. In the table engine the vertical cylinder of the beam engine was retained but the piston rod drove a crankshaft beneath by means of two return connecting rods. Its portability made it popular until the middle of the nineteenth century for driving workshops, but it has now almost completely disappeared. An example may be seen at the Science Museum.

The horizontal engine was introduced as early as 1802 by Richard Trevithick as one of a number of his experimental designs using high-pressure steam. Another high pressure design by Trevithick, but employing a vertical cylinder, is preserved in the Science Museum. The horizontal engine (Fig 9) was little exploited until after 1830 and did not become widespread until the 1850s. After this date, however, simple single-cylinder horizontal engines were produced in large numbers for use in breweries, saw mills, small engineering shops and many places where an easily maintained power unit was required. Firms such as Tangye of Birmingham made standard designs in a variety of sizes which could be installed either as a single cylinder version or with two identical cylinders, one on each side of the flywheel. An example of this latter type dating from 1885 is still used to power the Port of Bristol Authority workshop at Underfall Yard, Bristol (156/ST 572722).

The direct-acting vertical engine (Fig 9) with the crankshaft above the cylinder was patented in 1800 by Phineas Crowther of Newcastle-upon-Tyne but its only widespread application seems to have been for colliery winding in the Northumberland and Durham coalfield. One remaining example is preserved at Beamish Colliery (78/NZ 220537) under the care of the North of England Open Air Museum. The inverted vertical engine (Fig 9) with its crankshaft immediately below the cylinder was introduced in the 1840s by James Nasmyth (1808–90) as a logical derivation of his steam hammer design of 1839. It achieved considerable popularity as a small power source, particularly in the marine application of driving screw propellers. Various types of supports for the cylinder can be found, ranging from a single-side cast-iron frame with or without a turned steel column at the open side to a symmetrical 'A' shaped casting. Later versions, built in large numbers well into this century, have the connecting rod and crankshaft completely enclosed, in the same manner as a motor car engine, and operate at high speeds with pressure lubrication.

Despite this profusion of new engine layouts during the nineteenth century, the beam engine continued to be built with various modifications and one or two ingenious adaptations. One of these was the grasshopper engine (see Fig 9) patented in 1803 by William Fremantle, the same principle being employed by Oliver Evans in America at about the same time. In this design the piston rod was connected by a pin to one end of the beam while the other end was supported on two long back links which allowed it to rock backwards and forwards. The centre of the beam was constrained by radius arms and the drive to the connecting rod taken off at a point between the centre and the piston rod link. The major advantage of the engine was one of compactness. Another beam engine variant, introduced in 1805 by Matthew Murray (1765–1826), had the beam centred below the cylinder and crankshaft. Side rods connected the piston rod to one end of the beam while the other had a connecting rod driving upwards on to the crank. Its low centre of gravity made the engine (Fig 10) popular in paddle steamers, and an example may be seen in the tug *Reliant*, built in 1907 by J. T. Eltringham & Co of South Shields, and on view in the Neptune Hall of the National Maritime Museum at Greenwich.

By far the most significant advance in steam engine design in the nineteenth century was the introduction of the compound or multiple cylinder expansion principle, initially applied to the beam engine and later providing the basis for a wide variety of highly efficient direct-acting engines. As early as 1781 Jonathan Hornblower (1753–1815) had patented an engine with two cylinders in which the steam was introduced to the first direct from the boiler and was exhausted into a second cylinder of larger diameter where it continued to expand and do useful work on the piston. It was not found to be significantly more efficient than the contemporary Watt engine, but in 1804 Arthur Woolf (1776–1837) revived the idea using high-pressure

steam. Although reasonably successful, Woolf's engines (Fig 8) were not
widely adopted, being more expensive and complicated than the Cornish
engines of Trevithick with which they were compared. In 1845, however,
William McNaught of Glasgow introduced an ingenious and highly successful method (Fig 9) of compounding by adding a smaller diameter high-
pressure cylinder on the crank side of the beam of a conventional beam engine,
between its centre and the connecting rod. This avoided overstressing the
beam and, by replacing the old low pressure boiler with a high pressure one,
both power and economy were improved without the need for a completely
new engine. By the 1860s compound beam engines were widespread and
new engines were being built in the Woolf manner with cylinders side-by-
side driving on to the same end of the beam. Compounding enabled steam
to be expanded in the cylinders to many times its original volume with
minimal losses from condensation and leakage. The Ryhope engines
mentioned above are typical compound beam engines.

With high-pressure direct-acting engines, compounding (Fig 10) was still
more successful, eventually being achieved in three and even four stages
through cylinders of successively increasing volume. The triple-expansion
type with three cylinders mounted vertically and driving on to the crankshaft below found favour for marine use and also as a replacement for beam
engines in water pumping stations. Two of the largest land-based triples
(Plate 15) ever built are still in use at Kempton Park Waterworks, Hounslow
(170/TQ 110709), while another pair have recently ceased operation at
Otterbourne pumping station in Hampshire (168/SU 468233); both sets
were built by Worthington Simpson of Newark and date from the 1920s.

By the end of the nineteenth century the big textile mills of Lancashire
and Yorkshire were demanding higher and higher hps to drive their vast
numbers of machines and a specialised type of engine, the mill engine (Fig
14) was developed to satisfy this need. These engines were almost invariably
horizontal compounds and some were designed to produce as much as
4,000 hp. The two most popular layouts were the tandem-compound in
which the high and low pressure cylinders lay one behind the other with a
common piston rod, and the cross-compound in which the high pressure
cylinder drove one end of the crankshaft and the low pressure the other.
Between the two was the flywheel with its broad face cast in grooves for
the cotton drive-ropes that powered the mill. The engine of Dee Mill, Shaw,

15 Kempton Park Waterworks: two of the five triple-expansion pumping engines built by the Lilleshall Company in the early 1900s

near Rochdale (101/SD 945093), is an example of the ultimate in mill engine design. It is a twin-tandem compound, that is it has two piston rods each with a high and low pressure cylinder driving each end of the crankshaft. Built in 1906 by Scott & Hodgson Ltd of Guide Bridge, the 'Dee' engine has two 18 in diameter high pressure cylinders with Corliss semi-rotary valves and two low pressure cylinders of 42in with piston valves. It is preserved by the Northern Mill Engine Society in association with the owners, Courtaulds Ltd. A small tandem-compound mill engine by Pollitt & Wigzell of Sowerby Bridge is displayed in the Birmingham Museum of Science & Industry.

Fig 14 3,000 ihp triple-expansion mill engine — Hick, Hargreaves and Co Ltd, Bolton

In the 1880s a new demand arose for engines to power electrical dynamos. At first slow-speed engines were used to drive dynamos by belt but the advantages of direct coupling led to the introduction of a specialised type of engine capable of running at speeds in the region of 500 rpm. A number of these were made single-acting to avoid the reversal of load on the crankpin and thus eliminate the knocking which would develop unless impractically small bearing clearances were used. The most successful and widely adopted design of this type resulted from patents taken out in 1884 and 1885 by Peter William Willans (1851–92) for a central valve engine in which the steam was distributed by a piston valve inside the hollow piston rod. The valve was worked by an eccentric on the crankpin and the engine, which was a vertical, had a totally enclosed crankcase with splash lubrication. Simple, compound and triple expansion types were made in large numbers and ultimately in sizes up to 2,500 hp. Although extremely economical, they have almost completely disappeared from use and examples are much more difficult to find than are beam engines. Willans engines can be seen in the Science Museum, South Kensington and the Guinness Museum, St James's Gate, Dublin.

The introduction of the steam turbine in the 1880s and its rapid development in the following years rendered the Willans engine obsolete by the early 1900s, but another type of high-speed reciprocating engine was also rivalling it by that date. This came from the Bellis & Morcom company of Birmingham, which introduced a double-acting enclosed vertical engine in the mid-1890s in both compound and triple-expansion form, largely for powering small generators. It had forced lubrication and was extremely efficient. Large hp versions were built, up to 2,500 hp, but these could not compete with turbines. In small sizes, however, the Bellis & Morcom type of engine, made by a variety of manufacturers, is still used particularly in hospitals and laundries where low pressure steam is required for heating or process work. By generating steam at a high pressure and feeding it first through an engine, electricity can be generated at very small additional cost.

Before turning to the steam turbine and its development, let us consider a number of other types of reciprocating engine that may frequently be encountered by the industrial archaeologist in a variety of applications. So far we have dealt mainly with large engines designed for powering factories or major installations such as water pumping stations, but numerous steam engines were produced after about 1870, and well into the present century, to provide relatively small amounts of power at almost any point where it was needed. The most popular of these was based on the locomotive type of boiler on which the engine itself was mounted. Its most mobile form was the traction engine, consisting of a single-cylinder, or twin-cylinder compound, horizontal engine providing power both to move the engine and to drive machinery such as threshing machines. A similar type, known as the portable engine, was not self-propelled but had to be towed to where it was needed by horses or a traction engine. It was used mainly for powering saw mills and electricity generation at fairgrounds. A semi-portable form, although without wheels, consisting of a boiler with the engine mounted on it, found favour in saw mills as well as flour mills and in small, often rurally situated, factories, where a cheaply run engine of moderate hp was needed. A variation, known as the undertype, had the engine placed beneath the boiler in the same position as the cylinders of a railway locomotive. Rarely did these portable types of engine exceed 150 hp.

The patenting of a practical steam turbine in 1884 by C. A. Parsons (1854–1931) was one of the most significant events in the evolution of heat engines as prime movers, and marked the beginning of the end for the reciprocating steam engine. It also brought to fruition the dreams of scientists and engineers over many centuries who had been fascinated with this problem of rotary power. Between 1784 and 1884 nearly 200 patents were taken out in Britain alone for steam and gas turbines, some of them anticipating in principle designs which were ultimately to be successful. In the turbine the steam, instead of being used under pressure against a piston, is set in motion, and the conversion of this pressure energy into velocity or kinetic energy produces the rotation of the turbine shaft. Parsons* success lay in his appreciation of the problem of expanding the steam effectively through the turbine, a problem which he solved by dividing the pressure drop into many small stages, at each of which was an elemental turbine. Each of these turbines consisted of a ring of blades mounted on a long shaft, the rotor and the stator, which carried similar rows of blades projecting inwards between the rows of blades on the shaft. Steam admitted at one end of the stator flowed

* Parsons issued instructions that the apostrophe should be omitted in cases like this, preferring to offend those who knew than suffer those who did not.

parallel to the axis of the turbine, that is axially, between the blades of the rotor and stator alternately, eventually exhausting to atmosphere. In order to eliminate end thrust on the rotor bearings Parsons arranged a central admission point for the steam, whence it flowed through two identical sets of blades towards each end of the turbine.

The incentive behind the development of the steam turbine, like that behind the high speed reciprocating engine, was the need for an effective power source for electricity generation, and in this role it proved an immediate success. Indeed Parsons first turbine was direct-coupled to a 7·51 kW dynamo using steam at 80 lb per sq in and running at a speed of 18,000 rpm. The rate at which improvements were made by the original inventor was remarkable, and by 1900 1,250 kW units were in service, rivalling in power output and efficiency the best reciprocating engine generators. In 1897 the first practical marine application of the turbine was made by Parsons in the experimental *Turbinia* fitted with three axial flow turbines direct-coupled to three screw propellers. Steam from the boiler was led first to the high-pressure turbine on the starboard side, then passed to the intermediate pressure turbine on the port side and next to a low pressure turbine placed amidships before being exhausted to the condenser. A separate turbine on the central shaft drove the vessel astern. The spectacular introduction of the marine turbine to the assembled navies of the world at the 1897 Spithead review, when *Turbinia* raced up and down between the ranks of ships at an unprecedented 34·5 knots, established beyond all doubt its supremacy over the reciprocating engine. Exactly 10 years later the Cunard liner *Mauretania* of 38,000 tons attained 26.04 knots powered by steam turbines of 70,000 hp.

Two important Parsons turbine generating units are preserved in the Science Museum, South Kensington. These are his original 1884 unit with bipolar dynamo and the first condensing turbo-alternator of 100 kW built for the Cambridge Electric Lighting Company. Other Parsons turbines may be seen at Abbeydale industrial hamlet, Sheffield; Glasgow Art Gallery & Museum, Kelvingrove; and, appropriately, Newcastle-upon-Tyne Museum of Science & Engineering, where *Turbinia* is also preserved. Also at Glasgow Museum are an early De Laval turbo-generator and a high pressure and low pressure turbine from the Clyde steamer *King Edward* of 1901, the first commercial turbine-driven vessel in the world.

The steam engine, as we have seen, was the first effective power source to release man from his reliance on natural agencies—on his own muscles, the use of animals or on windmills and watermills. Power was available in almost unlimited quantities for the driving of machines and the early application of steam to transport in the form of ships and railways means that this one prime mover occupies a fundamental position in the expansion of industry and the development of industrial society in the last 250 years. Over this period the reciprocating steam engine has come to command a respect quite unique among machines, from a wide range of people who gain some aesthetic satisfaction from the sight, sound and smell of a steam engine in action. Today the industrial archaeologist, in tracing the evolution of the steam engine, can find numerous examples preserved which illustrate many of the major stages of development, although beam engines of one type or another are by far the most numerous. So far very few of the last generation of large steam engines have been kept and, although a number of mill engines, colliery winding and pumping engines are still in regular use, their numbers are decreasing rapidly. The Dee Mill engine at Rochdale is the exception which proves the rule but as yet no example of the big triple-expansion vertical pumping engines built in large numbers down to the 1920s has been scheduled for preservation. Similarly the steam turbine, much less interesting visually, does not have a wide enthusiast following, and only a few small and early examples have been preserved, as static exhibits in museums.

THE INTERNAL COMBUSTION ENGINE

The significant history of the internal combustion engine lies mainly in the period between the 1850s and the present day, although the experimental beginnings go back much further. Indeed the concept of burning fuel in the working cylinder is older than that of the steam engine itself, being ascribed to the Dutch scientist Christiaan Huygens (1629–95) who devised a machine using burning gunpowder to provide the expansive forces necessary to raise a piston. Cooling of the gases created a partial vacuum and atmospheric pressure forced the piston down. It was the substitution of gunpowder by steam, using an external fuel source, that was to lead to the development of a practicable engine in the early eighteenth century.

It was not until 1859 that an engine burning its fuel within the cylinder was devised to operate continuously under industrial conditions, but by then the steam engine was universally established and in an almost unassailable position. Earlier experimental machines had been built and an engine made in 1820 by the Rev W. Cecil of Cambridge using hydrogen as a fuel was perhaps the first internal combustion engine to work in Britain or, for that matter, in the world. Nothing came of it, however, nor of the dozens of patents for 'gas exploding' engines taken out in the first half of the nineteenth century.

Success was finally achieved by a Frenchman, Etienne Lenior (1822–1900), who in 1859 introduced a gas engine resembling in appearance a double-acting horizontal steam engine. A gas and air mixture was admitted at each end of the cylinder alternately but there was no compression. The mixture was introduced during the early part of each stroke, then fired by an electric spark and expanded during the remainder of the stroke. There were thus two explosions, one on each side of the piston, per revolution of the crank. While induction, ignition and expansion were taking place on one side of the piston, burnt gas was being exhausted at the other. Although small, ranging between $\frac{1}{2}$ and 3 hp, and consuming rather large quantities of gas, Lenoir's engine achieved a considerable measure of success, 300–400 being in use in France by the mid-1860s. An example can be seen in the Science Museum, South Kensington.

In 1862 another Frenchman, Alphonse Beau de Rochas (1815–91), obtained a patent for a gas engine employing what we now call the four-stroke cycle. He laid down a range of conditions for good efficiency, namely: the cylinder should have the greatest possible volume with the least possible cooling surface, there should be the greatest possible rapidity of expansion and ratio of expansion, and the greatest possible pressure in the cylinder at the beginning of expansion. These conditions led to the following sequence of events in his engine:

1 Suction or induction of the gas–air mixture during a complete outward stroke of the piston.
2 Compression during the following inward stroke.
3 Ignition at or near the dead point followed by combustion and expansion during the third stroke.

4 Exhausting of the burnt gases from the cylinder on the fourth and final inward stroke.

The cycle is then repeated. Beau de Rochas did not follow up his theory and it was left to a German engineer, Dr N. A. Otto (1832–91), to put it into practical operation.

During the 1860s Otto had developed an 'atmospheric' free piston gas engine bearing striking resemblances in its principles of operation to the Newcomen steam engines of a century and a half earlier. The piston, mounted in an open-topped vertical cylinder, was raised by the expansion of gases ignited beaneath it. Cooling and contraction of these gases resulted in the atmospheric pressure on top of the piston forcing it down. This was the working stroke, and a toothed rod, or 'rack', attached to the piston engaged in a gear wheel on a shaft converted its motion into rotary power suitable for driving machinery. Fuel consumption was substantially less than in Lenoir's engine and, after its introduction by the firm of Otto & Langen in 1867, it had soon driven almost all competitors off the market. In Britain Crossley Bros Ltd of Manchester produced the engine under licence in a variety of sizes and a number have been preserved in museums. Examples of the 2 hp type may be seen at South Kensington and Glasgow Art Gallery & Museum, while Bristol City Museum has a 4 hp version in store.

By 1876 Otto had produced a still more successful engine operating on the four-stroke cycle proposed by Beau de Rochas. The 'Otto Silent Engine' without doubt marked a milestone in the progress of the internal combustion engine, being the first really strong competitor to the steam engine and, in proving the practicability of the four-stroke cycle, forming the basis for the motor car engine of today. Crossley's took up this new Otto engine and produced a variety of sizes under licence. Large numbers have found their way into museums, as have similar slow-speed single-cylinder horizontal gas engines made by other British manufacturers. A number of types and sizes may be seen in the Birmingham Museum of Science & Industry, where a Tangye engine is usually running on gas.

In all these early four-stroke gas engines steam engine practice was followed to a large extent. They were usually slow-speed horizontals with admission of gas and air controlled by a slide valve. Although some engines used electric ignition, others relied upon a continuously burning flame inside a chamber in the cylinder wall. When the firing point arrived, the slide valve opened a slot exposing the flame to the mixture in the cylinder. Ignition of the gases, however, extinguished the flame itself so it was necessary to have a second one outside the chamber in order to re-ignite the internal flame. At the moment of ignition the external flame was shut off from the internal one. A later idea was the hot tube kept at bright red heat by an external flame.

The fuel used in most of the early gas engines was town gas, but gas from coke ovens, blast furnace gas and producer gas were also employed. By the end of the nineteenth century special gas producers, using coal, were being made for direct coupling to gas engines, thus making them independent of piped gas. In most designs the main piston of the engine was used to draw air into the producer. In the 1870s a number of engineers, notably in Austria and the United States, were experimenting with engines using an oil fuel instead of gas but little success resulted, largely because of difficulties in getting the oil into a sufficiently divided or atomised state to be easily combustible. The first really satisfactory design was the Priestman engine of 1886, which used paraffin (kerosene) as its fuel. The liquid was atomised by compressed air and vaporised in a vessel heated by exhaust gas before being drawn into the cylinder with the fresh air charge and ignited by electric spark. The Hornsby horizontal oil engine had a vaporiser at the end of the combustion chamber, on the cylinder head, and a special portable oil lamp was used to preheat it before starting, while in Crossley engines vaporisation was achieved in a spiral pipe encircling the oil lamp chimney. Once the engine was started and reached its operating temperature, the lamp was no longer required. All these early oil engines were slow-running single-cylinder water-cooled horizontals similar in general arrangement to both gas and steam engines of the period.

About 1890 a very different type of oil engine was designed by Herbert Ackroyd-Stuart (1864–1927), who owned an iron foundry at Bletchley where he conducted experiments with the advice of Prof William Robinson of University College, Nottingham. The engine had a combined vaporiser and explosion chamber forming part of the cylinder head. The vaporiser, which was in the shape of an elongated bulb, was maintained by the heat of combustion at a temperature high enough to vaporise the oil which was injected directly into it, and high enough to cause ignition of the fuel/air mixture at the end of compression. For starting purposes the vaporiser was heated with a blow lamp.

The Ackroyd-Stuart engine exhibited two features of great importance. It required no devices for igniting the inflammable mixture, once it had started, and the fuel was injected 'solid', that is, without the use of atomising air. These two features are characteristic of the modern high-speed oil engine, but it must be emphasised that the modern engine is fundamentally one of high compression, whereas the Ackroyd-Stuart design deliberately avoided high compression and provided auxiliary means for reaching the necessary ignition temperature. Lack of capital prevented Ackroyd-Stuart from carrying on his experiments and in 1891 he sold a licence to manufacture his engines to Ruston & Co of Lincoln, who made them successfully for a number of years.

Rudolph Diesel (1858–1913), a German engineer born in Paris, was responsible for taking the final step of developing an engine in which ignition took place solely by the heat generated by compression. His principal aims were to circumvent the two main sources of heat loss in an internal combustion engine—by controlling the maximum temperature, through the gradual introduction of the fuel, and by lowering the temperature of the exhaust gases. To these ends he designed an engine working on the four-stroke cycle in which pure air only was compressed by the piston to a very much higher degree than the mixture in any former type of oil engine. An injector pump then forced a minute but accurately determined quantity of oil into the combustion chamber, where it ignited spontaneously on contact with the compressed air. It was found that its maximum thermal efficiency was some 11 per cent higher than that of any other form of prime mover and that the engine worked well on a wide variety of petroleum oils. Initial disadvantages resulted from high weight, as the engine had to be solidly built to withstand pressures of up to thirty-five times atmospheric, but improved construction techniques had, by the 1920s, put the Diesel engine into a strong competitive position for both stationary and automotive uses.

It was Gottlieb Daimler (1834–1900) of Württemberg who successfully developed the small lightweight high-speed engine running on liquid fuel, in this case light petroleum spirit. In 1885 he patented a single-cylinder vertical engine with enclosed crankcase and flywheels. From this design all subsequent Daimler engines were derived and in two- and eventually four-cylinder versions this type of engine formed the basis for the evolution of the motor car. A suction-operated inlet valve was used with a mechanically worked exhaust valve, a governor being arranged to prevent the latter opening when engine revolutions exceeded a predetermined speed. Introduction of the fuel was not such a difficulty as with the oil engine, as petrol vaporises readily in the presence of air. Wick feed carburettors were soon to give way to jet feed types, particularly for road vehicles.

Almost exactly contemporary with Daimler's introduction of the high-speed engine in 1885, Karl Benz (1844–1929) was building his first motor vehicle. This incorporated a horizontal engine using petrol as a fuel and operating on the 'Otto' four-stroke cycle but at the slow speeds of a gas engine. It was the high-speed engine pioneered by Daimler which eventually triumphed, however, and although a number of ingenious variations and layouts were tried in the period before World War 1, the general arrangement of vertical water-cooled cylinders and enclosed crankcase is still by far the most popular type of motor car engine throughout the world. Numerous early motor cars are preserved in museums and often their engines can be examined closely. Notable collections include those of the National Motor Museum at Beaulieu in Hampshire; the Science Museum, South Kensington; the Herbert Art Gallery & Museum, Coventry; and Glasgow Transport Museum. For a real appreciation of the early motor car engine in operation, however, the London to Brighton road on the first Sunday in November, the occasion of the Veteran Car Club Run, enables one to see, hear and smell the faltering post-natal beginnings of the machine which has had such a fundamental effect on the lives of us all. The Historic Commercial Vehicle Club run takes place over the same route on the first Sunday in May.

Despite the fact that the internal combustion engine is so familiar, and indeed commonplace, in the everyday world, its origins and early years are as much the province of industrial archaeological enquiry as are those of the steam engine. The rate of development of internal combustion engines has been such that almost any example dating from before 1930 and still in use is a rarity. Paradoxically it is often the Otto-Crossley gas engine of the 1880s, slow-running and slow to wear out, which has survived to be preserved.

5 Coal

THE earliest miners were interested in flint, from which they made their tools, and to reach the best layers in the flint-bearing chalk, they excavated simple pits. These first mines, probably excavated by Mesolithic or Middle Stone Age Man of perhaps 10,000 years ago, were little more than simple holes in the ground; but by the Neolithic period, which ended about 2000 BC, much more sophisticated mines were being dug, with galleries extending from shafts to the flint-bearing levels. The flint mines of Europe were on or near the chalk outcrops in northern France, Belgium and southern England. In Norfolk the most extensive mining site, which is known as Grimes Graves, covers some 34 acres, but smaller remains survive at Cissbury in Sussex, Worthing and Chichester.

The succeeding Bronze Age saw the working of lead, tin and copper, and finally iron, which displaced the tin-copper alloy bronze as a toolmaking material. Coal too may have been worked at places where it outcropped and even possibly in small pits of shallow depth. It was of some small importance to the Romans in Britain but the Saxons and Danes appear to have disregarded coal almost entirely, using wood and peat to heat their dwellings. No mention of coal occurs in the Domesday survey of 1086, but by the time of Magna Carta in 1215 the industry had certainly started on the banks of the Rivers Tyne and Wear and the Firth of Forth, where coal was gathered from outcrops and occasionally mined.

Coal did not become a really important fuel until the sixteenth century, and in terms of industrial development it was not of major significance until the middle of the eighteenth. From then on, however, coal was far and away the most important of all the natural resources of Britain, providing heat for both the smelting and fashioning of metals and the generation of steam. Initially coal was not a popular fuel and for domestic use wood and charcoal were generally preferred. Only poor people living near the workings burnt coal. The impurities in coal which caused the noxious fumes so distasteful to the domestic user in a house with inadequate ventilation also caused problems to industry, so it was in a purified state, as coke, that coal was first used on a really large scale for industrial purposes. Thus coke was the first successful replacement of charcoal for iron smelting in 1709. Similarly, it was not until 1859 that the introduction of the brick arch into the fireboxes of railway locomotives enabled coal to be burnt satisfactorily. Previously coke had been used in all except small and relatively inefficient engines working in or near collieries.

This does not mean that coal had no industrial uses. Limeburners, bakers, brewers and glassmakers, for example, all adapted their processes to burn coal and, as the huge forested areas of England became decimated, the price of timber, coupled with the strategic timber requirements of the Royal Navy, stimulated an increase in the use of coal wherever possible. By the 1760s the coal industry was growing at a rapid rate, and it reached its peak in 1913; since then it has suffered a steady decline in the face of oil, and more recently natural gas and nuclear power. It is worth remembering, however, that most of the electricity generated in Britain comes from coal-fired power stations.

The first access to coal was at outcrops where it could be picked up on the ground, and on beaches where coal in cliffs was being constantly eroded. By the twelfth century small quarries and ditches were being dug, and in the thirteenth century, in addition to such opencast methods, coal was also being won from shallow drifts and bell-pits. Drifts were usually found in hilly districts and consisted of more or less horizontal tunnels or galleries cut into the hillsides and following the seams of coal. A number of privately owned drifts are still being worked under licence today, and although they are small by twentieth-century standards, they are much larger than their thirteenth-century predecessors. In areas such as the Forest of Dean in Gloucestershire there has been a continuous history of drift mining, and the 'free miners' of the Forest still exercise their medieval rights to mine coal (Plate 16). Their workings, although involving some modern equipment, are little altered from those of 5 centuries ago and include many of the basic techniques of mine operation. A reconstruction of a small drift mine can be seen at Blists Hill Open Air Museum, Ironbridge, Shropshire. Recently the National Coal Board has built a number of new large drift mines, notably in South Wales and Yorkshire.

Problems of ventilation and drainage limited the size of the early drift mines, but where coal lay at only a shallow depth below the surface, it was won by sinking bell-pits, a simple process involving little equipment

16 A free miner's working near Parkend, Forest of Dean, Gloucestershire

and no drainage or ventilation gear. Bell-pits are so called because, when viewed in section, they have the shape of bells. A pit was sunk like a well shaft to a shallow coal seam and the coal at the foot of the shaft was then taken. Next, it was cut away around the pit bottom in all directions until the sides were in danger of collapse. The pit was then abandoned and a new one started nearby. Bell-pits (Plate 17) were rarely more than 30ft deep, usually circular in plan, and often dug very close together. Very frequently they collapsed after their abandonment, so that areas of bell-pit working can now be recognised by a characteristic pock-marked surface to the ground made up of numerous circular depressions 20–30ft in diameter. Evidence of bell-pits can be found on many of the older worked coalfields, particularly in Derbyshire at Stretton, Wingerworth and Shipley, in Lancashire at Castercliff near Nelson, and in Shropshire on Brown Clee.

Where seams lay deeper than 20ft, bell-pits were wasteful of labour, so headings were cut out horizontally into coal for a short distance from the shaft bottom. Between these headings wide pillars of coal were left to support the roof. The arrangement was at first irregular in pattern, resulting in as much as half the coal being left behind, but it was soon recognised that it

17 Remains of bell-pits near Wakefield, Yorkshire

was both practicable and economical to divide the seams up into large pillars by roads driven at right-angles, and subsequently to follow up by extracting the pillars. This method of mining is known as bord-and-pillar or, more commonly, pillar-and-stall working (Fig 15). There were two distinct stages in the cutting of coal in this way. Initially, when the bords or stalls were being driven as working advanced from the pit bottom, the process was known as 'working in the whole'. The second stage, of extracting the pillars while retreating back towards the shaft was called 'working in the broken', although most miners would call this 'robbing the pillars on the retreat'. The method of removing pillars was to take slices off one side, the roof meanwhile being supported by timber props. When the whole of the pillar was cut away, the timber supports were withdrawn and the roof allowed to collapse.

Pillar-and-stall working became the standard method of coal extraction in all the major coalfields of Britain, and in Northumberland and Durham in particular continued well after nationalisation of the coal industry in 1947. The miner of the North-East, with his highly developed tradition of craftsmanship and skill, tended to be rather slow in adopting new mining techniques. The system of working, in which an individual miner or small group of men worked a stall also engendered a craft approach and perpetuated

METHODS OF WORKING COAL PLAN VIEW OF COAL SEAM

PILLAR-AND-STALL
1 Working in the whole

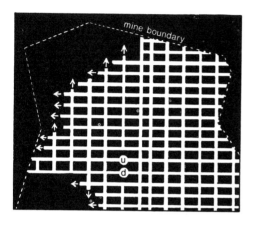

2 Working in the broken

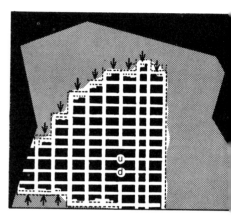

LONGWALL

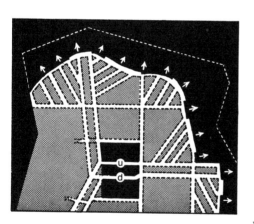

■	uncut coal
□	coal removed, roof still supported
▨	'goaf' or 'gob'- all coal removed, roof allowed to settle down gradually
▨	workings kept open with props
⬤ u	upcast shaft - foul air drawn out
⬤ d	downcast shaft - fresh air drawn in

N B Circulation of fresh air round the mine is controlled by air doors and ducts which have been omitted for clarity

Fig 15

this system of mining long after it had been replaced elsewhere by other techniques.

Pillar-and-stall working was a two-stage operation ideally suited to workings where there was not more than about 900ft of rock lying above the coal. Where depths were greater, there was a tendency for the overlying rock to crush the pillars as, or sometimes before, they were removed. There were also frequent problems of ventilation. To overcome these drawbacks, extraction in one operation was developed. Known as the longwall method, it originated in the late seventeenth century, probably in Shropshire, but did not come into widespread use until after 1850. In this system a wall of coal about 100yd long is won out and removed bodily in line. As the coal is taken away, any stone available is built into dry stone walls or packs 6–20ft wide arranged in parallel lines at right-angles to the advancing wall or face. The purpose of these walls is to support the roof after the layer of coal is removed and thus preserve it in a largely unbroken state. Longwall working is particularly suited to mechanical coal-cutting methods in seams which have layers of stone or shale within them.

Once mines had grown beyond the scale of the early drifts and bell-pits, the cutting of the coal itself became a relatively minor problem compared with those of shaft sinking and winding, ventilation and drainage. Indeed the finding of a solution to these last two difficulties was the major pre-occupation of miners and engineers from the end of the sixteenth century onwards. Until answers could be found, there were specific limits to the depth at which mines could be sunk and the distances to which workings extended from the pit bottom. The early miners on the exposed coalfields were working in known conditions. They could see where the coal was and assess the problems of working as they went along. Once mines away from the outcrops developed, shaft sinking became speculative and some means of discovering the presence of coal and any undesirable stratigraphical conditions above it became a necessity. As early as 1606 Huntington Beaumont, one of the first of the great coal entrepreneurs, who had extensive interests in Nottinghamshire and the North East, was demonstrating his 'art to boore with iron rodds to try the deepnesse and thicknesse of the cole'. This of course was much cheaper than digging trial shafts. In 1708 the cost of boring was said to be 15–20s a fathom, while sinking a shaft cost 50–60s a fathom. In 1804 James Ryan invented a boring technique which allowed cores to be extracted, and the application of steam power, first tried by Richard Trevithick, both speeded up and cheapened exploration.

Shaft sinking was usually carried out by hand picks and shovels and wedges for splitting rock. Later boring rods were employed, and in 1749 occurs one of the earliest references to the use of explosives, for a 210ft shaft near Halifax. Shafts were generally circular in section, 5–12ft in diameter, with about 7ft being the most common, though one shaft at New Rock Colliery, Somerset (166/ST 647505), in use until recently, is only 4ft 6in in diameter. Square or rectangular shafts were frequent on some coalfields as they could be easily and cheaply lined with wooden boards. Small rectangular shafts can still be found in the Forest of Dean, although often the timber lining has deteriorated, making them very dangerous to explore. Where water was a problem in a shaft, it was held back with 'tubbing' consisting of wooden planks arranged like the staves of a barrel or tub. The first cast-iron tubbing used in the Midlands was at Snibston Colliery in Leicestershire (121/SK 417145), sunk by George Stephenson in 1841–3. This can still be seen in the upcast shafts. Elsewhere brick lining was used, mostly with mortar but occasionally without. It was cheaper to lay bricks dry, and they could be used again when the shaft ceased production. A dry-lined shaft can be seen below the headgear from Farm Pit, Heath Hill, reconstructed at Blists Hill Open Air Museum, Ironbridge (119/SJ 694031).

There were various methods of raising coal up the shaft (Fig 16), of which the earliest was a simple hand winch or windlass, sometimes known as a 'jack roll' and similar to that used on a domestic well. The barrel of a windlass of this type, found in 1969 at the bottom of a shaft exposed on Stainsby Hag opencast site in Derbyshire, may be seen in the Mining Museum at Lound Hall Mining Training Centre, near Retford, Nottinghamshire (112/SK 701731). To improve the performance of the hand windlass, horse-driven cog-and-rung gins were introduced in the early seventeenth century. A vertical spindle was geared to the horizontal barrel of the winch, and the horse, attached to the spindle via a wooden pole, walked round the mouth of the pit to raise coal in small baskets known as corves or corfes. Towards the end of the seventeenth century further improvements were effected with the whim-gin, horse-whim or whimsy. This new winder had the rope drum mounted on a vertical shaft, which was erected some distance from the pit shaft. The horse walked round rotating the drum as in the cog-

OLLIERY WINDING GEAR

indlass or Jack Roll

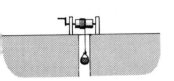

Cog and rung gin

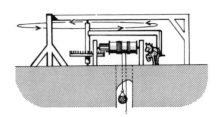

him-gin

ulleys

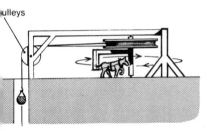

Steam whimsy

flat chains

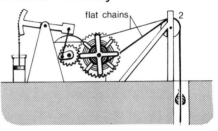

ertical steam winder

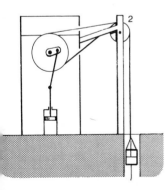

Horizontal steam winder with tandem headgear

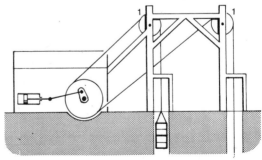

Fig 16

and-rung gin and the rope passed over a vertical pulley mounted on a wooden headgear over the shaft itself. Depending on the size of the mine, one, two or more horses were employed. Whim-gins were used until the early twentieth century in some places and a reconstructed example may be seen at the Nottingham Industrial Museum, Wollaton Park (112/SK 531393).

The use of water power for winding purposes occurred to a limited extent in Britain, initially with waterwheels mounted on horizontal shafts round which the winding rope was wound, and later using water balances. A waterwheel for winding coal was installed at Griff Colliery, Warwickshire, by John Smeaton (1724–92) in 1774, and in the North East non-rotative steam engines were used to raise water which was also used to power 'water gins'. No evidence survives of waterwheel winders but in South Wales, where water balances were used, a well preserved balance tower can be seen at Blaenavon (154/SO 250094). In a water balance coal was drawn up the shaft in a cage by the weight of a tub, filled with water at the pithead, which descended in a parallel shaft. When the water tub reached the bottom, the water was drawn off through a valve, a tram of coal was placed on top of the empty tub and then drawn up the shaft by the weight of another descending water-filled tub. An example from the Forest of Dean is displayed in the National Museum of Wales, Cardiff.

The earliest use for the steam engine, at the beginning of the eighteenth century, was for mine drainage, but it was not until 1784 that the first steam winder, a Watt engine, was erected, at Walker Colliery on Tyneside. The early steam winding engines were primitive and somewhat unreliable which encouraged the persistence of horse-gins at many small and poorly capitalised pits. One of the problems in tracing the introduction of steam winding in the late eighteenth century and early nineteenth results from the use of the word whimsy to describe a steam engine or a horse-gin, so that it is often difficult, if not impossible, to distinguish one from the other. What is certain, however, is that steam power was rapidly adopted, particularly in the large colleries of the Midlands and North East and that it remained the primary means of winding both coal and men until well after nationalisation in 1947. Electric power, introduced about 1906, has since 1947 become almost universal, and there are now thought to be less than twenty steam winders working in Britain, although a number of dead engines survive. Some have been preserved and others recorded on film.

18 Chimneys and pumping house, Jane Pit, Workington, Cumberland

Many of the early engines worked on the Newcomen atmospheric principle with open-top cylinders and timber beams, and by the end of the eighteenth century large numbers were being made, notably by the Coalbrookdale Company. A Newcomen-type winder used at Farme Colliery, Rutherglen, Scotland, between 1810 and 1915 is preserved at Glasgow Museum but is not on display at the time of writing. It has a 42in diameter cylinder with a stroke of 5ft 8in. By the mid-nineteenth century a standard layout of winding engines had developed. It comprised a drum on a horizontal shaft at each end of which was a crank; two horizontal cylinders, usually mounted on separate cast-iron bedplates, which also supported the crankshaft bearings, drove this shaft. The engineman had a control platform mounted above the cylinders, whence he could survey the whole engine-house and in many cases see the pithead too. Most engines that survive today are of this twin-cylinder horizontal type. Notable among these is the engine from Old Mills Colliery near Radstock in Somerset, built in 1861 by William Evans at Paulton Foundry and now preserved by Bristol City Museum. This engine, which is not on display, has cylinders of 26in bore and 5ft stroke, with a rope drum 12ft in diameter. A small horizontal engine with one cylinder and its crankshaft geared to the winding drum shaft instead of the more normal direct drive has been re-erected and is running on steam at the Blists Hill Open Air Museum, Ironbridge. The engine comes from Milburgh Pit near Broseley, Shropshire.

Of generally the same layout as twin-cylinder types is the large twin-tandem compound engine at Astley Green Colliery, Tyldesley, Lancashire (101/SJ 705999), built by Yates & Thom in 1908. In many ways it resembles a contemporary mill engine, with Corliss valve gear and a white tiled interior to the engine house. The engine is now out of use and may be scrapped, but there are hopes of preserving a twin-cylinder horizontal capstan engine once used in connection with maintenance of the shaft. The headstocks at Astley Green are typical of those built at larger collieries early this century, with four legs of lattice steel construction standing astride the top of the shaft.

A notable regional variation from the standard horizontal winding engine occurred in North East England, where vertical winding engines were common on the Northumberland and Durham coalfield. The direct-acting vertical engine with crankshaft mounted above the cylinder, patented in 1800 by Phineas Crowther of Newcastle-upon-Tyne, formed the basis for engines built by Thomas Murray and James Joicey for pit winders. One example, at Beamish Colliery (78/NZ 220537), is preserved by the North of England Open Air Museum. Built in 1855 by J. & G. Joicey of Newcastle-upon-Tyne, the engine occupies a tall stone-built engine-house (Plate 19), and the timber headstocks have two vertical legs astride the shaft and two almost horizontal members running back to be supported in the front of the engine-house. Other surviving vertical winders are at Elemore, County Durham (85/NZ 356456), and Old Glyn Pit near Pontypool (154/ST 265999), where there is also a beam engine of 1845 that was formerly used for pumping. Both the Pontypool engines were built by Neath Abbey Works.

The introduction of steam engines for winding resulted in new types of

19 Beamish Colliery, County Durham. Winding engine-house and headstock, 1855

winding rope being used. Those originally employed were round and made of hemp that consisted of several strands wrapped to form a composite rope. Flat ropes, in which the strands were stitched together side by side, were also extensively used, and had the advantage that during winding the rope could be wrapped layer upon layer on a narrow drum, thus varying the leverage. At the beginning of winding, with the load at the bottom of the shaft, the rope was wrapped around the smallest circumference of the drum and the empty basket or cage on its own rope at the top was wrapped round the largest. A similar form of continuously variable gearing can be seen on the winding drum at Astley Green Colliery, where a scroll on the side face of the drum feeds the cable from the small diameter at the beginning of the wind to the full diameter of the drum when the load is moving. In early coalmines, baskets or corves were wound up from the trams at the foot of the shaft on free-hanging hemp ropes, but owing to the twist on the rope they tended to spin round and sway from side to side. Thus the speed of winding had to be slow. To overcome this swaying, shaft guides were introduced in 1787, and baskets were attached to cross-bars which slid in wooden guides attached to the sides of the shaft.

20 Cymcynon Colliery, Mountain Ash, Glamorgan. A typical late nineteenth-century headgear, now demolished

The introduction of stranded iron wire ropes after about 1840 led to their being widely adopted for winding and also as shaft guides, two cables being hung down each side of the cage and stabilised by heavy weights in the shaft sump. In Shropshire particularly, with its local chain industry, flat wrought-iron chain was extensively used for winding purposes. Known as 'rattle chain', it was used in much the same way as flat hemp or wire rope, and wound on to a narrow drum. Despite the fact that wear in chain was difficult to detect and breakages were sudden and unexpected, rattle chain continued in use throughout the nineteenth century. Lengths can still be found all over the East Shropshire coalfield, used for a wide variety of purposes, including fencing.

In the late 1840s cages were introduced to replace corves for lifting coal up the shafts, and by 1860 most collieries of any size had them. Even so, corves were used as late as 1875 at William Pit, Whitehaven. An example is preserved at Lound Hall Mining Museum. The introduction of the cage, which was basically an open-sided box running on guides in the shaft, brought about the end of the primitive and dangerous methods of man-riding practised in many collieries. Often colliers merely clung to the rope to get up or down the shaft. Occasionally 'man engines' were used instead. The cage improved the efficiency of coal winding in mines greatly, as a load of coal could travel on rails in a truck or tram from where it had been cut at the coalface to the bottom of the shaft, run on to rails in the floor of the cage, be safely hauled to the surface and there be emptied while the cage returned underground with an empty truck. A typical small cage can be seen on the preserved Heath Hill Pit at Blists Hill Open Air Museum.

Having considered methods of mine operation, we must examine the two major problems facing the coalminer from the sixteenth century onwards— drainage and ventilation. The hand windlasses and horse-gins used for raising coal could also lift water, but there were obvious limitations to their capacity. By the end of the seventeenth century the size of coalmines and, for example, tin mines in Cornwall, was limited by the ability to keep them drained although in some collieries and lead mines quite effective use was made of underground ditches or drainage tunnels known in the North East as 'water gates', in the south as 'adits' and in parts of the Midlands, such as Derbyshire, as 'soughs'. These were clearly of little use for deep mines, and although wind and water power were used, it was the introduction of the steam engine after about 1712 that broke the deadlock. The steam engine was developed specifically for mine drainage and for the first half century or so of its existence did little else. The details of its development are considered in Chapter 4, as are some of the surviving examples which were used for mine drainage. These include the Hawkesbury engine now preserved at Dartmouth (188/SX 879515), which was originally installed in the 1720s at Griff Colliery, Warwickshire, and is the oldest steam engine in existence, and the atmospheric drainage engine at Elsecar (102/SE 390003) in the West Riding of Yorkshire. The Elsecar engine is preserved on its original site by the National Coal Board. Adjacent to the engine house is a timber headstock over a small shaft. Another atmospheric engine, of 1791, was acquired in 1917 from Pentrich Colliery, Derbyshire, by the Science Museum, where it is now preserved.

One of the most spectacular colliery sites and drainage engines is at

Prestongrange, East Lothian (62/NT 374737), on the B1348 road east of Musselburgh. At the centre of the site is the Cornish beam pumping engine by Harvey's of Hayle, Cornwall, which pumped water from the mine from 1874 to 1954. The beam weighs approximately 30 tons, is 33ft long and 6ft 4in deep at the centre. The single cylinder is 70in in diameter with a stroke of 12ft. The engine and its surroundings form the basis for a preservation scheme sponsored by East Lothian County Council with the assistance of the National Coal Board and various local organisations. It is intended to collect equipment and documentary material illustrating the history of coalmining in Scotland and display it in the recently restored colliery power house. Elsewhere it is difficult to find surface evidence of colliery drainage works, although here and there an engine-house survives. The massive house of Calcutta Colliery pumping engine near Thringstone, Leicestershire (121/SK 424183), is one example, and another, of rather Cornish appearance, may be seen at Nailsea in Somerset (165/ST 479691). In some coalfields engines were installed away from the collieries themselves to drain whole areas in which the various mine workings were connected by levels. An example was the scheme to drain the Fitzwilliam Barnsley Bed in South Yorkshire, of which the Elsecar engine was part. Similarly the Lloyds engine, Madeley Wood, near Ironbridge (119/SJ 690031), of which recognisable remains survive, drained a number of mines in the area.

Before turning to mine ventilation, we should mention an unusual form of coal extraction at Worsley in South Lancashire, which combined drainage levels and soughs with the mine workings themselves. The site has considerable historical significance in the early development of canals and is readily accessible to the visitor. The entrance to the Worsley Mine (Plate 21) is north of Worsley Road and west of the Delph (101/SD 748005). For further details of these extensive workings, see p344.

As mines grew in size, problems of ventilating them increased. In small workings the only gas with which the miner had to contend was 'stythe' or 'dampe', known now as blackdamp or chokedamp. It is a mixture of carbon dioxide and nitrogen which in large quantities will suffocate all coming into contact with it. Later, as mines became deeper, firedamp, a mixture of methane and air, was encountered and the era of the serious mine explosions began. Another explosive element in mines—the concentration of fine coaldust—was not known about until much later. Firedamp is produced

21 Entrance to the coalmines at Worsley, Lancashire. On the left is a 'starvationer' boat used on the underground canal system

during the decay of vegetable matter and its conversion into coal; it remains in the cleavage planes of the coal and the nearby rocks and is released as soon as the seam is worked. In mixture with air at concentrations of 5–15 per cent methane it is highly inflammable. By the late eighteenth century colliery explosions, often of great violence, were common, especially in Northumberland, Durham and South Wales. There were 643 explosions in the North East between 1835 and 1850, even after the introduction and widespread use of the safety lamp devised by Humphry (later Sir Humphry) Davy (1778–1829) in 1815.

The Society for Preventing Accidents in Coal Mines, formed in Sunderland in 1813, largely as a result of the Felling colliery disaster of the previous year in which ninety-two men and boys died, approached Davy, who expressed interest in the problem. He discovered the true nature of firedamp, the conditions under which it explodes and the rate of passage of flame through tubes of varying diameter. He found wire gauze in the form of a sleeve around the flame to be the most effective barrier. The gauze was made from iron wire ranging from $\frac{1}{40}$ to $\frac{1}{60}$ in diameter containing twenty-eight wires to the inch, or 748 apertures to the square inch. Two other men, Dr W. R. Clanny (1776–1850) and George Stephenson (1781–1848), the steam locomotive engineer, also devised safety lamps at about the same time. Miners' lamps are common in most industrial museums, but a particularly fine collection may be seen at Salford in the Science Museum in Buile Hill Park on Eccles Old Road. Another collection is maintained by the Protector Lamp and Lighting Company of Lansdowne Road, Morton, Eccles M30 9PH, which is accessible by appointment. Safety lamps reduced the incidence of explosions somewhat, but when they did occur in the bigger mines, the results were often catastrophic. In 1860 145 men died in the Risca Mine at Newport; in 1867 178 lives were lost at Ferndale Colliery in the Rhondda Valley. The causes of these two have since proved to be the ignition of coaldust, and today steps are taken to combat this by spreading stone dust in the mine workings.

    Most early mines relied on convection currents or natural air flow through two shafts for their ventilation. With increased size a forced ventilation system became necessary, and in the mid-seventeenth century the first reference to the use of a fire basket occurs, at Cheadle in North Staffordshire. Fire baskets and later ventilation furnaces were usually underground at the foot of the 'upcast' shaft. The upward movement of air due to the chimney effect of hot gases induced a downward flow in the 'downcast' shaft and the fresh air, circulated throughout the workings and controlled by trapdoors operated by boys, prevented dangerous concentrations of gas accumulating. A reconstruction of a surface ventilation fire and chimney may be seen at Blists Hill Open Air Museum, Ironbridge, and Brinsley Colliery, Nottinghamshire, still has the flues and furnace underground, though they have not been used since the nineteenth century. In Lancashire ventilation chimneys for underground furnaces could recently be seen at Clifton Colliery, Burnley, and Pewfall Colliery, Garswood. A surface ventilation furnace and chimney can still be seen at a drift mine at Trehafod in South Wales (154/ST 036910). The last recorded use of a fire basket was at Rock Pit, Shropshire, in 1965, and a surface furnace was used at Broseley Deep Pit, nearby, until 1941.

    These survivals were anachronisms, however, and various types of air pump were being installed at the larger collieries from the 1830s onwards. One of the most widely adopted in the 1870s was the Waddle fan, a centrifugal fan of up to 45ft in diameter powered by steam or later electricity at the relatively low speed of 70 rpm. The fan consisted of two parallel discs separated by backward curved blades. The centre of the disc was hollow and connected by a large-diameter pipe to the top of the upcast shaft. As the fan rotated, air was sucked in at the centre and expelled along the periphery. Between 1871 and 1896 220 Waddle fans were installed and a few still remain, though not now working. One was at Annesley, Nottinghamshire until recently, and another, from Ryhope Colliery, County Durham is preserved in the North of England Open Air Museum at Beamish. A Waddle fan at Abergorki Pit, Mountain Ash, Glamorgan (154/ST 050990), is also to be preserved.

Before mechanisation began in the latter part of the nineteenth century, and in many collieries years after then, the miner relied on pick, shovel and crowbar to get the coal. By about 1800 explosives were being used in shot-holes made with a chisel-ended iron bar, or, later in the century, by a hand drill. Loose gunpowder was poured into the hole and tamped with clay, using a tamping bar. A pricker or needle left in the hole when the clay was tamped in would then be withdrawn to allow a straw full of priming powder to be inserted. This was lit and burned for long enough to give the shot-lighter time to retire. A slow-burning fuse was invented by William Bickford in 1831 but many miners would not use it on grounds of expense.

A good selection of miners' tools is preserved in the North of England Open Air Museum, Beamish, which also has crackets or working stools and various types of protective headgear. Below ground mechanisation came slowly, and the steam engine, so valuable for pumping or winding, was out of the question as a source of power for coal-cutting machinery. The use of machinery in mines grew with the development of compressed air and electricity, particularly the latter, as sources of motive power. A com-pressed-air-powered coal cutter, using a toothed disc, was introduced in 1863 by Thomas Harrison, and established the principle of the rotary or con-tinuously moving cutter which applied until relatively recently. Three major types of cutting machines emerged, the first using a disc with teeth on its periphery, the second a continuous chain carrying cutters, similar to the chain saw used today for tree felling, and the third a rotating bar armed with cutters throughout its length. A variety of cutter-loaders have been tried in this century. The Meco-Moore was a widely adopted type, but it is now probably extinct; it travelled along the face cutting coal with two horizontal gibs, collected it and transferred it to a conveyor running parallel to the direction of the traverse.

The rate of change of technology in the coal industry, as in many others, makes the work of the industrial archaeologist difficult, particularly as much of the machinery is not easily accessible, and cannot easily be preserved *in situ*. Museums such as the one set up at Lound Hall near Retford in Nottinghamshire are to be welcomed, therefore, as a means of fostering interest within the industry itself. Another museum in which there is some National Coal Board interest is the Science Museum at Buile Hill Park, Salford, where a 'coalmine' constructed in the cellars of the museum includes a variety of equipment from various periods. Modern coal-cutting machinery is also exhibited and there is a lamp room with miners' electric lamps on charge ready for the visitor to use. The Department of Industry of the National Museum of Wales, Cardiff, also has a substantial coalmining section and is involved in on-site preservation in the South Wales coalfield (see Appendix 1). A Siskol percussive coal cutter, c1913, from Rock Pit, Ketley, Shropshire, is preserved at the Blists Hill Open Air Museum. It was recovered from the workings by the Shropshire Mining Club, a specialist organisation and the only one of its kind in Britain carrying out systematic exploration and archaeological survey work underground in the Coal Measures.

No study of the industrial archaeology of the coal industry would be complete without mention of the transport systems which developed to service it. Detailed consideration of canals and railways is given in other chapters, but it is worth remembering that the exploitation of coal was fundamental to the evolution of both. Canals in the Midlands and South Lancashire, for example, developed as a means of opening up coalfields. Associated with the canal were horse-drawn tramway systems connecting individual pitheads with canal basins. In the North East and South Wales tramways or plateways networked the coalfields, encouraged by the generally favourable gradient downhill from colliery to river or coastal wharf. Late in the nineteenth century railway companies such as the Bowes Railway in County Durham, the Hull & Barnsley in Yorkshire and, for example, the Taff Vale, Rhymney, Barry and Cardiff railways in South Wales, were built primarily to carry coal. As many as four separate railway companies occupied some valleys in South Wales in their anxiety to share in the carriage of coal to ports such as Penarth, Cardiff or Barry. The most dramatic remnants of the coal trade are to be found in the North East where there are still a few of the wharves, known as 'staithes', by means of which coal was shipped from wagon to vessel. The banks of the Tyne, later the Wear, and eventually such ports as Seaham Harbour, were the shipping points to which the wagonways led. The staithes originally served not only as gang-ways for loading, but also as storing places for the coal as mine owners found it desirable to keep a large part of their stock on the staithes, ready for immediate shipment, rather than at the pitheads, as shipmasters did not like delaying sailing while small wagon loads were brought from the colliery. The three distinctive features of the coal shipment industry were the staithes themselves, of which the best are at Seaham Harbour (85/NZ 435495), the chaldron wagons which ran on the wagonways and the coal drops which lowered the wagons over the holds of ships so that the coal could be dis-charged. A number of chaldron wagons and the last surviving coal drop, from Seaham, are preserved by the North of England Open Air Museum (Fig 17.). More modern staithes may be seen at Amble (71/NU 269049) and Blyth (78/NZ 3280).

The landscape changes wrought by the coal industry are of an infinitely broader scale than the effects of collieries and pit tips alone, and recognisable regional variations can still be seen. In South Wales the industry, crammed into the confines of narrow valleys, resulted in long straggling colliery villages of terrace houses, rarely more than three or four rows deep, strung out along the valley floors. Row upon row of Welsh slate roofs punctuated by tall nonconformist chapels lay among railway lines, many of which are now closed. In the North East the mining village was a new and distinct nucleated settlement generally fairly compact, well endowed with public houses but with perhaps fewer places of worship than in South Wales. Scotland and the Furness coast northwards to Whitehaven are noted for a preponderance of single-storey dwellings often rendered or pebble-dashed and invariably slate-roofed. The colliers of the Black Country or East Shropshire, however, where pits were often small, usually lived in semi-rural surroundings, their tile-roofed cottages scattered in little groups among smallholdings, overgrown waste tips and the dwellings of workers in other industries. Rarely is it possible to pick out the coalworker's house from that of the foundryman, iron puddler or chainmaker.

The North of England Open Air Museum has complete interiors from pitmen's cottages which can have changed little in half a century, but the

COAL DROP AT SEAHAM HARBOUR, CO DURHAM

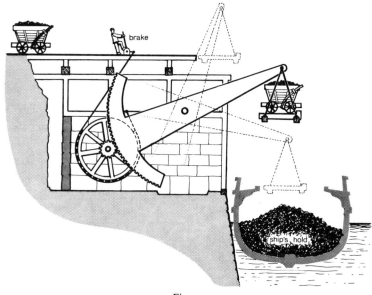

brake

ship's hold

Fig 17

same cannot be said for other mining areas. Miners' clothing, both working and best, is almost unrecorded. Similarly, material evidence of the living and working conditions of the population of mining areas is surprisingly scarce.

The coal industry, in fact, provides the industrial archaeologist with an outstanding challenge.

6 Iron and Steel

Iron and its alloy steel are at the root of our material civilisation. Bridges, railways, ships, motor vehicles, tall buildings, machinery, tinned foods, and reinforced concrete are just a few aspects of our existence today in which iron and steel play a fundamental role. The evolution of techniques for making iron and later steel in quantity are therefore of overwhelming significance in the development of industrialisation. From the industrial archaeological point of view the remains of the iron and steel industry present certain problems. Many early sites are often only physically identifiable by the waste products left behind, and analysis of the slags and a detailed knowledge of the ironworking process is needed before one can gain any indication of what originally went on. The Historical Metallurgy Society is devoting itself to the early history, not only of ironmaking but of many non-ferrous metal processes also. The eighteenth century and the first part of the nineteenth, a period in which rapid advances in iron and steel making took place, provide rather more in the way of physical evidence readily open to interpretation, though remains from, say, the 1860s onwards, have been to a great extent obliterated by recent advances in the industry. In this respect the iron and steel industry is typical of a number where evidence of earlier processes is much more complete than that of later. Anyway, age is not necessarily of special significance in determining the relative importance of sites.

The three commercially important forms of iron, in order of antiquity, are wrought iron, cast iron and steel. Wrought iron, for nearly 2,000 years the only form of the metal which was used, is an almost pure iron, ductile and easily shaped in the hot state by hammering or rolling. It is fibrous, has a high tensile strength and a resistance to corrosion far superior to the modern mild steel which has replaced it. Small quantities of slag in the iron contribute to these properties and act as a flux in welding which can be done when the iron is heated to the right temperature, and hammered or squeezed. This process is known as fire welding.

Cast iron, containing a much higher proportion of carbon than wrought iron (up to 3–4 per cent), is the product of melting iron to a completely liquid state and pouring it into moulds, where it solidifies. It has a crystalline structure, making it weak in tension but very strong in compression. It too is resistant to corrosion.

Steel has a wide variety of different forms but is basically an alloy of iron and carbon, but with less carbon than cast iron and more than wrought iron. Mild steel, the commonest form, contains not more than about 0·25 per cent carbon; it is ductile, strong in tension and can be forged, rolled and worked in much the same way as wrought iron. By varying the carbon content and subjecting it to heat treatment processes, steel can be hardened and tempered to give it additional strength and toughness. The addition of carbon to the outer surfaces produces a hard skin, a process known as case hardening. Today there are hundreds of different steels, each designed for a specific purpose and containing other elements such as manganese, nickel, chromium, molybdenum and tungsten. These alloy steels include high-speed steels, stainless steels and die steels.

Although iron is one of the most abundant elements in nature, it almost always occurs in association with oxygen in the form of iron oxides. There are two main types of commercially worked ores in Britain: stratified ores laid down on seabeds in the Carboniferous and Jurassic periods, and un-stratified ore found as nodules. Carboniferous ores occur in association with the Coal Measures, and are the clayband and blackband ores found in the Lowlands of Scotland, South Yorkshire, Derbyshire, the West Midlands and South Wales. They are of medium quality with about 30 per cent iron content and formed the basis for the iron industry of the eighteenth and early nineteenth centuries. Today most of the easily accessible Coal Measure iron deposits are worked out. Jurassic ores occur in a broad band stretching from the Cleveland Hills in North Yorkshire through Lincolnshire, Leicestershire, Northamptonshire and Oxfordshire, where the most important quarries are today, to the Cotswolds. They are of low quality, with often as little as 20 per cent of iron content, but are particularly easy to extract. An isolated pocket of richer Jurassic ore in the Weald of Kent formed the centre of the medieval iron industry, and was important until the sixteenth century when working ceased. The most important unstratified iron ore is haematite, which occurs in the Carboniferous as purple nodules of high iron content (about 50 per cent) and has been worked in Cumberland, the Furness district of

Lancashire, Glamorgan and the Forest of Dean.

Evidence of iron ore extraction is very widespread, particularly in North Yorkshire, the East Midlands and the haematite areas of North West England. In the Cleveland Hills of the North Riding mining was the normal technique, beginning in 1836, reaching a peak output in 1883, and declining gradually after World War I to cease completely in 1964. The largest mine, at Eston (86/NZ 560186) was opened by Bolckow, Vaughan & Company in 1851 to work the Main Seam, and formed the basis for the initial growth of the iron and steel industry of Teesside. It closed in 1949. The Main Seam was also worked from 1872 at North Skelton (86/NZ 675184), the last mine to work in Cleveland and, at 720ft to the shaft bottom, the deepest. At Boulby (86/NZ 760181) the Skinningrove Company operated a drift mine from 1903 to 1934, erecting for their workers a shanty town of corrugated-iron houses which became known as 'The Tin City'. The remains of the foundations and floors are still visible. In Rosedale (92/SE 723946) magnetic ironstone from the Kitchings and Garbutts deposits was worked from the 1850s until 1885. Up to the opening of the Rosedale branch railway in 1861 nearly 40,000 tons of ore had been taken from these mines by packhorse to the railway at Pickering, the last large-scale use in Britain of this form of transport.

In the East Midlands the Jurassic ores are at relatively shallow depths and have generally been worked by opencast methods. The early workings, dating from the 1850s, were located close to the outcrops, but as these became worked out, steam shovels, introduced in the mid-1890s, had to be used to move the increased depth of overburden. By 1916 dragline excavators capable of stripping 25ft of overburden were being used, to be followed in 1933 by electrically operated shovels which could handle up to 55ft. In 1951 the first British walking dragline capable of removing 100ft of overburden was introduced. Initially, no attempt was made to reinstate the worked-over areas and evidence of the first large-scale workings can still be seen in the form of ridges and furrows, with an amplitude of up to 20ft, resulting from the dumping of the overburden after the ore had been removed. Today the quarry areas are levelled and the top soil replaced, leaving an open landscape of large fenced fields devoid of trees and hedges. A steam excavator is preserved in working order by the North of England Open Air Museum, Beamish, County Durham.

The technique of ironstone quarrying has altered little over the last half century. An aspect which has changed, however, is the calcining of ore. The calcining process removes the volatiles, mostly carbon dioxide and water, thereby raising the percentage of iron in the ore. It was carried out on the floor of the quarry by burning coal mixed with ore before loading it for transport to the ironworks. Coal costs have made this process uneconomic in recent years and it is now no longer carried out. The sequence of events illustrated in Fig 18 shows how ironstone was worked in the 1920s. With the exception of the calcining stage, it can still be seen at numerous places in the East Midlands. A dragline excavator travelling parallel to the ironstone face (1 and 2) removes the topsoil and overburden. The overburden is dumped opposite the place from which it is taken on ground from which the iron-stone has already been removed. Topsoil is replaced and levelled, and the land restored to agricultural use. Having stripped a length of ironstone, the dragline dumps coal slack on the newly exposed surface. A steam navvy following behind digs out the ironstone and deposits it, with the slack inter-mingled, on lump coal spread out on the ground behind it. The whole heap is fired at intervals as the excavator advances. Calcination is complete in about 8 weeks (4), after which the ore is lifted into railway trucks and taken to the ironworks (5). At the end of the working face the excavators return to the starting point for another cut and the railway track is moved laterally forward to the edge of the new face. Today ore, which is usually blasted with explosives, is lifted straight from the bed of the quarry into railway trucks or lorries.

The principle of all conventional ironmaking processes involves the removal of the oxygen from the ore by reduction. Carbon in the form of charcoal or coke combines with the oxygen of the ore to release metallic iron and gases. In modern blast furnaces oil is also injected. Wrought iron was made by heating a mass of iron ore in a charcoal fire to create a spongy lump or bloom which could then be hammered into tools or weapons. The iron was not melted, the hammering or forging process being fundamental in the removal of many of the final impurities. This direct process was the only way of converting iron ore into metal until about the fifteenth century when furnaces of sufficient size, using hand or more often water-powered bellows, to increase the temperature, could melt the iron into a liquid state. This new iron, or cast iron, was probably at first an accidental by-product resulting

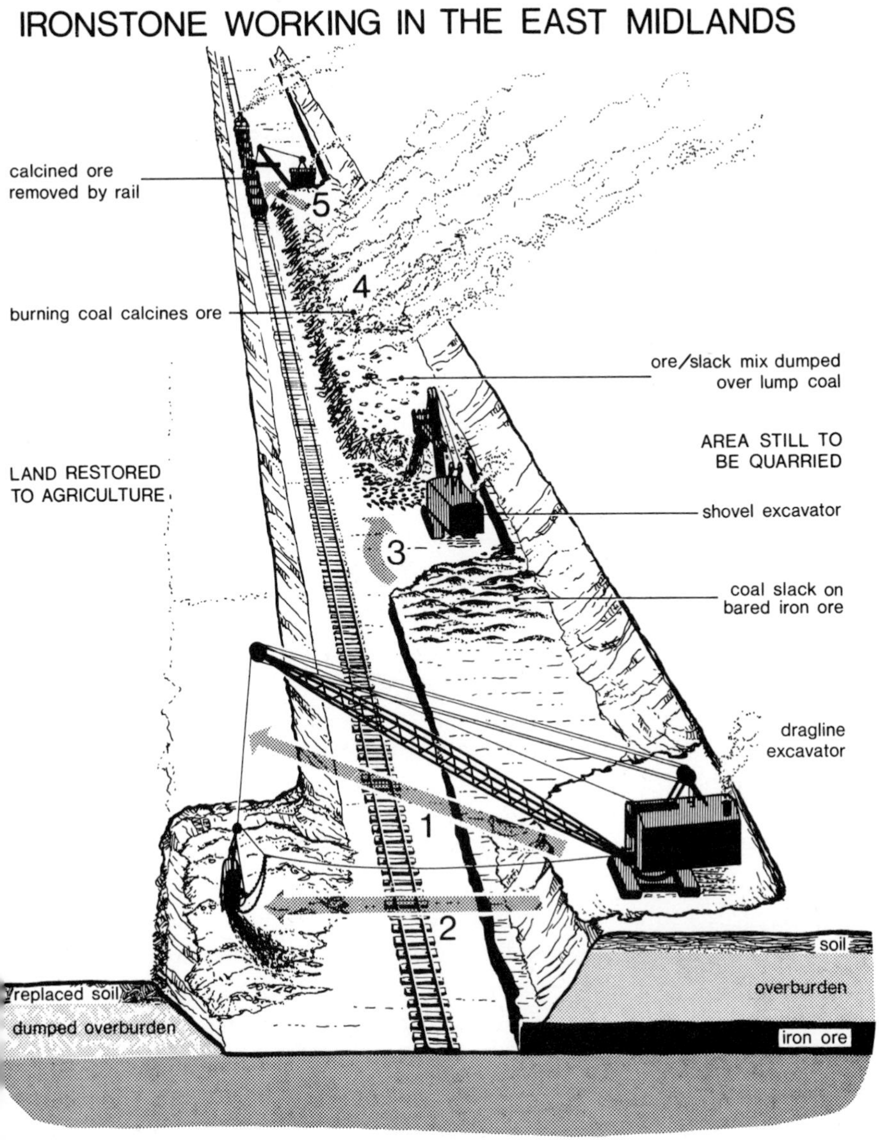

IRONSTONE WORKING IN THE EAST MIDLANDS

calcined ore
removed by rail

burning coal calcines ore

LAND RESTORED
TO AGRICULTURE

ore/slack mix dumped
over lump coal

AREA STILL TO
BE QUARRIED

shovel excavator

coal slack on
bared iron ore

dragline
excavator

soil

overburden

iron ore

replaced soil

dumped overburden

Fig 18

from the overheating of a bloomery furnace. It could not be shaped by hammering and its hard, brittle nature meant that there were at first no obvious uses to which it could be put. It was soon realised, however, that the production of cast iron could be a short cut to larger quantities of good quality wrought iron, and in this manner the iron smelting industry, based on the charcoal-fuelled blast furnace, came into existence.

The origin of the blast furnace is obscure but it is generally thought to have developed in what is now Belgium before AD 1400. The blast furnace enabled much larger quantities of iron to be produced than the old bloomery, as much as a ton in 24hr as compared with a few pounds previously. Cast iron from the blast furnace was run as a liquid into depressions in a bed of sand, the main runner being the sow and, for obvious reasons, the side branches being called pigs (Fig 19). Pig iron is still made, although now by machines, the size of the pig being determined by convenience of handling. By the sixteenth century objects such as firebacks, cannon and cannon balls were being cast, but cast iron remained of relatively minor importance until the early eighteenth century when it was to become the most vital of raw materials to the civil and mechanical engineer.

The primary object was still the production of wrought iron, which was achieved in two stages in the finery and chafery. During the smelting process the pig iron had absorbed a number of impurities, notably carbon, and, if the temperature was high enough, silicon. The finery was a charcoal-fired hearth, similar to a blacksmith's hearth, in which the iron was stirred at high temperature under a blast of air from bellows. The oxygen in the air blast combined first with the silicon, which was driven off in the form of SiO_2, and then with the carbon to form CO and CO_2. As the iron became purer, its melting temperature would rise, resulting in the coagulation of a spongy mass of iron in the hearth. This was hammered into a rectangular block weighing about $\frac{1}{2}$cwt before being transferred to the chafery. The chafery, unlike the finery, had no secondary blast of air and was simply for reheating the iron to forging temperature so that it could be fashioned into a shape suitable for marketing. The iron was not melted and no change in its chemistry occurred. Charcoal was the normal fuel in the chafery, but as iron absorbed very few impurities when in the solid state, it was in the chafery that the relatively 'dirty' fuel, coal, was first adopted. The finery and its ancillary equipment, of which the hammer was the most important, was known as a forge, a term which is still used today for any works where iron is fashioned. Strictly, the term originally applied only to the building containing the finery where wrought iron was manufactured.

The bloomery furnace, and the later finery and chafery, all needed hammers, both to beat the impurities out of the iron and to shape it. These were water-powered tilt hammers, each consisting of an iron hammer head on a wooden haft working on to an anvil. The tail of the haft was depressed by a series of cams on the axle of the waterwheel and, as the head was raised, it was pressed against a wooden spring beam which ensured that, when the cam released the hammer, it would fall with a considerable and consistent force. None of these early hammers survive in complete form, although the Weald & Downland Museum near Singleton in Sussex (181/SU 875130) has a hammer head and wheel shaft. Later, forging hammers known as helves were introduced for fashioning metal and some of these operated on the same basis as the early tilt hammers (Fig 22).

The importance of a supply of water for working tilt hammers applied equally to the blast furnace, where bellows had to operate continuously for weeks at a time. Indeed, water to power the bellows which blew the air into the furnace was a primary resource of the iron smelting and wrought-iron making industries, and an important factor in determining the general location and detailed siting of a furnace or forge. This significance can be fully appreciated from the fact that for every ton of iron smelted up to 4 tons of air were required. Today the pools which supplied the water-powered bellows and hammers of early ironworks are often the only tangible evidence of their existence, particularly in the South East, where the so-called 'hammer pond' is a familiar feature. Good examples, all in St Leonard's Forest, Sussex, are Hawkins Pond (182/TQ 217292), Hammer Pond (182/TQ 219289) and Slaugham Pond (182/TQ 248281). At each of these sites the earth dam survives intact, now carrying a minor road, and the drop necessary to provide adequate power and the quantity of water which had to be stored to ensure continuity of operation of the forge are well demonstrated.

The production of cast iron in blast furnaces expanded considerably during the sixteenth and seventeenth centuries, spreading from Sussex to the Midlands after 1561 and reaching the Lake District in 1711. The principle on which the blast furnace operated was relatively simple, although some of the chemical changes occurring within it during the smelting of a charge of

CHARCOAL BLAST FURNACE CUT OPEN TO SHOW INTERIOR

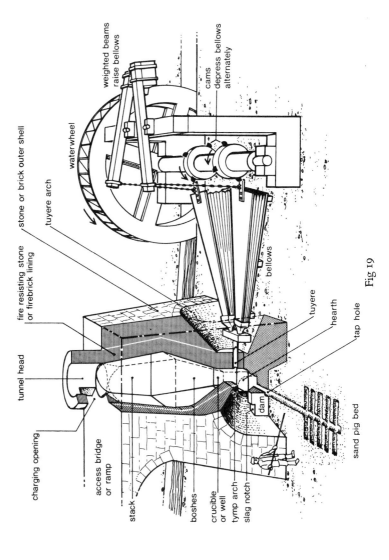

weighted beams
raise bellows

cams
depress bellows
alternately

waterwheel

stone or brick outer shell

tuyere arch

fire resisting stone
or firebrick lining

tunnel head

charging opening

access bridge
or ramp

stack

boshes

crucible
or well

tymp arch

slag notch

bellows

tuyere

hearth

dam

tap hole

sand pig bed

Fig 19

iron ore are quite complex and were probably not understood in any detail until the beginning of the nineteenth century. An early type of charcoal blast furnace is illustrated in Fig 19. In cross section it is shaped rather like a chimney with a narrow top to the stack widening gradually to the top of the boshes. The walls then slope inwards and become vertical in the hearth. There were numerous variations in this shape but the basic arrangement has been maintained down to today and still applies to modern steel-cased furnaces. The example illustrated has a square inside section to the stack; by the end of the seventeenth century blast furnaces were almost invariably circular in working section although still maintaining a rectangular outer shell.

The blast furnace operated continuously with iron ore and charcoal charged in at the top and gradually descending through the stack. In the upper part water and other volatiles such as carbon dioxide would be driven off and in the lower section the ore was reduced to metallic iron. The increase in diameter of the stack from top to bottom lessened the tendency for the charge to stick. At the top of the boshes the earthy impurities in the ore fused to form a slag and molten slag and iron were funnelled down into the hearth, where the denser metal lay at the bottom with the slag floating on top of it.

At the same time water-powered bellows blew air into the hearth through the tuyere (pronounced 'tweer') and this reacted with the charcoal to give carbon dioxide and heat and the carbon monoxide which reduced the ore by combination with the oxygen in it. As the iron trickled through this hottest part of the furnace around the tuyere, it would dissolve carbon out of the unburnt charcoal, which accounted for the high carbon content of the resulting cast iron. At intervals the slag was drawn off through the slag notch at one side of the fore arch, and when sufficient iron had accumulated in the bottom of the hearth, the clay plug in the tap hole was broken and the molten iron flowed out down a channel to the pig bed. During the sixteenth and seventeenth centuries most of the iron was run into pigs for eventual conversion into wrought iron, but if objects such as cannon were required, they were cast direct from the blast furnace. The direct technique of casting remained common until the latter part of the eighteenth century.

A typical site for one of these early furnaces would be on a fairly steep slope so that an access bridge or ramp, the 'bank' could easily be built from the hillside to the top of the stack for charging. The side of an existing watercourse was particularly suitable. At the foot of the slope there had to be ample space for the pig bed, which was often covered by a casting shed and the bellows, which might be 20–25ft long and 5ft wide at their outer ends. Other buildings associated with such a blast furnace were the charcoal store, which was usually a large barn-like building, and often an iron ore store. A particularly good example of an eighteenth-century charcoal blast furnace, where many of the ancillary buildings still survive, although in ruins, is at Duddon Bridge in the Lake District (88/SD 197884). The furnace was begun in 1736 and finally abandoned in 1867. Numerous other furnaces can be traced in the same area, including one at Newland (88/SD 299798) where the casting shed survives complete, and another on Leighton Beck, south-east of Arnside (89/SD 485778) where, although the furnace itself has disappeared, a large barn that was almost certainly the charcoal store can still be seen. At Charlcotte in Shropshire (129/SO 638861) is a well preserved blast furnace with an almost complete lining and cast-iron beams over the fore arch and tuyere arch supporting the stack. There are no ancillary buildings surviving on the site. Another good example, preserved by the Department of the Environment is at Bonawe in Argyllshire (35/NN 114770).

Charcoal was used exclusively as the fuel in all early blast furnaces, and this led to huge areas of the country being almost completely denuded of trees. Some furnaces consumed the wood from over 150 acres of forest in a year, with the result that the nation's timber resources, particularly in the South-East where there were the competing strategic needs of the Royal Navy, became seriously depleted. Before the end of the sixteenth century legislation was introduced to control the consumption of woodland and so, as the Wealden industry gradually died, ironmasters were driven to more remote sites in the border country of the River Severn, in Wales itself, the Lake District and Scotland, always seeking the vital combination of iron ore, wood for fuel and water for power.

What was to prove one of the major technological breakthroughs of the early Industrial Revolution occurred in the first decade of the eighteenth century with the perfection of a technique for smelting iron using coke as a fuel instead of the traditional charcoal. There had already been numerous attempts to use coal, of which the unsuccessful efforts of 'Dud' Dudley

(1599-1684) are the most notorious, but in none of these experiments was the fundamental problem of contamination of the iron by impurities in the coal overcome. The coke smelting process was developed in Coalbrookdale, Shropshire, in 1709 by the Quaker, Abraham Darby (1667-1717), who had recently come from Bristol to take over an existing charcoal blast furnace set up about 1638. The geological circumstances which led to Darby's success are significant and undoubtedly contributed greatly to the establishment of Coalbrookdale as a major centre of ironfounding technology by the second half of the eighteenth century. The key lay in the local 'clod' coal, which, although not a coking coal in the modern sense of the term, was ideal for iron smelting. The process of coke manufacture was essentially similar to that of charcoal burning in that coal was burned in conditions starved of oxygen in low mounds or clamps, thus driving off the volatile components. The clod coal of Shropshire is of relatively low rank, with a carbon content of 78–9 per cent, and will not 'cake' like normal good quality coking coal. It can, however, be successfully coked in large lumps and, of particular importance for iron smelting, it has an extremely low sulphur content. Thus clod coal produced a coke closer in its resemblance to charcoal than almost any other coal in Britain. It was indeed a fortunate coincidence that Darby should come to a place where an eminently suitable fuel occurred in close proximity to good quality clayband ironstones from the Coal Measures. An additional, although less significant factor was the availability of limestone, which was essential to the coke smelting process as a fluxing agent. It is likely that limestone was added to the blast furnace charge as early as the sixteenth century, and certainly by the beginning of the eighteenth the technique was well known. The object of the flux was to assimilate the various impurities in the iron ore, which could then be easily run off as slag.

Darby's technique was of immediate benefit to him, as the major output from his Coalbrookdale furnace consisted of cast-iron domestic products rather than pig iron for conversion to wrought-iron. There were initial difficulties, however, in using coke-smelted iron for this purpose, and the new smelting technique did not become widespread until the 1760s. By that time Coalbrookdale was thriving, using coke-smelted iron and also developments of foundry techniques patented by Abraham Darby in 1707. The patent for 'casting Iron-bellied Pots and other Iron-bellied Ware in

Sand only without Loam or Clay' contains no technical details but it may be assumed that Darby had devised what is basically the modern method of dry-sand moulding in conjunction with multi-part moulding boxes. The bellied pots for which Darby obtained a patent were three-legged cauldrons with a maximum diameter in the middle, and they were to become a typical early product of the Coalbrookdale Company which he formed.

By the second half of the eighteenth century Coalbrookdale's ironfounding expertise was widely known. As early as the 1720s Coalbrookdale had been casting cylinders for Newcomen steam engines in iron instead of the traditional brass. The first iron rails were cast there in 1767 and at the end of the following decade the components for the first iron bridge, the first civil engineering work in the world in which cast iron, or indeed iron of any type, played a structural role. By the end of the eighteenth century cast iron was accepted as the major raw material of the civil and mechanical engineer, to be used for steam engines, the columns and beams of mills and warehouses, tramway plates, bridges and aqueducts and innumerable smaller machinery components. Coke-fuelled blast furnaces were being built by the dozen, and in areas where the iron industry had hitherto been non-existent. Indeed the distribution of the iron industry was essentially a reflection of that remarkable geological coincidence which contributed so much to the Industrial Revolution in Britain and the nation's industrial supremacy in the succeeding century — the occurrence in the same series of measures, and often very near the surface, of ironstone and coal admirably suited to the available technical processes of coke manufacture and iron smelting. Coal of the clod type occurred in South Staffordshire in the famous 'Ten Yard' seam, in West and South Yorkshire, and in South Wales, where a denser and less reactive coke resulted in blast furnaces being generally taller than elsewhere. North Wales, Derbyshire and to a lesser extent Scotland also developed coke-based iron smelting, although in Scotland the 'splint' coals gave a rather lower yield coke and the great expansion of the iron industry there had to await further technological developments after 1820.

In 1760 there were perhaps ten blast furnaces using coke throughout Britain at sites including Cumberland and South Wales and the famous Carron foundry in Stirlingshire. Fourteen more were erected in the 1760s and early 1770s, but the greatest increase took place from 1775 onwards. By 1790 only twenty-five charcoal blast furnaces were still in operation

compared with eighty-one working on coke, of which thirty-five were
in the Midlands (twenty-four in Shropshire and eleven in Staffordshire).
The best results from coke smelting were not obtained until a stronger blast
could be developed than that provided by the old water-powered bellows.
In 1757 Isaac Wilkinson introduced cast-iron box bellows, to be followed
in 1760 by John Smeaton's invention of the cast-iron blowing cylinder,
which was basically a piston moving in a large diameter cylinder to provide
blast. Both these devices were water-powered, however; it was not until
the introduction by James Watt in 1775 of a steam blowing engine at John
Wilkinson's Willey furnaces in Shropshire that the coke blast furnace
became really efficient and, for the first time, was freed from its stream or
riverside site.

Evidence of this vital period in the development of ironmaking is readily
visible in the Coalbrookdale area of Shropshire (Plate 22). In the Dale itself
the now modified furnace in which Darby first smelted iron using coke
as a fuel (119/SJ 667047) is preserved by the Ironbridge Gorge Museum
Trust, and nearby is a small museum of ironfounding illustrating the
evolution of the cast-iron industry after 1709 and displaying examples of
the Coalbrookdale Company's products. The furnace itself (Plate 23), which
is one of Britain's primary industrial monuments, has cast-iron beams
supporting the fore arch, of which the lower two are from the original
charcoal blast furnace, one being dated 1638. The two upper beams date
from 1777 and were added by Abraham Darby III (1750–91), probably
to increase the capacity of the furnace sufficiently to cast the ribs of the
Iron Bridge. Lower down the valley of the Severn at Ironbridge are the
Bedlam furnaces (119/SJ 677034), which have recently been restored.
These furnaces date from 1757 and were some of the first to be built
specifically for coke smelting. Originally there were two furnaces side by
side, with bellows powered by waterwheels in wheelpits behind. Water
supply was extremely poor, however, and a steam engine was employed to
lift water from the nearby river to run the wheels. In every other respect
the Bedlam furnaces were a model of efficient layout, with tramways
running down-slope to the charging platform to feed in iron ore, coke
and limestone and a pig bed stretching almost to the banks of the Severn,
where there was a wharf against which the Severn trows (sailing barges)
could tie up. Like the Coalbrookdale Company, Bedlam was dependent

22 The blast furnace in Coalbrookdale, Shropshire, where Abraham Darby perfected the technique of smelting iron ore with coke in 1709. Excavation of the furnace site in the late 1950s

23 Abraham Darby blast furnace, Coalbrookdale, Shropshire. Detail of beams over forehearth

on water transport as a means of getting its iron—in this case good quality foundry iron—away to market.

At some date after their construction the Bedlam furnaces were modified to use a steam blowing engine, and today evidence of this can be seen in the form of the three tuyere arches, each of which still contains its cast-iron tuyere pipe. Air was conducted from the engine via the blast main, part of which remains at the back of the furnace, to the tuyeres by iron pipe. Although no tangible evidence of the engine can now be seen, two nine-teenth-century blowing engines are preserved by the Trust at the Blists Hill Open Air Museum about ½ mile downstream from Bedlam (119/SJ 693033). One consists of a pair of beam engines (Plate 24) driving a common crankshaft and flywheel. Known as *David* and *Sampson (sic)* these engines were built in 1851 by Murdock, Aitken of Glasgow for the Lilleshall Company of Oakengates, Shropshire. They worked until the 1950s and were eventually saved from destruction and re-erected at Blists Hill. Also at the Blists Hill museum are the remains of three mid-nineteenth century blast furnaces, with the houses that originally held two steam blowing engines (Plate 25). A vertical blowing engine, one of the last generation of recipro-cating steam blowing engines to be built before the introduction of modern electric turbo-blowers, has been reinstalled in one of these houses.

By the time these blowing engines were in use another major development in blast furnace technology had occurred, although, largely as a result of prejudice, superstition and old habits dying hard, it took a number of years to become universally accepted. All blast furnaces until the 1820s had depended on atmospheric air blown through tuyeres by water-powered bellows or steam blowing engines. In 1828, however, James Neilson (1792–1865) of Glasgow patented the technique of preheating the blast air using stoves with coal grates, which were installed and operated successfully on a furnace at the Clyde Ironworks in the early 1830s. They raised the air temperature substantially, achieving in due course a saving of 20 per cent in furnace fuel. In 1857 the process was further developed by E. A. Cowper, who applied successfully the regenerative principle used today. In the Cowper stove air on its way to the blast furnace is blown through and heated by checker-work columns of firebricks which have previously been heated by the combustion of waste gases from the same blast furnace. Using two or more stoves, heat is generated in one while air is blown through another. Alter-

25 Vertical blast-furnace blowing engine, preserved at the Blists Hill Open Air Museum, Ironbridge, Shropshire

nation of the flow assures a constant supply of hot air for the blast, which reaches a modern furnace at about 1,000 °C. Cowper stoves, introduced for the first time at Ormesby near Middlesbrough in 1860, are still used today, and their cylindrical forms with convex tops are a typical feature of most modern ironworks.

The application of hot blast, which was perhaps the greatest single improvement made to the technology of the blast furnace, resulted in a great increase in iron output and efficiency of fuel utilisation. It also meant that with the much higher temperatures involved, certain types of raw coal

24 Steam chests of the double-beam blast furnace blowing engines *David* and *Sampson* 1851, preserved at the Blists Hill Open Air Museum, Ironbridge, Shropshire

could be used instead of coke, and notably the blackband ironstones of Scotland with their splint coals. In South Wales, too, anthracite firing was used extensively after 1837, when George Crane introduced the process at Ynyscedwin. On-site evidence of cold and hot blast furnace practice is usually easy to find. Cold blast slag is of a glassy nature, has a conchoidal (shell-like) fracture, is usually blue and green, and is hard and valuable as hardcore or road metal. Hot blast slag on the other hand is a dull whitish grey and shaly, with a tendency to slake down to a fine mud when wet, although today it is also used extensively for aggregate and railway ballast. The coke smelting technique developed by Darby was acceptable when a perfect combination of raw materials was used, but there were distinct disadvantages when this was not the case. With a few exceptions, coke furnace pig when converted into *wrought* iron produced metal so brittle that it crumbled under the hammer. Much *cast* iron produced by coke furnaces also had a low strength, with a pronounced tendency to crack. The reason was that coke contained more impurities than charcoal, the quantity of ash was higher and sulphur and phosphorus were often present. In Britain the presence of phosphorus was a particular disadvantage, as many of the iron ore deposits which were being worked in the eighteenth century were themselves also phosphoric. In addition, not all the coal being used for coking had the same sulphur-free characteristics of the clod coal of Coalbrookdale.

The answer to the problem of poor quality cast iron was the remelting furnace in which coke-smelted pig could, in effect, be refined, thus improving its purity and homogeneity. The first remelting furnaces developed in Britain in the early eighteenth century were of the reverberatory type in which the iron did not come into direct contact with the fuel, which was usually coal. The name 'cupola' was given to these furnaces which were similar in general arrangement to puddling furnaces (see Fig 20). The modern cupola, which became the standard means of remelting iron, was devised in the 1790s by John Wilkinson (1728–1808) and consisted of a vertical shaft rather like a miniature blast furnace. It was used for melting iron, not for smelting, and in its smallest form often consisted of a barrel perhaps 3ft in diameter and 10ft high made of cast-iron staves held together with wrought-iron hoops. It was lined with refractory bricks or cement and fired with coke. A very early example, possibly dating from the 1820s, is preserved at the

RON PUDDLING FURNACE   CUT OPEN TO SHOW INTERIOR

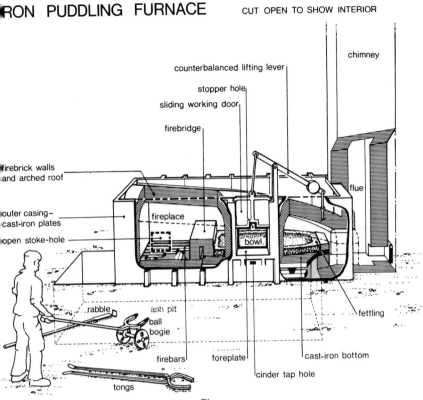

counterbalanced lifting lever

stopper hole

sliding working door

firebridge

chimney

firebrick walls
and arched roof

flue

outer casing–
cast-iron plates

fireplace

open stoke-hole

bowl

rabble   ash pit

ball
bogie

fettling

firebars   foreplate   cast-iron bottom

cinder tap hole

tongs

Fig 20

Blists Hill Open Air Museum.

A large late nineteenth-century cupola furnace is shown in Fig 21. It has a shell of rolled steel plates and a firebrick lining, and is similar in most respects to the modern cupola that is such a typical feature of foundry areas like the Black Country. Broken pig iron, scrap cast iron and coke were fed in at the charging level, and molten iron drawn off in small quantities at the tap hole as required. The iron would be either run down channels to moulds in a sand bed or caught in hand ladles and taken direct to the moulds. Although direct casting from the blast furnace continued for certain applications, the cupola almost completely replaced this technique by the end of the nineteenth century. Initially blast was provided by water-powered or even

CUPOLA FURNACE   CUT OPEN TO SHOW INTERIOR

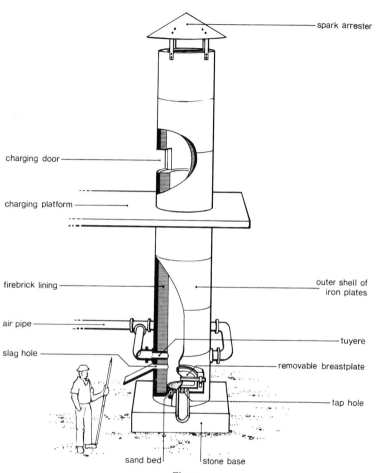

- spark arrester
- charging door
- charging platform
- firebrick lining
- outer shell of iron plates
- air pipe
- tuyere
- slag hole
- removable breastplate
- tap hole
- sand bed
- stone base

Fig 21

hand bellows, but now electric blowers are employed.

The other difficulty of making satisfactory *wrought* iron with coke-smelted pig was finally solved in the 1780s. Experiments with reverberatory furnaces using coal as a fuel were being conducted in Coalbrookdale in the 1760s by the brothers Thomas and George Cranage, who took out a patent for 'making pig or cast iron malleable—in a reverberatory or air furnace, with raw pit coal only' in 1766. For reasons unknown, this process and a similar one patented in 1783 by Peter Onions, were not brought into commercial use. Final success was achieved by Henry Cort (1740–1800) of Funtley, Hampshire, who patented a workable puddling furnace in 1784. Cort's process consisted essentially of stirring molten pig iron on the bed of a reverberatory furnace until, through the decarburising action (removal of the carbon content) of the air which circulated through the furnace, the pig became converted into malleable iron. In this process contact between the molten metal and the raw coal which was used as a fuel was avoided and blowing machinery could be dispensed with. An important contributory factor to Cort's success, however, was his use of grooved rolls which he included in his patents despite their previous use. The combination of the puddling furnace and the use of grooved rolls to produce iron bar led to an immediate and spectacular increase in the output of wrought iron and provided an additional stimulus to the changeover from charcoal to coke smelting of iron ore. Watercourses and slag can still be found at Cort's Funtley site (180/SU 550082) but no buildings or equipment survive.

There was, however, one major shortcoming of Cort's puddling process: it was wasteful of iron, which tended to combine with the sand floor of the furnace to form a useless siliceous slag. An initial improvement was effected by Samuel Rogers of Nantyglo, Monmouthshire, who in 1818 substituted a cast-iron plate and iron oxides for the sand bottom, but the real breakthrough came about 1830 as the result of the 'pig boiling' process developed by Joseph Hall (1789–1862) of Tipton, Staffordshire. Hall used a cast-iron tray for the bottom of the furnace, in which 'fettling' of oxidised compounds of iron such as cinder or mill scale was laid. The pig boiling process consisted of the decarburisation of the pig iron by contact with the molten oxidised compounds. These combined with the carbon in the pig to form carbon monoxide, which burst to the surface of the iron—hence the term boiling—where it burnt with blue flames known as 'puddlers' candles'. Hall's process, because the iron was molten, became known as 'wet' puddling, in contrast to 'dry' puddling, which was done on sand bottoms. The wet puddling process became universal, to the complete exclusion of Cort's and is the one practised today in the only works now producing wrought iron in Britain, Messrs Thomas Walmsley & Son of Atlas Forge, Bolton, Lancashire (101/SD 713084).

Fig 20 shows a typical nineteenth century wet puddling furnace of the type still used, although today oil instead of coal is the fuel. Flames from the fireplace on the left were drawn across the bowl of broken pig iron and up the flue. An initial period of melting took place in which most of the silicon, manganese and some of the phosphorus in the pig oxidised and passed into the cinder fettling. The damper in the flue was then partially closed to 'smother' the furnace while the remainder of the silicon and manganese and most of the phosphorus went into the slag. At this stage 'boiling' began with the carbon combining with oxygen and burning at the surface as puddlers' candles. Throughout this stage the puddler stirred the iron with a rabble until all the carbon had burnt off and the remaining phosphorus was removed. The iron was by now almost pure and, as its melting point rose, it coagulated to be gathered into four or five spongy balls and removed on a ball bogie to a hammer, where the liquid slag in the interstices would be hammered out and a roughly rectangular lump or bloom suitable for rolling would be formed. Hammering, or shingling as it was called, was initially carried out under a water-powered hammer or helve, of which there were three basic types (Fig 22), all of which were operated by cams on a water-wheel shaft. The type normally used for shingling was the nose or frontal helve, with a head of 5–8 tons in weight. At one end was the fulcrum and at the other the cams. Frequently these nose helves were steam-powered, but after the introduction of the steam hammer in 1839 by James Nasmyth (1808–90) they were gradually superseded and are now extinct. The other types of helve, used primarily for forging, will be considered later.

Once hammered into a rough bloom, the iron was ready for rolling, initially into a puddled bar or 'muck bar', and subsequently into smaller sections. Both the hammering and rolling processes were essential to improving the quality of the iron, which was sold according to the number of times it had been rolled. Thus muck bar, cut up, stacked in a pile, reheated in a mill furnace and re-rolled would become crown or merchant bar. The same process applied again produced *Best* iron, a further working resulted in *Best Best* or *BB* iron, and yet another rolling made the highest grade of all—*Best Best Best* or *BBB* iron.

Iron rolling had its origin in Britain in the slitting mills of the sixteenth and seventeenth centuries, which produced iron rod by cutting hammered plate into thin strips. From these developed the grooved rolls of the type

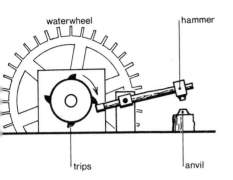

FORGING HAMMERS

Tail helve

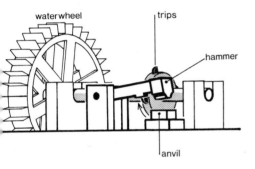

Belly helve

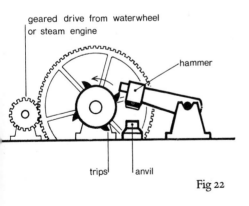

Nose helve

Fig 22

ROLLING MILL TYPES

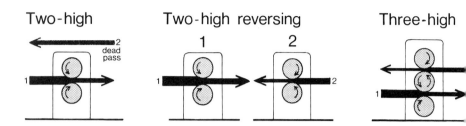

Continuous

Fig 23

patented by Cort in 1784, which produced iron in round or square section, depending on the shape of the grooves. Fig 23 illustrates the various types of roll, of which the two-high mill was common until the beginning of the nineteenth century. The problem with a two-high mill, particularly for thin section iron, was that, having passed through the rolls in one direction, it had to be returned to the beginning—the dead pass—before it could go through the rolls again, during which time it was continuously cooling. The answer was the three-high mill, in which a third roll, the same size as the other two was mounted above them. Thus a live pass could be made in each direction, the iron going out between the lower and middle rolls and returning between the middle and upper ones, work being done in both directions. Three-high mills are thought to have been introduced into Staffordshire before 1820, but they were not widespread until the 1860s. Also in the 1860s George Bedson of Manchester developed the continuous rolling mill (Fig 23) consisting of a number of two-high stands placed one behind the other. The reversing mill, in which the hot metal was passed backwards and forwards (Fig 23, stages 1 and 2), was introduced first at

Crewe locomotive works in 1866. A very old, probably eighteenth-century, two-high mill for making small section rounds can be seen at Wortley Top Forge (102/SK 294998) between Deepcar and Thurgoland near Sheffield, while Blists Hill Open Air Museum has a set of three-high rolls.

Before leaving the iron manufacturing industry it is worthwhile considering further some of the secondary ironworking processes so closely tied up with it. In both the manufacture of cast iron and wrought iron, continuations of the ironmaking process led through to the manufacture of finished articles. In the former case iron castings were initially made direct from the blast furnace and later by melting pig or scrap in a cupola furnace. Thus the foundry industry became separated from the smelting process and is now widely distributed throughout the country. Similarly with the wrought-iron industry rolled bar or rod of the appropriate quality was the usual end product of a puddling works. Numerous industries, however, used wrought iron as a raw material, some of them employing similar equipment to that found in the ironworks themselves. These are worth considering here.

An example is Top Forge at Wortley (102/SK 294998), already mentioned. Although parts of the surviving buildings may date from the seventeenth century, most of the machinery is nineteenth century, the period of the forge's greatest prosperity, when wrought-iron railway axles were made there. The oldest hammer, or helve, is nearest to the wall of the dam which once supplied the water power for its operation. The helve itself is of wrought iron (Plate 26) but originally it would have been of timber strengthened with iron hoops. It is of the belly helve type (Fig 22) with the cams on the shaft lifting the hammer between the fulcrum and the head. Wagon axles were made from faggots of 16in square iron bars heated to welding temperature and forged to shape under the hammers. A rolling mill was installed in the 1780s and iron puddling may have been carried out slightly later. All work ceased in 1912. The forge, which is being restored by the Sheffield Trades Historical Society is open to the public each Sunday (Plates 26 and 27).

Another preserved site where iron products were made is Finch Foundry at Sticklepath (175/SX 639940) near Okehampton in Devon. Here from 1814 until 1960 agricultural tools such as scythes, billhooks and shovels were made by successive generations of the Finch family. The machinery,

26 Wortley Top Forge, Yorkshire. Water-powered helve hammers

most of which is still in place, was powered by the River Taw and includes a pair of hammers of the tail helve type (Fig 22). A second waterwheel drove a fan to provide air to the various forges, while a third powered grinding wheels where the tools were sharpened. The foundry is being restored by the Finch Foundry Trust and much of the equipment can be seen in operation.

The availability of wrought iron in quantity from the end of the eighteenth century was almost as fundamental in its effects as that of cast iron produced by coke smelting a century earlier. The reputation of South Staffordshire bar, for example, became well established in the early years of the nineteenth century when Captain, later Sir, Samuel Brown (1776–1852) persuaded the Royal Navy to use iron chain instead of bulky hemp anchor cable. In 1813 he made a testing machine to measure the breaking stress of the iron and of the cable made from it. Today the remnants of the numerous chain shops linger on in the Cradley Heath area near Dudley where one or two works, such as those of Noah Bloomer (131/SJ 929862) still hammer-weld chain links by hand. A reconstructed chain forge can be seen at the

27 Wortley Top Forge. Eighteenth-century iron rolls

Avoncroft Museum Buildings, Stoke Prior, near Bromsgrove (131/SO 950684). Dudley Museum also has an 'oliver', the almost universally applied foot-operated hammer used in wrought-iron forges of the Black Country.

Samuel Brown developed further his interests in wrought iron, which he used for the chains of the Union Bridge near Berwick (64/NT 934510), and soon Telford was also using chains for his great suspension bridge at Menai. So great was the increased efficiency of production and volume of use of wrought iron in the early years of the nineteenth century that it dropped in price by 60 per cent between 1806 and 1830. From the mid-1820s rolled iron rails for the new steam railways were introduced. By the 1840s Brunel was using wrought-iron plate for his *Great Britain* steamship, and Stephenson was using wrought iron for the Britannia tubular bridge, the first of a whole generation of large wrought-iron railway bridges. About the same time the first wrought-iron girders were being fabricated from rolled flats, tees and angles riveted together, and these were making their appearance in large buildings by the late 1850s. A surviving example is in the Sheerness boat store of 1858 (172/TQ 910753). As a constructional material, wrought iron reigned supreme down to the end of the nineteenth century, almost completely ousting cast iron. It was itself soon to be superseded, however, by steel, which became available in quantity towards the end of the century and is almost universally used today.

Steel possesses a carbon content ranging from 0·1 to 1·7 per cent, depending upon its various applications, which initially were all related to its ability to take and keep a sharpened edge. These qualities were recognised from early times and it was made in very small quantities for such purposes as edging swords and tipping arrowheads. The first processes consisted of heating pure wrought iron in contact with charcoal so that it would absorb carbon. Subsequently numerous but not very successful attempts were made to manufacture steel direct from iron ore. In 1791, for example, Samuel Lucas heated a mixture of iron ore and reducing material such as charcoal, powdered bone or cow horn in a sealed crucible with the intention of producing steel. A similar process was devised in 1800 by David Mushet and another by John Hawkins as late as 1836.

The first reasonably successful means of producing anything more than the minutest quantities of steel was in the cementation furnace introduced early in the seventeenth century, probably from continental Europe. The process consisted of carburising wrought iron by sealing it in fireclay pots with a carbon-rich mixture, largely of charcoal, and heating it in a coal-fired reverberatory cementation furnace. The main improvement over earlier techniques was that the pots were sealed, thus ensuring good carburisation. The resulting steel, known as 'blister steel' because of its surface appearance, was generally of rather poor and inconsistent quality and lacked uniformity of composition through a section of the bar. A better quality was achieved by binding a number of bars into a 'faggot', heating and then forging and welding to give 'shear steel'. If the process was repeated, an even better 'double shear' steel was produced. After 1682 high quality Swedish iron was imported to Britain for conversion to steel, and cementation furnaces became established around Newcastle, the main centre of importation. It is in the North East that one of the few surviving cementation furnaces can be seen—the Derwentcote furnace (Plate 28) north-west of Hamsterley (78/NZ 131565), built in the early eighteenth century and used until 1880.

28 An eighteenth-century steel cementation furnace at Derwentcote, near Hamsterley, Co Durham

It is possible that the cementation process was brought from the North East to the Sheffield area, where in about 1742 Benjamin Huntsman (1704–76), a clockmaker from Doncaster, improved upon it with the 'crucible' technique in order to achieve a more uniform steel for springs and pendulums. After many failures, he finally found a method by which steel could be produced in a molten state. He melted bars of blister steel and subsequently iron and even scrap, with the addition of fluxes, in closed clay crucibles; the intense heat necessary was generated by coke. Two crucibles were placed in a chamber lined with firebrick, and the top of the furnace was closed by a cover of the same material, which was level with the floor of the melting house. A vaulted cellar gave access to the ash pit. Huntsman's process was

29 Crucible steel furnace, Abbeydale, Sheffield

far superior to those previously used and produced a uniform slag-free steel. In addition costs were reduced and output substantially increased.

Crucible steel was made at Abbeydale, near Sheffield, well into the present century (111/SK 326820) on a site now maintained by Sheffield City Museums (Plate 29). Here it is possible to trace the manufacture of steel edge tools from the raw materials to the finished product. The crucibles in which the steel was produced were made here and the workshop where the clay was kneaded with bare feet before being made into 'pots', as they were called, is still extant. The high quality steel was made from a charge of iron and scrap, and sometimes steel scrap or blister steel, which was heated in the pot for about 4hr before the carbon was added. The pot was then lifted from the furnace (Plate 30) and, after any slag had been skimmed off, the

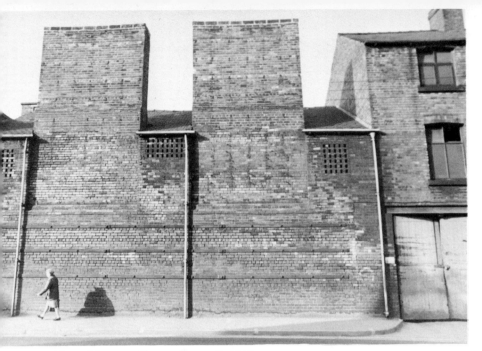

30 Crucible steel furnaces, Nursery Street, Sheffield

fluid metal was teemed into moulds and allowed to cool to a red heat before removal. When cold, the quality of the ingot was tested before being reheated and forged. At Abbeydale the reheating hearth has water-powered blowing cylinders and hammers under which the steel was sandwiched between outside layers of wrought iron. Thus great strength and reliability was given to the central cutting edge. There are various hand forges once used by craftsmen to temper and straighten the blades and also to manufacture other articles from bar steel made under the hammers. The grinding machinery was driven by an 18ft waterwheel, and during the nineteenth century a horizontal steam engine was added to provide power during times of water shortage. Adjacent to the grinding shop is the hafting and boring shop, which uses a further waterwheel to drive its machinery. In addition to this unique assemblage of workshops there is a large warehouse (now containing museum exhibits), offices, a row of workmen's cottages, and a manager's house built about the middle of the nineteenth century.

Not until the second half of the nineteenth century was steel made in quantities sufficient, and at prices cheap enough, to replace wrought iron

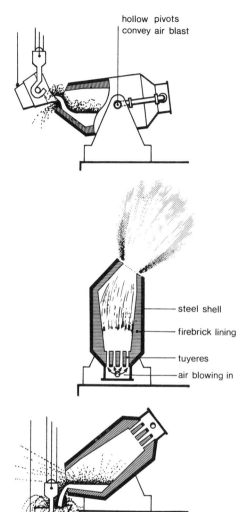

hollow pivots
convey air blast

steel shell

firebrick lining

tuyeres

air blowing in

BESSEMER CONVERTE

1 Charging with molten pig iron

2 Blowing air through the molten iron

3 Pouring out molten steel

Fig 24

for structural purposes, but after the introduction of the Bessemer converter in 1856, less than 15 years elapsed before the new material was beginning to be used extensively, firstly for railway rails and later for boiler plate and shipbuilding. The converter developed by Henry (later Sir Henry) Bessemer (1813–98) was extremely simple in construction and in the essential principles of its operation (Fig 24), being a trunnion-mounted container with a perforated bottom through which air was blown. The converter was first inclined to receive a charge of molten pig iron and then, with air blowing through the bottom, turned upright for air to pass through the iron to oxidise the carbon, silicon and manganese. As heat is given out by this reaction, the temperature of the iron actually increased. The progress of the reaction could be judged by the colour and character of the flames issuing from the mouth of the converter. When the process was completed, the blast was turned down and appropriate additions made to achieve the correct alloy composition. The steel was then poured into a ladle and into ingot moulds. An improvement of the Bessemer process was devised by Robert Mushet (1811–91), the pioneer of modern alloy steels such as high carbon, tungsten and manganese steel. He suggested the addition of manganese to remove the excess oxygen which had previously made Bessemer steel difficult to work.

The major disadvantage of the Bessemer process was that it could not remove phosphorus from the pig and, as the phosphorus in the ore accumulates in the iron, only very low phosphorus ores could be used, ruling out many of the chief sources of supply in Britain. The problem was eventually solved in 1879 by Sidney Gilchrist Thomas (1850–85) and his cousin Percy Gilchrist (1851–1935). It was known that lime would react with phosphorus to give calcium phosphate and so remove the phosphorus from the iron but, unfortunately, lime attacked the firebrick lining of the Bessemer converter. This problem was overcome by substitution of calcined dolomite bonded with fireclay as a lining for the converter. This new process was known as the 'basic' Bessemer process (because a chemically basic lining was used) to distinguish it from the original 'acid' Bessemer process. The terms 'acid' and 'basic' are still used for modern furnaces and refer still to the nature of the refractory lining.

The final major development in steelmaking technology during the nineteenth century occurred in the 1860s when C. W. (later Sir William) Siemens (1823–83), a German who became a naturalised British subject, introduced the regenerative open hearth furnace for converting pig iron into steel, using ore to assist in oxidising the excess carbon and other impurities. The furnace was in some ways similar to the puddling furnace, with flames being directed across the hearth, but the hot gas passes through checker brick regenerators before going up the chimney. The direction of combustion air and gas flow was reversed at intervals so that the incoming combustion air and producer gas were heated in the regenerator before being mixed and burnt in the hearth. Cold or molten pig iron, scrap or a mixture of all these could be charged into the open hearth furnace, which flexibility, together with its greater capacity, led to its gradually superseding the Bessemer converter. Later oil fuel replaced producer gas.

Throughout the whole period of the evolution of iron and steel making techniques the fundamental principles have been those of achieving reduction and oxidation, carburisation and decarburisation, and they apply today as strongly as they did for the Wealden Ironmasters of 4 centuries ago. For nearly 200 years, from the beginning of the eighteenth century until the 1870s, almost every new stage of development occurred in Britain, which by the early nineteenth century had achieved a degree of supremacy over all others in the field quite unprecedented and unrepeatable. The technological innovations of that period, besides giving Britain this commanding world position, had important effects inside the country by creating new regional concentrations of industry. Thus Darby and Cort transferred the iron industry to the coalfields, while Neilsen influenced the establishment of the industry in Scotland. Much British innovation assisted competitors too, so that by the end of the nineteenth century the output of the German iron and steel industry had surpassed that of Britain, helped to a great extent by the use of the Gilchrist and Thomas process for converting the rich phosphoric ores of Lorraine. The archaeology of the iron industry is therefore the archaeology of one of the most important aspects of Britain's past, of a period and of a range of technological processes fundamental in the growth of industrialisation throughout the world.

PRINCIPAL STAGES IN THE EARLY MANUFACTURE OF IRON AND STEEL

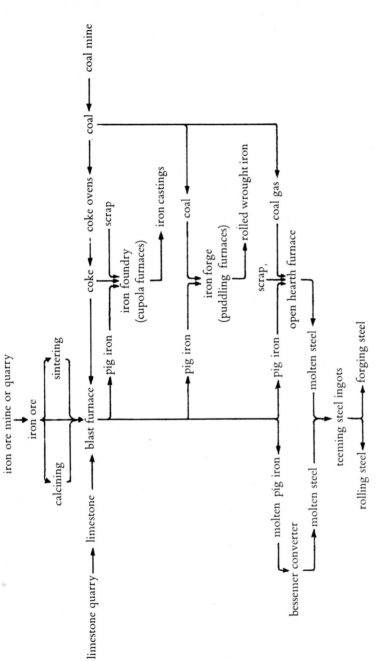

7 Engineering

THE Industrial Revolution was to a great extent a revolution in the techniques of making things, a revolution in methods of shaping wood and metal to produce machines which themselves were used to carry out other processes. There were, in effect, two stages in machine making, indeed two types of machine, which might be regarded as primary and secondary. The steam engine, as developed by Newcomen and later Watt, was a primary machine designed to carry out a specific function—initially the driving of a pump to lift water out of a mine. The limits on the efficiency of this primeval steam engine were twofold: firstly the theoretical concept which provided the basis for its design, and secondly, but at least as important, the practical limitations of available technology that applied to the way in which its components were made and assembled.

Early steam-engine making was the province of the millwright whose skills, developed over centuries in the building of windmills and watermills, were the most appropriate ones available. A Newcomen engine, built into a brick or masonry engine-house, using a massive timber beam as the link between steam cylinder and pump rods, was, generally speaking, within the already existing capacities of the millwright. The cylinder, and perhaps the boiler, were the parts of the engine that demanded the most of available technology. As the theoretical concept on which the steam engine was based became more sophisticated, so the demands on technology grew, and so too did the proportion of the total inefficiency of the engine which derived from the way in which it was built. Thus in 1774 when John Wilkinson (1728–1808), the celebrated ironmaster, patented his boring mill, initially used for guns but soon after for steam engine cylinders, he was making a major contribution to the efficiency of the steam engine. Up to this time an engine cylinder had been cast in brass or iron and its bore smoothed by a man rubbing it with rags and sand or by running the roughly cast barrel on a trolley over a boring head mounted on a rotating pole. Any irregularities in the cast bore were inevitably reflected in the finished section, as the flexibility of the pole allowed the cutter head to follow the path of least resistance. By mounting a cutter on a rotating bar which had bearings at each end, and devising a means of moving the cutter head along the bar, Wilkinson was able to bore a perfectly cylindrical barrel in the casting, which was bolted firmly to the bed of the machine. This boring mill was at least as important in the development of the steam engine as any of Watt's specific and recognised improvements; indeed the double-acting engine, depending as it did on a closed cylinder with a stuffing box around the piston rod, could not have been made without an accurately machined bore, and *that* could only be achieved on a boring mill.

Wilkinson's boring mill falls into the category of a secondary machine— one used to make other machines. It was also what would now be called a machine tool. The evolution of the machine tool was fundamental to the development of better and more efficient machines, and the men who built and used them were engineers rather than millwrights. In engineering a machine tool is a mechanical device concerned with the removal of metal or wood by turning, drilling, boring, milling, planing, shaping and grinding. During the nineteenth century machines were developed to carry out all these processes, sometimes automatically, that is, they could produce a complex sequence of cutting actions using information built into them rather than fed into them by a human operator. This growth of automatic machines and machine tools provided the basis for much of present-day manufacturing industry, saving not just on the numbers of men necessary to carry out a particular process but, much more important, saving on the number of *skilled* men required. The large-scale growth of manufacturing using automatic or semi-automatic tools was a phenomenon initially peculiar to the United States, where there was a great shortage of skilled manpower. It is no accident that the processes developed initially in the manufacture of small arms, which were to culminate in the introduction of production lines for making sewing machines, typewriters and motor cars, should occur first in the United States. The benefits in terms of cheap mass production were obvious, and already industrialised European countries, including Britain, took up these ideas enthusiastically. It is arguable whether these techniques were truly applicable in the context of a British labour force in view of the degradation of skill which they imply, and the first moves away from a production line system where each operative carries out a repetitive but unskilled task to a 'workshop' type of production environment are now being made, notably in Sweden and Holland.

The engineers who developed the first generation of machine tools during the eighteenth and nineteenth centuries were, in a very real sense, paving the way for the massive scales of production that we take for granted today, and the social and economic implications resulting from their innovations are at least as far-reaching as those deriving from other better recognised aspects of technological advance pioneered in the Industrial Revolution period. The machines they produced enabled other machines to be made more efficient, they enabled them to be made in quantity by making possible the large-scale production of identical components, and in doing *this* they were instrumental in establishing sets of engineering standards, relating to screw threads, for example, which allowed interchangeability of parts between one machine and another.

It is specifically with machine and production tools that this chapter is concerned; unfortunately they represent a much more difficult area of study for the industrial archaeologist than, for example, steam engines, canals or railways, not only because tools such as these were used in factories and workshops where they are often inaccessible but because they became obsolete relatively quickly and were easily scrapped. Many of the best examples of machine tools can now be found only in museums, while production equipment, which is generally very poorly documented, has tended to disappear almost completely. An added problem which applies particularly to production machinery of the last 80–90 years is its often highly sophisticated nature. Thus, appreciation of the significance of a particular machine is confined within the industry where it has been used; if there is no will to preserve it there, it is unlikely that any outside interest will have either sufficient knowledge or influence to secure its retention. Museums of technology tend to collect prime movers and easily understood pieces of manufacturing equipment which can be operated or their method of operation simulated in an easily comprehensible way. Rarely do they venture into the fields of complex production machinery, which makes the need for historical awareness in industry itself all the more critical.

As we have seen, machine tools are primarily concerned with cutting metal, taking on the processes previously carried out laboriously and imperfectly by a craftsman using hand tools. The earliest machine tools were the bow drill and the lathe. In the former a simple drilling bit was rotated by means of a string wrapped around the spindle of the drill and with each end fastened to the ends of a bow. Rapid oscillation of the bow resulted in a high speed backwards and forwards rotation being applied to the drill bit. In the early lathes rotation was provided in a similar manner, a string or cord wrapped round the workpiece being held by a bow or, more frequently, connected to a treadle beneath the lathe and a springy pole above. The advantage with the pole lathe was that the operator was left free to use both hands to hold the cutting tool against the work. String-operated drills and lathes are of pre-Christian origin and have been used until surprisingly recently in Britain. Bow lathes were used in watch and watch-case making workshops in the Clerkenwell area of London at least until 1970, and examples may be seen in a reconstruction of one of these shops in Liverpool Museum. Similarly the larger pole lathe in its most primitive form was the standard equipment of the chairmakers or bodgers active in the beech woods of Buckinghamshire around High Wycombe.

The first major improvement on the pole lathe came with the introduction of the mandrel lathe in the late sixteenth century. The drive was removed from the workpiece and fixed instead to a mandrel or spindle connected to a live centre which supported and rotated one end of the work, the other end running in a fixed centre. This type of drive also made possible the chuck in which work unsuitable for turning between centres could be held. By the early eighteenth century the mandrel, made of iron, was running in bearings cast of lead-tin alloy, although the frame of all but the smallest watch and instrument makers' lathes was still made of wood. Later in the century screw threads could be generated on a mandrel lathe in which both mandrel and workpiece were moved laterally across the cutting tool held stationary on the toolrest by the operator. A guide screw on the mandrel itself was engaged by a fixed key to drive the mandrel forward at a constant rate. To enable screwcutting to be carried out, an alternative to the inter-mittent drive afforded by a pole or bow had to be found, and two forms were applied to the mandrel lathe. The most common was a treadle-operated crank connected to a large flywheel which was grooved to take a drive cord, the advantage being that the operator could run the lathe himself. For larger lathes, however, such as those used by wheelwrights for turning wagon-wheel hubs, a separate drive wheel turned by one or even two boys was used.

The primitive screwcutting made possible by moving the mandrel and workpiece was greatly improved upon about 1770 by Jesse Ramsden (1735–1800), an instrument maker. The basis of Ramsden's lathe was to mount the cutting tool, ground to the profile of the thread, in a slide rest and propel it along the workpiece by means of a lead screw connected to the mandrel by a series of gear wheels. The number of threads per inch depended on the rates of the gears connecting the mandrel to the leadscrew and on the number of threads on the leadscrew itself. The first large-scale practical application of the screwcutting lathe resulted from the work of Henry Maudslay (1771–1831), an engineer who was to have a profound effect on the development of precision engineering and an overwhelming influence over his own and the succeeding generation of mechanical engineers. Indeed, much of the evolution of machine tools can be traced through the personal connections forged between Maudslay and his own employer Joseph Bramah (1748–1814) and those who subsequently worked for Maudslay Sons & Field, the firm he established in London. Born in Woolwich and employed in various workshops of the Arsenal from the age of twelve, Henry Maudslay rapidly gained a reputation for skill as a metalworker, a reputation which about 1790 gained him a position in the workshop of Joseph Bramah, already well established as a maker of permutation locks that, in improved form, are still made today. The influence which this brilliant Yorkshire inventor had on the young Maudslay must have been enormous, and the benefits which Bramah himself was later to derive from the ideas sparked off by his pupil represent a classic example of the cross-fertilisation on which much inventive genius was based. Bramah, besides inventing the lock on which most of his fame rested, also patented a rotary pump, and developed a highly successful hydraulic press, a beer pump and a machine for consecutively numbering banknotes which enabled the Bank of England to dismiss 100 clerks! His interest in hydraulics—as early as the 1770s he had designed a successful water closet which was standard for a century—led him to propose the transmission of hydraulic power from central generating stations by means of mains pipes under the streets to which customers could be connected, an idea later taken up in almost every large port in the country.

In this atmosphere of ideas Maudslay thrived and, probably jointly with Bramah, developed his screwcutting lathe. This comprised a slide rest mounted on a bed of two triangular-section bars, and a headstock carrying the live spindle or mandrel which was connected to the leadscrew by a pair of gears. This leadscrew drove the slide rest, referred to for many years as 'Maudslay's Carriage', on which the tool was clamped. The lathe was equipped with several leadscrews having different numbers of threads per inch so that screws of different pitch could be generated. By 1800 Maudslay had conceived the idea of using change wheels to avoid the need for alternative leadscrews. His screwcutting lathe of 1800, on view in the Science Museum, London, has twenty-eight change wheels, giving a range of 16 to 100 threads per inch.

After the introduction of the slide rest by Maudslay subsequent improvements in the lathe included the development by one of his pupils, Richard Roberts (1789–1864), of the four-step pulley and back gear which gave eight spindle speeds, and the self-acting traverse which enabled the tool to pass smoothly and automatically along the workpiece, driven by a long screw additional to the leadscrew and driven from the main spindle by a type of bevel gearing. Perhaps the most radical improvements, however, came as the result of American inventions, starting in the 1840s with the turret lathe in which a clamp holding as many as eight tools could be rotated to bring any one of them to bear on the workpiece by the simple operation of a locking lever. This was followed in 1873 by the automatic lathe, introduced by Christopher Spencer (1833–1922), in which movement of the cutting tools and turret was controlled by adjustable cams known as 'brain wheels'. The machine could be fed with bar stock and automatically manufactured components such as screws. A British automatic screw machine, patented by C. W. Parker in 1879, is in the collection of the Science Museum, London, while a similar machine is operated from time to time in the Birmingham Museum of Science and Industry. Other American contributions to lathe development in the late nineteenth century included the multi-spindle automatic lathe, in which a number of components could be made simultaneously, and the Norton quick-change gearbox, which eliminated the need to slip the drive belt from one pulley to another to change speed. At about the same time the introduction of high-speed steel for cutting tools greatly increased the productivity of the lathe and other machine tools and, because of the greater feed rates which were possible, resulted in much heavier and stiffer methods of construction.

To return to Henry Maudslay, his further contributions to the development of engineering and of machine tools were not concerned only with

31 Saw at Portsmouth naval dockyard for cutting lignum vitae. Installed in 1804 as part of Sir Marc Brunel's set of blockmaking machines

lathes but with standardisation and automatic machine tools, and in their own way anticipated American inventions by half a century. His table engine of 1807 was an example of a steam engine designed for standardised factory production and great portability, the first such engine to be produced in large numbers and the first widely available form of small steam power unit for factories that did not necessitate the complex installation procedures demanded by the house-built beam engine. Maudslay also pioneered the use of the surface plate as a contribution to accurate work by his employees, a carefully ground slab of cast iron being on every man's bench.

Far and away his most advanced pieces of work, however, were the forty-four machines he made to the designs of Marc Isambard Brunel

(1769–1849) for manufacturing pulley-blocks for the Royal Navy. At the instigation of Sir Samuel Bentham (1757–1831), Inspector General of Naval Works, Brunel was commissioned in 1801 to design equipment (Plate 31) capable of producing at least 100,000 blocks per year at a critical period in the war with Napoleonic France. The machines, designed by Brunel, were built by Maudslay, who doubtless contributed to their design. By 1808 the plant was in operation at Portsmouth, perhaps the first installation in the world in which machine tools were used for mass production. Output per year was 130,000 blocks, produced by ten unskilled men doing the work of 110 skilled men and saving the Admiralty £17,000 per annum for a capital outlay of £54,000. Driven by line-shafting from a 30 hp steam engine, the machines carried out the whole carefully programmed sequence of operations from sawing sections from elm logs, through the stages of mortising and drilling and turning the lignum vitae sheaves, to recessing for the metal bushes. Many of the machines remained in use for 145 years and several are preserved *in situ* in Portsmouth dockyard. Eight others are on view in the Science Museum, South Kensington. The Portsmouth blockmaking machinery established Maudslay's reputation beyond doubt, brought him a most valuable collaborator in the person of Joshua Field (1786–1863), a dockyard draughtsman who eventually became his partner, and, perhaps more important in terms of the long-term development of machine tools, made his firm the focal point for any aspiring young engineer anxious to train in an atmosphere of invention and innovation.

The most eminent of the engineers who worked for Maudslay were Richard Roberts (1789–1864), James Nasmyth (1808–90) and Sir Joseph Whitworth (1803–87). Roberts, as we have seen, made important contributions to lathe design but he was also responsible for making the spinning mule self-acting and for inventing a device for punching rivet holes in wrought-iron plate at exact intervals, in response to a request in 1847 from the builders of the great tubular girder bridges at Menai and Conway.

James Nasmyth was born in Edinburgh, son of a landscape artist and engineer. His early interest in ironmaking, brassfounding and engineering led him at the age of 21 to visit Maudslay at his Lambeth works, where he was taken on as an assistant, a position he held until shortly after Maudslay's death in February 1831. He set up on his own account at Edinburgh later that year and then moved to a small factory in Manchester. As his business expanded, he needed more space and took a 6 acre site at Patricroft, west of Manchester, bounded by the Bridgewater Canal, the Liverpool & Manchester Railway and a good road. There his engineering works grew up. In 1836 he invented the shaper, in which a piece of metal secured to a table is cut by a tool clamped to a horizontal ram that moves backwards and forwards over the workpiece, which in turn is traversed by a screw drive, either hand-operated or driven from the main shaft. Nasmyth's shaper in basic form is still used today, although there have been detail improvements. It is particularly suitable for planing small surfaces, cutting key-ways or producing any face which can be formed of straight-line elements. Nasmyth's most celebrated invention was the steam hammer, devised in response to the need for a 30in diameter paddle shaft for Brunel's *Great Britain* steamship. In the event the *Great Britain* was built with a screw propeller and Nasmyth's design of 1839 was not implemented until 2 years later. The only forging hammers available previously had been the water-powered tilt or trip hammers (Fig 22) which were severely limited in that they could only be lifted a relatively small height, and the force of their blows under gravity was not great nor could they be controlled. Nasmyth's hammer consisted simply of a vertically mounted steam cylinder supported on a type of A-frame with a hammer head fastened to the end of the piston rod projecting through the bottom of the cylinder. The anvil lay between the legs of the frame. Initially steam was used only to raise the hammer, which then fell under its own weight, when the steam was allowed to escape, but later versions were double-acting, the steam being applied above the piston to produce a more powerful and controllable blow. Later steam hammers, particularly those for fairly intricate forging work, had only one supporting pillar (Fig 25). There is a steam hammer of this latter type in the Underfall Yard workshops of the Port of Bristol Authority (156/ST 572722), while two large A-frame hammers, one of which is still in regular use, are involved in the wrought-iron puddling process still carried on at Walmsley's Atlas Forge in Bolton (101/SD 713084). Eccles Museum contains a wealth of information on James Nasmyth.

The third of Maudslay's eminent employees to make a name for himself in the machine tool field was Joseph Whitworth, a Mancunian who at the age of 22 left his work as a mechanic to come to London. In 1833 he rented a workshop in Manchester and set up as a toolmaker. By the Great Exhibi-

Fig 25 Morrison's patent double-acting steam hammer (from *The Circle of the Sciences,* Vol I, 882)

tion of 1851 this most prolific of all the machine tool manufacturers was able to exhibit twenty-three separate machines, in contrast to the two or three of most other makers, and by the 1862 Exhibition one quarter of the total space allotted to machine tools was occupied by Whitworth, the remainder containing the products of more than sixty other firms.

Whitworth was not so much an inventor of completely new tools or techniques as an improver of existing ones, and his work was based on the meticulous standards of precision which his years with Maudslay Sons &

Field had inculcated in him and an ability to experiment in a relentless and thorough manner. His initial improvements were made to lathes, and his patent of 1839 covered a split-nut which enabled the leadscrew to be engaged and disengaged at will. He also introduced the hollow box casting for lathe beds which was much more rigid than the triangular bars used by Maudslay and afforded good protection to the leadscrews. He produced a highly efficient planing machine based on previous designs by Richard Roberts and Joseph Clement (1779–1844), both Maudslay protégés, but whereas these early machines were hand-operated, Whitworth's was both power-driven and self-acting. In his 1842 machine the workpiece was clamped on a table which ran back and forth in a horizontal plane while a cutting tool mounted above it traversed the work a step at each stroke. His earliest design had a quick-return mechanism to make maximum use of the total operating time for cutting, but in the 1842 model the tool was mounted in a swivelling box that enabled it to be reversed at each stroke and cut the workpiece in *both* directions of travel.

Another area in which Whitworth's powers of pragmatically inspired improvement were put to good effect was in the development of precision measuring equipment, and here again the debt he owed to Maudslay is self-evident. In 1841 at the Institution of Civil Engineers Whitworth was advocating 'the general use of standard gauges, graduated to a fixed scale, as constant measures of size', which he pointed out would enable standard machine parts to be produced. Maudslay had already produced a bench micrometer, taking advantage of his knowledge of accurate screw-thread cutting and Whitworth developed this idea further and to greater degrees of accuracy, demonstrating in 1851 an instrument capable of measuring one-millionth of an inch.

Perhaps the most famous example of Whitworth's work was his standardisation of screw threads, which resulted from his famous paper *On a Uniform System of Screw Threads*, read in 1841. At this date the design of screws was chaotic, with no common formula for proportioning the number of threads per inch to their diameter. Whitworth's answer to the problem was characteristic, highly practical and overwhelmingly successful. Making an extensive collection of screw-bolts, as he described them, from numerous engineering works, he analysed their various characteristics in terms of pitch (the number of threads per inch), depth (the amplitude of the thread), and form (the shape of the thread). These he related to various diameters to discover maximum strength and durability. The depth of the thread in the various specimens he examined varied more than did the pitch, and the angle made by the sides of the thread was taken as an expression for the depth. The mean of the angle in the 1in diameter screws was found to be about 55 degrees, which was also nearly the mean in the remaining screws of all diameters which were examined. This angle he then adopted as his standard and in doing so a constant proportion was established between depth and pitch. The 'Whitworth' threads which resulted from this exhaustive survey were quickly and widely accepted and became the main threads used for engineering work in Britain until 1905, when the British Standard Fine Thread was introduced to cater for the need for finer pitches. The Whitworth, or BSW, thread continued in use alongside the BSF and small BA (British Association) threads as standard until 1949, when a new thread, the Unified Screw Thread, was introduced under BS 1580. Since then something of a return to the pre-Whitworth shambles has occurred, with a whole variety of Unified threads, of American origin, themselves being superseded by the Metric threads advocated by the International Standards Organisation. In addition numerous variations occur in the sizes and depths of hexagons for bolt heads and nuts.

There is no doubt that detailed analysis of screw threads and of wood-screw design can provide the industrial archaeologist with valuable dating evidence as, despite the introduction of standard types, there is enough variation in thread design, bolt head and nut shape and size, and materials used (iron or various types of steel), to enable reasonably accurate chronologies, if not absolute dates, to be worked out. Hand chased or leadscrew threads cut on a lathe can be differentiated from threads cut by tap or die, while the changeover from square bolt heads and nuts to hexagons deserves detailed examination. The use of coach bolts with domed heads of various sizes is yet another area of study. The wood screw, too, has been through numerous stages of development. Other types of specialised threads also had their standards, Whitworth's own work extending to cover pipe threads and spanners, as well as wire gauges.

Another important machine tool of the mid-nineteenth century was the milling machine. Milling is the removal of metal from a workpiece by passing it beneath or across a rotary cutting tool, in contrast to shaping or planing, where the tool is fixed. The concept of milling was certainly understood by the French clockmakers of the eighteenth century, who used small milling machines to cut gear wheels, but the credit for developing the miller as a commercial machine tool goes to a group of American engineer inventors of whom Eli Whitney (1765–1825) was the first and most important. In 1818 he made a small milling machine. This had a power-driven table, to carry the workpiece, moving horizontally below the cutter spindle and at right-angles to it. It was not until 1848, however, that a milling machine was manufactured for sale, designed by F. W. Howe (1822–91) for the Robbins & Lawrence Company of Vermont. This was followed in 1855 by the Lincoln miller, of which thousands were sold throughout the world. The problem of machining the helical flutes in twist drills, which began to replace the older flat drills during the 1850s and 1860s, inspired further refinements to the milling machine, the answer being found in 1862 by Joseph Brown of the Brown & Sharpe Company of Providence, Rhode Island. The machine he produced embodied all the basic features of the milling machine as we know it today, and with these features it deserved to be called a universal miller. Vertical adjustment of the workpiece using a screw-operated knee sliding in vertical guides, a spiral head geared to the feed mechanism to enable spirals to be cut, and provision for machining tapered spirals (necessary to make tapered reamers) were all included. Five of the original Number 1 model of Brown's miller were sold in Britain, and one is preserved in the Machine Tool Collection at the South Kensington Science Museum.

One further important machining process has still to be considered—the shaping of metals under abrasive stones, both natural and artificial. The development of the grinding machine was again largely the work of American engineers, although Nasmyth produced a grinder in 1845 with two 7ft diameter cast-iron wheels on which the abrasive stones were mounted. The introduction of artificial grindstones in the 1850s consisting of iron oxide, aluminium oxide or silica grits (emery), bonded with clay or rubber, accelerated the development of the grinder, which culminated in the introduction of a universal machine by Brown & Sharpe in 1876 in which most of the features of modern grinders were incorporated. The durability and cutting power of grinding wheels was greatly improved with the invention by E. A. Acheson in 1891 of carborundum, the name he gave to artificially produced silicon carbide. By the early 1900s grinding had become a well established technique for removing metal and sharpening cutting tools.

The failure after about 1870 of the British engineering industry to initiate major innovations in the design and manufacture of machine tools, textile machinery and production equipment is highly significant and marks a distinct terminal point in the hitherto steady progress of industrial growth. Some might say it marked the end of Britain's Industrial Revolution based on new ideas; from the end of the nineteenth century the United States and Germany took the lead in innovation in the manufacturing field. The industrial prosperity of this period in Britain was based on the techniques and skills, tools and equipment that had been used in the previous generation. Markets were easy to find and the incentive to devise new means of doing things had consequently diminished. But a completely new form of engineering industry was developing in the United States, an industry geared up to the production of large numbers of identical, relatively small, components, finished to fine tolerances on machines that required little skill from the operator. The significance of this quickly becomes apparent to the industrial archaeologist working in Britain. Firstly he finds machine tools of surprisingly obsolete design dating from the latter part of the nineteenth century. The Port of Bristol Authority's Underfall Yard workshop is an example with an almost complete range of machine tools of the mid-1880s, mainly of Manchester origin and still in occasional use. But an examination of the smaller precision mechanisms commonly in use in Britain reveals a different state of affairs. American sewing machines, typewriters, wall clocks and gramophones and German mechanical toys were finding their way into homes and offices. They were made by what came to be called 'The American System' of mass production. Brown & Sharpe micrometers, the ingenious pin tumbler cylinder locks invented by Linus Yale, Jnr, in 1865, and even American agricultural equipment can all be found without difficulty in this country. Eventually the change in approach came in Britain, a change accelerated by the technological demands of two world wars, but not before the demise of much of what the old order stood for. As Henry Ford launched into his 15 million Model 'T' motor cars, firms like Maudslay Sons & Field and James Watt & Company closed their doors for the last time.

8 Non-ferrous Metals

A NUMBER of non-ferrous metals were of increasing importance during the eighteenth and nineteenth centuries. Some, such as copper, tin and lead, had been known since antiquity, but others, of which zinc was the most important, were in effect 'new metals' from the point of view of their large-scale industrial application. All these metals were available in Britain, and the industries of mining or quarrying their ores, or in some cases the native metal itself, frequently enjoyed phenomenal rates of growth and prosperity. Just as often this was followed by total collapse, as deposits were worked out or cheaper foreign ores began to reach Britain in large quantities in the latter part of the nineteenth century. Of the four most important metals already mentioned, and of the less prolific deposits of gold and silver, only tin is mined in Britain today. This relict tin industry, however, with its two surviving mines, at South Crofty (189/SW 669409) and Geevor (189/SW 375345) in Cornwall, may form the basis for new expansion in the future as the high cost of overseas metal forces prospectors to look once again at the traditional sources of supply. A third mine may be opened in the Truro area. Samples from a shaft sunk west of Wheal Jane are being checked.

The requirements of industrialisation both expanded traditional demands for non-ferrous metals and created new ones. Thus copper, which had been used for coinage both in its pure state and alloyed with tin in the form of bronze, was needed for sheathing the hulls of wooden sailing ships and, of much greater importance, as a component with zinc for the alloy brass. The unprecedented demand for brass created by the growth of the Birmingham metal trades and engine and machine builders led to an enormous expansion in copper mining, quarrying and smelting in the late eighteenth and early nineteenth centuries. Thus copper production rose from about 2,000 tons per annum in 1700 to more than 7,000 tons by the end of the century. Similarly tin, used initially for making bronze, bell metal and solder, came into its own with the growth of the tinplate industry in the early years of the nineteenth century. The expansion of the lead industry, which occurred mainly in the middle of the nineteenth century, was not as rapid, but, like the others, it too eventually fell into decline.

Like iron and steel, the non-ferrous metal industries consist of three basic divisions—the mining of the ore, the conversion of that ore, using a fuel, to produce a refined metal, and the use of the metal to make a finished product. As with iron and steel, developments in technology and the economics of transport resulted in the various refining processes of the industry changing their location. Lead, tin and copper were already being smelted and refined, using mineral fuel, in reverberatory furnaces before the Industrial Revolution period, and, as the industry expanded, there was a growing tendency towards coalfield locations for smelting works. In the 1720s copper smelting was being transferred from sites near the copper mines in Cornwall to Swansea because coal was half the price in Wales, and in the smelting process much more fuel than ore was consumed. The technicalities of smelting also required that ore from different sources be mixed, an additional incentive to coalfield-located sites. As the main non-ferrous ores, unlike many of the iron ore deposits, tended to be located away from coal, considerable transport costs resulted, whichever way the system was worked. Thus Anglesey copper was generally smelted on the Lancashire coalfield, notably at St Helens, but some went as far afield as South Wales. By 1750 over half the total output of British copper was being smelted near Swansea, and it was a similar story with lead. Highly integrated organisations grew up, with partnerships having control of all stages of the process—the ore mining in one area, smelting and perhaps colliery owning in South Wales, and sometimes an interest in a rolling mill or metal manufactury in Birmingham. Thus the whole industry was being controlled by capitalists who had a national point of view and could balance the various components of the production process to determine the most satisfactory locations for their plant and to know which ore sources were profitable to work and which were not.

COPPER AND ZINC

Copper was perhaps the earliest metal known to Man, although it was not until it was alloyed with tin to form bronze hard enough for tools and weapons that it became widely used. In the Britain of the Industrial Revolution copper continued to be employed in its traditional role, for making bronze for a variety of purposes, but it was the widespread demand for brass, an alloy of copper and zinc, which resulted in the rapid growth of the industry, and for this reason it is worth considering the two metals together. There were a number of areas where copper occurred in workable quantities, of which parts of Cornwall and Devon, Anglesey and the Lake District were the most important. The ore is generally found in the form of a sulphide requiring a number of processes to convert it into metal. As many as fourteen separate stages were involved but this became simplified to about six during the early nineteenth century as the Webb process became universal. The ore was first roasted and then melted in furnaces with 'metal slag', a by-product from later stages in the process. This gave 'coarse metal' containing some 35 per cent copper, which was granulated by running it into a pit filled with water. The granulated coarse metal was then calcined (roasted) and subsequently melted with slag or ores rich in copper oxide. This resulted in metal containing about 75 per cent copper and 'metal slag'. The copper was run out of the furnace to make pigs which were transferred to a melting furnace and heated under vigorous air flow. The products of this stage were 'blister copper', about 95 per cent pure, and 'roaster slag'. The blister copper was tapped into sand moulds and further refined in a remelting furnace, where it was allowed to oxidise. The slag was skimmed off and the molten metal had charcoal or anthracite stirred into it with a green wood pole of birch or oak. This resulted in the copper seething as the gases were given off by the wood and becoming exposed to the deoxidising action of the charcoal or anthracite. All these various stages tended to concentrate the impurities in the slag, which was then removed, the final product being very pure copper. Purity was essential, any contaminants seriously impairing the mechanical properties of the metal. Thus even 0·2 per cent of oxygen in the finished copper resulted in brittleness.

Remains of the copper ore extraction industry are numerous although the various refining processes have left little in the way of tangible and comprehensible evidence on the ground. The Swansea valley on the other hand, perhaps one of Britain's most devastated industrial areas, shows what can result from unbridled development and subsequent decline of industries which produce large quantities of toxic or totally sterile by-products. The mining of copper in Britain on a large scale became established through the agency of a government-backed monopoly, The Society of Mines Royal, incorporated in 1568. With twenty-four shareholders, ten of whom were German, and between 300 and 400 German miners, the first workings were started near Keswick in Cumberland. The Crown received one-fifteenth of all copper produced and 10 per cent of any gold or silver. The only very early site identifiable as one worked by the Mines Royal is Goldscope Mine, Derwentwater, although most of the remains are probably of early nineteenth century date. An adit is visible (82/NY 228186) and there are shafts nearby (82/NY 226187). Over a mile of passages extend beneath Scope End, but these may well have been connected with lead mining as well as copper. Elsewhere in the Lake District more substantial remains can be seen not only of the mines themselves but of the plant used to concentrate the ore before it was taken for smelting. Like so many of these early metal mines, the sites are often highly dangerous, with small shafts often completely hidden in undergrowth. Very great caution must be exercised in exploring these areas. Underground workings should *never* be explored except with a local expert in charge.

Perhaps the most rewarding copper mine area is the valley of the Red Dell Beck, where the Coniston mines were established by the Mines Royal in 1599. Most of the present-day traces, however, are of nineteenth-century origin, dating from after 1834. The present youth hostel (88/SD 289986) is in the centre of the crushing and stamping works area, with the main workings away to the north-west. There are numerous adits, shafts and piles of slag, the remains of smelting carried out at the Low Mill site, 200 yd south of the hostel, in the 1890s. Initially the ore was picked over by hand, but by the middle of the nineteenth century mechanical 'jiggers' were being used to sort the grades of ore and there were various types of 'buddle' or separator. Even so, ore processing was a labour-intensive activity and some 600 people were employed, including a number of women and children, when the works was at its peak. Fortunately, water power was available in abundance and there were thirteen waterwheels in use in the 1850s. Before the railway reached Coniston in 1859, about 250 tons of ore a month were carried away to be sent out by ship from Greenodd (88/SD 315826), then the major port in the area. Subsequently ore was carried to Ulverston by rail. Decline set in soon after the great Rio Tinto mines started large-scale production in 1873, and with further competition from Chile developing after 1882, Coniston copper mining, like copper mining throughout Britain, soon came to an end. Other remains in the general area include the foundations of crushing houses, wheelpits, and settling beds at Tilberthwaite (88/NY 306007) built in the 1850s and 1860s.

Although the Mines Royal had interests there in the 1580s, copper mining on a large scale did not begin in Cornwall until the seventeenth century, the ores being shipped in increasing quantities from the 1690s to Bristol, Neath and Swansea although smaller quantities were smelted near the mines. Between 1700 and 1870 copper was of overwhelming importance in the Cornish economy, reaching a maximum output in the 1860s of 140,000 tons of ore per annum, to be followed by a steady decline as the workings became exhausted and cheaper foreign ores came into the country. Huge fortunes were made out of Cornish copper, both at the mining end of the industry and in the smelting works of Swansea where Cornish entrepreneurs had a large financial stake. There was one major attempt at smelting ore in Cornwall, however, at Hayle, and although the smelting and rolling plant has now gone, the area of Copperhouse (189/SW 568380) has canal dock walls built from copper slag or 'scoria' blocks 18in x 12in x 8in, which were provided free to the company's employees if they wished to build their own houses. Starting in the 1750s, the Cornish Copper Company's activities at Hayle lasted into the second decade of the nineteenth century, but the idea of smelting in Cornwall was basically unsound, some three to four times its own weight in coal being needed to smelt the copper ore and there being no local coalfield.

The archaeological evidence of copper mining in Cornwall is somewhat confusing, as many mines produced tin as well. The major areas of copper production are clearly defined, however, and included those of Redruth and Chacewater, another west and south-west of Redruth, the Marazion district, the Levant and Botallack mines north of St Just on the Land's End peninsula, the Porthtowan and St Agnes area and along the coast near St Austell north of Sticker. In the east of the county copper was also mined on Caradon Moor, north of Liskeard, and around Gunnislake and Callington. As the archaeology of the copper and tin industries, consisting largely of engine houses, waste tips, remains of crushing and stamping equipment and a few Cornish engines, is so inextricably intermixed, specific sites will be considered in the tin mining section of this chapter.

Perhaps the most spectacular of all the copper mining sites in Britain is Parys Mountain, Anglesey (106/SH 4490), which began as a series of small mines in the late 1760s but developed into a vast opencast quarry after the collapse of most of the mine workings. By the 1790s Parys Mountain was being systematically cut away by 1,500 men to form the largest copper workings in Europe, while the nearby hamlet and port of Amlwch (106/SH 449934) had grown into a small town from which the ore was shipped to Liverpool, Swansea and Holywell. Inferior ore, overcharged with sulphur, was roasted on the spot, the fumes destroying vegetation for miles around. This, together with the great chasm of the quarry itself, evoked descriptions of 'the awful spectacle of sublimity', 'the savage grandeur of the scene' and at the same time 'excited the most sublime ideas intermixed with sensations of terror' from all who saw it. By 1815 the balloon had burst, for copper prices had dropped and the best lodes were worked out. Revivals occured briefly at intervals down to 1883, when mining finally ceased, leaving the lunar landscape of today surmounted by an incongruous windmill tower (106/SH 444906) built in 1878 to assist a steam engine in draining the workings. A diorama of the Parys Mountain workings based on J. C. Ibbetston's late eighteenth-century watercolour may be seen in the National Museum of Wales, Cardiff.

Although zinc ores occur, often in association with lead, in a number of places in Britain, notably in Cumberland, Derbyshire, Durham, Somerset and North Wales, nowhere are they found in abundance, nor are they worked today. The most important ore is calamine, the carbonate of zinc, but the sulphide, known as blende or blackjack, has also been of commercial importance. The primary use for zinc found in Britain was for alloying with copper to make brass, but later, from the 1840s, the process of coating sheet iron or steel with the metal, known as galvanising, became increasingly important. The use of zinc for coating grew still further after the development of rolls for producing corrugated iron sheet at West Bromwich in 1844 and the widespread adoption of galvanised wire for fencing, while the development of electric batteries created a demand for the metal in a pure form as anodes.

Evidence of zinc extraction is sparse and difficult to identify, but in one of the major areas of working in Britain — the Mendip Hills of Somerset —'gruffy ground', as it is known locally, in the neighbourhood of Shipham and Rowberrow is probably the result of calamine working from the late sixteenth century onwards. A stone chimney some 20ft high in a field across the main street from Shipham parish church (165/ST 445574) could possibly be the remains of a processing plant where the calamine was calcined. Mendip calamine was used for the manufacture of brass, mainly in Bristol, the port where copper was brought in from Cornwall. It was used for wire making, very important for the carding of wool (see p243); and for sheet brass used in the production of pots and pans known as 'battery ware', the name arising from the fact that the brass was battered under water-powered hammers.

One of the first brass mills in the Bristol area was set up in 1702 by Abraham Darby at Baptist Mills, and when he moved to Coalbrookdale some 6 years later, it continued and expanded under the leadership of the remaining Quaker partners. In the succeeding 50 years more mills were established along the River Avon upstream towards Bath and on several of the tributary streams. Keynsham, the most suitable of these new sites, eventually became the headquarters of the company and was the last place in the Bristol region where brass goods were manufactured, ceasing production in 1927. In the eighteenth century, however, the Avon valley above Bristol was the technical centre of the brass industry and site remains can still be seen. At Keynsham itself are the remains of the brass mill with its weir (156/ST 657688) and at Saltford are the less significant remnants of a smaller site (156/ST 687671). The battery mill here closed in 1908, the last brass battery in the country, but the rolling mills remained, enjoying a brief revival during World War I, to close finally in 1924. Perhaps the most spectacular and archaeologically important site, however, is that north-west of Kelston (156/ST 695680), where the surviving walls and watercourses of a substantial works are dominated by the conical square-section towers of two annealing ovens in which brass battery could be heated to make it malleable again after becoming 'work-hardened' under the hammers.

Another site near Bristol of some importance is the Warmley Works (156/ST 668728) of William Champion, possibly the first place in Europe where metallic zinc or spelter was extracted on a commercial scale. It was established at Warmley about 1740, but had earlier origins in Bristol, where Champion took out a patent for deriving spelter from calamine. This was a breakthrough of some importance, as previously brass had been made by heating metallic copper and calamine together under a layer of powdered charcoal in a crucible. From 40lb of copper and 60lb of calamine (or blende) some 60lb of brass could be produced.

32 Warmley brass works near Bristol. The most substantial relic of William Champion's eighteenth-century works is this stone building incorporating black copper slag blocks

Champion's ability to separate metallic zinc, which was liable to volatise very readily during the extraction process, led to the manufacture of very fine brass, 'by the direct union of copper and zinc, care being taken to prevent the access of air to the materials while in fusion.' There is little on the Warmley site today which provides evidence of the technical aspects of Champion's activities, but several surviving buildings incorporate black scoria blocks as quoins (Plate 32). The site of the dam which impounded water for the waterwheels can still be traced, while from the dry bed of the millpond protrudes the remains of a seated statue of Neptune constructed entirely of slag blocks! Grottoes and ornamental walks separate the lake from Warmley House where Champion lived. The house is now used as council offices.

Although the brass industry of the Bristol region has become obsolete, with no Cornish copper being brought into the city docks and calamine mining on Mendip extinct, the area has continued to have associations with the production of zinc, which in its pure form was being used in Bristol in quantity for galvanising flat and corrugated sheet iron in the middle of the nineteenth century. Today zinc is produced in a modern plant developed at Avonmouth by the Imperial Smelting Corporation, in which a blast furnace is charged with roasted zinc ore concentrates and the vaporised zinc condensed on a continuously circulating stream of molten lead. By feeding lead-zinc concentrates into the furnace, lead also can be recovered.

TIN

Tin for alloying with copper to form bronze and with lead to produce pewter and various solders has been mined in Britain, mainly in Cornwall, for over 2,000 years, and tin ore, after iron, has perhaps been the most extensively worked metal-bearing mineral in the country. In the early nineteenth century successful experiments using tin-plated iron sheet to make cans for preserving food led to an enormous demand for tin, and today nearly half the world output of the metal goes into the making of 'tinplate'. Tin, of all metals, is one of the most familiar to everybody, although what is invariably called tin today is in fact tin-plated sheet steel. Tin is highly resistant to corrosion but is expensive and lacks strength. The result of coating a sheet of steel about 0.01in thick with a layer of tin perhaps only 20 millionths of an inch thick is a combination of sterility and strength ideal for food canning.

As was the case with much of the copper from Cornwall, so too the tin mined extensively in the Duchy found its way across the Bristol Channel, to the tinplate works of South Wales. Tinplate making was established there, at Pontypool and Cydweli, in the early eighteenth century and the process continued, but with steel replacing wrought iron, virtually unaltered down to the 1950s. Then the old hand mills finally gave way to modern strip mills, and an electrolytic tinning plant was set up at Ebbw Vale in 1948. A number of buildings used for the manufacture of tinplate can still be seen at Swansea, Pontardulais and Llanelli, for example, but most are now used for other industrial purposes and are of little interest to the industrial archaeologist. The site at Cydweli (152/SN 421079), however, is worthy of examination if only for the plaque on the wall above the door indicating that the works, 'the oldest in the Kingdom', were rebuilt in 1801. Cydweli was in fact preceded by Pontypool, but the site is nevertheless of considerable note and

33 Melingriffith water pump, Glamorgan. Double-beam pump powered by an undershot waterwheel and used to return water from the River Taff to the Glamorgan Canal

surprisingly complete, with brick buildings and chimneys still standing, many of early nineteenth-century date.

Perhaps the most notable surviving monument of the tinplate industry is the Melingriffith water pump (154/ST 142801). The Melingriffith tinplate works at Whitchurch, some 3 miles north-west of Cardiff, were powered by waterwheels using water from the River Taff, but problems arose as a result of the Glamorganshire Canal Company taking water from the river and causing stoppage of work in dry summers. The final answer, after years of litigation, came when the canal company agreed to take less water from the upper reaches of the Taff and to pay £700 for the manufacture and installation of a water-powered pump (Plate 33) to return water to the canal from the river below the works. Although in an advanced state of decay, the Melingriffith pump is still sufficiently complete for its method of operation to be made out. An undershot waterwheel drove, by means of two cranks and connecting rods, timber rocking beams that in turn operated the pistons in two cylinders, the water being drawn up alternately in each. The only other large pump of a similar nature in Britain is at Claverton near Bath (166/ST 791644), and that was used for lifting water from the River Avon into the Kennet & Avon Canal (see p77).

Far and away the most spectacular and widespread industrial archaeological remains of the tin industry, however, are in Cornwall, the county which for 2,000 years was Europe's major source of the metal. Reaching its peak in the second half of the nineteenth century, Cornish tin mining then began to feel the effects of overseas imports, mainly from Malaysia, and today, with the exception of the two sites mentioned at the beginning of this chapter, the mining industry is extinct. The legacy which tin mining has left the county in the form of derelict mine buildings is dramatic, and the characteristic stone pumping engine house, with its tapering chimney built into one corner, is a trademark of much of the Cornish landscape. The areas where the industry was concentrated were around Wendron, west of Truro, St Ives and, of particular importance, on the Land's End peninsula around St Just-in-Penwith. Tin was also mined in association with copper around Camborne, Gwenapp, St Day and Gunnislake, and even in predominantly copper areas like Redruth and Chacewater, substantial tin deposits were actively worked.

The tin mining industry has an important place in the history of technology, for it was the problems of draining tin mines which instigated much of the work on the development of steam pumping engines, initially by Savery and Newcomen and later in the form of improvements by Watt and Trevithick. Although the Boulton & Watt beam engine was extensively used in Cornish metal mines, it was the refined version of it, the 'Cornish engine' developed by Richard Trevithick (1771-1833), which found the greatest favour and which can still be seen at a number of mine sites today. Several have been preserved as a result of the efforts of the Cornish Engines Preservation Society, set up in 1935 with the immediate objective of preserving the 24in rotative beam winding engine at Levant copper mine near Land's End (189/SW 360340), the oldest surviving engine in Cornwall. Other engines preserved are the 80in cylinder pumping engine of Robinson's Shaft (189/SW

669409) within the buildings of South Crofty Mine at Pool and built at
Hayle in 1854, the 90in cylinder pumping engine at Taylor's Shaft, East
Pool (189/SW 679419), built in 1892 and also at Hayle, and the 30in rotative
beam-winding engine built at the Holman Foundry in Camborne in 1887
and preserved *in situ* alongside the A30 (T) at East Pool (189/SW 675416). In
1970 the Cornish Engines Preservation Society amalgamated with the Cornish Waterwheels Preservation Society to form the Trevithick Society, an
active body dedicated to the preservation and recording of industrial
archaeological sites in Cornwall. The engines mentioned above are now
administered by the National Trust.

Once one of the most important centres of the Cornish tin and copper
mining industry, Camborne still offers much for the visiting industrial
archaeologist. In the centre of the town, opposite the statue of Richard
Trevithick, is Holman's Museum (189/SW 647401), run by the firm that
manufactures mining equipment. Here is a large collection of mining tools,
a vertical steam engine of 1870, and models of Trevithick's steam engine
erected at Wheal Prosper in 1811 and of his double-acting water pressure
engine erected at Wheal Druid in 1800. Also preserved here is the rotative
beam engine of 1850 from Rostowrack used in the china clay pits there until
1953. In Camborne, too, is the School of Mines and the Literary Institution,
while ½ mile to the south-west at Penponds (189/SW 636389) is Richard
Trevithick's cottage.

The rich tin oxide ores from the Cornish mines required crushing and
concentrating before they could be smelted. Crushing was carried out under
stamps consisting of vertical wooden beams shod with iron which were
lifted by cams on a shaft and allowed to fall on to the ore fed into a box
below. The shaft with its cams was usually powered, through gears, by a
waterwheel or, less frequently, a steam engine. A working model of a set
of steam-powered stamps can be seen in Holman's Museum, Camborne.
Water-powered stamps or their remains can be seen at a number of sites,
including Nancledra (189/SW 500355), where there are eight stamps and an
18ft diameter waterwheel which were all in use until 1948.

Perhaps the only set of operational Cornish stamps in the world can be
seen at the Tolgus Tin Company's works (189/SW 690438) on the left-hand
side of the B3300 road out of Redruth to Portreath. Here is a complete and
working tin extraction plant which, until 1968, drew most of its raw material

from the waste coming from the deep mines of South Crofty and Geevor. Since then, mainly as the result of improved techniques of recovery from these mines, tin has been extracted from waste left at old mines, from beach sand at Gwithian and from ore received from the few surviving 'tributers', or miners working by themselves with the possible help of a son or relative. At the lower works are the stamps, at the upper works a rotary calciner, last used in 1940 to burn arsenic out of the tin ores, together with the rotating tables powered by waterwheels which separated the metalliferous material from the waste. The site, now somewhat commercialised, is run as a tourist attraction.

LEAD

Lead, like tin, has been mined and quarried in Britain for some 2,000 years and only in the last half century or so has it ceased to be worked. As with tin, foreign ores coming into Britain in increasing quantities in the early 1900s finally killed the remaining mines, although smelting and processing plants, relying on these overseas sources, have continued in operation. Unlike tin, which was largely concentrated in Cornwall, lead mining was much more widespread, with major working areas in Northumberland, Durham, Yorkshire, Derbyshire, North Wales, Shropshire and Somerset. The main uses for the metal during the eighteenth and nineteenth centuries were for roofing and guttering, water and gas pipes and general plumbing work, shot, and in the very purest form for the lead chambers used in the manufacture of sulphuric acid. It was also used extensively for the oxide (red lead) and the carbonate (white lead), both paint bases.

The most commonly worked lead ore was the sulphide, galena, which could be converted into metal in either specialised types of blast furnaces or in reverberatory furnaces. In some areas, notably the Mendip hills of Somerset, waste materials left behind by Roman lead smelters were reworked during the late nineteenth century, using more efficient processes.

The remains of lead mining and smelting and, to a lesser extent, the sites where lead was used commercially, provide some of the most rewarding areas of study for the industrial archaeologist. The period of working was often over many centuries and carried out within the framework of complex local laws. In Derbyshire and Somerset, for example, the lead working areas were divided into liberties within which miners could seek and mine ore

34 Snailbeach lead mines, Shropshire. Collapsed timber headgear

under specified conditions and subject to the surrendering to the landowner of dues relating to their output. Tools are abundant in museums such as Derby, Buxton and Sheffield and at the headquarters of the Peak District Mines Historical Society at Magpie Mine, Sheldon, Derbyshire (111/SK 173682), where there are also extensive surface remains. Some parts of the mining surface equipment are fairly conventional, and headstocks can be found in varying states of decay at a number of shaft mine sites, such as George's Shaft, Snailbeach (Plates 34 and 35), in Shropshire (118/SJ 375022). Elsewhere, in Derbyshire and the Dales of Yorkshire, for example, mine remains take the form of almost continuous fissures sometimes stretching over miles where the miners have followed a rake vein, as a vertical crevice

35 Snailbeach lead mines, Shropshire. Remains of ore separator with archimedean-screw feed

occupied by the ore was called. The extensiveness of lead mining, coupled with the remoteness of many of the sites and their easy accessibility, makes care and precaution in exploring them of very great importance. Often there are interesting remains underground, but the mines should not be entered without skilled and experienced guidance, which can often be found in specialist societies like the Peak District Mines Historical Society and the Shropshire Mining Club.

Once the ore was out of the ground, it still had a number of processes to undergo before it was converted into metallic lead. Remains of processing plants or, more correctly, the buildings which housed them, are prolific in many lead mining areas. They exhibit a number of regional differences in arrangement. Ore crushing was usually mechanised, with water-powered crushers. Perhaps the finest surviving lead mill site is in Weardale, County Durham (84/NY 927429), where the buildings and magnificent 33ft 8in iron waterwheel of the Killhope ore crushing plant are being preserved. Before this crushed ore could be fed into furnaces at least a proportion of the impurities had to be removed, so that the material eventually used was reasonably concentrated. This was achieved in a variety of ways, from picking over the ore by hand to various mechanised panning and washing operations. The latter techniques are used today but remains can be found at a number of sites of the predecessors of this modern equipment. One of the most common types of concentration equipment was the buddle, in which crushed ore in the form of a slurry was fed down a wooden trough or launder into the centre of a circular stone floor. As the ore flowed down and settled on the floor, its surface was brushed by rotating arms sometimes supporting heather. The buddling process relied simply on the fact that the heavy metal-laden fraction of the ore would settle first, near the mouth of the trough in the centre of the buddle, and the concentration would diminish rapidly towards the outer edges. Thus the centre of the filled buddle could be dug out and smelted, and the material at the outer edges thrown away. Remains of buddle floors can be found on Mendip near St Cuthbert's Lead Works, Priddy (165/ST 545508). The almost completely disintegrated skeleton of a jigging table with archimedean-screw feed, also used for ore washing and concentration, stands on the Snailbeach mining site in Shropshire (118/SJ 375022) (Plate 35).

Perhaps the most distinctive of all the site remains connected with the recovery of lead are those associated with smelting. In 1778 it was shown that lead was sublimed during the smelting of its ore, galena, and that the vapours settled in the flues and chimneys of the furnace or escaped to poison the surrounding grassland and surface water. It was also appreciated that a substantial proportion of the potentially usable lead in the ore was being lost. As the fumes were very finely divided, they settled slowly, so in order to retain them, very long flues with built-in partitions or obstructions were used to increase the time in the flue and provide sufficient surface area on which the fumes could precipitate. In some cases fine jets of water were tried in an attempt to assist settling. The most satisfactory arrangement seems to have been a long, almost horizontal flue with a vertical chimney at the end, but return flues and flues with chambers in them were also extensively used. Numerous variations on these themes can be found, defying almost any analysis of the optimum system, even if one was ever discovered. Frequently the nature of the terrain seems to have determined which type of flue was used. The flues have now often collapsed and are readily mistaken for culverts or drainage courses.

In open sites on the Pennines long single flues ran for distances of up to 2 miles from the furnace. One of very great length can be traced at Keld Heads Mill, Wensleydale (90/SE 077910). Here a Stokoe condenser was used in the flue about 160yd from the mill, consisting of a chamber filled with brushwood which was constantly sprayed with water. Between 4 and 6 per cent of the lead recovered at the smelt mill came from condensers of this type. Beyond the Stokoe condenser the flue continues for nearly 2 miles up on the moor beside Cobscar Smelter (90/SE 060930) and both share a common chimney. At Grassington High Mill (90/SE 025663) a double arrangement of Stokoe condensers can be found, with the walls of the two compartments substantially intact. At the Surrender smelt mill, Yorkshire (90/NY 988003), is another long flue extending from the union of two smaller flues from separate ore hearths, and at Lintzgarth mill, County Durham (84/NY 925430), two flues are carried on an arched bridge across a stream and a road to enter a condensing chamber. From the far side of the chamber the remains of a single flue run for some 1½ miles across the moor.

On restricted sites flues zigzagged or were banked, grid-iron fashion, with chambers at each return. Flues of this latter type (Plate 36) can be seen at Charterhouse-on-Mendip in Somerset (165/ST 504557), and there is a zigzag arrangement at Castleside smelter in County Durham (84/NZ 078485). The Wanlockhead site in Dumfriesshire (68/NS 855144) has a curious coiled system of flues nearly 1,000yd long and the remains of a condenser which held racks of pebbles and water-soaked coke filters. Wanlockhead is also notable for the water-powered pumping engine (see p76) used to drain the workings (Plate 37).

36 Lead precipitation flues, Charterhouse-on-Mendip, Somerset

37 Water bucket beam engine at Straitsteps lead mine, Wanlockhead, Dumfriesshire

Associated with these flues were chimneys, often of considerable height, many of which still survive. Some dominate the landscape for many miles, as at Smitham Hill, Mendip (165/ST 556547), where a chimney of very Cornish appearance has been recently restored. Another 'Cornish' type of chimney of circular section tops the long flue from Langley smelt mill, Northumberland (77/NY 841611), and there is a square section stack of squat appearance at Stone Edge mill, Derbyshire (111/SK 334670). Alport, Derbyshire (111/SK 223648) has a particularly corpulent chimney designed to receive the gases from four separate furnaces. Smelt mill chimneys in the mid-Pennines area also provide the inspiration for the band of enthusiasts who form the Earby Mines Research Group. They have repaired a number of chimneys, together with buddles and dressing floors, a horse gin and various pump rod chambers.

Before leaving chimneys and flues it is worth mentioning that other metal industries also used them to a certain extent in conjunction with the refining of tin and copper, as at Crews Hole, Bristol, where a copper works chimney survives (156/ST 625733), and also in the extraction of arsenic. In the latter case the flue played a twofold role in preventing the poisonous arsenious oxide from contaminating the countryside and by providing a means of recovery of the material for commercial use. At the Devon Great Consols mine (175/SX 425733), which was concerned initially with copper, arsenic had become the main source of income by the 1870s, as the chimney and flue system indicate. In Cornwall the Botallack tin mine (189/SW 363333) has a complete labyrinth of arsenic flues.

One product for which lead was extensively used—lead shot—required a highly specialised form of industrial building for its manufacture. By a process perfected in Bristol in the 1780s molten lead (mixed with arsenic to make it form hard and spherical globules) was poured through a perforated tray to fall up to 150ft into a vat of water. The droplets solidified as they fell and the water prevented them being damaged by impact. What was probably the first shot tower, built in Bristol in about 1787, was demolished in 1968 for the inevitable road widening, and this great loss, coupled with the

38 Shot tower in the works of Associated Lead, Chester

destruction soon after of the 174ft Elswick shot tower in Newcastle-upon-Tyne, means that there is now only one in existence in Britain (Plate 38), in the works of Associated Lead at Chester (109/SJ 415667). A shot tower that stood near Waterloo Bridge, London, was pulled down soon after the Festival of Britain in 1951.

OTHER NON-FERROUS METALS

Of the other non-ferrous metals which have been worked or processed in Britain, aluminium is perhaps the most important. A relatively 'modern' metal, it was considered semi-precious as recently as the 1890s and a century ago fetched £3 per ounce. The intensive demand for the metal, created particularly by the wartime aircraft industry, has made it the most important after iron/steel. The smelting industry in Britain uses imported bauxite (the ore, hydrated aluminium oxide) and because the process is electrical it is sited near sources of cheap electricity—for instance, in the Highlands of Scotland where hydroelectric generation makes smelting more economical than elsewhere. As with the smelting of copper in South Wales 150 years ago, the industry is located near its source of energy.

Although early aluminium smelters may only now be coming within the province of industrial archaeological investigation, gold mining installations in Wales provide a surprising wealth of site evidence. The gold mining industry was largely concentrated in Merionethshire north of the River Mawddach, and in Carmarthenshire. At Dolaucothi in Carmarthenshire, where the Romans had mined gold, there were revivals of activity in 1910 and the 1930s, the site (140/SN 670410) being finally abandoned in 1940. Although remains of the Roman workings, including an adit and watercourse, can still be seen, the only evidence of the recent mining is a concrete capped shaft. At Gwynfynydd (116/SH 735275) in Merioneth, however, there are substantial remains of the ore concentration plant, with steel pipes which brought water to a turbine, part of which still survives, and walls surrounding extensive working levels. The mine was worked from a number of levels, and there is a substantial headframe in one of them used for winding up and down an inclined shaft from levels lower down. Near the entrance to one of these adit levels is the strong room (116/SH 737282) where gold was stored before being transported to the mill. The site was first worked in 1864, reached its peak output in the 1901–4 period and finally closed in 1938.

9 Stone, Clay and Glass

THE iron industry, on which so much of Britain's industrial growth depended, relied on basic raw materials taken out of the ground—iron ore, limestone and coal for coking. So too did non-ferrous metal industries like those of tin, copper, zinc and lead. All these metal extraction industries, and their concomitant processing and refining, underwent radical changes in scale and technology during the Industrial Revolution period, which makes them a legitimate area of study for the industrial archaeologist. There were, however, other extractive industries, and manufacturing industries based on mineral or quarried raw materials, which also gained in importance during the same period. They used non-metallic raw materials, notably stone and clay. The stone industry, based largely on quarrying, was a traditional one which underwent more change as a result of increasing scale of operation than major advances in extractive technology. The products of quarrying in the form of stone for building continued to be used in the traditional manner. The main effects of industrialisation were to create enormous new demands on certain specialised sectors of the quarrying industry—for roofing slates from North Wales, for example—and it is these aspects of the industry on which this chapter will concentrate. Similarly demand for bricks, cement and later concrete was greatly stimulated by the building activity associated with industrialisation. The pottery and glass industries, also based on raw materials out of the ground, expanded enormously and developed new technologies. In the pottery industry, and largely as a result of the organisational innovations of Josiah Wedgwood (1730–95), not only were new manufacturing techniques introduced but a whole new approach to the basis of employment of workers akin to a 'production line' was devised, with specialist craftsmen each engaged on a limited area of the production process.

STONE AND CLAY FOR BUILDING

Even before the 'transport revolution', which occurred in parallel with the development of industrialisation, stone was carried enormous distances from the quarry to the place where it was used—Clipsham stone from Rutland to Windsor Castle, Purbeck 'marble' to Durham and many other cathedrals. With the completion of the Avon Navigation in 1727, Bath stone became even more extensively used, in London and Dublin, for example, and in the 1730s Ralph Allen built one of the first railways, to connect his Combe Down quarries overlooking Bath with the River Avon link to the outside world. The nineteenth century saw the real expansion of this long-distance transport of stone. The growth of London alone created enormous demands for stone, as it did for brick and slate also. Dartmoor granite was used for Rennie's London Bridge in the 1820s, Bazalgette's Victoria Embankment came largely from the quarries of Lundy Island, and Portland stone, already well established for the public buildings of the metropolis, became uniquely associated with the imperialist architectural *tours de force* of the Edwardian era.

Most stone is quarried, as opposed to being mined, and quarries, both working and abandoned, often yield useful information for the industrial archaeologist. Cranes, primitive railways, rock-sawing equipment, and curious little brick- or stone-built powder houses are among the site evidence to be found in disused stone quarries, which very often contain at least some other abandoned equipment too. A sandstone quarry in Bebington, Cheshire (109/SJ 315845), for example, possesses fishbelly rails on stone sleepers, thought to be part of the original track of the Liverpool & Manchester Railway and, until recently, there was also a steam-powered rock saw built in Vermont, USA.

In contrast to most building stones, Bath stone has since the 1850s usually been mined in underground galleries, many of great size. Only one, the Monks Park mine, is still in operation, but remains of others exist at Box and Corsham. The stone occurs in beds over 20ft thick, which were reached by shafts and inclines. The method of working was, in effect, the 'pillar and stall' technique in that huge stone pillars were left in the workings to support the roof as mining proceeded. The Bath stone was taken out in large blocks which were, until the 1940s, sawn by hand, but today a coal-cutting machine is used.

Of all the building materials quarried in the British Isles, Welsh slate has perhaps had the most geographically widespread use and its extraction has produced some strikingly spectacular landscapes of lunar quality. Before about 1820 North Wales slate was mainly used locally, but with the development of the canal network in England and later of railways, the easily won and highly tractable slate became the cheapest available roofing material over most of Britain. Huge quantities left North Wales on coastal schooners and by rail to cover acres of rooftops in every industrial town and city. Only in areas such as the West Riding of Yorkshire, Collyweston in Lincolnshire and Stonesfield in Oxfordshire could locally available 'slates'—in fact they are laminar limestone—hold their own. Welsh slates, and to a lesser extent Westmorland slates, were both cheap to quarry and dress and could be provided in accurate sizes of absolutely uniform quality which, in addition to the fact that they were relatively thin, made them ideal for the hundreds of thousands of standardised workers' houses which were being built throughout the nineteenth century.

Several parts of North Wales, even today, are still totally dominated by the slate industry, which once thrived there but is now almost dead. The huge Penrhyn complex (107/SH 6265) glowers over Bethesda and the entrance to Nant Ffrancon, massive piles of waste spilling over from the working levels high above the floor of the valley, and Blaenau Ffestiniog (109/SH 7046) is almost surrounded on the north and east by old quarry workings, together with underground mines. Perhaps the most spectacular and, to the industrial archaeologist, one of the most interesting areas of slate working is to the south-east of Llyn Padarn, in the Dinorwic Quarry at Gilfach Ddu, Llanberis (107/SH 5960). Here the North Wales Quarrying Museum has been set up, under the care of the National Museum of Wales, in the quarry workshop buildings.

First worked in 1809, the Dinorwic Quarry (Plate 39), like others in Caernarvonshire, enjoyed its greatest prosperity in the latter part of the nineteenth century, peak output being reached in 1900, when some 3,000 men were employed. The workshop buildings were erected in 1870 around a quadrangle, the main entrance being through a central archway surmounted by a clock with a face of slate. Behind towers the quarry, with terrace upon terrace of workings reaching up from the shores of Llyn Padarn 1,400 ft to the top of Elidir. It closed in 1969.

The museum occupies the old workshops or, to be more accurate, the old workshops *are* the museum, for they are little changed from when they were in use, and contain much of the original equipment. A woodworking

39 Llanberis slate quarry, Caernarvon

shop, pattern shop, foundries, smithies, fitting shops and locomotive sheds
made the quarries almost completely self-sufficient, enabling the company
to manufacture and maintain almost everything it required for the quarrying,
dressing and transport of the slate. All the machines were driven by line-
shafting from a single waterwheel of 50ft 5in diameter and 80 hp, which was
the sole prime mover from 1870 to 1925, when it was replaced by a Pelton
wheel that still drives some of the machinery. The foundry, dominated by a
huge hand-operated wooden crane of 1872, looks as it did when working,
with wooden patterns laid out for gear wheels, locomotive wheels, turn-
tables and numerous smaller items. At the four blacksmiths' hearths all the
hand tools for the quarry were made. The machine shop has lathes, a slotting
machine and a drill, most dating from early this century. Slate-sawing
tables can be seen and other aspects of the slate-dressing industry are to be
included as the museum develops. Outside a section of narrow gauge
railway along the shores of Llyn Padarn has been reinstated by a private
company to carry passengers.

Although Welsh slates were almost universal roofing material for the
houses and factories of nineteenth-century industrial Britain, by far the

majority of those buildings were built of brick rather than stone. Only in specific areas of Pennine Yorkshire and Lancashire did stone continue almost throughout, and even here invading terraces of red brick can often be seen. Elsewhere bricks were used for everything, the whole of the Midlands industrial area and all London but the centre being built of burnt clay from hundreds of brick-clay pits. It is in a way remarkable that something as large as a house is built of something as small as a brick but, as a manu-factured building unit, the brick had and still has a lot to offer, of which convenience of handling is the most important, being related to what a bricklayer can hold comfortably in one hand. The size of bricks has thus remained remarkably consistent. A curious exception were the bricks made by Sir Joseph Wilkes at his Measham brickworks in Leicestershire during the 1790s in an attempt to beat the brick tax introduced in 1784. Known locally as Wilkes' Gobs, these bricks, almost twice the size of normal ones, can still be seen in a number of houses in Measham (120/SK 334122) and nearby villages.

Wilkes' Gobs were only successful for a short time, as in 1803 bricks larger than 10in by 3in by 5in paid double the tax. The rate of duty was substantial, starting in 1784 at 2s 6d per 1,000 and reaching 5s in 1803, when tiles were also included. In 1833 the tile tax was repealed but 2 years later the duty on common bricks was raised to 5s 10d per 1,000. All taxes on bricks were removed in 1850, a considerable sacrifice of revenue by the government, which, in the year before the duty was repealed, collected charges on 1,800 million bricks.

Throughout the nineteenth century brickmaking continued to be the highly localised industry which it had always been, located near its market as the result of heavy transport charges on articles of low unit cost. Clay suitable for brickmaking is widespread and, as these clays are very varied, even in an industrial England, where uniformity was almost applauded in ordinary buildings, brick-built houses exhibit a surprising diversity of colour and texture.

Mechanisation of the brick-making process occurred progressively throughout the nineteenth century, although some of the first improvements, such as the compacting of clay under rollers, were introduced in the middle of the eighteenth. At that date bricks were hand-moulded and often fired in clamps in which the newly dried 'green' bricks were stacked with layers

40 Conical brick kiln, Nettlebed, Oxfordshire

of slack coal under a layer of earth. Later, updraught kilns were used, the bricks being stacked in a chamber with a fire below; temperatures were much higher, greater vitrification of the clay occurred and stronger and more durable bricks resulted. As with kilns for fine china, there is great variety to be found in the types of kiln built for brick and tile firing, both intermittent and continuous. The main problem with brick firing was that it was a batch process, both expensive in fuel and time. The breakthrough came with the introduction in 1858 of a form of continuous kiln by the German engineer Friedrich Hoffman (1818–1900). The Hoffman kiln was circular, with a tall central chimney, and consisted of a series of radiating chambers which could be charged, fired and unloaded in a continuous succession. The gas flow was so arranged that the exhaust from the bank being fired dried the 'green' bricks in the next bank and air passing over fired bricks in previous chambers cooled them, while providing preheated air for the chamber being fired. Kilns of this type are now becoming rare in

Britain; remains of one can be seen at Glencaise, Perthshire (55/NO 193206), and a very large example was demolished recently at Donnington, Shropshire, although a film of its operation is held by the Ironbridge Gorge Museum. Brickmaking, together with roof tile manufacture, is one of the industries well represented in the East Shropshire coalfield and one which this museum is anxious to have represented. A small brick and tile works at the Blists Hill Open Air Museum is currently being restored, as is the adjacent clay pit winding gear. A roof tile drying floor with underfloor flues has been reconstructed and a number of tile presses, which look rather like the fly-presses seen in engineering works, have been restored to working condition. Two circular Hoffmans dating from 1866 and 1873 at William Thomas's works at Wellington, Somerset, are unlikely to survive long, but the owners have co-operated with local industrial archaeologists to ensure proper recording.

   Another aspect of the tile industry which enjoyed enormous markets in the second half of the nineteenth century was the manufacture of decorative wall and floor tiles. Two of the largest makers, Maws and Craven Dunnill, had their works at Jackfield in the Ironbridge Gorge, and although the industry here is now extinct, buildings still survive and the companies' products can be seen in profusion in local buildings. Maws were in fact the largest tile manufacturers in the world at the end of the nineteenth century, producing floor and wall tiles which appear in nonconformist chapels, butchers' and game shops and stations on the London Underground. They were responsible for introducing the steam-driven tile press in 1873. Other major tile makers included Minton, Copeland and Doulton although the latter had a greater reputation for making terracotta, a material fired at a high temperature which could be moulded to intricate shapes. Unglazed terracotta and the glazed faience varieties were beloved of architects caught on the crest of the wave of Gothic revival. Without the ingenuity of the Victorian brick and tile makers, we would not have, or would have been spared, the Albert Memorial, Keble College Chapel and the Midland Hotel, Manchester.

   One remaining aspect of the building materials industry demands attention —the manufacture of cement and concrete. The huge increase in building works created a need not only for cement for ordinary constructional purposes but for hydraulic cements which would set in the absence of air.

In the early nineteenth century there were numerous so-called 'Roman' cements available, makers being stimulated by the London Building Act of 1774, which encouraged stucco facings for buildings, but more by the demands of canal, harbour and railway engineers. Parker's cement was one of the better patent 'Roman' cements and was used by Thomas Telford in the construction of Chirk Aqueduct (118/SJ 287373) because of its water-resistant properties. It was also employed by Marc Isambard Brunel (1769–1849) for the Thames Tunnel (161/TQ 352800).

The first really strong cement came in 1824 when Joseph Aspdin (1779–1855) patented a mixture called Portland cement, the name deriving not from any connection with Portland but probably from a desire to take advantage of the implied quality which the name Portland gave. Portland cement was at once a success. It was made by firing a clay and lime mixture at very high temperature in a type of bottle kiln quite unlike traditional limekilns.

Limekilns are amongst the most familiar and least studied of industrial archaeological sites. The majority were simply for burning lime for agricultural purposes, but these were usually small kilns often only a few feet high. Examination of a large-scale map of an area such as the Mendips reveals a limekiln in the corner of almost every field; exploration on the ground usually produces little more than a pile of rough stones. Coastal sites were quite common, too, and the North Devon and Somerset coasts have numerous limekilns which relied on South Wales coal brought across the Bristol Channel in sailing trows. Some of the Somerset kilns were on the foreshore; the trow ran up on to the beach, stayed there over low water while its coal was unloaded into horsedrawn carts, and left on the following tide. Although many large kilns were built for burning agricultural lime, most were for making lime cement. They are frequently found built into hillsides, in much the same manner as were blast furnaces in the eighteenth century, taking advantage of the high ground at the back for charging in the raw materials and the low front for withdrawing the burnt lime. Large numbers of this type of furnace can be found associated with limestone quarried along Wenlock Edge in Shropshire. A particularly well preserved group (Plate 41) stands in the designated site of the Black Country Museum, Dudley (131/SO 949917), alongside the A4123 Birmingham to Wolverhampton road. These kilns, dramatically depicted by J. M. W. Turner 150 years

41 Limekiln built in 1842 on the site of the Black Country Open Air Museum, Dudley

ago, were served by their own branch from the nearby canal, which provided an outlet for the lime. A much more modern kiln (Plate 42) of the split-shaft type stands at Betchworth in Surrey (170/TQ 208514).

Although concrete, consisting of a cement matrix and an aggregate of stones, is often regarded as a wholly modern material, it had its origins at least 2,000 years ago when it was used in Roman bridges and other engineering works. Mass lime concrete continued to be used intermittently for foundations, and in sea walls and breakwaters, until the nineteenth century, when the first attempts were made to develop its potential further. From the 1850s Portland cement was increasingly used instead of the older lime cements and, although this created problems because setting was so much more rapid, the vastly improved strength of the newer material stimulated numerous experiments in the application of concrete for building and civil engineering. Throughout the second half of the nineteenth century attempts were made, particularly in France, to develop concrete building techniques and eventually two rival Frenchmen, Edmond Coignet (1850–1915) and François Hennebique (1842–1921), perfected concrete con-

42 Split-shaft limekiln, 70ft high, at Betchworth, Surrey

struction systems for commercial use. Coignet developed the pioneering work of his father, François (1814–88), who proposed reinforcing the concrete with iron rods and beams and from 1890 onwards patented the use of reinforced concrete for pipes, tunnels, precast beams and piles. The Hennebique system was introduced to Britain when L. G. Mouchel opened an office in London in 1897 to exploit it under licence. It embraced columns, beams, floors and walls, all in reinforced concrete, and had no rival in Britain until Coignet introduced his system in 1904.

Early reinforced concrete structures are surprisingly rare and are seldom appreciated for what they are. One of the first large concrete-framed buildings, constructed on the Coignet principle, stands near the entrance to Bristol docks where three massive brick-clad tobacco bonds dominate the river (156/ST 567723), while a very early reinforced concrete bridge, the Free Bridge of 1908 (119/SJ 681033), crosses the Severn only ½ mile downstream from the pioneer iron bridge of 1779. What is perhaps the first concrete bridge in Britain, although made of mass concrete with no reinforcement, dates from the 1880s and crosses the River Axe at Seaton in Devon (177/SY 253900).

POTTERY

As with the manufacture of bricks and tiles, the pottery industry relies on clays which are fired in a kiln until vitrification occurs. The simplest possible classification would group pottery into earthenware, stoneware and porcelain, depending on the temperature of firing and quality of the clay and additional ingredients. Glazes are used for most pottery to make it impermeable and to produce decorative effects. Many are based on silica associated with other materials: thus lead glaze is silica and litharge, while others incorporate silica with alumina or felspar. The glaze is, in effect, a thin layer of glass fused on to the surface. Earthenware on the other hand, which is used for drain and sewer pipes among other things, was until recently glazed with common salt thrown into the kiln and allowed to vitrify on the articles being fired.

Clay suitable for pottery making is widespread in occurrence although widely variable in quality. Invariably, however, it requires pretreatment before it can be used. The first process is usually one of 'blunging', in which the clay is mixed with large quantities of water that is then sieved off from the resulting suspension. When in a stiff plastic form, it is then 'wedged', ie large pieces are thrown on top of each other to remove the air bubbles. Once in a suitable state for working, it may be used in three possible ways to make a pot. Firstly it can be pressed, in its plastic state, into a mould; secondly it can be thrown on a wheel; and thirdly it can be reduced to a liquid sludge and poured into a mould. The finished piece of pottery is then fired in a kiln to produce vitrification of the clay and, at high temperatures, impermeability. At lower firing temperatures glazing is essential.

Although clay for earthenware and stoneware is fairly widespread in its distribution, the raw materials of porcelain, the finest type of ceramic, occur only in limited areas. During the seventeenth century Chinese porcelain was being imported into Europe in increasing quantities, largely as the result of trading connections forged by the Dutch East India Company after its formation in 1609. The properties of Chinese porcelain, fine quality and whiteness, were at that date unattainable in Europe, but by the mid-seventeenth century were being imitated in Delft by the use of a soft clay body covered with tin enamel. By the latter part of the century this was, in its turn, being imitated in England at Bristol, Lambeth and Liverpool. Distinct and independent lines of development are then discernible in the evolution of fine pottery, with, on the one hand the continued production of this glassy, soft paste imitation porcelain, and on the other the production of true European porcelain. A third quite specific innovation, confined to England, was the production of bone china.

The discovery in Europe of the technique of making real hard porcelain represents one of those curious but by no means unique instances of a simultaneous technological innovation occurring in more than one place as the result of similar, but unconnected, thought processes. Friedrich Bottger (1682–1719), working in Meissen, near Dresden, had pioneered the use of china clay (kaolin) fused with a calcareous flux (marble or alabaster) at temperatures up to 1,400°C and on the basis of his work Meissen porcelain became supreme, and a closely guarded secret. In France the manufacture of porcelain began at Sèvres in 1768 as the result of persistent experiments pursued by P. J. Macquer (1718–84), while in the same year the independent experiments begun in 1745 by William Cookworthy (1705–80), a Plymouth chemist, resulted in the granting of the first English patent for true porcelain. He started manufacture in Plymouth using local timber as his fuel but moved to Bristol in 1770 to take advantage of plentiful coal supplies. By the 1780s the patents, which had been taken over in Bristol by Richard Champion (1743–91), were being challenged and porcelain manufacture began in Staffordshire. One of these Staffordshire potters was Josiah Wedgwood.

The mineral which provided the key to the porcelain secret was kaolin, the product of decomposition of granite. The components of granite are quartz, mica and felspar and it is a decomposition of the felspar (aluminium silicate) by a process known as kaolinisation which produces china clay. Most of the china clay found in Britain has come from the granite massif of Hensbarrow, north of St Austell in Cornwall, but the Lee Moor area on the slopes of Dartmoor above Plymouth has also been important. At first sufficient supplies could be found in small pits close to the surface, but as these became worked out and as demand grew, much larger and deeper clay excavations were carried out, reaching in recent years depths in excess of 400ft. By the mid-nineteenth century huge quantities were being sent to continental Europe, notably Hamburg and Antwerp, but the largest single market was Staffordshire, which by then had become firmly established as the pottery centre of Britain. The siting of the industry here, at such a long distance from the source of clay, is explained largely by supplies of fuel. The pottery industry is to a great extent located near its fuel supplies, which in this case was Staffordshire coal; the additional pull of this area was the already established tradition of pottery manufacture based on locally available clays.

To the industrial archaeologist the china clay area of Cornwall provides perhaps the most extreme example of a landscape of earlier exploitation, with huge pits separated by vast glistening white tips of the mica waste washed from the kaolin. Despite this, it is a man-made landscape which, perhaps more than any other, has a stark almost ghostly drama and magnificence about it. Like the tin mine engine-houses elsewhere in the county, the clay waste tips of St Austell are now a hallmark of the Cornish landscape.

Evidence of the clay processing can be seen in a number of places but nowhere is the range of equipment as complete as at Wheal Martyn (185/SX 004555), west of the A391 St Austell to Bodmin road. Closed in 1966, this is perhaps the last small family clayworking in Cornwall where all the intricate hydraulic processes connected with the separation and settling can still be seen complete. On the site is a 25ft diameter overshot waterwheel which by means of a crank drove a flat connecting rod that operated a pump through a bellcrank. This pump lifted the clay slurry and allowed it to flow through mica drags, from which the refined liquid gravitated to settling tanks and finally kiln tanks. As the water evaporated, the clay thickened and was finally spread on a floor, below which were flues from a coal fire. After drying for some 12hr the clay was cut from the pan and thrown into a storage shed alongside known as the linhay. The Wheal Martyn site is surprisingly complete, and, in addition to the equipment listed above, a large 35ft diameter waterwheel used to operate, by means of flat rods, another pump 2,000ft away. Shortly before it closed, Wheal

Martyn passed from the ownership of the Martyn family, who bought
the site in 1790, to English China Clays, which intends to develop there an
open air museum based on the conservation *in situ* of the surviving remains.
In addition a number of other sites are being preserved, including, at Park-
andillack clayworks near St Dennis (185/SW 945568), a 50in beam pumping
engine of 1852 complete with Cornish boilers and dog's pawmarks cast
into the iron beam! West of the engine is a 'button-hole launder', or wooden
box containing a number of plugs for draining the pit, and an extensive
series of micas.

Two other clayworks' pumping engines survive in Cornwall in addition
to the Rostowrack 22in engine preserved in Holman's Museum in Camborne. One, still in its original engine-house at Goonvean (185/SW 947552),
is a 50in Cornish beam pumping engine of 1863, and the other has been
removed from its original site at Greensplatt Clayworks, Garthew (185/SW
997554), and re-erected in a park-cum-museum open air site at Wendron
Forge (189/SW 680315). Another rare survival at Slip Chinastone Quarry,
also at Goonvean, is an overhead aerial ropeway still used for raising clay
out of a 250ft deep pit.

Having examined the origins of kaolin, the raw material of the porcelain
industry, let us consider the production end of the process and in particular
the main centre of pottery making in Britain—the 'five towns' of North
Staffordshire centred on Stoke-on-Trent. When in 1782 hard paste porcelain
was first made at New Hall near Shelton, Staffordshire was already well
established as a pottery-making centre. There was coal, a wide variety of
clays and a firm tradition of potting. Even in the late sixteenth century
Burslem and Hanley were producing jars, bottles and butter-pots, lead-
glazed and fired with coal dug by the potters themselves. By the 1680s a
second method of glazing became available with the introduction of salt
glaze from the Low Countries, but neither of these processes, when applied
over the common brown clay of the area, resulted in a product with the
appeal of Delft. Pale Shelton clays were used in the first steps towards a
finer white-bodied ware, and eventually a fine white salt-glazed stoneware
evolved from a white-burning clay mixed with fine grit and sand. It enjoyed
great popularity during the eighteenth century, being hard, translucent
and as near to porcelain as could be reached short of the real thing. John
Astbury (1688–1743) was instrumental in developing this ware and also

in utilising ground flint (silica) in the body material as a whitener. Initially the flint was ground dry under stamps rather like those used in Cornwall for crushing tin ore, but the problems of silica getting into the lungs of men working the crushers soon resulted in the development of a process for grinding underwater.

One of these flint mills is preserved in operational condition at Cheddleton in Staffordshire (110/SJ 974525). The original mill on this site was built as a corn mill, certainly before 1694 and probably much earlier. The present North Mill building dates from the 1750s or 1760s, and was probably built by the famous millwright and canal engineer James Brindley (1716–72). In the 1770s the original mill, by now known as South Mill, was converted for flint grinding also. Two undershot waterwheels driven by the River Churnet provide power for the grinding machinery, while set into the bank of the nearby Caldon Canal are kilns for calcining the flint. The Flint Mill Preservation Trust was formed in May 1967 and the mill opened to the public in April 1969.

Despite all these attempts during the eighteenth century to produce a superior form of stoneware, it was not until the introduction of real hard-paste porcelain, based on china clay, in the 1780s that Staffordshire began to produce wares of the highest quality. Even the introduction of this new technique might not have brought Staffordshire real fame and fortune had it not been for the entrepreneurial skill and organisational ability of Josiah Wedgwood (1730–95).

Brought up as a potter, Wedgwood set up on his own account at Burslem in 1759. One of his initial successes was a fine green-glazed ware, which he followed up by an improved stoneware evolved from earlier creamwares. Having obtained royal patronage, he called it Queen's ware and it was soon being made in dozens of potteries and used all over the country. Wedgwood never looked back. With newly introduced steam power to drive flint mills and lathes for producing refined shapes, the Staffordshire pottery industry was on the way towards rapid and large-scale expansion. But the expansion was not based solely on mechanisation and increased demand. Wedgwood developed a new works at Etruria in which to develop mechanised pottery manufacture, but he realized that to optimise the benefits which powered machinery afforded he had to press the division of labour to the maximum, with each distinct process identified and separated. He aimed at a production line process in which individual craftsmen expressed their skill in a limited field, arguing that this afforded them greater opportunities for developing their latent abilities. The specialisation within the labour force was geared to a graded pay structure ranging from 42s per week for an experienced modeller to 1s a week for the least skilled. There can be little doubt that Wedgwood's friendship with Matthew Boulton (1728–1809), the entrepreneurial half of the partnership with James Watt, stimulated many of the ideas he introduced. By the time of Wedgwood's death in 1795 the industrial revolution in the pottery industry was in full flood.

To travel through 'The Potteries' only 25 years ago was an experience shattering to the eye and the nose. Hundred upon hundred of bottle-shaped kilns stuck up through the skyline of smoke-blackened terrace houses. Today almost all those bottle kilns have disappeared as the industry has rationalised and adopted new techniques. Tunnel kilns, completely automated in their operation, have replaced the long established 'potbanks' with their bottle ovens and uncomplicated processes. As a result of this change, and in order to try and preserve something of the old methods, the Stafford-

43 Gladstone Pottery, Longton, now being preserved by the Staffordshire Pottery Industry Preservation Trust

shire Pottery Industry Preservation Trust was set up with the specific
objective of saving from demolition Gladstone Pottery (Plates 43-4) in
Longton (110/SJ 912434). The aim here is to create a museum in the existing
buildings, the best surviving example of a potbank, scarcely touched by
twentieth-century technology, where the old processes are being carried out.
Displays include not only the products but also contemporary information on the supply of materials and distribution of finished wares. A
project somewhat similar in concept is scheduled for another early group
of pottery buildings at Coalport on the banks of the River Severn in Shropshire (119/SJ 695024). Here the Ironbridge Gorge Museum Trust intends to
restore the works, together with their bottle kilns, where Coalport china
was made from the mid-eighteenth century down to the 1920s. The Coalport
company moved to Stoke and is now part of the Wedgwood Group
but the original pottery survives substantially intact and will be used as a
museum illustrating all aspects of the clay industries of the Ironbridge
Gorge, ranging from Coalport china to decorative floor and wall tiles.
The craftsman potter already established at the Blists Hill Open Air Museum
will move to Coalport, where the processes of manufacture of porcelain
will also be demonstrated.

GLASS

The earliest man-made glass dates from about 4000 BC, when it was used
in Egypt and Mesopotamia as a glaze for beads. By 1500 BC hollow glass
vessels were in use; they were probably made around a clay core which was
chipped away when the molten glass had solidified. At about the same date
small objects, such as pieces of jewellery, were being made in glass by
pressing between clay moulds, and finishing by grinding and polishing was
also becoming common. The high temperatures necessary to smelt the raw
materials for glass were achieved in simple furnaces, the glass being contained
in a crucible made of a refractory substance such as clay that had a higher
melting point than the glass itself. Possibly in the first century BC mouth
blowing of glass, using a blowing iron, was introduced, and this remained
the main method of glass forming for nearly 2,000 years. Blown glass vessels

44 Bottle ovens at Gladstone Pottery, one of the few remaining potbanks where
these once common features of the Potteries still survive

of Roman origin are quite common, and it was probably during the Roman occupation that glass was first made in Britain. Traces of Roman glass furnaces have been found at Wilderspool near Warrington and Caistor-by-Norwich. In the first century AD glassmakers had mastered the art of making clear transparent glass, a great improvement over the earlier opaque types, and delicate colours could be consistently achieved by adding a variety of chemical ingredients. Glazed windows were in use by the first century AD also, particularly in the north European areas of the Roman Empire.

Glass is a crypto-crystalline substance solidified from a variety of inorganic materials melted at high temperature, that is its molecular structure does not exhibit a crystalline pattern. Many different glasses, with properties varying according to the raw materials used, are made today. The main ingredients of almost all commercially important glass is silicon dioxide (SiO_2), often found in the form of sand. In its pure state very high temperatures (over 1,500 °C) are necessary to fuse silica, but glass which melts at much lower temperatures can be made by adding fluxing agents such as soda ash (Na_2CO_3) to the silica sand. The melting temperature can be reduced to about 800 °C by adding 25 per cent of soda ash but the resulting substance, waterglass (Na_2SiO_3), as its name implies, is soluble in water. Addition of a stabiliser such as limestone ($CaCO_3$) results in a non-soluble glass. An ordinary glass bottle or jar contains approximately 55 per cent sand, 25 per cent soda ash and 20 per cent limestone. To assist melting, 15–30 per cent of scrap glass or 'cullet' of the correct composition is usually added to the ingredients, which are known as the 'batch'.

Silica-soda-lime glasses are by far the most important group in terms of tonnages produced and variety of uses. The ingredients are cheap and easily obtained, the glass is well suited to shaping and it has good chemical-resistant properties. The colour of these glasses tends to be greenish, a result of the natural iron content of most sand, and in the case of old bottles where colour was immaterial the iron imparted an almost opaque blackish-green appearance. The cheapest bottle glass of the eighteenth or nineteenth centuries was of this crude and unrefined type. In evidence presented to the commissioners at an excise enquiry in 1831 it was stated that the materials used in common bottle glass were sand, soap-makers' waste, lime, common clay and ground bricks. Flint glass, from which tableware was produced, contained pearl-ash, litharge or red lead, Lynn or Alum Bay sand (particularly low in iron) or

'Yorkshire stones burnt and pulverised'.

Lead glasses have a high refractive index and electrical resistivity, and consist primarily of silica sand with as little iron as possible, potash and lead oxide. High quality table glass is made of lead glass, which, because its viscosity does not increase at a rapid rate during cooling, is particularly suitable for hand-made production; and also for engraving and cutting, an art that became highly developed in the late eighteenth century. Since the late seventeenth century lead glass has been used and known as 'English crystal'. Its constituents are more expensive than those of common glass, the amount of lead varying considerably—up to 92 per cent of lead oxide in some cases. A modern high-performance glass composed of high-purity silica sand and boric oxide is borosilicate glass. The boric oxide acts as a flux, permitting a reduction in alkali content that results in improved chemical stability and electrical properties. Developed early this century to cope with the problem of rain on hot railway signal-lamp lenses, boro-silicate glasses are now widely used where extreme thermal conditions occur, and their low coefficient of expansion and durability makes them ideal for industrial use and for ordinary heat-resistant domestic ovenware. Coloured glass is as old as glass itself but methods of production and knowledge of the chemical additives needed were at first crude and unscientific. Empirical methods, however subject to variation in the quality of the final product, produced some spectacular results, of which the rich glowing blues and reds of medieval church windows are the most notable examples surviving today.

There is little evidence available of the furnaces used by early glassmakers, but Theophilus in his *Diversum Artium Schedula* of the twelfth century AD describes a rectangular furnace divided into two unequal parts; in the smaller section the raw materials were heated to form a vitreous mass known as 'frit', which was broken up and melted in pots sunk in the hearth of the larger part of the furnace. Agricola in the mid-sixteenth century also describes furnaces in two parts: the oven-shaped fritting furnace, with pots for the molten glass arranged round a central hearth, and the annealing furnace, oblong in shape with a small hearth below the floor. Annealing is an essential stage in the manufacture of most glass. Because of its low thermal conductivity, the surface of glass cools and therefore shrinks more quickly and to a greater extent than the interior. If unchecked, enormous stresses would be set up within the object, leading to breakage, but this can be avoided by slow cooling at a controlled rate. This is annealing, which takes place in an oven or lehr. In a modern glassworks, for example, bottles pass slowly through the lehr on a conveyor belt and over a period of some 2hr the temperature is gradually reduced from about 540°C.

All early furnaces were fired by wood, the wood ash providing the necessary alkaline flux. One example of a type of wood-fired furnace introduced in the sixteenth century into Britain by French and Flemish glassworkers survives almost *in toto*. It was discovered in 1968 at Rosedale in the North Yorkshire Moors and later moved to the Rydedale Folk Museum, Hutton-le-Hole, near Helmsley, Yorkshire, where it was partially reconstructed and is on view to the public (86/SE 705900). The Rosedale glassworkers were perhaps the most isolated group among the numerous glassmaking families who came to England in large numbers in the 1560s and 1570s and set up furnaces in the heavily wooded areas of the Weald, and in Hampshire and Staffordshire. Fig 26 illustrates the probable original layout of the Rosedale furnace, which corresponds almost exactly with furnaces in use in Northern France in the late sixteenth century. Ingredients for the glass were heated in clay crucibles made on the site from locally available clay and baked in the side arches (F) of the furnace. The wood fuel was burnt in the central hearth (A), and burning gases circulated inside the chamber and through linnet holes or lunettes (E) into the side or wing arches. Glass was melted in crucibles (C) and the glassworkers standing at the side of the furnace inserted their pipes into the molten glass through holes (D). With the exception of a small access hole, these apertures would be stopped up with a clay filling during operation, the clay being broken away to allow removal of the crucibles for recharging. After fashioning, the glass, which in the case of the Rosedale furnace consisted largely of drinking vessels, bowls and similar utensils, was annealed in the side arches, and these were also used for fritting and heating the crucibles. The temperature of the wing arches could be controlled to some extent by partially or wholly closing the linnet holes from the hearth area.

Probably many other furnaces of this pattern were set up, mainly in southern England, where timber supplies were reasonably plentiful. Competition from the shipbuilding and iron industries was growing, however, and in 1615 there was a Royal Proclamation forbidding glassmakers to use wood for fuel. Availability of coal now became the chief locational factor,

THE ROSEDALE GLASS FURNACE
Presumed plan at working level

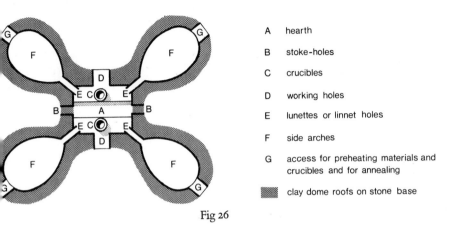

A   hearth

B   stoke-holes

C   crucibles

D   working holes

E   lunettes or linnet holes

F   side arches

G   access for preheating materials and crucibles and for annealing

▨   clay dome roofs on stone base

Fig 26

together with suitable sources of clay and the convenience of transport systems. The first coal-fired furnaces were probably modifications of the Rosedale pattern. During the seventeenth century a distinctive and completely new type of coal-fired furnace was developed in England, using the reverberatory process, in which the burning gases came into direct contact with glass in open crucibles. The English glassworks, consisting of a truncated cone up to 80ft high and with a base diameter of some 40–50ft provided the foundation for the industry on a large scale and was copied in Europe also. So significant was this furnace that it was included in Diderot's *Encyclopedie* in the late eighteenth century, one of the few pieces of British manufacturing technology specifically mentioned. The tall cone fulfilled a dual function, by providing cover for the glassworkers and a high level outlet for the furnace situated centrally on its floor. The grate was at approximately ground level, with a combined flue and ash tunnel running beneath it and extending across the building. The furnace would have between four and ten glass pots, with a flue between each. Immediately abreast of each pot and between two flues was an aperture called the working hole, used for introducing the raw materials and getting out the molten glass.

The furnace was fired by coal shovelled through a square fire hole on to a grate in the centre. The flames or smoke were directed towards the sides, around the glass pots, and discharged up the flues to escape into the central chimney of the cone itself. A ten-pot cone consumed 18–24 tons of coal per week. In addition to the principal furnace around which the glass blowers worked, there was also a small subsidiary furnace or 'glory hole' for softening vessels during fabrication when they were too large to be heated in one of the working holes. A long gallery, the lehr or annealing arch, opened at one end into the cone and the completed glassware was placed in this to cool gradually.

The crucibles in which the glass was melted had to be carefully made to prevent cracking in the intense heat of the furnace and to resist the solvent action of molten glass. They were commonly made of five parts Stourbridge clay, a very pure refractory clay notably free from lime and iron oxides, together with one part burnt clay or 'grog' obtained from old crucibles ground down to a powder.

Some five glass cones still survive in Britain, the most prominent monuments of the eighteenth- and nineteenth-century glass industry. The oldest of these, older indeed than any other cone in Europe, is at Catcliffe near Sheffield (103/SE 425887). It is the last survivor of at least six glasshouses known to have been built in the area in the eighteenth century at the height of the prosperity of the South Yorkshire glass industry. The industry became established in the Bolsterstone area in the mid-seventeenth century and by 1696 three glasshouses were in operation—one near Ferrybridge, probably at Glass Houghton, and two near Silkstone. William Fenney, works manager at Bolsterstone, left there in 1740 with a workman named Chatterton to start production in his own works at Catcliffe, $10\frac{1}{2}$ miles to the southeast. Two cones were erected and one of these survives today, substantially complete, 60ft high and with a base diameter of some 40ft. It has recently been restored. Excavation of the flue beneath the cone, which contains no remains of the furnace or ancillary buildings, has revealed that glass bottles were being made there down to the early 1900s when C. Wilcocks & Co owned the works, but flint glass and jugs, vases and flasks, often decorated with opaque white stripes, were known to have been made at least as late as the 1870s.

Of the numerous other glass manufacturers established in South Yorkshire during the nineteenth century little else remains, although a firm originally established at Worsborough Dale in 1828 is still active in Barnsley as Wood Bros Glass Co Ltd. The oldest surviving glass firm in the area, dating from 1751 and now known as Beatson Clark & Co Ltd of Masborough, Rotherham, has preserved many examples of the glassware produced in the nineteenth century, including very good examples of glass engraving.

In the North East, at Lemington, near Newcastle-upon-Tyne, is another glass cone (78/NZ 184646) which, although somewhat later in date than Catcliffe, provides a visual reminder of the industry that became important in the region from the early years of the seventeenth century, attracted primarily by cheap coal. In 1615 Sir Robert Mansel obtained a patent for making glass with coal, and, after trying to start a works in London and elsewhere, 'was enforced for his last refuge contrary to all men's opinion to make triall at Newcastle upon Tyne where after the expense of many thousand pounds that worke for window-glasse was effected with New-castle Cole'. Glassmakers from Lorraine came to Tyneside about this time also and by the end of the seventeenth century were working at South Shields, where plate glass became important. By the mid-nineteenth century glassmaking had become an important manufacturing industry in the North East, and flint glass, crown glass for glazing, and bottles were produced. The Wear glassworks, established at Sunderland in 1842, to produce a new kind of sheet glass called rolled-plate that was rather like unpolished plate glass, achieved a worldwide reputation after supplying the glazing for the Crystal Palace in 1851.

The Lemington Glassworks, famous in the nineteenth century for flint and crown glass, was founded in 1787 by 'a company of enterprising gentle-men (who) entered into the glass trade in Newcastle under the firm of the Northumberland Glass Company'. They were granted a lease of the site at Lemington and quickly erected their first glasshouse ,which was called 'the Northumberland Glasshouse'. Within a short time there were three more, including one which was very lofty and built of brick. This is the cone which still stands at Lemington. The site is now occupied by Glass Tubes & Com-ponents Ltd, but the cone is no longer used.

Other glass cones may be seen at Stourbridge, Worcestershire (130/SO 894864), and Alloa, Clackmannan (55/NS 881924), while in Bristol the truncated base of a glass cone of about 1780 has been converted into a restaurant for a new hotel (156/ST 592723). The incomplete remains of a cone also survive within the works of Pilkington Brothers, St Helens.

Comprehensive physical remains of the glass industry in the nineteenth century, when processes were changing rapidly, are hard to find today, but there are two excellent museum displays which, although they contain little actual manufacturing equipment, go a long way towards explaining the various techniques. The Pilkington Glass Museum at St Helens, Lancashire (100/SJ 498946), illustrates all the major stages in the development of the industry, concentrating particularly on the production of flat glass. The method of making plate glass of high quality by casting was introduced into Britain from France in 1773, when the British Cast Plate Glass Company, as it became called after 1798, was established at Ravenhead, St Helens. Part of the Ravenhead casting hall and works still stands within the Pilkington complex, and there are hopes of turning them into a museum to house some of the heavy equipment of flat glass making.

The second museum display of note is in the Science Museum, South Kensington, and was opened in 1968 as a gallery of glass technology. Two booklets prepared by the Glass Manufacturers' Federation, *Glass History* and *Making Glass*, are available at the museum. There is also a descriptive catalogue listing all the exhibits and illustrating many. Unlike the St Helens museum which contains fine representative collections of art glass, the Science Museum gallery concentrates almost entirely on the manufacturing techniques, with examples of various products to illustrate advancing glass technology. Although little glassmaking equipment survives, the everyday products of the industry over the last century and a half, particularly in the form of glass containers and window glass, are commonplace.

Glass wine bottles began to replace leather and earthenware ones in the second half of the seventeenth century. At first wine, like beer, was stored in barrels, and bottles were used mainly for carrying drink from the wine merchants to the tavern, for limited storage and for serving at table. The earliest glass bottles for this purpose were pale green and globular, and of light weight. Having no flat base they were usually 'wanded', that is en-encased in basketwork, or placed in metal stands on the table. In 1731 wanded bottles were advertised at 42s a gross and common black bottles at 20s a gross. The practice of having bottles embossed with a seal, often dated, grew up in the 1660s, and is a useful aid to tracing the evolution in the shape of wine bottles. Towards the end of the eighteenth century bottles became less globular, acquiring an angular shoulder between body and neck. At the same time the 'kick up', a concavity in the base of the bottle which aided stability and assisted annealing in the days before the development of the tunnel lehr, was increased in size. A fine collection of wine bottles, together with some bottle-making moulds, is exhibited in Harveys Wine Museum, Denmark Street, Bristol (156/ST 584729).

In the early seventeenth century it was discovered that beer could be kept almost indefinitely in bottles, and that, with a small amount of secondary fermentation occurring after bottling, it could actually improve in quality. The heavy taxation on glass was an initial restraint to the widespread adoption of bottles, but with the repeal in 1845 of the Excise Acts, which had imposed a tax of 8s 9d per cwt on glass bottles, the industry expanded rapidly.

A major problem with beer and the new carbonated soft drinks was to devise a satisfactory bottle closure. In 1872 the internal-screw stopper was patented by an Englishman, Henry Barrett, and in 1892 the familiar crown cork by an American, William Painter. Louis Pasteur's theories of food preservation were meanwhile put into practice in a Copenhagen brewery, which produced the first pasteurised beer. Earthenware bottles had been used by the early pioneers of soft drinks such as Jacob Schweppe, a Swiss who set up business in Bristol in 1794, but the wired-on cork closures were never satisfactory because they dried out and leaked. The egg-shaped glass bottle was introduced in 1814 to overcome this problem. It had to be stored on its side, thus keeping the cork moist. The egg bottle survived even after the introduction of the crown cork had made the shape and the need for flat storage unnecessary, and was in fact in use until the 1920s.

The best known and most successful internally stopped bottle, patented by Hiram Codd of Camberwell in 1875, had a glass marble pressed against a rubber ring in the bottle neck by the gas pressure in the drink. Codd bottles were used in Britain from the late 1870s until the 1930s, and between 1890 and 1914 were the most widely used containers for carbonated soft drinks. An exceptional collection of soft drink bottles, together with bottle equipment and gas making plant, was found recently in the works of J. B. Bowler of Corn Street, Bath, and is now being preserved by a newly formed trust.

Widespread preservation of food in glass containers began in the United States in the 1860s after the invention in 1858 of the screw-topped jar by

John Landis Mason. American domestic food-preserving jars are still known
as Mason jars. In Britain the similar Kilner jar did not come into general use
until the 1920s. Automatic jar manufacturing and filling machinery developed in the 1900s; it was followed in 1923 by the invention of the roll-on
closure and in 1926 by the pry-off cap still used today. Bottling of milk began
in the 1880s on a small scale, but it was not until the 1920s that pasteurised
milk deliveries in bottles replaced milk sold 'loose' from churns in the streets.
In 1934 bottled milk with a card disc closure was introduced in schools at a
cost of $\frac{1}{2}$d for one-third of a pint. Today the milk bottle has the more
hygenic foil cap and the wide-mouthed card-stoppered bottle has completely disappeared. Even the foil topped bottles of 5 years ago have now
given way to lightweight versions, with carefully contoured shoulders to
eliminate internal stresses.

The crown window-glass process was the earlier of the two chief methods
of making sheet glass by hand and was in common use until the early years
of the nineteenth century. Molten glass on a blowing iron was formed into a
large hollow sphere. Then a 'pontil' or solid iron rod was attached to it by a
nodule of the molten metal—glass is referred to as metal in a glassworks—
and the blowing iron then removed. Reheating the glass on the rotating
pontil reduced it to a soft and semi-molten state in which centrifugal force
caused it to flash into a disc. The thin fire-polished disc of glass was removed
from the pontil for annealing and then cut up into sheets. Every sheet made
by this method had a bull's-eye or 'crown' from which it took its name,
this being the point where the pontil had been attached. The sizes of pieces
of glass made by this method were severely restricted, and after about 1830
the process gave way to hand cylinder-glass making. Crown glass is easy to
recognise in window panes by the fine ripples and flow lines which form arcs
in its surface. The larger the radius of the arc the nearer the edge of the glass
disc was the sheet cut.

The hand-cylinder process of sheet glassmaking was brought to England
from Lorraine in 1832 by Lucas Chance. It was essentially a development of
the crown glass method, but instead of a sphere and then a disc of glass, an
elongated bulb was made 12–20in in diameter and 50–70in long. The ends of
the cylinder were removed, it was cut down its long side and, after reheating,
the glass was flattened in a flattening kiln. The sheets were much larger than
those of crown glass, were free from the central boss and were much

cheaper to make. In 1839 Sir James Chance (1814–1902) invented a method of grinding and polishing sheet glass, giving it the brilliancy and transparency of plate glass that had been similarly treated.

The third method of making sheet glass was to cast it in plates, a process developed in France in the 1680s and introduced to England in 1773. The great casting hall at the Ravenhead works, St Helens, where the technique became established, still partially survives as one of the largest industrial buildings of its day, 113yd long by 50yd wide. The method of making plate was to pour molten glass on to a flat table, first made of copper and later of cast iron, and when it had cooled and been annealed, over a period of about 10 days, the two faces of the glass were then ground and polished. A number of other firms were set up to cope with the enormous demand for flat glass as a result of the building explosion in early nineteenth-century Britain. The St Helens Crown Glass Company was formed in 1825, the Smethwick firm of Chance & Hartley brought continental glassmakers to blow cylinder glass in 1832 and in 1836 the great Union Plate Glass Works was set up at Pocket Nook, St Helens.

All these processes are well illustrated in the Pilkington Glass Museum, St Helens, and the glass technology gallery in the Science Museum, but little, if anything, survives of actual equipment. Modern manufacture of float glass and rolled sheet glass can be seen at the Pilkington works; visits for parties can be arranged through the curator of the museum. The float process, developed at St Helens in 1959, is one of the major advances in glassworking of recent years and consists of flowing glass on to a bath of molten tin to ensure a perfect under surface, the heat applied above producing a similar effect on the upper face. Ordinary sheet glass is also now made by a continuous process in which the molten 'metal' is drawn vertically from the melting pot between powered rollers.

10 Textiles

ONE of Man's earliest manufacturing techniques was the making of cloth by the spinning and weaving of animal and plant fibres. Before large-scale mechanised industrialisation began in Britain, the making of textiles was widely dispersed throughout the country and was of very great importance in the national economy. Wool, and later various woollen cloths, formed the largest export commodities from the medieval period through to the middle of the eighteenth century. International specialisations grew up between different production areas in Euope, and the fact that English wool was considered to be of the highest quality led merchants, particularly Flemish and Italian, to come in search of it. English taxation on wool exports led to a change in the trade as dyers and finishers abroad realised they could circumvent the tax by buying white undyed broadcloth instead of the wool itself. Broadcloth exports from the West of England rose dramatically, as did the lighter fabrics produced in East Anglia, though to a lesser extent, as they were not quite so popular. A large, rurally based cloth industry began to develop in the West of England—in Somerset, Gloucestershire and Wiltshire particularly—based on capitalist clothiers who bought wool, gave it out to hand-spinners and hand-weavers to convert into cloth, then carried out the fulling themselves and finally sent the cloth, undyed and unfinished, to Europe. In Yorkshire, which did not engage in the export market to such a great extent, the structure of the industry was somewhat different, as the clothiers, particularly in the Halifax area, were independent masters in their own right, owning their spinning wheels and weaving looms, buying wool and yarn and taking their pieces of cloth to the Cloth Hall every week for sale to merchants whom they faced as owners of the cloth they sold. The Cloth or Piece Halls of the West Riding became the symbols of an industry where the structure of production was based on a large number of masters, some of whom would be working in family units and others as employers of labour on a very small scale.

Before the coming of factories, therefore, a proletariat was already developing in many textile regions. Only in the West Riding of Yorkshire did the actual manufacturers have any degree of independence, though theirs was the independence of capital only. Elsewhere—in the West of England, around Norwich, in the worsted area around Bradford, Yorkshire, and in the Nottinghamshire stocking and lace manufacturing districts—the man who organised production and who owned the capital in production was the clothier or 'putter-out' of work, the cloth merchant or the hosier. As most of the capital in the industry was in the raw material and goods in various stages of processing, the merchant was able to control production throughout its course. He owned the materials right through the sequence of processes, paying spinners and weavers for their labour and often renting out the equipment, sometimes to many hundreds of dependent families. The structure of ownership which was later to characterise the factory system, therefore, already existed in several regions of the country in the days of the cottage-based industry, long before the development of modern machine processes.

In order to appreciate the significance of later innovations it is important to look at the processes through which textile fibres went during their conversion from raw material to finished cloth. The stages were substantially the same for all textiles, although here reference will be made mostly to wool, which was dominant before industrialisation. As will be seen later, a development in one branch of the textile industry often had very direct relevance to another, so that from the middle of the eighteenth century onwards the progress of the wool, cotton and to a certain extent flax (for linen) industry went hand in hand.

Wool textiles may be divided into woollens and worsteds. Woollens use short fibre or short staple wool, and worsteds longer staple. In both cases the wool is first washed and cleaned to remove natural grease and dirt, after which there are different techniques for the two fabrics. For woollen textiles the raw wool is 'carded' to lay the tangled fibres into roughly parallel strands so that they can be more easily drawn for spinning. Before the eighteenth century carding was done by hand using two oblong boards, each of which had on one of its sides projecting wires or nails. At first the heads of teasels were used but these were soon to be replaced by brass wire, though the term 'teasing' remained. (The demands of carding in the seventeenth century were, in fact, a great stimulus to the wire-making industry.) Washed raw wool was placed on the teeth of one carding board, and the other was repeatedly drawn over it in one direction, to disentangle the fibres. To get the wool off the cards, one board was turned round and again passed over the other; the teeth being set at an angle, this stripped the wool off the card. Many examples of hand cards survive and may be seen in, for example, Dumfries Burgh Museum; Bankfield Museum, Halifax; and the Museum & Art Gallery, Peel Park, Salford.

Wool used for worsted cloth required rather more thorough treatment, for the fibres had not only to be laid parallel to each other but also unwanted short staple wool had to be removed. This process was called combing. Two hand combs with tapered wooden teeth were used. A small quantity of wool was placed in the teeth of one of the combs, which was held firmly in a bracket while the other was drawn over it, pulling more and more wool out and collecting the longer fibres in its teeth. When most of the wool had become caught in the hand-held comb, the two were changed over and the process repeated. After combing, the long fibres were collected and joined into long slivers known as 'tops', which were sent for spinning. The remaining short staple fibres, called 'noils', were sold for woollens. When spun, combed wool produced a smooth fine worsted yarn, much harder than ordinary woollen yarns. Combing presented considerable difficulties for mechanisation and was the last section of the wool textile industry to be hand-worked, remaining so until after 1850. Hand combs may be seen in the Art Gallery & Museum, Cliffe Castle, Keighley, and the Bridewell Museum, Norwich.

After carding or combing, both woollens and worsteds were spun and, although different techniques of manipulating the fibres were employed, both involved the same equipment and went through the same processes. Spinning twists the fibres around each other and draws them together to form a yarn suitable for weaving into cloth. The most primitive technique was to use a spindle and distaff, in which the distaff or stick carrying the wool was held under one arm, often supported by a leather belt around the waist of the spinster. Strands of wool were pulled from the distaff and attached to the spindle, a small stick with a weight at one end. The spindle was suspended from the wool, given a twist with the finger to set it spinning, and the wool paid out slowly. When a length of yarn had been produced, it was wound round the spindle, the end caught in a notch to prevent it unwinding when suspended, and the process repeated.

The spinning wheel, which probably originated in the Far East, was a great improvement over the spindle and distaff and may be regarded as the first example of 'mechanisation' applied to the textile industry. In it the spindle was mounted horizontally in bearings and connected to a large flywheel by a driving band. This produced more consistent rotation of the spindle and speeded up the spinning process considerably. At first the large wheel was turned by hand, but later a treadle, connecting rod and crank on the wheelshaft were used—probably the first use of the common crank for developing rotary motion at least two centuries before Pickard and Watt 'rediscovered' it for the rotative steam engine. In the early type of spinning wheel known as the 'big wheel' or 'Jersey wheel' a piece of unspun wool was attached to the spindle and the large wheel turned by hand. The other hand holding the wool was pulled back slowly from the spindle paying out at a steady rate strands which were spun into yarn. When a length had been spun, the wheel was turned again to wind the yarn on to the body of the spindle. The process was then repeated.

Later a new type of spinning wheel, the Saxony wheel invented in 1555, largely supplanted the big wheel; it was an improvement as it both spun the yarn and wound it in at the same time, making the whole operation continuous. It was used for the spinning, usually of long fibres, until the late eighteenth century. The main section of the Saxony wheel was the U-shaped flyer that was attached to the spindle. The bobbin ran loose on the spindle shaft and was driven by a separate band from the flywheel. Thus yarn was spun continuously on the spindle and fed from the arms of the flyer to the bobbin rotating at a different speed. With all these methods of spinning, however, there was inconsistency of quality, as the results depended on the skill of the individual spinster, who had to pay out the right amount of wool to maintain an even thickness of yarn. As most of the women in a household learned to spin, this often meant that different qualities of yarn might be found even on the same spindle. This was an inconvenience to the weaver and an important incentive towards devising a machine that would produce consistent yarn. Spinning wheels are perhaps the most common evidence of pre-industrial textile manufacture to be found in museums today. In the Textile Machinery Museum, Tong Moor Road, Bolton, both Jersey and Saxony wheels are exhibited, and the Horner collection in the Ulster Museum, Belfast, contains spinning wheels from a number of countries.

Once a suitable yarn had been spun, the next process was to weave it into a cloth fabric on a loom. The traditional hand loom consisted of a frame carrying the longitudinal or 'warp' threads, which could be separated to allow the transverse 'weft' threads to pass alternately over and under them. This simplest form of interlacing of warp and weft is known as plain weave and was for centuries carried out on simple hand looms. The main obstacle to speeding up the process of weaving was the problem of moving the shuttle containing the weft yarn wound on a bobbin across the loom between the alternate warp yarns. The answer, when it came in the form of the 'flying shuttle', was one of the crucial inventions of the textile industry; it was remarkably simple in principle, cost very little and led to an enormous increase in hand-loom weaving, an increase which was to have tragic repercussions in the 1820s. With the exception of the stocking frame, which produced a knitted as opposed to a woven fabric, and which will be considered later, it was to be the first move in the sequence of events leading to the fully mechanised textile industry.

From the industrial archaeological point of view the chief features to examine are the textile machines themselves, the prime movers that drove them and the buildings that housed machines and workers. Of the textile machines a reasonably representative range has been preserved in museums, mainly in Lancashire and Yorkshire, but the prime movers—the water-wheels and steam engines that powered those machines—are somewhat harder to find. The technology of these sources of power has been considered in Chapters 3 and 4, but there were variants specific to the textile industry, such as the steam mill engine, which are worthy of additional passing reference. It is in the buildings, however, particularly those dating from the middle of the eighteenth century onwards, that the most prolific archaeological evidence of the industry lies. Indeed, of all the landscape changes brought about by the Industrial Revolution, the textile mill building is one of the most prominent. The evolution of the textile mill, almost from its earliest days, can be traced through surviving examples, in some of which were incorporated important innovations in constructional technique. In examining the industrial archaeology of textile manufacturing we will look first at the development of the machine itself and then at the buildings and power sources.

As we have seen, the bottleneck in the hand-weaving process was the speed at which the weft threads could be passed through the warp. The answer was found by John Kay (1704–c1780) who was born at Park near Bury in Lancashire. He was apprenticed into the weaving machinery trade and spent the whole of his working life involved with textile equipment. His 'fly' or 'flying shuttle' of 1733 (Patent No 542) consisted of boxes to hold the shuttle at each side of the loom connected by a long board, or 'shuttle race', along which the shuttle ran. Each box had a horizontal metal rod, and on each rod was a freely moving slide known as a 'picker'. Each picker was connected by a string tied to a stick or 'picking peg' held by the weaver. By jerking the picking peg from side to side, the weaver could throw the shuttle from one shuttle box to the other. Kay fitted wheels or rollers to some of his shuttles but later these were discarded and the term 'flying shuttle' was used. The operation of weaving became not only less tedious but output was often doubled.

There were a number of minor technical difficulties that slowed down the adoption of Kay's flying shuttle, an initial disbelief in its workability and considerable unwillingness by many weavers to pay the 15s per year which he charged for the use of his invention. However, it was widely taken up eventually, and had the effect of speeding up weaving and thereby substantially increasing the imbalance between the weaving and spinning processes. Even before his invention, four or five spinsters had been needed to supply one weaver, and the flying shuttle still further increased the incentive to devise a machine that would spin more than one or two threads at a time. Numerous hand looms, with and without flying shuttles, may be found in museums specialising in textile machinery, including the Bankfield Museum, Halifax, where they are demonstrated from time to time.

The first attempts at the mechanisation of spinning were made by Lewis Paul (d1759) and John Wyatt (1700–66) and patented in 1738. Their first machine, involving pairs of rollers to draw out the fibres, was unsuccessful, as were a number of variations on it produced in succeeding years, although the roller drawing principle was eventually used with great success. An experimental mill was built in Birmingham about 1741 and another in Northampton, but neither appears to have been very successful. A skein of yarn produced on a Paul & Wyatt machine is, however, preserved in Birmingham Museum & Art Gallery, and the Avery Historical Museum at Soho Foundry, Birmingham 40, besides its collection of wool scales and weights, has some documentary information on the two inventors.

It was not until the 1760s that James Hargreaves (c1719–78), a weaver of Stanhill near Blackburn, where his cottage still survives (95/SD 728277), developed a successful mechanism for spinning cotton on multiple spindles— initially eight and later sixteen. This was the spinning jenny, a hand-operated machine that fitted well into the domestically based spinning industry. The term 'jenny' is a simple corruption of the word 'engine', as is the 'gin' used in 'horse-gin', a term used in mining and for the machine that removed seeds from raw cotton. In the jenny a hand-driven wheel powered a number of spindles, and a clasp drew out the spun yarn from each of them at the same time. Having completed the drawing out, the clasp moved forward and the spun yarn was wound on to the 'cop', which, when full, became a cylindrical package of yarn with conical ends. The jenny (Plate 45) was, in effect, a mechanised Jersey wheel, as the spinning process was not continuous; but because of the larger number of spindles which it employed, output was very considerable. Jennies to be seen in most museums are of the improved variety, with a large number of spindles, but Higher Mill, Helmshore, in Lancashire (95/SD 777214), where a textile machinery museum is being established, has a jenny built a few years ago to the specification in Hargreaves'

45 Multiple-spindle spinning jenny in Bolton Textile Machinery Museum

original patent. A visitor to Higher Mill can see this and other equipment demonstrated.

There was considerable antagonism in Lancashire towards Hargreaves as a result of his invention, so he moved to Nottingham, where demand for cotton yarn for knitting in the stocking-frame was growing. Here he established a mill and in 1770, several years after his invention of the jenny, he finally took out a patent for it. The fact that Richard (later Sir Richard) Arkwright (1732–92) had patented a new device for spinning in 1769 may well have prompted this action by Hargreaves. Certainly Arkwright's machine proved much more suitable than the jenny for producing the fine cotton threads needed in knitting. Yet in Lancashire jennies became more and more popular for the weft yarn of cotton-linen woven fabrics and for all-cotton goods. In the woollen industry, too, the jenny was found to be an efficient means of spinning soft full yarns. Equally as important was the fact that it was cheap and could be used by cottage spinners and small manufacturers alike.

Richard Arkwright was born in Preston, Lancashire, apprenticed to a barber and subsequently set up in business on his own as a barber and wig-maker. He became interested in mechanisms and the problems of a satis-factory spinning machine and, in association with a clockmaker in Leigh named John Kay (not associated with the flying shuttle inventor), Ark-wright produced a prototype roller spinning machine for cotton. As with Hargreaves, hostility to Arkwright arose from those people already in the spinning industry who saw the machine as a threat to their livelihoods, so he too went to Nottingham and set up a business providing yarn for the knitting industry. He found a partner in a successful and well established hosiery manufacturer named Jedediah Strutt, and they established a small factory with a number of spinning machines driven by horse power. The yarns produced were most staisfactory for the hosiery industry, so in 1771 Arkwright moved to Cromford on the River Derwent in Derybshire and there set up a larger mill driven by water power. As a result of the use of this source of power, Arkwright's roller-spinning device became known as the water frame. On it was based the enormous development of factory spin-ning and the further fortunes of its inventor, who built numerous other mills, was knighted and became High Sheriff of Derbyshire. Of all the pioneer inventors in textiles during the eighteenth century, Arkwright had

46 Spinning mule developed by Samuel Crompton. Bolton Textile Machinery Museum

the least propitious beginning and derived the greatest benefits. He can really be described as the father of the factory system, an outstanding organiser of labour and machinery processing, ambitious, forceful and persevering.

A still more important advance in eighteenth-century spinning technology was still to come, however. This was the invention of the spinning mule (Plate 46) in 1779, in effect a combination of the jenny and the water frame, hence the name 'mule'. Its inventor Samuel Crompton (1753–1827) was born near Bolton, Lancashire, and began spinning on a jenny as a boy. His mule (Fig 27) was a great advance on either of the machines from which it derived—if in fact Crompton had any detailed knowledge of Arkwright's invention—and was particularly suitable for making fine yarns for muslin. The first mules had about thirty spindles but soon 130 were common. By moving the driving wheel to the centre, it was possible to operate still longer mules, and 400 spindle machines were built. Later machines carried

Fig 27 Mule spinning (from *The Circle of the Sciences,* Vol II, 609)

more than 1,000. In 1792 water power was applied at New Lanark Mills (Plate 47) in Scotland (61/NS 880425) for the first time to drive mules and this established large-scale factory mule spinning. Crompton's house near Bolton, 'Hall-i'-th'Wood' (101/SD 724116), still stands and is now a museum of the Crompton family. The Textile Machinery Museum in

47 Robert Owen's model town of New Lanark

Tong Moor Road, Bolton, includes water frames, Crompton's mule and other early textile machines. Mules may also be seen at Higher Mill, Helmshore, where there is an original Arkwright water frame from his Cromford mill. A pre-industrial water-powered textile mill in regular operation and open to visitors is the Esgair Moel Mill from Llantwrtyd, Brecknockshire, re-erected at the Welsh Folk Museum, St Fagans (154/ST 118772), in 1951. Here too may be seen a spinning mule, with eighty spindles, together with three hand looms and all the other equipment to convert raw wool into dyed and finished fabric.

Throughout this period of rapid development on the spinning side of the textile industry the hand loom for weaving fabric had remained virtually static, although there was a progressive increase in the use of the flying shuttle. There had been powered looms since the sixteenth century for weaving silk ribbons, but the general opinion among fabric weavers was that the hand loom involved too many independent actions requiring timing and skill to mechanise. The first breakthrough came in 1784 with the invention by Dr Edmund Cartwright (1743–1823), a Leicestershire rector, of a loom which could be powered, although he had never at the time seen a person weave! Cartwright's loom was by no means sophisticated, all its actions being rapid and harsh, particularly that of the shuttle, which was propelled by a powerful spring. Its main contribution was to prove the feasibility of powered looms, and other inventors were stimulated into carrying out further experiments. Cartwright looms of a more highly developed type were in use in Doncaster and Manchester in the 1790s, while in Scotland numerous inventors, including Robert Miller and J. L. Robertson of Glasgow, made improvements. The most significant improvement, however, was devised by William Horrocks of Stockport, who in 1813 introduced a means of varying the speed of separation of the warp threads so as to increase the period for the shuttle to pass through.

Between 1813 and 1820 the number of power looms in Britain increased from 2,400 to 14,150, but even then the bulk of woven cloth was still being produced by hand-loom weavers. The largest spinning mills employed 1,500 people, and almost all the preparatory processes, like carding, had been mechanised for wool and worsted, cotton, silk and flax. By 1820 there were 110,000 workers in spinning mills, but only 10,000 in weaving factories, and some of them were working traditional hand looms in factory buildings. As

Fig 28 Carding-engine for cotton (from *The Circle of the Sciences,* Vol II, 607)

power looms began to be improved mechanically, their numbers increased rapidly, so that the 2,000 looms per year installed between 1813 and 1820 had become 10,000 a year by the 1830s. Meanwhile the hand-loom weavers sank from being among the most prosperous workers in the country to some of the most poverty-stricken. The weavers' skills were no longer required, as in the factories the simple work of mending thread breakages and re-plenishing shuttles could be carried out by women and children. In the 1810s, first in the Midlands and subsequently in Lancashire and Yorkshire, the machine-smashing Luddites responded to these conditions, made all the more appalling by the general depression after the Napoleonic wars.

In other branches of the textile trade mechanisation took place during the late eighteenth and early nineteenth centuries also. At the preliminary pro-processing end, carding machines (Fig 28) were developed by a number of inventors; most worked on the roller principle, in which a large cylinder with wire teeth took the fibres round under a series of smaller 'worker' rollers running at a different speed, and they did the carding. Although these early carding machines were developed for cotton (Fig 29), it was not long before they were applied also to wool, where they were called 'scribblers'. Pattern weaving was also greatly improved after about 1800, with the introduction of the Jacquard attachment in which individual warp threads were lifted by a mechanism mounted above the loom and controlled by punched cards. The type of pattern depended on the 'programme' punched into the continuous strip of cards.

Fig 29 Carding, drawing and roving (from *The Circle of the Sciences,* Vol II, 608)

In the hosiery manufacturing industry, in which stockings were knitted by the looping together of threads to form an elastic fabric, the basic machine, the knitting-frame, had been developed as early as the 1590s by the Rev William Lee of Calverton near Nottingham. It was one of the most ingenious inventions in the textile industry and formed the basis for the early rise of the East Midlands as a hosiery area. The problem was one of looping threads into each other using a hooked needle, and the answer lay in developing a way of opening and closing the hook automatically to allow the loop to be made and the needle to be disengaged and then withdrawn without re-engagement. The crux of Lee's invention lay in a hook which was normally open but could be closed by pressure. By filing a slot in the shank of the needle, the point of the hook could sink into it upon closure and thus avoid any accidental catching of the loop. This is the bearded needle widely used in knitting machines today. A further development came with the mechanisation of rib knitting in 1758 by Jedediah Strutt. Rib-knitted hosiery was more closely fitting than plain-knitted but at the same time more elastic. Strutt's invention consisted of an additional set of needles added to the conventional stocking-frame which, operated in conjunction with the usual needles, had the effect of reversing the loop and producing a rib effect. A more fundamental development came in 1775 when the first warp knitting-machine was introduced. Previously loops had been formed in threads running across the width of the fabric (weft knitting), but the new machine, attributed to both J. Crane and J. Tarrett of Nottinghamshire, produced a knitted fabric which could be cut up and sewn into garments. By the 1850s rib knitting was being produced on powered circular machines, thus producing a tubular fabric for stockings, and about the same time M. Townsend of Nottingham patented the 'tumbler' or 'latch' needle, which was to be fundamental to the further progress of the knitting industry. Generally similar in appearance to the bearded needle, the latch needle had a hinged attachment to open and close the hook. All these and many more aspects of the technology of knitting can be seen in the large collection of machines held by Leicestershire Museums and on display at the Newarke Houses Museum, Newarke, Leicester.

Similarly the lace industry, so important in and around Nottingham, is well represented by machines on display at Nottingham Industrial Museum, Wollaton Hall, Nottingham. The basic step in the mechanisation of lace making had been made by John Heathcoat (1783–1861) in 1809, when he developed a machine (the bobbinet, later known as the plain net machine) capable of imitating almost exactly the hand-made pillow lace. He used a flat bobbin, resembling a disc, which could pass between the vertical warp threads and thus entwine the weft thread around them. In 1813 his machine was improved by John Lever, who adapted it to make patterned lace, using, if necessary, the Jacquard principle.

One major aspect of fabric production that has still to be considered is the finishing of the woven cloth. One of these finishing processes had been mechanised as early as the thirteenth century, when water-powered 'fulling' mills had replaced manual fulling of wool cloth. The process consisted of pounding the woven fabric in water with fuller's earth to felt it up and shrink it. It was relatively simple to devise water-powered hammers to carry out this work, cams on a shaft raising the heads in much the same manner as the tilt hammers used for ironworking. The effects on location of the industry were similar, too, resulting in an essentially urban-based craft moving out and dispersing to the fast-flowing streams of north Somerset, central Gloucestershire and west Wiltshire in the South West, and from towns like Beverley and York to the Pennine streams of the West Riding of Yorkshire. A number of fulling mills still survive and at Higher Mill, Helmshore

48 Higher Mill, Helmshore, Lancashire. An iron breastshot waterwheel with peripheral gearing and wooden floats

(95/SD 777214), the waterwheel (Plate 48) and fulling stocks can also be seen, as can the tenter hooks on which the cloth was subsequently stretched and dried and the rotary gig-mills containing teasels, which were used to raise the nap on the cloth. This was afterwards sheared, first by large hand-shears and later by a rotary device in action very similar to a cylinder lawnmower.

THE FIRST FACTORIES

The factory system that developed so rapidly in the textile industries at the end of the eighteenth century had its origins in 1702. In that year Thomas Cotchett (b1640) opened a three-storey silk spinning mill on the River Derwent in Derby in which he installed Dutch spinning or 'throwing' machinery. Although Cotchett's business failed and all but a few of the foundation arches of his building have disappeared (121/SK 354365), his mill has a good claim to the title of the first factory in that it was a single building with complex machinery, a source of power in its waterwheel, and accommodation for a number of employees. What was perhaps of more immediate importance was that his enterprise attracted the attention of the wealthy London silk merchant Thomas (later Sir Thomas) Lombe (1685–1739), and his half-brother John Lombe (1693?–1722), who worked for a time in Cotchett's Mill. Some years later, possibly after a visit to the highly advanced silk spinning areas of Italy, the Lombes built a much bigger factory in Derby near Cotchett's original building.

Here the three basic operations of converting the silk filament from the cocoon of the silkworm into a yarn suitable for weaving were carried on. The first stages, carried out before the silk arrived at the factory, consisted of unwinding the filament from the cocoon and rewinding it with others to form a skein. This skein was washed to remove the gummy matter known as sericin and was then ready for processing in Lombe's factory. Here it was wound on to bobbins on a winding machine; transferred to a second machine where the strands from several bobbins were wound on to a single bobbin, a process known as 'doubling'; and finally twisted together into a yarn on a third machine, a process known as 'throwing'. If the yarn was to be used for the weft in weaving, only a slight twist was put into it, but if for the warp, a stronger twist was applied. The weft yarn was called the 'tram' and the warp the 'organzine'.

The Lombes' factory in Derby was of unprecedented size, the throwing mill alone being five storeys high and 110ft long and accommodating over 300 workers. These were mainly women and children who reknotted the threads when they broke, a very frequent occurrence. A single large water-wheel operated over 25,000 movements in the machinery. The building established the form the textile mill was to take until well into the twentieth century, the name 'mill' itself deriving from the fact that all the early ones were water-powered. It remained in active use for silk until 1890, when part collapsed, and after a disastrous fire in 1910 the building was substantially altered. Today the original approach bridge and part of the tower survive, together with foundations in the river bank. The wrought-iron gates, dating from 1722, were re-sited in 1934 near the Borough Library in Wardwick, Derby.

Why the industry became established in Derby is difficult to explain. The main centre, occupied largely by refugee Huguenot weavers, was in the Spitalfields area (Plate 49) of London where, in and around Fournier Street

49 Silk weavers' garrets in Spitalfields, London

(160/TQ 338818), a considerable number of their houses with attic workshops still survive. The rise of the Nottingham framework knitting industry is the most likely reason for Cotchett and the Lombes coming to the East Midlands, and Derby may well have been chosen because of the power afforded by the waters of the Derwent. The Trent itself and tributaries like the Leen and Erewash would have been quite unsuitable. From Derby the silk industry spread to other centres after the expiration of the Lombe patent in 1732, and factories were established initially in Macclesfield, Stockport and Chesterfield, and later in Manchester, Salford, and Braintree in Essex where George Courtauld and his son Samuel founded the firm which is now world famous for man-made fibres.

In the first half of the eighteenth century, however, the silk industry's growth rate was relatively slow and, despite the fact that factories had been established, it played no part in the large-scale industrial progress in textiles that came later with cotton and wool. The reasons for this were the shortage

50 Silk weavers' houses in Macclesfield, Cheshire

of raw silk supplies, which were also expensive, and the competition from continental and eastern silks abroad, which destroyed the chance of appreciable export markets. The cotton industry on the other hand enjoyed unlimited supplies of raw material and, once the plantation system had developed fully in the American South, supplies that fell in price. Cotton fabric, an attractive and cheap alternative to wool, was able to penetrate the enormous and growing home market and at the same time, as a result of the fall in costs and prices as a result of technological innovations in the industry, to enjoy an almost unlimited export market. Cotton was also a tractable fibre lending itself to machine processes more readily than wool. Finally the cotton industry, for reasons which we shall examine shortly, had the good fortune to establish itself in Lancashire, which was not a traditional textile area and had none of the built-in restrictive practices to be found elsewhere. Thus it was cotton which stood in the forefront of industrial progress in the textile industry despite the fact that what might be called the first generation of true factories were for spinning silk.

THE DEVELOPMENT OF THE FACTORY BUILDING

The early silk mills and Arkwright's first cotton mills at Cromford were characterised by the fact that they contained novel machinery in buildings of essentially traditional construction. All the ingenious devices developed to convert fibre into cloth were of a size suitable for arrangement in rows watched over by relatively unskilled operatives. Eventually all could be powered from a rotating shaft that had at its input end a horse-gin in a few early examples, but more often a large waterwheel, and increasingly after about 1800 a rotative steam engine. The requirements of the factory were therefore large numbers of identical spaces, with reasonable natural lighting, arranged in such a way that power could easily be distributed to the machines. The outcome was a new form of building, taking the traditional constructional techniques of brick or stone load-bearing walls and timber beam-and-plank floors as its basis. Typically it was long and thin in plan, rarely more than 40ft deep, rising to four to six storeys, and with the line-shafting to carry power to the machines arranged parallel to the long axis and supported at or near ceiling height. This was basically the form the Lombes' mill had taken in 1721, and it was to survive virtually unaltered for two centuries.

Numerous fine examples of early textile mills still exist, although unfortunately Arkwright's Old Mill at Cromford (111/SK 298569), completed in 1772, has been so substantially altered, with the loss of two storeys, that it is almost unrecognisable. Masson Mill (111/SK 294573), however, built in 1783, is largely intact, the red-painted walls and white window surrounds a familiar feature on the A6(T) north of Cromford (Plate 51). Arkwright was associated with a number of other mills which, like those at Cromford, were located on streams that could provide power. At Cress-brook (111/SK 173728) the remains of his 1779 mill can be seen at the west end of the existing 1815 building, the latter a superb four-storey structure built by William Newton (Plate 52), one of the finest examples of the adoption of an enlarged domestic style for mills. It has twelve bays with a centrally placed four-bay pediment, hipped roof and a cupola that once held a bell to summon the workers.

An even finer example of this Georgian style may be seen in a number of silk mills in Macclesfield, notably Frost's Mill (110/SJ 918737) in the centre of the town (Plate 53) and the former silk mill on Chester Road, now the

51 Arkwright's Masson Mill, Cromford, Derbyshire

card factory of Henry and Leigh Slater (110/SJ 909737). This latter building
epitomises the large eighteenth-century mill—a rectangular and disciplined
brick box for machinery obeying to the letter the architectural rules of the
day. The Macclesfield card factory has four storeys and seventeen bays,
the centre five brought forward and supporting a pediment with central
clock, cupola and wind vane. In Hampshire the same style on a much smaller
scale can be seen in the beautiful red brick Witchurch silk mill (168/SU
464481), while in Cheshire, Quarry Bank Mill, Styal (101/SJ 834830), built
in 1784 by Samuel Greg of Belfast on a more complicated plan, has the same
graceful rhythm. A number of features typical of most of these early mills
are worthy of examination. Firstly the windows, which have small panes and
are usually of the sash type, often have cast-iron frames. Generally speaking

52 Cressbrook Mill, Derbyshire, a cotton mill of 1815 with later weaving sheds in front

the smaller window panes are the earlier, good examples being found at Calver Mill, Derbyshire (111/SK 245744), and Low Mill, Caton, in Lancashire (89/SD 527649). In the latter case the mill was built originally in 1784 and rebuilt after a fire in 1838, probably with the original windows. Tie irons of a disc or cruciform shape also are frequent, and in many cases appear to date from the construction of the building. These wall plates are tied by wrought-iron rods that pass right through the building and hold it together.

Inside, the floors consist of timber beams and boards sometimes supported by vertical timber pillars but more often by cast-iron ones of circular or cruciform section. The position of original line-shafting, if it has gone, can usually be traced from the positions of brackets or bracket-fixing holes either in the columns or on the ceiling beams. Occasionally the column itself is forked or has a bracket fixing cast on to it to support the bearing or 'plummer'

53 Frost's Mill, Macclesfield, Cheshire, like a number of other silk mills in the town, epitomises the translation of the Georgian domestic vernacular into the new textile factories

block. The position and size of watercourses are also worth noting, as they given an indication of the type of waterwheel used. In early mills the wheel was often centrally placed in the building with a vertical timber shaft taking the drive from the pit wheel up through the building to engage the horizontal line-shafts on each floor. Later, iron shafts and gearing were used. In smaller mills the waterwheel might be outside the building altogether, either completely exposed or housed in a small lean-to.

Although the general form of the multi-storey textile mill had been established at the beginning of the eighteenth century, a fundamental change in its technique of construction evolved in the 1780s and 1790s as a result of what we might now call a research programme. Arkwright's major partner in his Cromford venture was Jedediah Strutt, who had substantial silk interests in Derby and, after the dissolving of the partnership in 1781, took over completely the mills at Belper and Milford. These were greatly extended during the 1790s by Jedediah's son William Strutt (1756–1830), who systematically set about finding an answer to the problem of fire in these timber-floored buildings. Fires were frequent and usually disastrous, the complete destruction in 1791 of the enormous Albion flour mill in London providing the final incentive towards devising a solution. The first stage was reached in Strutt's calico mill in Derby, 1792–3, in which the floors were made of shallow brick arches of 9ft span springing from timber beams supported on cast-iron columns. The underside of the timber was coated with plaster to ensure that no surface that might catch fire would be exposed. Strutt produced more advanced versions at Milford in 1792–3 and Belper in 1793–5, but it was in fact a friend, Charles Bage, who took the next step by replacing the timber beam with a cast-iron one, so producing the world's first iron-framed building, a flax mill in Shrewsbury (118/SJ 500140). Although all Strutt's early buildings have now gone, the Marshall, Benyon & Bage flax mill, now used as a maltings, still stands at Ditherington, Shrewsbury. The modern factory had arrived and, although it was to be more than another 50 years before it became a completely frame structure and the load-bearing exterior walls disappeared to be replaced by curtain-wall cladding, the Shrewsbury flax mill must be regarded as one of the pioneer structures of the Industrial Revolution. Others quickly followed and, although the immediate descendants have been destroyed, Strutt's own response to the Bage building, his North Mill at Belper (111/

54 Anglo-Scotian Mills,
Beeston, Nottingham

SK 346480), completed in 1804, still survives as the most beautiful, sophisticated and technically perfect structure of its era. Now owned by English
Sewing Cotton Ltd, the mill is still in use and likely to remain so.

While these giant cotton and flax mills were developing so rapidly in
the early years of the nineteenth century, the wool textile industry was
stirring, too, although less violently. In the Stroud valleys of Gloucestershire
numerous mills, most of them relatively small, were being built in the warm
local stone, usually with interiors of conventional timber construction.
Similarly in west Wiltshire and north Somerset water-powered wool
mills appeared in considerable numbers. An exception to all the others is
Stanley Mill at Stonehouse near Stroud (156/SO 814043), which is of

cast-iron and brick 'fire-proof' construction. Built in 1813 to draw its power from the River Frome, Stanley Mill provides a remarkable combination of the functional use of brick panels and stone pilasters on its outside with traceried iron arches supporting iron floor beams on iron columns. By the 1820s the iron-framed textile mill had become well established, although it was not until the 1860s or even later that the building of mills with timber beams and floors died out. One reason may have been the failure of a number of cast-iron frame structures, such as the celebrated collapse of Lowerhouse Mill, Oldham, in 1844, and another the appreciation that, although iron itself was incombustible, if a fire did occur in an iron-framed building, the expansion of the members frequently resulted in the destruction of the shell of the building too.

It was to Lancashire that the cotton industry migrated in the late eighteenth and early nineteenth centuries, and there the factory continued to evolve. Large numbers of these buildings still survive, offering the industrial archaeologist an opportunity to examine in detail their evolution. Initially water, for power, washing and bleaching, was the major locational factor, with the result that mills tended to be situated in remote valleys of the Pennines where such site advantages outweighed problems of communication. With the introduction of steam power, however, new factors influenced location and the cotton industry became concentrated in towns stretching from Stockport in Cheshire north to Preston. These new cotton towns grew up on the Lancashire plain, still enjoying the water necessary for various finishing and bleaching processes, but having easier access to Liverpool for raw materials, to Manchester for marketing the finished products, to coal, and by virtue of the concentration of large numbers of mills to pools of skilled labour both for operating and maintaining the machinery.

An important example of this first phase of steam-powered mills survives in Orrell's Mill, Travis Street, Heaton Mersey, Stockport (101/SJ 867903), built in the mid-1830s by William (later Sir William) Fairbairn (1789–1874), the celebrated Manchester engineer. The mill has six storeys and the main spinning rooms are 280ft long by 50ft wide. Cast-iron columns and beams support the floors. Numerous less spectacular examples can be found in most of the textile towns, simple in shape and design, with rectangular windows regularly spaced and separated by almost their own width of brick wall.

From the 1860s onwards, and particularly after the widespread adoption of the American ring-spinning frame, cotton mills became much larger and were typically built of dark red brick with progressively increasing areas of glazing. The introduction of sprinkler systems for fire control necessitated high-level water tanks, which were at first simply placed on the roof of the mill, as at the 1851 Galgate silk mill at Ellel (94/SD 485557). By the late 1870s, however, it was more common to enclose the tank within the structure of a tower that frequently bore the name of the mill in white tile lettering.

The gradual recovery of the Lancashire cotton industry after the devastating effects of the American Civil War led eventually to a new boom in building, which, between about 1880 and 1920, brought the cotton mill to its ultimate state of development. Enormous brick-built spinning mills, often in shiny red Accrington brick with yellow brick detailing, great expanses of glass and highly ornamental towers, were built in large numbers, and they still dominate the skyline of most towns between Preston and Oldham. The demand created by large machinery for bigger and bigger spaces with fewer intermediate supports was satisfied by new constructional techniques employing initially fabricated wrought-iron beams and later, as at Centenary Mill, Preston (94/SD 551297), built in 1895, rolled steel beams and concrete floors. Less load was carried by the external walls, which in many cases became almost entirely glass, the brickwork being reduced to little more than mullions between large glazed panels. All-concrete construction was slow to be adopted in Britain, although it rapidly reached an advanced state of development abroad, notably in France. Concrete, however, was to bring the all-glass wall to the textile mill, one of the results of mushroom construction in which concrete pillars set well in from the skin of the building supported the floors on the cantilever principle. A good example is the Viyella factory designed by F. A. Broadhead on Castle Boulevard, Nottingham (112/SK 570394).

In parallel with the evolution of the mill's shape and structure came important changes in power transmission. The earliest water-powered mills had used timber millwork, transmitting the power by wooden shafts and gearing. In the latter part of the eighteenth century cast-iron shafting and gears were introduced, to be superseded by lightweight wrought-iron shafts revolving at higher speeds which were developed first by Fairbairn in the

FACTORY POWER TRANSMISSION

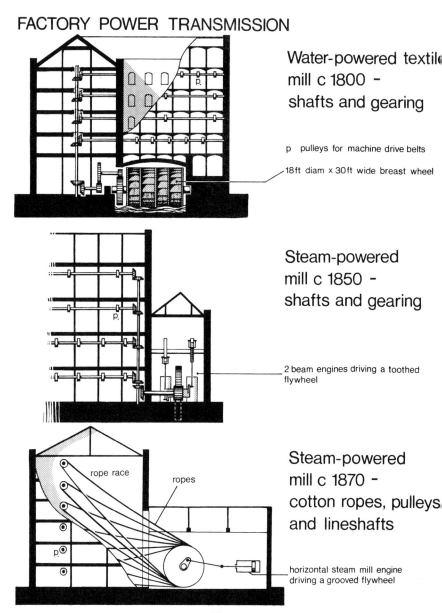

Water-powered textile mill c 1800 - shafts and gearing

p pulleys for machine drive belts

18 ft diam x 30 ft wide breast wheel

Steam-powered mill c 1850 - shafts and gearing

2 beam engines driving a toothed flywheel

Steam-powered mill c 1870 - cotton ropes, pulleys and lineshafts

rope race

ropes

horizontal steam mill engine driving a grooved flywheel

Fig 30

late 1820s. The greatest single advance came in the 1860s, when shaft drive was dispensed with altogether and ropes driven from the flywheel of the steam engine ran to each floor of the mill (see Fig 30). The flywheel face was grooved to take as many as thirty cotton ropes, which ran up through the rope race to drive the line-shafts at each floor. Ropes were mechanically efficient, cheap to install and maintain, and if a breakage occurred, the whole mill did not have to suspend production, as it did when a fault arose in a shaft-driven system. A specific type of engine evolved, too, in the steam mill engine, which became widespread in both Lancashire and Yorkshire. It was usually a horizontal compound with a variety of cylinder configurations (see Chapter 4 and Fig 14). A superb mill engine is preserved by the Northern Mill Engine Society at Dee Mill, Shaw, near Rochdale (101/SD 945093). Nearby is that other typical feature of all large steam textile mills—the pool, or mill 'lodge', in which condenser water was cooled and stored.

Although the spinning side of the textile industry produced a large and very individual style of mill building, the weaving of yarns into fabric resulted in an equally distinctive if less spectacular type of structure. Typically weaving was carried on in a single storey building, although in earlier mills looms occupied the ground floors of muli-storey spinning blocks. A good example of a weaving shed stands in front of Cressbrook Mill, Derbyshire (111/SK 173728), its roof of ridge-and-furrow form, with glazed north-lights on the steep-pitched faces and slates on the shallower sides. Wooden roof trusses with cast-iron columns were almost universal for weaving sheds, the looms being arranged in lines between the rows of columns on which line-shafts were carried. North-east Lancashire in particular abounds in weaving sheds mainly built in the latter part of the nineteenth century, when weaving became a speciality of towns like Nelson and Colne, Burnley, Blackburn, Preston and Clitheroe. In many ways the weaving shed, with its large ground floor area and good all-over lighting, formed the basis for the modern factory building to be seen on every inter-war trading estate and New Town.

On the east of the Pennines the early period of mill building, until, say, 1830, was generally similar to that on the west, although stone was almost universal as a building material. An early exception was Gott's Mill, Leeds (96/SE 291335), a large complex consisting of spinning mills and weavers' dwellings which was unfortunately demolished in the 1960s.

Just as exceptional, although for completely different reasons, was another Leeds mill, which happily still exists: Marshall's flax mill (96/SE 295326), completed in June 1840, is based on the Egyptian temple of Karnak. Designed by Bonomi and David Roberts, the single-storey preparing and spinning mill stretches 132yd along Marshall Street, and is 72yd in depth. The interior room of the Temple Mill, as it became known, covers some 2 acres, and slender cast-iron columns (which also act as drainpipes) support a ceiling 21ft high which has over 60 conical glass skylights 14ft in diameter rising above the roof. Along the façade stand squat columns flanking the windows, and supporting a massive Egyptianesque entablature, and to the north, set back slightly from the street line, is the office block added in 1843. The original chimney, built rather after the style of Cleopatra's needle, cracked in 1852 and was replaced by a conventional one. John Marshall (1765–1846), who built the Temple Mill and was also involved in the Shrewsbury flax mill of 1797, established his linen industry in Leeds in the early 1800s. The peak of its prosperity was exemplified by his Egyptian adventure of the 1840s but later, under a second generation, the business declined, to end finally in 1886. Temple Mill is now used by a mail order firm.

Two great complexes in Bradford epitomise the West Riding's position

55 The mill at Saltaire, Titus Salt's model village near Bradford, Yorkshire

56 Manningham Mills, Bradford, Yorkshire, built by Samuel Lister in the 1870s

57 The main entrance of Manningham Mills

in the textile industry in the second half of the nineteenth century, although, curiously enough, neither was concerned specifically with wool at the outset. Best known is Saltaire, the planned village surrounding mills, created by the model employer, social improver and philanthropist, Titus Salt (1803–76). Salt was born in Morley, near Bradford, and grew up in the worsted industry in partnership with his father at a time when the West Riding was beginning to outstrip the traditional centre of worsted manufacture in Norwich. His considerable business and inventive abilities enabled him to set up on his own, and by 1836 he owned four mills. His success in spinning the fibres of the South American Alpaca goat, previously regarded as unusable, led to a great increase in business at a time when a wide variety of differing warp and weft threads were being experimented with. By 1851 he had started a large new factory (Plate 55) on the River Aire outside Bradford around which he also built the new settlement of Saltaire, with its neat rows of houses for employees. By the 1870s a church, hospital, baths and schools had been added to form the complete model village which survives, virtually unaltered, today, a stage in the progress from New Lanark to Port Sunlight and Bournville.

The other major Bradford mill was built by Samuel C. Lister (1815–1906) at Manningham (96/SE 146348) and dates from 1873. Lister was an inventor and improver of processes, taking out more than 150 patents during his lifetime. Starting in the worsted industry, his major contributions included processes for combing wool and utilising waste silk, and it was on the strength of this latter technique that the great Manningham Mill complex developed (Plates 56 and 57). Velvet and plush were the main products which resulted from Lister's improvement of a Spanish loom for weaving pile cloth. The mill itself consists of two large six-storey blocks each capped by an ornamental and panelled parapet, and a series of lower buildings principally devoted to weaving. In the centre is the boiler house with a tall chimney resembling an Italian campanile.

11 The Chemical Industries

THE chemical industries present the industrial archaeologist with even greater problems than the engineering machinery discussed in Chapter 7, and for generally similar reasons. Not only are the processes of the industry fairly complex but the structures surviving from its past are often difficult to identify in the field. The very wide range of processes and plant can best be appreciated by reference to early textbooks on the subject like G. Martin's *Industrial Chemistry* (1925). The landscapes created by massive concentrations of chemical plant, in places like Widnes, for example, are among the most unattractive imaginable and, for this reason, derelict buildings and old waste tips of toxic materials are among the first to be removed in the interests of tidiness and public safety. An added difficulty results from the fact that the products of the chemical industry are rarely ends in themselves but are the raw materials for other manufacturing processes. The industry's evolution has therefore been governed by the demands of other industrial activities—of textile manufacturers for bleaches and dyes, of glassmakers for soda and of the fertiliser industry for sulphuric acid. To produce these chemicals, the industry demanded a wide variety of organic and inorganic raw materials, ranging from seaweed for alkalis and exotic foreign hardwoods for leather dyes to salt, copperas (derived from iron pyrites) and alum. Coal, besides providing the basis for town gas, was also an important raw material for many chemicals, although its main significance was as a fuel and as such an important factor in the location of chemical processes depending on heat. More recently oil has become an important, perhaps the most important, chemical base, its use extending back a surprisingly long way. Scottish oil shales were once the most important home source, but the vast quantities now used for fuel and chemical manufacturing purposes will nearly all continue to be imported until North Sea oil comes ashore in any quantity.

The varied nature of the chemical industry and its many products make systematic classification and examination difficult. Organic and inorganic raw materials were used, alkalis and acids were produced, and furnace techniques involving fusing and vitrification, evaporation resulting in crystallisation, and distillation were its most important processes. Two of the most industrially significant furnace processes of what is in essence part of the chemical industry, the manufacturer of pottery and of glass, have already been considered in Chapter 9, so it is primarily with crystallisation and distillation that we are concerned in this chapter.

Common salt, sodium chloride, has long been and still is an important raw material for many chemical products, although for centuries before the Industrial Revolution its extraction, mainly by evaporation, was geared to its sale as an end product in its own right for direct human consumption and for the preservation of fish and meat. Although solar evaporation was used to a limited extent in medieval times, only at Lymington in Hampshire was the technique practised in relatively recent years: there for about 16 weeks in the summer seawater was concentrated into a brine solution in evaporation ponds known as 'salterns' before being boiled in lead or brass pans to extract the crystalline salt. From September the brine obtained during the summer was evaporated, using Newcastle coal brought in by sea, an expensive process only made economic by the saving resulting from solar evaporation and the large nearby market of the Royal Navy at Portsmouth, which needed salt for preserving beef and pork on board ship. The Lymington salt industry reached its peak of production in the mid-eighteenth century, when 50,000 tons a year were being produced, and finally closed in 1865. The low banks that surrounded the evaporation pools can still be seen on Keyhaven and Pennington marshes (180/SZ 315923). Similar circular banks exist at Crosscanonby, near Maryport (82/NY 066401). Saltworkers' cottages stood nearby till recently.

The other main areas of salt extraction from seawater were the Firth of Forth, the Ayrshire coast around Saltcoats, and the estuary of the Tyne and the nearby coastal areas of Northumberland and Durham. The availability of cheap coal was a major locational factor, only the poorest quality slack, which was not worth the cost of transport far from the pithead, being used. It was often known as 'pancoal'. The process was carried out in heated pans made initially of lead but later of iron in which the water was evaporated until the salt crystallised, leaving behind a solution of calcium and magnesium salts known as 'bitterns'. In some areas, such as Lymington, the bitterns formed a profitable by-product in the form of Epsom salts, 4–5 tons being produced for every 100 tons of common salt. In Northumberland, Seaton Sluice (78/NZ 336768) was developed as a coal and salt port in the seventeenth century, and on the Firth of Forth east of Edinburgh the ancient salt centre of Prestonpans (its name derives from the process carried on there) continued seawater salt extraction down to 1959.

The discovery of rock salt in Cheshire about 1690 and on Teesside in 1863 provided the foundation for the modern British salt industry and the chemical processes based on it. Initially salt from natural brine wells had been evaporated in the Northwich and Middlewich areas of Cheshire, and near Droitwich in Worcestershire. The 'wich' place name ending is a strong, but not infallible, clue to the existence of a salt industry. The extensive mining in Cheshire—the great Marston Mine north of Northwich (101/SJ 6760) produced 110,000 tons in 1882—gave way to brine pumping, in which water was circulated through boreholes sunk into the salt deposits and brought back to the surface as a solution from which the salt could be evaporated or, more recently, used in the chemical industry direct. Evidence of the extensive subsidence caused by salt working can be seen around Northwich in the form of extensive pools or 'flashes', and to the east of the town are brine wells (110/SJ 7471). There is now only one active salt mine, at Winsford. South of Middlewich the main Crewe to Manchester railway line suffers constantly from the sinking of the ground surface above salt workings. Some of the finest surviving structures of the salt industry are in Winsford itself (110/SJ 599997). They are the timber sheds used for drying salt, and their construction, which is entirely of timber as metal fittings would corrode in the salt-laden atmosphere, provides an interesting example of the timber-framed tradition of domestic building carried through into industrial structures. To the north of the town at Winnington (110/SJ 6474) is the plant set up in 1873 by Ludwig Mond (1839–1909) and John Brunner (1842–1919) to produce synthetic soda by the Belgian Solvay or ammonia process. This largely replaced the Leblanc process discussed below. Brunner, Mond & Co Ltd became one of the four largest chemical manufacturers in Britain, and in 1926 amalgamated with the other three—The United Alkali Co, the British Dyestuffs Corporation and Nobel Industries—to form Imperial Chemical Industries. Winnington is the headquarters of the ICI Alkali Division and is well placed for supply of its basic raw materials of salt, limestone and coking coal.

SOAP

The growth of the wool and later cotton textile industries created new demands for soaps, bleaches, dyes and the mordants which fixed them. The two main types of soap used for cleaning fleeces and cloth were mixtures of fats or oils with mild alkalis, hard soap employing the alkali sodium carbonate (soda) and soft soap the alkali potassium carbonate (potash). These materials were boiled together for long periods to emulsify the ingredients, so a fuel, usually coal, was an additional requirement. From the thirteenth century onwards Bristol became an important soap-making centre based on the coincidence of local coal supplies and the great wool-producing areas of Gloucestershire, Somerset and Wiltshire. So important was the industry that the medieval writer Richard of Devizes wrote: 'At Bristol there is no one who is not, or has not been, a soap maker.' Today the industry in Bristol is extinct, although its major industrial monument— the exotic brick-built factory of Christopher Thomas & Brothers, makers of Puritan soap, at Broad Plain in the centre of the city (156/ST 597728)— dates only from the 1880s. The building, now used for storage, is one of the small collection of surviving structures which represent that curiously Bristolian style of commercial architecture, sometimes known colloquially as 'Bristol Byzantine', of the 1870s and 1880s.

Before the soap industry could reach an industrial scale of production, the problem of its raw materials had to be solved. Soda and potash were obtainable from the ashes of wood and seaweed and both were also increasingly in demand from glassmakers. Salts of sodium being much more plentiful in nature than those of potassium, and the most abundant of all being sodium chloride, it was natural that the latter should be seen as a possible source of soda for the soap industry; and the French chemist Nicholas Leblanc (1742–1806) in 1791 succeeded in developing a workable process for converting common salt into soda. In the earliest Leblanc process the first stage was the treatment of common salt with sulphuric acid to form sodium sulphate (saltcake) with the liberation into the atmosphere of hydrochloric acid gas, and the second stage the heating of the saltcake with coal or coke and limestone or chalk to produce crude sodium carbonate (ball soda) in solution and calcium sulphide and coal ash as waste products. Waste heat from the furnaces was used to evaporate the soda solution, producing 'soda ash' or anhydrous sodium carbonate. The stages may be represented simply thus:

1 Sodium chloride+Sulphuric acid=Sodium bisulphate+
   $NaCl$ H_2SO_4 $NaHSO_4$
   Hydrochloric acid
   HCl
2 Sodium chloride+Sodium bisulphate=Sodium sulphate+
   $NaCl$ $NaHSO_4$ Na_2SO_4
   Hydrochloric acid
   HCl

The first reaction begins at ordinary temperatures, but requires heat. The end product, 'saltcake' is melted with limestone or chalk and coal or coke:

3 Sodium sulphate+Carbon=Sodium sulphide+Carbon dioxide
   Na_2SO_4 $2C$ Na_2S $2CO_2$
4 Sodium sulphide+Calcium carbonate=Sodium carbonate+
   Na_2S $CaCO_3$ Na_2CO_3
   Calcium sulphide
   CaS

From these later reactions some carbon monoxide is produced and of course coal ash.

The first works in England to operate the Leblanc process was at Walker, east of Newcastle-upon-Tyne, using salt from a brine spring struck in the Walker Colliery. Various previous soda-making processes had been tried at this works but in 1823 it had become solely a Leblanc soda factory. In the same year the second works in the country was established, by James Muspratt (1821–71) in Liverpool. On both Merseyside and Tyneside the industries thrived, and both areas became important for soap making. As Leblanc soda making grew, however, there was a rising tide of protest in Widnes, St Helens, Jarrow, South Shields and other places against the pollution resulting from the release of hydrochloric acid gas into the atmosphere. As much as $12\frac{1}{2}$cwt of gas was produced from every ton of salt, and this flowed from the chimneys of the chemical works to defoliate the trees and poison livestock. The result of this agitation was the passing of the Alkali Works Act in 1863, which stipulated that at least 95 per cent of the hydrochloric acid gas had to be condensed. An alkali inspectorate was also set up to see that the law was obeyed. (This early involvement in clean air activity laid the foundation of the practical approach to problems that still exist in the UK, where enforcement of the 'best practical means' of abatement is preferred to the setting of arbitrary emission levels.)The enormous chimneys used by the soda factories to dissipate the gases—one at St Rollox, Glasgow, was 420ft high—had to be replaced by condensers most usually in the form of towers in which the gas passed upwards through beds of coke while water flowed down through them. The alkali manufacturers now had a new by-product, hydrochloric acid, with which to pollute rivers and streams instead of the atmosphere. Before long, however, all but the smallest works were using it for making bleach.

The soap industry of Merseyside, which developed in Widnes, Warrington and Liverpool, produced a wide range of products and eventually gave birth to a completely new industrial complex that was to become the home of one of the world's great soap combines. William Hesketh Lever (1851–1925) founded Port Sunlight (100/SJ 3484) on the Wirral or Cheshire side of the Mersey estuary in 1888, and developed there a factory and model village for his workpeople far in advance of anything previously built. Viscount Leverhulme, as he eventually became, was not a romantic idealist but a social realist as well as a successful businessman. He talked of the days when 'Workpeople will be able to live and be comfortable in semi-detached houses, with gardens back and front, in which they will be able to know more about the science of life than they can do in a back slum.' Port Sunlight was the realisation of this philosophy, the creation of an ideal community. Groups of 'Tudor' cottages with plenty of traditional half-timbering and moulded plasterwork were arranged in carefully contrived arcs around little greens and enclosed spaces at an average density of only eight dwellings per acre. In a way Port Sunlight did a disservice to the movement towards better workers' housing, for although it was important environmentally, it was not conceived with any thought of financial realism. The much more mundane Cadbury experiment at Bournville, near Birmingham (131/SP 0481), based on a return of 4 per cent on the investment in building in order to encourage local authorities to imitate it, had a greater influence on subsequent developments. The industrial archaeologist as a student of industrial landscapes should visit both. At Port Sunlight, in the Lady Lever Art Gallery, he will also find a fine portrait in oils of Thomas Telford.

BLEACHING AND DYEING

The demand for a chemical bleaching agent that was rapid in action was largely created by the cotton fabric side of the textile industry, which had grown beyond the stage where the natural action of sun, rain and wind on cloth spread out in bleachfields could cope with the enormous output. It was the bleaching action of chlorine, first recognised in 1785 by the French chemist C. L. Berthollet (1748–1822), which was eventually applied to fabrics. The manufacture of a chlorine-based bleach was first developed on a large scale by Charles Tennant (1768–1838), for which he set up the St Rollox chemical works in Glasgow in 1799. Previously sulphuric acid had been used to liberate chlorine from a mixture of common salt and manganese dioxide, but Tennant patented a solid compound of chlorine and lime known as chloride of lime or bleaching powder, which was less harmful to the people who made and used it than chlorine in aqueous solution. In 1800 Tennant was selling his bleaching powder at £140 per ton from his Glasgow factory. As the industry grew and techniques improved, the price dropped until in 1870 it had fallen to £8 10s per ton, presenting an enormous saving to cloth manufacturers. In the 1860s techniques for recovering chlorine from the waste hydrochloric acid of Leblanc soda plants were developed, and this eventually became not only the main means of producing bleach but in many cases the primary source of income for the Leblanc works.

Cleaned and bleached cloth often had to be dyed, but although the soap and bleach industries were revolutionised in the early nineteenth century, development of 'fast' dyes came much later. The principal dye-wares used throughout Europe were much the same as they had been for centuries and included vegetable-based materials such as saffron, turmeric, woad and logwood. A mill engaged in the logwood dye industry remained in use until 1964, and can still be seen at Keynsham in Somerset (156/ST 656679). Albert Mill, Keynsham (Plate 58), contains a logwood chipper and a set of stone edge-runners for crushing the wood chips, both powered by an external iron waterwheel of 18ft 6in diameter and 9ft width. The woods included fustics from Jamaica, South America, Greece and Turkey for yellow dyes; Brazilwood for pinks and reds; ebony to give olive green for glove leathers; and New Zealand Tanekaha to supply a golden brown colour.

In order to make the dye adhere to the fabric, mordants had to be used,

and some of them significantly altered the character and colour of the dyes themselves. One of the earliest was copperas, which itself was used for ink and black dye. Copperas was obtained from the oxidation and hydrolysis of iron pyrites (FeS_2), sometimes called 'fool's gold'. The process, carried out in large open pits initially at Queenborough on the Isle of Sheppey and at Deptford, took up to 5 years, the copperas liquors ($FeSO_4 . 7H_2O$) being led away to cisterns as the slow atmospheric oxidation took place. In the eighteenth century numerous works taking advantage of the pyrites found in locally mined coal grew up on Tyneside. Besides its use as a dye and mordant, copperas was also a source of 'oil of vitriol' or concentrated sulphuric acid, which resulted in a highly profitable by-product in the form of Venetian red, an iron oxide.

More important as a mordant was alum, a double sulphate of potassium and aluminium, which was produced first in England at Guisborough in Yorkshire in 1595. Alum shales outcrop extensively on the North Yorkshire coast and inland on the northern and eastern slopes of the Cleveland Hills. Huge quarries, as at Ravenscar (93/NZ 9701) and on the cliffs at Boulby (86/NZ 7519) and Kettleness (86/NZ 8415), were excavated during the nineteenth century to obtain the shales, which were subsequently calcined, usually in heaps on the floor of the quarry itself. The calcined shale was then put into stone leaching or lixiviation pits usually floored with large stone flags and the resulting liquor was evaporated in lead or iron pans over coal fires. Extensive remains of the alum extraction process have been excavated recently by the Teesside Industrial Archaeology Group on the edge of Boulby cliffs in North Yorkshire. Sandsend (86/NZ 862128), north of Whitby, has the scanty remains of a small wharf built for shipping out alum.

During the second half of the nineteenth century the dye industry changed rapidly as the result of work begun by W. H. Perkin (1838–1907) in 1856 while studying under A. W. von Hoffman (1818–92). Hoffman came to London from Giessen in Germany as the first superintendent of the Royal College of Chemistry, established in 1845. Hoffman and Perkin carried out pioneer work on coal-tar derivatives, and it was one of these, the first commercially successful synthetic dye, a mauve, that Perkin offered to

58 Stone edge-runners for crushing logwood, Albert Mill, Keynsham, Somerset

Pullar's of Perth in 1856. The subsequent history of the synthetic dye industry during the latter part of the nineteenth century provides an example of a technological takeover even more startling in its proportions than the American rise to pre-eminence in machine tool design in the same period.

Germany had led the world in pure organic chemistry for more than 20 years before Perkin's original discovery, Hoffman being one of her leaders. By the 1870s Germany had overtaken British output of aniline dyes. Between 1886 and 1900 the six largest German firms took out 948 British patents, whereas the six largest British firms took out only eighty-six. By 1900 Germany had 90 per cent of the world market. The prominence of the chemist in the German dye industry also provides a salutary indication of the appreciation of the need for high level research. In 1900 the six largest German firms employed some 18,000 workpeople, 1,360 commercial staff, 350 engineers and technologists and 500 chemists. At the same date there were less than forty chemists, of generally lower quality, employed in the whole British dyestuffs industry. By the interwar years German chemical pre-eminence had widened into pharmaceuticals, synthetic perfumes and flavouring, saccharine, synthetic rubber and numerous other products. After A. W. von Hoffman left London in 1865 to take up the Chair at Berlin, there was no chair of organic chemistry in Britain until 1874! Study of the Industrial Revolution is often preoccupied with technological innovation, growth and capture of world markets, especially when seen from the standpoint of Britain. The machine tool and chemical industries provide examples of how an advanced country with well established traditional techniques can fall back into a state of relative underdevelopment. The fact that Britain and the United States were forced into a position of having to catch up emphasised the importance of scientific and technical education and underlined the fact that the educational system necessary to provide scientists and science-based engineers needs to be set up a generation in advance.

SULPHURIC ACID

Sulphuric acid was one of the most important base chemicals of the 'chemical revolution' of the nineteenth century, being required in ever-increasing quantities. Indeed, its rate of consumption may be regarded as one of the measures of the commercial and industrial prosperity of a nation, so widely is it used. Both the Leblanc soda process and Tennant's bleach making depended on it, as did numerous subsequent developments. Knowledge of the acid dated back many centuries and descriptions of its distillation from green vitriol or ferrous sulphate ($FeSO_4 . 7H_2O$), itself derived from copperas, occur as early as 1570. Continuous manufacture in Britain probably began in Twickenham and Richmond in the 1730s and 1740s. A major advance came in 1746 when John Roebuck (1718–94) and Samuel Garbett (1717–1805) set up a sulphuric acid plant in Birmingham, probably to satisfy the increasing demand from local metal industries for the acid as a cleaner and stripper. In this and subsequent processes lead chambers were used (sulphuric acid does not attack lead) in which nitre or saltpetre (potassium nitrate, KNO_3) and pure sulphur were burned over a shallow depth of water on to which the fumes condensed. The process was repeated at intervals until the liquid had reached the required strength.

The availability of cheap sulphuric acid by the lead chamber process was one of the great inventions of the Industrial Revolution, making available soda instead of the more expensive potash for the soap and glass industries, freeing greater supplies of potassium salts for agriculture and, after 1845, being used directly in the manufacture of phosphatic fertilisers (superphosphates), which became the principal outlet for sulphuric acid. In addition it was used for the manufacture of bleach and explosives. After 1830, when Chilean saltpetre (sodium nitrate, $NaNO_3$) replaced the potassium salt, sulphuric acid became cheaper still. By the 1870s the lead chamber process had reached a state of great efficiency, with its main concentrations in the North East of England, Glasgow, Lancashire and London. Today the lead-chamber process is completely obsolete and remains of it are virtually non-existent, the high value of scrap lead encouraging rapid demolition. A direct contact process, eliminating the use of saltpetre, was propounded in the 1830s but not taken up commercially until 1914. A major producing area is now Teesside, using local supplies of anhydrite (calcium sulphate, $CaSO_4$), mined at Billingham.

GUNPOWDER

Gunpowder manufacture is not truly a chemical industry process, as it involves the mixing of sulphur, saltpetre (potassium nitrate) and charcoal (carbon) without any reaction occurring between them. Of Chinese invention, its first European use—probably as the result of re-invention—was in Germany in the mid-thirteenth century and it quickly spread from there. Its use for blasting purposes in England probably dates from the 1620s, and in Cornish mines from 1689. More sophisticated and controllable explosives, including dynamite and gelignite, replaced it during the nineteenth century. The industry developed in several areas of Britain and a number of sites still contain recognisable and comprehensible remains. In the Lake District at Blackbeck (89/SD 334859), near Bouth, lies the site of a mill operating from 1862 until 1928, which is now a caravan park. The approach lane was once a railway track from the Leven estuary. The office and weigh-house still survive at the site's entrance, and there are also some steam pipes from the original engine-house, water power not being used here. The Lowwood works of 1799 stood near Haverthwaite beside the River Leven (89/SD 347837), but is now substantially overgrown. More extensive remains can be seen, however, at Elterwater (89/NY 328048), with two waterwheel pits, now occupied by turbines, a number of the original buildings, edge-runners and a small howitzer used for testing powders in the grounds of Elterwater Hall. The industry started in the Lake District in 1764, using saltpetre imported from India and later Chile and Germany, sulphur from Italy and Sicily and charcoal from local birch and alder trees, although juniper was used at Lowwood. The last mill closed in 1937.

There is another important gunpowder site, currently the centre of a major conservation programme, at Faversham in Kent (172/TR 009613), where the Chart Mills are being restored. For some 300 years before the closure of the works in 1934 Faversham was a major centre of the gunpowder industry. Much of the buildings and machinery was destroyed but in the Home Works, oldest of all and once the Royal Gunpowder Factory, some of the plant survived. Known as Chart Mills, they contain two pairs of gunpowder mills consisting of edge-runners, each pair worked in tandem off a single large waterwheel. After some 30 years of neglect, restoration by the Faversham Society is now well in hand. Another area of gunpowder manufacture was Devon, where there were three factories working in 1890. Remains of one of these can be seen on Dartmoor, where the buildings have been incorporated into Powder Mills Farm (175/ST 628769), which stands north of the B3212 Princetown to Moretonhampstead road. The

59 Gun barrel proof house, Birmingham, built in 1813

walls of three wheelhouses and two tall chimneys can been seen on the moor behind the farm, while a small mortar once used for testing the powder stands by the farm entrance. Storage of gunpowder presented very special problems of security, and powder houses, usually small, substantially built brick or stone buildings, are a common feature of many mining and quarrying areas. The dangers arising from powder on board ships while they were in port was solved at Bristol by the construction of a powder house on the River Avon (156/ST 537765) at which ships could discharge any gunpowder before entering the crowded quays and wharves of the city.

PAPER

As with gunpowder, the manufacture of paper hardly qualifies for inclusion among the chemical industries, although since the 1870s at least the pulp from which it is produced has been boiled with various acid and alkaline reagents to purify it. Up to the beginning of the nineteenth century all paper products were made by hand, using a vat and hand mould. The raw material from which the paper pulp was derived was essentially rag, but during the latter half of the nineteenth century this was progressively replaced by cellulose fibre from coniferous trees. A variety of additives were mixed with the pulp to improve the quality of the finished paper, and of these, china clay, used to make high-quality dense white papers, is the most important. In the original hand processes a fibrous suspension, highly diluted in water, is contained in the vat. The vat man dips the hand mould, a fine wire screen surrounded by a wooden frame (the deckle), into the vat and lifts out some pulp from which the water is allowed to drain. The deckle is then removed and the mould with the fibrous web of pulp lying on it is passed to the couch man. He transfers the web on to a woollen felt. Further webs on felts are stacked on it and the whole transferred to a screw press where excess water is removed by pressing. Finally the webs are removed from the felts and hung in a loft for drying in the atmosphere.

The limitations of this batch type of process are obvious, and the demand for paper, which had been increasing with the spread of printing, was eventually satisfied by the Fourdrinier machine and cylinder mould. Henry Fourdrinier (1766–1854) developed a machine in the early years of the nineteenth century in which the pulp was fed continuously on to a moving belt of gauze through which water was allowed to drain. Successive squeezing eliminated further water from the web until it was strong enough to support itself, when it passed to a series of steam-heated rolls that eliminated the remaining undesirable moisture. A modern papermaking machine is usually of this basic Fourdrinier type, often several hundred feet long. The proportion of the machine involved in removing water from the web either by drainage or steam represents over 90 per cent of this total length. The speed at which paper, and more particularly multi-layer boards, can be produced is determined by the rate at which the water can be removed from the webs. A development in this field during the early 1960s was the 'Inverform' machine in which water was removed by gravity from below and by vacuum box from above the webs. The prototype of this machine is preserved in Bristol City Museum. A national papermaking collection developed by the industry at St Mary Cray in Kent has now been transferred to the North Western Museum of Science and Technology in Manchester.

The distribution of eighteenth- and nineteenth-century paper mills in the period before the industry became focused on a relatively small number of large production units was based on three primary locational factors. A source of rags was a major requirement, so the proximity of a large urban centre was essential, and this centre also provided a market for the finished paper. The third requirement was large quantities of clear water. In the Bristol area alone the Bristol Industrial Archaeological Society has identified thirty-eight sites of extinct paper mills in addition to the seven where production still continues. Most of these were located on streams such as the Chew and Axe, flowing from the Mendips. At Bathford (156/ST 790671) a small mill specialises in the production of 'India' papers for bibles and dictionaries, made on a single 84in machine. A 1912 horizontal-tandem compound mill engine by Wood Brothers of Sowerby Bridge drove the machinery until 1966, when the mill was converted to electric power. The engine remains *in situ*. Wookey Hole Mill, near Wells (165/ST 531466), owned by W. S. Hodgkinson & Co Ltd, is probably the largest hand-made paper mill in the world, dating back to 1610 or even earlier. It produces mould-made account books, deckle edge notepaper and paper for bank-notes. Of the abandoned mills in the area, numerous buildings survive, some converted to other purposes, but little equipment remains. At Slaughterford (156/ST 839738) a rag mill used for preparing the raw materials is now derelict but the iron waterwheel still survives.

RUBBER

The origins of the modern rubber industry are twofold, based on two quite distinct vegetable raw materials. One of these was gutta-percha, a tree gum from Malaya introduced in the 1840s for insulating purposes; it gained some importance in the manufacture of submarine telegraph cables and the first cables laid under the streets of London. Eventually the superior qualities of rubber made the harder and more brittle gutta-percha obsolete, but not before the irrepressible Victorian enthusiasm for anything new had resulted in household ornaments and even tableware being made of it. Several companies were formed, mainly in London, to process the gum, and the name of one of these, the S. W. Silver & Co Gutta Percha and Rubber Works, founded in 1852, is perpetuated in Silvertown (161/TQ 410800), between the Royal Victoria Dock and Woolwich Reach.

Rubber is made from the latex of a tree native to South America, its great attraction to European industrialists of the late eighteenth and early nineteenth centuries being its unique qualities of elasticity and impermeability. A patent was granted as early as 1820 to Thomas Hancock (1786–1865) for making rubber latex springs, and in 1823 Charles Macintosh (1766–1843), a Glasgow chemical manufacturer, patented a technique for dissolving rubber in coal-tar naptha, a by-product of the gas industry, and applying the solution to fabric. He set up a works in Manchester for making waterproof garments—the misspelt mackintosh. The problems of stickiness and perishability to which these early rubbers were prone was solved by the introduction of the 'vulcanisation' process, in which sulphur was mixed with the rubber. Developed in 1841 by Charles Goodyear (1800–66) in the United States, the process was offered to Macintosh in England, but Macintosh's partner Thomas Hancock worked out for himself how to vulcanise rubber and filed a British patent in 1844, beating Goodyear by days. Vulcanising resulted in a much more stable material and provided the foundation on which the rubber industry could expand, initially with products like rubberised fabrics and shoe soles and later on a bigger scale altogether as the result of the growth of the motor industry and the establishment of huge factories like Fort Dunlop on the outskirts of Birmingham.

Much of the equipment used in the mixing of the constituents of rubber, which in the case of tyres includes powdered carbon, was until recently surprisingly primitive. Masticators, rather like enormous mangles, are used and an early example, from an Avon factory in Wiltshire, is preserved in Bristol Museum. Calendering, introduced in 1836 and another basic manufacturing process, consists of rolling rubber into the surface of fabric under great pressure between a series of horizontal rollers arranged one above another. A variety of criteria have affected the distribution of the rubber industry in Britain but an unusual locational factor was responsible for the establishment of the industry in the Bradford on Avon and Melksham area of north-west Wiltshire—the availability of empty wool textile mills. The industry still occupies some of these, although its modern expansion has been based on new buildings on new and larger sites.

OIL

During the twentieth century the chemical industry has had a new raw material in oil, which has provided the basis for a vast range of products, including detergents, organic solvents, epoxy resins, sulphur, sulphuric acid and numerous plastics. Most of this industry is based on imported oil, but a few native sources are actively worked. In east Nottinghamshire around Eakring (112/SK 6762) and in north Leicestershire around Plungar (122/SK 7734) unmanned pumps may be seen lifting oil from wells. They are in effect beam engines—an electric motor driving one end, the other connected to the pump rods—and their characteristic movement has gained them the name 'nodding donkeys'.

The other main source, now no longer worked, was oil shale, of which the largest concentration in Britain occurs in the Lothians of Scotland. Exploitation began in 1851 when James Young (1811–83) a brilliant scientist who had assisted Faraday and later managed Tennant's chemical factory in Manchester, started mining the shale, from which he refined paraffin and paraffin wax. The industry grew slowly until 1864 when Young's patent lapsed, and by 1870 ninety-seven firms had been founded of which nearly a third had already failed. American competition after 1900 precipitated a decline and the industry finally became extinct in 1963. Remains are numerous, the most obvious being the waste tips known as 'bings'. At Torbane, near Bathgate, West Lothian (61/NS 953668), stands the bing from Young's pioneer enterprise of 1851; this incidentally is where the geological name Torbanite, applied to the oil shales, originated. At Broxburn (61/NT 087728) in 1862 the discovery of large shale deposits resulted in a boost to the Scottish oil industry. This village and nearby Winchburgh to the north are products of the industry, which has left a spectacular landscape of bings to the east of the B8020 road running between the two. The refinery, founded in 1883, was south of Broxburn at Pumpherston. In north Somerset oil shales were worked early this century on the sea cliffs east of Watchet at Kilve (164/ST 147439), where the remains of a distillation plant in the form of a brick tower still survive.

Perhaps the most spectacular source of oil in Britain, and one of the earliest to be commercially worked, can be seen in the so-called Tar Tunnel at Coalport, Shropshire (119/SJ 694025). Excavated in 1787, probably to give access to coal, the tunnel struck considerable quantities of natural bitumen, which were exploited well into the nineteenth century. Today the tunnel is administered by the Ironbridge Gorge Museum Trust and is accessible to visitors, who may view the cavernous 'tar' wells leading off the brick-lined tunnel at intervals along its length.

The sector of the chemical industry using oil for its raw material is perhaps too modern a development to form a legitimate area of study for the industrial archaeologist. As has been pointed out elsewhere, however, it is not absolute date that provides a criterion by which the industrial archaeologist can work, and in industries where the rate of change is rapid much of undoubted historical and archaeological significance will be lost if it is not recorded. Again the point about the complexity of the process must be made, as this places additional responsibility on industries themselves to ensure that there is a rational and comprehensive approach to the preservation of archival material and the maintenance of a record of evolution. To the industrial archaeologist engaged in the examination of the physical remains of the chemical industries this chapter can only provide the most generalised of indications on the directions in which to look. Certainly the obvious remnants of the industry vastly understate its importance in the industrial development of Britain and even if the opportunities for conservation of significant plant and buildings are limited, and probably in many cases difficult to justify, the need for the retention and study of documentary material is paramount.

12 Public Utilities

THE continuing and rapid proccesses of industrialisation throughout the nineteenth century had profound effects upon the way of life of the population. Industrialisation brought with it large-scale urbanisation, destroying the old balance between town and country and creating within the newly bulging towns horrifying conditions of overcrowding, squalor and disease. Liverpool's population increased from 82,000 in 1807 to 202,000 in 1831, and this before the massive immigration from Ireland after 1845. Leeds, at the centre of the West Riding woollen industry, climbed from 53,000 to 123,000 in the same period. In Birmingham, Glasgow, Manchester and Sheffield the pattern was the same, while London continued to maintain its superiority in size over all other towns.

The techniques of town living had become well established before this explosive growth in the early nineteenth century, but the sudden increase in scale, coupled with overcrowding, completely swamped the simple processes of water supply from wells, and of sewage disposal through open gutters (or, in the more enlightened towns, by 'rakers' or night-soil men). The water closet, patented by Joseph Bramah in 1778, could be little used because there were few proper sewers and often no regular water supply. Enormous pressures were put upon towns and their administrative systems, such as they were, but cholera epidemics, a prevailing *laisser faire* attitude to corporate initiative, a lack of adequate medical information and the total absence of any 'public service' technology all militated against reform and improvement. But reform did come, and a combination of private companies and, increasingly, local authorities, gradually brought about the provision of water, gas and drains, transport, housing and other urban necessities. From the mid-1830s towns had powers to supply water, by the 1840s to provide gas and in the 1870s and 1880s to build tramways and supply electric light. The Public Health Act of 1875 was only one of a large number of legislative moves to ensure proper sanitation and maintenance of good general living conditions.

With these developments came a new breed of professionals. The British Association of Gas Engineers, formed in 1863 under the famous sanitary

engineer Thomas Hawksley (1807–93), was followed 10 years later by the
Institution of Municipal Engineers. By the end of the century three more
professional groups had been formed to cover sanitary engineering (1895),
water supply (1896) and heating and ventilation (1897). Great works, privately
and publicly financed, sprang up in and around the expanding urban areas
and today provide some of the most tangible physical evidence of the
improvement in the quality of town life during the second half of the
nineteenth century.

WATER SUPPLY

A prime necessity of life and of many industries is water, and the need for
larger and better supplies, of which those concerned with public health were
the first to be aware, became generally recognised by the early nineteenth
century. The major sources of supply are rivers and lakes, reservoirs constructed specially to store water and pervious water-bearing rocks underground. Pumping stations for lifting water from deep wells are most
numerous in the Midlands and south-eastern England, although they also
occur in other places where water is taken from rivers. Large dams and
reservoirs are generally confined to mountainous country in Wales, Scotland
and the Pennines and often provide water for cities such as Birmingham,
Liverpool and Glasgow by long-distance aqueducts.

Some of the first large-scale water installations in Britain were built to
serve London in the early years of the seventeenth century. Under the
direction of one man, Hugh Myddelton (?1560–1631), and largely at his
personal expense, the New River, some 40 miles long was built to bring
spring water from Hertfordshire into the City. The New River Company
was the first of London's great water supply companies and the aqueduct,
much of which is still in use today, was formally opened on Michaelmas
Day, 1613, when water was let into the Round Pond at Clerkenwell. Traces
of the pond, together with remains of Smeaton's engine-house of c1768,
may be seen at the Metropolitan Water Board headquarters at New River
Head, Rosebery Avenue, Islington (160/TQ 313828). Of the conduit carrying the New River itself, a good section remains between Bullsmoor Lane,
Waltham Cross and Greens Lane, N4 (160/TQ 318878). A nineteenth-
century straightening, by which the New River is carried in a siphon pipe
across the Cuffley Brook, may be seen near Maidens Bridge, Forty Hill,

Enfield (160/TQ 343987). The old course is still traceable winding round Forty Hill. A further shortening, dating from 1859, runs between Myddleton Road (160/TQ 306916) and Hornsey High Street.

The New River Company, which took over the famous London Bridge Water Works, was soon to be followed by others, and by 1822 nine separate companies were serving the metropolis. This was reduced to eight in 1845, when the Southwark & Vauxhall company was formed by the amalgamation of two of them, and in 1902, after continued pressure from the London County Council, a single authority, the Metropolitan Water Board, was formed to take over them all.

The numerous companies set up in the early nineteenth century rarely had the capital to develop major sources of supply, especially where reservoirs or long aqueducts were required. Provision was generally intermittent, often with the water turned on for only an hour or two each day. This was very unsatisfactory where water was needed for street cleansing, fire-fighting, sewer-flushing and for public baths and wash-houses, the first of which had been opened in Liverpool in 1842. For these reasons most of the larger towns took over their private water companies, frequently following this with massive capital expenditure on reservoir or pumping schemes. Relatively few of the companies were large and efficient enough to resist these takeovers, although those serving Bristol, Portsmouth, south Staffordshire, and Sunderland and South Shields retained their independence.

In the early nineteenth century a number of Acts were passed authorising water undertakings to take water from rivers or to construct reservoirs without any restriction as to the rate of abstraction, but generally speaking the rights of riparian owners using water to power mills and factories were protected by defining minimum amounts of compensation water. Dams were at first constructed of earth, a watertight core of puddled clay being faced on both sides by filling material; on the water side stone pitching covered the face to prevent erosion, while the outer face was covered in soil and then grassed. To prevent water from passing under the dam, the clay core was set in a trench dug down to a watertight foundation such as rock or shale. The early earth dams were mainly in the Pennines, built to serve cities like Sheffield and Manchester. The first large masonry dam, on the River Vyrnwy in Montgomeryshire (117/SJ 018193) dates from 1881–92 and was built to serve Liverpool. It is 161ft high and 1,172ft long. Behind it on the lake side stands a remarkable turreted 'castle' containing the valve controls.

From the industrial archaeological point of view the most spectacular installations associated with water supply are the steam pumping engines built to lift water from wells or to pump it to high-level storage reservoirs. Engines were generally of the beam type, superbly finished and maintained, set in ornate and frequently quite exotic buildings, and surrounded by pools, trees and immaculately manicured formal gardens. Two such engines are preserved by the Bristol Waterworks Company at Blagdon in Somerset (165/ST 503600), and at Papplewick in Nottinghamshire (112/SK 582522) two riotously ornamental rotative beam engines (see Plate 12) by James Watt & Co have come into the care of a preservation trust. Papplewick pumping station was erected in 1883-5 to pump water out of the Bunter sandstone for the growing needs of Nottingham, and represents the ultimate in elaborate construction and setting. In Sunderland Ryhope pumping station (78/NZ 404525) is also being preserved, and in part of the adjacent boiler house a museum of water supply equipment is being established, again by a private preservation trust, in this case working in close liaison with Sunderland Museum. The four Cornish pumping engines at Kew Bridge waterworks, Brentford (170/TQ 188780), last worked in 1944; they are undoubtedly the finest single concentration of the breed in the world and are preserved by the Metropolitan Water Board, from whom permission to view can be obtained.

In the late nineteenth century and early twentieth vertical triple-expansion steam engines, similar in general layout to those used in ships, supplanted the beam type. A number are still in use, including two 1,008 hp Worthington-Simpson engines (see Plate 15) installed at Kempton Park Waterworks in 1928 and believed to be the largest land-based triples in Britain. The same works has five further triples built by the Lilleshall Company of Shropshire in 1900 but now out of use. At the opposite end of the scale a single triple, also by Lilleshall, can be seen by appointment at the Chelvey, Somerset, pumping station (165/ST 474679).

Reciprocating plunger or piston pumps were usual with most water pumping engines but towards the end of the nineteenth century centrifugal pumps, notably those made by Gwynne, were used increasingly. An extraordinary water pumping station, although now devoid of its original equipment, forms a noteworthy feature of Marshall Place, Perth (55/NO 121232).

Designed in 1830 by Dr Adam Anderson, then rector of Perth Academy and later Professor of Natural Philosophy at St Andrews, it has a central rotunda with drum and dome flanked by rectangular north and south wings and an annexe to the west. The drum and dome forming the reservoir are of cast iron decorated with Ionic pilasters and supplied by the Dundee Foundry Company. This remarkable essay in the assimilation of classical forms to functional needs is not only ingenious but a surprisingly satisfactory piece of design. Numerous other humbler water towers can be found all over Britain, often in commanding positions and visible for many miles because of their need to be higher than the area they are supplying. Low-lying south Lancashire has a number of good examples, notably Victoria Tower on Greetby Hill, near Ormskirk (100/SD 423087), and a neighbour east of Tower Hill (100/SD 423085) to the south. There is a fine concrete water tower at Newton-le-Willows near the M6 Motorway (100/SJ 599957), and a commanding brick and stone tower at Frith Heath, Godalming (170/SU 970445), in Surrey.

WASTE DISPOSAL

Disposal of town waste had become a major problem by the middle of the eighteenth century, and although London had since the 1660s, in theory at least, some sort of rubbish disposal organisation, most other cities had nothing at all. Rivers, streams or tidal estuaries and the sea provided the means of carrying away the unwanted detritus of urban humanity, and in some parts of Britain this situation still applies. The Thames was London's *cloaca maxima*, which was supposed to take away on each tide the city's waste products. The realisation that diseases such as cholera and typhoid were water-borne, and that all too often drinking water and waste water came into contact with each other, provided the great incentive to install sewers and sewage treatment plants. In two cholera epidemics in London in the middle of the nineteenth century nearly 20,000 people died, emphasising particularly the need for systematic methods not only of water supply and distribution but, more important, the disposal of waste water in underground pipes to areas away from the town, where it could be suitably treated.

In 1855 the Metropolitan Board of Works was created, with Sir Joseph Bazalgette (1819–91) as its engineer, to provide a system of sewers to prevent 'all or any part of the sewage within the Metropolis from flowing into the

Thames in or near the Metropolis'. Bazalgette's monumental undertaking provided the framework on which most of London's sewage disposal system still depends, and although much of it is below ground and not easily available for the industrial archaeologist to examine, some of the surviving surface remains exhibit a magnificence of conception and execution equal to the works of many a better known engineer. One of the main difficulties to be overcome in providing London with an efficient sewerage system was to carry the waste products away from the urban area itself, as most of the existing sewers flowed at right-angles to the Thames. Bazalgette's solution was to construct major sewers parallel with the river on each side of it—the Northern and Southern Outfalls—running to Barking in Essex and Crossness in Kent. Generally the gradient was sufficient for a gravity flow, but at intervals a pumping station was needed to achieve enough height to maintain an effective gradient. An example is at Greenwich High Road, Deptford (161/TQ 377772), where four beam pumping engines lifted low-level flow 18ft into the Southern Outfall. Only the Italianate pump house of 1864 now remains.

The often extravagant lengths to which the water supply companies went with their pumping stations were exceeded only by the works built by those authorities responsible for the eventual disposal of the waste. The Metropolitan Board of Works perpetrated two such works which, in all their elaborate mid-Victorian improbability, are quite without parallel. One, the Abbey Mills sewage pumping station in West Ham (161/TQ 388832), was built between 1865 and 1868 and originally housed eight beam engines, which were removed in the 1930s. The Venetian-Gothic style building with its exotic interior cast-iron work survives, however, a remarkable monument to the beginnings of the anti-pollution movement. Even more unlikely is the Southern Outfall pumping station in Thamesmead. Here the Crossness sewage treatment works (161/TQ 484811), also built in the mid-1860s, is still complete, with four 125hp beam engines by James Watt & Company. Now out of use and iced all over by hordes of invading pigeons, the incredible cast-iron tracery of the central octagonal framework supporting the beam floor has taken on the appearance of a fantastic petrified cathedral. While efforts are being made to preserve Crossness pumping station, three other sewage pumping installations, already safe in the hands of local authorities, are accessible to visitors. In Shrewsbury the Coleham (118/SJ 496121) beam pumping engines are preserved and run from time to time on electric power; built in 1900 by W. R. Renshaw of Stoke-on-Trent they were in use until 1970 and then taken over by Shrewsbury Museums. In Leicester, Abbey Lane pumping station (121/SK 589066), again with beam pumps (built by Gimson in the exotic manner), is being preserved as the focal point of a Museum of Technology for the East Midlands. Eastney sewage pumping station (181/SZ 675989) is one of a number that clear sewage and surface water from low-lying Portsea Island, on which Portsmouth stands. Originally two Clayton beam engines, installed in 1868, provided the power, but they were scrapped and replaced by two large compound engines by James Watt & Co, installed in 1886–7. These in turn became redundant in 1954, when four English Electric/Sulzer electric pumps took over the main load. The Watt engines and their engine-house have recently been restored by Portsmouth Museums and opened to the public as the nucleus of an industrial museum. Also on the site are three T2 type 170bhp Crossley double-ended (opposed-cylinder) gas engines driving Tangye centrifugal pumps. Dating from 1904, these engines are still maintained for standby use and may eventually be preserved.

As an example, Portsmouth illustrates very graphically the improvement in living conditions and reduction in mortality that resulted from better public health, largely brought about by good drains and sewers. The Sewage and Drainage of Towns Act of 1845 marked the beginning of steady progress in a town which had a particularly acute drainage problem, especially on Portsea Island, where the highest and most densely populated area was only 12ft above the level of ordinary tides. Two large pumping stations were built to pump effluent from the sewers, at Eastney in the 1860s and Stamshaw in the 1880s. By the 1950s fifteen more pumping stations had been built to cope with Portsmouth's sewage and drainage. Over that same period the death rate dropped from an excessively high 25·37 per 1,000 in 1851 when the population was 72,000, to one of the lowest for large towns of 18·9 in 1891, when the population stood at 159,251; by 1955, with 238,700 people in Portsmouth, the death rate stood at 10·76, though many other factors had come into play by then.

Disposal of domestic rubbish had been achieved in some towns by using scavengers who dumped the waste material in specified areas away from housing. In many places, however, it was left to rot in the streets. Systematic collection became widespread in the second half of the nineteenth century, but it was not until the introduction of destructors that there was an alternative to dumping. Even today a large number of local authorities dump their rubbish. The idea of a destructor is a simple one, involving the burning of rubbish at high temperature to destroy all organic matter and reduce it in bulk. A minimum sustained temperature of about 1,250°F is needed to achieve complete combustion of all noxious contents of the waste, and most early destructors fell far short of this. Charles Jones of Ealing, who erected the first destructor near London in 1883, was also the first to grapple with the problem of fumes given off by incomplete combustion, and in 1885 designed what was known as 'Jones' Fume Cremator. This did much to make destructors more acceptable to people living downwind of them, but it was not until forced draught, coke fuel and carefully designed combustion cells were developed in the 1890s that high temperature destruction of all organic material both eliminated the smell and reduced the waste to an innocuous clinker. Today destructors are widely used, and many of them, as examples of late Victorian public health engineering and architecture, could well bear more detailed examination by industrial archaeologists. So too could sewage treatment plants, once called sewage farms, of which numerous early examples are being modernised or replaced, with the destruction of what is frequently first-generation equipment. In towns, manhole covers frequently provide a clue to the type and design of the pipes beneath them and often bear the name or initials of the original authority responsible for construction. An almost completely extinct feature of sewage systems is the sewer gas lamp, built to burn fumes from the pipes below street level. An example of J. E. Webb's 'Patent Sewer Lamp' can be seen in Carting Lane, Strand, London WC2 (160/TQ 305806), and another, from Stourbridge, is preserved in the Blists Hill Open Air Museum, Ironbridge, Shropshire.

GAS

The first practical demonstration of the combustible possibilities offered by a mixture of coal gas and air is generally attributed to William Murdock (1754–1839), principal engine erector in Cornwall for the firm of Boulton & Watt. In 1792, the year after he had taken out a patent for a preservative treatment for ships' bottoms that had led him into various distillation experiments, Murdock generated gas from coal and lighted a room in his house in Redruth. Although numerous others had experimented with gas given off by 'cooking' coal in an oven, Murdock's particular and important contribution, on which the beginnings of a practical gas industry were founded, was his systematic investigation of the comparative behaviour of different classes of coal under conditions of varying temperature and times of carbonisation. Although there was little immediate interest in Murdock's experiments, news of parallel work in France being carried out by Philippe Lebon (1767–1804), and the active support of the celebrated Manchester chemist William Henry (1774–1836), encouraged him further and he resumed his work in 1801. In the following year he illuminated the Soho foundry of Boulton & Watt to commemorate the Peace of Amiens, and before long the company was marketing commercially a gas-making plant using Murdock's horizontal retort in which to carbonise the coal. Heat from a furnace was applied to the retort through flues, and crude gas rose to be carried away to a vertical condenser, where a jet of water precipitated the tar and washed it into a tar pit. The system was used extensively for lighting factories, whose owners were eager to adopt something more effective than the traditional candles or whale oil lamps.

In 1812 the first company selling gas from a central generating station through mains to independent consumers was formally established. It was the Gas Light & Coke Company, which by 1815 had built more than 26 miles of underground mains in London. By then gas was being made in tapered horizontal retorts, charged and discharged by scoops, long-handled shovels and rakes and purified by passing it through water to which lime had been added. After purification, a somewhat imperfect process until the 1840s, gas was transmitted through iron street mains to houses, factories and many public buildings, where initially it was used exclusively for lighting. Early gaslights can still be found with ceramic 'fish tail' burners on which the gas burned as an open wall-flame. Not until the 1840s was air mixed with gas to achieve more efficient combustion; the most obvious and familiar example of this was introduced by the chemist R. W. Bunsen (1811–99) in his Heidelberg laboratory in 1855. In the 1860s gas became more widely used than merely for lighting with the introduction of the water geyser in 1865, the gas ring in 1867 and the gas fire with radiants in 1880. Gas cooking was not common until the 1870s, and gas for heating houses on anything like a large scale did not become established until the early 1900s. By then the traditional stronghold of gas—lighting in streets and buildings— was being threatened by electric-arc and incandescent filament lamps, which were introduced commercially in the mid-1880s. The invention in 1885 of the incandescent gas-mantle by the Austrian Carl Auer von Welsbach (1858– 1929) enabled gas to hold its own and survive well into the mid-twentieth century, particularly in streets and railway stations, where lamps can still occasionally be found. To the industrial archaeologist gas-burning equip- ment offers an area of study worthy of energetic pursuit, as the rapid change- over from coal-produced gas to North Sea natural gas is resulting in the elimination of almost all equipment more than about 10 years old.

Similarly the conversion to natural supplies of gas has almost completely eliminated the traditional gasworks, and there are now very few carbonising plants in Britain. The basic processes of coal gas manufacture are still the same, comprising the destructive distillation of coal of low ash content in retorts which in most works today are vertical and mechanically charged. Gas from the retorts passes through various cleaning processes in which by- products such as coal tar and ammonia are recovered in 'washers' and 'scrubbers'. The gas is then pumped, using an 'exhauster', to a gasholder before being distributed to consumers at a controlled pressure. The approxi- mate composition of piped coal gas is usually 55 per cent hydrogen, 30 per cent methane and 10 per cent carbon monoxide, with small quantities of other gases.

Although coal-gas manufacturing equipment is rapidly disappearing, a few plants are still active. Some of these, like the gasworks at Biggar in Lanarkshire (68/NT 039377), are very small, with hand-fired retorts (Plate 60) and one gasholder. Gasholders, often misnamed 'gasometers', still have a storage role and are a familiar feature of many townscapes. The earliest gasholders were thought to present a danger from explosion, and gas companies were required to encase them in brick buildings. This curious idea, which in the event of a mishap would presumably have made every brick a projectile, was soon abandoned, and the riveted iron-plate cylindrical gasholder much as we know it today emerged to become one of the symbols —together with slag heaps and factory chimneys—of everything that was undesirable in the industrial landscape. Some early gasworks have a curious charm, like the one at Fakenham in Norfolk (125/TF 919293), which, it is

60 Hand-firing retorts at Girvan Gasworks, Ayrshire

hoped, will be preserved, or the other, already noted, at Biggar. What is probably the earliest surviving gasholder anywhere is at Fulham Gasworks, Sands End Lane (170/TQ 260768), dating from the 1830s. Another early example, with large spoked wheels over which the guiding chains roll, is at Dolgellau, Merionethshire (116/SH 729179). All these early gasholders consisted of cylindrical inverted 'bells' supported by gas pressure and sealed by water at the bottom. Later several sections of cylinder were telescoped one within another, a huge frame of cast-iron pillars and lattice girders acting as a support and guide. The No 3 gasholder at Fulham was a fine early example of ornate iron framing, and a later and very large example may be seen at Reading beside the River Kennet, near its junction with the Thames (169/SU 731738). Later gasholders dispensed with the fixed guides on pillars and worked with spiral rails on the side of each telescoping section or 'lift'. With the exception of preserved plant—assuming that Fakenham

gasworks *is* preserved—the gasholder is likely to be the only item associated
with the manufacturing side of the coal-gas industry that will survive in use.

Today we take electricity so much for granted that it is difficult to imagine
life without it. Not only is electrical energy fundamental to the standard of
living of us all but it is also the major source of power for industry. Electric
power has almost completely freed industry from the locational factors of
the past, which tied it to streams and rivers for water power or to the coalfields when steam was the major prime mover. Though a few activities
such as aluminium smelting, which consumes vast quantities of electricity,
tend to be deliberately located near the point of generation or to generate
for their own use, to almost every other industry, availability of an electricity
supply is taken for granted. As with gas, the provision of usable electrical
energy is a four-stage process comprising transport of fuel to the generating
station, generation, transmission and consumption. Also like gas, the first
electricity generating stations were mainly privately owned, of relatively
small scale and located near their markets. The creation of a National Grid
in the 1930s by which all power stations were linked, the nationalisation of
the electricity generating industry in 1948, and, above all, the enormous
increase in scale of generating plant, has made it much more economical
to locate power stations near the fuel source (usually coal) and transmit over
long distances by overhead power line. Thus the power axis of the country
has developed along the valley of the River Trent, with a string of large
base-load stations close to the East Midlands coalfield. The location of
nuclear power stations is governed by different factors, as the transport cost
of fuel is negligible. Those so far commissioned in Britain are, in effect,
market-located in that they are in coal-deficient areas. With the exception
of Trawsfynnyd in North Wales, they are located on estuarine or coastal
sites, for like traditional power stations they use steam turbines that need
condenser coolant water. For reasons of safety, however, in the event of an
accidental discharge of radioactive waste, nuclear power stations also tend
to be sited in fairly remote areas. The other form of electric power, hydro-
electricity, in which water turbines drive the generators, has been little
developed in England, although there are plants in Scotland and in North

Wales. The North Wales scheme, at Blaenau Ffestiniog, works in conjunction with Trawsfynydd nuclear power station. It is not possible easily to store high voltage electricity to meet the peak loads on power stations, but water can be stored, so that the hydroelectric station generates during peak times, while in the off-peak period the nuclear power station pumps water from a lower lake back to the upper one in readiness for the next peak period. This scheme allows the nuclear station to work at a very high load factor and at the same time makes available some 300mW of hydroelectric generating capacity for peak demand periods.

The electricity industry offers the industrial archaeologist some important remains at both the generating and consuming end of the energy chain, although for an industry which is so relatively new much in the way of equipment has already gone. The rapid rate of development of the technology of power generation, the changeover from direct to alternating current for consumers, and the postwar boom in efficient electrical appliances in the home has made almost any piece of electrical equipment more than 30 years old of historical interest.

The basis of all electrical power generated by mechanical means, as opposed to electrochemically in a battery, derives from the work of Michael Faraday (1791–1867), and was first demonstrated in 1831. On 17 October of that year he plunged a bar magnet into a coil of wire and generated, in his own words, 'a wave of electricity', and 11 days later he rotated a copper plate between the poles of a magnet and found that a current could be taken from the axis to the rim of the disc. Faraday's original experiment of holding the coil of wire stationary while varying the magnetic field forms in essence the basis of today's large power stations, although the bar magnet has been replaced by an electro-magnet and the coils are so arranged that their windings are cut by the magnetic field as the magnet rotates. Thus the mechanical energy required to turn the magnets is converted into electrical energy in the windings.

By the mid-1830s E. M. Clarke of London was manufacturing hand-powered generators on a commercial basis, but it was not until E. W. von Siemens (1816–92) took out a British patent for a two-pole shuttle armature in 1856 that a satisfactory small generator was available in Britain. In 1866 Henry Wilde and S. A. Varley in England and von Siemens in Germany had devised generators with electro-magnets and self-excited fields to create what they called 'dynamic electricity', meaning electricity generated by rotary motion. In the following year Charles Brooke (1804–79) used the compound term 'dynamo-electric' to describe all machinery which converted mechanical into electrical energy. The first dynamo of practical dimensions and capable of producing a continuous current was developed about 1870 by the Belgian Z. T. Gramme (1826–1901), and 3 years later the Gramme Company was able to supply a machine for public trial at Westminster, where it powered arc lights. Manufacture in Britain of a superior type of generator, developed in Switzerland by Emil Burgin, was carried out in the early 1880s by R. E. B. Crompton (1845–1940), who built over 400 of them. The first electricity for public electric lighting, at Godalming, in Surrey, in 1881, was, however, generated by a waterwheel. Taunton was another town that had an early public supply.

Crompton was one of the pioneers in Britain of commercial electric lighting using arc lamps in which a continuous electrical discharge was induced between the tips of two carbon rods. Initially his self-contained lighting units, consisting of a portable steam engine driving a generator by belt and powering a number of lights, were used for agricultural shows and fetes, but later they were installed in railway stations, the General Post Office in Glasgow, where two arc lamps replaced 180 gas jets, and in 1882 at the Mansion House in London. Here a combination of arc lamps and incandescent bulbs, developed by Joseph (later Sir Joseph) Wilson Swan (1828–1914) in Newcastle-upon-Tyne, was used. The incandescent filament lamp devised by Swan consisted of an evacuated glass bulb in which a current-carrying filament continuously glowed; although not as bright as the arc lamp, it was reliable and more suited to domestic applications. Almost simultaneously Thomas Alva Edison in the United States invented a similar lamp, which he patented in Britain. Subsequently Edison and Swan amalgamated and formed the Edison & Swan United Electric Light Company later known as the Ediswan Company, registered in 1883 with a capital of £1m. The factory established by Ediswan at Ponders End, Enfield, in 1886 has recently been redeveloped and virtually all the original buildings have gone. Fortunately the site was surveyed in 1969 by Enfield Archaeological Society. Incandescent lamps rapidly became popular and in 1881 were used in the House of Commons, on the Inman liner *City of Richmond*, on a train from London to Brighton, and in the Savoy theatre, where the stage was lit by 824 lamps, with a further 370 elsewhere in the building.

All these early installations had their own generators, but in 1882 the Edison Company opened its Holborn Viaduct generating station, initially to provide current for street lighting but later extended to serve private consumers. In 1887 the London Electric Supply Corporation was founded to put into effect a huge scheme devised by S. Z. de Ferranti (1864–1930), who believed that the satisfactory development of electric power hinged on generation in quantity. The power station, at Deptford (161/TQ 374779), was designed by Ferranti himself and included two alternators designed for 5,000V and powered by 1,250hp steam engines, and four with 10,000V windings coupled to a single 10,000hp engine. The first current was transmitted from Deptford in 1889, although the station was not in regular use until 1891. Today Deptford power station (Plate 61) is much altered from its first form, though most of the original buildings survive, and as such it is one of the earliest monuments of the electricity supply industry.

Throughout the 1890s power stations, usually relatively small, were built in many British cities by the newly formed electric light companies or to provide light and also current for street trams. Frequently one power station served both functions. In Bristol the original Central Electric Lighting Station building of 1893 (156/ST 594728) still survives on Temple Back, and across the road on Phillip Street is the Bristol Tramway Company's

61 Turbine hall, Deptford West power station, south-east London

power station building (156/ST 593729), built in the early 1900s. The latter is particularly interesting as one of the few stations in Britain built on the space-saving American principle, with its boilers on a floor above the engines and generators.

All these early power stations used reciprocating steam engines with either belt drive to the generators or in some cases direct-coupled crankshafts. The central-valve engine developed by P. W. Willans (1851–92) in the mid-1880s was the most widely used type, although by 1891 Bellis & Morcom of Birmingham were manufacturing smaller enclosed-crankcase high-speed verticals with forced lubrication that were ideal for generating work. Many of the latter can still be found, mainly dating from the 1920s and 1930s, generating electricity in hospitals. The problem with the reciprocating steam engine was developing sufficient speed to power a generator efficiently. The answer was the steam turbine, which was widely adopted soon after it had been invented by C. A. Parsons (1854–1931) in 1884. Today power stations use basically the same arrangement as that devised by Parsons, the steam turbine being direct-coupled to the alternator.

Initially most power stations distributed direct current on a two-wire system at 110V. This was later changed to a three-wire system at 220V offering 110V between each outer wire and the middle wire. As sytems expanded, it was found necessary to raise the voltage to 440 and 220 respectively, with electric lights operating at the lower voltage and the larger electric motors connected across the 440V wires. As the number of consumers grew, the current flowing in the mains became heavier, the mains themselves became longer and loss of power through voltage drop reached serious proportions. The answer, originally proposed by Ferranti, was to transmit high-voltage alternating current with minimal losses and to break down the voltage to consumers' requirements at local sub-stations and transformers. This system is the basis of our modern electricity supply network based on a National Grid of 400,000 and 275,000V. The area electricity boards distribute within their areas at 132,000V and below, reducing to 33,000V for heavy industry, 11,000V for light industry and 415/240V for farms and domestic users. National Grid lines are almost invariably carried on pylons for cheapness, although occasionally, as in the Wye valley, they may be underground to preserve scenic amenities. At 11,000V power is generally carried on wooden poles in country areas or underground in towns.

The industrial archaeology of the electricity industry illustrates the irrelevance of absolute age when examining the historical significance of a site, a process or a piece of equipment. It is the degree of obsolescence which matters and, in an industry changing as rapidly as electricity generation and supply, obsolescence can occur very quickly. In 1948, when the generating industry was nationalised, some 300 power stations supplied a maximum load of about 10,000mW. Today four times that load is supplied by less than 200 stations, and only two or three new ones are required each year compared with more than twenty that would have been needed under the technology of 20 years ago. Thus operating power stations of the 1920s and 1930s are almost primeval in terms of today's industry, and even stations built as recently as the late 1950s may only be used for peak loads. Few pre-war stations have their original turbines or generators, but a number have been re-equipped, with the result that it has been possible to retain the buildings. Many of these stations, erected by the old private supply companies, had distinctive architectural styles and detailing and, being built in a period of general depression, represent some of the few large-scale examples of building and engineering design of their period. The most distinctive feature in the majority of modern power stations is the hyperbolic concrete cooling tower, which enables condenser coolant water to be returned to source, usually a river, at an acceptable temperature. The first concrete cooling towers in Britain still survive at Lister Drive power station in Liverpool (100/SJ 387917); they date from the mid-1920s and appear minute by the standards of their majestic Trent valley successors. Other early towers may be seen at Croydon 'A' power station.

Efforts are now being consciously made to preserve aspects of the electricity supply industry, and a museum may eventually be set up to preserve important items of generating, transforming and transmission equipment. Numerous existing museums contain small electrical items such as early dynamos, motors, lighting and switchgear. Appropriately one of the largest collections is in the Newcastle-upon-Tyne Museum of Science & Engineering, where the work of C. A. Parsons, J. W. Swan and A. C. Reyrolle is well represented. Here, insulators, sections of cable, arc lamps and early incandescent bulbs abound. The most comprehensive range of material, however, is in the Science Museum, South Kensington.

URBAN TRAMWAYS

The availability of electricity and of efficient electric motors encouraged a mode of transport that had been developing since the 1860s in a number of British towns. Initially horse-drawn, the street tram had been introduced from the United States to Birkenhead in 1860 by George Francis Train, who laid a 5ft 2in gauge line with flanged rails from Woodside Ferry to Birkenhead Park, then a fashionable residential area. Other lines followed, including a route in London from Notting Hill Gate to Marble Arch, but most had been removed by 1862, largely because of the damage the up-standing edge of the 'step rail' was causing to the tyres of horse-drawn carriages. However, grooved rails and flanged wheels were substituted in Birkenhead and on another line in the Potteries, and proved highly success-ful. By the late 1860s the horse-drawn tram was becoming accepted as an efficient means of moving people in town streets, where a pair of horses could haul a tramcar seating forty-six and having the low rolling resistance of the rail-borne vehicle, while the traditional bus with two horses was limited to about twenty-six seats. There is little material evidence surviving today of the early period of tramway development, although Hull Transport Museum has a single-deck horse car of the type used by Train which was built in 1867 and ran on Ryde pier in the Isle of Wight.

Legislation allowing the widespread growth of street tramways came with the Tramways Act of 1870, which, in terms of the development of efficient and coordinated systems, was something of a mixed blessing. Two clauses in particular penalised the new tram-operating companies. Not only did they have to lay and maintain their own tracks but they were also responsible for the road surface between the rails and for 1ft 6in on each side of them. In addition the local authority had the power to purchase the whole system after 21 years, a right which then recurred every 7 years. This, not un-naturally, discouraged the tramway operators from installing expensive new capital equipment, for much expenditure would immediately make their takeover more attractive. The ultimate result of this bizarre state of affairs occurred in Bristol, where primitive open-top double-deck trams were still in use until the early 1940s, when they were replaced by buses. Bristol is still the only major British city without municipally owned transport.

Generally speaking, tramways were taken over by local authorities in the late nineteenth and early twentieth centuries, although by then it was often too late to develop any integrated inter-urban system on the American pattern because of gauge variations, though a surprisingly wide coverage was attained in Britain. By far the most popular was the standard 4ft 8½in used on railways although an ingenious variation found only in Glasgow, Huddersfield and Portsmouth involved a gauge of 4ft 7¾in. The reason for this was that conventional railway wagons could be run on the street tram tracks, thus giving them access to numerous industrial undertakings not normally enjoying a rail connection, but as the depth of flange on a railway wheel is greater than the depth of groove in a tram rail and the width of wheel tread substantially wider, the ¾in reduction in gauge allowed railway wagons to run on their wheel flanges along the flangeways of tram tracks. Elsewhere narrower gauges were used, 3ft 6in being universal in and around Birmingham and 4ft in the Potteries and north Staffordshire. One of Birmingham's narrow double-deck electric cars is preserved in the Birmingham Museum of Science & Industry, Newhall Street, Birmingham 3.

In 1879 mechanical power was permitted for trams under the Use of Mechanical Power on Tramways Act, but such severe restrictions were imposed for the protection of other road users, human and equine, that really imaginative developments were stultified at source. Despite the fact that 10mph was the maximum permitted speed, that all working parts had to be concealed from view and that machinery had to be practically silent, with no visible emission of smoke or steam, firms like Merryweather and Kitson produced reasonably successful steam engines for pulling trailer cars. A preserved example, from Portstewart in Northern Ireland, can be seen in Hull Transport Museum.

Electrification came in the 1880s in an experimental way and by the late 1890s had proved itself beyond all doubt as the best means of powering tramcars. At the start of large-scale electrification, in the late 1880s, there were some 800 route miles of tramway in Britain, and this had increased to 1,040 by 1900, the larger part still being horse- or steam-worked. Between 1900 and 1907 electric lines boomed and a total route mileage of 2,530 had been reached by the outbreak of World War I, the high point of the tramway era.

American practice considerably influenced the widespread development of electric tramways in Britain, although most of the initial experimental

work had been carried out in Germany by engineers such as Werner von
Siemens and Magnus Volk. Volk came to Britain in 1883 and built a 2ft 8½in
gauge electric railway along the seafront at Brighton from the Aquarium
(182/TQ 316038) to Black Rock. This odd little line, which still runs,
represents the first use of electric traction in Britain. Street trams proper
operated at about 600V DC, with current usually supplied to one (positive)
wire and, after passing through traction motors and lighting, being returned
to the power station through the (earthed) track rails. Trams had four wheels,
with two axle-mounted motors, but later large eight-wheel bogie cars were
introduced, notably in London, Glasgow and Liverpool. Current collection
was usually by trolley poles, but Glasgow and Leeds and some Birmingham
routes employed bow collectors, which obviated the needs for complicated
pointwork in the overhead wiring. In parts of London a conduit between
the rails carried the current.

The period from about 1900 to the outbreak of World War I in 1914
was the golden age of the tram, the first form of urban transport accessible
to the mass of the population. It was a harbinger of social change, continuing
and developing the work begun by the suburban railway services in enabling
people to move easily and cheaply between industrialised areas and their
homes in more pleasant surroundings. Every major town had a tramway,
and in Lancashire and Yorkshire particularly, end-on junctions of
innumerable independent systems enabled the diligent traveller with an eye
to economy rather than speed to make quite lengthy excursions. Thus the
Pier Head in Liverpool could form the start of a tram journey into the upper
Pennines beyond Rochdale by way of St Helens, Atherton, Bolton, Bury
and Heywood. Seven miles over the top was Hebden Bridge, terminus of
the West Riding network, running eastwards to beyond Leeds and Wakefield.
Suburban housing estates developed along tram routes, and cities like
Glasgow, Birmingham and Liverpool still reflect their one-time dependence
on trams in the wide central reservations of their main road approaches,
which once enabled trams to run completely separated from road traffic.
It was the incompatability of the tram with motor vehicles and its lack of
flexibility when compared to the bus that led to its decline and eventual
extinction. In addition the high cost of maintenance of track and overhead,
and the very low operating costs of the diesel bus, which began rapidly to
replace its petrol-driven predecessor in the late 1930s, made the tram in its

traditional form largely redundant. A few cities, notably Sheffield and Leeds, began programmes of tramway modernisation, with ideas of developing high-speed reserved-track systems, but changes of management and of political complexion killed these schemes and 1963 saw the last of Britain's trams withdrawn from the streets of Glasgow. Only in Blackpool can a near equivalent still be found, with streamlined single-deck cars operating along the seafront.

An interim phase between the tram and the complete domination of public road transport by the diesel bus has also recently come to an end with the withdrawal of the last trolleybuses in Bradford, which, with Leeds, had been the scene of the first regular services in 1911. Of German origin the 'railless tram' had the attraction of manoeuvrability in restricted town centres, quietness, speed, and in later years remarkable acceleration. Numerous tram systems were abandoned in favour of trolleybuses in the 1920s and 1930s, and new routes were being built well into the 1950s in several cities. Again, however, some of the shortcomings of the tram applied to the electric bus, the cost of overhead wires and pointwork in particular leading to their abandonment in favour of high-capacity diesel buses, now often operated by one man only. Today no trolleybus systems are working in Britain, although at least two operational museums are proposed and individual vehicles are preserved, notably at Bournemouth and Bradford.

Trams have always enjoyed a large enthusiast following, and at Crich in Derbyshire (111/SK 345548) the Tramway Museum Society operates a thriving museum where over forty cars from places as far apart as Glasgow, Sheffield, Southampton, Johannesburg and Oporto are preserved, many of them in running condition. A regular service is operated on a ½ mile track. Museums with collections of non-operational trams include the Glasgow Transport Museum and the London Transport Collection at Syon Park.

The period from the 1870s to 1914 represented the great age of public transport, and the tram and cheap-excursion train gave millions of people a mobility completely unknown before. Although the tram has disappeared and relatively few people go to the seaside by cheap-day excursion, a surprising number of working reminders of this pre-automobile age still survive. In the Isle of Man horse trams, introduced in 1876, still operate a summer service along the front at Douglas, providing a connection at the northern terminus with the Manx Electric Railway, a 3ft gauge rural tramway running to Ramsey. This itself connects with another electric line that connects Laxey to the summit of Snaefell. In North Wales a cable-operated 3ft 6in gauge tramway, opened in 1902, runs from Llandudno (107/SH 777827) to the 679ft summit of the Great Orme. Further south the Fairbourne Railway (116/SH 615128) in Merionethshire, a 1ft 3in gauge steam-operated miniature line, occupies the trackbed of a horse tramway opened in 1916 to connect with ferries across the Mawddach estuary.

Evidence of urban tramways is rapidly disappearing, although a large number of bus depots are merely tram sheds with the tracks removed, covered up or, occasionally, left *in situ*. A fine example of the smaller tram shed, with a section of 3ft 6in gauge track in front of it, can be seen near Chester General railway station (109/SJ 413668), while on the forecourt of Ashby-de-la-Zouch station (121/SK 355164) is the terminus trackwork of one of Britain's few real inter-urban lines—the Burton & Ashby Light Railway, operated initially by the Midland Railway and abandoned by the LMS in 1926. In London the Kingsway Tramway Subway (160/TQ 305817), built for single-deck cars in 1905–8 and deepened to take double-deckers in 1930–31, has been partially converted into a two-lane underpass. A rare survivor in Liverpool is a section of horse-tram track in Queen Square (100/SJ 346906) whose unusual features are a centre flangeway with a section of tread on each side (instead of the normal side flangeway) and rail joints made at an angle to reduce noise and wear. In many towns where trams were used in narrow streets the overhead wires were supported from buildings rather than from poles, and the cast-iron wall rosettes from which they hung can still be seen. They were particularly popular in Glasgow. In Liverpool a highly decorative rosette incorporating the city's emblem—'the liver bird'—can still be seen here and there.

MISCELLANEOUS PUBLIC UTILITIES

Numerous other public utilities provide the industrial archaeologist with fragmentary evidence of their development, although generally such evidence is on display in a museum rather than still in use. The introduction of the penny post by Rowland Hill in 1840, the first efficient large-scale postal service in the world, led to the building of post offices in all towns and many villages, and to cast-iron letterboxes appearing throughout the country. These have for long been objects of great affection, particularly the pillarboxes which appear in a variety of forms and bear several makers' names. The attractive 'Penfold' hexagonal boxes are relatively common, but less so are the dignified fluted pillarboxes found in Malvern, Worcestershire, and the magnificently crowned 'Liverpool specials' introduced in the 1860s to provide additional capacity for newspapers. A good example of the latter still stands on Edge Lane, Liverpool. Railway stations are a good source of early and unusual boxes.

The introduction of the successful electric telegraph in Britain, after many years of experiment, particularly in Germany, resulted from the collaboration of two complementary figures—the far-seeing William F. Cooke (1806–79) and the ingenious Charles Wheatstone (1802–75)—who installed a direct-reading system using five wires along the main line of the Great Western Railway between Paddington and West Drayton in 1839. Deflection of the needles on the telegraph instrument enabled any one of twenty letters to be indicated, but the high cost of laying five wires resulted in two-needle and even single-needle instruments being used on railways, where codes could be used. The best known of these telegraph codes, now the standard, was devised by the American Samuel F. B. Morse (1791–1872). The Science Museum has a fine collection of telegraphic equipment, including a remarkable two-needle instrument in the gothic style for use in the Palace of Westminster. The railways, which benefited directly from the introduction of the electric telegraph, became rapidly transformed in appearance, poles and wires following virtually every line. Indeed the railway was fundamental to the success of the telegraph system, as it could supply ready-made routes, with no problems of wayleaves for poles and wires, along which a nation-wide all-purpose communications network could be built. Thus the social changes the railway had helped to create by increasing the mobility of people were furthered by a new demand for the sending of personal messages.

The electric telegraph, perhaps the least recognised but certainly one of the most important nineteenth-century innovations in communication, was not in fact the first form of telegraphic system to be used regularly in Britain. There was, of course, the sixteenth-century system of hilltop bonfires, which gave warning of the approach of the Spanish Armada; and in the 1790s a series of hilltop telegraph stations were built to connect the Admiralty in London first with Deal and later with Portsmouth, Yarmouth and Plymouth. Initially shutters were used to transmit messages, but semaphore arms later replaced them. Today a number of stations remain, such as that on Chatley Heath, Surrey (170/TQ 089585), built in 1823 to replace an earlier wooden structure. Elsewhere the name Telegraph Hill is a common reminder of the system, while the sign of 'The Telegraph' inn on Putney Heath (170/TQ 233737) illustrates clearly the earlier signalling equipment. The London to Portsmouth telegraph, the last in use, finally closed on 31 December 1847.

The electric telegraph was to a great extent superseded, at first over relatively short distances, by the telephone developed from German experimental beginnings by Alexander Graham Bell (1847–1922) in America and patented in Britain in 1876. The first telephone exchange was established by a private company in London in 1879 and others quickly followed. Inter-urban lines were established and a countrywide network gradually developed, most of it in the hands of the National Telephone Company. In 1912 the General Post Office acquired all private telephone systems, with the exception of one that still operates in and around Kingston-upon-Hull in Yorkshire. The rapid rate of development of telephony, particularly since the introduction of subscriber trunk dialling in the 1950s, has resulted in most early exchange and transmission equipment disappearing, although numerous early handsets survive. Micro-wave transmitting, relay towers and multi-core cables have almost completely eliminated the poles and wires which were a feature, particularly of the Great North Road, in the inter-war period. The telephone kiosk, however, is still a link with the earlier days of the public telephone service, a distinguished piece of industrial design in cast iron by Sir Gilbert Scott (1880–1960), whose better known works include Liverpool Cathedral, Battersea power station and Waterloo Bridge.

The beginnings of modern fire-fighting by an organised fire brigade can be found in the first fire insurance companies set up in London shortly after the Great Fire of 1666. By the end of the eighteenth century almost every town and county had its own insurance company, some of which, as a result of their very direct pecuniary interest in reducing losses by fire, were beginning to operate their own fire-fighting forces. These companies issued plates to mark the properties insured with them, and many plates survive, illustrating the large number of companies. Fire engines, in the form of horse-drawn hand pumps, were used and numerous examples, mainly dating from the mid-nineteenth century, can be found in museums. An unusual small type of 'fire engine', developed by the Merryweather company, consisted of a manual pump with four carrying handles, which could be used in factories or country houses. An example can be seen in the Glasgow Museum of Transport. The replacement of manpower by steam was an obvious development, but initially this was only for powering the pumps. Throughout the second half of the nineteenth and well into the twentieth century the standard large fire engine, weighing up to 4 tons, was drawn by horses and had its pump powered by steam. Numerous examples of these engines, notably those built by Shand Mason and Merryweather, have been preserved in museums. Although self-propelled steam pumps had been tried, they were too heavy and cumbersome to be a success, and it was not until the early 1900s that the first petrol-driven fire engines began to supersede horse-drawn ones. For a short time petrol-engine-propelled fire engines with steam pumps were used, but before 1910 both road wheels and pumps were being powered by internal combustion engines. Of all the types of public service appliance, the fire engine has had greatest popular appeal, and large numbers are preserved in museums throughout Britain. They can be seen on display at Bristol, Glasgow, Leicester, Liverpool, the London Science Museum and Swindon, to name but a few. In Norwich the Norwich Union Insurance Group has a small museum relating to its work in fire insurance. Early fire stations, some with stables, bell turrets and smoke vents, can still be found, and deserve attention from the industrial archaeologist. The whole technology of built-in systems of the sprinkler type and automatic alarms is another area needing recording and documentation.

13 Roads and Bridges

THE development of the road system was intimately tied up with the growth of settlements, and early roads were simply paths from one village to another. They took the easiest, usually the driest, route, avoiding steep hills, dense woodland or land under crops. With the exception of Roman roads and new motor roads mainly built in the last 30 years, almost all the roads along which we travel today have their origin as primitive paths in a period when long-distance overland travel, let alone the wheeled vehicle, was virtually unknown.

A road, theoretically, is not a strip of land, but a right of passage and, during the Middle Ages, the keeping open of a way passable for travellers on horseback and for trains of packhorses was accomplished with varying degrees of success under manorial jurisdiction. As trade increased with the widening of the known world at the end of the fifteenth and the beginning of the sixteenth centuries, it became difficult for the roads to cope with the increasing traffic especially where this increase coincided with the breakdown of the manorial courts. A tenant who had recently secured his freedom from the agricultural and other servile duties imposed by customary law could hardly be expected to agree willingly to an increase in the amount of labour and time he spent on the highways of the manor.

This common law liability on the inhabitants of each parish to keep their roads in good repair was reinforced in 1555 by an Act of Parliament 'for the mending of highways'. Under the Act each parish had to choose annually a surveyor of highways, or waywarden, who was given power to call out the available labour of the village or town to work on the roads for 4 days per year. With various amendments, such as increasing the period of statute labour to 6 days and the granting of powers to levy rates up to 6d in the pound, the 1555 Act remained the basis of highway administration for nearly 300 years.

In some parishes this system worked fairly well. Where the roads of a parish were used by the inhabitants only, they received some attention in

316

turn, although perhaps not every year. When John Smith was waywarden he would naturally devote most time and labour to the roads he used, and perhaps neglect those used by Thomas Brown. But Thomas Brown would probably be surveyor before long, so things would even themselves out. In some parishes, however, a trunk route between two large towns might follow a parish road, and excessive wear and tear would result. In others a main road might cut across the corner of a parish, and although it would be used by long-distance travellers, its maintenance would still be the responsibility of the parishioners. In these situations the system of parish road maintenance fell into disrepute. On a porous, well drained subsoil heavily used but little cared for roads might stand the strain, but where the soil was of clay the road inevitably became, in the words of the time, 'deep and foundrous'. Stones might be laid on the surface but would soon sink into a sea of mud, to be followed by the wheels that rolled them in. Horses died, bogged down to their shoulders in mud. Roads were in places 60–100yd wide where travellers had attempted to skirt a treacherous area. As many as ten horses or oxen might be required to move a load of 1–1½ tons over heavy ground. In winter, haulage of heavy loads stopped altogether. In the early eighteenth century Daniel Defoe noted that it took 2–3 years to move a large tree trunk from the neighbourhood of Lewes to Chatham dockyard. A few miles would be achieved each summer, with as many as twenty-two oxen pulling the tree on a vehicle known as a tug, but by September the roads would be so soft that the journey would have to be abandoned until the following June.

It was these circumstances, repeated in greater or lesser degree all over the country, that led to the first turnpike Acts, under which tolls could be levied to repair the roads. The principle of making travellers pay a contribution towards the upkeep of the roads and bridges they used had been established as early as the twelfth century, some 400 years before the birth of the turnpike system. Grants of 'pavage' were made for the upkeep of roads and streets, and of 'pontage' for the construction and repair of bridges, usually by the king, to lords of manors or heads of religious houses, enabling them to collect tolls in specified areas. In 1279 Edward I granted pontage for 3 years to the 'bailiffs and good men' of Huntingdon, empowering them to collect tolls for the upkeep of the bridge. The great bridge at Swarkeston in Derbyshire, a fine surviving example of a medieval bridge (121/SK 369285), was the object of similar grants in the reigns of Edward II and Edward III. These grants may be called the forerunners of the turnpike Acts of later days, but they did not form the genesis of the system.

The first turnpike road resulted from an Act passed in 1663 empowering the justices of Hertfordshire, Huntingdonshire and Cambridgeshire to erect a gate in each county and levy tolls on the Great North Road. No further turnpike Act was passed until 1695–6 when Acts for the London to Harwich road and a section of road between Attleborough and Wymondham near Norwich were placed on the statute book. Increasing numbers of Acts followed in succeeding years, but 1706–7 established a precedent that was to become standard for all future turnpike roads. Instead of the local justices being empowered to become the road authority, a body, consisting usually of local gentry, was set up to act as turnpike trustees. In all cases where a road was turnpiked the initiative was local. Parliament did not decide that certain stretches of highway were more in need of extra care than others, but local people, interested in certain parts of the roads, formed themselves into committees, subscribed the legal expenses, petitioned Parliament, and, having obtained their Acts, became the trustees.

The key to the functioning of a turnpike trust was its power to raise tolls. At first toll lists were simple, but they gradually became more and more complicated as differential charges were introduced and various restrictions and allowances were made for wheel width, wheel construction, weight of lading, and number of draught beasts. On a few points there was general agreement between one trust and another. No tolls were levied on foot travellers, and tolls charged by the Acts were maxima, which could be lowered, but not raised, at the discretion of the trustees. The charges for horses, without vehicles, whether led, driven or ridden, varied between $\frac{1}{2}$d and 2d each. Cattle were generally charged 10d per score, and sheep and pigs 5d. The greatest variation occurred in the schedules of charges for vehicles, some forty separately identifiable goods and passenger vehicles appearing in the toll lists of the various Acts. In 1753 an Act prohibited the use of wagons with wheels less than 9in wide, unless drawn by oxen or less than five horses, and 2 years later another Act allowed 3 years' exemption from tolls for wagons with 9in wheels. In 1765 preferential treatment was given to wagons with the fore wheels on shorter axles than the rear wheels, on the grounds that a greater width of road would be effectively rolled, and in 1774 wagons with 16in wheels or rollers were given complete freedom from tolls for 5 years.

The period 1750–80 saw the greatest geographical expansion of turnpiking, although mileage increased at a slower rate down to the late 1830s. At this peak period most main roads, especially in England, were under the care of nearly 4,000 trusts whose responsibility covered some 22,000 miles of road out of an estimated total of 105,000 miles. Turnpikes were most numerous in heavily populated industrial areas, counties such as Suffolk and Essex having only some 10 per cent of their roads under trust maintenance. All other roads were still, of course, the responsibility of the parishes, and were generally in a poor state. It was not until 1835, after nearly 300 years, that the statute labour basis of maintenance was replaced by a rating system, with parishes formed into districts each covered by a district surveyor.

Throughout the eighteenth century highway legislation had been based on the supposition that it was impossible to keep roads in good repair without restrictions on the types of vehicle using them. Hence the idea prevailed that carts and wagons could be so constructed that they repaired rather than damaged the roads, with consequent agitation for broad rollers rather than wheels. At the root of all this was a fundamental lack of knowledge of any systematic or scientific approach to the construction or maintenance of the roads themselves. Credit for the introduction of new roadmaking techniques which, as the timings of the mail coaches indicated, revolutionised road travel, must go to three men—'Blind Jack' Metcalf, John Loudon Macadam, and Thomas Telford. John Metcalf (1717-1810) was born at Knaresborough, Yorkshire. He had been musician, jobmaster, fish dealer, recruiting agent, hosiery merchant, horsedealer, and possibly trader in smuggled tea before he took up roadmaking, with a contract to build some 3 miles of the Boroughbridge to Harrogate road, turnpiked in 1765. Blind from the age of six, Metcalf had an uncanny ability to assess the lie of the land and determine the most favourable route across it, gaining a picture by extensive walking or riding. When he retired in 1792, he had improved some 180 miles of road for a score or so of trusts in the West Riding of Yorkshire, south Lancashire and north Derbyshire. Metcalf was the first of the great road engineers to appreciate the need for a well drained, firm foundation. A smooth convex surface of stone and gravel was laid over bundles of ling or heather set on a foundation of prepared subsoil. Ditches on either side of the road, which was elevated between them, ensured the surface would be free-draining. This was a great advance in roadbuilding technique over contemporary practice, and although the amount of road he improved was relatively small, Metcalf's contribution was of fundamental significance.

Macadam (1756–1836) and Telford (1757–1834) were almost exact contemporaries whose chief work dates from a little later than that of 'Blind Jack'. Macadam's name is associated with the system of road surfacing using broken stone instead of gravel rather than the variations of his method that bear his name today. His plan was as follows: 'Now the principle of road-making I think the most valuable, is to put broken stone upon a road, which shall unite by its own angles, so as to form a solid hard surface.' This material, no stone of which was to exceed 6oz in weight, was to be laid to a depth of about 10in and be well consolidated. He did not care particularly what lay underneath, arguing that a subsoil base drained by side ditches and protected from rain penetration by a sound surface would support any weight. Great care had to be exercised in breaking stone for Macadam's roads. He insisted that surveyors trained in his system should be equipped with a pair of scales and a 6oz weight, or a 2in metal ring through which the stones had to pass. A 6in layer of these angular stones was laid as evenly as possible, followed by a further 6in some weeks later when the first had consolidated under traffic. A surface 18ft wide cost in the region of £88 per mile.

The relative cheapness of the Macadam system led to its adoption by the majority of turnpike trusts. By the late nineteenth century 'water-bound macadam' road was almost universal throughout Britain, and the name of its inventor had become part of the English language. Macadam himself became surveyor of the Bristol Trust in 1816, and by 1819 the 180 miles of road of this largest turnpike trust in the country were already well known for their admirable state of repair. The fact that, once improved, a macadamised road demanded much less maintenance than other roads attracted many trusts. Macadam was appointed Surveyor-General of the Metropolitan roads in 1827, and he and numerous members of his family advised dozens of trusts up and down the country in succeeding years.

Thomas Telford was one of the great civil engineers of his generation, a famous bridge and canal builder but mainly memorable perhaps as an improver of roads. The son of a shepherd and trained originally as a stone-mason, Telford was appointed Surveyor of Public Works for Shropshire in 1787. Besides undertaking a prodigious programme of bridge building, he gained wide experience of road work both in Shropshire and, later, in the Highlands of Scotland, where he built or improved many hundreds of miles of road as part of a scheme to bring life back to that depressed and depopulated region. Telford's system of road construction was similar to that developed in France in the 1770s by Pierre Trésaguet (1716–94). It consisted of laying a solid course of large stones on the prepared and level bed of the road 'in the form of a close neat pavement'. Over this was laid a 6in spread of hard broken stones, each as nearly cubical as possible, and on top of this again a 2in top layer of gravel. Great care had to be taken in laying the stone foundation and in applying the top surface of gravel, with its precisely specified 1 in 60 fall from the crown to the sides of the road. The cost of Telford's roads was relatively high because of the heavy foundation, and as a result they did not find as much favour as Macadam's 'elastic' system.

Nevertheless in 1815, when the Holyhead Road Commission was set up, Telford was called on to survey the route and engineer a new and efficient road out of the chaotic situation administered by no less than twenty-three separate turnpike trusts. South of Shrewsbury the major improvements consisted largely of easing gradients and building short by-passes to avoid narrow sections in villages. In Wales, however, a much more radical approach was needed, and the road as it stands today is a remarkable tribute to Telford's engineering skill. West of Bettws-y-Coed the existing route wound north along the Conway valley and then west beside the coast to Bangor. Even today the section of this old road through the Sychnant Pass (107/SH 750770) between Conway and Penmaenmawr is formidable; to the early mail coaches it was often impossible. Telford surveyed a new route westward from Bettws-y-Coed that included a winding ascent up the valley of the Llugwy to Capel Curig, a spectacular feat of road engineering rendered almost ordinary by the section which follows—from Llyn Ogwen through the Nant Ffrancon Pass. Here, without involving a gradient steeper than 1 in 22, Telford carefully edged his alignment up the steep side of the glacial valley towards its head. This is the real civil engineering that distinguished Telford from most contemporary road improvers, who did little more than remodel the surface of the existing alignment.

It is worthwhile reviewing the impact of turnpiking, its decline, and the remains of the turnpike era the industrial archaeologist can find on the ground today. Despite the obvious benefits, the new restrictions of gates on the 'King's Highway' were not without opposition and riots occurred in a number of places. Around Bristol in the 1730s and 1740s colliers from south Gloucestershire and farmers from north Somerset destroyed gates and burned tollhouses. In South Wales, too, farmers resisted turnpiking with force as late as the 1840s. This was the period of the 'Rebecca Riots', when gangs of small farmers, whose hardships resulting from economic depression were aggravated by the tolls, roamed Pembrokeshire and Carmarthenshire destroying the tollgates. The mob was usually led by a man in woman's clothes, named after Isaac's wife 'Rebecca' from *Genesis*, who receives the promise that her seed should possess the 'gate' of those who hate her. These local difficulties were usually shortlived, however, and the increasing number of travellers and carriers had by the 1820s, when Macadam's and Telford's improvements had become widespread, every reason to bless the new roads and their superior surfaces. For the first time for nearly 2,000 years the speed of long-distance land transport in Britain was limited by the capacity of the horse rather than the condition of the road. In 1784 the introduction of tightly scheduled mail coaches permitted the traveller to reach Birmingham from London in 12hr and Exeter in 17¼hr. By 1834 English coaches drove at an *average* speed of 9–10mph, only the severest winter weather causing dislocation of their services.

Generally speaking, it was not until well into the railway era that the turnpike trusts began to suffer financial difficulties, and at first some of them actually benefited from traffic attracted by the new lines. By the late 1840s, however, some trusts were appealing to the local justices for rates to be levied for the upkeep of roads, and in 1851 insolvent trusts were allowed to apply to the Secretary of State for provisional orders to reduce interest and extinguish arrears. Throughout the 1860s, 1870s and 1880s, the turnpike system was abolished as the various Acts expired. Most of these Acts were for specified periods, usually 21 years, and then subject to renewal. After 1831 this renewal became automatic under the terms of the Annual Continuance Acts, which extended for 1 year all Acts due to expire. An increasing number of trusts asked for their Acts to be excluded from the annual continuance process and in 1895 the last turnpike Act expired. The system had taken 232 years to grow, flourish briefly, and expire, and with its expiry came something of a decline in the standard of rural roads.

Visible evidence of turnpiking is still surprisingly common throughout much of Britain. Nothing much survives of the toll roads themselves, although occasionally road works may reveal an early nineteenth-century surface buried in the foundations of its modern counterpart. Similarly, and for obvious reasons, the gates have disappeared. There are, however, many hundreds of tollhouses and milestones and, here and there, signposts also. Most tollhouses date from the early nineteenth century, and frequently have a form which makes them instantly recognisable (Plates 62 and 63). The half-hexagonal end with windows giving a view in each direction down the road, the hipped roof often with a prominent overhang to the eaves, and the area of wall above the central window where the tollboard would originally have hung, are all typical features. Few tollhouses still have their boards. Notable examples which do are to be found at Steanor Bottom Bar, Todmorden in Lancashire (101/SD 945198) at the junction of Calderbrook Road and Rochdale Road, and on the Holyhead Road at Llanfair PG, Anglesey (107/SH 532715). The latter, a Telford tollhouse, has the veranda that typified a number of his other tollhouses and appeared less frequently

62 Tollhouse at the east end of Mythe Bridge, Tewkesbury, Gloucestershire

63 Tollhouse at Keswick, Cumberland

elsewhere, as at Ashton Gate, Bristol (156/ST 573717). A slate tollboard from a demolished tollhouse is mounted beside the A6(T) at Shardlow, Derbyshire (121/SK 442303); nearby are the abutments of the bridge across the Trent, swept away by floods in 1947.

The erection of milestones was a statutory responsibility of the turnpike trusts, although as early as 1698 parishes had been required to put signposts at crossroads. Few of these latter survive but long runs of milestones can still be seen, often beautifully maintained by the county highway authorities. Many trusts had distinctive patterns. Telford designed his own milestone for the Holyhead road—a chamfered tapering stone with a cast-iron plate. Others were made entirely of cast iron and frequently had a 'V' plan to make for ease of reading. A fine example by I. & F. Thornewill of Burton-on-Trent, dated 1828, is on show at the Staffordshire County Museum, Shugborough (119/SJ 991224), one of a series on the A50(T) between Uttoxeter and Newcastle-under-Lyme, of which many survive *in situ*. Numerous examples of the similar iron posts erected by the Bristol trust can be seen along the A38(T) between Bristol and Bridgwater. A distinctive cylindrical type (Plate 64) again in cast iron, occurs frequently in Derbyshire, the roads from Leek to Buxton and Ashbourne each having a substantially

64 Cast-iron milepost at Shardlow, Derbyshire

complete series. Signposts are less common, but notable examples include the very fine cast-iron Doric finger post in Bristol at the junction of the Bath and Wells roads (156/ST 599718) and the stone obelisk at Craven Arms, Shropshire (129/SO 433827). Although these early signs are reasonably safe from destruction, more recent examples, erected in the present century, are now becoming extremely rare and will almost certainly disappear with metrication and the adoption of international symbols. Even rarer survivals of the turnpike era, however, are the vehicle weighing machines introduced after an Act of 1741 put a levy of extra tolls on carts and wagons laden beyond certain specified limits. One at Woodbridge in Suffolk (150/TM 272491), operated on the steelyard principle, may owe something to the work of John Wyatt (1700–66), a prominent designer of weighing machines. The Woodbridge machine (Plate 66), mounted on the end wall of 'Ye Olde Bell and Steelyard', is suspended by a hook from a large pulley-block which is itself suspended from another block housed under a small roof. A small wooden platform is attached to the massive cantilever bracket that carries the steel yard, to enable the weighman to adjust the lead weight or poise and

65 Cast-iron road sign erected in 1913 by the Cheshire Automobile Club, Prenton, Cheshire

so effect a balance. The yard is some 20ft long but the load and fulcrum centres are only 2⅜in apart.

Although the introduction of motor vehicles brought about a new revolution in road construction, various attempts to improve on macadamisation were made in the nineteenth century. Tar was applied as early as 1845 in Nottingham and in the 1870s in Sheffield and Liverpool. Asphalt, a naturally occurring bitumen from Limmer in Hanover and later from Lake Asphalt in Trinidad, was also used, initially for paving and subsequently for road surfaces. Tar spraying of macadam roads was widely adopted as a way of combating the dust caused by the suction effect of rubber-tyred vehicles. Road surfaces in towns were generally made of granite setts after the 1830s, and huge quarries in Scotland, North Wales and Charnwood Forest, Leicestershire, were opened to supply the stone. Laid initially on sand and after about 1870 on concrete, these setts are still common, particularly in side streets. Sometimes they are laid in a fan pattern, as on the cab rank of Manchester Central station (101/SJ 837977). Wood blocks, with their advantage of quietness, were used in many towns from the 1840s down to the

66 Wagon-weighing machine based on the steelyard principle, Woodbridge, Suffolk

1920s, but have now almost completely disappeared. Special tracks for carts and wagons were frequently installed in dock areas. These consisted of large, well fitted blocks of granite laid railway-fashion in two lines to match the distance between the vehicle wheels, and separated by a band of ordinary setts. In 1825 they were laid in Commercial Road, London; a length in Exchange Street East, Liverpool, where the stones are known as 'wheelers', can still be seen.

Despite the massive modernisation of roads in recent years, they still provide a fruitful source of interest for the industrial archaeologist. Cast-iron kerbs and gullies, bollards and street signs survive in profusion, as in High Street, Dorking (170/TQ 166495), and more recent signs, often vitreous-enamelled, erected by the Automobile Association, Royal Automobile

Club, Cyclists' Touring Club and the various petrol companies etc, can still be seen though in rapidly declining numbers.

BRIDGES

From the industrial archaeologist's point of view bridge building, so intimately connected with the turnpike road movement, is a profitable area of study. In the mid-eighteenth century bridges were still the exceptional way of crossing large rivers, and many of those that did exist were of medieval origins and too narrow for horse-drawn vehicles. Fords and ferries predominated, and a large river like the Yorkshire Ouse, although having some twenty ferries, had only one bridge. Indeed it was not until 1888 that there was a general statutory obligation for public authorities to build bridges. A few bridges were maintained before 1750 by county quarter sessions or hundreds, but most were repaired by ancient and often inadequate endowments. The General Highway Act of 1773 allowed magistrates to make indictments in respect of bridges, which meant that counties were ultimately held responsible for upkeep. In Scotland the state-aided Commission for the Highland Roads, established in 1803 and with Thomas Telford as engineer, built some 1,200 in 25 years. With the rapid increase in traffic brought about by turnpiking, and the demand for shorter routes, a period of major bridge construction began in the latter years of the eighteenth century.

All bridges are based on one or more of three fundamental structural forms: the beam, of which the slab of rock or fallen tree trunk are the simplest forms; the arch, in which the deck is supported by a structure of wedge-shaped arch stones or voussoirs; and suspension, in which the deck is hung by suspenders from a continuous cable. In eighteenth-century Britain all important bridges were of the arch type, constructed on the empirical evidence available from earlier bridge builders and from buildings such as the great medieval cathedrals. At this period the first theories of arches were developed, notably in France where the Corps des Ingénieurs des Ponts et Chaussées under the guidance of Jean Rodolphe Perronet (1708–94) was applying scientific techniques to constructional problems. In Britain Robert Mylne (1734–1811) carried out much of the pioneer work on arch-bridge design, his first major work, Blackfriars Bridge, London, being completed in 1769. (It was replaced by the present wrought-iron structure in 1869.) In this bridge Mylne incorporated elliptical arches, an innovation in Britain; inverted arches in the piers between the springings of the two adjacent arches bearing on them; and the multiple or crocket wedge support for the timber bridge centres, which enabled the centring to be lowered gradually and any weakness in the arch itself to be detected at an early stage.

John Rennie (1761–1821) is much better known, but may be regarded as a successor to Mylne in the field of bridge building. Born at Phantassie, near East Linton, some 20 miles from Edinburgh, Rennie grew up in contact with the crafts of millwrighting, blacksmithing, stonemasonry and carpentry and learnt much about them from one of his father's tenants, Andrew Meikle (1719–1811), the celebrated mechanical engineer and windmill improver. After an education at Edinburgh University, which brought him into contact with leading scientific minds, Rennie established himself as an engineer working on canals, docks, steam engines, land drainage schemes, roads and mills, as well as some notable bridges. His most famous masonry bridges were Waterloo Bridge, London, completed in 1817 and now replaced by a reinforced-concrete beam structure; and London Bridge, completed in 1831 as successor to the famous medieval bridge and now removed to Havasu City, Arizona. The foundations of both these bridges were on piles built within cofferdams. Rennie's Waterloo and London Bridges, and his other Thames bridge, at Southwark, have all now been replaced, but Kelso bridge over the River Tweed, his first major structure, still stands at the southern approach to the town (70/NT 727336). It has five elliptical arches, each of 72ft span, and was virtually a small-scale prototype for Waterloo Bridge. Rennie's bridge-building abilities, like those of Telford a few years later, stood him in good stead for his work on canals in which, besides innumerable humble occupation crossings, mostly built to a standard design, he was responsible for a number of aqueducts, including the spectacular structure across the River Lune at Lancaster (89/SD 484638). These will be considered in Chapter 14. His standard bridges may be seen in profusion along the Lancaster Canal and the Kennet & Avon Canal. Most have walls curved on plan, so acting as arches springing from the buttress piers at each end; and in addition the walls are battered, making the whole bridge immensely strong.

Before turning to iron bridges, in which Rennie had been involved at
Southwark, a number of other surviving masonry structures are worth
noting. In Chester, Grosvenor Bridge across the Dee (109/SJ 403656),
designed by Thomas Harrison (1744–1829) and opened in 1832, has the
widest masonry span in Britain—200ft, with a rise of 40ft. The complete
arch has, in fact, a span of 230ft, as it extends into the abutments to carry the
thrust more effectively down to piling foundations. Harrison also designed
the elegant Skerton Bridge in Lancaster (89/SD 479623). Telford's masonry
bridges never reached the standards of structural elegance of his graceful
cast-iron bridges. His first major work, Montford Bridge (118/SJ 433153) of
1792, carrying the Holyhead road over the Severn west of Shrewsbury, is
very much in the eighteenth-century classical tradition, but his next, Tongue-
land Bridge (80/NX 693534) across the Dee near Kirkcudbright, with its
single 112ft span, is of considerable technical interest. Here Telford first
introduced hollow spandrels to lighten the load on the foundations, but,
instead of piercing with tunnels as Smeaton and Edwards had done, he
replaced the normal rubble fill with a series of parallel walls within the
spandrels themselves. Pierced spandrel bridges may be seen at Pontypridd,
Glamorgan (154/ST 074904), built in 1755 by William Edwards (1719–89),
and Coldstream, Northumberland (64/NT 848402), designed by John
Smeaton (1724–92) and completed in 1763. In the latter example the tunnels
are covered at the ends with ornamental discs. Returning to Telford and his
masonry bridges, Dean Bridge, Edinburgh (62/NT 243740), over the
Waters of Leith, completed in 1832, is perhaps his finest surviving stone
structure, while Over Bridge, Gloucester (143/SO 817196), is interesting
for its ingenuity. The splaying of the 150ft span arch, in which the two faces
of the bridge are in effect chamfered to form 'cow's horn voussoirs', is
based on Perronet's Pont de Neuilly over the Seine. Over Bridge is likely
to be demolished in the near future.

The completion in 1779 of the first metal bridge structure in the world,
the Iron Bridge (Plate 67) over the River Severn near Coalbrookdale in
Shropshire (118/SJ 673034), marked the beginning of the end of stone as the

67 The Iron Bridge, across the River Severn in Shropshire. Cast at the nearby
Coalbrookdale Works in 1779, this was the first major civil engineering work in the
world in which iron played a structural role

68 The Iron Bridge. Detail of arch showing dovetailing of radial members into ribs

major bridge-building material. The Iron Bridge derives all its structural principles from its stone predecessors and is, in effect a natural successor to the works of Edwards and Smeaton, who pioneered the reduction in self-weight of bridge structures. Like stone bridges, it has a compression arch, but close examination of the methods of construction reveals that techniques more appropriate to timber fabrication have been used in its assembly. The various components were designed to pass through one another and mortice or dove-tail together (Plate 68), and are secured by wedges. No bolts or rivets were used. The bridge has a span of 100ft and the rise is 45ft. There are five main ribs of 12in by 6½in section and 70ft long, virtually hinged at the springing and at the crown. They were cast in open sand moulds at the Coalbrookdale works of Abraham Darby.

Credit for the design of what is perhaps the most important monument of the Industrial Revolution in Britain is usually accorded to Thomas Farnolls Pritchard (d 1777), a Shrewsbury architect, who certainly prepared drawings for a 120ft flat-arched iron bridge as early as October 1775. In

69 Restoration of the Iron Bridge. Excavation of the north abutment and insertion of reinforced concrete strengthening

association with the ironmasters John Wilkinson (1728–1808) and Abraham Darby III (1750–91), Pritchard discussed schemes for a bridge, but his death in 1777 left the project entirely in Darby's hands. Who was responsible for the design of the 1779 bridge as constructed remains, therefore, something of a mystery.

There is no doubt, however, that the Iron Bridge proved to be an inspiration to other civil engineers. Thomas Telford used iron for the bridge at Buildwas, a few miles upstream from Coalbrookdale. The previous masonry bridge had been swept away by a flood in 1795 and Telford replaced it with a single iron span of 130ft weighing 173 tons, in contrast to the 378 tons of the first 1779 iron bridge. Buildwas Bridge (118/SJ 645044) survived until 1906, when it was replaced by the present steel structure.

Numerous designs for iron bridges were tried between 1795 and 1820. In 1796 a 236ft iron span was completed across the River Wear at Sunderland to the designs of Rowland Burdon, a local MP, who in the previous year had patented a system of construction involving separate openwork cast-iron voussoirs held together with wrought-iron straps instead of the ribs being cast complete, as at Ironbridge or Buildwas. The idea was not a complete success and two subsequent bridges built at Staines, 1802, and Yarm, 1805, collapsed soon after completion. Sunderland Bridge survived for half a century before requiring substantial modification and eventual replacement. Two bridges incorporating Burdon's patent still survive— at Spanish Town, Jamaica, 1801, and Newport Pagnell, Buckinghamshire, where Tickford Bridge (146/SP 877437) across the River Ouzel, completed in 1810, still carries the heavy traffic of the A50.

Open-frame voussoirs fell into disrepute as a result of these and other collapses, and Coalport Bridge of 1818 (119/SJ 702021) is an example of the return to ribs cast in complete sections. There are few eighteenth-century survivors of this type of construction, but those that do exist usually have characteristic features suggesting that the founders had some influence in the design. Thus the spans at Cound, Shropshire (118/SJ 556053), dated 1797 and presumably supplied to Telford, those at Bath over the Kennet & Avon Canal (156/ST 758654), one of two supplied to Rennie, and those at Tewkesbury (143/SO 893330), of unknown date, all have a diminishing circle motif in the outer ribs of the arches.

By 1815 really large iron bridges were being built, notably by Telford and Rennie. At Bettws-y-Coed (107/SH 799558) Telford's graceful arch provides a splendid example of the ironfounders' art. The outside ribs carry the legend, in finely proportioned openwork lettering, THIS ARCH WAS CONSTRUCTED IN THE SAME YEAR THE BATTLE OF WATERLOO WAS FOUGHT, across the full width of the arch. In the spandrels are enormous heraldic flowers—roses, thistles, shamrocks and leeks—a degree of decoration seldom seen in Telford's work. The arch was cast by William Hazledine at Plas Kynaston and erected by William Stuttle. Both their names are cast into the base of the balustrading. The Waterloo Bridge is surprisingly little known, perhaps because a good view of the arch involves scrambling down

70 Thomas Telford's cast-iron bridge of 1814 across the River Spey at Craigellachie, Banff

71 Cast-iron plaque Craigellachie Bridge: "Cast at Plas Kynaston, Ruabon, Denbighshire, 1814"

the river bank almost to water level. The effort is well worthwhile, however, and an examination of the underside of the arch reveals the sympathetic
way in which it has been strengthened and widened without destroying
its original character. In Scotland Telford's magnificently sited bridge at
Craigellachie (29/NJ 285452), with its ornamental castellated towers and
152ft arch of trussed iron ribs (Plates 70 and 71), has also been carefully reno-
vated in recent years, using new components and epoxy resin adhesives.
Similar large, although less spectacular, Telford bridges are Holt Fleet Bridge,
Ombersley, Worcestershire (130/SO 824634); Mythe Bridge, Tewkesbury
(143/SO 888337); and Galton Bridge, Smethwick (131/SP 015894). Un-
fortunately John Rennie's masterpiece in cast iron, the 240ft span Southwark
Bridge over the Thames, built between 1814 and 1819, no longer survives.
It was replaced by the present steel-arched bridge in 1922.

The need for spans larger than were feasible even with cast-iron bridges
became a real one by the 1820s, when the new roads and greatly increased
traffic created a demand for shorter and more direct routes. The suspension
bridge satisfied this need, and wrought iron, becoming readily available as a
result of Henry Cort's pioneer work in the 1780s on the development of the
puddling process, meant that for the first time material existed from which
suitable chains could be made. A number of suspension bridges were built in

72 Date plaque, Prince's Bridge, Salford, 1905

south Scotland. The greatest, with a span of 300ft, was completed in 1820 by Captain Samuel (later Sir Samuel) Brown, RN (1776–1852), and crossed the Tweed at Kelso. (It has since been demolished.) Brown had introduced the chain cable to the Royal Navy and in 1817 took out a patent for wrought-iron links which he incorporated in the Union Chain Bridge across the Tweed near Berwick (64/NT 934511). Completed in 1820, this earliest surviving suspension bridge has a span of 361ft and an 18ft deck hung from twelve wrought-iron chains. Major repairs have been undertaken on two occasions, the first in 1871–2 by the Berwick and Norham and Islandshire Turnpike Trustees and the second in 1902–3 by the Tweed Bridge Trustees, who now care for the bridge. A steel cable has been added on each side above the chains to help them support the platform. The tollhouse on the English side has been demolished (the bridge was made free in 1883) but that on the Scottish bank, which once belonged to the Berwickshire Turnpike Trust, still stands.

In 1819 the Act was passed for building Menai Bridge (107/SH 556714) to carry the Holyhead road from Anglesey to the mainland of Wales. Its designer, Thomas Telford, initially favoured a cast-iron arch construction similar to a scheme put forward in 1801 by Rennie, but Admiralty insistence on unobstructed navigation through the Straits resulted in his adopting the suspension principle, and on a scale far exceeding anything previously built. Work began on the piers in 1819 and on the manufacture of the iron chains in 1821. The links, each a little over 9ft long, were wrought at Upton Forge (118/SJ 560113) in Shropshire, sent to Hazledine's Coleham works in Shrewsbury for testing on a specially designed tensile machine and forwarded thence by canal to Chester and sea to Menai.

The Menai Bridge must be one of the most carefully built structures in the world. Telford, acutely conscious of the step he was taking into the unknown, tested each link of the sixteen suspension chains 100 per cent in excess of the calculated working load and then tested each complete chain in tension before final erection. The stones of the towers are dowelled together with iron pegs and the chains which they support run back 60ft into tunnels blasted in the rock. The main span is of 579ft, with a headroom of 100ft to satisfy Admiralty navigation requirements. Each of the main piers is 153ft high and is approached by a masonry viaduct of three arches on the Caernarvon side and four on the Anglesey side of the straits. Com-

pleted in 1826, like its smaller neighbour at Conway (107/SH 786777) on
the Chester road, Menai Bridge formed the last link in the road from
Holyhead to London. Despite Telford's care in design and construction,
various components have had to be replaced. In 1839 the unstiffened timber
deck was wrecked in a storm; a heavier timber deck lasted until 1893, when
Sir Benjamin Baker reconstructed it in steel; and this in turn was replaced
in 1940, when the tolls were also abolished and the chains replaced in high-
tensile steel.

The success of Menai encouraged others to build suspension bridges.
William Tierney Clark (1783–1852) designed the old Hammersmith Bridge,
built in 1827 and replaced 60 years later, and a beautiful 271ft span suspension
bridge at Marlow (159/SU 852862), completed in 1832 and still standing.
So is Clark's major work, the 666ft span suspension bridge at Budapest.
Victoria Bridge, Bath (156/ST 741650), across the River Avon, completed
in 1836 to the designs of J. Dredge, is of unusual construction, as the suspension rods from the catenary chains are inclined towards the piers instead
of being vertical, a device intended to increase structural stiffness. Undoubtedly the most spectacular of the great nineteenth-century suspension
bridges, however, is the epic Clifton Bridge (156/ST 564731), designed by
I. K. Brunel in the late 1820s and finally completed in modified form in
1864. The first moves to bridge the Avon gorge at Clifton date from 1753,
when William Vick, a Bristol wine merchant, bequeathed £1,000 to the
Society of Merchant Venturers with the instruction that it should be allowed
to accumulate to £10,000 when, it was hoped, a bridge could be built. By
1829 the amount had increased to £8,000, and a competition was held to
seek a suitable design. Numerous schemes were submitted, including an improbable gothic structure by Telford, who was one of the judges, and several
by Brunel. A modified Brunel design was finally selected, work began in
June 1831, the foundation stone was laid in 1836 and in 1840, when the
piers were substantially complete, money ran out. The chains were sold in
1853 to the South Devon Railway for use on Brunel's other major bridge,
the Royal Albert Bridge over the Tamar at Saltash (187/SX 435587). In
1859, when Brunel died, Clifton Bridge, the starting point of his independent engineering career, was no further advanced, but the prosperity of
the 1860s coupled with sorrow at the loss of a great engineer, at the relatively
early age of 53, revived interest in the scheme. A new company was formed

by some of the principal members of the Institution of Civil Engineers and,
utilising the chains from the recently demolished Hungerford suspension
bridge across the Thames, also designed by Brunel, they opened Clifton in
December 1864. With little modification it stands today, linking Gloucestershire and Somerset 245ft above the Avon. The span is 702ft 3in and the
total weight of ironwork 1,500 tons. Incidently, the piers of Brunel's
Hungerford Bridge still help to support today's rail and foot bridge between
Waterloo and Charing Cross.

The beam type of bridge had little application on roads in the nineteenth century, although it was extensively used on railways. Recently,
however, beam bridges in steel and prestressed concrete have appeared in
profusion on motorways and other modern roadworks. The early development of reinforced concrete was pursued largely in France by engineers
such as François Coignet (1814–88) and his son Edmond (1850–1915), and
François Hennebique (1842–1921). The structural use of concrete poured
in situ was adopted only slowly in England and no major bridge in the new
material appeared until after the World War I. A very early example still
survives across the River Axe at Seaton in Devon (177/SY 253900). It was
completed in 1877 and has a central span of 50ft. On a much larger scale the
Royal Tweed Bridge at Berwick (64/NT 995528), opened in 1928, exemp-
lifies the ponderous designs of the interwar years before prestressing brought
to concrete a supreme elegance and daring worthy of the great nineteenth-
century pioneers.

Before leaving road bridges altogether, a curious and somewhat bizarre
answer to the problems of spanning large rivers and at the same time maintaining headroom for navigation is worthy of brief mention. The transporter bridge, in effect an aerial ferry, had a brief period of popularity at
the end of the nineteenth century and beginning of the twentieth as a solution
to the problem in flat country or urban areas of low-level approach roads
making a fixed bridge impractical. By supporting a girder at high level
between two towers, vehicles could be carried across the gap on a platform
suspended by cables from a trolley running on rails above. The idea was
originally proposed by a British engineer in the 1870s, but was first put
into practice by the Frenchman F. Arnodin in 1893 at Portugalete, near
Bilbao, in Spain. Four transporter bridges were built in Britain and three
of these are still extant. The largest, in fact the largest in the world, crossed

the Mersey between Widnes and Runcorn. It was of the suspension type with a span of 1,000ft and was in use from 1905 until 1961, when the present high-level steel-arch structure replaced it.

In 1906 a smaller transporter bridge, also of suspension type, was completed across the Usk at Newport (155/ST 318863). Of 645ft span, it is still in regular use. The Middlesbrough transporter bridge (85/NZ 500213) is of a completely different form of construction, as its overhead deck is cantilevered, the outer ends being anchored with massive vertical cables. Opened in 1911, it has a span of 570ft and accommodation for 600 passengers and up to ten vehicles on the electrically propelled carriage. Much less known than these two is the privately owned transporter bridge across the River Mersey at Warrington (100/SJ 597877), connecting the two halves of the extensive soap and chemical works of Messrs Joseph Crosfield & Son Ltd. Compared with Newport and Middlesbrough, it is small, with a semi-cantilevered span of only 187ft. Built in 1916, and out of regular use since 1964, it was the last of the total of sixteen transporter bridges to be constructed.

14 Rivers and Canals

FROM the end of the Roman occupation until the mid-eighteenth century rivers were the main arteries of communication in Britain. They formed natural highways and were of paramount importance in influencing the settlement of people, the location of towns and the development of trade and commerce. Although susceptible to drought and flooding, rivers offered much greater reliability than roads, particularly where these crossed clay country. The Romans not only supplemented their comprehensive road system by river transport but sought to improve the latter with embankments. In the case of the Trent and the Witham they even cut a canal—the Fossdyke (Torksey Lock, 104/SK 837781 to Brayford Pool, Lincoln, 113/SK 970713)—in order to establish direct communication between them. A thousand years elapsed before any further improvements were carried out, although legislative procedures established rights of navigation over many rivers. There were numerous obstructions, however, shallows in dry weather, fishgarths for catching fish, and the dams and weirs of millowners being the major difficulties. In the sixteenth century eight Acts were passed dealing with rivers and the improvement of navigation, including one in 1571 to bring the River Lea to the north of London by making an artificial cut. By 1750, on the eve of the great era of canal building, Britain had 1,000 odd miles of navigable river, some of which, such as the Aire & Calder from 1699, had only been rendered navigable by the construction of cuts and pound locks. The early river engineers, such as Andrew Yarranton (1619–84?), had accumulated considerable experience of the problems of establishing navigations and their work, together with that of the fen drainers, provided the essential technological foundation for the canal engineers of later years.

A prominent feature of many improved rivers was the flashlock, which had its origins in the Middle Ages, often as a compromise between navigation and milling interests. Where water was impounded for a mill, a device was needed to pass boats through the weirs; and in between mills also, weirs were often necessary to maintain adequate depths of water for navigation. If a section of the weir was made removable, usually by the insertion of a gate, boats could pass through. These flashlocks, when opened, resulted in a powerful flush of water running downstream and boats simply 'shooting the rapids'. Those going upstream had to wait until the main force of water had subsided, when they were winched through the lock against the flow. The lock would then be closed and the water level allowed to build up for the next vessel. In a dry summer this might take several days and could, in extreme conditions, prevent navigation altogether. In many cases these flashlocks were replaced by pound locks, similar to those found on canals today, for flashlocks were highly dangerous and wasteful of time and water. A variation of the flashlock, usually known as a staunch, operated on a similar principle but was normally kept open to the river flow. Staunches were installed where flashlocks or pound locks were not always desirable, particularly on rivers with numerous mills, as impounded water would tend to back up the tailraces of waterwheels and reduce their efficiency. Also if a river was crossed by a ford, as, for example, at Tempsford on the Great Ouse (147/TL 161542), it was essential that the river level was not increased at the crossing point. The method of operation of staunches was even more tedious than that of flashlocks, a man usually preceding the boat to close the gates and allow sufficient water to build up.

Most flashlocks and staunches took the form of vertically hinged gates; these were rarely single but generally a pair of mitre gates like those on any canal lock. The angle between them was commonly 90 degrees, in contrast to the 120 or 130 degrees of canal and more modern river locks. In East Anglia guillotine staunches were sometimes used, and then the gate was raised vertically like a sash window and the boats passed underneath. A third and very simple type consisted of planks let into vertical slots in masonry walls, and was similar to the stop-planks commonly used on canals to isolate sections for repair. Perhaps the oldest form, however, was the beam and paddle weir, in which a beam was swung horizontally over a wooden cill across the bed of the lock. When closed, vertical boards or 'rimers' were put between beam and cill, and against these were set square planks with handles to hold back the water.

Most of the remaining flashlocks are decayed and ruinous, but a fine and nearly complete beam and paddle type can be seen on a small tributary of the Thames just below Eynsham Lock (158/SP 446089), Oxfordshire. Although traffic on this ½ mile navigation to Eynsham Wharf ceased in 1925, the beam still survives, bolted to the stop-post and supporting a foot-bridge. A substantially complete staunch on the Great Ouse may be seen at Castle Mills (147/TL 094509), with brickwork, c1840, intact and the decrepit remains of gates. Its purpose was to deepen the shallows below Castle Mills Lock, 300yd above. Tuddenham Mill Stream, a tributary of the Lark, which in turn flows into the Great Ouse, also has a well preserved gate staunch (135/TL 732729), with mitre gates, each with a single paddle (or sluice). There is a guillotine staunch, complete except for the spoked wheel used to lift the gate, at Bottisham Lode (135/TL 516651), which probably dates from the 1820s and was in use until navigation on this obscure tributary of the Cam ceased about 1900.

Like the navigable rivers, canals were chiefly used to move heavy bulky goods for which roads were unsuitable. Britain was slow to begin building canals, but, once started, quick to extend a network over much of England, with separate systems in Wales and Scotland. By 1850 the 1,000 miles of river navigation that had existed in 1750 had been expanded to a total of 4,250 miles as a result of canal building. The first canals were dug to connect or supplement existing river navigations or to link otherwise isolated agricultural or industrial communities with navigable water. The Newry Canal in Ireland, completed in 1742, was the first 'deadwater navigation' in the British Isles. It was followed in England by the Sankey Brook Navigation from the St Helens coalfield in south Lancashire to the River Mersey. Financed by Liverpool merchants, salt refiners and the town corporation, it was substantially complete by 1757 and can undoubtedly claim the distinction of being England's first canal. Its economic success was immediate and high dividends were paid. Soon after came the Bridgewater Canal, built by John Gilbert and James Brindley (1716–72) to connect the Duke of Bridgewater's collieries at Worsley with Manchester. On its completion in 1761, the price of coal in Manchester dropped by half. The canal revolution had begun.

James Brindley, the 'father of English canals', was born in Derbyshire and began work as an apprentice wheelwright and millwright at Sutton near Macclesfield. By 1742, at the age of twenty-six, he had his own business in Leek, where Brindley Mill (110/SJ 977570) survives as a memorial to his early career. His considerable abilities became well known in Staffordshire and brought him for the first time into contact with a canal scheme, to connect the Trent and Mersey rivers, for which he was asked to carry out a survey. The Trent and Mersey project was to remain a dream for some years, but it was his work in connection with it that brought Brindley to the notice of the Duke of Bridgewater and gained him his first definite commission for a canal. The 'Bridgewater', and the masonry aqueduct which Brindley designed to take his canal over the River Irwell, fired the imagination of the age. The three great arches carried the canal 38ft above the level of the river, enabling flats (sailing barges) to pass beneath. Completed in July 1761, it became a local wonder—'Vessels o'er vessels, water under water, *Bridgewater* triumphs – art has conquered nature.' It survived until 1893, when construction of the Manchester Ship Canal, which was built largely on the site of the Mersey & Irwell Navigation, necessitated its demolition. The abutments, however, can still be seen (101/SJ 767977), and give an indication of the massive construction. The replacement is a still more remarkable structure, a unique swinging aqueduct designed by Sir E. Leader Williams, engineer of the Ship Canal. A pivoted steel tank 235ft long, 18ft wide and 6ft deep provides a crossing for the Bridgewater 26ft above the Manchester Ship Canal. When passage of the ship canal is required, the tank is swung by hydraulic power on its central pier, the total weight of the span and its load of water being 1,450 tons. The first barge passed over Barton swing aqueduct on 21 August 1893, and Brindley's pioneer structure was then demolished.

At the west end of the Bridgewater Canal, Worsley Mine was an integral part of the project, and the line of the canal was continued into the vertical rock face at Worsley Delph (101/SD 748005) to form the basis of an underground network of waterways on which the coal was brought out. Underground channels known as soughs were in use before 1750 for draining coal workings north of Worsley, and it seems probable that these were adapted to give direct access by boat between the coalfaces and the main line canal. James Brindley was closely involved with the underground scheme in its early years, as was John Gilbert, the Duke's superintendent engineer, agent and surveyor, who was probably responsible for extending it in the years down to his death in 1795. The network grew continually until about 1840, when some 46 miles of underground waterways extended under Walkden and Farnworth. To tap deeper seams, separate systems were also dug at levels below the main line and connected to it by shafts; the deepest was 83ft below the level of the entrance tunnels. Further north a higher level system was connected to the main level by a 150yd underground inclined plane on which the boats were worked on wheeled cradles running on rails. At the Delph can be seen the two entrances to this system, cut about 30ft apart in the rock face. Note also the hand-crane with a wooden gib used for inserting the stop-planks (101/SD 747004) and the drydocks on the Bridgewater Canal. Examples of the long narrow boats, nicknamed 'starvationers', which were used in the tunnels can be seen in the North Western Museum of Science & Technology, 97 Grosvenor Street, Manchester.

Following the success of the Bridgewater the number of canals multiplied rapidly before 1773 and after 1787, the movement reaching a crescendo in the 'mania' of 1789–93. Three main types were developed—wide canals for some main lines, particularly those associated with rivers; narrow canals, with 7ft locks, for hilly inland routes that frequently suffered from poor water supplies; and tub-boat canals, where gradients were particularly steep. Wide canals were built mainly in Lancashire and Cheshire, in the East Midlands, and in the south wherever connection with tidal water was important. The gauge was usually about 14ft. The pattern of the narrow waterways was set by Brindley's Staffordshire & Worcestershire and Trent & Mersey canals, completed in 1772 and 1777 respectively. The need to economise on constructional costs where large numbers of locks and tunnels were needed resulted in major concentrations of narrow canals round Birmingham and also in South Wales. Tub-boat canals were built in Shropshire and the South West. Within these groups there were numerous minor variations, but, generally speaking, a *narrow boat* 70ft by 7ft could travel anywhere south of the Rivers Trent and Mersey, except on the tub-boat canals, and a *barge* 58ft by 13ft 6in anywhere north of that line. Larger barges worked on the river navigations.

The lack of uniformity in canal size and the total absence of planning prevented the canal network from ever being an integrated system. The geography of Britain meant heavily locked waterways, with consequent problems of water supply for summit levels; and many areas, notably much of Scotland, the far north of England and the south-west peninsula, were quite unsuited to artificial waterways. The web of canals was densest in the industrial Midlands where Birmingham, first entered by canal in 1772, became a focus of waterways. The estuaries of the Thames, Severn, Humber and Mersey were soon connected, the Pennines traversed, and London linked with the Midlands and North. In the south of England more than 430 miles of canal were dug, but with one or two exceptions few navigations paid dividends higher than 5 per cent. Of little industrial importance, the largely agricultural south did not have the traffic potential to make profits. By contrast such waterways as the Aire & Calder network, the Loughborough Navigation in Leicestershire and the Trent & Mersey Canal carried huge quantities of raw materials and manufactured goods. In 1824 the last two were paying dividends of 197 per cent and 75 per cent respectively. In South Wales too a series of short and generally unconnected canals provided for the thriving coal and iron trade of the valleys, stimulating the growth of coastal centres such as Cardiff and Newport, and supplying coking coal and iron ore to great ironworks complexes such as those at Merthyr Tydfil. The terrain in much of South Wales, and parts of the North East around the valleys of the Tyne and Wear, was totally unsuited to canal construction, however, and in these areas parallel development of horse tramroads began, to feed canals or rivers.

As already mentioned, the early canals were built as cheaply as possible. A typical Brindley canal, such as the Staffordshire & Worcestershire, follows the contours with hardly an embankment or cutting of any size upon it. The extra length resulting from their winding courses mattered little when boat-men's wages were low and effective competition non-existent. The threat of road and railway competition led to an increase in the efficiency and enterprise of waterways and to efforts at improvement. Harecastle Tunnel (110/SJ 837542 to 849517) on the Trent & Mersey canal was doubled in 1827, the new tunnel (16ft high and 14ft wide) taking only 3 years to build in contrast to the 11 years taken by the original bore (12ft high by 9ft 3in wide) of the 1770s. Engineering techniques had improved. In other cases routes were shortened, a notable example of the straightening of a contour canal being the Oxford, which was reduced from 91 to 77½ miles between 1829 and 1834. New canals themselves were made as straight as possible, even at the expense of considerable civil engineering work to maintain the level. Thus Telford's Birmingham & Liverpool Junction (now the Shrop-shire Union main line), completed in 1835, has long stretches of embank-ment and cutting, including the 2 mile long Tyrley Cutting (119/SJ 693315), the deepest in the country.

The obstacles facing canal engineers were overcome in a variety of ways. Locks were the normal method of climbing hills, tunnels and cuttings for going through them and aqueducts for crossing rivers or valleys. The river improvers with their flashlocks and staunches anticipated the common pound lock used on most canals in England. A century after its first known use in continental Europe, in 1373, the pound lock was in use on river navigations in Britain. It consisted of lifting or swinging gates enclosing a 'pound' of water of sufficient length to accommodate a boat. On the River Wey, made navigable from the Thames to Guildford, Surrey, under an Act of 1651, pound locks with turf sides, now reinforced, have survived in substantially original form, as at Papercourt (170/TQ 034568) and Walsham Gates (170/TQ 050578). Sheffield Lock on the Kennet Navigation, Berkshire (158/SU 649706), is also turf-sided (Plate 73).

On canals the lock evolved with a brick or masonry pound, generally rectangular in plan and of the minimum dimensions capable of handling the largest type of craft using the canal. Thus the smallest amount of water was consumed. In the Midlands a typical 'narrow' lock has a chamber 7ft wide and about 76ft long designed for boats of 6ft 10in beam and up to 72ft in length. The extra length of the chamber allows for the inward-opening bottom gates. The mode of operation is simple. A boat working down requires a full lock to enter. When the boat is in the chamber and the gates are closed, sluices, usually known in this context as paddles, at the lower end or tail of the lock are opened and as soon as the levels inside and outside are the same, the gates can be opened and the boat passes through. In locking up the procedure is followed in reverse.

Lock gates are generally of timber, oak being most commonly used, although on the Montgomeryshire and Ellesmere canals cast-iron gates were used in the early nineteenth century. A pair from the former canal can be seen at the Waterways Museum, Stoke Bruerne, Northamptonshire (146/SP 743500). The gates at the tail of the lock are the heavier because they extend the full depth of the lock, whereas those at the upper end or head need only be the depth of the upper pound of the canal. Double gates are generally used on river navigations and barge canals, but in narrow locks single top gates and double bottom gates are commonly found. Both upper and lower gates bed against a cill at the bottom of the chamber, the upper cill being

73 The turf-sided Sheffield Lock on the Kennet Navigation, Berkshire

exposed when the lock is empty. Cills are often made of timber, although concrete has been increasingly used in recent years. Gates have a vertical timber at the hinge end known as the heel post which fits into a hollow quoin in the masonry wall of the lock. Only a light iron strap is needed to maintain the gate in place as water pressure holds the heel post tightly into the quoin when the gate is closed. The outer end of the gate also has a vertical post called a breast or mitre post, which fits a rebate in the opposite wall of the lock or, in the case of double gates, the equivalent post of the partner gate. A gate is operated by a balance beam, which, as the name suggests,

74 Guillotine lock gate on the Shrewsbury Canal

provides the counterweight to the gate itself. Traditionally this beam was of timber but in many modern replacement gates rolled steel joists with concrete balance weights have been used. The guillotine gate (Plate 74) is not common on British canals, but examples can be found on the old Shropshire Canal section of the Shropshire Union north of Hadley (119/SJ 672133) and at King's Norton stop-lock at the junction of the Stratford-upon-Avon Canal with the Worcester & Birmingham (131/SP 053795). Modern guillotine gates can be seen on the Rivers Nene and Great Ouse, where their use more easily enables flood water to run through the lock.

Locks are filled and emptied by sluices, generally known as paddles but also called slackers in the Fens and cloughs in the North of England. Gate paddles fitted on the lock gates themselves are found at head and tail of most river navigation locks, and on the tail gates and occasionally head gates of canal locks. Ground paddles are mounted in the wall of the lock and admit water through culverts; they are generally used in combination with gate paddles at the head of a lock. Ground paddles used for drawing off water from a lock are rare features but can be seen on some of the wide locks on the stretch of the Grand Union between Napton and Birmingham. The paddle itself usually consists of a slab of elm that slides vertically in a frame across the sluice aperture. A wide variety of mechanisms for lifting or drawing paddles can be found, the most common being the rack and pinion arrangement incorporating a pawl to hold the paddle in the drawn position. Worm-and-nut gearing is used on the ground paddles of the Leeds & Liverpool Canal, and on the same navigation pivoted gate paddles can be found, a very rare feature. On the River Wey at Worsfold Gates, near Send, Surrey (170/TQ 016557), some paddles still operate in their most primitive form; they are lifted by hand and held in position by pegs through holes in the handles (Plate 75). Nearby are the Navigation's workshops, which are still in use. Nowadays, of course, many locks are mechanised, as on the Caledonian and Aire & Calder Canals and the Rivers Trent and Thames.

Groups or 'flights' of locks are commonly found on canals where great differences in level occur in a relatively short distance. The largest flight in Britain is at Tardebigge on the Worcester & Birmingham Canal, where thirty narrow locks raise the canal 217ft in about 2 miles. The summit lock at Tardebigge is, in fact, the deepest narrow lock in the country, with a fall

75 Peg-and-hole gate paddles at Worsfold Lock, on the Wey Navigation, Send, Surrey

of 14ft; this is exceptional and the average is 6–8ft. A flight almost equal to Tardebigge can be seen at Devizes, where the Kennet & Avon Canal climbs out of the Vale of Pewsey through twenty-nine wide locks. This flight is far more spectacular, however, as the locks are very close together and most of them in a straight line. At Combe Hay (166/ST 748604) on the Somersetshire Coal Canal one can see most of the locks of a flight of twenty-two completed in 1805 after the failure of a novel boat lift. The canal was closed in the 1890s, and later part of its bed was utilised for the Limpley Stoke to Hallatrow branch of the Great Western Railway, opened in 1910.

A variation on the simple flight of locks is the staircase, where the top gate of one lock forms the bottom gate of the one above. A notable example is to be seen at Foxton (133/SP 692895) where the Leicester line of the Grand Union Canal descends by means of two staircases, each of five locks. To economise in the use of water—always important to the canal operator— side-ponds were frequently built in association with staircases of locks, and these are used at Foxton. The side-pond consists of a chamber beside the locks at a level halfway between the upper and lower pounds and communicating with the pounds by culverts controlled by ground paddles (side-pond paddles). When a boat enters the full pound and the gates are closed, the side-pond paddle is opened first, until the levels equate and slightly less than half the water is in the side-pond. The side-pond paddle is then closed and the remainder of the water in the lock released into the lower pound in the normal way. The saving occurs when a boat locking up enters the empty lock, which can then be almost half-filled with water from the side-pond. Thus only the remaining half has to be drawn from the upper pond. A well known staircase of wide locks is Bingley 'Five Rise' (96/SE 108400) on the Leeds & Liverpool Canal (Plate 76). Here there are no side-ponds and water passes direct from chamber to chamber. The largest staircase in Britain, of eight locks, is at Banavie (35/NN 147770) on the Caledonian Canal.

A curious and unique flight of three locks is to be seen at Bratch (130/SO 867938) on the Staffordshire & Worcestershire Canal, where at first sight the locks appear to be arranged in a staircase. However, each lock has its own gates, the top gate of one lock being only a few feet from the lower gates of the lock above. Further south at Botterham (130/SO 860914) on

76 Rack and pinion sliding gate paddles, Bingley 'Five Rise' Locks, Leeds & Liverpool Canal

the same canal is a double lock or rise of normal type with a common gate between the two chambers, while to the north lies Compton top lock (130/SO 884989), said to be the first lock built by Brindley. It is interesting to speculate as to whether Brindley devised the principle of the staircase immediately after building the Bratch locks or whether he was already aware of continental examples, such as the staircase at Béziere on the Canal du Midi in France. Other locks of interest include the sectional cast-iron lock chambers at Beeston (109/SJ 554599) in Cheshire, devised by Telford to overcome the problems of soft sand (Plate 77), and Northgate Locks, Chester (109/SJ 403666), which are partly cut in solid rock. On the Staffordshire & Worcestershire Canal circular weirs instead of the normal straight cill type are used for the culverts that convey surplus water from the head to the tail of some of the locks.

Besides problems of water supply, long flights of locks imposed considerable delays to traffic, particularly where this was heavy. Thus from as early as the 1780s canal engineers sought means of replacing locks with other mechanisms such as inclined planes, lifts, and a variety of patent balance-lock and caisson devices. In Britain no inclined planes remain in use, but their overgrown alignments, often almost completely obscured by trees and undergrowth, can still be found here and there. There were twenty or so in

77 Cast-iron lock at Beeston, Cheshire, built by Telford to withstand the pressures of shifting sand

south-west England alone, notably on the Bude Canal and the Torrington Canal in north Devon, where remains of Ridd incline (163/SS 476217) can still be traced. On most of these the boats themselves—usually tub boats about 20ft long—were hauled up the inclines in cradles or water-filled caissons running on rails. Perhaps the most spectacular and well preserved canal incline, which was also used for tub boats, is that at Coalport in Shropshire (119/SJ 695028). There was a vertical fall of 207ft between the upper line of the canal and the point at the foot of the Severn Gorge where goods were transhipped from the tub boats into barges on the river. This incline fell into disuse about 1900, but its alignment has been cleared by the Ironbridge Gorge Museum Trust, which hopes eventually to have it operating again. The incline installed at Foxton, Leicestershire (133/SP 692895), in 1900 with the object of superseding the time-consuming staircase of locks is less easy to trace. The incline was of the counterbalanced type, with movable tanks or caissons on wheels into which the narrow boats were floated. A steam engine at the top provided the power, but trouble was experienced with subsidence of the rails, and the volume of traffic did not justify the expense of keeping a boiler constantly in steam with staff in attendance. The incline had ceased to be used regularly by 1910 and the machinery was sold for scrap in 1928. Today the original locks are still in active use, but the unfortunate incline is rapidly disappearing into a jungle of brambles.

The only canal lift still in use (Plate 78) in Britain is that at Anderton (101/SJ 647753), near Northwich. It allows boats to pass between the Trent & Mersey Canal and the River Weaver Navigation some 50ft below. A proposal for a lift had been put forward as early as 1865 by E. Leader Williams, engineer to the Weaver Navigation, with the idea of facilitating the interchange of traffic between the two waterways, but not until 1872 were the necessary Acts passed and Emmerson & Co given the lift contract. The design was by Edwin Clark of Clark, Standfield & Clark, consulting engineers of Westminster. As completed in 1875, the Anderton lift had two wrought-iron caissons 75ft by 15½ft by 5ft rising and falling a distance of 50ft 4in within a substantial tubular iron framework. Each caisson could take two narrow boats or one barge and weighed 240 tons with its water. The caissons were supported on 3ft diameter hydraulic rams, the two rams being connected by a 5in pipe. Removing 6in of water, weighing some 15 tons, from the lower caisson made the heavier upper caisson descend,

78 Anderton boat lift, Cheshire, connecting the Weaver Navigation with the Trent & Mersey Canal

and water passed through the transfer pipe to the other ram caused the second caisson to rise. The final lift of 4ft was achieved by closing the transfer pipe and connecting the upper press to a steam-powered hydraulic pump and accumulator. Although a press burst in 1882, the Anderton design was a good one and formed the basis for other lifts in France and Belgium. In 1903 electricity replaced steam power for the hydraulic pumps and in 1908 further substantial modifications dispensed with hydraulic operation altogether in order to simplify working and increase capacity. As rebuilt, the lift's caissons are counterbalanced by cast-iron weights and can be operated independently. Power is provided by an electric motor driving through gears. In 1913 the lift transferred a record 226,000 tons of traffic, more than would have been possible before reconstruction. Today it is still in regular use, mainly by pleasure boats, and a 'voyage' in it is a fascinating if slightly unnerving experience. One may make an excellent trip on a hire boat such as the *Lapwing* from Weston Docks, Runcorn (109/SJ 503830), up through the large 220ft x 41½ft locks of the Weaver to Anderton and up the lift, and then along the Trent & Mersey Canal through three tortuously narrow tunnels to the delightful little canal hamlet of Preston Brook. Here, at the junction of the Trent & Mersey and Bridgewater Canals (109/SJ 568806) one finds canal cottages, a large warehouse now used as a club, and a small roofed drydock.

On many canals there was no alternative to a tunnel when it came to cutting through hilly country. Canal tunnels are usually, although by no means always, on the summit level, crossing the watershed between one side of the navigation and the other. The first were on Brindley's Trent & Mersey Canal at Preston Brook (1,239yd, 109/SJ 570799), Saltersford (424yd, 101/SJ 624753), Barnton (572yd, 101/SJ 630749), and Harecastle. The latter, with its 2,880yd bore, carried the summit level under Harecastle Hill, the watershed between the valley of the Trent and the Cheshire plain. The original tunnel at Harecastle, like others on the canal, had a very small bore— only 9ft 3in wide and 12ft high (110/SJ 837542). Boats had to be legged through, the 'leggers' lying on narrow boards sprung out from either side of the boat and walking on the sides of the tunnel to push it through. In 1827 a new tunnel, parallel with the old, was completed to designs of Thomas Telford. It was of large section and had a towpath, but this has now been demolished. For some 90 years both tunnels were worked on a one-way system, but in 1918 colliery subsidence necessitated closure of the older bore.

Of even smaller section than the old Harecastle tunnel is Standedge tunnel (102/SE 006079 to 040120) on the Huddersfield Narrow Canal, which in places is only 8ft 6in high and 7ft 6in wide. Standedge, completed in 1811, is the longest canal tunnel in Britain (5,698yd) and on the highest summit above sea level. The 4¼ mile level through the Pennines between Diggle and Marsden is 645ft above Ordnance datum. Although the canal was abandoned in 1944, the tunnel is still navigable. A through passage in a properly organised party is an eerie experience, as the bore opens out at intervals into caverns blasted in the rock where boats can pass. A faint glimmer of light penetrates occasionally through the ventilation shafts, and the rumble of trains in the neighbouring railway tunnel sounds through the interconnecting galleries used by the engineers of half a century later to gain access to their workings. Several of the larger canal tunnels are now impassable, although in most cases their portals and ventilation shaft tops can still be traced. The 3,817yd Sapperton Tunnel in Gloucestershire, on the summit level of the Thames & Severn Canal beneath the Cotswolds, is waterless and in part collapsed. For some years before its closure in 1911 the canal had water supply problems, owing largely to the dry and porous limestone country through which it passed. The east portal (157/SO 966006) of Sapperton is one of the few canal tunnel entrances to have any architectural pretensions, with two niches (but no statues) flanked by finely cut pilasters. The west portal (157/SO 944034) by contrast is very simple.

The 3,795yd Lappal Tunnel between Halesowen and Selly Oak on the Birmingham Canal has, like Harecastle, suffered from mining subsidence and collapsed. So too has Norwood Tunnel, 2,895yd, on the Chesterfield Canal, and Butterley Tunnel, 3,063yd, on the Cromford Canal. The longest tunnel still in regular use on a through navigation in Britain was Blisworth (146/SP 729529 to 739503), 3,056yd, on the Grand Union Canal in Northamptonshire until the recent restoration of Parkhead locks put the 3,172yd Dudley Tunnel on a pleasure craft route. Blisworth Tunnel caused its builders a great deal of trouble, the first borings being a complete failure owing to excessive water finding its way into the workings. Work stopped in 1796, and it was not until 1802 that a new start was made with another tunnel on a slightly different line. This was eventually completed in March 1805, nearly 5 years after the rest of the canal had opened. Before the tunnel was finished, a double-track horse tramroad ran over the hill from Blisworth Wharf to what is now the foot of Stoke Bruerne locks. Time in the Blisworth area will be well spent in a visit to the Waterways Museum at Stoke Bruerne (146/SP 743500), where there are a number of open-air exhibits, including a boat-weighing machine, plus a unique collection of relics housed in an old grain warehouse covering the rich history of 200 years of canals and their people.

Of all the engineering works of the great canal builders, aqueducts have fired the imagination and excited the greatest wonder. Designed to bridge valleys that could not easily be negotiated by flight of locks, they were objects of incredulity at the time they were built. Many have survived the railway age, which had its own proliferation of great viaducts, with their splendour undiminished. Brindley's pioneer Barton Aqueduct—'the castle in the air', Smeaton called it—has already been mentioned. In fact it was the highest and visually most spectacular of Brindley's numerous aqueducts, most of which are squat brick or masonry structures providing little more than multiple culverts for the rivers underneath. The Dove Aqueduct (120/SK 269269) on the Trent & Mersey Canal near Burton-on-Trent is a typical example. With approaches it is 1¼ miles long and has twenty-three low arches. Others carry the Staffordshire & Worcestershire Canal over the Trent at Great Haywood (119/SJ 994229) and the Sow at Milford (119/SJ 973215).

William Edwards' precedent of pierced spandrels, which appeared in his graceful Pontypridd Bridge of 1755, was used by Benjamin Outram, engineer to the Peak Forest Canal, when he built Marple Aqueduct (101/SJ 956900) across the River Goyt. Designed to reduce the structure's self-weight, the holes also visually lighten and enhance the appearance of the aqueduct. For real elegance and panache, however, the masonry aqueducts of John Rennie are unsurpassed. Of classical proportions and detailing, his Dundas Aqueduct, a single-arch span carrying the Kennet & Avon Canal over the River Avon near Monkton Combe (166/ST 784625) in Somerset, blends into the steep wooded valley and completes the landscape in a very English way. The warm limestone provides a perfect medium for an architectural treatment of the structure appropriate to nearby Bath. Three miles to the south the canal recrosses the river at Avoncliff (166/ST 805600), but here neither the design nor the present condition of the structure are as good. The bed is dry, revealing the cement lining of the trough, while the stonework is covered with mysterious masons' marks. The sag in the centre of the river span is thought to have occurred soon after the aqueduct was completed in 1805. A larger and more severe example of Rennie's work is the Lune Aqueduct, Lancaster (89/SD 484639), which has five arches, each of 70ft span, carrying the Lancaster Canal 51ft above the surface of the river (Plate 79). Built in a hard grey sandstone, its top decorated with a handsome Doric cornice and balustrade, it too blends into the harsher north Lancashire landscape, a fine combination of functional simplicity and elegance in design. The architect, Alexander Stevens (1730–96), possibly collaborated with Rennie on its detailing.

The supreme heights of engineering accomplishment resulted from the use of cast iron in the building of aqueducts, although, unlike the first iron bridge, the earliest examples had an experimental lack of confidence. Possibly

79 John Rennie's aqueduct across the River Lune near Lancaster

the first use of the material was in a small aqueduct in Derby, now demolished, but here it only formed part of the whole structure. One month after the opening of this Derby aqueduct, in March 1796, Telford completed his crossing of the river at Longdon-on-Tern in Shropshire (118/SJ 617156) with the claim, 'I believe this to be the first aqueduct for the purposes of a navigable canal which has ever been composed of this metal.' Certainly in Telford's aqueduct (Plate 80) cast iron has real structural significance, not only in the construction of the trough itself but also in the supporting legs and partly cantilevered towpath. More important, however, was the opportunity Longdon gave Telford to test and demonstrate iron as a constructional material before building his masterpiece at Pont Cysyllte. Longdon-upon-Tern Aqueduct is a modest structure, with two full spans, one across the river, and two half spans springing from the brick and masonry abutments. The cast-iron sections are arranged in a similar manner to the voussoirs of a masonry arch and bolted together through flanges. The towpath is attached to the outside of the trough, which is thus of the minimum cross

80 Longdon-on-Tern Aqueduct, Shropshire, by Thomas Telford. The first iron aqueduct in the world, built in 1796

section necessary for a boat to pass, a design error that was not repeated at Pont Cysyllte. The problem with the Longdon arrangement was that great effort was needed to pull a boat through, as it was difficult for water to pass between the sides and bottom of the boat and the trough itself; at Pont Cysyllte the towpath projects inwards over a wide trough, leaving plenty of space for the water to pass.

Telford's great test came when he was resident engineer to William Jessop on the Ellesmere Canal. Here the problem was one of carrying the canal across the valleys of the Rivers Ceiriog and Dee as part of a project originally intended to tap the coal and iron district around Ruabon and the Irenant quarries near Valle Crucis, Llangollen. The aqueduct across the Ceiriog at Chirk (118/SJ 287372) has always been somewhat overshadowed by the proximity of its great neighbour, but on any other canal it would be regarded as an outstanding work. It has ten arches, each of 40ft span, carrying the canal 70ft above the river. Although the structure of the piers and arches is of stone and appears conventional in every respect, the trough itself consists of cast-iron plates, flanged and bolted together, which effectively tie in the side walls of the aqueduct. Telford appreciated that a puddle-clay-lined trough of the type used by Brindley, together with the massive masonry necessary to contain the pressure of water, would impose impossible weights on the foundations of the piers; hence the use of cast iron. The foundation stone of Chirk Aqueduct was laid on 17 June 1796 and it was completed in 1801.

The canal runs north from the aqueduct through the 459yd Chirk Tunnel (one of the first to have a towpath) towards the much larger valley of the Dee. Here, at Pont Cysyllte (117/SJ 271420), across the Vale of Llangollen, Telford carried the canal more than 120ft above the river on an aqueduct which has remained one of the great engineering achievements of all time. Compared with the alternative, of locks down each side of the valley, an aqueduct seems the obvious solution; it is the scale and sheer engineering elegance of that solution, however, which gives Pont Cysyllte a justified place amongst the industrial archaeological sights of Britain.

At Pont Cysyllte, as we have said, Telford adopted a trough construction entirely of cast iron, and the side sections, as at Longdon, are wedge-shaped to form an arch-like structure. Unlike Longdon, however, the trough is supported underneath by cross-braced cast-iron ribs (Plate 81), four beneath each span. The trough width is 11ft 10in and the deck of the towpath, 4ft 8in wide, is supported over the water surface on iron pillars. Cast-iron railings protect its outer edge, but on the opposite side the water level is only a few inches below the unprotected edge of the trough wall. Nineteen spans, each of 53ft, make a total length of 1,007ft between the approach embankments, the south one of which, with its height of 97ft at

81 Developed from Longdon, the trough sections of Telford's Pont Cysyllte Aqueduct are supported on cast-iron ribs

the tip, was the greatest earthwork in Britain at the time of its construction. The piers supporting the trough are of some interest in that, to reduce weight, they are of hollow construction from a height of 70ft upwards, with external walls only 2ft thick. Internal cross walls, used also in the hollow spandrels of Chirk Aqueduct and most of Telford's road bridges, provide the necessary structural stiffening. Today the Pont Cysyllte Aqueduct has much the same appearance as it did on its opening day in November 1805 and, although neglected and in ill-repair for many years, it is now scheduled as an ancient monument by the Department of the Environment and kept in a sound condition befitting perhaps the greatest single engineering epic of the canal age.

Another aqueduct worthy of notice is the Bearley (131/SP 162609) on the Stratford-upon-Avon Canal.

As the network of canals spread and the internal trade of the nation developed, a whole new transport industry supporting merchants, boatmen, suppliers of provisions, warehousemen, lock-keepers and lengthmen grew up also. This industry made its impact on the landscape in the form of new buildings ranging from tiny and uncompromisingly simple canal-side cottages to new townships with handsome mansions and warehouses. Few canal buildings exhibit any conscious architectural expression, and many of the smaller ones are a straightforward and economical translation of contemporary domestic traditions to new circumstances. Exceptions are inevitable and one only has to look at the Regency-style bridge-men's houses on the Gloucester & Berkeley Canal, the barrel-roofed Stratford-upon-Avon Canal cottages or the round-tower canal houses of the Thames & Severn to appreciate that here and there some architectural thought was involved. These are very much the exceptions, however, and the general rule, as exemplified by hundreds of little known and unpretentious structures, is in great contrast to the railway buildings of the following century.

At various places on the canal network junctions and transhipment points resulted in concentrations of canal-side buildings which in some cases have developed into independent communities. Some of these new towns of the canal era, small in comparison with the developments which were to occur in the age of the railways, still survive substantially intact and are among the earliest specialised industrial urban groupings in Britain. Perhaps the best known, and certainly the most highly developed of these communities, is

82 Wharf crane, Bumblehole Basin, Netherton, Dudley, Worcestershire

Stourport-on-Severn (130/SO 810710), built at the end of the eighteenth century as a trading and transhipment centre where the Staffordshire & Worcestershire Canal locks down to the River Severn. It became, in effect, an inland port between the Midlands and the sea, where goods could be transferred from canal narrow boats to river-going barges and sailing trows that voyaged down to Bristol and the South Wales ports. Here in Worcestershire Brindley 'caused a town to be erected, made a port and dockyards, built a new elegant bridge, established markets and made it the wonder not only of this county but of the nation at large.' Although the bridge was replaced by a larger cast-iron span during the nineteenth century, the centre of Stourport has changed little. It just survived the neglect following the decline of canals and is now reviving as a leisure boating centre. A fine brick ware-house with clock tower, stately merchants' houses and humble cottages all reflect the unselfconscious inspiration of the early Industrial Revolution. At Shardlow (121/SK 444304), near the junction of the Trent & Mersey Canal and the River Trent, stands another such point of interchange, built purely for commercial purposes but exhibiting through the architecture of its warehouses a functional beauty deriving from the simple use of traditional building materials. Warehouses of a more spectacular scale may be seen at

Ellesmere Port, in Cheshire (109/SJ 405775), another junction, between the Wirral line of Jessop and Telford's Ellesmere & Chester Canal and the River Mersey. Dating originally from 1795, Ellesmere Port continued to grow until the 1850s, suffered a temporary relapse, and thrived again after the completion of the Manchester Ship Canal in the 1890s, although its prosperity then no longer came from inland canal traffic. Unfortunately Telford's great general warehouse, one of the finest structures on Britain's waterways, has now gone, destroyed by fire in 1970, but other impressive structures still survive and the general arrangement and layout of the port and its facilities are worthy of examination.

Today much of the canal network, the larger part of which is no longer used at all for commercial purposes, is undergoing a transformation. Groups of enthusiasts working in cooperation with the British Waterways Board are energetically putting many of the more scenic routes back into commission for leisure purposes; the names and addresses of the leading societies and coordinating bodies are given in Appendix 3. Already the northern section of the Stratford-upon-Avon Canal is operational again, restored from a state of complete dereliction, and working parties are active on canals such as the Peak Forest, the Kennet & Avon and the Caldon. Moreover, the amenity value of waterways is also being recognised by local authorities, and enterprising conservation schemes have been carried out in the Little Venice area of Paddington; at Farmer's Bridge, Birmingham, the junction of the Birmingham Canal Navigation main line and the Birmingham & Fazeley Canal; and at the nearby Gas Street basin. Tree planting, landscaping and the rehabilitation of derelict canal-side cottages all contribute to the success of schemes which amply demonstrate that the canal in an urban area does not have to be an eyesore.

Although the future of the narrow canal system must lie in amenity usage, there are a number of commercial waterways actively in operation and employing in many cases up-to-date cargo-handling techniques. Centred on the Humber are the Aire & Calder Navigation, giving access for 540 ton barges to Leeds and Wakefield, and the Sheffield & South Yorkshire and Trent Navigations, running to Rotherham and Nottingham respectively. The Weaver Navigation can take sizeable ships, as can the Gloucester & Sharpness Ship Canal, a link in the navigation of the Severn up to Stourport. The South East has the Thames and the River Lee. Only on these kinds of waterway, and of course the Manchester Ship Canal, can further cargo-carrying developments be expected. On the majority of inland navigations the commercial traffic which brought them into existence in the second half of the eighteenth century has gone for ever, and only the archaeological remains reflect the buoyant enthusiasm, panache and grinding labour of the canal promoters, their engineers and navvies.

15 Railways

THE railway captured the imagination of the people as did no other form of industrial technology. In the country of origin of the steam locomotive, the UK, and elsewhere too, the opening of a new railway line was almost always an occasion for festivities and rejoicing. A century or more later the demise of steam on British Railways in the late 1960s evoked a wave of nostalgia quite without precedent. Today more than 900 steam railway locomotives are preserved in Britain in museums, on privately owned branch lines, or merely on short stretches of track where they can be put into steam for a few hours at a weekend. The railway was the first form of transport with which the mass of the populace had any contact, and as such it has been regarded as rightfully subject to both public criticism and affection. Criticism of railways and their methods of operation has always been a fashionable sport, while affection, of almost equally long standing, has centred largely around the mystique of the steam locomotive. Much of the enormous bibliography which railways have generated is also devoted to steam power, so in this chapter the civil engineering works, the 'real estate' of the railways, will be considered primarily.

The idea of using rails for vehicular traffic dates back much further than the steam locomotive, and this early period, which might be called the 'prehistory' of railways, can be a fruitful area of study for the industrial archaeologist. The profusion of field remains and frequent wealth of documentary and cartographic information has enabled a remarkably complete picture to be built up of the role of the railway before the coming of steam power. Specifically archaeological evidence has made a major contribution. The first use of rails in Britain was probably in the late sixteenth century in Shropshire, Nottinghamshire and Northumberland. In these areas lines were built for moving coal relatively short distances to rivers or the coast, where boats could load it. The rails were made of wood, as at first were the wheels that ran on them. Not until the second quarter of the eighteenth century were iron wheels employed and wooden rails faced with iron plates to reduce wear.

The first known use of iron rails was in 1767. Cast at Coalbrookdale in Shropshire, they were thereafter used extensively on local lines in and around coal workings and also in South Wales. They were 'edge rails', designed for use with flanged wheels, and were probably laid on timber cross sleepers. In the 1780s iron rails of an 'L' section—with the flange cast on the rail instead of on the wheel—were introduced and quickly became popular. In South Wales, for example, some 300 route miles of this 'plateway' were in use in the early years of the nineteenth century, and in Shropshire, the birthplace of the iron edge rail, the L section plates became almost universal (Plate 83). The new rails were supposedly stronger than the edge rails, but it is doubtful if the other claimed benefit—that the vehicles could be used off the rails in colliery yards—was found to be particularly useful.

A note on terminology is relevant here, as a variety of sometimes conflicting nomenclature has been applied to these early pre-locomotive railways. All were technically railways, in that the vehicles ran on rails, although the term 'railroad' was more widely used before 1830 and was later adopted as standard in North America. In the North of England particularly, where edge rails were favoured, 'waggonway' was used, and this persisted until relatively recently. Elsewhere, however, 'tramroad', 'dramroad' and 'tramway' were after 1790 applied specifically to lines employing L section rails. The origin of these terms is uncertain, but they possibly derive from

83 Dual-gauge cast-iron plateway, Coalbrookdale, Shropshire

the old German or Scandinavian words for a beam of wood, a 'traam', which might have been the rail. Certainly 'trammy' and 'tram' were applied to the vehicles themselves in the sixteenth century. There is no evidence to support the theory that 'tramroad' had any connection with the name of Benjamin Outram, one of the chief protagonists of the cast-iron rail. Later in the nineteenth century, of course, the word tramway was revived in a different context, to describe the new passenger-carrying street tramways, first horse-drawn and later electrically propelled. Yet another word specifically applied to the early railways using L section iron rails was 'plateway', from which the modern term 'platelayer' originates.

   Three distinct forms of pre-locomotive railway developed before 1830 and all were in operation side by side at the outbreak of the steam-powered railway revolution. The first type, as we have seen, comprised lines built and usually owned by coalowners to connect their collieries with existing river or sea transport. Successors to these are still operated, as conventional railways, by the National Coal Board in County Durham, one of the longest systems being the Bowes Railway, with lines radiating south-westwards from Jarrow Staithes (78/NZ 353650) towards Pontop. The second type of tramway was built as an adjunct to a canal and was usually owned by the canal company. Tramways were less restricted by topography than canals, and from the 1780s onwards were built in large numbers as feeders to canal branches. The third variety came into being on 26 July 1803 when the Surrey Iron Railway was opened as a double-track public tramway from the Thames at Wandsworth to Croydon, 9 miles away. This line, which was seen as a possible first stage in a route from London to Portsmouth, heralded the era of public lines promoted as common carriers by separate railway companies.

   Of the colliery-owned and operated lines, numerous remains survive, particularly in the North East. One of these remains, at Tanfield in County Durham, is the Causey Arch, built in 1727 and generally accepted as the oldest existing railway bridge (78/NZ 220537). It is a spectacular masonry structure about 60ft high, its span of 103ft the fifth largest of any masonry railway bridge in Britain. Near Whitfield, also south of the Tyne, early eighteenth-century tramway earthworks are to be seen at High Spen (78/NZ 137596).

   One of the earliest surviving railway buildings is a weigh-house of 1799 at Brampton Sands, Cumberland (76/NY 550600), on the alignment of the Brampton Railway, an extension of the Tindale Fell Waggonway opened about 1775. Near Kirkhouse, cuttings and embankments are easily traceable (76/NY 567599), while the earthworks of the Parker waggonway, south of Whitehaven harbour, can be seen at Monkwray Brow (82/NX 969167). This line, owned by Sir James Lowther, was opened in 1738.

The 6 mile Middleton Colliery Railway in Leeds, dating from 1758, was built under Parliamentary Acts and is thus claimed to be the first officially authorised railway. Not a great deal can be seen of the original alignment, but the incline, known as the 'Old Run', can still be traced and stone sleepers are visible on Hunslet Moor where they have been re-used as platform edging. Three miles of the railway are operated with steam locomotives by the Middleton Railway Trust. Some of the line is protected by the National Trust.

Lines feeding canals are well represented archaeologically and, unlike the colliery lines, which are mainly in the north, they are concentrated primarily in midland and southern England where the canal network was densest. One of the earliest examples ran from the Froghall basin terminus of the Caldon Canal in Staffordshire (111/SK 028477) to limestone quarries at Cauldon Lowe. The canal itself, a branch from the Trent & Mersey, at Etruria passes through the Churnet valley and some of the finest scenery in north Staffordshire. It is being restored by the Caldon Canal Society. Remains of the tramway, built originally in 1777, and realigned in 1783 and again in 1802 (by John Rennie), are numerous. At Woodcock there is a ruined bridge and at Whiston a complete bridge, an embankment and the remains of one of the three self-acting inclined planes (111/SK 029476).

In Derbyshire extensive remains can be seen of the Peak Forest tramway engineered by Benjamin Outram and opened in 1796 from Bugsworth (now politely renamed Buxworth) basin (111/SK 020820) to Chapel-en-le-Frith and limestone quarries at Doveholes. The 85yd tunnel at Chapel Milton (111/SK 058817) must be the earliest railway tunnel in the world. Much of the alignment can be traced, including long lines of stone sleeper blocks. A wagon is preserved in York Railway Museum.

Another well preserved line extended from Willesley on the Ashby-de-la-Zouch Canal in Leicestershire to limestone quarries at Ticknall and Cloud Hill in Derbyshire. The best sites are in Ticknall itself, where a bridge crosses the main street (121/SK 356240) and a 138yd cut-and-cover tunnel has been put in to preserve the amenities of the approach to Calke Abbey (121/SK 355238). On the Somersetshire Coal Canal sparse remains can be seen of an inclined plane tramway that was laid as a temporary link at Combe Hay (166/ST 748604) while a flight of twenty-two locks was being built. The alignment of a similar type of tramway, later used as a bridle path, links the two ends of Blisworth Tunnel (146/SP 729529 to 739503). It was used between 1800 and 1805 to connect the two ends of the canal while the tunnel itself was under construction. A permanent inclined plane for the transhipment of goods from canal boats to wagons connected the terminus of the Tavistock Canal above Morwellham with quays on the River Tamar 247ft below (187/SX 446698). It was opened in 1817. The remains of slate sleepers are preserved in the Morwellham Quay Centre for Recreation & Education.

Of the lines built to link sections of canal, the longest was the Cromford & High Peak Railway in Derbyshire, opened in 1831 to join the Cromford Canal with the Peak Forest Canal near Whaley Bridge. Tapping the lime-stone resources of the Peak, it spanned 34 miles of central Derbyshire, reaching at its summit a height of 1,266ft above sea level. Inclines connected the central sections with the termini. Much of the line, which was using steam locomotives as early as 1834, remained in use as a railway rather than a tramway until 1967. Miles of its trackbed can be walked, including the two great inclines—Middleton and Sheep Pasture. At Middleton Top (111/SK 275552) the steam winding engine is preserved.

The biggest mileage of canal-owned tramways was in South Wales, where almost all the companies had extensive feeder networks. The Monmouth-shire Canal, for example, owned 14 route miles of railway, comprising nine separate lines. A particular advantage many of these coal-carrying lines enjoyed was that the down gradient favoured the loaded trains. There is a bridge at Blaenavon in Prince Street, and a milepost at Abersychan. Also in Monmouthshire, although not on canal-owned lines, are the 2,050ft Pwll-Ddu Tunnel, opened in 1815 partly through old mine workings (141/SO 248114), and a fine bridge carrying an incline (Plate 84) on the Redbrook branch of the Monmouth Railway, opened in 1812 (142/SO 537103).

It was inevitable that the success of the tramway as an aid to canal and river transport should result in its use as a common carrier in its own right

84 Tramway incline bridge in the Wye Valley at Redbrook, Monmouthshire

for providing cross-country links. The Surrey Iron Railway of 1803 was the first and others followed quickly. By the 1820s several of these horse-drawn public railways were being authorised each year, mainly for freight haulage, although as early as 1807 the Oystermouth Railway running along the coast between Swansea and the Mumbles was carrying fare-paying passengers. It is important to appreciate that the railway proved its value, and perhaps even its superiority over the canal, before the introduction of steam power, and that by the mid 1820s inter-city routes were being pro-posed. Lines such as the Sirhowy (1802), the Severn & Wye (1809), the Mansfield & Pinxton (1817) and the Stratford & Moreton (1821) were all conceived as horse railways, and as such were highly successful. Some of their major civil engineering works remain, such as the bridge across the River Avon at Stratford (144/SP 205548) now used as a footbridge. Some re-erected track of the Surrey Iron Railway can be seen on its original alignment at Purley Rotary Field (170/TQ 316622) and some more, though not on the old route, at the *Joliffe Arms* (170/TQ 290543) and outside Wallington branch library (170/TQ 288638). In Ayrshire there are notable tramway bridge remains at Fairlie (67/NS 383369), where the Kilmarnock & Troon Railway crossed the River Irvine, and the remains of an early skew bridge on the Doura branch of the Ardrossan & Johnstone Railway (59/NS 338423).

It took just 25 years for the locomotive to prove itself the most suitable means of applying the power of steam to railways. Richard Trevithick (1771–1833) built what is generally considered to be the first steam railway locomotive at the Coalbrookdale Ironworks in Shropshire in 1802, and 2 years later operated a similar machine successfully on the Penydarran Railway in South Wales (154/ST 083969). For a quarter of a century the locomotive developed spasmodically, in competition with the use of stationary steam engines to haul trains with cables, until in 1829 the railway engineer George Stephenson, in an effort to decide which form of power to apply to the Liverpool & Manchester Railway, then in an advanced stage of construction, proved beyond all doubt that the steam engine should move with the train. The Rainhill trials of 1829, won by Stephenson's own *Rocket*, were the turning point in the fortunes of the locomotive and the effective beginning of the railway revolution.

A number of 'pre-Rainhill' locomotives are preserved, and they demonstrate clearly the evolution of design. Trevithick was a pioneer of high-pressure steam in stationary engines—that is engines operating at a pressure of 20–25lb per sq in—and it was this use of high pressure that provided the key to the successful development of the locomotive. The great size of the low-pressure beam engine, and more particularly its enormous condensing apparatus, prevented its use as a mobile power source. Trevithick's own locomotive, which has not survived, employed a horizontal cylinder of small bore and long stroke rather like his stationary engines. Similarly other early locomotives were adaptations of available high pressure designs. *Wylam Dilly* in the Royal Scottish Museum, Edinburgh, and *Puffing Billy* in the Science Museum, London, both dating from 1812–13, are in effect grasshopper engines on wheels, whereas the Hetton Colliery locomotive of 1822, preserved at the York Railway Museum, and the Killingworth locomotive in the Newcastle Museum of Science & Engineering have the more direct form of drive of the Maudslay table engine. By the late 1820s locomotives were being built with pistons connected directly to their wheels through piston and connecting rods. *Sans Pareil* and *Rocket*, both contenders at Rainhill and both preserved in the Science Museum, London, are of this type. More important at this date, however, was the way in which the boiler was developing, with numerous tubes between firebox and smokebox giving it a good steaming rate. It was primarily the superiority of its boiler

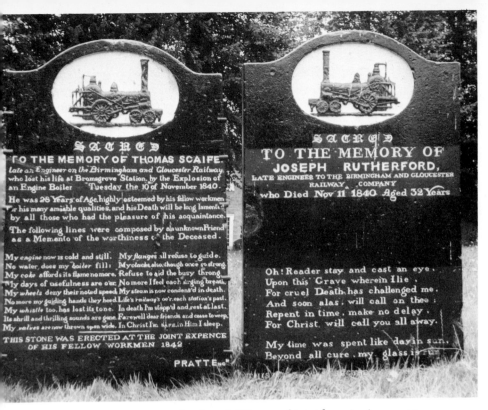

SACRED
TO THE MEMORY OF THOMAS SCAIFE,
late an Engineer on the Birmingham and Gloucester Railway,
who lost his life at Bromsgrove Station, by the Explosion of
an Engine Boiler   Tuesday the 10 of November 1840.

He was 28 Years of Age, highly esteemed by his fellow workmen
for his many amiable qualities, and his Death will be long lamented
by all those who had the pleasure of his acquaintance.

The following lines were composed by an unknown Friend
as a Memento of the worthiness of the Deceased.

My engine now is cold and still.   My flanges all refuse to guide.
No water does my boiler fill;   My coke also, though once so strong,
My coke affords its flame no more.   Refuse to aid the busy throng,
My days of usefulness are o'er.   No more I feel each urging breath.
My wheels deny their noted speed.   My steam is now condens'd in death.
No more my guiding hands they heed.   Life's railway's o'er, each station's past.
My whistle too, has lost its tone.   In death I'm stopp'd and rest at last.
Its shrill and thrilling sounds are gone.   Farewell dear friends and cease to weep,
My valves are now thrown open wide.   In Christ I'm safe, in Him I sleep.

THIS STONE WAS ERECTED AT THE JOINT EXPENCE
OF HIS FELLOW WORKMEN 1842

PRATT Enc.

SACRED
TO THE MEMORY OF
JOSEPH   RUTHERFORD,
LATE ENGINEER TO THE BIRMINGHAM AND GLOUCESTER
RAILWAY,   COMPANY
who Died Nov 11 1840. Aged 32 Years

Oh! Reader stay, and cast an eye,
Upon this Grave wherein I lie.
For cruel Death has challenged me,
And soon alas, will call on thee;
Repent in time, make no delay,
For Christ, will call you all away.

My time was spent like day in sun.
Beyond all cure, my glass is run.

85 Gravestones in Bromsgrove Churchyard, Worcestershire, of two enginemen on
the Birmingham & Gloucester Railway killed by a boiler explosion in 1840

that gave *Rocket* the edge over its competitors at Rainhill. Within 5 years
Stephenson engines such as *Northumbrian* and *Planet* had established the
general form of the locomotive, which was to survive virtually unaltered
until the demise of steam power on British Rail in the 1960s.

The success of the steam locomotive was very much a personal triumph
for George Stephenson (1781–1848) and his son Robert (1803–1859). In
1825 the elder Stephenson had engineered the first public railway on which
steam locomotion was used, although initially only on a small scale, between
Stockton & Darlington. Five years later he built the Liverpool & Manchester,
the first railway to carry passengers and the first to be completely steam-
worked from the beginning. Both were built to the now standard gauge of
4ft 8½in. The origins of this gauge are obscure but it seems likely to have
evolved from the tramways of the North East, a natural derivation from the

width between pairs of horse-drawn cartwheels. The Stephensons were unrivalled as railway engineers in the early 1830s, and it was their appreciation that one day all local lines would be joined together in a nationwide network that led to the adoption of the 4ft 8½in gauge throughout most of the country. Only one major line, the Great Western, brainchild of the brilliant engineer Isambard Kingdom Brunel, did not adopt standard gauge.

Lines such as the Stockton & Darlington and the Liverpool & Manchester, and other contemporaries like the Canterbury & Whitstable and the Leicester & Swannington, had been built to satisfy specific local requirements for the haulage of goods, but in the event the traffic pattern was quite different; passenger receipts were more than double freight takings on the L & MR right down to the mid-1840s, and the national consciousness suddenly became aware that big profits were there for the taking. By 1836 nearly 2,000 route miles of railway had been sanctioned, including most of what were to become the major trunk routes focused on London. The first of these was Stephenson's superbly engineered London & Birmingham, to be quickly followed by routes from the capital to Southampton, Brighton

86 Gatekeeper's cottage at Glenfield level crossing, Leicester & Swannington Railway, 1832. Demolished

and Bristol, by an extension of the L & BR northwards into Lancashire, and by a collection of small lines which eventually linked London with York, the North East and Scotland. Three of these—the Midland Counties, the Birmingham & Derby Junction and the North Midland—amalgamated in 1844 to form the Midland Railway, one of the largest companies not to have a London terminus, a fact which was significantly to alter the skyline of the Euston Road a quarter of a century later.

The 'railway revolution' born out of the success of lines like the Liverpool & Manchester and London & Birmingham got going in earnest in the 1840s. It was one of the most remarkable phenomena of the whole period of Britain's industrialisation. The landscape changes the railway brought about were more widespread and more fundamental than those created by any other industry, and this is reflected today in the profusion of remains. The direct effects could be seen in terms of embankments and cuttings, viaducts and tunnels, on the one hand, and by new towns such as Crewe and Swindon, which were creations of the railway companies themselves, on the other. Less direct but just as obvious was the increase in general economic activity brought about by the improvement in transport, a trend that had begun with canals and accelerated rapidly with the coming of railways. Railways performed the same basic economic function as canals, shifting bulk goods at low cost. In addition, however, they offered the equivalent, on a larger scale, of the best eighteenth-century post roads, which provided rapid communication for people, mail and specialised freight.

The enormous impact the railway had on the economy and the scale of its development are worth studying. To the success of the second-generation steam railways—early main lines like the London & Brimingham of 1838 and the Great Western of 1841—may be directly attributed the enormous boom in railway building which reached a peak in 1848, when 1,253 miles were opened. The peak years for sanctioning construction were 1845 (2,816 miles), 1846 (4,540 miles) and 1847 (1,295 miles). Many lines promoted in these frantic years of the mid-1840s were never built, so that by 1851, when a total of 12,698 miles had been sanctioned, only a little over half (6,803 miles) had been completed. This in itself was a formidable figure. During the years 1846–8 railway investment was absorbing 5–7 per cent of the national income, about half the total capital investment and equivalent to about two-thirds of the value of all exports. It entailed a wage

bill of £16 million for a construction force of 250,000, and by 1850 there
were 60,000 employees running the new railways. The significance of railway building in the national economy was such that during the late 1840s
and the 1850s the railway industry itself could be regarded as a major factor
in determining the cyclic movements of the economy. Iron, coal and brick
prices moved in parallel with the timing of railway contracts; indeed the
demands of the railways were almost solely responsible for the enormous
growth in iron rolling mills during the 1850s and 1860s. By 1850 railway
locomotives were burning 1 million tons of coal a year, and, although this
was only some 2 per cent of national production, the railway-stimulated
industries all consumed their share too. Railway development led directly
to increased urban growth, while the railway industry itself became one of
the greatest breeding grounds of the new technocrats who were to be the
mainstay of Victorian industrial might. The effect on other transport
systems was cataclysmic. By the 1850s the long-distance road coach had been
virtually eliminated and most canals rendered unprofitable. There was a
real deterioration in road conditions in many parts of Britain as the turnpike trusts were wound up and road maintenance became again the responsibility of a reluctant parish.

With the completion of the Great Northern main line between King's
Cross and York in 1852, nearly all the major routes of the modern railway
system in England had been developed. All the major industrial areas, cities
and ports were linked by a network which, although its individual components belonged to dozens of separate companies, could be regarded as a
national railway system. There was still much filling in of the gaps to be
undertaken, however, and both Wales and Scotland, with the exception of
the industrial lowlands, were virtually without railway lines. By 1914, its
approximate peak, the total network of the United Kingdom was 23,000
miles. The £1,300 million invested in the system had created the most
expensive, extravagant, wasteful and at the same time spectacular symbol of
Victorian success.

British railways were very costly to build, and at an average of £40,000
per mile were three or four times as expensive as American and most conti-
netal systems. They became an engineer's paradise, with lavish standards of
finish to major bridges and viaducts, tunnel portals and stations. There were
real reasons, however, for the heroic quality of much railway engineering

RAILWAYS 377

and architecture, particularly in the late 1830s and early 1840s. Firstly, engineers such as the Stephensons and Brunel, while consciously designing for the future, had to allow for the limited locomotive tractive effort and relatively underdeveloped mechanical knowledge of their day. So they built lines with easy gradients—the London & Birmingham had a ruling gradient of 1 in 330—and therefore committed themselves to building heavy earthworks. Secondly, there was the problem of making the railway a socially acceptable means of travel, and this was solved by magnificent termini, architecturally acceptable in a city environment, line-side stations of a vernacular or domestic style often beautifully attuned to their geographical and social surroundings, and major engineering structures handled with a panache and yet sympathy for landscape unequalled to this day. Euston or Temple Meads had the same function as the airline terminals of today, being designed not merely to book the passenger on to a train but to inflate his ego, enhance the prestigiousness of the railway experience, and reassure him that it was not as dangerous as he imagined.

Both the Stockton & Darlington and the Liverpool & Manchester railways were built before this attitude had become fashionable—they were after all built primarily as goods lines. On the S & DR stone sleeper blocks can still be seen on disused inclines at Brusselton (85/NZ 195255) and Etherley and there are the earthworks of abandoned stretches of the line at Low Etherley (85/NZ 170289) and North Leaze. A fine stone three-arch bridge by Ignatius Bonomi crosses the River Skerne at Darlington North Road (85/NZ 289157); this is perhaps the first bridge of the steam age, and although it has been widened, the south face is original. Another bridge, of cast and wrought iron, crossed the River Gaunless near West Auckland but it was removed in 1901 and can now be seen in the York Railway Museum—one of the first pieces of conscious industrial archaeological preservation. Here too is an S & DR chaldron wagon, very like the thousands that worked the colliery lines of the North East until relatively recently; examples can also be seen at the North of England Open Air Museum, Beamish. Two locomotives from the line—*Locomotion* of 1825 and *Derwent* (Plate 87) of the late 1830s—are preserved at Darlington Bank Top Station (85/NZ 294140).

The masonry arch in a variety of shapes and sizes was by far the commonest type of railway bridge structure until the 1860s and 1870s, when fabricated

87 Stockton & Darlington locomotive *Derwent* preserved at Darlington Station

girders began to appear. The Liverpool & Manchester has two fine masonry viaducts by George Stephenson in the nine-arch Sankey Viaduct near Warrington (100/SJ 569947) carrying tracks 70ft above the valley floor, and a smaller one of four arches at Newton-le-Willows (100/SJ 591954). On the same railway the skew arch bridge carrying the main Liverpool to Warrington road over the line at Rainhill (100/SJ 491914) has been widened, but the basic structure of the arch with its intricate compound curves is still intact beneath the present deck. Little remains of early station buildings, although the original L & MR eastern terminus at Liverpool Road, Manchester (101/SJ 830978) still has some of the original offices and reception areas. Line-side buildings were domestic in style, influenced if anything by contemporary road and canal architecture. The cottage situated in Bridge Road, St Johns, Stockton- on-Tees, on the S & DR, and claimed to be the first railway booking office, is now administered by Teesside Museums. There is a building with more obvious lineage at Bagworth (121/SK 446091) on the Leicester & Swannington Railway, opened in 1832; with its half-hexagonal end and panel for a non-existent tollboard, it is a perfect replica of a contemporary tollhouse and is now, since the demolition of the gem at Glenfield, the only one of its kind on the line and a curious example of the transfer of style from one transport system to another.

The remains of the first inter-city main lines, like the London & Birmingham and Great Western, are surprisingly common, and as spectacular today as when J. C. Bourne recorded them in his dramatic series of lithographs of the early 1840s. At Tring, Hertfordshire (159/SP 940137) the great cutting (Plate 88) is 2½ miles long and 60ft deep, and at Roade another bites 70ft deep into the Northamptonshire hills (146/SP 750525). The greatest work on the L & BR, however, is Kilsby Tunnel (133/SP 565715 to 578697); nearly 1½ miles long it is marked on the surface by the brick towers of its ventilating shafts, the largest of which are 60ft in diameter. All these works reflect

88 Tring cutting, Hertfordshire, cut in the late 1830s for the main line of the London & Birmingham Railway and subsequently opened out to four-track width

George Stephenson's insistence on gentle gradients; had the line been built 20 years later, Kilsby Tunnel could have been avoided altogether.

Stations on the L & BR have not fared so well. The destruction of the Euston arch, Philip Hardwick's magnificent gateway to the world's first main line railway, was a major loss. It is perhaps some consolation that Euston's demise was a major contributory factor towards creating an informed and articulate lobby prepared to argue the case for preservation. Indeed the industrial archaeologist of the future may well look back on the loss of Euston as the first great sacrificial price that had to be paid before other monuments of Britain's industrial heritage could be spared. North of Euston, however, at Camden, stands a very tangible memorial to the early days of the L & BR—the roundhouse locomotive shed (160/TQ 282843) designed by George Stephenson and built in 1837 at the head of the mile-long incline up from the terminus itself. Initially the trains were cable-hauled out of Euston, locomotives taking over at Camden for the journey north. Hardwick's other terminus building, at Curzon Street, Birmingham (131/SP 080871), with its Ionic columned façade and office block substantially intact, maintains a dignity and presence truly monumental in character amid the grimmest of urban surroundings. Birmingham could ill afford its loss.

Another early main line built in the grand manner, and of which considerable evidence survives today, was the Great Western connecting Bristol with the Metropolis. Conceived in Bristol and engineered by Isambard Kingdom Brunel, only 30 years old when the railway's Act was passed in 1836, the Great Western was part of a splendid vision, the child of a brief spell when Bristol recalled its former glories and saw itself again as the Gateway to the West. Brunel alone among the engineers of his period rethought the railway from basic principles and argued that in engineering terms a much wider gauge—he adopted 7ft—would provide a better ride, permit higher speeds, give greater carrying capacity and allow much more latitude for future development than 4ft 8½in. There can be no doubt that he was right, in engineering terms, but unfortunately there were other factors to be considered. Goods and passengers had to be changed wherever the standard and broad gauge met, and there was no possibility of through-running trains or rolling stock. By the end of the nineteenth century, when Britain had the second densest rail network in the world (after Belgium), the Great Western had to capitulate and change to the standard gauge, an operation which was completed in 1892.

The journey west from Paddington is a triumphant succession of major civil engineering works culminating in the minute (by modern standards) but still surprisingly complete terminus at Temple Meads, Bristol. The first Paddington station has gone, replaced by the magnificent multiple-aisle transepted train shed of 1854, designed by Matthew Digby Wyatt. The transepts give the whole roof structure a remarkably complex appearance, but they did once fulfil a useful purpose, providing clearance for carriage traversers, now extinct mechanisms for moving individual vehicles laterally from one track to another.

The first major work westwards from Paddington is Hanwell Viaduct (160/TS 150840) spanning the valley of the Brent in eight yellow brick arches and demonstrating in a restrained way Brunel's predilection for the Egyptian style, to be seen also in his Clifton suspension bridge at Bristol. The arms of Lord Wharncliffe were placed on the south face in honour of one of the staunchest supporters of the Great Western Bill in Parliament. At Maidenhead comes the first crossing of the Thames (159/SU 901810), on two 128ft semi-elliptical arches, their rise of only 24ft 6in making them the flattest brick arches constructed at that date. Westwards again the line passes through the great cutting at Sonning (159/SU 759743), originally planned as a tunnel some 2 miles long, before reaching Reading and the route up the Thames valley towards Didcot (Plate 89). In following the Thames the line departs from the traditional route to the west, taken by the Bath Road and the Kennet & Avon Canal, to pursue a more northerly course across north Wiltshire to a summit west of Wootton Bassett. The descent into the valley of the Avon through the 2 mile tunnel at Box is the climax of the line. Box Tunnel, with its gradient of 1 in 100, was to be for Brunel what Kilsby had been for the Stephensons—the civil engineering *tour de force* of the line, the one major work on the successful completion of which the railway depended. In addition to the engineering problems of this greatest railway tunnel so far attempted (it killed over 100 men during construction) almost every conceivable bad omen was called down upon it, with predictions of wholesale death and disaster for any who ventured inside. But the tunnel was completed, 9 months behind schedule, in the summer of 1841. At its western end (156/ST 829689) Brunel, always susceptible to a setting in which to make a grand gesture, created a portal that

89 Great Western Railway broad-gauge standard-gauge goods transfer shed, Didcot, Berkshire

epitomises the early railway age and the man. Its dignified architectural style and enormous proportions sit perfectly in the cutting east of the Bath Road, which the railway here rejoins. Only Brunel could stage-manage this supreme advertisement for the new Great Western Railway at the entrance to that 'monstrous and extraordinary, most dangerous and impracticable tunnel at Box'. West of Box the line continues its descent towards Bath, which it enters through a beautifully finished cutting along the edge of Sydney Gardens and a great viaduct of seventy-three arches on which stands the station, now much altered. Between Bath and Bristol are five more tunnels (there were originally seven but two were opened out in 1894), a twenty-eight arch viaduct at Twerton and four large bridges now all substantially modified. In Bristol itself is the grand finale, the terminus at Temple Meads, the most complete early railway terminus in the world, with its 72ft span timber-roofed train shed and Tudor-style office block fronting on to Temple Gate. Although the train shed is fulfilling a new function as a car park for the later Temple Meads, completed in the 1870s, the office block is virtually unused and under threat of demolition for the inevitable road widening. No railway station extant today is more deserving of preservation.

An aspect of any major railway project, for which no real precedents in other forms of transport existed, was the provision of repair and maintenance facilities for locomotives and rolling stock. On the London & Brimingham a works was established approximately halfway along the line at Wolverton, and on the Great Western a similar 'green field' situation was chosen by Brunel about a mile north of the market town of Swindon in north Wiltshire. On Brunel's Great Western over 70 of the total of 118 route miles had a ruling gradient of less than 1:1,000, on 40 more this was increased to 1:750 and only in the western section, between Wootton Basset and Bath, were steep gradients encountered at all, the 3 miles including Box tunnel involving the sharpest section at 1:100. The choice of Swindon as a suitable place to set up a locomotive works thus stemmed not only from its approximate mid-point position. It was a place where locomotives suitable for the heavy gradients of the western section could be changed and also, as an added advantage, a point where the projected branch to Gloucester and Cheltenham could meet the main line.

Swindon was the first of the major railway towns, for Wolverton was eventually to be eclipsed by Crewe. Despite Swindon's enormous industrial diversification in the last 10 years or so, it retains something of the flavour of the Great Western about it. Neat terraces of workers' houses faced in the local stone were built by the railway company around the entrance to the works on the south side of the line, and these, together with the institute and church, formed a new town second only perhaps to Saltaire near Bradford as an example of planned urban development. One of these railway-built buildings, possibly designed by Brunel himself, houses the Great Western Railway Museum, which contains a small but comprehensive collection of locomotives, including the replica broad-gauge *North Star*, and innumerable small items which add up to form the complex organism that was a railway. The Great Western name is still kept alive by numerous preservation societies, and its locomotives and stock are run at Didcot by the Great

Western Society, on the Dart Valley Railway in Devon and on the Severn Valley Railway, centred on Bridgnorth, Shropshire.

Curiously, some of the most widespread pieces of archaeological evidence of the early days of the Great Western are sections of broad-gauge rail designed by Brunel and made redundant by standardisation of gauge. Brunel designed his broad-gauge track with a continuous longitudinal timber sleeper beneath each rail to give good but resilient support, and these longitudinals were tied every 15ft and the ties initially piled into the trackbed. On the timbers were laid rolled-wrought-iron rails of 'top hat' section fixed down by bolts through the base flange or 'brim' of the hat. It seems probable that Brunel devised this particular section to give maximum strength for a minimum amount of iron, and also possibly to arrive at a section that could be rolled satisfactorily without suffering the lamination experienced on other types of rolled iron rail at this period. With the eventual adoption of standard 'I' section bullhead rails, first in iron and later steel, the 'bridge rail', as Brunel's rail was called, became redundant; but it was re-used for fencing stakes and as such can be found all over the old Great Western system, as far west as Cornwall and Pembrokeshire and north-west in Cheshire on the line to Birkenhead Woodside. A similar rolled section, although probably not re-used rail, can be seen in the roof girders of the Swindon railway works drawing office. Another type of rail, used on the Great Western and by some standard-gauge companies and devised by W. H. Barlow, aimed at dispensing with the longitudinal timber baulk altogether, the rail being laid directly into the ballast. Of an expanded 'top-hat' section with a base width of 12in, it was not a great success, but sections of the rail can still be found quite frequently in the form of gate-posts to goods and coal yards, mainly on old Great Western lines.

Although few other railways were to be built throughout to the standards of the Great Western, dozens of major engineering structures and thousands of minor ones dotted the immense network of lines which grew up through-out the remainder of Victoria's reign. Some 25,000 bridges were added by the railways to the British landscape between 1830 and 1860 alone. The majority still survive, many in substantially original condition and most still in use. A number of bridge types have already been mentioned and the point made that in the early period of railway building brick or masonry arch structures were by far the most numerous. The largest masonry span in Britain is the 181ft Ballochmyle Viaduct (67/NS 508254), built in 1848 on the Glasgow & South Western Railway between Kilmarnock and Dumfries to the designs of the Scottish engineer John Miller. Almost as spectacular is the seven-arch Victoria Bridge across the River Wear in Sunderland (78/NZ 396575), completed in 1838 by the Durham Junction Railway, with a largest span of 161ft.

Most major brick and stone-arch bridges on British railways have multiple arches with spans ranging from 25 to 50ft. A fine early example with unusually large spans of 60ft is the twenty-arch Dutton Viaduct (109/SJ 583764) built by George Stephenson and Joseph Locke to carry the Grand Junction Railway linking Birmingham with Manchester and Liverpool across the valley of the River Weaver in Cheshire. By far the longest arch structure, however, was built as late as the 1880s, when the Midland Railway put in its alternative route to the Soar valley line running from Kettering via Oakham and Melton Mowbray to Nottingham through the rich Jurassic iron-ore fields of east Leicestershire. Harringworth Viaduct (133/SP 914975) across the Welland Valley, Rutland's only major industrial monument, is some 3,500ft long and has eighty-two brick arches. It is little used today except by occasional mineral trains.

By the end of the nineteenth century almost all bridges were being built in wrought iron or steel, but concrete was just sufficiently developed and accepted as a building material to be used in some of the last viaducts constructed on British lines. There is an example at Glenfinnan (35/NM 910813) on the Mallaig extension of the West Highland Railway, opened in 1898, which has twenty-one arches each of 50ft span and is built on a curve of 12 chains radius (Plate 90). The concrete is not reinforced but simply poured into timber form-work, the curve being achieved by tapering the piers so that simple semi-cylindrical arches could be used. To allow for any possible differential settlement of the piers, a sliding joint consisting of two steel plates is incorporated in the crown of each arch, but no noticeable movement has occurred since the bridge was built.

Of the variety of metal bridges built to carry railways, the earliest large-span types were beam structures made in the form of tubular or plate girders. The Britannia tubular bridge (107/SH 542710) built by the Chester & Holyhead Railway across the Menai Straits was the most important of these, not merely as a railway structure but as a landmark in the evolution of

90 Mass-concrete viaduct at Glenfinnan on the Mallaig extension of the West Highland Railway, 1898

civil engineering. It marked the first use of the beam principle for a long span bridge, and its design and construction was the culmination of the model experiments carried out by William Fairbairn (1789–1874) and their translation into usable theoretical terms by Eaton Hodgkinson (1789–1861). Robert Stephenson, engineer to the Chester & Holyhead, approached Fairbairn, a shipbuilder and engineer of Millwall, London, as early as April 1845 regarding the desirable shape of the tubular deck of a wrought-iron suspension bridge he was proposing. By December of 1845 Fairbairn, in consultation with Hodgkinson, who was later appointed Professor of Mechanical Principles of Engineering at University College, London, had evolved a rectangular section beam design, cellular at the top and bottom to resist any possible collapse through compression or failure through tension. Fairbairn advocated the use of the tubes as simple beam structures, suggesting that chains would be unnecessary. A one-sixth scale model of one of the tubes was tested to destruction before the eventual design was arrived at and construction of the Menai bridge and its smaller neighbour at Conway (107/SH 787776) could begin. Conway was built first as the tubes were smaller and only had to be raised some 18ft. It proved a useful trial run for the larger-scale and much more hazardous operation at Menai. Both bridges consisted of a pair of parallel tubes, each containing a single track. At Menai Stephenson was able to avoid heavy underwater engineering by siting the central pier on the Britannia rock in the middle of the Straits. By early 1846 the working drawings for the piers were well advanced, at a period when Stephenson was still considering the use of chains. The piers, were, in fact, built considerably higher than the level of the tubes and the holes through their tops for the chains that were never used are a feature of the bridge today. As at Conway, the tubes were built on shore and floated into position, hydraulic rams being used to elevate them. When all were raised, they were riveted end to end to form a pair of continuous beams, 1,511ft long, Stephenson himself driving the last rivet on 5 March 1850, so completing the world's longest span bridge at that time and also, at £600,000, the most costly. The bridge carried main line traffic to and from Holyhead until July 1970, when a fire in wooden staging inside the tubes resulted in their distortion beyond all hope of repair. Today a steel-arch structure sits, far from happily, between the piers, and the most important single monument of wrought-iron bridge building and early structural theory in the world is gone. Conway still survives, however, and, although strengthened with intermediate piers near each end, illustrates the constructional technique, but it has neither the dimensions nor the grandeur of the great Menai Bridge.

Slightly later in the 1850s wrought iron was used for an ingenious railway bridge designed by I. K. Brunel to carry the line of the South Wales Railway over the Wye at Chepstow (156/ST 539941). The two parallel main spans, of 300ft, consisted of plate girders supported by chains from piers at each end, but instead of carrying the chains back to an anchor point on the ground, Brunel held the piers apart by wrought-iron tubes 8ft in diameter. The tubes could not support themselves over this distance, so they were in turn supported from the bridge deck by wrought-iron A frames. Brunel's Chepstow Bridge was replaced by the present lattice steel structure in 1962, but the much more sophisticated design which derived from it still carries the old Great Western main line across the Tamar from Devon into Cornwall.

The River Tamar represented the most formidable obstacle to the westward progress of the Cornwall Railway from Plymouth and, as at

Menai, the exacting Admiralty stipulations about clearance for heights for shipping had to be met to the letter. Brunel was faced at Saltash with the problem of bridging 1,000ft of tidal water at a height of 100ft. The design eventually decided upon owed something to Chepstow, but here the tubes were elliptical in section, arched in profile and self-supporting. Besides withstanding the inward pull of the suspension chains, they shared with the chains the load of the bridge deck. Each of the spans is of 445ft, the composite truss, consisting of tube, catenary chains, suspender rods and deck, being 70ft deep at its centre and containing 1,600 tons of wrought iron.

The problem of the central pier was solved by using a 37ft diameter cylinder or caisson—the 'Great Cylinder', weighing about 300 tons— which was lowered vertically through the water and mud to rest on the bed rock of the estuary floor. The whole end of the cylinder was sealed off by the use of an airtight bulkhead, and in this pressurised space the foundations of the masonry pier were built. This was the first example of the use of a pressurised caisson for underwater work. Saltash Bridge (Plate 91) was opened to traffic by Prince Albert on 2 May 1859 but by then Brunel, who had gone abroad for his health before the second span had been raised, was within a few months of death. He returned to cross his bridge on a couch placed on a flat truck. Four months later he died and the inscriptions on the piers of Saltash Bridge, 'I. K. BRUNEL – ENGINEER – 1859', were placed there in his memory by the grateful directors of the Cornwall Railway.

By the 1860s wrought-iron bridges were becoming numerous. In the main they utilised fabricated plate 'I' section girders for small spans and lattice girders over greater distances. A fine example of a large wrought-iron girder bridge is to be seen at Runcorn (100/SJ 509835), where the L & NWR main line to Liverpool crosses the Mersey (and the later Manchester Ship Canal) on three 305ft spans. The bridge was completed in 1863. At Charing Cross a nine-span wrought-iron lattice girder bridge designed by Sir John Hawkshaw was opened in the following year on the site of Brunel's Hungerford suspension footbridge, which had been acquired by the South Eastern Railway and demolished. In later years Charing Cross Bridge was widened to carry three further tracks. Wrought-iron, sometimes in combination with cast iron, was also used for a series of remarkable and elegant lattice girder viaducts that crossed steep valleys at high level. The first of them, built at

91 Brunel's Royal Albert Bridge, Saltash, spanning the Tamar between Devon and Cornwall

Crumlin, Monmouthshire, in 1857, had ten 150ft spans in the form of lattice beams known as Warren triangular girders after Captain James Warren, who, with W. T. Manzoni, patented the system in 1848. The essence of the design is that no members in the girders are subjected to bending stresses, only to simple tension and compression. The piers were made of cast-iron columns braced laterally and diagonally with wrought-iron rods, giving the whole viaduct a delicate and ethereal quality which belied its strength. Crumlin Viaduct has been dismantled, as have two of basically similar design built in 1859 at Belah, Westmorland, and Deepdale, County Durham. Only Meldon Viaduct in Devon (175/SX 565924), built by the London & South Western Railway and completed in 1874, survives as a representative of the lattice girder and pier type of construction.

The final and in some respects greatest period of railway bridge building came very late in the evolution of the network and was part of a move to

shorten existing and often circuitous routes. The last barriers to direct railway
communication were the great estuaries of the Tay, the Forth and the Severn,
estuaries which were not to be tackled by the roadbuilders until nearly a
century later. The first major railway bridge of this type was completed
across the Tay in 1878, and in the following year, as a result of design and
construction faults, was swept away in a gale with the loss of seventy-five
lives. It was a wrought-iron lattice girder structure like its successor which
stands today, the last of the great wrought-iron bridges and, with a total
length of 10,711ft, the longest railway bridge in Britain. The present bridge
was designed by W. H. Barlow and opened on 20 June 1887. Beside it can
still be seen the stumps of the piers of Bouch's narrow and spindly creation.
The second Tay Bridge was the first civil engineering work in Britain in
which an effort was made to calculate and allow for lateral wind pressure.
It was designed to resist 56lb per sq ft, giving a generous margin of safety
and resulting in a rather solid and ungraceful structure. The next estuary to
be tackled was the Severn, which was crossed in two places. The first crossing
was completed in 1879 near Sharpness with a wrought-iron bowstring
girder bridge, 4,161ft long and carrying a single track. It was hardly a trunk
route bridge, however, being designed mainly to give access to the Forest
of Dean coalfield, and after being struck and badly damaged by a barge in
1960, it was subsequently demolished. The main crossing of the Severn
came much lower down the estuary in the form of Britain's longest tunnel,
opened in the 1880s.

The bridging of the Firth of Forth was the grand finale for the nineteenth-
century bridge builders. It was the largest cantilever bridge in the world
when opened in March 1890, and the first large civil engineering structure
to be built in mild steel instead of the traditional wrought iron. The scheme
to bridge the Forth started in earnest in 1873 when the Forth Bridge Company, a consortium of the North British, Midland, and Great Northern
railways, was formed. Thomas Bouch, designer of the first Tay Bridge was
appointed engineer and work had already started on an enormous suspension
bridge when the Tay disaster occurred. Work on the Forth Bridge came to a
standstill, the suspension bridge scheme was dropped and two new engineers,
Benjamin Baker and John Fowler, were appointed in place of Bouch. In 1882
the contract was let for a cantilever bridge based on three towers made of
12ft diameter steel tubes rising 361ft above high water. From each tower

the lattice-braced cantilevers stretch out towards those of the next tower, the connection being made by two suspended lattice girder spans. Approach spans at each end are of conventional lattice girders on tapered granite piers. The central tower stands on the little island of Inch Garvie but the other two have concrete bases built in caissons; wrought-iron caissons 70ft in diameter were in fact sunk into the clay bed of the Firth under each of the four tubes of the towers. The Forth Bridge has a total length of 8,296ft.

In addition to the main types there were a number of minor types of railway bridge in Great Britain. Some were quite numerous but have now gone, like Brunel's timber viaducts in Devon and Cornwall, of which only the masonry piers can be seen here and there. Wooden viaducts still run across the Mawddach estuary south of Barmouth (116/SH 624150) and further north on the same line at Penrhyndeudraeth (116/SH 619384). Cast iron, too, was used as a bridge-building material surprisingly late in the railway age. At Ironbridge, Shropshire, the Albert Edward Bridge of 1863 is still in use (118/SJ 661038); it was designed by John Fowler, later of Forth Bridge fame, and cast by the nearby Coalbrookdale Company. In Derby an even later cast-iron arch, of 1878, crosses Friargate (121/SK 347364). Built by the Great Northern Railway, it was cast in the Derby foundry of Andrew Handyside, and exhibits *par excellence* the decorative possibilities of cast iron; the parapet panels and spandrels are full of floral ornament and also display the town's coat of arms, all cast in relief.

The large number of viaducts on British railways reflects the need for well graded, direct routes across undulating country, the same factors that resulted in so many tunnels. In towns, too, viaducts and tunnels are numerous, the obvious answers to high land costs. Paradoxically, tunnels in particular are nowhere near as common on lines in the mountainous areas of Wales and Scotland, where the economic incentive for a direct route was usually low and the topography so severe that circuitous valley-located routes involving minimum engineering works and therefore minimum expenditure were the norm. It must be remembered too that many of the lines in Wales and Scotland were built late in the railway era after the first flush of extravagance had died away. Thus there is only one tunnel in Wales over 2 miles long, at Blaenau Ffestiniog (107/SH 687505 to 697469), and there are none at all in Scotland. Britain's major railway tunnels are therefore concentrated in the Pennines and lowland England, cutting through what in many places appear to be insignificant hills. Kilsby Tunnel through the North-amptonshire uplands has already been mentioned as an example of a shallow depth bore made necessary by Stephenson's stringent gradient requirements. Another early Stephenson tunnel, the first railway tunnel in the world over a mile in length, is at Glenfield in Leicestershire (121/SK 545065 to 561061) on the Leicester & Swannington Railway, opened in 1832. Its narrow single-track bore is now closed. Quite unavoidable, however, was the tunnel under the Pennines at Woodhead (102/SK 114999 to SE 156023) between Man-chester and Sheffield, completed in 1845 after a 7 year saga of death and disease in the workings and the shanty navvy encampments on Pikenaze Moor above. Built initially for a single track, it was later duplicated, and then in the 1950s replaced altogether by a modern double track tunnel put in to accommodate the 1,500V DC electrification scheme initiated by the London & North Eastern Railway. The stark portals can be seen, however, and one of the bores is now doing useful work carrying a power line that would otherwise have necessitated unsightly pylons across the moors.

To the industrial archaeologist the most obvious evidence of tunnels is their portals and, on the longer bores, their ventilating shafts. Unlike the canal builders the railway engineers used tunnels as an excuse for architectural extravagance, of which numerous examples can still be seen. The south portal of Primrose Hill Tunnel (160/TQ 276843) on the London & Birming-ham 1½ miles out of Euston is Italianate in style, while at Shugborough in Staffordshire (119/SJ 982216 to 988216) one end of the tunnel is castellated and the other Egyptianesque. In the latter case the cosmetic architectural treatment, like that of the adjacent bridges, was required by the Earl of Lichfield, owner of the estate through which the line passed. Two other 'fortified' portals are to be found at Redhill (121/SK 496308) on the Midland main line between Leicester and Derby and at Grosmont (86/NZ 829051) on the abandoned alignment of Stephenson's Whitby & Pickering Railway. At Bramhope, Yorkshire, the 2 mile tunnel on the Harrogate line has an ornate castellated north portal (96/SE 256438) which is reproduced on a smaller scale at nearby Otley Churchyard (96/SE 202455) as a memorial to the men killed during its construction.

Britain's longest railway tunnel came late in the railway era and, like the longest bridges, spanned an estuary. From the 1850s the mouth of the Severn had been an obstacle to rail traffic between South Wales and London, which had to travel via Gloucester. In 1863 the first attempt at a shorter route was completed with the opening of the Bristol & South Wales Union Railway to New Passage (155/ST 544864) and a ferry connection to Portskewett and the South Wales Railway. Little remains of this venture today other than the stone landward section of the original timber pier and the flourishing New Passage Hotel. At Blackrock on the Monmouthshire side (155/ST 514881) two bridges and an overgrown cutting are all that remain of the connection with the main line. A tunnel as the final answer to crossing the Severn by rail was devised as early as the 1860s, taken up by the Great Western Railway in 1872, and eventually completed in 1886 at a cost of more than £1½ million. The Severn Tunnel when completed represented the ultimate in the engineers' fight against adversity. A natural freshwater stream, the Great Spring, was broken into and the workings were flooded by the river, delaying operations for about 3 years. The Great Spring has had to be pumped ever since, initially by steam engines and now by electricity. At Sudbrook (155/ST 507874) the huge 29ft shaft through which most of the Great Spring water is pumped can still be seen, but the six superb 70in Cornish beam pumps have been scrapped.

The design of passenger railway stations presented engineers and architects with considerable problems, for they were working in a field where no precedents existed. The logistics of handling large numbers of people arriving and departing simultaneously represented something completely new, and demanded a particular type of building combining all the basic functions in a logical and well articulated way. Thus the *layout* of stations is peculiar to the nature of railways themselves and represents a response to a specific challenge. In architectural terms, however, the designers of railway stations exhibited less originality, and, although the great roofs of termini were undoubtedly allied closely to the function of the station, the treatment of façades, of booking office blocks and of railway hotels was frequently pedestrian and derivative in the extreme. On the other hand the railway companies were responsible for some very good architecture both in large city stations and simpler rural surroundings. Railway architecture has become a study in itself and railway buildings, which often reflected the relative wealth and desire for prestige of their owners, illustrate in microcosm many of the essentials of Victorian architectural thought. As we have seen, the first railways required little in the way of buildings, but as early as 1830 the

termini of the Liverpool & Manchester Railway, of which the Manchester
one still survives, had the essentials of booking office, waiting rooms and a
sheltered platform for the passengers. By the late 1830s the U-shaped
terminus station that was to become the standard had evolved, with arrival
and departure platforms linked by a cross platform containing the entrances,
waiting rooms and offices. An early example, now demolished, was Nine
Elms, designed by Sir William Tite. Brunel's Temple Meads, Bristol, is
another, which happily still exists.

Most early termini had one arrival and one departure platform, often
separated by a number of tracks on which empty rolling stock could be
stored. As traffic increased, the area of sidings in the centre was reduced and
further platforms added. This happened at King's Cross (160/TQ 303831),
the London terminus of the Great Northern Railway, which was designed
by Lewis Cubitt and opened in 1852. King's Cross is a classic terminus,
its simple brick façade penetrated by the arches of the double train shed
behind expressing so perfectly its 'arrival' and 'departure' functions. Cubitt's
claim that the station would fulfil itself architecturally through 'the largeness
of some of its features, its fitness for its purpose, and its characteristic expression of that purpose' is admirably demonstrated.

Much more typical in London and other major provincial termini has
been the combination of the hotel with the station offices in the transverse
section of the U, resulting in the train shed being completely obscured.
Nowhere is the duality of function and treatment better demonstrated than
at St Pancras (160/TQ 302829), the terminus built by the Midland Railway
when it finally gained access to the capital in the late 1860s. Both components
of the station are larger than life; the iron and glass train shed by W. H.
Barlow and the Butterley Company is enormous, its span of 240ft then
being the largest in the world, and in front Sir Gilbert Scott's romantic red
brick Victorian Gothic hotel is, in its architect's words 'possibly too good for
its purpose'! St Pancras is still, happily, an operating station dominating the
Euston Road, the ultimate expression of Victorian confidence and the might
of the railway.

Other London termini incorporating hotels are Paddington (where
Philip Hardwick's building of 1854 is architecturally interesting as an early
example of French Renaissance and Baroque influence in England), Charing
Cross, Cannon Street, Liverpool Street and Marylebone. The last named,

where the hotel now provides the headquarters for the British Railways Board, shows a marked disparity in size between the huge hotel block and the miniature station behind it. Marylebone, the terminus of the last main line into London, was built in the late 1890s by the Manchester, Sheffield & Lincolnshire Railway, which, to celebrate its new-found status, changed its name to the Great Central Railway in 1897. Today Marylebone only handles suburban traffic, the main line to the north through Rugby, Leicester and Nottingham having gone after little more than 60 years of life.

Through stations presented peculiar problems of design, particularly when, as was often the case, the town lay on one side of the railway. It was considered undesirable for passengers to have to cross the lines, so there was sometimes just one long single platform for both up and down trains. At Reading and Slough Brunel built stations of this type, with up and down station buildings both on the south side of the line, and at Derby Francis Thompson did much the same along the street side of an immense 1,050ft long platform (121/SK 363355). Although there were clearly some advantages in this type of layout for the passengers, the operating difficulties were considerable, since trains had to cross each others' paths on entering and leaving the station. Only one survives today in operational form, at Cambridge (135/TL 462573), the GWR stations having been rebuilt, and those at Derby, Chester General, Huddersfield and Newcastle having been given extra platforms. Thompson's Chester station of 1848 (109/SJ 413669) still retains its great façade—over 1,000ft of vaguely Venetian symmetry in stone-faced brick punctuated by little towers. The awning was added later.

Almost every conceivable architectural style can be found somewhere in British railway stations. Initially classicism was favoured, as at Euston and Birmingham Curzon Street (131/SP 080871), and it later spread to Huddersfield (102/SE 144169), Monkwearmouth, Sunderland (78/NZ 396577) and, finest of all, Newcastle Central (78/NZ 245638). Huddersfield, by J. P. Pritchett, is an example of a station (Plate 92) planned to be balanced by the same architect's designs in other adjacent buildings, in this case the George Hotel and Lion Arcade in St George's Square. Similarly at Stoke-on-Trent (110/SJ 879456) R. A. Stent matched the second Stoke station with the neo-Jacobean North Stafford Hotel on the opposite side of the square, while in Ashby-de-la-Zouch, Leicestershire (121/SK 355163), the frontage of the beautiful little Grecian station of 1849 (now disused) was part of a grand

92 The newly cleaned façade of Huddersfield Station, designed by J. P. Pritchett

plan to develop a spa town. Perhaps the last purely classical station façade is that of the also disused Bath Green Park (166/SO 745647), built in the early 1870s as the terminus of the Midland's branch from Mangotsfield and the Somerset & Dorset Railway.

The Tudor style appears in Bristol Temple Meads and Shrewsbury (118/SJ 494129) but is exemplified in its purest form in the Carlisle Citadel station of 1847, designed by Sir William Tite and described as Britain's 'finest piece of railway architecture in the sixteenth century collegiate style'. 'Jacobean' stations are mainly small, as at Maldon, Essex (162/TL 853077), and Stone, Staffordshire (119/SJ 896346), although an unusually large railway building in this style is the old General Office of the Bristol & Exeter Railway beside the approach to Temple Meads station in Bristol (156/ST 596724), completed in 1854 to the designs of S. C. Fripp. The Italian idiom was used by Tite in the late 1830s on the London & Southampton Railway and the original Southampton terminus (180/SU 422109) survives intact (see also Gosport station, Plate 93). Campaniles in the same vein appeared in the pumping stations installed by Brunel on his 'atmospheric' railway along the south Devon coast, but only Starcross (176/SX 977819), dating from 1846, is in anything like complete condition.

From an architectural point of view the stations of cities and larger towns

93 Ruinous colonnade of William Tite's Gosport Station, Hampshire

must be considered in the context of the other public buildings, with which they often compare well. It is in small towns and villages, however, that railway architecture really comes into its own, and where stations and often other railway buildings most frequently reflect the characteristics of individual companies. Their variety is enormous, but careful observation of the works of a particular railway will soon reveal similarities of style and frequent use of standardised components. Indeed one of the major contributions made by the larger British railway companies was in the development of prefabricated buildings based on a range of standardised components. Thus throughout the territory of the Midland Railway, for example, from St Pancras to Carlisle and Lincoln to Avonmouth, one may find signal boxes, station waiting rooms, level crossing gates, platform lamps and awnings fitting into one style. The typical Midland signal box was of unit construction, comprising standard timber posts, beams and panels that could be built in any number of bays, depending on the number of signal and point levers in the frame. Waiting rooms, too, were of standard design and, although usually built of brick, included standard components such as doors, bargeboards and cast-iron window frames. It is in this field of what might be called 'vernacular railway architecture' that much interest lies, and where, as the result of the great reduction in the number of passenger stations over the last 10 years, considerable recording and preservation effort is needed. Fortunately railways have received the àttentions of innumerable enthusiastic devotees anxious to record every detail of a particular system, and although their efforts have tended to be concentrated mainly on locomotives and rolling stock, other aspects of railway operations are receiving increasing attention.

The whole field of operational railway preservation is in itself a remarkable phenomenon, which has resulted in a number of lines being kept running after official closure and others being revived and brought back into use, sometimes after many years of complete dereliction. The first line in the country to be saved by enthusiast interests was the Talyllyn Railway, which in 1951 had been brought to the point of closure by declining slate traffic and road competition. Built in 1865 to serve slate quarries at Bryn Eglwys, it was opened for goods in the same year and for passengers in 1866. Today the 2ft 3in gauge line, covering the $6\frac{3}{4}$ miles from Wharf Station, Tywyn (127/SH 586005), to Abergynolwyn (127/SH 671064), carries over 130,000 passengers each season. Also at Tywyn is a narrow-gauge railway museum. Other operating narrow-gauge railways in Wales include the Festiniog, running from Porthmadog (116/SH 571384) to Dduallt; the Welshpool & Llanfair Light Railway, based at Llanfair Caerinion, Montgomeryshire (117/SJ 106068); and the Vale of Rheidol, British Rail's only steam-operated line, which runs from Aberystwyth (127/SN 585815) to Devil's Bridge (127/SN 738769). Also in Wales and unique in Britain is the Snowdon Mountain Railway, a 2ft $7\frac{1}{2}$in gauge rack line that climbs from Llanberis (107/SH 583597) to a height of 3,493ft. It was opened in 1896 and operates with 0-4-2T inclined boiler locomotives of Swiss manufacture.

Standard-gauge preservation schemes are widespread throughout the country and vary enormously in their aims and methods of operation. Most are concerned primarily with running steam locomotives and, although ostensibly 'preservation societies', few go further than preserving locomotives and stock in original condition. Some, such as the Keighley & Worth Valley, based at Haworth (96/SE 035373) in the West Riding of Yorkshire, and the Bluebell Railway centred on Sheffield Park Station (183/TQ 404237) in Sussex, include locomotives and rolling stock painted in non-original liveries, whilst others like the Dart Valley Railway at Buckfastleigh (188/SX 746663), Devon, and the Severn Valley at Bridgnorth (130/SO 715926), Shropshire, maintain locomotives and rolling stock in the colours of their old owners. It is perhaps a little regrettable that, despite all this wealth of interest in railway preservation, as yet no line has been retained as a living example of how it used to be operated, with appropriate locomotives, stock, signal and telegraph equipment and so on.

16 Ports and Shipping

THE Industrial Revolution in Britain needed good internal transport systems, but equally important was the provision of facilities for import and export. The 'workshop of the world' was dependent on trade, and by the middle of the nineteenth century over 40 per cent of the entire world output of traded manufactured goods were produced in Britain, through whose ports passed over a quarter of total international trade. Over 90 per cent of British exports were composed of manufactured goods, which comprised only 7 per cent of imports. At no other time has one country so dominated the world economy. First canals and then railways gave manufacturers access to the coast, where sophisticated ports developed to handle goods in and out. Capital at least equal to that absorbed by canals was invested in the construction of these ports, although it was spread over a longer period.

In 1700 British trade was concentrated very heavily on London, which handled over 80 per cent of the nation's imports, 70 per cent of her exports and no less than 86 per cent of her re-exports. Defoe remarked that London 'sucked the vitals of trade in this island to itself'. In 1700 also London opened its first 'wet dock' at Rotherhithe. Previously London, like all other ports, had been entirely tidal, with ships either tying up at wharves and lying on the bottom over low tide or mooring in the river and being loaded and unloaded by lighter. The Rotherhithe wet dock consisted of a basin with entrance locks through which ships could pass into an area of water at constant level. There cargoes could be transferred safely and quickly between ship and shore. In Bristol, Britain's second port after London, ships made their way laboriously up the River Avon to the wharves of the city, where they lay on the bottom over low water. Bristol's exceptional tidal range, which is 42ft at Portishead near the mouth of the river, meant that a ship in port would be grounded twice a day, and vessels trading regularly with the city had to have specially strengthened hulls.

It could take as long as 4 months to turn a ship round in Bristol, and many had their backs broken while they were there. In 1712 a wet dock was completed lower down the Avon at Sea Mills (155/ST 550760) and, although long disused, substantial evidence of it can still be seen in the form of a masonry wall and entrance lock. Sea Mills never became a real competitor to Bristol itself, being too far away from the commercial centre, and eventually it was used only by whaling ships, whose unwholesome cargoes were not welcome in the city.

The new trading activity of the eighteenth century, much of it transoceanic, led to rapid growth in other west coast ports. This growth was most dramatic in Liverpool. Defoe in 1720 thought its expansion 'one of the wonders of Britain . . . what it may grow to in time I know not'. At the end of the sixteenth century there had been fewer than 200 houses there and the Dee estuary, with Chester at its head, took prominence over the Mersey. By 1700 Liverpool's population was between 5,000 and 7,000, but it had reached 10,000 by 1720 and 30,000 by 1750—and canals had not yet connected the town with the heart of industrial England. Bristol also doubled its population in the first half of the eighteenth century, reaching 90,000 by 1750, but then growth slackened as the port lost ground first to Liverpool and then Glasgow. Liverpool's first wet dock was completed in 1715 and a further six were added in the succeeding century.

In Glasgow improvements in the Clyde were made by John Golborne between 1773 and 1781 and by the Clyde Trust after 1809; and on the east coast Hull, with its Baltic trade and close waterway connections with the West Riding, had formed a dock company by 1774 and opened three inter-connected docks by 1829. Completely new ports were also created, often for specific purposes, such as coal shipment. Seaham (85/NZ 435495) was the creation of the Marquess of Londonderry, who had coal interests in County Durham. On the west coast Maryport (82/NY 030365) in Cumberland developed for similar reasons.

Other new ports were canal-inspired, like Grangemouth (61/NS 925825), opened in 1777, at the eastern end of the Forth & Clyde Canal, or Goole (98/SE 745230), opened in 1826 at the Humber end of the Aire & Calder Navigation.

Between 1753 and 1830 some 370 acres of wet docks were provided in England alone. Harbour commissioners or trustees were formed at numerous places round the coast to put port finance on a firmer basis and carry out improvements in response to the growth of trade. They engaged outstanding civil engineers to advise them, including such illustrious names as John Smeaton (1724–92) and John Rennie (1761–1821). Rennie alone was involved in over seventy harbour schemes. Not surprisingly the struggle with the sea to provide safe harbourage for ships led to many technological discoveries, including steam dredging, hollow walls and the diving bell. Although the cost of improvements was enormous, most of them enjoyed a much longer life than other works of the period, particularly the canals, which were soon to be ruined by railways. Their long-term usefulness, coupled frequently with very high standards of workmanship and materials, have meant that large numbers of port installations have survived to the present. As yet relatively little work has been done on the industrial archaeology of ports, which, with today's rapid rate of change in shipping techniques and increase in vessel sizes, are likely to undergo radical alterations in the next few years. The closure of Bristol's city docks in favour of concentrating traffic at Avonmouth can only be a few years away, and in Liverpool plans are already in hand to shut down all docks south of the Pier Head.

As an example of a port complex now almost completely extinct but offering much of interest to the industrial arcaeologist, the estuary of the Lune in Lancashire is worthy of examination. Before the late seventeenth century the port of Lancaster confined itself mainly to coastal trade, but shortly after 1700 the opportunity was taken of widening its scope to includes the West Indies. Warehouses were built in large numbers along St George's Quay (94/SD 474623), and several of mid-eighteenth century date still survive, their gable walls complete with wooden beam cranes or 'lucams', which were used for hoisting goods to upper floors. Some merchants built dwelling houses, of which several remain, but the most notable reflection of Lancaster's importance as a port in the eighteenth century is the fine Custom House, erected in 1764 to the design of Richard Gillow. A number of streets running back from the quay area to Cable Street were laid out around 1800, with names like Antigua Street, Barbadoes Street and Jamaica Street, but these have long gone, swept away by the railway in 1849.

Also in the early eighteenth century Sunderland Point (94/SD 426560), which lies between the Lune estuary and Morecambe Bay, was promoted as an outport for Lancaster by Robert Lawson, a prominent local merchant. Here ships too big to make the difficult passage up to Lancaster itself could moor; a jetty was built and moderate prosperity enjoyed for a few years. The village is little changed today, with its two terraces of houses accessible from Overton by a causeway submerged by the tide twice daily. According to legend the first bale of cotton to reach Lancashire was landed at Sunderland Point, to begin the industry for which the county was to become most famous. Across the river from Sunderland Point was Glasson (94/SD 445562), a safer anchorage, which soon took over as the unloading point for cargoes that were then shipped by lighter to Lancaster. In 1751 the port commissioners placed a chain and mooring stone there, and in 1791 a wet dock large enough to accommodate twenty-five merchant ships was completed. In 1826 Glasson Dock was linked with the Lancaster Canal, which necessitated the construction of a large inner basin. In 1834 a patent slip was laid down, in 1836 a grid-iron or frame on which ships could be repaired at low water was put in, and in 1838 a graving dock was opened. Today Glasson is the home only of pleasure craft and the odd surviving Morecambe Bay prawn boats or 'nobbies', the graving dock filling with rubbish, and the fine five-storey warehouse demolished for car parking. Yet the place has an air of former glory, and, like Lancaster itself, exudes the atmosphere of a once important port.

There is little remaining today in Bristol docks of eighteenth-century date with the possible exception of one or two small warehouses at the south end of Broad Quay. The whole harbour, which was tidal until the early nineteenth century, was completely remodelled by William Jessop, who installed an entrance basin—Cumberland Basin (156/ST 570723)—with lock gates, and in effect created a huge wet dock occupying the whole of the bed of the River Avon and its tributary the Frome for over a mile upstream. River water was diverted down a new specially excavated channel, the New Cut. These enormous works were completed in 1809 and for a time enabled Bristol to compete with the up-and-coming Liverpool. As the size of ships increased, however, problems of access along the tortuous Avon arose, and Jessop's entrance locks were soon found to be too small. I. K. Brunel, who had recently brought the Great Western Railway into the city, was called in by the Bristol Dock Company to carry out improvements, which he completed in 1848. A new south entrance lock (156/ST 570723), whose chamber can still be seen, was built for Cumberland Basin, and improvements made to the dredging system by the use of a steam-powered cable-hauled scraper. The engine of this boat is preserved in Bristol City Museum, where there is also a model of the complete vessel. By the 1860s problems of increased shipping sizes arose again and the Port of Bristol Authority, the then municipal owners of the docks, undertook to build a new and larger north entrance lock, which is in use today.

Bristol city docks are still in use and contain a wealth of material of relevance to the industrial archaeologist. Their life cannot be long, however, as the newer docks built after 1877 at the confluence of the Avon with the Bristol Channel—Avonmouth and the smaller Portishead (1879)—have for nearly a century been the focal points of Bristol's port activities. At the entrance to Cumberland Basin in the shadow of a modern road swing-bridge is a grid-iron, installed in 1884 for the repair of small vessels, while over the entrance lock and Brunel's now redundant lock of the 1840s are two wrought-iron girder swing bridges. The first of these, dating from 1848, was installed by Brunel and is thought to be the earliest wrought-iron girder bridge in existence, if not the first ever constructed. The second bridge, built over the new entrance lock in the 1870s, is almost identical.

Like many ports in the nineteenth century Bristol used, and to a small extent still uses, hydraulic power to drive the numerous ancillary installations like lock gates, capstans and cranes. The hydraulic press, consisting of a small hand pump and reservoir connected to a hydraulic cylinder and ram, had been patented in 1795 by Joseph Bramah and was soon to be widely adopted for engineering work and, as modified by Matthew Murray (1765–1826) of Leeds, for baling cloth. In 1812 Bramah proposed the installation of hydraulic power mains on a municipal basis, with a central generating station and users paying by meter for the power they used. Although this far-sighted idea was not adopted for a further 65 years, it was in essence the basis for numerous dock installations. Both Bramah and Murray developed hydraulic cranes but it was the work of William (later Sir William) George Armstrong (1810–1900), whose first hydraulic crane was erected in Newcastle in 1846, that made hydraulic power widely acceptable both in docks and elsewhere. Armstrong devised the weight-loaded hydraulic accumulator to provide sufficient head, air vessels to balance the fluctuations between supply and demand and smooth out pump pulsations, and the hydraulic jigger (consisting of a jack with pulley sheaves mounted at each end) by means of which the effective stroke could be multiplied and excessively long jack cylinders obviated.

The first public hydraulic supply was installed in Hull in 1877, to be followed in London by the installations of the Wharves & Warehouses Steam Power & Hydraulic Pressure Company, which in 1883 operated some 7 miles of mains on both sides of the Thames. In the following year this company was absorbed into the London Hydraulic Power Company, which by the 1930s supplied over 8,000 separate hydraulic machines through 184 miles of mains. About half this number of machines are at present supplied. Elsewhere many of the large public hydraulic-power companies have closed, in Hull because of war damage, and in Liverpool as recently as 1970 as the result of a dwindling consumer demand. The Glasgow and Manchester systems have also closed down recently. (An electrically powered hydraulic generator pump is on display, working in the local history gallery of the City of Liverpool Museums.)

By the standards of these installations, that at Bristol is small, supplying power only for the port authority's own use. The generating station is near the Cumberland Basin at the Underfall Yard (156/ST 572722), where there are three electrically driven pumps by Fullerton, Hodgart & Barclay of Paisley. A brick accumulator tower near the generating station is no longer used, but outside is a modern steel tower where the weight can be seen falling and rising intermittently as water is taken from the mains and then replenished. The system is used regularly for the older swing bridges of Cumberland Basin and the lock gates. A few hydraulic cranes may still be seen in the city docks, but they are now out of use. Prince's Street Bridge (156/ST 586723), although not now hydraulically powered, also has a small booster accumulator tower.

Numerous examples of hydraulically operated machinery can still be seen in most ports of any size, the accumulator tower usually being the most obvious clue to their existence. Of these, the campanile-style tower standing between the entrance locks at Grimsby (105/TA 281113), Lincoln-shire, must be the most spectacular. Dating from the early 1850s, it is 313ft high and was built by the Manchester, Sheffield & Lincolnshire Railway to provide a head for the hydraulic mains of the port and support a freshwater tank for ships. It is not an accumulator tower in the true sense of the term, but an artificial head of water for the hydraulic mains, consisting of a 33,000 gallon tank into which water was pumped by a steam engine. The enormous cost of providing a tower like that at Grimsby was instrumental in the development of the accumulator proper, in which a large weight is

raised on a piston to create the same sort of pressure. The Grimsby tower
now serves only as a television relay station and for supplying water to wash
down the fish pontoon. Other towers may be seen in Liverpool docks and
at Glasgow.

Numerous bridges are still powered by hydraulics, including the
famous swing bridge across the Tyne at Newcastle (78/NZ 253637)
built by Armstrong in 1876, and several swing bridges on the Manchester
Ship Canal, including the Barton Aqueduct and the adjacent road bridge
(101/SJ 766976). The best known of all, Tower Bridge, London (160/TQ
337802), an engineering masterpiece and architectural absurdity to the
designs of Horace Jones, architect to the City of London, and John Wolfe
Barry, was opened in 1894. Construction was by William Arrol, with
hydraulic equipment supplied by Armstrong's of Newcastle. There are four
hydraulic engines to each 1,070 ton bascule leaf, and in ordinary working
only one engine to each leaf is used, the other six engines being in gear and
running idle with water circulating through their cylinders and valves. The
four accumulators were until recently charged by a pair of double-tandem-
compound steam engines, each of 360hp, but these are now out of use and
hydraulic supply is drawn from the London Hydraulic Power Company's
mains. Each tower also has hydraulic lifts giving public access to the high-
level pedestrian deck. Visitors may at present see all this equipment by
appointment, but eventually electric power may be installed or the bridge
itself demolished in favour of a fixed bridge of higher traffic capacity. The
very improbability of this worldwide tourist attraction justifies its preservation; how appropriate that it should retain its hydraulic equipment rather
than become still more of a sham, with electric motors or perhaps no power
at all.

The growth of trade through British ports in the early years of the nineteenth century necessitated a completely new approach to the provision of
port installations, particularly warehousing (Plate 94). Traditionally quayside warehouses had been relatively small, of up to four storeys, and with
timber floors supported on timber beams presenting problems of load
capacity and fire risk. The warehouses in Lancaster, already mentioned,
typify what might be called the 'pre-industrial' warehouse building. Other
examples may be seen in ports as far apart as King's Lynn, Norfolk; Boston,
Lincolnshire (Plate 95); Bideford and Exeter in Devon (where appropriately

94 Mid-nineteenth-century warehouses at Gloucester Docks

95 Late eighteenth-century warehouses at Boston, Lincolnshire

some warehouse buildings form part of a developing and wide-ranging maritime museum). One of the King's Lynn buildings, incidentally, on Nelson Street overlooking Mill Fleet, provides a fine example of a new use for an old industrial building, for here the granaries have been sensitively converted into offices. In Portsoy, Banffshire (30/NJ 589665) a group of miscellaneous harbour buildings have been converted into council houses.

Bristol also has a number of early warehouses of traditional construction, alongside others which represent the transition to a larger scale of port building that developed mainly in London and Liverpool. One of these transitional warehouses is J. & R. Bush's tea bond on Prince Street (156/ST 586725), overlooking the traditional heart of the city's harbour at the junction of the Avon and Frome. Dating from the 1830s, it is a five-storey structure with timber floors supported by cast-iron columns. The boldly featured stone exterior, with its prominent string courses and arch-headed windows, heralded a more exotic style of Bristol warehouse that developed after 1850, but in terms of constructional technique nothing more advanced was built in the port until the great tobacco bonds of the early 1900s. The city docks continued to be provided with relatively small warehouses, appropriate to the size of ships trading there, of which a few classic examples survive. Two beside Bathurst Basin (156/ST 587722) exhibit in a restrained way the polychrome brickwork and ogee arches which typified large numbers of buildings in the Victoria Street area in the third quarter of the nineteenth century, a style which has since become known, with some architectural inexactitude, as 'Bristol Byzantine'. The prize example of the style is on Welsh Back (156/ST 588726), built in 1869 to the designs of two local architects, Archibald Ponton and W. V. Gough. It epitomises Bristol Byzantine at its most exotic and yet, despite its unusual outside appearance, the internal structure is of conventional timber joists and floorboards. The building is now a jazz club.

London's early wet docks, like that at Rotherhithe, had no warehousing of their own—indeed the Rotherhithe Dock had a double row of poplar trees round the basin as a protection against wind. Similarly Brunswick Dock, Blackwall, opened in 1790, was chiefly intended for the safe accommodation of the East India Company's ships, and the only building of note was the masting house. Not until the opening of the West India docks in 1802 was a system of warehousing provided, solving at once two major problems—

the difficulty of unloading ships in tidal water and, by the provision of a
Customs wall, the pilfering of cargoes, which had been causing merchants
grave concern.

The origins of large-scale port warehousing may still be seen, in a somewhat diminished state, in St Katharine Dock, London. The purpose of the
dock was to provide both an unloading place for ships and quayside warehousing as close as possible to the commercial heart of London. The St
Katharine Dock Company Act was passed in 1825 for an enclosed wet dock
system immediately to the east of the Tower of London (160/TQ 339805).
Thomas Telford was chief engineer, with Philip Hardwick (1792–1870) as
architect. The two major criteria which Telford and Hardwick had to apply
in developing the 23-acre site were the need to obtain as much quayside
length as possible for unloading purposes and the provision of the maximum
amount of warehouse storage space. Room had also to be made for several
vessels docking together as, unlike today, arrival times were very dependent
on the weather. The final design consisted of two irregularly shaped docks
each linked to a smaller entrance basin, although here the originally intended
second entrance lock was never built. In having all its warehouses built up
to the water's edge, St Katharine Dock was unique. Normal practice was
to have an open quay, transit sheds and a road between the water and the
warehouses. The idea at St Katharine's, however, was to save double handling
by taking goods straight from the ship's hold to the appropriate floor of the
warehouse by means of overhead cranes.

The result was a magnificent range of six-storey warehouses, cubelike,
compact and functional, with a ground floor arcade of giant cast-iron Doric
columns and full-height round-headed blank arches embracing the windows
above. Most were designed by Thomas Telford but the block on the west
side facing the Tower Bridge approach is by Hardwick. Architecturally
their importance lies in the combination of utilitarian function and a classical
discipline of design, and they represent an important stage in the development of buildings adapted specifically to the large-scale requirements of
the nineteenth century. The constructional technique of the initial buildings
was in fact fairly conventional, with timber floors, but the central block,
added in the late 1850s, had an iron frame and stone slab floors. After
suffering extensive bomb damage in 1940, after which several of the warehouses were demolished, St Katharine Dock was eventually closed in

October 1968 and the site is now the centre for an ambitious redevelopment scheme under the auspices of the Greater London Council which involves the retention of most of the surviving buildings and dock area.

Although London has always retained its lead as Britain's major port, the eighteenth and nineteenth centuries saw Liverpool take Bristol's place as the second most important, with Hull, Glasgow and at the end of the period, Manchester, all overtaking her also. Liverpool's small cluster of wet docks near what is now called the Pier Head formed the basis for the remarkable linear development of docks, now exceeding 7 miles in length which is illustrated in Fig 31. The evolution of this dock estate during the nineteenth century was influenced by a number of factors, including the need for more dock and warehouse space as traffic increased, the building of larger vessels, the coming of steamships, and the need for greater security, which led to the separation of the dock area from the city. In much of this development the central figure was Jesse Hartley, who was dock engineer from 1824 until his death in 1860 and whose indelible stamp still characterises much of Liverpool's dockland. This linear development and need for greater security was emphasised by the great wall that Hartley built on the landward side of the dock estate and alongside which the present Dock Road runs. Entrances were protected by huge sliding gates and towers that have all the appearance of miniature fortifications. Only Stanley Dock, opened in 1848, lies outside the wall, but this was because it formed the link between the main dock system and the Leeds & Liverpool Canal. By the time of Hartley's death the line of docks stretched from Canada Dock on the northern edge of Liverpool to Brunswick Dock in the south, the latter the first dock to be built by Hartley himself.

Undoubtedly Hartley's masterpiece is Albert Dock (100/SJ 342897), close to the traditional heart of the port and immediately south of the Pier Head. Albert Dock (Plate 96) is the logical extension of the principle established in St Katharine Dock, London, in the late 1820s, but here the rectangle of open water is surrounded by an almost complete wall of warehousing coming right up to the edge of the quay, although still retaining the arcade with cast-iron columns at ground floor level. The columns are modelled on Greek Doric prototypes and are hollow drums 12ft 6in in circumference and 15ft high. Encased with walls of brick, the five floors of the warehouses are supported on iron columns, the spaces between them spanned by cast-iron

THE GROWTH OF THE LIVERPOOL DOCK SYSTEM
1760-1960

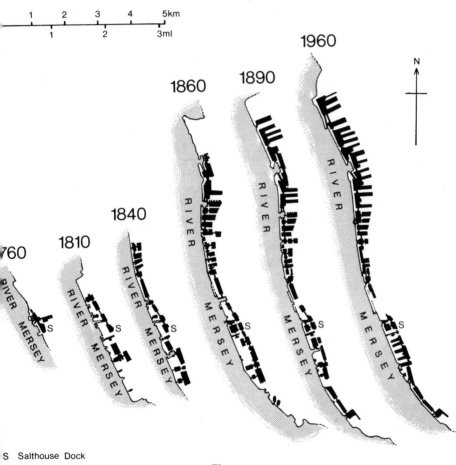

S Salthouse Dock

Fig 31

96 Albert Dock, Liverpool.
Colonnade with cast-iron
columns

beams of inverted-Y section tied laterally with wrought-iron tension rods.
From these beams spring the brick arches of the floors (Plate 97), the whole
method of construction evolving directly from the pioneer work of Strutt
and Bage in Derbyshire and Shrewsbury at the end of the eighteenth century.
At Albert Dock, however, even the roof trusses are of iron, and the roof
itself is made of wrought-iron plates. Tucked into the north-east corner is
the Dock Traffic Office, dating, like the warehouses, from the mid-1840s
but in this case designed by Philip Hardwick, who had collaborated with
Telford at St Katharine Dock and meanwhile built a triumphal arch at
Euston. Hardwick's design for Euston seems to have influenced him in
Liverpool, and the Tuscan portico of the Dock Traffic Office, entirely
constructed in cast-iron, symbolises *par excellence* Victorian commercial
achievement and self-confidence.

97 Albert Dock, Liverpool. Interior of warehouse showing cast-iron columns and beams with brick vaulting

Granite, brick and iron are the materials for the monumental mass of the Albert Dock warehouses, the ultimate demonstration of the maritime prosperity of the Port of Liverpool. Today they stand disused, ships having outgrown the dock facilities, and multi-storey warehouses having lost their *raison d'être* in a world of containers and fork-lift trucks. Their colossal bulk rising above the Mersey Wall presents every planner or would-be conservationist with a problem, for while it is easy to save a watermill or even a reasonably sized railway station, the supreme monuments to Victorian industrial and commercial might have become commercial white elephants in areas of high land values. They are too big to retain and yet their retention is essential. They could be turned into maritime museums or a polytechnic —'Pierhead Poly' has been proposed—or into offices, small workshops, even residential accommodation. Perhaps a combination of all of these is the answer, but fundamental to achieving the right solution is the need for just a fraction of the spirit of adventure, confidence and imagination that gave birth to Albert Dock over 130 years ago. What J. A. Picton in 1875 described as 'a hideous pile of naked brickwork' in his *Memorials of Liverpool* can now

413

be appreciated as one of the supreme archaeological monuments to the rise of the first industrial nation.

Albert Dock, however, is not the only site of industrial archaeological significance in the Port of Liverpool. Whole areas of the city are rich in dockland archaeology. Within the estate are swing bridges, including cast-iron examples designed by Hartley at Albert, Salthouse and Wapping Docks, and a curious timber footbridge across the entrance to Canning Dock (100/SJ 342899), supposedly by John Rennie. Similarly the warehouses and transit sheds, particularly those of the Hartley era, are almost universally of a monumental scale and impeccable standard of construction. By contrast much of the private warehousing inland from the Dock Road is mean and penny-pinching. Despite the Liverpool Warehouse Act of 1843, which introduced reduced premiums for brick and iron structures, many were still built with timber floors up to the latter part of the nineteenth century. Other worthwhile sites include Hartley's Victoria Tower (100/SJ 333922), completed in 1848 at the entrance to Salisbury Dock (Plate 98) and the Floating Landing Stage (100/SJ 337904) at the Pier Head by G. Fosbery Lyster and Sir William Cubitt (1876). Victoria Tower, built of the same grey granite as his other dock works, is unmistakably Hartley, the stone blocks carefully dressed and fitted together like a jigsaw puzzle. It carries an unusual six-faced clock and bell to ring out warnings. The Landing Stage, on the other hand, is much more utilitarian. Built on iron pontoons and originally nearly $\frac{1}{2}$ mile long, it was the place from which Liverpool's transatlantic liners departed—Cunard and White Star until they moved to Southampton, Canadian Pacific more recently. Now it is only used regularly by the ferries and the packet boats to the Isle of Man.

Unlike London, Liverpool had no other major function during the nineteenth century and first part of the twentieth than being a port, so the down-town part of the city, more so than any other in Britain, reflects a deep involvement with ships and commerce even today. Marine insurance offices, shipping company offices, dockside pubs, warehouses and merchants' houses are all still there, some still thriving but others in the final stages of decay. The Sailors' Home in Canning Place (100/SJ 345900), dating originally from the 1840s, came into this last category. Externally a fair representation of Hardwick Hall, its cast-iron inside closely resembled an American penitentiary. It has now been demolished. In a healthier state is

98 Victoria Tower, Liverpool Docks, built of the random granite blocks favoured by Jesse Hartley

the Albany (100/SJ 340906) on Old Hall Street, dating from 1858 and one of the finest of the Victorian office blocks that grew up immediately inland from the waterfront. It is built round a courtyard that is spanned by a delicate cast-iron bridge reached by a spiral staircase. The yard provides light to the inner offices, as do skylights above galleries at each side of the building.

The industrial archaeologist in dockland has unrivalled opportunities for the discovery of obscure and obsolete equipment in addition to the more obvious large-scale installations. Winches and hand cranes frequently bear makers' names cast into them, as do iron mooring bollards. Cranes alone (Plate 99) are worthy of detailed examination, as almost any which are not electrically powered may be regarded as obsolete. Harwich (150/TM 262325) has what is probably the oldest crane (Plate 100) in Britain, dated 1666; it consists of a fixed wooden house containing a treadmill and a swinging jib

99 Albert Dock, Liverpool.
Cast-iron swinging-jib crane

100 Treadmill-powered seventeenth-century quayside crane preserved at Harwich, Essex

mounted on heavy framing at one end and turning through 180 degrees. It has been moved from its original site in the original harbour area. Steam cranes were introduced about the same time as Armstrong was experimenting with hydraulic power, but few of either type now survive. A heavy lift steam crane with riveted wrought-iron plate jib dating from the 1870s (156/ST 584722) can be seen in Bristol, and there is a smaller example in Dover. Electric cranes, introduced in the 1890s, are now almost universal, although the earlier types, like the one at Southampton dated 1893, are becoming increasingly scarce.

To enable ships to navigate coastal waters safely, lighthouses have been provided from ancient times, but it was not until the eighteenth century that there was any systematic approach to the design of either the tower or the light it carried. John Smeaton (1724–92), who built the third Eddystone Lighthouse 14 miles from Plymouth in 1759, was one of the first to examine the civil engineering problems, and his dovetailing of the core stones of the tower became a standard technique. Smeaton's light continued in use at the Eddystone until 1882, when it was decided to build a new tower on a different part of the reef because the foundation rock was becoming undermined. Smeaton's lighthouse was then re-erected on Plymouth Hoe (187/SX 478538), where it may still be visited. In 1836 Parliament transferred all English lighthouses to the care of Trinity House, while in Scotland the Commissioners for Northern Lighthouses, established in 1786, were responsible for a number of notable lights.

SHIPBUILDING

During the first century or more of industrialisation in Britain the nation's trade was handled by sailing ships that changed relatively little in design or size. Shipbuilding was an industry steeped in tradition and slow to respond to new requirements. It was no accident that Captain James Cook (1728–79) circumnavigated the world in what was basically a Whitby collier. This was the best type of vessel available to the British Admiralty, so it was used for the job. Towards the end of the eighteenth century came a gradual move to improve ship design led by the French, although later the North Americans took the lead in merchant shipbuilding. Despite conservatism of design and constructional techniques the British merchant fleet grew enormously during the eighteenth century, the total tonnage rising from 323,000 tons in 1700 to reach the 1 million ton mark by 1788.

There were, however, improvements to individual parts of ships and to the techniques of constructing them. In the 1780s copper sheathing of the wooden hulls to prevent attack by the Teredo ship worm was introduced, while in the early 1800s Sir Marc Isambard Brunel, father of I. K. Brunel, designed mass-production machine tools for the manufacture of pulley blocks (see p186).

Although the first steam paddle boat to run commercially, the *Comet*, designed by Henry Bell (1767–1830), had indicated the potential of the new form of power as early as 1812 on the Clyde, it was some years before steam navigation had any real impact. In April 1838 the 703 ton *Sirius* made the first transatlantic crossing mainly by using its steam engine, beating by a few days the paddle steamer *Great Western*. Designed by I. K. Brunel, the *Great Western* was the first ship built specifically for the transatlantic trade. She was 236ft long and weighed 4,000 tons, but the hull was basically of tradi-tional timber construction although heavily strengthened with iron knees and bolts. Not until the hulls of ships were built completely of iron could the potential of the steam engine be fully realised.

The first iron vessel had been launched into the River Severn at Preens Eddy below Ironbridge as early as 1787. Designed and built by the local ironmaster John Wilkinson (1728–1808), it was no more than a barge, probably of similar general appearance and constructional technique to the mid-nineteenth century iron tub boat preserved on the Shropshire Canal in the Blists Hill Open Air Museum (119/SJ 694034). The demand of the steam engine prompted active investigation of the possibilities of iron hulls and this fact, coupled with the success of Brunel's *Great Western* in 1838, encouraged both her owners and designer to think on a completely new and unprecedented scale when planning their next ship. That ship was the *Great Britain*, the first screw-propelled all-iron merchant ship to enter Atlantic service. Designed by Brunel, she was the largest ship afloat when Prince Albert launched her in Bristol on 19 July 1843. Unlike most vessels then and now *Great Britain* was not built on a slipway but in a drydock that had been specially built to accommodate her enormous bulk. That dock still exists, holding once more the ship to which it gave birth (158/ST 578724). After a varied but successful career involving a number of alterations to engines and rig, *Great Britain's* active life ended in 1886 when she was abandoned as a hulk in the Falkland Islands. Then, a century and a quarter after her launching, she was returned to Bristol showing signs of age but not of any major deterioration, a remarkable testimony to the skill and workmanship of her builders. The Great Britain Steamship Preservation Project, which raised the money to salvage the ship, is now actively engaged on her restoration, which visitors to Bristol are welcome to see.

Although the *Great Britain* in her dock is perhaps the most spectacular combination of maritime and shipbuilding archaeology to be found anywhere, there are numerous other remains of significance to the industrial archaeologist. Unfortunately shipbuilding tends to produce few lasting remains other than the ships themselves, and the adoption of prefabrication and welding techniques in an industry that since the 1920s has been in an almost perpetual state of flux and reorganisation has meant that there is often little of significance left to see. There is ample evidence of the products themselves, however, in the form of models in museums like Glasgow, Sunderland, Liverpool and Bristol, and in the Science Museum, South Kensington, the Maritime Museum at Exeter, and the National Maritime Museum, Greenwich. Other evidence is available in the form of plans and drafts, and in the records of Lloyd's.

Naval shipbuilding has left more to posterity than the merchant ship side of the industry. In addition to HMS *Victory* at Portsmouth and the cruiser *Belfast* in the Pool of London, efforts are now being made to preserve the hull of HMS *Warrior*, the first British armoured battleship, launched in 1860, and now part of an oil pipeline jetty at Pembroke. The Naval dockyards, too, are rich in important structures relating to both the building of ships and their subsequent operation. The four dockyards at Portsmouth, Chatham, Sheerness and Plymouth (Devonport) all contain an assortment of buildings of all periods from the seventeenth century onwards, including stores, docks, workshops, barracks, foundries, ropewalks, dwellings and chapels. Particularly important are the No 53 Boat Store at Chatham (172/TQ 765700), built in 1813 for building and repairing men-of-war; the cast- and wrought-iron framed boathouse of 1858 at Sheerness (172/TQ 910753); and the cast-iron framed fire station, previously a storehouse, at Portsmouth (180/SU 630005). The Sheerness boathouse is one of the earliest known multi-storey iron-frame buildings, and was designed by

Colonel G. T. Greene, Director of Engineering and Architectural Works at the Admiralty from 1850 to 1864. It is a frame building, ie the whole structure is supported by its frame, and the external walls are non-loadbearing panels of standardised form. Beams supporting the floors are fabricated from wrought-iron plate and angle riveted together to form H girders, the earliest known large building in Britain where this form of construction occurs. Since 1960 the Navy has stopped using Sheerness Dockyard, but at the others access may be obtained by special permission.

One remaining aspect of the industrial archaeology of ships and shipping is worthy of mention because it is a rapidly developing field offering some considerable possibilities for research. Submarine archaeology has forged ahead in recent years with the improvements made in self-contained diving apparatus, and although most of its practitioners have so far been largely concerned with wrecks, the possibilities for underwater surveying and recording in the industrial archaeological field are obvious. Recording and excavation underwater can be as accurate and thorough as on land, and the information recoverable from the 'closed site' of a well preserved wreck is often very great. The standards of surveying, recording and plotting of finds are at a relatively elementary stage in Britain, but the Committee for Nautical Archaeology, founded in 1964, is endeavouring to coordinate and systematise the approach to this new field of research and eliminate some of the regrettable unscientific exploration of sites that has occurred so far.

17 Conclusion

In this review of the major industries an attempt has been made to link processes and the stages of their evolution with the surviving visual evidence. This has not always been posisble, however, with the result that imbalances occur which in no way reflect the relative importance of various industrial activities. Thus the chemical industry, of enormous and generally unrecognised importance throughout the Industrial Revolution, has received less than its due because the physical remains, or at any rate the significant and comprehensible ones, have virtually disappeared. The present state of industrial archaeological knowledge, together with the variability of individual enthusiasms, contributes to this problem; canals and railways are more inspiring than lead-chamber sulphuric acid plants, even supposing any still exist. With the increasing amount of disciplined and well organised work within the field of industrial archaeological recording, however, these enthusiast imbalances are being redressed, particularly as local societies build up comprehensive surveys of the whole range of sites within their own areas.

Numerous industries have not been mentioned at all, but this does not mean to say that they have no archaeological significance. Food processing, clothing, and boot and shoe making are some of the areas which have been neglected but, in the case of the latter, a detailed analysis of the industry in and around Northampton will reveal through surviving buildings the transition from a domestic to a factory-based industry in the mid-nineteenth century. This change occurred to some extent as a result of the introduction of American-made sewing machines, initially for closing the uppers but later for sole and welt sewing. Examples can be seen in Northampton Museum. In the 'domestic' system the uppers were cut and stitched together (closed) at a central premises and then sent out to hand-sewers working usually in sheds at the bottom of their gardens. These 'shops' can still be seen in many Northamptonshire towns and villages. By the end of the nineteenth century the processes had all been gathered together into factories, with the cutting of the leather (clicking) and closing on the top floor where there was most light and the machines were not heavy, lasting and attaching on the floor below and at the bottom the leather stores and heavy cutting presses. This simple functionalism, with the work flowing down through the building, still exists in some Northampton factories. Thus the physical evidence of buildings and to a lesser extent machines exists to illustrate the stages in the transition from a cottage industry to that ultimate in mid-nineteenth century shoe factories, the Manfield Building in Campbell Square, Northampton (133/SP 755609). To find out *why* shoes are made in Northampton requires evidence of a completely different type. Only a detailed analysis of documentary sources and a thorough appreciation of a range of geographical factors will build up the picture of coinciding elements—of cattle for leather, perhaps of oak trees providing bark for tanning, of agrarian unrest and unemployment associated with enclosure—creating the conditions for the growth of the industry. Northamptonshire tended at first to specialise in cheaper shoes, as the top end of the market was largely the province of London-based shoemakers located near their discerning customers. Northamptonshire shoemakers prospered on army contracts, initially for Cromwell's New Model Army, and eventually gaining a virtual monopoly of all service footwear. All this, but particularly the relation of the physical evidence to other sources, is the concern of the industrial archaeologist.

Besides the evidence of its own specific technology, the brewing industry affords the industrial archaeologist an opportunity to examine functionalism in building design and construction at its purest. In addition the appreciation of the role which many of the spectacular structural elements, particularly of maltings, play in both urban and rural landscapes is a refined aesthetic experience in its own right. Malting as an essential part of the brewing process has been carried on both at the brewery itself or in separate establishments. The process consists of encouraging barley to germinate and thereby change its starch content into sugar, at which stage the process is arrested in drying kilns. Before the development of large-scale breweries, malting was a local and very small-scale activity carried out in almost every town. Even so, some had marked concentrations of small malthouses. Marshfield in Gloucestershire, for example, had dozens, and the characteristic perforated tiles from the drying floors are commonplace there.

The development of large-scale maltings, often separate from the breweries themselves, in the second half of the nineteenth century resulted in some of the most visually stimulating and dynamic examples of functional building to emerge during the Industrial Revolution. East Anglia and the Home

Counties, areas not noted for their high degree of industrialisation, are rich in these sophisticated and often beautiful buildings. The main part of the structure usually has three or more floors for the germination process, often with floor to ceiling heights of only 6ft or even less, with small rectangular windows louvred to serve as vents. Very typically there are tie irons passing through the building whose presence is evident on the exterior in the form of tie plates—huge crosses or discs of cast iron regularly spaced along the façades. Attached are the kilns with their tall pyramidal roofs and cowls. The architectural personality of these structures derives from the common ingredients of functional elements often combined with great size (Plate 101), so that they make their presence felt in the landscape in a very positive but honest and unobtrusive sort of way. Often, because of their rural situation, it is difficult to associate them with an industrial process at all; they are more an extension of the agricultural tradition of building.

Their extensive floor areas and attractive proportions have led to some highly successful conversions of disused maltings to new purposes. Best known are the Snape, Suffolk, maltings now a hall for the Aldeburgh Music Festival (137/TM 392575), while in Newmarket a much larger maltings is occupied by a colour-processing laboratory. The oasthouse in which hops are dried, also for brewing, is another distinctive structure common in Kent but also to be found in Worcestershire and Herefordshire.

101 Late nineteenth-century maltings at Ipswich Docks, Suffolk

Cylindrical kilns with their characteristic wind vane cowls are, generally speaking, older than the rectangular type; both are in demand for conversion to dwellings. This functional simplicity extends, too, to some of the older whisky distilleries in Scotland, of which the main concentration is in Strath Spey. The malting process is basically the same and the characteristic cowled pyramidal roofs can still be seen here and there.

Town breweries also have an architecture all their own, with pronounced tendencies towards simple and symmetrical Georgian proportions continuing well into the second half of the nineteenth century. External features typically include clocks or clock towers, weather vanes, large lettering proclaiming the name of the firm or the brew and more functional details such as cranes, or 'lucams', above loading bays. Bullard's Anchor Brewery in Norwich (126/TG 231088), dating mainly from the late 1860s, has strongly emphasised arch-headed windows and doors with iron frames, while the somewhat later Tadcaster, Yorkshire, brewery of John Smith's (97/SE 484433), with its ornamental ironwork and spectacular chimney (Plate 102), represents a less common Victorian ornateness. Young's Ram Brewery in Wandsworth (170/TQ 256747) is even more remarkable, with its two working beam engines, of 1835 and 1867, used for driving mashing and milling machinery, as well as coopers' and farriers' shops and stables. Horses are still used regularly for local deliveries.

These are examples of industries that make a visible contribution to the urban or rural landscape and are therefore important not only for the intrinsic characteristics of their own processes but for their role in creating the personality of an area. The industrial archaeologist in studying landscapes is involved in the analysis of their personalities, which depends not only on collecting and collating detailed field evidence and relating it to documentary sources but also on a subtler aesthetic appreciation of the components of that landscape in terms of building materials, of the size and shape of windows, the pitch of roofs, the depths of mouldings and string courses, the design of rainwater goods, the types of paving and road surfacing. Here the work of the industrial archaeologist is wedded immutably with the field evidence, and only by exhaustive and detailed examination of large numbers of structures can he isolate the components that make up the personality of an area. Industrial landscapes, even of the late nineteenth century, possess as much visual variety, structural and architectural indi-

102 John Smith's Tadcaster Brewery, Yorkshire, 1883

viduality as do their rural predecessors, in which the regional variations of the vernacular tradition have long been accepted. The industrial archaeologist in extracting from the surviving buildings and other features of the landscape the specific characteristics that in total create its personality is carrying out a vital archaeological function, and providing what may be the only basis for defining rational conservation policies. He can only analyse those characteristics after recording in painstaking detail large numbers of individual structures and comparing the results. Students of vernacular architecture have long used a system of building record cards which enables a basic tabulation of constructional details, materials, etc, to be made. The technique is as valid for industrial buildings, particularly housing, and the results of analysis contribute in the same way not only to our knowledge of social conditions but also to an understanding of the intangible visual characteristics of an area.

The Industrial Revolution was characterised, we are told, by uniformity and standardisation, by identical machine-made artefacts that could be produced in large numbers. This is to a great extent true, and it poses a peculiar problem of both recording and preservation. It is particularly important to preserve the *typical*, as this represents as closely as possible what conditions were really like, but it is only by the most diligent processes of archaeological investigation that the characteristics of the typical can be isolated. Having defined a typical row of pitmens' cottages or silk weavers' garrets, the industrial archaeologist is faced with the even greater problem of justifying their retention *because* they are typical, ordinary and everyday. It is only by a detailed knowledge of what those typical characteristics are that a credible case can be made on industrial archaeological grounds.

In South Wales David Anderson and Jeremy Lowe of the Welsh School of Architecture in Cardiff have been able to analyse in detail the characteristics of numerous workers' houses, although unfortunately this has often had to be done in advance of or during the demolition of these houses. They have been able to build up a picture, based largely on the collection of massive quantities of field evidence, of the evolution of house types, providing an insight into the social conditions of the area and the development of techniques of building construction. Now they are able to use their mass of accumulated information as a means of dating, or at least establishing a relative chronology, on the basis of field evidence alone. In their

103 Carpenters' Row, Coalbrookdale, Shropshire. Workers cottages built in the 1790s and now being restored by the Ironbridge Gorge Museum Trust

Iron Industry Housing Papers No 2 they examine two cottages, one in Coed-penmaen and the other in Gelligaer, which they describe as 'prototypes', drawing conclusions from a wide variety of constructional features that are compared with other buildings in the area. The absence of beams in the floor construction, the provision of three fireplaces and the use of wall structure above the first floor windows they see in one cottage as being advanced for the late eighteenth century, but the dimensions, particularly of the span, the extensive use of oak and the heavy complex roof suggest an early date, probably before 1811. They recognise both cottages as the continuation of a much earlier seventeenth-century tradition. Physical and documentary evidence combine to pin down the date and their accumulated survey information indicates the coexistence in South Wales in about 1810 of three forms of floor structure—cross-beams alone, cross-beams and joists, and joists alone. They are thus able to make observations based on the collection of comparative evidence, as would the archaeologist of any other period.

The industrial archaeologist, then, can have a valid place in both the processes of data collection and interpretation. The sources available to him are wide, demanding a disciplined and well organised approach but offering in return a vivid insight into the past. This variety of material and documentary evidence and its direct relevance to current society is the key to the involvement of so many people in industrial archaeological investigation, and offers in many ways much wider opportunities for making a fruitful contribution than those afforded to the average amateur digging on a conventional archaeological excavation. The future strength of industrial archaeology rests in this integrated but inter-disciplinary nature of the study, drawing its expertise from a wide range of sources in order to analyse all the available evidence. Few economic historians would today consider writing about industrial sites if they have not examined the physical remains, which is progress in itself, but industrial archaeology offers more than adding an extra dimensional quality to documentary source material. It is the meeting point of people whose motivating interests range from history to complex technologies, from geography or mining geology to architecture or the pure unalloyed aesthetic enjoyment of functional buildings, but whose common inspiration is the physical evidence of the Industrial Revolution, the material heritage of our contemporary culture.

Appendices:
1 Gazetteer of Sites

The majority of the sites listed in this gazetteer are mentioned in the text and a page reference is given with each entry, where appropriate. The gazetteer is arranged under eight regions and within each region the sites are listed in the order of the chapters in this book. There is no standard form of presentation; the information is provided in the form likely to be most convenient to the reader. The geographical descriptions refer to the old (pre-April 1974) county and county borough boundaries. Map numbers refer to the Ordnance Survey 1in series, an index to which appears on the back cover of all Ordnance Survey sheets. Grid references are presented in the standard form with the grid letters followed by a six-figure reference. In some cases, where an area rather than a specific point is referred to, a four-figure reference is given indicating the kilometre square within which the site comes.

Sites mentioned in the gazetteer which do *not* appear in the text are listed at the end of the appropriate sub-section in italics.

The eight gazetteer regions are

1 Scotland
2 North West England (Cumberland, Westmorland, Lancashire, The Isle of Man and Cheshire)
3 North East England (Northumberland, Durham and Yorkshire)
4 The West Midlands (Shropshire, Staffordshire, Herefordshire, Worcestershire, Warwickshire)
5 The East Midlands (Derbyshire, Nottinghamshire, Lincolnshire, Leicestershire, Rutland, Northamptonshire)
6 The South East (Huntingdonshire, Cambridgeshire, Norfolk, Suffolk, Oxfordshire, Buckinghamshire, Bedfordshire, Hertfordshire, Essex, Berkshire, Greater London, Hampshire, Surrey, Sussex and Kent)
7 The South West (Gloucestershire, Somerset, Wiltshire, Cornwall, Devon, Dorset)
8 Wales

ACCESS TO SITES

Most of the sites described in the text and listed in the gazetteer are on private property, and although the majority can be viewed from public areas, access to them is by courtesy of the owners. It must be remembered that in many cases owners are unaware of the significance of their buildings or plant. Visitors are advised to make prior arrangement and on no account to regard access as automatically forthcoming. Although some firms welcome individual visitors and even parties, others do not, and often for reasons of safety cannot permit entry to their sites. Remember too that in, for example, derelict mining areas where public access is not restricted there may be hidden shafts or workings. Keep a sharp lookout for these and *never* enter derelict mines without guidance from a local expert who has permission and knows the site well.

1 SCOTLAND

WIND AND WATER POWER

Site	Map	Grid ref	Page
Click Mill, Orkney	6	HY 290200	66
Wanlockhead water pump, Dumfries	68	NS 855144	76
Preston Mill, East Lothian	63	NT 595779	78
Alford watermill, Aberdeen	*39*	*NJ 612167*	
Carluke windmill, Lanark	*61*	*NS 849508*	
Hilton windmill, Aberdeen	*40*	*NJ 942342*	
Mouswald windmill, Dumfries	*74*	*NY 053736*	
Shortrigg windmill, Dumfries	*75*	*NY 162744*	

STEAM AND INTERNAL COMBUSTION POWER

	Map	Grid ref	Page
Prestongrange pumping engine, East Lothian	62	NT 374737	103

COAL

	Map	Grid ref	Page
Prestongrange pumping engine, East Lothian	62	NT 374737	138

IRON AND STEEL

	Map	Grid ref	Page
Bonawe furnace, Argyllshire	35	NN 114770	154
Carron Ironworks, Stirlingshire	*61*	*NS 880825*	
Dalmellington Ironworks, Ayrshire	*67*	*NS 480060*	
Muirkirk Ironworks, Ayrshire	*67*	*NS 697268*	

ENGINEERING

	Map	Grid ref
Barblues Forge, Airdrie, Lanark	*61*	*NS 803675*
Eagle Foundry, Port Dundas, Glasgow	*60*	*NS 592666*
London Road Foundry, Edinburgh	*62*	*NT 273744*
Macfarlane's Saracen Foundry, Glasgow	*60*	*NS 592683*

2 NORTH-WEST ENGLAND

Site	Map	Grid ref	Page
Worsley Delph, Lancs	101	SD 748005	138
Salford Museum, Buile Hill	101	SJ 799996	140

IRON AND STEEL

Duddon Furnace, Furness, Lancs	88	SD 197884	154
Newland Furnace, Lancs	88	SD 299798	154
Leighton, Arnside, Lancs	89	SD 485778	154

ENGINEERING

Walmsley's Atlas Forge, Bolton, Lancs	101	SD 713084	188

NON-FERROUS METALS

Goldscope copper mine, Derwentwater	82	NY 228186	
		& 226187	197
Coniston copper mine	88	SD 289986	197
Greenodd copper mine, Lancs	88	SD 315826	197
Tilberthwaite copper mine, Lancs	88	NY 306007	197
Chester shot tower	109	SJ 415667	213

STONE, CLAY AND GLASS

Pilkington Glass Museum, St Helens, Lancs	100	SJ 498946	238

TEXTILES

Hargreaves' cottage, Stanhill, Lancs	95	SD 728277	248
Higher Mill, Helmshore, Lancs	95	SD 777214	248
Frost's Mill, Macclesfield, Cheshire	110	SJ 918737	260
Card factory, Macclesfield, Cheshire	110	SJ 909737	261
Styal Mill, Cheshire	101	SJ 834830	261
Galgate Mill, Lancs	94	SD 485557	267
Centenary Mill, Preston, Lancs	94	SD 551247	267
Dee Mill, Shaw, Rochdale, Lancs	101	SD 945093	269

CHEMICALS

Crosscanonby	82	NY 066401	274
Marston salt mine, Northwich, Cheshire	101	SJ 6760	275
Salt sheds, Winsford, Cheshire	110	SJ 599997	275
Winnington, ICI Works, Cheshire	110	SJ 6474	275
Port Sunlight, Cheshire	100	SJ 3484	278

Site	*Map*	*Grid ref*		*Page*
Blackbeck gunpowder mill, Westmorland	89	SD	334859	284
Haverthwaite gunpowder mill, Westmorland	89	NY	328048	284

PUBLIC SERVICES

Water towers, Ormskirk, Lancs	100	SD	423087	
		&	423085	295
Water tower, Newton-le-Willows, Lancs	100	SJ	599957	295
Lister Drive power station, Liverpool	100	SJ	387917	307
Tram depot, Chester	109	SJ	413668	312
Horse tram track, Queen Square, Liverpool	100	SJ	346906	312

ROADS AND BRIDGES

Tollhouse, Todmorden, Lancs	101	SD	945198	323
Central Station, Manchester	101	SJ	837977	326
Grosvenor Bridge, Chester	109	SJ	403656	330
Warrington transporter bridge, Lancs	100	SJ	597877	340
Skerton Bridge, Lancaster	89	SD	479623	330

RIVERS AND CANALS

Barton Aqueduct, Bridgewater Canal, Lancs	101	SJ	767977	344
Worsley Delph, Lancs	101	SD	748005	344
Worsley Delph, Wharf Crane, Lancs	101	SD	747004	345
Beeston Cast-iron Lock, Cheshire	109	SJ	554599	353
Northgate Locks, Chester	109	SJ	403666	353
Anderton boat lift, Cheshire	101	SJ	647753	354
Preston Brook canal hamlet, Cheshire	109	SJ	568806	356
Barnton Tunnel, Cheshire	110	SJ	630749	356
Saltersford Tunnel, Cheshire	101	SJ	624753	356
Harecastle Tunnel, Staffs	110	SJ	837542	346
Marple Aqueduct, Cheshire	101	SJ	956900	358
Lune Aqueduct, Lancaster	89	SD	484639	358
Ellesmere Port warehouses, Cheshire	109	SJ	405775	364

RAILWAYS

Viaduct, Earlestown, Lancs	100	SJ	569947	378
Viaduct, Newton-le-Willows, Lancs	100	SJ	591954	378
Skew-arch bridge, Rainhill, Lancs	100	SJ	491914	378
Liverpool Road Station, Manchester	101	SJ	830978	378

Site	Map	Grid ref		Page
Dutton Viaduct, Cheshire	109	SJ	583764	385
Runcorn Viaduct, Cheshire	100	SJ	509835	388
Chester General Station	109	SJ	413669	395
Huskisson memorial, Newton-le-Willows, Lancs	*100*	*SJ*	*606955*	

PORTS AND SHIPPING

Maryport Harbour, Cumberland	82	NY	030365	401
St George's Quay, Lancaster	94	SD	474623	402
Sunderland Point, nr Lancaster	94	SD	426560	402
Glasson Dock, nr Lancaster	94	SD	445562	403
Barton Swing Aqueduct, Lancs	101	SJ	766976	406
Albert Dock, Liverpool	100	SJ	342897	410
Canning Dock, Liverpool	100	SJ	342899	414
Victoria Tower, Liverpool	100	SJ	333922	414
Floating Landing Stage, Liverpool	100	SJ	337904	414
Sailors' Home, Liverpool (demol)	100	SJ	345900	414
The Albany, Liverpool	100	SJ	340906	415

MISCELLANEOUS SITES

Arighi Bianchi iron-fronted store, Macclesfield, Cheshire	*110*	*SJ*	*920737*
Oriel Chambers, Liverpool, curtain wall office	*100*	*SJ*	*341904*
St George's (cast-iron) Church, Everton, Liverpool	*100*	*SJ*	*355925*
St Michael's (cast-iron) Church, Aigburth, Liverpool	*100*	*SJ*	*369871*

3 NORTH EAST ENGLAND

WIND AND WATER POWER

Killhope Lead Mill, Durham	84	NY	827429	74
Lothersdale Watermill, Yorks	95	SD	959459	74
Foster Beck Watermill, Pateley Bridge, Yorks	91	SD	148664	74
Abbeydale industrial hamlet, Sheffield	111	SK	325820	78
Shepherd Wheel, Sheffield	111	SK	317854	78
High Mill, Skipton, Yorks	95	SD	989518	78

STEAM AND INTERNAL COMBUSTION POWER

Elsecar pumping engine, Yorks	102	SE	390003	84
Ryhope pumping station, Sunderland	78	NZ	403523	102
Beamish winding engine, Durham	78	NZ	220537	110

Site	Map	Grid ref	Page
COAL			
Beamish winding engine, Durham	78	NZ 220537	134
Elemore winding engine, Durham	85	NZ 356456	134
Elsecar pumping engine, Yorks	102	SE 390003	137
Ryhope Colliery, Sunderland	78	NZ 399534	141
Seaham Harbour, Durham	85	NZ 435495	143
Amble Harbour, Northumberland	71	NU 269049	143
Blyth Harbour, Northumberland	78	NZ 3280	143
IRON AND STEEL			
Eston ironstone mines	86	NZ 560186	147
North Skelton ironstone mines	86	NZ 675184	147
Boulby ironstone quarries	86	NZ 760181	147
Rosedale ironstone quarries	92	SE 723946	147
Wortley Forge, Yorks	102	SK 294998	169
Union Bridge, nr Berwick	64	NT 934510	171
Abbeydale industrial hamlet, Yorks	111	SK 326820	174
Hamsterley steel cementation furnace, Durham	78	NZ 131565	172
NON-FERROUS METALS			
Keld Heads lead mill, Yorks	90	SE 077910	209
Cobscar lead mill, Yorks	90	SE 060930	210
Grassington High Mill, Yorks	90	SE 025663	210
Surrender lead mill, Yorks	90	NY 988003	210
Lintzgarth lead mill, Durham	84	NY 925430	210
Castleside lead mill, Durham	84	NZ 078485	210
Langley lead mill, Northumberland	77	NY 841611	211
STONE, CLAY AND GLASS			
Ryedale Folk Museum, Hutton-le-Hole, Yorks	86	SE 705900	234
Catcliffe glass cone, Yorks	103	SE 425887	236
Lemington glass cone, Newcastle-upon-Tyne	78	NZ 184646	237
TEXTILES			
Gott's Mill, Leeds (demol)	96	SE 291335	269
Marshall's Mill, Leeds	96	SE 295326	270
Manningham Mills, Bradford	96	SE 146348	272

4 THE WEST MIDLANDS
WIND AND WATER POWER

Site	Map	Grid ref		Page
Compton Lock, Worcs	130	SO	884989	353
Coalport inclined plane, Shropshire	119	SJ	695028	354
Dove Aqueduct, Burton-on-Trent, Staffs	120	SK	269269	358
Great Haywood Aqueduct, Staffs	119	SJ	994229	358
Milford Aqueduct	119	SJ	973215	358
Longden-upon-Tern Aqueduct, Shropshire	118	SJ	617156	359
Chirk Aqueduct, Shropshire	118	SJ	287372	360
Stourport, inland port, Worcs	130	SO	810710	363
Stretton Aqueduct, Staffs	*119*	*SJ*	*873107*	

RAILWAYS

Site	Map	Grid ref		Page
Froghall basin terminus, Caldon Canal, Staffs	111	SK	028477	369
Remains of tramway bridge, Woodcock, Staffs	111	SK	070480	369
Tramway bridge, Whiston, Staffs	111	SK	029476	369
Curzon Street Station, Birmingham	131	SP	080871	380
Albert Edward Bridge, Ironbridge, Shropshire	118	SJ	661038	391
Shugborough Tunnel, Staffs	119	SJ	982216	392
		to	988216	395
Stoke-on-Trent Station, Staffs	110	SJ	879456	396
Shrewsbury Station	118	SJ	494129	396
Stone Station, Staffs	119	SJ	896346	399
Bridgnorth Station, Shropshire	130	SO	715926	000

5 THE EAST MIDLANDS
WIND AND WATER POWER

Site	Map	Grid ref		Page
Maud Foster windmill, Boston, Lincs	114	TF	333447	61
Burgh-le-Marsh windmill, Lincs	114	TF	504650	61
Alford windmill, Lincs	114	TF	457766	61
Sibsey windmill, Lincs	114	TF	344510	61
Heckington windmill, Lincs	113	TF	145436	61

STEAM AND INTERNAL COMBUSTION POWER

Site	Map	Grid ref		Page
Papplewick pumping station, Notts	112	SK	583522	101
Abbey Lane pumping station, Leicester	121	SK	589066	101

COAL

Site	Map	Grid ref		Page
Snibston Colliery, Leics	121	SK	417145	130
Lound Hall Mining Museum, Notts	112	SK	701731	130

6 THE SOUTH EAST

Holton windmill, Suffolk	137	TM 402776	56
Pitstone windmill, Bucks	159	SP 945157	56
Wheatley windmill, Oxon	158	SP 589052	57
West Wittering windmill, Sussex	181	SZ 797972	57
Willingham windmill, Cambs	135	TL 404697	57
Cranbrook windmill, Kent	172	TQ 779359	57
St Margaret's Bay windmill, Kent	173	TR 363435	57
Bembridge windmill, Isle of Wight	180	SZ 640875	58
Herne windmill, Kent	173	TR 184665	59
Great Bardfield windmill, Essex	148	TL 681308	59
Polegate windmill, Sussex	183	TQ 581041	59
Selsey windmill, Sussex	181	SZ 843933	59
West Wratting windmill, Cambs	148	TL 604510	59
Burwell windmill, Cambs	135	TL 590665	60
Outwood windmill, Surrey	170	TQ 327456	60
Saxted Green windmill, Suffolk	137	TM 254644	63
Great Chishill windmill, Cambs	148	TL 413388	63
Cross-in-Hand windmill, Sussex	183	TQ 558218	63
Wicken Fen windmill, Cambs	135	TL 562706	65
Horsey windmill, Norfolk	126	TG 457223	65
Berney Arms windmill, Norfolk	126	TG 465051	65
Woodbridge tide mill, Suffolk	150	TM 276847	74
Deben Watermill, Wickham Market, Suffolk	*150*	*TM 306566*	
Drinkstone windmill, Suffolk	*136*	*TL 964622*	
Morden snuff mills, Merton	*170*	*TQ 262686*	

STEAM AND INTERNAL COMBUSTION POWER

Ram Brewery, Wandsworth, London	170	TQ 256747	92
Stretham pump, Cambs	135	TL 517730	93
Eastney pumping station, Portsmouth	181	SZ 675989	102
Kempton Park pumping station, Hounslow, London	170	TQ 110709	112
Otterbourne pumping station, Hants (demol)	168	SU 468233	112

IRON AND STEEL

Weald and Downland Open Air Museum, Sussex	181	SU 875130	151
Hawkins Pond, Sussex	182	TQ 217292	151
Hammer Pond, Sussex	182	TQ 219289	151
Slaugham Pond, Sussex	182	TQ 248281	151

Cort's furnace site, Funtley, Hants	180	SU 550082	165
Sheerness boatsheds, Kent	172	TQ 910753	172

STONE, CLAY AND GLASS

Betchworth limekilns, Surrey	170	TQ 208514	222

TEXTILES

Fournier Street silk weavers' houses, London	160	TQ 338818	258
Silk mill, Whitchurch, Hants	168	SU 464481	261
Yarn Mill, Cowgate, Norwich (now Jarrold's)	*126*	*TG 235092*	

CHEMICALS

Faversham gunpowder mills, Kent	172	TR 009613	284

PUBLIC SERVICES

Water supply ponds, Islington, London	160	TQ 313828	292
New River conduit, London	160	TQ 318878	292
	160	TQ 343987	293
	160	TQ 306916	293
Kew Bridge water pumping station, Brentford, London	170	TQ 188780	294
Water tower, Godalming, Surrey	170	SU 970445	295
Sewage pumping station, Greenwich	161	TQ 377772	296
Abbey mills sewage pumping station, West Ham	161	TQ 388832	296
Crossness sewage pumping station, Thamesmead	161	TQ 484811	296
Eastney sewage pumping station, Portsmouth	181	SZ 675989	297
Webb sewer lamp, Carting Lane, London	160	TQ 305806	298
Fakenham Gasworks, Norfolk	125	TF 919293	300
Fulham Gasworks, London	170	TQ 260768	301
Reading Gasworks, Berkshire	169	SU 731738	301
Deptford power station, London	161	TQ 374779	305
Volk's Electric Railway, Brighton, Sussex	182	TQ 316038	310
Kingsway tram subway, London	160	TQ 305817	312
Semaphore station, Chatley Heath, Surrey	170	TQ 089585	314

ROADS AND BRIDGES

Wagon-weighing machine, Woodbridge, Suffolk	150	TM 272491	325
Tickford Bridge, Newport Pagnell, Bucks	146	SP 877437	334
Marlow suspension bridge, Bucks	159	SU 852862	338

Site	Map	Grid ref		Page
RIVERS AND CANALS				
Eynsham flash lock, Oxon	158	SP	446089	343
Castle Mills staunch, Beds	147	TL	094509	343
Tuddenham Mill stream, staunch	135	TL	732729	343
Bottisham Lode, staunch	135	TL	516651	343
Papercourt turf locks, R. Wey, Surrey	170	TQ	034568	347
Walsham gates	170	TQ	050578	347
Worsfold gates, nr Send, Surrey	170	TQ	016557	350
Sheffield turf lock, Berkshire	158	SU	649706	347
RAILWAYS				
Surrey Iron Railway track, Purley	170	TQ	316622	371
		TQ	290543	371
Surrey Iron Railway track, Wallington	170	TQ	288638	371
Tring cutting, Herts	159	SP	940137	379
Camden roundhouse, London	160	TQ	282843	380
Hanwell Viaduct, Middlesex	160	TQ	150804	381
Maidenhead Viaduct, Berks	159	SU	901810	381
Sonning cutting, Berks	159	SU	759743	381
Primrose Hill Tunnel, London (South portal)	160	TQ	276843	392
Kings Cross Station, London	160	TQ	303831	394
St Pancras Station, London	160	TQ	302829	394
Cambridge Station	135	TL	462573	395
Maldon Station, Essex	162	TL	853077	396
Southampton (L&SR) Station	180	SU	422109	396
Sheffield Park Station, Sussex	183	TQ	404237	398
Battle Station, Sussex	*184*	*TQ*	*755156*	
PORTS AND SHIPPING				
Tower Bridge, London	160	TQ	337802	406
St Katharine's Dock, London	160	TQ	339805	409
Dockside crane, Harwich	150	TM	262325	415
Chatham boat store	172	TQ	765700	419
Sheerness boatshed	172	TQ	910753	419
Portsmouth dockyard storehouse	180	SU	630005	419
Cutty Sark, Greenwich	*171*	*TQ*	*383781*	
HMS Victory, Portsmouth	*180*	*SU*	*630001*	

Site	Map	Grid ref		Page
CHEMICALS				
Salt evaporation pools, Lymington, Hants	180	SZ	315923	274
Soap factory, Broad Plain, Bristol	156	ST	597728	276
Logwood Mill, Keynsham, Somerset	156	ST	656679	279
Powder Mills Farm, nr Princetown, Devon	175	ST	628769	284
Powder House, Bristol	156	ST	537765	285
Bathford paper mill, Somerset	156	ST	790671	287
Wookey Hole paper mill, Somerset	165	ST	531466	287
Slaughterford rag mill, Glos	156	ST	839738	287
Oil shale extraction plant, Kilve, Somerset	164	ST	147439	289
PUBLIC SERVICES				
Blagdon water pumping station, Somerset	165	ST	503600	294
Chelvey water pumping station, Somerset	165	ST	474679	294
Bristol electricity power stations	156	ST	594728	
		&	593728	305
ROADS AND BRIDGES				
Ashton Gate tollhouse, Bristol	156	ST	573717	324
Cast-iron finger post, Bristol	156	ST	599718	325
Over Bridge, Gloucester	143	SO	817196	330
Iron bridges over Kennet & Avon Canal, Bath	156	ST	758654	334
Iron bridge, Tewkesbury, Glos	143	SO	893330	334
Mythe Bridge, Tewkesbury, Glos	143	SO	888337	336
Victoria Bridge, Bath	156	ST	741650	338
Clifton suspension bridge, Brsitol	156	ST	564731	338
Royal Albert Bridge, Saltash, Cornwall..	187	SX	435587	338
Seaton, concrete bridge, Devon	177	SY	253900	339
RIVERS AND CANALS				
Combe Hay locks, Somerset	166	ST	748604	351
Ridd incline, Devon	163	SS	476217	354
Sapperton Tunnel, Glos	157	SO	966006	
		to	944034	357
Dundas Aqueduct, Monkton Combe, Somerset	166	ST	784625	358
Avoncliff Aqueduct, Somerset	166	ST	805600	358
Devizes Locks, Kennet & Avon Canal, Wilts	*167*	*ST*	*980615*	

Site	Map	Grid ref	Page

8 WALES

Site	Map	Grid ref	Page

Site	Map	Grid ref		Page
RAILWAYS				
Pwll-Ddu tramway tunnel, Mon	141	SO	248114	370
Tramway bridge, Redbrook, Mon	142	SO	537103	370
Penydarran Tramway remains	154	ST	083969	372
Britannia Bridge, Caernarvonshire	107	SH	542710	385
Conway Bridge, Caernarvonshire	107	SH	787776	386
Barmouth timber viaduct, Merioneth	116	SH	624150	391
Penrhyndeudraeth timber viaduct, Merioneth	116	SH	619384	391
Ffestiniog Tunnel, Merioneth	107	SH	687505	391
		to	697469	
Blackrock Pier, Mon	155	ST	514881	393
Sudbrook pumping station, Mon	155	ST	507874	393
Tywyn Station, Merioneth	127	SH	586005	398
Abergynolwyn Station, Merioneth	127	SH	671064	398
Porthmadog Station (FR), Caernarvon	116	SH	571384	398
Llanfair Caereinion Station, Montgomery	117	SJ	106068	398
Aberystwyth Station (V of RR), Cardigan	127	SN	585815	398
Devil's Bridge Station, Cardigan	127	SN	738769	398
Llanberis station, Snowdon Railway, Caernarvon	107	SH	583597	398
Tramway Bridge, Aberdare	*154*	*SN*	*997037*	

2 Museums of Industry

MUSEUMS OF INDUSTRY

The following are the principal museums holding industrial, technological and transport material. They are listed alphabetically by place and the entries in column two refer to the type of industrial material in the collection—thus 'textiles' means textile machinery and so on.

ANSTRUTHER (Fife) Scottish Fisheries Museum, St Ayles, Harbourhead, Anstruther Tel: Anstruther 628	Scottish fisheries
BANGOR (Caernarvon) Penrhyn Castle Locomotive and Industrial Museum, Penrhyn Castle, Bangor	Railways, slate transport
BEAMISH (County Durham) North of England Open Air Museum, Beamish Hall, Stanley, County Durham Tel: Stanley (02073) 3586	Industry and social history of the North East
BEAULIEU (Hampshire) Buckler's Hard Maritime Museum, Buckler's Hard, Beaulieu, Brockenhurst Tel: Buckler's Hard 203	Maritime
National Motor Museum, Palace House, Beaulieu Tel: Beaulieu 374	Motor vehicles
BIRMINGHAM Avery Historical Museum, W. & T. Avery Ltd, Soho Foundry, Birmingham 40 Tel: (021) 558 1112	Company museum, weighing (appointment preferred)

451

Museum of Science & Industry,   Science, engineering, transport
Newhall Street, Birmingham B3 1RZ
Tel: (021) 236 1022
Sarehole Mill, Cole Bank Road,   Watermill
Hall Green, Birmingham
(administered by City Museum & Art Gallery)
Tel: (021) 777 6612

BLACKBURN (Lancashire)   Textiles
Lewis Museum of Textile Machinery,
Exchange Street, Blackburn
Tel: (0254) 59511

BRADFORD (Yorkshire)   Textiles, engineering, transport
Industrial Museum, Moorside Mills,
Moorside Road, Eccleshill, Bradford

BRISTOL
Blaise Castle House Museum,   Local crafts, watermill (Stratford Mill)
Henbury, Bristol BS10 7QS
Tel: (0272) 625378
City Museum,   Industry (mainly in store), maritime,
Queen's Road, Bristol BS8 1RL   transport
Tel: (0272) 299771
Harvey's Wine Museum   Company Museum, wine, bottles
12 Denmark Street, Bristol
Tel: (0272) 20164

CAMBORNE (Cornwall)
Holman Museum, (Holman Brothers Ltd) Mining engineering, local industry
Camborne
School of Mines Museum, Camborne   Mining engineering

CARDIFF
National Museum of Wales,   Welsh industry, mining, steel, tinplate,
Cathays Park, Cardiff CF1 3NP   quarrying, shipping
Tel: (0222) 26241
Welsh Folk Museum, St Fagans,   Welsh craft industries,
Cardiff CF5 6XB   woollen mill, tannery
Tel: (0222) 561357

CASTLETOWN (Isle of Man)
Nautical Museum, Bridge Street,
Castletown (administered by the
Manx Museum)

Maritime. Schooner-rigged yacht
Peggy, 1789

COALBROOKDALE (*see* Telford)

COVENTRY
Herbert Art Gallery & Museum,
Jordan Well, Coventry CV1 5QP
Tel: (0203) 25555

Road transport, textiles, aeronautics

CRICH (Derbyshire)
Tramway Museum, Matlock Road,
Crich, near Matlock, Derbyshire DE4 5DP
Tel: (077 385) 2565
(Grid ref: 111 SK 345548)

Trams

DERBY
Museum of Industry & Technology,
Silk Mill Lane, Derby

Local industry, textiles, aeronautics

ECCLES (Lancashire)
Monks Hall Museum,
42 Wellington Road, Eccles,
Lancashire M30 0NP
Tel: (061) 789 4372

Nasmyth machiney

EDINBURGH
Royal Scottish Museum,
Chambers Street, Edinburgh EH1 1JF
Tel: (031) 225 7534

Science, engineering, transport,
aeronautics, mining

EXETER (Devon)
Exeter Maritime Museum, The Quay,
Exeter EX2 4AN
Tel: (0392) 58075

Maritime, mainly sailing craft

GLASGOW

Art Gallery & Museum, Kelvingrove, Glasgow C3 Tel: (041) 334 1134	Maritime engineering
Museum of Transport, 25 Albert Drive, Glasgow S1 Tel: (041) 423 8000	Transport

HALIFAX (Yorkshire)

Bankfield Museum & Art Gallery, Akroyd Park, Halifax Tel: (0422) 54823	Textiles
West Yorkshire Folk Museum, Shibden Hall, Shibden, Halifax Tel: (0422) 52246	Local industry, transport

HARTLEBURY (Worcestershire)

Worcestershire County Museum, Hartlebury Castle, nr Kidderminster Tel: Hartlebury 416	Local industry, carpets, transport

HARTLEPOOL (County Durham)

Maritime Museum, Northgate, Hartlepool	Maritime, fishery

HULL (Yorkshire)

Maritime Museum, Pickering Road, Hessle Road, Kingston upon Hull Tel: (0482) 51936	Maritime
Transport & Archaeology Museum, 36 High Street, Kingston upon Hull Tel: (0482) 27625	Transport

IRONBRIDGE (see Telford)

LEICESTER

Museum of Technology, Abbey Lane Pumping Station, Corporation Road, Leicester Tel: (0533) 61330	Industry of the East Midlands, transport
Railway Museum, London Road, Stoneygate, Leicester	Railways

LIVERPOOL
Merseyside County Museums,
William Brown Street, Liverpool L3 8EN
Tel: (051) 207 0001

Land transport, maritime

LLANBERIS (Caernarvon)
North Wales Quarrying Museum,
Llanberis
Tel: Llanberis 630

Slate quarrying, iron founding,
engineering

LONDON
National Maritime Museum,
Romney Road, Greenwich,
London SE10 9NF
Tel: (01) 858 4422

Maritime

Science Museum,
Exhibition Road, South Kensington,
London SW7 2DD
Tel: (01) 589 6371

Science, technology, industry

MAIDSTONE (Kent)
Tyrwhitt-Drake Museum of Carriages,
Archbishop's Stables, Mill Street,
Maidstone
Tel: (0622) 54497

Carriages

MANCHESTER
North Western Museum of Science &
Industry,
97 Grosvenor Street,
Manchester M1 7HF
Tel: (061) 273 6636

Science, industry of the North West,
textiles

NEWCASTLE-UPON-TYNE
Museum of Science & Engineering,
Exhibition Park, Great North Road,
Newcastle NE2 4PZ
Tel: (0632) 20737

Engineering, maritime, mining,
transport

NOTTINGHAM
Industrial Museum,
Wollaton Hall, Courtyard Buildings,

Local industry, textiles (lace)

Nottingham NG8 2AE
Tel: (0602) 284602

OXFORD   Scientific instruments
Museum of the History of Science,
Old Ashmolean Building, Broad Street,
Oxford OX1 3AZ
Tel: (0865) 43997

READING (Berkshire)   Farm and craft technology, rural
Museum of English Rural Life,   industry
Whiteknights Park, Reading RG6 2AG
Tel: (0734) 85123, ext 475

ST HELENS (Lancashire)   Company museum,
Pilkington Glass Museum,   history of glassmaking
Prescot Road, St Helens WA10 3TT
Tel: (0744) 28882

SALFORD (Lancashire)   Coalmining, local industry
Science Museum, Buile Hill Park,
Eccles Old Road, Salford M6 8GL
Tel: (061) 736 1832

SHUGBOROUGH (Staffordshire)   Local industry, transport
Staffordshire County Museum,
Shugborough, Stafford ST17 0XB
Tel: Little Haywood 388

STOKE BRUERNE (Northamptonshire) Inland waterways
Waterways Museum, nr Towcester
Tel: Northampton (0604) 862229

STOKE PRIOR (Worcestershire)   Museum of buildings
Avoncroft Museum of Buildings,
nr Bromsgrove, B60 4JR
Tel: Bromsgrove 31363

STREET (Somerset)   Company museum, footwear
Clarks Shoe Museum,   manufacture
Street
Tel: (0458 4) 3131, ext 2681 & 2557

SUNDERLAND (County Durham)   Restored railway station, local history
Monkwearmouth Station Museum,
North Bridge Street,
Sunderland
Tel: (0783) 7705
Public Museum & Art Gallery,   Maritime, local industry
Borough Road, Sunderland SR1 1PP
Tel: (0783) 70417

SWANSEA   Local industry
Industrial Museum of South Wales,
Victoria Road, Swansea

SWINDON (Wiltshire)   Great Western Railway
Great Western Railway Museum,
Faringdon Road, Swindon
Tel: (0793) 27211

TELFORD (Salop)   Open Air Industrial Museum,
Blists Hill Open Air Museum   iron, coal, clay, the Iron Bridge
Coalbrookdale Museum & Furnace Site
Ironbridge Gorge Museum Trust, Church
Hill, Ironbridge, Telford, Salop TF8 7RE
Tel: (095 245) 3522

TOWYN (Merioneth)   Narrow-gauge railways
Narrow Gauge Railway Museum,
Wharf Station, Towyn

WEST DEAN (Sussex)   Open-air museum of buildings
Weald & Downland Open Air Museum,
Singleton, Chichester
Tel: Liphook 723104

YORK   Railways
Railway Museum, Queen Street,
York YO1 1HT
Tel: (0904) 53022

3 Industrial Archaeological Organisations

ABERGAVENNY & DISTRICT STEAM SOCIETY
Secretary, 15 Elm Drive, Llanellen, Abergavenny, Mon

ABERTAY HISTORICAL SOCIETY: IA SECTION
Secretary: 21 Strawberry Bank, Dundee DD2 1BH

ANTIQUARIAN HOROLOGICAL SOCIETY
Secretary: 35 Northampton Square, Clerkenwell, London EC1

ASSOCIATION FOR INDUSTRIAL ARCHAEOLOGY
Secretary: Church Hill, Ironbridge, Telford, Salop TF8 7RE
Tel: 095-245 3522

ASSOCIATION OF COUNTY COUNCILS
Secretary: 66a Eaton Square, London SW1W 9BH
Tel: 01-235 5173

ASSOCIATION OF DISTRICT COUNCILS
Secretary: 25 Buckingham Gate, London SW1E 6LE
Tel: 01-828 7425

ASSOCIATION OF METROPOLITAN AUTHORITIES
Secretary: 36 Old Queen Street, London SW1H 9JE
Tel: 01-930 9861

BASINGSTOKE IA GROUP
Chairman: 103 Maldive Road, Basingstoke, Hants

BATH & CAMERTON ARCHAEOLOGICAL SOCIETY
Secretary: 61 Pulteney Street, Bath

BATH UNIVERSITY: CENTRE FOR THE STUDY OF THE HISTORY OF
  TECHNOLOGY
Director: School of Humanities and Social Sciences,
Claverton Down, Bath BA2 7AY

BATLEY MUSEUM SOCIETY: IA GROUP
Secretary: 16 High Cote, Riddleston, Keighley, Yorks

BERKSHIRE ARCHAEOLOGICAL SOCIETY: IA GROUP
Secretary: 2 Eldon Road, Reading RG1 4DH

BIRMINGHAM & WARWICKSHIRE ARCHAEOLOGICAL SOCIETY: IA
   RESEARCH GROUP
Secretary: Dept of Industrial Administration, University of Aston in Birmingham,
Maple House, 158 Corporation Street, Birmingham 4

BRADFORD ARCHAEOLOGY GROUP, IA SECTION
Secretary: Bradford Industrial Museum, Moorside Mills, Moorside
Road, Bradford BD2 3HP

BRADFORD UNIVERSITY, IA UNIT
Secretary: The University, Richmond Road, Bradford BD7 1DP

BRISTOL INDUSTRIAL ARCHAEOLOGICAL SOCIETY (BIAS)
Secetary: Hunter's Hill, Oakfield Road, Keynsham, Bristol BS18 1JQ

BRITISH COUNCIL
Director: 65 Davies Street, London W1Y 2AA
Tel: 01-499 8011

BRITISH LIBRARY BOARD
Press Officer: Store Street, London WC1E 7DG
Tel: 01-636 0755

BRITISH LIBRARY LENDING DIVISION
Boston Spa, Wetherby, Yorkshire LS23 7BQ
Tel: 0937 843434

BRITISH MUSEUM LIBRARY
Bloomsbury, London WC1
Tel: 01-636 1555

BRITISH MUSEUM NEWSPAPER LIBRARY
Colindale Avenue, London NW9
Tel: 01-205 4788, 6039

BRITISH RAILWAYS BOARD
222 Marylebone Road, London NW1
Tel: 01-262 3232

BRITISH RECORD SOCIETY
Secretary: Dept of History, The University, Keele, Staffs

BRITISH RECORDS ASSOCIATION
Secretary: The Charterhouse, Charterhouse Square, London EC1
Tel: 01-253 0436

BRITISH SOCIETY FOR THE HISTORY OF SCIENCE
Asst Secretary: 47 Belgrave Square, London SW1X 8QX
Tel: 01-235 6111

BRITISH TRANSPORT FILMS
Melbury House, Melbury Terrace, London NW1
Tel: 01-262 3232

BRITISH TRANSPORT HISTORICAL RECORDS
66 Porchester Road, London W2
Tel: 01-262 6711

BRITISH TOURIST AUTHORITY
239 Marylebone Road, London NW1 5QT
Tel: 01-262 0141

BRUNEL SOCIETY
Secretary: Brunel Technical College, Ashley Down, Bristol BS7 9BU

BUSINESS ARCHIVES COUNCIL
Secretary: 63 Queen Victoria Street, London EC4

CAMBRIDGE SOCIETY FOR IA
Secretary: 4 Springfield Road, Cambridge CB4 1AD

CARNEGIE UNITED KINGDOM TRUST
Secretary: Comely Park House, Dunfermline, Fife KY12 7EJ
Tel: 0383 21445

CHESTER & DISTRICT IA SOCIETY
Secretary: Sunnycot, 1 Ash Grove, Little Sutton, Wirral, Cheshire L66 1PP

CIVIC TRUST
Director: 17 Carlton House Terrace, London SW1Y 5AW
Tel: 01-930 0914

CLACKMANNANSHIRE FIELD STUDIES SOCIETY: IA SECTION
Secretary: 26 Victoria Street, Alloa, Clackmannanshire

COMMITTEE FOR NAUTICAL ARCHAEOLOGY
Secretary: The Institute of Archaeology, University of London, 31-34 Gordon Square,
   London WC1
Tel: 01-387 6052

CONSULTATIVE PANEL FOR THE PRESERVATION OF BRITISH TRANS-
PORT RELICS
Secretary: 32 Russell Road, London W14

CORNWALL ARCHAEOLOGICAL SOCIETY: IA SUB-COMMITTEE
Secretary: 6 Godolphin Way, Newquay

COUNCIL FOR BRITISH ARCHAEOLOGY
Director: 8 St Andrew's Place, Regent's Park, London NW1 4LB

COUNCIL FOR BRITISH ARCHAEOLOGY: GROUP 2: IA SECTION
Secretary: Maesflas, Llanafan, Aberystwyth, Cardiganshire

COUNCIL FOR NAUTICAL ARCHAEOLOGY
Secretary: Institute of Archaeology, University of London, 31-34 Gordon Square,
   London WC1H 0PY
Tel: 01-387 6052

COUNCIL FOR SMALL INDUSTRIES IN RURAL AREAS
35 Camp Road, Wimbledon Common. London SW19

COUNTRYSIDE COMMISSION
1 Cambridge Gate, London NW1 4JY
Tel: 01-935 5533

COUNTRYSIDE COMMISSION FOR SCOTLAND
Director: Battleby, Redgorton, Perth
Tel: 0738 27921

CRAFTS ADVISORY COMMITTEE
Secretary: 12 Waterloo Place, London SW1
Tel: 01-839 5263

CUMBERLAND AND WESTMORLAND ANTIQUARIAN & ARCHAEO-
LOGICAL SOCIETY: IA COMMITTEE
Joint Secretaries: M. Davies-Shiel, Lilac Cottage, Lake Road, Bowness-on-Winder-
mere, and Dr J. D. Marshall, Department of History, University of Lancaster

DEPARTMENT OF THE ENVIRONMENT
Directorate of Ancient Monuments & Historic Buildings, 2 Marsham Street, London
SW1P 3EB. Chief Inspector of Ancient Monuments & Historic Buildings, Fortress
House, 23 Savile Row, London W1X 2AA
Tel: 01-734 6010.
See also Historic Buildings Council; National Monuments Record. Royal Commission
on Historical Monuments

DERBYSHIRE ARCHAEOLOGICAL SOCIETY: IA SECTION
Sectional Secretary: 48A Sandbed Lane, Belper, Derby

DEVON IA SURVEY
Secretary: Dartington Amenity Research Trust, Central Office, Shinner's Bridge,
Dartington, Totnes

DEVONSHIRE ASSOCIATION: IA SECTION
Secretary: 18 Margaret Park, Hartley Vale, Plymouth, PL3 5RR

DORSET NATURAL HISTORY & ARCHAEOLOGICAL SOCIETY: IA
GROUP
Secretary: 20 Martel Close, Broadmayne, Dorchester

DURHAM IA GROUP
Secretary: 26 Bede Terrace, Bowburn, Durham

DURHAM UNIVERSITY GROUP FOR IA
Secretary: Dunelm House, New Elvet, Durham

EAST LOTHIAN ANTIQUARIAN & FIELD NATURALISTS' SOCIETY
Secretary: Hadley Court, Sidegate, Haddington

EAST RIDING AGRICULTURAL MACHINERY PRESERVATION SOCIETY
Secretary: Louvain, Rowley Road, Little Weighton, Hull

EAST YORKSHIRE LOCAL HISTORY SOCIETY
Secretary: Purey Cust Chambers, York, YO1 2EJ

ENFIELD ARCHAEOLOGICAL SOCIETY
Hon. Secretary: 23 Uvedale Road, Enfield, Middlesex

ENGLISH LAKES COUNTIES TOURIST BOARD
Ellerthwaite, Windermere, Westmorland
Tel: Windermere 4444

ENGLISH TOURIST BOARD
4 Grosvenor Gardens, London, SW1W 0DU
Tel: 01-730 3400

EUROPEAN ARCHITECTURAL HERITAGE YEAR, 1975
(United Kingdom Secretariat)
17 Carlton House Terrace, London, SW1Y 5AW
Tel: 01-930 0914

EXETER IA GROUP
Secretary: 5 Elmgrove Road, Topsham, Exeter, EX3 0EQ

FAVERSHAM SOCIETY
Secretary: 42 Newton Road, Faversham, Kent

FIELD STUDIES COUNCIL
9 Devereux Court, London WC2

FINCH FOUNDRY TRUST
Secretary: Sticklepath, Okehampton, Devon

FORFAR & DISTRICT HISTORICAL SOCIETY
Secretary: 7 Wyllie Street, Forfar

GEORGIAN GROUP
Secretary: 2 Chester Street, London, SWiX 7BB
Tel: 01-235 3081

GLOUCESTERSHIRE SOCIETY FOR IA
Secretary: 6 & 7 Montpelier Street, Cheltenham

'GREAT BRITAIN' PROJECT
The British Centre, Quality House, Quality Court, Chancery Lane, London WC2
(and Great Western Dock, Bristol). Concerned with SS *Great Britain*.

GREATER LONDON IA SOCIETY (GLIAS)
Secretary: 69 St. Peter's Road, Croydon, Surrey, CR0 1HS

(CALOUSTE) GULBENKIAN FOUNDATION
United Kingdom and British Commonwealth Branch
Director: 98 Portland Place, London, WiN 4ET
Tel: 01-636 5313-7

HAMPSHIRE FIELD CLUB & ARCHAEOLOGICAL SOCIETY
Secretary: Dept of Archaeology, University of Southampton, SO9 5NH

HIGHLANDS & ISLANDS DEVELOPMENT BOARD
Bridge House, Bank Street, Inverness
Tel: 0463 34171

HISTORIC AIRCRAFT PRESERVATION SOCIETY
Secretary: 7 Baker Street, London Wi

HISTORIC BUILDINGS BUREAU
Caxton House, Tothill Street, London, SWi

HISTORIC BUILDINGS COUNCIL (ENGLAND)
Secretary: Queen Anne's Mansions, Queen Anne's Gate, London, SWi

HISTORIC BUILDINGS COUNCIL (SCOTLAND)
Secretary: 21 Hill Street, Edinburgh 2

HISTORIC BUILDINGS COUNCIL (WALES)
Secretary: Welsh Office, Summit House, Windsor Place, Cardiff CFi 3BQ

HISTORIC COMMERCIAL VEHICLE CLUB
1 Pembury House, Abbey Park, Beckenham, Kent
Tel: 01-650 2896

HISTORICAL ASSOCIATION
Secretary: 59A Kennington Park Road, London SE11 4JH
Tel: 01-735 3901

HISTORICAL METALLURGY SOCIETY
Secretary: Dept of Economic History, The University, Sheffield, S10 2TN

HISTORICAL MODEL RAILWAY SOCIETY
Secretary: 18 Beverley Gardens, Great Woodley, Romsey, Hampshire, SO5 8TA

HUDDERSFIELD IA SOCIETY
Secretary: 119 Coniston Avenue, Dalton, Huddersfield

INDUSTRIAL STEAM PRESERVATION GROUP
Chairman: 146 Milner Close, Hunslet Grange, Leeds 10

INLAND WATERWAYS ASSOCIATION
Gen Secretary: General Office, 114 Regent's Park Road, London, NW1
Tel: 01-586 2556, 2510

INLAND WATERWAYS PROTECTION SOCIETY
Secretary: Gorse-side, Cartledge Lane, Holmsfield, Sheffield, S18 5SB
Telephone: 0742 138352

INSTITUTE OF ARCHAEOLOGY
Secretary & Registrar: University of London, 31-34 Gordon Square, London,
   WC1H 0PY
Tel: 01-387 6052

INSTITUTE OF CHEMICAL ENGINEERS
Gen Secretary: 16 Belgrave Square, London, SW1

INSTITUTE OF MARINE ENGINEERS
Secretary: Memorial Building, 76 Mark Lane, London, EC3

INSTITUTE OF PATENTEES & INVENTORS
Secretary: 207–8 Abbey House, Victoria Street, London, SW1

INSTITUTE OF QUARRYING
Secretary: 62-4 Baker Street, London, W1

INSTITUTE OF TRANSPORT
Secretary: 80 Portland Place, London, W1

INSTITUTION OF CIVIL ENGINEERS
Secretary: Great George Street, London, SW1
Panel for Historic Engineering Works (PHEW): address above

INSTITUTION OF ELECTRICAL ENGINEERS
Secretary: Savoy Place, London, WC2

INSTITUTION OF HIGHWAY ENGINEERS
Secretary: 14 Queen Anne's Gate, London, SW1

INSTITUTION OF MECHANICAL ENGINEERS
Secretary: 1 Birdcage Walk, London, SW1

INSTITUTION OF MINING & METALLURGY
Secretary: 44 Portland Place, London, W1

INSTITUTION OF MINING ENGINEERS
Secretary: 3 Grosvenor Crescent, London, SW1

INSTITUTION OF PLANT ENGINEERS
Secretary: 138 Buckingham Palace Road, London, SW1

INSTITUTION OF PRODUCTION ENGINEERS
Secretary: 10 Chesterfield Street, London, W1

INSTITUTION OF STRUCTURAL ENGINEERS
Secretary: 11 Upper Belgrave Street, London. SW1
Historical Group, Secretary's address as above

INSTITUTION OF WATER ENGINEERS
Secretary: 6–8 Sackville Street, London, W1

INTERNATIONAL COUNCIL OF MUSEUMS
(British National Committee)
Secretary: Science Museum, London, SW7
Tel: 01-589 6371

INTERNATIONAL INSTITUTE FOR CONSERVATION OF HISTORIC AND
ARTISTIC WORKS
Secretary General: 608 Grand Buildings, Trafalgar Square, London, SC2N 5HN
Tel: 01-839 5975

IRISH SOCIETY FOR IA
Secretary: 34 Lakelands Close, Blackrock, Co Dublin

IRON & STEEL INSTITUTE
Secretary: 4 Grosvenor Gardens, London, SW1

IRONBRIDGE GORGE MUSEUM TRUST
Director: Church Hill, Ironbridge, Telford, Shropshire, TF8 7RE

ISLE OF MAN NATURAL HISTORY & ANTIQUARIAN SOCIETY FIELD
   SECTION: IA GROUP
Secretary: c/o Manx Museum, Douglas, IOM

ISLE OF MAN TOURIST BOARD
13 Victoria Street, Douglas, IOM
Tel: 0624 4323

KINGSTON POLYTECHNIC IA SOCIETY
Secretary: Kingston Polytechnic, Penrhyn Road, Kingston-upon-Thames, Surrey

KIRKCALDY NATURALISTS' SOCIETY
Secretary: 55 King Street, Kirkcaldy, Fife

LANCASHIRE & CHESHIRE ANTIQUARIAN SOCIETY
Secretary: c/o The Portico Library, Mosley Street, Manchester, M2 3HY

LEICESTERSHIRE INDUSTRIAL HISTORY SOCIETY
Secretary: 'Three Gables', Queen Street, Markfield, Leicester

LIBRARY ASSOCIATION
Secretary: 7 Ridgmount Street, London, SC1E 7AE
Tel: 01-636 7543

LINCOLNSHIRE LOCAL HISTORY SOCIETY: IA GROUP
Secretary: Museum of Lincolnshire Life, Burton Road, Lincoln

MAIDSTONE AREA IA GROUP
Secretary: 15 Hermitage Lane, Barming, Maidstone

MANCHESTER REGION IA SOCIETY
Secretary: North-Western Museum of Science and Technology, 97 Grosvenor Street,
    Manchester, M1 7HF

MARITIME TRUST
Director: 53 Davies Street, London, W1Y 1FH

(WILLIAM) MORRIS SOCIETY
Secretary: 25 Lawn Crescent, Kew, Surrey

MUSEUMS ASSOCIATION
Secretary: 87 Charlotte Street, London, W1P 2BX
Tel: 01-636 4600

NATIONAL CENTRAL LIBRARY
Librarian & Secretary: Store Street, London, WC1
Tel: 01-636 0755

NATIONAL COUNCIL ON INLAND TRANSPORT
Secretary: 396 City Road, London, EC1
Tel: 01-837 9145

NATIONAL FILM ARCHIVE
81 Dean Street, London, W1V 6AA

NATIONAL HERITAGE: THE MUSEUM ACTION MOVEMENT
Secretary: 202 Great Suffolk Street, London, SE1
Tel: 01-407 7411

NATIONAL LENDING LIBRARY FOR SCIENCE & TECHNOLOGY
Boston Spa, Yorkshire

NATIONAL MONUMENTS RECORD (INCLUDING NATIONAL BUILDING RECORD)
Curator: Fortress House, 23 Savile Row, London, W1X 1AB
Tel: 01-743 6010

NATIONAL RECORD OF INDUSTRIAL MONUMENTS
University of Bath, Claverton Down, Bath, Somerset

NATIONAL REFERENCE LIBRARY OF SCIENCE & INVENTION
Bayswater Division, 10 Porchester Gardens, London, W2
Tel: 01-727 3022
Holborn Division, 25 Southampton Buildings, London, WC2
Tel: 01-405 8721

NATIONAL REGISTER OF ARCHIVES
Quality House, Quality Court, Chancery Lane, London, WC2
Tel: 01-242 3205

NATIONAL TRUST
42 Queen Anne's Gate, London, SW1H 9AS
Tel: 01-930 0211

NATIONAL TRUST FOR SCOTLAND
5 Charlotte Square, Edinburgh, EH2 4DU
Tel: 031-225 2184

NEWCOMEN SOCIETY FOR THE STUDY OF THE HISTORY OF ENGIN-
    EERING AND TECHNOLOGY
Secretary: Science Museum, London, SW7
Tel: 01-589 1793

NEWCOMEN SOCIETY
Midlands Branch
Hon Secretary: 147 Whirlowdale Road, Sheffield, S7 2NG
Tel: 0742-367960

NORFOLK IA STUDY GROUP
Secretary: 2 Mill Corner, Hingham, NOR 23X

NORTHAMPTONSHIRE IA GROUP
Secretary: 17 Mayfield Road, Northampton, NN3 2RE

NORTHERN CAVERN & MINE RESEARCH SOCIETY
Secretary: 33 Gledhow Avenue, Roundhay, Leeds, L58 1LD

NORTHERN MILL ENGINE SOCIETY
Secretary: 2 Brocklebank Road, Rochdale, Lancashire

NORTH EAST IA SOCIETY
Secretary: 26 Bede Terrace, Bowburn, Durham, DH6 5DT

NORTH WEST TOURIST BOARD
119 The Piazza, Piccadilly Plaza, Piccadilly, Manchester, M1 4AN
Tel: 061 236 0393

NORTH-WESTERN SOCIETY FOR IA & HISTORY
Secretary: Merseyside County Museum, William Brown Street, Liverpool, L3 8EN

NORTHUMBRIA TOURIST BOARD
Prudential Building, 140-150 Pilgrim Street, Newcastle-upon-Tyne, NE1 6TH
Tel: 0632 28795

PEAK DISTRICT MINES HISTORICAL SOCIETY
Secretary: Riverdale Farm, Coombs Road, Bakewell, Derbyshire

PEMBROKESHIRE COUNTY MUSEUM, FRIENDS OF: IA GROUP
Secretary: The Pembrokeshire County Museum, The Castle, Haverfordwest, Pembrokeshire

PILGRIM TRUST
Secretary: Fielden House, Little College Street, London, SW1P 3SH
Tel: 01-839 4727

POOLE (WEA) IA GROUP
Secretary: 18 Parkstone Avenue, Parkstone, Poole, Dorset, BH14 9LR

PORTSMOUTH POLYTECHNIC: IA SOCIETY
Secretary: 111 High Street, Portsmouth, PO1 2HL

PUBLIC RECORD OFFICE
Keeper of Public Records: Chancery Lane, London WC2
Tel: 01-405 0741

RAILWAY & CANAL HISTORICAL SOCIETY
Secretary: 38 Station Road, Wylde Green, Sutton Coldfield

REDDITCH IA SOCIETY
Secretary: 127 Beaumont Road, Bourneville, Birmingham

RICKMANSWORTH HISTORICAL SOCIETY
Secretary: 66 The Queens Drive, Rickmansworth, Herts

ROCHDALE SOCIETY FOR STUDY OF HISTORY OF INDUSTRY &
TECHNOLOGY
Secretary: 298 Hatfield, Ashfield Valley, Rochdale, Lancs

ROYAL AERONAUTICAL SOCIETY
Secretary: 4 Hamilton Place, London, W1

ROYAL COMMISSION ON HISTORICAL MANUSCRIPTS
Secretary: Quality House, Quality Court, Chancery Lane, London, WC2
Tel: 01-242 2981

ROYAL COMMISSION ON HISTORICAL MONUMENTS (ENGLAND)
Secretary: Fortress House, 23 Savile Row, London, W1X 1AB
Tel: 01-734 6010

ROYAL COMMISSION ON THE ANCIENT & HISTORICAL MONUMENTS
OF SCOTLAND
(including the National Monuments Record of Scotland)
52/54 Melville Street, Edinburgh, EH3 7HF
Tel: 031-225 5994-5

ROYAL COMMISSION ON ANCIENT & HISTORICAL MONUMENTS
(WALES)

Secretary: Edleston House, Queens Road, Aberystwyth, Cardiganshire
Tel: 0970-2256

ROYAL INSTITUTE OF BRITISH ARCHITECTS
Secretary: 66 Portland Place, London, W1

RYHOPE ENGINES TRUST
Secretary: 3 Leominster Road, Sunderland, SR2 9HG

SADDLEWORTH HISTORICAL SOCIETY
Secretary: 'Ceann', Frixeland Lane, Greenfield, near Oldham

SALISBURY & SOUTH WILTSHIRE IA SOCIETY
Secretary: 34 Countess Road, Amesbury, Salisbury, Wilts

SCIENCE MUSEUM LIBRARY
Keeper: London, SW7
Tel: 01-589 6371

SCOTTISH DEVELOPMENT DEPARTMENT (HISTORIC BUILDINGS)
Argyle House, Lady Lawson Street, Edinburgh, EH3 9SD

SCOTTISH RECORD OFFICE
Register House, Edinburgh
Tel: 031-556 6585

SCOTTISH SOCIETY FOR IA
Secretary: Teachers' Centre, Bronshill Road, Alloa, Clackmannanshire

SCOTTISH TOURIST BOARD
23 Ravelston Terrace, Edinburgh, EH4 3EU
Tel: 031-332 2433

SHROPSHIRE MINING CLUB
Secretary: 5 Beech Drive, Shifnal, Shropshire

SMALL INDUSTRIES COUNCIL FOR RURAL AREAS OF SCOTLAND
Secretary: 27 Walker Street, Edinburgh

SOCIETY FOR FOLK LIFE STUDIES
Secretary: National Museum of Antiquities of Scotland, Queen Street, Edinburgh, EH2 1JD
Tel: 031-556 8921

SOCIETY FOR MEDIEVAL ARCHAEOLOGY
Secretary: University College, Gower Street, London, WC1E 6BT
Tel: 01-387 7050 Ext. 476

SOCIETY FOR NAUTICAL RESEARCH
Hon Secretary: National Maritime Museum, Greenwich, London, SE10

SOCIETY FOR POST-MEDIEVAL ARCHAEOLOGY
Secretary: Passmore Edwards Museum, Stratford, London, E15 4LZ

SOCIETY FOR THE PROTECTION OF ANCIENT BUILDINGS
Secretary: 55 Great Ormond Street, London, WC1N 3JA
Tel: 01-405 2646

SOCIETY OF ARCHIVISTS
Secretary: County Record Office, County Hall, Hertford
Tel: 099 25 4242

SOMERSET IA SOCIETY
Chairman: Somerset Education Museum & Art Service, Weir Lodge, Staplegrove Road, Taunton

SOUTHAMPTON UNIVERSITY IA GROUP
Secretary: Heathermount, Moor Hill, West End, Southampton

SOUTH-EAST WALES IA SOCIETY
Secretary: The Library, University College of Swansea, SA2 8PP

STAFFORDSHIRE IA SOCIETY
Secretary: 4 The Oval, Stafford

STANDING COMMISSION ON MUSEUMS & GALLERIES
Secretary: 2 Carlton Gardens, London, SW1
Tel: 01-930 0995

STANDING CONFERENCE FOR LOCAL HISTORY
26 Bedford Square, London, WC1
Tel: 01-636 4966

SUNDERLAND IA GROUP
Secretary: 3 Broxbourne Terrace, Sunderland

SURREY ARCHAEOLOGICAL SOCIETY
Secretary: Castle Arch, Guildford, Surrey

SUSSEX IA SOCIETY
Secretary: Albion House, Cobourg Place, Hastings, Sussex

TEESSIDE IA GROUP
Secretary: 8 Loweswater Crescent, Stockton-on-Tees, Teesside

TYNE IA GROUP
Secretary: 1 Regents Drive, Tynemouth

VICTORIAN SOCIETY
Secretary: 29 Exhibition Road, London, SW7
Tel: 01-589 7203

WALES TOURIST BOARD
Welcome House, High Street, Llandaff, Cardiff, DF5 2YZ
Tel: 0222 567701

WATFORD & DISTRICT INDUSTRIAL HISTORY SOCIETY
Secretary: 23 St Lawrence Way, Bricket Wood, Hertfordshire

WEST COUNTRY TOURIST BOARD
Trinity Court, Southernhay East, Exeter, EX1 1QS
Tel: 0392 76351

WEST LOTHIAN COUNTY HISTORY SOCIETY
Secretary: Norwood, Woodend by Winchburgh, West Lothian

WEST WILTSHIRE INDUSTRIAL ARCHAEOLOGICAL SOCIETY
Secretary: Hope Cottage, Station Road, Holt, Trowbridge, Wiltshire

Tel: North Trowbridge 782234

WILTSHIRE ARCHAEOLOGICAL & NAT. HIST. SOCIETY (IA COMMITTEE)
Secretary: Wyndhams, Shrewton, Salisbury, Wiltshire

WOLVERHAMPTON POLYTECHNIC: STUDY CENTRE FOR INDUS-
TRIAL ARCHAEOLOGY & BUSINESS HISTORY OF THE WEST MIDLANDS
Secretary: The Polytechnic, Wolverhampton

WOLVERTON & DISTRICT ARCHAEOLOGICAL SOCIETY
Secretary: 13 Vicarage Walk, Stoney Stafford, Wolverton, Buckinghamshire

YORKSHIRE ARCHAEOLOGICAL SOCIETY: INDUSTRIAL HISTORY
SECTION
Secretary: 307 Spen Lane, Leeds, LS16 5BD

YORKSHIRE TOURIST BOARD
312 Tadcaster Road, York, YO2 2HF
Tel: 0904 67961

Bibliography

The following is a selective list of books and pamphlets relevant to the general themes of industrial archaeology in Britain. The first sections relate to the chapter divisions of this book and are followed by regional works broken down under the same headings as in Appendix 1.

Industrial Archaeology

Bracegirdle, Brian etc. *The Archaeology of the Industrial Revolution* (Heinemann, 1973). Excellent photographs provide a good visual insight into industrial sites in Britain

Buchanan, R. A. *Industrial Archaeology in Britain* (Pelican, 1972). Compact and comprehensive study of the subject with basic list of sites

Cossons, Neil and Hudson, Kenneth. *Industrial Archaeologist's Guide 1971-73* (David & Charles, Newton Abbot, 1971). A state of the subject message, updating the 1969-70 Guide

Hudson, Kenneth. *Industrial Archaeology* (John Baker, 1963). The pioneer work on the subject

Industrial Archaeology (Bratton Publishing, Edinburgh, quarterly), edited by J. Butt, Department of Economic History, University of Strathclyde, McCance Building, Richmond Street, Glasgow C1

Pannell, J. P. M. *The Techniques of Industrial Archaeology* (David & Charles, Newton Abbot, 1966; new edition, J. K. Major, 1973). Basic practical techniques of field-work

Raistrick, Arthur. *Industrial Archaeology: An Historical Survey* (Eyre Methuen, 1972). Emphasises the traditional archaeological element in industrial archaeology to produce a chronologically broad but thematically narrow study

General Background on the Industrial Revolution Period

Ashton, T. S. *The Industrial Revolution, 1760–1830* (Oxford University Press, first published 1948). Still the standard text

Chaloner, W. H., and Musson, A. E. *Industry & Technology* (Vista, 1963). A visual history of the Industrial Revolution

Chambers, J. D., and Mingay, G. E. *The Agricultural Revolution: 1750–1850* (Batsford, 1966)

Cossons, Neil, (ed). *Rees's Manufacturing Industry, 1802–19*, 5 volumes (1819; edited version, David & Charles, Newton Abbot, 1973). A five-volume condensation from Rees's *Cyclopedia* containing in alphabetical form the references on industry and technology

Derry, T. K., and Williams, T. I. *A Short History of Technology* (Oxford University Press, 1960)

Engineering Heritage volumes 1 and 2 (Heinemann, on behalf of the Institution of Mechanical Engineers, 1963 and 1966). Contain articles from *The Chartered Mechanical Engineer* covering a wide range of historical aspects of engineering

Hartwell, R. M. *Causes of the Industrial Revolution in England* (Methuen, 1967). Analyses the causal factors. In a condensed form by the same author is *The Industrial Revolution in England,* Historical Association pamphlet (London 1965, bibliography revised 1968)

Jordan, R. F. *Victorian Architecture* (Pelican, 1965). A comprehensive review of buildings in Victorian Britain

Klingender, Francis D. *Art and the Industrial Revolution,* edited and revised by Sir Arthur Elton (Adams and Mackay, 1968 and Paladin paperback, 1972). The artists' point of view, admirably interpreted

Mathias, Peter. *The First Industrial Nation: An Economic History of Britain, 1700–1914* (Methuen, 1969). Reviews the economic and political progress of Britain through the Industrial Revolution

Minchinton, W. E. *The Growth of English Overseas Trade in the Seventeenth and Eighteenth Centuries* (Methuen, 1969). Reviews the 'Commercial Revolution' which preceded industrialisation

Pevsner, N. *Pioneers of Modern Design* (Pelican, 1960). The birth and history of the Modern Movement in architecture and design

Rees, W. *Industry Before the Industrial Revolution* (University of Wales Press, 1968). A detailed account of industrial activity in Britain before the Industrial Revolution with particular reference to the organisation of metal mining

Richards, J. M. *The Functional Tradition in Early Industrial Buildings* (Architectural Press, 1958; reprinted 1968). Still unsurpassed as the apotheosis of industrial architecture

Singer, C., Holmyard, E. J., Hall, A. R., and Williams, T. I. (eds). *A History of Technology,* 5 volumes (Oxford University Press, 1954–8), of which volumes 4 and 5 are the most relevant to the industrial archaeologist. The outstanding work on the development of technology available in a shortened single volume form is Derry, T. K. and Williams, T. I. *A Short History of Technology* (Oxford University Press, 1960)

Tarn, J. N. *Working Class Housing in Nineteenth Century Britain* (Lund Humphries for the Architectural Association, 1971)

Wind and Water Power

Reynolds, John. *Windmills and Watermills* (Hugh Evelyn, 1970). An admirably illustrated review of wind and watermills, not only in Britain

Transactions of the International Molinological Society (secretary of the United Kingdom group, J. K. Major, 2 Eldon Road, Reading, Berkshire). Papers on wind and watermills throughout the world

Wailes, Rex. *The English Windmill* (Routledge and Kegan Paul, 1967). A history of the development of windmills in England. Numerous papers on windmills, by the same author appear in the *Transactions of the Newcomen Society*

Steam and Internal Combustion Power

Barton, D. B. *The Cornish Beam Engine: A Survey of Its History and Development . . . from 1800 to the Present Day* (D. B. Barton, Truro, 1965). Covers the origins of this specialised type of steam engine with numerous biographies of the engines themselves and their day-to-day working

Dickinson, H. W. *James Watt – Craftsman and Engineer* (Cambridge, 1935) Still the best of several works on Watt

Dickinson, H. W. *A Short History of the Steam Engine* (first published 1936, reprinted by Cass, 1963, with a new introduction by A. E. Musson). The classic work on the evolution of the steam engine

Evans, A. F. *The History of the Oil Engine . . . 1680–1930* (Sampson Low, 1932). Describes all the basic types with index of important patents

Rolt, L. T. C. *Thomas Newcomen: The Prehistory of the Steam Engine* (David & Charles, Macdonald, Dawlish and London, 1963). Biography of the steam engine pioneer. More details are in numerous issues of the *Transactions of the Newcomen Society*

Watkins, George. *The Stationary Steam Engine* (David & Charles, Newton Abbot, 1968). A well illustrated review of steam engine types in Britain

Watkins, George. *Textile Mill Engines,* two volumes (David & Charles, Newton Abbot, 1970 and 1971). A detailed study on this specialised species of engine

Coal

Atkinson, F. *The Great Northern Coalfield 1700–1900* (Durham County Local History Society, 1966). A brief history of the Durham and Northumberland Coalfield which provides an insight into the lives of the men who worked in it

Galloway, R. L. *A History of Coal Mining in Great Britain* (originally published in 1882; reprinted, David & Charles, Newton Abbot, 1970). The best easily accessible nineteenth-century view of the coal industry

Griffin, A. R. *Coalmining* (Longman, 1971). Reviews the development of mining technology

Guide to the Coalfields (published annually by the *Colliery Guardian*). Contains an index with maps of every operational mine in Britain

Nef, J. U. *The Rise of the British Coal Industry,* two volumes (Routledge, 1932). Still the classic work on the history of the industry, with plenty of statistics

Trueman, A. *The Coalfields of Great Britain* (Arnold, 1954). Accounts of the geology of the British coalfields

Iron and Steel

Agricola, G. *De Re Metallica,* English translation by J. C. and L. M. Hoover (Dover, New York, 1950). This sixteenth-century manual on mining and metallurgy provides an admirable background on the state of early technology

Bulletin of the Historical Metallurgy Society. This contains excellent papers on all aspects of the history of metals, largely in Britain. The *Bulletin* and details of the membership of the Society may be obtained from C. R. Blick, Honorary Treasurer, Historical Metallurgy Society, 147 Whirlowdale Road, Sheffield, S7 2NG

Alexander, W. and Street, A. *Metals in the Service of Man* (Pelican, first published 1944 but subsequent editions come up to date). A review of the significance of metals, ferrous and non-ferrous, in the life of man

Ashton, T. S. *Iron and Steel in the Industrial Revolution* (Manchester, 1924). The standard general work on the economic history of the industry

Gale, W. K. V. *The British Iron and Steel Industry* (David & Charles, Newton Abbot, 1967). An account of the technology of the industry, largely in the Industrial Revolution period.

Gale, W. K. V. *Iron & Steel* (Longman, 1969). Similar to the above with a brief note on some sites of interest

Gloag, J. and Bridgwater, D. *A History of Cast Iron in Architecture* (Architectural Press, 1958). Well illustrated account of the architectural and some structural uses of cast-iron

Griffith's Guide to the Iron Trade of Great Britain (1873; with a new introduction by W. K. V. Gale, David & Charles, Newton Abbot, 1968)

Lister, R. *Decorative Wrought Ironwork in Great Britain* (Bell, 1957). Covers the largely pre-industrial use of wrought iron

Lister, R. *Decorative Cast Ironwork in Great Britain* (Bell, 1960). The use of cast iron for decorative and architectural purposes, mainly after 1750

Raistrick, A. *Dynasty of Ironfounders: The Darbys of Coalbrookdale* (Longman, 1953; reprinted David & Charles, Newton Abbot, 1970). The standard work on the development of the Coalbrookdale Company

Schubert, H. R. *History of the British Iron & Steel Industry from c 450 BC to AD 1775* (Routledge, 1957). Covers the early history of the industry

Trinder, B. *The Darbys of Coalbrookdale* (Phillimore, Chichester, 1974). A brief account of the Coalbrookdale ironmasters and their work

Engineering

Armytage, W. H. G. *A Social History of Engineering* (Faber, 1970). An account of technological developments, especially in Britain, and their interactions with society

Burstall, A. F. *A History of Mechanical Engineering* (Faber, 1963). Mechanisms from earliest times to 1960

Gilbert, K. R. *The Machine Tool Collection* (Science Museum, London, 1966). A catalogue of exhibits with historical introduction

Greaves, W. F. and Carpenter, J. H. *A Short History of Mechanical Engineering* (Longman, 1969). An elementary account of the major engineering innovations with biographical sketches.

Pendred, L. St. L. *British Engineering Societies* (British Council, 1947). A brief account of the Institutions of Civil, Mechanical and Electrical Engineers

Rolt, L. T. C. *The Mechanicals: Progress of a Profession* (Heinemann, for the Institution of Mechanical Engineers, 1967). A history of the Mechanicals over 120 years

Westcott, G. F. (comp). *Synopsis of Historical Events: Mechanical and Electrical Engineering etc,* revised by H. P. Spratt (Science Museum, London, 1960)

Non-ferrous Metals

Aitchison, L. *A History of Metals,* 2 volumes (Macdonald & Evans, 1960). A wide-ranging survey of metals and their uses from earliest times

Barton, D. B. *A History of Tin Mining and Smelting in Cornwall* (D. B. Barton, Truro, 1967) and *A History of Copper Mining in Cornwall and Devon,* 2nd ed (1968) provide a detailed account of the most important non-ferrous metals area in Britain

Clough, R. T. *The Lead Smelting Mills of the Yorkshire Dales* (published by the author, Keighley, 1962). A detailed survey, with numerous drawings, of the surviving remains of the industry

Cocks, E. J. and Walters, B. *A History of the Zinc Smelting Industry in Britain* (Harrap, 1968). A brief historical background precedes a more detailed coverage of commercial and technical developments with particular reference to the Imperial Smelting Corporation

Day, J. *Bristol Brass* (David & Charles, Newton Abbot, 1973). The history of the most important brass-making area in Britain

Gough, J. W. *Mines of Mendip* (Oxford University Press, 1930; reprinted David & Charles, Newton Abbot, 1967). One of the earliest regional works on lead mining and smelting

Hamilton, H. *The English Brass and Copper Industries* (reprinted Cass, 1967). The standard work on the industry

Hedger, E. S. *Tin in Social and Economic History* (Arnold, 1964). A general history of the tin industry

Kirkham, N. *Derbyshire Lead Mining Through the Centuries* (D. B. Barton, Truro, 1968)

Morgan Rees, D. *Mines, Mills and Furnaces* (National Museum of Wales, Cardiff, 1969). Non-ferrous metal industries of Wales are covered with considerable reference to surviving remains

Raistrick, A. *Lead Mining in the Mid-Pennines* (D. B. Barton, Truro, 1973). In effect a sequel to A. Raistrick and B. Jennings. *A History of Lead in the Pennines* (Longman, 1966)

Stone, Clay and Glass

Barnard, J. *Victorian Ceramic Tiles* (Studio Vista, 1972). A history of decorative tile making during the nineteenth century

Barton, R. M. *A History of the Cornish China-Clay Industry* (D. B. Barton, Truro, 1966)

Clifton-Taylor, A. *The Pattern of English Building* (Batsford, 1962). A classic on building materials

Davey, N. *A History of Building Materials* (Phoenix, 1961)

Hudson, K. *The History of English China Clays* (David & Charles, Newton Abbot, 1966)

Hudson, K. *The Fashionable Stone* (Adams & Dart, Bath, 1972). A history of Bath stone

Hudson, K. *Building Materials* (Longman, 1972). Reviews the stone, slate, brick, tile and concrete industries with sections on minor building materials

Janson, S. E. *Glass Technology* (Science Museum, London, 1969). Descriptive catalogue of the glass technology collections

Richards, J. M. *The Functional Tradition in Early Industrial Buildings* (Architectural Press, 1958; reprinted 1968)

Thomas, J. *The Rise of the Staffordshire Potteries* (Adams & Dart, Bath, 1971)

Textiles

Baines, E. *History of the Cotton Manufacture in Great Britain* (1835; reprinted, Cass, 1966)

Bischoff, J. *A Comprehensive History of the Woollen and Worsted Manufacture* (1842; reprinted Cass, 1968)

Chapman, S. D. *The Early Factory Masters* (David & Charles, Newton Abbot, 1967). The development of the factory-based textile industry of the East Midlands

English, W. *The Textile Industry* (Longman, 1969). An account of the evolution of textile manufacture in Britain

Hills, R. L. *Power in the Industrial Revolution* (Manchester University Press, 1970). Concerned particularly with the use of power in the textile industry

Mantoux, P. *The Industrial Revolution in the Eighteenth Century* (1928; revised edition, Cape, 1961). Pays particular attention to the role of the textile industry in the Industrial Revolution

The Chemical Industries

Campbell, W. A. *The Chemical Industry* (Longman, 1971). Reviews the whole range of chemical manufacturing, particularly during the nineteenth century

Clow, A. and N. L. *The Chemical Revolution* (Batchworth, 1952). A general work on the role of the chemical industry in the broader processes of industrialisation

Haber, L. F. *The Chemical Industry during the Nineteenth Century* (Oxford University Press, 1958)

Hardie, D. W. F. and Pratt, J. D. *A History of the Modern British Chemical Industry* (Pergamon, 1966). The development of chemical processes from the beginning of the Industrial Revolution to the present, including brief accounts of important chemical firms and trade associations

Miall, S. *History of the British Chemical Industry* (Benn, 1931)

Taylor, F. S. *A History of Industrial Chemistry,* two volumes (Heinemann, 1957). Covers the rise of chemical industries up to 1780 in volume 1 and through the nineteenth century to today in volume 2

Public Utilities

Bett, W. H. and Gillham, J. C. *Great British Tramway Networks* (Light Railway Transport League, London, 1962). Reviews the growth and decline of the street tramway in Britain

Dunsheath, P. *A History of Electrical Engineering* (Faber, 1962)

Farrugia, J. Y. *The Letter Box* (Centaur, Sussex, 1969). A detailed history of letter-boxes and their design

O'Dea, W. T. *The Social History of Lighting* (Routledge, 1958)

Steward, E. C. *Town Gas* (Science Museum, London, 1958). A brief account of the introduction of town gas

Roads and Bridges

Beckett, D. *Bridges* in Great Buildings of the World Series (Hamlyn, 1969). A general history of bridge building

Bird, A. *Roads & Vehicles* (Longman, 1969). Concerned mainly with vehicles rather than road development

Copeland, J. *Roads and Their Traffic, 1750–1850* (David & Charles, Newton Abbot, 1968)

Hopkins, H. J. *A Span of Bridges* (David & Charles, Newton Abbot, 1970). An engineering history of the bridge

Jackman, W. T. *The Development of Transportation in Modern England* (1916; reprinted, Cass, 1962). Despite its age, Jackman's classic on transport development is still valuable

Law, H. *Construction of Common Roads: A Rudimentary Treatise* (1855; reprinted Kingsmead, Bath, 1970). A basic account of nineteenth-century road building methods

Mare, E. de. *The Bridges of Britain* (Batsford, 1954). The evolution of the bridge seen largely through the eyes of the architect and aesthete

Rolt, L. T. C. *Thomas Telford* (Longman, 1958). An admirable biography of the great engineer with good coverage of his road and bridge building activities

Rivers and Canals

Hadfield, C. *British Canals: An Illustrated History* (David & Charles, Newton Abbot, 1969). The standard general history of British canals and the navigable rivers associated with them

Hadfield, C. (ed). *Canals of the British Isles Series* (David & Charles, Newton Abbot, various dates). The whole country is now covered by this excellent series of regional histories, many of which have been written by Charles Hadfield, who is also general editor for the series

Nicholson's Guides to Waterways (British Waterways Board, London, various dates). These official guides to BWB Waterways cover England and Wales in four volumes: 1 South-East; 2 North-West; 3 South-West; 4 North-East. Detailed maps of all navigable waterways identify every lock and bridge

Rolt, L. T. C. *Navigable Waterways* (Longman, 1969). A general account of canal development with some reference to surviving sites of significance

Railways

Appleton, J. H. *The Geography of Communications in Great Britain* (University of Hull, 1962). The geographical implications of transport networks and their development in Britain

Baxter, B. *Stone Blocks and Iron Rails* (David & Charles, Newton Abbot, 1966). An account of the evolution of tramways in Britain, with a gazetteer of sites

Coleman, T. *The Railway Navvies* (Pelican, 1968). A highly readable account which brings alive the men who built the railways.

Ellis, H. *British Railway History,* two volumes (Allen & Unwin, 1954 and 1959). Volume 1 covers the period 1830 to 1876, volume 2 from 1877 to 1947. A most readable account of the development of the British railway system

Journal of the Railway & Canal Historical Society (published quarterly). Details of the Society and the *Journal* from the Secretary, 174 Station Road, Wylde Green, Sutton Coldfield, B73 5LE

Lewis, M. J. T. *Early Wooden Railways* (Routledge, 1970). A detailed and comprehensive study of the earliest type of railed transport

Morgan, B. *Railway Relics* (Ian Allan, Shepperton, 1969). An account of surviving railway civil and mechanical engineering remains in Britain with gazetteer

Ottley, G. *A Bibliography of British Railway History* (Allen & Unwin, 1965). A massive compilation of railway literature

Rolt, L. T. C. *Isambard Kingdom Brunel* (Longman, 1957, and Pelican, 1970). Not only the life of a great engineer but an outstanding biography in its own right

Simmons, J. *The Railways of Britain: An Historical Introduction* (Routledge, 1961). A comprehensive general account of the development of railways in Britain

Thomas, D. St J. (ed). *Regional History of the Railways of Great Britain* (David & Charles, Newton Abbot, various dates). A new comprehensive series of regional histories by various authors

Transport History. Journal published three times a year by Bratton Publishing, Edinburgh. Editor, Baron F. Duckham, University of Strathclyde. Covers all aspects of transport history

Ports and Harbours

Bracegirdle, B. and Miles, P. H. *Thomas Telford* (David & Charles, Newton Abbot, 1973). Illustrates a number of Telford's harbour works

Glynn, J. *Construction of Cranes and Machinery: A Rudimentary Treatise* (1854; reprinted Kingsmead, Bath, 1970). Useful work on small cranes frequently found on docks and canal wharves

McNeil, I. *Hydraulic Power* (Longman, 1972). Covers many applications of hydraulic power but with considerable emphasis on harbours

Mountfield, S. *Western Gateway* (Liverpool University Press, 1965). A history of the Mersey Docks & Harbour Board

Sennett, R. and Oram, H. J. *The Marine Steam Engine* (Longman, 1915). The standard work

Regional Publications

Although some regional publications have been mentioned in the preceding subject bibliography, the following are concerned with industrial archaeology in specific regional or local areas of Britain. Many contain gazetteers of sites. The most comprehensive, although by no means complete, is the *Regional Industrial Archaeology* series published by David & Charles. There are numerous gazetteers published as pamphlets, of which a selected sample is included. Information on a particular area and on the availability of specifically local literature can best be obtained through an appropriate industrial archaeological society (see Appendix 3)

Scotland

Bracegirdle, B. and Miles, P. H. *Thomas Telford* (David & Charles, Newton Abbot, 1973). Many Scottish illustrations

Butt, J. *The Industrial Archaeology of Scotland* (David & Charles, Newton Abbot, 1967)

Butt, J., Donnachie, I. L. and Hume, J. R. *Industrial History in Pictures: Scotland* (David & Charles, Newton Abbot, 1968)

Donnachie, I. *The Industrial Archaeology of Galloway* (David & Charles, Newton Abbot, 1971)

Lindsay, J. *The Canals of Scotland* (David & Charles, Newton Abbot, 1968)

Thomas, J. *Scottish Railway History in Pictures* (David & Charles, Newton Abbot, 1967)

North-west England

Ashmore, O. *The Industrial Archaeology of Lancashire* (David & Charles, Newton Abbot, 1969)

Davies-Shiel, M. and Marshall, J. D. *The Industrial Archaeology of the Lake Counties* (David & Charles, Newton Abbot, 1969)

Hadfield, C. and Biddle, G. *The Canals of North-West England*, two volumes (David & Charles, Newton Abbot, 1970)

Hughes, Q. *Seaport – Architecture and Townscape in Liverpool* (Lund Humphries, 1964)

Sharp, D. (ed) *Manchester* (Studio Vista, 1969). A gazetteer of architecturally significant buildings

North-east England

Atkinson, F. *The Great Northern Coalfield 1700–1900* (Durham County Local History Society, 1966)

Atkinson, F. (ed). *Industrial Archaeology: Top Ten Sites in North East England* (Frank Graham, Newcastle, 1971). A gazetteer of the more important sites in the North-East

Clough, R. T. *The Lead Smelting Mills of the Yorkshire Dales* (published by the author, Keighley, 1962)

Duckham, B. F. *The Yorkshire Ouse* (David & Charles, Newton Abbot, 1973)

Raistrick, A. and Jennings, B. *A History of Lead in the Pennines* (Longman, 1966)

Raistrick, A. *Lead Mining in the Mid-Pennines* (D. B. Barton, Truro, 1973)

Singleton, F. *Industrial Revolution in Yorkshire* (Dalesman Publishing, Clapham via Lancaster, Yorkshire, 1970)

The West Midlands

Copeland, R. *Cheddleton Flint Mill and the History of Pottery Milling, 1726–1900* (Cheddleton Flint Mill Preservation Trust, 1969)

Hadfield, C. *The Canals of the West Midlands* (David & Charles, Newton Abbot, 1969)

Raistrick, A. *Dynasty of Ironfounders: The Darbys of Coalbrookdale* (Longman, 1953; reprinted David & Charles, Newton Abbot, 1970)

Timmins, S. (ed). *The Resources, Products, and Industrial History of Birmingham and the Midland Hardware District* (1866; new edition, Cass, 1967)

Trinder, B. *The Industrial Revolution in Shropshire* (Phillimore, Chichester, 1973)

Trinder, B. *The Darbys of Coalbrookdale* (Phillimore, Chichester, 1974)

The East Midlands

Chapman, S. D. *The Early Factory Masters* (David & Charles, Newton Abbot, 1967)

Hadfield, C. *The Canals of the East Midlands* (David & Charles, Newton Abbot, 1966)

Harris, H. *The Industrial Archaeology of the Peak District* (David & Charles, Newton Abbot, 1971)

Kirkham, N. *Derbyshire Lead Mining Through the Centuries* (D. B. Barton, Truro, 1968)

Nixon, F. *The Industrial Archaeology of Derbyshire* (David & Charles, Newton Abbot, 1969)

Smith, D. M. *The Industrial Archaeology of the East Midlands* (David & Charles, Newton Abbot, 1965)

Starmer, G. H. (ed). *Industrial Archaeology: Northamptonshire* (Northampton Museums & Art Gallery, 1970)

The South-east

Ashdown, J., Bussell, M. and Carter, P. *A Survey of Industrial Monuments in Greater London* (Thames Basin Archaeological Observers' Group, 1969). A gazetteer of sites

Branch Johnson, W. *Industrial Monuments in Hertfordshire* (Hertfordshire County Council, 1967). A gazetteer of sites

Branch Johnson, W. *The Industrial Archaeology of Hertfordshire* (David & Charles,

Newton Abbot, 1970)

Hadfield, C. *The Canals of South & South East England* (David & Charles, Newton Abbot, 1969)

Hall, P. G. *The Industries of London* (Hutchinson, 1962)

Industrial Archaeology in Enfield (Enfield Archaeological Society, 1971)

Laws, P. *Industrial Archaeology in Bedfordshire* (Bedfordshire County Council, 1967). A gazetteer of major sites in the county

Wilson, A. *London's Industrial Heritage* (David & Charles, Newton Abbot, 1967)

The South-west

Barton, D. B. *The Cornish Beam Engine* (D. B. Barton, Truro, 1965)

Barton, D. B. *A History of Copper Mining in Cornwall and Devon* (D. B. Barton, Truro, 1966)

Barton, D. B. *A History of Tin Mining and Smelting in Cornwall* (D. B. Barton, Truro, 1967)

Barton, R. M. *A History of the Cornish China Clay Industry* (D. B. Barton, Truro, 1966)

Booker, F. *The Industrial Archaeology of the Tamar Valley* (David & Charles, Newton Abbot, 1967)

Buchanan, R. A. and Cossons, Neil. *The Industrial Archaeology of the Bristol Region* (David & Charles, Newton Abbot, 1969)

Buchanan, R. A. and Cossons, Neil. *Industrial History in Pictures: Bristol* (David & Charles, Newton Abbot, 1970)

Hadfield, C. *The Canals of South-West England* (David & Charles, Newton Abbot, 1967)

Harris, H. *The Industrial Archaeology of Dartmoor* (David & Charles, Newton Abbot, 1968)

Hudson, K. *The Industrial Archaeology of Southern England* (David & Charles, Newton Abbot, 1965)

Hudson, K. *The History of English China Clays* (David & Charles, Newton Abbot, 1969)

Industrial Archaeology in Gloucestershire (Gloucestershire Society for Industrial Archaeology and Gloucestershire Community Council, 1973). A gazetteer of sites in the new administrative county

Minchinton, W. E. (ed). *Industrial Archaeology in Devon* (Dartington Amenity Research Trust, 1968). A comprehensive gazetteer of sites

Ponting, K. E. *The Woollen Industry of South-West England* (Adams & Dart, Bath, 1971)

Tann, J. *Gloucestershire Woollen Mills* (David & Charles, Newton Abbot, 1967)

Wales

Hadfield, C. *The Canals of South Wales and the Border* (David & Charles, Newton Abbot, 1967)

Jenkins, J. G. *The Welsh Woollen Industry* (National Museum of Wales, Cardiff, 1969)

Lewis, W. J. *Lead Mining in Wales* (University of Wales, 1967)

Minchinton, W. E. *The British Tinplate Industry* (Oxford University Press, 1957)

Morgan Rees, D. *Mines, Mills and Furnaces* (National Museum of Wales, Cardiff, 1969)

Thomas, W. G. *Amgueddfa, Bulletin of the National Museum of Wales, No 10* (Cardiff, 1972). Preserving industrial sites in Wales

Index

THE BEDSIDE BOOK

THE BEDSIDE BOOK

A MISCELLANY
for
THE QUIET HOURS

selected and arranged
by

ARTHUR STANLEY

———

LONDON
VICTOR GOLLANCZ LTD
14 Henrietta Street
W.C.

First published September 1932
Second impression November 1932
Third impression December 1932
Fourth impression December 1932
Fifth impression December 1933
Sixth impression September 1935
Seventh impression October 1936
Eighth impression October 1938
Ninth impression (first cheap edition) November 1939
Tenth impression January 1940
Eleventh impression September 1940

TO

THE OTHER SLEEPERS

IN

"OUR DEN"

INSCRIPTION
FOR AN OLD BED

No tale I tell
Of ill or well,
But this I say :
Night treadeth on day,
And for worst or best,
Right good is rest.

WILLIAM MORRIS

FOREWORD

This book is founded on my belief that a need of my own is probably shared by others. Whether we indulge ourselves in the luxury of reading in bed (like Pepys, reading ourselves asleep) or refrain from it as an objectionable habit, it may be found an advantage to have at hand a book offering a variety of consolation, information and entertainment in that part of our dwelling where we are most free from the invasions of the outside world. The virtuous objector to reading in bed will protest that he goes there to sleep, but even he may one day be sworn of my company; for there are many people who remain in bed besides those who do not want to get up, and I have had in mind the involuntary bed-user. It is hoped also that this book may sometimes be found useful out of bed— that it may be a friendly companion on journeys by land or sea and on other suitable occasions which the ingenious reader will discover for himself.

I have endeavoured to provide a reasonable variety of matter within the limits of my scheme, which extends in time from the writers of Ancient Egypt to authors now living and in character of material from the Bible to Mr. Punch. While I remain staunch in my loyalty to venerable bed-fellows like Lucretius, Burton, Browne and Montaigne, to whom so many candles have been sacrificed by preceding generations, I have (as will be seen) made other friends both old and new. The maker of a book of this kind is lucky if he satisfies himself: he should not have the effrontery to expect the same satisfaction on the part of his readers. The good anthologist is not so much a guide as a friend, and who can hope to be a friend of all the world? We begin by overloading our argosies. We

7

pack a great cargo of legacies from the dead and gifts from the living, but we are soon throwing things overboard to lighten the ship, perhaps making flotsam and jetsam of goods for which a ready merchant is waiting at the wharf. But it is not to be supposed that the critics have been reading in bed all these years without discovering some principles to guide the bedside anthologist. They tell us, for example, that the proper bed-book should be continually interesting, un-dramatic, not too exciting, and that it should be one that can be begun anywhere and dropped anywhere. I approve of all these nocturnal regulations, and have endeavoured to obey them. They are stated here in order that my readers may reflect on the frailty of human nature, and have the pleasure of finding out for themselves by means of these tests my errors of inclusion and exclusion.

Sometimes we find the land of sleep as full of briars as this work-a-day world. Perhaps our experience in both depends to some extent on what we bring into them. If so, our last thoughts as we approach the misty frontier should be bright rather than gloomy; and it may be an advantage to close our eyes at a moment when our minds have been cheered by the gracious companionship of some friendly writer. A good night, then, brother or sister—may the sleep-tide carry you gently to a land of peace, and may you meet only those kindly Dreams that pass the Gate of Horn!

A. S.

CONTENTS

FIRST PART
§ I CURFEW

Evening, thou that bringest all that bright morning scattered, thou bringest the sheep, the goat, and the child back to its mother.

SAPPHO (Trans. EDWIN M. COX)

For though the day be never so long
At last the bell ringeth to evensong.

STEPHEN HAWES

Ut quotidie sero signe pulsu ad preces Deo fundendas quisque invitaretur, atque occlusis foribus domorum ultra vagari amplius vetitum admoneretur.

ORDER MADE AT SYNOD OF CAEN, 1061

§ I CURFEW ANCIENT AND MODERN

1. CURFEW CUSTOM

Contrary to the general notion, it appears that no " curfew law " was ever enacted in England. There was, however, long before the Norman Conquest a curfew " custom " which was followed by the English as well as by other European peoples as a precaution against fire. There is for example, an old tradition that a curfew bell was rung every evening at Carfax in Oxford during the reign of Alfred the Great and that at its ringing all persons were expected to cover their fires, shut up their houses and go to bed. The medieval Church gave the weight of its authority to this beneficial custom, and somewhat improved upon it when a Synod at Caen (1061), held by the Duke's authority and attended by Bishops, Abbots and Barons, ordered that a bell should be rung every evening, at hearing of which prayer should be offered, and all people should get within their houses and shut their doors. We are told the object in view was " protection from night thieves," and nothing appears to have been said about fires or lights. Thus the old custom became a police regulation and also a call to evening prayer. Doubtless the sanction of the Church facilitated the enforcement of the old English curfew and extended its scope in England after the Norman conquest. But it was not, as has been said so often, a punishment inflicted by William I on a conquered people. If we can believe William of Malmesbury, Henry I allowed the use of candles at court after curfew ; but kings will be kings, or at least they would in those days.

In London, in Edward III's reign, the bells of St. Martin's-le-Grand rang curfew for the closing of the city gates and the shutting of all taverns. Before the end of the 14th century the Great Bell of Bow had become the Common Bell of London, and curfew was then rung by the whole peal of Bow. The Customary Records of London for the year 1495 show that curfew custom was then strictly enforced in the city :—" yf ther be anye paryshe clerke that ryngeth curfewe after the curfewe be ronge at Bowe Chyrche, or Saint Brydes Chyrche, or Saint Gyles without Cripelgat, *all suche to be presented* " (that is, the offending clerk was to be summoned to appear before the Quest—or Court—of Wardmote). Another typical record is furnished by the Articles of Faversham settled in 1531 :—" Imprimis, the sexton, or his sufficient deputy, shall lye in the church steeple ; and at eight o'clock every night shall ring the curfewe by the space of a quarter of an hour, with such bell as of old time hath been accustomed." The curfew was evidently a municipal rather than a state institution.

Curfew is still rung in several English towns and villages throughout the year—in some places at 8 o'clock, in others at 9 o'clock, and this variation of time has existed for at least four centuries. In the Middle Ages curfew ringing began at Michaelmas and ended at Lady Day.

2. CURFEW LAW

The first English " curfew law " (strictly speaking) is probably to be found in the Regulations issued by the Board of Trade during the European War and known as

" The Curfew Order," which sought to reduce the consumption of gas and electricity in order to save coal. By virtue of this order (which came into operation on April 2, 1918) the following provisions applied throughout Great Britain :

No lights to be used in shop fronts.
No hot meals to be served and no food cooked in hotels,
restaurants, clubs, or public eating-places between 9-30
p.m. and 5 a.m. and no light to be exhibited in the
dining-room of such places after 10 p.m. No gas or
electric current to be consumed on the stage or in the
auditorium of any place of entertainment between 10-30
at night and 1 p.m. on the following day.

The most recent " curfew law " (which was only of short duration) seems to take us back to Medieval times. This was enacted during the post-war troubles in Ireland when an order of local application was issued on August 30, 1920 by the Competent Military Authority under the Defence of the Realm Regulations requiring that " *every person shall remain indoors between the hours of 10-30 o'clock p.m. and 5 o'clock a.m., unless provided with a Permit in writing.*"

A. S.

ADVICE TO SHEPHERDS

Shepherds all, and maidens fair,
Fold your flocks up, for the air
'Gins to thicken, and the sun
Already his great course has run

15

See the drew-drops how they kiss
Every little flower that is,
Hanging on their velvet heads,
Like a rope of crystal beads.
See the heavy clouds low falling,
And bright Hesperus down calling
The dead night from underground,
At whose rising, mists unsound,
Damps and vapours fly apace,
Hovering o'er the wanton face
Of these pastures, where they come
Striking dead both bud and bloom.
Therefore from such danger lock
Every one his lovèd flock ;
And let your dogs lie loose without,
Lest the wolf come, as a scout
From the mountain, and ere day
Bear a kid or lamb away ;
Or the crafty, thievish fox
Break upon your simple flocks.
To secure yourselves from these,
Be not too secure in ease.
So shall you good shepherds prove,
And deserve your master's love.
Now, good night ! may sweetest slumbers
And soft silence fall in numbers
On your eyelids : so, farewell ;
Thus I end my evening knell.

JOHN FLETCHER

" Open, ye everlasting gates ! " they sung ;
" Open, ye Heavens, your living doors ! let in
The great Creator, from his work returned
Magnificent, his six days' work, a World !
Open, and henceforth oft ; for God will deign
To visit oft the dwellings of just men
Delighted, and with frequent intercourse
Thither will send his wingèd messengers
On errands of supernal grace." So sung
The glorious train ascending. He through Heaven,
That opened wide her blazing portals, led
To God's eternal house direct the way—
A broad and ample road, whose dust is gold
And pavement stars, as stars to thee appear
Seen in the Galaxy, that milky way
Which nightly as a circling zone thou seest
Powdered with stars. And now on Earth the seventh
Evening arose in Eden—for the sun
Was set, and twilight from the east came on,
Forerunning night—when at the holy mount
Of Heaven's high-seated top, the imperial throne
Of Godhead, fixed for ever firm and sure,
The Filial Power arrived, and sat him down
With his great Father ; for he also went
Invisible, yet stayed (such privilege
Hath Omnipresence) and the work ordained,
Author and end of all things, and, from work
Now resting, blessed and hallowed the seventh Day,
As resting on that day from all his work ;
But not in silence holy kept : the harp
Had work, and rested not ; the solemn pipe

And dulcimer, all organs of sweet stop,
All sounds on fret by string or golden wire,
Tempered soft tunings, intermixed with voice
Choral or unison; of incense clouds,
Fuming from golden censers, hid the Mount.
Creation and the Six Days' acts they sung.

MILTON (from *Paradise Lost*, Bk. VII)

TO EVENING

Methinks I see thee in the streaky west,
With matron-step slow-moving, while the night
Treads on thy sweeping train; one hand employ'd
In letting fall the curtain of repose
On bird and beast, the other charg'd for man
With sweet oblivion of the cares of day:
Not sumptuously adorn'd, nor needing aid,
Like homely featur'd night, of clust'ring gems;
A star or two, just twinkling on thy brow,
Suffices thee; save that the moon is thine
No less than her's, not worn indeed on high
With ostentatious pageantry, but set
With modest grandeur in thy purple zone,
Resplendent less, but of an ampler round
Come then, and thou shalt find thy vot'ry calm,
Or make me so. Composure is thy gift.

COWPER (from *The Task*)

18

A NOCTURNAL REVERIE

In such a night, when every louder wind
Is to its distant cavern safe confin'd ;
And only gentle zephyr fans his wings,
And lonely Philomel, still waking, sings ;
Or from some tree, fam'd for the owl's delight,
She, hollowing clear, directs the wand'rer right :
In such a night, when passing clouds give place,
Or thinly vail the Heav'ns mysterious face ;
When in some river, overhung with green,
The waving moon and trembling leaves are seen ;
When freshen'd grass now bears itself upright,
And makes cool banks to pleasing rest invite
Whence springs the woodbind, and the bramble-rose,
And where the sleepy cowslip shelter'd grows ;
Whilst now a paler hue the foxglove takes,
Yet chequers still with red the dusky brakes :
When scatter'd glow-worms, but in twilight fine,
Shew trivial beauties, watch their hour to shine ;
Whilst Salisbury stands the test of every light,
In perfect charms, and perfect virtue bright :
When odours, which declin'd repelling day,
Thro' temp'rate air uninterrupted stray ;
When darken'd groves their softest shadows wear,
And falling waters we distinctly hear ;
When thro' the gloom more venerable shows
Some ancient fabrick, awful in repose,
While sunburnt hills their swarthy looks conceal,
And swelling haycocks thicken up the vale :
When the loos'd horse now, as his pasture leads,
Comes slowly grazing thro' th' adjoining meads,
Whose stealing pace, and lengthen'd shade we fear,

Till torn up forage in his teeth we hear :
When nibbling sheep at large pursue their food,
And unmolested kine re-chew the cud ;
When curlews cry beneath the village-walls,
And to her straggling brood the partridge calls ;
Their shortliv'd jubilee the creatures keep,
Which but endures whilst tyrant man does sleep ;
When a sedate content the spirit feels,
And no fierce light disturbs, whilst it reveals,
But silent musings urge the mind to seek
Something, too high for syllables to speak ;
Till the free soul to a compos'dness charm'd,
Finding the elements of rage disarm'd,
O'er all below a solemn quiet grown,
Joys in th' inferior world, and thinks it like her own :
In such a night let me abroad remain,
Till morning breaks, and all's confus'd again ;
Our cares, our toils, our clamours are renew'd,
Or pleasures, seldom reach'd, again pursu'd.

ANNE, COUNTESS OF WINCHILSEA

SONG FOR THE SPINNING WHEEL

Swiftly turn the murmuring wheel !
Night has brought the welcome hour,
When the weary fingers feel
Help, as if from faery power ;
Dewy night o'ershades the ground ;
Turn the swift wheel round and round !

20

Now, beneath the starry sky,
Couch the widely-scattered sheep ;—
Ply the pleasant labour, ply !
For the spindle, while they sleep,
Runs with speed more smooth and fine,
Gathering up a trustier line.

Short-lived likings may be bred
By a glance from fickle eyes ;
But true love is like the thread
Which the kindly wool supplies,
When the flocks are all at rest
Sleeping on the mountain's breast.

WORDSWORTH

TO A SKYLARK

Hail to thee, blithe Spirit !
  Bird thou never wert,
That from heaven, or near it,
  Pourest thy full heart
In profuse strains of unpremeditated art.

Higher still and higher
  From the earth thou springest
Like a cloud of fire ;
  The blue deep thou wingest,
And singing still dost soar, and soaring ever singest.

In the golden lightning
  Of the sunken sun,
O'er which clouds are brightening
  Thou dost float and run,
Like an unbodied joy whose race is just begun.

The pale purple even
　　Melts around thy flight ;
Like a star of heaven
　　In the broad daylight
Thou art unseen, but yet I hear thy shrill delight :

Keen as are the arrows
　　Of that silver sphere,
Whose intense lamp narrows
　　In the white dawn clear
Until we hardly see, we feel that it is there.

All the earth and air
　　With thy voice is loud,
As, when night is bare,
　　From one lonely cloud
The moon rains out her beams, and heaven is over-flow'd.

What thou art we know not
　　What is most like thee ?
From rainbow clouds there flow not
　　Drops so bright to see
As from thy presence showers a rain of melody . . .

Teach me half the gladness
　　That thy brain must know ;
Such harmonious madness
　　From my lips would flow,
The world should listen then, as I am listening now !

SHELLEY

WHAT THE THRUSH SAID TO THE POET

O thou whose face has felt the Winter's wind,
Whose eye has seen the snow-clouds hung in mist,
And the black elm-tops 'mong the freezing stars,
To thee the Spring will be a harvest time.
O thou, whose only book has been the light
Of supreme darkness which thou feedest on
Night after night when Phoebus was away,
To thee the Spring shall be a triple morn.
O fret not after knowledge—I have none,
And yet my song comes native with the warmth.
O fret not after knowledge—I have none,
And yet the Evening listens. He who saddens
At thought of idleness cannot be idle,
And he's awake who thinks himself asleep.

KEATS

NIGHT

The sun descending in the west,
The evening star does shine ;
The birds are silent in their nest,
And I must seek for mine.
The moon, like a flower
In heaven's high bower,
With silent delight
Sits and smiles on the night.

Farewell, green fields and happy grove,
Where flocks have ta'en delight ;
Where lambs have nibbled, silent move
The feet of angels bright.

Unseen they pour blessing,
And joy without ceasing,
On each bud and blossom,
On each sleeping bosom.

They look in every thoughtless nest,
Where birds are covered warm;
They visit caves of every beast,
To keep them all from harm.
If they see any weeping
That should have been sleeping,
They pour sleep on their head,
And sit down by their bed.

WILLIAM BLAKE

EVENING IN THE VILLAGE

Now the light o' the west is a-turn'd to gloom,
An' the men be at huome vrom ground;
An' the bells be a-zenden āl down the Coombe
A muoanen an' dyen sound.
An' the wind is still,
An' the house-dogs da bark,
An' the rooks be a-vled to the elems high an' dark,
An' the water da roar at mill.

An' out droo yander cottage's winder-piane
The light o' the candle da shoot,
An' young Jemmy the blacksmith is down the liane
A-playen his jarmen-flute.

24

An' the miller's man
Da zit down at his ease
'Pon the girt wooden seat that is under the trees,
Wi' his pipe an' his cider can.

Tha'da zay that tis zom'hat in towns to zee
Fresh fiazen vrom day to day :
Tha' mid zee em var me, ef the two or dree
I da love should but smile an' stay.
Zoo gi'e me the sky,
An' the air an' the zun,
An' a huome in the dell wher the water da run,
An' there let me live an' die.

WILLIAM BARNES

MAGDALEN

Magdalen at Michael's gate
  Tirlèd at the pin ;
On Joseph's thorn sang the blackbird,
  ' Let her in ! Let her in ! '

' Hast thou seen the wounds ? ' said Michael,
  'Know'st thou thy sin ? '
' It is evening, evening,' sang the blackbird,
  ' Let her in ! Let her in ! '

' Yes, I have seen the wounds,
  And I know my sin ! '
' She knows it well, well, well,' sang the blackbird,
  ' Let her in ! Let her in ! '

25

'Thou bringest no offerings,' said Michael.
  'Nought save sin.'
And the blackbird sang, 'she is sorry, sorry, sorry,
  'Let her in ! Let her in !'

When he had sung himself to sleep,
  And night did begin,
One came and open'd Michael's gate,
  And Magdalen went in.

HENRY KINGSLEY

INVOCATION

I am he that walks with the tender and growing
  night,
I call to the earth and sea half-hid by the night.
Press close, bare-bosomed night—press close, magnetic
  nourishing night !
Night of south winds—night of the large few stars.
Still nodding night—mad naked summer night.
Smile, O voluptuous cool-breath'd earth !
Earth of the slumbering and liquid trees !
Earth of departed sunset—earth of the mountains misty-
  topt !
Earth of the vitreous pour of the full moon just tinged with
  blue !
Earth of shine and dark mottling the tide of the river !
Earth of the limpid grey of clouds brighter and clearer for
  my sake !
Far-swooping elbow'd earth—rich apple-blossom'd
  earth—
Smile, for your lover comes.

WALT WHITMAN

LOVE SIGHT

When do I see thee most, belovèd one ?
When in the light the spirits of mine eyes
   Before thy face, their altar, solemnise
The worship of that love thro' thee made known ?
Or when, in the dusk hours (we two alone),
   Close-kissed, and eloquent of still replies
   Thy twilight-hidden glimmering visage lies,
And my soul only sees thy soul its own ?

O love, my love ! if I no more should see
Thyself, nor on the earth the shadow of thee,
   Nor image of thine eyes in any spring,—
How then should sound upon Life's darkening slope
The ground-whirl of the perish'd leaves of Hope,
   The wind of Death's imperishable wing ?

D. G. ROSSETTI

TWILIGHT CALM

Oh pleasant eventide !
Clouds on the western side
Grow grey and greyer, hiding the warm sun :
The bees and birds, their happy labours done,
   Seek their close nests and bide.

Screened in the leafy wood
The stock-doves sit and brood :
The very squirrel leaps from bough to bough
But lazily ; pauses ; and settles now
   Where once he stored his food.

One by one the flowers close,
            Lily and dewy rose
Shutting their tender petals from the moon :
The grasshoppers are still ; but not so soon
            Are still the noisy crows. . . .

            From far the lowings come
            Of cattle driven home :
From farther still the wind brings fitfully
The vast continual murmur of the sea,
            Now loud, now almost dumb. . . .

            Remote, each single star
            Comes out, till there they are
All shining brightly. How the dews fall damp
While close at hand the glow-worm lights her lamp,
            Or twinkles from afar.

            But evening now is done
            As much as if the sun
Day-giving had arisen in the East—
For night has come ; and the great calm has ceased,
            The quiet sands have run.

CHRISTINA ROSSETTI

VESPERS

O blackbird, what a boy you are !
How you do go it !
Blowing your bugle to that one sweet star—
How you do blow it !

And does she hear you, blackbird boy, so far ?
Or is it wasted breath ?
" Good Lord ! she is so bright
To-night ! "
The blackbird saith.

T. E. BROWN

EVENING

Already evening ! In the duskiest nook
   Of yon dusk corner, under the Death's-head,
   Between the alembics, thrust this legended,
And iron-bound, and melancholy book,
For I will read no longer. The loud brook
   Shelves his sharp light up shallow banks thin-spread
   The slumbrous west grows slowly red, and red :
Up from the ripened corn her silver hook
The moon is lifting : and deliciously
   Along the warm blue hills the day declines :
The first star brightens while she waits for me,
And round her swelling heart the zone grows tight :
   Musing, half-sad, in her soft hair she twines
The white rose, whispering, ' He will come to-night ! '

EARL OF LYTTON

TWILIGHT ON EGDON HEATH

The distant rims of the world and of the firmament
seemed to be a division in time no less than a division in
matter. The face of the heath by its mere complexion

29

added half an hour to evening ; it could in like manner retard the dawn, sadden noon, anticipate the frowning of storms scarcely generated, and intensify the opacity of a moonless midnight to a cause of shaking and dread.

In fact, precisely at this transitional point of its nightly roll into darkness the great and particular glory of the Egdon waste began, and nobody could be said to understand the heath who had not been there at such a time. It could best be felt when it could not clearly be seen, its complete effect and explanation lying in this and the succeeding hours before the next dawn : then, and only then did it tell its true tale. The spot was, indeed, a near relation of night, and when night showed itself an apparent tendency to gravitate together could be perceived in its shades and the scene. The sombre stretch of rounds and hollows seemed to rise and meet the evening gloom in pure sympathy, the heath exhaling darkness as rapidly as the heavens precipitated it. And so the obscurity in the air and the obscurity in the land closed together in a black fraternization towards which each advanced half-way.

The place became full of a watchful intentness now ; for when other things sank brooding to sleep the heath appeared slowly to awake and listen. Every night its Titanic form seemed to await something ; but it had waited thus, unmoved, during so many centuries, through the crises of so many things, that it could only be imagined to await one last crisis—the final overthrow.

It was a spot which returned upon the memory of those who loved it with an aspect of peculiar and kindly congruity. Smiling champaigns of flowers and fruit hardly do this, for they are permanently harmonious only with an existence of better reputation as to its issues than the present. Twilight combined with the scenery of Egdon

Heath to evolve a thing majestic without severity, impressive without showiness, emphatic in its admonitions, grand in its simplicity. The qualifications which frequently invest the façade of a prison with far more dignity than is found in the façade of a palace double its size lent to this heath a sublimity in which spots renowned for beauty of the accepted kind are utterly wanting. Fair prospects wed happily with fair times ; but alas, if times be not fair ! Men have oftener suffered from the mockery of a place too smiling for their reason than from the oppression of surroundings oversadly tinged. Haggard Egdon appealed to a subtler and scarcer instinct, to a more recently learnt emotion, than that which responds to the sort of beauty called charming and fair.

THOMAS HARDY (from *The Return of the Native*)

AN EVENING IN SUSSEX

Ah, Hesperus ! the even falls
From silences to silences,
As when a diver drops at ease
Far down the waters to the halls
Of Thetis and her silver seas,
Beholding through the delicate mist
The colours shifting by degrees
From purple into amethyst.

Across the pure pellucid dale
The shingled spire so darkly stands
Against the gold and crimson bands,
Methinks it were not hard to tell

31

How points the clock his brazen hands,
Or if the arrow warns us well,
The vane that looks across the lands
The rising winds to sentinel.

Hark in the twilight !—was it sound
Of bell, or bird, or rustling tree ?
It is the children, homeward bound,
Some little comrade they have crowned
The monarch of their revelry ;
Their laughter floats along the hill,
The laughter dies, and all is still.
What horseman comes so late to ride
The solitary stages ? Now
His hoofs are on the steep hill-side,
Now loud and full upon the brow,
Now faintly dying down the hollow :
How many a mile the moon has shown,
Fast dwindling on the friendly stone,
And yet and yet his steed must follow
The road that runs, so white and lone,
Between dark avenues of trees,
Towards the southern villages.

The heavens are like a deep lagoon
In some unfathomable sea,
Where with majestic sail the moon
Sweeps, like a galleon, to the tune
Of oarsmen bending silently.
Her full bright face is clear and cold,
As silver touched with palest gold ;
Her liveried henchmen of the night,
Rose-tinged and gold, and chrysolite,

Move on her errands manifold,
And come and pass and ply their wings
In sweet ethereal wanderings.

Unto what thing shall I compare
So sweet a sight, so strange, so rare,
Or fruit, or flower, or lady fair?
Around her, in a girdling band,
White companies of clouds are spread,
As in the North snow mountains stand,
Encompassing a silver land
Upon a blue lake islanded;
Or moving now before her face,
As babes that in the twilight play
About their mother's feet, nor less
As goats around their shepherdess
In most delightful pastures stray.

The light is on the laurel leaves;
With such a glow it seems to fall
Upon the gables and the eaves,
It looks so pure, so chaste, so holy,
That I could half believe the Hall
Were some old convent mystical,
Haunted by cloistered melancholy.

Come to me, gentle lady mine,
That hast not any part or name
In this our mortal world,—divine
And yet most tender; come the same
As I have seen thee when the beams
Grew softer in the silent grace
Of thy sweet coming; with the face

That I have worshipped in my dreams,
Come to me ! 'Tis the hour ; and now
There's something tells me thou art near,
It is thy footfall I can hear ;
Thy lips are pressed upon my brow ;
Thy breath is in the garden scents
That float so softly in the air ;
And all of nature seems to wear
The impress of thy lineaments.

Say not it is the rustling tree,
Whose leaves the soulless breezes stir
Amid the beech-wood ! Come to me !
It is thy voice that bids me be
Thy poet, thine interpreter.
Or if indeed in yon white star,
Where love and life and beauty are
More true, more tender, more intense,
Thy spiritual home I see,
Stretch out thine hand and bear me hence !
O blessèd Lady, take me far
Unto the haunts of innocence !
So for a little space I flee
From my false self, and dwell with thee.

W. J. COURTHOPE

A DAY'S COACHING IN SCOTLAND

Where have I been this perfect summer day,—
Or *fortnight* is it, since I rose from bed,
Devoured that kippered fish, the oatmeal bread,
And mounted to this box ? O bowl away,

Swift stagers, through the dusk ; I will not say
' Enough,' nor care where I have been or be,
Nor know one name of hill, or lake, or lea,
Or moor, or glen ! Were not the clouds at play
Nameless among the hills, and fair as dreams ?
On such a day we must love things, not words,
And memory take or leave them as they are.
On such a day ! What unimagined streams
Are in the world, how many haunts of birds,
What fields and flowers,—and what an evening Star !

EDWARD DOWDEN

THE TRYST

Long are the hours the sun is above,
But when evening comes I go home to my love.

I'm away the daylight hours and more,
Yet she comes not down to open the door.

She does not meet me upon the stair,—
She sits in my chamber and waits for me there.

As I enter the room she does not move :
I always walk straight up to my love ;

And she lets me take my wonted place
At her side, and gaze in her dear dear face.

There as I sit, from her head thrown back
Her hair falls straight in a shadow black.

35

Aching and hot as my tired eyes be,
She is all that I wish to see.

And in my wearied and toil-dinned ear,
She says all things that I wish to hear.

Dusky and duskier grows the room,
Yet I see her best in the darker gloom.

When the winter eves are early and cold,
The firelight hours are a dream of gold.

And so I sit here night by night,
In rest and enjoyment of love's delight.

But a knock at the door, a step on the stair
Will startle, alas, my love from her chair.

If a stranger comes she will not stay :
At the first alarm she is off and away.

And he wonders, my guest, usurping her throne,
That I sit so much by myself alone.

ROBERT BRIDGES

IN THE CHESTNUT WOODS

Where still Varenna wears her cypress-crown
   At eve amid the chestnut-woods I lay ;
The twilight lingered with the little town,
   Then round by Cadenabbia stole away :

The dim woods darkened at the set of day;
Yet where the forest-shadows lowering frown
   Like fairies with their lamps the fire-flies stray,
Lighting their lanterns as the sun goes down.

There in the dusk, in silence resting there,
Was it a Spirit-Voice I heard declare—
   Some Pixy of the Woods that stopped to say—
' Eternal are the skies and infinite;
Eternal are the stars that shine so bright;
   But here a little while the fire-flies play.'

SAMUEL WADDINGTON

THE LATE LARK

A late lark twitters from the quiet skies
And from the west,
Where the sun, his day's work ended,
Lingers as in content,
There falls on the old, gray city
An influence luminous and serene,
A shining peace.
The smoke ascends
In a rosy-and-golden haze. The spires
Shine and are changed. In the valley
Shadows rise. The lark sings on. The sun,
Closing his benediction,
Sinks, and the darkening air
Thrills with a sense of the triumphing night—
Night with her train of stars
And her great gift of sleep.

So be my passing !
My task accomplish'd and the long day done,
My wages taken, and in my heart
Some late lark singing,
Let me be gather'd to the quiet west,
The sundown splendid and serene,
Death.

W. E. HENLEY

IN THE HEART OF THE HILLS

In the warm blue heart of the hills
  My beautiful beautiful one
Sleeps where he laid him down
  Before the journey was done.

All the long summer day
  The ghosts of noon draw nigh,
And the tremulous aspens hear
  The footing of winds go by.

Down to the gates of the sea,
  Out of the gates of the west,
Journeys the whispering river
  Before the place of his rest.

The road he loved to follow
  When June came by his door,
Out through the dim blue haze
  Leads, but allures no more.

The trailing shadows of clouds
   Steal from the slopes and are gone :
The myriad life in the grass
   Stirs, but he slumbers on ;

The inland-wandering tern
   Skriel as they forage and fly ;
His loons on the lonely reach
   Utter their querulous cry

Over the floating lilies
   A dragon-fly tacks and steers ;
Far in the depth of the blue
   A martin settles and veers ;

To every roadside thistle
   A gold-brown butterfly clings ;
But he no more companions
   All the dear vagrant things.

The strong red journeying sun,
   The pale and wandering rain,
Will roam on the hills together
   And find him never again.

Then twilight falls with the touch
   Of a hand that soothes and stills,
And a swamp-robin sings into light
   The lone white star of the hills.

Alone in the dusk he sings,
   And a burden of sorrow and wrong
Is lifted up from the earth
   And carried away in his song.

Alone in the dusk he sings,
    And the joy of another day
Is folded in peace and borne
    On the drift of years away.

But there in the heart of the hills
    My beautiful weary one
Sleeps where I laid him down ;
    And the long sweet night is begun.

BLISS CARMAN

THE END OF THE DAY

I hear the bells at eventide
    Peal slowly one by one,
Near and far off they break and glide,
    Across the stream float faintly beautiful
    The antiphonal bells of Hull ;
The day is done, done, done,
    The day is done.

The dew has gathered in the flowers
    Like tears from some unconscious deep,
The swallows whirl around the towers,
    And light runs out beyond the long cloud bars,
    And leaves the single stars ;
'Tis time for sleep, sleep, sleep,
    'Tis time for sleep.

The hermit thrush begins again,
    Timorous eremite,

That song of risen tears and pain,
  As if the one he loved was far away ;
   ' Alas ! another day—— '
' And now Good-night, Good-night,' ' Good-night.'

DUNCAN C. SCOTT

EVENSONG

Thrush, sing clear, for the spring is here :
Sing, for the summer is near, is near.

All day long thou hast plied thy song,
Hardly hid from the hurrying throng :

Now the shade of the trees is laid
Down the meadow and up the glade :

Now when the air grows cool and rare
Birds of the cloister fall to prayer :

Here is the bed of the patient dead,
Shoulder by shoulder, head by head.

Sweet bells swing in the tower, and ring
Men to worship before their King.

See they come as the grave bells hum,
Restless voices awhile are dumb :

More and more on the sacred floor
Feet that linger about the door :

Sweet sounds swim through the vaulting dim,
Psalm and canticle, vesper hymn.

That is the way that mortals pray :
Which is the sweeter ? Brown bird, say !

Which were best for me ? Both are blest ;
Sing thy sweetest and leave the rest.

A . C . BENSON

CHIMES

Brief, on a flying night,
  From the shaken tower,
A flock of bells take flight,
  And go with the hour.

Like birds from the cote to the gales,
  Abrupt—O hark !
A fleet of bells set sails,
  And go to the dark.

Sudden the cold airs swing
  Alone, aloud,
A verse of bells takes wing
  And flies with the cloud.

ALICE MEYNELL

IN ROMNEY MARSH

As I went down to Dymchurch Wall,
  I heard the South sing o'er the land ;
I saw the yellow sunlight fall
  On knolls where Norman churches stand

And ringing shrilly, taut and lithe,
  Within the wind a core of sound,
The wire from Romney town to Hythe
  Alone its airy journey wound.

A veil of purple vapour flowed
  And trailed its fringe along the Straits ;
The upper air like sapphire glow'd ;
  And roses fill'd Heaven's central gates.

Masts in the offing wagg'd their tops ;
  The swinging waves peal'd on the shore;
The saffron beach, all diamond drops
  And beads of surge, prolong'd the roar.

As I came up from Dymchurch Wall,
  I saw above the Down's low crest
The crimson brands of sunset fall,
  Flicker and fade from out the west.

Night sank : like flakes of silver fire
  The stars in one great shower came down ;
Shrill blew the wind ; and shrill the wire
  Rang out from Hythe to Romney town.

The darkly shining salt sea drops
  Streamed as the waves clashed on the shore ;
The beach, with all its organ stops
  Pealing again, prolong'd the roar.

JOHN DAVIDSON

43

THE CITY

Full of Zeus the cities : full of Zeus the harbours : full of
Zeus are all the ways of men

What domination of what darkness dies this hour,
And through what new, rejoicing, winged, ethereal power
O'erthrown, the cells opened, the heart released from
    fear
Gay twilight and grave twilight pass. The stars appear
O'er the prodigious, smouldering, dusky, city flare.
The hanging gardens of Babylon were not more fair
Than these blue flickering glades, where childhood in its
    glee
Re-echoes with fresh voice the heaven-lit ecstasy.
Yon girl whirls like an eastern dervish. Her dance is
No less a god-intoxicated dance than his,
Though all unknowing the arcane fire that lights her feet,
What motions of what starry tribes her limbs repeat.
I, too, firesmitten, cannot linger : I know there lies
Open somewhere this hour a gate to Paradise,
Its blazing battlements with watchers thronged, O where ?
I know not, but my flame-winged feet shall lead me
    there.
O, hurry, hurry, unknown shepherd of desires,
And with thy flock of bright imperishable fires
Pen me within the starry fold, ere the night falls
And I am left alone below immutable walls.
Or am I there already, and is it Paradise
To look on mortal things with an immortal's eyes ?
Above the misty brilliance the streets assume
A night-dilated blue magnificence of gloom
Like many-templed Nineveh tower beyond tower ;

And I am hurried on in this immortal hour.
Mine eyes beget new majesties : my spirit greets
The trams, the high-built glittering galleons of the streets
That float through twilight rivers from galaxies of light.
Nay, in the Fount of Days they rise, they take their flight,
And wend to the great deep, the Holy Sepulchre.
Those dark misshapen folk to be made lovely there
Hurry with me, not all ignoble as we seem,
Lured by some inexpressible and gorgeous dream.
The earth melts in my blood. The air that I inhale
Is like enchanted wine poured from the Holy Grail.
What was that glimmer then ? Was it the flash of wings
As through the blinded mart rode on the King of Kings ?
O stay, departing glory, stay with us but a day,
And burning seraphim shall leap from out our clay,
And plumed and crested hosts shall shine where men
    have been,
Heaven hold no lordlier court than earth at College Green.
Ah, no, the wizardry is over ; the magic flame
That might have melted all in beauty fades as it came.
The stars are far and faint and strange. The night draws
    down.
Exiled from light, forlorn, I walk in Dublin Town
Yet had I might to lift the veil, the will to dare,
The fiery rushing chariots of the Lord are there,
The whirlwind path, the blazing gates, the trumpets
    blown,
The halls of heaven, the majesty of throne by throne,
Enraptured faces, hands uplifted, welcome sung
By the thronged gods, tall, golden-coloured, joyful,
    young.

GEORGE RUSSELL ("A.E.")

NOD

Softly along the road of evening,
    In a twilight dim with rose,
Wrinkled with age, and drenched with dew,
    Old Nod, the shepherd, goes.

His drowsy flock streams on before him,
    Their fleeces charged with gold,
To where the sun's last beam leans low
    On Nod the shepherd's fold.

The hedge is quick and green with briar,
    From their sand the conies creep ;
And all the birds that fly in heaven
    Flock singing home to sleep.

His lambs outnumber a noon's roses,
    Yet, when night's shadows fall,
His blind old sheep-dog, Slumber-soon,
    Misses not one of all.

His are the quiet steeps of dreamland,
    The waters of no-more-pain,
His ram's bell rings 'neath an arch of stars,
    " Rest, rest, and rest again."

                              WALTER DE LA MARE

FAREWELL

Look thy last on all things lovely,
Every hour. Let no night
Seal thy sense in deathly slumber
    Till to delight

Thou have paid thy utmost blessing ;
Since that all things thou wouldst praise
Beauty took from those who loved them
    In other days.

WALTER DE LA MARE

THE COUNTRY BEDROOM

My room's a square and candle-lighted boat,
In the surrounding depths of night afloat,
My windows are the portholes, and the seas
The sound of rain on the dark apple-trees.

Sea monster-like beneath, an old horse blows
A snort of darkness from his sleeping nose,
Below among drowned daisies. Far off, hark !
Far off one owl amidst the waves of dark.

FRANCES CORNFORD

IN THE COOL OF THE EVENING

I thought I heard Him calling. Did you hear
A sound, a little sound ? My curious ear
Is dinned with flying noises, and the tree
Goes—whisper, whisper, whisper silently
Till all its whispers spread into the sound
Of a dull roar. Lie closer to the ground,
The shade is deep and He may pass us by,
We are so very small, and His great eye,
Customed to starry majesties, may gaze
Too wide to spy us hiding in the maze :

47

Ah, misery ! the sun has not yet gone
And we are naked : He may look upon
Our crouching shame, may make us stand upright
Burning in terror—O that it were night !
He may not come. . . . What ? listen, listen, now—
He is here ! lie closer. . . . *Adam, where art thou ?*

JAMES STEPHENS

EVENING SCENTS

No evening scents, I think, have the fascination of the
delicate fragrance of the evening primroses, especially
that of the commonest variety. Those pale moons irradiate
the twilight with their sweet elusive perfumes. Like the
flowers themselves their scent as night draws in becomes
full of mystery and holds our imagination captive. And
the scent of limes, what an exquisite scent this is—as
exquisite as the music of the trees. To me the loveliest
music in the world is the music of the evening breeze in the
lime trees on a July evening. Each one of us, I suppose,
dreams their own dreams and reads their own thoughts
in the wondrously varied music of trees. Just as with the
music of bells. 'He that hears bells will make them sound
what he list ; as the soul thinketh, so the bell clinketh.'
The sound of the wind amongst beeches is a glorious
sound, deep, rich and full. It is magnificent, but it is
a song of this earth. The music of limes is a far-away
melody reaching to the stars, a music which sweeps our
thoughts to those stupendous flowers set by Almighty
God in the gardens of space.

ELEANOUR SINCLAIR ROHDE (from
The Scented Garden)

FOREFATHERS

Here they went with smock and crook,
   Toiled in the sun, lolled in the shade,
Here they mudded out the brook
   And here their hatchet cleared the glade.
Harvest-supper woke their wit,
Huntsman's moon their wooings lit.

From this church they led their brides,
   From this church themselves were led
Shoulder-high ; on these waysides
   Sat to take their beer and bread.
Names are gone—what men they were
These their cottages declare.

Names are vanished, save the few
   In the old brown Bible scrawled ;
These were men of pith and thew,
   Whom the city never called ;
Scarce could read or hold a quill,
Built the barn, the forge, the mill.

On the green they watched their sons
   Playing till too dark to see,
As their fathers watched them once,
   As my father once watched me ;
While the bat and beetle flew
On the warm air webbed with dew.

Unrecorded, unrenowned,
   Men from whom my ways begin,
Here I know you by your ground

But I know you not within—
All is mist, and there survives
Not a moment of your lives.

Like the bee that now is blown
   Honey-heavy on my hand,
From the toppling tansy-throne
   In the green tempestuous land,—
I'm in clover now, nor know
Who made honey long ago.

                              EDMUND BLUNDEN

AT DUSK

Left to the stars the sky,
   Left to the sea the sand,
Softly the small waves drop
   Hand on white hand :
Where murmuring hills are steep
Countless musicians keep
   Tryst, among wild, dim valleys
Lost in sleep.

Their music binds a world
   Of alien fields unknown,
Stirs among cloud-hung peaks
   Lovely and lone.
Far and remote they seem,
Playing their endless theme—
   Thin threads of sound come trembling back,
Dream upon dream.

                    ENID, COUNTESS OF KINNOULL

THE PRINCE OF SLEEP

I met at eve the Prince of Sleep,
His was a still and lovely face;
He wandered through a valley steep,
   Lovely in a lonely place.

His garb was grey of lavender,
About his brows a poppy-wreath
Burned like dim coals, and everywhere
   The air was sweeter for his breath.

His twilight feet no sandals wore,
His eyes shone faint in their own flame,
Fair moths that gloomed his steps before
   Seemed letters of his lovely name.

His house is in the mountain ways,
A phantom house of misty walls,
Whose golden flocks at evening graze,
   And witch the moon with muffled calls.

Upwelling from his shadowy springs
Sweet waters shake a trembling sound,
There flit the hoot-owl's silent wings,
   There hath his web the silkworm wound.

Dark in his pools clear visions lurk,
And rosy, as with morning buds,
Along his dales of broom and birk
   Dreams haunt his solitary woods.

I met at eve the Prince of Sleep,
His was a still and lovely face;
He wandered through a valley steep,
   Lovely in a lonely place.

WALTER RAMAL

THE VALLEY OF BELLS

Monotonous ringing, far away, a solitary bell.
Where ? For whom ? By whom ? There's nobody here
    to tell.
Noon, silent summer noon. The flowers
Droop in the heat. Cloudless, blue, blue sky.
Haze on the convent spire. White, heat haze.
Not a stir on the leaves, not a fluttering butterfly.

Heavy, breathless noon. Even the cows
Sleepy-eyed, cease their tinkling tune
And drowse in the shade of the trees.
All things drowse in the lonely Siesta noon.

Twelve ! Listen. Awake, awake peals
The angelus bell. No stir, no answer here.
Pray, pray, an echo rings from the church
Far below. They're pealing and ringing far and near.

Awake, awake. Have you heard, oh idle one ?
Why do you dream, lying all day, supine ?
Up, up and pray. With your lips to the earth,
Oh, beware, beware, you're drinking the Lotus wine.

Bells, bells, I hear you long ago,
In a far away home, hushing the shrill street cries
In the fetid, smoky air of a northern town ;
Pealing and mingling with all its labouring noise.

I'm still in the valley here. They've ceased. But no.
The little convent bell ! 'tis late, 'tis late.
Hurry, sister, hurry ; the hour is past.
Ring out, little bell. The noon will never wait.

Silence again. Drowsy summer day.
No stir, no answer here. The sun will creep
Soon enough to the western sky. And the bees, hush!
They hum and drone. " Sleep, stranger, sleep."

And still monotonous, far away, a solitary bell.
Why is it ringing now? There's nobody here to tell.

IRENE HAUGH

SOLITUDE

This is a lonely place,
And old in dreams; the woods
Fold in their wide embrace
Unravished solitudes.

Here, while still evening falls
And the grey light grows less,
Peace builds the shadowy walls
Of ancient quietness.

Her hands uprear the gloom,
And evermore round me
The vast unshuttered room
Of night grows silently.

She has such mighty guests
To furnish for and keep,
For here old Saturn rests,
And Time comes home to sleep.

R. G. T. COVENTRY

MADONNA OF THE EVENING FLOWERS

All day long I have been working,
Now I am tired.
I call : " Where are you ? "
But there is only the oak tree rustling in the wind.
The house is very quiet,
The sun shines in on your books,
On your scissors and thimble just put down.
But you are not there.
Suddenly I am lonely :
Where are You ?
I go about searching.
Then I see you,
Standing under a spire of pale blue larkspur,
With a basket of roses on your arm.
You are cool, like silver,
And you smile.
I think the Canterbury bells are playing little tunes,
You tell me that the peonies need spraying,
That the columbines have overrun all bounds,
That the pyrus japonica should be cut back and rounded
You tell me these things.
But I look at you, heart of silver,
White heart-flame of polished silver,
Burning beneath the blue steeples of the larkspur,
And I long to kneel instantly at your feet,
While all about us peal the loud, sweet, Te Deums of the
    Canterbury bells.

AMY LOWELL

LIGHTS OUT

I have come to the borders of sleep,
The unfathomable deep
Forest where all must lose
Their way, however straight,
Or winding, soon or late ;
They cannot choose

Many a road and track
That, since the dawn's first crack,
Up to the forest brink,
Deceived the travellers
Suddenly now blurs,
And in they sink.

Here love ends,
Despair, ambition ends,
All pleasure and all trouble,
Although most sweet or bitter,
Here ends in sleep that is sweeter
Than tasks most noble.

There is not any book
Or face of dearest look
That I would not turn from now
To go into the unknown
I must enter and leave alone
I know not how.

The tall forest towers;
Its cloudy foliage lowers
Ahead, shelf above shelf;
Its silence I hear and obey
That I may lose my way
And myself.

EDWARD THOMAS

THE MIDLANDS

Black in the summer night my Cotswold hill
  Aslant my window sleeps, beneath a sky
Deep as the bedded violets that fill
  March woods with dusky passion. As I lie
Abed between cool walls I watch the host
  Of the slow stars lit over Gloucester plain,
And drowsily the habit of these most
  Beloved English lands moves in my brain,
While silence holds dominion of the dark,
Save when the foxes from the spinneys bark.

I see the valleys in their morning mist
  Wreathed under limpid hills in moving light,
Happy with many a yeoman melodist;
  I see the little roads of twinkling white
Busy with fieldward teams and market gear
  Of rosy men, cloth-gaitered, who can tell
The many-minded changes of the year,
  Who know why crops and kine fare ill or well;
I see the sun persuade the mist away,
Till town and stead are shining to the day.

I see the wagons move along the rows
  Of ripe and summer-breathing clover-flower,
I see the lissom husbandman who knows
  Deep in his heart the beauty of his power,
As lithely pitched, the full-heaped fork bids on
  The harvest home. I hear the rickyard fill
With gossip as in generations gone,
  While wagon follows wagon from the hill.
I think how, when our seasons all are sealed,
Shall come the unchanging harvest from the field.

I see the barns and comely manors planned
  By men who somehow moved in comely thought,
Who, with a simple shippon to their hand,
  As men upon some godlike business wrought ;
I see the little cottages that keep
  Their beauty still where since Plantagenet
Have come the shepherds happily to sleep,
  Finding the loaves and cups of cider set ;
I see the twisted shepherds, brown and old,
Driving at dusk their glimmering sheep to fold.

And now the valleys that upon the sun
  Broke from their opal veils, are veil'd again,
And the last light upon the wolds is done,
  And silence falls on flock and fields and men ;
And black upon the night I watch my hill,
  And the stars shine, and there an owly wing
Brushes the night, and all again is still,
  And, from this land of worship that I sing,
I turn to sleep, content that from my sires
I draw the blood of England's midmost shires.

JOHN DRINKWATER

SWALLOW SONG

O little hearts, beat home, beat home!
  Here is no place to rest;
Night darkens on the falling foam
  And on the fading west.
O little wings, beat home, beat home!
Love may no longer roam.

Oh, Love has touched the fields of wheat,
  And Love has crowned the corn,
And we must follow Love's white feet
  Through all the ways of morn:
Through all the silver roads of air
We pass and have no care.

The silver roads of Love are wide,
O winds that turn, O stars that guide!
Sweet are the ways that Love hath trod
Through the clear skies that reach to God,
But in the cliff-grass Love builds deep
A place where wandering wings may sleep.

MARJORIE PICKTHALL

IN LAMPLIGHT

Now that the chill October day is declining
Pull the blinds, draw each voluminous curtain,
Till the room is full of gloom and of the uncertain
Gleams of firelight on polished edges shining.

Then bring the rosy lamp to its wonted station
On the dark-gleaming table. In that soft splendour
Well-known things of the room, grown deep and tender,
Gather round, a mysterious congregation :
Pallid sheen of the silver, the bright brass fender,
The wine-red pool of carpet, the bowl of roses,
Lustrous-hearted, crimsons and purples looming
From dusky rugs and cushions. Nothing discloses
The unseen walls, but the broken, richly-glooming
Gold of frames and opulent wells of mingling
Dim colours gathered in darkened mirrors. And breaking
The dream-like spell, and your deep chair forsaking
You go, perhaps, to the shelves and, slowly singling
Some old rich-blazoned book, return. But the gleaming
Spells close round you again and you fall to dreaming,
Eyes grown dim, the book on your lap unheeded.

                              MARTIN ARMSTRONG

FIRST PART
§ II THE EVENING POST

The post is the consolation of life.

VOLTAIRE

Blessed is he who is made happy by the sound of a rat-tat !

THACKERAY

The chief interest of a study of the great letter-writers is that it introduces us, not to literary works, but to persons. This is the triumph of letter-writing, that it keeps a more delicate image alive and presents us with a subtler likeness of the writer than we can find in the more formal achievements of authorship.

SIR WALTER RALEIGH (1861-1922)

§ II THE EVENING POST

LETTERS FROM CICERO

1. *To his friend Atticus* (*in Epirus*) B.C. 60.

Believe me there is nothing at this moment of which I stand so much in need as a man with whom to share all that causes me anxiety; a man to love me; a man of sense to whom I can speak without affectation, reserve, or concealment. For my brother is away—that most open-hearted and affectionate of men. Metellus is not a human being, but

"Mere sound and air, a howling wilderness."

While you, who have so often lightened my anxiety and my anguish of soul by your conversation and advice, who are ever my ally in public affairs, my confidant in all private business, the sharer in all my conversations and projects—where are you? So entirely am I abandoned by all, that the only moments of repose left me are those which are spent with my wife, pet daughter and sweet little Cicero. For as to those friendships with the great, and their artificial attractions, they have indeed a certain glitter in the outside world, but they bring no private satisfaction. And so, after a crowded morning *levée*, as I go down to the forum surrounded by troops of friends, I can find no one out of all that crowd with whom to jest freely, or into whose ear I can breathe a familiar sigh. Therefore I wait for you, I long for you, I even urge on you to come; for I have many anxieties, many pressing cares, of which I think, if I once had your ears to listen to me, I could unburden myself in the conversation of a single walk. And of my private anxieties, indeed, I shall conceal all the stings and vexations, and not trust them to this letter and an unknown letter-carrier. These, however—for I don't want you to be made too anxious—are not very painful : yet they are persistent and worrying, and are not put to rest by the advice or conversation of any friend. But in regard to the Republic I have still the same courage and purpose, though it has again and again of its own act eluded treatment. For should I put briefly what has occurred since you left, you would certainly exclaim that the Roman empire cannot be maintained much longer. . . . You now understand in what stormy water we are : and as from what I have written to you in such strong terms you have a view also of what I have not written. Come back to me, for it is time you did. And though the state of affairs to which I invite you is one to be avoided, yet let your value for me so far prevail, as to induce you to come there even in these vexatious circumstances. For the rest I will take care that due warning is given, and a notice put up in all places, to prevent you being entered on the census as absent ; and to get put on the census just before the lustration is the mark of your true man of business. So let me see you at the earliest possible moment. Farewell.

20 January, in the Consulship of Q. Metellus and L. Afranius. (*Written from Rome.*)

2. *To his brother Quintus* (*in Britain*) B.C. 54.

When you receive a letter from me by the hand of an amanuensis, you may be sure that I have not even a little leisure ; when by my own a little. For let me tell you that in regard to causes and trials in court, I have never been closer tied, and that, too, at the most unhealthy season

of the year, and in the most oppressively hot weather. . . .
How glad I was to get your letter from Britain ! I was
afraid of the ocean, afraid of the coast of the island. The
other parts of the enterprise I do not under-rate ; but
yet they inspire more hope than fear, and it is the
suspense rather than any positive alarm that renders me
uneasy. You, however, I can see, have a splendid subject
for description, topography, natural features of things and
places, manners, races, battles, your commander himself—
what themes for your pen ! I will gladly, as you request,
assist you in the points you mention, and will send you
the verses you ask for. But, look you ! I think you are
keeping me in the dark. Tell me, my dear brother, what
Caesar thinks of my verses. For he wrote before to tell me
he had read my first book. Of the first part, he said that
he had never read anything better even in Greek : the
rest, up to a particular passage, somewhat " careless "—
that is his word. Tell me the truth is it the subject-matter
or the " style " that he does not like ? You needn't be
afraid : I shall not admire myself one whit the less. On
this subject speak like a lover of truth, and with your
usual brotherly frankness. (*Written from Rome.*)

LETTERS OF CICERO
(Trans. E. S. SHUCKBURGH)

PLINY TO TACITUS

(*Describing the Eruption of Vesuvius*, 79 A.D.)

Your request that I would send you an account of my
uncle's end, so that you may transmit a more exact relation
of it to posterity, deserves my acknowledgments ; for if
his death shall be celebrated by your pen, the glory of it,

I am aware, will be rendered for ever deathless. For notwithstanding he perished, as did whole peoples and cities, in the destruction of a most beautiful region, and by a misfortune memorable enough to promise him a kind of immortality ; notwithstanding he has himself composed many and lasting works ; yet I am persuaded, the mentioning of him in your immortal writings, will greatly contribute to eternize his name. . . . The more willingly do I undertake, nay, solicit, the task you set me.

He was at that time with the fleet under his command at Misenum. On the 24th of August, about one in the afternoon, my mother desired him to observe a cloud of very unusual size and appearance. He had sunned himself, then taken a cold bath, and after a leisurely luncheon was engaged in study. He immediately called for his shoes and went up an eminence from whence he might best view this very uncommon appearance. It was not at that distance discernible from what mountain this cloud issued, but it was found afterwards to be Vesuvius . . .

My uncle, true savant that he was, deemed the phenomenon important and worth a nearer view. He ordered a light vessel to be got ready, and gave me the liberty, if I thought proper, to attend him. I replied I would rather study ; and, as it happened, he had himself given me a theme for composition. As he was coming out of the house he received a note from Rectina, the wife of Bassus, who was in the utmost alarm at the imminent danger (his villa stood just below us, and there was no way to escape but by sea) ; she earnestly entreated him to save her from such deadly peril. He changed his first design and what he began with a philosophical, he pursued with an heroical turn of mind. He ordered large galleys to be launched, and went himself on board one, with the intention of assisting not only Rectina, but many others; for the villas stand extremely thick upon that beautiful coast. Hastening to the place from whence others were flying, he steered his direct course to the point of danger, and with such freedom from fear, as to be able to make and dictate his observations upon the successive motions and figures of that terrific object.

And now cinders, which grew thicker and hotter the nearer he approached, fell into the ships, then pumice-stones too, with stones blackened, scorched, and cracked by fire, then the sea ebbed suddenly from under them, while the shore was blocked up by landslips from the mountains. . . .

In the meanwhile Mount Vesuvius was blazing in several places with spreading and towering flames, whose refulgent brightness the darkness of the night set in high relief. But my uncle, in order to soothe apprehensions, kept saying that some fires had been left alight by the terrified country people, and what they saw were only deserted villas on fire in the abandoned district. After this he retired to rest . . . On being aroused, he came out, and returned to Pomponianus and the others, who had sat up all night. They consulted together as to whether they should hold out in the house, or wander about in the open. For the house now tottered under repeated and violent concussions, and seemed to rock to and fro as if torn from its foundations. In the open air, on the other hand, they dreaded the falling pumice-stones, light and porous though they were; yet this, by comparison, seemed the lesser danger of the two; a conclusion which my uncle arrived at by balancing reasons and the others by balancing fears. They tied pillows upon their heads with napkins; and this was their whole defence against the showers that fell round them.

It was now day everywhere else, but there a deeper darkness prevailed than in the most obscure night; relieved, however, by many torches and divers illuminations. They thought proper to go down upon the shore to observe from close at hand if they could possibly put out to sea, but they found the waves still run extremely high and contrary. There my uncle having thrown himself down upon a disused sail, repeatedly called for, and drank, a draught of cold water; soon after, flames, and a strong smell of sulphur, which was the forerunner of them dispersed the rest of the company in flight; him they only aroused. He raised himself up with the assistance of two of his slaves, but instantly fell; some unusually gross vapour, as I conjecture, having obstructed his breathing and blocked his windpipe, which was not only naturally weak and constricted, but chronically inflamed. When day dawned again (the third from that he last beheld) his body was found entire and uninjured, and still fully clothed as in life; its posture was that of a sleeping, rather than a dead man.

Meanwhile my mother and I were at Misenum. But this has no connection with history, and your inquiry went no farther than concerning my uncle's death. I will therefore put an end to my letter. Suffer me only to add, that I have faithfully related to you what I was either an eye-witness of myself, or heard at the time, when report speaks most truly. You will select what is most suitable to your purpose; for there is a great difference between a letter, and an history; between writing to a friend, and writing for the public. Farewell.

PLINY THE YOUNGER (*Letters VI*. 16. Trans. W. MELMOTH and W. M. L. HUTCHINSON—Loeb Classical Library)

EGYPTIAN CORRESPONDENCE

Letter from Corbolon to Heraclides (Second Century)

Corbolon to Heraclides, greeting. I send you the key by Horion and the piece of the lock by Onnophris, the camel-driver of Apollonius. I enclosed in the former packet a pattern of white-violet colour. I beg you to be good enough to match it and buy me two drachmas' weight, and send it to me at once by any messenger you can find, for the tunic is to be woven immediately. I received everything you told me to expect by Onnophris safely. I send you by the same Onnophris six quarts of good apples. I thank all the gods to think that I came upon Plution in the Oxyrhynchite nome. Do not think that I took no trouble about the key. The reason is that the smith is a long way from us. I wonder that you did not see your way to let me have what I asked you to send by Corbolon, especially when I wanted it for a festival. I beg you to buy me a silver seal and to send it me with all speed. Take care that Onnophris buys me what Irene's mother told me. I told him that Syntrophus said that nothing more should be given to Amarantus on my account. Let me know what you have given him that I may settle accounts with him. Otherwise I and my son will come for this purpose. I had the large cheeses from Corbolon. I did not however want large ones, but small. Let me know of anything that you want and I will gladly do it. Farewell. Payni the 1st. —Send me an obol's worth of cake for my nephew.

A Boy's Letter (Second Century)

Theon to his father Theon, greeting. It was a fine thing of you not to take me with you to the city! If you won't take me with you to Alexandria I won't write you a letter or speak to you or say good-bye to you; and if you go to Alexandria I won't take your hand nor ever greet you again. That is what will happen if you won't take me. Mother said to Archelaus, " It quite upsets him to be left behind." It was good of you to send me presents . . . on the 12th, the day you sailed. Send me a lyre, I implore you. If you don't, I won't eat, I won't drink; there now !

To a Wife-Sister (Second Century)

Serenus to his beloved sister Isidora, many greetings. Before all else I pray for your health, and every day and evening I perform the act of veneration on your behalf to Thöeris who loves you. I assure you that ever since you left me I have been in mourning, weeping by night and lamenting by day. Since we bathed together on Phaophi 12, I never bathed nor anointed myself until Athur 12. You sent me letters which would have shaken a stone, so much did your words move me. Instantly I answered you and gave the letter sealed to the messenger on the 12th, together with letters for you. . . . See how many times I have sent to you ! Whether you are coming or not, let me know.

Cornelius to Hierax (Second Century)

Cornelius to his sweetest son, Hierax, greeting. All our household warmly salutes you and all those with you. Regarding the man about whom you write to me so often, claim nothing until I come to you auspiciously in company with Vestinus and the donkeys. For if the gods will I shall arrive quickly after Mecheir is over, since at present I have urgent affairs on hand. Take care not to offend any of the persons at home, and give your undivided attention to your books, devoting yourself to learning, and then they will bring you profit. Receive by Onnophris the white robes which are to be worn with the purple cloaks, the others you should wear with the myrtle-coloured ones. I shall send you by Anoubas both the money and the monthly supplies and the other pair of scarlet cloaks. You won me over by the dainties, and I will send you the price of these two by Anoubas ; until however Anoubas arrives, you must pay for the provisions of yourself and your household out of your own money, until I send you some. For the month of Tubi there is for yourself what you like, for Phronimus 16 drachmae, for Abascantus and his companions and Myron 9 drachmae, for Secundas 12 drachmae. Send Phronimus to Asclepiades in my name, and let him obtain from him an answer to the letter which I wrote to him, and send it. Let me know what you want. Good-bye, my son.

Invitation to a Festival (*Third Century*)

Greeting, my dear Serenia, from Petosiris. Be sure, dear, to come up on the 20th for the birthday festival of the god, and let me know whether you are coming by boat or by donkey, in order that we may send for you accordingly. Take care not to forget. I pray for your continued health.

OXYRHYNCHUS PAPYRI

(Trans. GRENFELL AND HUNT)

FROM THE EMPEROR JULIAN TO EVAGRIUS,
THE RHETORICIAN

(*Making him the present of a small estate. Written from Constantinople in the year 362 A.D.*)

A small estate of four fields, in Bithynia, was given to me by my grandmother, and this I give as an offering to your affection for me. It is too small to bring a man any great benefit on the score of wealth or to make him appear opulent, but even so it is a gift that cannot wholly fail to please you, as you will see if I describe its features to you one by one. And there is no reason why I should not write in a light vein to you who are so full of the graces and amenities of culture. It is situated not more than twenty stades from the sea, so that no trader or sailor with his chatter and insolence disturbs the place. Yet it is not wholly deprived of the favours of Nereus, for it has a constant supply of fish, fresh and still gasping; and if you walk up on to a sort of hill away from the house, you will see the sea, the Propontis and the islands, and the city that bears the name of the noble Emperor [Constantinople]; nor will you have to stand meanwhile on seaweed and brambles, or be annoyed by the filth that is always thrown out on to seabeaches and sands, which is so very unpleasant and even unmentionable; but you will stand on smilax and thyme and fragrant herbage. Very peaceful it is to lie down there and glance into some book, and then, while resting one's eyes, it is very agreeable to gaze at the ships and the sea. When I was still hardly more than a boy I thought that this was the most delightful summer place, for it has, moreover, excellent springs and a charming bath and garden and

72

trees. When I had grown to manhood I used to long for my old manner of life there and visited it often, and our meetings there did not lack talks about literature. Moreover there is there, as a humble monument of my husbandry, a small vineyard that produces a fragrant, sweet wine, which does not have to wait for time to improve its flavour. You will have a vision of Dionysus and the Graces. The grapes on the vine, and when they are being crushed in the press, smell of roses, and the new made wine in the jars is a " rill of nectar," if one may trust Homer. Then why is not such a vine as this abundant and growing over very many acres ? Perhaps I was not a very industrious gardener. But since my mixing bowl of Dionysus is inclined to soberness, and calls for a large proportion of the nymphs [i.e., of water], I only provided enough for myself and my friends—and they are very few. Well then, I now give this to you as a present, dear heart, and though it be small, as indeed it is, yet it is precious as coming from a friend to a friend, " from home, homeward bound," in the words of the wise poet Pindar. I have written this letter in haste, by lamplight, so that, if I have made any mistakes, do not criticise them severely or as one rhetorician would another.

(From *The Works of the Emperor Julian*. Trans. W. C. WRIGHT—Loeb Classical Library)

SAINT AUGUSTINE TO NEBRIDIUS

I read your letter by lamplight after supper. I had gone to bed, but not (as it happened) to sleep; so I meditated, lying on my bed. These were my inmost thoughts—Augustine talking to Augustine, so to speak—Is it really true, I asked myself, as Nebridius says, that we are happy ? No, indeed; for he himself would not be so bold as to deny that we are foolish; and, though fools are not beyond the reach of blessing, we know that we can suffer no greater misfortune than the lack of wisdom—perhaps, indeed, no other misfortune. *Letters* (Trans. A. S.)

A 15TH-CENTURY LOVE AFFAIR

(From the Young Lady's Mother to the Young Gentleman)

To my worshipful Cousin JOHN PASTON, Be this Bill delivered, &c.

Cousin, I recommend me unto you, Thanking you heartily for the great cheer ye made me, and all my Folks, the last time that I was at Norwich; and ye promised me, that ye would never break the matter to Margery unto such time, as ye and I were at a point. But ye have made her such an Advocate for you, that I may never have rest night nor day, for calling and crying upon to bring the said matter to effect, &c.

And Cousin, upon Friday is Saint Valentine's day, and every Bird chuseth him a Mate; and if it like you to come on Thursday at night, and so purvey you, that ye may abide there till Monday, I trust to God, that ye shall so speak to mine husband; and I shall pray, that we shall bring the matter to a conclusion, &c.

For, Cousin, " it is but a simple Oak,
" That cuts down at the first stroke."

for ye will be reasonable I trust to God, which have you ever in his merciful keeping, &c.

By your Cousin DAME ELIZABETH BREWS otherwise shall be called by God's Grace. 14th February, 1477.

74

(From the Young Lady to the Young Gentleman)

Unto my right well beloved Valentine, JOHN PASTON,
   Esquire, be this Bill delivered, &c.

Right reverend and worshipful, and my right well
beloved Valentine, I recommend me unto you, full heartily
desiring to hear of your welfare, which I beseech Almighty
God long for to preserve unto his pleasure, and your
heart's desire.

And if it please you to hear of my welfare, I am not in
good health of body, nor of heart, nor shall be till I hear
from you ; for there knows no creature, what pain that I
endure, and for to be dead I dare it not discover.

And my Lady my Mother hath laboured the matter to
my father full diligently, but she can no more get than ye
know of, for the which God knoweth I am full sorry. But
if that ye love me, as I trust verily that ye do, ye will not
leave me therefore.

And if ye command me to keep me true wherever
      I go,
I wis I will do all my might you to love, and never
      no mo.

   And if my Friends say, that I do amiss,
      They shall not me let so for to do,
   Mine heart me bids evermore to love you,
      Truly over all earthly thing,
   And if they be never so wrath,
      I trust it shall be better in time coming.

No more to you at this time, but the Holy Trinity have
you in keeping ; and I beseech you that this bill be not
seen of none earthly Creature save only yourself, &c.

75

And this Letter was endited at Topcroft, with full heavy heart, &c.

By your own,

MARGERY BREWS.

TOPCROFT.

To my Right Well beloved Cousin JOHN PASTON, Esquire, be this Letter delivered, &c.

Right worshipful and well beloved Valentine, in my most humble wise, I recommend me unto you, &c. And heartily I thank you for the letter, which that ye send me by John Beckerton, whereby I understand and know, that ye be purposed to come to Topcroft in short time, and without any errand or matter, but only to have a conclusion of the matter betwixt my father and you, I would be most glad of any Creature alive, so that the matter might grow to effect. And whereas ye say, and if ye come and find the matter no more towards you than ye did aforetime, ye would no more put my father and my Lady my Mother to no cost nor business, for that cause a good while after, which causeth my heart to be full heavy; and if that ye come, and the matter take to none effect, then should I be much more sorry, and full of heaviness.

And as for myself I have done, and understand in the matter that I can or may, as God knoweth; and I let you plainly understand, that my father will no more money part withal in that behalf, but an hundred pounds and fifty marks which is right far from the accomplishment of your desire.

Wherefore, if that ye could be content with that Good, and my poor Person, I would be the merriest maiden on ground; and if ye think nor yourself so satisfied, or that ye might have much more Good, as I have understood

76

by you afore; good, true, and loving Valentine, that ye take no such labour upon you, as to come more for that matter. But let what is, pass, and never more to be spoken of, as I may be your true Lover and Beadwoman during my life.

No more unto you at this time, but Almighty Jesu preserve you both body and soul, &c.

By your Valentine,

MARGERY BREWS.

TOPCROFT.

(*From the Young Gentleman*)

To my right worshipful Mother MARGARET PASTON.

Right worshipful Mother, after all duties of recommendation, in as humble wise as I can, I beseech you of your daily blessing. Mother, please it you to weet, that the cause that Dame Elizabeth Brews desireth to meet with you at Norwich, and not at Langley, as I appointed with you at my last being at Mawtby, is by my means, for my brother Thomas Jermyn, which knoweth nought of the match, telleth me, that the Causey ere ye can come to Bokenham Ferry is so overflown that there is no man that may scarcely pass it, though he be right well horsed; which is no meet way for you to pass over, God forbid it. But all things reckoned, it shall be less cost to you to be at Norwich, as for a day or tweyn and pass not, than to meet at Langley, where everything is dear; and your horse may be sent home again the same Wednesday.

Mother, I beseech you for divers causes, that my Sister Anne may come with you to Norwich; Mother, the matter is in a reasonable good way, and I trust with God's mercy, and with your good help, that it shall take effect better to mine advantage than I told you of at Norwich; for I believe there is not a kinder woman living than I shall have to my Mother in law, if the matter take, nor yet a kinder Father in law than I shall have, though he be hard to me as yet.

All the circumstances of the matter, which I trust to tell you at your coming to Norwich, could not be written in three leaves of paper, and ye know my poor head well enough, I may not write long, wherefore I ferry over all things till I may await on you myself. I shall do tun into your place a dozen Ale, and Bread according, against Wednesday. If Sym might be spared it were well done, that he were at Norwich on Wednesday in the morning at market. Dame Elizabeth Brews shall lie at John Cook's; if it might please you, I would be glad that she might dine in your house on Thursday, for there should you have most secret talking.

And Mother, at the reverence of God, beware that ye be so purveyed for, that ye take no cold by the way towards Norwich, for it is the most perilous March, that ever was seen by any man's days now living; and I pray to Jesu to preserve you and yours.

Written at Topcroft, the 8th day of March.

Your Son and humble Servant,

JOHN PASTON.

TOPCROFT.

Saturday, 8th of March, 1477.

(From *The Paston Letters*)

FROM THE DUCHESS OF MILAN (BEATRICE D'ESTE) TO THE DUCHESS OF MANTUA (ISABELLA D'ESTE)

Villa Nova, Val di Ticino,
18th March, 1491.

I am now here at Villa Nova, where the loveliness of the country and the balmy sweetness of the air make me think we are already in the month of May, so warm and splendid is the weather we are enjoying ! Every day we go out riding with the dogs and falcons, and my husband and I never come home without having enjoyed ourselves exceedingly in hunting herons and other water-fowl. I cannot say much of the perils of the chase, since game is so plentiful here that hares are to be seen jumping out at every corner—so much so, that often we hardly know which way to turn to find the best sport. Indeed, the eye cannot take in all one desires to see, and it is scarcely possible to count up the number of animals that are to be found in this neighbour-hood. Nor must I forget to tell you how every day Messer Galeazzo and I, with one or two other courtiers, amuse ourselves playing at ball after dinner, and we often talk of your Highness, and wish that you were here. I say all this, not to diminish the pleasure that I hope you will have when you do come by telling you what you may expect to find here, but in order that you may know how well and happy I am, and how kind and affectionate my husband is, since I cannot thoroughly enjoy any pleasure or happiness unless I share it with you. And I must tell you that I have had a whole field of garlic planted for your benefit, so that when you come, we may be able to have plenty of your favourite dishes !

(Trans. JULIA CARTWRIGHT)

A KING'S LOVE LETTERS

(Written by Henry VIII to Anne Boleyn in the year 1528 when the King was seeking a Papal pronouncement annulling his marriage with Katharine of Aragon)

My mistress and friend, my heart and I surrender ourselves into your hands, beseeching you to hold us commended to your favour, and that by absence your affection to us may not be lessened : for it would be a great pity to increase our pain, of which absence produces enough and more than I could ever have thought could be felt, reminding us of a point in astronomy which is this : the longer the days are, the more distant is the sun, and nevertheless the hotter ; so is it with our love, for by absence we are kept a distance from one another, and yet it retains its fervour, at least on my side ; I hope the like on yours, assuring you that on my part the pain of absence is already too great for me ; and when I think of the increase of that which I am forced to suffer, it would be almost intolerable, but for the firm hope I have of your unchangeable affection for me : and to remind you of this sometimes, and seeing that I cannot be personally present with you, I now send you the nearest thing I can to that, namely, my picture set in bracelets, with the whole of the device, which you already know, wishing myself in their place, if it should please you. This is from the hand of your loyal servant and friend,

H. R.

On turning over in my mind the contents of your last letters, I have put myself into great agony, not knowing how to interpret them, whether to my disadvantage, as I understand them in some others, beseeching you earnestly to let me know expressly your whole mind as to the love between us two. It is absolutely necessary for me to obtain this answer, having been for above a whole year stricken with the dart of love, and not yet sure whether I shall fail or find a place in your heart and affection, which last point has prevented me for some time past from calling you my mistress; because, if you only love me with an ordinary love, that name is not suitable for you, because it denotes a singular love, which is far from common. But if you please to do the office of a true loyal mistress and friend, and to give up yourself body and heart to me, who will be, and have been, your most loyal servant, (if your rigour does not forbid me) I promise you that not only shall the name be given you, but also that I will take you for my only mistress, casting off all others besides you out of my thoughts and affections and serve you only. I beseech you to give an entire answer to this my rude letter, that I may know on what and how far I may depend. And if it does not please you to answer me in writing, appoint some place where I may have it by word of mouth, and I will go thither with all my heart.

No more, for fear of tiring you.

Written by the hand of him who will willingly remain yours,

H. R.

The reasonable request of your last letter, with the pleasure also that I take to know them true, causeth me to send you these news. The legate whom we most desired, arrived at Paris on Sunday or Monday last past, so that I trust by the next Monday to hear of his arrival at Calais; and then I trust within a while after to enjoy that which I have so long longed for, to God's pleasure, and both our comforts.

No more to you at this present, mine own darling, for lack of time, but that I would you were in mine arms, or I in yours, for I think it long since I kissed you.

Written after the killing of a hart, at eleven of the clock, minding, with God's grace, to-morrow, mighty timely, to kill an other, by the hand, which, I trust, shortly shall be yours.

HENRY R.

FROM SAINT TERESA TO DON FRANCISCO DE SALCEDO, AVILA

Valladolid, Sept. 1568.

Glory be to God, after having written seven or eight unavoidable business letters, a short time remains for me to refresh myself by sending you these few lines telling you what a comfort yours were to me. Do not fancy you are wasting time by writing to me, for I need it occasionally, provided that you do not repeat so often that you are growing old, which cuts me to the heart. As if the lives of young men were guaranteed ! Please God, you will live until I die and then I shall ask Him to summon you promptly lest I should be without you in heaven . . .

The 6 ducats you say you would give to see me seem a very dear bargain, but I would pay far more to see you— in fact, you are worth much more, for who sets any value on a poor, insignificant little nun who lives in poverty ? *You*, who can give *aloja*,[1] rolls, radishes, and lettuces

[1] A favourite drink in Spain at the time. A. S.

82

from your own garden (and I know that you are the "errand boy" who brings us apples) would naturally fetch a higher price. The *aloja* here is said to be very good, but for want of Francisco de Salcedo we do not know what it tastes like and probably never shall.

I have told Antonia to write to you as I have no time for more. Abide with God!

Your unworthy and sincere servant,

TERESA DE JESUS, *Carmelite.*

A BAD START

(Letter written on board a ship of the Spanish Armada to the Venetian Ambassador in Madrid)

On the 14th of this month, while the Armada was off Cape Finisterre, despatches were sent to his Majesty, and with them I wrote to your Lordship a particular account of our voyage down to that date. After that, partly to meet the galleys which were ordered to wait us in Mugia, a port four leagues distant from the Cape; partly to take on board some provisions and supplies which the Governor of that Kingdom (Galicia), the Marquis of Seralvo, was to prepare for us, we drew in as far as the island of Cesarga. There, on the 17th, we were joined by the galleys which his Excellency had sent to Corunna for provisions and water, as both were running short; and to land some sick, who are now in considerable numbers, especially after the storm of the 19th and 20th which the Armada encountered. The flagship, thirty-five others, and almost all the transports and carvels, came into Corunna, before the storm reached its height. The rest of the fleet, partly owing to its falling away to lee, and being unable to make the port, and partly to the dark night which settled down, remained out-side. The night was a tempestuous one, with wind, rain, and a heavy sea. The following day, Monday, the ship of Don Alonzo de Leyva and the flagship of Don Oquendo put into the port of Baris, one much damaged, the other having carried away mainmast, sails, and yards. On Tuesday twelve others arrived at Biucco, among them the *Labbia* uninjured. On Wednesday the Admiral Recalde sailed into Corunna with other twelve ships and two galleys, among them the *Regazzona* uninjured; yesterday other three. So that up to this hour thirty ships and two galleasses are missing. The storm was one of those great winter storms. It has greatly discouraged the fleet, and above all the commander.

We shall be obliged to wait here till we have news of the missing ships. Some scouts have been sent out this evening to look for them.

Corugna, 24th June 1588.

CALENDAR OF STATE PAPERS
(*Venetian Series, VIII*, 681)

LETTERS FROM DEAN SWIFT

1. *A Letter to " Varina " (Miss Jane Waring)*

April 29, 1696.

MADAM,

Impatience is the most inseparable quality of a lover, and indeed of every person who is in pursuit of a design whereon he conceives his greatest happiness or misery to depend. It is the same thing in war, in courts, and in common business. Everyone who hunts after pleasure, or fame, or fortune, is still restless and uneasy till he has hunted down his game ; and all this is not only very natural, but something reasonable too, for a violent desire is little better than a distemper, and therefore men are not to blame in looking after a cure. I find myself hugely infected with this malady, and am easily vain enough to believe it has some very good reasons to excuse it. For indeed, in my case, there are some circumstances which will admit pardon for more than ordinary disquiets. That dearest object upon which all my prospect of happiness entirely depends, is in perpetual danger to be removed for ever from my sight. Varina's life is daily wasting, and though one just and honourable action could furnish health to her, and unspeakable happiness to us both, yet some power that repines at human felicity has that influence to hold her continually doating upon her cruelty, and me upon the cause of it. This fully convinces me of what we are told, that the miseries of man's life are all beaten out on his own anvil. Why was I so foolish to put my hopes and fears into the power or management of another ? Liberty is doubtless the most valuable blessing of life ; yet we are fond to fling it away on those who have been these five thousand years using us ill. Philosophy advises to keep our desires and prospects of happiness as much as we can in our own breasts, and independent of anything without. He that sends them abroad is likely to have as little quiet as a merchant whose stock depends upon winds, and waves, and pirates, or upon the words and faith of creditors, every whit as dangerous and inconstant as the other . . . Would to God you had treated and scorned me from the beginning. It was your pity opened the first way to my misfortune; and now your love is finishing my ruin. In one fortnight I must take eternal farewell of Varina, and (I wonder) will she weep at parting, a little to justify her poor pretences of some affection to me? And will my friends still continue reproaching me for the want of gallantry, and neglecting a close siege? How comes it that they all wish us married together, they knowing my circumstances and yours extremely well, and I am sure love you too much, if it be only for my sake, to wish you anything that might cross your interest or your happiness?

Surely, Varina, you have but a very mean opinion of the joys that accompany a true, honourable, unlimited love; yet either nature and our ancestors have highly deceived us, or else all other sublunary things are dross in comparison. Is it possible you can be yet insensible to the prospect of a rapture and delight so innocent and exalted? Trust me, Varina, Heaven has given us nothing else worth the loss of a thought. Ambition, high appearances, friends, and fortune, are all tasteless and insipid when they come in competition; yet millions of such glorious minutes are we perpetually losing, for ever losing, irrecoverably losing, to gratify empty forms and wrong notions, and affected coldnesses and peevish humour. These are the unhappy encumbrances which we who are distinguished from the vulgar do fondly create to torment ourselves. The only felicity permitted to human life we clog with tedious circumstances and barbarous formality. By Heaven, Varina, you are more experienced, and have less virgin innocence than I. Would not your conduct make one think you were highly skilled in all the little politic methods of intrigue? Love, with the gall of too much discretion, is a thousand times worse than with none at

86

all. It is a peculiar part of nature which art debauches, but cannot improve. We have all of us the seeds of it implanted in ourselves, and they require no helps from courts or fortune to cultivate and improve them. To resist the violence of our inclinations in the beginning, is a train of self-denial that may have some pretences to set up for a virtue ; but when they are grounded at first upon reason, when they have taken firm root and grown up to a height, it is folly—folly as well as injustice, to withstand their dictates ; for this passion has a property peculiar to itself, to be most commendable in its extremes, and it is as possible to err in the excess of piety as of love.

These are the rules I have long followed with you, Varina ; and had you pleased to imitate them, we should both have been infinitely happy. The little disguises, and affected contradictions of your sex were all (to say the truth) infinitely beneath persons of your pride and mine ; paltry maxims that they are, calculated for the rabble of humanity. O Varina, how imagination leads me beyond myself and all my sorrows ! It is sunk, and a thousand graves lie open ! No, Madam, I will give you no more of my unhappy temper, though I derive it all from you.

Farewell, Madam, and may love make you a while forget your temper to do me justice. Only remember that, if you still refuse to be mine, you will quickly lose him that has resolved to die as he has lived—all yours

JON. SWIFT.

2. News for Stella.

Do you know that about our town we are mowing already and making hay, and it smells so sweet as we walk through the flowery meads; but the hay-making nymphs are perfect drabs, nothing so clean and pretty as farther in the country. There is a mighty increase of dirty wenches in straw hats since I knew London. I staid at home till five o'clock, and dined with Dean Atterbury: then went by water to Mr. Harley's, where the Saturday club was met, with the addition of the Duke of Shrewsbury. I whispered Lord Rivers, that I did not like to see a stranger among us: and the rogue told it aloud: but Mr. Secretary said, the Duke writ to have leave: so I appeared satisfied, and so we laughed. Mr. Secretary told me the Duke of Buckingham had been talking to him much about me, and desired my acquaintance. I answered, it could not be: for he had not made sufficient advances. Then the Duke of Shrewsbury said, he thought that Duke was not used to make advances. I said I could not help that; for I always expected advances in proportion to men's quality, and more from a Duke than other men. The Duke replied, that he did not mean anything of his quality; which was handsomely said enough; for he meant his pride: and I have invented a notion to believe that nobody is proud. At ten all the company went away; and from ten till twelve Mr. Harley and I sat together, where we talked through a great deal of matters I had a mind to settle with him, and then walked, in a fine moonshine night, to Chelsea, where I got by one. Lord Rivers conjured me not to walk so late; but I would, because I had no other way; but I had no money to lose. . . .

Morning. I sat up late last night, and waked late to-day ; but will now answer your letter in bed before I go to town, and I will send it to-morrow ; for perhaps you mayn't go so soon to Wexford.—No, you are not out in your number ; the last was Number 14, and so I told you twice or thrice ; will you never be satisfied ? What shall we do for poor Stella ? Go to Wexford, for God's sake : I wish you were to walk there by three miles a-day, with a good lodging at every mile's end. Walking has done me so much good, that I cannot but prescribe it often to poor Stella. . . . O faith, I should be glad to be in the same kingdom with M D., however, although you were at Wexford. But I am kept here by a most capricious fate, which I would break through, if I could do it with decency or honour.—To return without some mark of distinction, would look extremely little : and I would likewise gladly be somewhat richer than I am. I will say no more, but beg you to be easy, till Fortune take her course, and to believe that M D's felicity is the great end I aim at in my pursuits. And so let us talk no more on this subject, which makes me melancholy, and that I would fain divert. Believe me, no man breathing at present has less share of happiness in life than I : I do not say I am unhappy at all, but that everything here is tasteless to me for want of being as I would be. And so a short sigh, and no more of this.

(From *Journal to Stella*)

THOMAS GRAY TO HIS MOTHER

Lyons, Oct. 13, 1739

It is now almost five weeks since I left Dijon, one of the gayest and most agreeable little cities of France, for Lyons its reverse in all these particulars. It is the second in the kingdom in bigness and rank, the streets excessively narrow and nasty ; the houses immensely high and large ; (that, for instance, where we are lodged, has twenty-five rooms on a floor, and that for five stories) it swarms with inhabitants like Paris itself, but chiefly a mercantile people, too much given up to commerce to think of their own, much less of a stranger's diversions. We have no acquaintance in the town, but such English as happen to be passing through here, in their way to Italy and the South, which at present happen to be near thirty in number. It is a fortnight since we set out from hence upon a little excursion to Geneva. We took the longest road, which lies through Savoy, on purpose to see a famous monastery, called the grand Chartreuse, and had no reason to think our time lost. After having travelled seven days very slow (for we did not change horses, it being impossible for a chaise to go post in these roads) we arrived at a little village, among the mountains of Savoy, called Echelles ; from thence we proceeded on horses, who are used to the way, to the mountain of the Chartreuse : It is six miles to the top ; the road runs winding up it, commonly not six feet broad ; on one hand is the rock, with woods of pine trees hanging over head ; on the other, a monstrous precipice, almost perpendicular, at the bottom of which rolls a torrent, that sometimes tumbling among the fragments of stone that have fallen from on high, and sometimes precipitating itself down vast descents with a noise like thunder, which is still made greater by the echo from the mountains on each side, concurs to form one of the most solemn, the most romantic, and the most astonishing scenes I ever beheld : Add to this the strange views made by the craggs and cliffs on the other hand ; the cascades that in many places throw themselves from the very summit down into the vale, and the river below ; and many other particulars impossible to describe ; you will conclude we had no occasion to repent our pains. This place St. Bruno chose to retire to, and upon its very top founded the aforesaid Convent, which is the superior of the whole order. When we came there, the two fathers, who are commissioned to entertain strangers, (for the rest must neither speak one to another, nor to any one else) received us very kindly ; and set before us a repast of dried fish, eggs, butter, and fruits, all excellent in their kind, and extremely neat. They pressed us to spend the night there, and to stay some days with them ; but this we could not do, so they led us about their house, which is, you must think, like a little city ; for there are 100 fathers, besides 300 servants, that make their clothes, grind their corn, press their wine, and do every thing among themselves : The whole is quite orderly and simple ; nothing of finery, but the wonderful decency, and the strange situation, more than supply the place of it. In the evening we descended by the same way, passing through many clouds that were then forming themselves on the mountain's side. Next day we continued our journey by Chamberry, which, though the chief city of the Dutchy, and residence of the king of Sardinia, when he comes into this part of his dominions, makes but a very mean and insignificant appearance ; we lay at Aix, once famous for its hot baths, and the next night at

Anneçy; the day after, by noon, we got to Geneva. I have not time to say any thing about it, nor of our solitary journey back again.

Turin, Nov. 7, 1739

I am this night arrived here, and have just set down to rest me after eight days tiresome journey: For the three first we have had the same road we before past through to go to Geneva; the fourth we turned out of it, and for that day and the next travelled rather among than upon the Alps; the way commonly running through a deep valley by the side of the river Arc, which works itself a passage, with great difficulty and a mighty noise, among vast quantities of rocks, that have rolled down from the mountain tops. The winter was so far advanced, as in great measure to spoil the beauty of the prospect; however, there was still somewhat fine remaining amidst the savageness and horrour of the place: The sixth we began to go up several of these mountains; and as we were passing one, met with an odd accident enough: Mr. Walpole had a little fat black spaniel, that he was very fond of, which he sometimes used to set down, and let it run by the chaise side. We were at that time in a very rough road, not two yards broad at most; on one side was a great wood of pines, and on the other a vast precipice; it was noon-day, and the sun shone bright, when all of a sudden, from the wood-side, (which was as steep upwards, as the other part was downwards) out rushed a great wolf, came close to the head of the horses, seized the dog by the throat, and rushed up the hill again with him in his mouth. This was done in less than a quarter of a minute; we all saw it, and yet the servants had not time to draw their pistols, or do any thing to save the dog. If he had not been there, and the creature had thought fit to lay hold of one of the horses, chaise, and we, and all must inevitably have tumbled above fifty fathoms perpendicular down the precipice. The seventh we came to Lanebourg, the last town in Savoy; it lies at the foot of the famous mount Cenis, which is so situated as to allow no room for anyway but over the very top of it. Here the chaise was forced to be pulled to pieces, and the baggage and that to be carried by mules: We ourselves were wrapped up in our furs, and seated upon a sort of matted chair, without legs, which is carried upon poles in the manner of a bier and so began to ascend by the help of eight men. It was six miles to the top, where a plain opens itself about as many more in breadth, covered perpetually with very deep snow, and in the midst of that a great lake of unfathomable depth, from whence a river takes its rise, and tumbles over monstrous rocks quite down the other side of the mountain. The descent is six miles more, but infinitely more steep than the going up; and here the men perfectly fly down with you, stepping from stone to stone with incredible swiftness, in places where none but they could go three paces without falling. The immensity of the precipices, the roaring of the river and torrents that run into it, the huge craggs covered with ice and snow, and the clouds below you and about you, are objects it is impossible to conceive without seeing them; and though we had heard many strange descriptions of the scene, none of them at all came up to it. We were but five hours in performing the whole, from which you may judge of the rapidity of the men's motion. We are now got into Piedmont, and stopped a little while at La Ferriere, a small village about three quarters of the way down, but still among the clouds, where we began to hear a new language spoken round about us; at last we got quite down, went through the Pás de Suse, a narrow road among the Alps, defended by two fortresses, and lay at Bossolens : Next evening thro' a fine avenue of nine miles in length, as straight as a line, we arrived at this city.

WILLIAM COWPER TO LADY HESKETH

Olney, Feb. 9, 1786.

MY DEAR COUSIN,

I have been impatient to tell you that I am impatient to see you again ... And now, my dear, let me tell you once more, that your kindness in promising us a visit has charmed us both—I shall see you again—I shall hear your voice, we shall take walks together ; I will shew you my prospects, the hovel, the alcove, the Ouse, and its banks, every thing that I have described. I anticipate the pleasure of those days not very far distant, and feel a part of it at this moment. Talk not of an inn ! Mention it not for your life ! We have never had so many visitors but we could easily accommodate them all ; though we have received Unwin, and his wife, and his sister, and his son, all at once. My dear, I will not let you come till the end of May, or beginning of June, because before that time my green-house will not be ready to receive us, and it is the only pleasant room belonging to us. When the plants go out, we go in. I line it with mats, and spread the floor with mats ; and there you shall sit with a bed of mignonette at your side, and a hedge of honeysuckles, roses, and jasmine ; and I will make you a bouquet of myrtle every day. Sooner than the time I mention the country will not be in complete beauty. And I will tell you what you shall find at your first entrance. *Imprimis*, as soon as you have entered the vestibule, if you cast a look on either side of you, you shall see on the right hand a box of my making. It is the box in which have been lodged all my Hares, and in which lodges Puss at present. But he, poor fellow, is worn out with age, and promises to die before you can see him. On the right hand, stands a cupboard, the work of the same Author. It was once a dove-cage, but I transformed it. Opposite to you stands a table, which I also made. But a merciless servant having scrubbed it until it became paralytic, it serves no purpose now but of ornament ; and all my clean shoes stand under it. On the left hand, at the farther end of this superb vestibule, you will find the door of the parlour, into which I will conduct you, and where I will introduce you to Mrs. Unwin, unless we should meet her before, and where we will be as happy as the day is long. Order yourself, my Cousin, to the Swan at Newport, and there you shall find me ready to conduct you to Olney . . .

Adieu ! my dearest, dearest Cousin.

The Lodge, Nov. 10, 1787

I have a kitten, my dearest Cousin, the drollest of all creatures that ever wore a cat's skin. Her gambols are not to be described, and would be incredible, if they could. In point of size she is likely to be a kitten always, being extremely small of her age, but time I suppose, that spoils every thing, will make her also a cat. You will see her I hope before that melancholy period shall arrive, for no wisdom that she may gain by experience and reflection hereafter, will compensate the loss of her present hilarity. She is dressed in a tortoise-shell suit, and I know that you will delight in her.

Mrs. Throckmorton carries us to-morrow in her chaise

to Chicheley. The event however must be supposed to depend on elements, at least on the state of the atmosphere, which is turbulent beyond measure. Yesterday it thundered, last night it lightened, and at three this morning I saw the sky as red as a city in flames could have made it. I have a leech in a bottle that foretells all these prodigies and convulsions of nature. No, not as you will naturally conjecture by articulate utterance of oracular notices, but by a variety of gesticulations, which here I have not room to give an account of. Suffice it to say, that no change of weather surprises him, and that in point of the earliest and most accurate intelligence, he is worth all the barometers in the world. None of them all indeed can make the least pretence to foretell thunder—a species of capacity of which he has given the most unequivocal evidence. I gave but sixpence for him, which is a groat more than the market price, though he is in fact, or rather would be, if leeches were not found in every ditch, an invaluable acquisition.

The Lodge, June 27, 1788

For the sake of a longer visit, my dearest Coz, I can be well content to wait. The country, this country at least, is pleasant at all times, and when winter is come, or near at hand, we shall have the better chance for being snug. I know your passion for retirement indeed, or for what we call *deedy* retirement, and the Frogs[1] intending to return to Bath with their mother, when her visit at the Hall is over, you will then find here exactly the retirement in question. I have made in the orchard the best winter-walk in all the parish, sheltered from the east, and from the north-east, and open to the sun, except at his rising, all the day. Then we will have Homer and Don Quixote:

[1] Cowper's friends the Throckmortons. A. S.

96

and then we will have saunter and chat and one laugh more before we die. Our orchard is alive with creatures of all kinds ; poultry of every denomination swarms in it, and pigs, the drollest in the world ! . . .

I must tell you a feat of my dog Beau. Walking by the river-side, I observed some water-lilies floating at a little distance from the bank. They are a large white flower, with an orange coloured eye, very beautiful. I had a desire to gather one, and, having your long cane in my hand, by the help of it endeavoured to bring one of them within my reach. But the attempt proved vain, and I walked forward. Beau had all the while observed me very attentively. Returning soon after toward the same place, I observed him plunge into the river, while I was about forty yards distant from him ; and, when I had nearly reached the spot, he swam to land with a lily in his mouth, which he came and laid at my foot.

Mr. Rose, whom I have mentioned to you as a visitor of mine for the first time soon after you left us, writes me word that he has seen my ballads against the slave-mongers, but not in print. . . . There is but one of them with which I am myself satisfied, though I have heard them all well spoken of. But there are very few things of my own composition, that I can endure to read, when they have been written a month, though at first they seem to me to be all perfection.

Mrs. Unwin, who has been much the happier since the time of your return hither has been in some sort settled, begs me to make her kindest remembrance. Yours, my dear, most truly.

WILLIAM BLAKE TO THOMAS BUTTS

[Postmark Sept. 23, 1800]

DEAR FRIEND OF MY ANGELS,

We are safe arrived at our cottage without accident or hindrance, tho' it was between eleven and twelve o'clock at night before we could get home, owing to the necessary shifting of our boxes and portfolios from one chaise to another. We had seven different chaises and as many different drivers. All upon the road was chearfulness and welcome; tho' our luggage was very heavy there was no grumbling at all. We travel'd thro' a most beautiful country on a most glorious day. Our cottage is more beautiful than I thought it, and also more convenient, for tho' small it is well proportion'd, and if I should ever build a Palace it would be only my cottage enlarged. Please to tell Mrs. Butts that we have dedicated a chamber for her service, and that it has a very fine view of the sea. Mr. Hayley receiv'd me with his usual brotherly affection. My wife and sister are both very well, and courting Neptune for an embrace, whose terrors this morning made them afraid, but whose mildness is often equal to his terrors. The villagers of Felpham are not meer rustics; they are polite and modest. Meat is cheaper than in London, but the sweet air and the voices of winds, trees and birds, and the odours of the happy ground, makes it a dwelling for immortals. Work will go on here with God speed.—A roller and two harrows lie before my window. I met a plow on my first going out at my gate the first morning after my arrival, and the Plowboy said to the Plowman, " Father, the gate is open." I have begun to work, and find that I can work with greater pleasure than ever. Hope soon to give you a proof that Felpham is propitious to the Arts.

God bless you ! I shall wish for you on Tuesday evening as usual. Pray give my and my wife and sister's love and respects to Mrs. Butts ; accept them yourself, and believe me, for ever,

Your affectionate and obliged friend,

WILLIAM BLAKE.

Felpham,

Jany. 10, 1802

DEAR SIR,

Your very kind and affectionate letter and the many kind things you have said in it, call'd upon me for an immediate answer ; but it found my wife and myself so ill, and my wife so very ill, that till now I have not been able to do this duty. . . .

But you have so generously and openly desired that I will divide my griefs with you, that I cannot hide what it is now become my duty to explain.—My unhappiness has arisen from a source which, if explor'd too narrowly, might hurt my pecuniary circumstances, as my dependence is on engraving at present, and particularly on the engravings I have in hand for Mr. H. : and I find on all hands great objections to my doing anything but the meer drudgery of business, and intimations that if I do not confine myself to this, I shall not live ; this has always pursu'd me. You will understand by this the source of all my uneasiness. . . . I am not ashamed, afraid, or averse to tell you what ought to be told : that I am under the direction of messengers from Heaven, daily and nightly ; but the nature of such things is not, as some suppose, without trouble or care. Temptations are on the right hand and left; behind, the sea of time and space roars and follows swiftly; he who keeps not right onward is lost, and if our footsteps slide in clay, how can we do otherwise than fear and tremble? but I should not have troubled you with this account of my spiritual state, unless it had been necessary in explaining the actual cause of my uneasiness, into which you are so kind as to enquire; for I never obtrude such things on others unless question'd, and then I never disguise the truth.—But if we fear to do the dictates of our angels, and tremble at the tasks set before us; if we refuse to do spiritual acts because of natural fears or natural desires! Who can describe the dismal torments of such a state!—I too well remember the threats I heard!—" If you, who are organised by Divine Providence for spiritual communion, refuse, and bury your talent in the earth, even tho' you should want natural bread, sorrow and desperation pursues you thro' life, and after death shame and confusion of face to eternity. Every one in eternity will leave you, aghast at the man who was crown'd with glory and honour by his brethren, and betray'd their cause to their enemies. You will be call'd the base Judas who betray'd his friend!"— Such words would make any stout man tremble, and how then could I be at ease? But I am now no longer in that state, and now go on again with my task, fearless, and tho' my path is difficult, I have no fear of stumbling while I keep it. . . . Naked we came here, naked of natural things, and naked we shall return; but while cloth'd with the Divine mercy, we are richly cloth'd in spiritual and suffer all the rest gladly. Pray give my love to Mrs. Butts and your family.

I am, Yours sincerely,

WILLIAM BLAKE.

A LETTER FROM CHARLES LAMB

TO JOHN BATES DIBDIN

(A city clerk who had gone to Hastings for his health)

Friday, some day in June, 1826

DEAR D.—My first impulse upon opening your letter was pleasure at seeing your old neat hand, nine parts gentlemanly, with a modest dash of the clerical: my second thought, natural enough this hot weather, am I to answer all this? why 'tis as long as those to the Ephesians and Galatians put together—I have counted the words for curiosity. But then Paul has nothing like the fun which is ebullient all over yours. I don't remember a good thing (good like yours) from the 1st Romans to the last of the Hebrews. I remember but one Pun in all the Evangely, and that was made by his and our master: Thou art Peter (that is Doctor Rock) and upon this rock will I build &c.; which sanctifies Punning with me against all gain-sayers. I never knew an enemy to puns who was not an ill-natured man. Your fair critic in the coach reminds me of a Scotchman who assured me that he did not see much in Shakespeare. I replied, I dare say *not*. He felt the equivoke, looked awkward and reddish, but soon returned to the attack, by saying that he thought Burns was as good as Shakespeare: I said that I had no doubt he was—to a *Scotchman*. We exchanged no more words that day.— Your account of the fierce faces in the Hanging, with the presumed interlocution of the Eagle and the Tyger, amused us greatly. You cannot be so very bad, while you can pick mirth off from rotten walls. But let me hear you have escaped out of your oven. May the form of the fourth person who clapt invisible wet blankets about the shoulders of Shadrach, Meschach and Abednego, be with you in the fiery trial. But get out of the frying-pan. Your business, I take it, is bathing, not baking.

Let me hear that you have clamber'd up to Lover's Seat; it is as fine in that neighbourhood as Juan Fernandez, as lonely too, when the fishing boats are not out; I have sat for hours, staring upon a shipless sea. The salt sea is never so grand as when it is left to itself. One cock-boat spoils it. A sea-mew or two improves it. And go to the little church, which is a very protestant Loretto, and seems dropt by some angel for the use of a hermit, which was at once parishioner and a whole parish. It is not too big. Go in the night, bring it away in your portmanteau, and I will plant it in my garden. It must have been erected in the very infancy of British Christianity, for the two or three first converts; yet hath it all the appertenances of a church of the first magnitude, its pulpit, its pews, its baptismal font; a cathedral in a nutshell. Seven people would crowd it like a Caledonian Chapel. The minister that divides the word there, must give lumping pennyworths. It is built to the text of two or three assembled in my name. It reminds me of the grain of mustard seed. If the glebe land is proportionate, it may yield two potatoes. Tythes out of it could be no more split than a hair. Its first fruits must be its last, for 'twould never produce a couple. It is truly the strait and narrow way, and few there be (of London visitants) that find it. The still small voice is surely to be found there if anywhere. A sounding board is merely there for ceremony. It is secure from earthquakes, not more from sanctity than size, for 'twould feel a mountain thrown upon it no more than a taper-worm would. Go and see, but not without your spectacles. By the way, there's a capital farm house two thirds of the way to the Lover's Seat, with

incomparable plum cake, ginger beer, etc. Mary bids me
warn you not to read the anatomy of Melancholy in your
present *low way*. You'll fancy yourself a pipkin, or a
headless bear, as Burton speaks of. You'll be lost in
a maze of remedies for a labyrinth of diseasements, a
plethora of cures. Read Fletcher ; above all the Spanish
Curate, the Thief or Little Night-walker, the Wit without
Money, and the Lover's Pilgrimage. Laugh and come
home fat. Neither do we think Sir T. Browne quite the
thing for you just at present. Fletcher is as light as Soda
water. Browne and Burton are too strong potions for an
invalid. And don't thumb or dirt the books. Take care
of the bindings. Lay a leaf of silver paper under 'em, as
you read them. And don't smoke tobacco over 'em, the
leaves will fall in and burn or dirty their namesakes. If
you find any dusty atoms of the Indian Weed crumbled
up in the Beaumont and Fletcher they are *mine*. But then,
you know, so is the Folio also. A pipe and a comedy of
Fletcher's the last thing of a night is the best recipe
for light dreams and to scatter away nightmares. *Probatum
est*. But do as you like about the former. Only cut the
Baker's. You will come home else all crust ; Rankings must
chip you before you can appear in his counting house.
And my dear Peter Fin Junior, do contrive to see the sea
at least once before you return. You'll be ask'd about it in
the Old Jewry. It will appear singular not to have seen
it. And rub up your Muse, the family Muse, and send us
a rhyme or so. Don't waste your wit upon that damn'd
dry Salter. I never knew but one Dry Salter who could
relish those mellow effusions, and he broke. You knew
Tommy Hill, the wettest of dry salters. Dry Salters, what
a word for this thirsty weather ! I must drink after it.
Here's to thee, my dear Dibdin, and to our having you

again snug and well at Colebrooke, but our nearest hopes
are to hear again from you shortly. An epistle only a
quarter as agreeable as your last, would be a treat.

Yours most truly

C. LAMB.

FIRST PART
§III A BUNCH OF POPPIES

Yet here, this one night, thou may'st rest with me,
Thy bed green branches. Chestnuts soft have I
And mealy apples, and our fill of cheese.
Already, see, the far-off chimneys smoke,
And deeper grow the shadows of the hills.

    C. S. CALVERLEY (after VIRGIL, Eclogue I)

Who shall silence all the airs and madrigals that whisper
  softness in chambers?

      MILTON (*Areopagitica*)

Oh sleep ! it is a gentle thing,
Beloved from pole to pole !
To Mary Queen the praise be given !
She sent the gentle sleep from Heaven,
That slid into my soul.

    COLERIDGE (*The Ancient Mariner*)

§ III A BUNCH OF POPPIES

SONG

Let not the sluggish sleep
Close up thy waking eye,
Until with judgment deep
Thy daily deeds thou try :
He that one sin in conscience keeps
When he to quiet goes,
More venturous is than he that sleeps
With twenty mortal foes.

WILLIAM BYRD

THE LOVER ASKS FOR SLEEP

Come, Sleep, O Sleep ! the certain knot of peace,
  The baiting place of wit, the balm of woe,
The poor man's wealth, the prisoner's release,
  Th' indifferent judge between the high and low :
With shield of proof shield me from out the prease
  Of those fierce darts despair at me doth throw :
O make in me those civil wars to cease ;
  I will good tribute pay, if thou do so,
Take thou of me smooth pillows, sweetest bed,
  A chamber deaf to noise and blind to light,
A rosy garland, and a weary head :
  And if these things, as being thine by right,
Move not thy heavy grace, thou shalt in me,
Livelier than elsewhere, Stella's image see.

SIR PHILIP SIDNEY

O Night, the ease of care, the pledge of pleasure,
Desire's best mean, harvest of hearts affected,
The seat of peace, the throne which is erected
  Of human life to be the quiet measure ;
  Be victor still of Phoebus' golden treasure,
Who hath our sight with too much sight infected,
Whose light is cause we have our lives neglected,
  Turning all nature's course to self displeasure.
  These stately stars in their now shining faces,
With sinless sleep, and silence wisdom's mother,
  Witness his wrong, which by thy help is eased.
Thou art, therefore, of these our desert places
  The sure refuge ; by thee and by no other
My soul is blest, sense joy'd, and fortune raised.

SIR PHILIP SIDNEY

SLEEP IN SICKNESS

Care-charming Sleep, thou easer of all woes,
Brother to Death, sweetly thyself dispose
On this afflicted prince : fall like a cloud,
In gentle showers : give nothing that is loud
Or painful to his slumbers ; easy, sweet,
And as a purling stream, thou Son of Night,
Pass by his troubled senses ; sing his pain
Like hollow murmuring wind or silver rain,
Into this prince gently, O gently slide
And kiss him into slumber like a bride.

BEAUMONT AND FLETCHER (from Valentinian)

THE EVE OF PHILIPPI

(*Scene—Within the Tent of Brutus*)

BRUTUS : The deep of night is crept upon our talk,
And nature must obey necessity ;
Which we will niggard with a little rest.
There is no more to say ?
CASSIUS :   No more, Good night ;
Early to-morrow will we rise, and hence.
BRUTUS : Lucius ! [*Enter* LUCIUS]—My gown.
    [*Exit* LUCIUS.]—Farewell, good Messala :
Good night, Titinius :—Noble, noble Cassius,
Good night, and good repose.
CASSIUS :   O my dear brother !
This was an ill beginning of the night :
Never come such division 'tween our souls !
Let it not, Brutus.
BRUTUS :   Everything is well.
CASSIUS : Good night, my lord.
BRUTUS :   Good night, good brother.
TITINIUS, MESSALA : Good night, Lord Brutus.
BRUTUS :   Farewell, every one.
            [*Exeunt* CASSIUS, TITINIUS, *and* MESSALA.]
            Re-enter LUCIUS, *with the gown*.
Give me the gown. Where is thy instrument ?
LUCIUS : Here in the tent.
BRUTUS.   What, thou speak'st drowsily ?
Poor knave, I blame thee not ; thou art o'er-watch'd.
Call Claudius, and some other of my men ;
I'll have them sleep on cushions in my tent !
LUCIUS : Varro and Claudius !
                Enter VARRO *and* CLAUDIUS.
VARRO : Calls my lord ?

BRUTUS : I pray you, sirs, lie in my tent and sleep ;
It may be, I shall raise you by-and-by
On business to my brother Cassius.
VARRO : So please you, we will stand and watch your
    pleasure.
BRUTUS : I will not have it so ; lie down, good sirs ;
It may be, I shall otherwise bethink me.
Look, Lucius, here's the book I sought for so ;
I put it in the pocket of my gown.

                 [VARRO *and* CLAUDIUS *lie down*.]
LUCIUS : I was sure your lordship did not give it me.
BRUTUS : Bear with me, good boy, I am much forgetful
Canst thou hold up thy heavy eyes awhile,
And touch thy instrument a strain or two ?
LUCIUS : Ay, my lord, an't please you.
BRUTUS :   It does, my boy :
I trouble thee too much, but thou art willing.
LUCIUS : It is my duty, sir.
BRUTUS : I should not urge thy duty past thy might ;
I know young bloods look for a time of rest.
LUCIUS : I have slept, my lord, already.
BRUTUS : It was well done ; and thou shalt sleep again ;
I will not hold thee long : if I do live,
I will be good to thee. [*Music*]
This is a sleepy tune :—O murderous slumber !
Layest thou thy leaden mace upon my boy,
That plays thee music ?—Gentle knave, good night ;
I will not do thee so much wrong to wake thee.
If thou dost nod, thou break'st thy instrument ;
I'll take it from thee ; and, good boy, good night.
Let me see, let me see ;—is not the leaf turn'd down,
Where I left reading ? Here it is, I think.

             SHAKESPEARE (from *Julius Cæsar*)

FRIENDSHIP'S CONSOLATION

When to the sessions of sweet silent thought
I summon up remembrance of things past,
I sigh the lack of many a thing I sought,
And with old woes new wail my dear time's waste :
Then can I drown an eye, unused to flow,
For precious friends hid in death's dateless night,
And weep afresh love's long since cancelled woe,
And moan the expense of many a vanished sight :
Then can I grieve at grievances foregone,
And heavily from woe to woe tell o'er
The sad account of fore-bemoanèd moan,
Which I new pay as if not paid before.
   But if the while I think on thee, dear friend,
   All losses are restored and sorrows end.

SHAKESPEARE

TO MUSIQUE, TO BECALME HIS FEVER

Charm me asleep, and melt me so
   With thy Delicious Numbers ;
That being ravisht, hence I goe
   Away in easy slumbers.
     Ease my sick head,
     And make my bed,
  Thou power that canst sever
    From me this ill :
    And quickly still :
    Though thou not kill
     My Fever.

Thou sweetly canst convert the same
 From a consuming fire,
Into a gentle-licking flame,
 And make it thus expire.
  Then make me weep
  My paines asleep;
 And give me such resposes,
  That I, poore I,
  May think, thereby,
  I live and die
  'Mongst Roses.

Fall on me like a silent dew,
 Or like those Maiden show'rs,
Which, by the peepe of day, doe strew
 A Baptime o're the flowers,
  Melt, melt my paines,
  With thy soft straines;
 That having ease me given,
  With full delight,
  I leave this light;
  And take my flight
  For Heaven.

ROBERT HERRICK

THE POET ASKS FOR SLEEP

A flock of sheep that leisurely pass by,
One after one; the sound of rain, and bees
Murmuring; the fall of rivers, winds, and seas,
Smooth fields, white sheets of water, and pure sky.
I've thought of all by turns; and yet do lie
Sleepless; and soon the small bird's melodies

Must hear first utter'd from my orchard trees,
And the first cuckoo's melancholy cry.
Even thus last night, and two nights more, I lay
And could not win thee, Sleep ! by any stealth :
So do not let me wear to-night away :
Without Thee what is all the morning's wealth ?
Come, blessèd barrier between day and day,
Dear mother of fresh thoughts and joyous health !

WORDSWORTH

ASIA REPLIES TO THE VOICE IN THE AIR

My soul is an enchanted Boat,
  Which, like a sleeping swan, doth float
Upon the silver waves of thy sweet singing ;
  And thine doth like an angel sit
  Beside the helm conducting it,
Whilst all the winds with melody are ringing.
  It seems to float ever, for ever,
  Upon that many-winding river,
  Between mountains, woods, abysses,
  A Paradise of wildernesses !
Till, like one in slumber bound,
Borne to the ocean, I float down, around,
Into a sea profound, of ever-spreading sound.

SHELLEY (from Prometheus Unbound)

TO SLEEP

O soft embalmer of the still midnight,
  Shutting with careful fingers and benign
Our gloom-pleased eyes embowered from the light
  Enshaded in forgetfulness divine,

O soothest Sleep ! if so it please thee, close
  In midst of this thine hymn my willing eyes,
Or wait the Amen, ere thy poppy throws
  Around my bed its lulling charities.
  Then save me, or the passèd day will shine
Upon my pillow, breeding many woes ;
  Save me from curious conscience, that still hoards
Its strength for darkness, burrowing like a mole ;
  Turn the key deftly in the oilèd wards,
And seal the hushèd casket of my soul.

KEATS

LAST SONNET

Bright star, would I were steadfast as thou art—
  Not in lone splendour hung aloft the night,
And watching, with eternal lids apart,
  Like Nature's patient sleepless Eremite,
The moving waters at their priestlike task
  Of pure ablution round earth's human shores,
Or gazing on the new soft-fallen mask
  Of snow upon the mountains and the moors.—
No—yet still steadfast, still unchangeable,
  Pillowed upon my fair love's ripening breast,
To feel for ever its soft fall and swell,
  Awake for ever in a sweet unrest ;
Still, still to hear her tender-taken breath,
And so live ever—or else swoon to death.

KEATS

A NIGHT SONG

Oh ! do you wake, or do you sleep
   With window to the full-moon'd sky ?
Oh ! have you lost, or do you keep
   A thought of all the day gone by ?
Or are you dead to all you knew
Of life, the while I live to you ?

May air, o'er wallside roses brought,
   Of charming gardens give you dreams ;
May rustling leaves beguile your thought
   With dreams of walks by falling streams.
And on your lids be light that yields
Bright dream-clouds over daisied fields.

Our meeting hour of yesterday
   To me, now deep in waning night,
Seems all a glory pass'd away
   Beyond a year—time's longsome flight.
Though night seems far too short to weigh
Your words and deeds of yesterday.

While rise or sink the glittering stars
   Above dim woods, or hillock brows,
There, out within the moonpaled bars,
   In darksome bunches sleep your cows.
So sweetly sleep, asleep be they
Until you meet the opening day.

                WILLIAM BARNES

NIGHT THOUGHTS

The crackling embers on the hearth are dead ;
  The indoor note of industry is still ;
  The latch is fast ; upon the window-sill
The small birds wait not for their daily bread;
The voiceless flowers—how quietly they shed
  Their nightly odours ; and the household rill
  Murmurs continuous dulcet sounds that fill
The vacant expectation, and the dread
Of listening night. And haply now She sleeps,
  For all the garrulous noises of the air
Are hushed in peace ; the soft dew silent weeps,
  Like hopeless lovers for a maid so fair :—
Oh ! that I were the happy dream that creeps
  To her soft heart, to find my image there.

HARTLEY COLERIDGE

A SUMMING UP

I have lived and I have loved ;
I have waked and I have slept ;
I have sung and I have danced ;
I have smiled and I have wept ;
I have won and wasted treasure ;
I have had my fill of pleasure ;
And all these things were weariness,
And some of them were dreariness.
And all these things, but two things,
Were emptiness and pain :
And Love—it was the best of them ;
And Sleep—worth all the rest of them.

CHARLES MACKAY

SLEEPLESS DREAMS

Girt in dark growths, yet glimmering with one star,
   O night, desirous as the nights of youth !
   Why should my heart within thy spell, forsooth,
Now beat, as the bride's finger-pulses are
Quickened within the girdling golden bar ?
   What wings are these that fan my pillow smooth ?
   And why does Sleep, waved back by Joy and Ruth,
Tread softly round and gaze at me from far ?

Nay, night deep-leaved ! And would Love feign in thee
   Some shadowy palpitating grove that bears
   Rest for man's eyes and music for his ears ?
O lonely night ! art thou not known to me,
A thicket hung with masks of mockery
   And watered with the wasteful warmth of tears ?

D. G. ROSSETTI

INVITATION TO SLEEP

Come, blessed sleep, most full, most perfect, come :
   Come, sleep, if so I may forget the whole ;
   Forget my body and forget my soul,
Forget how long life is and troublesome.
Come, happy sleep, to soothe my heart or numb,
   Arrest my weary spirit or control :
   Till light be dark to me from pole to pole,
And winds and echoes and low songs be dumb
Come, sleep, and lap me into perfect calm,
   Lap me from all the world and weariness :

Come, secret sleep, with thine unuttered psalm,
   Safe sheltering in a hidden cool recess :
Come, heavy dreamless sleep, and close and press
Upon mine eyes thy fingers dropping balm.

CHRISTINA ROSSETTI

LOVE IN DREAMS

Love hath his poppy-wreath,
   Not Night alone.
I laid my head beneath
   Love's lilied throne :
Then to my sleep he brought
   This anodyne—
The flower of many a thought
   And fancy fine :
A form, a face, no more ;
   Fairer than truth ;
A dream from death's pale shore ;
   The soul of youth :
A dream so dear, so deep,
   All dreams above,
That still I pray to sleep—
   Bring Love back, Love !

J. A. SYMONDS

TO SLEEP

O Sleep, O tranquil son of noiseless Night,
   Of humid, shadowy Night ; O dear repose
   For wearied men, forgetfulness of woes
Grievous enough the bloom of life to blight !

118

Succour this heart that hath outworn delight,
    And knows no rest ; these tirèd limbs compose ;
    Fly to me, Sleep ; thy dusky vans disclose
Over my languid eyes, then cease thy flight.
Where, where is Silence, that avoids the day ?
    Where the light dreams, that with a wavering tread
    And unsubstantial footing follow thee ?
Alas ! in vain I call thee ; and these grey,
    These frigid shades flatter in vain. O bed,
    How rough with thorns ! O nights, how harsh to me !

J. A SYMONDS (from the Italian)

TO THE GENIUS OF ETERNAL SLUMBER

Sleep, thou art named eternal ! Is there then
    No chance of waking in thy noiseless realm ?
    Come there no fretful dreams to overwhelm
The feverish spirits of o'erlaboured men ?
Shall conscience sleep where thou art ; and shall pain
    Lie folded with tired arms around her head ;
    And memory be stretched upon a bed
Of ease, whence she shall never rise again ?
O Sleep, that art eternal ! Say, shall Love
    Breathe like an infant slumbering at thy breast ?
        Shall hope there cease to throb ; and shall the smart
Of things impossible at length find rest ?
Thou answerest not. The poppy-heads above
        Thy calm brows sleep. How cold, how still thou art !

J. A. SYMONDS

119

Home, home from the horizon far and clear,
  Hither the soft wings sweep ;
Flocks of the memories of the day draw near
  The dovecote doors of sleep.

O, which are they that come through sweetest light
  Of all these homing birds ?
Which with the straightest and the swiftest flight ?
  Your words to me, your words !

ALICE MEYNELL

A PRAYER TO THE BOY-GOD

What sin was mine, sweet, silent boy-god, Sleep,
Or what, poor sufferer, have I left undone,
That I should lack thy guerdon, I alone ?
Quiet are the brawling streams : the shuddering deep
Sinks, and the rounded mountains feign to sleep.
The high seas slumber pillowed on Earth's breast ;
All flocks and birds and beasts are stilled in rest,
But my sad eyes their nightly vigil keep . . .
  O ! if beneath the night some happier swain,
Entwined in loving arms, refuse thy boon
In wanton happiness,—come hither soon,
Come hither, Sleep. Let happier mortals gain
The full embrace of thy soft angel wing :
But touch me with thy wand, or hovering
Above mine eyelids sweep me with thy train.

W. H. FYFE (after STATIUS)

FALSE SLEEP

Ah, Sleep, to me thou com'st not in the guise
Of one who brings good gifts to weary men,
Balm for bruised hearts and fancies alien
To unkind truth, and drying for sad eyes.
I dread the summons to that fierce assize
Of all my foes and woes, that waits me when
Thou mak'st my soul the unwilling denizen
Of thy dim troubled house where unrest lies.

My soul is sick with dreaming, let it rest.
False Sleep, thou hast conspired with Wakefulness,
I will not praise thee, I too long beguiled
With idle tales. Where is thy soothing breast?
Thy peace, thy poppies, thy forgetfulness?
Where is thy lap for me so tired a child?

LORD ALFRED DOUGLAS

THE BAT

In broad daylight
He should not be:
Yet toward and froward,
Froward and toward
He weaves a flight.
Who will guide him back to his cave,
A little bat astray,
Where he'll rest on the breast of night,
Away from day's bright miscreation?
The linnet throbs through the air,
The magpie coquettes with day,
The rook caws " Time to be gone,"
And travels on;

While toward and froward,
Froward and toward,
The bat . . . a fathom
Of flight . . . weaves.

PADRAIC COLUM

BED-TIME

I mind, love, how it ever was this way :
   That I would to my task ; and soon I'd hear
Your little fluttering sigh, and you would say,
   " It's bed-time, dear."

So you would go and leave me at my work ;
   And I would turn to it with steady will,
And wonder why the room had grown so dark,
   The night so chill.

Betimes I'd hear the whisper of your feet
   Upon the stair ; and you would come to me,
All rosy from your dreams, and take your seat
   Upon my knee.

" Poor tired boy ! " you'd say. But I would miss
   The lonely message of your eyes, and so
Proffer the hasty bribery of a kiss,
   And let you go.

But now, dear heart, that you have scaled the stair
   To that dim chamber far above the sun,
I fumble with my futile task, nor care
   To get it done.

For all is empty since you said good-night
   (So spent you were, and weary with the day!)
And on the hearth the ashes of delight
   Lie cold and grey.

Ah, sweet my love, could I but wish you down
   In that white raiment which I know you wear;
And hear once more the rustle of your gown
   Upon the stair;

Could I but have you, drowsily sweet, to say
   The tender little words that once I knew—
How gaily would I put my work away
   And go with you.

RALPH M. JONES

A MEMORY

Each night beside my bed
   My mother sang so tenderly and low,
While I with snuggling head
   Floated away on slumber's quiet flow.—
   There are no songs like hers of long ago.

Each night until I slept
   A little while beside my bed she stayed;
And then away she crept
   While through the fields of wonderland I strayed
   There are no pray'rs like those my mother prayed.

Long years ago, she died.
    But sometimes when the silence seals the day,
And slumber's dreamful tide
    Begins to bear me on its homeward way,
    I think I hear her sing, I hear her pray.

ARTHUR L. SALMON

FALLING ASLEEP

Voices moving about in the quiet house :
Thud of feet and a muffled shutting of doors :
Everyone yawning. Only the clocks are alert.

Out in the night there's autumn-smelling gloom
Crowded with whispering trees ; across the park
A hollow cry of hounds like lonely bells :
And I know that the clouds are moving across the moon ;
The low, red, rising moon. Now herons call
And wrangle by their pool ; and hooting owls
Sail from the wood above pale stooks of oats.

Waiting for sleep, I drift from thoughts like these ;
And where to-day was dream-like, build my dreams.
Music . . . there was a bright white room below,
And someone singing a song about a soldier,
One hour, two hours ago : and soon the song
Will be " *last night* " ; but now the beauty swings
Across my brain, ghost of remembered chords
Which still can make such radiance in my dream
That I can watch the marching of my soldiers,
And count their faces ; faces ; sunlit faces.

124

Falling asleep ... the herons, and the hounds. ...
September in the darkness; and the world
I've known; all fading past me into peace.

SIEGFRIED SASSOON

A LITTLE SOUND

A little sound—
Only a little, a little—
The breath in a reed,
A trembling fiddle;
The trumpet's ring,
The shuddering drum;
So all the glory, bravery, hush
Of music come.

A little sound—
Only a stir and a sigh
Of each green leaf
Its fluttering neighbour by;
Oak on to oak,
The wide, dark forest through—
So o'er the watery wheeling world
The night-winds go.

A little sound—
Only a little, a little,
The thin high drone
Of the simmering kettle,
The gathering frost,
The click of needle and thread;
Mother, the fading wall, the dream,
The drowsy bed.

WALTER DE LA MARE

DON'T FORGET THE VIOLET

For him that may not slepe for sickness set this herbe in water, and at even let him soke well hys fete in the water to the ancles. When he goeth to bed bind of this herbe to his temples, and he shal slepe wel by the grace of God.

ANTHONY ASCHAM (from *A Little Herbal*, 1550)

AN OLD SLEEPING BAG

A Bag to smell unto for melancholy or to cause one to sleep.
Take drie rose leaves, keep them close in a glass which will keep them sweet, then take powder of mints, powder of cloves in a gross powder, and put the same to the rose leaves, then put all these together in a bag, and take that to bed with you, and it will cause you to sleep, and it is good to smell unto at other times.

A New Herbal (1578)

CONCLUSION TO *THE GARDEN OF CYRUS*

But the quincunx of heaven runs low, and 'tis time to close the five ports of knowledge. We are unwilling to spin out our awaking thoughts into the phantasms of sleep, which often continueth precogitations; making cables of cobwebs, and wildernesses of handsome groves. Beside Hippocrates hath spoke so little, and the oneiro-critical masters have left such frigid interpretations from plants, that there is little encouragement to dream of paradise itself. Nor will the sweetest delight of gardens afford much comfort in sleep; wherein the dulness of that sense shakes hands with delectable odours; and though in the bed of Cleopatra, can hardly with any delight raise up the ghost of a rose.

Night, which Pagan theology could make the daughter of Chaos, affords no advantage to the description of order : although no lower than that mass can we derive its genealogy. All things began in order, so shall they end, and so shall they begin again; according to the Ordainer of order and mystical mathematics of the city of heaven.

Though Somnus in Homer be sent to rouse up Agamemnon, I find no such effects in these drowsy approaches of sleep. To keep our eyes open longer, were but to act our Antipodes. The huntsmen are up in America, and they are already past their first sleep in Persia. But who can be drowsy at that hour which freed us from everlasting sleep ? or have slumbering thoughts at that time, when sleep itself must end, and as some conjecture all shall awake again.

SIR THOMAS BROWNE

COLERIDGE'S COMMENT ON THE FORE-GOING

" *To keep our eyes open longer,*" *etc.* Think you that there ever was such a reason given before for going to bed at midnight; to wit, that if we did not, we should be *acting* the part of our antipodes ! And then—" *The Huntsmen are up in America* "—what life, what fancy ! Does the whimsical knight give us, thus, the *essence* of gunpowder tea, and call it an *opiate* ?

M S. Notes in a copy of Browne's Works

This is an article for the reader to think of when he or she is warm in bed, a little before he goes to sleep, the clothes at his ear, and the wind moaning in some distant crevice.

" Blessings," exclaimed Sancho, " on him that first invented sleep ! It wraps a man all round like a cloak." It is a delicious moment certainly—that of being well nestled in bed, and feeling that you shall drop gently to sleep. The good is to come, not past : the limbs have been just tired enough to render the remaining in one posture delightful : the labour of the day is done. A gentle failure of the perceptions comes creeping over one : the spirit of consciousness disengages itself more and more, with slow and hushing degrees like a mother detaching her hand from that of her sleeping child ; the mind seems to have a balmy lid closing over it, like the eye ; 'tis closing ;— 'tis more closing ;—'tis closed. The mysterious spirit has gone to take its airy rounds . . .

In the course of the day few people think of sleeping, except after dinner ; and then it is often rather a hovering and nodding on the borders of sleep than sleep itself . . .

The most complete and healthy sleep that can be taken in the day is in summer-time, out in a field. There is, perhaps, no solitary sensation so exquisite as that of slumbering on the grass or hay, shaded from the hot sun by a tree, with the consciousness of a fresh but light air running through the wide atmosphere, and the sky stretching far overhead upon all sides. Earth, and heaven, and a placid humanity seem to have the creation to themselves. There is nothing between the slumberer and the naked and glad innocence of nature.

Next to this, but at a long interval, the most relishing snatch of slumber out of bed is the one which a tired person takes before he retires for the night, while lingering in his sitting-room. The consciousness of being very sleepy, and of having the power to go to bed immediately, gives great zest to the unwillingness to move. Sometimes he sits nodding in his chair; but the sudden and leaden jerks of the head, to which a state of great sleepiness renders him liable, are generally too painful for so luxurious a moment; and he gets into a more legitimate posture, sitting sideways with his head on the chair-back, or throwing his legs up at once on another chair, and half reclining. It is curious, however, to find how long an inconvenient posture will be borne for the sake of this foretaste of repose. The worst of it is, that on going to bed the charm sometimes vanishes; perhaps from the colder temperature of the chamber; for a fireside is a great opiate.

Speaking of the painful positions into which a sleepy lounger will get himself, it is amusing to think of the more fantastic attitudes that so often take place in bed. If we could add anything to the numberless things that have been said about sleep by the poets, it would be upon this point. Sleep never shows himself a greater leveller. A man in his waking moments may look as proud and self-possessed as he pleases. He may walk proudly, he may sit proudly, he may eat his dinner proudly; he may shave himself with an air of infinite superiority; in a word, he may show himself grand and absurd upon the most trifling occasions. But sleep plays the petrifying magician. He arrests the proudest lord as well as the humblest clown in the most ridiculous postures: so that if you could draw a grandee from his bed without waking him, no limb-twisting fool in a pantomime should create wilder laughter. The toy with the string between its legs is hardly a posture-master more extravagant. Imagine a despot lifted up to the gaze of his valets, with his eyes shut, his mouth open, his left hand under his right ear, his other twisted and hanging helplessly before him like an idiot's, one knee lifted up, and the other leg stretched out, or both knees huddled up together ; what a scarecrow to lodge majestic power in ! . . .

Sleep is most graceful in an infant ; soundest, in one who has been tired in the open air ; completest, to the seaman after a hard voyage ; most welcome, to the mind haunted with one idea ; most touching to look at, in the parent that has wept ; lightest, in the playful child ; proudest, in the bride adored.

LEIGH HUNT

A RAILWAY SLEEPER

If the people of Milo did well to put up a statue in gold to the man that invented wheels, so should we also put one up in Portland stone or plaster to the man that invented rails, whose property it is not only to increase the speed and ease of travel, but also to bring on slumber as can no drug : not even poppies gathered under a waning moon. The rails have a rhythm of slight falls and rises . . . they make a loud roar like a perpetual torrent ; they cover up the mind with a veil.

HILAIRE BELLOC (from *The Path to Rome*)

LULLABIES

From Old English Song Books

Retire, my thoughts, unto your rest again,
Your proffered service may incur disdain,
The dice are cast, and if the gamesters please,
I'll take my chance and rest myself at ease.

WEELKES' Madrigalls, 1597

O sleep, fond Fancy, sleep, my head thou tirest
With false delight of that which thou desirest.
Sleep, sleep, I say, and leave my thoughts molesting,
Thy master's head hath need of sleep and resting.

BENNET'S Madrigalls, 1599

Weep you no more, sad fountains ;
    What need you flow so fast ?
Look how the snowy mountains
    Heaven's sun doth gently waste !
But my Sun's heavenly eyes
        View not your weeping,
        That now lies sleeping
Softly, now softly lies
        Sleeping.

Sleep is a reconciling,
    A rest that peace begets ;
Doth not the sun rise smiling
    When fair at even he sets ?
Rest you then, rest, sad eyes !
        Melt not in weeping,
        While she lies sleeping
Softly, now softly lies
        Sleeping.

DOWLAND'S Book of Ayres, 1603

131

Sing lullabies, as women do,
   With which they charm their babes to rest ;
And lullaby can I sing too,
   As womanly as can the best.
With lullaby they still the child ;
And, if I be not much beguil'd,
Full many wanton babes have I,
Which must be still'd with lullaby.

First lullaby my youthful years :
   It is now time to go to bed :
For crooked age, and hoary hairs,
   Have wore the haven within mine head.
With lullaby then youth be still,
With lullaby content thy will ;
Since courage quails, and comes behind,
Go sleep, and so beguile thy mind

Next lullaby my gazing eyes,
   Which wonted were to glance apace ;
For ev'ry glass may now suffice
   To shew the furrows in my face.
With lullaby then wink awhile ;
With lullaby your looks beguile ;
Let no fair face, or beauty bright,
Entice you efte with vain delight.

And lullaby my wanton will,
   Let reason's rule now rein thy thought,
Since all too late I find by skill,
   How dear I have thy fancies bought ;

With lullaby now take thine ease,
With lullaby thy doubt appease;
For, trust in this, if thou be still,
My body shall obey thy will.

GEORGE GASCOIGNE

LULLABY FOR TITANIA

FIRST FAIRY

You spotted snakes with double tongue,
　　Thorny hedgehogs, be not seen;
Newts, and blind-worms, do no wrong;
　　Come not near our fairy queen.

CHORUS

　　Philomel with melody
　　Sing in our sweet lullaby;
Lulla, lulla, lullaby; lulla, lulla, lullaby!
Never harm, nor spell, nor charm,
　　Come our lovely lady nigh!
　　So good-night, with lullaby.

SECOND FAIRY

Weaving spiders, come not here;
　　Hence, you long-legg'd spinners, hence;
Beetles black, approach not near;
　　Worm, nor snail, do no offence.

133

Philomel with melody
Sing in our sweet lullaby;
Lulla, lulla, lullaby; lulla, lulla lullaby .
Never harm, nor spell, nor charm,
Come our lovely lady nigh!
So good-night, with lullaby.

SHAKESPEARE (from *Midsummer Night's Dream*)

GOLDEN SLUMBERS

Golden slumbers kiss your eyes,
Smiles awake you when you rise!
Sleep, pretty wantons; do not cry,
And I will sing a lullaby:
Rock them, rock them, lullaby!

Care is heavy, therefore sleep you;
You are care, and care must keep you.
Sleep, pretty wantons; do not cry,
And I will sing a lullaby:
Rock them, rock them, lullaby!

THOMAS DEKKER

LULLABY FOR WANDERERS

Softly Night's wings closing in have enfolded the mountains,
Hardly a breath is astir in the slumbering trees;
Snug in the heart of the forest the song-birds are silent—
Rest is at hand for the weary ones—sleep and have ease!

GOETHE (Trans. A. S.)

CRADLE SONG

Sleep, sleep, beauty bright,
Dreaming in the joys of night !
Sleep, sleep ; in thy sleep
Little sorrows sit and weep.

Sweet babe, in thy face
Soft desires I can trace,
Secret joys and secret smiles
Little pretty infant wiles.

As thy softest limbs I feel,
Smiles as of the morning steal
O'er thy cheek, and o'er thy breast
Where thy little heart doth rest.

O, the cunning wiles that creep
In thy little heart asleep !
When thy little heart shall wake,
Then the dreadful light shall break.

WILLIAM BLAKE

A SERENADE

" Lullaby, oh, lullaby ! "
Thus I heard a father cry,
" Lullaby, oh, lullaby !
The brat will never shut an eye ;
Hither come, some power divine !
Close his lids, or open mine ! "

" Lullaby, oh, lullaby !
What the devil makes him cry ?
   Lullaby, oh, lullaby !
Still he stares—I wonder why,
Why are not the sons of earth
Blind, like puppies, from the birth ? "

   " Lullaby, oh, lullaby ! "
Thus I heard the father cry ;
   " Lullaby, oh, lullaby !
Mary, you must come and try !—
Hush, oh, hush, for mercy's sake—
The more I sing, the more you wake ! "

   " Lullaby, oh, lullaby !
Fie, you little creature, fie !
   Lullaby, oh, lullaby !
Is no poppy-syrup nigh ?
Give him some, or give him all,
I am nodding to his fall ! "

   " Lullaby, oh, lullaby !
Two such nights, and I shall die !
   Lullaby, oh, lullaby !
He'll be bruised, and so shall I,—
How can I from bedposts keep,
When I'm walking in my sleep ? "

   " Lullaby, oh, lullaby !
Sleep his very looks deny—
   Lullaby, oh, lullaby ;
Nature soon will stupefy—
My nerves relax,—my eyes grow dim—
Who's that fallen—me or him ? "

THOMAS HOOD

136

SWEET AND LOW

Sweet and low, sweet and low,
   Wind of the western sea,
Low, low, breathe and blow,
   Wind of the western sea !
Over the rolling waters go,
Come from the dying moon, and blow,
   Blow him again to me ;
While my little one, while my pretty one,
    sleeps.

Sleep and rest, sleep and rest,
   Father will come to thee soon :
Rest, rest, on mother's breast,
   Father will come to thee soon ;
Father will come to his babe in the nest,
Silver sails all out of the west
   Under the silver moon :
Sleep, my little one, sleep, my pretty one,
    sleep.

TENNYSON

WILLIE WINKIE

Wee Willie Winkie
   Rins through the toun,
Up stairs and down stairs
   In his nicht-gown,
Tirling at the window,
   Crying at the lock,
   Are the weans in their bed,
   For it's now ten o'clock ? "

Hey, Willie Winkie,
   Are ye coming ben ?
The cat's singing grey thrums
   To the sleeping hen ;
The dog's spelder'd on the floor,
   And disna gie a cheep ;
But here's a waukrife laddie
   That winna fa' asleep.

Onything but sleep, you rogue !
   Glow'ring like the moon,
Rattling in an airn jug
   Wi' an airn spoon,
Rumblin', tumblin' 'round about,
   Crawing like a cock,
Skirlin' like a kenna-what,
   Wauk'nin' sleeping folk.

Hey, Willie Winkie,
   The wean's in a creel !
Wamblin' aff a body's knee
   Like a very eel,
Ruggin' at the cat's lug,
   Rav'llin' a' her thrums—
Hey, Willie Winkie,
   See, there he comes !

Wearied is the mither
   That has a stoorie wean,
A wee stumpie stousie
   That canna rin his lane

That has a battle aye wi' sleep,
  Before he'll close an e'e ;
But a kiss fra aff his rosy lips
  Gies strength anew to me.

WILLIAM MILLER

THE WEE CROODLIN' DOO [1]

Will ye no fa' asleep the nicht,
  Ye restless little loun ?
The sun has lang been oot o' sicht
  An' gloamin's dark'nin' doon.
There's claes to mend, the house to clean—
  This nicht I'll no win through,
An' yet ye winna close yer een—
  Ye wee croodlin' doo !

Spurrin' wi yer restless feet,
  My very legs are sair,
Clautin' wi' yer buffy hands,
  Touslin' mammy's hair.
I've gi'en ye meat wi' sugar sweet,
  Yer little crappie's fu' ;
Cuddle doon, ye stourie loun—
  Ye wee croodlin' doo !

Now, hushaba, my little pet,
  Ye've a' the warld can gi'e ;
Ye're just yer mammy's lammie yet,
  An' daddy's ae e'e.

[1] Croodling doo = cooing dove.

139

Will ye never close yer een ?
   There's the bogle-boo !
Ye dinna care a single preen,
   Ye wee croodlin' doo !

Twistin' roun' an' roun' again,
   Warslin' aff my lap,
An' pussy on the hearthstane,
   As sound as ony tap ;
Dickie birdie gane to rest—
   A' asleep but you,
Nestle into mammy's breast,
   Ye wee croodlin' doo !

Happit cosy, trig, an' sweet,
   Fifty bairns are waur,
An' ye'se get fotties for yer feet
   At the Big Bazaar.
An' ye shall hae a hoodie braw
   To busk yer bonnie broo,
" Cockle shells an' silver bells,"
   My wee croodlin' doo !

Gude be praised, the battle's by,
   An' sleep has won at last,
How still the puddlin' feetie lie,
   The buffy hands at rest !
An' saftly fa's the silken fringe
   Aboon thy een o' blue ;
Blessin's on my bonnie bairn—
   My wee croodlin' doo !

JAMES THOMSON (b. 1825)

LULLABY OF A MOUNTAIN WOMAN

(*To an old Irish air*)

Little gold head, my house's candle,
You will guide all wayfarers that walk this mountain.

Little soft mouth that my breast has known,
Mary will kiss you as she passes.

Little round cheek, O silk of the thistle,
Jesus will lay his hand upon you.

Mary's kiss on my child's red mouth,
Christ's little hand on my darling's cheek !

House be still, and ye little grey mice,
Lie close, lie close, lest ye break his slumber.

Moths on the window, fold your wings,
Little black chafers, silence your humming.

Plover and curlew, fly not over my house,
Do not speak, wild barnacle, passing over this mountain.

Things of the mountain that wake in the night-time,
Be still, be still, for my little one sleeps.

PADRAIC H. PEARSE

GOOD NIGHT

Sleep sweetly in this quiet room
O thou—whoe'er thou art—
And let no mournful yesterdays
Disturb thy peaceful heart ;
Nor let to-morrow mar thy rest
With dreams of coming ill.
Thy Maker is thy Changeless Friend :
His love surrounds thee still.
Forget thyself and all the world,
Put out each garish light.
The stars are shining overhead—
Sleep sweetly, then. Good night !

ANONYMOUS

FIRST PART

§ IV LODGINGS FOR THE NIGHT

Matthew, Mark, Luke, and John
Bless the bed that I lie on !
  Four corners to my bed,
  Five angels there be spread ;
    Two at my head,
    Two at my feet,
One at my heart my soul to keep.

The White Paternoster

  Bona sera ai vivi ;
  E riposo ai morti poveri ;
  Bon viaggio ai naviganti ;
  E bona notte a tutti quanti !

Old Song (15th century)

Here my " master " comes : he has poked out all the house-fires, has looked to all the bolts, has ordered the whole male and female crew to their chambers ; and begins to blow my candles out, and says, " Time, Sir George, to go to bed ! Twelve o'clock ! "

" Bless me ! So indeed it is." And I close my book, and go to my rest, with a blessing on those around me now asleep.

THACKERAY (*The Virginians*)

§ IV LODGINGS FOR THE NIGHT

DISCOUNT FOR CASH

A few days afterwards we set out on our return to Florence. We lay one night at a place on this side Chioggia, on the left hand as you go toward Ferrara. Here the host insisted upon being paid before we went to bed, and in his own way; and when I observed that it was the custom everywhere else to pay in the morning, he answered : " I insist on being paid overnight, and in my own way." I retorted that men who wanted everything their own way ought to make a world after their own fashion, since things were differently managed here. Our host told me not to go on bothering his brains, because he was determined to do as he had said. Tribolo stood trembling with fear, and nudged me to keep quiet, lest they should do something worse to us; so we paid them in the way they wanted, and afterwards we retired to rest. We had, I must admit, the most capital beds, new in every particular, and as clean as they could be. Nevertheless I did not get one wink of sleep, because I kept on thinking how I could revenge myself. At one time it came into my head to set fire to his house; at another to cut the throats of four fine horses which he had in the stable; I saw well enough that it was easy for me to do all this; but I could not see how it was easy to secure myself and my companion. At last I resolved to put my things and my comrade's on board the boat; and so I did. When the towing-horses had been harnessed to the cable, I ordered the people not to stir before I returned, for I had left a pair of slippers in my bedroom. Accordingly I went back to the inn and called our host, who told me he had nothing to do with us, and that we might go to Jericho. There was a ragged stable-boy about, half asleep, who . . . asked me for a tip, and I gave him a few Venetian coppers, and told him to make the barge man wait till I had found my slippers and returned. I went upstairs, took out a little knife as sharp as a razor, and cut the four beds that I found there into ribbons. I had the satisfaction of knowing I had done a damage of more than fifty crowns. Then I ran down to the boat with some pieces of the bed-covers in my pouch, and bade the bargee start at once without delay. We had not gone far before my gossip Tribolo said that he had left behind some little straps belonging to his carpet-bag, and that he must be allowed to go back for them. I answered that he need not take thought for a pair of little straps, since I could make him as many big ones as he liked. He told me I was always joking, but that he must really go back for his straps. Then he began ordering the bargee to stop, while I kept ordering him to go on. Meanwhile I informed my friend what kind of trick I had played our host, and showed him specimens of the bed-covers and other things, which threw him into such a quaking fright that he roared out to the bargee : " On with you, on with you, as quick as you can ! " and never thought himself quite safe until we reached the gates of Florence.

When we arrived there, Tribolo said : " Let us bind our swords up, for the love of God ; and play me no more of your games, I beg ; for all this while I've felt as though my guts were in the saucepan." I made answer : " Gossip Tribolo, you need not tie your sword up, for you have never loosed it " ; and this I said at random, because I never once had seen him act the man upon that journey. When he heard the remark, he looked at his sword and cried out : " In God's name, you speak true ! Here it is tied, just as I arranged it before I left my house." My gossip deemed that I had been a bad travelling companion to him, because I resented affronts and defended myself against folk who would have done us injury. But I deemed that he had acted a far worse part with regard to me by never coming to my assistance at such pinches. Let him judge between us who stands by and has no personal interest in our adventures.

BENVENUTO CELLINI (from *Autobiography*—
Trans. J. A. SYMONDS)

ADVICE FROM A TUDOR DOCTOR

Whole men of what age or complexion soever they be of, should take their natural rest and sleep in the night : and to eschew meridial sleep. But if need should compel a man to sleep after his meat : let him make a pause, and then let him stand and lean and sleep against a cupboard, or else let him sit upright in a chair and sleep. To bedward be you merry or have merry company about you, so that to bedward no anger nor heaviness, sorrow nor pensifulness do trouble or disquiet you. In the night let the windows of your house, especially of your chamber, be closed. When you be in your bed lie a little while on your left side, and sleep on your right side. Let your night cap be of scarlet : and this I do advertise you, to cause to be made a good thick quilt of cotton, or else of pure flocks or of clean wool, and let the covering of it be of white fustian, and lay it on the feather-bed that you do lie on ; and in your bed lie not too hot nor too cold, but in a temperance.

Old ancient Doctors of Physic say seven hours of sleep in summer and nine in winter is sufficient for any man; but I do think that sleep ought to be taken as the complexion of man is. When you do rise in the morning, rise with mirth and remember God.

ANDREW BORDE (from A Compendious Regyment, 1557)

CHARGING THE WATCH

DOGBERRY : Are you good men and true?

VERGES : Yea, or else it were pity but they should suffer salvation, body and soul.

DOGBERRY : Nay, that were a punishment too good for them, if they should have any allegiance in them, being chosen for the prince's watch.

VERGES: Well, give them their charge, neighbour Dogberry.

DOGBERRY : First, who think you the most desartless man to be constable?

FIRST WATCH : Hugh Otecake, sir, or George Seacole; for they can write and read.

DOGBERRY : Come hither, neighbour Seacole. God hath blessed you with a good name : to be a well-favoured man is the gift of fortune; but to write and read comes by nature.

SECOND WATCH : Both which, master constable,—

DOGBERRY : You have : I knew it would be your answer. Well, for your favour, sir, why, give God thanks, and make no boast of it; and for your writing and reading, let that appear when there is no need of such vanity. You are thought here to be the most senseless and fit man for the constable of the watch; therefore bear you the lantern. This is your charge : you shall comprehend all vagrom men ; you are to bid any man stand, in the prince's name.

SECOND WATCH : How if a' will not stand ?

DOGBERRY : Why, then, take no note of him, but let him go ; and presently call the rest of the watch together, and thank God you are rid of a knave.

VERGES : If he will not stand when he is bidden, he is none of the prince's subjects.

DOGBERRY : True, and they are to meddle with none but the prince's subjects. You shall also make no noise in the streets ; for for the watch to babble and to talk is most tolerable and not to be endured.

WATCH : We will rather sleep than talk : we know what belongs to a watch.

DOGBERRY : Why, you speak like an ancient and most quiet watchman ; for I cannot see how sleeping should offend : only, have a care that your bills be not stolen. Well, you are to call at all the ale-houses, and bid those that are drunk get them to bed.

WATCH : How if they will not ?

DOGBERRY : Why, then, let them alone till they are sober : if they make you not then the better answer, you may say they are not the men you took them for.

WATCH : Well, sir.

DOGBERRY : If you meet a thief, you may suspect him, by virtue of your office, to be no true man ; and, for such kind of men, the less you meddle or make with them, why, the more is for your honesty.

WATCH : If we know him to be a thief, shall we not lay hands on him ?

DOGBERRY : Truly, by your office, you may ; but I think they that touch pitch will be defiled : the most peaceable way for you, if you do take a thief, is to let him show himself what he is, and steal out of your company.

149

VERGES : You have been always called a merciful man, partner.

DOGBERRY : Truly, I would not hang a dog by my will, much more a man who hath any honesty in him.

VERGES : If you hear a child cry in the night, you must call to the nurse and bid her still it.

WATCH : How if the nurse be asleep and will not hear us ?

DOGBERRY : Why, then, depart in peace, and let the child wake her with crying ; for the ewe that will not hear her lamb when it baes will never answer a calf when he bleats.

VERGES : 'Tis very true.

DOGBERRY : This is the end of the charge . . . Well, masters, good night : an there be any matter of weight chances, call up me : keep your fellows' counsels and your own ; and good night. Come, neighbour.

WATCH : Well, masters, we hear our charge : let us go sit here upon the church-bench till two, and then all to bed.

SHAKESPEARE (from *Much Ado about Nothing*)

ANGLERS AT HODDESDON

PISCATOR : 'Tis enough, honest scholar, come let's to supper. Come, my friend Coridon, this trout looks lovely, it was twenty-two inches when it was taken, and the belly of it looked some part of it as yellow as a marigold, and part of it as white as a lily, and yet, methinks, it looks better in this good sauce.

CORIDON : Indeed, honest friend, it looks well, and tastes well, I thank you for it, and so does my friend Peter, or else he is to blame.

PETER : Yes, and so I do, we all thank you, and when we

have supped, I will get my friend Coridon to sing you a song, for requital.

CORIDON : I will sing a song, if anybody will sing another ; else, to be plain with you, I will sing none : I am none of those that sing for meat, but for company : I say, *'Tis merry in hall, when men sing all.*

PISCATOR : I'll promise you I'll sing a song that was lately made at my request by Mr. William Basse, one that hath made the choice songs of The Hunter in his Career, and of Tom of Bedlam, and many others of note ; and this that I will sing is in praise of angling.

CORIDON : And then mine shall be the praise of a countryman's life ; what will the rest sing of ?

PETER : I will promise you, I will sing another song in praise of angling to-morrow night ; for we will not part till then, but fish to-morrow, and sup together, and the next day every man leave fishing, and fall to his business.

VIATOR : 'Tis a match ; and I will provide you a song or a catch against then too, that shall give some addition of mirth to the company ; for we will be merry.

PISCATOR : 'Tis a match, my masters ; let's e'en say grace, and turn to the fire, drink the other cup to wet our whistles, and so sing away all sad thoughts. Come on, my masters, who begins ? I think it best to draw cuts and avoid contention.

PETER : It is a match. Look the shortest cut falls to Coridon.

CORIDON : Well, then, I will begin : for I hate contention. (CORIDON *sings*.) . . .

PISCATOR : Well sung, Coridon, this song was sung with metal, it was choicely fitted to the occasion ; I shall love you for it as long as I know you : I would you were a brother of the Angle, for a companion that is cheerful and free from swearing and scurrilous discourse, is worth gold. I'll love such mirth as does not make friends ashamed to look upon one another next morning : nor men (that cannot well bear it) to repent the money they spend when they be warmed with drink : and take this for a rule, you may pick out such times and such companions, that you may make yourselves merrier for a little than a great deal of money : for then it is the company and not the charge that makes the feast : and such a companion you prove, I thank you for it. But I will not compliment you out of the debt that I owe you, and therefore I will begin my song, and wish it may be as well liked. (PISCATOR *sings*.) . . .

CORIDON : Well sung, brother, you have paid your debt in good coin. We anglers are all beholden to the good man that made this song : come, hostess, give us more ale, and let's drink to him. And now let's every one go to bed, that we may rise early ; but first let's pay our reckoning, for I will have nothing to hinder me in the morning, for I will prevent the sun-rising.

PETER : A match. Come, Coridon, you are to be my bed-fellow. I know, brother, you and your scholar will lie to-gether. But where shall we meet to-morrow night ? for my friend Coridon and I will go up the water towards Ware.

PISCATOR : And my scholar and I will go down towards Waltham.

CORIDON : Then let's meet here, for here are fresh sheets that smell of lavender ; and I am sure we cannot expect better meat or better usage.

PETER : 'Tis a match. Goodnight to everybody !

PISCATOR : And so say I.

VIATOR : And so say I.

IZAAK WALTON (from *The Compleat Angler*)

1668. *June* 11 (*Thursday*). By a happy mistake, and
that looked like an adventure, we were carried out of our
way to a town where we would lye, since we could not go
so far as we would. And there with great difficulty come
about ten at night to a little inn, where we were fain to go
into a room where a pedlar was in bed, and made him rise ;
and there wife and I lay, and in a truckle-bed Betty
Turner and Willett.[1] But good beds, and the master of the
house a sober, understanding man, and I had good discourse with him about this country's matters, as wool, and
corne, and other things. By and by to bed, glad of this
mistake, because, it seems, had we gone on as we intended,
we could not have passed with our coach, and must have
lain on the Plain all night.

12*th* (*Friday*). Up, finding our beds good, but lousy ;
which made us merry.

Diary of Samuel Pepys

ROBINSON MAKES THE BEST OF IT

What to do with myself at night I knew not, nor indeed
where to rest, for I was afraid to lie down on the ground,
not knowing but some wild beast might devour me,
though, as I afterwards found, there was really no need
for those fears.

However, as well as I could, I barricaded myself round
with the chest and boards that I had brought on shore, and
made a kind of hut for that night's lodging. As for food,

---

[1] These were the daughter of Pepys' " Cozen Turner " and Mrs. Pepys' maid.
The truckle or trundle bed was a low bedstead on wheels, which was run under
the principal bed when not in use. A. S.

I yet saw not which way to supply myself, except that I had seen two or three creatures like hares run out of the wood where I shot the fowl.

I now began to consider that I might yet get a great many things out of the ship which would be useful to me, and particularly some of the rigging and sails, and such other things as might come to land; and I resolved to make another voyage on board the vessel, if possible . . .

Having got my second cargo on shore—though I was fain to open the barrels of powder, and bring them by parcels, for they were too heavy, being large casks—I went to work to make me a little tent with the sail and some poles which I cut for that purpose : and into this tent I brought everything that I knew would spoil either with rain or sun; and I piled all the empty chests and casks up in a circle round the tent, to fortify it from any sudden attempt, either from man or beast.

When I had done this, I blocked up the door of the tent with some boards within, and an empty chest set up on end without; and spreading one of the beds upon the ground, laying my two pistols just at my head, and my gun at length by me, I went to bed for the first time, and slept very quietly all night.

DEFOE (from *Robinson Crusoe*)

LIBERTY HALL

Scene 1. Room in an Alehouse

(MARLOW, HASTINGS, TONY LUMPKIN AND LANDLORD.)

MARLOW : This house promises but a poor reception; though perhaps the landlord can accommodate us.

LANDLORD : Alack, master ! we have but one spare bed in the whole house.

TONY : And, to my knowledge, that's taken up by three lodgers already. (*After a pause, in which the rest seem disconcerted.*) I have it. Don't you think, Stingo, our landlady could accommodate the gentlemen by the fireside, with—three chairs and a bolster ?

HASTINGS : I hate sleeping by the fireside.

MARLOW : And I detest your three chairs and a bolster.

TONY : You do, do you ?—then, let me see—what if you go on a mile farther, to the Buck's Head ; the Old Buck's Head, on the hill, one of the best inns in the whole country ?

HASTINGS : O ho ! so we have escaped an adventure for this night, however.

LANDLORD (*apart to* TONY) : Sure, you ben't sending them to your father's as an inn, be you ?

TONY : Mum, you fool you. Let them find that out. (*To them*) You have only to keep on straight forward, till you come to a large old house by the road side. You'll see a pair of large horns over the door. That's the sign. Drive up the yard and call stoutly about you.

HASTINGS : Sir, we are obliged to you. The servants can't miss the way ?

TONY : No, no ; but I tell you, though, the landlord is rich, and going to leave off business ; so he wants to be thought a gentleman, saving your presence, he ! he ! He'll be for giving you his company ; and, ecod ! if you mind him, he'll persuade you that his mother was an alderman, and his aunt a justice of peace.

LANDLORD : A troublesome old blade, to be sure ; but he keeps as good wines and beds as any man in the whole country.

MARLOW : Well, if he supplies us with these, we shall want no further connection. We are to turn to the right did you say ?

TONY : No, no ; straight forward, I'll just step myself, and show you a piece of the way. (*To the* LANDLORD Mum !

Scene 2. *Mr. Hardcastle's House*

(*Enter* HARDCASTLE.)

HARDCASTLE : Gentlemen, once more you are heartily welcome. Which is Mr. Marlow ? Sir, you are heartily welcome. It's not my way, you see, to receive my friends with my back to the fire. I like to give them a hearty reception in the old style at my gate. I like to see their horses and trunks taken care of.

MARLOW (*aside*) : He has got our names from the servants already. (*To him*) We approve your caution and hospitality, sir. (*To* HASTINGS) I have been thinking, George, of changing our travelling dresses in the morning. I am grown confoundedly ashamed of mine.

HARDCASTLE : I beg, Mr. Marlow, you'll use no ceremony in this house.

HASTINGS : I fancy, Charles, you're right : the first blow is half the battle. I intend opening the campaign with the white and gold.

HARDCASTLE : Mr. Marlow—Mr. Hastings—gentlemen —pray, be under no restraint in this house. This is Liberty Hall, gentlemen. You may do just as you please here.

MARLOW : Yet, George, if we open the campaign too fiercely at first, we may want ammunition before it is over. I think to reserve the embroidery to secure a retreat.

HARDCASTLE : Your talking of a retreat, Mr. Marlow, puts me in mind of the Duke of Marlborough, when we went to besiege Denain. He first summoned the garrison——

MARLOW : Don't you think the *ventre d'or* waistcoat will do with the plain brown ?

HARDCASTLE : He first summoned the garrison, which might consist of about five thousand men——

HASTINGS : I think not : brown and yellow mix but very poorly.

HARDCASTLE : I say, gentlemen, as I was telling you, he summoned the garrison, which might consist of about five thousand men——

MARLOW : The girls like finery.

HARDCASTLE : Which might consist of about five thousand men, well appointed with stores, ammunition, and other implements of war. Now, says the Duke of Marlborough to George Brooks, that stood next to him—you must have heard of George Brooks—I'll pawn my dukedom, says he, but I take that garrison without spilling a drop of blood. So——

MARLOW : What, my good friend, if you gave us a glass of punch in the meantime, it would help us to carry on the siege with vigour.

HARDCASTLE : Punch, sir ! (*Aside*) This is the most unaccountable kind of modesty I ever met with.

MARLOW : Yes, sir, punch. A glass of warm punch, after our journey, will be comfortable. This is Liberty Hall, you know.

GOLDSMITH (from *She Stoops to Conquer*)

THE DIFFICULTY OF GETTING UP

I talked of the difficulty of rising in the morning. Dr. Johnson told me " that the learned Mrs. Carter, at that period when she was eager in study, did not awake as early as she wished, and she therefore had a contrivance, that, at a certain hour, her chamber-light should burn a string to which a heavy weight was suspended, which then fell with a strong sudden noise : this roused her from sleep, and then she had no difficulty in getting up." But I said *that* was my difficulty ; and wished there could be some medicine invented which would make one rise without pain, which I never did, unless after lying in bed a very long time. Perhaps there may be something in the stores of Nature which could do this. I have thought of a pully to raise me gradually ; but that would give me pain, as it would counteract my internal inclination. I would have something that can dissipate the *vis inertiæ*, and give elasticity to the muscles. As I imagine that the human body may be put, by the operation of other substances, into any state in which it has ever been ; and as I have experienced a state in which rising from bed was not disagreeable, but easy, nay, sometimes agreeable ; I suppose that this state may be produced, if we knew by what. We can heat the body, we can cool it ; we can give it tension or relaxation ; and surely it is possible to bring it into a state in which rising from bed will not be a pain.

BOSWELL (from *Life of Samuel Johnson*)

A little light food at intervals during the night is said to be a cure for insomnia. A small table by the bedside would accommodate a dish of the following

HERBACEOUS TREAT

To make this condiment, your poet begs
The pounded yellow of two hard-boil'd eggs ;
Two boil'd potatoes, pass'd through kitchen sieve,
Smoothness and softness to the salad give ;
Let onion atoms lurk within the bowl,
And, half-suspected, animate the whole.
Of mordant mustard add a single spoon,
Distrust the condiment that bites so soon ;
But deem it not, thou man of herbs, a fault,
To add a double quantity of salt ;
Four times the spoon with oil from Lucca brown,
And twice with vinegar procured from town ;
And, lastly, o'er the flavoured compound toss
A magic soupçon of anchovy sauce.
Oh, green and glorious ! Oh, herbaceous treat !
'Twould tempt the dying anchorite to eat :
Back to the world he'd turn his fleeting soul,
And plunge his fingers in the salad-bowl !
Serenely full, the epicure would say,
Fate cannot harm me, I have dined to-day

SYDNEY SMITH

A FERRYMAN'S HUT

Loch Katrine, August 27, 1803

We caroused our cups of coffee, laughing like children at the strange atmosphere in which we were : the smoke came in gusts, and spread along the walls and above our heads in the chimney, where the hens were roosting like light clouds in the sky. We laughed and laughed again, in spite of the smarting of our eyes, yet had a quieter pleasure in observing the beauty of the beams and rafters gleaming between the clouds of smoke. They had been crusted over and varnished by many winters, till, where the firelight fell upon them, they were as glossy as black rocks on a sunny day cased in ice. When we had eaten our supper we sate about half an hour, and I think I had never felt so deeply the blessing of a hospitable welcome and a warm fire. When I went to bed, the mistress, desiring me to " go ben," attended me with a candle, and assured me that the bed was dry, though not " sic as I had been used to." . . .

The walls of the whole house were of stone unplastered. It consisted of three apartments—the cow-house at one end, the kitchen or house in the middle, and the spence at the other end. The rooms were divided, not up to the rigging, but only to the beginning of the roof, so that there was a free passage for light and smoke from one end of the house to the other.

I went to bed some time before the family. The door was shut between us, and they had a bright fire, which I could not see ; but the light it sent up among the varnished rafters and beams, which crossed each other in almost as intricate and fantastic a manner as I have seen the under-boughs of a large beech-tree withered by the depth of the shade above, produced the most beautiful effect that can be conceived. It was like what I should suppose an under-ground cave or temple to be, with a dripping or moist roof, and the moonlight entering in upon it by some means or other, and yet the colours were more like melted gems. I lay looking up till the light of the fire faded away, and the man and his wife and child had crept into their bed at the other end of the room. I did not sleep much, but passed a comfortable night, for my bed, though hard, was warm and clean : the unusualness of my situation prevented me from sleeping. I could hear the waves beat against the shore of the lake ; a little " syke " close to the door made a much louder noise ; and when I sate up in my bed I could see the lake through an open window-place at the bed's head. Add to this, it rained all night.

DOROTHY WORDSWORTH
(from Recollections of a Tour made in Scotland)

TWO FALLACIES

1. *That we should rise with the lark*

At what precise minute that little airy musician doffs his night gear, and prepares to tune up his unseasonable matins, we are not naturalists enough to determine. But for a mere human gentleman—that has no orchestra business to call him from his warm bed to such preposterous exercises—we take ten, or half after ten (eleven, of course, during this Christmas solstice), to be the very earliest hour at which he can begin to think of abandoning his pillow. To think of it, we say ; for to do it in earnest, requires another half hour's good consideration. Not but there are pretty sun-risings, as we are told, and such like gawds, abroad in the world, in summer time especially, some hours before what we have assigned ; which a gentleman may see, as they say, only for getting up. But, having been tempted once or twice, in earlier life, to assist at those ceremonies, we confess our curiosity abated. We are no longer ambitious of being the sun's courtiers, to attend at his morning levees. We hold the good hours of the dawn too sacred to waste them upon such observances ; which have in them, besides, something Pagan and Persic. To say truth, we never anticipated our usual hour, or got up with the sun (as 'tis called), to go a journey or upon a foolish whole day's pleasuring, but we suffered for it all the long hours after in listlessness and headaches ; Nature herself sufficiently declaring her sense of our presumption, in aspiring to regulate our frail waking courses by the measures of that celestial and sleepless traveller. We deny not that there is something sprightly and vigorous, at the outset especially, in these break-of-day excursions. It is flattering to get the start of a lazy world ; to conquer death by proxy in his image. But the seeds of sleep and mortality are in us ; and we pay usually in strange qualms, before night falls, the penalty of the unnatural inversion. Therefore, while the busy part of mankind are fast huddling on their clothes, are already up and about their occupations, content to have swallowed their sleep by wholesale ; we chose to linger a-bed, and digest our dreams. It is the very time to re-combine the wandering images, which night in a confused mass presented ; to snatch them from forgetfulness ; to shape, and mould them. Some people have no good of their dreams. Like fast feeders, they gulp them too grossly, to taste them curiously. We love to chew the cud of a fore-gone vision : to collect the scattered rays of a brighter phantasm, or act over again, with firmer nerves, the sadder nocturnal tragedies ; to drag into daylight a struggling and half-vanishing nightmare ; to handle and examine the terrors, or the airy solaces. We have too much respect for these spiritual communications, to let them go so lightly. We are not so stupid, or so careless, as that Imperial forgetter of his dreams, that we should need a seer to remind us of the form of them. They seem to us to have as much significance as our waking concerns ; or rather to import us more nearly as more nearly we approach by years to the shadowy world whither we are hastening. We have shaken hands with the world's business ; we have done with it ; we have discharged ourself of it. Why should we get up ? we have neither suit to solicit nor affairs to manage. The drama has shut in upon us at the fourth act. We have nothing here to expect, but in a short time a sick bed, and a dismissal. We delight to anticipate death by such shadows as night affords. We are already half acquainted with ghosts. We were never much in the world. Disappointment early struck a dark veil between us and its dazzling illusions. Our spirits showed grey before our hairs. The mighty changes of the world already appear as but the vain stuff out of which dramas are composed. We have asked no more of life than what the mimic images in play-houses present us with. Even those types have waxed fainter. Our clock appears to have struck. We are SUPERANNUATED. In this dearth of mundane satisfaction, we contract politic alliances with shadows. It is good to have friends at court. The abstracted media of dreams seem no ill introduction to that spiritual presence, upon which in no long time we expect to be thrown. We are trying to know a little of the usages of that colony ; to learn the language, and the faces we shall meet with there, that we may be the less awkward at our first coming among them. We willingly call a phantom our fellow, as knowing we shall soon be of their dark companionship. Therefore, we cherish dreams. We try to spell in them the alphabet of the invisible world; and think we know already, how it shall be with us. Those uncouth shapes, which, while we clung to flesh and blood, affrighted us, have become familiar. We feel attenuated into their meagre essences, and have given the hand of half-way approach to incorporeal being. We once thought life to be something; but it has unaccountably fallen from us before its time. Therefore we choose to dally with visions. The sun has no purposes of ours to light us to. Why should we get up?

2. *That we should lie down with the lamb*

We could never quite understand the philosophy of this arrangement, or the wisdom of our ancestors in sending us for instructions to these woolly bedfellows. A sheep, when it is dark, has nothing to do but to shut his silly eyes, and sleep if he can. Man found out long sixes.— Hail candle-light! without disparagement to sun or moon, the kindliest luminary of the three—if we may not rather style thee their radiant deputy, mild viceroy of the moon! —We love to read, talk, sit silent, eat, drink, sleep, by candle-light. They are everybody's sun and moon. This is our peculiar and household planet. Wanting it, what savage unsocial nights must our ancestors have spent, wintering in caves and unillumined fastnesses! They must have lain about and grumbled at one another in the dark. What repartees could have passed, when you must have felt about for a smile, and handled a neighbour's cheek to be sure that he understood it? This accounts for the seriousness of the elder poetry. It has a sombre cast (try Hesiod or Ossian) derived from the tradition of those unlantern'd nights. Jokes came in with candles. We wonder how they saw to pick up a pin, if they had any. How did they sup? what a melange of chance carving they must have made of it!—here one had got a leg of a goat, when he wanted a horse's shoulder—there another had dipt his scooped palm in a kid-skin of wild honey, when he meditated right mare's milk. There is neither good eating nor drinking in fresco. Who, even in these civilised times, has never experienced this, when at some economic table he has commenced dining after dusk, and waited for the flavour till the lights came? The senses absolutely give and take reciprocally. Can you tell pork from veal in the dark? or distinguish Sherris from pure Malaga? Take away the candle from the smoking man; by the glimmering of the left ashes, he knows that he is still smoking, but he knows it only by an inference; till the restored light, coming in aid of the olfactories, reveals to both senses the full aroma. Then how he redoubles his puffs! how he burnishes!—There is absolutely no such thing as reading, but by a candle. We have tried the affectation of a book at noon-day in gardens, and in sultry arbours; but it was labour thrown away. Those gay motes in the beam come about you, hovering and teazing, like so many coquets, that will have you all to their self, and are jealous of your abstractions. By the midnight taper, the writer digests his meditations. By the same light we must approach to their perusal, if we would catch the flame, the odour. It is a mockery, all that is reported of the influential Phoebus. No true poem ever owed its birth to the sun's light. They are abstracted works:

" *Things that were born, when none but the still night*
And his dumb candle, saw his pinching throes."

165

Marry, daylight—daylight might furnish the images, the crude material; but for the fine shapings, the true turning and filing (as mine author hath it) they must be content to hold their inspiration of the candle. The mild internal light that reveals them, like fires on the domestic hearth, goes out in the sunshine. Night and silence call out the starry fancies. Milton's Morning Hymn on Paradise, we would hold a good wager, was penned at midnight; and Taylor's richer description of a sunrise smells decidedly of the taper. Even ourself, in these our humbler lucubrations, tune our best measured cadences (Prose has her cadences) not unfrequently to the charm of the drowsier watchman, "blessing the doors"; or the wild sweep of winds at midnight. Even now a loftier speculation than we have yet attempted courts our endeavours. We would indite something about the Solar System.—*Betty, bring the candles!*

CHARLES LAMB (from *Popular Fallacies*)

A TRAVELLER IN THE EAST

I. *My First Night*

We had ridden on for some two or three hours—the stir and bustle of our commencing journey had ceased—the liveliness of our little troop had worn off with the declining day, and the night closed in as we entered the great Servian forest. Through this our road was to last for more than a hundred miles. Endless and endless now on either side the tall oaks closed in their ranks, and stood gloomily lowering over us, as grim as an army of giants with a thousand years' pay in arrear. One strived, with listening ear, to catch some tidings of that forest-world within—some stirring of beasts, some night-bird's scream ; but all was quite hushed, except the voice of the cicadas that peopled every bough, and filled the depths of the forest through and through with one same hum everlasting—more stilling than very silence. . .

Long before midnight we reached the hamlet in which we were to rest for the night ; it was made up of about a dozen clay huts standing upon a small tract of ground hardly won from the forest. . . . . The burdens unstrapped from the pack-saddles very quickly furnished our den : a couple of quilts spread upon the floor with a carpet-bag at the head of each, became capital sofas. . . . Soon there was tea before us, with all its welcome fragrance ; and as we reclined on the floor we found that a portmanteau was just the right height for a table. The duty of candlesticks was ably performed by a couple of intelligent natives : the rest of the villagers stood by the open doorway at the lower end of the room, and watched our banquet with grave and devout attention.

The first night of your first campaign (though you be but a mere peaceful campaigner) is a glorious time in your life. It is so sweet to find one's self free from the stale civilisation of Europe ! Oh, my dear ally, when first you spread your carpet in the midst of these Eastern scenes, do think for a moment of those your fellow-creatures that dwell in squares, and streets, and even (for such is the fate of many !) in actual country-houses ; think of the people that are " presenting their compliments," and " request-ing the honour," and " much regretting "—of those that are pinioned at dinner-tables, or stuck up in ball-rooms, or cruelly planted in pews—ay, think of these, and so remembering how many poor devils are living in a state of utter respectability, you will glory the more in your own delightful escape.

But, with all its charms, a mud floor (like a mercenary match) does certainly promote early rising. Long before daybreak we were up and had breakfasted ; afterwards there was nearly a whole tedious hour to endure, whilst the horses were laden by torch-light ; but this had an end, and then our day's journey began.

2. *My First Bivouac*

We heard at a little distance the brawling of a rivulet, and on the banks of this it was determined to establish our bivouac ; we soon found the stream, and following its course for a few yards came to a spot which was thought to be fit for our purpose. . . .

My servants busied themselves in unpacking the baggage, as though we had arrived at an hotel—Shereef and his helpers unsaddled their cattle. We had left Tiberias without the slightest idea that we were to make our way to Jerusalem along the desolate side of the Jordan, and my servants (generally provident in those matters) had brought with them only, I think, some unleavened bread, and a rocky fragment of goat's-milk cheese. These treasures were produced. Tea, and the contrivances for making it, were always a standing part of my baggage. My men gathered in circle round the fire. The Nazarene was in a false position, from having misled us so strangely, and he would have shrunk back, poor devil, into the cold and outer darkness, but I made him draw near, and share the luxuries of the night. My quilt and my pelisse were spread, and the rest of my people had all their *capotes* or pelisses, or robes of some sort, which furnished their couches. The men gathered in circle, some kneeling, some sitting, some lying reclined around our common hearth, Sometimes on one, sometimes on another, the flickering light would glare more fiercely. Sometimes it was the good Shereef that seemed the foremost as he sat with venerable beard, the image of manly piety—unknowing of all geography, unknowing where he was, or whither he might go, but trusting in the goodness of God, and the clenching power of fate, and the good star of the Englishman. Sometimes, like marble, the classic face of the Greek Mysseri would catch the sudden light, and then again, by turns, the ever perturbed Dthemetri, with his odd Chinaman's eye, and bristling, terrier-like moustache, shone forth illustrious.

I always liked the men who attended me on these Eastern travels, for they were all of them brave, cheery-hearted fellows, and, although their following my career brought upon them a pretty large share of those toils and hardships which are so much more amusing to gentlemen than to servants, yet not one of them ever uttered or hinted a syllable of complaint, or even affected to put on an air of resignation. I always liked them, but never perhaps so much as when they were thus grouped together under the light of the bivouac fire. I felt towards them as my comrades, rather than as my servants, and took delight in breaking bread with them, and merrily passing the cup. . . .

At length we thought it well to seek for sleep. Our plans were laid for keeping up a good watch through the night. My quilt, and my pelisse, and my cloak were spread out so that I might lie spokewise, with my feet towards the central fire. I wrapped my limbs daintily round, and gave myself orders to sleep like a veteran soldier. But my attempt to sleep upon the earth that God gave me was more new and strange than I had fancied it. I had grown used to the scene which was before me whilst I was sitting or reclining by the side of the fire; but now that I laid myself down at full length, it was the deep, black mystery of the heavens that hung over my eyes—not an earthly thing in the way from my own very forehead right up to the end of all space. I grew proud of my boundless bedchamber. I might have " found sermons " in all this greatness (if I had I should surely have slept), but such was not then my way. If this cherished Self of mine had built the universe, I should have dwelt with delight on " the wonders of creation." As it was, I felt rather the vainglory of my promotion, from out of mere rooms and houses, into the midst of that grand, dark, infinite palace.

And then, too, my head, far from the fire, was in cold latitudes, and it seemed to me strange that I should be lying so still and passive, whilst the sharp night-breeze walked free over my cheek, and the cold damp clung to my hair, as though my face grew in the earth, and must bear with the footsteps of the wind and the falling of the dew, as meekly as the grass of the field. And so, when, from time to time, the watch quietly and gently kept up the languishing fire, he seldom, I think, was unseen to my restless eyes. Yet, at last, when they called me, and said that the morn would soon be dawning, I rose from a state of half-oblivion, not much unlike to sleep, though sharply qualified by a sort of vegetable's consciousness of having been growing still colder and colder for many and many an hour.

A. W. KINGLAKE (from *Eothen*)

Tom had never been in London, and would have liked to have stopped at the Belle Savage, where they had been put down by the Star, just at dusk, that he might have gone roving about those endless, mysterious, gas-lit streets, which, with their glare and hum and moving crowds excited him so that he couldn't talk even. But as soon as he found that the Peacock arrangement would get him to Rugby by twelve o'clock in the day, whereas otherwise he wouldn't be there till the evening, all other plans melted away; his one absorbing aim being to become a public schoolboy as fast as possible, and six hours sooner or later seeming to him of the most alarming importance.

Tom and his father had alighted at the Peacock, at about seven in the evening, and having heard with unfeigned joy the paternal order at the bar of steaks and oyster-sauce for supper in half-an-hour, and seen his father seated cosily by the bright fire in the coffee-room, with the paper in his hand, Tom had run out to see about him, had wondered at all the vehicles passing and repassing, and had fraternised with the boots and ostler, from whom he ascertained that the Tally-ho was a tip-top goer, ten miles an hour including stoppages, and so punctual, that all the road set their clocks by her.

Then being summoned to supper, he had regaled himself in one of the bright little boxes of the Peacock coffee-room, on the beef-steak and unlimited oyster-sauce, and brown stout (tasted then for the first time—a day to be marked for ever by Tom with a white stone); had at first attended to the excellent advice which his father was bestowing on him from over his glass of steaming brandy-and-water, and then begun nodding, from the united effects of the stout, the fire, and the lecture. Till the Squire observing Tom's state, and remembering that it was nearly nine o'clock, and that the Tally-ho left at three, sent the little fellow off to the chambermaid, with a shake of the hand (Tom having stipulated in the morning before starting, that kissing should now cease between them) and a few parting words. Tom was carried off by the chambermaid in a brown study, from which he was roused in a clean little attic, by that buxom person calling him a little darling, and kissing him as she left the room ; which indignity he was too much surprised to resent.

THOMAS HUGHES (*Tom Brown's School Days*)

THE SARACEN'S HEAD

" I say," remonstrated Bob Sawyer, looking in at the coach window, as they pulled up before the door of the Saracen's Head, Towcester, " this won't do, you know."

" Bless me," said Mr. Pickwick, just awakening from a nap, " I'm afraid you're wet."

" Oh, you are, are you ? " returned Bob. " Yes, I am a little that way. Uncomfortably damp, perhaps."

Bob did look dampish, inasmuch as the rain was streaming from his neck, elbows, cuffs, skirts and knees ; and his whole apparel shone so with the wet that it might have been mistaken for a full suit of prepared oilskin.

" I *am* rather wet," said Bob, giving himself a shake, and casting a little hydraulic shower around, like a New-foundland dog just emerged from the water.

" I think it's quite impossible to go on to-night," interposed Ben.

"Out of the question, sir," remarked Sam Weller, coming to assist in the conference; "it's a cruelty to animals, sir, to ask 'em to do it. There's beds here, sir," said Sam, addressing his master, "everything clean and comfortable. Wery good little dinner, sir, they can get ready in half an hour—pair of fowls, sir, and a weal cutlet; French beans, 'taturs, tart, and tidiness. You'd better stop vere you are, sir, if I might recommend. Take adwice, sir, as the doctor said."

The host of the Saracen's Head opportunely appeared at this moment, to confirm Mr. Weller's statement relative to the accommodation of the establishment, and to back his entreaties with a variety of dismal conjectures regarding the state of the roads, the doubt of fresh horses being to be had at the next stage, the dead certainty of its raining all night, the equally mortal certainty of its clearing up in the morning, and other topics of inducement familiar to innkeepers.

"Well," said Mr. Pickwick; "but I must send a letter to London by some conveyance, so that it may be delivered the very first thing in the morning, or I must go forward at all hazards."

The landlord smiled his delight. Nothing could be easier than for the gentleman to inclose a letter in a sheet of brown paper, and send it on, either by the mail or the night coach from Birmingham. If the gentleman were particularly anxious to have it left as soon as possible, he might write outside, "To be delivered immediately," which was sure to be attended to; or "pay the bearer half-a-crown extra for instant delivery," which was surer still.

"Very well," said Mr. Pickwick, "then we will stop here."

" Lights in the Sun, John; make up the fire; the gentlemen are wet!" cried the landlord. " This way, gentlemen; don't trouble yourselves about the postboy now, sir.
I'll send him to you when you ring for him, sir. Now,
John, the candles."

DICKENS (from Pickwick Papers)

DISTURBANCES AT HEILBRONN

We were in bed by ten, for we wanted to be up and
away on our tramp homeward with the dawn. I hung
fire, but Harris went to sleep at once. I hate a man who
goes to sleep at once; there is a sort of indefinable something about it which is not exactly an insult, and yet is an
insolence; and one which is hard to bear, too. I lay there
fretting over this injury, and trying to go to sleep; but the
harder I tried the wider awake I grew. I got to feeling
very lonely in the dark, with no company but an undigested
dinner. My mind got a start by-and-by, and began to
consider the beginning of every subject which has ever
been thought of; but it never went further than the
beginning: it was touch and go; it fled from topic to
topic with a frantic speed. At the end of an hour my head
was in a perfect whirl, and I was dead tired, fagged out.

The fatigue was so great that it presently began to make
some head against the nervous excitement; while imagining myself wide awake, I would really doze into momentary unconsciousnesses, and come suddenly out of
them with a physical jerk which nearly wrenched my
joints apart—the delusion of the instant being that I was
tumbling backwards over a precipice. After I had fallen
over eight or nine precipices and thus found out that

174

one half of my brain had been asleep eight or nine times without the wide-awake, hard-working other half suspecting it, the periodical unconsciousnesses began to extend their spell gradually over more of my brain-territory, and at last I sank into a drowse which grew deeper and deeper and was doubtless just on the very point of becoming a solid, blessed, dreamless stupor, when—what was that?

My dulled faculties dragged themselves partly back to life, and took a receptive attitude. Now out of an immense, a limitless distance, came a something which grew and grew, and approached, and presently was recognisable as a sound—it had rather seemed to be a feeling, before. This sound was a mile away, now—perhaps it was the murmur of a storm; and now it was nearer—not a quarter of a mile away; was it the muffled rasping and grinding of distant machinery? No, it came still nearer; was it the measured tramp of a marching troop? But it came nearer still, and still nearer—and at last it was right in the room: it was merely a mouse gnawing the woodwork. So I had held my breath all that time for such a trifle.

Well, what was done could not be helped; I would go to sleep at once and make up the lost time. That was a thoughtless thought. Without intending it—hardly knowing it—I fell to listening intently to that sound, and even unconsciously counting the strokes of the mouse's nutmeg-grater. Presently I was deriving exquisite suffering from this employment, yet maybe I could have endured it if the mouse had attended steadily to his work; but he did not do that; he stopped every now and then, and I suffered more while waiting and listening for him to begin again than I did while he was gnawing. Along at first I was mentally offering a reward of five—six—seven—ten dollars for that mouse; but towards the last I was offering rewards which were entirely beyond my means. I close-reefed my ears—that is to say, I bent the flaps of them down, and furled them into five or six folds, and pressed them against the hearing-orifice—but it did no good: the faculty was so sharpened by nervous excitement that it was become a microphone, and could hear through the overlays without trouble.

My anger grew to a frenzy. I finally did what all persons before me have done, clear back to Adam—resolved to throw something. I reached down and got my walking-shoes, then sat up in bed and listened, in order to exactly locate the noise. But I couldn't do it; it was as unlocatable as a cricket's noise; and where one thinks that that is, is always the very place where it isn't. So I presently hurled a shoe at random, and with a vicious vigour. It struck the wall over Harris's head and fell down on him; I had not imagined I could throw so far. It woke Harris, and I was glad of it until I found he was not angry; then I was sorry. He soon went to sleep again, which pleased me; but straightway the mouse began again, which roused my temper once more. I did not want to wake Harris a second time, but the gnawing continued until I was compelled to throw the other shoe. This time I broke a mirror—there were two in the room—I got the largest one of course. Harris woke again, but did not complain, and I was sorrier than ever. I resolved that I would suffer all possible torture before I would disturb him a third time.

The mouse eventually retired, and by-and-by I was sinking to sleep, when a clock began to strike; I counted till it was done, and was about to drowse again when another clock began; I counted; then the two great Rathhaus clock angels began to send forth soft, rich, melodious blasts from their long trumpets. I had never heard anything that was so lovely, or weird, or mysterious —but when they got to blowing the quarter-hours, they seemed to me to be overdoing the thing.

MARK TWAIN (from A Tramp Abroad)

THE ENGLISH INN

1. *The Open Arms*

A night in a good inn gives repose a quality of stimulus. Sleep and food have here a flavour that is absent from sleep and food at a friend's house. The inn waits at the end of the journey as certainly as your friend's house ; yet its shelter and food come always with an agreeable sensation of accident and surprise. Too, you have at your inn all that your friend can give you, with many more conveniences and a wider range of entertainment ; and with all this you are yet at the full centre of fluid life. In your friend's house you are shut away, but in the inn you are a looker-on at goings and comings ; you are in contact with the present and you touch hands with the wraiths of the past and the substantial mementoes of their days ; and from your seat in the lounge you view the world as through a loophole of retreat. I begrudge my sixpence or shilling for the inspection of the mansions of the great, with their Keep Off the Grass and Please Do Not Touch ; I consider five pounds a trifle for the privilege of spending a night at the George of Glastonbury, the Feathers of Ludlow, the Lygon Arms of Broadway, or the Spread Eagle of Thame, where I am free to look and touch, and to walk unhindered up lordly staircases and to command a retinue of servitors. The ordinary Englishman's home is not in any sense— and never was—his castle. An officer or bailiff with the proper warrant may enter it when he chooses. But the Englishman's inn—say, the Angel, at Grantham, or the King Arthur, at Tintagel—is a castle, and every sojourner is its lord. He may feel its traditions in his blood as certainly as the children of a great house feel the traditions of their territory.

Your old inn is a many-pointed star, at each point touching great event or pleasing anecdote. A single inn may evoke memories of Izaak Walton, Charles I, Walter Scott, Drunken Barnaby, Bolingbroke, George Borrow, Jonathan Swift; and all these memories and traditions are yours. Isn't it worth five pounds to sit down to dinner with that company, or to trip over that same unseen stair in the dark passages that sent Celia Fiennes to her hands and knees? Or to use that room at the Angel, Grantham, where Richard signed Buckingham's death-warrant in 1483; or sleep in that oaken four-poster at the Saracen's Head, Southwell, where Charles slept his last night of freedom before surrendering to the Scotch; or to sleep in the rooms where slept those shadowy but urgently-living creatures of our novelists? . . To get the full savour of an old inn you should come to it at night, and best of all a winter night, or twilight, when the mists are rising and the soul is low, and a log fire and a dinner seem to be the twin stars of human aspiration. All of us know those moments, and that is why inns were made—to stand upon the pilgrim's way with an understanding smile for the pilgrim's weakness. They are a sign to us to shed austerity and vigilance, and to meet and mingle with our fellows; to turn from our various occasions, lofty or low, and to

ease our common needs and common anxieties in kindly
communion.

THOMAS BURKE (from *The Book of the Inn*)

2. *The Inn of the Future*

The more general means of transit will be the air, and
there will be special air hotels. As distance will be a mere
matter of minutes, they will occur only at wide intervals
in such places as popular taste may dictate. They will be
large and modern. The inn has adapted itself to many
changes, but it will not be able to adapt itself to this. As
soon as the air becomes everybody's road, those inns that
happen to be in the selected spots will be able to do
nothing but pull down and rebuild in accordance with the
new idea. Those that are outside the air-track will have to
close, and possibly become, as many did in the railway-
age, private houses . . .

And so, farewell the inn. There may be some who will
regret its passing, but life is a series of adjustments, of
getting used to what is, while we are still regretting what
was ; and before we know where we are we shall be
wondering how we ever put up with its easy, intimate
homeliness. We shall congratulate ourselves on having
escaped out of the Dark Ages. The old will tell tales of
having cans of hot water brought to their bedrooms.
They will tell of going four days without a bath, despite
thirty desperate dashes to the bath-room. They will
tell how, if you wanted a meal, you had to take it within
a given two hours fixed by the inn, or go without. They
will tell of the standardised lunch. They will tell of the
game of Bedroom Bell, played between guest and servants, the game being to see who gave way first, the

Ringer or the Rung; a game that guests seldom won.
They will tell of the desiccated drawing-rooms for Ladies
Only. And the young will sit and wonder why the old
fools were so spineless and so rooted in custom as to
accept these things.

THOMAS BURKE (from *The English Inn*)

NIGHT CAPS

*If your Landlord does not know his business, you can
teach him the following method of making*

INN KEEPERS' PUNCH

Dissolve about seven ounces of lump sugar in one pint
of boiling water, add forty grains of citric acid, seven or
eight drops of essence of lemon, and (when well mixed)
half of a pint of rum, a quarter of a pint of brandy, and
a glass of sherry.

*If you are a Prohibitionist, you may like to know
about a cold weather temperance drink with a kick in it
– not sufficient to throw you off your balance. It is
called*

STINGER

Its ingredients are :—2 lbs. Loaf Sugar, $\frac{1}{2}$ oz. Essence
of Cayenne, $\frac{1}{2}$ oz. Essence of Ginger, $\frac{1}{2}$ oz. Tartaric Acid,
3 Lemons—rind and juice. Peel the lemons and boil the
rind for ten minutes in half a pint of water. Strain and add
the rest of the ingredients with two quarts of boiling

water. Stir until all is dissolved. This makes about four
bottles of concentrated essence to be taken in the proportion of about two tablespoonfuls to a tumbler of hot
water.

OXFORD NIGHT CAPS

IN(N)S AND OUTS OF THE LAW

(By a Solicitor)

Assuming you are a traveller, an innkeeper is bound
to receive you at any hour of day or night if he has a
vacant bedroom, and you arrive "in proper condition"
and are able and willing to pay a reasonable sum for your
accommodation. If all the bedrooms are occupied, it will
not do to say you don't object to sleep in the coffee-room ;
you must go away. You can properly be denied the use
of a vacant bedroom if you are a chimney sweep in your
business costume, if you are drunk, or if you bring a large
dog and refuse to be parted from him.

An innkeeper must take good care of his guests' person
and property and must indemnify his guest for injury
to the person or theft of goods if he or his servants have
been careless in the matter. If you are beaten by another
guest, that is your own affair ; and if you hang your watch
on the stairs or decorate with your jewels the dressing-
table of an unlocked bedroom, your landlord will not be
responsible for such eccentricities. The rights of the inn
are attached to your sacred office of " traveller." If you
stay long enough to abandon this character, the landlord
can turn you out.

It has been decided that a lady in " rational " dress has no claim against an innkeeper who refuses to serve her in the coffee-room, provided he offers to serve her in the bar parlour (*R. v. Sprague*, 1899). It does not appear that a lady in " irrational " dress would have any stronger claim.

A NIGHT OUT IN THE DOLOMITES

(*A True Story*)

About 6 o'clock on a September evening we found ourselves in the wild and beautiful valley of Angoraz at the foot of the Passo di Miel, which leads up to the great Pala Plateau. We had seen no reason why two girls should not pass on foot in one day from the Val di San Lucano to San Martino in the Val di Castrozza ; but through a series of mishaps we had lost about three hours of precious daylight. The most difficult part of our journey was yet to come, and the sinking sun warned us that San Martino would be beyond our reach. We decided to spend the night at the Club Hut on the Rosetta Pass.

After a stiff climb up very steep and slippery slabs of rock we reached the top of the pass about 7 o'clock, and another quarter of an hour brought us to the signpost on the edge of the wide stone-covered Plateau. From this point our way was supposed to be sufficiently marked with painted stakes and heaps of stones (locally called " Stone Men.") We found these of little use, for the evening clouds were now down, hugging the peaks which should have been our landmarks and sweeping in bewildering drifts along the level of the Plateau. The whole region appeared to be a mass of limestone slabs and loose stones. To the south-west a momentary break in the clouds showed us the foot of a small glacier on our left front. From the bearings we had taken earlier in the day I felt sure that our way lay across the foot of that glacier. My companion thought differently ; and, as she had been there before and I had not, I gave in. We set off in the opposite direction, climbing and descending what seemed to be an interminable series of hillocks. The stakes and Stone Men seemed to lead us in all directions, and were more a hindrance than a help. After a while the clouds broke, and we saw a mountain straight ahead which we knew was not in our direction. We turned back. Daylight was now fading, but the Plateau began to slope downwards, which was encouraging. We found more waymarks, but soon lost them in the gathering darkness. Our frequent shouts received no reply.

We were now nearly dead beat, and agreed that we could not possibly go on. We clambered into a gully, where a tiny snow-drift promised a supply of water—a welcome discovery, as we had long since thrown out our water to lighten our packs. Thankful to get rid of my rucsac and sit down, I lost no time in getting out the spirit lamp, lighting it, boiling the kettle and making tea. It was now about 9 o'clock. We decided to spend the night in the gully, although it seemed very stony and unattractive. We tried to clear a space to lie on, but whenever we moved a sharp stone we found a sharper one underneath. Huddled close together for warmth and covered by our rain-coats, we spent a restless night, neither of us sleeping for more than a few minutes at a time. These snatches of sleep were, in my case, filled with vivid pictures of the day—our fruitless search for breakfast at

5.30 a.m., the late arrival of the carriage, the detour to Agordo to obtain breakfast and provisions, the broken bridge at Taibon, the long trudge in stifling heat up the San Lucano valley, the welcome shelter of the pine woods, the wooden bowls full of creamy milk at the alpine dairy, the little meadow bright with gentians and pansies, the steep rocks of the Pass, the all-embracing clouds and the wilderness of stones.

Even had our beds been more comfortable, we should have been wakened by the cold. We were wet as well as cold, for our clothing had been saturated by the damp mist. Before midnight a bitter wind came whistling through the gully. Winds were busy in the upper air also, making bright moments in the sky. At one time we watched the Great Bear being chased by swift clouds, at another we admired the lovely jewels of the Milky Way hanging above our heads. At frequent intervals we boiled our precious kettle. We did not hesitate to mix our drinks, but used everything we had—tea, chocolate, milk, brandy—and just as day was beginning to dawn, we had a final beverage comprising all that was left of my nice strong English peppermints. Thus we disposed of the last of our snow-water and the last of our methylated spirit. In the faint light, as we gathered our scattered belongings together, I saw the dry bottom of our little pool—it gave me a shock. It was lined with the dirtiest of dirt! Stiff and tired, though warmed and refreshed by our peppermint soup, we started off once more. My companion, climbing first out of the gully, cried " Cima Rosetta ! ", and joining her I saw straight ahead a jagged Dolomite peak rising above the mist. In front of us lay the path to the Hut, not a stone's throw away.

BERTHA SMITH

184

SEA-LODGINGS

I. A Leith Sloop (1776)

I made my way, by Linlithgow, to Edinburgh, and got on board a Leith sloop bound for Newcastle. We had no sooner got down the Firth of Forth to the open sea than we met a heavy swell, and presently encountered a violent gale which soon tore our sails to shivers, drove us far out of sight of land, and put our crew in a great bustle and dilemma. In this small vessel the crew and passengers amounted to twenty-six. For these latter there was no accommodation. The boat upon deck was full of the sick, covered by an old sail, and the rest were obliged to sit or lie down in any corner where they could find room. The first night was a sickly, suffocating one; and for three more nights and three days there was little or no amendment of our situation. On board this sloop there were only two beds that were not stowed with goods; and, from my wanting rest so long before I left Edinburgh, I crept into one of them as soon as I could, but found it so low that I could not lie on my side or easily turn over. So I could get no sleep; and, to mend the matter, I had not been long in this wretched bed till an infant was put in beside me, its mother being dismally sick in the boat upon deck; and the child fell exclusively into my charge. I nursed it as well as I could during the whole voyage; and I think, had I not done so, it must have died.

THOMAS BEWICK

II. An American Trader (1840)

(a) Roughing it off the Horn

The decks were covered with snow, and there was a constant driving of sleet. In fact, Cape Horn had set in with good earnest. In the midst of all this, and before it became dark, we had all the studding-sails to make up and stow away, and then to lay aloft and rig in all the booms fore and aft, and coil away the tacks, sheets, and halyards. This was pretty tough work for four or five hands, in the face of a gale which almost took us off the yards, and with ropes so stiff with ice that it was almost impossible to bend them. I was nearly half an hour out on the end of the fore yard, trying to coil away and stop down the top-mast studding-sail tack and lower halyards. It was after dark when we got through, and we were not a little pleased to hear four bells struck, which sent us below for two hours, and gave us each a pot of hot tea with our cold beef and bread, and, what was better yet, a suit of thick, dry clothing, fitted for the weather, in place of our thin clothes, which were wet through and now frozen stiff.

This sudden turn, for which we were so little prepared, was as unacceptable to me as to any of the rest ; for I had been troubled for several days with a slight tooth-ache, and this cold weather, and wetting and freezing were not the best things in the world for it.

When we went on deck at eight bells, it had stopped snowing, and there were a few stars out, but the clouds were still black, and it was blowing a steady gale. Just before midnight, I went aloft and sent down the mizen royal yard, and had the good luck to do it to the satisfaction of the mate, who said it was done " out of hand and shipshape." The next four hours below were but little relief to me, for I lay awake in my berth, the whole time, from the pain in my face, and heard every bell strike, and at four o'clock, turned out with the watch, feeling little spirit for the hard duties of the day. Bad weather and hard work at sea can be borne up against very well, if one only has spirit and health; but there is nothing brings a man down, at such a time, like bodily pain and want of sleep. There was, however, too much to do to allow time to think; for the gale of yesterday, and the heavy seas we met with a few days before, while we had yet ten degrees more southing to make, had convinced the captain that we had something before us which was not to be trifled with, and orders were given to send down the long top-gallant masts. It was an interesting sight to see our noble ship, dismantled of all her top-hamper of long tapering masts and yards, and boom pointed with spear-head, which ornamented her in port; and all that canvas, which a few days before had covered her like a cloud, from the truck to the water's edge, spreading far out beyond her hull on either side, now gone; and she, stripped, like a wrestler for the fight. It corresponded, too, with the desolate character of her situation;—alone, as she was, battling with storms, wind, and ice, at this extremity of the globe, and in almost constant night.

(b) Full Sail at Night

One night, while we were in the tropics, I went out to the end of the flying-jib-boom, upon some duty, and, having finished it, turned round, and lay over the boom for a long time, admiring the beauty of the sight before me. Being so far out from the deck, I could look at the ship, as at a separate vessel;—and there rose up from the water, supported only by the small black hull, a pyramid of canvas, spreading out far beyond the hull, and towering up almost, as it seemed in the indistinct night air, to the clouds. The sea was as still as an inland lake; the light trade wind was gently and steadily breathing from astern; the dark blue sky was studded with the tropical stars;

187

there was no sound but the rippling of the water under the stem ; and the sails were spread out, wide and high ; the two lower studding-sails stretching, on each side, far beyond the deck ; the top-mast studding-sails, like wings to the top-sails ; the top-gallant studding-sails spreading fearlessly out above them ; still higher, the two royal studding-sails, looking like two kites flying from the same string ; and highest of all, the little sky-sail, the apex of the pyramid, seeming actually to touch the stars, and to be out of reach of human hand. So quiet, too, was the sea, and so steady the breeze, that if these sails had been sculptured marble, they could not have been more motionless. Not a ripple upon the surface of the canvas ; not even a quivering of the extreme edges of the sail—so perfectly were they distended by the breeze. I was so lost in the sight, that I forgot the presence of the man who came out with me, until he said (for he too, rough old man-of-war's-man as he was, had been gazing at the show,) half to himself, still looking at the marble sails— " How quietly they do their work ! "

R. H. DANA (from *Two Years Before the Mast*)

III. *An Atlantic Liner* (1925)

He explored the steamer. It was to him, the mechanic, the most sure and impressive mechanism he had ever seen; more satisfying than a Rolls, a Delauney-Belleville, which to him had been the equivalents of a Velasquez. He marvelled at the authoritative steadiness with which the bow mastered the waves; at the powerful sweep of the lines of the deck and the trim stowing of cordage. He admired the first officer, casually pacing the bridge. He wondered that in this craft which was, after all, but a floating iron egg-shell, there should be the roseate music-room,

the smoking-room with its Tudor fireplace—solid and
terrestrial as a castle—and the swimming-pool, green-
lighted water washing beneath Roman pillars. He climbed
to the boat deck, and some never-realised desire for sea-
faring was satisfied as he looked along the sweep of gang-
ways, past the huge lifeboats, the ventilators like giant
saxophones, past the lofty funnels serenely dribbling black
woolly smoke, to the forward mast. The snow-gusts along
the deck, the mysteriousness of this new world but half
seen in the frosty lights, only stimulated him. He shivered
and turned up his collar, but he was pricked to imagina-
tiveness, standing outside the wireless-room, by the
crackle of messages springing across bleak air-roads
ocean-bounded to bright snug cities on distant plains.

" I'm at sea ! "

He tramped down to tell Fran—he was not quite sure
what it was that he wanted to tell her, save that steamers
were very fine things indeed, and that ahead of them, in the
murk of the horizon, they could see the lanes of England.

She, in their cabin with its twin brass beds, its finicking
imitations of grey-blue French prints on the panelled
walls, was amid a litter of shaken-out frocks, heaps of
shoes, dressing gowns, Coty Powder, three gift copies of
The Perennial Bachelor, binoculars, steamer letters,
steamer telegrams, the candy and the Charles & Company
baskets of overgrown fruit and tiny conserves with which
they were to help out the steamer's scanty seven meals a
day, his dress-shirts (of which he was to, and certainly
would not, put on a fresh one every evening), and French
novels (which she was to, and certainly wouldn't, read in
a stately, aloof, genteel manner every day on deck). . . .

Round and round the deck. The long stretch on the
starboard side, filled with deck chairs, with rug-wadded

passengers turning a pale green as the sea rose, with wind-ruffled magazines, cups left from teatime, and children racing with toy carts. The narrow passage aft, where the wind swooped on them, pushing them back, and the steamer dipped so that they had to labour uphill, bending forward, their limbs of lead. But, as they toiled, a glimpse of ship mysteries that were stirring to land-bound imaginations. They looked down into a hatchway—someone said there were half a dozen Brazilian cougars being shipped down there—and along a dizzy aerial gangway to the after-deck and the wheelhouse and a lone light in the weaving darkness. They saw the last glimmer of the streaky wake stretching back to New York. . . .

He awoke, bewildered, at two in the morning. The storm had come ; the steamer was pitching abominably. . . . He lay awake. In the watery light from the transom he saw the sheen of her silver toilet things on the dresser. He thought of this tremendous steamer, pounding the waves. He thought of the modern miracle of the radio, up above, of the automatic electric steering apparatus. Yet on the bridge were sailors, unautomatic, human, eternal. The ship, too, was eternal, as a vehicle of man's old voyaging. Its creaking seemed to him like the creaking of an ancient Greek trireme.

But while his thoughts reached out thus for things heroic, he heard her placid breathing and he smelled not the sea gale but perfume that came from little crystal vials among her silver toilet-things that were vaster than the hull of the steamer, stronger than the storm.

He felt that he would never sleep again.

He closed his great fist, tight. Then it relaxed, and he was asleep.

SINCLAIR LEWIS (from Dodsworth)

" SHOWING A LEG "

In Nelson's time, when His Majesty's ships were in harbour, ladies were allowed to sleep on board. The sailors were required to get up at the usual hour, but the ladies might please themselves. A nice problem of discipline thus arose. A solution was found in the fact that the ladies wore their stockings in bed, while the men slept bare-footed. If (as usually happened) all the sailors did not appear punctually on deck, it was necessary for the Boatswain to search for defaulters. He went along the bunks calling out " Show a leg ! show a leg." The owner of a bare leg was promptly dealt with ; but any leg wearing a stocking was allowed to return where it came from, and doubtless the Boatswain would apologize to the lady in nautical terms. Evidently our sailors, being such innocent fellows, never thought of borrowing the ladies' stockings.

A. S.

BAD COMPANIONS

1. *Pulex Irritans*

This is the Latin name for the homely English flea. Those who are fond of French phrases may call him *pousse-pour-tous*. His love of dirt and darkness suggests that he is not a person of culture, but he has his luxurious side, being also fond of warmth, cosiness and quiet situations. Though a great believer in indoor exercise, he is no fresh air fiend. If you keep your windows and doors wide open and lie on your bed quite naked in a thorough draught, he will keep away from you all night, but he will not accept responsibility for any inconvenience caused to you by such arrangements. Long ago he paid us the compliment of giving up his wings in order to cultivate our society and that of other mammals. His athletic powers, which attracted the attention of Socrates, are very considerable. It is true that he can jump into the air to a height sixty-four times his length, his record on the level being two hundred times his length; but these figures become less impressive if we remember his length is only about one-sixteenth of an inch and that of his wife (truly his " better half ") one-tenth of an inch. As a race the P.I. are highly intelligent, and our grandparents often paid sixpence to see one of their teams drawing a dainty coach. They are nimble folk and make very lively companions, but it is a mistake to cultivate their society, as they have been known to abuse human hospitality in a distressing manner, causing the most pain to those with whom they are most familiar. There is nothing P.I. likes better (after meals) than a game of hide-and-seek, and he seldom gives in until he is compelled to rest by pressure from a piece of soap. The average life of the P.I. is only about five weeks; but he lives merrily, if not long.

2. *Cimex Lectularius*

There is little to be said in favour of the C.L. His appearance, his odour, his habits and his pet name— bug—are all equally unattractive. Let us say at once that he is not really an Englishman. We are told he was introduced into England in the time of Charles II, an event which marks the extremity of the English taste for foreign importations in the 17th century. For diet the C.L. prefers human blood, but at a pinch will nibble at grain, seed, flour and soft woods such as deal. Apparently he has no objection to long waits between meals, and has been known to live for twelve months without food. He is a night-worker, spending his days lazily in cracks and crevices. His nature is bloodthirsty and his influence degrading. He is worthy of capital punishment, and this sentence should be executed on all his household. You must find out his residence and insert a soothing mixture into all its apertures, say soft soap and paraffin. Benzine is good also, but dangerous, being inflammable. Boiling water will do ; but it must be really boiling, not merely hot.

Early in March is said to be the best time for a bug-hunt, but few people will hesitate to poach in the close season. As a counter-attraction for the C.L. you may hang a bunch of pepperwort on your bedstead, but it is long odds he will like you better.

3. *Anopheles*

This name suggests some Greek hero of the Trojan war, and seems rather high-sounding for a small insect. Those who have travelled in Italy will perhaps remember the mosquito as *Signora Zanzara*, a name which suits this little lady very well. She is truly an enemy of Sleep ; for, if her bites do not keep you awake, her trumpetings probably will. It is said that the purpose of her shrill note is to call her mate and let him know where she is ; but why must this love business be conducted in our bedrooms ? Signor Zanzara is not so good a buzzer. Jove-like he drinks nectar (of flowers), and he is a fruit-eater. He seems to have some little respect for human beings ; but perhaps his principles are vegetarian. When in a country which you have to share with the Zanzare, undress with your windows tightly closed, put out the light before you open them, and beware of careless servants who overlook holes in the mosquito curtains or draw them shutting an enemy inside.

The little mosquito has had the audacity to dispute with man for possession of a considerable portion of the earth's surface. Indeed we surrendered large tracts of territory to these little pests, who were in a fair way to become conquerors of the tropical world. It looked as if it was possible for the mosquito in its capacity of malaria-carrier to have destroyed the human race. It was found there were only two ways of stamping out malaria —to exterminate man or to exterminate the mosquito. Naturally we desired to adopt the latter alternative. The issue was decided in 1897 when Sir Ronald Ross found the malaria organism in the stomach of a dapple-winged mosquito. This was one of the greatest discoveries ever made by man; compared with it Columbus' discovery of America resembles the finding of sixpence in the gutter.

It is only fair to the mosquitoes to say that their bite is normally harmless in itself. They have no malicious motive—they merely want some food—and the microbe is introduced incidentally. If they are carrying it, they cannot help passing it on. After all, they take the risk of getting something unpleasant from us. That was a sad ending to the story in Goldsmith's *Elegy* :—

> " The man recovered of the bite,
> The dog it was that died."

A. S.

CONCERNING BITES

1. *Prevention*

Rub into the skin of the exposed parts of your body the following mixture :—

> Naphtha — 4 parts.
> Oil of citronella — 1 part.
> Oil of eucalyptus — 1 part.
> Oil of peppermint — 1 part.

2. *Cure*

The reaction of human beings to bites and curative applications varies greatly, but most people will obtain relief if they apply Tincture of Iodine to the afflicted spot soon after the bite has been received.

A. S.

A NIGHTLY ARMOUR

Against small foes that fly, creep, crawl, and/or bite

Make a bag of strongest artificial silk about seven feet long and about three feet wide with casing for running string at top. Cut out a piece of same material of size and shape suitable for hood, making one casing along edges of top and sides (for running string to draw round face) and another casing along bottom edge (for running string to draw round neck). Stitch lower edge of hood to top of bag at centre of back. Insert running strings. Provide a piece of mosquito netting sufficient to cover the face loosely and amply. Before getting into the bag remove boots or shoes and any other apparel or decorations you may be wearing likely to cause damage. Otherwise, clothing may be worn according to taste, provided there is room for it. If you intend to use other coverings, such as bedclothes, you will (unless you are a Sack Race Blue) place the bag in position beneath these before getting into it, otherwise you would have to perform certain difficult movements. These might be very amusing, but it would be wasteful to provide such entertainment in the absence of spectators. Examine the bag carefully before you get in. It may be already inhabited. When in the bag place the face netting loosely over your face and tuck in the edges underneath the hood. Then draw tight and securely fasten the neck strings and face strings of the hood. The edges of the netting should then be amply covered. Lastly, draw tight and securely fasten the neck strings of the bag, keeping your hands well inside while doing so. You can then lie down and go to sleep. When you wish to get up in the morning untie the strings, remove the face netting and get out of the bag delicately. Thoroughly shake netting, bag and hood, examine them carefully and remove any foreign bodies discovered. Then fold or roll up bag, hood and netting and cover and keep secure till next required. This contrivance is equally suitable for indoor and outdoor use. It has been tested many times in varying climates and found efficient. It is not fool-proof, and any user relying upon it without following strictly all the above instructions is liable to be punished with bites *according to taste*.

A. S.

A BASKET OF BUGS

I believe I am the only surviving basket-maker who,
during the 'sixties and early 'seventies, made, in the ordinary
course of his work, the wicker bug-traps then surviving in
use in middle-class families. Such, as I remember, were
placed in every bed in my great-grandfather's house
in Whitechapel and in my grandfather's house in Spitalfields. In order to preserve specimens of this quaint instrument I made one for exhibition in our Cambridge
Museum of Archæology and Ethnology, and another for
the London Museum of Pestology. . . . The trap was placed
behind the bolster and between it and the head of the
bed—the iron bed had not then been invented. The little
anthropophagi after their nightly meal would retire to
digest between the interstices of the wicker trap. The
housemaid in the morning would take the trap into the
yard or garden and shake out the victims, who would meet
a violent death under her feet. She would then replace the
trap in position for the following night's service.

THOMAS OKEY (from *A Basketful of Memories*)

EXECUTION IN THE PALACE

Among the records preserved in the College of Pestology
(52 Bedford Square, W.C.) is a receipt for two guineas
paid in July 1827 to the Bug-Destroyer to His Majesty
King George IV for destroying bugs in four bedsteads.

A. S.

THE ACCOMPANIMENT

The soloist engaged in such an exquisite performance as the act of sleeping should be provided with a fitting and harmonious accompaniment. Your ordinary sleeper will very likely share the opinion of the crusty old gentleman who, being asked by the barber how he liked his hair cut, replied " In silence." But more finished performers will have it that the beauty of sleep is intensified by certain sounds heard first consciously, then subconsciously. The sound of a storm at night is exhilarating to some, but many find such a powerful orchestra too violent an accompaniment. Lesser winds make sweeter music for most of us, using trees for instruments. Poplars near a house will send on windy nights a soothing pattering sound through the open windows. Wind in pine trees is to some of us a sobbing melancholy sound—to others, more fortunate, it may be a pleasing croon. For ourselves, we sleep most happily on a rainy night ; for there is a spout from the roof close to our bedroom window down which the rain slips very pleasantly, making a soothing sound like *googly-goo*. The sound of the sea will be pleasing to some, though we ourselves have often been kept awake by that melancholy roar which retreating waves send up from a pebbly beach. But it is surely pleasant to sleep by a quiet river. What a lovely sleep we had once at Landeck in Tyrol ! The tall windows were thrown open, and our eyes shut themselves unwillingly against a wide sky glittering with stars. Below us the living waters of the Inn went by melodiously all night long like dancers dancing in tune. It is likely that all audible sounds give form and colour to our dreams, no matter how little we remember them when we awake.

If you are unaccustomed to sleep in the open air, you will do wisely to make a careful survey of your surroundings before settling down. If you are in the neighbourhood of cows, you will find that their grazing, which seems such a quiet affair in daytime, sounds at night exactly like stout sheets being torn asunder. Again, hotels at Railway Junctions, though very convenient for the catching of early trains, are often impossible sleeping-places. Goods traffic is much handled at night, and the clash of waggons meeting each other is no less startling than the shrieks of locomotives. You will probably hear plenty of both. Our sleep, however, may become attuned to anything by custom. The kindly owner of a noisy factory, which was working at night, had in his employment a mechanic who lived near and was seriously ill. A message was sent to the man's wife to say that night-work would be stopped if that would make the patient sleep better. " If they stop the works," she said ; " he won't sleep a wink."

A. S.

SOLVITUR AMBULANDO

There is nothing more conducive to sleep than fresh air and exercise. If Sleep refuses her gift because during the day you have withheld these offerings, it is never too late to make amends. Don't go to bed just yet, or if already there get up, dress yourself and go for a short walk. If it be dark, wet and windy, good and well ; groping through the darkness and battling with wind and rain will make you more fit for sleep. If the moon be shining clearly out of a windless sky, the quiet beauty of the night will give you almost a foretaste of sleep. In any case you will very likely add something notable to your experiences. The night-walker is at least sure of one reward—a comforting feeling of superiority to the " folk in housen." Don't go far, don't walk fast, and go to bed at once when you return.

A. S.

BOOKS AT NIGHT

The great moment of the day is come. One stands watching the last sweep of violet into dun above the line of the hill, one sees how the flowers are falling one and all into a grey mist of confusion through which the little evening wind faintly whispers. Beyond the gate on the rough among the bracken, that has been amber-coloured all day and now is stretching a pale cloud to the horizon, two farmers are talking :

" Well, good-night."

" Good-night."

Now the only sound in all the world is the running stream, you turn down the path, open the door, find your way by the light of the fire to the lamp, light it, and then turn. The books crowd in upon you, they are pressing, urgent, upon every side. As you stand by one of the bookcases there is a glorious instant of indecision that you would prolong if nature would but allow it, then the book, almost without deliberate consciousness, is in your hand, your chair is drawn to the blaze, and with a sigh of content you are off and away. So, as the House has my Books and my Books have me, this last prayer to their presiding god :

Command the Roofe, great Genius, and from thence
Into this house powre downe thy influence,
That through each room a golden pipe may run
Of living water by thy Benizon.
Fulfill the Larders, and with strengthening bread
Be ever more these Bynns replenishèd.
Next, like a Bishop consecrate my ground,
That luckie Fairies here may dance their Round :
And after that, lay downe some silver pence,
The Master's charge and care to recompence.
Charme then the chambers ; make the beds for ease
More than for peavish pining sicknesses.
Fix the foundation fast, and let the Roofe
Growold with time, but yet keepe weather-proofe.

HUGH WALPOLE (from *Reading*)

WHAT SIR HARRY THINKS

It's nice to get up in the morning when the sun begins to
   shine,
At four or five or six o'clock in the good old summer time ;
But when the snow is snowing, and it's murky overhead—
It's nice to get up in the morning—but it's nicer to lie
   in your bed !

SIR HARRY LAUDER

MORNING

'Tis the hour when white-horsed Day
Chases Night her mares away ;
When the Gates of Dawn (they say)
   Phoebus opes :

And I gather that the Queen
May be uniformly seen,
Should the weather be serene,
   On the slopes.

When the ploughman, as he goes
Leathern-gaitered o'er the snows,
From his hat and from his nose
   Knocks the ice;
And the panes are frosted o'er,
And the lawn is crisp and hoar,
As has been observed before
   Once or twice.

When arrayed in breastplate red
Sings the robin, for his bread,
On the elmtree that hath shed
   Every leaf;
While, within, the frost benumbs
The still sleepy schoolboy's thumbs,
And in consequence his sums
   Come to grief.

But when breakfast-time hath come,
And he's crunching crust and crumb,
He'll no longer look a glum
   Little dunce;
But be brisk as bees that settle
On a summer rose's petal:
Wherefore, Polly, put the kettle
   On at once.

C. S. CALVERLEY

SECOND PART

§ I SMALL TALK IN THE CARAVANSERAI

§ 1. Little Playthings

§ 2. These from the Land of *Nods*

A halt on the journey, a rest, a drink from the well, and the caravan moves on at the setting of the stars.

OMAR KHAYYÁM

" The time has come," the Walrus said,
    " To talk of many things :
Of shoes—and ships—and sealing wax—
    Of cabbages—and kings——"

LEWIS CARROLL (*Through the Looking-glass*)

§1. LITTLE PLAYTHINGS

WASSAIL

The old English merrymakings on New Year's Eve were of very ancient origin. The Head of the House assembled his family around a bowl of spiced ale (comically called "Lamb's Wool"). After the Head had drunk the health of all, the bowl was passed round and each person before drinking said the Saxon words *waes hál* (i.e. "be whole "="be well "="good health"). The children of the poor carried round the neighbourhood a bowl decorated with ribbons, begging the means of filling it with "Lamb's Wool." They announced their presence with

A WASSAIL SONG

"Here we come a wassailing,
    Among the leaves so green,
Here we come a wandering,
    So fair to be seen.

Love and joy come to you,
And to you your wassail too,
And God bless you and send you
                a happy New Year !

We are not daily beggars,
    That beg from door to door ;
But we are neighbours' children,
    Whom you have seen before.

Here we have a little purse
    Of stretching leather skin,
A little from your money bags
    Would line it well within.

So bring us out a table,
    And spread it with a cloth ;
And bring us out a mouldy cheese,
    And some of your Christmas loaf.

God bless the master of this house,
    Likewise the mistress too,
And all the little children,
    That round the table go !

Love and joy come to you,
And to you your wassail too,
And God bless you and send you
    a happy New Year ! ”

The Loving Cup filled with sweetened and spiced wine
handed round at the Feasts of the City of London Companies is the true descendant of the Wassail Bowl ; but
those who wish for a proper wassailing after the old style
will take note of the following

RECIPE

Put into a bowl ½lb. of Lisbon sugar ; pour on it 1 pint
of warm beer ; grate a nutmeg and some ginger into it ;
add 5 additional pints of beer ; stir well ; sweeten to
taste ; cover up and keep covered for 3 hours ; then add
4 thin slices of toasted bread and 4 roasted apples which

will float pleasantly on the top. You can then begin
wassailing, or, if you prefer to bottle the mixture and
drink it unceremoniously, it will be ready for use in a
few days in an effervescent state.

A. S.

A FOURTEENTH CENTURY DISH

Take hens and pork, and boil them together. Take the
flesh and hew it small, and grind it all to dust. Take grated
bread, and mix it with the broth, and add to it yolks of
eggs. Boil it, and put therein powder of ginger sugar,
saffron, and salt—and look that it be stiff.

Cookery Book of King Richard II

SLEEPING AND WAKING:

(*Love and love*)

Sleep, wayward thoughts, and rest you with my Love.
  Let not my Love be with my love dis-eased.
Touch not, proud hands, lest you her anger move,
  But pine you with my longings long displeased.
Thus while she sleeps I sorrow for her sake,
So sleeps my Love, and yet my love doth wake . .

My love doth rage, and yet my Love doth rest.
  Fear in my love, and yet my Love secure.
Peace in my Love, and yet my love oppressed,

Impatient yet of perfect temperature.
Sleep, dainty Love, while I sigh for thy sake.
So sleeps my Love, and yet my love doth wake.

From DOWLAND's *Booke of Ayres*, 1597

GET BORN ON A SUNDAY

Sunday's child is full of grace,
Monday's child is full in the face,
Tuesday's child is solemn and sad,
Wednesday's child is merry and glad,
Thursday's child is inclined to thieving,
Friday's child is free in giving,
Saturday's child works hard for his living.

A Cornish Rhyme

ROMANCE

My mother said that I never should
Play with the gipsies in the wood.
I told my mother that if I could
I'd play with the gipsies in the wood.
I went to the sea, but couldn't get across,
So I paid ten shillings for an old blind horse.
I jumped on his back, was off in a crack,
And came at last to the woodman's track.
The wood was dark and the grass was green.
Up came Sally with a tambourine.

Old English Game Song

BIBO AND CHARON

When Bibo thought fit from the world to retreat,
As full of champagne as an egg's full of meat,
He wak'd in the boat ; and to Charon he said,
He would be row'd back, for he was not yet dead,
" Trim the boat, and sit quiet," stern Charon replied,
" You may have forgot, you were drunk when you died."

MATTHEW PRIOR

STELLA'S BIRTHDAY
(1720)

All travellers at first incline
Where'er they see the fairest sign,
And if they find the chambers neat,
And like the liquor and the meat,
Will call again, and recommend
The Angel Inn to every friend.
And though the painting grows decay'd,
The house will never lose its trade :
Nay, though the treach'rous tapster, Thomas,
Hangs a new Angel two doors from us,
As fine as daubers' hands can make it,
In hopes that strangers may mistake it,
We think it both a shame and sin
To quit the true old Angel Inn.

Now this is Stella's case in fact,
An angel's face a little crack'd.
(Could poets or could painters fix
How angels look at thirty-six :)

This drew us in at first to find
In such a form an angel's mind ;
And every virtue now supplies
The fainting rays of Stella's eyes.
See, at her levee crowding swains,
Whom Stella freely entertains
With breeding, humour, wit, and sense,
And puts them to so small expense ;
Their minds so plentifully fills,
And makes such reasonable bills,
So little gets for what she gives,
We really wonder how she lives !
And had her stock been less, no doubt
She must have long ago run out.

 Then who can think we'll quit the place,
When Doll hangs out a newer face ;
Or stop and light at Chloe's Head,
With scraps and leavings to be fed.

 Then, Chloe, still go on to prate
Of thirty-six and thirty-eight ;
Pursue your trade of scandal picking,
Your hints that Stella is no chicken.
Your innuendoes when you tell us
That Stella loves to talk with fellows ;
And let me warn you to believe
A truth, for which your soul should grieve :
That should you live to see the day
When Stella's locks must all be grey,
When age must print a furrowed trace
On every feature of her face ;
Though you and all your senseless tribe,
Could art, or time, or nature bribe
To make you look like beauty's queen

And hold for ever at fifteen ;
No bloom of youth can ever blind
The cracks and wrinkles of your mind ;
All men of sense will pass your door,
And crowd to Stella's at fourscore.

SWIFT

A GENTLE ECHO ON WOMAN

(*In the Doric Manner*)

SHEPHERD. Echo, I ween, will in the wood reply,
  And quaintly answer questions : shall I try ?
ECHO.   Try.
SHEPHERD : What must we do our passion to express ?
ECHO.   Press.
SHEPHERD. How shall I please her, who ne'er loved
  before ?
ECHO.   Be Fore.
SHEPHERD : What moves women when we them address ?
ECHO :   A dress.
SHEPHERD : Say, what can keep her chaste whom I adore ?
ECHO :   A door.
SHEPHERD : If music softens rocks, love tunes my lyre.
ECHO :   Liar.
SHEPHERD : Then teach me, Echo, how shall I come by
  her.
ECHO :   Buy her.
SHEPHERD : When bought, no question I shall be her
  dear ?

ECHO :   Her deer.

SHEPHERD : But deer have horns : how must I keep her
  under ?

ECHO :   Keep her under.

SHEPHERD : But what can glad me when she's laid on bier ?

ECHO :   Beer.

SHEPHERD : What must I do when women will be kind ?

ECHO :   Be kind.

SHEPHERD : What must I do when women will be cross ?

ECHO :   Be cross.

SHEPHERD : Lord, what is she that can so turn and wind ?

ECHO :   Wind.

SHEPHERD : If she be wind, what stills her when she
  blows ?

ECHO :   Blows.

SHEPHERD : But if she bang again, still should I bang her ?

ECHO :   Bang her.

SHEPHERD : Is there no way to moderate her anger ?

ECHO :   Hang her.

SHEPHERD : Thanks, gentle Echo ! right thy answers tell
  What woman is and how to guard her well.

ECHO :   Guard her well.

SWIFT

SOMETHING ABOUT NOTHING

I am now trying an experiment very frequent among
modern authors, which is to write upon nothing ; when
the subject is utterly exhausted, to let the pen still move
on : by some called the ghost of wit, delighting to walk

after the death of its body. And to say the truth, there seems to be no part of knowledge in fewer hands than that of discerning when to have done. By the time that an author has written out a book he and his readers are become old acquaintance, and grow very loth to part; so that I have sometimes known it to be in writing as in visiting, where the ceremony of taking leave has employed more time than the whole conversation before. The conclusion of a treatise resembles the conclusion of human life, which has sometimes been compared to the end of a feast, where few are satisfied to depart; for men will sit down after the fullest meal, though it be only to doze or to sleep out the rest of the day. But in this latter I differ extremely from other writers; and shall be too proud if, by all my labours, I can have anyways contributed to the repose of mankind in times so turbulent and unquiet as these. Neither do I think such an employment so very alien from the office of a wit as some would suppose. For, among a very polite nation in Greece, there were the same temples built and consecrated to Sleep and the Muses; between which two deities they believed the strictest friendship was established.

SWIFT (from *Tale of a Tub*)

MRS. MARY BLAIZE

Good people all, with one accord,
   Lament for Madam Blaize,
Who never wanted a good word—
   From those who spoke her praise.

The needy seldom pass'd her door,
    And always found her kind;
She freely lent to all the poor—
    Who left a pledge behind.

She strove the neighbourhood to please
    With manners wondrous winning;
And never followed wicked ways—
    Unless when she was sinning.

At church, in silks and satins new,
    With hoop of monstrous size,
She never slumbered in her pew—
    But when she shut her eyes.

Her love was sought, I do aver,
    By twenty beaux and more;
The King himself has followed her—
    When she has walk'd before.

But now, her wealth and finery fled,
    Her hangers-on cut short-all:
The doctors found, when she was dead,—
    Her last disorder mortal.

Let us lament, in sorrow sore,
    For Kent Street well may say,
That had she lived a twelvemonth more,—
    She had not died to-day.

                                GOLDSMITH

214

SOME OLD RIDDLES

The Highway

When Caesar did this Isle invade,
I first experienc'd royal aid ;
Nay, now to Majesty belong,
Tho' subject to the vulgar throng ;
Who with uncivil usage treat,
And trample me beneath their feet ;
With heavy burdens me oppress,
And money gain by my distress ;
Yet all their insults I endure,
While they my given bruises cure ;
I am in every country found,
And traverse all the kingdom round :
Say what's my name, that's so well known,
I am a common proverb grown.

A Tree

In spring I look gay,
Deck'd in comely array,
In summer more clothing I wear :
When colder it grows,
I fling off my clothes,
And in winter quite naked appear.

A Peach

Midst numbers round I spy'd a beauty fair,
More charming than her circling sisters were :
With blushing cheek the tempter of me stood,
At last I cropt her bloom and suck'd her blood ;
Sweet meat she was, but neither flesh nor bone,
Yet in her tender heart she had a stone.

A Comb

I am white at the neck as Susannah the fair,
Tho' my body sometimes is all cover'd with hair;
As a flounder am flat, as a beetle am blind,
Yet good services do to the race of mankind;
The copses and coverts I traverse each day,
To drive from their holds and destroy beasts of prey;
Having two rows of teeth for engagement design'd,
They all fly before me like chaff before wind;
Now tell but my name, ye mammas or misses,
And those who stand by shall reward you with kisses.

A Pair of Shoes

Tho' good fellows we are,
We can't hope to be sav'd;
From our very first day,
To our last we're enslav'd,
Our office is hardest,
And food sure the worst,

Being crammed with raw flesh,
Till we're ready to burst;
Tho' low in our state,
Ev'n Kings we support;
And at balls have
The principal share of the sport.

A Doll

Like Lady Patch, in diff'rent dress,
   I either sex can ape;
And like her, all mankind confess,
   Have comeliness and shape;

Had she the innocence of me,
    And I her air and parts,
She would a perfect goddess be,
    And I should gain more hearts.

A Fan

Come hear and see a tawdry thing,
Fluttering with expanded wing;
Like the lark that upward tends,
And like her too, when she descends
Toss'd by the owner to and fro,
Her beauty and its own to show;
Suff'ring much at ball and play
And working ev'ry holiday;
But what is still more strange to tell,
When by Belinda manag'd well,
Its pow'r th' admiring youth perplexes,
For her it cools, but burns Alexis.

From *A New Riddle Book*, 1778

SOME OLD RHYMES

The Wish

Oh that I were where I would be!
Then should I be where I am not;
But where I am, there I must be,
And where I would be I can not.

If

If all the world was apple-pie
   And all the sea was ink,
And all the trees were bread and cheese,
   What should we do for drink?
It's enough to make an old man
   Scratch his head and think.

A Candle Burning

Little Nan Etticoat
In a white petticoat
And a red nose:
The longer she stands
The shorter she grows.

ANONYMOUS

KITTY OF COLERAINE

As beautiful Kitty one morning was tripping,
   With a pitcher of milk from the fair of Coleraine,
When she saw me she stumbled, the pitcher it tumbled,
   And all the sweet butter-milk watered the plain.

O, what shall I do now, 'twas looking at you, now,
   Sure, sure, such a pitcher I'll not meet again.
'Twas the pride of my dairy, O, Barney M'Leary,
   You're sent as a plague to the girls of Coleraine.

I sat down beside her—and gently did chide her,
　That such a misfortune should give her such pain,
A kiss then I gave her—before I did leave her,
　She vowed for such pleasure she'd break it again.

'Twas hay-making season, I can't tell the reason,
　Misfortunes will never come single,—that's plain,
For, very soon after poor Kitty's disaster,
　The devil a pitcher was whole in Coleraine.

E. LYSAGHT

HOUSEHOLD HINTS

Luncheon for an Invalid

Put bread crumbs and red currant, or any other jelly,
alternately into a tumbler, and when nearly half full, fill
it up with milk.

The Bustard

will probably thrive well on the same food as the turkey.
It is seldom reared ; but, as its flesh has ever been considered most delicious, it appears particularly worthy of
the attention of those who aim at variety and novelty.

FOR AUTHORS DESIRING IMMORTALITY

How to make Permanent Ink

Rub down, in a small mortar, 5 scruples of lunar caustic,
with one drachm of gumarabic, 1 scruple of sap green, and
one ounce of rain water.

From MRS. DALGAIRNS' *Practice of Cookery, &c.*, 1829

Miss Blofield, Professor of the Terpsichorean Positions, exercises in families and schools where dancing cannot be conscientiously admitted. Miss B. begs to state that her system of exercises may be practised with perfect safety, on account of the great gentleness of the method pursued.

Advertisement in 1834

FAITHLESS SALLY BROWN

Young Ben he was a nice young man,
 A carpenter by trade ;
And he fell in love with Sally Brown,
 That was a lady's maid.

But as they fetch'd a walk one day,
 They met a press-gang crew ;
And Sally she did faint away,
 Whilst Ben he was brought to.

The Boatswain swore with wicked words,
 Enough to shock a saint,
That though she did seem in a fit,
 'Twas nothing but a feint.

" Come, girl," said he, " hold up your head,
 He'll be as good as me ;
For when your swain is in our boat,
 A boatswain he will be."

So when they'd made their game of her,
   And taken off her elf,
She rous'd, and found she only was
   A coming to herself.

" And is he gone, and is he gone ? "
   She cried, and wept outright :
" Then I will to the water-side,
   And see him out of sight."

A waterman came up to her,
   " Now, young woman," said he,
" If you weep on so, you will make
   Eye-water in the sea."

" Alas ! they've taken my beau Ben,
   To sail with old Benbow " ;
And her woe began to run afresh,
   As if she'd said, Gee woe !

Says he, " They've only taken him
   To the Tender-ship, you see " ;
" The Tender-ship," cried Sally Brown,
   " What a hard-ship that must be ! "

" Oh ! would I were a mermaid now,
   For then I'd follow him ;
But—Oh ! I'm not a fish-woman,
   And so I cannot swim.

" Alas ! I was not born beneath
   The virgin and the scales,
So I must curse my cruel stars,
   And walk about in Wales."

Now Ben had sail'd to many a place
    That's underneath the world;
But in two years the ship came home,
    And all her sails were furl'd.

But when he call'd on Sally Brown,
    To see how she got on,
He found she'd got another Ben,
    Whose Christian name was John.

" Oh, Sally Brown, Oh, Sally Brown,
    How could you serve me so,
I've met with many a breeze before,
    But never such a blow ! "

Then reading on his 'bacco box,
    He heav'd a heavy sigh,
And then began to eye his pipe,
    And then to pipe his eye.

And then he tried to sing, " All's Well,"
    But could not, though he tried;
His head was turn'd, and so he chew'd
    His pigtail till he died.

His death, which happened in his berth,
    At forty-odd befell;
They went and told the sexton, and
    The sexton toll'd the bell.

THOMAS HOOD

THE BRUTES

I think I could turn and live with animals, they are so
    placid and self-contain'd ;
I stand and look at them sometimes half the day long.
They do not sweat and whine about their condition ;
They do not lie awake in the dark and weep for their
    sins ; . . .
Not one is dissatisfied—not one is demented with the
    mania of owning things ; . . .
Not one is respectable or industrious over the whole earth.

WALT WHITMAN (from *Song of Myself*)

AN OXFORD IDYLL

Ah little mill, you're rumbling still,
    Ah sunset flecked with gold !
Ah deepening tinge, ah purple fringe
    Of lilac as of old !
Ah hawthorn hedge, ah light-won pledge
    Of kisses warm and plenty,
When she was true, and twenty-two,
    And I was two-and-twenty.
I don't know how she broke her vow—
    She said that I was " horty " ;
And there's the mill a-goin' still,
    And I am five-and-forty.
And sooth to tell, 'twas just as well,
    Her aitches were uncertain ;
Her ways though nice, not point-device ;
    Her father liked his " Burton."

But there's a place you cannot trace,
　　So spare the fond endeavour—
A cloudless sky, where Kate and I
　　Are twenty-two for ever.

T. E. BROWN

ENGLISH MADE IN GERMANY

Inscription on a receptacle for cigar-ash

NOTIS !

Every defilement of the carpet with cigar-ash is forbidden to the severest. He who nevertheless finds himself guilty of such a one will be punished irrevocably with house-arrest.

(From a German-made article, 19th century)

INSCRIPTION ON A MEMORIAL TABLET NEAR MÜRREN

Erected in memory of Miss —— who was killed by lightning on this spot by her sorrowing sister.

(Copied on the spot)

FOOTNOTES TO HISTORY (1914–1918)

Mr. Punch watches the Great War

THE BULL-DOG BREED

Scene : The English shore.

OFFICER : " Now, my lad, do you know what you are placed here for ? "

RECRUIT : " To prevent the henemy from landin', Sir."

OFFICER : " And do you think that you could prevent him landing all by yourself ? "

RECRUIT : " Don't know, Sir, I'm sure. But I'd have a dam good try ! "

Punch (Sept. 30, 1914)

THE SKEELY SKIPPER

FIRST TRAWLER SKIPPER (to friend who is due to sail by next tide) : " Are ye takin' any precautions against these submarines, Jock ? "

SECOND SKIPPER : " Ay ! Although I've been in the habit o' carryin' my bits o' bawbees wi' me, I went an' bankit them this mornin', an' am no takin' ma best oilskins or ma noo seaboots."

FIRST SKIPPER : " Oh, you're a' richt, then. Ye'll have practically naethin' tae lose but yer life."

Punch (July 14, 1915)

TIME AND TASTE

THE PESSIMIST (morbidly) : " I tell yer wot it is. This ere War's goin' to last five years."

THE OTHER : " Why not make it fifty, and *thoroughly* enjoy yourself ? "

Punch (July 21, 1915)

SUBALTERN : " Donnez-moi, s'il vous plait, du pain, de la beurre et de la fromage, pour la messe."

MADAME : " Pour la messe ! Mon Dieu, quelle religion ! "

Punch (July 21, 1915)

MAKING THE MOST OF IT

COSTER'S LADY (pointing to a friend who has just passed) : " Yes, she's off to the cinema again, and I don't blame her. Make the most of it, I say. Who knows ? We may be 'aving peace upon us at any moment ! "

Punch (August 25, 1915)

FAITH IN THE FORCE

MISTRESS : " Well, Cook, if you and the other maids are at all nervous of the Zeppelins, you can have your beds removed into the basement."

COOK : " No, thank you, ma'am. We have every confidence in the policeman at the gate."

Punch (March 10, 1915)

AN AWKWARD SITUATION

YOUNG LADY VISITOR (at private hospital) : " Can I see Lieutenant Barker, please ? "

MATRON : " We do not allow ordinary visiting. May I ask if you are a relative ? "

YOUNG LADY (boldly) : " Oh, yes ! I'm his sister."

MATRON : " Dear me. I'm very glad to meet you. I'm *his mother*."

Punch (April 5, 1916)

PET OF THE PLATOON : " I didn't half tell off our Sergeant just now. I called him a knock-kneed, pigeon-toed, swivel-eyed monkey, and said he ought to go to a night school."

ECSTATIC CHORUS : " And what did he say ? "

BILL (after a pause) : " Well, as a matter of fac', I don't think he quite heard me."

Punch (January 24, 1917)

FIDO DOES (WITHOUT) HIS BIT

ANGRY LADY (on being told that Fido's favourite biscuits are now unobtainable) : " Nothing but these ! Really this war is getting beyond a joke ! "

Punch (August 15, 1917)

CIRCUMSTANCES ALTER CASES

MEDICAL OFFICER (London practitioner in private life, addressing military patient) : " Would you come to me with such a trivial complaint in private life ? "

PRIVATE : " No, Sir. I should send for you."

Punch (August 21, 1918)

SOME THOUGHTS ON EXAMINATIONS

Doctor Johnson said that questioning is not the mode of conversation among gentlemen. Doctor Johnson left Oxford without a degree.

The brilliant man who did not know and the learned

man who did not think met in the Second Class and
disliked each other. The poet sat in the Third and
laughed.

The nightingale got no prize at the poultry show.

WISHES AT A GARDEN PARTY

I wish I loved the Human Race ;
I wish I loved its silly face ;
I wish I liked the way it walks ;
I wish I liked the way it talks ;
And when I'm introduced to one
I wish I thought *What Jolly Fun* !

SIR WALTER RALEIGH (1861–1922)
(from *Laughter from a Cloud*)

RÉCHAUFFÉ FIN DE SIÈCLE

(from a novel published in 1897)

Love, alas ! when smitten with the sword of indifference,
dieth soon, but once struck on the tunnelled cheek of
secrecy with the hand of pity there leaves a scar of indelible
intolerance, until wiped out for ever with the curative
balsam of battled freedom . . .

" Speak ! Irene ! Wife ! Woman ! Do not sit in silence
and allow the blood that now boils in my veins to ooze
through cavities of unrestrained passion and trickle down
to drench me with its crimson hue ! " . . .

228

It was at this stage, too, that Lady Dunfern was made to taste of the dish of fanciful wish in which she often dipped her slender fingers to sprinkle her body of dishonesty. She got time now to brood over her actions of silly execution and hatch them with heated hunger . . .

She had at last been cast on the mercy of a world of icy indifference to facts of long standing, and made to taste of the stagnant waters of pity, which flung their muddy drops of rancid rascality on the face of dogmatic dread . . .

He was tempted to invest in the polluted stocks of magnified extension, and when their banks seemed swollen with rotten gear, gathered too often from the winds of wilful wrong, how the misty dust blinded his sense of sight and drove him through the field of fashion and feeble effeminacy, which he once never meant to tread, landing him on the slippery rock of smutty touch, to wander into its hidden cavities of ancient fame . . .

AMANDA M'KITTRICK ROS
(from *Irene Iddesleigh*)

ABSIT NOMEN !

Rebecca flung about the town
Without a thought of settling down.
Her features most distinctly classy
Began to grow a little *passé*.
She vowed to husband her resources,
And summoned all her female forces
To advertise her hand and heart
Upon the London marriage mart.
Although her charms were slightly aged,
Rebecca soon became engaged.
Charles suited well her dearest fancy,

And was indeed a fine fiancy.
Her rivals incommoded were—
(Whatever could he see in her?)
Bewitching were her smiles and prattles
When Charles produced his list of chattels,
And told without the slightest swank
The size of his account at Bank,
Described his country seat at Wantage
With grounds laid out to great advantage,
His diamonds with frequent facets,
His cellars full of liquid assets,
His car that ran like a torpedo,
His yacht at Cannes, his house at Lido.
They motored, dined, and danced and swam,
They rowed on Isis, Thames and Cam;
They flew abroad for winter sports,
They sunbathed in the shortest shorts.
But when the wedding day approached
Fear in Rebecca's heart encroached.
A fly was in the festive ointment—
She failed to keep her church appointment.
It was, she said, a rotten shame
She should be asked to change her name.
Her friends might call her jilt or flirt—
She could not marry Mr. Dyrt.

ANONYMOUS

NANNY

I sing a long-neglected dame.
Let plays and poets all proclaim
The wonder of the Mother's name,
    And even that of Granny;

Let others tell with loud hurrahs
The general praises of papas—
I hymn the Mother of Mammas,
   I sing the British Nanny.
Not every pink and girlish thing
   That pushes round a pram,
The ancient rock-like NURSE I sing,
   Britannia's virgin dam,
That, old as mountains and as stout,
From child to child is passed about
Till childless yet, she passes out,
   The lonely British Nanny.

For she it was that from the first
Refused to judge us by our worst;
We might be yelling fit to burst—
   She crooned a cheerful ditty;
Our very aunts could not deny
That we were small and ugly fry,
But she with fond prophetic eye
   Maintained that we were pretty.
Alone of all the human race
   She took the kind of view
Of our importance, brain and face,
   That we would have men do;
And I can never quite forget
No other person I have met
Considered me a perfect pet,
   So here's a health to Nanny!

The artless prattle of a child
Drives everybody nearly wild,
And who that for an hour beguiled
   A babe however clever

For all the riches of the rich
Would undertake a life in which
They lived at that exacting pitch
  Ten hours a day for ever ?
Though even in the mother's joys
  A grander cycle dawns
When we grow more like little boys
  And less like little prawns,
Our Nanny, in a nobler strain,
Would have us at our worst remain,
A babe for ever pink and plain,
  Herself for ever Nanny.

Alas ! the twig becomes a bough ;
We do not need a Nanny now ;
Forgetting her who showed us how,
  We walk to death or glory ;
And whether Fate blows cold or hot,
Whatever women shape our lot,
It's safe to say a Nurse will not
  Be mentioned in the story.
Some other baby far away
  Is hers to soothe or slap.
Some Nelson's in the bath to-day,
  Some Shelley in her lap ;
And when I think on this small star
How many mighty men there are,
I call for wine and drain a jar
  To England's noble Nannies.

A. P. HERBERT

232

VERSES THAT RHYME

(if read as intended)

There was a young fellow of *St. Bartholomew's*
Whose car went by fits and by *St. Startholomew's*
   Till a chap named *St. John*
   Overhauled the *t. John*
And fitted it out with spare *St. Partholomew's*.

ANONYMOUS

A LIMERICK

There was once a young rascal called Denny
Who sold all his clothes for a penny ;
   When the folk went to church
   He was left in the lurch,
But he said I shall go without any.

ANONYMOUS

TEMPER

" Blow out the light," they said, they said
   (She'd got to the very last page) ;
" Blow out the light," they said, they said,
" It's dreadfully wicked to read in bed " ;
Her eyes grew black and her face grew red
   And she blew in a terrible rage.

She put out the moon, she did, she did,
  So frightfully hard she blew,
She put out the moon, she did, she did ;
Over the sky the darkness slid,
The stars all scuttled away and hid—
  (A very wise thing to do).

But please don't whisper the tale about,
  She'd get into trouble, she would ;
Please don't whisper the tale about,
If anyone else should ever find out
She'd get into trouble without a doubt,
  And now she's *ever* so good.

ROSE FYLEMAN

§ 2. THESE FROM THE LAND OF *NODS*

Our good Homer sometimes nods.

HORACE (*Ars Poetica*)

MORTAL STARS

O eyes, O mortal stars,
    The authors of my harms,
That in slumbering wage wars
    To kill me with sweet charms ;
If closed you do annoy me,
Being open you'd destroy me.

From *Ferrabosco's Ayres*, 1609

THE SLUGGARD

'Tis the voice of the sluggard ; I hear him complain,
" You have wak'd me too soon, I must slumber again."
As the door on its hinges, so he on his bed,
Turns his sides, and his shoulders, and his heavy head.

" A little more sleep, and a little more slumber,"
Thus he wastes half his days and his hours without
        number ;
And when he gets up, he sits folding his hands,
Or walks about sauntering, or trifling he stands.

I pass'd by his garden, and saw the wild brier,
The thorn and the thistle grow broader and higher ;
The clothes that hang on him are turning to rags ;
And his money still wastes till he starves or he begs.

I made him a visit, still hoping to find
He had took better care for improving his mind :
He told me his dreams, talk'd of eating and drinking ;
But scarce reads his Bible, and never loves thinking.

Said I then to my heart, " Here's a lesson for me,"
That man's but a picture of what I might be ;
But thanks to my friends for their care in my breeding ;
Who taught me betimes to love working and reading.

ISAAC WATTS

THE SAINT PURSUED

Hark ! she bids all her friends adieu ;
Some angel calls her to the spheres ;
Our eyes the radiant saint pursue
Through liquid telescopes of tears.

ISAAC WATTS (from lines
On the sudden death of Mrs. Mary Peacock)

POOR SOUTH

Poor South ! Her books get fewer and fewer,
She was never much given to literature.

J. GORDON COOGLER

A WORD FOR THE WORM

O may Thy powerful word
   Inspire the feeble worm
To rush into Thy kingdom, Lord,
   And take it as by storm.

          From *The Wesleyan Hymn-Book*

TO GENTLE READERS

And now, kind friends, what I have wrote,
   I hope you will pass o'er,
And not criticise as some have done
   Hitherto herebefore.

          JULIA MOORE

A POETICAL THOUGHT

O Moon, when I gaze on thy beautiful face,
Careering along through the boundaries of space,
The thought has often come into my mind
If I ever shall see thy glorious behind.

          ANONYMOUS

A WARNING TO TOURISTS

But most avoid Italia's coast,
Where ev'ry sentiment is lost,
Where Treach'ry reigns, and base Disguise,
And Murder—looking to the skies,
While sordid Selfishness appears
In low redundancy of fears.
O ! What can Music's voice bestow
Of sculptur'd grace, or Titian glow,
To recompense the feeling mind
For British virtues left behind ?

ANONYMOUS (*c.* 1790)

PAOLO AND FRANCESCA

Twice had he seen her since the Prince was gone,
On some small matter needing unison ;
Twice linger'd, and convers'd, and grown long friends
But not till now where no one else attends.—
" May I come in ? " said he :—it made her start,—
That smiling voice ;—she colour'd, press'd her heart
A moment, as for breath, and then with free
And usual tone said,—" O yes, certainly."

LEIGH HUNT (from *The Story of Rimini*)

A CRITICISM OF LEIGH HUNT

O crimini !
What a nimini-pimini
Story of Rimini !

THEODORE HOOK (from *Letter from a Cockney*)

238

DIABOLUS EX MACHINA

Now, when the rustic wears the social smile,
Released from day and its attendant toil,
And draws his household round their evening fire,
And tells the oft-told tales that never tire :
Or where the town's blue turrets dimly rise,
And manufacture taints the ambient skies,
The pale mechanic leaves the labouring loom,
The air-pent hold, the pestilential room,
And rushes out, impatient to begin
The stated course of customary sin :
Now, now, my solitary way I bend
Where solemn groves in awful state impend,
And cliffs, that boldly rise above the plain,
Bespeak, blest Clifton, thy sublime domain.

HENRY KIRKE WHITE (from *Clifton Grove*)

A GOOD GOER

To horse ! to horse ! my coal-black steed
   Paws the ground and snuffs the air !
There's not a foal of Arab's breed
   More knows what he must bear ;
On the hill he will not tire,
Swifter as it waxes higher ;
In the march he will not slacken,
On the plain be overtaken,
In the wave he will not sink,
Nor pause at the brook's side to drink ;

In the race he will not pant,
In the combat he'll not faint ;
On the stones he will not stumble
Time nor toil will make him humble ;
In the stall he will not stiffen,
But be wingèd as a griffin,
Only flying with his feet :
And will not such a voyage be sweet ?

BYRON (from *The Deformed Transformed*)

A PUZZLER

" Now, little Edward, say why so :
My little Edward, tell me why."—
" I cannot tell, I do not know."—
" Why, this is strange," said I.

WORDSWORTH (from *Anecdote for Fathers*)

ENOUGH OF IT

And thus continuing, she said,
" I had a son, who many a day
Sailed on the sea ; but he is dead ;
In Denmark he was cast away ;
And I have travelled far as Hull to see
What clothes he might have left, or other property."

WORDSWORTH (from *The Sailor's Mother*)

A NASTY PUSH

By that lake whose gloomy shore
Skylark never warbles o'er,
Where the cliff hangs high and steep,
Young St. Kevin stole to sleep.
" Here at least," he calmly said,
" Woman ne'er shall find my bed."
Ah ! the good Saint little knew
What that wily sex can do . . .
Even now, while calm he sleeps,
Kathleen o'er him leans and weeps.
Fearless, she had tracked his feet
To this rocky wild retreat ;
And when morning met his view,
Her mild glances met it too.
Ah ! your Saints have cruel hearts !
Sternly from his bed he starts,
And with rude, repulsive shock,
Hurls her from the beetling rock.

THOMAS MOORE (from *Irish Melodies*)

A QUESTION

Little girl, have you finished your daily employ
   With industry, patience and care ?
If so, lay your head on your pillow with joy,
   No thorn to disturb shall be there.

JANE TAYLOR (1804)

CHARLES AND THE INSECTS

1. *The Bee*

Ah, cruel Charles, how could'st thou take
  Captive that bee, amid the flow'r,
Which gaily left its home to make
  Sweet honey at the morning hour . . .

O, thou hast crushed, hard-hearted boy,
  The little weak industrious thing ;
How could'st thou wantonly destroy—
  Ha ! dost thou feel its venom'd sting ?

Well may'st thou shriek, weep, pout, and low'r,
  That hadst no pity on the bee—
Tho' but an insect it had pow'r
  To make thee rue thy cruelty.

2. *The Moth*

When Charles with his loved parents sat
In social and amusing chat,
Candles shone bright, bright glow'd the fire,
And Lydia touch'd the tuneful lyre.

And now as loud the sweet harp rung,
And Charles with his fond sister sung,
A sprightly moth its wings outspread
And humm'd and buzz'd around each head . . .

She hovers round and round the light,
Nor dreams its glare is deadly bright,
Then darts amid the flame, most blest,
To bask in such a Phoenix' nest . . .

Lydia and Charles, O, be aware,
That pleasure often proves a gilded snare :
The flames of vice, tho' clad in lovely tints most bright,
Are but the guide to realms of everlasting night.

J. F. PENNIE (1822)

THE FEMALE FRIEND

In this imperfect, gloomy scene
    Of complicated ill,
How rarely is a day serene,
    The throbbing bosom still !
Will not a beauteous landscape bright,
    Or music's soothing sound,
Console the heart, afford delight,
    And throw sweet peace around ?
They may, but never comfort lend
Like an accomplish'd female friend ! . . .

As orbs revolve and years recede,
    As seasons onward roll,
The fancy may on beauties feed,
    With discontented soul !
A thousand objects bright and fair
    May for a moment shine,
Yet many a sigh and many a tear
    But mark their swift decline ;
While lasting joys the man attend
Who has a faithful female friend !

CORNELIUS WHUR (1837)

SECOND PART

§II A LIGHT REPAST

SECOND PART

Dost thou think, because thou art virtuous, there shall be no more cakes and ale ?

SHAKESPEARE (*Twelfth Night*)

I live in a constant endeavour to fence against the evils of life by mirth, being firmly persuaded that every time a man smiles—but much more so when he laughs—it adds something to this Fragment of Life.

STERNE (Dedication of *Tristram Shandy*)

Damn braces ! Bless relaxes !
I hate scarce smiles. I love laughing.

BLAKE

§ II A LIGHT REPAST

TO HIS COY MISTRESS

Had we but world enough, and time,
This coyness, lady, were no crime.
We would sit down, and think which way
To walk, and pass our long love's day.
Thou by the Indian Ganges' side
Should'st rubies find : I by the tide
Of Humber would complain. I would
Love you ten years before the Flood,
And you should, if you please, refuse
Till the conversion of the Jews.
My vegetable love should grow
Vaster than empires, and more slow.
An hundred years should go to praise
Thine eyes, and on thy forehead gaze :
Two hundred to adore each breast :
But thirty thousand to the rest ;
An age at least to every part,
And the last age should shew your heart.
For, lady, you deserve this state,
Nor would I love at lower rate.

But at my back I always hear
Time's wingèd chariot hurrying near :
And yonder all before us lie
Deserts of vast eternity.
Thy beauty shall no more be found ;
Nor, in thy marble vault, shall sound
My echoing song ; then worms shall try
That long-preserv'd virginity :

And your quaint honour turn to dust,
And into ashes all my lust.
The grave's a fine and private place,
But none, I think, do there embrace,
   Now, therefore, while the youthful hue
Sits on thy skin like morning dew,
And while thy willing soul transpires
At every pore with instant fires,
Now let us sport us while we may;
And now, like amorous birds of prey,
Rather at once our Time devour,
Than languish in his slow-chapt power.
Let us roll all our strength and all
Our sweetness up into one ball,
And tear our pleasures with rough strife
Thorough the iron gates of life.
Thus, though we cannot make our Sun
Stand still, yet we will make him run.

MARVELL

AFTERNOON TEA IN 1816

Some innuendoes more had pass'd,
Till out the scandal came at last.
" Come then, I'll tell you something more,"
Says she,—" Eliza, shut the door.—
I would not trust a creature here,
For all the world, but you, my dear.
Perhaps it's false—I wish it may,
—But let it go no further, pray."
" O," says mamma, " You need not fear,
We never mention what we hear."

" Indeed we shall not, Mrs. G."
Says I, again, impatiently :
And so, we drew our chairs the nearer,
And whispering, lest the child should hear her,
She told a tale, at least too *long*,
To be repeated in a song ;
We, panting every breath between,
With curiosity and spleen.
And how we did enjoy the sport !
And echo every faint report,
And answer every candid doubt,
And turn her motives inside out,
And holes in all her virtues pick,
Till we were sated, almost sick.
　　—Thus having brought it to a close,
In great good humour, we arose.
Indeed, 'twas more than time to go,
Our boy had been an hour below.
So, warmly pressing Mrs. G.
To fix a day to come to tea,
We muffled up in cloke and plaid,
And trotted home behind the lad.

JANE TAYLOR

JUAN'S EDUCATION

But that which Donna Inez most desired,
　　And saw into herself each day before all
The learned tutors whom for him she hired,
　　Was, that his breeding should be strictly moral :

Much into all his studies she enquired,
    And so they were submitted first to her, all,
Arts, sciences, no branch was made a mystery
To Juan's eyes, excepting natural history.

The languages, especially the dead,
    The sciences, and most of all the abstruse.
The arts, at least all such as could be said
    To be the most remote from common use,
In all these he was much and deeply read;
    But not a page of any thing that's loose,
Or hints continuation of the species,
Was ever suffer'd, lest he should grow vicious.

His classic studies made a little puzzle,
    Because of filthy loves of gods and goddesses,
Who in the earlier ages raised a bustle,
    But never put on pantaloons or bodices;
His reverend tutors had at times a tussle,
    And for their Aeneids, Iliads, and Odysseys,
Were forced to make an odd sort of apology,
For Donna Inez dreaded the Mythology. . . .

Juan was taught from out the best edition,
    Expurgated by learned men, who place,
Judiciously, from out the schoolboy's vision,
    The grosser parts; but fearful to deface
Too much their modest bard by this omission,
    And pitying sore his mutilated case,
They only add them all in an appendix,
Which saves, in fact, the trouble of an index. . . .

The Missal too (it was the family Missal)
  Was ornamented in a sort of way
Which ancient mass-books often are, and this all
  Kinds of grotesques illumined ; and how they,
Who saw the figures on the margin kiss all,
  Could turn their optics to the text and pray,
Is more than I know—but Don Juan's mother
Kept this herself, and gave her son another.

Sermons he read, and lectures he endured,
  And homilies, and lives of all the saints ;
To Jerome and to Chrysostom inured,
  He did not take such studies for restraints ;
But how faith is acquired, and then ensured,
  So well not one of the aforesaid paints
As Saint Augustine in his fine Confessions,
Which make the reader envy his transgressions.

This, too, was a seal'd book to little Juan—
  I can't but say that his mamma was right,
If such an education was the true one.
  She scarcely trusted him from out her sight ;
Her maids were old, and if she took a new one
  You might be sure she was a perfect fright,
She did this during even her husband's life—
I recommend as much to every wife.

                                BYRON (from *Don Juan*)

THE MERMAID TAVERN

Souls of poets dead and gone,
What Elysium have ye known,
Happy field or mossy cavern,
Choicer than the Mermaid Tavern?
Have ye tippled drink more fine
Than mine host's Canary wine?
Or are fruits of Paradise
Sweeter than those dainty pies
Of venison? O generous food!
Dressed as though bold Robin Hood
Would, with his Maid Marian,
Sup and bowse from horn and can.

I have heard that on a day
Mine host's sign-board flew away,
Nobody knew whither, till
An astrologer's old quill
To a sheepskin gave the story,
Said he saw you in your glory,
Underneath a new old sign
Sipping beverage divine,
And pledging with contented smack
The Mermaid in the Zodiac!

Souls of poets dead and gone,
What Elysium have ye known,
Happy field or mossy cavern,
Choicer than the Mermaid Tavern?

KEATS

GRANDPAPA

This is a portrait. Here one can
  Descry those purely human features
Whereby, since first the world began,
Man has with ease distinguished Man
  From humbler fellow-creatures
And seldom, whatso'er his shape,
Mistaken him for Dog or Ape.

Inspect this subject well, and note
  The whiskers centrally divided,
The silken stock about his throat,
The loose but elegant frock-coat,
  The boots (elastic-sided),
And you'll at once remark: "Ah, ha!
" This must, of course, be Grandpapa! "

'Tis he, of feudal types the last,
  By all his peers revered, respected;
His lines in pleasant places cast
Where churls saluted as he pass'd
  And maidens genuflected,
And, if he chanced to meet the Vicar,
The latter's pulse would beat the quicker. . . .

In politics it was his rule
  To be broadminded but despotic;
In argument he kept quite cool
Knowing a man to be a fool
  And most unpatriotic
Who differed from the views that he
Had cherished from the age of three.

I well remember, as a child,
   How much his moods perplexed and awed me
At times irate, at others mild,
Alternately he frowned and smiled,
   Would censure or applaud me,
And either pat me on the head
Or send me screaming off to bed.

If I was late for morning pray'rs
   I saw dire retribution looming ;
Though stealthily I crept downstairs
And knelt and smelt the study chairs
   While Grandpa's voice kept booming,
I knew I should be soundly trounced
After the Blessing was pronounced.

Once I recall—a sad affair—
   When, as a child of years still tender,
I chanced to sit in *his* armchair,
He seized me roughly by the hair
   And flung me in the fender.
He had such quaint impulsive ways ;
I didn't sit again for days.

Dear Grandpapa—I see him yet,
   My friend, philosopher and guide, too,
A personality, once met,
One could not possibly forget,
   Though lots of people tried to—
Founder of a distinguished line,
And worthy ancestor of mine !

HARRY GRAHAM (from *Strained Relations*)

DON QUIXOTE AND THE LIONS

" Give me that helmet, friend," said the knight, "for if I understand anything of adventures, I descry one yonder that obliges me to arm."

The gentleman in green, hearing this, looked about to see what was the matter, but could perceive nothing but a waggon, which made towards them; and by the little flags about it, he judged it to be one of the king's carriages, and so he told Don Quixote. . . . By this time the waggon was come up with them, attended only by the carter, mounted on one of the mules, and another man that sat on the forepart of the waggon. Don Quixote making up to them, " Whither go ye, friends ? " said he. " What waggon is this ? What do you convey in it ? And what is the meaning of these colours ? "—" The waggon is mine," answered the waggoner: " I have there two brave lions, which the general of Oran is sending to the king our master, and these colours are to let the people understand that what goes here belongs to him. . . " What ! " said Don Quixote, with a scornful smile, " lion whelps against me ! Against me those puny beasts ! . . . In despite of those enchanters that have sent them to try me, I will make the creatures know, in the midst of this very field, who Don Quixote de la Mancha is." . . Then turning about to the keeper, " Sirrah ! you rascal you," said he, " either open your cages immediately, or I vow to God, I will pin thee to the waggon with this lance."— " Good sir," cried the waggoner, seeing this strange apparition in armour so resolute, "for mercy's sake, do but let me take out our mules first, and get out of harm's way with them as fast as I can, before the lions get out ; for if they should once set upon the poor beasts, I should be undone for ever; for alas! that cart and they are all I have in the world to get a living with." ..

Sancho, hearing this, came up to his master with tears in his eyes, and begged him not to go about this fearful undertaking .. "Good your worship," cried he, "I peeped even now through the grates of the cage, and I am sure I saw the claw of a true lion, and such a claw as makes me think the lion that owns it must be as big as a mountain." "Alas, poor fellow!" said Don Quixote, "thy fear will make him as big as half the world. Retire, Sancho, and leave me, and if I chance to fall here, thou knowest our old agreement; repair to Dulcinea—I say no more." ..

Now while the keeper took time to open the foremost cage, Don Quixote stood debating with himself, whether he had best make his attack on foot or on horseback; and upon mature deliberation, he resolved to do it on foot, lest Rozinante, not used to lions, should be put into disorder. Accordingly he quitted his horse, threw aside his lance, grasped his shield, and drew his sword; then advancing with a deliberate motion, and an undaunted heart, he posted himself just before the door of the cage, commending himself to heaven, and afterwards to his lady Dulcinea. ..

The keeper observing the posture Don Quixote had put himself in, and that it was not possible for him to prevent letting out the lions, without incurring the resentment of the desperate knight, set the door of the foremost cage wide open, where the male lion lay, who appeared of a monstrous bigness and of a hideous frightful aspect. The first thing he did was to roll and turn himself round in his cage; in the next place, he stretched out one of his paws, put forth his claws, and roused himself. After that he gaped and yawned for a good while, and showed his

dreadful fangs, and then thrust out half a yard of broad
tongue, and with it licked the dust out of his eyes and
face. Having done this, he thrust his head quite out of the
cage, and stared about with his eyes that looked like two
live coals of fire ; a sight and motion enough to have
struck terror into temerity itself. But Don Quixote only
regarded it with attention, wishing his grim adversary
would leap out of his hold, and come within his reach, that
he might exercise his valour, and cut the monster piecemeal. To this height of extravagance had his folly transported him ; but the generous lion, more gentle than arro-
gant, taking no notice of his vapouring and bravadoes,
after he had looked about him a while, turned his tail, and
having showed Don Quixote his posteriors, very con-
tentedly lay down again in his apartment.

Don Quixote, seeing this, commanded the keeper to
rouse him with his pole, and force him out whether he
would or no. " Not I, indeed, sir," answered the keeper :
" I dare not do it for my life ; for if I provoke him, I am
sure to be the first he will tear to pieces. Let me advise
you, sir, to be satisfied with your day's work . . . You have
shown enough the greatness of your courage. No man is
obliged to do more than challenge his enemy, and wait for
him in the field. If he comes not, that is his own fault, and
the scandal is his, as the honour the challenger's."

" 'Tis true," replied Don Quixote. " Come, shut the
cage-door, honest friend, and give me a certificate under
thy hand, in the amplest form thou canst devise, of what
thou hast seen me perform ; how thou didst open the
cage for the lion ; how I expected his coming, and he did
not come out ; how, upon his not coming out then, I
staid his own time, and instead of meeting me, he turned
tail and lay down. I am obliged to do no more. So,

IB   257

enchantments, avaunt! and heaven prosper truth, justice, and knight-errantry! Shut the door, as I bid thee, while I make signs to those that ran away from us, and get them to come back, that they may have an account of this exploit from thy own mouth."

The keeper obeyed, and at last Sancho observed the signal of the white flag, and calling out to the rest, "Hold," cried he, "my master calls to us; I will be hanged if he has not got the better of the lions."

At this they all faced about, and, recovering a little from their fright, they leisurely rode back and came up to the waggon.

"Well, Sancho," said Don Quixote to his squire, "what dost thou think of this? Can enchantment prevail over true fortitude? No, these magicians may perhaps rob me of success, but never of my invincible greatness of mind."

CERVANTES (Trans. P. A. MOTTEUX)

A MIDNIGHT REVEL

(*Enter Sir Toby Belch and Sir Andrew Aguecheek*)

SIR TO.: Approach, Sir Andrew: not to be a-bed after midnight is to be up betimes; and 'diluculo surgere,' thou know'st,—

SIR AND.: Nay, by my troth, I know not: but I know, to be up late is to be up late.

SIR TO.: A false conclusion: I hate it as an unfilled can. To be up after midnight and to go to bed then, is early: so that to go to bed after midnight is to go to bed betimes. Does not our life consist of the four elements?

Sir And. : Faith, so they say; but I think it rather consists of eating and drinking.

Sir To. : Thou'rt a scholar; let us therefore eat and drink.
Marian, I say! a stoup of wine!

(*Enter Clown*)

Sir And. : Here comes the fool, i' faith.

Clo. : How now, my hearts! did you never see the picture
of ' we three ' ?

Sir To. : Welcome, ass! Now let's have a catch.

Sir And. : By my troth, the fool has an excellent breast.
I had rather than forty shillings I had such a leg, and so
sweet a breath to sing, as the fool has. In sooth, thou wast
in very gracious fooling last night, when thou spokest
of Pigrogromitus, of the Vapians passing the equinoctial
of Queubus : 'twas very good, i' faith. I sent thee sixpence
for thy leman : hadst it ?

Clo. : I did impeticos thy gratillity; for Malvolio's nose
is no whipstock; my lady has a white hand, and the
Myrmidons are no bottle-ale houses.

Sir And. : Excellent! why, this is the best fooling, when
all is done. Now, a song!

Sir To. : Come on; there is sixpence for you : let's have
a song.

Sir And. : There's a testril of me too : if one knight give
a——

Clo. : Would you have a love-song, or a song of good life ?

Sir To. : A love-song, a love-song.

Sir And. : Ay, ay : I care not for good life.

Clo. [*Sings.*]

> *O Mistress mine, where are you roaming ?*
> *O, stay and hear ; your true love's coming,*
>   *That can sing both high and low :*

> *Trip no further, pretty sweeting ;*
> *Journeys end in lovers meeting,*
> *Every wise man's son doth know.*

SIR AND. : Excellent good, i' faith.
SIR TO. : Good, good.
CLO. [*Sings.*]

> *What is love ? 'tis not hereafter ;*
> *Present mirth hath present laughter ;*
> *What's to come is still unsure ;*
> *In delay there lies no plenty ;*
> *Then come kiss me, sweet and twenty,*
> *Youth's a stuff will not endure.*

SIR AND. : A mellifluous voice, as I am true knight.
SIR TO. : A contagious breath.
SIR AND. : Very sweet and contagious i' faith.
SIR TO. : To hear by the nose, it is dulcet in contagion.
But shall we make the welkin dance indeed ? shall we
rouse the night-owl in a catch that will draw three souls
out of one weaver ? shall we do that ?
SIR AND. : An you love me, let's do't : I am dog at a
catch.
CLO. : By'r lady, sir, and some dogs will catch well.
SIR AND. : Most certain. Let our catch be ' Thou
knave.'
CLO. : ' Hold thy peace, thou knave,' knight ? I shall be
constrained in't to call thee knave, knight.
SIR AND. : 'Tis not the first time I have constrained one
to call me knave. Begin, fool ; it begins ' Hold thy peace.'
CLO. : I shall never begin if I hold my peace.
SIR AND. : Good, i' faith. Come, begin.

[*They sing a catch.*]

(Enter Maria)

MAR. : What a caterwauling do you keep here! If my lady have not called up her steward Malvolio and bid him turn you out of doors, never trust me.

SIR TO. : My lady's a Cataian, we are politicians, Malvolio's a Peg-a-Ramsey, and 'Three merry men we be.' Am not I consanguineous? am I not of her blood? Tillyvally. Lady! [*Sings.*] '*There dwelt a man in Babylon, lady, lady!*'

CLO. : Beshrew me, the knight's in admirable fooling.

SIR AND. : Ay, he does well enough if he be disposed, and so do I too : he does it with a better grace, but I do it more natural.

SIR TO. : [*Sings.*] '*O, the twelfth day of December,*'—

MAR. : For the love o' God, peace!

(Enter Malvolio)

MAL. : My masters, are you mad? or what are you? Have you no wit, manners, nor honesty, but to gabble like tinkers at this time of night? Do ye make an alehouse of my lady's house, that ye squeak out your coziers' catches without any mitigation or remorse of voice? Is there no respect of place, persons, nor time in you?

SIR TO. : We did keep time, sir, in our catches. Sneck up!

MAL. : Sir Toby, I must be round with you. My lady bade me tell you, that, though she harbours you as her kinsman, she's nothing allied to your disorders. If you can separate yourself and your misdemeanours, you are welcome to the house; if not, an it would please you to take leave of her, she is very willing to bid you farewell.

SIR TO. : '*Farewell, dear heart, since I must needs be gone.*'

MAR. : Nay, good Sir Toby.

CLO. : '*His eyes do show his days are almost done.*'

MAL. : Is't even so?

261

SIR TO.: ' *But I will never die.*'

CLO.: Sir Toby, there you lie.

MAL.: This is much credit to you.

SIR TO.: ' *Shall I bid him go ?* '

CLO.: ' *What an if you do ?* '

SIR TO.: ' *Shall I bid him go, and spare not ?* '

CLO.: ' *O no, no, no, no, you dare not.*'

SIR TO.: Out o' tune, sir : ye lie. Art any more than a steward ? Dost thou think, because thou art virtuous, there shall be no more cakes and ale ?

CLO.: Yes, by Saint Anne, and ginger shall be hot i' the mouth too.

SIR TO.: Thou'rt i' the right. Go, sir, rub your chain with crumbs. A stoup of wine, Maria !

MAL.: Mistress Mary, if you prized my lady's favour at any thing more than contempt, you would not give means for this uncivil rule : she shall know of it, by this hand. [*Exit.*]

MAR.: Go shake your ears.

SIR AND.: 'Twere as good a deed as to drink when a man's a-hungry, to challenge him the field, and then to break promise with him and make a fool of him.

SIR TO.: Do't, knight : I'll write thee a challenge ; or I'll deliver thy indignation to him by word of mouth.

MAR.: Sweet Sir Toby, be patient for to-night : since the youth of the count's was today with my lady, she is much out of quiet. For Monsieur Malvolio, let me alone with him : if I do not gull him into a nayword, and make him a common recreation, do not think I have wit enough to lie straight in my bed : I know I can do it . . . For this night, to bed, and dream on the event. Farewell. [*Exit.*]

SIR TO.: Good night, Penthesilea.

SIR AND.: Before me, she's a good wench.

SIR TO. : She's a beagle, true-bred, and one that adores me : what o' that ?

SIR AND. : I was adored once too.

SIR TO. : Let's to bed, knight. Thou hadst need send for more money.

SIR AND. : If I cannot recover your niece, I am a foul way out.

SIR TO. : Send for money, knight : if thou hast her not i' the end, call me cut.

SIR AND. : If I do not, never trust me, take it how you will.

SIR TO. : Come come, I'll go burn some sack ; 'tis too late to go to bed now : come, knight ; come, knight.

SHAKESPEARE (from *Twelfth Night*)

REMINISCENCES

(Sir John Falstaff, Justice Shallow and Silence)

FAL. : I am glad to see you, by my troth, Master Shallow.

SHAL. : O, Sir John, do you remember since we lay all night in the windmill in Saint George's field ?

FAL. : No more of that, good Master Shallow, no more of that.

SHAL. : Ha ! 'twas a merry night. And is Jane Nightwork alive ?

FAL. : She lives, Master Shallow.

SHAL. : She never could away with me.

FAL. : Never, never ; she would always say she could not abide Master Shallow.

SHAL. : By the mass, I could anger her to the heart. She was then a *bona-roba*. Doth she hold her own well ?

FAL. : Old, old, Master Shallow.

SHAL. : Nay, she must be old ; she cannot choose but be old ; certain she's old ; and had Robin Nightwork by old Nightwork before I came to Clement's Inn.

SIL. : That's fifty-five years ago.

SHAL. : Ha, cousin Silence, that thou hadst seen that that this knight and I have seen ! Ha, Sir John, said I well ?

FAL. : We have heard the chimes at midnight, Master Shallow.

SHAL. : That we have, that we have, that we have.

SHAKESPEARE (from *Henry IV, Part 2*)

A SAILOR'S WOOING

Scene—A Room in Foresight's House
(*Enter Ben, a young sailor, and Prue, a country girl*)

BEN : Come, mistress, will you please to sit down ? for an you stand astern a that'n, we shall never grapple together.—Come, I'll haul a chair ; there, an you please to sit I'll sit by you.

PRUE : You need not sit so near one ; if you have anything to say I can hear you farther off, I an't deaf.

BEN : Why, that's true, as you say ; nor I an't dumb ; I can be heard as far as another ;—I'll heave off to please you.—(*Sits further off.*) An we were a league asunder, I'd undertake to hold discourse with you, an 'twere not a main high wind indeed, and full in my teeth. Look you, forsooth, I am, as it were, bound for the land of matrimony ; 'tis a voyage, d'ye see, that was none of my seeking, I was commanded by father, and if you like of it mayhap

264

I may steer into your harbour. How say you, mistress? The short of the thing is, that if you like me, and I like you, we may chance to swing in a hammock together.

PRUE: I don't know what to say to you, nor I don't care to speak with you at all.

BEN: No? I'm sorry for that.—But pray, why are you so scornful?

PRUE: As long as one must not speak one's mind, one had better not speak at all, I think, and truly I won't tell a lie for the matter.

BEN: Nay, you say true in that, 'tis but a folly to lie: for to speak one thing, and to think just the contrary way, is, as it were, to look one way and row another. Now, for my part, d'ye see, I'm carrying things above board, I'm not for keeping anything under hatches,—so that if you ben't as willing as I, say so a' God's name, there's no harm done. Mayhap you may be shamefaced? some maidens, tho'f they love a man well enough, yet they don't care to tell'n so to's face: if that's the case, why silence gives consent.

PRUE: But I'm sure it is not so, for I'll speak sooner than you should believe that; and I'll speak truth, though one should always tell a lie to a man; and I don't care, let my father do what he will; I'm too big to be whipped; so I'll tell you plainly I don't like you, nor love you at all, nor never will, that's more: so, there's your answer for you; and don't trouble me no more, you ugly thing!

BEN: Look you, young woman, you may learn to give good words however, I spoke you fair, d'ye see, and civil.— As for your love or your liking, I don't value it of a rope's end;—and mayhap I like you as little as you do me.— What I said was in obedience to father; gad, I fear a whipping no more than you do. But I tell you one thing, if you should give such language at sea you'd have a cat o' nine-tails laid across your shoulders. Flesh! who are you? You heard t'other handsome young woman speak civilly to me, of her own accord: whatever you think of yourself, gad, I don't think you are any more to compare to her than a can of small beer to a bowl of punch.

PRUE: Well, and there's a handsome gentleman, and a fine gentleman, and a sweet gentleman, that was here, that loves me, and I love him; and if he sees you speak to me any more he'll thrash your jacket for you, he will, you great sea-calf!

BEN: What, do you mean that fair-weather spark that was here just now? will he thrash my jacket?—let'n— let'n. But an he comes near me, mayhap I may giv'n a salt eel for's supper, for all that. What does father mean to leave me alone as soon as I come home, with such a dirty dowdy? Sea-calf! I an't calf enough to lick your chalked face, you cheese-curd, you!—Marry thee! 'oons, I'll marry a Lapland witch as soon, and live upon selling contrary winds and wrecked vessels.

PRUE: I won't be called names, nor I won't be abused thus, so I won't. If I were a man (Cries), you durst not talk at this rate;—no, you durst not, you stinking tar-barrel! . . .

BEN: Tar-barrel? let your sweetheart there call me so if he'll take your part, your Tom Essence, and I'll say something to him; gad, I'll lace his musk doubtlet for him! I'll make him stink! he shall smell more like a weasel than a civet cat afore I ha' done with 'en.

(Enter Mrs. Foresight and Mrs. Frail)

MRS. FORE.: Bless me, what's the matter, miss? What, does she cry?—Mr. Benjamin, what have you done to her?

266

BEN : Let her cry : the more she cries, the less she'll—she has been gathering foul weather in her mouth, and now it rains out at her eyes.

MRS. FORE. : Come, miss, come along with me, and tell me, poor child.

MRS. FRAIL : Lord, what shall we do ? there's my brother Foresight and Sir Sampson coming.—Sister, do you take miss down into the parlour, and I'll carry Mr. Benjamin into my chamber, for they must not know that they are fallen out.—Come, sir, will you venture yourself with me ?

(Looking kindly at him)

BEN : Venture, mess, and that I will, though 'twere to sea in a storm.

(Exeunt)

CONGREVE (from *Love for Love*)

DOCTOR JOHNSON AND THE PIG

I told him, in one of my latest visits to him, of a wonderful learned pig, which I had seen at Nottingham ; and which did all that we have observed exhibited by dogs and horses. The subject amused him. ' Then,' said he, ' the pigs are a race unjustly calumniated. *Pig* has, it seems, not been wanting to *man*, but *man* to *pig*. We do not allow time for his education, we kill him at a year old.' Mr. Henry White, who was present, observed that if this instance had happened in or before Pope's time, he would not have been justified in instancing the swine as the lowest degree of groveling instinct. Dr. Johnson seemed pleased with the observation, while the person who made it proceeded to remark that great torture must have been employed ere the indocility of the animal could have been subdued.—' Certainly,' said the Doctor, ' but (turning to me) how old is your pig ? ' I told him three years old. ' Then,' said he, ' the pig has no cause to complain ; he would have been killed the first year if he had not been educated.'

ANNA SEWARD (from BOSWELL'S *Life of Johnson*)

MR. JORROCKS ARRIVES

The clear bright beauty of the day, combined with the attraction of a stranger coming to fill so important a situation as master of fox-hounds, drew many to the Datton railway station who were previously unacquainted even with the name of ' Jorrocks '. . .

All the flys, hack horses, donkeys, and ponies, were bespoke as usual ; and many set out at noon to secure good berths at the station. . . Precisely at three-quarters of a minute before three, a wild shrill whistle, that seemed to issue from the bowels of the earth and to run right up into mid-air, was heard at the back of Shavington Hill, and, in an instant, the engine and long train rounded the base, the engine smoking and snorting like an exasperated crocodile. Nearer and nearer it comes with a thundering sort of hum that sounds throughout the country. The wondering ploughman stops his team. The cows and sheep stand staring with astonishment, while the horses take a look, and then gallop about the fields, kicking up their heels and snorting with delight. The guard's red coat on the engine is visible—next his gold hatband appears—

268

now we read the 'Hercules' on the engine, and anon it pulls up with a whiff, a puff, and a whistle, under the slate-covered shed, to give the Hercules his water, and set down and take up passengers and goods. Seven first-class passenger carriages follow the engine, all smart, clean, and yellow, with appropriate names on each door panel—The Prince Albert, Queen Victoria, and the Prince of Wales, The Venus, The Mercury, The Comet, and The Star; next come ten second-class ones, green, with covered tops and half-covered sides, but in neither set is there anything at all like the Jorrocks party. Cattle-pens follow, holding sheep, swine, donkeys, and poultry; then come an open platform with a broken britzka, followed by a curious looking nondescript one horse vehicle, containing a fat man in a low-crowned hat, and a versatio, or re-versible coat, with the preferable side outwards. Along with him were two ladies muffled up in cloaks, and at the back was a good looking servant-maid. From the bottom of the carriage swung a couple of hams, and a large warm-ing pan. 'Pray is Mr. Jorrocks here?' inquired the elegant M.C., who had persuaded the station-master to let him in upon the line, riding his white charger near the door of the first-class carriage, and raising his hat as he spoke; but getting no answer, he continued his interrogatory down the whole set until he came to the end, when casting a despairing glance at the cattle pens, he was about to wheel round, when the gentleman in the versatio coat, in a very stentorian voice, roared out, 'I say, Sir! Bain't this the 'Andley Cross station?' 'It is, Sir,' replied Captain Doleful, in his most dignified manner, 'The Datton station for Handley Cross at least.'

'Then I want to land,' responded the same sweet voice.

'Here's a gentleman wants to be down,' observed

Captain Doleful to the scarlet-coated guard, who came bustling past with a pen of Cochin-Chinas to put upon the train.

' Yes, a gentleman and two ladies,' roared our friend ; ' Mister and Missis Jorrocks in fact, and Miss Jorrocks ! ' . . .

Thereupon the Captain beckoned the guard, and Mr. Jorrocks, standing up in the vehicle, looking very like a hay-stack with a hat on the top, bounded to the ground. Mrs. Jorrocks, in a black velvet bonnet lined with pink satin, and her body all shrouded in a sea green silk cloak, then accepted the offer of the Captain's arm, and descended with caution and due state, while Belinda, with the spring of youth and elasticity in her limbs, bounded on to the foot-way beyond the rail. Benjamin, who was asleep in the horse-box, being considerately kicked awake by Mr. Jorrocks, the porters cut off the last joints of the train, when away it went, hissing and snorting through the quiet country, leaving our party to the undisturbed observation of the Handley Cross company.

ROBERT SMITH SURTEES (from *Handley Cross*)

THE BRUISERS OF ENGLAND

Let no one sneer at the bruisers of England—what were the gladiators of Rome, or the bullfighters of Spain, in its palmiest days, compared to England's bruisers ? Pity that ever corruption should have crept in amongst them—but of that I wish not to talk ; let us still hope that a spark of the old religion, of which they were the priests, still lingers in the breasts of Englishmen. There they come, the bruisers, from far London, or from wherever else they might chance to be at the time, to the great rendezvous in the old city; some came one way, some another: some of tip-top reputation came with peers in their chariots, for glory and fame are such fair things that even peers are proud to have those invested therewith by their sides; others came in their own gigs, driving their own bits of blood, and I heard one say: " I have driven through at a heat the whole hundred and eleven miles, and only stopped to bait twice." Oh, the blood-horses of old England! but they, too, have had their day—for everything beneath the sun there is a season and a time.

So the bruisers of England are come to be present at the grand fight speedily coming off; there they are met in the precincts of the old town, near the field of the chapel, planted with tender saplings at the restoration of sporting Charles, which are now become venerable elms, as high as many a steeple; there they are met at a fitting rendezvous, where a retired coachman, with one leg, keeps an hotel and a bowling-green. I think I now see them upon the bowling-green, the men of renown, amidst hundreds of people with no renown at all, who gaze upon them with timid wonder. Fame, after all, is a glorious thing, though it lasts only for a day. There's Cribb, the champion of England, and perhaps the best man in England; there he is, with his huge massive figure, and face wonderfully like that of a lion. There is Belcher, the younger, not the mighty one, who is gone to his place, but the Teucer Belcher, the most scientific pugilist that ever entered a ring, only wanting strength to be, I won't say what. He appears to walk before me now, as he did that evening, with his white hat, white greatcoat, thin genteel figure, springy step, and keen, determined eye. Crosses him, what a contrast! grim, savage, Shelton, who has a civil word for nobody, and a hard blow for anybody—hard! one blow, given with the proper play of his athletic arm, will unsense a giant. Yonder individual, who strolls about with his hands behind him, supporting his brown coat lappets, under-sized, and who looks anything but what he is, is the king of the light weights, so called—Randall! the terrible Randall, who has Irish blood in his veins; not the better for that, nor the worse; and not far from him is his last antagonist, Ned Turner, who, though beaten by him, still thinks himself as good a man, in which he is, perhaps, right, for it was a near thing; and "a better shentleman," in which he is quite right, for he is a Welsh-man. But how shall I name them all? they were there by dozens, and all tremendous in their way. There was Bulldog Hudson, and fearless Scroggins, who beat the conqueror of Sam the Jew. There was Black Richmond—no, he was not there, but I knew him well; he was the most dangerous of blacks, even with a broken thigh. There was Purcell, who could never conquer till all seemed over with him. There was—what! shall I name thee last? ay, why not? I believe that thou art the last of all that strong family still above the sod, where mayst thou long continue—true piece of English stuff, Tom of Bedford—sharp as Winter, kind as Spring.

Hail to thee, Tom of Bedford, or by whatever name it may please thee to be called, Spring or Winter. Hail to thee, six-foot Englishman of the brown eye, worthy to have carried a six foot bow at Flodden, where England's yeomen triumphed over Scotland's king, his clans and chivalry. Hail to thee, last of England's bruisers, after all the many victories which thou hast achieved—true English victories, unbought by yellow gold; need I recount them? nay, nay! they are already well known to fame—sufficient to say that Bristol's Bull and Ireland's Champion were vanquished by thee, and one mightier still, gold itself, thou didst overcome; for gold itself strove in vain to deaden the power of thy arm; and thus thou didst proceed till men left off challenging thee, the unvanquishable, the incorruptible. 'Tis a treat to see thee, Tom of Bedford, in thy " public " in Holborn way, whither thou hast retired with thy well-earned bays. 'Tis Friday night, and nine by Holborn clock. There sits the yeoman at the end of his long room, surrounded by his friends; glasses are filled, and a song is the cry, and a song is sung well suited to the place; it finds an echo in every heart—fists are clenched, arms are waved, and the portraits of the mighty fighting men of yore, Broughton, and Slack, and Ben, which adorn the walls, appear to smile grim approbation, whilst many a manly voice joins in the chorus.

GEORGE BORROW (from *Lavengro*)

NEWS FROM THE FRONT (1812)

" You must remember, Captain, time's passing; the placards are all out; must be at press before one o'clock to-night; the morning edition is everything with us. You were at the first parallel, I think ? "

" Devil a bit o' me knows. Just ring that bell near you; them's elegant oysters; and you're not taking your drop of liquor; here's a toast for you; ' May——' whoop—raal Carlingfords upon my conscience. See now, if I won't hit that little black chap up there, the first shot."

Scarcely were the words spoken, when a little painted

bust of Shakespeare fell in fragments on the floor as an oyster shell laid him low.

A faint effort at a laugh at the eccentricities of his friend was all the poor editor could accomplish, while Mike's triumph knew no bounds.

" Didn't I tell you ? But come now, are you ready ? Give the pen a drink, if you won't take one yourself."

" I'm ready, quite ready," responded the editor.

" Faith, and it's more nor I am. See now, here it is : The night was murthering dark ; you could not see a stim."

" Not see a—a what ? "

" A stim ! bad luck to you ; don't you know English ? Hand me the hot water. Have you that down yet ? "

" Yes. Pray proceed."

" The Fifth Division was orthered up bekase they were fighting chaps ; the Eighty-eighth was among them ; the Rangers—oh ! upon my soul, we must drink the Rangers. Here, devil a bit o' me will go on till we give them all the honours—hip—begin."

" Hip," sighed the luckless editor, as he rose from his chair, obedient to the command.

" Hurra—hurra—hurra ! Well done ! there's stuff in you yet, ould foolscap ! the little bottle's empty—ring again, if you plaze."

" Really, Mr. Free, I see no prospect of our ever getting done."

" The saints in heaven forbid," interrupted Mike piously ; " the evening's young, and drink plenty ; here, now, make ready ! "

The editor once more made a gesture of preparation.

" Well, as I was saying," resumed Mike, " it was pitch dark when the columns moved up, and a cold raw night with a little thin rain falling. Have you that down ? "

" Yes. Pray go on."

" Well, just as it might be here at the corner of the trench I met Doctor Quill. ' They're waiting for you, Misther Free,' says he, ' down there. Picton's asking for you.' ' Faith, and he must wait,' says I . . ."

" But, my dear sir," interposed Mr. Meekins, " pray *do* remember this is somewhat irrelevant. In fifteen minutes it will be 12 o'clock."

" I know it, ould boy, I know it. I see what you're at. You were going to observe how much better we'd be for a broiled bone." . .

" Nothing of the kind, I assure you. I protest that here we are for two hours at work, and we haven't got to the foot of the great breach."

" And wasn't the army three months and a half in just getting that far, with a battering train, and mortars, and the finest troops ever were seen ? and there you sit, a little fat creature, with your pen in your hand, grumbling that you can't do more than the whole British army. Take care you don't provoke me to beat you ; for I am quiet till I am roused. But, by the Rock O' Cashel——"

" For mercy's sake, Mr. Free——"

" Well, sit down then, and don't be bothering me about sieges, and battles, and things you know nothing about."

" I protest," rejoined Mr. Meekins, " that, had you not sent to my office intimating your wish to communicate an account of the siege, I never should have thought of intruding myself upon you. Once for all, sir, . . . I would beg you to recollect that, on the faith of your message to me, I have announced an account of the storming of Ciudad Rodrigo for our morning edition. Are you prepared, may I ask, for the consequences of my disappointing ten thousand readers ? "

275

" It's little I care for one of them. I never knew much of reading myself."

" If you think to make a jest of me——" interposed Mr. Meekins, reddening with passion.

" A jest of you ! Troth, it's little fun I can get out of you ; you're as tiresome a creature as ever I spent an evening with. See, now, I told you before not to provoke me : we'll have a little more drink ; ring the bell : who knows but you'll turn out better by-and-by ? "

CHARLES LEVER (from *Charles O'Malley*)

BOB SAWYER'S PARTY

" Does Mr. Sawyer live here ? " said Mr. Pickwick, when the door was opened.

" Yes," said the girl, " first floor. It's the door straight afore you, when you gets to the top of the stairs." Having given this instruction, the handmaid, who had been brought up among the aboriginal inhabitants of South-wark, disappeared, with the candle in her hand, down the kitchen stairs : perfectly satisfied that she had done everything that could possibly be required of her under the circumstances.

Mr. Snodgrass, who entered last, secured the street door, after several ineffectual efforts, by putting up the chain ; and the friends stumbled upstairs, where they were received by Mr. Bob Sawyer, who had been afraid to go down, lest he should be waylaid by Mrs. Raddle.

" How are you ? " said the discomfited student. " Glad to see you—take care of the glasses." This caution was

276

addressed to Mr. Pickwick, who had put his hat in the tray.

" Dear me," said Mr. Pickwick, " I beg your pardon."

" Don't mention it, don't mention it," said Bob Sawyer. " I'm rather confined for room, here, but you must put up with all that, when you come to see a young bachelor. Walk in. You've seen this gentleman before, I think ? " Mr. Pickwick shook hands with Mr. Benjamin Allen, and his friends followed his example. They had scarcely taken their seats when there was another double knock.

" I hope that's Jack Hopkins ! " said Mr. Bob Sawyer. " Hush. Yes, it is. Come up, Jack ; come up."

A heavy footstep was heard upon the stairs, and Jack Hopkins presented himself. He wore a black velvet waist-coat, with thunder-and-lightning buttons ; and a blue striped shirt, with a white false collar.

" You're late, Jack ? " said Mr. Benjamin Allen.

" Been detained at Bartholomew's," replied Hopkins.

" Anything new ? "

" No, nothing particular. Rather a good accident brought into the casualty ward."

" What was that, sir ? " inquired Mr. Pickwick.

" Only a man fallen out of a four pair of stairs' window ; —but it's a very fair case—very fair case indeed."

" Do you mean that the patient is in a fair way to re-cover ? " inquired Mr. Pickwick.

" No," replied Hopkins carelessly. " No, I should rather say he wouldn't. There must be a splendid opera-tion though, to-morrow—magnificent sight if Slasher does it."

" You consider Mr. Slasher a good operator ? " said Mr. Pickwick.

" Best alive," replied Hopkins. " Took a boy's leg out of the socket last week—boy ate five apples and a ginger-bread cake—exactly two minutes after it was all over, boy said he wouldn't lie there to be made game of, and he'd tell his mother if they didn't begin."

" Dear me ! " said Mr. Pickwick, astonished.

" Pooh ! That's nothing, that ain't," said Jack Hopkins. " Is it, Bob ? "

" Nothing at all," replied Mr. Bob Sawyer.

" By the bye, Bob," said Hopkins, with a scarcely per-ceptible glance at Mr. Pickwick's attentive face, " we had a curious accident last night. A child was brought in, who had swallowed a necklace."

" Swallowed what, sir ? " interrupted Mr. Pickwick.

" A necklace," replied Jack Hopkins. " Not all at once, you know, that would be too much—*you* couldn't swallow that, if the child did—eh, Mr. Pickwick, ha ! ha ! " Mr. Hopkins appeared highly gratified with his own pleasan-try ; and continued. " No, the way was this. Child's parents were poor people who lived in a court. Child's eldest sister bought a necklace ; common necklace, made of large black wooden beads. Child, being fond of toys, cribbed the necklace, hid it, played with it, cut the string, and swallowed a bead. Child thought it capital fun, went back next day, and swallowed another bead."

" Bless my heart," said Mr. Pickwick, " what a dreadful thing ! I beg your pardon, sir. Go on."

" Next day, child swallowed two beads ; the day after that, he treated himself to three, and so on, till in a week's time he had got through the necklace—five-and-twenty beads in all. The sister, who was an industrious girl, and seldom treated herself to a bit of finery, cried her eyes out at the loss of the necklace : looked high and low for it ;

but, I needn't say, didn't find it. A few days afterwards, the family were at dinner—baked shoulder of mutton, and potatoes under it—the child, who wasn't hungry, was playing about the room, when suddenly there was heard a devil of a noise, like a small hailstorm. ' Don't do that, my boy,' said the father. ' I ain't doin' nothing,' said the child. 'Well, don't do it again,' said the father. There was a short silence, and then the noise began again, worse than ever. ' If you don't mind what I say, my boy,' said the father, ' you'll find yourself in bed, in something less than a pig's whisper.' He gave the child a shake to make him obedient, and such a rattling ensued as nobody ever heard before. ' Why, dam'me, it's *in* the child ! ' said the father, ' he's got the croup in the wrong place ! ' ' No, I haven't, father,' said the child, beginning to cry, ' it's the necklace ; I swallowed it, father.'—The father caught the child up, and ran with him to the hospital ; the beads in the boy's stomach rattling all the way with the jolting ; and the people looking up in the air, and down in the cellars, to see where the unusual sound came from. He's in the hospital now," said Jack Hopkins, " and he makes such a devil of a noise when he walks about, that they're obliged to muffle him in a watchman's coat, for fear he should wake the patients ! "

" That's the most extraordinary case I ever heard of," said Mr. Pickwick, with an emphatic blow on the table.

" Oh, that's nothing," said Jack Hopkins; " is it, Bob?"

" Certainly not," replied Mr. Bob Sawyer.

" Very singular things occur in our profession, I can assure you, sir," said Hopkins.

" So I should be disposed to imagine," replied Mr. Pickwick.

279

After supper, another jug of punch was put upon the table, together with a paper of cigars, and a couple of bottles of spirits. . .

" Now, Betsy," said Mr. Bob Sawyer, with great suavity, and dispersing at the same time, the tumultuous little mob of glasses the girl had collected in the centre of the table : " now, Betsy, the warm water. Be brisk, there's a good girl."

" You can't have no warm water," replied Betsy.

" No warm water ! " exclaimed Mr. Bob Sawyer.

" No," said the girl, with a shake of the head which expressed a more decided negative than the most copious language could have conveyed. " Missis Raddle said you warn't to have none."

The surprise depicted on the countenances of his guests imparted new courage to the host.

" Bring up the warm water instantly—instantly ! " said Mr. Bob Sawyer, with desperate sternness.

" No. I can't," replied the girl ; " Missis Raddle raked out the kitchen fire afore she went to bed, and locked up the kittle."

" Oh, never mind ; never mind. Pray don't disturb yourself about such a trifle," said Mr. Pickwick, observing the conflict of Bob Sawyer's passions, as depicted in his countenance, " cold water will do very well."

" Oh, admirably," said Mr. Benjamin Allen.

" My landlady is subject to some slight attacks of mental derangement," remarked Bob Sawyer with a ghastly smile ; " and I fear I must give her warning."

" No, don't," said Ben Allen.

" I fear I must," said Bob with heroic firmness. " I'll pay her what I owe her, and give her warning to-morrow

morning." Poor fellow! how devoutly he wished he
could! . .

"Now," said Jack Hopkins, "just to set us going again,
Bob, I don't mind singing a song." And Hopkins, incited
thereto, by tumultuous applause, plunged himself at
once into "The King, God bless him," which he sang as
loud as he could, to a novel air, compounded of the
"Bay of Biscay" and "A Frog he would." The chorus
was the essence of the song; and, as each gentleman
sang it to the tune he knew best, the effect was very striking
indeed.

It was at the end of the chorus to the first verse, that
Mr. Pickwick held up his hand in a listening attitude, and
said, as soon as silence was restored:

"Hush! I beg your pardon. I thought I heard somebody calling from upstairs."

A profound silence immediately ensued; and Mr. Bob
Sawyer was observed to turn pale.

"I think I hear it now," said Mr. Pickwick. "Have the
goodness to open the door."

The door was no sooner opened than all doubt on the
subject was removed.

"Mr. Sawyer! Mr. Sawyer!" screamed a voice from
the two-pair landing.

"It's my landlady," said Bob Sawyer, looking round
him with great dismay. "Yes, Mrs. Raddle."

"What do you mean by this, Mr. Sawyer?" replied
the voice, with great shrillness and rapidity of utterance.
"Ain't it enough to be swindled out of one's rent, and
money lent out of pocket besides, and abused and in-
sulted by your friends that dares to call themselves men:
without having the house turned out of the window, and
noise enough made to bring the fire-engines here, at

two o'clock in the morning?—Turn them wretches away."

"You ought to be ashamed of yourselves," said the voice of Mr. Raddle, which appeared to proceed from beneath some distant bed-clothes.

"Ashamed of themselves!" said Mrs. Raddle. "Why don't you go down and knock 'em every one downstairs? You would if you was a man."

"I should if I was a dozen men, my dear," replied Mr. Raddle, pacifically, "but they've the advantage of me in numbers, my dear."

"Ugh, you coward!" replied Mrs. Raddle, with supreme contempt. "*Do* you mean to turn them wretches out, or not, Mr. Sawyer?"

"They're going, Mrs. Raddle, they're going," said the miserable Bob. "I am afraid you'd better go," said Mr. Bob Sawyer to his friends. "I *thought* you were making too much noise."

"It's a very unfortunate thing," said the prim man. "Just as we were getting so comfortable too!.. It's hardly to be borne—hardly to be borne, is it?"

"Not to be endured," replied Jack Hopkins; "let's have the other verse, Bob. Come, here goes!"

"No, no, Jack, don't," interposed Bob Sawyer; "it's a capital song, but I am afraid we had better not have the other verse. They are very violent people, the people of the house."

"Shall I step upstairs, and pitch into the landlord?" inquired Hopkins, "or keep on ringing the bell, or go and groan on the staircase? You may command me, Bob."

"I am very much indebted to you for your friendship and good nature, Hopkins," said the wretched Mr. Bob

Sawyer, " but I think the best plan to avoid any further dispute is for us to break up at once."

" Now, Mr. Sawyer ! " screamed the shrill voice of Mrs. Raddle, " *are* them brutes going ? "

DICKENS (from *Pickwick Papers*)

DINNER BY PROXY

" Is that the little gentleman from Blunderstone ? "

" Yes, ma'am," I said.

" What name ? " inquired the lady.

" Copperfield, ma'am," I said.

" That won't do," returned the lady. " Nobody's dinner is paid for here, in that name."

" Is it Murdstone, ma'am ? " I said.

" If you're Master Murdstone," said the lady, " why do you go and give another name first ? "

I explained to the lady how it was, who then rang a bell, and called out, " William ! show the coffee-room ! " upon which a waiter came running out of a kitchen on the opposite side of the yard to show it, and seemed a good deal surprised when he found he was only to show it to me.

It was a large, long room with some large maps in it. I doubt if I could have felt much stranger if the maps had been real foreign countries, and I cast away in the middle of them. I felt it was taking a liberty to sit down, with my cap in my hand, on the corner of the chair nearest the door; and when the waiter laid a cloth on purpose for me, and put a set of castors on it, I think I must have turned red all over with modesty.

He brought me some chops and vegetables, and took the covers off in such a bouncing manner that I was afraid I must have given him some offence. But he greatly relieved my mind by putting a chair for me at the table, and saying, very affably, " Now six-foot ! come on ! "

I thanked him, and took my seat at the board ; but found it extremely difficult to handle my knife and fork with anything like dexterity, or to avoid splashing myself with the gravy, while he was standing opposite, staring so hard, and making me blush in the most dreadful manner every time I caught his eye. After watching me into the second chop, he said :

" There's half a pint of ale for you. Will you have it now ? "

I thanked him and said " Yes." Upon which he poured it out of a jug into a large tumbler, and held it up against the light, and made it look beautiful.

" My eye ! " he said. " It seems a good deal, don't it ? "

" It does seem a good deal," I answered with a smile. For it was quite delightful to me to find him so pleasant. He was a twinkling-eyed, pimple-faced man, with his hair standing upright all over his head ; and as he stood with one arm a-kimbo, holding up the glass to the light with the other hand, he looked quite friendly.

" There was a gentleman here, yesterday," he said— " a stout gentleman, by the name of Topsawyer—perhaps you know him ? "

" No," I said, " I don't think——"

" In breeches and gaiters, broad-brimmed hat, grey coat, speckled choker," said the waiter.

" No," I said bashfully, " I haven't the pleasure——"

" He came in here," said the waiter, looking at the light through the tumbler, " ordered a glass of this ale—

would order it—I told him not—drank it, and fell dead. It was too old for him. It oughtn't to be drawn ; that's the fact."

I was very much shocked to hear of this melancholy accident, and said I thought I had better have some water.

" Why, you see," said the waiter, still looking at the light through the tumbler, with one of his eyes shut up, " our people don't like things being ordered and left. It offends 'em. But *I'll* drink it, if you like. I'm used to it, and use is everything. I don't think it'll hurt me, if I throw my head back, and take it off quick. Shall I ? "

I replied that he would much oblige me by drinking it, if he thought he could do it safely, but by no means otherwise. When he did throw his head back, and take it off quick, I had a horrible fear, I confess, of seeing him meet the fate of the lamented Mr. Topsawyer, and fall lifeless on the carpet. But it didn't hurt him. On the contrary, I thought he seemed the fresher for it.

" What have we got here ? " he said, putting a fork into my dish. " Not chops ? "

" Chops," I said.

" Lord bless my soul ! " he exclaimed, " I didn't know they were chops. Why, a chop's the very thing to take off the bad effects of that beer ! Ain't it lucky ? "

So he took a chop by the bone in one hand, and a potato in the other, and ate away with a very good appetite, to my extreme satisfaction. He afterwards took another chop, and another potato ; and after that another chop and another potato. When he had done, he brought me a pudding, and having set it before me, seemed to ruminate, and to become absent in his mind for some moments.

" How's the pie ? " he said, rousing himself.

" It's a pudding," I made answer.

" Pudding ! " he exclaimed. " Why, bless me, so it is ! What ! " looking at it nearer. " You don't mean to say it's a batter-pudding ! "

" Yes, it is indeed."

" Why, a batter-pudding," he said, taking up a table-spoon, " is my favourite pudding ! Ain't that lucky. Come on, little 'un, and let's see who'll get most."

The waiter certainly got most. He entreated me more than once to come in and win, but what with his table-spoon to my tea-spoon, his despatch to my despatch, and his appetite to my appetite, I was left far behind at the first mouthful, and had no chance with him. I never saw anyone enjoy a pudding so much, I think ; and he laughed, when it was all gone, as if his enjoyment of it lasted still.

DICKENS (from *David Copperfield*)

CHILDREN AT A WEDDING

Flora had a great scarlet and gold church service. As soon as she opened it, she disconcerted me by saying aloud, to an imaginary female friend, " My dear, there is going to be a collection ; and I have left my purse on the piano."

At this time, also, Gus, seeing that the business was well begun, removed to the further end of the pew, sat down on the hassock, and took from his trousers' pocket a large tin trumpet.

I broke out all over in a cold perspiration as I looked at him. He saw my distress, and putting it to his lips, puffed out his cheeks. Flora administered comfort to me. She

286

said, " You are looking at that foolish boy. Perhaps he won't blow it, after all. He mayn't if you don't look at him. At all events, he probably won't blow it till the organ begins ; and then it won't matter so much." . .

I wish those dear children (not meaning them any harm) had been, to put it mildly, at play on the village green, that blessed day.

When I looked at Gus again, he was still on the hassock, threatening propriety with his trumpet. I hoped for the best. Flora had her prayer-book open, and was playing the piano on each side of it, with her fingers. After a time she looked up at me, and said out loud—

" I suppose you have heard that Archy's cat has kittened ? "

I said, " No."

" Oh, yes, it has," she said. " Archy harnessed it to his meal cart, which turns a mill, and plays music when the wheels go round ; and it ran downstairs with the cart ; and we heard the music playing as it went ; and it kittened in the wood-basket immediately afterwards ; and Alwright says she don't wonder at it ; and no more do I ; and the steward's room boy is going to drown some. But you mustn't tell Archy, because, if you do, he won't say his prayers ; and if he don't say his prayers, he will—etc., etc." Very emphatically, and in a loud tone of voice.

This was very charming. If I could only answer for Gus, and keep Flora busy, it was wildly possible that we might pull through. If I had not been a madman, I should have noticed that Gus had disappeared.

He had. And the pew door had never opened, and I was utterly unconscious. Gus had crawled up, on all fours, under the seat of the pew, until he was opposite the calves of his sister's legs, against which calves, *horresco*

287

referens, he put his trumpet and blew a long shrill blast. Flora behaved very well and courageously. She only gave one long, wild shriek, as from a lunatic in a padded cell at Bedlam, and then, hurling her prayer-book at him, she turned round and tried to kick him in the face.

This was the culminating point of my misfortunes. After this, they behaved better.

HENRY KINGSLEY (from *Ravenshoe*)

A BLACK AFFAIR

The skipper was the first to discover the mischief, and he came on deck and published the news in a voice which struck a chill to all hearts.

" Where's that black devil got to ? " he yelled.

" Anything wrong, sir ? " asked Sam anxiously.

" Come and look here," said the skipper. He led the way to the cabin, where the mate and one of the crew were already standing, shaking their heads over the parrot.

" What do you make of that ? " demanded the skipper fiercely.

" Too much dry food, sir," said Sam, after due deliberation.

" Too much what ? " bellowed the skipper.

" Too much dry food," repeated Sam firmly. " A parrot—a grey parrot—wants plenty o' sop. If it don't get it, it moults."

" It's had too much *cat*," said the skipper fiercely, " and you know it, and overboard it goes."

" I don't believe it was the cat, sir," interposed the other man ; " it's too soft-hearted to do a thing like that."

288

" You can shut your jaw," said the skipper reddening. " Who asked you to come down here at all ? "

" Nobody saw the cat do it," urged the mate.

The skipper said nothing, but, stooping down, picked up a tail feather from the floor, and laid it on the table. He then went on deck followed by the others, and began calling, in seductive tones, for the cat. No reply forthcoming from the sagacious animal, which had gone into hiding, he turned to Sam, and bade him call it.

" No, sir, I won't 'ave no 'and in it," said the old man. " Putting aside my liking for the animal, *I'm* not going to 'ave anything to do with the killing of a black cat."

" Rubbish ! " said the skipper.

" Very good, sir," said Sam, shrugging his shoulders, " you know best, o' course. You're eddicated and I'm not, an' p'raps you can afford to make a laugh o' such things. I knew one man who killed a black cat an' he went mad. There's something very pecooliar about that cat o' ours."

" It knows more than we do," said one of the crew, shaking his head. " That time you—I mean we—ran the smack down, that cat was expecting of it 'ours before. It was like a wild thing."

" Look at the weather we've 'ad—look at the trips we've made since he's been aboard," said the old man. " Tell me it's chance if you like, but I *know* better."

The skipper hesitated. He was a superstitious man even for a sailor, and his weakness was so well known that he had become a sympathetic receptacle for every ghost story, which, by reason of its crudeness or lack of corroboration, had been rejected by other experts. He was a perfect reference library for omens, and his interpretations of dreams had gained for him a widespread reputation.

KB   289

"That's all nonsense," he said, pausing uneasily; "still, I only want to be just. There's nothing vindictive about me, and I'll have no hand in it myself. Joe, just tie a lump of coal to that cat and heave it overboard."

"Not me," said the cook, following Sam's lead, and working up a shudder. "Not for fifty pun in gold. I don't want to be haunted."

"The parrot's a little better now, sir," said one of the men, taking advantage of his hesitation, "he's opened one eye."

"Well, I only want to be just," repeated the skipper. "I won't do anything in a hurry, but, mark my words, if the parrot dies that cat goes overboard."

Contrary to expectations, the bird was still alive when London was reached, though the cook, who from his connection with the cabin had suddenly reached a position of unusual importance, reported great loss of strength and irritability of temper. It was still alive, but failing fast on the day they were to put to sea again; and the fo'c's'l in preparation for the worst, stowed their pet away in the paint-locker and discussed the situation.

Their council was interrupted by the mysterious behaviour of the cook, who, having gone out to lay in a stock of bread, suddenly broke in upon them more in the manner of a member of a secret society than a humble but useful unit of a ship's company.

"Where's the cap'n?" he asked in a hoarse whisper, as he took a seat on the locker with the sack of bread between his knees.

"In the cabin," said Sam, regarding his antics with some disfavour. "What's wrong, cookie?"

"What d'yer think I've got in here," asked the cook, patting the bag.

The obvious reply to this question was, of course, bread; but as it was known that the cook had departed specially to buy some, and that he could hardly ask a question involving such a simple answer, nobody gave it.

"It come to me all of a sudden," said the cook, in a thrilling whisper. "I'd just bought the bread and left the shop, when I see a big black cat, the very image of ours, sitting on a doorstep. I just stooped down to stroke its 'ed when it come to me."

"They will sometimes," said one of the seamen.

"I don't mean that," said the cook, with the contempt of genius. "I mean the idea did. Ses I to myself, 'You might be old Satan's brother by the look of you; an' if the cap'n wants to kill a cat, let it be you,' I ses. And with that, before it could say Jack Robinson, I picked it up by the scruff o' the neck and shoved it in the bag."

"What, all in along of our bread?" said the previous interrupter in a pained voice.

"Some of yer are 'ard ter please," said the cook, deeply offended.

"Don't mind him, cook," said the admiring Sam. "You're a masterpiece, that's what you are."

"Of course, if any of you've got a better plan——" said the cook generously.

"Don't talk rubbish, cook," said Sam; "fetch the two cats out and put 'em together."

"Don't mix 'em," said the cook warningly; "for you'll never know which is which agin if you do."

He cautiously opened the top of the sack and produced his captive, and Satan, having been relieved from his prison, the two animals were carefully compared.

"They're as like as two lumps o' coal," said Sam

slowly. " Lord, what a joke on the old man. I must tell the mate o' this ; he'll enjoy it."

" It'll be all right if the parrot don't die," said the dainty pessimist, still harping on his pet theme. " All that bread spoilt, and two cats aboard."

"Don't mind what he ses," said Sam; "you're a brick, that's what you are. I'll just make a few holes in the lid o' the boy's chest, and pop old Satan in. You don't mind, do you, Billy ? "

" Of course he don't," said the other men indignantly.

Matters being thus agreeably arranged, Sam got a gimlet, and prepared the chest for the reception of its tenant, who, convinced that he was being put out of the way to make room for a rival, made a frantic fight for freedom.

" Now get something 'eavy and put on the top of it," said Sam, having convinced himself that the lock was broken ; " and, Billy, put the noo cat in the paint-locker till we start ; it's home-sick."

The boy obeyed, and the understudy was kept in durance vile until they were off Limehouse, when he came on deck and nearly ended his career there and then by attempting to jump over the bulwark into the next garden. For some time he paced the deck in a perturbed fashion, and then, leaping on the stern, mewed plaintively as his native city receded farther and farther from his view.

" What's the matter with old Satan," said the mate, who had been let into the secret. " He seems to have something on his mind."

" He'll have something round his neck presently," said the skipper grimly.

The prophecy was fulfilled some three hours later, when he came up on deck ruefully regarding the remains of a bird whose vocabulary had once been the pride of its native town. He threw it overboard without a word, and then, seizing the innocent cat, who had followed him under the impression that it was about to lunch, produced half a brick attached to a string, and tied it round his neck. The crew, who were enjoying the joke immensely, raised a howl of protest.

" The *Skylark*'ll never have another like it, sir," said Sam solemnly. " That cat was the luck of the ship."

" I don't want any of your old woman's yarns," said the skipper brutally. " If you want the cat, go and fetch it."

He stepped aft as he spoke, and sent the gentle stranger hurtling through the air. There was a " plomp " as it reached the water, a bubble or two came to the surface, and all was over.

" That's the last o' that," he said turning away.

The old man shook his head. " You can't kill a black cat for nothing," said he, " mark my words ! "

. . . .

The night, which had been dirty, cleared somewhat, and the bright crescent of the moon appeared above a heavy bank of clouds, as the cat, which had by dint of using its back as a lever at length got free from that cursed chest, licked its shapely limbs, and came up on deck. After its stifling prison, the air was simply delicious.

" Bob ! " yelled the skipper suddenly.

" Ay, ay, sir ! " said the look-out, in a startled voice.

" Did you mew ? " inquired the skipper.

" Did I *wot*, sir ? " cried the astonished Bob.

" Mew," said the skipper sharply, " like a cat ? "

" No, sir," said the offended seaman. " What 'ud I want to do that for ? "

" I don't know what you want to for," said the skipper,

looking round him uneasily. "There's some more rain coming, Bob."

"Ay, ay, sir," said Bob.

"Lot o' rain we've had this summer," said the skipper, in a meditative bawl.

"Ay, ay, sir," said Bob. "Sailing-ship on the port bow, sir."

The conversation dropped, the skipper, anxious to divert his thoughts, watching the dark mass of sail as it came plunging out of the darkness into the moonlight until it was abreast of his own craft. His eyes followed it as it passed his quarter, so that he saw not the stealthy approach of the cat which came from behind the companion, and sat down close by him. For over thirty hours the animal had been subjected to the grossest indignities at the hands of every man on board the ship except one. That one was the skipper, and there is no doubt but that its subsequent behaviour was a direct recognition of that fact. It rose to its feet, and crossing over to the unconscious skipper, rubbed its head affectionately and vigorously against his leg.

From simple causes great events do spring. The skipper sprang four yards, and let off a screech which was the subject of much comment on the barque which had just passed. When Bob, who came shuffling up at the double, reached him he was leaning against the side, incapable of speech, and shaking all over.

"Anything wrong, sir?" inquired the seaman anxiously, as he ran to the wheel.

The skipper pulled himself together a bit, and got closer to his companion.

"Believe me or not, Bob," he said at length, in trembling accents, "just as you please, but the ghost of that

294

—— cat, I mean the ghost of that poor affectionate animal which I drowned, and which I wish I hadn't, came and rubbed itself up against my leg."

" Which leg ? " inquired Bob, who was ever careful about details.

" What the blazes does it matter which leg ? " demanded the skipper, whose nerves were in a terrible state. " Ah, look—look there ! "

The seaman followed his outstretched finger, and his heart failed him as he saw the cat, with its back arched, gingerly picking its way along the side of the vessel.

" I can't see nothing," he said doggedly.

"Can't you see anything, cook ?" demanded the skipper.

" It may be fancy, sir," faltered the cook, lowering his eyes, " but it does seem to me as though I can see a little misty sort o' thing there. Ah, now it's gone."

" No, it ain't," said the skipper. " The ghost of Satan's sitting there. The case seems to have fallen on its tail. It appears to be howling something dreadful."

The men made a desperate effort to display the astonishment suitable to such a marvel, whilst Satan, who was trying all he knew to get his tail out, cursed freely. How long the superstitious captain of the *Skylark* would have let him remain there will never be known, for just then the mate came on deck and caught sight of it before he was quite aware of the part he was expected to play.

" Why the devil don't you lift the thing off the poor brute," he yelled, hurrying up towards the case.

" What, can *you* see it, Dick ? " said the skipper impressively, laying his hand on his arm.

" *See* it ? " retorted the mate. " D'ye think I'm blind ? Listen to the poor brute. I should—oh ! "

He became conscious of the concentrated significant gaze of the crew. Five pairs of eyes speaking as one, all saying " idiot " plainly, the boy's eyes conveying an expression too great to be translated.

Turning, the skipper saw the bye-play, and a light slowly dawned upon him. But he wanted more, and he wheeled suddenly to the cook for the required illumination.

The cook said it was a lark. Then he corrected himself and said it wasn't a lark, then he corrected himself again and became incoherent. Meantime the skipper eyed him stonily, while the mate released the cat and good-naturedly helped to straighten its tail.

It took fully five minutes of unwilling explanation before the skipper could grasp the situation. He did not appear to fairly understand it until he was shown the chest with the ventilated lid ; then his countenance cleared, and, taking the unhappy Billy by the collar, he called sternly for a piece of rope.

W. W. JACOBS (from *A Black Affair*)

SUMMER SORROWS OF THE SUPER-RICH

In the course of each summer it is my privilege to do some visiting in the class of the super-rich. By this I mean the kind of people who have huge estates at such fashionable places as Nagahucket, and Dogblastit, and up near Lake Owatawetness, where the country is so beautifully wild that it costs a thousand dollars an acre. . . .

Now you would think that the people who live in these great places are happy. They are not. They have troubles of which you and I and the ordinary people never dream. They come out to the wilderness to rough it, and to snatch a brief four months' vacation between the strain of the Riviera and the pressure of New York, and then, right in the happiest season of the summer, they come up against desperate problems. . . .

Problem No. 1. What to do to amuse the butler in the evening?

It seems that he doesn't play bridge. The butler who was here last year was always quite content if he could be provided with a game of bridge, and except for a run to New York now and then and a trip to see his brother in Vancouver in the middle of the summer, he stayed on the place without a break and seemed quite satisfied.

But the new man Jennings doesn't care for cards. He says quite frankly that it is not a matter of conscience and that he doesn't mind cards in the house, but that they simply don't interest him. So what can one do?

Problem No. 2. How to get the chauffeur's collars starched?

It appears that there have been very great difficulties at Dogblastit about this. It is very hard to get the kind of gloss that Ransome likes on his collars. There is, of course, an electric laundry in the basement of Dogblastit itself, but unfortunately the laundry maids who do the work in it will not undertake any collars over 11 inches long. They say they simply won't undertake them.

The experiment was made of bringing up a laundress from Boston, but it was found that she wouldn't undertake to starch anything at such a high altitude. She can only do her work at from 500 to 800 feet above the sea. Beyond that, she said, she could do nothing.

They tried also sending Ransome's collars by express to New York, but this was quite unsatisfactory, because the express people threw them about so roughly. More than once they were seen actually throwing the packet of Ransome's collars right from the platform of Dogblastit station into the express car. The only feasible thing up to now has been to have Ransome take one of the cars and drive his collars either to New York or to Philadelphia. The objection is that it takes up so much of his time, especially as he always likes to drive his boots over to Burlington, Vermont, once a week, where he can get them properly treated.

Problem No. 3. What to get for the cook to read on Sunday?

The trouble is, she doesn't care for fiction. She evidently is a woman of literary culture, somehow, because she said one day that she had read the whole of Shakespeare and thought it very good. In the library of Dogblastit itself, which is a really beautiful room done in Japanese oak with leaded windows to represent the reading room of a settler's cabin, there are practically no books that suit the cook. In fact, there are nothing but the Blue Book (one needs that to look up people in) and the Pink Book and the Red Book, and of course the Automobile Rude Book and then some Guide Books such as *The Perfect Bartender*, and the *Gentleman's Collar* and *Cocktails for All Occasions*.

Beyond that there are, of course, all the new books—the new fiction—because there is a standing order with Spentano to send up fifty pounds of new fiction by express once a week. None of the guests of the house ever care to read any book more than three weeks old, as they are quite worthless for conversation.

An order was sent to Boston for the Harvard Classics, but the cook says she doesn't care for the way they are selected. The only compromise so far is to get her books about the South Seas. She says she is just crazy over the South Sea literature. So we have given her *Six Weeks in the Marquesas Islands* and *Four Days in Fiji, Half Hours in Hoo-Poo*. But all that will only last her less than seven weeks, and after that we don't know what to do. . .

My visits with my fashionable friends have been so much disturbed by perpetual conversation on these problems that I have decided to give them up altogether and to get back into my own class of society. I have some friends, real ones, who have a wooden house on an island where there is no electric light within twenty miles and where they use rain water out of a barrel.

They have coal-oil lanterns to see by; they wear flannel collars and they pass the soap from one room to another as it is needed. The men cut the firewood, as required, and never keep more than half an hour's supply on hand, and the girls do all the work because help can't be got and they know ten different ways of cooking canned salmon.

I am going back there.

STEPHEN LEACOCK (from *Winnowed Wisdom*)

The burglar stepped inside the window quickly, and then he took his time. A burglar who respects his art always takes his time before taking anything else.

The house was a private residence. By its boarded front door and untrimmed Boston ivy the burglar knew that the mistress of it was sitting on some ocean-side piazza telling a sympathetic man in a yachting cap that no one had ever understood her sensitive, lonely heart. He knew by the light in the third-story front windows, and by the lateness of the season, that the master of the house had come home, and would soon extinguish his light and retire. For it was September of the year and of the soul, in which season the house's good man comes to consider roof gardens and stenographers as vanities, and to desire the return of his mate and the more durable blessings of decorum and the moral excellencies.

The burglar lighted a cigarette. The guarded glow of the match illuminated his salient points for a moment. He belonged to the third type of burglars.

This third type has not yet been recognised and accepted. The police had made us familiar with the first and second. Their classification is simple. The collar is the distinguishing mark.

When a burglar is caught who does not wear a collar he is described as a degenerate of the lowest type, singularly vicious and depraved, and is suspected of being the desperate criminal who stole the handcuffs out of Patrolman Hennessy's pocket in 1878 and walked away to escape arrest.

The other well-known type is the burglar who wears a collar. He is always referred to as a Raffles in real life. He is invariably a gentleman by daylight, breakfasting in a dress suit, and posing as a paper-hanger, while after dark he plies his nefarious occupation of burglary. His mother is an extremely wealthy and respected resident of Ocean Grove, and when he is conducted to his cell he asks at once for a nail file and the *Police Gazette*. He always has a wife in every State in the Union and fiancées in all the Territories, and the newspapers print his matrimonial gallery out of their stock of cuts of the ladies who were cured by only one bottle after having been given up by five doctors, experiencing great relief after the first dose.

The burglar wore a blue sweater. He was neither a Raffles nor one of the chefs from Hell's Kitchen. The police would have been baffled had they attempted to classify him. They have not yet heard of the respectable, unassuming burglar who is neither above nor below his station.

This burglar of the third class began to prowl. He wore no masks, dark lanterns, or gum shoes. He carried a 38-calibre revolver in his pocket, and he chewed peppermint gum thoughtfully.

The furniture of the house was swathed in its summer dust protectors. The silver was far away in safe-deposit vaults. The burglar expected no remarkable " haul." His objective point was that dimly lighted room where the master of the house should be sleeping heavily after whatever solace he had sought to lighten the burden of his loneliness. A " touch " might be made there to the extent of legitimate fair, professional profits—loose money, a watch, a jewelled stick-pin—nothing exorbitant or beyond reason. He had seen the window left open and had taken the chance.

The burglar softly opened the door of the lighted room.

The gas was turned low. A man lay in the bed asleep. On the dresser lay many things in confusion—a crumpled roll of bills, a watch, keys, three poker chips, crushed cigars, a pink silk hair bow, and an unopened bottle of bromo-seltzer for a bulwark in the morning.

The burglar took three steps toward the dresser. The man in the bed suddenly uttered a squeaky groan and opened his eyes. His right hand slid under his pillow, but remained there.

" Lay still," said the burglar in conversational tone. Burglars of the third type do not hiss. The citizen in the bed looked at the round end of the burglar's pistol and lay still.

" Now hold up both your hands," commanded the burglar.

The citizen had a little, pointed, brown-and-grey beard, like that of a painless dentist. He looked solid, esteemed, irritable, and disgusted. He sat up in bed and raised his right hand above his head.

" Up with the other one," ordered the burglar. " You might be amphibious and shoot with your left. You can count two, can't you ? Hurry up, now."

" Can't raise the other one," said the citizen with a contortion of his lineaments.

" What's the matter with it ? "

" Rheumatism in the shoulder."

" Inflammatory ? "

" Was. The inflammation has gone down."

The burglar stood for a moment or two, holding his gun on the afflicted one. He glanced at the plunder on the dresser and then, with a half-embarrassed air back at the man in the bed. Then he, too, made a sudden grimace.

" Don't stand there making faces," snapped the

302

citizen, bad-humouredly. " If you've come to burgle why don't you do it ? There's some stuff lying around."

" 'Scuse me," said the burglar, with a grin ; " but it just socked me one, too. It's good for you that rheumatism and me happens to be old pals. I got it in my left arm, too. Most anybody but me would have popped you when you wouldn't hoist that left claw of yours."

" How long have you had it ? " inquired the citizen.

" Four years. I guess that ain't all. Once you've got it, it's you for a rheumatic life—that's my judgment."

" Ever try rattlesnake oil ? " asked the citizen interestedly.

" Gallons," said the burglar. " If all the snakes I've used the oil of was strung out in a row they'd reach eight times as far as Saturn, and the rattles could be heard at Valparaiso, Indiana, and back."

" Some use Chiselum's Pills," remarked the citizen.

" Fudge ! " said the burglar. " Took 'em five months. No good. I had some relief the year I tried Finkelham's Extract, Balm of Gilead poultices, and Pott's Pain Pulverizer ; but I think it was the buckeye I carried in my pocket what done the trick."

" Is yours worse in the morning or at night ? " asked the citizen.

" Night," said the burglar ; " just when I'm busiest. Say, take down that arm of yours—I guess you won't— Say ! did you ever try Blickerstaff's Blood Builder ? "

" I never did. Does yours come in paroxysms or is it a steady pain ? "

The burglar sat down on the foot of the bed and rested his gun on his crossed knee.

" It jumps," said he. " It strikes me when I ain't looking for it. I had to give up second-story work because

I got stuck sometimes half-way up. Tell you what—I don't believe the bloomin' doctors know what is good for it."

" Same here. I've spent a thousand dollars without getting any relief. Yours swell any ? "

" Of mornings. And when it's goin' to rain—great Christopher ! "

" Me, too," said the citizen. " I can tell when a streak of humidity the size of a tablecloth starts from Florida on its way to New York. And if I pass a theatre where there's an ' East Lynne' matinée going on, the moisture starts my left arm jumping like a toothache."

" It's undiluted—hades ! " said the burglar.

" You're dead right," said the citizen.

The burglar looked down at his pistol and thrust it into his pocket with an awkward attempt at ease.

" Say, old man," he said constrainedly, " ever try opodeldoc ? "

" Slop ! " said the citizen angrily. " Might as well rub on restaurant butter."

" Sure," concurred the burglar. " It's a salve suitable for little Minnie when the kitty scratches her finger. I'll tell you what ! We're up against it. I only find one thing that eases her up. Hey ? Little old sanitary, ameliorating, lest-we-forget Booze. Say—this job's off—'scuse me—get on your clothes and let's go out and have some. 'Scuse the liberty, but—ouch ! There she goes again ! "

" For a week," said the citizen, " I haven't been able to dress myself without help. I'm afraid Thomas is in bed, and——"

" Climb out ! " said the burglar, " I'll help you get into your duds."

The conventional returned as a tidal wave and flooded the citizen. He stroked his brown-and-grey beard.

" It's very unusual——" he began.

" Here's your shirt," said the burglar, " fall out. I know a man who said Omberry's Ointment fixed him in two weeks so he could use both hands in tying his four-in-hand."

As they were going out the door the citizen turned and started back.

" Liked to forgot my money," he explained ; " laid it on the dresser last night."

The burglar caught him by the right sleeve.

" Come on," he said, bluffly. " I ask you. Leave it alone. I've got the price. Ever try witch hazel and oil of wintergreen ? "

O. HENRY (from Sixes and Sevens)

THE OLDEST JOKE

Many investigators have speculated as to the character of the first joke ; and as speculation must our efforts remain. But I personally have no doubt whatever as to the subject-matter of that distant pleasantry ; it was the face of the other person involved. I don't say that Adam was caustic about Eve's face or Eve about Adam's : that is improbable. Nor does matrimonial invective even now ordinarily take this form. But after a while, after cousins had come into the world, the facial jest began ; and by the time of Noah and his sons the riot was in full swing. In every rough and tumble among the children of Ham.

Shem, and Japheth, I feel certain that crude and candid personalities fell to the lot, at any rate, of the little Shems.

So was it then ; so is it still to-day. No jests are so rich as those that bear upon the unloveliness of features not our own. The tiniest street urchins in dispute always—sooner or later—devote their retorts to the distressing physiognomy of the foe. Not only are they conforming to the ancient convention, but they show sagacity too, for to sum up an opponent as " Face," " Facey," or " Funny Face," is to spike his gun. There is no reply but the cowardly *tu quoque*. He cannot say, " My face is not comic, it is handsome " ; because that does not touch the root of the matter. The root of the matter is your opinion of his face as deplorable.

Not only is the recognition of what is odd in an opponent's countenance of this priceless value in ordinary quarrels among the young and the ill-mannered (just as abuse of the opposing counsel is the best way of covering the poverty of one's own case at law), but the music-hall humorist has no easier or surer road to the risibilities of most of his audience. Jokes about faces never fail, and are never threadbare. Sometimes I find myself listening to one who has been called—possibly the label was self-imposed—the Prime Minister of Mirth, and he invariably enlarges upon the quaintness of somebody's features, often, for he is the soul of impartiality, his own ; and the first time, now thirty years ago, that I ever entered a music-hall (the tiny stuffy old Oxford at Brighton, where the chairman with the dyed hair—it was more purple than black—used to sit amid a little company of bloods whose proud privilege it was to pay for his refreshment), another George, whose surname was Beauchamp, was singing

306

about a siren into whose clutches he had or had not fallen, who had

an indiarubber lip
Like the rudder of a ship.

—So you see there is complete continuity.

But the best example of this branch of humour is beyond all question that of the Two Macs, whose influence, long though it is since they eclipsed the gaiety of the nation by vanishing, is still potent. Though gone they still jest : or, at any rate, their jests did not all vanish with them : the incorrigible veneration for what is antique displayed by low comedians takes care of that. " I saw your wife at the masked ball last night," the first Mac would say, in his rich brogue. " My wife was at the ball last night," the other would reply in a brogue of deeper richness, " but it wasn't a masked ball." The first Mac would then express an overwhelming surprise, as he countered with the devastating question, " Was *that* her face ? "

" You're not two-faced, anyway. I'll say that for you," was the apparently magnanimous concession made by one comedian to another in a recent farcical play. The other was beginning to express his gratification when the speaker continued : " If you were, you wouldn't have come out with that one." Again, you observe, there is no answer to this kind of attack. Hence, I suppose, its popularity. And yet, perhaps, to take refuge in a smug sententiousness, and remark crisply, " Handsome is as handsome does," should now and then be useful. But it requires some self-esteem.

There is no absolute need, however, for the face joke to be applied to others to be successful. Since, in spite of the complexion creams, " plumpers," and nose-machines advertised in the papers, faces will continue to be here and there somewhat Gothic, the wise thing for their owners is to accept them and think of other things, or console themselves before the unflattering mirror with the memory of those mortals who have been both quaint-looking and gifted. Wiser still perhaps to make a little capital out of the affliction. Public men who are able to make a jest of the homeliness of their features never lose by it. President Wilson's public recital of the famous lines on his countenance (which I personally find not impossibly unprepossessing) did much to increase his popularity.

> As a beauty I am not a star,
> There are others more handsome by far.
> But my face, I don't mind it,
> For I keep behind it ;
> It's the people in front get the jar.

And an English bishop, or possibly dean, came, at last, very near earth when in a secular address he repeated his retort to the lady who had commented upon his extraordinary plainness : "Ah, but you should see my brother." There is also the excellent story of the ugly man before the camera, who was promised by the photographer that he should have justice done to him. "Justice !" he exclaimed. "I don't want justice ; I want mercy."

The great face joke, as I say, obviously came first. Because there were in the early days none of the materials for the other staple quips—such as alcohol, and sausages, and wives' mothers. Faces, however, were always there. And not even yet have the later substitutes ousted it. Just as Shakespeare's orator, "When he is out," spits, so does the funny man, in similar difficulties, if he is wise, say, "Do you call that a face ?" and thus collects his thoughts for fresh sallies. If all " dials " were identical, Mr. George Graves, for example, would be a stage bankrupt ; for, resourceful as he is in the humour of quizzical disapproval, the vagaries of facial oddity are his foundation stone.

Remarkable as are the heights of grotesque simile to which all the Georges have risen in this direction, it is, oddly enough, to the other and gentler sex that the classic examples (in my experience) belong. At a dinner-party given by a certain hospitable lady who remained something of an *enfant terrible* to the end of her long life, she drew the attention of one of her guests, by no means too cautiously, to the features of another guest, a bishop of great renown. " Isn't his face," she asked, in a deathless sentence, " like the inside of an elephant's foot ? " I have not personally the honour of this divine's acquaintance, but all my friends who have met or seen him assure me that the similitude is exact. Another lady, happily still living, said of the face of an acquaintance, that it was " not so much a face, as a part of her person which she happened to leave uncovered, by which her friends were able to recognise her." A third, famous for her swift analyses, said that a certain would-be beauty might have a title to good looks but for a " rush of teeth to the head." I do not quote these admirable remarks merely as a proof of woman's natural kindliness, but to show how even among the elect—for all three speakers are of more than common culture—the face joke holds sway.

E. V. LUCAS (from *Mixed Vintages*)

The grill-room clock struck eleven with the respectful unobtrusiveness of one whose mission in life is to be ignored. When the flight of time should really have rendered abstinence and migration imperative the lighting apparatus would signal the fact in the usual way.

Six minutes later Clovis approached the supper-table, in the blessed expectancy of one who has dined sketchily and long ago.

" I'm starving," he announced, making an effort to sit down gracefully and read the menu at the same time.

" So I gathered," said his host, " from the fact that you were nearly punctual. I ought to have told you that I'm a Food Reformer. I've ordered two bowls of bread-and-milk and some health biscuits. I hope you don't mind."

Clovis pretended afterwards that he didn't go white above the collar-line for the fraction of a second.

" All the same," he said, " you ought not to joke about such things. There really are such people. I've known people who've met them. To think of all the adorable things there are to eat in the world, and then to go through life munching sawdust and being proud of it."

" They're like the Flagellants of the Middle Ages, who went about mortifying themselves."

" They had some excuse," said Clovis. " They did it to save their immortal souls, didn't they ? You needn't tell me that a man who doesn't love oysters and asparagus and good wines has got a soul, or a stomach either. He's simply got the instinct for being unhappy highly developed."

Clovis relapsed for a few golden moments into tender

intimacies with a succession of rapidly disappearing oysters.

" I think oysters are more beautiful than any religion," he resumed presently. " They not only forgive our unkindness to them ; they justify it, they incite us to go on being perfectly horrid to them. Once they arrive at the supper-table they seem to enter thoroughly into the spirit of the thing. There's nothing in Christianity or Buddhism that quite matches the sympathetic unselfishness of an oyster. Do you like my new waistcoat ? I'm wearing it for the first time to-night."

" It looks like a great many others you've had lately, only worse. New dinner waistcoats are becoming a habit with you."

" They say one always pays for the excesses of one's youth ; mercifully that isn't true about one's clothes. My mother is thinking of getting married."

" Again ! "

" It's the first time."

" Of course, you ought to know. I was under the impression that she'd been married once or twice at least."

" Three times, to be mathematically exact. I meant that it was the first time she'd thought about getting married ; the other times she did it without thinking. As a matter of fact, it's really I who am doing the thinking for her in this case. You see, it's quite two years since her last husband died."

" You evidently think that brevity is the soul of widowhood."

" Well, it struck me that she was getting moped, and beginning to settle down, which wouldn't suit her a bit. The first symptom that I noticed was when she began to complain that we were living beyond our income. All decent people live beyond their incomes nowadays, and those who aren't respectable live beyond other people's. A few gifted individuals manage to do both."

" It's hardly so much a gift as an industry."

" The crisis came," returned Clovis, " when she suddenly started the theory that late hours were bad for one, and wanted me to be in by one o'clock every night. Imagine that sort of thing for me, who was eighteen on my last birthday."

" On your last two birthdays, to be mathematically exact."

" Oh, well, that's not my fault. I'm not going to arrive at nineteen as long as my mother remains at thirty-seven. One must have some regard for appearances."

" Perhaps your mother would age a little in the process of settling down."

" That's the last thing she'd think of. Feminine reformations always start in on the failings of other people. That's why I was so keen on the husband idea."

" Did you go as far as to select the gentleman, or did you merely throw out a general idea, and trust to the force of suggestion ? "

" If one wants a thing done in a hurry one must see to it oneself. I found a military Johnny hanging round on a loose end at the club, and took him home to lunch once or twice. He's spent most of his life on the Indian frontier building roads, and relieving famines and minimizing earthquakes, and all that sort of thing that one does do on frontiers. He could talk sense to a peevish cobra in fifteen native languages, and probably knew what to do if you found a rogue elephant on your croquet-lawn ; but he was shy and diffident with women. I told my mother privately that he was an absolute woman-hater ; so, of course, she laid herself out to flirt all she knew, which isn't a little."

" And was the gentleman responsive ? "

" I hear he told some one at the club that he was looking out for a Colonial job, with plenty of hard work, for a young friend of his, so I gather that he has some idea of marrying into the family."

" You seem destined to be the victim of the reformation, after all."

Clovis wiped the trace of Turkish coffee and the beginnings of a smile from his lips, and slowly lowered his dexter eyelid. Which, being interpreted, probably meant " I *don't* think ! "

" SAKI " (from *The Chronicles of Clovis*)

SPORT AT THE RACES

The races had by this time begun with a competition known as the " Hop, Step, and Lep " ; this, judging by the yells was a highly interesting display, but as it was conducted between two impervious rows of onlookers, the aristocracy on the fish-boxes saw nothing save the occasional purple face of a competitor, starting into view above the wall of backs like a jack-in-the-box. For me, however, the odorous sanctuary of the fish-boxes was not to be. I left it guarded by Slipper with a cart-whip of flail-like dimensions, as disreputable an object as could be seen out of low comedy, with someone's old white cords on his bandy legs, butcher boots three sizes too big for him, and a black eye. The small boys fled before him ; in the glory of his office he would have flailed his own mother off the fish-boxes had occasion served.

I had an afternoon of decidedly mixed enjoyment. My stewardship blossomed forth like Aaron's rod, and added to itself the duties of starter, handicapper, general referee, and chucker-out, besides which I from time to time strove with emissaries who came from Philippa with messages about water and kettles. Flurry and I had to deal single-handed with the foot-races (our brothers in office being otherwise engaged at Mr. Sheehy's), a task of many difficulties, chiefest being that the spectators all swept forward at the word "Go!" and ran the race with the competitors, yelling curses, blessings, and advice upon them, taking short cuts over anything and everybody, and mingling inextricably with the finish. By fervent applications of the whips, the course was to some extent purged for the quarter-mile, and it would, I believe, have been a triumph of handicapping had not an unforeseen disaster overtaken the favourite—old Mrs. Knox's bath-chair boy. Whether, as was alleged, his braces had or had not been tampered with by a rival was a matter that the referee had subsequently to deal with in the thick of a free fight; but the painful fact remained that in the course of the first lap what were described as "his galluses" abruptly severed their connection with the garments for whose safety they were responsible, and the favourite was obliged to seek seclusion in the crowd.

The tug-of-war followed close on this *contretemps*, and had the excellent effect of drawing away, like a blister, the inflammation set up by the grievances of the bath-chair boy. I cannot at this moment remember of how many men each team consisted; my sole aim was to keep the numbers even, and to baffle the volunteers, who, in an ecstasy of sympathy, attached themselves to the tail of the rope at moments when their champions weakened. The rival forces dug their heels in and tugged in an uproar that drew forth the innermost line of customers from Mr. Sheehy's porter tent, and even attracted " the quality " from the haven of the fish-boxes, Slipper, in the capacity of Squire of Dames, pioneering Lady Knox through the crowd with the cart-whip, and with language whose nature was providentially veiled, for the most part, by the din. The tug-of-war continued unabated. One team was getting the worst of it, but hung doggedly on, sinking lower and lower till they gradually sat down ; nothing short of the trump of judgment could have conveyed to them, that they were breaking rules, and both teams settled down by slow degrees on to their sides, with the rope under them, and their heels still planted in the ground, bringing about complete deadlock. I do not know the record duration for a tug-of-war, but I can certify that the Cullinagh and Knockranny teams lay on the ground at full tension for half-an-hour, like men in apoplectic fits, each man with his respective adherents howling over him, blessing him, and adjuring him to continue.

With my own nauseated eyes I saw a bearded country-man, obviously one of Mr. Sheehy's best customers, fling himself on his knees beside one of the combatants, and kiss his crimson and streaming face in a rapture of en-couragement. As he shoved unsteadily past me on his return journey to Mr. Sheehy's, I heard him informing a friend that " he cried a handful over Danny Mulloy, when he seen the poor brave boy so shtubborn, and, indeed, he couldn't say why he cried."

" For good-nature, ye'd cry," suggested the friend.

" Well, just that, I suppose," returned Danny Mulloy's

315

admirer resignedly ; " indeed, if it was only two cocks ye seen fightin' on the road, yer heart'd take part with one o' them ! "

I had begun to realise that I might as well abandon the tug-of-war and occupy myself elsewhere, when my wife's much harassed messenger brought me the portentous tidings that Mrs. Yeates wanted me at the tent at once. When I arrived I found the tent literally bulging with Philippa's guests ; Lady Knox, seated on a hamper, was taking off her gloves, and loudly announcing her desire for tea, and Philippa, with a flushed face and a crooked hat, breathed into my ear the awful news that both the cream and the milk had been forgotten.

" But Flurry Knox says he can get me some," she went on ; " he's gone to send people to milk a cow that lives near here. Go out and see if he's coming."

I went out and found, in the first instance, Mrs. Cadogan, who greeted me with the prayer that the divil might roast Julia McCarthy, that legged it away to the races like a wild goose, and left the cream afther her on the servants' hall table. " Sure, Misther Flurry's gone looking for a cow, and what cow would there be in a backwards place like this ? And look at me shtriving to keep the kettle simpering on the fire, and not as much coals undher it as'd redden a pipe ! "

" Where's Mr. Knox ? " I asked.

" Himself and Slipper's galloping the counthry like the deer. I believe it's to the house above they went, sir."

I followed up a rocky hill to the house above, and there found Flurry and Slipper engaged in the patriarchal task of driving two brace of coupled and spancelled goats into a shed.

" It's the best we can do," said Flurry briefly ; " there

isn't a cow to be found, and the people are all down at the sports. Be d——d to you, Slipper, don't let them go from you!" as the goats charged and doubled like football players.

"But goats' milk!" I said, paralysed by horrible memories of what tea used to taste like at Gib.

"They'll never know it!" said Flurry, cornering a venerable nanny; "here, hold this divil, and hold her tight!"

I have no time to dwell upon the pastoral scene that followed. Suffice it to say, that at the end of ten minutes of scorching profanity from Slipper, and incessant warfare with the goats, the latter had reluctantly yielded two small jugfuls, and the dairymaids had exhibited a nerve and skill in their trade that won my lasting respect.

"I knew I could trust *you*, Mr. Knox!" said Philippa, with shining eyes, as we presented her with the two foaming beakers. I suppose a man is never a hero to his wife, but if she could have realised the bruises on my legs, I think she would have reserved a blessing for me also.

What was thought of the goats' milk I gathered symptomatically from a certain fixity of expression that accompanied the first sip of the tea, and from observing that comparatively few ventured on second cups. I also noted that, after a brief conversation with Flurry, Miss Sally poured hers secretly on to the grass.

E. Œ. SOMERVILLE AND MARTIN ROSS
(from *The Irish R.M.*)

" O illustrious person," said Kai Lung very earnestly, " this is evidently an unfortunate mistake. Doubtless you were expecting some exalted Mandarin to come and render you homage, and were preparing to overwhelm him with gratified confusion by escorting him yourself to your well-appointed abode. Indeed, I passed such a one on the road, very richly apparelled, who inquired of me the way to the mansion of the dignified and upright Lin Yi. By this time he is perhaps two or three li towards the east."

" However distinguished a Mandarin he may be, it is fitting that I should first attend to one whose manners and accomplishments betray him to be of the Royal House," replied Lin Yi, with extreme affability. " Precede me, therefore, to my mean and uninviting hovel, while I gain more honour than I can reasonably bear by following closely in your elegant footsteps, and guarding your Imperial person with this inadequate but heavily-loaded weapon."

Seeing no chance of immediate escape, Kai Lung led the way, instructed by the brigand, along a very difficult and bewildering path, until they reached a cave hidden among the crags. Here Lin Yi called out some words in the Miaotze tongue, whereupon a follower appeared, and opened a gate in the stockade of prickly mimosa which guarded the mouth of the den. Within the enclosure a fire burned, and food was being prepared. At a word from the chief, the unfortunate Kai Lung found his hands seized and tied behind his back, while a second later a rough hemp rope was fixed round his neck, and the other end tied to an overhanging tree.

Lin Yi smiled pleasantly and critically upon these preparations, and when they were complete dismissed his follower.

"Now we can converse at our ease and without restraint," he remarked to Kai Lung. "It will be a distinguished privilege for a person occupying the important public position which you undoubtedly do; for myself, my instincts are so degraded and low-minded that nothing gives me more gratification than to dispense with ceremony."

To this Kai Lung made no reply, chiefly because at that moment the wind swayed the tree, and compelled him to stand on his toes in order to escape suffocation.

"It would be useless to try to conceal from a person of your inspired intelligence that I am indeed Lin Yi," continued the robber. "It is a dignified position to occupy, and one for which I am quite incompetent. In the sixth month of the third year ago, it chanced that this unworthy person, at that time engaged in commercial affairs at Knei Yang, became inextricably immersed in the insidious delights of quail-fighting. Having been entrusted with a large number of taels with which to purchase elephants' teeth, it suddenly occurred to him that if he doubled the number of taels by staking them upon an exceedingly powerful and agile quail, he would be able to purchase twice the number of teeth, and so benefit his patron to a large extent. This matter was clearly forced upon his notice by a dream, in which he perceived one whom he then understood to be the benevolent spirit of an ancestor in the act of stroking a particular quail, upon whose chances he accordingly placed all he possessed. Doubtless evil spirits had been employed in the matter; for, to this person's great astonishment the

319

quail in question failed in a very discreditable manner at the encounter. Unfortunately, this person had risked not only the money which had been entrusted to him, but all that he had himself become possessed of by some years of honourable toil and assiduous courtesy as a professional witness in law cases. Not doubting that his patron would see that he was himself greatly to blame in confiding so large a sum of money to a comparatively young man of whom he knew little, this person placed the matter before him, at the same time showing him that he would suffer in the eyes of the virtuous if he did not restore this person's savings, which but for the presence of the larger sum, and a generous desire to benefit his patron, he would never have risked in so uncertain a venture as that of quail-fighting. Although the facts were laid in the form of a dignified request instead of a demand by legal means, and the reasoning carefully drawn up in columns on fine parchment by a very illustrious writer, the reply which this person received showed him plainly that a wrong view had been taken of the matter, and that the time had arrived when it became necessary for him to make a suitable rejoinder by leaving the city without delay."

"It was a high-minded and disinterested course to take," said Kai Lung with great conviction, as Lin Yi paused. "Without doubt evil will shortly overtake the avaricious-souled person at Knei Yang."

"It has already done so," replied Lin Yi. "While passing through this forest in the season of Many White Vapours, the spirits of his bad deeds appeared to him in misleading and symmetrical shapes and drew him out of the path and away from his bowmen. After suffering many torments, he found his way here, where, in spite of our continual care, he perished miserably and in great bodily pain. . . . But I cannot conceal from myself, in spite of your distinguished politeness, that I am becoming intolerably tiresome with my commonplace talk."

" On the contrary," replied Kai Lung, " while listening to your voice I seemed to hear the beating of many gongs of the finest and most polished brass. I floated in the Middle Air, and for the time I even became unconscious of the fact that this honourable appendage, though fashioned, as I perceive, out of the most delicate silk, makes it exceedingly difficult for me to breathe."

" Such a thing cannot be permitted," exclaimed Lin Yi, with some indignation, as with his own hands he slackened the rope, and, taking it from Kai Lung's neck, fastened it round his ankle. " Now, in return for my uninviting confidences, shall not my senses be gladdened by a recital of the titles and honours borne by your distinguished family ? Doubtless, at this moment many Mandarins of the highest degree are anxiously awaiting your arrival at Knei Yang, perhaps passing the time by outdoing one another in protesting the number of taels each would give rather than permit you to be tormented by fire-brands, or even to lose a single ear."

" Alas ! " replied Kai Lung, " never was there a truer proverb than that which says, ' It is a mark of insincerity of purpose to spend one's time in looking for the sacred Emperor in the low-class tea-shops.' Do Mandarins or the friends of Mandarins travel in mean garments and unattended ? Indeed, the person who is now before you is none other than the outcast Kai Lung, the story-teller, one of degraded habits and no very distinguished or reputable ancestors. His friends are few, and mostly of the criminal class ; his wealth is not more than some six or eight cash, concealed in his left sandal ; and his entire stock-in-trade consists of a few unendurable and badly told stories, to which, however, it is his presumptuous intention shortly to add a dignified narrative of the high-born Lin Yi, setting out his domestic virtues and the honour which he has reflected upon his house, his valour in war, the destruction of his enemies, and, above all, his great benevolence and the protection which he extends to the poor and those engaged in the distinguished arts."

" The absence of friends is unfortunate," said Lin Yi thoughtfully, after he had possessed himself of the coins indicated by Kai Lung, and also of a much larger amount concealed elsewhere among the story-teller's clothing.

ERNEST BRAMAH (from *The Wallet of Kai Lung*)

SECOND PART

§ III STAR DUST

Bright thoughts are the gems of noble minds.

SIR THOMAS BROWNE

The true harvest of my daily life is somewhat as intangible and indescribable as the tints of morning or evening. It is a little star-dust caught, a segment of the rainbow which I have clutched.

THOREAU (*Walden*)

"Can you emit sparks?" said the cat to the ugly duckling in the fairy tale, and the poor abashed creature had to admit that it could not.

A. BIRRELL (*Res Judicatae*)

§III STAR DUST

THOUGHTS WORTH REMEMBERING

Others, too, having done what men may, have borne what men must.

> Speech of Nicias to the Athenian Army

Wise men learn more from fools than fools learn from wise men.

> CATO

We cannot prevent the black birds of evil from flying over our heads, but we can prevent them from building their nests in our hair.

> *Chinese Proverb*

He who goes to the hills goes to his mother.

> *Indian Saying*

Of law there can be no less acknowledged than that her seat is in the bosom of God, her voice the harmony of the world, all things in heaven and earth do her homage,—the very least in feeling her care, and the greatest as not exempted from her power.

> HOOKER

Man is a name of honour for a king.

> CHAPMAN

What a deal of cold business doth a man mis-spend the better part of life in ! In scattering compliments, tendering visits, gathering and venting news, following feasts and plays, making a little winter-love in a dark corner.

BEN JONSON

Old friends are best. King James used to call for his old shoes : they were easiest for his feet.

King James said to the fly, Have I three kingdoms, and thou must needs fly into my eye ?

SELDEN

> Only the actions of the just
> Smell sweet and blossom in their dust.

SHIRLEY

Act nothing in furious passion ; it's putting to sea in a storm.

Almost twenty years since, I heard a profane jest, and still remember it. How many pious passages of a far later date have I forgotten ! It seems my soul is like a filthy pond, wherein fish die soon, and frogs live long.

Some admiring what motives to mirth infants meet with in their silent and solitary smiles, have resolved (how truly I know not) that then they converse with angels.

THOMAS FULLER

No man can make another man to be his slave, unless he hath first enslaved himself to life and death, to pleasure and pain, to hope or fear ; command these passions, and you are freer than the Parthian Kings.

Stay but till to-morrow, and your present sorrow will be weary, and will lie down to rest.

JEREMY TAYLOR

A man that should call every thing by its right name, would hardly pass the streets without being knocked down as a common enemy.

Hope is generally a wrong guide, though it is very good company by the way.

The best party is but a kind of conspiracy against the rest of the nation.

LORD HALIFAX

You will never enjoy the world aright till the sea itself floweth in your veins, till you are clothed with the heavens and crowned with the stars.

THOMAS TRAHERNE

Friendship is to be purchased only by friendship. A man may have authority over others ; but he can never have their heart but by giving his own.

BISHOP WILSON (1663–1755)

In faith and hope the world will disagree,
But all mankind's concern is charity.

· · · ·

Is there no bright reversion in the sky
For those who greatly think, or bravely die ?

POPE

Statesmen and beauties are very rarely sensible of the gradations of their decay ; and, too sanguinely hoping to shine on in their meridian, often set with contempt and ridicule.

Cunning is the dark sanctuary of incapacity.

LORD CHESTERFIELD

The English have a hundred religions, but only one sauce.

VOLTAIRE

There is nothing so ridiculous that has not at some time been said by some philosopher.

GOLDSMITH

There is more pleasure in building castles in the air than on the ground.

GIBBON

If the world were good for nothing else, it is a fine subject for speculation.

HAZLITT

God created man in his image, and man has not been slow in returning the compliment.

HEINE

Our dead are never dead to us until we have forgotten them ; they can be injured by us, they can be wounded.

GEORGE ELIOT

We need examples of people who, leaving Heaven to decide whether they are to rise in the world, decide for themselves that they will be happy in it, and have resolved to seek not greater wealth but simple pleasure, not higher future but deeper felicity—to make the first of possessions self-possession.

RUSKIN

There is no room for sweeping denunciations or trenchant criticisms in the dealings of a world whose falsehoods and veracities are separated by so very thin a barrier.

BISHOP STUBBS (1825–1901)

Business is really more agreeable than pleasure ; it interests the whole mind, the aggregate nature of man more continuously, and more deeply. But it does not *look* as if it did.

WALTER BAGEHOT

To himself every one is an immortal ; he may know that he is going to die, but he can never know that he is dead.

SAMUEL BUTLER (1835–1902)

Vulgarity is an inadequate conception of the art of living.

BISHOP CREIGHTON

Education is an admirable thing, but it is well to remember from time to time that nothing that is worth knowing can be taught.

The soul is born old but grows young. That is the comedy of life. The body is born young and grows old. That's life's tragedy.

OSCAR WILDE

The soul is dyed the colour of its leisure thoughts.

DEAN INGE

The difficult is that which can be done immediately, the impossible that which takes a little longer.

NANSEN

Whoever it was who searched the heavens with his telescope and found no God would not have found the human mind if he had searched the brain with a microscope.

Truth is a jewel which should not be painted over ; but it may be set to advantage and shown in a good light.

Life is not a spectacle or a feast ; it is a predicament.

To understand oneself is the classic form of consolation ; to elude oneself is the romantic.

GEORGE SANTAYANA

JOTTINGS BY LEONARDO

Who injures others regards not himself.

Why does the eye see a thing more clearly in dreams than the imagination when awake ?

In rivers, the water that you touch is the last of what has passed and the first of that which comes : so with time present.

Thou, O God, dost sell unto us all good things at the price of labour.

As a well-spent day brings happy sleep, so life well used brings happy death.

Note-Books of Leonardo da Vinci

(Trans. E. MCCURDY)

SOME PROVERBS

The best preacher is the heart ; the best teacher is time ; the best book is the world ; the best friend is God.

Before fording the river, do not curse the alligator's mother.

If fate throws a knife at you, there are two ways of catching it—by the blade and by the handle.

The dogs bark but the caravan passes.

God does not smite with both hands.

If the weather is fine, take your cloak ; if it rains, do as you please.

Hope is a good breakfast but a bad supper.

The gods sell all things at a fair price.

No man can be happy without a friend, nor be sure of him till he's unhappy.

Genius is one part inspiration and three parts perspiration.

Do right, and fear no man ; don't write, and fear no woman.

By the road called Straight we come to the house called Beautiful.

He who speaks the truth must have one foot in the stirrup.

No one but God and I knows what is in my heart.

The stars make no noise.

Night is a good herdsman, she brings all creatures home.

From poverty to profusion is a hard journey, but the way back is easy.

You can count the number of apples on one tree, but you cannot count the number of trees in one apple.

HOT AND COLD

She is my joy, she is my care and woe,
She is my pain, she is my ease therefor
She is my death, she is my life also,

She is my salve, she is my wound so sore :
In fine, she hath the hand and knife
That both may save and end my life.

EDWARD DE VERE, EARL OF OXFORD

THE BEST OF SHYLOCK

TUBAL : There came divers of Antonio's creditors in my company to Venice. . . One of them showed me a ring that he had of your daughter for a monkey.

SHYLOCK : Out upon her ! Thou torturest me, Tubal. It was my turquoise. I had it of Leah when I was a bachelor ! I would not have given it for a wilderness of monkeys.

SHAKESPEARE (from *Merchant of Venice*)

OTHER SHAKESPEARIAN ITEMS

There was a star danced, and under that was I born. Cousins, God give you joy !

(From *Much Ado About Nothing*)

A good leg will fall ; a straight back will stoop ; a black beard will turn white ; a curled pate will grow bald ; a fair face will wither ; a full eye will wax hollow : but a good heart, Kate, is the sun and the moon ; or rather the sun and not the moon ; for it shines bright and never changes, but keeps his course truly.

(From *Henry V*)

Weariness
Can snore upon the flint, when resty sloth
Finds the down pillow hard.

(From *Cymbeline*)

They say miracles are past : and we have our philosophical
persons to make modern and familiar things supernatural
and causeless. Hence is it that we make trifles of terrors,
ensconcing ourselves into seeming knowledge, when we
should submit ourselves to an unknown fear.

(From *All's Well that Ends Well*)

Let never day nor night unhallow'd pass,
But still remember what the Lord hath done.

(From *2 Henry VI*)

To Thee I do commend my watchful soul
Ere I let fall the windows of mine eyes :
Sleeping and waking, O, defend me still !

(From *Richard III*)

ELIZABETHAN CRITICISM

1. *Homage to Chaucer*

Truly I know not, whether to mervaile more, either
that he in that mistie time, could see so clearely, or that
wee in this cleare age, walke so stumblingly after him.

SIR PHILIP SIDNEY

2. *Satirical Observations on certain " lines in Mr. Shakespeare's vayne "*

Ey marry, Sir, these have some life in them ! Let this
duncified worlde esteeme of Spencer and Chaucer, I'le

333

worshipp sweet Mr. Shakespeare and to honour him will lay his Venus and Adonis under my pillowe, as we reade of one (I doe not well remember his name, but I am sure he was a Kinge), slept with Homer under his bed's heade.

ANONYMOUS (from *The Returne from Parnassus*,
a play acted by students of St. John's College,
Cambridge, 1601)

CORYATE DISCOVERS THE FORK

I observed a custom in all those Italian cities and towns through the which I passed, that is not used in any other country that I saw in my travels. The Italians do always at their meals use a little fork when they cut their meat. The reason of this their curiosity is, because the Italian cannot by any means endure to have his dish touched with fingers, seeing all men's fingers are not alike clean.

THOMAS CORYATE (from *Crudities*, 1611)

GIPSY SONG

The faery beam upon you,
The stars to glister on you ;
   A moon of light
   In the noon of night,
Till the fire-drake hath o'ergone you !
The wheel of fortune guide you,
The boy with the bow beside you ;
   Run aye in the way
   Till the bird of day,
And the luckier lot betide you !

BEN JONSON

334

INFORMATIONS OF BEN JONSON TO W. D.

when he came to Scotland on foot

That Shakspear wanted Arte :

That he told Cardinal depperon at his being in France anno 1613 who shew him his translations of Virgill that they were naught :

Shakspear in a play brought in a number of men saying they had suffered Shipwrack in Bohemia wher yr is no sea neer by some 100 miles :

S. P. Sidney was no pleasant man in countenance, his face being spoiled with Pimples :

Queen Elizabeth never saw herself after she became old in a true Glass. they painted her & sometymes would vermilion her nose, she had allwayes about Christmas evens set dice, that threw sixes or five, & she knew not they were other, to make her win & esteame herself fortunate :

A Cook, who was of ane evill lyfe, when a minister told him he would to hell, askt what torment was yr, being answered fyre, fire (said he) that is my Playfellow.

From *Notes made by William Drummond of Hawthornden,* 1619

HOW SHAKESPEARE STRUCK A CONTEMPORARY

Hee was (indeed) honest, and of an open, and free nature : had an excellent *Phantsie* ; brave notions, and gentle expressions : wherein he flow'd with that facility that sometime it was necessary he should be stop'd.

BEN JONSON (from *Discoveries,* 1641)

335

IF ALL BE TRUE

If all be true that I do think,
There are five reasons we should drink;
Good wine; a friend; or being dry;
Or lest we should be by and by;
Or any other reason why.

HENRY ALDRICH

NIGHT-WORK

Now Mayors and Shrieves are hush'd and satiate lay,
Yet eat in dreams, the custard of the day;
While pensive poets painful vigil keep,
Sleepless themselves, to give their readers sleep.

POPE (from The Dunciad)

TWO RIVERS

Says Tweed to Till—
" What gars ye rin sae still ? "
Says Till to Tweed—
" Though ye rin with speed
And I rin slaw,
For ae man that ye droon
I droon twa."

ANONYMOUS

AN UNSATISFACTORY POSITION

" I wish I had not known so much of this affair," added
my uncle Toby, " or that I had known more of it."

STERNE (from Tristram Shandy)

A BLOCK IN PICCADILLY

I have been twice going to stop my coach in Piccadilly (and the same has happened to Lady Aylesbury), thinking there was a mob; and it was only nymphs and swains sauntering or trudging. T'other morning, i.e. at two o'clock, I went to see Mrs. Garrick and Miss Hannah More at the Adelphi, and was stopped five times before I reached Northumberland House; for the tides of coaches, chariots, curricles, phaetons, &c., are endless. Indeed, the town is so extended, that the breed of chairs is almost lost; for Hercules and Atlas could not carry anybody from one end of this enormous capital to the other.

HORACE WALPOLE (from Correspondence)

HORACE'S CHOICE

I had rather be put into the round-house for a wrong-headed quarrel, than sup quietly at eight o'clock with my grandmother.

HORACE WALPOLE

EPIGRAM ON BEAUTY

You say that Celia's face combines
The lily and the rose;
True, on her cheek the former pines,
The latter tips her nose.

ANONYMOUS (18th Century)

TWO HEADS BETTER THAN ONE

See, one physician, like a sculler, plies,
The patient lingers and by inches dies.
But two physicians, like a pair of oars,
Waft him more swiftly to the Stygian shores.

ANONYMOUS

SAYINGS OF SAMUEL JOHNSON

Whoever thinks of going to bed before twelve o'clock is a scoundrel.

The happiest part of a man's life is what he passes lying awake in bed in the morning.

Hope is itself a species of happiness, and, perhaps, the chief happiness which this world affords.

Sir, when a man is tired of London, he is tired of life; for there is in London all that life can afford.

If a man does not make new acquaintance as he advances through life, he will soon find himself left alone. A man, Sir, should keep his friendship in constant repair.

Sorrow is a kind of rust of the soul, which every new idea contributes in its passage to scour away.

Grief is a species of idleness.

Small debts are like small shot; they are rattling on every side, and can scarcely be escaped without a wound; great debts are like cannon; of loud noise, but little danger.

The highest panegyric that private virtue can receive is the praise of servants.

BOSWELL (from *Life of Johnson*)

GOOD SHOTS FROM A WITTY CAN(N)ON

A Welcome Gift

I thank God, who has made me poor, that he has made me merry.

Improvement in Modern Travel

The Scotchman now eats his porridge at home in the morning and scratches himself in Piccadilly ere set of sun.

Sleepy Sermons

Is sin to be taken from men, as Eve was from Adam, by casting them into a deep slumber?

SYDNEY SMITH

SOME CURES FOR THE BLUES

1. Live as well as you dare.
2. Go into the shower-bath.
3. Amusing books.
4. Be as busy as you can.
5. See as much as you can of those friends who respect and like you.
6. Compare your lot with that of other people.
7. Be as much as you can in the open air without fatigue.
8. Don't be too severe upon yourself.

SYDNEY SMITH (from Correspondence)

EAU DE COLOGNE

In Köln, a town of monks and bones,
And pavements fang'd with murderous stones,
And rags, and hags, and hideous wenches ;
I counted two and seventy stenches,
All well defined, and several stinks !
Ye Nymphs that reign o'er sewers and sinks,
The river Rhine, it is well known,
Doth wash your city of Cologne ;
But tell me, Nymphs ! what power divine
Shall henceforth wash the river Rhine ?

COLERIDGE

SOUVENIR

Jenny kiss'd me when we met,
   Jumping from the chair she sat in ;
Time, you thief ! who love to get
   Sweets into your list, put that in.
Say I'm weary, say I'm sad ;
   Say that health and wealth have miss'd me ;
Say I'm growing old, but add—
   Jenny kiss'd me !

LEIGH HUNT

POETRY

Poetry awakens and enlarges the mind by a thousand
unapprehended combinations of thought. It lifts the veil
from the hidden beauty of the world. The great secret of

morals is love ; or a going out of our own nature, and an identification of ourselves with the beautiful which exists in thought, action, or person, not our own. A man to be greatly good must imagine intensely and comprehensively ; he must put himself in the place of another and of many others ; the pains and pleasures of his species must become his own. The great instrument of moral good is the imagination. Poetry enlarges the circumference of the imagination and strengthens the faculty which is the organ of the moral nature of man, in the same manner as exercise strengthens a limb.

SHELLEY (from *A Defence of Poetry*)

WHY NOT ?

My brain is dull, my sight is foul,
I cannot write a verse, or read,—
Then Pallas, take away thine Owl,
And let us have a Lark instead.

THOMAS HOOD

SAYINGS OF EMERSON

In every work of genius we recognise our own rejected thoughts ; they come back to us with a certain alienated majesty.

Let us treat the men and women well : treat them as if they were real : perhaps they are.

341

It is always so pleasant to be generous, though very vexatious to pay debts.
Our chief want in life is, somebody who shall make us do what we can.

THE NIGHT SHADOWS

A wonderful fact to reflect upon, that every human creature is constituted to be that profound secret and mystery to every other. A solemn consideration, when I enter a great city by night, that every one of those darkly clustered houses encloses its own secret; that every room in every one of them encloses its own secret; that every beating heart in the hundreds of thousands of breasts there, is, in some of its imaginings, a secret to the heart nearest it! . . . In any of the burial-places of this city through which I pass, is there a sleeper more inscrutable than its busy inhabitants are, in their innermost personality, to me, or than I am to them?

DICKENS (from *Tale of Two Cities*)

EPITAPH IN DERRY CATHEDRAL ON A YOUNG CURATE WHO DIED DURING AN EPIDEMIC OF TYPHUS

Down through our crowded lanes and closer air,
O friend, how beautiful thy footsteps were!
When through the fever's waves of fire they trod,
A form was with thee like the Son of God.

342

'Twas but one step for those victorious feet
From their day's walk unto the golden street;
And they who watch'd that walk so bright and brief
Have marked this marble with their hope and grief.

ARCHBISHOP ALEXANDER

DISTICHS

I

Wisely a woman prefers to a lover a man who neglects her,
This one may love her some day, some day the lover will
not.

II

Maidens, why do you worry in choosing whom you shall
marry,
Choose whom you may, you'll find you've got somebody
else!

JOHN HAY

A MEMORY OF " CUMMY "

(*Stevenson's Nurse*)

How well I remember her lifting me out of bed, carrying me to the window, and showing me one or two lit
windows up in Queen Street across the dark belt of
gardens; where also, we told each other, there might be
sick little boys and their nurses waiting, like us, for the
morning.

R. L. STEVENSON (from *Memories and Portraits*)

343

Of those who have thus survived themselves most completely, left a sort of personal seduction behind them in the world, and retained, after death, the art of making friends, Montaigne and Samuel Johnson certainly stand first.

If your morals make you dreary, depend upon it they are wrong.

There is no duty we so much underrate as the duty of being happy.

Absences are a good influence in love and keep it bright and delicate.

No man is useless while he has a friend.

To-morrow's travel will carry you, body and mind, into some different parish of the infinite.

THE NIGHT HAS A THOUSAND EYES

The night has a thousand eyes,
  And the day but one;
Yet the light of the bright world dies
  With the dying sun.

The mind has a thousand eyes,
  And the heart but one;
Yet the light of a whole life dies
  When love is done.

F. W. BOURDILLON

SEEING BETWEEN THE LINES

What we have inherited from our fathers and mothers is not all that walks in us ! There are all sorts of dead ideas and lifeless old beliefs. They have no tangibility, but they haunt us all the same and we cannot get rid of them. Whenever I take up a newspaper I seem to see Ghosts gliding between the lines.

IBSEN (from *Ghosts*)

ONE WORLD

The worlds in which we live are two—
The world " I am " and the world " I do."
The worlds in which we live at heart are one,—
The world " I am " the fruit of " I have done " ;
And underneath these worlds of flower and fruit
The world " I love " the only living root.

H. VAN DYKE

GOOD COUNSEL

To awaken each morning with a smile brightening my face ; to greet the day with reverence for the opportunities it contains ; to approach my work with a clean mind ; to hold ever before me, even in the doing of little things, the Ultimate Purpose toward which I am working ; to meet men and women with laughter on my lips and love in my heart; to be gentle, kind, and courteous through all the hours; to approach the night with weariness that ever woos sleep and the joy that comes from work well done—this is how I desire to waste wisely my days.

THOMAS DEKKER

Give me a man that is not dull,
When all the world with rifts is full;
But unamazed dares clearly sing,
Whenas the roof's a-tottering;
And, though it falls, continues still
Tickling the cittern with his quill.

ROBERT HERRICK

My soul, sit thou a patient looker-on;
Judge not the play before the play is done.
Her plot hath many changes; every day
Speaks a new scene; the last act crowns the play.

FRANCIS QUARLES

Though all the winds of doctrine were let loose to play upon the Earth, so Truth be in the field, we do injuriously to misdoubt her strength. Let her and Falsehood grapple. Whoever knew Truth put to the worse in a free and open encounter?

MILTON

What I spent I had,
What I saved I lost,
What I gave I have.

Old German Motto

Honey and the honeycomb, roses and violets, are yet in
the Earth. The Sun and Moon yet reign in Heaven, and
the lesser lights keep up their pretty twinklings. Meats
and drinks, sweet sights and sweet smells, a country walk,
spring and autumn, follies and repentance, quarrels and
reconcilements, have all a sweetness by turns.

CHARLES LAMB

It is hard to believe long together that anything is worth
while unless there is some eye to kindle in common with
our own, some brief word uttered now and then to imply
that what is infinitely precious to us is precious alike to
another mind.

GEORGE ELIOT

A CAPITAL LETTER

(*from a School-boy to his Uncle*)

S.O.S., L.S.D., R.S.V.P.

ANONYMOUS

347

A CHILD'S PRAYER

Make me, dear Lord, polite and kind
    To every one, I pray.
And may I ask you how you find
    Yourself, dear Lord, to-day?

JOHN BANISTER TABB

A BAD LOT

From Witches, Warlocks and Wurricoes,
From Ghoulies, Ghosties and Long-leggity Beasties,
From all Things that go bump in the night—
    Good Lord deliver us!

A Cornish Litany

SECOND PART

§ IV DREAMLAND

There are two Gates of the dark Underworld. Through the Horn Gate kindly and true Visions throng unhindered; but by that other, fashioned of glistening Ivory, go forth Dreams false and evil.

VIRGIL (Aeneid, Bk. VI)

Saint Francis and Saint Benedict
Blesse thys House from Wicked Wight,
From the Nightmare and the Goblin that is hight!
Goodfellow Robin keepe it
From all evil Spirites, Fayries, Wezles, Bats and Ferryts,
From Curfew Time till the next Prime!

An Old House-Blessing

§1. DREAM POETRY

FAUSTUS' VISION OF HELEN

Was this the face that launched a thousand ships
And burnt the topless towers of Ilium ?
Sweet Helen, make me immortal with a kiss.
Her lips suck forth my soul ; see where it flies !—
Come, Helen, come, give me my soul again.
Here will I dwell, for heaven is in these lips,
And all is dross that is not Helena.
I will be Paris, and for love of thee,
Instead of Troy, shall Wittenberg be sacked :
And I will combat with weak Menelaus,
And wear thy colours on my plumèd crest :
Yea, I will wound Achilles in the heel,
And then return to Helen for a kiss,
Oh, thou art fairer than the evening air
Clad in the beauty of a thousand stars ;
Brighter art thou than flaming Jupiter
When he appeared to hapless Semele :
More lovely than the monarch of the sky
In wanton Arethusa's azured arms ;
And none but thou shall be my paramour.

MARLOWE (from *Faustus*)

SLEEP SIGHT

How would, I say, mine eyes be blessèd made
By looking on thee in the living day,
When in dead night thy fair imperfect shade

351

Through heavy sleep on sightless eyes doth stay?
All days are nights to see, till I see thee,
And nights bright days, when dreams do show me thee.

SHAKESPEARE (from *Sonnet XLIII*)

TO THE MEMORY OF HIS SECOND WIFE[1]

Methought I saw my late espousèd Saint
   Brought to me like Alcestis from the grave,
   Whom Jove's great Son to her glad Husband gave,
   Rescu'd from death by force though pale and faint.
Mine as whom washt from spot of child-bed taint
   Purification in the old Law did save,
   And such as yet once more I trust to have
   Full sight of her in Heaven without restraint,
Came vested all in white, pure as her mind:
   Her face was vail'd, yet to my fancied sight,
   Love, sweetness, goodness, in her person shin'd
So clear, as in no face with more delight.
   But O as to embrace me she enclin'd
   I wak'd, she fled, and day brought back my night.

MILTON

DREAMS

Dreams are but interludes which Fancy makes;
When monarch Reason sleeps, this mimic wakes:
Compounds a medley of disjointed things,
A mob of cobblers, and a court of kings:

[1] As Milton had become blind some years before his second marriage, this was the first time he *saw* his second wife, who died soon after giving birth to a daughter. A. S.

Light fumes are merry, grosser fumes are sad :
Both are the reasonable soul run mad ;
And many monstrous forms in sleep we see,
That neither were, nor are, nor e'er can be.
Sometimes forgotten things long cast behind
Rush forward in the brain, and come to mind.
The nurse's legends are for truths received,
And the man dreams but what the boy believed.
Sometimes we but rehearse a former play,
The night restores our actions done by day ;
As hounds in sleep will open for their prey.
In short, the farce of dreams is of a piece,
Chimeras all ; and more absurd or less.

DRYDEN (from *The Cock and the Fox*)

ST. CATHERINE ASLEEP

You pleasing dreams of love and sweet delight,
Appear before this slumbering Virgin's sight :
Soft visions set her free
From mournful piety ;
Let her sad thoughts from heaven retire ;
And let the melancholy love
Of those remoter joys above
Give place to your more sprightly fire ;
Let purling streams be in her fancy seen,
And flowery meads and vales of cheerful green ;
And in the midst of deathless groves
Soft sighing wishes lie,
And smiling hopes fast by,
And just beyond them ever-laughing loves.

DRYDEN (from *Tyrannic Love*)

MB   353

A THOUGHT OF BEAUTY

A thing of beauty is a joy for ever :
   Its loveliness increases ; it can never
   Pass into nothingness ; but still will keep
   A bower quiet for us, and a sleep
Full of sweet dreams, and health, and quiet breathing.

                   KEATS (from *Endymion*)

BOAT-SONG OF THE HIGHLANDERS IN CANADA

Listen to me as when you heard our father
   Sing long ago the songs of other shores,
Listen to me and then in chorus gather
   All your deep voices as you pull your oars—
   Fair these broad meads, these hoary woods are grand,
   But we are exiles from our native land.

From the lone shieling of the misty island
   Mountains divide us and the waste of seas ;
Yet still the blood is strong, the heart is Highland,
   And we in dreams behold the Hebrides.

                        ANONYMOUS

DREAM-PEDLARY

If there were dreams to sell,
 What would you buy?
Some cost a passing bell;
 Some a light sigh,
That shakes from Life's fresh crown
Only a rose-leaf down.
If there were dreams to sell,
Merry and sad to tell,
And the crier rang the bell,
 What would you buy?

A cottage lone and still,
 With bowers high,
Shadowy, my woes to still,
 Until I die.
Such pearl from Life's fresh crown
Fain would I shake me down.
Were dreams to have at will,
This would best heal my ill,
 This would I buy.

THOMAS LOVELL BEDDOES

PRAYER IN SLEEP

Prayer goeth forth in sleep as true
And pauseless as the pulses do.

ELIZABETH BARRETT BROWNING

THE BLESSĖD DAMOZEL

The blessėd damozel leaned out
  From the gold bar of Heaven ;
Her eyes were deeper than the depth
  Of waters stilled at even ;
She had three lilies in her hand,
  And the stars in her hair were seven.

Her robe, ungirt from clasp to hem,
  No wrought flowers did adorn,
But a white rose of Mary's gift,
  For service meetly worn ;
Her hair that lay along her back
  Was yellow like ripe corn.

Her seemed she scarce had been a day
  One of God's choristers ;
The wonder was not yet quite gone
  From that still look of hers ;
Albeit, to them she left, her day
  Had counted as ten years.

(To *one* it is ten years of years.
  . . . Yet now, and in this place,
Surely she leaned o'er me—her hair
  Fell all about my face . . .
Nothing : the autumn-fall of leaves.
  The whole year sets apace.)

It was the rampart of God's house
  That she was standing on ;
By God built over the sheer depth

The which is Space begun ;
So high, that looking downward thence
   She scarce could see the sun.

It lies in Heaven, across the flood
   Of ether, as a bridge.
Beneath, the tides of day and night
   With flame and darkness ridge
The void, as low as where this earth
   Spins like a fretful midge.

Around her, lovers, newly met
   'Mid deathless love's acclaims,
Spoke evermore among themselves
   Their heart-remembered names ;
And the souls mounting up to God
   Went by her like thin flames.

And still she bowed herself and stooped
   Out of the circling charm,
Until her bosom must have made
   The bar she leaned on warm,
And the lilies lay as if asleep
   Along her bended arm.

From the fixed place of Heaven she saw
   Time like a pulse shake fierce
Through all the worlds. Her gaze still strove
   Within the gulf to pierce
Its path ; and now she spoke as when
   The stars sang in their spheres.

The sun was gone now ; the curled moon
    Was like a little feather
Fluttering far down the gulf ; and now
    She spoke through the still weather.
Her voice was like the voice the stars
    Had when they sang together.

(Ah sweet ! Even now, in that bird's song,
    Strove not her accents there,
Fain to be hearkened ? When those bells
    Possessed the mid-day air,
Strove not her steps to reach my side
    Down all the echoing stair ?)

D. G. ROSSETTI

DREAMS

It looks as if in dreams the soul was free,
    No bodily limit checks its absolute play ;
Then why doth it not use its liberty,
    And clear a certain way
To further truth beyond the actual sea ?

It is not so ; for when, with loosened grip,
    The warder sense unlocks the visible hold,
Then will my soul from forth its chamber slip,
    An idiot blithe and bold,
And into vacancy of folly skip ;

Or aimless wander on the poppied floor
    Of gaudy fields, or, scarce upon the street,
Return unto the grim, familiar door,
    And, coward, crave retreat,
As who had never been outside before.

What boots it that I hold the chartered space,
    If I but fill it with th' accustomed forms,
And load its breathless essence with the trace
    Of casual-risen storms,
And drag my chain along the lovely place ?

O, but if God would make a deep suspense,
    And draw me perfect from th' adhesive sheath :
If all the veils and swathings of pretence,
    Dropt from me, sunk beneath,
Then would I get me very far from hence.

I'd come to Him with one swift arrow-dart,
    Aimed at the zenith of th' o'erbrooding blue ;
Straight to the centre of His awful heart
    The flight long-winged and true
Should bear me rapt through all the spheres that part.

But as it is, it is a waste of rest.
    God uses not the occasion : on the rock
Stands prone my soul, a diver lean undrest,
    And looks, and fears the shock,
And turns and hides its shame with some poor sorry jest.

                                        T. E. BROWN

A DREAM

Beneath the loveliest dream there coils a fear :
Last night came she whose eyes are memories now ;
Her far-off gaze seemed all forgetful how
Love dimmed them once, so calm they shone and clear.
" Sorrow," I said, " has made me old, my dear ;
'Tis I, indeed, but grief can change the brow :
Beneath *my* load a seraph's neck might bow,
Vigils like mine would blanch an angel's hair."
Oh, then I saw, I saw the sweet lips move !
I saw the love-mists thickening in her eyes—
I heard a sound as if a murmuring dove
Felt lonely in the dells of Paradise ;
But when upon my neck she fell, my love,
Her hair smelt sweet of whin and woodland spice.

T. WATTS-DUNTON

AD AMICAM

When from the blossoms of the noiseful day
   Unto the hive of sleep and hushèd gloom
Throng the dim-wingèd dreams—what dreams are they
   That with the wildest honey hover home ?
Oh, they that have from many thousand thoughts
   Stolen the strange sweet of ever-blossomy you,
A thousand fancies in fair-coloured knots
   Which you are inexhausted meadow to.
Ah, what sharp heathery honey, quick with pain,
   Do they bring home ! It holds the night awake
To hear their lovely murmur in my brain ;

And Sleep's wings have a trouble for your sake.
Day and you dawn together : for, at end,
   With the first light breaks the first thought—
     " My friend ! "

FRANCIS THOMPSON

RENOUNCEMENT

I must not think of thee ; and, tired yet strong,
   I shun the thought that lurks in all delight—
   The thought of thee—and in the blue Heaven's height,
And in the sweetest passage of a song.

Oh, just beyond the fairest thoughts that throng
   This breast, the thought of thee waits, hidden yet
     bright ;
   But it must never, never come in sight ;
I must stop short of thee the whole day long.

But when sleep comes to close each difficult day,
   When night gives pause to the long watch I keep,
     And all my bonds I needs must loose apart.

Must doff my will as raiment laid away,—
   With the first dream that comes with the first sleep
     I run, I run, I am gathered to thy heart.

ALICE MEYNELL

SONG

She comes not when Noon is on the roses—
    Too bright is Day.
She comes not to the Soul till it reposes
    From work and play.

But when Night is on the hills, and the great Voices
    Roll in from sea.
By starlight and by candlelight and dreamlight
    She comes to me.

HERBERT TRENCH

PROMISE

Be not so desolate
Because thy dreams have flown
And the hall of the heart is empty
And silent as stone,
As age left by children
Sad and alone.

Those delicate children,
Thy dreams, still endure :
All pure and lovely things
Wend to the Pure.
Sigh not : unto the fold
Their way was sure.

Thy gentlest dreams, thy frailest,
Even those that were
Born and lost in a heart-beat,

Shall meet thee there.
They are become immortal
In shining air.

The unattainable beauty
The thought of which was pain,
That flickered in eyes and on lips
And vanished again :
That fugitive beauty
Thou shalt attain.

The lights innumerable
That led thee on and on,
The Masque of Time ended,
Shall glow into one.
It shall be with thee for ever
Thy travel done.

GEORGE RUSSELL ("A. E.")

TO L. H. B. (1894–1915)

Last night for the first time since you were dead
I walked with you, my brother, in a dream.
We were at home again beside the stream
Fringed with tall berry bushes, white and red.
" Don't touch them : they are poisonous," I said.
But your hand hovered, and I saw a beam
Of strange, bright laughter flying around your head ;
And as you stooped I saw the berries gleam,
" Don't you remember ? We called them Dead Man's
    Bread."

I woke and heard the wind moan and the roar
Of the dark water tumbling on the shore.
Where—where is the path of my dream for my eager feet ?
By the remembered stream my brother stands
Waiting for me with berries in his hands:
" These are my body. Sister, take and eat."

KATHERINE MANSFIELD

COUNTING SHEEP

Half-awake I walked
A dimly-seen sweet hawthorn lane
Until sleep came ;
I lingered at a gate and talked
A little with a lonely lamb.
He told me of the great still night,
Of calm starlight,
And of the lady moon, who'd stoop
For a kiss sometimes ;
Of grass as soft as sleep, of rhymes
The tired flowers sang :
The ageless April tales
Of how, when sheep grew old,
As their faith told,
They went without a pang
To far green fields, where fall
Perpetual streams that call
To deathless nightingales.
    And then I saw, hard by,
A shepherd lad with shining eyes,
And round him, gathered one by one
Countless sheep, snow-white ;

364

More and more they crowded
With tender cries,
Till all the field was full
Of voices and of coming sheep.
Countless they came, and I
Watched, until deep
As dream-fields lie
I was asleep.

WILLIAM KERR

§ 2. PROSE

ARTEMIDORUS ON DREAMS

A dream is a motion of fiction of the soul in a diverse form, signifying either good or evil to come.

Thus :—

1. To have the head of a lion, a wolf, a panther, or elephant instead of his own, is good : for he which attempteth things beyond his power, and hath this dream shall attain unto great dignity and honour. Many desiring offices and places of honour after this dream have obtained them. To dream you have the head of a dog, horse or ass, or such four-footed beast, is servitude, pain and misery. To have a bird's head argues one shall not stay long in this country.

2. To see a great fish in the sea is good for no man, the dolphin excepted ; but out of the sea every fish and great monster is good, for they can hurt no more, nor save themselves : and therefore besides that our dream signifies that our enemies cannot hurt us. Notwithstanding, the dolphin being out of the sea is not good, but signifieth the death of some of our good friends.

3. To see all the stars clear and fair is good for a traveller and for all business. Such stars as vanish and go out of the sky is poverty and forsaking to the rich ; for you must imagine that the sky signifieth the house of him that dreams. To eat the stars is not good, except to astrologers and sooth-sayers.

4. Mixed or compounded dreams are very doubtful, and cannot be easily understood or expounded, which is a great grief to many.

Dreams are notable means of discovering our own

inclinations. The wise man learns to know himself, as well by the night's black mantle as the scorching beams of the day : in sleep we have the naked and natural thoughts of our souls : outward objects interpose not, either to shuffle in occasional cogitations, or hale out the included fancy. The mind is then shut up in the burrow of the body. The Indians, when their kings went to their sleep used to pray that they might have happy dreams and withal consult well for their subjects' benefit ; as if the night had been a time wherein they might grow good and wise. And certainly the wise man is the wiser for his sleeping, if he can order well in the day,—and every dream the eyeless night presents him is to be counted of. Dreams may to a wise observer be of special benefit. I would neither depend upon any to incur a prejudice, nor yet cast any away in a prodigal neglect and scorn. I find it of one that, having been troubled with the paining spleen, he dreamt if he opened a certain vein between two of his fingers he should be cured, which he awaking did, and amended. But indeed I would rather believe this than to be drawn to practice after it.

(Trans. R. WOOD)

KING MILINDA ASKS ABOUT DREAMS

" Venerable Nâgasena, when a man dreams a dream, is he awake or asleep ? "

" Neither the one, O king, nor yet the other. But when his sleep has become light, and he is not yet fully conscious, in that interval it is that dreams are dreamt. When a man is in deep sleep, O king, his mind has returned home like a bird that has re-entered its nest, and a mind thus shut in does not act. A mind hindered in its action knows not evil and good, and he who knows not has no dreams. Just, O king, as in the darkness and gloom, where no light is, no shadow will fall even on the most burnished mirror, so when a man is in deep sleep his mind has returned into itself and acts not, knowing neither good nor evil. As the mirror, O king, are you to regard the body, as the darkness sleep, as the light the mind."

"Venerable Nâgasena, is there a beginning, a middle, and an end of sleep?"

"Yes, O king, there is. The feeling of oppression and inability in the body—of weakness, slackness, inertness—that is the beginning, of sleep. The light "monkey's sleep" in which a man still guards his scattered thoughts —that is the middle of sleep. When the mind has entered into itself—that is the end of sleep. And it is in the middle stage that dreams are dreamt. Just, O king, as when a man self-restrained with collected thoughts, stedfast in the faith, unshaken in wisdom, plunges deep into the woods far from the sound of strife, and thinks over some subtle matter, he there, tranquil and at peace, will master the meaning of it—just so a man still watchful, not fallen into sleep, but dozing will dream a dream.

The Questions of King Milinda (Trans. from the
Pâli by T. W. RHYS DAVIDS)

THE SACRED SLEEP

The soul has a twofold life, a lower and a higher. In sleep that soul is freed from the constraint of the body, and enters, as one emancipated, on its divine life of intelligence. Then, as the noble faculty which beholds

368

objects as they are—the objects in the world of intelligence—stirs within, and awakens to its power, who can be surprised that the mind, which contains in itself the principles of all that happens, should, in this its state of liberation, discern the future in those antecedent principles which will make that future what it is to be ? The nobler part of the soul is thus united by abstraction to higher natures, and becomes a participant in the wisdom and foreknowledge of the gods.

Recorded examples of this are numerous and well authenticated ; instances occur, too, every day. Numbers of sick, by sleeping in the temple of Aesculapius, have had their cure revealed to them in dreams vouchsafed by the god. Would not Alexander's army have perished but for a dream in which Dionysus pointed out the means of safety ? Was not the siege of Aphutis raised through a dream sent by Jupiter Ammon to Lysander ? The night-time of the body is the day-time of the soul.

IAMBLICHUS

ST. AUGUSTINE RELATES A DREAM

It chanced at Carthage that the rhetorician Eulogius, who had been my disciple in that art, being (as he himself, after our return to Africa, told us the story) in course of lecturing to his disciples on Cicero's rhetorical books, as he looked over the portion of reading which he was to deliver on the following day, fell upon a certain passage, and not being able to understand it, was scarce able to sleep for the trouble of his mind : in which night, as he dreamed, I expounded to him that which he did not understand ; nay, not I, but my likeness, while I was unconscious of the thing and far away beyond sea, it might be

369

doing, or it might be dreaming, some other thing, and not in the least caring for his cares. In what way these things come about I know not; but in what way soever they come, why do we not believe it comes in the same way for a person in a dream to see a dead man, as it comes that he sees a living man? both, no doubt, neither knowing nor caring who dreams of their images, or where or when.

From *De Cura pro Mortuis Habenda* (Oxford Library of the Fathers, XVII)

A MYSTERY OF SLEEP

There yet live in my memory the images of such things, as my ill custom there fixed; which haunt me, strengthless when I am awake: but in sleep, not only so as to give pleasure, but even to obtain assent, and what is very like reality. Yea, so far prevails the illusion of the image, in my soul and in my flesh, that, when asleep, false visions persuade to that which when waking, the true cannot. Am I not then myself, O Lord my God! And yet there is so much difference betwixt myself and myself, within that moment wherein I pass from waking to sleeping, or return from sleeping to waking! Where is reason then, which, awake, resisteth such suggestions? And should the things themselves be urged on it, it remaineth unshaken. Is it clasped up with the eyes? is it lulled asleep with the senses of the body? And whence is it that often even in sleep we resist, and mindful of our purpose, and abiding most chastely in it, yield no assent to such enticement? And yet so much difference there is, that when it happeneth otherwise, upon waking we return to peace of conscience: and by this very difference discover that we did not, what yet we be sorry that in some way it was done in us.

Confessions of St. Augustine (Trans. E. B. PUSEY)

THE HAPPY DREAMER

I thank God for my happy dreams, as I do for my good rest; for there is a satisfaction in them unto reasonable desires, and such as can be content with a fit of happiness; and surely it is not a melancholy conceit to think we are all asleep in this World, and that the conceits of this life are as meer dreams to those of the next, as the Phantasms of the night to the conceits of the day. There is an equal delusion in both, and the one doth but seem to be the emblem or picture of the other: we are somewhat more than our selves in our sleeps, and the slumber of the body seems to be but the waking of the soul. It is the ligation of sense, but the liberty of reason; and our waking conceptions do not match the Fancies of our sleeps. At my Nativity my Ascendant was the watery sign of Scorpius; I was born in the Planetary hour of Saturn, and I think I have a piece of that Leaden Planet in me. I am no way facetious, nor disposed for the mirth and galliardise of company; yet in one dream I can compose a whole Comedy, behold the action, apprehend the jests, and laugh my self awake at the conceits thereof. Were my memory as faithful as my reason is then fruitful, I would never study but in my dreams; and this time also would I chuse for my devotions: but our grosser memories have then so little hold of our abstracted understandings, that they forget the story, and can only relate to our awaked souls, a confused and broken tale of that that hath passed. Aristotle, who hath written a singular Tract *Of Sleep*, hath not, methinks, thoroughly defined it ; nor yet Galen, though he seem to have corrected it ; for those Noctambuloes and night-walkers, though in their sleep, do yet injoy the action of their senses. We must therefore say that there is something in us that is not in the jurisdiction of Morpheus ; and that those abstracted and estatick souls do walk about in their own corps, as spirits with the bodies they assume, wherein they seem to hear, see, and feel, though indeed the Organs are destitute of sense, and their natures of those faculties that should inform them. Thus it is observed, that men sometimes, upon the hour of their departure, do speak and reason above themselves ; for then the soul, beginning to be freed from the ligaments of the body, begins to reason like her self, and to discourse in a strain above mortality.

We term sleep a death ; and yet it is waking that kills us, and destroys those spirits that are the house of life. 'Tis indeed a part of life that best expresseth death ; for every man truely lives, so long as he acts his nature, or some way makes good the faculties of himself. Themistocles, therefore, that slew his Soldier in his sleep, was a merciful Executioner : 'tis a kind of punishment the mildness of no laws hath invented : I wonder the fancy of Lucan and Seneca did not discover it. It is that death by which we may be literally said to dye daily ; a death which Adam dyed before his mortality ; a death whereby we live a middle and moderating point between life and death : in fine, so like death, I dare not trust it without my prayers, and an half adieu unto the World, and take my farewell in a Colloquy with God.

SIR THOMAS BROWNE (from *Religio Medici*)

Now I saw in my dream, that by this time the pilgrims were got over the Enchanted Ground, and entering into the country of Beulah whose air was very sweet and pleasant, the way lying directly through it, they solaced themselves there for a season. Yea, here they heard continually the singing of birds, and saw every day the flowers appear in the earth, and heard the voice of the turtle in the land. In this country the sun shineth night and day; wherefore this was beyond the Valley of the Shadow of Death, and also out of the reach of Giant Despair, neither could they from this place so much as see Doubting Castle. Here they were within sight of the city they were going to, also here met them some of the inhabitants thereof; for in this land the Shining Ones commonly walked, because it was upon the borders of heaven, So I saw, that as I went on, there met them two men, in raiment that shone like gold; also their faces shone as the light.

These men asked the pilgrims whence they came; and they told them. They also asked them where they had lodged, what difficulties and dangers, what comforts and pleasures they had met in the way; and they told them. Then said the men that met them, You have but two difficulties more to meet with, and then you are in the city.

Christian then, and his companion, asked the men to go along with them; so they told them they would But, said they, you must obtain it by your own faith. So I saw in my dream that they went on together, until they came in sight of the gate.

Now, I further saw, that betwixt them and the gate was a river, but there was no bridge to go over; the river was very deep. At the sight, therefore, of this river, the pilgrims were much stunned; but the men that went with them said, You must go through, or you cannot come at the gate. Then they took courage, and the enemy was after that as still as a stone, until they were gone over. Christian therefore presently found ground to stand upon, and so it followed that the rest of the river was but shallow. Thus they got over...

Now you must note that the city stood upon a mighty hill, but the pilgrims went up that hill with ease, because they had these two men to lead them up by the arms; also, they had left their mortal garments behind them in the river, for though they went in with them, they came out without them. They, therefore, went up here with much agility and speed, though the foundation upon which the city was framed was higher than the clouds. They, therefore, went up through the regions of the air, sweetly talking as they went, being comforted, because they safely got over the river, and had such glorious companions to attend them.

Now while they were thus drawing towards the gate, behold a company of the heavenly host came out to meet them. . There came out also at this time to meet them, several of the King's trumpeters, clothed in white and shining raiment, who, with melodious noises and loud, made even the heavens to echo with their sound. These trumpeters saluted Christian and his fellow with ten thousand welcomes from the world; and this they did with shouting, and sound of trumpet.

This done, they compassed them round on every side; some went before, some behind, and some on the right hand, some on the left (as it were to guard them through the upper regions), continually sounding as they went, with melodious noise, in notes on high : so that the very sight was to them that could behold it, as if heaven itself was come down to meet them. Thus, therefore, they walked on together ; and as they walked, ever and anon these trumpeters, even with joyful sound, would, by mixing their music with looks and gestures, still signify to Christian and his brother, how welcome they were into their company, and with what gladness they came to meet them ; and now were these two men, as it were, in heaven, before they came at it, being swallowed up with the sight of angels, and with hearing of their melodious notes. Here also they had the city itself in view, and they thought they heard all the bells therein to ring, to welcome them thereto. But above all, the warm and joyful thoughts that they had about their own dwelling there, with such company, and that for ever and ever. Oh, by what tongue or pen can their glorious joy be expressed ! And thus they came up to the gate.

Now I saw in my dream that these two men went in at the gate : and lo, as they entered, they were transfigured, and they had raiment put on that shone like gold. There were also that met them with harps and crowns, and gave them to them—the harps to praise withal, and the crowns in token of honour. Then I heard in my dream that all the bells in the city rang again for joy.

BUNYAN (from *The Pilgrim's Progress*)

READING VIRGIL IN BED

After the lassitude of a day, spent in the strolling manner, which is usual with men of pleasure in this town, and with a head full of a million of impertinencies, which had danced round it for ten hours together, I came to my lodging, and hastened to bed. My valet-de-chambre knows my university-trick of reading there ; and he, being a good scholar for a gentleman, ran over the names of Horace, Tibullus, Ovid, and others, to know which I would have. Bring Virgil, said I ; and, if I fall asleep, take care of the candle. I read the Sixth Book over with the most exquisite delight, and had gone half through it a second time, when the pleasant ideas of Elysian fields, deceased worthies walking in them, sincere lovers enjoying their languishment without pain, compassion for the unhappy spirits who had mispent their short day-light, and were exiled from the seats of bliss for ever ; I say, I was deep again in my reading, when this mixture of images had taken place of all others in my imagination before, and lulled me into a dream, from which I am just awake, to my great disadvantage. The happy mansions of Elysium, by degrees, seemed to be wafted from me, and the very traces of my late waking thoughts began to fade away, when I was cast by a sudden whirlwind upon an island, encompassed with a roaring and troubled sea, which shaked its very centre, and rocked its inhabitants as in a cradle. The islanders lay on their faces without offering to look up, or hope for preservation ; all her harbours were crowded with mariners, and tall vessels of war lay in danger of being driven to pieces on her shores. Bless me, said I, why have I lived in such a manner, that the convulsion of nature should be so terrible to me, when I feel in myself that the better part of me is to survive it ? Oh ! may that be in happiness.

STEELE (from *The Tatler*)

ON DREAMS

Our dreams are great instances of that activity which is natural to the human soul, and which it is not in the power of sleep to deaden or abate. When the man appears tired and worn out with the labours of the day, this active part in his composition is still busied and unwearied. When the organs of sense want their due repose and necessary reparations, and the body is no longer able to keep pace with that spiritual substance to which it is united, the soul exerts herself in her several faculties, and continues in action till her partner is again qualified to bear her company. In this case dreams look like the relaxations and amusements of the soul, when she is disencumbered of her machine ; her sports and recreations, when she has laid her charge asleep.

In the second place, dreams are an instance of that agility and perfection which is natural to the faculties of the mind, when they are disengaged from the body. The soul is clogged and retarded in her operations, when she acts in conjunction with a companion that is so heavy and unwieldy in its motions. But in dreams it is wonderful to observe with what a sprightliness and alacrity she exerts herself. The slow of speech make unpremeditated harangues, or converse readily in languages that they are but little acquainted with. The grave abound in pleasantries, the dull in repartees and points of wit. There is not a more painful action of the mind than invention ; yet in dreams it works with that ease and activity, that we are not sensible when the faculty is employed. . .

There is another circumstance, which, methinks, gives us a very high idea of the nature of the soul, in regard to what passes in dreams : I mean that innumerable multitude and variety of ideas which then arise in her. Were that active watchful being only conscious of her own existence at such a time, what a painful solitude would her hours of sleep be? Were the soul sensible of her being alone in her sleeping moments after the same manner that she is sensible of it while awake, the time would hang very heavy on her, as it often actually does when she dreams that she is in such solitude.

But this observation I only make by the way. What I would here remark, is that wonderful power in the soul of producing her own company on these occasions. She converses with numberless beings of her own creation, and is transported into ten thousand scenes of her own raising. She is herself the theatre, the actors, and the beholder. This puts me in mind of a saying which I am infinitely pleased with, and which Plutarch ascribes to Heraclitus, " That all men, whilst they are awake, are in one common world ; but that each of them, when he is asleep, is in a world of his own." The waking man is conversant in the world of nature ; when he sleeps he retires to a private world that is particular to himself. There seems something in this consideration that intimates to us a natural grandeur and perfection in the soul, which is rather to be admired than explained.

I must not omit that argument for the excellency of the soul, which I have seen quoted out of Tertullian, namely its power of divining in dreams. That several such divinations have been made, none can question who believes the holy writings, or who has but the least degree of a common historical faith; there being innumerable instances of this nature in several authors, both ancient and modern, sacred and profane. Whether such dark presages, such visions of the night, proceed from any latent power in the soul during this her state of abstraction, or from any communication with the Supreme Being, or from any operation of subordinate spirits, has been a great dispute among the learned ;—the matter of fact is, I think, incontestable, and has been looked upon as such by the greatest writers, who have never been suspected either of superstition or enthusiasm.

I do not suppose that the soul in these instances is entirely loose and unfettered from the body ; it is sufficient, if she is not so far sunk and immersed in matter, nor entangled and perplexed in her operations with such motions of blood and spirits, as when she actuates the machine in its waking hours. The corporeal union is slackened enough to give the mind more play. The soul seems gathered within herself, and recovers that spring which is broke and weakened, when she operates more in concert with the body.

The speculations I have here made, if they are not arguments, they are at least strong intimations not only of the excellency of a human soul, but of its independence on the body ; and if they do not prove, do at least confirm those two great points, which are established by many other reasons that are altogether unanswerable.

ADDISON (from *The Spectator*)

DREAMS OF MEN AND ANIMALS

Seeking the cause of our dreams—what it is that makes our former sensations repeat themselves—we notice that we do not dream during profound sleep, for then we are completely unconscious, asleep without and within. But our inner consciousness falls asleep last and wakens first, because it is more lively, more active, and more easily disturbed than our outer consciousness. Consequently it is during periods of light or incomplete sleep that we dream, renewing our former sensations, especially those on which we have reflected in our waking hours. Then our inner consciousness, unable to operate on actual sensations while our outer consciousness is quiescent, concerns itself with past sensations. The most vivid will be those which have been most frequently apprehended, and the more vivid the sensation the more extraordinary will be the scene presented. Hence our dreams are very often either terrifying or extremely pleasant.

Our outer consciousness need not be entirely dormant in order that our inner consciousness should operate—it is enough that it be quiescent. Although we are accustomed to give ourselves up as a matter of course to expected sleep, we do not always readily do so. Our bodies, relaxed and extended, may be quite motionless ; our eyes under their closed lids see nothing in the darkness ; our ears tell us nothing, so quiet is our chamber, so silent is the night ; —we are entirely at rest, yet no part of us is entirely lulled. Then, when we have no thoughts, our outer consciousness being inactive, our inner consciousness assumes control, and presents us with grotesque images and tumbling shadows. We become spectators in sleep's theatre. If we are in good health we receive pleasant impressions, but otherwise it is different—we see old hags and dreadful ghosts which seem to speak to us and which succeed one another with startling rapidity. It is like a magic lantern show which fills our brain then empty of other images, and these phantoms are the more lively, the more numerous and the more unpleasant in proportion as our faculties are out of order, our nerves upset and our bodies enfeebled ; for the effects of real sensations being greater in illness than in health, the images of such sensations which the renewal of these effects produces must also be more vivid and more unpleasant.

We remember our dreams just as we remember actual sensations that we have recently received, and the only difference here between the lower animals and ourselves is that we are able to distinguish between dream sensations and actual sensations. Into this operation of our memory (which involves a comparison) the idea of time enters. The lower animals, however, being unable to make this comparison, cannot distinguish between their dreams and their actual experiences ; so that to them all that they have dreamt appears to have actually happened.

BUFFON (from *Sur la Nature des Animaux*—
Trans. A.S.)

BOCCACCIO'S DREAM

Scarcely had I closed my eyes, if indeed time can be reckoned any more in sleep than in heaven, when my Fiammetta seemed to have led me into the meadow. . . I sprang to embrace her.

" Do not spill the water ! Ah ! you have spilt a part of it."

I then observed in her hand a crystal vase. A few drops were sparkling on the sides and running down the rim : a few were trickling from the base and from the hand that held it.

" I must go down to the brook," said she, " and fill it again as it was filled before."

What a moment of agony was this to me ! Could I be

certain how long might be her absence? She went: I was
following: she made a sign for me to turn back: I dis-
obeyed her only an instant: yet my sense of disobedience,
increasing my feebleness and confusion, made me lose
sight of her. In the next moment she was again at my side
with the cup quite full. I stood motionless: I feared my
breath might shake the water over. I looked her in the
face for her commands—and to see it—to see it so calm, so
beneficent, so beautiful. I was forgetting what I had
prayed for, when she lowered her head, tasted of the cup,
and gave it me. I drank; and suddenly sprang forth
before me, many groves and palaces and gardens, and
their statues and their avenues, and their labyrinths of
alaternus and bay, and alcoves of citron, and watchful
loopholes in the retirements of impenetrable pomegran-
ate. Farther off, just below where the fountain slipt away
from its marble hall and guardian gods, arose, from their
beds of moss and drosera and darkest grass, the sisterhood
of oleanders, fond of tantalising with their bosomed
flowers and their moist and pouting blossoms the little
shy rivulet, and of covering its face with all the colours of
the dawn. My dream expanded and moved forward. I
trod again the dust of Posilipo, soft as the feathers in the
wings of Sleep. I emerged on Baia; I crossed her innumerable arches; I loitered in the breezy sunshine of her mole;
I trusted the faithful seclusion of her caverns, the keepers
of so many secrets; and I reposed on the buoyancy of her
tepid sea. Then Naples, and her theatres and her churches
and grottoes and dells and forts and promontories, rushed
forward in confusion, now among soft whispers, now
among sweetest sounds, and subsided, and sank, and disappeared. Yet a memory seemed to come fresh from every
one: each had time enough for its tale, for its pleasure,

for its reflection, for its pang. As I mounted with silent steps the narrow staircase of the old palace, how distinctly did I feel against the palm of my hand the coldness of that smooth stonework, and the greater of the cramps of iron in it!

" Ah me! is this forgetting? " cried I anxiously to Fiammetta.

" We must recall these scenes before us," she replied: " such is the punishment of them. Let us hope and believe that the apparition, and the compunction which must follow it, will be accepted as the full penalty, and that both will pass away almost together."

I feared to lose anything attendant on her presence: I feared to approach her forehead with my lips: I feared to touch the lily on its long wavy leaf in her hair, which filled my whole heart with fragrance. Venerating, adoring, I bowed my head at last to kiss her snow-white robe, and trembled at my presumption. And yet the effulgence of her countenance vivified while it chastened me. I loved her—I must not say *more* than ever—*better* than ever; it was Fiammetta who had inhabited the skies. As my hand opened toward her,

" Beware! " said she, faintly smiling; " beware, Giovanni! Take only the crystal; take it, and drink again."

" Must all be then forgotten? " said I sorrowfully.

" Remember your prayer and mine, Giovanni. Shall both have been granted—O how much worse than in vain? "

Although the water gave me strength and comfort, and somewhat of celestial pleasure, many tears fell around the border of the vase as she held it up before me, exhorting me to take courage, and inviting me with more than exhortation to accomplish my deliverance. She came nearer, more tenderly, more earnestly; she held the dewy globe with both hands, leaning forward, and sighed and shook her head, drooping at my pusillanimity. It was only when a ringlet had touched the rim, and perhaps the water (for a sunbeam on the surface could never have given it such a golden hue) that I took courage, clasped it, and exhausted it. Sweet as was the water, sweet as was the serenity it gave me—alas! that also which it moved away from me was sweet!

"This time you can trust me alone," said she, and parted my hair, and kissed my brow. Again she went toward the brook; again my agitation, my weakness, my doubt, came over me: nor could I see her while she raised the water, nor knew I whence she drew it. When she returned, she was close to me at once: she smiled: her smile pierced me to the bones: it seemed an angel's. She sprinkled the pure water on me; she looked most fondly; she took my hand; she suffered me to press hers to my bosom, but, whether by design I cannot tell, she let fall a few drops of the chilly element between.

"And now, O my beloved!" said she, "we have consigned to the bosom of God our earthly joys and sorrows. The joys can not return, let not the sorrows. These alone would trouble my repose among the blessed."

"Trouble thy repose! Fiammetta! Give me the chalice!" cried I—"not a drop will I leave in it, not a drop."

"Take it!" said that soft voice. "O now most dear Giovanni! I know thou hast strength enough; and there is but little—at the bottom lies our first kiss."

"Mine! didst thou say, beloved one? and is that left thee still?"

384

" *Mine*," said she, pensively ; and as she abased her head, the broad leaf of the lily hid her brow and her eyes ; the light of heaven shone through the flower.

" O Fiammetta ! Fiammetta ! " cried I in agony, " God is the God of mercy, God is the God of love—can I, can I ever ? " I struck the chalice against my head, unmindful that I held it ; the water covered my face and my feet. I started up, not yet awake, and I heard the name of Fiammetta in the curtains.

W. S. LANDOR (from *The Pentameron*)

NIGHT-FANCIES

My night-fancies have long ceased to be afflictive. I confess an occasional nightmare ; but I do not, as in early youth, keep a stud of them. Fiendish faces, with the extinguished taper, will come and look at me ; but I know them for mockeries, even while I cannot elude their presence, and I fight and grapple with them. For the credit of my imagination, I am almost ashamed to say how tame and prosaic my dreams are grown. They are never romantic, seldom even rural. They are of architecture and of buildings—cities abroad, which I have never seen and hardly have hope to see. I have traversed, for the seeming length of a natural day, Rome, Amsterdam, Paris, Lisbon —their churches, palaces, squares, market-places, shops, suburbs, ruins, with an inexpressible sense of delight— a map-like distinctness of trace, and a daylight vividness of vision, that was all but being awake.—I have formerly travelled among the Westmoreland fells—my highest

Alps,—but they are objects too mighty for the grasp of my dreaming recognition; and I have again and again awoke with ineffectual struggles of the inner eye, to make out a shape, in any way whatever, of Helvellyn. Methought I was in that country, but the mountains were gone. The poverty of my dreams mortifies me. There is Coleridge, at his will can conjure up icy domes, and pleasure-houses for Kubla Khan, and Abyssinian maids, and songs of Abara . . . to solace his night solitudes—when I cannot muster a fiddle. Barry Cornwall has his tritons and his nereids gambolling before him in nocturnal visions, and proclaiming sons born to Neptune—when my stretch of imaginative activity can hardly, in the night season, raise up the ghost of a fish-wife. To set my failures in somewhat a mortifying light—it was after reading the noble Dream of this poet, that my fancy ran strong upon these marine spectra; and the poor plastic power, such as it is, within me set to work to humour my folly in a sort of dream that very night. Methought I was upon the ocean billows at some sea nuptials, riding and mounted high with the customary train sounding their conchs before me (I myself, you may be sure, the *leading god*), and jollily we went careering over the main, till just where Ino Leucothea should have greeted me (I think it was Ino) with a white embrace, the billows gradually subsiding fell from a sea roughness to a sea calm, and thence to a river motion, and that river (as happens in the familiarisation of dreams) was no other than the gentle Thames, which landed me in the wafture of a placid wave or two, alone, safe and inglorious, somewhere at the foot of Lambeth palace.

The degree of the soul's creativeness in sleep might furnish no whimsical criterion of the quantum of poetical

faculty resident in the same soul waking. An old gentleman, a friend of mine, and a humorist, used to carry this
notion so far, that when he saw any stripling of his
acquaintance ambitious of becoming a poet, his first
question would be,—" Young man, what sort of dreams
have you ? " I have so much faith in my old friend's
theory, that when I feel that idle vein returning upon me,
I presently subside into my proper element of prose, remembering those eluding nereids, and that inauspicious
inland landing.

CHARLES LAMB

A POET'S DREAM

The fifth canto of Dante pleases me more and more—it
is that one in which he meets with Paolo and Francesca.
I had passed many days in rather a low state of mind, and
in the midst of them I dreamt of being in that region of
Hell. The dream was one of the most delightful enjoy-
ments I ever had in my life. I floated about the whirling
atmosphere (as it is described) with a beautiful figure to
whose lips mine were joined, as it seemed for an age—and
in the midst of all this cold and darkness I was warm—
even flowery tree tops sprung up and we rested on them
sometimes with the lightness of a cloud, till the wind
blew us away again. I tried a Sonnet upon it—there are
fourteen lines but nothing of what I felt in it—O that
I could dream it every night !

KEATS (from a Letter written
at Wentworth Place in 1819)

THE VISION

How frequently does his form visit my mind's eye in slumber and in wakefulness, in the light of day, and in the night watches; but last night I saw him in his beauty and his strength; he was about to speak, and my ear was on the stretch, when at once I awoke, and there was I alone, and the night storm was howling amidst the branches of the pines which surround my lonely dwelling : " Listen to the moaning of the pine, at whose root thy hut is fastened,"— a saying that, of wild Finland, in which there is wisdom ; I listened, and thought of life and death.

GEORGE BORROW (from *Lavengro*)

THE QUEEN'S CROQUET-GROUND

(*part of Alice's dream*)

When the procession came opposite to Alice, they all stopped and looked at her, and the Queen said severely, " Who is this ? " She said it to the Knave of Hearts, who only bowed and smiled in reply.

" Idiot ! " said the Queen, tossing her head impatiently ; and, turning to Alice, she went on, " What's your name, child ? "

" My name is Alice, so please your Majesty," said Alice very politely ; but she added, to herself, " Why, they're only a pack of cards, after all. I needn't be afraid of them ! "

" And who are *these* ? " said the Queen, pointing to the three gardeners who were lying round the rose-tree ;

for, you see, as they were lying on their faces, and the pattern on their backs was the same as the rest of the pack, she could not tell whether they were gardeners, or soldiers, or courtiers, or three of her own children.

"How should *I* know?" said Alice, surprised at her own courage. "It's no business of *mine*."

The Queen turned crimson with fury, and, after glaring at her for a moment like a wild beast, began screaming, "Off with her head! Off——"

"Nonsense!" said Alice, very loudly and decidedly, and the Queen was silent.

The King laid his hand upon her arm, and timidly said "Consider, my dear: she is only a child!"

The Queen turned angrily away from him, and said to the Knave "Turn them over!"

The Knave did so, very carefully, with one foot.

"Get up!" said the Queen in a shrill, loud voice, and the three gardeners instantly jumped up, and began bowing to the King, the Queen, the royal children, and everybody else.

"Leave off that!" screamed the Queen. "You make me giddy." And then, turning to the rose-tree, she went on, "What *have* you been doing here?"

"May it please your Majesty," said Two, in a very humble tone, going down on one knee as he spoke, "we were trying——"

"*I* see!" said the Queen, who had meanwhile been examining the roses. "Off with their heads!" and the procession moved on, three of the soldiers remaining behind to execute the unfortunate gardeners, who ran to Alice for protection.

"You shan't be beheaded!" said Alice, and she put them into a large flower-pot that stood near. The three soldiers wandered about for a minute or two, looking for them, and then quietly marched off after the others.

" Are their heads off ? " shouted the Queen.

" Their heads are gone, if it please your Majesty ! " the soldiers shouted in reply.

" That's right ! " shouted the Queen. " Can you play croquet ? "

The soldiers were silent, and looked at Alice, as the question was evidently meant for her.

" Yes ! " shouted Alice.

" Come on, then ! " roared the Queen, and Alice joined the procession, wondering very much what would happen next.

" It's—it's a very fine day ! " said a timid voice at her side. She was walking by the White Rabbit, who was peeping anxiously into her face.

" Very," said Alice :—" Where's the Duchess ? "

" Hush ! hush ! " said the Rabbit in a low, hurried tone. He looked anxiously over his shoulder as he spoke, and then raised himself upon tiptoe, put his mouth close to her ear, and whispered " She's under sentence of execution."

" What for ? " said Alice.

" Did you say ' What a pity ' ? " the Rabbit asked.

" No, I didn't," said Alice : " I don't think it's at all a pity. I said ' What for ? ' "

" She boxed the Queen's ears——" the Rabbit began. Alice gave a little scream of laughter. " Oh, hush ! " the Rabbit whispered in a frightened tone. " The Queen will hear you ! You see she came rather late, and the Queen said——"

" Get to your places ! " shouted the Queen in a voice of

thunder, and people began running about in all directions, tumbling up against each other ; however, they got settled down in a minute or two, and the game began.

LEWIS CARROLL (from *Alice in Wonderland*)

TWO DREAMS

1. *The Pig in the Dining-Room*

Mrs. Atlay, wife of a late Bishop of Hereford, dreamed one night that there was a pig in the dining-room of the palace. She came downstairs, and in the hall told her governess and children of the dream before family prayers. When these were over, nobody who was told the story having left the hall in the interval, she went into the dining-room and there was the pig. It was proved to have escaped from the sty after Mrs. Atlay got up.

2. *The Lost Cheque*

Mr. A., a barrister, sat up one night to write letters, and about half-past twelve went out to put them in the post. On undressing he missed a cheque for a large sum, which he had received during the day. He hunted everywhere in vain, went to bed, slept, and dreamed that he saw the cheque curled round an area railing not far from his own door. He woke, got up, dressed, walked down the street and found his cheque in the place he had dreamed of. In his opinion he had noticed it fall from his pocket as he walked to the letter-box, without consciously remarking it and his deeper memory awoke in slumber.

ANDREW LANG (from *A Book of Dreams and Ghosts*)

THIRD PART

§I THE ANCIENT WORLD

I know nothing can conduce more to letters than to examine the writings of the Ancients. They opened the gates, and made the way that went before us.

BEN JONSON

We go to our favourite classical author, as it were for conversation with a friend; and we discover that these benevolent antique minds reflect our own thoughts, but in a richer maturity. Their friendship never fails us, and their serene philosophy brings us reconciliation—and how often do we need it !—with mankind and with ourselves.

SAINTE-BEUVE

§ 1. EGYPT AND THE EAST

THE COMING FORTH BY DAY

(*Hymn to the Rising Sun*)

" Homage to thee, O Rā, when thou risest. Thou art adored by me when thy beauties are before mine eyes, and when thy radiance falleth upon my body. Thou stridest over the heavens in peace, and all thy foes are cast down ; the never-resting stars sing hymns of praise unto thee, and the stars which rest, and the stars which never fail glorify thee as thou sinkest to rest in the horizon of Manu, O thou who art beautiful at morn and at eve, O thou lord who livest and art established, O my lord !

" Homage to thee, O thou who art Rā when thou risest, and Ten when thou settest in beauty. Thou risest and shinest on the back of thy mother Nut, O thou who art crowned king of the gods ! Nut doeth homage unto thee, and everlasting and never-changing order embraceth thee at morn and at eve. Thou stridest over the heaven, being glad of heart, and the Lake of Testes is content thereat. . . Rā hath a fair wind ; the boat goeth forth and sailing along it cometh into port. The gods of the south and of the north, of the west and of the east, praise thee, O thou divine substance, from whom all forms of life come into being. Thou sendest forth the word, and the earth is flooded with silence, O thou only One, who didst dwell in heaven before ever the earth and the mountains came into existence. O Runner, O Lord, O only One, thou maker of things which are, thou hast fashioned the tongue of the company of the gods, thou hast produced whatsoever cometh forth from the waters, and thou springest up from them over the flooded land of the Lake of Horus. Let me snuff the air which cometh forth from thy nostrils, and the north wind which cometh forth from thy mother Nut. O make thou to be glorious my shining form, O Osiris, make thou to be divine my soul! Thou art worshipped in peace, O lord of the gods, thou art exalted by reason of thy wondrous works. Shine thou with thy rays of light upon my body day by day, upon me, Osiris the scribe, the teller of the divine offerings of all the gods, the overseer of the granary of the lords of Abydos, the royal scribe in truth who loveth thee ; Ani, victorious in peace. . .

"Hail, thou Disk, thou lord of rays, who risest on the horizon day by day! Shine thou with thy beams of light upon the face of Osiris Ani, who is victorious ; for he singeth hymns of praise unto thee at dawn, and he maketh thee to set at eventide with words of adoration. May the soul of Osiris Ani, the triumphant one, come forth with thee into heaven, may he cleave his path among the never-resting stars. . .

"Homage to thee, O thou who risest in thy horizon as Rā, thou reposest upon law which changeth not nor can it be altered. Thou passest over the sky, and every face watcheth thee and thy course, for thou hast been hidden from their gaze. Thou dost shew thyself at dawn and at eventide day by day. The boat, wherein is thy Majesty, goeth forth with might ; thy beams shine upon all faces ; the number of thy red and yellow rays cannot be known, nor can thy bright beams be told. The lands of the gods, and the eastern lands of Punt must be seen, ere that which is hidden in thee may be measured. Alone and by thyself thou dost manifest thyself when thou comest into being above the sky. May Ani advance, even as thou dost advance ; may he never cease to go forward, even as thy Majesty ceaseth not to go forward, even though it be for a moment; for with strides dost thou in one little moment pass over the spaces which would need hundreds of thousands and millions of years for man to pass over ; this thou doest, and then dost thou sink to rest. Thou puttest an end to the hours of the night, and thou dost count them, even thou ; thou endest them in thine own appointed season, and the earth becometh light. Thou settest thyself before thy handiwork in the likeness of Rā ; thou risest in the horizon " . . .

And the god saith :—

" Thou shalt come forth into heaven, thou shalt pass over the sky, thou shalt be joined unto the starry deities. . . . Thou shalt behold Horus on the standing-place of the pilot of the boat, and Thoth and Maāt shall stand one upon each side of him. All the gods shall rejoice when they behold Rā coming in peace to make the hearts of the shining ones to live, and Osiris Ani, victorious, the scribe of the divine offerings of the lords of Thebes, shall be along with them ! "

From *The Book of the Dead*
(Trans. SIR E. A. WALLIS BUDGE)

A SONG FROM PALESTINE

(Sung during the arraying of the Bride before leaving her parents' house)

' O Sabha, Darling, 'tis to thee we sing :
  In lyric song our voices rise and fall.
We hear thy Father calling, Sabha, Dear,
  We hear thy Father's gentle loving call.

'O Sabha of the trustful sable eyes,
　　Eyes dark as night, so calm, so deep, so rare :
We hear thy Brother call thee, Sabha, Dear—
　　We hear thy Brother call thee, Sabha, Fair.

'O Sabha of the rippling golden hair ;
　　Gold, living gold, its every curling tress :
Let not our sorrow cloud thy faithful heart,
　　Let not our sorrow that dear heart distress.

'With softest sound of rhythmic melody
　　The anklets tinkle on thy Mother's feet.
Sabha, we hear thy Father's Brother call,
　　We hear thy Father's Brother call thee, Sweet.

'The anklets tinkle, Sabha, on thy feet,
　　Making soft melody within the hall.
Sabha, we hear thy Mother's Brother call—
　　O Love, we hear thy Mother's Brother call.

'We clasp the bracelet on thy white round arm,
　　Less round and white the silvery moon appears.
Thine eyes are tenderer than the camel's eyes,
　　And hers compare with liquid wells of tears.

'Behold the scarlet shoes upon thy feet,
　　Each dainty foot lost in a dainty shoe,
Fair as the moon as full thy face is fair.
　　More fair than moon thy form, more pure than
　　dew.

' I clasp these priceless gems around thy neck,
  They hide the Breast so far more dear to me ;
My steed, my camel for thy sake I'd sell,
  My choicest treasure I'd pour out for thee.'

From DALMAN'S *Palästinischer Diwan*
(Trans. H. BARNES)

FROM THE PERSIAN

On her delicate cheeks the ringlets flutter with the breath of my sigh, in the same manner that the reflexion of the hyacinth in the water quivers with the blowing of the breeze. When she walks there is a pleasant tremor of the body from head to foot, just like the quivering of the roses on a tender rose-branch.

My sweetheart has entered the hut, and the bird of my heart has remained bewildered. The candle is put into the lantern, and the moth is left outside fluttering.

Take care, the sleep of non-existence will overtake you at last ; for the coming and going of the breath is but the rocking of the cradle.

When the wind waves thy dark ringlets, thy rosy face glows still more. One may say, it has in hand a fan of raven's feather, and by the movement of the fan it makes the fire blaze.

Translated by M. N. KUKA

THE GUEST

The householder, when the day's work is finished, shall rest awhile in the evening. He shall sit before his dwelling, during the time required for the milking of a cow, in readiness for the arrival of an unexpected guest.

From a Hindu Law-Book

The reward for honouring a guest is heavenly bliss and immunity from misfortunes. The householder shall converse kindly with his guest and gladden him with milk and eatables. He shall offer to his guest a room, a bed, a mattress, a pillow with a cover, and ointment and what else may be necessary. The reception of guests is an everlasting sacrifice offered by the householder. He who entertains guests for one night obtains earthly happiness, a second night gains the middle air, a third heavenly bliss, a fourth the world of unsurpassable happiness. Many nights procure endless worlds. A guest who can repeat the whole Veda (together with the supplementary books) is worthy to receive a cow.

From Aphorisms on the Sacred Laws of the Hindus
(Trans. GEORG BÜHLER)

THE INDIAN'S PRAYER

O Supreme Ruler, all-pervading and all-supporting, O endowed Messengers of God, make our wills wise rulers of our thoughts and deeds that we may abide in happiness. Let winds be favourable to us. Let the seas send forth soft vapours to form clouds sweet as honey. And on land make the herbs and plants to flourish for our well-being. Let day and night be pleasant to us. Let our father, the Sun, pour down happiness. May the Almighty Lord Indra, owner of heaven and the wide regions, the great Creator, be gracious to us and give us peace.

From the *Rigveda*

INDIAN APHORISMS

The sage who excludes from his mind external objects, who restrains senses, mind and understanding, from whom desire, fear and wrath have departed is, indeed, for ever released from birth and death. He, knowing the great Lord of all worlds and the Friend of all beings, attains tranquillity.

From *Bhagavadgîtâ* (Trans. K. T. TELANG)

Health is the greatest of gifts, contentment the best riches ; trust is the best of relationships. He who has tasted the sweetness of solitude and tranquillity is free from fear and free from sin, while he tastes the sweetness of drinking in the law. He who walks in the company of fools suffers a long way ; company with fools, as with an enemy, is always painful; company with the wise is pleasure, like meeting with kinsfolk. Therefore, one ought to follow the wise, the learned, the much enduring, the dutiful, the elect : one ought to follow such a good and wise man, as the moon follows the path of the stars.

From *Dhammapada* (Trans. F. MAX MÜLLER)

A DREAM IN WINTER

Cold, cold the year draws to its end,
The crickets and grasshoppers make a doleful chirping.
The chill wind ceases its violence.
My wandering love has no coat to cover him.
He gave his embroidered furs to the Lady of Lo,
But from me his bedfellow he is quite estranged.
Sleeping alone in the depth of the long night
In a dream I thought I saw the light of his face.
My dear one thought of our old joys together,
He came in his chariot and gave me the front reins.
I wanted so to prolong our play and laughter,
To hold his hand and go back with him in his coach.
But when he had come he would not stay long,
Nor stop to go with me to the Inner Chamber.
Truly without the falcon's wings to carry me
How can I rival the flying wind's swiftness?
I go and lean at the gate and think of my grief,
My falling tears wet the double gates.

> From the Chinese, 1st Century B.C.
> (Trans. A. WALEY)

HOW GOES THE NIGHT?

How goes the night?
Midnight has still to come.
Down in the court the torch is blazing bright;
I hear far off the throbbing of the drum.

How goes the night?
The night is not yet gone.

I hear the trumpets blowing on the height :
The torch is paling in the coming dawn.

How goes the night ?
The night is past and done.
The torch is smoking in the morning light,
The dragon banner floating in the sun.

> From the Chinese, 9th Century B.C.
> (Trans. HELEN WADDELL)

FROM AN OLD PILLOW-BOOK

One has been expecting someone, and rather late at
night there is a stealthy tapping at the door. One sends a
maid to see who it is, and lies waiting, with some slight
flutter of the breast. But the name one hears when she returns is that of someone completely different, who does
not concern one at all. Of all depressing experiences, this
is by far the worst. . . .

Of course, what I really like is a house where there is no
fuss about the front gate, and no one particularly minds
whether it is midnight or morning. Then one can go out to
the front of the house and talk to whoever it may be—
perhaps one of the princes, or of the lords attached to his
Majesty's service—sit all through a winter's night with
the shutters open, and after the guest has gone, watch him
make his way into the distance. If he leaves just at daybreak, this is very agreeable, particularly if he plays upon
his flute as he goes. Then, when he is out of sight, one does

not hurry to go to bed, but discusses the visitor with someone, reviews the poems he made, and so gradually falls to
sleep.

SEI SHŌNAGON, 10th Century

(Trans. A. WALEY)

THE RIVER OF HEAVEN

He is coming, my long-desired lord, whom I have been
waiting to meet here, on the banks of the River of Heaven.
. . . The moment of loosening my girdle is nigh.

Over the Rapids of the Everlasting Heaven, floating in
his boat, my lord will doubtless deign to come to me this
very night.

From the day that the autumn wind began to blow (I
kept saying to myself), "Ah, when shall we meet?"—
but now my beloved, for whom I waited and longed, has
come indeed!

On the River of Heaven, at the place of the august ferry,
the sound of the water has become loud : perhaps my long-
awaited lord will soon be coming in his boat.

When I see the water-grasses of the River of Heaven
bend in the autumn wind (I think to myself): "The time
for our meeting seems to have come."

When I feel in my heart a sudden longing for my husband, then on the River of Heaven the sound of the rowing
of the night-boat is heard, and the plash of the oars
resounds.

When autumn comes, and the river-mists spread over
the Heavenly Stream, I turn toward the river and long ;
and the nights of my longing are many!

Hikoboshi and Tanabata-tsumé are to meet each other

to-night ;—ye waves of the River of Heaven, take heed that ye do not rise !

On the River of Heaven a sound of plashing can be distinctly heard : is it the sound of the rippling made by Hikoboshi quickly rowing his boat ?

Perhaps this evening shower is but the spray flung down from the oar of Hikoboshi, rowing his boat in haste.

From to-morrow alas ! after having put my jewel-bed in order, no longer reposing with my lord, I must sleep alone !

Oh, ferryman, make speed across the stream !—my lord is not one who can come and go twice in a year !

From the Japanese (Trans. LAFCADIO HEARN)

WHEN EVENING COMES

When evening comes
I will leave the door open beforehand and
    then wait
For him who said he would come
To meet me in my dreams.

By way of pretext
I said " I will go
And look at
The condition of the bamboo fence " ;
But it was really to see you !

From the Japanese (YAKAMOCHI, d. 785 A.D.
                            —Trans. A. WALEY)

§ 2. GREECE

PRIAM GOES TO ACHILLES

And the messenger of Zeus stood beside Priam and spake softly unto him, and trembling came upon his limbs : " Be of good cheer in thy heart, O Priam son of Dardanos, and be not dismayed for anything, for no evil come I hither to forebode to thee, but with good will. I am the messenger of Zeus to thee, who, though he be afar off, hath great care and pity for thee. The Olympian biddeth thee ransom noble Hector and carry gifts to Achilles that may gladden his heart : go thou alone, let none other of the Trojans go with thee. Only let some elder herald attend on thee to guide the mules and the smooth-wheeled waggon to carry back to the city the dead man whom noble Achilles slew. Let not death be in thy thought, nor any fear; such guide shall go with thee, even the slayer of Argus, who shall lead thee until his leading bring thee to Achilles. . ."

Then the old man made haste to go up into his car, and drave forth from the doorway and the echoing portico. In front the mules drew the four-wheeled wain, and wise Idaios drave them ; behind came the horses which the old man urged with the lash at speed along the city : and his friends all followed lamenting loud as though he were faring to his death. And when they were come down from the city and were now on the plain, then went back again to Ilios his sons and marriage kin. But the two coming forth upon the plain were not unbeheld of far-seeing Zeus. But he looked upon the old man and had compassion on him, and straightway spake unto Hermes his dear son : " Hermes, since unto thee especially is it dear to companion men, and thou hearest whomsoever thou wilt, go forth and so guide Priam to the hollow ships of the Achaians that no man behold or be aware of him, among all the Danaans' host, until he come to the son of Peleus."

Thus spake he, and the Messenger, the slayer of Argus, was not disobedient unto his word. . . When they were come to the towers and trench of the ships, there were the sentinels just busying them about their supper. Then the Messenger, the slayer of Argus, shed sleep upon them all, and straightway opened the gates and thrust back the bars, and brought within Priam and the splendid gifts upon his wain and spake aloud : " Old sire, go thou in and clasp the knees of Peleus' son, and entreat him for his father's sake and his mother's of the lovely hair and for his child's sake that thou mayest move his soul."

Thus Hermes spoke, and departed unto high Olympus. But Priam leapt from the car to the earth, and left Idaios in his place ; he stayed to mind the horses and mules ; but the old man made straight for the house where Achilles dear to Zeus was wont to sit. And therein he found the man himself, and his comrades sate apart. But they were unaware of great Priam as he came in, and so stood he anigh and clasped in his hands the knees of Achilles, and kissed his hands, terrible, man-slaying, that slew many of Priam's sons. And as when a grievous curse cometh upon a man who in his own country hath slain another and escapeth to a land of strangers, to the house of some rich man, and wonder possesseth them that look on him—so Achilles wondered when he saw godlike Priam, and the rest wondered likewise, and looked upon one another. Then Priam spake and entreated him, saying : " Bethink thee, O Achilles like to gods, of thy father that is of like years with me, on the grievous pathway of old age. Him haply are the dwellers round about entreating evilly, nor is there any to ward from him ruin and bane. Nevertheless while he heareth of thee as yet alive he rejoiceth in his heart, and hopeth withal day after day that he shall see his dear son returning from Troy-land. But I, I am utterly unblest, since I begat sons the best men in wide Troyland, but declare unto thee that none of them is left. He who was yet left and guarded city and men, him slewest thou but now as he fought for his country, even Hector. For his sake come I unto the ships of the Achaians that I may win him back from thee, and I bring with me untold ransom. Yea, fear thou the gods, Achilles, and have compassion on me, even me, bethinking thee of thy father. Lo, I am yet more piteous than he, and have braved what none other man on earth have braved before, to stretch forth my hand toward the face of the slayer of my sons."

Thus spake he, and stirred within Achilles desire to make lament for his father. And he touched the old man's hand and gently moved him back. And as they both bethought them of their dead, so Priam for man-slaying Hector wept sore as he was fallen before Achilles feet, and Achilles wept for his own father, and now again for Patroklos, and their moan went up throughout the house. But when noble Achilles had satisfied him with lament, and the desire thereof departed from his heart and limbs, straightway he sprang from his seat, and raised the old man by his hand, pitying his hoary head and hoary beard, and spake unto him winged words and said: "Ah hapless! many ill things verily thou hast endured in thy heart. How durst thou come alone to the ships of Achaians and to meet the eyes of the man who hath slain full many of thy brave sons? of iron verily is thy heart.

But come then set thee on a seat, and we will let our sorrows lie quiet in our hearts, for all our pain, for no avail cometh of chill lament. This is the lot the gods have spun for miserable men, that they should live in pain; yet themselves are sorrowless. . . Keep courage, and lament not unabatingly in thy heart. For nothing wilt thou avail by grieving for thy son, neither shalt thou bring him back to life or ever some new evil come upon thee."

Then made answer unto him the old man, godlike Priam : " Bid me not to a seat, O fosterling of Zeus, so long as Hector lieth uncared for at the huts, but straightway give him back that I may behold him with mine eyes ; and accept thou the great ransom that we bring. So mayest thou have pleasure thereof, and come unto thy native land, since thou hast spared me from the first."

Then fleet-footed Achilles looked sternly upon him and said : " No longer chafe me, old sire ; of myself am I minded to give Hector back to thee, for there came to me a messenger from Zeus, even my mother who bare me, daughter of the Ancient One of the Sea. . . Thy son, old sire, is given back as thou wouldest and lieth on a bier and with the break of day thou shalt see him thyself as thou carriest him " . . .

Now all other gods and warriors lords of chariots slumbered all night, by soft sleep overcome. But not on the Helper Hermes did sleep take hold as he sought within his heart how he should guide forth king Priam from the ships unespied of the trusty sentinels. And he stood above his head and spake a word to him : " Old sire, no thought then hast thou of any evil, seeing thou yet sleepest among men that are thine enemies, for that Achilles spared thee. Truly now hast thou won back thy dear son, and at great price. But for thy life will thy sons thou hast left behind be offered threefold ransom, if but Agamemnon Atreus' son be aware of thee, and aware be all the Achaians."

Thus spake he, and the old man feared, and roused the herald. And Hermes yoked the horses and mules for them, and himself drave them lightly through the camp, and none was aware of them.

But when they came to the ford of the fair-flowing river, (even eddying Xanthos, begotten of immortal Zeus) then Hermes departed up to high Olympus, and Morning of the saffron robe spread over all the earth. And they with wail and moan drave the horses to the city, and the mules drew the dead. Nor marked them any man or fair-girdled woman until Kassandra, peer of golden Aphrodite, having gone up upon Pergamos, was aware of her dear father as he stood in the car, and the herald that was crier to the town. Then beheld she him that lay upon the bier behind the mules, and thereat she wailed and cried aloud throughout all the town : " O men and women of Troy, come ye hither and look upon Hector, if ever while he was alive ye rejoiced when he came back from battle, since great joy was he to the city and all the folk."

Thus spake she, nor was man or woman left within the city, for upon all came unendurable grief. And near the gates they met Priam bringing home the dead. First bewailed him his dear wife and lady mother, as they cast them on the fair-wheeled wain and touched his head ; and around them stood the throng and wept.

From HOMER'S *Iliad*, Bk. XXIV.
(Trans. LANG, LEAF and MYERS)

Now when they were come to the beautiful stream of
the river, where truly were the unfailing cisterns, and
bright water welled up free from beneath, and flowed
past, enough to wash the foulest garments clean, there the
girls unharnessed the mules from under the chariot, and
turning them loose they drove them along the banks of
the eddying river to graze on the honey-sweet clover.
Then they took the garments from the wain, in their
hands, and bore them to the black water, and briskly trod
them down in the trenches, in busy rivalry. Now when
they had washed and cleansed all the stains, they spread
all out in order along the shore of the deep even where the
sea, in beating on the coast, washed the pebbles clean.
Then having bathed and anointed them well with olive
oil, they took their mid-day meal on the river's banks,
waiting till the clothes should dry in the brightness of the
sun. Anon, when they were satisfied with food, the
maidens and the princess, they fell to playing at ball,
casting away their tires, and among them Nausicaa of the
white arms began the song. And even as Artemis, the
archer, moveth down the mountain, either along the
ridges of lofty Taygetus or Erymanthus, taking her pastime in the chase of boars and swift deer, and with her
the wild wood-nymphs disport them, the daughters of
Zeus, lord of the Aegis, and Leto is glad at heart, while
high over all she rears her head and brows, and easily
may she be known—but all are fair ; even so the girl unwed
outshone her maiden company.

But when now she was about going homewards, after
yoking the mules and folding up the goodly raiment, then
grey-eyed Athene turned to other thoughts, that so

Odysseus might awake, and see the lovely maiden, who should be his guide to the city of the Phaeacian men. So then the princess threw the ball at one of her company; she missed the girl, and cast the ball into the deep eddying current, whereat they all raised a piercing cry. Then the goodly Odysseus awoke and sat up, pondering in his heart and spirit:

"Woe is me! to what men's land am I come now? say, are they froward, and wild, and unjust, or are they hospitable, and of godfearing mind? How shrill a cry of maidens rings round me, of the nymphs that hold the steep hill-tops, and the river-springs, and the grassy water meadows! It must be, methinks, that I am near men of human speech. Go to, I myself will make trial and see."

Therewith the goodly Odysseus crept out from under the coppice, having broken with his strong hand a leafy bough from the thick wood, to hold athwart his body, that it might hide his nakedness withal. And forth he sallied like a lion mountain-bred, trusting in his strength, who fares out blown and rained upon, with flaming eyes; amid the kine he goes or amid the sheep or in the track of the wild deer; yea, his belly bids him go even to the good homestead to make assay upon the flocks. Even so Odysseus was fain to draw nigh to the fair-tressed maidens, all naked as he was, such need had come upon him. But he was terrible in their eyes, being marred with the salt sea foam, and they fled cowering here and there about the jutting spits of shore. And the daughter of Alcinous alone stood firm, for Athene gave her courage of heart, and took all trembling from her limbs. So she halted and stood over against him, and Odysseus considered whether he should clasp the knees of the lovely maiden, and so make

412

his prayer, or should stand as he was, apart, and beseech her with smooth words, if haply she might show him the town, and give him raiment. And as he thought within himself, it seemed better to stand apart, and beseech her with smooth words, lest the maiden should be angered with him if he touched her knees: so straightway he spake a sweet and cunning word :

" I supplicate thee, O queen, whether thou art a goddess or a mortal! If indeed thou art a goddess of them that keep the wide heaven ; to Artemis, then, the daughter of great Zeus, I mainly liken thee, for beauty and stature and shapeliness. But if thou art one of the daughters of men who dwell on earth, thrice blessed are thy father and thy lady mother, and thrice blessed thy brethren. Surely their souls ever glow with gladness for thy sake, each time they see thee entering the dance, so fair a flower of maidens. But he is of heart the most blessed beyond all other who shall prevail with gifts of wooing, and lead thee to his home. Never have mine eyes beheld such an one among mortals, neither man nor woman ; great awe comes upon me as I look on thee. Yet in Delos once I saw as goodly a thing : a young sapling of a palm tree springing by the altar of Apollo. For thither too I went, and much people with me, on that path where my sore troubles were to be. Yea, and when I looked there upon, long time I marvelled in spirit,—for never grew there yet so goodly a shoot from ground,—even in such wise as I wonder at thee, lady, and am astonied and do greatly fear to touch thy knees, though grievous sorrow is upon me. Yesterday, on the twentieth day, I escaped from the wine-dark deep, but all that time continually the wave bare me, and the vehement winds drave, from the isle Ogygia. And now some god has cast me on this shore, that here too, methinks, some evil may betide me : for I trow not that trouble will cease ; the gods ere that time will yet bring many a thing to pass. But, queen, have pity on me, for after many trials and sore to thee first of all am I come, and of the other folk, who hold this city and land, I know no man. Nay show me the town, give me an old garment to cast about me, if thou hadst, when thou camest here, any wrap for the linen. And may the gods grant thee all thy heart's desire: a husband and a home, and a mind at one with his may they give—a good gift, for there is nothing mightier and nobler than when man and wife are of one heart and mind in a house, a grief to their foes, and to their friends great joy, but their own hearts know it best."

Then Nausicaa of the white arms answered him, and said : " Stranger, forasmuch as thou seemest no evil man nor foolish—and it is Olympian Zeus himself that giveth weal to men, to the good and to the evil, to each one as he will, and this thy lot doubtless is of him, and so thou must in anywise endure it :—and now, since thou hast come to our city and our land, thou shalt not lack raiment, nor aught else that is the due of a hapless suppliant, when he has met them who can befriend him. And I will show thee the town, and name the name of the people. The Phaeacians hold this city and land, and I am the daughter of Alcinous, great of heart, on whom all the might and force of the Phaeacians depend."

Thus she spake, and called to her maidens of the fair tresses : " Halt, my maidens, whither flee ye at the sight of a man ? Ye surely do not take him for an enemy ? That mortal breathes not, and never will be born, who shall come with war to the land of the Phaeacians, for they are very dear to the gods. Far apart we live in the wash of the waves, the outermost of men, and no other mortals are conversant with us. Nay, but this man is some helpless one come hither in his wanderings, whom now we must kindly entreat, for all strangers and beggars are from Zeus, and a little gift is dear. So, my maidens, give the stranger meat and drink, and bathe him in the river, where withal is a shelter from the winds."

So she spake, but they had halted and called each to the other, and they brought Odysseus to the sheltered place, and made him sit down, as Nausicaa bade them, the daughter of Alcinous, high of heart. Beside him they laid a mantle, and a doublet for raiment, and gave him soft olive oil in the golden cruse, and bade him wash in the streams of the river. . .

Then they went apart and told all to their lady. But with the river water the goodly Odysseus washed from his skin the salt scurf that covered his back and broad shoulders, and from his head he wiped the crusted brine of the barren sea. But when he had washed his whole body, and anointed him with olive oil, and had clad himself in the raiment that the unwedded maidens gave him, then Athene, the daughter of Zeus, made him greater and more mighty to behold, and from his head caused deep curling locks to flow, like the hyacinth flower. . .

Then to the shore of the sea went Odysseus apart, and sat down, glowing in beauty and grace, and the princess marvelled at him.

From HOMER'S Odyssey, Bk. VI.
(Trans. BUTCHER and LANG)

It was these men and their like who made Athens great.
With them, as with few among Greeks, words cannot
exaggerate the deeds that they have done. Such an end as
we have here seems indeed to show us what a good life is,
from its first signs of power to its final consummation.
For even where life's previous record showed faults and
failures it is just to weigh the last brave hour of devotion
against them all. There they wiped out evil with good and
did the city more service as soldiers than they did her
harm in private life. There no hearts grew faint because
they loved riches more than honour; none shirked the
issue in the poor man's dream of wealth. All these they
put aside to strike a blow for the city. Counting the quest
to avenge her honour as the most glorious of all ven-
tures, and leaving Hope, the uncertain goddess, to send
them what she would, they faced the foe as they drew
near him in the strength of their own manhood; and when
the shock of battle came, they chose rather to suffer the
uttermost than to win life by weakness. So their memory
has escaped the reproaches of men's lips, but they bore
instead on their bodies the marks of men's hands, and in
a moment of time, at the climax of their lives, were rapt
away from a world filled, for their dying eyes, not with
terror but with glory.

Such were the men who lie here and such the city that
inspired them. We survivors may pray to be spared their
bitter hour, but must disdain to meet the foe with a spirit
less triumphant. Let us draw strength, not merely from
twice-told arguments—how fair and noble a thing it is to
show courage in battle—but from the busy spectacle of
our great city's life as we have it before us day by day,

falling in love with her as we see her, and remembering that all this greatness she owes to men with the fighter's daring, the wise man's understanding of his duty, and the good man's self-discipline in its performance—to men who sacrificed their lives as the best offerings on her behalf. So they gave their bodies to the commonwealth and received, each for his own memory, praise that will never die, and with it the grandest of all sepulchres, not that in which their mortal bones are laid, but a home in the minds of men, where their glory remains fresh to stir to speech or action as the occasion comes by. For the whole earth is the sepulchre of famous men; and their story is not graven only on stone over their native earth, but lives on far away, without visible symbol, woven into the stuff of other men's lives. For you now it remains to rival what they have done.

Therefore I do not mourn with the parents of the dead who are here with us. I will rather comfort them. For they know that they have been born into a world of manifold chances and that he is to be accounted happy to whom the best lot falls—the best sorrow, such as is yours to-day, or the best death, such as fell to these, for whom life and happiness were cut to the self-same measure. I know it is not easy to give you comfort. I know how often in the joy of others you will have reminders of what was once your own, and how men feel sorrow, not for the loss of what they have never tested, but when something that has grown dear to them has been snatched away. But you must keep a brave heart in the hope of other children, those who are still of age to bear them. For the newcomers will help you to forget the gap in your own circle, and will help the city to fill up the ranks of its workers and its soldiers. For no man is fitted to give fair and honest advice in council if he has not, like his fellows, a family at stake in the hour of the city's danger. To you who are past the age of vigour I would say: count the long years of happiness so much gain to set off against the brief space that yet remains, and let your burden be lightened by the glory of the dead. For the love of honour alone is not staled by age, and it is by honour, not, as some say, by gold, that the helpless end of life is cheered.

THUCYDIDES (*History*, Bk. II—
Trans. A. E. ZIMMERN)

A TALK BY THE RIVER

PHAEDRUS : Where shall we sit and read?

SOCRATES : Let us turn aside here and go along the Ilissus; then we can sit down quietly wherever we please.

PHAEDRUS : I am fortunate, it seems, in being barefoot; you are so always. It is easiest then for us to go along the brook with our feet in the water, and it is not unpleasant, especially at this time of the year and the day.

SOCRATES : Lead on then, and look out for a good place where we may sit.

PHAEDRUS : Do you see that very tall plane tree?

SOCRATES : What of it?

PHAEDRUS : There is shade there and moderate breeze and grass to sit on, or, if we like, to lie down on.

SOCRATES : Lead the way.

PHAEDRUS : Tell me, Socrates, is it not from some place along here by the Ilissus that Boreas is said to have carried off Oreithyia?

SOCRATES : Yes, that is the story.

PHAEDRUS : Well, is it from here ? The streamlet looks very pretty and pure and clear and fit for girls to play by.

SOCRATES : No, the place is about two or three furlongs farther down, where you cross over to the precinct of Agra. . . But, my friend, while we were talking, is not this the tree to which you were leading us ?

PHAEDRUS : Yes, this is it.

SOCRATES : By Hera, it is a charming resting place. For this plane tree is very spreading and lofty, and the tall and shady willow is very beautiful, and it is in full bloom, so as to make the place most fragrant ; then, too, the spring is very pretty as it flows under the plane tree, and its water is very cool, to judge by my foot. And it seems to be a sacred place of some nymphs and of Achelous, judging by the figurines and statues. Then again, if you please, how lovely and perfectly charming the breeziness of the place is ! and it resounds with the shrill summer music of the chorus of cicadas. But the most delightful thing of all is the grass, as it grows on the gentle slope, thick enough to be just right when you lay your head on it. So you have guided the stranger most excellently, dear Phaedrus.

PHAEDRUS : You are an amazing and most remarkable person. For you really do seem exactly like a stranger who is being guided about, and not like a native. You don't go away from the city, out over the border, and it seems to me you don't go outside the walls at all.

SOCRATES : Forgive me, my dear friend. You see, I am fond of learning. Now the country places and the trees won't teach me anything, and the people in the city do. But you seem to have found the charm to bring me out. For as people lead hungry animals by shaking in front of them a branch of leaves or some fruit, just so, I think, you, by holding before me discourses in books, will lead me all

419

over Attica and wherever else you please. So now that I have come here, I intend to lie down, and do you choose the position in which you think you can read most easily, and read. . . We have plenty of time, apparently ; and besides, the locusts seem to be looking down upon us as they sing and talk with each other in the heat. Now if they should see us not conversing at mid-day, but, like most people, dozing, lulled to sleep by their song because of our mental indolence, they would quite justly laugh at us, thinking that some slaves had come to their resort and were slumbering about the fountain at noon like sheep. But if they see us conversing and sailing past them unmoved by the charm of their Siren voices, perhaps they will be pleased and give us the gift which the gods bestowed on them to give to men.

PHAEDRUS : What is this gift ? I don't seem to have heard of it.

SOCRATES : It is quite improper for a lover of the Muses never to have heard of such things. The story goes that these locusts were once men, before the birth of the Muses, and when the Muses were born and song appeared, some of the men were so overcome with delight that they sang and sang, forgetting food and drink, until at last unconsciously they died. From them the locust tribe afterwards arose, and they have this gift from the Muses, that from the time of their birth they need no sustenance, but sing continually, without food or drink, until they die, when they go to the Muses and report who honours each of them on earth. They tell Terpsichore of those who have honoured her in dances, and make them dearer to her ; they gain the favour of Erato for the poets of love, and that of the other Muses for their votaries, according to their various ways of honouring them ; and to

420

Calliope, the eldest of the Muses, and to Urania who is next to her, they make report of those who pass their lives in philosophy and who worship these Muses who are most concerned with heaven and with thought divine and human and whose music is the sweetest. So for many reasons we ought to talk and not sleep in the noontime.

PHAEDRUS : Yes, we ought to talk.

A PRAYER OF SOCRATES

Grant to me that I may be made beautiful in my soul within, and that all external possessions be in harmony with my inner man. May I consider the wise man rich, and may I have such wealth as only the self-restrained man can bear or endure.

From PLATO'S *Phaedrus* (Trans. H. N. FOWLER—
Loeb Classical Library)

REST OUT OF DOORS

So, I and Eucritus and the fair Amyntichus, turned aside into the house of Phrasidamus, and lay down with delight in beds of sweet tamarisk and fresh cuttings from the vines, strewn on the ground. Many poplars and elm-trees were waving over our heads, and not far off the running of the sacred water from the cave of the nymphs warbled to us : in the shimmering branches the sun-burnt grasshoppers were busy with their talk, and from afar the little owl cried softly out of the tangled thorns of the blackberry; the larks were singing and the hedge-birds, and

the turtle-dove moaned; the bees flew round and round
the fountains, murmuring softly; the scent of late summer
and of the fall of the year was everywhere; the pears fell
from the trees at our feet, and apples in number rolled
down at our sides, and the young plum-trees were bent to
the earth with the weight of their fruit.

THEOCRITUS (*Idyll* VII—
Trans. WALTER PATER)

SAYINGS OF EPICTETUS

It is not easy to gain the attention of effeminate young
men, for you cannot take custard by a hook.

How do we act in a voyage? What is in my power?
To choose the pilot, the sailors, the day, the time of day.
Afterwards comes a storm. What have I to care for? My
part is performed. The subject belongs to another, to the
pilot. But the ship is sinking: what then have I to do?
That which alone I can do: I am drowned, without fear,
without clamour, or accusing God; but as one who knows
that what is born must likewise die. For I am not eternity,
but a man; a part of the whole, as an hour is of the day.
I must come like an hour, and like an hour must pass away.
What signifies it whether by drowning or by a fever?
For, in some way or other, pass I must.

You see that Caesar hath procured us a profound peace;
there are neither wars nor battles, nor great robberies
nor piracies, but we may travel at all hours, and sail from
east to west. But can Caesar procure us peace from a

fever too ? From a shipwreck ? From a fire ? From an earthquake ? From a thunderstorm ? Nay, even from love ? He cannot. From grief ? From envy ? No, not from any one of these. But the doctrine of philosophers promises to procure us peace from these too. And what doth it say ? " If you will attend to me, O mortals, wherever you are, and whatever you are doing, you shall neither grieve nor be angry, nor be compelled nor restrained ; but you shall live impassive, and free from all." Shall not he who enjoys this peace, proclaimed, not by Caesar (for how should he have it to proclaim ?) but by God, through reason, be contented when he is alone reflecting and considering : " To me there can now no ill happen ; there is no thief nor earthquake. All is full of peace, all full of tranquillity ; every road, every city, every assembly. My neighbour, my companion, unable to hurt me."

Ought we not when we are digging and ploughing and eating to sing this hymn to God ?—" Great is God, who has given us such implements with which we shall cultivate the earth : great is God, who has given us hands, the power of swallowing, a stomach, imperceptible growth, and the power of breathing while we sleep." This is what we ought to sing on every occasion, and to sing the greatest and most divine hymn for giving us the faculty of comprehending these things and using a proper way. I am a rational creature, and I ought to praise God : this is my work ; I do it, nor will I desert this post, so long as I am allowed to keep it ; and I exhort you to join in this same song.

(Trans. E. CARTER)

(*Note by the Author :*—The following matter is intended to have an attraction independent of any originality of subject. This attraction is in the veiled reference underlying all the details of my narrative; they parody the cock-and-bull stories of ancient poets, historians, and philosophers. As I have no truth to put on record, having lived a very humdrum life, I fall back on falsehood—but falsehood of a more consistent variety; for I now make the only true statement you are to expect—that I am a liar. My subject is, then, what I have neither seen, experienced, nor been told, what neither exists nor could conceivably do so.)

1. *The Land of Vines*

Starting on a certain date from the Pillars of Heracles, I sailed with a fair wind into the Atlantic. The motives of my voyage were a certain intellectual restlessness, a passion for novelty, a curiosity about the limits of the ocean and the peoples who might dwell beyond it. This being my design, I provisioned and watered my ship on a generous scale. My crew amounted to fifty, all men whose interests, as well as their years, corresponded with my own. I had further provided a good supply of arms, secured the best navigator to be had for money, and had the ship—a sloop—specially strengthened for a long and arduous voyage.

For a day and a night we were carried quietly along by the breeze, with land still in sight. But with the next day's dawn the wind rose to a gale, with a heavy sea and dark sky; we found ourselves unable to take in sail. We surrendered ourselves to the elements, let her run, and were storm-driven for more than eleven weeks. On the eightieth day the sun came out quite suddenly, and we found ourselves close to a lofty wooded island, round which the waves were murmuring gently, the sea having almost fallen by this time. We brought her to land, disembarked, and after our long tossing lay a considerable time idle on shore ; we at last made a start, however, and leaving thirty of our number to guard the ship I took the other twenty on a tour of inspection.

We had advanced half a mile inland through woods, when we came upon a brazen pillar, inscribed in Greek characters—which however were worn and dim—"Heracles and Dionysus reached this point." Not far off were two footprints on rock ; one might have been an acre in area, the other being smaller ; and I conjecture that the latter was Dionysus's, and the other Heracles's ; we did obeisance, and proceeded. Before we had gone far, we found ourselves on a river which ran wine ; it was very like Chian ; the stream full and copious, even navigable in parts. This evidence of Dionysus's sojourn was enough to convince us that the inscription on the pillar was authentic. Resolving to find the source, I followed the river up, and discovered, instead of a fountain, a number of huge vines covered with grapes ; from the root of each there issued a trickle of perfectly clear wine, the joining of which made the river. It was well stocked with great fish, resembling wine both in colour and taste ; catching and eating some, we at once found ourselves intoxicated ; and indeed when opened the fish were full of wine-lees ; presently it occurred to us to mix them with ordinary water fish, thus diluting the strength of our spirituous food.

We now crossed the river by a ford, and came to some

vines of a most extraordinary kind. Out of the ground
came a thick well-grown stem; but the upper part was a
woman, complete from the loins upward. They were
like our painters' representations of Daphne in the act of
turning into a tree just as Apollo overtakes her. From the
finger-tips sprang vine twigs, all loaded with grapes; the
hair of their heads was tendrils, leaves, and grape-clusters.
They greeted us and welcomed our approach, talking
Lydian, Indian, and Greek, most of them the last. They
went so far as to kiss us on the mouth; and whoever was
kissed staggered like a drunken man. But they would not
permit us to pluck their fruit, meeting the attempt with
cries of pain. Some of them made further amorous advances; and two of my comrades who yielded to these
solicitations found it impossible to extricate themselves
again from their embraces; the man became one plant
with the vine, striking root beside it; his fingers turned
to vine twigs, the tendrils were all round him, and em-
bryo grape-clusters were already visible on him.

We left them there and hurried back to the ship, where
we told our tale, including our friends' experiment in
viticulture. Then after taking some casks ashore and filling
them with wine and water we bivouacked near the beach,
and next morning set sail before a gentle breeze.

2. The Isle of Dreams

Very soon we seemed quite close to the Isle of Dreams,
though there was a certain dimness and vagueness about
its outline; but it had something dreamlike in its very
nature; for as we approached it receded, and seemed to
get further and further off. At last we reached it and
sailed into Slumber, the port, close to the ivory gates

where stands the temple of the Cock. It was evening when we landed, and upon proceeding to the city we saw many strange dreams. But I intend first to describe the city, as it has not been done before ; Homer indeed mentions it, but gives no detailed description.

The whole place is embowered in wood, of which the trees are poppy and mandragora, all thronged with bats ; this is the only winged thing that exists there. A river, called the Somnambule, flows close by, and there are two springs at the gates, one called Wakenot, and the other Nightlong. The rampart is lofty and of many colours, in the rainbow style. The gates are not two, as Homer says, but four, of which two look on to the plain Stupor; one of them is of iron, the other of pottery, and we were told that these are used by the grim, the murderous, and the cruel. The other pair face the sea and port, and are of horn—it was by this that we had entered—and of ivory. On the right as you enter the city stands the temple of Night, which deity divides with the Cock their chief allegiance ; the temple of the latter is close to the port. On the left is the palace of Sleep. He is the governor, with two lieutenants, Nightmare, son of Whimsy, and Flittergold, son of Fantasy. A well in the middle of the market-place goes by the name of Heavyhead ; beside which are the temples of Deceit and Truth. In the market also is the shrine in which oracles are given, the priest and prophet, by special appointment from Sleep, being Antiphon the dream-interpreter.

The dreams themselves differed widely in character and appearance. Some were well-grown, smooth-skinned, shapely, handsome fellows, other rough, short, and ugly ; some apparently made of gold, others of common cheap stuff. Among them some were found with wings, and other

427

strange variations; others again were like the mummers in a pageant, tricked out as kings or gods or what not. Many of them we felt that we had seen in our world, and sure enough these came up and claimed us as old acquaintance; they took us under their charge, found us lodgings, entertained us with lavish kindness, and, not content with the magnificence of this present reception, promised us royalties and provinces. Some of them also took us to see our friends, doing the return trip all in the day.

For thirty days and nights we abode there—a very feast of sleep.

LUCIAN (Trans. H. W. FOWLER and
F. G. FOWLER)

APOLLONIUS AND KING PORUS

While they were thus talking, the strain of the hymn sung to the flute fell upon their ears, and Apollonius asked the king what was the meaning of their ode. " The Indians," he answered, " sing their admonitions to the king, at the moment of his going to bed; and they pray that he may have good dreams, and rise up propitious and affable towards his subjects." " And how," said Apollonius, " do you, O king, feel in regard to this matter? For it is yourself I suppose that they honour with their pipes." " I don't laugh at them," he said, " for I must allow it because of the law, although I do not require any admonition of the kind: for in so far as a king behaves himself with moderation and integrity, he will bestow, I imagine, favours on himself rather than on his subjects."

After this conversation they laid themselves down to repose ; but when the day dawned, the king himself went to the chamber in which Apollonius and his companions were sleeping, and gently stroking the bed he addressed the sage, and asked him what he was thinking about. " For," he said, " I don't imagine you are asleep, since you drink water and despise wine." Said the other : " Then you don't think that those who drink water go to sleep ? " " Yes," said the king, " they sleep, but with a very light sleep, which just sits upon the tips of their eyelids, as we say, but not upon their minds." " Nay, with both do they sleep," said Apollonius, "and perhaps more with the mind than with the eyelids. For unless the mind is thoroughly composed, the eyes will not admit of sleep either. For note how madmen are not able to go to sleep because their mind leaps with excitement, and their thoughts run coursing hither and thither, so that their glances are full of fury and morbid impulse, like those of the dragons who never sleep. . . But those who drink water, as I do, see things as they really are, and they do not record in fancy things that are not ; and they go to bed with a clear, pure soul and welcome sleep, and are neither buoyed up by the bubbles of their own private luck, nor scared out of their wits by any adversity. For the soul meets both alternatives with equal calm, if it be sober and not overcome by either feeling ; and that is why it can sleep a delightful sleep untouched by the sorrows which startle others from their couches.

And more than this, as a faculty of divination by means of dreams, which is the divinest and most godlike of human faculties, the soul detects the truth all the more easily when it is not muddied by wine, but accepts the message unstained and scans it carefully. Anyhow, the explainers of dreams and visions, those whom the poets call interpreters of dreams, will never undertake to explain any vision to anyone without having first asked the time when it was seen. For if it was at dawn and in the sleep of morning-tide, they calculate its meaning on the assumption that the soul is then in a condition to divine soundly and healthily, because by then it has cleansed itself of the stains of wine. But if the vision was seen in the first sleep or at midnight, when the soul is still immersed in the lees of wine and muddied thereby, they decline to make any suggestions, if they are wise. . . And I could mention many oracles, held in repute by Greeks and barbarians alike, where the priest utters his responses from the tripod after imbibing water and not wine. So you may consider me also as a fit vehicle of the god, O king, along with all who drink water. For we are rapt by the nymphs and are bacchantic revellers in sobriety."

From PHILOSTRATUS' *Life of Apollonius* (Trans.
F. C. CONYBEARE—Loeb Classical Library)

DAPHNIS AND CHLOE

It was the beginning of spring, and all the flowers of the lawns, meadows, valleys and hills were now blowing. All was fresh and green. Now was there humming of bees, and chanting of melodious birds, and skipping of newborn lambs ; the bees hummed in the meadows, the birds warbled in the groves, the lambs skipt on the hills. And now, when such a careless joy had filled those blest and happy fields, Daphnis and Chloe, as delicate and young folks will, would imitate the pleasant things they heard and saw. Hearing how the birds did chant it, they began to carol too, and seeing how the lambs skipt, tript their light and nimble measures. Then, to emulate the bees, they fall to cull the fairest flowers ; some of which in toysome sport they cast in one another's bosoms, and of some platted garlands for the Nymphs ; and always keeping near together, had and did all things in common ; for Daphnis often gathered in the straggling sheep, and Chloe often drove the bolder venturous goats from the crags and precipices ; and sometimes to one of them the care of both the flocks was left while the other did intend some pretty knack or toysome play.

For all their sports were sports of children and of shepherds. Chloe, scudding up and down and here and there picking up the windlestraws, would make in plats a cage for a grasshopper, and be so wholly bent on that, that she was careless of her flocks. Daphnis on the other side having cut the slender reeds and bored the quills or intervals between the joints, and with his soft wax joined and fitted one to another, took no care but to practise or devise some tune even from morning to the twilight. Their wine and their milk and whatsoever was brought from home to the fields, they had still in common. And a man might sooner see all the cattle separate from one another than he should Chloe and Daphnis asunder.

But while they are thus playing away their time to sweeten pleasure, afterwards Love in good earnest kindled up this fire. A wolf that had a kennel of whelps was come often ravenous upon the neighbouring fields, and had borne away from other flocks many cattle, because she needed much prey to keep herself and those cubs. The villagers therefore meet together, and in the night they dig ditches a fathom wide and four fathom deep; of the earth flung up they scatter the more part all abroad at a good distance, and laying over-cross the chasm long, dry, and rotten sticks, they strow them over with the earth that did remain, to make the ground like it was before; that if a hare do but offer to run there, she cannot choose but break those rods that were as brittle as the stubble, and then does easily make it known that that indeed was not true, but only counterfeited soil. Many such trap-ditches were now digged in the mountains and the fields; yet they could not take this wolf (for she could perceive them because of the sophistic and commentitious ground), but many of their sheep and goats were there destroyed, and there wanted but a little that Daphnis too was not slain. And it was on this chance.

Two he-goats were exasperated to fight, and the shock was furious. One of them, by the violence of the very first butt, had one of his horns broke. Upon the pain and grief of that, all in a fret, and mighty chafe he betakes himself to flight, but the victor, pursuing him close, would not let him take breath. Daphnis was vexed to see the horn broke and that kind of malapertness of the goat. Up he catches a cudgel, and pursues the pursuer. But as it frequently happens when one hastes away as fast as possibly he can and the other with ardency pursues, there was no certain prospect of the things before them, but into the trap-ditch both fall, first the goat, then Daphnis. And indeed it was only this that served to save poor Daphnis, that he flundered down to the bottom a-cockhorse on the rough goat. There in a lamentable case he lay, waiting if perchance it might be somebody to draw him out. Chloe seeing the accident, away she flies to the

ditch, and finding he was alive, calls for help to a herdsman of the adjoining fields. When he was come, he
bustled about for a long cord, which holding, Daphnis
might be drawn up ; but finding none, Chloe in a tearing
haste pulls off her stomacher or breastband, gives him it
to let down, and standing on the pitbrim, they both began
to draw and hale ; and Daphnis, holding fast by it, nimbly
followed Chloe's line, and so ascended to the top. They
drew up too the wretched goat, which now had both his
horns broke (so fiercely did the revenge of the vanquished
pursue him); and they gave him to the herdsman to sacrifice, as a reward of the rescue and redemption of their
lives. And if anybody missed him at home, they would say
it was an invasion of wolves. And so returned to see after
their sheep and goats.

And when they had found that all were feeding orderly,
both goats and sheep, sitting down upon the trunk of an
oak they began curiously to search whether he had hurt
any limb in that terrible fall. But nothing was hurt,
nothing bloodied ; only his hair and the rest of his body
were dirtied by mud and the soil which covered over and
hid the trap. And therefore they thought it best before the
accident was made known to Lamo and Myrtale, that he
should wash himself in the cave of the Nymphs.

And coming there together with Chloe, he gave her his
scrip and his shirt to hold, and standing by the spring fell
to washing himself from top to toe. Now his hair was long
and black, and his body all brown and sunburnt, insomuch that the one seemed to have taken colour from the
shadow of the tother ; and to Chloe's eye he seemed of a
sweet and beautiful aspect, and when she wondered that
she had not deemed him such before, she thought it must
be the washing that was the cause of it. And when she

washed his back and shoulders the flesh yielded so softly and gently to her hand, that again and again she privily touched herself to see if hers were more delicate than his. Sunset now coming on, they drove home their flocks, and that night there was but one thing in Chloe's mind, and that the wish she might see Daphnis at his washing again.

When they came out to pasture in the morning, and Daphnis, sitting down under the oak where they were wont, played his pipe and watched the flocks that lay around as if to listen to the music of it, Chloe, sitting close by, although she looked well after her sheep, looked better after Daphnis. And piping there, he seemed again to her goodly and beautiful to look to, and wondering again, she thought the cause must be the music ; and so, when he was done, took the pipe from him and played, if haply she herself might be as beautiful. Then she asked him if he would come again to the bath, and when she persuaded him, watched him at it ; and as she watched, put out her hand and touched him ; and before she went home had praised his beauty, and that praise was the beginning of love.

LONGUS (Trans. GEORGE THORNLEY, revised by
J. M. EDMUNDS—Loeb Classical Library)

THE SPINNING WOMAN

Morning and evening, sleep she drove away,
    Old Platthis,—warding hunger from the door,
And still to wheel and distaff hummed her lay
    Hard by the gates of Eld, and bent and hoar ;
Plying her loom until the dawn was grey,
    The long course of Athene did she tread :

434

With withered hand by withered knee she spun
　　Sufficient for the loom of goodly thread,
Till all her work and all her days were done.
　　And in her eightieth year she saw the wave
　　Of Acheron,—old Platthis,—kind and brave.

LEONIDAS (Trans. A. LANG)

LITTLE POEMS FROM THE GREEK ANTHOLOGY

(Trans. F. A. WRIGHT)

TO ASTER

Thou gazest on the stars ·
　　Would I might be,
O star of mine, the skies
　　With myriad eyes
　　　　To gaze on thee.

PLATO

EPITAPH ON TIMAS: A GIRL WHO DIED BEFORE HER MARRIAGE DAY

Behold the dust of Timas dead ;
　　She knew not wedlock's hour,
For ere that day her golden head
　　Passed to the Dark Maid's bower.
Yea, she has gone, and all her comrades fair
Have shorn with flashing steel the radiance of
　　their hair.

SAPPHO

A DEDICATION

Old Satyra and Melo bring
The Muses dear their offering :
Melo the flute that oft did please
Her father Antigenides
Whereon her lips would swiftly race,
And with it, see, this boxwood case.
To Satyra this pipe belongs,
Sweet minstrel of a lover's songs,
Companion of the evening revel
Fast bound with wax to make it level,
With it content she played through all the night
Till the sun came and smote the doors with light.

LEONIDAS

SPRING SONG

Now swallows build beneath the eaves,
And shape anew their rounded home ;
Now meadows smile with tender leaves,
    And know that spring has come.

Now is the hour for ships to go,
    And lightly o'er the billows leap ;
While winter winds no longer blow
    Or vex the ocean deep.

Come then, ye shipmen, hoist the sail,
    And from its nest the anchor haul ;
Coil the wet ropes and take the gale ;
    Lo I, Priapus, call.

ANTIPATER

EPITAPHS AND EPIGRAMS FROM THE GREEK ANTHOLOGY

(Trans. J. W. MACKAIL)

I. Epitaphs

Philip his father laid here the twelve-years-old child, his high hope, Nicoteles.

I am the tomb of one shipwrecked; but sail thou; for even while we perished, the other ships sailed on over the sea.

Mariner, ask not whose tomb I am here, but be thine own fortune a kinder sea.

I am the grave of Biton, O wayfarer; and if leaving Torone thou goest even to Amphipolis, tell Nicagoras that the wind from Strymon at the setting of the Kids lost him his only son.

I, Brotachus of Gortyna, a Cretan, lie here, not having come hither for this, but for traffic.

I, Dionysius of Tarsus, lie here at sixty, having never married; and I would that my father had not.

Thou who passest on the path, if haply thou dost mark this monument, laugh not, I pray thee, though it is a dog's grave; tears fell for me, and the dust was heaped above me by a master's hands, who likewise engraved these words on my tomb.

437

No longer, poor partridge migrated from the rocks, does thy woven house hold thee in its thin withies, nor under the sparkle of fresh-faced Dawn dost thou ruffle up the edges of thy basking wings ; the cat bit off thy head, but the rest of thee I snatched away, and she did not fill her greedy jaw ; and now may the earth cover thee not lightly but heavily, lest she drag out thy remains.

II. *Epigrams*

I know that I am mortal and ephemeral ; but when I scan the multitudinous circling spirals of the stars, no longer do I touch earth with my feet, but sit with Zeus himself, and take my fill of the ambrosial food of gods.

If that which bears all things bears thee, bear thou and be borne ; but if thou art indignant and vexest thyself, even so that which bears all things bears thee.

SONG OF THE TROZENIAN WOMEN

(Phædra, unable to avoid her destiny, has gone to hang herself in the Castle)

Could I take me to some cavern for mine hiding,
　　In the hill-tops where the Sun scarce hath trod ;
Or a cloud make the home of mine abiding,
　　As a bird among the bird-droves of God !
　　　Could I wing me to my rest amid the roar
　　　Of the deep Adriatic on the shore,

438

Where the waters of Eridanus are clear,
    And Phaëthon's sad sisters by his grave
Weep into the river, and each tear
        Gleams, a drop of amber, in the wave.

To the strand of the Daughters of the Sunset,
    The Apple-tree, the singing and the gold ;
Where the mariner must stay him from his onset,
    And the red wave is tranquil as of old ;
        Yea, beyond that Pillar of the End
        That Atlas guardeth, would I wend ;
Where a voice of living waters never ceaseth
    In God's quiet garden by the sea,
And Earth, the ancient life-giver, increaseth
        Joy among the meadows, like a tree.

EURIPIDES (from *Hippolytus*—
Trans. G. MURRAY)

HERACLITUS

They told me, Heraclitus, they told me you were dead,
They brought me bitter news to hear and bitter tears to
    shed.
I wept as I remember'd how often you and I
Had tired the sun with talking and sent him down the sky.

And now that thou art lying, my dear old Carian guest,
A handful of grey ashes, long, long ago at rest,
Still are thy pleasant voices, thy nightingales, awake ;
For Death, he taketh all away, but them he cannot take.

CALLIMACHUS, Ep. II (Trans. WILLIAM CORY)

§3. ROME

SLEEP AND DEATH

Sleep occurs when the substance of the soul has been disturbed throughout the several members, and has partly seceded from the body (as being driven forth abroad,) and has partly, as being more concentrated, retreated into the interior of the body; for then, at length, when the frame is in this state, the limbs are relaxed and lose their power. Since there is no doubt but that this our vital sense exists in us by means of the soul, which sense when sleep hinders from being exerted, we must then suppose that our soul is disturbed, and expelled from the body; but not wholly, for if it were all withdrawn, the body would lie steeped in the eternal cold of death, as, in that case, no part of the soul would remain latent in the members, (concealed, as fire lies hidden under thick ashes,) whence the sense might be suddenly rekindled throughout the limbs, and flame, as it were, rise from secret heat.

But by what means this change from wakefulness to sleep is produced, and how the soul may be disturbed, and the body languish, I will explain. Do you, my friend take care that I may not pour out my words to the winds.

In the first place, it necessarily happens that the body since it is touched by the breezes of the air to which it is exposed, must be externally assailed and harassed by the frequent impulse of that air; and, for this reason, almost all animated bodies are covered with hide, or even with shells, or with hard skin, or bark. This same air, likewise, impinges on the interior part of the body of animals, when, as they breathe, it is drawn in and respired. For which reason, when the body is affected from both causes, and when assaults penetrate through the small pores of our frame to its primary parts and first elements, a labefactation, as it were, takes place by degrees throughout our members; for the positions of the elements of the body and mind are disturbed, so that part of the soul is drawn forth from them, and part retires hidden into the interior; part also, dispersed throughout the limbs, cannot remain united together, nor perform its ordinary motions mutually with other parts; for nature obstructs the communications and passages, and therefore, the motions of the atoms being changed, sense wholly fails. And since there remains nothing that can, as it were, prop up the limbs, the body becomes weak, and all its members languish; the arms and the eye-lids fall, and the hams often subside with a sinking lassitude, and relax their strength.

When the mind and body are merely at rest together in sleep, no one will feel concern for himself and his life; for, for our parts, our sleep might thus be eternal; nor does any care for ourselves affect us; and yet, at that season, the atoms, throughout our limbs, withdraw to no great distance from sensible motions, and the man who is suddenly roused from sleep quickly recollects himself. Death, then, we must consider to be of far less concern to us, if less can be than that which we see to be nothing. For a greater separation of the atoms of matter takes place in death, nor does any man awake when once the cold pause of life has overtaken him. . . . Why do you groan and weep at the thought of death? For if your past and former life has been an object of gratification to you, and all your blessings have not, as if poured into a leaky vessel, flowed away and

been lost without pleasure, why do you not, O unreasonable man, retire like a guest satisfied with life, and take
your undisturbed rest with resignation ? But if those
things, of which you have had the use, have been wasted
and lost, and life is offensive to you, why do you seek to
incur further trouble, which may all again pass away and
end in dissatisfaction ? . . Yield then, with submissive
feelings, to that which is stronger than thou ; for it is
necessary. . . The matter of which thou art made is
wanted by nature that succeeding generations may grow
up from it ; all which, however, when they have passed
their appointed term of life, will follow thee ; and so have
other generations, before these, fallen into destruction ;
and other generations, not less certainly than thyself,
will fall. Thus shall one thing never cease to rise from
another ; and thus is life given to none in possession, but
to all only for use.

LUCRETIUS (from *De Rerum Natura*—
Trans. J. S. WATSON)

THE BEGINNING OF MUSIC

To imitate with the mouth the liquid voices of birds
was practised long before men could play melodious tunes,
and delight the ear with music. The whistling of the
zephyr through the empty reeds first taught the rustics
to blow through hollow stalks. Then by degrees they
learned the sweet plaintive notes, which the pipe, pressed
by the fingers of the players, pours forth—the pipe,
which is now found through all the pathless groves and

woods and glades, through the solitary haunts and divine resting-places of the shepherds. (Thus time by degrees suggests every discovery, and skill evolves it into the regions of light and fame.) These melodies softened the hearts of those swains, and delighted them when they were satisfied with food; for then every thing affords pleasure.

LUCRETIUS (from *De Rerum Natura*—
Trans. J. S. WATSON)

SULPICIA'S BIRTHDAY

Juno of the birthday, receive the holy piles of incense which the accomplished maid's soft hand now offers thee. To-day she is thine wholly; most joyfully she has decked herself for thee, to stand before thy altar a sight for all to see. 'Tis in thee, goddess, she bids us find the reason for this apparelling. Yet there is one that in secret she desires to please. Then, hallowed one, be kind, and let none pluck apart the lovers : but forge, I prithee, like fetters for the youth. Thus shalt thou match them well. There is no maid that he, or man that she might serve more fitly. And may no watchful guard surprise their wooings, but Love suggest a thousand ways for his outwitting. Bow assent and come in all the sheen of purple palla. They are making offering to thee, holy goddess, thrice with cake and thrice with wine, and the mother eagerly enjoins upon her child what she must pray for. But she, now mistress of herself, sues for another thing in the silence of her heart. She burns as the altar burns with the darting flames, nor, even

443

though she might, would she be whole. Be grateful, Juno, so that, when the next year comes, this love, now of long standing, may be there unchanged to meet their prayers.

CATULLUS (Trans. J. P. POSTGATE
—Loeb Classical Library)

THE COUNTRY LIFE

O husbandmen, too dear to Fortune, if they know their own blessedness ! For them of herself, far from the clash of arms, all-righteous Earth pours from her soil an easy sustenance. If no high mansion with proud portals discharge from all the palace its huge tide of early visitants, if they never stare at door-posts variously inlaid with beauteous tortoise-shell, and dresses tricked with gold, and statues of Corinthian brass, and if white wool is not stained with the Assyrian drug, nor the usefulness of the olive's fair oil adulterated with cassia ; yet, repose without a care, and a life that knows not what disappointment is, a life enriched with manifold treasures—yet ease with wide domains, caverns, and living lakes, and Tempe's cool vale, and the lowing of oxen, and soft slumber beneath the trees, are theirs ; with them are woodland glades and the wild-beasts' haunt, and a band of youths inured to toil, and accustomed to little ; the sacred rites of Heaven, and reverend sires : Justice, as she departed from earth, planted among them her latest footsteps.

For myself, may the lovely Muses first above all else, they whose mysteries I bear, smitten with o'erwhelming passion, take me to themselves, and show me the paths of heaven, and its stars, the various eclipses of the sun and labours of the moon, from whence the earthquake springs, by what force it is that deep seas learn to swell and burst their barriers, and again of themselves sink back into their place ; why winter suns make so much haste to dip in Ocean, or what obstacle it is that clogs the course of the lingering nights. But if, to prevent me from having the power to approach these regions of nature, chill blood around my heart shall prove a barrier, may the fields of the country delight me, and the streams that water the valleys ; rivers and forests may I love, all inglorious though I be. Oh, where are those plains, and the stream of Spercheus and Taygetus haunted by the revels of Spartan maids ! Oh, who will set me down in the cool dells of Haemus, and shield me with the branches' boundless shade ! Happy is he who has been able to learn the causes of things, and has cast beneath his feet all fears, and inexorable Fate, and the roar of greedy Acheron ! Blest too is he who knows the rural gods, Pan, and Silvanus old, and sister-nymphs ! Not him the fasces of the Roman People, nor the monarch's purple can sway, and the discord that drives brethren to mutual treachery, or the Dacian sweeping down from his confederated Danube, nor the Roman state, and the kingdoms doomed to fall ; and never is he pained through pity for him that is destitute, or envies him that has great possessions. Those fruits that the boughs afford, the fruits that of itself, of its own free will, the country bears, he gathers ; and has never seen laws carved on steel, and the maddening forum, or the archives of the Roman People. Other men vex with oars the perilous seas, and rush to take the sword : they press their way into courts and through kingly portals : one assails with ruin a city and its hapless household gods, that he may drink from a jewelled cup, and sleep on Tyrian purple ; another hoards up wealth, and broods over the gold he has buried in the earth ; one is amazed and dazzled at the eloquence of the Rostra ; one the applause of commons and patricians, redoubled as it is along the rows of the theatre, sets agape with the shock of joy ; some delight to steep themselves in brother's blood, and exchange for a place of exile their homes and pleasant thresholds, and seek a fatherland that lies beneath another sun. The husbandman with his crooked plough furrows the soil ; from this comes the work for the year ; by this he maintains his country and little grandsons, by this his herds of oxen, and his bullocks that have served him well. And there is never a time of rest ; for either in fruits the season richly abounds, or in the offspring of cattle, or in the sheaf of Ceres' stalk, and loads the furrows with increase, and overflows the barns. Then winter comes ; in the olive-mill is bruised the berry of Sicyon, the swine come home, well satisfied with mast, the forest gives the fruit of the arbutus, and Autumn drops his various produce, and on the sunny cliffs the mellowing vintage basks.

Meanwhile his dear children hang about his lips, his stainless house preserves its purity ; his cows hang down their udders fraught with milk, and fat kids on the smiling lawn with levelled horns against each other strive. The sire himself keeps holy-day, and stretched along the grass, where is a kindled altar in the midst and his companions wreathe the wine-bowl, with a libation invokes thee, O Father of the wine-press, and for the masters of his cattle sets upon an elm the target, for a match at the flying dart, and their wondrous hardy limbs they strip for the rustic wrestling bout. This life of yore the antique Sabines lived, and Remus too, and his brother ; so, I ween, brave

446

Etruria grew, and Rome became the beauty of the world ;
and, one within herself, encompassed with her bulwarks
seven heights. Likewise, before the Cretan king held
sceptred sway, and before an impious age banqueted on
slaughtered bullocks, this was the life that Saturn passed
on earth, the monarch of the golden age ; nor yet too had
they heard the clarion blare, nor sword-blades ring, when
placed on anvils hard.

But we in our career have traversed o'er a vast expanse
of plain, and now 'tis time to loosen from the yoke our
horses' smoking necks.

From VIRGIL'S *Georgics*, Bk. II
(Trans. J. LONSDALE and S. LEE)

WINTER NIGHT

See, deep in glistening snow Soracte stands ;
No more the straining woods their load uphold,
The streams are frozen with the piercing cold ;
Pile on the hearth the chill-dispersing brands,
Pour out the Sabine wine, four winters old.

Leave to the gods all else ; when they allay
The winds that battle on the seething seas,
The ancient ashes and the cypress trees
Will shake no longer ; count as gain each day
That Fortune grants ; but never think to tease

Its secret from to-morrow. Now, ere yet
Morose old age thy bloom of beauty stain,
Sweet love and dances thou must not disdain,
Nor shun the places where most oft are met
Whispers of tenderness, when night again

447

Brings back the trysting hour, and laughs betray
The merry maid in some far corner hid,
Whose ring or bracelet has been snatched, in play
Which she invites, while feigning to forbid.

HORACE, *Odes*, I. 9 (Trans. F. COUTTS
and W. H. POLLOCK)

THE ROMAN PEASANT

How happy in his low degree,
　How rich, in humble poverty, is he,
Who leads a quiet country life ;
Discharg'd of business, void of strife,
　And from the griping scrivener free ! . .
Sometimes beneath an ancient oak,
　Or on the matted grass he lies :
No God of Sleep he need invoke ;
　The stream, that o'er the pebbles flies,
　With gentle slumber crowns his eyes.
The wind that whistles through the sprays,
　Maintains the concert of the song :
And hidden birds with native lays
　The golden sleep prolong.
But when the blast of winter blows,
　And hoary frost invests the year,
Into the naked woods he goes,
　And seeks the tusky boar to rear,
　With well-mouth'd hounds and pointed
　　　spear ! . .

Amidst his harmless, easy joys,
   No anxious care invades his health,
Nor love his peace of mind destroys,
   Nor wicked avarice of wealth.
But, if a chaste and pleasing wife,
To ease the business of his life,
Divides with him his household care,
Such as the Sabine matrons were,
Such as the swift Apulian's bride,
   Sunburnt and swarthy though she be,
Will fire for winter nights provide,
   And—without noise—will oversee
   His children and his family :
And order all things till he come,
Sweaty and overlabour'd, home.

DRYDEN (after HORACE, Epode 2)

A CAPTIVE OF LOVE

What makes my bed seem hard, seeing it is soft ?
Or why slips down the coverlet so oft ?
Although the nights be long, I sleep not though
My sides are sore with tumbling to and fro.
Were Love the cause, it's like I should descry him ;
Or lies he close, and shoots where none can spy him ?
'Twas so he struck me with a slender dart ;
'Tis cruel Love turmoils my captive heart.
Yielding or struggling, do we give him might ?
Let's yield : a burden easily borne is light !

MARLOWE (after OVID, Elegies, I. 2)

THE NOISES OF ROME

Why am I brought so oft, and by what charm,
To dry Nomentum and this humble farm ?
For poor men, Sparsus, who would find a space
For sleep or thinking, Rome affords no place.
You claim to think ; but all deny your right,
By morn schoolmasters, baker's men by night ;
Armies of copper-smiths, a thousand strong,
Go hammer, hammer, hammer, all day long.
Your money-changers here, a lazy horde,
Rattle gold coins upon their dirty board ;
There ponderous mallets, pounding Spanish rock
For lumps of gold, the midnight chamber shock.
Add to the noise Bellona's drunken crew,
The shipwrecked mariner, the begging Jew,
Ay, and blind beggars, selling matches, too !
He who can tell how many clamours keep
The weary Roman from his noonday sleep
Can count the brazen instruments as soon
Of those who beat their gongs to help the Moon.
You, Sparsus, of these plagues can nothing tell,
Who, far-removed, in dainty villa dwell,
And on the slumbering hills look down at home,
To see your farm and vineyards both in Rome.
Your grapes are large as what Falernum stores ;
Your house so spacious you may drive indoors ;
No noise breaks in upon your sleep at night ;
By day naught wakes you but admitted light.
For me the laughter of the passing crowd,
All Rome beneath my bedroom, shrill and loud,
Disgust me with some ever fresh alarm :
Hence, when I wish to sleep, I seek this farm.

MARTIAL—(XII. 57—Trans. W. J. COURTHOPE)

Antonius being thus inclined, the last and extremest mischief of all other (to wit, the love of Cleopatra) lighted on him, who did waken and stir up many vices yet hidden in him, and were never seen to any : and if any spark of goodness or hope of rising were left him, Cleopatra quenched it straight, and made it worse than before. The manner how he fell in love with her was this. Antonius, going to make war with the Partians, sent to command Cleopatra to appear personally before him when he came into Cilicia, to answer unto such accusations as were laid against her, being this : that she had aided Cassius and Brutus in their war against him. The messenger sent unto Cleopatra, to make this summons unto her, was called Dellius ; who when he had thoroughly considered her beauty, the excellent grace and sweetness of her tongue, he nothing mistrusted that Antonius would do any hurt to so noble a lady, but rather assured himself, that within few days she should be in great favour with him. Thereupon he did her great honour, and persuaded her to come into Cilicia, as honourably furnished as she could possible ; and bade her not to be afraid at all of Antonius, for he was a more courteous lord than any that she had ever seen. Cleopatra on the other side, believing Dellius' words, and guessing by the former access and credit she had with Julius Caesar and C. Pompey (the son of Pompey the Great) only for her beauty, she began to have good hope that she might more easily win Antonius. For Caesar and Pompey knew her when she was but a young thing, and knew not then what the world meant : but now she went to Antonius at the age when a woman's beauty is at the prime, and she also of best judgment. So she furnished herself with a world of gifts, store of gold and silver, and of riches and other sumptuous ornaments, as is credible enough she might bring from so great a house, and from so wealthy and rich a realm as Egypt was. But yet she carried nothing with her wherein she trusted more than in herself, and in the charms and enchantment of her passing beauty and grace. Therefore, when she was sent unto by divers letters, both from Antonius himself and also from his friends, she made so light of it, and mocked Antonius so much, that she disdained to set forward otherwise, but to take her barge in the river of Cydnus; the poop whereof was of gold, the sails of purple, and the oars of silver, which kept stroke in rowing after the sound of the music of flutes, howboys, cithernes, viols, and such other instruments as they played upon in the barge. And now for the person of her self, she was laid under a pavilion of cloth of gold of tissue, apparelled and attired like the goddess Venus, commonly drawn in picture: and hard by her, on either hand of her, pretty fair boys apparelled as painters do set forth god Cupid, with little fans in their hands, with the which they fanned wind upon her. Her ladies and gentlewomen also, the fairest of them, were apparelled like the nymphs Nereids (which are the mermaids of the waters) and like the Graces; some steering the helm, others tending the tackle and ropes of the barge, out of the which there came a wonderful passing sweet savour of perfumes, that perfumed the wharf's side, pestered with innumerable multitudes of people. Some of them followed the barge all along the river-side: others also ran out of the city to see her coming in. So that in the end, there ran such multitudes of people one after another to see her, that Antonius was left post alone in the market-place, in his imperial seat, to give audience: and there went a

rumour in the people's mouths, that the goddess Venus
was come to play with the god Bacchus, for the general
good of all Asia. When Cleopatra landed, Antonius sent to
invite her to supper to him. But she sent him word again,
he should do better rather to come and sup with her.
Antonius therefore, to shew himself courteous unto her
at her arrival, was contented to obey her, and went to
supper to her : where he found such passing sumptuous
fare, that no tongue can express it. But amongst all other
things he most wondered at the infinite number of lights
and torches hanged on the top of the house, giving light
in every place, so artificially set and ordered by devices,
some round, some square : that it was the rarest thing to
behold that eye could discern, or that ever books could
mention. The next night Antonius, feasting her, contended
to pass her in magnificence and fineness ; but she over-
came him in both. So that he himself began to scorn
the gross service of his house, in respect of Cleopatra's
sumptuousness and fineness. And when Cleopatra found
Antonius' jests and slents to be but gross and soldier-
like, in plain manner, she gave it him finely, and without
fear taunted him thoroughly. Now her beauty (as it is
reported) was not so passing as unmatchable of other
women, nor yet such as upon present view did enamour
men with her : but so sweet was her company and conversation, that a man could not possibly but be taken.
And besides her beauty, the good grace she had to talk and
discourse, her courteous nature that tempered her words
and deeds, was a spur that pricked to the quick. Furthermore, besides all these, her voice and words were marvellous pleasant : for her tongue was an instrument of
music to divers sports and pastimes, the which she easily
turned into any language that pleased her. She spake unto

453

few barbarous people by interpreter, but made them answer her self, or at the least the most part of them ; as the Æthiopians, the Arabians, the Troglodytes, the Hebrews, the Syrians, the Medes, and the Parthians, and to many others also, whose languages she had learned. Whereas divers of her progenitors, the kings of Egypt, could scarce learn the Egyptian tongue only, and many of them forgot to speak the Macedonian.

Now Antonius was so ravished with the love of Cleopatra, that though his wife Fulvia had great wars, and much ado with Caesar for his affairs, and that the army of the Parthians (the which the king's lieutenants had given to the only leading of Labienus) was now assembled in Mesopotamia, ready to invade Syria ; yet (as though all this had nothing touched him) he yielded himself to go with Cleopatra unto Alexandria, where he spent and lost in childish sports (as a man might say) and idle pastimes, the most precious thing a man can spend (as Antiphon saith), and that is, time. For they made an order between them, which they called *Amimetobian* (as much to say, no life comparable and matchable with it), one feasting each other by turns, and in cost exceeding all measure and reason.

From PLUTARCH'S *Lives*

(Trans. SIR THOMAS NORTH from the French of AMYOT)

SOME MEDITATIONS OF MARCUS AURELIUS CONCERNING HIMSELF

Betimes in the morning say to thy selfe, This day I shall have to doe with an idle curious man, with an unthankfull man, a railer, a crafty, false, or an envious man ; an unsociable uncharitable man. All these ill qualities have hapned unto them, through ignorance of that which is truly good and truly bad. But I that understand the nature of that which is good, that it onely is to be desired, and of that which is bad, that it onely is truly odious and shameful : who know moreover, that this transgressor, whosoever he be, is my kinsman, not by the same blood and seed, but by participation of the same reason, and of the same divine particle ; How can I either be hurt by any of those, since it is not in their power to make me incurre anything that is truly reproachfull ?

Let it be thy earnest and incessant care as a Romane and a man to performe whatsoever it is that thou art about, with true and unfained gravity, naturall affection, freedome and justice : and as for all other cares, and imaginations, how thou mayest ease thy minde of them. Which thou shalt doe ; if thou shalt goe about every action as thy last action, free from all vanitie, all passionate and wilfull aberration from reason, and from all hypocrisie, and selfe-love, and dislike of those things, which by the fates or appointment of God have hapned unto thee.

If thou shalt finde any thing in this mortall life better then righteousnesse, then truth, temperance, fortitude, and in generall better then a minde contented both with those things which according to right and reason shee doth, and in those, which without her will and knowledge happen unto thee by the Providence ; If I say, thou canst finde out any thing better then this ; apply thy selfe unto it with thy whole heart, and that which is best wheresoever thou dost finde it, injoy freely.

They seeke for themselves private retiring places, as countrey villages, the sea shoare, mountains ; yea thou thy selfe art wont to long much after such places. But all this thou must know proceeds from simplicitie in the highest degree. At what time soever thou wilt, it is in thy power, to retire into thy selfe, and to bee at rest, and free from all businesses.

Whatsoever is now present, and from day to day hath its existence ; all objects of memories, and the mindes and memories themselves, incessantly consider, all things that are, have their being by change, and alteration. Use thy selfe therefore often to meditate upon this, that the Nature of the Universe delights in nothing more, then in altering those things that are, and in making others like unto them. So that wee may say, that whatsoever is, is but as it were the seed of that which shall be.

Let this be thy only joy, and thy only comfort, from one sociable kinde action without intermission to passe unto another, God being ever in thy minde.

Hee that seeth the things that are now, hath seene all that either was ever, or ever shall be, for all things are of one kinde ; and all like one unto another. Meditate often upon the connexion of all things in the world ; and upon the mutuall relation that they have one unto another.

How all things upon Earth are pesle mesle ; and how miraculously things contrary one to another, concurre to the beautie and perfection of this Universe.

Remember, that to change thy minde upon occasion, and to follow him that is able to rectifie thee, is equally ingenuous, as to finde out at the first what is right and just, without helpe.

O my soule, the time I trust will be when thou shalt be good, simple, single, more open and visible then that body by which it is inclosed. Thou wilt one day be sensible of their happinesse, whose end is love.

In the morning when thou findest thyselfe unwilling to rise, consider with thyselfe presently it is to goe about a mans worke that I am stirred up. Am I then yet unwilling to goe about that, for which I myselfe was borne and brought forth into this world ? Or was I made for this, to lay me downe, and make much of myself in a warme bed ?

From *The Golden Book*
(Trans. MERIC CASAUBON, 1634)

§ 4. GÖTTERDÄMMERUNG

That ancient world perished; and all the while, side by side with it, a new world was growing up ... Even through the long swoon of art which is usually thought of as following the darkness of the third century, the truth was that art was transforming itself into new shapes and learning a new language. The last wisdom of the Neo-Platonic philosophy was barely said when the Church of the Holy Wisdom rose in Constantinople, the most perfect work of art that has yet been known in organic beauty of design and splendour of ornament; and when Justinian by his closure of the schools of Athens marked off, as by a precise line, the end of the ancient world, in the Greek monasteries of Athos new types of beauty were being slowly wrought out which passed outward from land to land, transfiguring the face of the world as they went.

It is only in the growth and life of that new world that the decay and death of the old can be regarded with equanimity, or can in a certain sense be historically justified; for Greek civilization was and still is so incomparable that its loss might otherwise fill the mind with despair, and seem to be the last irony cast by fate against the idea of human progress. But it is the law of all Nature, from her highest works to her lowest, that life only comes by death; " she replenishes one thing out of another," in the words of the Roman poet, " and does not suffer anything to be begotten before she has been recruited by the death of something else."

J. W. MACKAIL (from Introduction to *Selections
from the Greek Anthology*)

B.C. AND A.D.

Soles occidere et redire possunt:
Nobis, cum semel occidit brevis lux,
Nox est perpetua una dormienda.

CATULLUS, V.

Behold, I shew you a mystery ! The trumpet shall sound, and the dead shall be raised incorruptible ; for this mortal must put on immortality. Then shall be brought to pass the saying that is written: "Death is swallowed up in victory."

I CORINTHIANS (A.V.)

THIRD PART

§ II ROMANCE AND FAIRIES

So whan I saw I might not slepe
Til now late, this other nyght
Upon my bedde I sat upryght
And bad oon reché me a book,
A ròmaunce, and he hit me took
To rede, and dryve the nyght away.

CHAUCER

Sweet friends, to bed ! . . .
To bed ; 'tis almost fairy time.

SHAKESPEARE (*Midsummer Night's Dream*)

§11 ROMANCE AND FAIRIES

THE SEVEN SLEEPERS

Among the insipid legends of ecclesiastical history, I am tempted to distinguish the memorable fable of the Seven Sleepers ; whose imaginary date corresponds with the reign of the younger Theodosius and the conquest of Africa by the Vandals. When the emperor Decius persecuted the Christians, seven noble youths of Ephesus concealed themselves in a spacious cavern in the side of an adjacent mountain ; where they were doomed to perish by the tyrant, who gave orders that the entrance should be firmly secured with a pile of huge stones. They immediately fell into a deep slumber, which was miraculously prolonged, without injuring the powers of life, during a period of one hundred and eighty-seven years. At the end of that time, the slaves of Adolius, to whom the inheritance of the mountain had descended, removed the stones, to supply materials for some rustic edifice ; the light of the sun darted into the cavern, and the seven sleepers were permitted to awake. After a slumber, as they thought, of a few hours, they were pressed by the calls of hunger ; and resolved that Jamblichus, one of their number, should secretly return to the city, to purchase bread for the use of his companions. The youth (if we may still employ that appellation) could no longer recognise the once familiar aspect of his native country ; and his surprise was increased by the appearance of a large cross, triumphantly erected over the principal gate of Ephesus. His singular dress and obsolete language confounded the baker, to whom he offered an ancient medal of Decius as the current coin of the empire; and Jamblichus, on the suspicion of a secret treasure, was dragged before the judge. Their mutual inquiries produced the amazing discovery that two centuries were almost elapsed since Jamblichus and his friends had escaped from the rage of a Pagan tyrant. The bishop of Ephesus, the clergy, the magistrates, the people, and, as it is said, the emperor Theodosius himself, hastened to visit the cavern of the Seven Sleepers; who bestowed their benediction, related their story, and at the same instant peaceably expired. The origin of this marvellous fable cannot be ascribed to the pious fraud and credulity of the *modern* Greeks, since the authentic tradition may be traced within half a century of the supposed miracle. James of Sarug, a Syrian bishop, who was born only two years after the death of the younger Theodosius, has devoted one of his two hundred and thirty homilies to the praise of the young men of Ephesus. Their legend before the end of the sixth century was translated from the Syriac into the Latin language, by the care of Gregory of Tours. The hostile communions of the East preserve their memory with equal reverence; and their names are honourably inscribed in the Roman, the Abyssinian, and the Russian calendar. Nor has their reputation been confined to the Christian world. This popular tale, which Mahomet might learn when he drove his camels to the fairs of Syria, is introduced, as a divine revelation, into the Koran. The story of the Seven Sleepers has been adopted, and adorned, by the nations, from Bengal to Africa, who profess the Mahometan religion; and some vestiges of a similar tradition have been discovered in the remote extremities of Scandinavia. This easy and universal belief, so expressive of the sense of mankind, may be ascribed to the genuine merit of the fable itself. We imperceptibly advance from youth to age without observing the gradual but incessant change of human affairs, and, even in our larger experience of history, the imagination is accustomed, by a perpetual series of causes and effects, to unite the most distant revolutions. But, if the interval between two memorable æras could be instantly annihilated—if it were possible, after a momentary slumber of two hundred years, to display the *new* world to the eyes of a spectator who still retained a lively and recent impression of the *old*—his surprise and his reflections would furnish the pleasing subject of a philosophical romance.

GIBBON (from *Decline and Fall of the Roman Empire*, Ch. 33)

THE MARRIAGE OF PSYCHE

Men sailed no longer to Paphos, to Cnidus or Cythera, to the presence of the goddess Venus; her sacred rites were neglected, her images stood uncrowned, the cold ashes were left to disfigure her forsaken altars. It was to a maiden that men's prayers were offered, to a human countenance they looked, in propitiating so great a godhead: when the girl went forth in the morning they strewed flowers on her way, and the victims proper to that unseen goddess were presented as she passed along. This conveyance of divine worship to a mortal kindled meantime the anger of the true Venus. " Lo ! now the ancient parent of nature," she cried, " the fountain of all elements ! Behold me, Venus, benign mother of the world, sharing my honours with a mortal maiden, while my name, built up in heaven, is profaned by the mean things of earth !

Shall a perishable woman bear my image about with her ? In vain did the shepherd of Ida prefer me ! Yet shall she have little joy, whosoever she be, of her usurped and unlawful loveliness ! " Thereupon she called to her that winged, bold boy, of evil ways, who wanders armed by night through men's houses, spoiling their marriages ; and stirring yet more by her speech his inborn wantonness, she led him to the city and showed him Psyche as she walked.

" I pray thee," she said, " give thy mother a full revenge. Let this maid become the slave of an unworthy love." Then, embracing him closely, she departed to the shore and took her throne upon the crest of the wave. And lo ! at her unuttered will, her ocean-servants are in waiting : the daughters of Nereus are there singing their song, and Portunus, and Salacia, and the tiny charioteer of the dolphin, with a host of Tritons leaping through the billows. And one blows softly through his sounding seashell, another spreads a silken web against the sun, a third presents the mirror to the eyes of his mistress, while the others swim side by side below, drawing her chariot. Such was the escort of Venus as she went upon the sea.

Psyche meantime, aware of her loveliness, had no fruit thereof. All people regarded and admired, but none sought her in marriage. It was but as upon the finished work of the craftsman that they gazed upon that divine likeness. Her sisters, less fair than she, were happily wedded. She, even as a widow, sitting at home, wept over her desolation, hating in her heart the beauty in which all men were pleased.

And the king, supposing that the gods were angry, inquired of the oracle of Apollo, and Apollo answered him thus : " Let the damsel be placed on the top of a certain mountain, adorned as for the bed of marriage and of death. Look not for a son-in-law of mortal birth ; but for that evil serpent-thing, by reason of whom even the gods tremble and the shadows of Styx are afraid."

So the king returned home and made known the oracle to his wife. For many days she lamented, but at last the fulfilment of the divine precept was urgent upon her, and the company was made ready to conduct the maiden to her deadly bridal. And now the nuptial torch gathers dark smoke and ashes ; the pleasant sound of the pipe changes into a cry ; the marriage hymn concludes in a sorrowful wailing. Below her yellow wedding-veil the bride shook away her tears : insomuch that the whole city was afflicted together at the ill-luck of the stricken house.

But the mandate of the god impelled the hapless Psyche to her fate, and, those solemnities being ended, the funeral of the living soul goes forth, all the people following. Psyche, bitterly weeping, assists not at her marriage but at her own obsequies, and while the parents hesitate to accomplish a thing so unholy the daughter cries to them : " Wherefore torment your luckless age by long weeping ? This was the prize of my extraordinary beauty ! When all people celebrated us with divine honours, and with one voice named the *New Venus*, it was then ye should have wept for me as one dead. Now at last I understand that that one name of Venus has been my ruin. Lead me and set me upon the appointed place. I am in haste to submit to that well-omened marriage, to behold that goodly spouse. Why delay the coming of him who was born for the destruction of the whole world ? "

She was silent, and with firm step went on the way. And they proceeded to the appointed place on a steep mountain, and left there the maiden alone, and took their way homewards dejectedly. The wretched parents, in their close-shut house, yielded themselves to perpetual night; while to Psyche, fearful and trembling and weeping sore upon the mountain-top, comes the gentle Zephyrus. He lifts her gently, and, with vesture floating on either side, bears her by his own soft breathing over the windings of the hills, and sets her lightly among the flowers in the bosom of a valley below.

Psyche, in those delicate grassy places, lying sweetly on her dewy bed, rested from the agitation of her soul and arose in peace. And lo! a grove of mighty trees, with a fount of water, clear as glass, in the midst; and hard by the water, a dwelling-place, built not by human hands but by some divine cunning. One recognized, even at the entering, the delightful hostelry of a god. Golden pillars sustained the roof, arched most curiously in cedar-wood and ivory. The walls were hidden under wrought silver:—all tame and woodland creatures leaping forward to the visitor's gaze. Wonderful indeed was the craftsman, divine or half-divine, who by the subtlety of his art had breathed so wild a soul into the silver. The very pavement was distinct with pictures in goodly stones. In the glow of its precious metal the house is its own daylight, having no need of the sun. Well might it seem a place fashioned for the conversation of gods with men!

Psyche, drawn forward by the delight of it, came near, and her courage growing, stood within the doorway. One by one, she admired the beautiful things she saw; and, most wonderful of all! no lock, no chain, nor living guardian protected that great treasure-house. But as she gazed there came a voice—a voice, as it were unclothed of its bodily vesture—" Mistress ! " it said, " all these things are thine. Lie down, and relieve thy weariness, and rise again for the bath when thou wilt. We thy servants, whose voice thou hearest, will be beforehand with our service, and a royal feast shall be ready."

And Psyche understood that some divine care was providing, and, refreshed with sleep and the bath, sat down to the feast. Still she saw no one; only she heard words falling here and there, and had voices alone to serve her. And the feast being ended, one entered the chamber and sang to her unseen, while another struck the chords of a harp, invisible with him who played on it. Afterwards, the sound of a company singing together came to her, but still so that none was present to sight; yet it appeared that a great multitude of singers was there.

And the hour of evening inviting her, she climbed into the bed; and as the night was far advanced, behold a sound of a certain clemency approaches her. Then, fearing for her maidenhood, in so great solitude, she trembled, and more than any evil she knew dreaded that she knew not. And now the husband, that unknown husband, drew near, and ascended the couch, and made her his wife; and lo! before the rise of dawn he had departed hastily. And the attendant voices ministered to the needs of the newly married. And so it happened with her for a long season.

WALTER PATER (from *Marius the Epicurean*)

THE DEAD AT CLONMACNOIS
(*From the Irish*)

In a quiet water'd land, a land of roses,
    Stands Saint Kieran's city fair;
And the warriors of Erin in their famous generations
    Slumber there.

There beneath the dewy hillside sleep the noblest
  Of the clan of Conn,
Each below his stone with name in branching Ogham
  And the sacred knot thereon.

There they laid to rest the seven Kings of Tara,
  There the sons of Cairbrè sleep—
Battle-banners of the Gael that in Kieran's plain of
    crosses
  Now their final hosting keep.

And in Clonmacnois they laid the men of Teffia,
  And right many a lord of Breagh ;
Deep the sod above Clan Creidè and Clan Conaill,
  Kind in hall and fierce in fray.

Many and many a son of Conn the Hundred-fighter
  In the red earth lies at rest ;
Many a blue eye of Clan Colman the turf covers,
  Many a swan-white breast.

T. W. ROLLESTON

THE LITTLE BLACK ROSE

The little black rose shall be red at last ;
What made it black but the March wind dry,
And the tear of the widow that fell on it fast ?
It shall redden the hills when June is nigh.

The Silk of the Kine shall rest at last ;
What drove her forth but the dragon-fly ?

In the golden vale she shall feed full fast
With her mild gold horn and slow dark eye.

The wounded wood dove lies dead at last !
The pine long bleeding it shall not die !
This song is secret—mine ear it passed
In a wind on the plains at Athenry.

AUBREY DE VERE

THE COMPLAINT OF TROILUS FOR CRESSIDA REMOVED TO THE GRECIAN CAMP

On morwe, as sone as day bigan to clere,
This Troilus gan of his slep t'abreyde,
And to Pandàre, his ownè brother dere,
' For love of God,' full pitousliche he seyde,
' As go we sen the paleis of Criseyde :
For sin we yit may han no morè feste,
So lat us sen her paleis at the leste ! ' . .

Therwith whan he was war and gan biholde
How shet was every window of the place,
As frost, him thoughte, his hertè gan to colde ;
For-which with chaungèd dedlich palè face,
Withouten word he forth-by gan to pace ;
And, as God wolde, he gan so fastè ride,
That no wight of his contenaunce espi'de.

471

Than seide he thus : ' O paleis desolat,
O hous, of houses whilom best y-hight,
O paleis empty and disconsolat,
O thou lantèrne of which queynt is the light,
O paleis, whilom day that now art night,
Wel oughtestow to falle, and I to dye,
Sin she is went that wont was us to gye !

' O paleis, whilom crowne of houses alle,
Enluminèd with sonne of allé blisse !
O ring, fro which the ruby is out-falle,
O cause of wo, that cause hast been of lisse !
Yit, sin I may no bet, fayn wolde I kisse
Thy coldè dorès, dorste I for this route :
And far-wel shrine, of which the seynt is oute ! ' . .

Fro thennèsforth he rideth up and down,
And everything com him to rèmembraunce
As he rod for-by places of the town
In which he whilom hadde al his plesàunce.
' Lo, yonder saw I last my lady daunce !
And in that templè with her ẏen clere
Me caughtè first my rightè lady dere ! ' . .

Upon the wallès faste ek wolde he walke,
And on the Grekès cost he woldè see,
And to himself right thus he woldè talke,
' Lo, yonder is myn ownè lady free !
Or ellès yonder ther the tentès be !
And thennèscom'th this eir that is so swote,
That in my soule I fele it doth me bote !

472

'And, hardily, this wind, that more and more
Thus stoundemele encresseth in my face,
Is of my lady's depê sikês sore !
I preve it thus, for in non other space
Of al this town, save only in this place,
Fele I no wind that souneth so lik peyne :
It seith, " Allas ! why twinnêd be we tweyne ? " '

CHAUCER (from Troilus and Cressida)

THE GOOD OLD TIMES

In tholdê dayês of the Kyng Arthòur,
Of which that Britons speken greet honòur,
All was this land fulfild of faêrye.
The elf queene with hir joly compaignye
Dauncêd ful ofte in many a grenê mede.
This was the olde opinion as I rede,—
I speke of manye hundred yeres ago,—
But now kan no man se none elvês mo.

CHAUCER (from Wife of Bath's Tale)

THE END OF A GREAT LOVE STORY

Then came Sir Bors de Ganis, and said, My Lord Sir
Launcelot, what think ye for to do, now to ride in this
realm ? wit thou well ye shall find few friends. Be as be
may, said Sir Launcelot, keep you still here, for I will
forth on my journey, and no man nor child shall go with
me. So it was no boot to strive, but he departed and rode

473

westerly, and there he sought a seven or eight days, and at the last he came to a nunnery, and then was queen Guenever ware of Sir Launcelot as he walked in the cloister, and when she saw him there she swooned thrice, that all the ladies and gentlewomen had work enough to hold the queen up. So when she might speak, she called ladies and gentlewomen to her, and said, Ye marvel, fair ladies, why I make this fare. Truly, she said, it is for the sight of yonder knight that yonder standeth : wherefore, I pray you all, call him to me. When Sir Launcelot was brought to her, then she said to all the ladies, Through this man and me hath all this war been wrought, and the death of the most noblest knights of the world ; for through our love that we have loved together is my most noble lord slain. Therefore, Sir Launcelot, wit thou well I am set in such a plight to get my soul's health ; and yet I trust, through God's grace, that after my death to have a sight of the blessed face of Christ, and at doomsday to sit on his right side, for as sinful as ever I was are saints in heaven. Therefore, Sir Launcelot, I require thee and beseech thee heartily, for all the love that ever was betwixt us, that thou never see me more in the visage ; and I command thee on God's behalf, that thou forsake my company, and to thy kingdom thou turn again and keep well thy realm from war and wrack. For as well as I have loved thee, mine heart will not serve me to see thee ; for through thee and me is the flower of kings and knights destroyed. Therefore, Sir Launcelot, go to thy realm, and there take thee a wife, and live with her with joy and bliss, and I pray thee heartily pray for me to our Lord, that I may amend my mis-living. Now, sweet madam, said Sir Launcelot, would ye that I should return again unto my country, and there to wed a lady ? Nay, madam, wit you well that shall I never do : for I shall never be so false to you of that I have promised, but the same destiny that ye have taken you to, I will take me unto, for to please Jesu, and ever for you I cast me specially to pray. If thou wilt do so, said the queen, hold thy promise; but I may never believe but that thou wilt turn to the world again. Well, madam, said he, ye say as pleaseth you, yet wist you me never false of my promise, and God defend but I should forsake the world as ye have done. For in the quest of the Sancgreal I had forsaken the vanities of the world, had not your lord been. And if I had done so at that time with my heart, will, and thought, I had passed all the knights that were in the Sancgreal, except Sir Galahad my son. And therefore, lady, sithen ye have taken you to perfection, I must needs take me to perfection of right. For I take record of God, in you I have had mine earthly joy. And if I had found you now so disposed, I had cast me to have had you into mine own realm.

But sithen I find you thus disposed, I insure you faithfully I will ever take me to penance, and pray while my life lasteth, if that I may find any hermit either grey or white that will receive me. Wherefore, madam, I pray you kiss me, and never no more. Nay, said the queen, that shall I never do, but abstain you from such works. And they departed. But there was never so hard an hearted man, but he would have wept to see the dolour that they made. For there was lamentation as they had been stung with spears, and many times they swooned. And the ladies bare the queen to her chamber, and Sir Launcelot awoke, and went and took his horse, and rode all that day and all that night in a forest, weeping. And at the last he was ware of an hermitage and a chapel stood betwixt two cliffs, and then he heard a little bell ring to mass, and

475

thither he rode and alight, and tied his horse to the gate, and heard mass, .. and there he served God day and night with prayers and fastings. And thus upon a night there came a vision to Sir Launcelot, and charged him, in remission of his sins, to haste him unto Almesbury,— And by then thou come there, thou shalt find queen Guenever dead : and therefore take thy fellows with thee, and purvey them of an horse bier, and fetch thou the corpse of her, and bury her by her husband the noble king Arthur. So this vision came to Launcelot thrice in one night.

Then Sir Launcelot rose up or day, and told the hermit. It were well done, said the hermit, that ye made you ready, and that ye disobey not the vision. Then Sir Launcelot took his seven fellows with him, and on foot they went from Glastonbury to Almesbury, the which is little more than thirty miles. And thither they came within two days, for they were weak and feeble to go. And when Sir Launcelot was come to Almesbury, within the nunnery, queen Guenever died but half an hour before. . . Then Sir Launcelot saw her visage, but he wept not greatly, but sighed. And so he did all the observance of the service himself, both the Dirige, and on the morn he sang mass. And there was ordained an horse bier : and so with an hundred torches ever burning about the corpse of the queen, and ever Sir Launcelot with his eight fellows went about the horse bier singing and reading many an holy orison, and frankincense upon the corpse incensed. Thus Sir Launcelot and his eight fellows went on foot from Almesbury unto Glastonbury : and when they were come to the chapel and the hermitage, there she had a Dirige with great devotion. And on the morn the hermit, that sometime was Bishop of Canterbury, sang the mass of

476

Requiem with great devotion : and Sir Launcelot was the
first that offered, and then all his eight fellows. And then
she was wrapped in cered cloth of Raines, from the top to
the toe in thirty fold, and after she was put in a web of
lead, and then in a coffin of marble. And when she was put
in the earth, Sir Launcelot swooned, and lay long still, and
never after eat but little meat, nor drank, till he was dead.
. . So at a season of the night they went all to their beds,
for they all lay in one chamber. And so after midnight,
against day, when Sir Bors and his fellows came to his bed
they found him stark dead, and he lay as he had smiled,
and the sweetest savour about him that ever they felt.
Then was there weeping and wringing of hands, and the
greatest dole they made that ever made men. And on the
morn the bishop did his mass of Requiem ; and after the
bishop and all the nine knights put Sir Launcelot in the
same horse bier that queen Guenever was laid in tofore
that she was buried : and so the bishop and they altogether went with the corpse of Sir Launcelot daily, till
they came to Joyous Gard, . . and ever they had a
hundred torches burning about him ; and so within
fifteen days they came to Joyous Gard. And there they
laid his corpse in the body of the quire, and sang and
read many psalters and prayers over him and about him ;
and ever his visage was laid open and naked, that all folk
might behold him ; for such was the custom in those
days, that all men of worship should so lie with open
visage till that they were buried. And right thus as they
were at their service, there came Sir Ector de Maris, that
had seven year sought all England, Scotland, and Wales,
seeking his brother Sir Launcelot.

And when Sir Ector heard such noise and light in the
quire of Joyous Gard, he alight and put his horse from

him, and came into the quire, and there he saw men
sing and weep. And they all knew Sir Ector, but he knew
not them. Then went Sir Bors unto Sir Ector, and told
him how there lay his brother Sir Launcelot dead. And
then Sir Ector threw his shield, sword, and helm from
him ; and when he beheld Sir Launcelot's visage he fell
down in a swoon. And when he awaked it were hard any
tongue to tell the doleful complaints that he made for his
brother. Ah, Launcelot, he said, thou were head of all
christian knights ; and now I dare say, said Sir Ector, thou
Sir Launcelot, there thou liest, that thou were never
matched of earthly knight's hand ; and thou were the
courtiest knight that ever bare shield ; and thou were the
truest friend to thy lover that ever bestrode horse ; and
thou were the truest lover of a sinful man that ever loved
woman ; and thou were the kindest man that ever strake
with sword ; and thou were the goodliest person ever came
among press of knights ; and thou was the meekest man
and the gentlest that ever ate in hall among ladies ; and
thou were the sternest knight to thy mortal foe that ever
put spear in the rest.

SIR THOMAS MALORY (from *Le Morte Darthur*)

THE ESCAPE OF NICOLETTE

It befel in the fair summer time, in the month of May,
when the long days are warm and the nights are blissful
and still, that Nicolette lay on her bed, and watched the
moon shine clear through her window, and likewise heard
the nightingale sing in the garden. Then was she mindful
of her friend Aucassin whom she loved so well. Now the

478

old woman who guarded her slept full soundly; so she arose and tired herself in a goodly tunic of silk that she had at hand, and took up napkins and sheets of the bed and knotted one to the other, and very featly she made a rope as long as she could and tied it to a pillar of the window. Therewith she let herself down unto the ground and caught her raiment in both hands, behind and before, and tucked it up because there was much dew on the grass, and so made her way through the moonlit garden.

Her locks were fair and curly, her eyes bright and smiling, her face of a good length, her nose high and well set, her lips more red than cherry or rose in summer, her teeth white and small; her breasts so firm that they bore up her tunic as they had been two large nuts; so slim she was that your two hands might have girdled her waist, and the daisy-flowers that brake beneath her toes and bent above them seemed black against her feet, so very white was this maiden.

Quietly she unlocked the postern gate and passed into the streets of Beaucaire, and keeping within the shadows of the houses (for the moon shone very clearly) she went on till that she came to the tower where Aucassin was shut up. She crouched behind one of the pillars, and putting her ear to a chink in the wall, heard Aucassin making a great dole and sorrowing for his sweet friend.

When she had listened to him long enough she began to speak.

Now Aucassin was filled with dismay when he heard Nicolette tell how she would go away to another land, because his father hated her. " Fair sweet friend," said he, " indeed you shall not go away, for that would kill me."

While he was so saying, the town watch were searching the streets with their swords drawn under their cloaks.

Now the sentinel on the tower (who was a gallant man and kindly withal) heard them talking of Nicolette and saying that she must be put to death.

" Alas ! " he thought, " what a pity to slay so fair a maiden ! It were a kindness to make her ware of this danger."

And very cleverly the sentinel began to sing. Now his song was a warning to Nicolette, but the watch took it for an old ballad that he sang to himself.

" Ah ! " said Nicolette, " may the souls of your father and mother have sweet repose, because of those gentle and gracious words. If it so please God, I shall now make myself safe."

So she wrapped her cloak full closely about her, and crouching in the deep shadow deftly hid herself until the watch had passed. Then she tarried no longer, but took leave of her dear Aucassin, and, climbing the castle wall which was of a great age and partly broken, so came to a narrow place between the high wall and the steep moat. Now the moat was of a great depth and full of darkness, and Nicolette was sorely afraid.

" Alas ! " thought she, " if I fall in this perilous place I shall break my neck, and if I go back I shall be taken to prison as soon as the sun shines."

So she made the sign of the cross, and slid down to the bottom of the moat, which was dried up. Her dainty feet and her fair hands were sorely cut and bruised, but she faced the other side bravely and clomb up with much pain, and came at length to the top. At a bowshot from the moat lay a great forest, and hither Nicolette made her way. Now in this forest dwelt beasts of a savage kind and baneful serpents, and at first she feared to enter it, thinking these would devour her. Then she remembered the terrible Count of Beaucaire. If she went back to the town she would be taken to his prison, and perchance afterwards she would be burned to death. So she entered the great forest, and, lying down in a bushy place, she fell asleep. When she awoke the birds were singing gaily all round her, and she was ware of a company of herd boys who had driven their beasts into the forest and were eating their breakfast at a beautiful spring near by. Nicolette arose and ran towards them.

" Fair youths," she called out, " may God have you in His keeping ! "

" And may God bless you also ! " replied one who was more ready of tongue than the others.

Then Nicolette begged them that they seek out Aucassin, the son of Count Garin of Beaucaire, and have him to come hunting in that forest, for that he would find there a beast he would not lose the chance of taking for all the wealth in the world.

> *Aucassin and Nicolette* (from the Old French
> —Trans. A. s.)

HOW BRUIN THE BEAR WAS SPED OF
REYNARD THE FOX

Now is Bruin gone on his way toward the Fox in a stout mood, which supposed well that the Fox should not have beguiled him. As he came in a dark wood in a forest where Reynard had a bypath when he was hunted, there beside was a high mountain and land, and there must Bruin go over in the middle for to go to Maleperduys. For

Reynard had many a dwelling place, but the Castle of Maleperduys was the best and the safest burrow that he had. There lay he in, when he had need and was in any dread or fear. Now when Bruin was come to Maleperduys, he found the gate fast shut. Then went he before the gate, and sat upon his tail, and called : " Reynard, be ye at home? I am Bruin. The King hath sent me for you that you should come to Court, for to plead your cause. He hath sworn there by his God, come ye not or bring I you not with me for to abide such right and sentence as shall be there given, it shall cost you your life. He will hang you or set you on the rack. Reynard, do by my counsel, and come to the Court."

Reynard lay within the gate, as he oft was wont to do, for the warmth of the sun. When Reynard heard Bruin, then went he inward into his hole. For Maleperduys was full of holes—here one hole and there another, and yonder another—narrow, crooked and long, with many ways to go out, which he opened and shut after that he had need. When he had brought any prey home, or wist that any sought him for his misdeeds and trespasses, then he ran and hid him from his enemies into his secret chambers that they could not find him : by which he deceived many a beast that sought him. And then thought Reynard in himself how he might best bring the Bear to trouble, and that *he* abode in credit.

In this thought Reynard came out, and said : " Bruin, uncle, ye be welcome ! I heard you well before, but I was in mine evensong—therefore have I the longer tarried a little. Dear uncle, he hath done to you no good service, and I owe him no thanks that hath sent you over this long hill ; for I see that ye be also weary that the sweat runneth down by your cheeks. It was no need : I had nevertheless come to Court to-morrow; and I sorrow now the less, for your wise counsel shall well help me in the Court. And could the King find none less messenger but you for to send hither? That is great wonder. For, next the King, ye be the most gentle, and richest of levies and of land. I would well that we were now at the Court, but I fear me that I shall not well know how to go thither, for I have eaten so much new food that methinketh my belly will break or cleave asunder, and because the food was new I ate the more."

Then spake the Bear: " Dear nephew, what food have ye eaten that made you so full? "

" Dear uncle, what I ate, what might it help you if I told you? I ate but simple food. A poor man is no Lord, that may ye know, uncle, by me. We poor folk must eat oftimes such as we gladly would not eat if we had better. They were great honeycombs; which I must needs eat for hunger. They have made my belly so great that I can nowhere endure."

Bruin then spake anon: " Alas, Reynard, what say ye! Set ye so little by honey? I prize and love it above all food. Dear Reynard, help me that I might get a deal of this honey, and as long as I live I shall be to you a true friend, and abide by you, as far as ye help me that I may have a part of this honey."

" Bruin, uncle, I would have supposed that ye had jested therewith."

" So help me God, Reynard, nay. I should not gladly jest with you."

Then spake the red Reynard: " Is it then earnest, that ye love so well the honey? I shall see that you have so much that ten of you should not eat it at one meal, might I get therewith your friendship."

"Not we ten, Reynard nephew!" said the Bear. "How should that be? Had I all the honey that is between this and Portugal, I should well eat it alone."

Reynard said: "What say ye, uncle? Hereby dwelleth a husbandman named Lantfert, which hath so much honey that ye could not eat it in seven years; which ye shall have in your hold if ye will be to me friendly and helping against mine enemies in the King's Court."

Then promised Bruin the Bear to him that, if he might have his belly full, he would truly be to him before all other a faithful friend.

Hereof laughed Reynard the knave, and said: "If ye would have seven amber barrels full, I shall well get them, and help you to have them." These words pleased the Bear so well, and made him so much to laugh that he could not well stand.

Then thought Reynard: "This is good luck; I shall lead him thither that he shall laugh *by measure*."

Reynard said then: "This matter may not be long delayed. I must pain myself for you. Ye shall well understand the very favour and goodwill that I bear toward you. I know none in all my lineage that I now would labour for thus sore."

That thanked him the Bear, and thought he tarried long.

"Now, uncle, let us go a good pace, and follow ye me. I shall make you to have as much honey as ye may bear." The Fox meant, of good strokes; but the caitiff marked not what the Fox meant; and they went so long together that they came unto Lantfert's yard. Then was Sir Bruin merry.

Now hark of Lantfert. If it is true what men say,

Lantfert was a strong carpenter of great timber, and had brought the day before into his yard a great oak, which he begun to cleave. And, as men be accustomed, he had smitten two wedges therein one after the other, in such wise the oak was wide open. Whereof Reynard was glad, for he had found it exactly as he wished, and said to the Bear all laughing : " See now well sharply to it ! In this tree is so much honey that it is *without measure.* Try if ye can come therein ; and eat but little, for, though the honey-combs be sweet and good, yet beware that ye eat not too many, but take of them *by measure,* that ye catch no harm in your body ; for, sweet uncle, I should be blamed if they did you any harm."

" What, Reynard, cousin, trouble yourself not for me ! Ween ye that I were a fool ? "

" *Measure* is good in all food," Reynard said. " Ye say truth. Wherefore should I trouble myself ? Go to the end, and creep therein ! "

Bruin the Bear hasted sore toward the honey, and trode in with his two foremost feet, and put his head over his ears into the cleft of the tree. And Reynard sprang lightly and brake out the wedges of the tree. Then helped the Bear neither flattering ne chiding : he was fast shut in the tree. Thus hath the nephew, with deceit, brought his uncle in prison in the tree, in such wise as he could not get out with might ne with craft, head ne foot.

What profiteth Bruin the Bear that he strong and hardy is ? That may not help him. He saw well that he was beguiled. He began to howl, and to bellow, and scratched with the hinder feet, and made such a noise and rumour that Lantfert came out hastily, and knew nothing what this might be ; and brought in his hand a sharp hook. Bruin the Bear lay in the cleft of the tree in great fear and

dread, and held fast his head, and nipped both his fore-
feet. He struggled, he wrestled, and cried ; and all was for
naught. He wist not how he might get out.

WILLIAM CAXTON (from *Reynard the Fox*—
modernised by W. S. STALLYBRASS)

THOMAS OF ERCILDOUNE

(*who slept for seven years*)

True Thomas lay on Huntley bank ;
    A ferlie spied he wi' his ee ;
There he saw a lady bright
    Come riding doun by the Eildon Tree.

Her skirt was o' the grass green silk,
    Her mantle o' the velvet fine ;
At ilka tett o' her horse's mane,
    Hung fifty siller bells and nine.

True Thomas he pu'd aff his cap,
    And louted low doun on his knee :
' Hail to thee, Mary, Queen of Heaven !
    For thy peer on earth could never be.'

' O no, O no, Thomas,' she said,
    ' That name does not belong to me ;
I'm but the Queen o' fair Elfland,
    That hither have come to visit thee.

' Harp and carp, Thomas,' she said ;
    ' Harp and carp along wi' me ;

486

And if ye dare to kiss my lips,
    Sure of your body I shall be.'

' Betide me weal, betide me woe,
    That weird shall never daunten me.'
Syne he has kiss'd her on the lips,
    All underneath the Eildon Tree.

' Now ye maun go wi' me,' she said,
    ' Now, Thomas, ye maun go wi' me ;
And ye maun serve me seven years,
    Through weal or woe as may chance to be.

She's mounted on her milk-white steed,
    And she's ta'en Thomas up behind ;
And aye, whene'er her bridle rang,
    The steed gaed swifter than the wind.

O they rade on, and farther on,
    The steed gaed swifter than the wind ;
Until they reach'd a desert wide,
    And living land was left behind.

' Now, Thomas, light doun, light doun,' she said,
    ' And lean your head upon my knee ;
Abide ye there a little space,
    And I will show you ferlies three.

' O see ye not yon narrow road,
    So thick beset wi' thorns and briars ?
That is the Path of Righteousness,
    Though after it but few enquires.

'And see ye not yon braid, braid road,
   That lies across the lily leven?
That is the Path of Wickedness,
   Though some call it the road to Heaven.

'And see ye not yon bonny road
   That winds about the ferny brae?
That is the road to fair Elfland,
   Where thou and I this night maun gae.

'But, Thomas, ye sall haud your tongue,
   Whatever ye may hear or see;
For speak ye word in Elfin-land,
   Ye'll ne'er win back to your ain countrie.'

O they rade on, and further on,
   And they waded rivers abune the knee;
And they saw neither sun nor moon,
   But they heard the roaring of a sea. . .

Syne they came to a garden green,
   And she pu'd an apple frae a tree:
'Take this for thy wages, Thomas,' she said;
   'It will give thee the tongue that can never lee.'

'My tongue is my ain,' then Thomas he said;
   'A gudely gift ye wad gie to me!
I neither dought to buy or sell
   At fair or tryst where I might be.

'I dought neither speak to prince or peer,
   Nor ask of grace from fair ladye!'—
'Now haud thy peace, Thomas,' she said,
   'For as I say, so must it be.'

He has gotten a coat of the even cloth,
  And a pair o' shoon of the velvet green ;
And till seven years were come and gane,
  True Thomas on earth was never seen.

ANONYMOUS

THE FAIRY FROLIC

All sing :

By the moon we sport and play,
With the night begins our day :
As we dance the dew doth fall :
Trip it, little urchins all !
Lightly as the little bee,
Two by two, and three by three :
And about go we, and about go we ! . .

First Fairy :

I do come about the copse
Leaping upon flowers' tops ;
Then I get upon a fly,
She carries me above the sky,
And trip and go.

Second Fairy :

When a dewdrop falleth down,
And doth light upon my crown,
Then I shake my head and skip,
And about I trip.

489

All sing :
Round about, round about, in a fine ring a,
Thus we dance, thus we dance and thus we sing a ;
Trip and go, to and fro, over this green a,
All about, in and out, for our brave Queen a.

ANONYMOUS (from *The Maid's Metamorphosis*, 1600)

FAIRY PUNISHMENT

Pinch him, pinch him, black and blue,
Saucy mortals must not view
What the Queen of Stars is doing,
Nor pry into our fairy wooing.
  Pinch him blue—
  And pinch him black—
  Let him not lack
Sharp nails to pinch him blue and red
Till sleep has rocked his addle head.
For the trespass he hath done,
Spots o'er all his flesh shall run.

    JOHN LYLY (from *Endymion*)

SONG OF THE FAIRY QUEEN

Hark all you ladies that do sleep !
The Fairy Queen Proserpina
Bids you awake and pity them that weep !
  You may do in the dark
  What the day doth forbid ;
  Fear not the dogs that bark,
  Night will have all hid.

But, if you let your lovers moan,
The Fairy Queen Proserpina
Will send abroad her fairies every one
    That shall pinch black and blue
    Your white hands and fair arms,
    That did not kindly rue
    Your paramours' harms.

In myrtle arbours on the downs
The Fairy Queen Proserpina
This night by moonshine, leading merry rounds,
    Holds watch with sweet Love,
    Down the dale, up the hill,
    No plaints nor griefs may move
    Their holy vigil.

All you that will hold watch with Love,
The Fairy Queen Proserpina
Will make you fairer than Diana's dove.
    Roses red, lilies white,
    And the clear damask hue
    Shall on your cheeks alight.
    Love will adorn you.

All you that love or loved before !
The Fairy Queen Proserpina
Bids you increase that loving humour more !
    They that have not yet fed
    On delight amorous—
    She vows that they shall lead
    Apes in Avernus.

ANONYMOUS, 16th century

She is the fairies' midwife, and she comes
In shape no bigger than an agate-stone
On the fore-finger of an alderman,
Drawn with a team of little atomies
Athwart men's noses as they lie asleep ;
Her waggon-spokes made of long spinners' legs,
The cover of the wings of grasshoppers,
The traces of the smallest spider's web,
The collars of the moonshine's watery beams,
Her whip of cricket's bone, the lash of film,
Her waggoner a small grey-coated gnat,
Not half so big as a round little worm
Prick'd from the lazy finger of a maid ;
Her chariot is an empty hazel-nut
Made by the joiner squirrel or old grub,
Time out o' mind the fairies' coachmakers.
And in this state she gallops night by night
Through lovers' brains, and then they dream of love ;
O'er courtiers' knees, that dream on court'sies straight,
O'er lawyers' fingers, who straight dream on fees,
O'er ladies' lips, who straight on kisses dream,
Which oft the angry Mab with blisters plagues,
Because their breaths with sweetmeats tainted are :
Sometime she gallops o'er a courtier's nose,
And then dreams he of smelling out a suit ;
And sometime comes she with a tithe-pig's tail
Tickling a parson's nose as a' lies asleep,
Then dreams he of another benefice :
Sometime she driveth o'er a soldier's neck,
And then dreams he of cutting foreign throats,
Of breaches, ambuscadoes, Spanish blades,

Of healths five-fathom deep ; and then anon
Drums in his ear, at which he starts and wakes,
And being thus frighted swears a prayer or two
And sleeps again.

SHAKESPEARE (from *Romeo and Juliet*)

NEWS OF THE DUKE

They say he is already in the Forest of Arden, and a
many merry men with him ; and there they live like the
old Robin Hood of England ; they say many young
gentlemen flock to him every day, and fleet the time
carelessly, as they did in the golden world.

SHAKESPEARE (from *As You Like It*)

HOBGOBLINS, &c.

A bigger kind there is of them called with us hobgoblins,
and Robin Goodfellows, that would in those superstitious
times grind corn for a mess of milk, cut wood, or do any
manner of drudgery work. They would mend old irons in
those Æolian isles of Lipari, in former ages, and have been
often seen and heard. Tholosanus calls them Trullos and
Getulos, and saith, that in his days they were common in
many places of France. Dithmarus Bleskenius, in his description of Iceland, reports for a certainty, that almost in
every family they have yet some such familiar spirits ; and
Fœlix Malleolus affirms as much, that these Trolli or
Telchines are very common in Norway, and seem to do

drudgery work ; to draw water, dress meat, or any such thing. Another sort of these there are, which frequent forlorn houses, which the Italians call foliots, most part innoxious. They will make strange noises in the night, howl sometimes pitifully, and then laugh again, cause great flame and sudden lights, fling stones, rattle chains, shave men, open doors and shut them, fling down platters, stools, chests, sometimes appear in the likeness of hares, crows, black dogs, etc.

ROBERT BURTON (from *Anatomy of Melancholy*)

COMUS LEADS IN THE REVELLERS

The star that bids the shepherd fold
Now the top of heaven doth hold ;
And the gilded car of day
His glowing axle doth allay
In the steep Atlantic stream :
And the slope sun his upward beam
Shoots against the dusky pole,
Pacing toward the other goal
Of his chamber in the east.
Meanwhile, welcome joy and feast,
Midnight shout and revelry,
Tipsy dance and jollity.
Braid your locks with rosy twine,
Dropping odours, dropping wine.
Rigour now is gone to bed ;
And Advice with scrupulous head,
Strict Age, and sour Severity,
With their grave saws, in slumber lie.

We, that are of purer fire,
Imitate the starry quire,
Who, in their nightly watchful spheres,
Lead in swift round the months and years.
The sounds and seas, with all their finny drove,
Now to the moon in wavering morrice move;
And on the tawny sands and shelves
Trip the pert fairies and the dapper elves.
By dimpled brook and fountain-brim,
The wood-nymphs, decked with daisies trim,
Their merry wakes and pastimes keep:
What hath night to do with sleep?

MILTON (from *Comus*)

ADVICE FROM A GHOST

'Tis late and cold, stir up the fire;
Sit close and draw the table nigher;
Be merry and drink wine that's old,
A hearty medicine 'gainst a cold.
Your beds of wanton down the best,
Where you shall tumble to your rest.
Call for the best the house may ring,
Sack, white, and claret let them bring,
And drink apace, whilst breath you have;
You'll find but cold drink in the grave;
Plover, partridge for your dinner,
And a capon for the sinner,
You shall find ready when you're up,
And your horse shall have his sup.
Welcome, welcome, shall fly round,
And I shall smile, though underground.

JOHN FLETCHER (from *The Lover's Progress*)

THE FAIRY'S FUNERAL

I was walking alone in my garden; there was great stillness among the branches and flowers, and more than common sweetness in the air; I heard a low and pleasant sound, and I knew not whence it came. At last I saw the broad leaf of a flower move, and underneath I saw a procession of creatures, of the size and colour of green and grey grasshoppers, bearing a body laid out on a rose-leaf, which they buried with songs, and then disappeared. It was a fairy funeral.

WILLIAM BLAKE (from GILCHRIST'S
Life of Blake)

THE OLD GODS

For the stricken heart of Love
This visible nature, and this common world,
Is all too narrow; yea, a deeper import
Lurks in the legend told my infant years
Than lies upon that truth we live to learn;
For fable is Love's world, his home, his birth-place;
Delightedly dwells he 'mong fays and talismans,
And spirits; and delightedly believes
Divinities, being himself divine
The intelligible forms of ancient poets,
The fair humanities of old religion,
The Power, the Beauty, and the Majesty,
That had her haunts in dale, or piny mountain,
Or forest by slow stream, or pebbly spring,
Or chasms, and wat'ry depths; all these have vanish'd.
They live no longer in the faith of reason!

But still the heart doth need a language, still
Doth the old instinct bring back the old names,
And to yon starry world they now are gone,
Spirits or gods, that used to share this earth
With man as with their friend.

SCHILLER (from *The Piccolomini—*
Trans. COLERIDGE)

KILMENY

‘ Kilmeny, Kilmeny, where have you been ?
Long hae we sought baith holt and den ;
By linn, by ford, and green-wood tree,
Yet you are halesome and fair to see.
Where gat you that joup o’ the lily scheen ?
That bonnie snood of the birk sae green ?
And these roses, the fairest that ever were seen ?
Kilmeny, Kilmeny, where have you been ? ’ . .

In yon green-wood there is a waik,
And in that waik there is a wene,
And in that wene there is a maike,
That neither has flesh, blood nor bane ;
And down in yon green-wood he walks his lane.

In that green wene Kilmeny lay,
Her bosom happ’d wi’ flowerets gay ;
But the air was soft and the silence deep,
And bonnie Kilmeny fell sound asleep.
She kenn’d nae mair, nor open’d her e’e,
Till waked by the hymns of a far countrye . .

They clasped her waist and her hands sae fair,
They kiss'd her cheek and they kemed her hair,
And round came many a blooming fere,
Saying, ' Bonny Kilmeny, ye're welcome here ! ' . .

They bore her away, she wist not how,
For she felt not arm nor rest below ;
But so swift they wain'd her through the light,
'Twas like the motion of sound or sight ;
They seem'd to split the gales of air,
And yet nor gale nor breeze was there.
Unnumber'd groves below them grew,
They came, they pass'd, and backward flew,
Like floods of blossoms gliding on,
In moment seen, in moment gone.
O, never vales to mortal view
Appear'd like those o'er which they flew !
That land to human spirits given,
The lowermost vales of the storied heaven ;
From thence they can view the world below,
And heaven's blue gates with sapphires glow,
More glory yet unmeet to know.
They bore her far to a mountain green,
To see what mortal never had seen ;
And they seated her high on a purple sward,
And bade her heed what she saw and heard,
And note the changes the spirits wrought,
For now she lived in the land of thought . .

With distant music, soft and deep,
They lull'd Kilmeny sound asleep ;
And when she awaken'd, she lay her lane,
All happ'd with flowers, in the green-wood wene.

When seven lang years had come and fled,
When grief was calm, and hope was dead ;
When scarce was remember'd Kilmeny's name,
Late, late in a gloamin' Kilmeny came hame ! . .

When a month and a day had come and gane,
Kilmeny sought the green-wood wene ;
There laid her down on the leaves sae green,
And Kilmeny on earth was never mair seen.
But O, the words that fell from her mouth
Were words of wonder, and words of truth !
But all the land were in fear and dread,
For they kendna whether she was living or dead.
It wasna her hame, and she couldna remain ;
She left this world of sorrow and pain,
And return'd to the land of thought again.

JAMES HOGG

PROUD MAISIE

Proud Maisie is in the wood,
    Walking so early ;
Sweet Robin sits on the bush,
    Singing so rarely.

" Tell me, thou bonny bird,
    When shall I marry me ? "
" When six braw gentlemen
    Kirkward shall carry ye."

" Who makes the bridal bed,
    Birdie say truly ? "
" The grey-headed sexton
    That delves the grave duly.

" The glow-worm o'er grave and stone
    Shall light thee steady ;
The owl from the steeple sing
    ' Welcome, proud lady.' "

SIR WALTER SCOTT

MUSIC AT SEA

Around, around, flew each sweet sound,
Then darted to the Sun ;
Slowly the sounds came back again,
Now mixed, now one by one.

Sometimes a-dropping from the sky
I heard the sky-lark sing ;
Sometimes all little birds that are,
How they seemed to fill the sea and air
With their sweet jargoning !

And now 'twas like all instruments,
Now like a lonely flute ;
And now it is an angel's song
That makes the heavens be mute.

It ceased; yet still the sails made on
A pleasant noise till noon,
A noise like of a hidden brook
In the leafy month of June,
That to the sleeping woods all night
Singeth a quiet tune.

COLERIDGE (from *The Ancient Mariner*)

LA BELLE DAME SANS MERCI

' O what can ail thee, knight-at-arms,
   Alone and palely loitering?
The sedge is wither'd from the lake,
   And no birds sing.

' O what can ail thee, knight-at-arms,
   So haggard and so woe-begone?
The squirrel's granary is full,
   And the harvest's done.

' I see a lily on thy brow
   With anguish moist and fever dew;
And on thy cheek a fading rose
   Fast withereth too.'

' I met a lady in the meads,
   Full beautiful—a faery's child,
Her hair was long, her foot was light,
   And her eyes were wild.

'I made a garland for her head,
  And bracelets too, and fragrant zone;
She look'd at me as she did love,
  And made sweet moan.

'I set her on my pacing steed
  And nothing else saw all day long,
For sideways would she lean, and sing
  A faery's song.

'She found me roots of relish sweet,
  And honey wild and manna dew,
And sure in language strange she said,
  "I love thee true!"

'She took me to her elfin grot,
  And there she wept and sigh'd full sore;
And there I shut her wild, wild eyes
  With kisses four.

'And there she lullèd me asleep,
  And there I dream'd—Ah! woe betide!
The latest dream I ever dream'd
  On the cold hill's side.

'I saw pale kings and princes too,
  Pale warriers, death-pale were they all;
Who cried—"La belle Dame sans Merci
  Hath thee in thrall!"

'I saw their starved lips in the gloam
  With horrid warning gapèd wide,
And I awoke and found me here
  On the cold hill's side.

' And this is why I sojourn here
   Alone and palely loitering,
Though the sedge is wither'd from the lake,
   And no birds sing.'

KEATS

THE DEATH OF THE PHOENIX

O'er the broad nest her silver wings
Shook down their wasteful glitterings ;
Her brinded neck high-arched in air
Like a small rainbow faded there ;
But brighter glowed her plumy crown
Mouldering to golden ashes down ;
With fume of sweet woods, to the skies,
Pure as a Saint's adoring sighs,
Warm as a prayer in Paradise,
Her life-breath rose in sacrifice !
The while with shrill triumphant tone
Sounding aloud, aloft, alone,
Ceaseless her joyful deathwail she
Sang to departing Araby !
   Deep melancholy wonder drew
Tears from my heartspring at that view.
Like cresset shedding its last flare
Upon some wistful mariner,
The Bird, fast blending with the sky,
Turned on me her dead-gazing eye
Once—and as surge to shallow spray
Sank down to vapoury dust away !

GEORGE DARLEY (from *Nepenthe*)

JOHNNIE KIGARROW

My brother and I went down to Wales,
And listened by night to the Welshman's tales :
I was but seven and he was ten.
We sat on the knees of the farmer's men
After the whole day's work was done ;
And I was friends with the farmer's son.
His hands were rough, his arms were strong,
His mouth was merry and loud for song :
Each night, when set by the ingle-wall,
He was the merriest man of them all.
I would catch at his beard and say
All the things I had done in the day—
Tumbled boulders over the force,
Swum in the river and fired the gorse—
' Half the side of the hill ! ' quoth I :—
' Tut ! ' cried he, ' and didn't you die ?
How was it, then, you saved your marrow ?
Didn't you meet with Johnnie Kigarrow ? '
' No ! ' said I, ' and who will he be ?
And what will be Johnnie Kigarrow to me ? '
The farmer's son said under his breath,
' Johnnie Kigarrow may be your death !
Listen you here, and keep you still—
Johnnie Kigarrow bides under the hill ;
Twloch barrow stands over his head ;
He shallows the river to make his bed :
Boulders roll when he stirs a limb ;
And the gorse on the hills belongs to him !
And if so be one fires his gorse,
He's out of his bed, and he mounts his horse.

Off he sets : at the first long stride
He is halfway over the mountain side :
At a second stride he's across the barrow,
And has you fast, has Johnnie Kigarrow!'

Half I laughed and half I feared,
As I upped and tugged at the strong man's beard,
And bragged as brave as a boy could be—
'So?' but, you see, 'he didn't catch *me*!'

Fear took hold of me : what had I done?
High as the roof rose the farmer's son :
How the sight of him froze my marrow!
'I,' he cried, 'am Johnnie Kigarrow!'

Well, you wonder, what was the end?
Never forget ;—he'd called me 'friend'!
Mighty of limb, and hard, and brown :
Quickly he laughed, and set me down.
'Heh!' said he, 'but the squeak was narrow,
Not to be caught by Johnnie Kigarrow!'

Now, I hear, after years gone by,
Nobody knows how he came to die.
He strode out one night of storm :
'Get you to bed, and keep you warm!'
Out into darkness so went he :
Nobody knows where his bones may be.

Only I guess—if tongue let go
Truth that once—how perhaps *I* know.
Twloch river and Twloch barrow
Cover the sleep of Johnnie Kigarrow.

LAURENCE HOUSMAN

THE STOLEN CHILD

Where dips the rocky highland
Of Sleuth Wood in the lake,
There lies a leafy island
Where flapping herons wake
The drowsy water rats;
There we've hid our faery vats,
Full of berries,
And of reddest stolen cherries.
Come away, O human child!
To the waters and the wild
With a faery, hand in hand,
For the world's more full of weeping than
*   you can understand.*

Where the wave of moonlight glosses
The dim grey sands with light,
Far off by farthest Rosses
We foot it all the night,
Weaving olden dances,
Mingling hands and mingling glances
Till the moon has taken flight;
To and fro we leap
And chase the frothy bubbles,
While the world is full of troubles
And is anxious in its sleep.
Come away, O human child!
To the waters and the wild
With a faery, hand in hand,
For the world's more full of weeping than
*   you can understand.*

Where the wandering water gushes
From the hills above Glen-Car,
In pools among the rushes
That scarce could bathe a star,
We seek for slumbering trout
And whispering in their ears
Give them unquiet dreams ;
Leaning softly out
From ferns that drop their tears
Over the young streams,
Come away, O human child !
To the waters and the wild
With a faery, hand in hand,
For the world's more full of weeping than
*   you can understand.*

Away with us he's going,
The solemn-eyed :
He'll hear no more the lowing
Of the calves on the warm hillside
Or the kettle on the hob
Sing peace into his breast,
Or see the brown mice bob
Round and round the oatmeal-chest.
For he comes, the human child,
To the waters and the wild
With a faery, hand in hand,
From a world more full of weeping than
*   he can understand.*

                          W. B. YEATS

THE TWILIGHT OF THE FAIRIES

The new Spirit of Chivalry made a shift to support itself for a time, when reason was but dawning, as we may say, and just about to gain the ascendant over the portentous spectres of the imagination. Its growing splendour, in the end, put them all to flight, and allowed them no quarter even amongst the poets . . . Thus at length the magic of the old romances was perfectly dissolved. They began with reflecting an image indeed of the feudal manners, but an image magnified and distorted by unskilful designers. Common sense being offended with these perversions of truth and nature (still accounted the more monstrous, as the antient manners, they pretended to copy after, were now disused, and of most men forgotten) the next step was to have recourse to *allegories*. . . . Under this form the tales of faery kept their ground, and even made their fortune at Court, where they became for two or three reigns the ordinary entertainment of our princes. But reason, in the end (assisted however by party and religious prejudices), drove them off the scene, and would endure these *lying wonders*, neither in their own proper shape, nor as masked in figures.

Henceforth, the taste of wit and poetry took a new turn, and fancy, that had wantoned it so long in the world of fiction, was now constrained, against her will, to ally herself with strict truth, if she would gain admittance into reasonable company. What we have gotten by this revolution, you will say, is a great deal of good sense. What we have lost, is a world of fine fabling ; the illusion of which is so grateful to the *Charmed Spirit* ; that, in spite of philosophy and fashion, *Faery* Spenser still ranks highest among the Poets—I mean with all those who are either come of that house or have any kindness for it.

RICHARD HURD, Bishop of Worcester
(from *Letters on Chivalry and Romance*, 1762)

THIRD PART

§ III FRIENDS OLD AND NEW

Life is to be fortified by many friendships.

SYDNEY SMITH

Intercourse with books is my comfort in solitude. For diverting my troublesome fancies there is no resource like that of books ; they easily turn my thoughts to themselves and drive out the others. They always receive me with the same welcome.

MONTAIGNE

§ III FRIENDS OLD AND NEW

§ 1. OUT-OF-DOOR POEMS

BARLEY-BREAK

(*The Elizabethan form of ' Prisoners' Base '*)

Now is the month of maying,
When merry lads are playing,
Each with his bonny lass,
Upon the greeny grass.

The Spring clad all in gladness,
Doth laugh at Winter's sadness,
And to the bag-pipe's sound
The nymphs tread out their ground.

Fie then ! why sit we musing,
Youth's sweet delight refusing ?
Say, dainty nymphs, and speak,
Shall we play barley-break ?

ANONYMOUS (1595)

SONG OF AUTOLYCUS

When daffodils begin to peer,
  With heigh ! the doxy over the dale,
Why, then comes in the sweet o' the year ;
  For the red blood reigns in the winter's pale.

511

The white sheet bleaching on the hedge,
  With heigh ! the sweet birds, O how they sing !
Doth set my pugging tooth on edge ;
  For a quart of ale is a dish for a king. . .

Jog on, jog on, the foot-path way,
  And merrily hent the stile-a :
A merry heart goes all the day,
  Your sad tires in a mile-a.

SHAKESPEARE (from *Winter's Tale*)

THOUGHTS IN A GARDEN

How vainly men themselves amaze
To win the palm, the oak, or bays,
And their uncessant labours see
Crown'd from some single herb or tree,
Whose short and narrow-vergèd shade
Does prudently their toils upbraid ;
While all the flowers and trees do close
To weave the garlands of repose.

Fair Quiet, have I found thee here,
And Innocence thy sister dear !
Mistaken long, I sought you then
In busy companies of men :
Your sacred plants, if here below,
Only among the plants will grow :
Society is all but rude
To this delicious solitude. . .

What wondrous life in this I lead !
Ripe apples drop about my head ;
The luscious clusters of the vine
Upon my mouth do crush their wine ;
The nectarine and curious peach
Into my hands themselves do reach ;
Stumbling on melons, as I pass,
Ensnared with flowers, I fall on grass.

Meanwhile the mind, from pleasure less,
Withdraws into its happiness ;
The mind, that ocean where each kind
Does straight its own resemblance find ;
Yet it creates, transcending these,
Far other worlds, and other seas ;
Annihilating all that's made
To a green thought in a green shade.

MARVELL

DAFFODILS

I wandered lonely as a cloud
That floats on high o'er vales and hills,
When all at once I saw a crowd,
A host, of golden daffodils ;
Beside the lake, beneath the trees,
Fluttering and dancing in the breeze.

Continuous as the stars that shine
And twinkle on the milky way,
They stretched in never-ending line
Along the margin of a bay :

Ten thousand saw I at a glance,
Tossing their heads in sprightly dance.

The waves beside them danced ; but they
Out-did the sparkling waves in glee :
A poet could not but be gay,
In such a jocund company ;
I gazed—and gazed—but little thought
What wealth the show to me had brought :

For oft, when on my couch I lie
In vacant or in pensive mood,
They flash upon that inward eye
Which is the bliss of solitude ;
And then my heart with pleasure fills,
And dances with the daffodils.

WORDSWORTH

HYMN TO PAN

O thou, whose mighty palace roof doth hang
From jagged trunks, and overshadoweth
Eternal whispers, glooms, the birth, life, death
Of unseen flowers in heavy peacefulness ;
Who lovest to see the Hamadryads dress
Their ruffled locks where meeting hazels darken ;
And through whole solemn hours dost sit, and hearken
The dreary melody of bedded reeds—
In desolate places, where dank moisture breeds

The pipy hemlock to strange overgrowth,
Bethinking thee, how melancholy loth
Thou wast to lose fair Syrinx—do thou now,
By thy love's milky brow,
By all the trembling mazes that she ran,
Hear us, great Pan!

O thou, for whose soul-soothing quiet turtles
Passion their voices cooingly 'mong myrtles,
What time thou wanderest at eventide
Through sunny meadows, that outskirt the side
Of thine enmosséd realms: O thou, to whom
Broad-leavéd fig-trees even now foredoom
Their ripened fruitage; yellow-girted bees
Their golden honey-combs; our village leas
Their fairest-blossomed beans and poppied corn;
The chuckling linnet its five young unborn,
To sing for thee; low-creeping strawberries
Their summer coolness; pent-up butterflies
Their freckled wings; yea, the fresh-budding year
All its completions—be quickly near,
By every wind that nods the mountain pine,
O forester divine!

Thou, to whom every Faun and Satyr flies
For willing service; whether to surprise
The squatted hare while in half-sleeping fit;
Or upward ragged precipices flit
To save poor lambkins from the eagle's maw;
Or by mysterious enticement draw
Bewildered shepherds to their path again;
Or to tread breathless round the frothy main

515

And gather up all fancifullest shells
For thee to tumble into Naiads' cells,
And, being hidden, laugh at their out-peeping ;
Or to delight thee with fantastic leaping,
The while they pelt each other on the crown
With silvery oak-apples, and fir-cones brown—
By all the echoes that about thee ring,
Hear us, O satyr king !

O Hearkener to the loud-clapping Shears,
While ever and anon to his shorn peers
A ram goes bleating : Winder of the Horn,
When snouted wild-boars, routing tender corn,
Anger our huntsmen : Breather round our farms,
To keep off mildews, and all weather harms :
Strange Ministrant of undescribèd sounds,
That come a-swooning over hollow grounds,
And wither drearily on barren moors :
Dread Opener of the Mysterious Doors
Leading to universal knowledge—see,
Great Son of Dryope,
The many that are come to pay their vows,
With leaves about their brows !

Be still the unimaginable lodge
For solitary thinkings : such as dodge
Conception to the very bourne of heaven,
Then leave the naked brain ! be still the leaven,
That spreading in this dull and clodded earth,
Gives it a touch ethereal—a new birth !
Be still a symbol of immensity ;
A firmament reflected in a sea ;

An element filling the space between ;
An unknown—but no more ! We humbly screen
With uplift hands our foreheads, lowly bending,
And, giving out a shout most heaven-rending,
Conjure thee to receive our humble Paean
Upon thy Mount Lycean !

KEATS (from Endymion)

LINDEN LEA

'Ithin the woodlands, flow'ry gleäded,
   By the woak tree's mossy moot,
The sheenèn grass bleädes, timber-sheäded,
   Now do quiver under voot ;
An' birds do whissle auver head,
An' water's bubblèn in its bed,
An' there vor me the apple tree
Do leän down low in Linden Lea.

When leaves that leätely wer a-springèn
   Now do feäde 'ithin the copse,
An' painted birds do hush ther zingèn
   Up upon the timber's tops ;
An' brown-leaf'd fruit's a-turnèn red,
In cloudless zunsheen, auver head,
Wi' fruit vor me, the apple tree
Do leän down low in Linden Lea.

Let other vo'k meäke money vaster
   In the aïr o' dark-room'd towns,
I don't dread a peevish meäster ;
   Though noo man do heed my frowns,

I be free to goo abrode,
Or teäke ageän my hwomeward road
To where, vor me, the apple tree
Do leän down low in Linden Lea.

WILLIAM BARNES

FOUR DUCKS ON A POND

Four ducks on a pond,
A grass-bank beyond,
A blue sky of spring,
White clouds on the wing ;
What a little thing
To remember for years—
To remember with tears !

WILLIAM ALLINGHAM

MAY-DAY ON MAGDALEN TOWER

Morn of the year, of day and May the prime !
    How fitly do we scale the steep dark stair
    Into the brightness of the matin air
To praise with chanted hymn and echoing chime,
Dear Lord of Light, thy lowlihead sublime
    That stooped erewhile our life's frail weed to wear !
    Sun, cloud, and hill, all things Thou framest so fair,
With us are glad and gay, greeting the time.

The college of the lily leaves her sleep ;
  The greỳ tower rocks and trembles into sound,
    Dawn-smitten Memnon of a happier hour ;
Through faint-hued fields the silver waters creep ;
  Day grows, birds pipe, and robed anew and crowned,
    Green Spring trips forth to set the world aflower.

SIR HERBERT WARREN

MARCH THOUGHTS FROM ENGLAND

O that I were lying under the olives,
Lying alone among the anemones !
Shell-colour'd blossoms they bloom there and scarlet,
Far under stretches of silver woodland,
Flame in the delicate shade of the olives.

O that I were lying under the olives !
Grey grows the thyme on the shadowless headland,
The long low headland, where white in the sunshine
The rocks run seaward. It seems suspended
Lone in an infinite gulf of azure.

There were I lying under the olives,
Might I behold come following seaward,
Clear brown shapes in a world of sunshine,
A russet shepherd, his sheep too, russet.
Watch them wander the long grey headland
Out to the edge of the burning azure.
O that I were lying under the olives !
So should I see the far-off cities
Glittering low by the purple water,
Gleaming high on the purple mountain ;
See where the road goes winding southward.

519

It passes the valleys of almond blossom,
Curves round the crag o'er the steep-hanging orchards,
Where almond and peach are aflush 'mid the olives—
Hardly the amethyst sea shines through them—
Over it cypress on solemn cypress
Lead to the lonely pilgrimage places. . .

Would I were listening under the olives !
So should I see in an airy pageant
A proud chivalrous pomp sweep by me ;
Hear in high courts the joyous ladies
Devising of Love in a world of lovers ;
Hear the song of the Lion-hearted,
A deep-voiced song—and O ! perchance,
Ghostly and strange and sweet to madness,
Rudel sing the Lady of Tripoli.

MARGARET L. WOODS

THE WAY THROUGH THE WOODS

They shut the road through the woods
   Seventy years ago.
Weather and rain have undone it again,
   And now you would never know
There was once a road through the woods
   Before they planted the trees.
It is underneath the coppice and heath,
   And the thin anemones.
   Only the keeper sees
That, where the ring-dove broods,
   And the badgers roll at ease,
There was once a road through the woods.

Yet, if you enter the woods
  Of a summer evening late,
When the night-air cools on the trout-ringed pools
  Where the otter whistles his mate,
(They fear not men in the woods
  Because they see so few)
You will hear the beat of a horse's feet
  And the swish of a skirt in the dew,
  Steadily cantering through
The misty solitudes,
  As though they perfectly knew
The old lost road through the woods . .
But there is no road through the woods.

RUDYARD KIPLING

IN A MEADOW

  This is the place
Where far from the unholy populace
The daughter of Philosophy and Sleep
  Her court doth keep,
Sweet Contemplation. To her service bound
  Hover around
The little amiable summer airs,
  Her courtiers.

  The deep black soil
Makes mute her palace-floors with thick trefoil;
The grasses sagely nodding overhead
  Curtain her bed;

And lest the feet of strangers overpass
   Her walls of grass,
Gravely a little river goes his rounds
   To beat the bounds.

   No bustling flood,
To make a tumult in her neighbourhood,
But such a stream as knows to go and come
   Discreetly dumb.
Therein are chambers tapestried with weeds
   And screen'd with reeds ;
For roof the waterlily-leaves serene
   Spread tiles of green.

   The sun's large eye
Falls soberly upon me where I lie ;
For delicate webs of immaterial haze
   Refine his rays.
The air is full of music none knows what,
   Or half-forgot ;
The living echo of dead voices fills
   The unseen hills.

   I hear the song
Of cuckoo answering cuckoo all day long ;
And know not if it be my inward sprite
   For my delight
Making remember'd poetry appear
   As sound in the ear :
Like a salt savour poignant in the breeze
   From distant seas.

Dreams without sleep,
And sleep too clear for dreaming and too deep;
And Quiet very large and manifold
    About me roll'd;
Satiety, that momentary flower,
    Stretch'd to an hour:
These are her gifts which all mankind may use,
    And all refuse.

J. S. PHILLIMORE

WASHING DAY

The washing hangs upon the line,
Between the prunus and the arch
(Where tender leaves of rambler thrust),
On this gay day in middle March.

The washing bellies in the breeze,
Across the clothes blue shadows go,
Above the house the lark sings high,
Before me, see, two aprons blow.

To watch the patterns move criss-cross,
Cast from the branches of the pear;
For symphony the song of birds,
And daffodils beside my chair;—

These are the simple joys of life;
With rippling clothes put out to dry,
Reflecting cleanliness and light
Beneath a wide and changing sky.

THEODORA ROSCOE

TEWKESBURY ROAD

It is good to be out on the road, and going one knows not
    where,
  Going through meadow and village, one knows not
    whither nor why;
Through the grey light drift of the dust, in the keen cool
    rush of the air,
  Under the flying white clouds, and the broad blue lift
    of the sky;

And to halt at the chattering brook, in the tall green fern
    at the brink
  Where the harebell grows, and the gorse, and the fox-
    gloves purple and white;
Where the shy-eyed delicate deer troop down to the pools
    to drink,
  When the stars are mellow and large at the coming on of
    the night.

O ! to feel the warmth of the rain and the homely smell of
    the earth
  Is a tune for the blood to jig to, a joy past power of
    words;
And the blessed green comely meadows seem all a-ripple
    with mirth
  At the lilt of the shifting feet, and the dear wild cry of
    the birds.

JOHN MASEFIELD

THE STARLING LAKE

My sorrow that I am not by the little dūn
By the lake of the starlings at Rossès under the hill,
And the larks there, singing over the fields of dew,
Or evening there and the sedges still.
For plain I see now the length of the yellow sand,
And Lissadell far off and its leafy ways,
And the holy mountain whose mighty heart
Gathers into it all the coloured days.
My sorrow that I am not by the little dūn
By the lake of the starlings at evening when all is still,
And still in whispering sedges the herons stand.
'Tis there I would nestle at rest till the quivering moon
Uprose in the golden quiet over the hill.

SEUMAS O'SULLIVAN

§ 2. INDOOR POEMS

TO LADY ANNE FITZPATRICK,

when about five years old, with a present of shells (1772)

O nymph, compar'd with whose young bloom
    Hebe's herself an ancient fright;
May these gay shells find grace and room
    Both in your baby-house and sight!
Shells! What are shells? you ask, admiring
    With stare half pleasure half surprise;
And fly with nature's art, enquiring
    In dear mamma's all-speaking eyes.

525

Shells, fairest Anne, are playthings, made
  By a brave god call'd Father Ocean,
Whose frown from pole to pole's obey'd,
  Commands the waves, and stills their motion.
From that old sire a daughter came,
  As like mamma, as blue to blue ;
And, like mamma, the sea-born dame
  An urchin bore, not unlike you.
For him fond grand-papa compels
  The floods to furnish such a state
Of corals and of cockleshells,
  Would turn a little lady's pate.
The chit has tons of bawbles more ;
  His nurs'ry's stuff'd with doves and sparrows ;
And litter'd is its azure floor
  With painted quivers, bows, and arrows.
Spread, spread your frock ; you must be friends ;
  His toys shall fill your lap and breast :
To-day the boy this sample sends,
  And some years hence he'll send the rest.

HORACE WALPOLE, EARL OF ORFORD

THE SPIRIT OF BEAUTY

Spirit of beauty, that dost consecrate
  With thine own hues all thou dost shine upon
  Of human thought or form, where art thou gone ?
Why dost thou pass away and leave our state,
This dim vast vale of tears, vacant and desolate ?
    Ask why the sunlight not for ever
    Weaves rainbows o'er yon mountain river ;

Why aught should fail and fade that once is shown;
    Why fear and dream and death and birth
    Cast on the daylight of this earth
    Such gloom; why man has such a scope
For love and hate, despondency and hope.

No voice from some sublimer world hath ever
    To sage or poet these responses given:
    Therefore the names of Demon, Ghost, and Heaven,
Remain the records of their vain endeavour;
Frail spells, whose uttered charm might not avail to sever,
    From all we hear and all we see,
    Doubt, chance, and mutability.
Thy light alone, like mists o'er mountains driven,
    Or music by the night wind sent
    Through strings of some still instrument,
    Or moonlight on a midnight stream,
Gives grace and truth to life's unquiet dream.

Love, Hope, and Self-esteem, like clouds, depart
    And come, for some uncertain moments lent.
    Man were immortal, and omnipotent,
Didst thou, unknown and awful as thou art,
Keep with thy glorious train firm state within his heart.
    Thou messenger of sympathies,
    That wax and wane in lover's eyes;
Thou, that to human thought art nourishment,
    Like darkness to a dying flame!
    Depart not as thy shadow came:
    Depart not—lest the grave should be,
Like life and fear, a dark reality.

        .   .   .   .   .

The day becomes more solemn and serene
   When noon is past : there is a harmony
   In autumn, and a lustre in its sky,
Which through the Summer is not heard or seen,
As if it could not be, as if it had not been !
     Thus let thy power, which like the truth
     Of Nature on my passive youth
Descended, to my onward life supply
    Its calm, to one who worships thee,
    And every form containing thee,
     Whom, SPIRIT fair, thy spells did bind
To fear himself, and love all human kind.

       SHELLEY (from *Hymn to Intellectual Beauty*)

TO MR. AND MRS. ——, A SON

Out of the deep, my child, out of the deep,
Where all that was to be, in all that was,
Whirl'd for a million aeons thro' the vast
Waste dawn of multitudinous-eddying light—
Out of the deep, my child, out of the deep,
Thro' all this changing world of changeless law,
And every phase of ever-heightening life,
And nine long months of antenatal gloom,
With this last moon, this crescent—her dark orb
Touch'd with earth's light—thou comest, darling boy ;
Our own ; a babe in lineament and limb
Perfect, and prophet of the perfect man ;
Whose face and form are hers and mine in one,
Indissolubly married like our love ;

Live, and be happy in thyself, and serve
This mortal race thy kin so well, that men
May bless thee as we bless thee, O young life
Breaking with laughter from the dark ; and may
The fated channel where thy motion lives
Be prosperously shaped, and sway thy course
Along the years of haste and random youth
Unshatter'd ; then full-current thro' full man ;
And last in kindly curves, with gentlest fall,
By quiet fields, a slowly-dying power,
To that last deep where we and thou are still.

TENNYSON (from *De Profundis*)

THE POPE SPEAKS OF POMPILIA

First of the first,
Such I pronounce Pompilia, then as now
Perfect in whiteness : stoop thou down, my child,
Give one good moment to the poor old Pope
Heart-sick at having all his world to blame—
Let me look at thee in the flesh as erst,
Let me enjoy the old clean linen garb,
Not the new splendid vesture ! Armed and crowned,
Would Michael, yonder, be, nor crowned nor armed,
The less pre-eminent angel ? Everywhere
I see in the world the intellect of man,
That sword, the energy his subtle spear,
The knowledge which defends him like a shield—
Everywhere ; but they make not up, I think,
The marvel of a soul like thine, earth's flower
She holds up to the softened gaze of God !

529

It was not given Pompilia to know much,
Speak much, to write a book, to move mankind,
Be memorized by who records my time.
Yet if in purity and patience, if
In faith held fast despite the plucking fiend,
Safe like the signet stone with the new name
That saints are known by,—if in right returned
For wrong, most pardon for worst injury,
If there be any virtue, any praise—
Then will this woman-child have proved—who knows?—
Just the one prize vouchsafed unworthy me,
Seven years a gardener of the untoward ground
I till,—this earth, my sweat and blood manure
All the long day that barrenly grows dusk:
At least one blossom makes me proud at eve
Born 'mid the briers of my enclosure! Still
(Oh, here as elsewhere, nothingness of man!)
Those be the plants, imbedded yonder South
To mellow in the morning, those made fat
By the master's eye, that yield such timid leaf,
Uncertain bud, as product of his pains!
While—see how this mere chance-sown cleft-nursed seed
That sprang up by the wayside 'neath the foot
Of the enemy, this breaks all into blaze,
Spreads itself, one wide glory of desire
To incorporate the whole great sun it loves
From the inch-height whence it looks and longs! My
    flower,
My rose I gather for the breast of God.

BROWNING (from *The Ring and the Book*)

530

A CHILD'S LAUGHTER

All the bells of heaven may ring,
All the birds of heaven may sing,
All the wells on earth may spring,
All the winds on earth may bring
    All sweet sounds together ;
Sweeter far than all things heard,
Hand of harper, tone of bird,
Sound of woods at sundown stirred,
Welling water's winsome word,
    Wind in warm wan weather.

One thing yet there is, that none
Hearing ere its chime be done
Knows not well the sweetest one
Heard of man beneath the sun,
    Hoped in heaven hereafter ;
Soft and strong and loud and light,
Very sound of very light
Heard from morning's rosiest height,
When the soul of all delight
    Fills a child's clear laughter.

Golden bells of welcome rolled
Never forth such notes, nor told
Hours so blithe in tones so bold,
As the radiant mouth of gold
    Here that rings forth heaven.
If the golden-crested wren
Were a nightingale—why, then,
Something seen and heard of men
Might be half as sweet as when
    Laughs a child of seven.

SWINBURNE

531

Onward :—thro' baffled hopes, thro' bootless prayers,
With strength that sinks, with high task half begun,
Things great desired, things lamentable done,
Vows writ in water, blows that beat the air.
Oh ! I have guessed the end ; the end is fair.
Not with these weak limbs is thy last race run ;
Not all thy vision sinks with this low sun ;
Not all thy spirit swoons in this despair.
Look how thine own soul, throned where all is well,
Smiles to regard thy days disconsolate ;
Yea ; since herself she wove the worldly spell,
Doomed thee for lofty gain to low estate ;—
Sown with thy fall a seed of glory fell ;
Thy heaven is in thee, and thy will thy fate.

F. W. H. MYERS

TO MILTON—BLIND

He who said suddenly, " Let there be light ! "
To thee the dark deliberately gave ;
That those full eyes might undistracted be
By this beguiling show of sky and field,
This brilliance, that so lures us from the Truth.
He gave thee back original night, His own
Tremendous canvas, large and blank and free,
Where at each thought a star flashed out and sang.
O blinded with a special lightning, thou
Hadst once again the virgin Dark ! and when
The pleasant flowery sight, which had deterred

532

Thine eyes from seeing, when this recent world
Was quite withdrawn ; then burst upon thy view
The elder glory ; space again in pangs,
And Eden odorous in the early mist,
That heaving watery plain that *was* the world ;
Then the burned earth, and Christ coming in clouds.
Or rather a special leave to thee was given
By the high power, and thou with bandaged eyes
Wast guided through the glimmering camp of God.
Thy hand was taken by angels who patrol
The evening, or are sentries to the dawn,
Or pace the wide air everlastingly.
Thou wast admitted to the presence, and deep
Argument heardest, and the large design
That brings this world out of the woe to bliss.

STEPHEN PHILLIPS

THE FAIR CHIVALRY

Ah, see the fair chivalry come, the companions of Christ !
White Horsemen, who ride on white horses, the Knights
of God !
They, for their Lord and their Lover who sacrificed
All save the sweetness of treading where He first trod !

These, through the darkness of death, the dominion of
night,
Swept, and they woke in white places at morning tide :
They saw with their eyes, and sang for joy of the sight,
They saw with their eyes the Eyes of the Crucified.

533

Now, whithersoever He goeth, with Him they go :
White Horsemen, who ride on white horses, oh, fair to
    see !
They ride, where the Rivers of Paradise flash and flow,
White Horsemen, with Christ their Captain : for ever He !

LIONEL JOHNSON

WISHES FOR WILLIAM

These things I wish you for our friendship's sake :
A sunburnt thatch, a door to face the sun
At westering, the noise of homing rooks,
A kind, old, lazy chair, a courtly cat
To rub against your knees,
Shelves of well-chosen books—
I wish you these.

I wish you friends whose wisdom makes them kind,
Well leisured friends to share your evening's peace,
Friends who can season knowledge with a laugh.
A hedge of lavender, a patch of thyme,
With sage and marjoram and rosemary,
A damask rosebush and a hive of bees,
And cabbages that hold the morning dew,
A blackbird in the orchard boughs—all these
And—God bless you.

Children, no matter whose, to wait for you
With flower faces at your garden gate,
And one to watch the clock with eager eyes,
Saying, " He's late—he's late."

W. M. LETTS

§3. LOVE POEMS

THE APPEAL:

An Earnest Suit to his Unkind Mistress, not to Forsake him

And wilt thou leave me thus?
Say nay, say nay, for shame!
To save thee from the blame
Of all my grief and grame.
And wilt thou leave me thus?
        Say nay! say nay!

And wilt thou leave me thus,
That hath loved thee so long
In wealth and woe among:
And is thy heart so strong
As for to leave me thus?
        Say nay! say nay!

And wilt thou leave me thus,
That hath given thee my heart
Never for to depart
Neither for pain nor smart:
And wilt thou leave me thus?
        Say nay! say nay!

And wilt thou leave me thus,
And have no more pitye
Of him that loveth thee?
Alas, thy cruelty!
And wilt thou leave me thus?
        Say nay! say nay!

SIR THOMAS WYATT

THE SHIP OF LOVE

My galley, chargèd with forgetfulness,
  Through sharpè seas in winter nights doth pass
'Tween rock and rock ; and eke my foe, alas,
  That is my lord, steereth with cruelness :
And every hour, a thought in readiness,
  As though that death were light in such a case,
  An endless wind doth tear the sail apace
  Of forcèd sighs and trusty fearfulness.
A rain of tears, a cloud of dark disdain,
  Have done the wearied cords great hinderance ;
  Wreathèd with error and with ignorance,
The stars be hid that lead me to this pain ;
  Drowned is reasòn, that should be my comfòrt,
  And I remain despairing of the port.

SIR THOMAS WYATT

THE ROYAL LOVER

I grieve, yet dare not shew my discontent,
  I love, and yet am forc'd to seem to hate ;
I do, yet dare not say I ever meant,
  I seem stark mute, but inwardly do prate.
    I am, and not, I freeze, and yet am burn'd,
    Since from myself my other self I turn'd.

My care is like my shadow in the sun,
  Follows me flying, flies when I pursue it ;
Stands and lies by me, does what I have done ;
  This too familiar care doth make me rue it.
    No means I find to rid him from my breast,
    Till by the end of things it be supprest.

Some gentler passions steal into my mind,
   For I am soft, and made of melting snow;
Or, be more cruel, love, and so be kind,
   Let me or float or sink, be high or low;
     Or let me live with some more sweet content,
     Or die, and so forget what love e'er meant.

QUEEN ELIZABETH (from *Ashmol. Mus. MSS.*
6989–781)

LOVE THE FULFILMENT

Love is life's end (an end, but never ending)
   All joys, all sweets, all happiness awarding;
Love is life's wealth (ne'er spent, but ever spending),
   More rich by giving, taking by discarding;
Love's life's reward, rewarded in rewarding:
     Then from thy wretched heart fond care remove;
     Ah! should thou live but once love's sweets to prove,
     Thou wilt not love to live unless thou live to love.

ANONYMOUS (from *Brittain's Ida*, 1628)

THE LOVER PLAINETH IN WINTER

   O western wind, when wilt thou blow
     That the small rain down can rain?
   Christ, that my love were in my arms
     And I in my bed again!

ANONYMOUS (16th Century)

1. *Lullaby*

" Sleep, baby mine," Desire's nurse Beauty singeth ;
" Thy cries, O baby, set mine head on aching."
The babe cries, " Way ! thy love doth keep me waking."

" Lully, lully, my babe ! Hope cradle bringeth
Unto my children, always good rest taking."
The babe cries " Way ! thy love doth keep me waking."

" Since, baby mine, from me thy watching springeth,
Sleep then a little ; pap Content is making."
The babe cries " Nay ! for that abide I waking."

2. *Complaint*

Thou blind man's mark, thou fool's self-chosen snare,
Fond fancy's scum, and dregs of scattered thought :
Band of all evils ; cradle of causeless care ;
Thou web of will, whose end is never wrought :
Desire ! Desire ! I have too dearly bought,
With price of mangled mind, thy worthless ware ;
Too long, too long, asleep thou hast me brought,
Who should my mind to higher things prepare.
But yet in vain thou hast my ruin sought ;
In vain thou mad'st me to vain things aspire ;
In vain thou kindlest all thy smoky fire ;
For Virtue hath this better lesson taught,—
Within myself to seek my only hire,
Desiring nought but how to kill Desire.

3. *Farewell*

Leave me, O Love, which reachest but to dust;
And thou, my mind, aspire to higher things;
Grow rich in that which never taketh rust;
Whatever fades, but fading pleasure brings.
Draw in thy beams, and humble all thy might
To that sweet yoke, where lasting freedoms be;
Which breaks the clouds, and opens forth the light
That doth both shine, and give us sight to see.
O take fast hold; let that light be thy guide
In this small course which birth draws out to death,
And think how evil becometh him to slide,
Who seeketh heav'n and comes of heav'nly breath.
Then farewell, world; thy uttermost I see:
Eternal Love, maintain thy Life in me.

SIR PHILIP SIDNEY

THE TRUE BEAUTY

O how much more doth beauty beauteous seem
By that sweet ornament which truth doth give!
The Rose looks fair, but fairer we it deem
For that sweet odour which doth in it live.
The Canker-blooms have full as deep a dye
As the perfumèd tincture of the Roses,
Hang on such thorns, and play as wantonly
When summer's breath their maskèd buds discloses:

539

But—for their virtue only is their show—
They live unwoo'd and unrespected fade,
Die to themselves. Sweet Roses do not so ;
Of their sweet deaths are sweetest odours made.
   And so of you, beauteous and lovely youth,
    When that shall vade, my verse distils your truth.

SHAKESPEARE

ETERNAL LINES

Shall I compare thee to a Summer's day ?
Thou art more lovely and more temperate :
Rough winds do shake the darling buds of May,
And Summer's lease hath all too short a date :
Sometime too hot the eye of heaven shines,
And often is his gold complexion dimm'd ;
And every fair from fair sometime declines,
By chance or nature's changing course untrimm'd :
But thy eternal Summer shall not fade
Nor lose possession of that fair thou owest ;
Nor shall Death brag thou wanderest in his shade,
When in eternal lines to time thou growest :
   So long as men can breathe, or eyes can see,
    So long lives this, and this gives life to thee.

SHAKESPEARE

A NIGHT OF WAITING

Good night, good rest ! Ah, neither be my share :
She bade good night that kept my rest away ;
And daff'd me to a cabin hang'd with care,
To descant on the doubts of my decay.
  "Farewell," quoth she, "and come again to-morrow " :
  Fare well I could not, for I supp'd with sorrow.

Yet at my parting sweetly did she smile,
In scorn or friendship, nill I conster whether :
May be she joy'd to jest at my exile,
May be again to make me wander thither :
  "Wander," a word for shadows like myself,
  As take the pain, but cannot pluck the pelf.

Lord, how mine eyes throw gazes to the east !
My heart doth charge the watch ; the morning rise
Doth cite each moving sense from idle rest.
Not daring trust the office of mine eyes,
  While Philomela sings, I sit and mark,
  And wish her lays were tunèd like the lark ;

For she doth welcome daylight with her ditty,
And drives away at last dark dreaming night ;
The night so pack'd, I post unto my pretty ;
Heart hath his hope and eyes their wishèd sight ;
  Sorrow made solace, solace mix'd with sorrow ;
  For why ? She sigh'd, and bade me come to-morrow.

Were I with her, the night would post too soon;
But now are minutes added to the hours;
To spite me now, each minute seems a moon;
Yet not for me—Shine sun to succour flowers!
    Pack night, peep day; good day, of night now borrow;
    Short, night, to-night, and length thyself, to-morrow!

ANONYMOUS (from *The Passionate Pilgrim*, 1599)

NOBLE LOVE

It is the counterpoise that minds
To fair and virtuous things inclines;
It is the gust we have and sense
Of every noble excellence;
It is the pulse by which we know
Whether our souls have life or no;
And such a soft and gentle fire
As kindles and inflames desire;
Until it all like incense burns
And unto melting sweetness turns.

RICHARD FLECKNOE

HIGH AND LOW

Were I as base as is the lowly plain,
And you, my love, as high as heaven above,
Yet should the thoughts of me your humble swain
Ascend to heaven in honour of my love.

Were I as high as heaven above the plain,
And you, my love, as humble and as low
As are the deepest bottoms of the main,
Wheresoe'er you were, with you my love should go.
Were you the earth, dear love, and I the skies,
My love should shine on you like to the sun,
And look upon you with ten thousand eyes,
Till heaven waxed blind, and till the world were done.
   Wheresoe'er I am, below, or else above you,
   Wheresoe'er you are, my heart shall truly love you.

J. SYLVESTER (1602)

MY LADY'S TEARS

   I saw my Lady weep,
And Sorrow proud to be advancèd so
In those fair eyes where all perfections keep.
   Her face was full of woe ;
But such a woe (believe me) as wins more hearts
Than Mirth can do with her enticing parts.

   Sorrow was there made fair,
And Passion wise ; Tears a delightful thing ;
Silence beyond all speech, a wisdom rare :
   She made her sighs to sing,
And all things with so sweet a sadness move
As made my heart at once both grieve and love.

543

O fairer than aught else
The world can show, leave off in time to grieve !
Enough, enough : your joyful look excels :
    Tears kill the heart, believe.
O strive not to be excellent in woe,
Which only breeds your beauty's overthrow.

From JOHN DOWLAND'S *Third and Last*
                        Book of Songs or Airs, 1603

THE THOUGHT

If you do love as well as I,
Then every minute from your heart
        A thought doth part ;
And wingèd with desire doth fly
Till it hath met, in a straight line,
        A thought of mine
So like to yours, we cannot know
Whether of both doth come, or go,
        Till we define
Which of us two, that thought doth owe.

I say then, that your thoughts which pass,
Are not so much the thoughts you meant,
        As those I sent :
For as my image in a glass
Belongs not to the glass you see,
        But unto me ;
So when your fancy is so clear
That you would think you saw me there,
        It needs must be
That it was I did first appear.

544

Likewise, when I send forth a thought,
My reason tells me, 'tis the same
    Which from you came,
And which your beauteous image wrought.
Thus while our thoughts by turns do lead,
    None can precede ;
And thus, while in each other's mind
Such interchangèd forms we find,
    Our loves may plead
To be of more than vulgar kind.

May you then often think on me,
And by that thinking know 'tis true
    I thought on you ;
I in the same belief will be :
While, by this mutual address,
    We will possess
A love must live, when we do die,
Which rare and secret property
    You will confess,
If you do love as well as I.

LORD HERBERT OF CHERBURY

SONGS

I.

O were my Love yon lilac fair,
    Wi' purple blossoms to the spring,
And I a bird to shelter there,
    When wearied on my little wing ;

How I wad mourn when it was torn
    By autumn wild and winter rude !
But I wad sing on wanton wing
    When youthfu' May its bloom renew'd.

O gin my Love were yon red rose
    That grows upon the castle wa',
And I mysel a drap o' dew
    Into her bonnie breast to fa' ;
O there, beyond expression blest,
    I'd feast on beauty a' the night ;
Seal'd on her silk-saft faulds to rest,
    Till fley'd awa' by Phoebus' light.

2.

O, wert thou in the cauld blast
    On yonder lea, on yonder lea,
My plaidie to the angry airt,
    I'd shelter thee, I'd shelter thee.
Or did Misfortune's bitter storms
    Around thee blaw, around thee blaw,
Thy bield should be my bosom
    To share it a', to share it a'.

Or were I in the wildest waste,
    Sae black and bare, sae black and bare,
The desert were a Paradise,
    If thou wert there, if thou wert there.
Or were I monarch of the globe,
    Wi' thee to reign, wi' thee to reign,
The brightest jewel in my crown
    Wad be my queen, wad be my queen.

BURNS

ROSE AYLMER

Ah, what avails the sceptred race !
    Ah, what the form divine,
What every virtue, every grace !
    Rose Aylmer, all were thine.

Rose Aylmer, whom these wakeful eyes
    May weep, but never see,
A night of memories and sighs
    I consecrate to thee.

W. S. LANDOR

AMOR OMNIA VINCIT

Our love is not a fading, earthly flower :
Its wingèd seed dropped down from Paradise,
And, nursed by day and night, by sun and shower,
Doth momently to fresher beauty rise :
To us the leafless autumn is not bare,
Nor winter's rattling boughs lack lusty green.
Our summer hearts make summer's fulness, where
No leaf, or bud, or blossom may be seen :
For nature's life in love's deep life doth lie,
Love,—whose forgetfulness is beauty's death,
Whose mystic key these cells of Thou and I
Into the infinite freedom openeth,
And makes the body's dark and narrow grate
The wind-flung leaves of Heaven's palace-gate.

JAMES RUSSELL LOWELL

A BIRTHDAY

My heart is like a singing bird
   Whose nest is in a watered shoot;
My heart is like an apple-tree
   Whose boughs are bent with thickset fruit:
My heart is like a rainbow shell
   That paddles in a halcyon sea;
My heart is gladder than all these
   Because my love is come to me.

Raise me a dais of silk and down;
   Hang it with vair and purple dyes;
Carve it in doves and pomegranates,
   And peacocks with a hundred eyes;
Work it in gold and silver grapes,
   In leaves and silver fleurs-de-lys;
Because the birthday of my life
   Is come, my love is come to me.

CHRISTINA ROSSETTI

THE SOURCE OF LOVE

My eyes for beauty pine,
   My soul for Goddès grace:
No other care nor hope is mine
   To heaven I turn my face.

One splendour thence is shed
   From all the stars above:
'Tis namèd when God's name is said,
   'Tis Love, 'tis heavenly Love.

And every gentle heart,
That burns with true desire,
Is lit from eyes that mirror part
Of that celestial fire.

ROBERT BRIDGES

SONG

The nightingale has a lyre of gold,
    The lark's is a clarion call,
And the blackbird plays but a boxwood flute,
    But I love him best of all.

For his song is all of the joy of life,
    And we in the mad, spring weather,
We two have listened till he sang
    Our hearts and lips together.

W. E. HENLEY

NIGHT IS FALLEN

Night is fallen within, without,
    Come, Love, soon!
I am weary of my doubt.
The golden fire of the Sun is out,
    The silver fire of the Moon.

Love shall be
A child in me

When they are cinders grey,
With the earth and with the sea,
With the star that shines on thee.
And the night and day.

MARY E. COLERIDGE

THE HAPPY NIGHT

I have loved to-night ; from love's last bordering steep
  I have fallen at last with joy and forgotten the shore ;
  I have known my love to-night as never before,
I have flung myself in the deep, and drawn from the deep,
And kissed her lightly, and left my belovèd to sleep.
  And now I sit in the night and my heart is still :
  Strong and secure ; there is nothing that's left to will,
There is nothing to win but only a thing to keep.

And I look to-night, completed and not afraid,
  Into the windy dark where shines no light ;
And care not at all though the darkness never should fade,
  Nor fear that death should suddenly come to-night.
Knowing my last would be surely my bravest breath,
I am happy to-night : I have laughed to-night at death.

J. C. SQUIRE

550

§4. PROSE

TWO KINDS OF HUNTING

1. *Hunting by Water*

Fishing is a kind of hunting by water, be it with nets, weeles, baits, angling, or otherwise, and yields all out as much pleasure to some men as dogs or hawks, when they draw their fish upon the bank. James Dubravius, that Moravian, in his book telleth how, travelling by the highway side in Silesia, he found a nobleman, " booted up to the groins," wading himself, pulling the nets, and labouring as much as any fisherman of them all : and when some belike objected to him the baseness of his office, he excused himself, " that if other men might hunt hares, why should not he hunt carps ? " Many gentlemen in like sort with us will wade up to the arm-holes upon such occasions, and voluntarily undertake that to satisfy their pleasure, which a poor man for a good stipend would scarce be hired to undergo. Plutarch speaks against all fishing, " as filthy, base, illiberal employment, having neither wit nor perspicacity in it, nor worth the labour." But he that shall consider the variety of baits for all seasons, and pretty devices which our anglers have invented, peculiar lines, false flies, several sleights, etc., will say, that it deserves like commendation, requires as much study and perspicacity as the rest, and is to be preferred before many of them. Because hawking and hunting are very laborious, much riding, and many dangers accompany them ; but this is still and quiet : and if so be the angler catch no fish, yet he hath a wholesome walk to the brookside, pleasant shade by the sweet silver streams ; he hath good air, and sweet smells of fine fresh meadow flowers, he hears the melodious harmony of birds, he sees the swans, herons, ducks, waterhorns, coots, etc., and many other fowl, with their brood, which he thinketh better than the noise of hounds, or blast of horns, and all the sport that they can make.

2. *Hunting the Dear*

'Tis most true, many gentlewomen are so nice, they scorn all suitors, crucify their poor paramours, and think nobody good enough for them, as dainty to please as Daphne herself. One while they will not marry, as they say at least (when as they intend nothing less), another while not yet, when 'tis their only desire, they rave upon it. She will marry at last, but not him : he is a proper man indeed, and well qualified, but he wants means : another of her suitors hath good means, but he wants wit ; one is too old, another too young, too deformed, she likes not his carriage : a third too loosely given, he is rich, but base born : she will be a gentlewoman, a lady, as her sister is, as her mother is : she is all out as fair, as well brought up, hath as good a portion, and she looks for as good a match, as Matilda or Dorinda : if not, she is resolved as yet to tarry, so apt are young maids to boggle at every object, so soon won or lost with every toy, so quickly diverted, so hard to be pleased. In the meantime, one suitor pines away, languisheth in love, another sighs and grieves, she cares not. They take a pride to prank up themselves, to make young men enamoured to dote on them, and to run mad for their sakes. All suit and service is too little for them, presents too base. As Atalanta they must be overrun, or not won. Many young men are as obstinate, and as curious in their choice, as tyrannically proud, insulting, deceitful, false-hearted, as irrefragable and peevish on the other side, Narcissus-like. Echo wept and wooed him by all means above the rest, Love me for pity, or pity me for love, but he was obstinate, " he would rather die than give consent." Psyche ran whining after Cupid, but he rejected her nevertheless. Thus many lovers do hold out so long, doting on themselves, stand in their own light, till in the end they come to be scorned and rejected, as Narcissus was himself. They begin to be contemned themselves of others, as he was of his shadow, and take up with a poor curate, or an old serving-man at last, that might have had their choice of right good matches in their youth. Yet this is a common humour, will not be left, and cannot be helped.

ROBERT BURTON (from *Anatomy of Melancholy*)

OLD SONGS

PISCATOR : Look, under that broad *Beech tree* I sate down, when I was last this way a fishing, and the birds in the adjoyning Grove seemed to have a friendly contention with an Eccho, whose dead voice seemed to live in a hollow tree, near to the brow of that Primrose-hill ; there I sate viewing the silver-streams glide silently towards their center, the tempestuous Sea, yet sometimes opposed by rugged roots and pebble stones which broke their waves and turned them into foam : and sometimes I beguil'd time by viewing the harmless Lambs, some leaping securely in the cool shade, whilst others sported themselves in the chearful Sun ; and saw others craving comfort from the swoln Udders of their bleating Dams. . . As I left this place, and entered into the next field, a second pleasure entertained me, 'twas a handsome milk-maid, that had not yet attain'd so much age and wisdom as to load her mind with any fears of many things that will never be (as too many men too often do) but she cast away all care, and sung like a *Nightingale* : her voice was good, and the Ditty fitted for it ; 'twas that smooth song which was made by *Kit Marlow*, now at least fifty years ago ; and the Milk-maid's Mother sung an answer to it, which was made by Sir *Walter Rawleigh* in his younger days. They were old fashioned Poetry, but choicely good, I think much better than the strong lines that are now in fashion in this critical age. Look yonder ! on my word, yonder they both be a milking again : I will give her the *Chub*, and perswade them to sing those two songs to us.

IZAAK WALTON (from *The Compleat Angler*)

THE WARFARING CHRISTIAN

Good and evil we know in the field of this world grow up together almost inseparably ; and the knowledge of good is so involved and interwoven with the knowledge of evil, and in so many cunning resemblances hardly to be discerned, that those confused seeds which were imposed upon Psyche as an incessant labour to cull out, and sort asunder, were not more intermixed. It was from out the rind of one apple tasted, that the knowledge of good and evil, as two twins cleaving together, leaped forth into the world. And perhaps this is that doom which Adam fell into of knowing good and evil, that is to say of knowing good by evil. As therefore the state of man now is ; what wisdom can there be to choose, what continuance to forbear without the knowledge of evil ? He that can apprehend and consider vice with all her baits and seeming pleasures, and yet abstain, and yet distinguish, and yet prefer that which is truly better, he is the true warfaring Christian. I cannot praise a fugitive and cloistered virtue, unexercised and unbreathed, that never sallies out and sees her adversary, but slinks out of the race, where that immortal garland is to be run for, not without dust and heat. Assuredly we bring not innocence into the world, we bring impurity much rather; that which purifies us is trial, and trial is by what is contrary.

MILTON (from *Areopagitica*)

THE NEGLECT OF PREACHING

I shall produce certain instances to show the great neglect of preaching now among us.

These may be reduced under two heads. First, men's absence from the service of the church; and secondly, their misbehaviour when they are here.

The first instance of men's neglect is in their frequent absence from the church.

There is no excuse so trivial that will not pass upon some men's consciences to excuse their attendance at the public worship of God. Some are so unfortunate as to be always indisposed on the Lord's day, and think nothing so unwholesome as the air of a church. Others have their affairs so oddly contrived, as to be always unluckily prevented by business. With some it is a great mark of wit and deep understanding to stay at home on Sundays. Others again discover strange fits of laziness, that seize them particularly on that day, and confine them to their beds. Others are absent out of mere contempt of religion. And, lastly, there are not a few who look upon it as a day of rest, and therefore claim the privilege of their cattle, to keep the Sabbath by eating, drinking, and sleeping, after the toil and labour of the week. Now in all this the worst circumstance is, that these persons are such whose companies are most required, and who stand most in need of a physician.

Secondly, Men's great neglect and contempt of preaching appear by their misbehaviour when at church.

If the audience were to be ranked under several heads, according to their behaviour when the word of God is delivered, how small a number would appear of those who receive it as they ought! How much of the seed then sown would be found to fall by the wayside upon stony ground, or among thorns ; and how little good ground there would be to take it ! A preacher cannot look round from the pulpit without observing that some are in a perpetual whisper, and by their air and gesture give occasion to suspect that they are in those very minutes defaming their neighbour. Others have their eyes and imagination constantly engaged in such a circle of objects, perhaps to gratify the most unwarrantable desires, that they never once attend to the business of the place ; the sound of the preacher's words does not so much as once interrupt them. Some have their minds wandering among idle, worldly, or vicious thoughts. Some lie at catch to ridicule whatever they hear, and with much wit and humour provide a stock of laughter by furnishing themselves from the pulpit. But of all misbehaviour, none is comparable to that of those who come here to sleep. Opium is not so stupefying to many persons as an afternoon sermon. Perpetual custom hath so brought it about that the words of whatever preacher become only a sort of uniform sound at a distance, than which nothing is more effectual to lull the senses. For that it is the very sound of the sermon which bindeth up their faculties is manifest from hence because they all awake so very regularly as soon as it ceaseth, and with much devotion receive the blessing.

SWIFT (from *A Sermon on Sleeping in Church*)

A RAMBLE FROM RICHMOND TO LONDON

I lay one night last week at Richmond ; and being restless, not out of dissatisfaction, but a certain busy inclination one sometimes has, I rose at four in the morning, and took boat for London, with a resolution to rove by boat and coach for the next four-and-twenty hours, till the many different objects I must needs meet with should tire my imagination, and give me an inclination to a repose more profound than I was at that time capable of. I beg people's pardon for an odd humour I am guilty of, and was often that day, which is saluting any person whom I like, whether I know him or not. This is a particularity would be tolerated in me, if they considered that the greatest pleasure I know I receive at my eyes, and that I am obliged to an agreeable person for coming abroad into my view, as another is for a visit of conversation at their own houses.

The hours of the day and night are taken up in the cities of London and Westminster, by people as different from each other as those who are born in different centuries. Men of six o'clock give way to those of nine, they of nine to the generation of twelve ; and they of twelve disappear, and make room for the fashionable world, who have made two o'clock the noon of the day.

When we first put off from shore, we soon fell in with a fleet of gardeners, bound for the several market ports of

London; and it was the most pleasing scene imaginable to see the cheerfulness with which those industrious people plied their way to a certain sale of their goods. The banks on each side are as well peopled, and beautified with as agreeable plantations, as any spot on the earth; but the Thames itself, loaded with the product of each shore, added very much to the landscape. It was very easy to observe by their sailing, and the countenances of the ruddy virgins, who were supercargoes, the parts of the town to which they were bound. There was an air in the purveyors for Covent-garden, who frequently converse with morning rakes, very unlike the seeming sobriety of those bound for Stocks-market.

Nothing remarkable happened in our voyage; but I landed with ten sail of apricot-boats, at Strand-bridge, after having put in at Nine-Elms, and taken in melons, consigned by Mr. Cuffe, of that place, to Sarah Sewell and Company, at their stall in Covent-garden. We arrived at Strand-bridge at six of the clock, and were unloading; when the hackney-coachmen of the foregoing night took their leave of each other at the Dark-house, to go to bed before the day was too far spent. . .

The day of people of fashion began now to break, and carts and hacks were mingled with equipages of show and vanity; when I resolved to walk it out of cheapness; but my unhappy curiosity is such, that I find it always my interest to take coach; for some odd adventure among beggars, ballad-singers, or the like, detains and throws me into expense. It happened so immediately: for at the corner of Warwick-street, as I was listening to a new ballad, a ragged rascal, a beggar who knew me, came up to me, and began to turn the eyes of the good company upon me, by telling me he was extremely poor, and should die in the street for want of drink, except I immediately would have the charity to give him sixpence to go into the next ale-house and save his life. He urged, with a melancholy face, that all his family had died of thirst. All the mob have humour, and two or three began to take the jest; by which Mr. Sturdy carried his point, and let me sneak off to a coach. As I drove along, it was a pleasing reflection to see the world so prettily checkered since I left Richmond, and the scene still filling with children of a new hour. This satisfaction increased as I moved towards the city; and gay signs, well-disposed streets, magnificent public structures and wealthy shops adorned with contented faces, made the joy still rising till we came into the centre of the city, and centre of the world of trade, the Exchange of London. As other men in the crowds about me were pleased with their hopes and bargains, I found my account in observing them, in attention to their several interests. I, indeed, looked upon myself as the richest man that walked the Exchange that day; for my benevolence made me share the gains of every bargain that was made. . . When I came to my chambers, I writ down these minutes; but was at a loss what instruction I should propose to my reader from the enumeration of so many insignificant matters and occurrences; and I thought it of great use, if they could learn with me to keep their minds open to gratification, and ready to receive it from any thing it meets with. This one circumstance will make every face you see give you the satisfaction you now take in beholding that of a friend; will make every object a pleasing one; will make all the good which arrives to any man an increase of happiness to yourself.

STEELE (from the *Spectator*)

THE ADVENTURES OF A SHILLING

" I was born " (says he) " on the side of a mountain, near a little village of Peru, and made a voyage to England in an ingot, under the convoy of Sir Francis Drake. I was, soon after my arrival taken out of my Indian habit, refined, naturalised, and put into the British mode, with the face of Queen Elizabeth on one side, and the arms of the country on the other. Being thus equipped, I found in me a wonderful inclination to ramble, and visit all parts of the new world into which I was brought. The people very much favoured my natural disposition, and shifted me so fast from hand to hand, that before I was five years old, I had travelled into almost every corner of the nation. But in the beginning of my sixth year, to my unspeakable grief, I fell into the hands of a miserable old fellow, who clapped me into an iron chest, where I found five hundred more of my own quality who lay under the same confinement. The only relief we had, was to be taken out and counted over in the fresh air every morning and evening. After an imprisonment of several years, we heard somebody knocking at our chest, and breaking it open with a hammer. This we found was the old man's heir, who, as his father lay a-dying, was so good as to come to our release : he separated us that very day. What was the fate of my companions I know not ; as for myself, I was sent to the apothecary's shop for a pint of sack. The apothecary gave me to an herb-woman, the herb-woman to a butcher, the butcher to a brewer, and the brewer to his wife, who made a present of me to a nonconformist preacher. After this manner I made my way merrily through the world; for, as I told you before, we shillings love nothing so much as travelling. I sometimes fetched in a shoulder of mutton, sometimes a play-book, and often had the satisfaction to treat a Templar at a twelvepenny ordinary or carry him, with three friends, to Westminster Hall.

"In the midst of this pleasant progress which I made from place to place, I was arrested by a superstitious old woman, who shut me up in a greasy purse, in pursuance of a foolish saying, 'That while she kept a Queen Elizabeth's shilling about her, she should never be without money.' I continued here a close prisoner for many months, till at last I was exchanged for eight and forty farthings.

"I thus rambled from pocket to pocket till the beginning of the civil wars, when to my shame be it spoke, I was employed in raising soldiers against the king : for being of a very tempting breadth, a sergeant made use of me to inveigle country fellows, and list them in service of the parliament.

"As soon as he had made one man sure, his way was to oblige him to take a shilling of a more homely figure, and then practise the same trick upon another. Thus I continued doing great mischief to the crown, till my officer, chancing one morning to walk abroad earlier than ordinary, sacrificed me to his pleasures, and made use of me to seduce a milk-maid. This wench bent me, and gave me to her sweetheart applying more properly than she intended the usual form of, ' To my love and from my love.' This ungenerous gallant, marrying her within a few days after, pawned me for a dram of brandy, and drinking me out next day, I was beaten flat with a hammer, again set a-running.

"After many adventures, which it would be tedious to relate, I was sent to a young spendthrift, in company with the will of his deceased father. The young fellow, who I found was very extravagant, gave great demonstrations of joy at the receiving of the will; but opening it, he found himself disinherited and cut off from the possession of a fair estate, by virtue of my being made a present to him. This put him into such a passion, that after having taken me in his hand, and cursed me, he squirred me away from him as far as he could fling me. I chanced to light in an unfrequented place under a dead wall, where I lay undiscovered and useless, during the usurpation of Oliver Cromwell.

"About a year after the king's return, a poor cavalier that was walking there about dinner-time, fortunately cast his eye upon me, and, to the great joy of us both, carried me to a cook's shop, where he dined upon me, and drank the king's health. When I came again into the world, I found that I had been happier in my retirement than I thought, having probably, by that means, escaped wearing a monstrous pair of breeches.[1]

" Being now of great credit and antiquity, I was rather looked upon as a medal than an ordinary coin; for which reason a gamester laid hold of me and converted me to a counter, having got together some dozens of us for that use. We led a melancholy life in his possession, being busy at those hours wherein current coin is at rest, and partaking the fate of our master, being in a few moments valued at a crown, a pound, or a sixpence, according to the situation in which the fortune of the cards placed us. I had at length the good luck to see my master break, by which means I was again sent abroad under my primitive denomination of a shilling.

" I shall pass over many other accidents of less moment,

[1] A fancied resemblance, from the disposition of the arms of England and Ireland on Commonwealth coins. A. S.

and hasten to that fatal catastrophe, when I fell into the hands of an artist, who conveyed me under ground, and with an unmerciful pair of shears, cut off my titles, clipped my brims, retrenched my shape, rubbed me to my inmost ring, and, in short, so spoiled and pillaged me, that he did not leave me worth a groat. You may think what a confusion I was in, to see myself thus curtailed and disfigured. I should have been ashamed to have shown my head, had not all my old acquaintance been reduced to the same shameful figure, excepting some few that were punched through the belly. In the midst of this general calamity, when everybody thought our misfortune irretrievable, and our case desperate, we were thrown into the furnace together, and (as it often happens with cities rising out of a fire) appeared with greater beauty and lustre than we could ever boast of before. What has happened to me since this change of sex which you now see, I shall take some other opportunity to relate. In the meantime, I shall only repeat two adventures, as being very extraordinary, and neither of them having ever happened to me above once in my life. The first was, my being in a poet's pocket, who was so taken with the brightness and novelty of my appearance, that it gave occasion to the finest burlesque poem in the British language, entitled from me, 'The Splendid Shilling.'[1] The second adventure, which I must not omit, happened to me in the year 1703, when I was given away in charity to a blind man; but indeed this was by a mistake, the person who gave me having heedlessly thrown me into the hat among a pennyworth of farthings."

ADDISON (from the *Tatler*)

---

[1] By John Phillips. A. S.

As long as the cruelty of Maximin was confined to the illustrious senators, or even to the bold adventurers who in the court or army expose themselves to the caprice of fortune, the body of the people viewed their sufferings with indifference, or perhaps with pleasure. But the tyrant's avarice, stimulated by the insatiate desires of the soldiers, at length attacked the public property. Every city of the empire was possessed of an independent revenue, destined to purchase corn for the multitude, and to supply the expenses of the games and entertainments. By a single act of authority, the whole mass of wealth was at once confiscated for the use of the Imperial treasury. The temples were stripped of their most valuable offerings of gold and silver, and the statues of gods, heroes, and emperors, were melted down and coined into money. These impious orders could not be executed without tumults and massacres, as in many places the people chose rather to die in defence of their altars, than to behold in the midst of peace their cities exposed to the rapine and cruelty of war. The soldiers themselves, among whom this sacrilegious plunder was distributed, received it with a blush ; and, hardened as they were in acts of violence, they dreaded the just reproaches of their friends and relations. Throughout the Roman world a general cry of indignation was heard, imploring vengeance on the common enemy of human kind ; and at length, by an act of private oppression, a peaceful and unarmed province was driven into rebellion against him.

The procurator of Africa was a servant worthy of such a master, who considered the fines and confiscations of the rich as one of the most fruitful branches of the Imperial revenue. An iniquitous sentence had been (A.D. 237, April) pronounced against some opulent youths of that country, the execution of which would have stripped them of far the greater part of their patrimony. In this extremity, a resolution that must either complete or prevent their ruin, was dictated by despair. A respite of three days, obtained with difficulty from the rapacious treasurer, was employed in collecting from their estates a great number of slaves and peasants, blindly devoted to the commands of their lords, and armed with the rustic weapons of clubs and axes. The leaders of the conspiracy, as they were admitted to the audience of the procurator, stabbed him with the daggers concealed under their garments, and, by the assistance of their tumultuary train, seized on the little town of Thysdrus, and erected the standard of rebellion against the sovereign of the Roman empire. They rested their hopes on the hatred of mankind against Maximin, and they judiciously resolved to oppose to that detested tyrant, an emperor whose mild virtues had already acquired the love and esteem of the Romans, and whose authority over the province would give weight and stability to the enterprise. Gordianus, their proconsul, and the object of their choice, refused, with unfeigned reluctance, the dangerous honour, and begged with tears that they would suffer him to terminate in peace a long and innocent life, without staining his feeble age with civil blood. Their menaces compelled him to accept the Imperial purple, his only refuge indeed against the jealous cruelty of Maximin ; since, according to the reasoning of tyrants, those who have been esteemed worthy of the throne deserve death, and those who deliberate have already rebelled.

The family of Gordianus was one of the most illustrious

of the Roman senate. On the father's side, he was descended from the Gracchi; on his mother's from the emperor Trajan. A great estate enabled him to support the dignity of this birth, and, in the enjoyment of it, he displayed an elegant taste and beneficent disposition. The palace in Rome, formerly inhabited by the great Pompey, had been, during several generations, in the possession of Gordian's family. It was distinguished by ancient trophies of naval victories, and decorated with the works of modern painting. His villa on the road to Praeneste was celebrated for baths of singular beauty and extent, for three stately rooms of an hundred feet in length, and for a magnificent portico, supported by two hundred columns of the four most curious and costly sorts of marble. The public shows exhibited at his expense, and in which the people were entertained with many hundreds of wild beasts and gladiators, seemed to surpass the fortune of a subject; and whilst the liberality of other magistrates was confined to a few solemn festivals in Rome, the magnificence of Gordian was repeated, when he was aedile, every month in the year, and extended, during his consulship, to the principal cities of Italy. He was twice elevated to the last-mentioned dignity, by Caracalla and by Alexander; for he possessed the uncommon talent of acquiring the esteem of virtuous princes without alarming the jealousy of tyrants. His long life was innocently spent in the study of letters and the peaceful honours of Rome; and, till he was named proconsul of Africa by the voice of the senate and the approbation of Alexander, he appears prudently to have declined the command of armies and the government of provinces. As long as that emperor lived, Africa was happy under the administration of his worthy representative; after the barbarous Maximin had usurped the throne, Gordianus alleviated the miseries which he was unable to prevent. When he reluctantly accepted the purple, he was above fourscore years old; a last and valuable remains of the happy age of the Antonines, whose virtues he revived in his own conduct and celebrated in an elegant poem of thirty books. With the venerable proconsul, his son, who had accompanied him into Africa as his lieutenant, was likewise declared emperor. His manners were less pure, but his character was equally amiable with that of his father. Twenty-two acknowledged concubines, and a library of sixty-two thousand volumes, attested the variety of his inclinations, and from the productions which he left behind him, it appears that the former as well as the latter were designed for use rather than ostentation. The Roman people acknowledged in the features of the younger Gordian the resemblance of Scipio Africanus, recollected with pleasure that his mother was the grand-daughter of Antoninus Pius, and rested the public hope on those latent virtues which had hitherto, as they fondly imagined, lain concealed in the luxurious indolence of a private life.

EDWARD GIBBON (from *Decline and Fall of the Roman Empire*)

THE ENGLISH MAIL-COACH
(1805—1815)

From eight p.m., to fifteen or twenty minutes later, imagine the mails assembled on parade in Lombard Street, where, at that time, and not in St. Martin's-le-Grand, was seated the General Post-Office. In what exact strength we mustered I do not remember; but, from the length of each separate *attelage*, we filled the street, though a long one, and though we were drawn up in double file. On *any* night the spectacle was beautiful. The absolute perfection of all the appointments about the carriages and the harness, their strength, their brilliant cleanliness, their beautiful simplicity—but, more than all, the royal magnificence of the horses—were what might first have fixed the attention. Every carriage, on every morning in the year, was taken down to an official inspector for examination—wheels, axles, linchpins, pole, glasses, lamps, were all critically probed and tested. Every part of every carriage had been cleaned, every horse had been groomed, with as much rigour as if they belonged to a private gentleman; and that part of the spectacle offered itself always. But the night before us is a night of victory; and, behold! to the ordinary display, what a heart-shaking addition !— horses, men, carriages, all are dressed in laurels and flowers, oak-leaves and ribbons. The guards, as being officially his Majesty's servants, and of the coachmen such as are within the privilege of the post-office, wear the royal liveries of course; and as it is summer (for all the *land* victories were naturally won in summer), they wear, on this fine evening, these liveries exposed to view without any covering of upper coats. Such a costume, and the elaborate arrangement of the laurels in their hats, dilate their hearts, by giving to them openly a personal connection with the great news, in which already they have the general interest of patriotism. That great national sentiment surmounts and quells all sense of ordinary distinctions. Those passengers who happen to be gentlemen are now hardly to be distinguished as such except by dress; for the usual reserve of their manner in speaking to the attendants has on this night melted away. One heart, one pride, one glory, connects every man by the transcendent bond of his national blood. The spectators, who are numerous beyond precedent, express their sympathy with these fervent feelings by continual hurrahs. Every moment are shouted aloud by the post-office servants, and summoned to draw up, the great ancestral names of cities known to history through a thousand years—Lincoln, Winchester, Portsmouth, Gloucester, Oxford, Bristol, Manchester, York, Newcastle, Edinburgh, Glasgow, Perth, Stirling, Aberdeen—expressing the grandeur of the empire by the antiquity of its towns, and the grandeur of the mail establishment by the diffusive radiation of its separate missions. Every moment you hear the thunder of lids locked down upon the mail-bags. That sound to each individual mail is the signal for drawing off, which process is the finest part of the entire spectacle. Then come the horses into play. Horses ! can these be horses that bound off with the action and gestures of leopards ? What stir !—what sea-like ferment !—what a thundering of wheels !—what a trampling of hoofs !— what a sounding of trumpets !

THOMAS DE QUINCEY

THE GREAT MOMENT

" I want to tell you something," I said : " I want to tell you all."

" Speak, Lucy ; come near ; speak ! . ."

Before I had half done, he held both my hands, he consulted my eyes with a most piercing glance : there was something in his face which tended neither to calm nor to put me down ; he forgot his own doctrine, he forsook his own system of repression when I most challenged its exercise. I think I deserved strong reproof : but when have we our deserts ? I merited severity ; he looked indulgence. To my very self I seemed imperious and unreasonable; he smiled, betraying delight. Warm, jealous, and haughty, I knew not till now that my nature had such a mood : he gathered me near his heart. I was full of faults ; he took them and me all home. For the moment of utmost mutiny he reserved the one deep spell of peace. . .

We walked back to the Rue Fossetti by moonlight— such moonlight as fell on Eden—shining through the shades of the Great Garden, and haply gilding a path glorious for a step divine—a Presence nameless. Once in their lives some men and women go back to these first fresh days of our great Sire and Mother—taste that grand morning's dew—bathe in its sunrise.

CHARLOTTE BRONTË (from Villette)

THE DEATH OF A BIRD

The bird, however hard the frost may be, flies briskly to his customary roosting-place, and, with beak tucked into his wing, falls asleep. He has no apprehensions ; only the hot blood grows colder and colder, the pulse feebler as he sleeps, and at midnight, or in the early morning, he drops from his perch—dead.

Yesterday he lived, and moved, responsive to a thousand external influences, reflecting earth and sky in his small brilliant brain as in a looking-glass ; also he had a various language, the inherited knowledge of his race, and the faculty of flight, by means of which he could shoot, meteor-like, across the sky, and pass swiftly from place to place ; and with it such perfect control over all his organs, such marvellous certitude in all his motions, as to be able to drop himself plumb down from the tallest tree-top, or out of the void air, on to a slender spray, and scarcely cause its leaves to tremble. Now, on this morning, he lies stiff and motionless; if you were to take him up and drop him from your hand, he would fall to the ground like a stone or a lump of clay—so easy and swift is the passage from life to death in wild nature! But he was never miserable.

W. H. HUDSON (from *Birds in Town and Village*)

GOOD COMPANY

It is enough to lie on the sward in the shadow of green boughs, to listen to the songs of summer, to drink in the sunlight, the air, the flowers, the sky, the beauty of all. Or upon the hill-tops to watch the white clouds rising over the curved hill-lines, their shadows descending the slope. Or on the beach to listen to the sweet sigh as the smooth sea runs up and recedes. It is lying beside the immortals, in-drawing the life of the ocean, the earth, and the sun.

I want to be always in company with these, with earth, and sun, and sea, and stars by night. The pettiness of house-life—chairs and tables—and the pettiness of observances, the petty necessity of useless labour, useless because productive of nothing, chafe me the year through.

I want to be always in company with the sun, and sea, and earth. These, and the stars by night, are my natural companions.

RICHARD JEFFERIES (from *The Story of my Heart*)

IN ENGLAND NOW

Every morning, early, through the misty air of spring, she walked over the fields (to St. Chad's). The path was familiar and beloved; past the mill, through flats of mare's-tail and king-cup steeped in moist, marshy odours. At this early hour the millpond lay tranced as in the quiet of evening. On its glassy flats the roach rose lazily with sucking dimples that spread to rings. Sometimes the burning blue of a kingfisher that haunted the willow-roots passed with a flash that brought her heart into her mouth. Above the pool a field of cowslips. The low sun raked their pale clusters with a keener fire; their gusty vinous odour mounted to her brain. Then the edge of the larch-wood, piercingly green, younger than anything on earth. Within its curved shadow dew lay late; the cropped turf was bloomed with it; and there, unconscious of her coming, crouched the little huddled shapes of rabbits nibbling against time. It was almost as if they could hear her smile. Suddenly the nibbling ceased; the warm bodies lay like scattered stones. One drummed his feet, and all vanished with a clumsy, unhurried reluctance. They did not seem very much afraid of her. She was sorry that they mistrusted her at all. Couldn't they see, the silly things, that she loved them.

FRANCIS BRETT YOUNG (from *Portrait of Clare*)

572

THIRD PART

§ IV TRAVELLERS' JOY

" How many miles to Babylon ? "
" Three score and ten."
" Can I get there by candle-light ? "
" Yes ! If your legs are long."

Old English Game Song

In every land thy feet may tread
Time like a veil is round thy head.
Only the land thou seek'st with me
Never hath been nor yet shall be.

SIR HENRY NEWBOLT

§ IV TRAVELLERS' JOY

TO BABYLON BY CANDLELIGHT

It is by candlelight one enters Babylon ; and all roads lead to Babylon, provided it is by candlelight one journeys. It was by candlelight that John Milton read Diodorus, and by the Third Book he had voyaged beyond the Cape of Hope and now was past Mozambic, and already felt freshly blowing on his face

> *Sabean odours from the spicie shore*
> *Of Arabie the blest.*

It was by candlelight that the sea coast of Bohemia was discovered, and the finding of it made a winter's tale. Baghdad is not a city to be seen by day ; candlelight is the only illumination for all Arabian nights.

One sees most by candlelight, because one sees little. There is a magic ring, and in it all things shine with a yellow shining, and round it wavers the eager dark. This is the magic of the lyrics of the twelfth century in France, lit candles in " a casement ope at night," starring the dusk in Babylon ; candles flare and gutter in the meaner streets, Villon's lyrics, these ; candles flame in its cath-edral-darkness, Latin hymns of the Middle Ages, of Thomas of Celano and Bernard of Morlaix. For if Bab-ylon has its Quartier Latin, it has also its Notre Dame. The Middle Ages are the Babylon of the religious heart.

Every literature has its Babylon. Or rather, like that other Babylon, not of the spirit, Babylon is one, and all nations have drunk of her wine. She, too, is the haven desired of " everyone that saileth any whither" by reason of her costliness, her merchandise of gold and precious stones and pearls, of fine linen and purple and silk and scarlet, thyine wood and ivory, cinnamon and incense, wine and souls of men ; and this Babylon too will have fallen when the sound of the flute is no more heard in her, and " the light of a candle shall shine no more at all." All languages are spoken in Babylon, yet with the same accent ; here are gateways of the Moors in Spain, Venetian waterways, streets of Old Paris, and over all the undiscerning twilight. All men meet in Babylon who go on pilgrimages, for all roads end in Babylon, the Road of the San Grael, the Road of the Secret Rose.

HELEN WADDELL (from Introduction to
Lyrics from the Chinese)

THE INTERIOR OF CATHAY

Upon leaving the capital and travelling ten miles, you come to a river named Pulisangan, which discharges itself into the ocean, and is navigated by many vessels entering from thence, with considerable quantities of merchandise. Over this river there is a very handsome bridge of stone, perhaps unequalled by any other in the world. Its length is three hundred paces, and its width eight paces ; so that ten mounted men can, without inconvenience, ride abreast. It has twenty-four arches, supported by twenty-five piers erected in the water, all of serpentine stone, and built with great skill.

On each side, and from one extremity to the other, there is a handsome parapet, formed of marble slabs and pillars arranged in a masterly style. At the beginning of the ascent the bridge is something wider than at the summit, but from the part where the ascent terminates, the sides run in straight lines and parallel to each other. Upon the upper level there is a massive and lofty column, resting upon a tortoise of marble, and having near its base a large figure of a lion, with a lion also on the top. Towards the slope of the bridge there is another handsome column or pillar, with its lion, at the distance of a pace and a half from the former; and all the spaces between one pillar and another, throughout the whole length of the bridge, are filled up with slabs of marble, curiously sculptured, and mortised into the next adjoining pillars, forming altogether a beautiful spectacle. These parapets serve to prevent accidents that might otherwise happen to passengers.

Upon leaving the fortress of Thaigin, and travelling about twenty miles, you come to a river called the Karamoran [Yellow River], which is of such magnitude, both in respect to width and depth, that no solid bridge can be erected upon it. Its waters are discharged into the ocean. On its banks are many cities and castles, in which a number of trading people reside, who carry on an extensive commerce. The country bordering upon it produces ginger, and silk also in large quantities.

Of birds the multitude is incredible, especially of pheasants, which are sold at the rate of three for the value of a Venetian groat. Here likewise grows a species of large cane, in infinite abundance, some of a foot and others a foot and a half in circumference, which are employed by the inhabitants for a variety of useful purposes.

Having crossed this river and travelled three days' journey, you arrive at a city named Ka-chan-fu, whose inhabitants are idolaters. They carry on a considerable traffic, and work at a variety of manufactures. The country produces in great abundance silk, ginger, and many drugs that are nearly unknown in our part of the world. Here they weave gold tissues, as well as every other kind of silken cloth. We shall speak in the next place of the noble and celebrated city of Ken-zan-fu, in the kingdom of the same name.

Departing from Ka-chan-fu, and proceeding eight days' journey in a westerly direction, you continually meet with cities and commercial towns, and pass many gardens and cultivated grounds, with abundance of the mulberry-tree that contributes to the production of silk. The inhabitants in general worship idols, but there are also found here Nestorian Christians, Turkomans, and Saracens.

The wild beasts of the country afford excellent sport and a variety of birds also are taken.

At the end of eight days you arrive at the city of Ken-zan-fu, which was anciently the capital of an extensive, noble, and powerful kingdom, the seat of many kings, highly descended and distinguished in arms. At the present day it is governed by a son of the Great Khan, named Mangalu, upon whom his father has conferred the sovereignty.

It is a country of great commerce, and eminent for its manufactures. Raw silk is produced in large quantities, and tissues of gold and every other kind of silk are woven there. At this place likewise they prepare every article necessary for the equipment of an army. All species of provisions are in abundance, and to be procured at a moderate price. . .

In a plain, about five miles from the city, stands a beautiful palace belonging to King Mangalu, embellished with many fountains and rivulets, both within and on the outside of the buildings. There is also a fine park, surrounded by a high wall, with battlements, enclosing an extent of five miles, where all kinds of wild animals, both beasts and birds, are kept for sport. In its centre is this spacious palace, which, for symmetry and beauty, cannot be surpassed. It contains many marble halls and chambers, ornamented with paintings and beaten gold and the finest azure. Mangalu, pursuing the footsteps of his father, governs his principality with strict equity, and is beloved by his people. He also takes much delight in hunting and hawking.

Travelling westward three days, from the residence of Mangalu, you still find towns and castles, whose inhabitants subsist by commerce and manufactures, and where there is an abundance of silk. At the end of these three days you enter upon a region of mountains and valleys, which lie within the province of Kun-kin.

This tract, however, has no want of inhabitants, who are worshippers of idols and cultivate the earth. They live also by the chase, the land being much covered with woods. In these are found many wild beasts, such as tigers, bears, lynxes, fallow-deer, antelopes, stags, and many other animals, which are made to turn to good account. This region extends to the distance of twenty days' journey, during which the way lies entirely over mountains and through valleys and woods, but containing towns where travellers may find convenient accommodation.

From *Travels of Marco Polo*
(Trans. MARSDEN and KOMROFF)

And now will I tell you of lands and countries and isles that are beyond the land of Cathay; And therefore he that will go from Cathay to Inde . . . shall go through a kingdom that is called Cadile, the which is a great land. And there groweth a manner of fruit great as gourds, and when it is ripe they open it and find therein a beast with flesh and blood, and bone, and it is like to a little lamb without wool. And men of that country eat that beast and the fruit also. And that is a great marvel. . .

In this land also are great apples of noble smell and noble savour, and men may find of them on a cluster an hundred and more and the leaves of the trees are two foot long and some longer. And in that country are trees bearing gariofles and nutmegs, and great nuts of Inde, and other divers spiceries. And there are vines that bear so great bobbs of grapes that a strong man may uneasily bear one of them.

And in that land are many griffins, more than in any country else. And some men say they have the shape of an eagle before, and behind the shape of a lion, and sickerly they say sooth.

. . .

I, John Maundeville Knight (although I be unworthy) have passed many lands and many isles and countries and searched many full strange places, and have been in many a full good honourable company, and now I am comen home, maugre myself, to rest, for gowts that me distreynen and put an end to my labour, against my will God knoweth.

SIR JOHN MANDEVILLE (from *Voiage and Travaile*
—Cotton MS., *c.* 1400)

CONVERSATION FOR FLEMISH TRAVELLERS

(14th Century)

GUEST : God be here, dame !

HOSTESS : Fellow, ye be welcome.

GUEST : May I have a bed here within ?—May I here be lodged ?

HOSTESS : Yea, well and cleanly, even though were ye twelve, all on horseback.

GUEST : Nay, but we three. Is there to eat here within ?

HOSTESS : Yea, enough, God be thanked.

GUEST : Bring it to us. Give hay to the horses, and straw them well ; but see that they be watered. . .
Dame, what owe we ? We have been well eased.

HOSTESS : We shall reckon to-morrow, and shall pay also, that ye shall hold you pleased.

GUEST : Bring us to sleep ; we been merry.

HOSTESS : Well, I go. Ye shall rest. Janet light the candle ; and lead them there above ; and bear them hot water for to wash their feet ; and cover them with cushions ; see that the stable be well shut.

From a Flemish Phrase-Book compiled at Bruges

(Trans. WM. CAXTON)

ERASMUS TRAVELS IN GERMANY

I left Bâle relaxed and worn out as one out of favour with the gods. The river part of my journey was well enough, save for the heat of the sun. We dined at Breisach. Dinner abominable. Foul smells and flies in swarms. We were kept waiting half an hour while the precious banquet was preparing. There was nothing that I could eat, every dish filthy and stinking. At night we were turned out of the boat into a village—the name I forget, and I would not write it if I remembered. It nearly made an end of me. There were sixty of us to sup together in a tavern, a medley of human animals in one small heated room. It was ten o'clock, and, oh! the dirt and the noise, especially after the wine had begun to circulate. The cries of the boatmen woke us in the morning. I hurry on board un-supped and unslept. At nine we reached Strasburg, when things mended a little. From Strasburg we went on to Speyer. My English horse had broken down, a wretch of a blacksmith having burnt his foot with a hot shoe. I escaped the inn at Speyer and was entertained by my friend the Dean. Two pleasant days with him, thence in a carriage to Worms and so on to Mentz, where I was again lodged by a Cathedral canon. So far things had gone tolerably with me. The smell of the horses was disagree-able and the pace was slow, but that was the worst. At a village further on I call on my friend Christopher, the wine-merchant, to his great delight. On his table I saw the works of Erasmus. He invited a party to meet me, sent the boatmen a pitcher of wine and promised to let them off the customs duty as a reward for having brought him so great a man. Imagine a wine-merchant reading my books and given to the study of the Muses. Christ said the publicans and harlots would go into the kingdom of heaven before the Pharisees. Priests and monks live for their bellies, and vintners take to literature. But, alas, the red wine which he sent to the boatmen took the taste of the bargeman's wife, a red-faced sot of a woman. She drank it to the last drop, and then flew to arms and almost murdered a servant wench with oyster-shells. Then she rushed on deck, tackled her husband, and tried to pitch him overboard. There is vinal energy for you !

At the hotel at Cologne I ordered breakfast at ten o'clock, with a carriage and pair to be ready immediately after. I went to church, came back to find no breakfast, and a carriage not to be had. My horse being disabled, I tried to hire another. I was told this could not be done either. I saw what it meant. I was to be kept at Cologne, and I did not choose to be kept; so I ordered my poor nag to be saddled, lame as he was, with another for my servant, and I started on a five hours' journey for the Count of New Eagle. I had five pleasant days with the Count, whom I found a young man of sense. A carriage had been ordered for me for the next morning. The Count would not take leave of me overnight, meaning to see me before I started. The night was wild. I rose before dawn to finish off some work. At seven, the Count not appearing, I sent to call him. He came, and protested that I must not leave his house in such weather. I must have lost half my mind when I went to Cologne. My evil genius now carried off the other half. Go I would, in an open carriage, with wind enough to tear up oak-trees. It came from the south and charged with pestilence. Towards evening wind changed to rain. I reached Aix shaken to pieces by the bad roads. I should have done better on my lame horse.

Letter of ERASMUS (1518)

ENGLAND AS SEEN BY FOREIGNERS IN QUEEN ELIZABETH'S TIME

1. A Dutch Physician, 1560

At my first arrival at Dover, and so along my journey toward London, which I dispatched partly upon horseback and partly by water, I saw and noted many things able to ravish and allure any man in the world, with desire to travel and see that so noble a country. Frankly to utter what I think of the incredible courtesy and friendliness in speech and affability used in this famous realm, I must needs confess it doth surmount and carry away the prick and price of all others. And beside this, the neat cleanliness, the exquisite fineness, the pleasant and delightful furniture in every point for household, wonderfully rejoiced me ; their chambers and parlours strawed over with sweet herbs refreshed me ; their nosegays finely intermingled with sundry sorts of fragrant flowers in their bedchambers and privy rooms, with comfortable smell cheered me up and entirely delighted all my senses. And this do I think to be the cause that Englishmen, living by such wholesome and exquisite meat, and in so wholesome and healthful air be so fresh and clean coloured : their faces, eyes and countenance carrying with it and representing a portly grace and comeliness, giveth out evident tokens of an honest mind ; in language very smooth and allective, but yet seasoned and tempered within the limits and bonds of moderation, not bombasted with any unseemly terms or enforced with any clawing flatteries or allurements. At their tables although they be very sumptuous, and love to have good fare, yet neither use they to overcharge themselves with excess of drink, neither thereto greatly provoke and urge others, but suffer every man to drink in such measure as best pleaseth himself, which drink being either Ale or Beer, most pleasant in taste and wholesomely relished, they fetch not from foreign places, but have it among themselves brewed. As touching their populous and great haunted cities, the fruitfulness of their ground and soil, their lively springs and mighty rivers, their great herds and flocks of cattle, their mysteries and art of weaving and cloth-making, their skilfulness in shooting, it is needless here to discourse— seeing the multitude of merchants exercising the traffic and art of merchandise among them, and ambassadors also sent thither from foreign Princes, are able abundantly to testify that nothing needful and expedient for man's use and commodity lacketh in that most noble island.

LEVINUS LEMNIUS
(from *The Touchstone of Complexions*)

2. An Antwerp Merchant, 1575

The people are bold, courageous, ardent, and cruel in war, fiery in attack and having little fear of death; they are not vindictive, but very inconstant, rash, vain-glorious, light, and deceiving, and very suspicious, especially of foreigners, whom they despise. They are full of courtly and affected manners and words, which they take for gentility, civility, and wisdom. They are eloquent and very hospitable; they feed well and delicately, and eat a great deal of meat; and as the Germans pass the bounds of sobriety in drinking, these do the same in eating, for which the fertility of the country affords them sufficient means, although in general the fruits have not such strength and virtue as in France or the Netherlands for the want of hot sun. Even the grass, as the herbalists say, is not so nourishing, whereby the meat is in consequence softer and not so firm, although they have a great abundance of it ; but it is well-tasted enough.

The people are not so laborious and industrious as the Netherlanders or French, and the most toilsome, difficult, and skilful works are chiefly performed by foreigners as among the idle Spaniards. They have a great many sheep which bear fine wool, of which for these 200 years they have learnt to make fine cloth. They keep many lazy servants, and also many wild animals for their pleasure, rather than trouble themselves to cultivate the land. The island which they inhabit is very large, and abounds with fish ; they have likewise the best harbours in Christendom. They are also rich in ships ; nevertheless they do not catch as many fish as they require, so that they are obliged to buy more from their neighbours ; but they do catch a great quantity of herrings, of which they send away every year more than five or six hundred lasts to Italy and elsewhere. . .

Although the women there are entirely in the power of their husbands except for their lives, yet they are not kept so strictly as they are in Spain or elsewhere. . . They are well-dressed, fond of taking it easy, and commonly leave the care of household matters and drudgery to their servants. They sit before their doors, decked out in fine clothes, in order to see and be seen by the passers-by. . The rest of their time they employ in walking and riding, in playing at cards or otherwise, in visiting their friends and keeping company, conversing with their equals (whom they term *gosseps*) and their neighbours, and making merry with them at child-births, christenings, churchings, and funerals ; and all this with the permission and knowledge of their husbands, as such is the custom.

The women are beautiful, fair, well-dressed and modest, which is seen there more than elsewhere, as they go about the streets without any covering either of huke or mantle, hood, veil, or the like. Married women only wear a hat both in the street and in the house; those unmarried go without a hat, although ladies of distinction have lately learnt to cover their faces with silken masks or vizards, and feathers,—for indeed they change very easily, and that every year, to the astonishment of many.

EMANUEL VAN METEREN
(from *History of the Netherlands*)

3. A Brandenburg Lawyer, 1598

The soil is fruitful and abounds with cattle, which inclines the inhabitants rather to feeding than ploughing, so that near a third part of the land is left uncultivated for grazing. The climate is most temperate at all times, and the air never heavy, consequently maladies are scarcer, and less physic is used there than anywhere else. . . The general drink is ale, which is prepared from barley, and is excellently well tasted, but strong and what soon fuddles. . .

The English are serious like the Germans, lovers of show; followed wherever they go by whole troops of servants, who wear their masters' arms in silver fastened to their left arms, and are not undeservedly ridiculed for wearing tails hanging down their backs. They excel in dancing and music, for they are active and lively, though of a thicker make than the French; they cut their hair close on the middle of the head, letting it grow on either side; they are good sailors and better pirates, cunning, treacherous, and thievish; above 300 are said to be hanged annually at London; beheading with them is less infamous than hanging; they give the wall as the place of honour: hawking is the common sport with the gentry. They are more polite in eating than the French, consuming less bread but more meat, which they roast in perfection; they put a great deal of sugar in their drink; their beds are covered with tapestry, even those of farmers; they are often molested with the scurvy, said to have first crept into England with the Norman Conquest; their houses are commonly of two stories, except in London, where they are of three and four, though but seldom of four; they are built of wood, those of the richer sort with bricks, their roofs are low, and where the owner has money, covered with lead. They are powerful in the field, successful against their enemies, impatient of anything like slavery; vastly fond of great noises that fill the ear, such as the firing of cannon, drums, and the ringing of bells, so that in London it is common for a number of them that have got a glass in their heads to go up into some belfry, and ring the bells for hours together, for the sake of exercise. If they see a foreigner very well made, or particularly handsome, they will say, " It is a pity he is not an Englishman."

PAUL HENTZNER
(from *Itinerary of Travels in England*, etc.)

I
Northward Ho !

(An account of the First Voyage of Master John Davis
undertaken in June, 1585, for the Discovery of the
North West Passage)

The 19th of July we fell into a great whirling and brust-
ling of a tide, setting to the northwards ; and sailing about
half a league we came into a very calm sea, which bent to
the south-south-west. Here we heard a mighty great
roaring of the sea, as if it had been the breach of some
shore, the air being so foggy and full of thick mist, that
we could not see the one ship from the other, being a very
small distance asunder ; so the captain and the master,
being in distrust how the tide might set them, caused the
Moonshine to hoist out her boat and to sound, but they
could not find ground in three hundred fathoms and
better. Then the captain, master, and I went towards the
breach to see what it should be, giving charge to our
gunners that at every blast they should shoot off a musket
shot, to the intent we might keep ourselves from losing
them ; then coming near to the breach, we met many
islands of ice floating, which had quickly compassed us
about. Then we went upon some of them, and did perceive that all the roaring which we heard was caused only by
the rolling of this ice together. Our company seeing us not
to return according to our appointment, left off shooting
muskets and began to shoot falconets, for they feared
some mishap had befallen us ; but before night we came
aboard again, with our boat laden with ice, which made

very good fresh water. Then we bent our course toward the north, hoping by that means to double the land.

The 20th, as we sailed along the coast, the fog brake up, and we discovered the land, which was the most deformed, rocky, and mountainous land that ever we saw, the first sight whereof did show as if it had been in form of a sugar loaf, standing to our sight above the clouds, for that it did show over the fog like a white liste [edge] in the sky, the tops altogether covered with snow, and the shore beset with ice a league off into the sea, making such irksome noise as that it seemed to be the true pattern of desolation, and after the same our captain named it the land of desolation.

The 21st the wind came northerly and overblew, so that we were constrained to bend our course south again, for we perceived that we were run into a very deep bay, where we were almost compassed with ice, for we saw very much towards the north-north-east, west, and south-west ; and this day and this night we cleared ourselves of the ice, running south-south-west along the shore.

Upon Thursday, being the 22nd of this month, about three of the clock in the morning, we hoisted out our boat, and the captain, with six sailors, went towards the shore, thinking to find a landing-place, for the night before we did perceive the coast to be void of ice to our judgment ; and the same night we were all persuaded that we had seen a canoe rowing along the shore, but afterwards we fell in some doubt of it, but we had no great reason so to do. The captain, rowing towards the shore willed the master to bear in with the land after him ; and before he came near the shore, by the space of a league, or about two miles, he found so much ice that he could not get to land by any means. Here our mariners put to their lines to see if they could get any fish, because there were so many seals upon the coast, and the birds did beat upon the water, but all was in vain : the water about this place was very black and thick, like to a filthy standing pool ; we sounded, and had ground in 120 fathoms. While the captain was rowing to the shore our men saw woods upon the rocks, like to the rocks of Newfoundland, but I could not discern them ; yet it might be so very well, for we had wood floating upon the coast every day, and the *Moonshine* took up a tree at sea not far from the coast, being sixty foot of length and fourteen handfuls about, having the root upon it. After this, the captain came aboard, the weather being very calm and fair, we bent our course toward the south with intent to double the land.

The 23rd we coasted the land which did lie east-north-east and west-south-west.

The 24th, the wind being very fair at east, we coasted the land which did lie east and west, not being able to come near the shore by reason of the great quantity of ice. At this place, because the weather was somewhat cold by reason of the ice, and the better to encourage our men, their allowance was increased. The captain and the master took order that every mess, being five persons, should have half a pound of bread and a can of beer every morning to breakfast. The weather was not very cold, but the air was moderate, like to our April weather in England. When the wind came from the land or the ice it was somewhat cold, but when it came off the sea it was very hot.

The 25th of this month we departed from sight of this land at six of the clock in the morning, directing our course to the north-westward, hoping in God's mercy to find our desired passage, and so continued above four days.

The 29th of July we discovered land in 64 degrees 15 minutes of latitude, bearing north-east from us. The wind being contrary to go to the north-westwards, we bare in with this land to take some view of it, being utterly void of the pester of ice, and very temperate. Coming near the coast we found many fair sounds and good roads for shipping, and many great inlets into the land, whereby we judged this land to be a great number of islands standing together. Here, having moored our barque in good order we went on shore upon a small island to seek for water and wood. Upon this island we did perceive that there had been people, for we found a small shoe and pieces of leather sewed with sinews and a piece of fur, and wool like to beaver. Then we went upon another island on the other side of our ships, and the captain, the master, and I, being got up to the top of a high rock, the people of the country having espied us made a lamentable noise, as we thought, with great outcries and screechings : we, hearing them, thought it had been the howling of wolves. At last I hallooed again, and they likewise cried; then we, perceiving where they stood—some on the shore, and one rowing in a canoe about a small island fast by them—we made a great noise, partly to allure them to us and partly to warn our company of them. Whereupon M. Bruton and the master of his ship, with others of their company, made great haste towards us, and brought our musicians with them from our ship, purposing either by force to rescue us, if needs should so require, or with courtesy to allure the people. When they came unto us we caused our musicians to play, ourselves dancing and making many signs of friendship. At length there came ten canoes from the other islands, and two of them came so near the shore where we were that they talked with us, the other being in their boats a pretty way off. Their pronunciation was very hollow through the throat, and their speech such as we could not understand, only we allured them by friendly embracings and signs of courtesy. At length one of them, pointing up to the sun with his hand, would presently strike his breast so hard that we might hear the blow. This he did many times before he would any way trust us. Then John Ellis, the master of the *Moonshine*, was appointed to use his best policy to gain their friendship, who struck his breast and pointed to the sun after their order, which when he had divers times done they began to trust him, and one of them came on shore, to whom we threw our caps, stockings, and gloves, and such others things as then we had about us, playing with our music, and making signs of joy, and dancing. So the night coming we bade them farewell, and went aboard our barques.

JOHN JANES

(from HAKLUYT'S *Principal Navigations*, etc.)

2

A Worthy Fight

Performed in the voyage from Turkey by five ships of London, against eleven galleys and two frigates of the King of Spain's, at Pantalarea, within the Straits, Anno 1586

The merchants of London, being of the incorporation for the Turkey trade, having received intelligences and advertisements from time to time that the King of Spain, grudging at the prosperity of this kingdom, had not only of late arrested all English ships, bodies, and goods in

Spain, but also, maligning the quiet traffic which they used, to and in the dominations and provinces under the obedience of the Great Turk, had given orders to the captains of his galleys in the Levant to hinder the passage of all English ships, and to endeavour by their best means to intercept, take, and spoil them, their persons and goods; they hereupon thought it their best course to set out their fleet for Turkey in such strength and ability for their defence that the purpose of their Spanish enemy might the better be prevented, and the voyage accomplished with greater security to the men and ships. For which cause, five tall and stout ships appertaining to London, and intending only a merchant's voyage, were provided and furnished with all things belonging to the seas, the names whereof were these :—

1. The *Merchant Royal*, a very brave and goodly ship, and of great report.
2. The *Toby*.
3. The *Edward Bonaventure*.
4. The *William and John*.
5. The *Susan*.

These five departing from the coast of England in the month of November, 1585, kept together as one fleet till they came as high as the isle of Sicily, within the Levant. And there, according to the order and direction of the voyage, each ship began to take leave of the rest, and to separate himself, setting his course for the particular port whereunto he was bound. . . But before they divided themselves, they altogether consulted of and about a certain and special place for their meeting again after the lading of their goods at their several ports. And in conclusion, the general agreement was to meet at Zante, an island near to the main continent of the west part of

Morea, well known to all the pilots, and thought to be the fittest place for their rendezvous. . .

It fell out that the *Toby*, which was bound for Constantinople, had made such good speed, and gotten such good weather, that she first of all the rest came back to the appointed place of Zante, and not forgetting the former conclusion, did there cast anchor, attending the arrival of the rest of the fleet, which accordingly (their business first performed) failed not to keep promise. . .

Thus in good order they left Zante and the Castle of Grecia, and committed themselves again to the seas, and proceeded in their course and voyage in quietness, without sight of any enemy till they came near to Pantalarea, an island so called betwixt Sicily and the coast of Africa ; into sight whereof they came the 13th day of July, 1586. And the same day, in the morning, about seven of the clock, they descried thirteen sails in number, which were of the galleys lying in wait of purpose for them in and about that place. As soon as the English ships had spied them, they, by-and-bye, according to a common order, made themselves ready for a fight. In the meantime, the galleys more and more approached the ships, and in their banners there appeared the arms of the isles of Sicily and Malta, being all as then in the service and pay of the Spaniard. Immediately both the Admirals of the galleys sent from each of them a frigate to the Admiral of our English ships, which being come near them, the Sicilian frigate first hailed them, and demanded of them whence they were ; they answered that they were of England, the arms whereof appeared in their colours. Whereupon the said frigate expostulated with them, and asked why they delayed to send or come with their captains and pursers to Don Pedro de Leiva, their General, to acknowledge their duty and obedience to him, in the name of the Spanish king, lord of those seas. Our men replied and said that they owed no such duty nor obedience to him, and therefore would acknowledge none... They also demanded of the frigate whence she and the rest of the galleys were. The messenger answered, " We are of Malta, and for mine own part, my name is Cavalero. These galleys are in service and pay to the King of Spain, under the conduct of Don Pedro de Leiva, a nobleman of Spain who hath been commanded hither by the king with this present force and army of purpose to intercept you. You shall therefore," quoth he, " do well to repair to him to know his pleasure ; he is a nobleman of good behaviour and courtesy, and means you no ill." The captain of the English Admiral, whose name was Master Edward Wilkinson, replied and said, " We purpose not at this time to make trial of Don Pedro his courtesy, whereof we are suspicious and doubtful, and not without good cause " ; using withal good words to the messenger, and willing him to come aboard him, promising security and good usage, that thereby he might the better know the Spaniard's mind. Whereupon he indeed left his frigate and came aboard him, whom he entertained in friendly sort, and caused a cup of wine to be drawn for him, which he took, and began, with his cap in his hand and with reverent terms, to drink to the health of the Queen of England, speaking very honourably of Her Majesty, and giving good speeches of the courteous usage and entertainment that he himself had received in London. . . At the last he entreated to have the merchant of the Admiral carried by him as a messenger to the General, that so he might be satisfied and assured of their minds by one of their own company. But Master Wilkinson would agree to no such thing ; although Richard Rowit, the merchant himself, seemed willing to be employed in that message, and laboured by reasonable persuasions to induce Master Wilkinson to grant it—as hoping to be an occasion by his presence and discreet answers to satisfy the General, and thereby to save the effusion of Christian blood, if it should grow to a battle. And he seemed so much the more willing to be sent, by how much deeper the oaths and protestations of this Cavalero were, that he would (as he was a true knight and a soldier) deliver him back again in safety to his company. Albeit, Master Wilkinson, who, by his long experience, had received sufficient trial of Spanish inconstancy and perjury, wished him in no case to put his life and liberty in hazard upon a Spaniard's oath ; but at last, upon much entreaty, he yielded to let him go to the General, thinking indeed that good speeches and answers of reason would have contented him, whereas, otherwise, refusal to do so might peradventure have provoked the more discontentment.

Master Rowit, therefore, passing to the Spanish General, the rest of the galleys, having espied him, thought, indeed, that the English were rather determined to yield than to fight, and therefore came flocking about the frigate, every man crying out. . . And the Spanish General, being come to the galley wherein he was, showed himself to Master Rowit in his armour, his guard of soldiers attending upon him, in armour also, and began to speak very proudly in this sort : " Thou Englishman, from whence is your fleet ? Why stand ye aloof off ? know ye not your duty to the Catholic king, whose person I here represent ? Where are your bills of lading, your letters, passports, and the chief of your men ? Think ye my attendance in these seas to be in vain, or my person to no purpose?" .. These words of the Spanish General were not so outrageously pronounced, as they were mildly answered by Master Rowit, who told him that they were all merchantmen, using traffic in honest sort, and seeking to pass quietly, if they were not urged further than reason. .. And as touching his commandment aforesaid for the acknowledging of duty in such particular sort, he told him that, where there was no duty owing there none should be performed, assuring him that their whole company and ships in general stood resolutely upon the negative, and would not yield to any such unreasonable demand, joined with such imperious and absolute manner of commanding. "Why, then," said he, "if they will neither come to yield, nor show obedience to me in the name of my king, I will either sink them or bring them to harbour; and so tell them from me." With that the frigate came away with Master Rowit, and brought him aboard to the English Admiral again, according to promise, who was no sooner entered in but by-and-bye defiance was sounded on both sides. The Spaniards hewed off the noses of the galleys, that nothing might hinder the level of the shot; and the English, on the other side, courageously prepared themselves to the combat, every man, according to his room, bent to perform his office with alacrity and diligence. In the meantime a cannon was discharged from out the Admiral of the galleys, which being the onset of the fight, was presently answered by the English Admiral with a culverin; so the skirmish began, and grew hot and terrible. There was no powder nor shot spared, each English ship matched itself in good order against two Spanish galleys, besides the inequality of the frigates on the Spanish side. . . . Thus the fight continued furious and sharp, and doubtful a long time to which part the victory would incline, till at last the Admiral of the galleys of Sicily began to warp from the fight, and to hold up her side for fear of sinking, and after her went also two others in like case, whom all the sort of them enclosed, labouring by all their means to keep them above water, being ready by the force of English shot which they had received to perish in the seas. And what slaughter was done among the Spaniards the English were uncertain, but by a probable conjecture apparent afar off they supposed their loss was so great that they wanted men to continue the charging of their pieces; whereupon with shame and dishonour, after five hours spent in the battle, they withdrew themselves. And the English, contented in respect of their deep lading rather to continue their voyage than to follow in the chase, ceased from further blows, with the loss of only two men slain amongst them all, and another hurt in his arm, whom Master Wilkinson, with his good words and friendly promises did so comfort that he nothing esteemed the smart of his wound, in respect of the honour of the victory and the shameful repulse of the enemy.

Thus, with dutiful thanks to the mercy of God for His gracious assistance in that danger, the English ships proceeded in their navigation. And coming as high as Algiers, a port town upon the coast of Barbary, they made for it, of purpose to refresh themselves after their weariness, and to take in such supply of fresh water and victuals as they needed. They were no sooner entered into the port but immediately the king thereof sent a messenger to the ships to know what they were. With which messenger the chief master of every ship repaired to the king, and acquainted him not only with the state of their ships in respect of merchandise, but with the late fight which they had passed with the Spanish galleys, reporting every particular circumstance in word as it fell out in action; whereof the said king showed himself marvellous glad, entertaining them in the best sort, and promising abundant relief of all their wants; making general proclamation in the city, upon pain of death, that no man, of what degree or state soever he were, should presume either to hinder them in their affairs or to offer them any manner of injury in body or goods; by virtue whereof they despatched all things in excellent good sort with all favour and peaceableness.

The English, having received this good justice at the king's hands, and all other things that they wanted or could crave for the furnishing of their ships, took their leave of him, and of the rest of their friends that were resident in Algiers, and put out to sea, looking to meet with the second army of the Spanish king, which waited for them about the mouth of the Strait of Gibraltar, which they were of necessity to pass. But coming near to the said strait, it pleased God to raise, at that instant, a very dark and misty fog, so that one ship could not discern another if it were forty paces off, by means whereof, together with the notable fair Eastern winds that then blew most fit for their course, they passed with great speed through the strait, and might have passed, with that good gale, had there been five hundred galleys to withstand them and the air never so clear for every ship to be seen. But yet the Spanish galleys had a sight of them, when they were come within three English miles of the town, and made after them with all possible haste; and although they saw that they were far out of their reach, yet in a vain fury and foolish pride, they shot off their ordnance and made a stir in the sea as if they had been in the midst of

them, which vanity of theirs ministered to our men notable matter of pleasure and mirth, seeing men to fight
with shadows and to take so great pains to so small
purpose.

But thus it pleased God to deride and delude all the
forces of that proud Spanish king, which he had provided
of purpose to distress the English ; who, notwithstanding,
passed through both his armies,—in the one, little hurt,
and in the other, nothing touched, to the glory of His
immortal name, the honour of our prince and country,
and the just commendation of each man's service performed in that voyage.

PHILIP JONES
(from HAKLUYT'S *Principal Navigations,* etc.)

OF TRAVELLING IN GENERAL

For my part, I think variety to be the most pleasing
thing in the world, and the best life to be, neither con-
templative alone, nor active altogether, but mixed of both.
God would have made eternal spring, had he not known,
that the divers seasons would be not only most profitable
to the works of nature, but also most pleasant to his
creatures, while the cold winter makes the temperate
spring more wished. Such is the delight of visiting foreign
countries, charming all our senses with most sweet variety.
They seem to me most unhappy, and no better than prisoners, who from the cradle to old age, still behold the
same walls, faces, orchards, pastures, and objects of the
eye, and still hear the same voices and sounds beat in
their ears ; not the song of the cuckoo, nor the craking
of the crows, nor the howling of wolves, nor the bellowing

of oxen, nor the bleying of sheep, no nor the sweet voices of larks and nightingales, if they be shut up in a cage, do so much please us at home, as the variety of all, composed of divers tunes, delights us in the fields abroad. In like sort, it is manifest that all the other senses are not so much pleased with any thing, as variety. They are in some measure happy, who having but one house, yet have change of chambers, to remove as the season of the year changeth : but I judge lawyers and officers more happy, who have their terms to live in the city, and their vacations to return into the country, so often (as it were) renewing their marriage days : and of all, I judge the nomads most happy, (the comparison holding in other things) who live in tents, and so by removing, not only escape the heat of summer, the cold of winter, the want of pastures, all diseases, and all unpleasing things, but at their pleasure, enjoy all commodities of all places.

Let us imitate the storks, swallows, and cranes, which like the nomads yearly fetch their circuits, and follow the sun, without suffering any distemper of the seasons. The fixed stars have not such power over inferior bodies as the wandering planets. Running water is sweet, but standing pools stink : take away idleness, and the bait of all vice is taken away. Men were created to move, as birds to fly ; what they learn by nature, that reason joined to nature teacheth us. Nothing can be added to the worthy praises of him as the poet saith :

> *Who many men's manners hath seen,*
> *And hath in many cities been.*

In one word, I will say what can be said upon this subject ; every soil is to a valiant man his own country, as the sea to the fishes. We are citizens of the whole world, yea, not of this world, but of that to come. All our life is a pilgrimage. God for his only begotten Son's sake (the true Mercury of travellers) bring us that are here strangers safely into our true country.

FYNES MORYSON (from *Itinerary*, 1617)

THE ROAD TO THE HIGHLANDS

The road which we travelled had become wild and open as soon as we had left Glasgow a mile or two behind us, and was growing more dreary as we advanced. Huge continuous heaths spread before, behind, and around us in hopeless barrenness, now level and interspersed with swamps, green with treacherous verdure, or sable with turf, or, as they call them in Scotland, peat-bogs, and now swelling into huge heavy ascents, which wanted the dignity and form of hills, while they were still more toilsome to the passenger. There were neither trees nor bushes to relieve the eye from the russet livery of absolute sterility. The very heath was of that stinted, imperfect kind which has little or no flower, and affords the coarsest and meanest covering, which, as far as my experience enables me to judge, Mother Earth is ever arrayed in. Living thing we saw none, except occasionally a few straggling sheep of a strange diversity of colours, as black, bluish, and orange. The sable hue predominated, however, in their faces and legs. The very birds seemed to shun these wastes,—and no wonder, since they had an easy method of escaping from them ; at least, I only heard the monotonous and plaintive cries of the lapwing and curlew, which my companions denominated the peasweep and whaup. . .

The few miserable hovels that showed some marks of human habitation were now of still rarer occurrence ; and at length, as we began to ascend an uninterrupted swell of moorland, they totally disappeared. The only exercise which my imagination received was when some particular turn of the road gave us a partial view, to the left, of a large assemblage of dark-blue mountains stretching to the north and north-west, which promised to include within their recesses a country as wild, perhaps, but certainly differing greatly in point of interest, from that which we now travelled. The peaks of this screen of mountains were as wildly varied and distinguished as the hills which we had seen on the right were tame and lumpish ; and while I gazed on this Alpine region I felt a longing to explore its recesses. . .

The road, which had ascended for six or seven English miles, began now to descend for about the same space, through a country which, neither in fertility or interest, could boast any advantage over that which we had passed already, and which afforded no variety, unless when some tremendous peak of a Highland mountain appeared at a distance. We continued, however, to ride on without pause ; and even when night fell and overshadowed the desolate wilds which we traversed, we were, as I understood from Mr. Jarvie, still three miles and a bittock distant from the place where we were to spend the night.

The night was pleasant, and the moon afforded us good light for our journey. Under her rays, the ground over which we passed assumed a more interesting appearance than during the broad daylight, which discovered the extent of its wasteness. The mingled light and shadows gave it an interest which naturally did not belong to it, and, like the effect of a veil flung over a plain woman, irritated our curiosity on a subject which had in itself nothing gratifying.

The descent, however, still continued, turned, winded, left the more open heaths, and got into steeper ravines, which promised soon to lead us to the banks of some brook or river, and ultimately made good their presage. We found ourselves at length on the bank of a stream which rather resembled one of my native English rivers than those I had hitherto seen in Scotland. It was narrow, deep, still, and silent; although the imperfect light, as it gleamed on its placid waters, showed also that we were now among the lofty mountains which formed its cradle. "That's the Forth," said the Bailie, with an air of reverence which I have observed the Scotch usually pay to their distinguished rivers. . .

The Forth, however, as far as the imperfect light permitted me to judge, seemed to merit the admiration of those who claimed an interest in its stream. A beautiful eminence of the most regular round shape, and clothed with copsewood of hazels, mountain-ash, and dwarf-oak, intermixed with a few magnificent old trees, which, rising above the underwood, exposed their forked and bared branches to the silver moonshine, seemed to protect the sources from which the river sprung. If I could trust the tale of my companion,—which, while professing to disbelieve every word of it, he told under his breath, and with an air of something like intimidation,—this hill, so regularly formed, so richly verdant, and garlanded with such a beautiful variety of ancient trees and thriving copsewood, was held by the neighbourhood to contain, within its unseen caverns, the palaces of the fairies : a race of airy beings, who formed an intermediate class between men and demons, and who, if not positively malignant to humanity, were yet to be avoided and feared, on account of their capricious, vindictive, and irritable disposition.

"They ca' them," said Mr. Jarvie, in a whisper, "*Daoine Schie*, whilk signifies, as I understand, men of peace,—meaning thereby to make their gude-will. And we may e'en as weel ca' them that too, Mr. Osbaldistone; for there's nae gude in speaking ill o' the laird within his ain bounds." But he added presently after, on seeing one or two lights which twinkled before us, "It's deceits o' Satan, after a', and I fearna to say it; for we are near the manse now, and yonder are the lights in the Clachan of Aberfoil."

SIR WALTER SCOTT (from *Rob Roy*)

JOHNSON AND BOSWELL IN THE WESTERN ISLES

Glenelg, September 1, 1773.

It grew dusky, and we had a very tedious ride for what was called five miles, but I am sure would measure ten. We had no conversation. I was riding forward to the inn at Glenelg, on the shore opposite to Skye, that I might take proper measures before Dr. Johnson, who was now advancing in dreary silence, Hay leading his horse, should arrive. Vass also walked by the side of his horse, and Joseph followed behind; as therefore he was thus attended, and seemed to be in deep meditation, I thought there could be no harm in leaving him for a little while. He called me back with a tremendous shout, and was really in a passion with me for leaving him. I told him my intentions, but he was not satisfied, and said, " Do you know, I should as soon have thought of picking a pocket as doing so."—BOSWELL : " I am diverted with you, sir." —JOHNSON : " Sir, I could never be diverted with incivility : doing such a thing makes one lose confidence in him who has done it, as one cannot tell what he may do next." His extraordinary warmth confounded me so much that I justified myself but lamely to him, yet my intentions were not improper. . .

We came on to the inn at Glenelg. There was no provender for our horses, so they were sent to grass, with a man to watch them. A maid showed us up-stairs into a room damp and dirty, with bare walls, a variety of bad smells, a coarse black greasy fir table, and forms of the same kind ; and out of a wretched bed started a fellow from his sleep, like Edgar in *King Lear*: " Poor Tom's a-cold." . .

Our bad accommodation here made me uneasy and almost fretful. Dr. Johnson was calm. I said he was so from vanity.—JOHNSON : " No, sir, it is from philosophy." It pleased me to see that the Rambler could practise so well his own lessons.

I resumed the subject of my leaving him on the road, and endeavoured to defend it better. He was still violent upon that head, and said, " Sir, had you gone on, I was thinking that I should have returned with you to Edinburgh, and then have parted from you, and never spoken to you more."

I sent for fresh hay, with which we made beds for ourselves, each in a room equally miserable. Like Wolfe, we had " a choice of difficulties." Dr. Johnson made things easier by comparison. At Macqueen's last night, he observed, that few were so well lodged in a ship. To-night, he said, we were better than if we had been upon the hill. He lay down buttoned up in his great coat : I had my sheets spread on the hay, and my clothes and great coat laid over me by way of blankets.

Thursday, September 2.

I had slept ill. Dr. Johnson's anger had affected me much. I considered that without any bad intention I might suddenly forfeit his friendship, and was impatient to see him this morning. I told him how uneasy he had made me by what he had said, and reminded him of his own remark at Aberdeen, upon old friendships being hastily broken off. He owned he had spoken to me in a passion ; that he would not have done what he had threatened ; and that if he had he should have been ten times worse than I ; that forming intimacies would indeed be " limning the water," were they liable to such sudden dissolution ; and he added, " Let's think no more on't."

Skye, September 12.

Miss Flora Macdonald (for so I shall call her) told me she heard upon the mainland, as she was returning home about a fortnight before, that Mr. Boswell was coming to Skye, and one Mr. Johnson, a young English buck, with him. He was highly entertained with this fancy. Giving an account of the afternoon which we passed, at Anoch, he said, " I, being a *buck*, had miss in to make tea."—He was rather quiescent to-night, and went early to bed. I was in a cordial humour, and promoted a cheerful glass. The punch was excellent. Honest Mr. Macqueen observed that I was in high glee, " my *governor* being gone to bed." . . . I slept in the same room with Dr. Johnson. Each had a neat bed, with tartan curtains, in an upper chamber.

The room where we lay was a celebrated one. Dr. Johnson's bed was the very bed in which the grandson of the unfortunate King James the Second lay, on one of the nights after the failure of his rash attempt in 1745-6, while he was eluding the pursuit of the emissaries of Government, which had offered thirty thousand pounds as a reward for apprehending him. To see Dr. Samuel Johnson lying in that bed, in the Isle of Skye, in the house of Miss Flora Macdonald, struck me with such a group of ideas as it is not easy for words to describe, as they passed through the mind. He smiled, and said, " I have had no ambitious thoughts in it." . . . At breakfast he said he would have given a good deal rather than not have lain in that bed. I owned he was the lucky man ; and observed, that without doubt it had been contrived between Mrs. Macdonald and him. She seemed to acquiesce, adding, " You know young *bucks* are always favourites of the ladies." He spoke of Prince Charles being here, and asked Mrs. Macdonald " *Who* was with him ? We were told, madam, in England, there was one Miss Flora Macdonald with him." She said, "They were very right"; and perceiving Dr. Johnson's curiosity, though he had delicacy enough not to question her, very obligingly entertained him with a recital of the particulars which she herself knew of that escape, which does so much honour to the humanity, fidelity, and generosity of the Highlanders. Dr. Johnson listened to her with placid attention, and said, " All this should be written down."

Ostig, September 29.

After a very good sleep, I rose more refreshed than I had been for some nights. We were now at but a little distance from the shore, and saw the sea from the windows, which made our voyage seem nearer. Mr. Macpherson's manners and address pleased us much. He appeared to be a man of such intelligence and taste as to be sensible of the extraordinary powers of his illustrious guest. He said to me : " Dr. Johnson is an honour to mankind ; and, if the expression may be used, is an honour to religion."

Col, who had gone yesterday to pay a visit at Camuscross, joined us this morning at breakfast. Some other gentlemen also came to enjoy the entertainment of Dr. Johnson's conversation. The day was windy and rainy, so that we had just seized a happy interval for our journey last night. We had good entertainment here, better accommodation than at Corrichatachin, and time enough to ourselves. The hours slipped along imperceptibly. We talked of Shenstone. Dr. Johnson said he was a good layer-out of land, but would not allow him to approach excellence as a poet. He said, he believed he had tried to read all his Love Pastorals, but did not get through them. . . . He was this afternoon full of critical severity, and dealt about his censures on all sides. . .

While he was in this mood, I was unfortunate enough, simply perhaps, but I could not help thinking, undeservedly, to come within " the whiff and wind of his fell sword." I asked him, if he had ever been accustomed to wear a night-cap. He said, " No." I asked, if it was best not to wear one.—JOHNSON : " Sir, I had this custom by chance, and perhaps no man shall ever know whether it is best to sleep with or without a night-cap."—Soon afterwards, he was laughing at some deficiency in the Highlands and said, " One might as well go without shoes and stockings."—Thinking to have a little hit at his own deficiency, I ventured to add, " Or without a night-cap, sir."

But I had better have been silent; for he retorted directly. "I do not see the connection there (laughing). Nobody before was ever foolish enough to ask whether it was best to wear a night-cap or not. This comes of being a little wrong-headed."—He carried the company along with him; and yet the truth is, that if he had always worn a night-cap, as is the common practice, and found the Highlanders did not wear one, he would have wondered at their barbarity; so that my hit was fair enough.

BOSWELL (from *Journal of a Tour to the Hebrides*)

EXCURSIONS AT GRASMERE

Sunday, 27th June, 1800.—After tea we rowed down to Loughrigg Fell, visited the white foxglove, gathered wild strawberries, and walked up to view Rydale. We lay a long time looking at the lake; the shores all dim with the scorching sun. The ferns were turning yellow, that is here and there one was quite turned. We walked round by Benson's wood home. The lake was now most still, and reflected the beautiful yellow and blue and purple and grey colours of the sky. We heard a strange sound in the Bainriggs wood, as we were floating on the water; it *seemed* in the wood, but it must have been above it, for presently we saw a raven very high above us. It called out, and the dome of the sky seemed to echo the sound. It called again and again as it flew onwards, and the mountains gave back the sound, seeming as if from their centre; a musical bell-like answering to the bird's hoarse voice. We heard both the call of the bird, and the echo, after we could see him no longer.

Friday Evening, 29*th August*, 1800.—We walked over the hill by the firgrove. I sate upon a rock, and observed a flight of swallows gathering together high above my head. They flew towards Rydale. We walked through the wood over the stepping-stones. The lake of Rydale very beautiful, partly still. John and I left Wm. to compose an inscription ; that about the path. We had a very fine walk by the gloomy lake. There was a curious yellow reflection in the water, as of corn fields. There was no light in the clouds from which it appeared to come.

(*Saturday Morning*, 30*th August*.)— . . . William finished his Inscription of the Pathway, then walked in the wood ; and when John returned, he sought him, and they bathed together. I read a little of Boswell's *Life of Johnson*. I went to lie down in the orchard. I was roused by a shout that Anthony Harrison was come. We sate in the orchard till tea time. Drank tea early, and rowed down the lake, which was stirred by breezes. We looked at Rydale, which was soft, cheerful, and beautiful. We then went to peep into Langdale. The Pikes were very grand. We walked back to the view of Rydale, which was now a dark mirror. We rowed home over a lake still as glass, and then went to George Mackareth's to hire a horse for John. A fine moonlight night. The beauty of the moon was startling, as it rose to us over Loughrigg Fell. We returned to supper at 10 o'clock.

DOROTHY WORDSWORTH (from *Journals*)

THE BRUGES-GHENT CANAL

Nothing can be more refreshing than to float thus at ease, the awning screening us from the sun, and the pleasant breezes fanning our temples ; . . . cottages constantly varying the shores, which are particularly gay at this season, interspersed with fruit-tree blossom and the broom flower ; goats tethered on the grassy banks, under the thin line of elms ; a village with a pretty church, midway on the journey ; . . . the air delightfully refreshed by the rain ; the banks, again low, allow the eye to stretch beyond the avenue ; corn looking well, rich daisy-clad pastures, and here alive with grasshoppers ; large village on both sides of the canal, bridge between, from which letters are dropped into the barge, as we pass, by means of a shoe. A sale at a Thames-like château; we take on purchasers with their bargains—chests of drawers, bed and chamber furniture of all sorts—barge crowded ; Catholic priests do not scruple to interlard their conversation with oaths ; the three Towers of Ghent, seen through the misty air in the distance under the arch of the canal bridge, give a fine effect to this view; drawing nearer and gliding between villages and châteaux, the architecture looks very rich.

MARY WORDSWORTH

(from *Journal of a Tour in Belgium*, 1823)

SEVILLE

As it was my intention to remain at Seville for some months, I determined to hire a house, in which I conceived I could live with more privacy, and at the same time more economically than in a posada. It was not long before I found one in every respect suited to me. It was situated in the Plazuela de la Pila Seca, a retired part of the city, in the neighbourhood of the cathedral, and at a short distance from the gate of Xeres; and in this house, on the arrival of Antonio and the horses, which occurred within a few days, I took up my abode.

I was now once more in beautiful Seville, and had soon ample time and leisure to enjoy its delights and those of the surrounding country; unfortunately, at the time of my arrival, and indeed for the next ensuing fortnight, the heaven of Andalusia, in general so glorious, was overcast with black clouds, which discharged tremendous showers of rain, such as few of the Sevillians, according to their own account, had ever seen before. This extraordinary weather had wrought no little damage in the neighbourhood, causing the Guadalquivir, which, during the rainy season, is a rapid and furious stream, to overflow its banks and to threaten an inundation. It is true that intervals were occurring when the sun made his appearance from his cloudy tabernacle, and with his golden rays caused everything around to smile, enticing the butterfly forth from the bush, and the lizard from the hollow tree, and I invariably availed myself of these intervals to take a hasty promenade.

O how pleasant it is, especially in springtide, to stray along the shores of the Guadalquivir. Not far from the city, down the river, lies a grove called Las Delicias, or the Delights. It consists of trees of various kinds, but more especially of poplars and elms, and is traversed by long shady walks. This grove is the favourite promenade of the Sevillians, and there one occasionally sees assembled whatever the town produces of beauty or gallantry. There wander the black-eyed Andalusian dames and damsels,

clad in their graceful silken mantillas ; and there gallops
the Andalusian cavalier, on his long-tailed thick-maned
steed of Moorish ancestry. As the sun is descending, it is
enchanting to glance back from this place in the direction
of the city ; the prospect is inexpressibly beautiful. Yonder
in the distance, high and enormous, stands the Golden
Tower, now used as a toll-house, but the principal bulwark
of the city in the time of the Moors. It stands on the shore
of the river like a giant keeping watch, and is the first
edifice which attracts the eye of the voyager as he
moves up the stream to Seville. On the other side, opposite the tower, stands the noble Augustine convent, the
ornament of the faubourg of Triana, whilst between the
two edifices rolls the broad Guadalquivir, bearing on its
bosom a flotilla of barks from Catalonia and Valencia.
Farther up is seen the bridge of boats which traverses the
water. The principal object of this prospect, however, is the
Golden Tower, where the beams of the setting sun seem to
be concentrated as in a focus, so that it appears built of
pure gold, and probably from that circumstance received
the name which it now bears. Cold, cold must the heart be
which can remain insensible to the beauties of this magic
scene, to do justice to which the pencil of Claude himself
were barely equal. Often have I shed tears of rapture
whilst I beheld it, and listened to the thrush and the
nightingale piping forth their melodious songs in the
woods, and inhaled the breeze laden with the perfume of
the thousand orange gardens of Seville.

GEORGE BORROW (from *The Bible in Spain*)

THE ISLE OF APHRODITE

(*Cyprus*)

The isle is beautiful : from the edge of the rich, flowery fields on which I trod, to the midway sides of the snowy Olympus, the ground could only here and there show an abrupt crag or a high straggling ridge that upshouldered itself from out of the wilderness of myrtles, and of a thousand bright-leaved shrubs that twined their arms together in lovesome tangles. The air that came to my lips was warm and fragrant as the ambrosial breath of the goddess, infecting me—not (of course) with a faith in the old religion of the isle, but with a sense and apprehension of its mystic power—a power that was still to be obeyed— obeyed by me ; for why otherwise did I toil on with sorry horses to " where, for HER, the hundred altars glowed with Arabian incense, and breathed with the fragrance of garlands ever fresh " ?

I passed a sadly disenchanting night in the cabin of a Greek priest—not a priest of the goddess, but of the Greek Church : there was but one humble room, or rather shed, for man, and priest, and beast. The next morning I reached Baffa (Paphos), a village not far distant from the site of the temple. There was a Greek husbandman there who (not for emolument, but for the sake of the protection and dignity which it afforded) had got leave from the man at Limesol to hoist his flag as a sort of deputy-provision-ary-subvice-pro-acting-consul of the British sovereign. The poor fellow instantly changed his Greek head-gear for the cap of consular dignity, and insisted upon accompanying me to the ruins. I would not have stood this if I could have felt the faintest gleam of my yesterday's pagan piety, but I had ceased to dream, and had nothing to dread from any new disenchanters.

The ruins (the fragments of one or two prostrate pillars) lie upon a promontory, bare and unmystified by the gloom of surrounding groves. My Greek friend in his consular cap stood by, respectfully waiting to see what turn my madness would take now that I had come at last into the presence of the old stones. If you have no taste for research, and can't affect to look for inscriptions, there is some awkwardness in coming to the end of a merely senti-mental pilgrimage, when the feeling which impelled you has gone : in such a strait you have nothing to do but to laugh the thing off as well as you can—and, by-the-bye, it is not a bad plan to turn the conversation (or rather allow the natives to turn it) towards the subject of hidden treasures. This is a topic on which they will always speak with eagerness ; and if they can fancy that you, too, take an interest in such matters, they will not only begin to think you perfectly sane, but will even perhaps give you credit for some more than human powers of forcing dark Earth to show you its hoards of gold.

When we returned to Baffa, the vice-consul seized a club, with the quietly determined air of a brave man re-solved to do some deed of note. He went into the yard ad-joining his cottage, where there were some thin, thought-ful, canting cocks, and serious, low-church-looking hens, respectfully listening, and chickens of tender years so well brought up as scarcely to betray in their conduct the careless levity of youth. The vice-consul stood for a moment quite calm—collecting his strength ; then suddenly he rushed into the midst of the congregation and began to deal death and destruction on all sides ; he spared neither sex nor age. The dead and dying were immediately removed

617

from the field of slaughter, and in less than an hour, I think, they were brought to the table, deeply buried in mounds of snowy rice.

A. W. KINGLAKE (from *Eothen*)

THE ARABIAN DAYS

Damascus Prepares for the Pilgrimage

There is every year a new stirring of this goodly Oriental city in the days before the Haj ; so many strangers are passing in the bazaars, of outlandish speech and clothing from far provinces. The more part are of Asia Minor, many of them bearing overgreat white turbans that might weigh more than their heads : the most are poor folk of a solemn countenance, which wander in the streets seeking the bakers' stalls, and I saw that many of the Damascenes could answer them in their own language. The town is moved in the departure of the great Pilgrimage of the Religion and again at the home-coming, which is made a public spectacle ; almost every Moslem household has some one of their kindred in the caravan.

In the markets there is much taking up in haste of wares for the road. The tent-makers are most busy in their street, overlooking and renewing the old canvas of hundreds of tents, of tilts and the curtains for litters ; the curriers in their bazaar are selling apace the water-skins and leathern buckets and saddle-bottes, *matara* or *zemzemîeh* ; the carpenters' craft are labouring in all haste for the Haj, the most of them mending litter-frames.

618

The Good Traveller

The traveller must be himself, in men's eyes, a man worthy to live under the bent of God's heaven, and were it without a religion : he is such who has a clean human heart and long-suffering under his bare shirt ; it is enough, and though the way be full of harms, he may travel to the ends of the world. Here is a dead land, whence, if he die not, he shall bring home nothing but a perpetual weariness in his bones. The Semites are like to a man sitting in a cloaca to the eyes, and whose brows touch heaven. Of the great antique humanity of the Semitic desert, there is a moment in every adventure, wherein a man may find to make his peace with them, so he know the Arabs. The sour Wahaby fanaticism has in these days cruddled the hearts of the nomads, but every Beduin tent is sanctuary in the land of Ishmael (so there be not in it some cursed Jael). If the outlandish person come alone to strange nomad booths, let him approach boldly, and they will receive him.

The Red House

Before the sunset we came to our white tents pitched beside the ruinous kella, without door and commonly abandoned. Dàr-el-Hamra, " the red house." Ruddy is that earth and the rocks whereof this water-castle is built. High and terrible it showed in the twilight in this desolation of the world.

Sun and Moon

The summer's night at end, the sun stands up as a crown of hostile flames from that huge covert of inhospitable sandstone bergs ; the desert day dawns not little and little, but it is noontide in an hour. The sun, entering as a tyrant upon the waste landscape, darts upon us a torment of fiery beams, not to be remitted till the far-off evening.—No matins here of birds ; not a rock partridge-cock, calling with blithesome chuckle over the extreme waterless desolation. Grave is that giddy heat upon the crown of the head; the ears tingle with a flickering shrillness, a subtle crepitation it seems, in the glassiness of this sun-stricken nature : the hot sand-blink is in the eyes, and there is little refreshment to find in the tents' shelter ; the worsted booths leak to this fiery rain of sunny light. Mountains looming like dry bones through the thin air stand far around about us : the savage flank of Ybba Moghrair, the high spire and ruinous stacks of el-Jebâl, Chebàd, the coast of Helwàn ! Herds of weak nomad camels waver dispersedly, seeking pasture in the midst of this hollow fainting country, where but lately the swarming locusts have fretted every green thing. This silent air burning about us we endure breathless till the assr: when the dazing Arabs in the tents revive after their heavy hours. The lingering day draws down to the sun-setting ; the herdsmen, weary of the sun, come again with the cattle, to taste in their menzils the first sweetness of mirth and repose.—The day is done, and there rises the nightly freshness of this purest mountain air : and then to the cheerful song and the cup at the common fire. The moon rises ruddy from that solemn obscurity of jebel like a mighty beacon :—and the morrow will be as this day, days deadly drowned in the sun of the summer wilderness.

CHARLES DOUGHTY
(from *Travels in Arabia Deserta*)

AN AUSTRALIAN ROBINSON

I found myself on my legs upon the beach, though hardly able to move from exhaustion of mind and body. When at length I had recovered sufficiently to walk about, I made a hasty survey of the little island or sandbank upon which I found myself. Thank God, I did not realise at that moment that I should have to spend a soul-killing *two and a half years* on that desolate, miscroscopical strip of sand ! . .

The great thing was to ward off the dull agony, the killing depression, and manias generally. Fortunately I was of a very active disposition, and as a pastime I took to gymnastics, even as I had at Montreux. I became a most proficient tumbler and acrobat, and could turn two or three somersaults on dashing down from the sloping roof of my hut ; besides, I became a splendid high jumper, with and without pole. Another thing I interested myself in was the construction of a sun-dial. . .

I also played the part of Neptune in a very extraordinary way. I used to wade out to where the turtles were, and on catching a big six-hundred pounder, I would calmly sit astride on his back. Away would swim the startled creature, mostly a foot or so below the surface. When he dived deeper I simply sat far back on the shell, and then he was forced to come up. I steered my queer steeds in a curious way. When I wanted my turtle to turn to the left, I simply thrust my foot into his right eye, and *vice-versâ* for the contrary direction. My two big toes placed simultaneously over both his optics caused a halt so abrupt as almost to unseat me. Before the wet season commenced I put a straw thatch on the roof of my hut, as before stated, and made my quarters as snug as possible. And it was a very necessary precaution, too, for sometimes it rained for days at a stretch. It never kept me indoors, however, and I took exercise just the same, as I didn't bother about clothes, and I rather enjoyed the shower bath. I was always devising means of making life more tolerable, and amongst other things I made a sort of swing, which I found extremely useful in beguiling time. I would also practise jumping with long poles. One day I captured a young pelican, and trained him to accompany me in my walks and help me in my fishing operations. He also acted as a decoy. Frequently I would hide myself in some grass, whilst my pet bird walked a few yards away to attract his fellows. Presently he would be joined by a whole flock, many of which I shot with my bow and arrows, or lassoed. But for my dog—my almost human Bruno—I think I must have died. I used to talk to him just as though he were a human being. We were absolutely inseparable. I preached long sermons to him from Gospel texts. I told him in a loud voice all about my early life and school-days at Montreux; I recounted to him my adventures from the fatal meeting with Poor Peter Jensen in Singapore ; I sang little *chansons* to him, and among these he had his favourites as well as those he disliked cordially. If he did not care for a song, he would set up a pitiful howl.

LOUIS DE ROUGEMONT (from *Adventures*)

A DESCENT INTO ITALY

1. *Above Val Tellina*

Our evening drive was swift and exciting. An impetuous horse whirled us down a steep vine-clad hill, rounding the zigzags at a pace which made perils by mountains sink into insignificance compared to the perils by road. Near a beautiful waterfall tumbling from the opposite hills, the Malero was leapt by a bold arch, and for some time we ran along a terrace, high above the strong glacier torrent.

From the last brow overlooking the Val Tellina the eye rests on one of those wonderful landscapes which tell the southward-bound traveller that he has reached his goal and is at last in Italy.

The great barrier is crossed, and the North is all behind us. The face of the earth, nay the very nature of the air, has changed, colours have a new depth, shadows a new sharpness. From the deep-green carpet of the smooth valley to the crowns of the sunset-flushed hills, all is wealth and luxuriance. No more pines stand stiff in regimental ranks to resist the assaults of winter and rough weather. No mountain rhododendrons collect all their strength in a few tough short shoots, and push themselves forward like hardy skirmishers of the vegetable world into the very abode of snow. Here the " green things of the earth " are all at home and at peace, not as in some high Graubünden valley waging unequal war in an enemy's country. The beeches cluster in friendly companies on the hills. The chestnut-forest rejoicing in a green old age spreads out into the kindly air broad, glossy branches, the vines toss their long arms here and there in sheer exuberance of life. Even on the roadside wall the lizards run in and out amongst beds of cyclamen and tenderest ferns and mosses. The hills seem to stand back and leave room for the sunshine; and the broad, shining town of Sondrio, girt by towers and villas, wears, after the poor hamlets of the mountains, a stately air, as if humanity too shared in the general well-being.

623

Near Cevio the landscape takes a more romantic character. The valley-walls close in and bend, and huge knobs of ruddy-grey rock thrust themselves forward. The river, confined to a narrow bed, alternately lies still in pools, whose depth of blue no comparison can express, or rushes off over the white boulders in a clear sparkling dance. Chestnut-trees hang from the crags overhead ; higher on the hills every ledge is a stripe of verdure fringed with the delicate shapes of the birch and larch. In the far distance a snow-peak in the range above Val Leventina gleams behind the folds of the nearer mountains. . . . The waters at our feet are transparent depths of colour, half sapphire and half emerald, indescribable, and, the moment the eye is taken away, inconceivable, so that every glance becomes a fresh surprise. In the foreground on either bank of the stream are frescoed walls and mossy house-roofs ; beyond is a summer-house supported by pillars, and a heavily laden peach-orchard lit with a blaze of sunflowers. At the gate of Val Bavona a white village glistens from amidst its vineyards. Sheer above it two bold granite walls rise out of the verdure, and form the entrance to a long avenue of great mountain shapes. Behind these foremost masses the hills fall valley-wards in noble and perfectly harmonious lines. Each upper cliff flows down into a slope of chestnut-muffled boulders in a curve, the classical beauty of which is repeated by the vine-tendrils at its feet. In the distance the snows of the Basodine seen through the sunny haze gleam, like a golden halo, on the far-off head of the mountain.

Is human interest wanted to give completeness and a motive to the picture ? As daylight faded I have watched

the swinging torches and low chaunt of those who carried
the Host to some passing soul. In the morning-glow I have
seen a white-robed procession pour slowly with banners
and noise of bells from the yet dark village, then suddenly
issuing into the sunshine, surge, a living wave of brightness, over the high-arched bridges.

D. W. FRESHFIELD (from *Italian Alps*)

NIGHT IN VENICE

Night in Venice! Night is nowhere else so wonderful,
unless it be in winter among the high Alps. But the nights
of Venice and the nights of the mountains are too different
in kind to be compared.

There is the ever-recurring miracle of the full moon
rising, before day is dead, behind San Giorgio, spreading a
path of gold on the lagoon, which black boats traverse
with the glow-worm lamp upon their prow; ascending the
cloudless sky and silvering the domes of the Salute; pouring vitreous sheen upon the red lights of the Piazzetta;
flooding the Grand Canal, and lifting the Rialto higher
in ethereal whiteness; piercing but penetrating not the
murky labyrinth of *rio* linked with *rio* through which we
wind in light and shadow, to reach once more the level
glories and the luminous expanse of heaven beyond
Misericordia.

This is the melodrama of Venetian moonlight; and if a
single impression of the night has to be retained from one
visit to Venice, those are fortunate who chance upon a full
moon of fair weather. Yet I know not whether some

quieter and soberer effects are not more thrilling. To-night, for example, the waning moon will rise late through veils of *scirocco*. Over the bridges of San Cristoforo and San Gregorio, through the deserted Calle di Mezzo, my friend and I walk in darkness, pass the marble basements of the Salute, and push our way along its Riva to the point of the Dogana. We are out at sea alone, between the Canal-ozzo and the Giudecca. A moist wind ruffles the water and cools our forehead. It is so dark that we can only see San Giorgio by the light reflected on it from the Piazzetta. The same light climbs the Campanile of St. Mark, and shows the golden angel in a mystery of gloom. The only noise that reaches us is a confused hum from the Piazza. Sitting and musing there, the blackness of the water whispers in our ears a tale of death. And now we hear a splash of oars, and gliding through the darkness comes a single boat. One man leaps upon the landing-place without a word and disappears. There is another wrapped in a military cloak asleep. I see his face beneath me, pale and quiet. The *barcaruolo* turns the point in silence. From the darkness they came; into the darkness they have gone. It is only an ordinary incident of coastguard service. But the spirit of the night has made a poem of it.

Even tempestuous and rainy weather, though melan-choly enough, is never sordid here. There is no noise from carriage traffic in Venice, and the sea-wind preserves the purity and transparency of the atmosphere. It had been raining all day, but at evening came a partial clearing. I went down to the Molo, where the large reach of the lagoon was all moon-silvered, and San Giorgio Maggiore dark against the bluish sky, and Santa Maria della Salute domed with moon-irradiated pearl, and the wet slabs of the Riva shimmering in moonlight, the whole misty sky, with its clouds and stellar spaces, drenched in moon-light, nothing but moonlight sensible except the tawny flare of gas-lamps and the orange lights of gondolas afloat upon the waters. On such a night the very spirit of Venice is abroad. We feel why she is called Bride of the Sea.

Take yet another night. There had been a representation of Verdi's *Forza del Destino* at the Teatro Malibran. After midnight we walked homeward through the Mer-ceria, crossed the Piazza, and dived into the narrow *calle* which leads to the *traghetto* of the Salute. It was a warm moist starless night, and there seemed no air to breathe in those narrow alleys. The gondolier was half asleep. Eustace called him as we jumped into his boat, and rang our *soldi* on the gunwale. Then he arose and turned the ferro round, and stood across towards the Salute. Silently, insensibly, from the oppression of confinement in the airless streets to the liberty and immensity of the water and the night we passed. It was but two minutes ere we touched the shore and said good-night, and went our way and left the ferryman. But in that brief passage he had opened our souls to everlasting things—the freshness, and the darkness, and the kindness of the brooding, all enfolding night above the sea.

J. A. SYMONDS (from *A Venetian Medley*)

THE GLAMOUR OF THE SEA

1. *The East*

" And this is how I see the East. I have seen its secret places and have looked into its very soul ; but now I see it always from a small boat, a high outline of mountains, blue and far in the morning ; like faint mist at noon ; a jagged

627

wall of purple at sunset. I have the feel of the oar in my hand, the vision of a scorching blue sea in my eyes. And I see a bay, a wide bay, smooth as glass and polished like ice, shimmering in the dark. A red light burns far off upon the gloom of the land, and the night is soft and warm. We drag at the oars with aching arms, and suddenly a puff of wind, a puff faint and tepid and laden with strange odours of blossoms, of aromatic wood, comes out of the still night—the first sigh of the East on my face. That I can never forget. It was impalpable and enslaving, like a charm, like a whispered promise of mysterious delight. . . . When I opened my eyes again the silence was as complete as though it had never been broken. I was lying in a flood of light, and the sky had never looked so far, so high, before. I opened my eyes and lay without moving.

" And then I saw the men of the East—they were looking at me. The whole length of the jetty was full of people. I saw brown, bronze, yellow faces, the black eyes, the glitter, the colour of an Eastern crowd. And all these beings stared without a murmur, without a sigh, without a movement. They stared down at the boats, at the sleeping men who at night had come to them from the sea. Nothing moved. The fronds of palms stood still against the sky. Not a branch stirred along the shore, and the brown roofs of hidden houses peeped through the green foliage, through the big leaves that hung shining and still like leaves forged of heavy metal. This was the East of the ancient navigators, so old, so mysterious, resplendent and sombre, living and unchanged, full of danger and promise. And these were the men. I sat up suddenly. A wave of movement passed through the crowd from end to end, passed along the heads, swayed the bodies, ran along the jetty like a ripple on the water, like a breath of wind on

a field—and all was still again. I see it now—the wide
sweep of the bay, the glittering sands, the wealth of green
infinite and varied, the sea blue like the sea of a dream, the
crowd of attentive faces, the blaze of vivid colour—the
water reflecting it all, the curve of the shore, the jetty, the
high-sterned outlandish craft floating still, and the three
boats with the tired men from the West sleeping, unconscious of the land and the people and of the violence of
sunshine. They slept thrown across the thwarts, curled
on bottom-boards, in the careless attitudes of death. The
head of the old skipper, leaning back in the stern of the
long-boat, had fallen on his breast, and he looked as
though he would never wake. Farther out old Mahon's
face was upturned to the sky, with the long white beard
spread out on his breast, as though he had been shot where
he sat at the tiller ; and a man, all in a heap in the bows
of the boat, slept with both arms embracing the stem-
head and with his cheek laid on the gunwale. The East
looked at them without a sound.

" I have known its fascination since ; I have seen the
mysterious shores, the still water, the lands of brown
nations, where a stealthy Nemesis lies in wait, pursues,
overtakes so many of the conquering race, who are proud
of their wisdom, of their knowledge, of their strength.
But for me all the East is contained in that vision of my
youth. It is all in that moment when I opened my young
eyes on it. I came upon it from a tussle with the sea—and
I was young—and I saw it looking at me. And this is all
that is left of it ! Only a moment ; a moment of strength, of
romance, of glamour—of youth ! . . . A flick of sunshine
upon a strange shore, the time to remember, the time for
a sigh, and—good-bye !—Night—Good-bye . . . ! "

He drank.

" Ah ! The good old time—the good old time. Youth and the sea. Glamour and the sea ! The good, strong sea, the salt, bitter sea, that could whisper to you and roar at you and knock your breath out of you."

He drank again.

" By all that's wonderful it is the sea, I believe, the sea itself—or is it youth alone ? Who can tell ? But you here —you all had something out of life : money, love—whatever one gets on shore—and, tell me, wasn't that the best time, that time when we were young at sea ; young and had nothing, on the sea that gives nothing, except hard knocks—and sometimes a chance to feel your strength— that only—what you all regret ? "

And we all nodded at him : the man of finance, the man of accounts, the man of law, we all nodded at him over the polished table that like a still sheet of brown water reflected our faces, lined, wrinkled ; our faces marked by toil, by deceptions, by success, by love ; our weary eyes looking still, looking always, looking anxiously for something out of life, that while it is expected is already gone— has passed unseen, in a sigh, in a flash—together with the youth, with the strength, with the romance of illusions.

2. *The Old River*

The day was ending in a serenity of still and exquisite brilliance. The water shone pacifically ; the sky, without a speck, was a benign immensity of unstained light ; the very mist on the Essex marshes was like a gauzy and radiant fabric, hung from the wooded rises inland, and draping the low shores in diaphanous folds. Only the gloom to the west, brooding over the upper reaches, became more sombre every minute, as if angered by the approach of the sun.

And at last, in its curved and imperceptible fall, the sun sank low, and from glowing white changed to a dull red without rays and without heat, as if about to go out suddenly, stricken to death by the touch of that gloom brooding over a crowd of men.

Forthwith a change came over the waters, and the serenity became less brilliant but more profound. The old river in its broad reach rested unruffled at the decline of day, after ages of good service done to the race that peopled its banks, spread out in the tranquil dignity of a waterway leading to the uttermost ends of the earth. We looked at the venerable stream not in the vivid flush of a short day that comes and departs for ever, but in the august light of abiding memories. And indeed nothing is easier for a man who has, as the phrase goes, " followed the sea " with reverence and affection, than to evoke the great spirit of the past upon the lower reaches of the Thames. The tidal current runs to and fro in its unceasing service, crowded with memories of men and ships ithad borne to the rest of home or to the battles of the sea. It had known and served all the men of whom the nation is proud, from Sir Francis Drake to Sir John Franklin, knights all, titled and untitled —the great knights-errant of the sea. It had borne all the ships whose names are like jewels flashing in the night of time, from the *Golden Hind* returning with her round flanks full of treasure, to be visited by the Queen's Highness and thus pass out of the gigantic tale, to the *Erebus* and *Terror*, bound on other conquests—and that never returned. It had known the ships and the men. They had sailed from Deptford, from Greenwich, from Erith—the adventurers and the settlers ; kings' ships and the ships

of men on 'Change ; captains, admirals, the dark " inter-
lopers " of the Eastern trade, and the commissioned
" generals " of East India fleets. Hunters for gold or pur-
suers of fame, they all had gone out on that stream, bearing
the sword, and often the torch, messengers of the might
within the land, bearers of a spark from the sacred fire.
What greatness had not floated on the ebb of that river
into the mystery of an unknown earth ! . . . The dreams of
men, the seed of commonwealths, the gems of empires.

The sun set ; the dusk fell on the stream, and lights
began to appear along the shore. The Chapman lighthouse, a three-legged thing erect on a mud-flat, shone
strongly. Lights of ships moved in the fairway—a great
stir of lights going up and going down. And farther west
on the upper reaches the place of the monstrous town was
still marked ominously on the sky, a brooding gloom in
sunshine, a lurid glare under the stars.

JOSEPH CONRAD
(1. from *Youth*. 2. from *Heart of Darkness*)

A ROMAN PILGRIMAGE

The sun was conquering me, and I was looking hope-
lessly for a place to sleep, when a cart drawn by two oxen
at about one mile an hour came creaking by. The driver
was asleep, his head on the shady side. The devil tempted
me, and without one struggle against temptation, nay with
cynical and congratulatory feelings, I jumped up behind,
and putting my head also on the shady side (there were
soft sacks for a bed) I very soon was pleasantly asleep.

We lay side by side for hour after hour, and the day

rose on to noon; the sun beat upon our feet, but our heads were in the shade and we slept heavily a good and honest sleep: he thinking that he was alone, but I knowing that I was in company (a far preferable thing), and I was right and he was wrong. And the heat grew, and sleep came out of that hot sun more surely than it does out of the night air in the north. But no dreams wander under the noon.

From time to time one or the other of us would open our eyes drowsily and wonder, but sleep was heavy on us both, and our minds were sunk in calm like old hulls in the dark depths of the sea where there are no storms.

We neither of us really woke until, at the bottom of the hill which rises into Acquapendente, the oxen stopped. This halt woke us up; first me and then my companion. He looked at me a moment and laughed. He seemed to have thought all this while that I was some country friend of his who had taken a lift; and I, for my part, had made more or less certain that he was a good fellow who would do me no harm. I was right, and he was wrong. I knew not what offering to make him to compensate him for his trouble which his heavy oxen had taken. After some thought I brought a cigar out of my pocket, which he smoked with extreme pleasure. The oxen meanwhile had been urged up the slow hill, and it was in this way that we reached the famous town of Acquapendente. But why it should be called famous is more than I can understand. It may be that in one of those narrow streets there is a picture or a church, or one of those things which so attract unbelieving men. To the pilgrim it is simply a group of houses. Into one of these I went, and, upon my soul, I have nothing to say of it except that they furnished me with food. . .

The road was interminable, and the crest, from which I promised myself the view of the crater-lake, was always just before me, and was never reached. A little spring, caught in a hollow log, refreshed a meadow on the right. Drinking there again, I wondered if I should go on or rest; but I was full of antiquity, and a memory in the blood, or what not, impelled me to see the lake in the crater before I went to sleep: after a few hundred yards this obsession was satisfied.

I passed between two banks, where the road had been worn down at the crest of the volcano's rim; then at once, far below, in a circle of silent trees with here and there a vague shore of marshy land, I saw the Pond of Venus: some miles of brooding water, darkened by the dark slopes around it. At its hither end a hill, that had once been a cone in the crater, stood out all covered with a dense wood. It was the Hill of Venus. There was no temple, nor no sacrifice, nor no ritual for the Divinity, save this solemn attitude of perennial silence; but under the influence which still remained and gave the place its savour, it was impossible to believe that the gods were dead. There were no men in that hollow; nor was there any memory of men, save of men dead these thousand of years. There was no life of visible things. The mind released itself and was in touch with whatever survives of conquered but immortal Spirits.

Thus ready for worship, and in a mood of adoration; filled also with the genius which inhabits its native place and is too subtle or too pure to suffer the effect of time, I passed down the ridge-way of the mountain rim, and came to the edge overlooking that arena whereon was first fought out and decided the chief destiny of the world.

For all below was the Campagna. Names that are at the

origin of things attached to every cleft and distant rock
beyond the spreading level, or sanctified the gleams of
rivers. There below me was Veii ; beyond, in the Wall of
the Apennines, only just escaped from clouds, was
Tibur that dignified the ravine at the edge of their rising ;
that crest to the right was Tusculum, and far to the
south, but clear on a mountain answering my own, was the
mother of the City, Alba Longa. The Tiber, a dense,
brown fog rolling over and concealing it, was the god of
the wide plain. There and at that moment I should have
seen the City. I stood up on the bank and shaded my eyes,
straining to catch the dome at least in the sunlight ; but
I could not, for Rome was hidden by the low Sabinian
hills.

HILAIRE BELLOC (from *The Path to Rome*)

SAN ANTONIO OF THE RIO MADEIRA

Where we were anchored, San Antonio was in view,
about five miles up stream. Where at the end of that
reach of river a line of tremulous light, which we thought
was the cataracts, bridged the converging palisades of the
jungle, in the trees of the right bank it was sometimes
easy to believe there was a glint of white buildings. But
looking again, to reassure your sight, the apparition of
dwellings vanished. At night, in the quiet, sometimes the
ears could detect the shudder of the weighty rapids by
San Antonio ; but it was merely a tremor felt ; there was
no sound. The village remained to us for some time just
that uncertain gleam by day, and the rapids but a minute
reduction of a turmoil that was far. For in that languorous

heat we counted miles differently, and it was pleasanter to suspect than to go and prove, and much easier.

One day I went. When in a small boat the jungle towered. The river, too, had a different character. From the shore, or from the big *Capella*, the river was an expanse of light, an impression of shining peace. Whenever you got close to its surface it became alive and menacingly intimate. Our little boat seemed to roll in the powerful folds of a monster which wallowed ponderously and without ceasing. The trees afloat, charging down swiftly and in what one felt was an ominous quiet, stood well above our tiny craft.

We steered close in-shore to avoid the drifting wood and the set of the current. The jungle's sheer height, confusion, and intensity were more awesome than when seen from the steamer. Not many of the trees were of great beam, but their consistent height, with the lianas in a wreck from the far overhanging cornice, dwarfed our boat to an unimportant straw. At times the forest had a selvage of cane, and growths of arrow grass, bearing long white plumes twelve feet above us, and a pair of fan-shaped leaves resembling palm leaves. . .

The little huddle of San Antonio's white houses is on slightly rising ground, and the lambent green of the jungle is beside them and over them. The foliage presses the village down to the river. Like every Amazonian town and village, it appears, set in that forest, as rare a human foothold as a ship in mid-ocean ; a few lights and a few voices in the dark and interminable wastes. So I landed from our little craft elated with a sense of luckily acquired security.

The white embowered village, the leaping fountains and the rocks, the air in a flutter with the shock of

ponderous water collapsing, the surmounting island in mid-
stream with its coronet of palms, the half-naked Indians
idling among the Bolivian rubber boats hauled up to the
foreshore below, the unexplored jungle which closed in
and framed the scene, the fierce sun set in the rounded
amplitude of the clouds of the rains, made the tropical
picture which was the right reward for a great journey.
I had come down long weeks of empty leisure, in which the
mind got farther and farther away from the cities where
time is so carefully measured and highly valued. The
centre of the ultimate wilderness was more than a matter of
fact. It was now a personal conviction which needed no
verification.

H. M. TOMLINSON (from *The Sea and the Jungle*)

THE GOLDEN JOURNEY

We who with songs beguile your pilgrimage
    And swear that Beauty lives though lilies die,
We Poets of the proud old lineage
    Who sing to find your hearts, we know not why,—

What shall we tell you ? Tales, marvellous tales
    Of ships and stars and isles where good men rest,
Where nevermore the rose of sunset pales,
    And winds and shadows fall toward the West :

And there the world's first huge white-bearded kings
    In dim glades sleeping, murmur in their sleep,
And closer round their breasts the ivy clings,
    Cutting its pathway slow and red and deep.

And how beguile you ? Death has no repose
   Warmer and deeper than that Orient sand
Which hides the beauty and bright faith of those
   Who made the Golden Journey to Samarkand.

And now they wait and whiten peaceably,
   Those conquerors, those poets, those so fair :
They know time comes, not only you and I,
   But the whole world shall whiten, here or there ;

When those long caravans that cross the plain
   With dauntless feet and sound of silver bells
Put forth no more for glory or for gain,
   Take no more solace from the palm-girt wells ;

When the great markets by the sea shut fast
   All that calm Sunday that goes on and on :
When even lovers find their peace at last,
   And Earth is but a star, that once had shone.

               J. E. FLECKER (from *Prologue*)

FOURTH PART

§1 MOON AND STARS

Canst thou bind the sweet influences of Pleiades, or loose the bands of Orion? Canst thou bring forth Mazzaroth in his season? Or canst thou guide Arcturus with his sons? Knowest thou the ordinances of heaven? Canst thou set the dominion thereof in the earth?

JOB xxxix. (A.V.)

When in heaven the stars about the bright moon shine clear to see, when the air is windless and all the peaks appear and the tall headlands and glades and from heaven breaketh open the infinite air and all the stars are seen, then the shepherd's heart is glad.

HOMER (*Iliad*)

The massy shoulder of Orion came heaving up . . . first one bright star, then another; then the gleaming girdle. . . . As the constellation rose, so presently new vigour entered into the trees, the sap moved, the buds thrust forth, the new leaf came, and the nightingale travelling up from the south sang in the musical April nights.

RICHARD JEFFERIES (*Bevis*)

§I MOON AND STARS

THE PROBLEM OF THE HEAVENS

The generations of men observed that the pageant of heaven and the seasons of the year came round in regular succession, and they could not discover the causes of these movements. Hence they sought refuge by leaving all this in the hands of the gods, supposing everything to be guided by them. And they placed the gods' abode in the heavens, because night and moon were seen to revolve through the sky—moon, day and night and night's grave stars, night-wandering meteors, clouds and sun, rain and snow, winds, lightnings, hail, and the loud blasts of thunder.

O unhappy race of men, to charge such doings to the gods, ascribing to them bitter wrath! What groans did our forefathers thus beget for themselves, what wounds for us, what tears for future generations! It is no mark of piety to be seen often with veiled head approaching every altar, falling prostrate on the ground and spreading out the palms before the statues of the gods, or sprinkling their altars with the flowing blood of beasts, linking vow to vow—true piety it is to be able to look upon all things with a mind at peace. Yet, when we lift our eyes to the heavenly regions of the upper world, to the ether filled with glittering stars, and think of the journeys of sun and moon, then another misgiving suddenly arises in our hearts already burdened with other ills—the fear that perchance the gods have an unlimited power over us, if indeed they are able to roll the bright stars in their various motions. And we are sorely puzzled, finding no answer to these questions—whether there was ever a birth-time of the world, whether there is to be an end of it, whether the heavenly ramparts will be unable to endure the strain of this mysterious motion or whether endowed with ever-lasting existence they can glide on through never-ending time, defying the strong powers of immeasurable ages. Again, what human mind does not quail with fear of the gods, what human limbs do not sink with terror, when the scorched earth shakes with the thunderbolt's appalling shock and the great sky resounds with rumblings? Do not the nations then tremble and their proud rulers shrink smitten with terror, lest for some evil deed or some proud word the solemn day of punishment be now come? When too, the utmost fury of a violent wind strikes the sea and sweeps over its waters the admiral of a fleet with his mighty legions and his elephants, does he not beseech the gods' peace with vows, does he not tremble and pray for an end of the storm and for favouring breezes; but all in vain, since none the less he is often seized by the hurricane and driven upon the shoals of death? So does some hidden power constantly trample upon us, treading underfoot the noble rods and cruel axes of human author-ity, holding them in derision. Again, when the earth quakes beneath our feet, and cities rock or fall, what wonder if mortal men abase themselves and acknow-ledge that the gods have marvellous powers—sufficient to govern all things!

LUCRETIUS (*De Rerum Natura,* V—Trans. A. S.)

THE HARPER OF DIDO

Sweet soundeth the golden harp with the song of the
    long-haired Iopas,
For Atlas the Great was his teacher. Now sings he of
    moonrise and moonset,
Now tells of the Sun and his toiling, of men and of beasts
    the beginnings—
Of lightning and storm, Arcturus, of Hyades wet and
    the Bear-stars;
Why Winter hurries the Sun to his bed in the deeps of the
    ocean,
When nights are so heavy with darkness, so gloomy and
    tardy in passing.

VIRGIL (Æneid, Bk. I—Trans. A. S.)

HOW THE EARTH WAS MADE

A few stars are known which are hardly bigger than the
earth, but the majority are so large that hundreds of thousands of earths could be packed inside each and leave
room to spare ; here and there we come upon a giant star
large enough to contain millions of millions of earths. And
the total number of stars in the universe is probably something like the total number of grains of sand on all the sea-
shores of the world. Such is the littleness of our home in
space when measured up against the total substance of
the universe.

This vast multitude of stars are wandering about in

space. A few form groups which journey in company, but the majority are solitary travellers. And they travel through a universe so spacious that it is an event of almost unimaginable rarity for a star to come anywhere near to another star. For the most part each voyages in splendid isolation, like a ship on an empty ocean. In a scale model in which the stars are ships, the average ship will be well over a million miles from its nearest neighbour, whence it is easy to understand why a ship seldom finds another within hailing distance.

We believe, nevertheless, that some two thousand million years ago this rare event took place, and that a second star, wandering blindly through space, happened to come within hailing distance of the sun. Just as the sun and moon raise tides on the earth, so this second star must have raised tides on the surface of the sun. But they would be very different from the puny tides which the small mass of the moon raises in our oceans; a huge tidal wave must have travelled over the surface of the sun, ultimately forming a mountain of prodigious height, which would rise ever higher and higher as the cause of the disturbance came nearer and nearer. And, before the second star began to recede, its tidal pull had become so powerful that this mountain was torn to pieces and threw off small fragments of itself, much as the crest of a wave throws off spray. These small fragments have been circulating around their parent sun ever since. They are the planets, great and small, of which our earth is one.

SIR JAMES JEANS (from *The Mysterious Universe*)

644

Each living cell that floats in protoplasm has a kind of protecting membrane round it; and of such is our intellect to us who float in cosmic protoplasm, and are being perpetually bombarded by stellar and universal influences that, though we know it not, pierce through and through the thinking cell that is man. They come to us by night and by day, the messages and communications for which we have been so ardently longing; not in the childish articulate language we have sought to impose on the spheres, but in a manner far subtler, more cogent, more irresistible, than if they had been words spoken from the very crown of the sky.

Our earth being poised in the centre of the universe, where all is centre; living and developing there like a child in its mother's womb, must of necessity be in constant communication, communion, symbiosis with the universe. Nothing can happen there that has not its effect, reverberation, on the earth. In the entire universe the elements are everywhere the same as on our own globe; few in number and unvarying, however distant a star may be and whatever its temperature. In the whole Cosmos our spectroscope reveals nothing that we have not; when the presence of unknown gases or substances was suspected, indications furnished by the stars themselves helped our chemists to identify similar bodies on the earth. Behind solid matter, behind gases and fluids that hide it, lurks the electron, perpetual, eternal, universal, immortal; the most infinitely little of the infinitely little, and yet propelling the infinitely great. The limitless All, with its nebulæ, galaxies, vast hidden spaces that even light cannot reach, with its new worlds that suddenly spring into being, floats in the ether, most inevitable of all the fluids and the one of which we know least; the ether whose waves will transmit through eternity, through measureless areas of millions of light-years, the flash of light sent by a star so remote that most of the worlds will be dead or extinct before it can reach them.

M. MAETERLINCK

(from *The Magic of the Stars*—Trans. A. SUTRO)

THE MARINER'S BENEDICTION

In his loneliness and fixedness he yearneth towards the journeying Moon, and the stars that still sojourn, yet still move onward; and every where the blue sky belongs to them, and is their appointed rest, and their native country and their own natural homes, which they enter unannounced, as lords that are certainly expected, and yet there is a silent joy at their arrival. By the light of the Moon he beholdeth God's creatures of the great calm —their beauty and their happiness. He blesseth them in his heart.

COLERIDGE

(from *The Ancient Mariner*—Prose Argument)

VOICES OF THE NIGHT

I remember nothing better than the time when in the south country I was first able to look out night after night over woods and fields, with nothing but one small country town halfway between my window and the

646

Downs and the sea twenty-five miles away; to hear the fox's bark, the hoot of owls, and the song of nightingales answering one another away down the valley. A vixen's scream is surely the most unearthly of night noises, just as the purr of the nightjar and the stick-and-comb chatter of the landrail are the most homely and soothing; though even the vixen's scream is not much less startling than, heard within a few yards, the screech of the white owl. But the sound of sounds of the night is the hoot of the brown owl. That long-drawn, deep music of the night, the voice and vigour of life unseen, comes from the heart of the wood.

These sounds of night belong to an open window. But to know other sounds, to learn what can be the noise or the silence of darkness, you must walk by night alone. It has fallen to my lot to spend many hours at all times of the night alone, in English woods and fields, and I have heard many sounds and have seen sights I should never have known so well in any other way. The grunts and squeals of badgers at their earth only a few yards away up the hill; rats cracking hazel-nuts in the trees above my head; an otter taking the water of a stream in a place where no otter was ever found by hounds. Songs of birds; I have heard the cuckoo often, and the wood-pigeon once, and snatches of other song, lark's and chaffinch's and robin's, —sometimes it seemed as if the bird sang without thought, sometimes as if it was suddenly angered or alarmed. Mallard on the wing, curlew, whimbrel; the whee-yoh of widgeon, the screwy calls of coot, the lapping noises of duck feeding on ooze, though these, too, may be sounds of the day as well.

Yet they are sounds to be heard more clearly and more separately by night; and as for sights, only he who has walked many hours in the dark knows that there are few nights in the summer when he will not see the horizon leap with lightning, and that winter lightning is not much less common. And that the cold glory of moonlight over wood and field is only part of the night ; the deepness of night is over a man when the moon is down, and he waits under the dome of stars to hear and to see ; to listen for the owl and the fox ; to watch Vega swing behind the naked oak, and Orion with his jewelled sword journeying high above the southern hills.

ERIC PARKER (from *English Wild Life*)

HOUSES OF THE SUN

Thousands of years ago the Chaldean astronomers saw the Sun as a traveller through the heavens who stayed in certain houses on his way, and Job (A.V. xxxviii. 32) gives the name " Mazzaroth " to the great series of hostels provided for this illustrious traveller. Along the curving road which he apparently followed (his orbit or ecliptic) certain groups of stars were seen in association with his movement. This starry pathway across the sky was called the Zodiac or " animal circle " (Greek, *zodiacos*), for all the constellations in it with one exception (*Libra*) were seen as figures of living creatures. Within this zone, it was noticed, lay the track of other lesser travellers—the moon and the five planets known to the ancients (we can now see eight under favourable conditions). So the Zodiac was divided into twelve Houses or " Signs " (one for each month of the year), a twelfth part of the whole circular band being assigned to each of its twelve star-groups or constellations. Each sign was given an appropriate symbol and a name. The names are :

SPRING. *Aries* (the Ram), *Taurus* (the Bull), *Gemini* (the Twins) ;

SUMMER. *Cancer* (the Crab), *Leo* (the Lion), *Virgo* (the Virgin) ;

AUTUMN. *Libra* (the Scales), *Scorpio* (the Scorpion), *Sagittarius* (the Archer) ;

WINTER. *Capricornus* (the Goat), *Aquarius* (the Water-carrier), and *Pisces* (the Fishes). They are easily remembered by the help of this old rhyme :

> *The Ram, the Bull, the Heavenly Twins,*
> *And next the Crab the Lion shines,*
> *The Virgin and the Scales,*
> *The Scorpion, Archer and Sea-goat,*
> *The Man that bears the watering-pot,*
> *And Fish with glittering tails.*

Or, if you prefer a more stately measure, by the following verses :

> *Behold our orbit as through twice six signs*
> *Our central Sun apparently inclines :*
> *The Golden Fleece his pale ray first adorns,*
> *Then tow'rds the Bull he winds and gilds his horns ;*
> *Castor and Pollux then receive his ray ;*
> *On burning Cancer then he seems to stay ;*
> *On flaming Leo pours the liquid shower ;*
> *Then faints beneath the Virgin's conquering power ;*
> *Now the just Scales weigh well both day and night ;*
> *The Scorpion then receives the solar light ;*

649

Then quivered Chiron clouds his wintry face,
And the tempestuous Sea-goat mends his pace ;
Now in the water Sol's warm beams are quench'd,
Till with the Fishes he is fairly drench'd.
These twice six signs successively appear,
And mark the twelve months of the circling year.

The symbols are mostly conventional pictures. Thus, the symbol for *Aquarius* is the Egyptian character for water. The origin of the signs for *Leo, Capricornus,* and *Virgo* is obscure.

The Sun stays for a month (i.e., a solar month, a little longer than a lunar month) in each of his Houses ; or, more properly speaking, he spends this time in passing through each. The House of the Sun on any particular day can easily be ascertained. Imagine the twelve star-groups as represented by the hours marked on the dial of a watch, the first constellation (*Aries*) being one o'clock. If there is a full moon, and the moon is in the second constellation (*Taurus*), then the Sun must be on the *opposite* side of the ecliptic in the eighth constellation (*Scorpio*). If the moon is not full, observe the constellation which is in the south at midnight, and the Sun will be in its opposite.

" The first point of *Aries* " was the Vernal Equinox, when the Sun crossed the equator going north and days and nights are equal throughout the world. This point was fixed according to the position of the *Aries* star-group in relation to the Sun at the time (several thousand years ago) when the ancients provided these Houses for the Sun. It happens, however, that the Sun does not now enter *Aries* exactly in accordance with this old man-made time-table, for the equinoctial points have a continuous westerly motion or " drift," the direction of the earth's axis with reference to the stars changing slowly. Consequently the pole-star of one age is not the pole-star of another. Hipparchus, a Greek astronomer of the second century B.C., discovered that the year of the seasons was shorter than the solar year. It seemed that the equinoxes stepped forward a little (" preceded ") to meet the Sun. This phenomenon, known as the precession of the equinoxes, was first explained by Newton, who found it was due to the attraction of the sun and moon on the bulging equator of the earth. Our planet rotates like a wobbly spinning top, whose slanting axis rotates as the top spins. It takes nearly 26,000 years to make one complete wobble. As a result of this behaviour the signs of the Zodiac no longer correspond to its star-groups. Each sign has " backed " into the constellation west of it, so that the sign of *Aries* is now in the constellation of *Pisces*. The equinoctial points have been moving slowly westward since the ancient astronomers assigned these Houses to the Sun, but it is satisfactory to know that, when a cycle of about 26,000 years has been completed, the Sun will once more enter *Aries* punctually at the Vernal Equinox.

A. S.

THE MAN IN THE MOON

Look out for a dusky form on the western side of the moon when it is eight days old, and if you have the eye of a lunarian you will see the Man in the Moon ; and you will (in such case) also observe the thornbush carried on his back and the small dark figure of his little dog. It is difficult to say how he got there. As to his identity, the

popular view common to many nations has connected him
with the Sabbath-breaker whose short history is recorded
in the Bible. " While the children of Israel were in the
wilderness they found a man that gathered sticks upon
the Sabbath day" (*Numbers*, Chap. xv). They brought the
culprit to Moses and Aaron, and he was stoned to death
without the camp. This punishment would seem to be
both severe and conclusive. The mediæval mind, however, was not content with it, and embellished the story
with the addition of perpetual banishment to the cold
regions of the moon, recording a curse pronounced in the
following terms : " As you regarded not *Sunday* on
earth, you shall keep a perpetual *Moonday* in heaven."
These mediæval writers, in whom the historic sense was
but feebly developed, quite overlooked the fact that the
position of Man in the Moon was already occupied by
Cain, who—condemned to be a fugitive on earth—was
generally understood to have taken refuge in the moon.
It is true that Beatrice " smiled a little " when Dante
asked for an explanation of those dusky marks on the
moon which made folk on earth " tell the tale of Cain "
(*Par*. II). In spite of the learned explanations he then
received, Dante later on decorates his verse with this
legend, poetically describing moonset in these words :
" Cain and his thorns already touch the wave." But,
whoever he was, it is clear that there was somebody in the
moon with a bush or a bundle of sticks, and Bottom the
weaver, preparing his play for Duke Theseus, was careful
to provide Moonshine by means of a man with a bush of
thorns.

There are some people who see a sort of facial expression on the moon at the full, and to these the Man in the
Moon is nothing more than this jolly round face. There are

others who object to this view as a derogation of the moon's manhood, since it causes the Man in the Moon to dwindle like the Cheshire cat in *Alice in Wonderland*, leaving us nothing but a smile. Truly, as Lyly says in his Prologue to *Endymion*, " there liveth none under the sun that knows what to make of the Man in the Moon." It is likely that the only people who know the truth of the matter are *lunatics*, properly so called.

A. S.

THE GREAT BEAR

Last night Jones was walking down with me from Staple Inn to Clifford's Inn, about 10 o'clock, and we saw the Great Bear standing upright on the tip of his tail which was coming out of a chimney pot. Jones said it wanted attending to. I said :

" Yes, but to attend to it properly we ought to sit up with it all night, and if the Great Bear thinks that I am going to sit by his bed-side and give him a spoonful of barley-water every ten minutes, he will find himself much mistaken."

SAMUEL BUTLER (from Note-Books)

TOM OF BEDLAM

The moon's my constant mistress,
And the lonely owl my marrow ;
  The flaming drake
  And the night-crow make
Me music to my sorrow.

I know more than Apollo,
For oft, when he lies sleeping,
  I see the stars
   At mortal wars
In the wounded welkin weeping,

The moon embrace her shepherd,
And the Queen of Love her warrior,
  While the first doth horn
   The star of morn,
And the next the heavenly farrier.

With a host of furious fancies
Whereof I am commander,
  With a burning spear
   And a horse of air
To the wilderness I wander;

By a knight of ghosts and shadows
I summoned am to tourney
  Ten leagues beyond
   The wide world's end—
Methinks it is no journey.

ANONYMOUS

A COMPLAINT BY NIGHT

Alas, so all things now do hold their peace!
  Heaven and earth disturbèd in no thing;
The beasts, the air, the birds their song do cease,
  The nightès car the stars about doth bring;

Calm is the sea ; the waves work less and less :
   So am not I, whom love, alas ! doth wring,
Bringing before my face the great increase
   Of my desires, whereat I weep and sing,
In joy and woe, as in a doubtful case.
   For my sweet thoughts sometime do pleasure bring ;
But by and by, the cause of my disease
   Gives me a pang that inwardly doth sting,
When that I think what grief it is again
To live and lack the thing should rid my pain.

EARL OF SURREY (after PETRARCH)

A TALK BY MOONLIGHT

(*Enter* LORENZO and JESSICA.)

LORENZO : The moon shines bright : in such a night as
   this,
When the sweet wind did gently kiss the trees
And they did make no noise, in such a night
Troilus methinks mounted the Trojan walls
And sigh'd his soul toward the Grecian tents,
Where Cressid lay that night.
JESSICA :   In such a night
Did Thisbe fearfully o'ertrip the dew
And saw the lion's shadow ere himself
And ran dismay'd away.
LORENZO :   In such a night
Stood Dido with a willow in her hand
Upon the wild sea banks and waft her love
To come again to Carthage.

JESSICA :   In such a night
Medea gather'd the enchanted herbs
That did renew old Æson.
LORENZO :   In such a night
Did Jessica steal from the wealthy Jew
And with an unthrift love did run from Venice
As far as Belmont.
JESSICA :   In such a night
Did young Lorenzo swear he loved her well,
Stealing her soul with many vows of faith
And ne'er a true one.
LORENZO :   In such a night
Did pretty Jessica, like a little shrew,
Slander her love, and he forgave it her.

SHAKESPEARE (from *Merchant of Venice*)

WINTER NIGHTS

Now winter nights enlarge
The number of their hours ;
And clouds their storms discharge
Upon the airy towers.
Let now the chimneys blaze
And cups o'erflow with wine,
Let well-tuned words amaze
With harmony divine !
Now yellow waxen lights
Shall wait on honey love
While youthful revels, masques,
    and courtly sights,
Sleep's leaden spells remove.

656

This time doth well dispense
With lovers' long discourse ;
Much speech hath some defence,
Though beauty no remorse.
All do not all things well ;
Some measures comely tread
Some knotted riddles tell,
Some poems smoothly read.
The summer hath his joys,
And winter his delights,
Though love and all his pleasures
   are but toys,
They shorten tedious nights.

THOMAS CAMPION

HYMN TO DIANA

Queen and huntress, chaste and fair,
  Now the sun is laid to sleep,
Seated in thy silver chair,
    State in wonted manner keep :
     Hesperus entreats thy light,
     Goddess excellently bright !

Earth, let not thy envious shade
  Dare itself to interpose ;
Cynthia's shining orb was made
    Heaven to clear when day did close :
     Bless us then with wishèd sight,
     Goddess excellently bright !

Lay thy bow of pearl apart,
    And thy crystal-shining quiver;
Give unto the flying hart
    Space to breathe, how short soever :
        Thou that mak'st a day of night—
        Goddess excellently bright !

BEN JONSON

A SONNET OF THE MOON

Look how the pale Queen of the silent night
Doth cause the ocean to attend upon her,
And he as long as she is in his sight,
With his full tide is ready her to honour :
But when the silver waggon of the Moon
Is mounted up so high he cannot follow,
The sea calls home his crystal waves to moan,
And with low ebb doth manifest his sorrow ;
So you, that are the sovereign of my heart,
Have all my joys attending on your will ;
My joys low-ebbing when you do depart,
When you return, their tide my heart doth fill ;
    So as you come, and as you do depart,
    Joys ebb and flow within my tender heart.

CHARLES BEST (1602)

NIGHT-PIECE, TO JULIA

Her eyes the glow-worm lend thee,
The shooting stars attend thee;
    And the elves also,
    Whose little eyes glow
Like the sparks of fire, befriend thee.

No will-o'-the-wisp mislight thee;
Nor snake or slow-worm bite thee:
    But on, on thy way
    Not making a stay,
Since ghost there's none to affright thee.

Let not the dark thee cumber;
What though the moon does slumber?
    The stars of the night
    Will lend thee their light,
Like tapers clear without number.

Then, Julia, let me woo thee,
Thus, thus to come unto me:
    And when I shall meet
    Thy silvery feet,
My soul I'll pour into thee.

ROBERT HERRICK

MIDNIGHT

All things are hushed, as Nature's self lay dead ;
The mountains seem to nod their drowsy head,
The little birds in dreams their songs repeat,
And sleeping flowers beneath the night-dew sweat ;
Even lust and envy sleep, yet love denies
Rest to my soul and slumber to my eyes.

                                    DRYDEN

A NIGHT-PIECE

————The sky is overcast
With a continuous cloud of texture close,
Heavy and wan, all whitened by the Moon,
Which through that veil is indistinctly seen,
A dull, contracted circle, yielding light
So feebly spread that not a shadow falls
Chequering the ground—from rock, plant, tree, or
    tower.
At length a pleasant instantaneous gleam
Startles the pensive traveller while he treads
His lonesome path, with unobserving eye
Bent earthwards ; he looks up—the clouds are split
Asunder,—and above his head he sees
The clear Moon, and the glory of the heavens.
There, in a black-blue vault she sails along,
Followed by multitudes of stars, that, small
And sharp, and bright, along the dark abyss
Drive as she drives : how fast they wheel away,
Yet vanish not !—the wind is in the tree,

But they are silent ;—still they roll along
Immeasurably distant ; and the vault,
Built round by those white clouds, enormous clouds,
Still deepens its unfathomable depth.
At length the Vision closes ; and the mind,
Not undisturbed by the delight it feels,
Which slowly settles into peaceful calm,
Is left to muse upon the solemn scene.

WORDSWORTH

LUCY

The stars of midnight shall be dear
To her ; and she shall lean her ear
In many a secret place
Where rivulets dance their wayward round,
And beauty born of murmuring sound
Shall pass into her face.

WORDSWORTH

SONNET TO NIGHT

Mysterious Night ! when our first parent knew
  Thee from report divine, and heard thy name,
  Did he not tremble for this lovely frame,
This glorious canopy of light and blue ?
Yet 'neath a curtain of translucent dew,
  Bathed in the rays of the great setting flame,
  Hesperus with the host of heaven came,
And lo ! Creation widened in man's view.

Who could have thought such darkness lay concealed
Within thy beams, O Sun! or who could find,
  Whilst flow'r and leaf and insect stood revealed,
That to such countless orbs thou mad'st us blind!
  Why do we then shun Death with anxious strife?
  If Light can thus deceive, wherefore not Life?

JOSEPH BLANCO WHITE

ALL THROUGH THE NIGHT
(*To an old Welsh air*)

Deep the silence round us spreading,
  All through the night;
Dark the path that we are treading
  All through the night.
  Still the coming day discerning,
  By the hope within us burning,
  To the dawn our footsteps turning,
  All through the night.

Star of faith, the dark adorning
  All through the night,
Leads us fearless toward the morning
  All through the night.
  Though our hearts be wrapt in sorrow
  From the hope of dawn we borrow
  Promise of a glad to-morrow
  All through the night.

ANONYMOUS

THE PERSIAN MOON

Ah, Moon of my Delight who know'st no wane,
The Moon of Heaven is rising once again :
  How oft hereafter rising shall she look
Through this same Garden after me—in vain !

EDWARD FITZGERALD
(after OMAR KHAYYÁM)

THE SLEEPER

At midnight, in the month of June,
I stand beneath the mystic moon.
An opiate vapour, dewy, dim,
Exhales from out her golden rim,
And, softly dripping, drop by drop,
Upon the quiet mountain top,
Steals drowsily and musically
Into the universal valley.
The rosemary nods upon the grave ;
The lily lolls upon the wave ;
Wrapping the fog about its breast,
The ruin moulders into rest,
Looking like Lethe, see ! the lake
A conscious slumber seems to take,
And would not, for the world, awake.
All Beauty sleeps !—and lo ! where lies
Irene, with her Destinies !
O lady bright ! can it be right—
This window open to the night ?

The wanton airs, from the tree-top,
Laughingly through the lattice drop—
The bodiless airs, a wizard rout,
Flit through thy chamber in and out,
And wave the curtain canopy
So fitfully—so fearfully—
Above the closed and fringèd lid
'Neath which thy slumb'ring soul lies hid,
That, o'er the floor and down the wall,
Like ghosts the shadows rise and fall !
Oh, lady dear, hast thou no fear ?
Why and what art thou dreaming here ?
Sure thou art come o'er far-off seas,
A wonder to these garden trees !
Strange is thy pallor ! strange thy dress,
Strange, above all, thy length of tress,
And this all solemn silentness !

The lady sleeps ! Oh, may her sleep,
Which is enduring, so be deep !
Heaven have her in its sacred keep !
This chamber changed for one more holy,
This bed for one more melancholy,
I pray to God that she may lie
For ever with unopen'd eye
While the pale sheeted ghosts go by !

My love, she sleeps ! Oh, may her sleep
As it is lasting, so be deep !
Soft may the worms about her creep !
Far in the forest, dim and old,
For her may some tall vault unfold—

Some vault that oft has flung its black
And wingèd panels fluttering back,
Triumphant, o'er the crested palls
Of her grand family funerals—
Some sepulchre, remote, alone,
Against whose portal she hath thrown,
In childhood, many an idle stone—
Some tomb from out whose sounding door
She ne'er shall force an echo more,
Thrilling to think, poor child of sin !
It was the dead who groan'd within.

EDGAR ALLAN POE

MOON MAGIC

What, there's nothing in the moon noteworthy ?
Nay : for if that moon could love a mortal,
Use, to charm him (so to fit a fancy),
All her magic ('tis the old sweet mythos)
She would turn a new side to her mortal,
Side unseen of herdsman, huntsman, steersman—
Blank to Zoroaster on his terrace,
Blind to Galileo on his turret,
Dumb to Homer, dumb to Keats—him, even !
Think the wonder of the moonstruck mortal—
When she turns round, comes again in heaven,
Opens out anew for worse or better !
Proves she like some portent of an iceberg
Swimming full upon the ship it founders,
Hungry with huge teeth of splintered crystals ?

Proves she as the paved work of a sapphire
Seen by Moses when he climbed the mountain ?
Moses, Aaron, Nadab and Abihu
Climbed and saw the very God, the Highest,
Stand upon the paved work of a sapphire.
Like the bodied heaven in his clearness
Shone the stone, the sapphire of that paved work,
When they ate and drank and saw God also !
What were seen ? None knows, none ever shall know.
Only this is sure—the sight were other,
Not the moon's same side, born late in Florence,
Dying now impoverished here in London.
God be thanked, the meanest of his creatures
Boasts two soul-sides—one to face the world with,
One to show a woman when he loves her !

BROWNING

SOHRAB AND RUSTUM

So, on the bloody sand, Sohrab lay dead.
And the great Rustum drew his horseman's cloak
Down o'er his face, and sate by his dead son.
    And night came down over the solemn waste,
And the two gazing hosts, and that sole pair,
And darken'd all ; and a cold fog, with night,
Crept from the Oxus. Soon a hum arose,
As of a great assembly loosed, and fires
Began to twinkle through the fog : for now
Both armies moved to camp, and took their meal :
And Rustum and his son were left alone.

But the majestic River floated on,
Out of the mist and hum of that low land,
Into the frosty starlight, and there moved,
Rejoicing, through the hush'd Chorasmian waste,
Under the solitary moon : he flow'd
Right for the Polar Star, past Orgunjè,
Brimming, and bright, and large : then sands begin
To hem his watery march, and dam his streams,
And split his currents ; that for many a league
The shorn and parcell'd Oxus strains along
Through beds of sand and matted rushy isles—
Oxus forgetting the bright speed he had
In his high mountain cradle in Pamere,
A foil'd circuitous wanderer :—till at last
The long'd-for dash of waves is heard, and wide
His luminous home of waters opens, bright
And tranquil, from whose floor the new-bathed stars
Emerge, and shine upon the Aral Sea.

MATTHEW ARNOLD

LUCIFER IN STARLIGHT

On a starred night Prince Lucifer uprose.
Tired of his dark dominion swung the fiend
Above the rolling ball in cloud part screened,
Where sinners hugged their spectre of repose.
Poor prey to his hot fit of pride were those.
And now upon his western wing he leaned,
Now his huge bulk o'er Afric's sands careened,
Now the black planet shadowed Arctic snows.

Soaring through wider zones that pricked his scars
With memory of the old revolt from Awe,
He reached a middle height, and at the stars,
Which are the brain of heaven, he looked, and sank.
Around the ancient track marched, rank on rank,
The army of unalterable law.

GEORGE MEREDITH

LULLABY

Lullaby, oh, lullaby !
Flowers are closed and lambs are sleeping ;
Lullaby, oh, lullaby !
Stars are up, the moon is peeping ;
Lullaby, oh, lullaby !
While the birds are silence keeping,
(Lullaby, oh, lullaby !)
Sleep, my baby, fall a-sleeping,
Lullaby, oh, lullaby !

CHRISTINA ROSSETTI

SONG

Let the red dawn surmise
What we shall do,
When this blue starlight dies
And all is through.

668

If we have loved but well
   Under the sun,
Let the last morrow tell
   What we have done.

BLISS CARMAN

THE STATUE OF KING CHARLES AT CHARING CROSS

Sombre and rich, the skies ;
Great glooms, and starry plains.
Gently the night wind sighs ;
Else a vast silence reigns.

The splendid silence clings
Around me : and around
The saddest of all kings
Crowned, and again discrowned.

Comely and calm, he rides
Hard by his own Whitehall :
Only the night wind glides :
No crowds, nor rebels, brawl.

Gone, too, his Court ; and yet,
The stars his courtiers are :
Stars in their stations set ;
And every wandering star.

669

Alone he rides, alone,
The fair and fatal king :
Dark night is all his own,
That strange and solemn thing.

Which are more full of fate :
The stars ; or those sad eyes ?
Which are more still and great :
Those brows ; or the dark skies ?

Although his whole heart yearn
In passionate tragedy :
Never was face so stern
With sweet austerity.

Vanquished in life, his death
By beauty made amends :
The passing of his breath
Won his defeated ends.

Brief life and hapless ? Nay :
Through death, life grew sublime.
Speak after sentence ? Yea :
And to the end of time.

Armoured he rides, his head
Bare to the stars of doom :
He triumphs now, the dead,
Beholding London's gloom.

Our wearier spirit faints,
Vexed in the world's employ :
His soul was of the saints ;
And art to him was joy.

King, tried in fires of woe !
Men hunger for thy grace :
And through the night I go,
Loving thy mournful face.

Yet when the city sleeps ;
When all the cries are still :
The stars and heavenly deeps
Work out a perfect will.

LIONEL JOHNSON

THE BUSH, MY LOVER

The camp-fire gleams resistance
  To every twinkling star ;
The horse-bells in the distance
  Are jangling faint and far ;
Through gum-boughs lorn and lonely
  The passing breezes sigh ;
In all the world are only
  My star-crowned Love and I.

The still night wraps Macquarie ;
  The white moon, drifting slow,
Takes back her silver glory
  From watching waves below ;
To dalliance I give over,
  Though half the world may chide,
And clasp my one true Lover
  Here on Macquarie side.

The loves of earth grow olden
  Or kneel at some new shrine ;
Her locks are always golden—
  This brave Bush-Love of mine ;

And for her star-lit beauty,
    And for her dawns dew-pearled,
Her name in love and duty
    I guard against the world. . .

If we some white arms' folding,
    Some warm, red mouth should miss—
Her hand is ours for holding,
    Her lips are ours to kiss ;
And closer than a lover
    She shares our lightest breath,
And droops her great wings over
    To shield us to the death.

The winds of Dawn are roving,
    The river-oaks astir—
What heart were lorn of loving
    That had no Love but her ?
Till last red stars are lighted
    And last winds wander West,
Her troth and mine are plighted—
    The Lover I love best !

WILLIAM OGILVIE

ACQUAINTED WITH THE NIGHT

I have been one acquainted with the night.
I have walked out in rain and back in rain.
I have outwalked the furthest city light.

I have looked down the saddest city lane.
I have passed by the watchman on his beat
And dropped my eyes unwilling to explain.

I have stood still and hushed the sound of feet
When far away an interrupted cry
Came over houses from another street,

But not to call me back or say good-bye;
And further still at an unearthly height
One luminary clock against the sky

Proclaimed the time was neither wrong nor right.
I have been one acquainted with the night.

ROBERT FROST

THE POOR GIRL'S MEDITATION
(*Translated from the Irish*)

I am sitting here,
Since the moon rose in the night;
Kindling a fire,
And striving to keep it alight:
The folk of the house are lying
In slumber deep;
The geese will be gabbling soon:
The whole of the land is asleep.

May I never leave this world
Until my ill-luck is gone:
Till I have cows and sheep,
And the lad that I love for my own:

I would not think it long,
The night I would lie at his breast,
And the daughters of spite, after that,
Might say the thing they liked best.

Love covers up hate,
If a girl have beauty at all :
On a bed that was narrow and high,
A three-month I lie by the wall :
When I bethought on the lad
That I left on the brow of the hill,
I wept from dark until dark
And my cheeks have the tear-tracks still.

And, O, young lad that I love,
I am no mark for your scorn :
All that you know of me is
Undowered I was born :
And if I've no fortune in hand,
Nor cattle nor sheep of my own,
This I can say, O lad,
I am fitted to lie my lone !

PADRAIC COLUM

MOONLIT APPLES

At the top of the house the apples are laid in rows,
And the skylight lets the moonlight in, and those
Apples are deep-sea apples of green. There goes
  A cloud on the moon in the autumn night.

A mouse in the wainscot scratches, and scratches, and then
There is no sound at the top of the house of men
Or mice ; and the cloud is blown, and the moon again
  Dapples the apples with deep-sea light.

They are lying in rows there, under the gloomy beams ;
On the sagging floor ; they gather the silver streams
Out of the moon, those moonlit apples of dreams,
  And quiet is the steep stair under.

In the corridors under there is nothing but sleep.
And stiller than ever on orchard boughs they keep
Tryst with the moon, and deep is the silence, deep
  On moon-washed apples of wonder.

JOHN DRINKWATER

OLD FIRES

The fire burns low
Where it has burned ages ago,
Sinks and sighs
As it has done to a hundred eyes
Staring, staring
At the last cold smokeless glow.

Here men sat
Lonely and watched the golden grate
Turn at length black ;
Heard the cooling iron crack :
Shadows, shadows,
Watching the shadows come and go.

And still the hiss
I hear, the soft fire's sob and kiss,
And still it burns
And the bright gold to crimson turns,
Sinking, sinking,
And the fire shadows larger grow.

O dark-cheeked fire,
Wasting like spent heart's desire,
You that were gold,
And now crimson will soon be cold—
Cold, cold,
Like moon-shadows on new snow.

Shadows all,
They that watched your shadows fall.
But now they come
Rising around me, grave and dumb. . .
Shadows, shadows,
Come as the fire-shadows go.

And stay, stay,
Though all the fire sink cold as clay,
Whispering still,
Ancestral wise Familiars—till,
Staring, staring,
Dawn's wild fires through the casement glow.

JOHN FREEMAN

LOVE'S CAUTION

Tell them, when you are home again
   How warm the air was now ;
How silent were the birds and leaves,
   And of the moon's full glow ;
And how we saw afar
   A falling star :
It was a tear of pure delight
   Ran down the face of Heaven this happy night.

Our kisses are but love in flower,
   Until that greater time
When, gathering strength, those flowers take wing,
   And Love can reach his prime.
And now, my heart's delight,
   Good night, Good night :
Give me the last sweet kiss—
   But do not breathe at home one word of this !

W. H. DAVIES

THE MOON

Thy beauty haunts me, heart and soul,
   Oh thou fair Moon, so close and bright ;
Thy beauty makes me like the child,
   That cries aloud to own thy light :
The little child that lifts each arm,
To press thee to her bosom warm.

Though there are birds that sing this night
   With thy white beams across their throats,
Let my deep silence speak for me
   More than for them their sweetest notes :
Who worships thee till music fails
Is greater than thy nightingales.

                                    W. H. DAVIES

NIGHT RHAPSODY

How beautiful it is to wake at night,
When over all there reigns the ultimate spell
Of complete silence, darkness absolute,
To feel the world, tilted on axle-tree,
In slow gyration, with no sensible sound,
Unless to ears of unimagined beings,
Resident incorporeal or stretched
In vigilance of ecstasy among
Ethereal paths and the celestial maze.
The rumour of our onward course now brings
A steady rustle, as of some strange ship
Darkling with soundless sail all set and amply filled
By volume of an ever-constant air,
At fullest night, through seas for ever calm,
Swept lovely and unknown for ever on.

How beautiful it is to wake at night,
Embalmed in darkness watchful, sweet, and still,
As is the brain's mood flattered by the swim
Of currents circumvolvent in the void,
To lie quite still and to become aware
Of the dim light cast by nocturnal skies

On a dim earth beyond the window-ledge,
So, isolate from the friendly company
Of the huge universe which turns without,
To brood apart in calm and joy awhile
Until the spirit sinks and scarcely knows
Whether self is, or if self only is
For ever . . .

        How beautiful to wake at night,
Within the room grown strange, and still, and sweet,
And live a century while in the dark
The dripping wheel of silence slowly turns ;
To watch the window open on the night,
A dewy silent deep where nothing stirs,
And, lying thus, to feel dilate within
The press, the conflict, and the heavy pulse
Of incommunicable sad ecstasy,
Growing until the body seems outstretched
In perfect crucifixion on the arms
Of a cross pointing from last void to void,
While the heart dies to a mere midway spark.

All happiness thou holdest, happy night,
For such as lie awake and feel dissolved
The peaceful spice of darkness and the cool
Breath hither blown from the ethereal flowers
That mist thy fields ! O happy, happy wounds,
Conditioned by existence in humanity,
That have such powers to heal them ! slow sweet sighs
Torn from the bosom, silent wails, the birth
Of such long-treasured tears as pain his eyes,
Who, waking, hears the divine solicitudes
Of midnight with ineffable purport charged.

How beautiful it is to wake at night,
Another night, in darkness yet more still,
Save when the myriad leaves on full-fledged boughs,
Filled rather by the perfume's wandering flood
Than by dispansion of the still sweet air,
Shall from the furthest utter silences
In glimmering secrecy have gathered up
An host of whisperings and scattered sighs,
To loose at last a sound as of the plunge
And lapsing seethe of some Pacific wave,
Which, risen from the star-thronged outer troughs,
Rolls in to wreathe with circling foam away
The flutter of the golden moths that haunt
The star's one glimmer daggered on wet sands.

So beautiful it is to wake at night!
Imagination, loudening with the surf
Of the midsummer wind among the boughs,
Gathers my spirit from the haunts remote
Of faintest silence and the shades of sleep,
To bear me on the summit of her wave
Beyond known shores, beyond the mortal edge
Of thought terrestrial, to hold me poised
Above the frontiers of infinity,
To which in the full reflux of the wave
Come soon I must, bubble of solving foam,
Borne to those other shores—now never mine
Save for a hovering instant, short as this
Which now sustains me ere I be drawn back—
To learn again, and wholly learn, I trust,
How beautiful it is to wake at night.

ROBERT NICHOLS

THE PERSIAN FLUTE

Persian shepherd by a waterfall
Piping to please himself among his goats,
Gave me this flute, that now upon my wall
Hangs, hollow exile, prisoning its notes.

Its heart is broken ; silent are its strains.
I cannot wake the little Persian flute.
It does not, will not, know me ; it remains
Beneath my fingers obstinately mute.

Yet this slim reed, when stars were overhead,
And dusk was vocal with the bleating flocks,
Sent up its pure and melancholy thread
Of music by the river and the rocks.

I thought that I should wake that note again
With one clear echo of the hills apart,
And summon Persia to an English lane,—
I had not reckoned with a broken heart.

Shall we go back together, my flute and I,
To find again the shepherd of Shalil,
And when the planet Venus travels high
Above the myrtle grove of Murdafil

Make each our separate music ? For I too
Am silent sometimes, thinking of those stars,
That solitude, those evenings waning blue,
And the lost beauty of the plains of Fars.

V. SACKVILLE-WEST

NIGHT

An odorous shade lingers, the fair day's ghost,
  And the frail moon now by no wind is tost,
And shadow-laden scents of tree and grass
  Build up again a world our eyes have lost.

Now all the wood is but a murmured light
  Where leaf on leaf falls softly from the height;
The hidden freshness of the river seems
  A breath that mingles with the breath of night.

And time and shade and silence seem to say
  Close now your eyes nor fear to die with day;
For if the daylight win to earth again,
  Will not its beauty also find a way?

And flower and stream and forest, will they not
  Bring back to-morrow, as to-day they brought,
This shadow-hidden scent—this odorous shade?
  Yea, and with more abiding memories fraught.

SEUMAS O'SULLIVAN
(from the French of HENRI DE RÉGNIER)

THE NIGHT WILL NEVER STAY

The night will never stay,
The night will still go by,
Though with a million stars
You pin it to the sky ;
Though you bind it with the blowing
    wind
And buckle it with the moon,
The night will slip away
Like sorrow or a tune.

ELEANOR FARJEON

FOURTH PART

§ II GOOD BEDFELLOWS

They are never alone that are accompanied by noble thoughts.

SIR PHILIP SIDNEY (*Arcadia*)

Good company and good discourse are the very sinews of virtue.

IZAAK WALTON

Please you, draw near!

SHAKESPEARE (*Tempest*)

§ II GOOD BEDFELLOWS

A GIFT OF GOD

A wyf is Goddès giftè verraily ;
Alle othere manere giftès hardily,
As londès, rentès, pasture, or commùne,
Or moeblès, alle been giftès of Fortùne,
That passen as a shadow on a wal ;
But dredèlees, if pleynly speke I shal,
A wyf wol laste and in thyn hous endure,
Wel lenger than thee list, paràventure.

CHAUCER (from Merchant's Tale)

A TALK AT URBINO

(in the year 1506)

[The Speakers are :—
PIETRO BEMBO (afterwards Cardinal), a Venetian humanist,
called "The Dictator of the Renascence."
CESARE GONZAGA, a kinsman of the Duchess and friend of
Castiglione (the author).
GASPARE PALLAVICINO, a gay young courtier.
EMILIA PIA, a lively companion of the Duchess.
GIULIANO DE' MEDICI, son of Lorenzo the Magnificent and
friend of Castiglione.
ELISABETTA GONZAGA (the Duchess), wife of Guidobaldo,
Duke of Urbino.]

Messer PETER BEMBO *said*: Since the beauties, which we
daily see with these our dim eyes in bodies subject to corruption, that nevertheless be nothing else but dreams

and most thin shadows of beauty, seem unto us so well favoured and comely, that oftentimes they kindle in us a most burning fire, and with such delight, that we reckon no happiness may be compared to it, that we feel otherwhile through the only look which the beloved countenance of a woman casteth at us : what happy wonder, what blessed abashment may we reckon that to be, that taketh the souls, which come to have a sight of the heavenly beauty ? what sweet flame ? What great incense may a man believe that to be, which ariseth of the fountain of the sovereign and right beauty ? . .

Then the Lord CESAR GONZAGA : The way (*quoth he*) that leadeth to this happiness is so steep (in my mind) that (I believe) it will be much a do to get to it.

The Lord GASPAR *said* : I believe it be hard to get up for men, but impossible for women.

The Lady EMILIA *laughed and said* : If ye fall so often to offend us, I promise you, ye shall be no more forgiven.

The Lord GASPAR *answered* : It is no offence to you, in saying, that women's souls be not so purged from passions as men's be, nor accustomed in beholdings as Messer Peter hath said, is necessary for them to be, that will taste of the heavenly love. Therefore it is not read that ever woman hath had this grace : but many men have had it, as Plato, Socrates, Plotinus, and many other. . .

Here answered the Lord JULIAN : In this point men shall nothing pass women, for Socrates himself doth confess that all the mysteries of love which he knew, were oped unto him by a woman, which was Diotima. And the angel that with the fire of love imprinted the five wounds in Saint Francis, hath also made some women worthy of the same print in our age. You must remember moreover that Saint Mary Magdalen had many faults forgiven her, because she loved much : and perhaps with no less grace than Saint Paul, was she many times through Angelic love haled up to the third heaven. And many other (as I showed you yesterday more at large) that for love of the name of Christ have not passed upon life, nor feared torments, nor any other kind of death how terrible and cruel ever it were. And they were not (as Messer Peter will have his Courtier to be) aged, but soft and tender maidens, and in the age, when he saith that sensual love ought to be borne withal in men.

The Lord GASPAR *began to prepare himself to speak, but the* DUCHESS: "Of this" (*quoth she*) "let Messer Peter be judge, and the matter shall stand to his verdite, whether women be not as meet for heavenly love as men. But because the plead between you may happen be too long, it shall not be amiss to defer it until to-morrow."

"Nay, to-night," *quoth the Lord* CESAR GONZAGA.

"And how can it be to-night ? " *quoth the* DUCHESS.

The Lord CESAR *answered*: "Because it is day already," and showed her the light that began to enter in at the clefts of the windows.

Then every man rose to his feet with much wonder, because they had not thought that the reasonings had lasted longer than the accustomed wont, saving only that they were begun much later, and with their pleasantness had deceived so the Lords' minds, that they wist not of the going away of the hours. And not one of them felt any heaviness of sleep in his eyes, the which often happeneth when a man is up after his accustomed hour to go to bed. When the windows then were opened on the side of the Palace that hath his prospect toward the high top of Mount Catri, they saw already risen in the East a fair morning like unto the colour of roses, and all stars voided, saving only the sweet Governess of the heaven, Venus, which keepeth the bounds of the night and the day, from which appeared to blow a sweet blast, that filling the ear with a biting cold, began to quicken the tunable notes of the pretty birds, among the hushing woods of the hills at hand. Whereupon they all, taking their leave with reverence of the Duchess, departed toward their lodgings, without torch, the light of the day sufficing.

From *Il Cortegiano* of CASTIGLIONE
(Trans. SIR THOMAS HOBY, 1561)

BITS OF BURTON

Remedies against Discontent

Many grievances there are which happen to mortals in this life and many good remedies to mitigate and oppose them, many divine precepts to counterpoise our hearts, special antidotes both in scriptures and humane authors, which who so will observe, shall purchase much ease and quietness unto himself. I will point at a few :—

Be sober and watch.
Recompence good for evil.
Love one another.
Know thy self.
Beware of " Had I wist."
Speak well of friends.
If thou seest ought amiss in another, mend it in thyself.
Be not proud or popular.
Cast not off an old friend.

Take heed of a reconciled enemy.
If thou come as a guest, stay not too long.
Make not a fool of thy self to make others merry.
Live merrily as thou canst.
Go as thou wouldst be met : sit as thou wouldst be found.

The Advantage of Music

Music is a roaring-meg against melancholy, to rear and
revive the languishing soul ; " affecting not only the ears,
but the very arteries, the vital and animal spirits, it erects
the mind, and makes it nimble." Labouring men that sing
to their work, can tell as much, and so can soldiers when
they go to fight, whom terror of death cannot so much
affright, as the sound of trumpets, drum, fife, and such
like music animates. It makes a child quiet, the nurse's
song; and many times the sound of a trumpet on a sudden, bells ringing, a carman's whistle, a boy singing some
ballad tune early in the street, alters, revives, recreates
a restless patient that cannot sleep in the night, etc. In a
word, it is so powerful a thing that it ravisheth the soul.

Enjoyment out of doors

The most pleasant of all outward pastimes is to make a
petty progress, a merry journey now and then with some
good companions : to visit friends, see cities, castles, towns,
to walk amongst orchards, gardens, bowers, mounts, and
arbours, artificial wildernesses, green thickets, arches,
groves, lawns, rivulets, fountains and such like pleasant
places, brooks, pools, fishponds, betwixt wood and water,
in a fair meadow, by a river side, to disport in some

pleasant plain, park, run up a steep hill sometimes, or sit in a shady seat must needs be a delectable recreation.

A Good Friend

Tobacco, divine, rare, superexcellent tobacco, which goes far beyond all the panaceas, potable gold, and philosopher's stones, a sovereign remedy to all diseases.

From *Anatomy of Melancholy* (1621)

MR. PEPYS GOES TO EPSOM

July 14th, 1667. Up, and my wife, a little before four, and by and by Mrs. Turner come to us by agreement, and she and I staid talking below while my wife dressed herself, which vexed me that she was so long about it, keeping us till past five o'clock before she was ready. She ready ; and taking some bottles of wine and beer and some cold fowle with us into the coach, we took coach and four horses which I had provided last night, and so away. A very fine day, and so towards Epsum. The country very fine, only the way very dusty. We got to Epsum by eight o'clock, to the well ; where much company, and there we 'light, and I drank the water : I did drink four pints. Here I met with divers of our town, among others with several of the tradesmen of our office, but did talk but little with them, it growing hot in the sun, and so we took coach again and to the towne, to the King's Head. Here we called for drink, and bespoke dinner. W. Hewer rode with us, and I left him and the women, and myself walked to church, where few people, contrary to what I expected, and none I knew, but all the Houblons, brothers,

and them after sermon I did salute. We parted to meet
anon, and I to my women, and there to dinner, a good
dinner, and were merry. After dinner we all lay down (the
day being wonderful hot) to sleep, and each of us took a
good nap, and then rose. We took coach and to take the
ayre. W. Hewer's horse broke loose, and we had the sport
to see him taken again. Then I carried them to see my
cozen Pepys' house, and 'light and walked round about it,
and they like it, as indeed it deserves, very well, and is a
pretty place ; and then I walked them to the wood hard
by, and there got them in the thickets till they had lost
themselves, and I could not find the way into any of the
walks in the wood, which indeed are very pleasant, if I
could have found them. At last got out of the wood again ;
and I, by leaping down the little bank coming out of the
wood, did sprain my right foot, which brought me great
present pain ; but presently, with walking, it went away
for the present. And so the women and W. Hewer and I
walked upon the Downes, where a flock of sheep was ; and
the most pleasant and innocent sight that ever I saw in my
life. We find a shepherd and his little boy reading, far
from any houses or sight of people, the Bible to him ; so
I made the boy read to me, which he did, with the forced
tone that children do usually read, that was mighty pretty,
and then I did give him something, and went to the father
and talked with him ; and I find he had been a servant in
my cozen Pepys' house, and told me what was become of
their old servants. He did content himself mightily in my
liking his boy's reading, and did bless God for him the
most like one of the old patriarchs that ever I saw in my
life, and it brought those thoughts of the old age of the
world in my mind for two or three days after. We took
notice of his woollen knit stockings of two colours mixed,

and of his shoes shod with iron shoes, both at the toe and heels, and with great nails in the soles of his feet, which was mighty pretty : and, taking notice of them, " Why," says the poor man, " the downes, you see, are full of stones, and we are faine to shoe ourselves thus ; and these," says he, " will make the stones fly till they sing before me." I did give the poor man something, for which he was mighty thankful, and I tried to cast stones with his horne crooke. He values his dog mightily, that would turn a sheep any way which he would have him when he goes to fold them : told me there was about eighteen scoare sheep in his flock, and that he hath four shillings a week the year round for keeping of them. So we posted thence with mighty pleasure in the discourse we had with this poor man ; and Mrs. Turner, in the common fields here, did gather one of the prettiest nosegays that ever I saw in my life.

So to our coach and through Mr. Minnes's wood, and looked upon Mr. Evelyn's house ; and so over the common, and through Epsum towne to our inne, in the way stopping a poor woman with her milk-pail, and in one of my gilt tumblers did drink our bellyfulls of milk, better than any creame ; and so to our inne and there had a dish of creame, but it was sour and so had no pleasure in it ; and so paid our reckoning and took coach, it being about seven at night, and passed and saw the people walking with their wives and children to take the ayre ; and we set out for home, the sun by and by going down, and we in the cool of the evening all the way with much pleasure home, talking and pleasing ourselves with the pleasure of this day's work, Mrs. Turner mightily pleased with my resolution, which, I tell her, is never to keep a country-house, but to keep a coach, and with my wife on the

Saturday to go sometimes for a day to this place, and then quit to another place; and there is more variety and as little charge, and no trouble, as there is in a country-house. Anon it grew dark, and as it grew dark we had the pleasure to see several glow-wormes, which was mighty pretty, but my foot begins more and more to pain me, which Mrs. Turner, by keeping her warm hand upon it, did much ease; but so that when we come home, which was just at eleven at night, I was not able to walk from the lane's end to my house without being helped, which did trouble me, and therefore to bed presently.

Other Adventures

16th January, 1660.

After dinner we went to the Green Dragon, on Lambeth Hill, and there we sang of all sorts of things, and I ventured with good success upon things at first sight, and after that I played on my flageolet, and staid there till nine o'clock, very merry and drawn on with one song after another till it came to be so late. So parted, and thence home, where I found my wife and maid a-washing. I staid up till the bell-man came by with his bell just under my window as I was writing of this very line, and cried, "Past one of the clock, and a cold, frosty, windy morning." I then went to bed, and left my wife and the maid a-washing still.

25th May, 1660.

Got on shore when the King did, who was received by General Monk with all imaginable love and respect upon his entrance upon the land of Dover. Infinite the crowd of people and the horsemen, citizens and noblemen of all sorts. The Mayor of the town came and gave him his white staff, the badge of his place, which the King did give him again. The Mayor also presented him from the town a very rich Bible, which he took and said it was the thing that he loved above all things in the world.

12th December, 1660.

With J. Spicer to his office and took £100, and by coach with it as far as my father's, where I called to see them, and my father did offer me six pieces of gold, in lieu of six pounds that he borrowed of me the other day, but it went against me to take it of him and therefore did not, though I was a little troubled that I did not. Thence home, and took out this £100 and sealed it up with the other [of] last night, it being the first £200 that ever I saw together of my own in my life. For which God be praised. So to my Lady Batten and sat an hour or two, and talked with her daughter and people in the absence of her father and mother and my wife to pass away the time. After that home and to bed, reading myself asleep, while the wench sat mending my breeches by my bedside.

9th July, 1663.

Abroad, it raining, to Blackfriars, and there went into a little alehouse, and here I kissed three or four times the maid of the house, who is a pretty girl but very modest.

30th November, 1664.

(Lord's Day.) Up, and this morning put on my new, fine, coloured cloth suit, with my cloake lined with plush, which is a dear and noble suit, costing me about £17.

My wife busy in going with her woman to a hot-house to bathe herself, after her long being within doors in the dirt, so that she now pretends to a resolution of being hereafter very clean. How long it will hold I can guess.

25th March, 1667.

(Lady Day.) . . . By and by to dinner, a poor dinner, my wife and I, at Sir W. Pen's, and then he and I before to the King's playhouse; and by and by comes Mr. Lowther and his wife and mine, and into a box, forsooth, neither of them being dressed, which I was almost ashamed of. Sir W. Pen and I in the pit, and here saw " The Mayden Queene," which indeed the more I see the more I like, and is an excellent play, and so done by Nell, her merry part, as cannot be better done in nature, I think.

31st May, 1669.

Up very betimes, and so continued all the morning with W. Hewer upon examining and stating my accounts, in order to the fitting myself to go abroad beyond sea, which the ill condition of my eyes, and my neglect for a year or two, hath kept me behindhand in . . . Being called by my wife, we to the Park, Mary Batelier, and a Dutch gentleman, a friend of hers, being with us. Thence to " The World's End," a drinking-house by the Park; and there merry, and so home late.

And this ends all that I doubt I shall ever be able to do with my own eyes in the keeping of my Journal, I being not able to do it any longer, having done now so long as to undo my eyes almost every time that I take a pen in my hand ; and therefore whatever comes of it I must forbear . .

And so I betake myself to that course, which is almost as much as to see myself go into the grave : for which and all the discomforts that will accompany my being blind, the good God prepare me !

From Diary of Samuel Pepys

AN INTERRUPTED CONFERENCE

Word was brought that the tea-table was set in the library, which is a gallery on a ground-floor, with an arched door at one end opening into a walk of limes ; where, as soon as we had drunk tea, we were tempted by fine weather to take a walk which led us to a small mount of easy ascent, on the top whereof we found a seat under a spreading tree. Here we had a prospect on one hand of a narrow bay or creek of the sea, enclosed on either side by a coast beautified with rocks and woods, and green banks and farm-houses. At the end of the bay was a small town, placed upon the slope of a hill, which, from the advantage of its situation, made a considerable figure. Several fishing-boats and lighters, gliding up and down on a surface as smooth and bright as glass, enlivened the prospect. On the other side, we looked down on green pastures, flocks, and herds basking beneath in sunshine, while we, in our superior situation, enjoyed the freshness of air and shade.

Here we felt that sort of joyful instinct which a rural scene and fine weather inspire; and proposed no small pleasure in resuming and continuing our conference without interruption till dinner. But we had hardly seated ourselves and looked about us when we saw a fox run by the foot of our mount into an adjacent thicket. A few minutes after, we heard a confused noise of the opening of hounds, the winding of horns, and the roaring of country squires. While our attention was suspended by this event, a servant came running, out of breath, and told Crito that his neighbour Ctesippus, a squire of note, was fallen from his horse, attempting to leap over a hedge, and brought into the hall, where he lay for dead. Upon which we all rose, and walked hastily to the house, where we found Ctesippus just come to himself, in the midst of half a dozen sun-burnt squires, in frocks, and short wigs, and jockey boots. Being asked how he did, he answered it was only a broken rib. With some difficulty Crito persuaded him to lie on a bed till the chirurgeon came. These fox-hunters, having been up early at their sport, were eager for dinner, which was accordingly hastened. They passed the afternoon in a loud rustic mirth, gave proof of their religion and loyalty by the healths they drank, talked of hounds, and horses, and elections, and country affairs, till the chirurgeon, who had been employed about Ctesippus, desired he might be put into Crito's coach, and sent home, having refused to stay all night.

Our guests being gone, we reposed ourselves after the fatigue of this tumultuous visit, and next morning assembled again at the seat on the mount.

Now Lysicles, being a nice man and a *bel esprit*, had an infinite contempt for the rough manners and conversation of fox-hunters, and could not reflect with patience that he had lost, as he called it, so many hours in their company. I flattered myself, said he, that there had been none of this species remaining among us : strange that men should be diverted with such uncouth noise and hurry or find pleasure in the society of dogs and horses! How much more elegant are the diversions of the town!

There seems, replied Euphranor, to be some resemblance between fox-hunter and free-thinkers; the former exerting their animal faculties in pursuit of game, as you gentlemen employ your intellectuals in the pursuit of truth. The kind of amusement is the same, although the object be different.

GEORGE BERKELEY, Bishop of Cloyne
(from *Alciphron*)

A DISTURBED HOUSEHOLD

" Were one sure," said my father to himself, scratching his eyebrow, " that the child was expiring, one might as well compliment my brother Toby as not—and it would be a pity, in such a case, to throw away so great a name as *Trismegistus* upon him—but he may recover."

" No, No," said my father to Susannah, " I'll get up."
" There is no time," cried Susannah, " the child's as black as my shoe."

" *Trismegistus*," said my father—" But stay! Thou art a leaky vessel, Susannah," added my father, " Canst thou carry *Trismegistus* in thy head, the length of the gallery without scattering? "

" Can I ? " cried Susannah, shutting the door in a huff.

" If she can, I'll be shot," said my father, bouncing out of bed in the dark, and groping for his breeches.

Susannah ran with all speed along the gallery.

My father made all possible speed to find his breeches. Susannah got the start, and kept it. " 'Tis *Tris*—something," cried Susannah. " There is no christian-name in the world," said the curate, " beginning with *Tris*—but *Tristram*."

" Then 'tis *Tristram-gistus*," quoth Susannah.

" There is no *gistus* to it, noodle !—'tis my own name," replied the curate, dipping his hand, as he spoke, into the basin. " *Tristram !* " said he, &c., &c., &c., &c., so *Tristram* was I called, and *Tristram* shall I be to the day of my death.

My father followed Susannah, with his night-gown across his arm, with nothing more than his breeches on, fastened through haste with but a single button, and that button through haste thrust only half into the button-hole.

" She has not forgot the name ? " cried my father, half opening the door.

" No, no," said the curate, with a tone of intelligence.

" And the child is better," cried Susannah.

" And how does your mistress ? "

" As well," said Susannah, " as can be expected."

" Pish ! " said my father, the button of his breeches slipping out of the button-hole—So that whether the interjection was levelled at Susannah, or the button-hole—whether Pish was an interjection of contempt or an interjection of modesty, is a doubt, and must be a doubt till I shall have time to write the three following favourite chapters, that is, my chapter of *chamber-maids*, my chapter of *pishes*, and my chapter of *button-holes*.

All the light I am able to give the reader at present is this, that the moment my father cried Pish ! he whisk'd himself about—and with his breeches held up by one hand, and his night-gown thrown across the arm of the other, he turned along the gallery to bed, something slower than he came.

I wish I could write a chapter upon sleep.

A fitter occasion could never have presented itself, than what this moment offers, when all the curtains of the family are drawn—the candles put out—and no creature's eyes are open but a single one, for the other has been shut these twenty years, of my mother's nurse.

It is a fine subject!

And yet, as fine as it is, I would undertake to write a dozen chapters upon button-holes, both quicker and with more fame, than a single chapter upon this.

Button-holes! there is something lively in the very idea of 'em—and trust me, when I get amongst 'em—You gentry with great beards look as grave as you will—I'll make merry work with my button-holes—I shall have 'em all to myself—'tis a maiden subject—I shall run foul of no man's wisdom or fine sayings in it.

But for sleep—I know I shall make nothing of it before I begin—I am no dab at your fine sayings in the first place —and in the next, I cannot for my soul set a grave face upon a bad matter, and tell the world—'tis the refuge of the unfortunate—the enfranchisement of the prisoner— the downy lap of the hopeless, the weary, and the broken-hearted; nor could I set out with a lie in my mouth, by affirming, that of all the soft and delicious functions of our nature, by which the great Author of it, in his bounty, has been pleased to recompense the sufferings where-with his justice and his good pleasure has wearied us— that this is the chiefest (I know pleasures worth ten of it);

or what a happiness it is to man, when the anxieties and passions of the day are over, and he lies down upon his back, that his soul shall be so seated within him, that whichever way she turns her eyes, the heavens shall look calm and sweet above her—no desire—or fear—or doubt that troubles the air, nor any difficulty past, present, or to come, that the imagination may not pass over without offence, in that sweet secession.

" God's blessing," said Sancho Pança, " be upon the man who first invented this self-same thing called sleep— it covers a man all over like a cloak." Now there is more to me in this, and it speaks warmer to my heart and affections, than all the dissertations squeez'd out of the heads of the learned together upon the subject.—Not that I altogether disapprove of what Montaigne advances upon it—'tis admirable in its way—(I quote by memory).

The world enjoys other pleasures, says he, as they do that of sleep, without tasting or feeling it as it slips and passes by. We should study and ruminate upon it, in order to render proper thanks to him who grants it to us. For this end I cause myself to be disturbed in my sleep, that I may the better and more sensibly relish it. And yet I see few, says he again, who live with less sleep, when need requires ; my body is capable of a firm, but not of a violent and sudden agitation—I evade of late all violent exercises—I am never weary with walking—but from my youth, I never liked to ride upon pavements, I love to lie hard and alone, and even without my wife—This last word may stagger the faith of the world—but remember, " La Vraisemblance " (as Bayle says in the affair of *Liceti*) " n'est pas toujours du Côté de la Verité." And so much for sleep.

———

"If my wife will but venture him, brother Toby, Trismegistus shall be dress'd and brought down to us, whilst you and I are getting our breakfasts together."

"Go, tell Susannah, Obadiah, to step here."

"She is run upstairs," answered Obadiah, "this very instant, sobbing and crying, and wringing her hands as if her heart would break."

"We shall have a rare month of it," said my father, turning his head from Obadiah, and looking wistfully in my uncle Toby's face for some time, "we shall have a devilish month of it, brother Toby," said my father, setting his arms a-kimbo, and shaking his head, "fire, water, women, wind, brother Toby!"

"'Tis some misfortune," quoth my uncle Toby.

"That it is," cried my father, "to have so many jarring elements breaking loose, and riding triumph in every corner of a gentleman's house. Little boots it to the peace of a family, brother Toby, that you and I possess ourselves, and sit here silent and unmoved, whilst such a storm is whistling over our heads."

"And what's the matter, Susannah?"

"They have called the child Tristram, and my mistress is just got out of an hysterick fit about it—No—'tis not my fault," said Susannah—"I told him it was *Tristram-gistus.*"

"Make tea for yourself, brother Toby," said my father, taking down his hat, but how different from the sallies and agitations of voice and members which a common reader would imagine! For he spake in the sweetest modulation, and took down his hat with the genteelest movement of limbs that ever affliction harmonised and attuned together.

"Go to the bowling-green for corporal Trim," said my uncle Toby, speaking to Obadiah, as soon as my father left the room.

STERNE (from *Tristram Shandy*)

AN EARLY MORNING FRISK

One night when Beauclerk and Langton had supped at a tavern in London, and sat till about three in the morning, it came into their heads to go and knock up Johnson, and see if they could prevail on him to join them in a ramble. They rapped violently at the door of his chambers in the Temple, till at last he appeared in his shirt, with his little black wig on the top of his head, instead of a nightcap, and a poker in his hand, imagining, probably, that some ruffians were coming to attack him. When he discovered who they were, and was told their errand, he smiled, and with great good humour agreed to their proposal : " What, is it you, you dogs ! I'll have a frisk with you." He was soon drest, and they sallied forth together into Covent-Garden, where the greengrocers and fruiterers were beginning to arrange their hampers, just come in from the country. Johnson made some attempts to help them ; but the honest gardeners stared so at his figure and manner, and odd interference, that he soon saw his services were not relished. They then repaired to one of the neighbouring taverns, and made a bowl of that liquor called *Bishop*, which Johnson had always liked ; while in joyous contempt of sleep, from which he had been roused, he repeated the festive lines,

" *Short, O short then be thy reign,*
And give us to the world again ! "

They did not stay long, but walked down to the Thames, took a boat, and rowed to Billingsgate. Beauclerk and Johnson were so well pleased with their amusement, that they resolved to persevere in dissipation for the rest of the day : but Langton deserted them, being engaged to breakfast with some young Ladies. Johnson scolded him for " leaving his social friends, to go and sit with a set of wretched *un-idea'd* girls." Garrick being told of this ramble, said to him smartly, " I heard of your frolick t'other night. You'll be in the Chronicle." Upon which Johnson afterwards observed, " *He* durst not do such a thing. His *wife* would not *let* him ! "

BOSWELL (from *Life of Johnson*)

A BALL AT BATH

10th June, 1780.

In the evening was the last ball expected to be at Bath this season, and, therefore, knowing we could go to no other, it was settled we should go to this. Of our party were Mrs. Byron and Augusta, Miss Philips, and Charlotte Lewis.

Mrs. Byron was placed at the upper end of the room by Mr. Tyson, because she is honourable, and her daughter next to her. I, of course, the lowest of our party ; but the moment Mr. Tyson had arranged us, Augusta arose, and nothing would satisfy her but taking a seat not only next to, but below me ; nor could I, for my life, get the better of the affectionate humility with which she quite supplicated me to be content. She was soon after followed by Captain Brisbane, a young officer who had met her in

Spring Gardens, and seemed much struck with her, and was now presented to her by Mr. Tyson for her partner.

Captain Brisbane is a very pretty sort of young man, but did not much enliven us. Soon after I perceived Captain Bouchier, who, after talking some time with Mrs. Thrale, and various parties, made up to us, and upon Augusta's being called upon to dance a minuet, took her place, and began a very lively sort of chit-chat.

Just before she went to dance her minuet, upon my admiring her bouquet, which was the most beautiful in the room, she tore from it the only two moss-roses in it, and so spoilt it all before her exhibition, merely that I might have the best of it.

Country dances were now preparing, and Captain Bouchier asked me for the honour of my hand, but I had previously resolved not to dance, and, therefore, declined his offer. But he took, of the sudden, a fancy to prate with me, and therefore budged not after the refusal.

He told me this was the worst ball for company there had been the whole season ; and, with a wicked laugh that was too significant to be misunderstood, said, " And, as you have been to no other, perhaps you will give this for a specimen of a Bath ball ! "

He told me he had very lately met with Hannah More, and then mentioned Mrs. Montagu and Mrs. Carter, whence he took occasion to say most high and fine things of the ladies of the present age,—their writings, and talents ; and I soon found he had no small reverence for us blue-stockings.

About this time, Charlotte, who had confessedly dressed herself for dancing, but whose pretty face had by some means been overlooked, drawled towards us, and asked me why I would not dance ?

"I never intended it," said I; "but I hoped to have seen you."

"No," said she, yawning, "no more shall I,—I don't choose it."

"Don't you?" said Captain Bouchier, drily, "why not?"

"Why, because I don't like it."

"O fie!" cried he; "consider how cruel that is."

"I must consider myself," said she, pertly; "for I don't choose to heat myself this hot weather."

Just then, a young man came forward, and requested her hand. She coloured, looked excessively silly, and walked off with him to join the dancers.

When, between the dances, she came our way, he plagued her, à la Sir Clement.

"Well," cried he, "so you have been dancing this hot night! I thought you would have considered yourself better?"

"Oh," said she, "I could not help it—I had much rather not;—it was quite disagreeable to me."

"No, no,—pardon me there!" said he maliciously; "I saw pleasure dance first in your eyes; I never saw you look more delighted: you were quite the queen of smiles!"

She looked as if she could have killed him: and yet, from giddiness and good-humour, was compelled to join in the laugh.

After this we went to tea. When that was over, and we all returned to the ball-room, Captain Bouchier followed me, and again took a seat next mine, which he kept, without once moving, the whole night.

From *Diary of Frances Burney, Madame D'Arblay*

CAROLUS REX

A pretty severe fit of indisposition which, under the name of a nervous fever, has made a prisoner of me for some weeks past, and is but slowly leaving me, has reduced me to an incapacity of reflecting upon any topic foreign to itself. Expect no healthy conclusions from me this month, reader; I can offer you only sick men's dreams.

And truly the whole state of sickness is such; for what else is it but a magnificent dream for a man to lie-a-bed, and draw daylight curtains about him; and, shutting out the sun, to induce a total oblivion of all the works which are going on under it? To become insensible to all the operations of life, except the beatings of one feeble pulse?

If there be a regal solitude, it is a sick-bed. How the patient lords it there; what caprices he acts without control! how king-like he sways his pillow—tumbling, and tossing, and shifting, and lowering, and thumping, and flatting, and moulding it, to the ever-varying requisitions of his throbbing temples!

He changes sides oftener than a politician. Now he lies full length, then half length, obliquely, transversely, head and feet quite across the bed; and none accuses him of tergiversation. Within the four curtains he is absolute. They are his Mare Clausum. . .

He has put on the strong armour of sickness, he is wrapped in the callous hide of suffering; he keeps his sympathy, like some curious vintage, under trusty lock and key, for his own use only.

He lies pitying himself, honing and moaning to himself; he yearneth over himself; his bowels are even melted within him, to think what he suffers ; he is not ashamed to weep over himself.

He is for ever plotting how to do some good to himself ; studying little stratagems and artificial alleviations.

He makes the most of himself ; dividing himself, by an allowable fiction, into as many distinct individuals as he hath sore and sorrowing members. Sometimes he meditates—as of a thing apart from him—upon his poor aching head, and that dull pain which, dozing or waking, lay in it all the past night like a log, or palpable substance of pain, not to be removed without opening the very skull, as it seemed to take it thence. Or he pities his long, clammy, attenuated fingers. He compassionates himself all over ; and his bed is a very discipline of humanity, and tender heart.

He is his own sympathizer ; and instinctively feels that none can so well perform that office for him. He cares for few spectators to his tragedy. Only that punctual face of the old nurse pleases him, that announces his broths and his cordials. He likes it because it is so unmoved, and because he can pour forth his feverish ejaculations before it as unreservedly as to his bed-post. . .

Household rumours touch him not. Some faint murmur, indicative of life going on within the house, soothes him, while he knows not distinctly what it is. He is not to know anything, not to think of anything. Servants gliding up or down the distant staircase, treading as upon velvet, gently keep his ear awake, so long as he troubles not himself further than with some feeble guess at their errands. Exacter knowledge would be a burthen to him ; he can just endure the pressure of conjecture. He opens his eye faintly at the dull stroke of the muffled knocker, and closes it again without asking " Who was it ? " He is flattered by a general notion that inquiries are making after him, but he cares not to know the name of the inquirer. In the general stillness, and awful hush of the house, he lies in state, and feels his sovereignty.

To be sick is to enjoy monarchal prerogatives. Compare the silent tread and quiet ministry, almost by the eye only, with which he is served—with the careless demeanour, the unceremonious goings in and out (slapping of doors, or leaving them open) of the very same attendants, when he is getting a little better—and you will confess that from the bed of sickness (throne let me rather call it) to the elbow-chair of convalescence, is a fall from dignity, amounting to a deposition.

CHARLES LAMB (from " The Convalescent ")

A " FANCY " OVERTURE

Joe and I could not settle about the method of going down. He said there was a caravan, he understood, to start from Tom Belcher's at two, which would go there *right out* and back again the next day. Now I never travel all night, and said I should get a cast to Newbury by one of the mails. Joe swore the thing was impossible, and I could only answer that I had made up my mind to it. In short, he seemed to me to waver, said he only came to see if I was going, had letters to write, a cause coming on the day after, and faintly said at parting (for I was bent on setting out that moment)—" Well, we meet at Philippi?" I made the best of my way to Piccadilly. The mail coach stand was bare. " They are all gone," said I—" this is always the way with me—in the instant I lose the future—if I had not stayed to pour out that last cup of tea, I should have been just in time ; "—and cursing my folly and ill-luck together, without inquiring at the coach-office whether the mails were gone or not, I walked on in despite, and to punish my own dilatoriness and want of determination. At any rate, I would not turn back : I might get to Hounslow, or perhaps farther, to be on my road the next morning. I passed Hyde Park corner (my Rubicon), and trusted to fortune. Suddenly I heard the clattering of a Brentford stage, and the fight rushed full upon my fancy. I argued (not unwisely) that even a Brentford coachman was better company than my own thoughts (such as they were just then), and at his invitation mounted the box with him. . . . The Bath mail I had set my mind upon, and I had missed it, as I miss everything else, by my own absurdity, in putting the will for the deed, and aiming at ends without employing means. " Sir," said he of the Brentford, " the Bath mail will be up presently, my brother-in-law drives it, and I will engage to stop him if there is a place empty." I almost doubted my good genius ; but, sure enough, up it drove like lightning, and stopped directly at the call of the Brentford Jehu. I would not have believed this possible, but the brother-in-law of a mail-coach driver is himself no mean man. I was transferred without loss of time from the top of one coach to that of the other, desired the guard to pay my fare to the Brentford coachman for me as I had no change, was accommodated with a great coat, put up my umbrella to keep off a drizzling mist, and we began to cut through the air like an arrow. The mile-stones disappeared one after another, the rain kept off ; Tom Turtle the trainer sat before me on the coach-box, with whom I exchanged civilities as a gentleman going to the fight ; the passion that had transported me an hour before was subdued to pensive regret and conjectural musing on the next day's battle ; I was promised a place inside at Reading, and upon the whole, I thought myself a lucky fellow. Such is the force of imagination ! On the outside of any other coach on the 10th of December, with a Scotch mist drizzling through the cloudy moonlight air, I should have been cold, comfortless, impatient, and, no doubt, wet through ; but seated on the Royal mail, I felt warm and comfortable, the air did me good, the ride did me good, I was pleased with the progress we had made, and confident that all would go well through the journey. When I got inside at Reading, I found Turtle and a stout valetudinarian, whose costume bespoke him one of the FANCY, and who had risen from a three months' sick bed to get into the mail to see the fight. They were intimate, and we fell into a lively discourse. My friend the trainer was confined in his topics to fighting dogs and men, to bears and badgers ; beyond this he was " quite chap-fallen," had not a word to throw at a dog, and indeed very wisely fell asleep, when any other game was started. The whole art of training (I, however, learnt from him) consists in two things, exercise and abstinence, abstinence and exercise, repeated alternately and without end. . . . We had now but a few miles to our destination, and the first thing I did on alighting at Newbury, both coaches stopping at the same time, was to call out, " Pray is there a gentleman in that mail of the name of P——s ? " " No," said Joe, borrowing something of the vein of Gilpin, " for I have just got out." " Well ! " says he, " this is lucky ; but you don't know how vexed I was to miss you ; for," added he, lowering his voice, " do you know when I left you I went to Belcher's to ask about the caravan, and Mrs. Belcher said very obligingly, she couldn't tell about that, but there were two gentlemen who had taken places by the mail and were gone on in a landau, and she could frank us. It's a pity I didn't meet with you ; we could then have got down for nothing. . ."

Our present business was to get beds and supper at an inn ; but this was no easy task. The public-houses were full, and where you saw a light at a private house, and people poking their heads out of the casement to see what was going on, they instantly put them in and shut the window, the moment you seemed advancing with a sus-pitious overture for accommodation. Our guard and coachman thundered away at the outer gate of the Crown for some time without effect—such was the greater noise within ; and when the doors were unbarred, and we got admittance, we found a party assembled in the kitchen round a good hospitable fire, some sleeping, others drink-ing, others talking on politics and on the fight. A tall English yeoman (something like Matthews in the face, and quite as great a wag)—

A lusty man to ben an abbot able,

—was making such a prodigious noise about rent and taxes, and the price of corn now and formerly that he had prevented us from being heard at the gate. The first thing I heard him say was to a shuffling fellow who wanted to be off a bet for a shilling glass of brandy and water—" Con-found it, man, don't be *insipid* ! " Thinks I, that is a good phrase. It was a good omen. He kept it up so all night, nor flinched with the approach of morning. He was a fine fellow, with sense, wit, and spirit, a hearty body and a joyous mind, free-spoken, frank, convivial—one of that true English breed that went with Harry the Fifth to the

714

siege of Harfleur—"standing like greyhounds in the slips," &c. We ordered tea and eggs (beds were soon found to be out of the question), and this fellow's conversation was *sauce piquante*. It did one's heart good to see him brandish his oaken towel and to hear him talk. He made mince-meat of a drunken, stupid, red-faced, quarrelsome, *frowsy* farmer, whose nose "he moralised into a thousand similes," making it out a firebrand like Bardolph's. "I'll tell you what, my friend," says he, " the landlady has only to keep you here to save fire and candle. If one was to touch your nose, it would go off like a piece of charcoal." At this the other only grinned like an idiot, the sole variety in his purple face being his little peering grey eyes and yellow teeth ; called for another glass, swore he would not stand it ; and after many attempts to provoke his humorous antagonist to single combat, which the other turned off (after working him up to a ludicrous pitch of choler) with great adroitness, he fell quietly asleep with a glass of liquor in his hand, which he could not lift to his head. . . . The morning dawns ; that dim but yet clear light appears, which weighs like solid bars of metal on the sleepless eyelids ; the guests dropped down from their chambers one by one—but it was too late to think of going to bed now.

WILLIAM HAZLITT (from *The Fight*)

THE TRUE GENTLEMAN

It is almost a definition of a gentleman to say that he is one who never inflicts pain. This description is both refined and, as far as it goes, accurate. He is mainly occupied in merely removing the obstacles which hinder the free and unembarrassed action of those about him; and he concurs with their movements rather than takes the initiative himself. His benefits may be considered as parallel to what are called comforts or conveniences in arrangements of a personal nature: like an easy chair or a good fire, which do their part in dispelling cold and fatigue, though nature provides both means of rest and animal heat without them. The true gentleman in like manner carefully avoids whatever may cause a jar or a jolt in the minds of those with whom he is cast;—all clashing of opinion, or collision of feeling, all restraint, or suspicion, or gloom, or resentment; his great concern being to make every one at their ease and at home. He has his eyes on all his company; he is tender towards the bashful, gentle towards the distant, and merciful towards the absurd; he can recollect to whom he is speaking; he guards against unreasonable allusions, or topics which may irritate; he is seldom prominent in conversation, and never wearisome. He makes light of favours while he does them, and seems to be receiving when he is conferring. He never speaks of himself except when compelled, never defends himself by a mere retort, he has no ears for slander or gossip, is scrupulous in imputing motives to those who interfere with him, and interprets everything for the best. He is never mean or little in his disputes, never takes un-fair advantage, never mistakes personalities or sharp say-ings for arguments, or insinuates evil which he dare not say out. From a long-sighted prudence, he observes the maxim of the ancient sage, that we should even conduct ourselves towards our enemy as if he were one day to be our friend. He has too much good sense to be affronted at insults, he is too well employed to remember injuries, and too indolent to bear malice. He is patient, forbearing and resigned, on philosophical principles; he submits to pain, because it is inevitable, to bereavement, because it is irreparable, and to death, because it is his destiny. If he engages in controversy of any kind his disciplined intellect preserves him from the blundering discourtesy of better, perhaps, but less educated minds; who, like blunt weapons, tear and hack instead of cutting clean, who mistake the point in argument, waste their strength on trifles, misconceive their adversary and leave the question more involved than they find it. He may be right or wrong in his opinion, but he is too clear-headed to be unjust; he is as simple as he is forcible, and as brief as he is decisive. Nowhere shall we find greater candour, consideration, indulgence: he throws himself into the minds of his opponents, he accounts for their mistakes. He knows the weakness of human reason as well as its strength.

CARDINAL NEWMAN (from *The Idea of a University*)

DINNER WITH A BACHELOR

I expected Miss Matty to jump at this invitation; but, no! Miss Pole and I had the greatest difficulty in persuading her to go. She thought it was improper; and was even half annoyed when we utterly ignored the idea of any impropriety in her going with two other ladies to see her old lover. Then came a more serious difficulty. She did not think Deborah would have liked her to go. This took us half a day's good hard talking to get over; but, at the first sentence of relenting, I seized the opportunity, and wrote and dispatched an acceptance in her name—

717

fixing day and hour, that all might be decided and done with . . .

She was in a state of silent agitation all the way to Woodley. She had evidently never been there before; and, although she little dreamt I knew anything of her early story, I could perceive she was in a tremor at the thought of seeing the place which might have been her home, and round which it is probable that many of her innocent girlish imaginations had clustered. It was a long drive there, through paved jolting lanes. Miss Matilda sat bolt upright, and looked wistfully out of the windows, as we drew near the end of our journey. The aspect of the country was quiet and pastoral. Woodley stood among fields; and there was an old-fashioned garden, where roses and currant bushes touched each other, and where the feathery asparagus formed a pretty background to the pinks and gillyflowers; there was no drive up to the door: we got out at a little gate, and walked up a straight box-edged path. " My cousin might make a drive, I think," said Miss Pole, who was afraid of earache, and had only her cap on.

" I think it is very pretty," said Miss Matty, with a soft plaintiveness in her voice, and almost in a whisper; for just then Mr. Holbrook appeared at the door, rubbing his hands in very effervescence of hospitality. He looked more like my idea of Don Quixote than ever, and yet the likeness was only external. His respectable housekeeper stood modestly at the door to bid us welcome; and while she led the elder ladies upstairs to a bedroom, I begged to look about the garden. My request evidently pleased the old gentleman; who took me all round the place, and showed me his six-and-twenty cows, named after the different letters of the alphabet. . .

When he and I went in, we found that dinner was nearly ready in the kitchen,—for so I suppose the room ought to be called, as there were oak dressers and cupboards all round, an oven by the side of the fireplace, and only a small Turkey carpet in the middle of the flag-floor. . .

When the ducks and green peas came, we looked at each other in dismay ; we had only two-pronged, black handled forks. It is true, the steel was as bright as silver ; but what were we to do ? Miss Matty picked up her peas, one by one, on the point of the prongs, much as Aminé ate her grains of rice after her previous feast with the Ghoul. Miss Pole sighed over her delicate young peas as she left them on one side of her plate untasted ; for they *would* drop between the prongs. I looked at my host : the peas were going wholesale into his capacious mouth, shovelled up by his large round-ended knife. I saw, I imitated, I survived ! My friends, in spite of my precedent, could not muster up courage enough to do an ungenteel thing ; and, if Mr. Holbrook had not been so heartily hungry, he would probably have seen that the good peas went away almost untouched.

After dinner, a clay pipe was brought in, and a spittoon ; and, asking us to retire to another room, where he would soon join us, if we disliked tobacco-smoke, he presented his pipe to Miss Matty, and requested her to fill the bowl. This was a compliment to a lady in his youth ; but it was rather inappropriate to propose it as an honour to Miss Matty, who had been trained by her sister to hold smoking of every kind in utter abhorrence. But if it was a shock to her refinement, it was also a gratification to her feelings to be thus selected ; so she daintily stuffed the strong tobacco into the pipe ; and then we withdrew.

"It is very pleasant dining with a bachelor," said Miss Matty, softly, as we settled ourselves in the counting-house. "I only hope it is not improper; so many pleasant things are!"

ELIZABETH GASKELL (from *Cranford*)

ON GETTING UP ON COLD MORNINGS

Some people say it is a very easy thing to get up of a cold morning. You have only, they tell you, to take the resolution; and the thing is done. This may be very true; just as a boy at school has only to take a flogging, and the thing is over. But we have not at all made up our minds upon it; and we find it a very pleasant exercise to discuss the matter, candidly, before we get up. This, at least, is not idling, though it may be lying. It affords an excellent answer to those who ask how lying in bed can be indulged in by a reasoning being,—a rational creature. How? Why, with the argument calmly at work in one's head, and the clothes over one's shoulder. Oh—it is a fine way of spending a sensible, impartial half-hour.

If these people would be more charitable they would get on with their argument better. But they are apt to reason so ill, and to assert so dogmatically, that one could wish to have them stand round one's bed, of a bitter morning, and *lie* before their faces. They ought to hear both sides of the bed, the inside and out. If they cannot entertain themselves with their own thoughts for half-an-hour or so, it is not the fault of those who can. . .

On my first movement towards the anticipation of getting up I find that such parts of the sheets and bolster

720

as are exposed to the air of the room are stone cold. On opening my eyes, the first thing that meets them is my own breath rolling forth, as if in the open air, like smoke out of a chimney. Think of this symptom. Then I turn my eyes sideways and see the window all frozen over. Think of that. Then the servant comes in. " It is very cold this morning, is it not ? "—" Very cold, sir."— " Very cold indeed, isn't it ? "—" Very cold indeed, sir."—" More than usually so, isn't it, even for this weather ? " (Here the servant's wit and good-nature are put to a considerable test, and the inquirer lies on thorns for the answer.) " Why, sir . . . I think it *is*." (Good creature ! There is not a better or more truth-telling servant going.) " I must rise, however—get me some warm water."—Here comes a fine interval between the departure of the servant and the arrival of the hot water; during which, of course, it is of " no use ? " to get up. The hot water comes. " Is it quite hot ? "—" Yes, sir."— " Perhaps too hot for shaving ; I must wait a little ? "— " No, sir ; it will just do." (There is an over-nice propriety sometimes, an officious zeal of virtue, a little troublesome.) " Oh—the shirt—you must air my clean shirt ;—linen gets very damp this weather."—" Yes, sir." Here another delicious five minutes. A knock at the door. " Oh, the shirt—very well. My stockings—I think the stockings had better be aired too."—" Very well, sir. Here another interval. At length everything is ready, except myself.

LEIGH HUNT

EL DORADO

To be truly happy is a question of how we begin and not of how we end, of what we want and not of what we have. An aspiration is a joy for ever, a possession as solid as a landed estate, a fortune which we can never exhaust and which gives us year by year a revenue of pleasurable activity. To have many of these is to be spiritually rich. Life is only a very dull and ill-directed theatre unless we have some interests in the piece ; and to those who have neither art nor science, the world is a mere arrangement of colours, or a rough footway where they may very well break their shins. It is in virtue of his own desires and curiosities that any man continues to exist with even patience, that he is charmed by the look of things and people, and that he wakens every morning with a renewed appetite for work and pleasure.

R. L. STEVENSON (from *El Dorado*)

DARK HOURS

In the ordinary way I have to woo my sleep, and that is one reason why I have read so many books, chasing Morpheus down innumerable labyrinths of eighteenth-century moralising or twentieth-century introspection. Those no-sooner-have-I-touched-the-pillow people are past my comprehension. There is something suspiciously bovine about them. When they begin to yawn about half-past ten, as they always do when I am with them (and I make you a present of the inevitable comment,) I feel that they forfeit all right to be considered as fellow-creatures, spirits

here for a season that they may exchange confidences at
the hour when all the beasts that perish are fast asleep.
I do not complain about having to approach sleep so
stealthily, tip-toeing through a chapter or so. After all, this
is only to prolong the day, and I cannot help thinking that
such a reluctance to part for ever from the day, though it
be only an unconscious reluctance, is proof of an affectionate nature, unwilling to dismiss a servant, however poor a
thing. Nor do I complain—though I like it less—about
waking too early, beginning the day before it is fairly
ready for me, nothing but a grey little monster with the
chill on it and still opposed to all our nobler activities.
I have been told that as the years wither me away, I shall
have more and more of these early wakings, and I cannot
say that the prospect pleases me. But for the moment I will
submit to it without complaint, for there are worse things,
and all this last week I have been suffering from them. I
have been finding myself awake, not at the end of one
day nor at the beginning of another, but sometime between them, in the mysterious dark hours.

Now this I do most bitterly resent. I have accustomed
myself to prolonging the day, and I will try hard to resign
myself to beginning it before it is worth beginning, but
this other thing, this awful interloping piece of time,
neither honest to-day nor splendid to-morrow, is a horror.
You suddenly wake up, open your eyes, expecting welcome daylight and the morning's post and the savour of
breakfast, only to discover that it is still dark, that nothing
is happening. You roll over, turn back then over again,
curl your legs up, stretch them out, push your hands under
the pillow, then take them out, all to no purpose ; sleep
will not come. You have been thrust, a dreadfully alert
consciousness, into some black No Man's Land of time.

Reading, for once, fails as a resource. Frequently your eyes are so tired that the lines of print become blurred and run into one another. But even if you have no difficulty in seeing, it is still hard to read because all the savour seems to have departed from literature. You feel as if you were trying to attack a dish of cold potatoes. Even a new play by Shakespeare would leave you indifferent. I remember spending one very hot night in a London hotel. The place was full and I was a late-comer, so that I was given a tiny bed-room not far from the roof and looking out on nothing but a deep narrow court. I got off to sleep very quickly, but awoke about two and then vainly tossed and turned. There was nothing for it but to read, and I switched on my light. As a rule I have a book in my bag, but this night I was completely bookless, and the only reading matter in the room was that supplied by two evening papers. I had already glanced through these papers, but now I had to settle down to read them as I have never read evening papers before or since. Every scrap of print, sports gossip, society chit-chat, City Notes, small advertisements, was steadily devoured. There I was, in my hot little aerie, reading those silly paragraphs about Lord A leaving town or Miss B the musical comedy star making puddings, while the night burned slowly away. For weeks afterwards the sight of an evening paper made me feel depressed.

J. B. PRIESTLEY (from *The Dark Hours*)

MONTAIGNE

The True Friendship

I cannot allow other common friendships to be placed in the same line with ours. I have as much knowledge of them as another, and of the most perfect of their kind, but I should not advise any one to measure them with the same rule ; he would be much mistaken. In those other friendships one has to walk with the bridle in one's hand, prudently and cautiously: the knot is not tied so tightly but that it will cause some misgiving. " Love him," said Chilo, " as if you had one day to hate him ; hate him, as if you had to love him." This precept which is so abominable in this sovereign and commanding friendship, is of salutory use in the common and customary friendships to which must be applied the saying that Aristotle was so fond of, " Oh my friends ! there is no friend."

In this noble intercourse, good offices and benefits, the feeders of other friendships, deserve not even to be taken into account, by reason of the complete blending of our wills. For even as the love I bear to myself is not increased by the succour I give myself in time of need, whatever the Stoics may say, and as I feel no gratitude to myself for the service I do myself; so the union of such friends, being truly perfect, makes them lose the sense of such duties, and hate and banish from their minds these words that imply separation and distinction : benefit, obligation, gratitude, request, thanks, and the like. Everything being actually in common between them, wills, thoughts, opinions, possessions, wives, children, honour, and life, and their agreement being such that they are but one soul in two bodies, according to the very apt definition of Aristotle, they can neither lend nor give anything to one another. That is why the makers of laws, in order to honour marriage with some imaginary resemblance to this divine alliance, interdict all donations between husband and wife; meaning to infer therefrom that all should belong to each of them, and that they have nothing to divide and share out between them.

If, in the friendship of which I speak, one could give to the other, it would be the one who received the benefit that lays his friend under an obligation. For, as each of them studies above all to benefit the other, it is he who furnishes the matter and occasion that plays the liberal part, by giving his friend the satisfaction of doing that to him which he most desires.

When the philosopher Diogenes was in want of money he used to say that he redemanded it of his friends, not that he demanded it. And to show how that works in practice, I will relate a singular example from antiquity.

Eudamidas of Corinth had two friends, Charixenus a Sicyonian and Aretheus a Corinthian. When on his death-bed, being poor, and his two friends rich, he made his will after this manner: " My legacy to Aretheus is that he maintain my mother and support her in her old age; to Charixenus, that he give my daughter in marriage, and provide her with as good a dowry as he is able to afford; and in case one of them chance to die I appoint his survivor to take his place." They who first saw this testament laughed at it; but when the heirs were informed of it, they accepted it with a singular satisfaction. And one of them, Charixenus, dying five days later, leaving Aretheus at liberty to take his place, the latter supported the mother with great care, and of five talents he had in his estate, he gave two and a half as a marriage portion to his only daughter and two and a half to the daughter of Eudamidas and the two weddings took place on the same day.

This example is very complete, except for one objection, namely the number of friends. For that perfect friendship of which I speak is indivisible: each one gives himself so wholly to his friend, that there remains to him nothing to divide with another; on the contrary he grieves that he is not double, triple, or fourfold, and that he has not several souls and several wills, to confer them all on the object of his love.

Common friendships are capable of being shared : we may love one for his handsome exterior, another for his easy-going manners, another again for his liberality; this one for his fatherly and that one for his brotherly ways, and so forth ; but this friendship which possesses the soul and dominates it with absolute power, cannot possibly be split in two. If two at the same time entreated your assistance, to which of them would you hasten ? If they required of you opposite services, how would you arrange it? If one of them imparted to you a secret that it would be useful for the other to know, how would you solve the difficulty ?

The unique and paramount friendship dissolves all other obligations. The secret that I have sworn not to reveal to another, I may without perjury communicate to one who is not another : that is myself. It is miracle enough to divide oneself into two, and they know not the greatness of it who speak of dividing oneself into three. Nothing is extreme that has its like. And he who supposes that I can equally love each of two, and that they can love one another and me as much as I love them, makes a multiple brotherhood of a thing that is most one and united, and of which even one is the rarest thing in the world to find.

The sequel of that story agrees very well with what I was saying, for Eudamidas makes it a kindness and a favour to his friends to employ them for his needs. He leaves them heirs to his liberality, which consists in giving into their hands the means of benefiting him. And without doubt the power of friendship is much more richly evident in his action than in that of Aretheus.

In short, these are delights which are not to be imagined by one who has not tasted them; and therefore I highly honour the answer of a young soldier to Cyrus, who inquired of him what he would take for a horse that had just enabled him to win the prize in a race, and whether he would exchange it for a kingdom : " No indeed, Sire, but I would willingly part with it to gain a friend, if I could find a man worthy of such alliance." Not a bad answer, " if I could find "; for it is easy to find men fit for a superficial acquaintance. But in the other kind, where we exhibit the very depths of our heart and make no reservations, truly all the springs of action must be perfectly clear and true.

A Gascon Library

I never travel without books, either in peace or in war-time. Yet many days, and even months, will pass without my using them. . .

When at home I resort a little more frequently to my library, from which I can quite easily overlook my household. It is over the entry, and I see below me my garden, my farm-yard, my court-yard, and into most parts of my house. There I turn over now one book, now another, without order or plan, in a desultory way. At one time I muse, at another I make notes and dictate, walking to and fro, my fancies, such as these.

It is on the third story of a tower [1]; on the first is my chapel, on the second a bedroom with its accompaniment, where I often lie down, to be alone. Above it is a large wardrobe. Formerly this was the most useless place in my establishment. There I spend most of the days of my life, and most of the hours of the day ; I am never there at night. Adjoining the library is a rather neat study, in which a fire may be kindled in winter, very pleasantly lighted by a window. And if I did not fear the trouble more than the expense, the trouble that drives me from every kind of business, I could easily join to each side, on the same level, a gallery, a hundred paces long and twelve broad, having found all the walls raised, for another purpose, to the necessary height.

Every place of retirement requires a place for walking. My thoughts go to sleep if I sit still. My mind will not move unless stirred by my legs. All who study without a book are in the same plight.

My library is circular in shape, the only flat side being that needed for my table and chair ; it being rounded I can see all my books at a glance, arranged about me on five rows of shelves. From this room I have three open and extensive views ; and it offers sixteen paces of empty space in diameter.

In winter I am not there so continually, for my house is perched upon an eminence, as its name implies, and no room is more exposed to the winds than this, which,

1 The tower here described is still standing on its hill in Périgord. A. S.

being rather difficult of access and a little out of the way, I like, both for the benefit of the exercise and because I can keep people at a distance.

Pain and Pleasure

We are naturally so feeble that we cannot enjoy things in their native purity and simplicity. The elements we live on are corrupted ; and so are the metals : even gold must be debased with some other matter to fit it for our use. . .

Of the pleasures and good things we enjoy not one is exempt from some mixture of evil and discomfort. . . Our keenest pleasure appears, as it were, to groan and lament. Would you not think it were dying of anguish ? Nay, when we compose a picture of it at its highest point : we deck it out with sickly and painful epithets and qualities, languor, softness, weakness, faintness, *morbidezza*; a great testimony to their consanguinity and consubstantiality.

In profound joy there is more seriousness than gaiety ; in the highest and fullest contentment more soberness than merriment. " Even felicity, unless it be tempered, overwhelms " (Seneca). Happiness grinds us down.

That is the meaning of an old Greek line which says " that the gods sell us all the good things they give us;" that is to say, that they give us none pure and perfect and that we do not buy at the price of some evil.

Toil and pleasure, very unlike by nature, are however joined together by some sort of natural connexion.

Socrates said that some god tried to mix in one lump and

to confound pain and pleasure; but that, unable to succeed, he bethought himself to couple them at least by the tail.

Metrodorus said that in sadness there is some alloy of pleasure. I know not whether he meant something else, but for my part I imagine there is a certain amount of purpose, acquiescence, and satisfaction in nursing one's melancholy; I mean besides the desire for approval which may be mixed up with it. There is a little shade of daintiness and delicacy that smiles upon and flatters us in the very lap of melancholy.

Of Sleeping

Reason commands us ever to walk along the same path, but not at the same pace; and, although the wise man should not permit his human passions to turn him from the right course, he may indeed, without prejudice to his duty, leave it to them to hasten or retard his steps and not plant himself like an immovable and impassive Colossus. Though Virtue herself should put on flesh and blood, I believe her pulse would beat more strongly when marching to an attack than when going to dinner: nay, it is necessary that she should be subject to emotion and heat. For that reason I have remarked as a rare thing to see great men, when engaged in the loftiest enterprises and the most important affairs, keep themselves so entirely in trim, as not even to curtail their sleep.

Alexander the Great, on the day assigned to that furious battle against Darius, slept so profoundly and so late in the morning, that Parmenion was obliged to enter his chamber, and, approaching his bed, call him two or three times by name to awaken him, the moment to go to battle being so urgent.

The Emperor Otho, having resolved to kill himself, on that same night, when he had settled his domestic affairs, divided his money among his servants, and sharpened the edge of a sword wherewith he intended to take his own life, staying only to know if each of his friends had retired in safety, fell into so sound a sleep, that his chamber-servants heard him snore.

The death of that Emperor has many points in common with that of the great Cato, and particularly that just mentioned: for, Cato being ready to make away with himself, whilst awaiting news to be brought him whether the Senators whom he was sending away had evacuated the port of Utica, began to sleep so soundly that he could be heard breathing from the next room : and when the man he had sent to the port awakened him to tell him that the Senators were prevented by a storm from conveniently setting sail, he sent yet another, and, resettling himself in his bed, again began to slumber until the second messenger assured him of their departure.

We may also compare with that of Alexander his behaviour in that great and dangerous storm which threatened him through the sedition of Metellus the Tribune, when the latter insisted on publishing the decree recalling Pompey with his army to the city, on the occasion of Catiline's conspiracy ; which decree Cato alone opposing, high words and violent threats passed between him and Metellus in the Senate. But it was on the next day that the matter was to be put into execution in the Forum, where Metellus, besides being favoured by the common people and by Caesar, then conspiring in Pompey's interest, was to appear accompanied by many alien slaves and desperate gladiators, Cato being fortified by his courage alone. His friends and relations and many worthy people were consequently in great anxiety about him, some of whom spent the night together without any desire to sleep, eat or drink, on account of the danger they saw threatening him, his wife and sisters especially did nothing but weep and fret in his house, whilst he, on the contrary, comforted everybody, and after having supped in his usual manner, retired to his couch, and slept a very sound sleep till morning, when one of his fellow tribunes roused him to go to the skirmish.

The knowledge we possess of the greatness of this man's courage, throughout the rest of his life, may enable us to judge in all sureness that his conduct proceeded from a soul so far raised above such accidents, that he disdained to allow this one to cause him any more uneasiness than any ordinary event.

In the naval battle which Augustus won against Sextus Pompeius in Sicily, when on the point of entering into conflict, he was sunk in so deep a sleep, that his friends had to rouse him to give the signal for attack. This gave occasion to M. Antonius to reproach him afterwards, that he had not had the heart even to behold with open eyes the array of his army, and that he had not dared to appear before his soldiers until Agrippa came to announce to him the victory he had gained over his enemies.

But as to the young Marius, who did still worse, for on the day of his last battle against Sylla, after having marshalled his army and given the word and signal for battle, he lay down to rest in the shade of a tree, and slept so heavily that he could hardly be awakened by the rout and flight of his own men, having seen nothing of the battle; they say it was because he was so extremely spent with fatigue and the want of sleep, that nature could hold out no longer.

On the subject of sleep, the physicians will determine whether it is so necessary that our life depends on it: for we hear indeed that King Perseus of Macedon, when prisoner at Rome, was brought to his death by being prevented from sleeping; but Pliny instances cases of people who lived a long time without sleep. In Herodotus we read of nations where men sleep and wake by half-years. And they who wrote the life of the sage Epimenides say that he slept for fifty-seven years on end.

Is Death an Evil?

Theodorus replied to Lysimachus, who was threatening to kill him, " Thou wilt do a great thing in doing what a Spanish fly could do ! " Most of the philosophers are seen to have either designedly anticipated, or hastened and aided their own death. How many men of the people we see led to their death, and that not a simple death, but attended with ignominy and sometimes with cruel tortures, and exhibiting such assurance, the one through stubbornness, the other through a natural simplicity, that we may perceive no change from their ordinary demeanour; settling their domestic affairs, commending themselves to their friends, singing, preaching, and talking to the people, nay, sometimes jesting and drinking to their acquaintances, as cheerfully as Socrates.

A man who was being led to the gibbet said " For goodness' sake don't go by such and such a street, where I shall run the risk of being collared by a tradesman for an old debt." Another entreated the hangman " not to touch his neck, for he was so ticklish he would shake with laughter." Another replied to his confessor, who was promising him that he should sup that night with our Lord, " You may go yourself, for I am fasting." Another, having called for drink, and the hangman drinking before him, said he would not drink after him for fear of catching the pox. Everybody has heard the story of the man of Picardy who, when on the ladder, was presented with a girl, with the offer (as our justice sometimes permits) that, if he would marry her, his life should be spared ; he, having considered her for a while and perceived that she halted, said, " Tie up ! Tie up ! she limps." The same tale is current of a man in Denmark who was condemned to lose his head ; being on the scaffold he was offered the same condition, but refused it on the ground that the girl they offered him had flabby cheeks and too sharp a nose. . .

Fortune does us neither good nor harm : she only holds out to us the seed and the matter of good or harm, which our soul, more powerful than she, turns and applies as she pleases, being sole cause and mistress of her happy or unhappy condition.

Essays (Trans. E. J. TRECHMANN)

SOME THOUGHTS OF PASCAL

We rate human reason so highly that no matter what privileges we have, we are not content unless we stand well with our fellows. This, we think, is the finest position in the world; and those who place man on a level with the brutes still wish to be admired and believed in by men, for their feelings convince them of the greatness of man more powerfully than their reason convinces them of his vileness.

Man may be overwhelmed by a natural force, but he is nobler than his destroyer; for man knows that Nature has this power, while Nature knows nothing.

Justice and Truth are of too fine a quality to be measured by our clumsy human instruments.

We are conscious of beauty when there is a harmonious relation between something in our nature and the quality of the object which delights us.

Whoever will know fully the vanity of man has but to consider the causes and the effects of love. Its cause is unknown: its effects are over-powering. This unknown something is so intangible a matter that we cannot analyse it. Yet it moves the whole world, princes, armies, and people. If Cleopatra's nose had been shorter, how many countries would have had a different history!

From *Pensées* (Trans. A. S.)

ADVICE FROM AN ARCHBISHOP

(Letter to a Young Nephew, advising him to go to Court)

Jan. 7, 1713

I am not surprised at your disliking it—one feels constrained with people whom one knows but little or not at all, and one does badly that which one is not accustomed to do. Our self-esteem is apt to assert itself when we control our dispositions without making much progress. You are accustomed to a simple life, made easy and acceptable by the friendship of those around you, and this spoils you. You must grow accustomed to mental fatigue in the world as to bodily fatigue in camp. The longer you postpone the labour of making acquaintance with the world the harder it will grow, not to say impossible. You run the risk of very decided failure after a certain age ; and if you give it up entirely, you will spend your life in obscurity, without any distinguished friends, without credit or position, without any reward for your service, or any means of helping your family. So it is important that you should at once break the ice courageously and patiently. Ease will gradually come with practice. You will not be shy when you know everybody and everybody knows you, when you are accustomed to the new ways and are qualified to enter into familiar conversation with those around you. As soon as you have made friends with a few worthy, highly-esteemed people, they will admit you into their society, and by degrees you will get all you want. You will be courteous to every one, you will pay customary civilities to individuals, while for real society you will limit yourself to true

Z_B

friends. In these you must look not merely for goodness, but for a certain standing and position. . .

As for Paris, keep some hours to yourself for work; avoid suppers, which are prolonged too late and upset all the next day; try to save some part of your mornings for yourself. Read, and reflect on what you read. I am quite aware that you cannot always be so regular; good nature to friends must sometimes lay you open to invasion, society and the habits of the age demand it; but while giving up something to your friends' amusement, you must rescue those hours without which you would do nothing to make you worthy of their friendship.

FÉNÉLON (Trans. A. s.)

SAYINGS OF LA BRUYÈRE

A fine face is the loveliest thing we can see, and the voice of a friend makes our sweetest music.

The most delightful intercourse a man can have is with a lovely woman who has the qualities of a gentleman.

A delicate thought is the finest product, and, as it were, the flower of the soul.

(Trans. A.s.)

ROUSSEAU

Father and Son

I know not how I learned to read; I recollect only my first reading, and its effect on me. From this time I date my continuing knowledge of myself. There was in the house a collection of romances which had belonged to my mother, and my father and I sat down to read them after supper. My father's object, at first, was merely to instruct me in reading by means of amusing books ; but we both became so interested in these adventures that we read by turns without relaxation, and often spent whole nights in that occupation. We could never stop till we got to the end of the book. Sometimes my father, hearing the swallows outside the window, would jump up, exclaiming " Let us go to bed ; I am more of a child than you."

A Night in the Open

It is certainly a hardship to pass one's nights in the street, and this happened to me several times at Lyons. I decided to spend my few remaining sous on food rather than on lodgings, for I thought I should die sooner from want of food than from want of sleep. I was surprised to find that in this unfortunate situation I was neither sad nor uneasy. I felt no misgivings about the future, and lying on the ground or stretched out on a bench I slept as peacefully as on a bed of roses. I remember one delightful night I spent outside the city, on a roadside by the Rhone or the Saône—I forget which. Above the road some terraced gardens faced the river. It had been a hot day, and the evening was very pleasant. The withered grass was wet with dew. The setting sun had filled the sky with crimson clouds, making lovely reflexions in the river. It was a serene and windless night, fresh but not too cold. The trees above the gardens were full of nightingales calling to each other. I walked about in a kind of ecstasy, giving myself up to delightful sensations, but not without a sigh of regret that I must enjoy this happiness alone. Absorbed in my reverie, I walked far into the night without noticing that I was tired. At length I did so, and lay down on the slab of a kind of niche or false door let into a wall. My bed was canopied by overhanging branches, and a nightingale, perched above my head, sang me to sleep. I awoke refreshed. It was broad day-light, and I beheld again the river, the friendly trees and the pleasant fields. I got up and shook off my drowsiness. I soon felt hungry, and with a light heart I made for the town, resolved to spend the two coins I had left on a good breakfast.

The Nightingale Again

It was on the 9th of April, 1756, that I left cities never to reside in them again. Madame d'Épinay came and took us in her carriage. My little retreat was furnished with simplicity and taste. Although the weather was cold (for there had been more snow) there was already some growth, and I saw both violets and primroses. Trees were beginning to bud, and on the night of my arrival the nightingale sang his first song hard by my window, for the house was on the edge of a wood. After a light sleep, forgetting my change of abode, I fancied myself still in the Rue de Grenelle until the twittering of the birds gave me a start and I exclaimed " At last my wishes are fulfilled."

The first thing I did was to give myself up to the impressions of my rural surroundings. Instead of setting my things in order indoors I began to plan my walks abroad, and by the next day I had become familiar with every path, every grove and every corner of the grounds. The more I explored this delightful retreat, the more I felt satisfied with it. This wild, or rather solitary, spot seemed to me to be the end of the world. It had beauty of a kind hardly to be found in the neighbourhood of a city, and no one suddenly transferred there would imagine that he was within four leagues of Paris.

The Lake of Bienne

I have ever been passionately fond of water, and the sight of it throws me into a delightful reverie, although often without a definite object. When the weather was fine, immediately after getting out of bed, I never failed to run to the terrace to breathe the fresh and invigorating morning air, and feast my eyes on this lovely lake, its shores and its mountains. I can easily understand why the inhabitants of cities, who (surrounded by walls) see nothing but the streets and their crimes, have little faith, but it is not so easy to see how country people—especially those in remote places—can be without it. How comes it that these do not a hundred times a day elevate their souls in ecstasy to the Author of the wonders which they see? For my part,—especially when I rise wearied from want of sleep—long habit inclines me to this elevation, which does not give me the trouble of thinking. This is when my eyes can behold the ravishing spectacle of nature. In my chamber I pray less frequently, and less fervently, but at the view of a fine landscape I feel myself moved, yet by what I am unable to tell. I have somewhere read of a wise bishop who came across an old woman whose only prayer consisted in the single interjection Oh! " Good mother," said he to her, " continue always to pray thus. Your prayer is better than ours."

From *Confessions* (Trans. A. S.)

741

Wisdom is to the mind what meat is to the body.

Perfect valour consists in doing without a witness all that we should be capable of doing before the whole world.

We are much nearer loving those that hate us, than those who love us more than we like.

No person is either so happy or so unhappy as he imagines.

Happiness lies in imagination, not in possession ; we are made happy by obtaining, not what others think desirable, but what we ourselves think so.

The greatest faults are those of Great Men.

To praise great actions with sincerity, may be said to be taking part in them.

AMIEL

A dream is an excursion into the world beyond, a temporary deliverance from our human prison. When we dream we are a theatre in which various scenes are staged, and we are at the same time involuntary spectators of the performance. We are then passive and without personality—the playthings of unknown forces and invisible powers.

A man who lives habitually in a state of dreaming is hardly alive; but a man who never dreams can know his own character only when it is formed, knowing nothing of the genesis of personality—he will be like a crystal without a crystal-gazer. Dreams are rare in old age, for they arise from our vital energy, being indeed, the flower of organic life.

Thought represents the highest point in the series of ascending changes which we call Nature. If our thoughts are turned inward—if we look within ourselves—we shall be fully compensated for what we miss of the outside world; for our compensation will be no less than that privilege of self-direction which is our true liberty. Our dreams, throwing everything into confusion and removing all limits, make us realise how severe are the conditions of the higher existence. It is, however, by means of our conscious and voluntary thoughts that we are capable of knowing and doing. Let us dream, then, to satisfy our psychological curiosity and our desire for diversion; but let us not despise thought, which gives us power and dignity. Let us begin like wise men of the East, but let us end like wise men of the West, for each has one half of wisdom.

.   .   .   .

Our greatness depends upon our needs. Tell me what you wish for and I will tell you what you are. You will reply, perhaps, that resignation is better than aspiration. That is true, but not of a resignation which is passive, melancholy, and unmanly—it is true only of a resignation which is compelling and serene, resulting from an act of will. The former is negative, nothing more than regret: the latter is a possession of the mind and includes hope. Consider this, and you will see that your resignation may be in reality an aspiration.

.   .   .   .

The surface of the sand is indented with little spots, and heavy clouds hang in the sky. The sea, veined tawny and green, has taken on a work-a-day aspect. It goes about its business without threat and without tenderness. As I walk along the shore I come across a heap of shell-fish about to crumble, and I perceive that the sand dunes may well be the detritus of the organic life of past ages, pyramids built up by millions of generations of little fishes, who have laboured on these shores as good workmen of God. If, then, sand-hills and mountains are the dust of beings who have preceded us, how can we doubt that our death will be as useful as our life—how doubt that nothing that has ever flourished can be lost? A mutual lending and serving seems to be a law of life. But the strong exploit or destroy the weak, and this concrete inequality of parts, in spite of the abstract equality of the whole, leaves us with disquieting thoughts of divine justice.

.   .   .   .

The secret of remaining young in spite of old age and white hairs is to preserve our enthusiasm, and this we can do by means of meditation and goodwill—in short by maintaining harmony in ourselves. When everything has its proper place in our minds we are able to stand in equilibrium with the rest of the world. A solemn enthusiasm for the order and beauty of the universe, an elevated mind and a serene benevolence—these things are, perhaps, the very foundations of wisdom.

From *Fragments d'un Journal Intime* (Trans. A. S.)

SAINTE-BEUVE

A Plea for Quiet Books

A friend who, after having seen much of the world, has withdrawn from it almost entirely, and judges at a distance—as it were from the shore—the swift whirlpool in which the rest of us are tossed about, lately wrote to me about certain rough estimates I had made of contemporary writings: "What you say of our 'sublimities' interests me very much. Certainly they are sublime. What they lack is calm and freshness, as it were a little cold water to cool our burning palates." This quality of freshness and delicacy, this clearness of emotion and sobriety of speech, this soft and quiet shading, as they disappear on all hands from actual life and the imaginative writings now produced, become all the more precious when we meet them in obscurity, and in those pleasing compositions in which they were last reflected. It would be a mistake to suppose that it is a sign of weakness or degeneracy to regret these vanished charms—these flowers which, it would appear, could bloom only in the very last days of an order of society now passed away. The softly-tinted pictures of which we speak presuppose a kind of taste and culture which democratic civilisation could not have abolished without loss, unless something analogous were to reappear later on. Modern society, when it shall have become a little more settled and better defined, will also have its element of repose, its cool, mysterious nooks, its shades favourable to refined sentiment, a few tolerably ancient forests, a few undiscovered fountains. It will admit into its seemingly uniform framework a thousand varieties of thought, and many a rare form of inner life : otherwise it will be, in one respect, far inferior to the civilisation which preceded it, and will hardly meet the needs of a whole family of souls. In a progressive age, in times confused and incoherent like the present, it is natural to aim at what seems most important, to follow the general movement, and everywhere, even in literature, to strike boldly, aim high, and shout through trumpets or speaking-tubes. The modest graces will, perhaps, eventually, come back and come with an expression appropriate to their new surroundings. I would fain believe it; but while hoping for the best, I feel sure that it will not be to-morrow that their sentiments and their speech will once more prevail. Meanwhile, we realise that something is wanting, and suffer accordingly. We betake ourselves, in our hours of *ennui* to the perfumes of the past—a past only of yesterday, which, nevertheless, will not return.

From *Portraits de Femmes* (Trans. A. S.)

FOURTH PART

§ III A SANCTUARY OF QUIET

e la sua volontate è nostra pace :
    ella è quel mare, al qual tutto si move
    ciò ch' ella crea e che natura face.

DANTE (*Paradiso*, III)

Truth hath a quiet breast.

SHAKESPEARE (*Richard II*)

§ III A SANCTUARY OF QUIET

A BALLAD OF GOOD COUNSEL

Flee fro the press, and dwelle with sothfastnesse,
Suffice thine owen thing, though it be small ;
That thee is sent receive in buxumnesse,
The wrastling for this worlde axeth a fall ;
Here is none home, here is but wildernesse.
Forth, pilgrim, forth ! Forth, beast, out of thy stall !
Know thy countrèy, look up, thank God of all ;
Hold the high way, and let thy ghost thee lede,
And truthé shall deliver, it js no drede.

CHAUCER (from " Truth ")

GARMENT FOR A FAIR LADY

Her gown should be of goodliness
Well ribboned with renown,
Purfilled [1] with pleasure in ilk place
Furrèd with fine fashòn. [2]

Her belt should be of benignity
About her middle met ;
Her mantle of humility,
To thole [3] both wind and wet.

Her hat should be of fair having,
And her tippèt of truth,
Her ruffet of good pansing [4]
Her neck-ribbòn of ruth.

---

[1] Bordered.   [2] Good manners.   [3] Endure.   [4] Fair thought.

Her sleeves should be of esperance
To keep her from despair ;
Her gloves of the good governance
To guide her fingers fair.

Her shoon should be of sickerness,[1]
For then she would not slide ;
Her hose of honesty I guess,
I should for her provide.

Would she put on this garment gay,
I durst swear by my seel
That she wore never green nor grey
Suited her half so weel.

ROBERT HENRYSON

MEDITATION IN WINTER

In to these dirk and drumlie days,
When sabill all the hewin arrays
With misty vapours, clouds, and skies,
Nature all courage me denies
Of sangis, ballads, and of plays.

When that the night does lenthin hours,
With wind, with hail, and heavy showers,
My dulè spreit does lurk for schoir [2] ;
My heart for languor does forloir
For lack of Summer with his flowers.

1 Security.   2 Cower for dread.

750

I walk, I turn, sleep may I not;
I vexèd am with heavy thought;
This world all o'er I cast about,
And ay the mair I am in doubt,
The mair that I remeid have sought.

I am assailed on every side.
Despair says ay :—" In time provide,
And get some thing whereon to leif,
Or with great trouble and mischèif
Thou shall in to this court abide."

And then says Age :—" My friend, come near,
And be not strange, I thee requeir!
Come, brother, by the hand me take :
Remember thou hast compt to make
Of all thy time thou spended here." . .

For fear of this all day I drowp;
No gold in kist, nor wine in cowp,
No lady's beauty, nor luif's bliss
May let me to remember this,
How glad that ever I dine or sowp.

Yet, when the night begins to short,
It does my spreit some part comfòrt,
Of thought oppressèd with the showers.
Come, lusty Summer! with thy flowers,
That I may live in some disport!

WILLIAM DUNBAR

751

AN OLD CAROL

I sing of a maiden that is makèless;
King of all kings to her son she owes,

> He came all so still
> Where His mother was,
> As dew in Aprill
> That falleth on the grass;

> He came all so still
> Where His mother lay,
> As dew in Aprill
> That falleth on the spray;

> He came all so still
> To His mother's bower,
> As dew in Aprill
> That falleth on the flower.

> Maiden and Mother
> Was never none but she;
> Well might such a Lady
> Goddis Mother be.

ANONYMOUS (15th Century)

THE OBSCURE NIGHT

Upon an obscure night
Fevered with love in love's anxiety
(O hapless-happy plight!)
I went, none seeing me,
Forth from my house where all things be.

By night, secure from sight,
And by the secret stair, disguisedly
(O hapless-happy plight!)
By night, and privily,
Forth from my house where all things quiet be.

Blest night of wandering,
In secret, where by none might I be spied,
Nor I see anything;
Without a light or guide,
Save that which in my heart burnt in my side.

That light did lead me on,
More surely than the shining of noontide,
Where well I knew that one
Did for my coming bide;
Where He abode, might none but He abide.

O night that didst lead thus,
O night more lovely than the dawn of light,
O night that broughtest us,
Lover to lover's sight,
Lover with loved in marriage of delight!

Upon my flowery breast
Wholly for Him, and save Himself for none,
There did I give sweet rest
To my belovèd one;
The fanning of the cedars breathed thereon.

When the first moving air
Blew from the tower and waved His locks aside,
His hand, with gentle care,
Did wound me in the side,
And in my body all my senses died.

All things I then forgot,
My cheek on Him who for my coming came;
All ceased, and I was not,
Leaving my cares and shame
Among the lilies, and forgetting them.

From the Spanish of ST. JOHN OF THE CROSS
(Trans. ARTHUR SYMONS)

A LOVER'S COMPLAINT

If care or skill could conquer vain desire,
Or reason's reins my strong affection stay,
Then should my sighs to quiet breast retire
And shun such sights as secret thoughts betray;
   Uncomely love, which lurks now in my breast,
   Should cease, my grief by wisdom's power oppress'd.
But who can leave to look on Venus' face,
Or yieldeth not to Juno's high estate?
What wit so wise as gives not Pallas place?
These virtues rare the Gods did yield a mate.
   Save her alone, who yet on earth doth reign,
   Whose beauty's string no God can well distrain.
What worldly wight can hope for heavenly hire,
When only sighs must make his secret moan?
A silent suit doth seld to grace aspire.
My hapless hap doth roll the restless stone.

EDWARD DE VERE, EARL OF OXFORD

FROM "THE FAERY QUEEN"

1. *Care In Heaven*

And is there care in heaven? And is there love
In heavenly spirits to these creatures base
That may compassion of their evils move?
There is—or else more wretched were the case
Of men than beasts: but O th' exceeding grace
Of Highest God that loves His creatures so,
And all His works with mercy doth embrace,
That blessèd angels He sends to and fro,
To serve to wicked man, to serve his wicked foe!

How oft do they their silver bowers leave
To come to succour us that succour want!
How oft do they with golden pinions cleave
The flitting skies, like flying pursuivant,
Against foul fiends to aid us militant!
They for us fight, they watch and duly ward,
And their bright squadrons round about us plant;
And all for love and nothing for reward:
O, why should Heavenly God to men have such regard!

2. *The End of the Passage*

What if some little pain the passage have
That makes frail flesh to fear the bitter wave;
Is not short pain well borne, that brings long ease,
And lays the soul to sleep in quiet grave?
Sleep after toil, port after stormy seas,
Ease after war, death after life, doth greatly please.

SPENSER

THE PILGRIM'S WAY

Give me my scallop-shell of quiet,
My staff of faith to walk upon,
My scrip of joy, immortal diet,
　　My bottle of salvation,
My gown of glory, hope's true gage ;
And thus I'll take my pilgrimage.
Blood must be my body's balmer ;
　　No other balm will there be given ;
Whilst my soul, like quiet palmer,
　　Travelleth towards the land of heaven ;
Over the silver mountains,
Where spring the nectar fountains—
　　　　There will I kiss
　　　　The bowl of bliss,
And drink mine everlasting fill
Upon every milken hill.
My soul will be a-dry before ;
But, after, it will thirst no more.

　　　　　　　　　SIR WALTER RALEIGH (b. 1552)

THE SCENTED GARDEN

And because the Breath of Flowers is farre Sweeter in
the Aire (where it comes and goes like the Warbling of
Musick) than in the hand, therefore nothing is more fit
for that delight than to know what be the Flowers and
Plants that doe best perfume the Aire. Roses Damask and
Red are fast Flowers of their Smells, so that you may
walke by a whole Row of them and find Nothing of their
Sweetnesse ; yea, though it be in a Morning's Dew.
Bayes likewise yeeld no Smell as they grow ; Rosemary

756

little ; nor Sweet-Marjoram. That which above all Others
yeelds the Sweetest Smell in the Aire is the Violet;
specially the White-double Violet, which comes twice a
Yeare, about the middle of Aprill, and about Bartholo-
mew-tide. Next to that is the Muske-Rose ; then the
Strawberry-Leaves dying, with a most excellent Cordiall
Smell. Then the Flower of the Vines ; it is a little dust,
like the dust of a Bent, which growes upon the Cluster in
the first comming forth. Then Sweet Briar. Then Wall-
Flowers, which are very Delightfull, to be set under a
Parler or Lower Chamber Window. Then Pincks and
Gilly-Flowers, specially the Matted Pinck and Clove
Gilly-Flower. Then the Flowers of the Lime tree. Then
the Honey-suckles, so they be somewhat a-farre off. Of
Beane Flowers I speake not, because they are Field
Flowers. But those which perfume the Aire most de-
lightfully, not passed by as the rest, but being Trodden
upon and Crushed, are Three : that is, Burnet, Wild-
Time, and Water-Mints. Therefore you are to set whole
Allies of them, to have the Pleasure when you walke or
tread.

BACON (from *Of Gardens*)

CONTENT

Art thou poor, yet hast thou golden slumbers ?
        O sweet content !
Art thou rich, yet is thy mind perplexèd ?
        O punishment !
Dost thou laugh to see how fools are vexèd
To add to golden numbers, golden numbers ?
O sweet content ! O sweet, O sweet content !

Work apace, apace, apace, apace ;
Hence labour bears a lovely face ;
Then hey nonny nonny, hey nonny nonny !

Canst drink the waters of the crispèd spring ?
O sweet content !
Swimm'st thou in wealth, yet sink'st in thine own tears?
O punishment !
Then he that patiently want's burden bears
No burden bears, but is a king, a king !
O sweet content ! O sweet, O sweet content !

Work apace, apace, apace, apace ;
Honest labour bears a lovely face ;
Then hey nonny nonny, hey nonny nonny !

THOMAS DEKKER

ALMS FOR MORPHEUS

Sleep must be procured, by nature or art. It moistens
and fattens the body, concocts, and helps digestion (as we
see in dormice, and those Alpine mice that sleep all
Winter), which Gesner speaks of, when they are so found
sleeping under the snow in the dead of Winter, as fat as
butter. It expels cares, pacifies the mind, refresheth the
weary limbs after long work. To procure this sweet moist-
ening sleep, it's best to take away the occasions (if it be
possible) that hinder it, and then to use such inward or
outward remedies, which may cause it.—Sacks of worm-
wood, mandrake, henbane, roses made like pillows and
laid under the patient's head, are mentioned by Cardan
and Mizaldus, " to anoint the soles of the feet with the

758

fat of a dormouse, the teeth with ear wax of a dog, swine's gall, hare's ears " : charms, etc.

Many cannot sleep for Witches and Fascinations, which are too familiar in some places. But the ordinary causes are heat and dryness, which must first be removed ; a hot and dry brain never sleeps well : grief, fears, cares, expectations, anxieties, great businesses, and all violent perturbations of the mind must in some sort be qualified, before we can hope for any good repose. He that sleeps in the day time, or is in suspense, fear, any way troubled in mind, or goes to bed upon a full stomack, may never hope for quiet rest in the night. Inns and such like troublesome places are not for sleep ; one calls Ostler, another Tapster, one cries and shouts, another sings, whoops and halloos. Who, not accustomed to such noises, can sleep amongst them ? He that will intend to take his rest must go to bed with a secure and composed mind, in a quiet place : and if that will not serve, or may not be obtained, to seek then such means as are requisite. To lie in clean linen and sweet ; before he goes to bed, or in bed, to hear sweet musick, to read some pleasant author till he be asleep, to have a bason of water still dropping by his bedside, or to lie near that pleasant murmur, some flood-gates, arches, falls of water, like London Bridge, or some continuate noise which may benumb the senses. As a gentle noise to some procures sleep, so silence in a dark room and the will itself is most available to others. Andrew Borde commends a good draught of strong drink before one goes to bed; I say, a nutmeg and ale, or a good draught of muscadine, with a toast and nutmeg, or a posset of the same, which many use in a morning, but, methinks, for such as have dry brains, are much more proper at night ; some prescribe a sup of vinegar as they go to bed, a spoonful saith Aêtius, because it rarifies melancholy, and procures an appetite to sleep. If in the midst of the night when they lie awake, which is usual to toss and tumble, and not sleep, Ranzovius would have them if it be in warm weather, to rise and walk three or four turns (till they be cold) about the chamber, and then go to bed again.

Against fearful and troublesome dreams the best remedy is to eat a light supper, and of such meats as are easy of digestion; no Hare, Venison, Beef, &c., not to lie on his back, not to meditate or think in the day time of any terrible objects, or especially talk of them before he goes to bed. Ptolemy, King of Egypt, had posed the 70 interpreters in order, and asked the nineteenth man, what would make one sleep quietly in the night, he told him the best way was to have divine and celestial meditations, and to use honest actions in the day time.

ROBERT BURTON (from *Anatomy of Melancholy*)

A GOOD-NIGHT

Close now thine eyes, and rest secure;
Thy soul is safe enough; thy body sure;
   He that loves thee, he that keeps
And guards thee, never slumbers, never sleeps.
The smiling conscience in a sleeping breast
   Has only peace, has only rest:
   The music and the mirth of kings
Are all but very discords, when she sings:
   Then close thine eyes and rest secure;
No sleep so sweet as thine, no rest so sure.

FRANCIS QUARLES

VIRTUE

Sweet day so cool, so calm, so bright,
The bridal of the earth and sky,
The dew shall weep thy fall to-night,
    For thou must die.

Sweet rose, whose hue, angry and brave,
Bids the rash gazer wipe his eye,
Thy root is ever in its grave,
    And thou must die.

Sweet spring, full of sweet days and roses,
A box where sweets compacted lie,
My music shows ye have your closes,
    And all must die.

Only a sweet and virtuous soul,
Like seasoned timber, never gives ;
But though the whole world turn to coal,
    Then chiefly lives.

GEORGE HERBERT

THE PULLEY

When God at first made Man,
Having a glass of blessings standing by—
Let us (said He) pour on him all we can ;
Let the world's riches, which dispersèd lie,
    Contract into a span.

So strength first made a way,
Then beauty flow'd, then wisdom, honour, pleasure :
When almost all was out, God made a stay,
Perceiving that, alone of all His treasure,
　　　Rest in the bottom lay.

For if I should (said He)
Bestow this jewel also on My creature,
He would adore My gifts instead of Me,
And rest in Nature, not the God of Nature ;
　　　So both should losers be.

Yet let him keep the rest,
But keep them with repining restlessness ;
Let him be rich and weary, that at least,
If goodness lead him not, yet weariness
　　　May toss him to My breast.

GEORGE HERBERT

FLOWERS AND MEN

As many herbs and flowers with their fragrant sweet
smells do comfort and as it were revive the spirits and
perfume a whole house ; even so such men as live vir-
tuously, labouring to do good, and to profit the Church of
God and the commonwealth do as it were send forth a
pleasing savour of sweet instructions, not only to that
time wherein they live and are fresh, but being dry,
withered and dead, cease not in all after ages to do as
much or more.

JOHN PARKINSON (from *Paradisus*, 1629)

ON THE SEPULCHRAL URNS FOUND IN
NORFOLK

Now since these dead bones have already out-lasted the living ones of Methuselah, and in a yard under ground, and thin walls of clay, out-worn all the strong and specious buildings above it; and quietly rested under the drums and tramplings of three conquests: what prince can promise such diuturnity unto his relics? Time, which antiquates antiquities, and hath an art to make dust of all things, hath yet spared these minor monuments. In vain we hope to be known by open and visible conservatories, when to be unknown was the means of their continuation, and obscurity their protection. . .

What song the Syrens sang, or what name Achilles assumed when he hid himself among women, though puzzling questions, are not beyond all conjecture. What time the persons of these ossuaries entered the famous nations of the dead, and slept with princes and counsellors, might admit a wide solution. But who were the proprietaries of these bones, or what bodies these ashes made up, were a question above antiquarism; not to be resolved by man, nor easily perhaps by spirits, except we consult the provincial guardians, or tutelary observators. Had they made as good provision for their names, as they have done for their relics, they had not so grossly erred in the art of perpetuation. But to subsist in bones, and be but pyramidally extant, is a fallacy in duration. . .

And therefore, restless inquietude for the diuturnity of our memories unto present considerations seems a vanity almost out of date, and superannuated piece of folly. We cannot hope to live so long in our names, as some have done in their persons. . . . To be nameless in worthy deeds, exceeds an infamous history.

But the iniquity of oblivion blindly scattereth her poppy, and deals with the memory of men without distinction to merit of perpetuity. Who can but pity the founder of the pyramids? Herostratus lives that burnt the temple of Diana, he is almost lost that built it. Time hath spared the epitaph of Adrian's horse, confounded that of himself. In vain we compute our felicities by the advantage of our good names, since bad have equal durations, and Thersites is like to live as long as Agamemnon. Who knows whether the best of men be known, or whether there be not more remarkable persons forgot, than any that stand remembered in the known account of time? Without the favour of the everlasting register, the first man had been as unknown as the last, and Methuselah's long life had been his only chronicle.

Oblivion is not to be hired. The greater part must be content to be as though they had not been, to be found in the register of God, not in the record of man. Twenty-seven names make up the first story before the flood, and the recorded names ever since contain not one living century. The number of the dead long exceedeth all that shall live. The night of time far surpasseth the day, and who knows when was the equinox? . .

Darkness and light divide the course of time, and oblivion shares with memory a great part even of our living beings; we slightly remember our felicities, and the smartest strokes of affliction leave but short smart upon us. Sense endureth no extremities, and sorrows destroy us or themselves. To weep into stones are fables. Afflictions induce callosities; miseries are slippery, or fall like snow upon us, which notwithstanding is no unhappy stupidity.

To be ignorant of evils to come, and forgetful of evils past is a merciful provision in nature, whereby we digest the mixture of our few and evil days, and, our delivered senses not relapsing into cutting remembrances, our sorrows are not kept raw by the edge of repetitions. . .

In vain do individuals hope for immortality, or any patent from oblivion, in preservations below the moon : men have been deceived even in their flatteries, above the sun, and studied conceits to perpetuate their names in heaven. The various cosmography of that part hath already varied the names of contrived constellations ; Nimrod is lost in Orion, and Osyris in the dog-star. While we look for incorruption in the heavens, we find they are but like the earth ;—durable in their main bodies, alterable in their parts ; whereof, beside comets and new stars, perspectives begin to tell tales, and the spots that wander about the sun, with Phaeton's favour, would make clear conviction.

There is nothing strictly immortal, but immortality. Whatever hath no beginning, may be confident of no end —which is the peculiar of that necessary essence that cannot destroy itself ;—and the highest strain of omnipotency, to be so powerfully constituted as not to suffer even from the power of itself : all others have a dependent being and within the reach of destruction. But the sufficiency of Christian immortality frustrates all earthly glory, and the quality of either state after death, makes a folly of posthumous memory. God, who can only destroy our souls and hath assured our resurrection, either of our bodies or names, hath directly promised no duration. Wherein there is so much of chance, that the boldest expectants have found unhappy frustration ; and to hold long subsistence, seems but a scape in oblivion. But man is a noble animal, splendid in ashes, and pompous in the grave, solemnising nativities and deaths with equal lustre, nor omitting ceremonies of bravery in the infamy of his nature.

SIR THOMAS BROWNE (from *Urnes found in Brampton Field, Norfolk, anno* 1667)

OLD AGE

The seas are quiet when the winds give o'er ;
So calm are we when passions are no more.
For then we know how vain it was to boast
Of fleeting things, so certain to be lost.
Clouds of affection from our younger eyes
Conceal that emptiness which age descries.

The soul's dark cottage, batter'd and decay'd,
Lets in new light through chinks that Time hath made :
Stronger by weakness, wiser men become
As they draw near to their eternal home.
Leaving the old, both worlds at once they view
That stand upon the threshold of the new.

EDMUND WALLER

ALL IS BEST

All is best, though we oft doubt
What the unsearchable dispose
Of Highest Wisdom brings about,
And ever best found in the close.

MILTON (from *Samson Agonistes*)

THE WISH

Well then ; I now do plainly see
This busy world and I shall ne'er agree.
The very honey of all earthly joy
Does, of all meats, the soonest cloy ;
   And they, methinks, deserve my pity
Who for it can endure the stings,
The crowd, and buzz, and murmurings
    Of this great hive, the city.

Ah yet, ere I descend to the grave,
May I a small house and large garden have ;
And a few friends, and many books, both true,
Both wise, and both delightful too !
   And since love ne'er will from me flee,
A mistress moderately fair,
And good as guardian angels are,
    Only beloved, and loving me !

O fountains ! when in you shall I
Myself eased of unpeaceful thoughts espy ?
O fields ! O woods ! when, when shall I be made
The happy tenant of your shade ?
   Here's the spring-head of pleasure's flood ;
Here's wealthy Nature's treasury,
Where all the riches lie that she
    Has coined and stamped for good.

Pride and ambition here
Only in far-fetched metaphors appear ;
Here nought but winds can hurtful murmurs scatter,
And nought but echo flatter.

The gods, when they descended, hither
From heaven did always choose their way ;
And therefore we may boldly say
That 'tis the way too thither.

How happy here should I
And one dear she live, and embracing die !
She who is all the world, and can exclude
In deserts solitude.
I should have then this only fear :
Lest men, when they my pleasures see,
Should hither throng to live like me,
And so make a city here.

COWLEY

FITNESS FOR SOLITUDE

The truth of the matter is, that neither he who is a fop
in the world is a fit man to be alone ; nor he who has set
his heart much upon the world, though he have never so
much understanding ; so that solitude can be well fitted
and set right, but upon a very few persons. They must
have enough knowledge of the world to see the vanity of
it, and enough virtue to despise all vanity ; if the mind be
possest with any lust or passion, a man had better be in a
fair, than in a wood alone. They may, like petty thieves,
cheat us perhaps, and pick our pockets, in the midst of
company ; but like robbers, they use to strip and bind or
murder us, when they catch us alone. This is but to retreat from men, and to fall into the hands of devils. It is
like punishment of parricides among the Romans, to be
sew'd into a bag, with an ape, a dog, and a serpent.

COWLEY (from Essay on Solitude)

THE REVIVAL

Unfold, unfold ! take in his light,
Who makes thy cares more short than night.
The joys which with his day-star rise
He deals to all but drowsy eyes ;
And, what the men of this world miss,
Some drops and dews of future bliss.

Hark how his winds have changed their note,
And with warm whispers call thee out !
The frosts are past, the storms are gone,
And backward life at last comes on.
   The lofty groves in express joys
   Reply unto the turtle's voice ;
   And here in dust and dirt, oh, here
   The lilies of his love appear !

VAUGHAN

THE NIGHT

Through that pure virgin-shrine,
That sacred veil drawn o'er thy glorious noon,
That men might look and live, as glow-worms shine
   And face the moon :
   Wise Nicodemus saw such light
   As made him know his God by night.

   Most blest believer he !
Who in that land of darkness and blind eyes

Thy long-expected healing wings could see
    When thou didst rise,
  And, what can never more be done,
  Did at midnight speak with the Sun !

  O who will tell me, where
He found thee at that dead and silent hour ?
What hallowed solitary ground did bear
    So rare a flower
  Within whose sacred leaves did lie
  The fulness of the Deity ?

  No mercy-seat of gold,
No dead and dusty cherub, nor carved stone,
But his own living works did my Lord hold
    And lodge alone ;
  Where trees and herbs did watch and peep
  And wonder, while the Jews did sleep.

  Dear Night ! this world's defeat ;
The stop to busy fools ; care's check and curb ;
The day of spirits ; my soul's calm retreat
    Which none disturb !
  Christ's progress, and his prayer-time ;
  The hours to which high heaven doth chime.

  God's silent, searching flight :
When my Lord's head is fill'd with dew and all
His locks are wet with the clear drops of night ;
    His still, soft call ;
  His knocking-time ; the soul's dumb watch,
  When spirits their fair kindred catch.

Were all my loud, evil days
Calm and unhaunted as is thy dark tent,
Whose peace but by some angel's wing or voice
   Is seldom rent;
  Then I in heaven all the long year
  Would keep, and never wander here.

  But living where the sun
Doth all things wake, and where all mix and tire
Themselves and others, I consent and run
   To every mire;
  And by this world's ill-guiding light,
  Err more than I can do by night.

  There is in God (some say)
A deep, but dazzling darkness; as men here
Say it is late and dusky, because they
   See not all clear.
  O for that night! where I in him
  Might live invisible and dim.

VAUGHAN

A QUIET SOUL

Thy soul within such silent pomp did keep,
  As if humanity were lull'd asleep;
So gentle was thy pilgrimage beneath,
  Time's unheard feet scarce make less noise,
  Or the soft journey which a planet goes:
Life seem'd all calm as its last breath.

771

A still tranquillity so hush'd thy breast,
As if some Halcyon were its guest,
And there had built her nest ;
It hardly now enjoys a greater rest.

JOHN OLDHAM

FRUITS OF SOLITUDE

Ignorance

It is admirable to consider how many millions of people come into, and go out of the world, ignorant of themselves, and of the world they have lived in.

If one went to see Windsor Castle, or Hampton Court, it would be strange not to observe and remember the situation, the building, the gardens, fountains, etc., that make up the beauty and pleasure of such a seat. And yet few people know themselves ; no, not their own bodies, the houses of their minds, the most curious structure of the world ; a living walking tabernacle : nor the world of which it was made, and out of which it is fed ; which would be so much our benefit, as well as our pleasure, to know. We cannot doubt of this when we are told that the invisible things of God are brought to light by the things that are seen; and consequently we read our duty in them as often as we look upon them, to him that is the great and wise Author of them if we look as we should do.

The world is certainly a great and stately volume of natural things ; and may be not improperly styled the hieroglyphics of a better : But, alas ! how very few leaves of it do we seriously turn over ! This ought to be the subject of the education of our youth, who, at twenty when they should be fit for business, know little or nothing of it.

Friendship

There can be no friendship where there is no freedom. Friendship loves a free air, and will not be penned up in straight and narrow enclosures. It will speak freely, and act so too ; and take nothing ill where no ill is meant ; nay, where it is, 'twill easily forgive, and forget too, upon small acknowledgments.

A true friend unbosoms freely, advises justly, assists readily, adventures boldly, takes all patiently, defends courageously, and continues a friend unchangeably.

They have a right to censure, that have a heart to help : the rest is cruelty, not justice.

Happiness

We are apt to call things by wrong names. We will have prosperity to be happiness, and adversity to be misery. If thou wouldest be happy, bring thy mind to thy condition and have an indifferency for more than what is sufficient.

Religion

Men may tire themselves in a labyrinth of search, and talk of God : but if we would know him indeed, it must be from the impressions we receive of him; and the softer our hearts are, the deeper and livelier those will be upon us.

WILLIAM PENN (from *Some Fruits of Solitude*)

ON EQUANIMITY

It is certain that to enjoy life and health as a constant feast, we should not think pleasure necessary, but, if possible, to arrive at an equality of mind. It is as mean to be overjoyed upon occasions of good fortune, as to be dejected in circumstances of distress. Laughter in one condition is as unmanly as weeping in the other. We should not form our minds to expect transport on every occasion, but know how to make it enjoyment to be out of pain. Ambition, envy, vagrant desire, or impertinent mirth will take up our minds, without we can possess ourselves in that sobriety of heart which is above all pleasures, and can be felt much better than described. But the ready way, I believe, to the right enjoyment of life, is by a prospect towards another to have but a very mean opinion of it.

STEELE (from *Spectator*)

SONG

How sweet I roamed from field to field,
    And tasted all the summer's pride
Till I the Prince of Love beheld
    Who in the sunny beams did glide !

He shewed me lilies for my hair,
    And blushing roses for my brow ;
He led me through his gardens fair
    Where all his golden pleasures grow.

With sweet May-dews my wings were wet,
    And Phoebus fired my vocal rage;
He caught me in his silken net,
    And shut me in his golden cage.

He loves to sit and hear me sing;
    Then, laughing, sports and plays with me;
Then stretches out my golden wing,
    And mocks my loss of liberty.

WILLIAM BLAKE

FAREWELL TO THE RIVER

I thought of Thee, my partner and my guide,
    As being past away—vain sympathies!
    For backward, Duddon, as I cast my eyes,
I see what was, and is, and will abide;
Still glides the Stream, and shall for ever glide;
    The Form remains, the Function never dies;
    While we, the brave, the mighty and the wise,
We Men, who in our morn of youth defied
    The elements, must vanish;—be it so!
Enough if something from our hand have power
To live and act and serve the future hour;
    And if, as toward the silent tomb we go,
Through love, through hope, and faith's
        transcendent dower
    We feel that we are greater than we know.

WORDSWORTH (from *The River Duddon:*
A Series of Sonnets)

Reader, would'st thou know what true peace and quiet mean; would'st thou find a refuge from the noises and clamours of the multitude; would'st thou enjoy at once solitude and society; would'st thou possess the depth of thine own spirit in stillness, without being shut out from the consolatory faces of thy species; would'st thou be alone and yet accompanied; solitary, yet not desolate; singular, yet not without some to keep thee in countenance; a unit in aggregate; a simple in composite; come with me into a Quakers' Meeting.

Dost thou love silence deep as that " before the winds were made " ? go not out into the wilderness, descend not into the profundities of the earth; shut not up thy casements; nor pour wax into the little cells of thy ears, with little-faith'd self-mistrusting Ulysses. Retire with me into a Quakers' Meeting.

For a man to refrain even from good words, and to hold his peace, it is commendable; but for a multitude it is great mastery.

What is the stillness of the desert compared with this place ? what the uncommunicating muteness of fishes ? Here the goddess reigns and revels. " Boreas, and Cesias, and Argestes loud," do not with their interconfounding uproars more augment the brawl—nor the waves of the blown Baltic with their clubbed sounds—than their opposite (Silence her sacred self) is multiplied and rendered more intense by numbers, and by sympathy. She too hath her deeps, that call unto deeps. Negation itself hath a positive more and less; and closed eyes would seem to obscure the great obscurity of midnight.

There are wounds which an imperfect solitude cannot

heal. By " imperfect " I mean that which a man enjoyeth himself. The perfect is that which he can sometimes attain in crowds, but nowhere so absolutely as in a Quakers' Meeting. Those first hermits did certainly understand this principle, when they retired into Egyptian solitudes, not singly but in shoals, to enjoy one another's want of conversation. The Carthusian is bound to his brethren by his agreeing spirit of incommunicativeness. On secular occasions, what so pleasant as to be reading a book through a long Winter evening, with a friend sitting by—say, a wife—he, or she, too (if that be probable), reading another, without interruption, or oral communication ?—can there be no sympathy without the gabble of words ? Away with this inhuman, shy, single, shade-and-cavern-haunting solitariness ! Give me, Master Zimmermann, a sympathetic solitude.

To pace alone in the cloisters or side-aisles of some cathedral, time-stricken ;

> *Or under hanging mountains,*
> *Or by the fall of fountains ;*

is but a vulgar luxury compared with that which those enjoy who come together for the purposes of more complete, abstracted solitude. This is the loneliness " to be felt." The Abbey Church of Westminster hath nothing so solemn, so spirit-soothing, as the naked walls and benches of a Quakers' Meeting. Here are no tombs, no inscriptions,

> *—Sands, ignoble things,*
> *Dropt from the ruin'd sides of kings—*

but here is something which throws Antiquity herself into the foreground—SILENCE—eldest of things—language of old Night—primitive Discourser—to which the insolent decays of mouldering grandeur have but arrived by a violent, and, as we may say, unnatural progression.

> *How reverend is the view of these hush'd heads,*
> *Looking tranquillity!*

Nothing-plotting, nought-caballing, unmischievous synod! convocation without intrigue! parliament without debate! what a lesson dost thou read to council, and to consistory! If my pen treat of you lightly, (as haply it will wander,) yet my spirit hath gravely felt the wisdom of your custom, when sitting among you in deepest peace, which some out-welling tears would rather confirm than disturb, I have reverted to the times of your beginnings, and the sowings of the seed by Fox and Dewesbury. . .

Frequently the Meeting is broken up without a word having been spoken. But the mind has been fed. You go away with a sermon not made with hands. You have been in the milder caverns of Trophonius; or as in some den, where that fiercest and savagest of all wild creatures, the TONGUE, that unruly member, has strangely lain tied up and captive. You have bathed with stillness. O, when the spirit is sore fretted, even tired to sickness of the janglings and nonsense-noises of the world, what a balm and a solace it is to go and seat yourself for a quiet half hour upon some undisputed corner of a bench, among the gentle Quakers!

Their garb and stillness conjoined present a uniformity, tranquil and herd-like—as in the pasture— "forty feeding like one."

The very garments of a Quaker seem incapable of receiving a soil; and cleanliness in them to be something more than the absence of its contrary. Every Quakeress is a lily ; and when they come up in bands to their Whitsun conferences, whitening the easterly streets of the metropolis, from all parts of the United Kingdom, they show like troops of the Shining Ones.

CHARLES LAMB (from *A Quakers' Meeting*)

WHY DISTANT OBJECTS PLEASE

Whatever is placed beyond the reach of sense and knowledge, whatever is imperfectly discerned, the fancy pieces out at its leisure ; and all but the present moment, but the present spot, passion claims for its own, and brooding over it with wings outspread, stamps it with an image of itself. Passion is lord of infinite space, and distant objects please because they border on its confines and are moulded by its touch. When I was a boy, I lived within sight of a range of lofty hills, whose blue tops blending with the setting sun had often tempted my longing eyes and wandering feet. At last I put my project in execution, and on a nearer approach, instead of glimmering air woven into fantastic shapes, found them huge lumpish heaps of discoloured earth. I learnt from this (in part) to leave " Yarrow unvisited," and not idly to disturb a dream of good !

Distance of time has much the same effect as distance of place. It is not surprising that fancy colours the prospect of the future as it thinks good, when it even effaces the forms of memory. Time takes out the sting of pain ; our sorrows after a certain period have been so often steeped in a medium of thought and passion that they

" unmould their essence " ; and all that remains of our
original impressions is what we would wish them to have
been. Not only the untried steep ascent before us, but the
rude, unsightly masses of our past experience presently
resume their power of deception over the eye: the golden
cloud soon rests upon their heads, and the purple light of
fancy clothes their barren sides! Thus we pass on, while
both ends of our existence touch upon Heaven! There is
(so to speak) " a mighty stream of tendency " to good in
the human mind, upon which all objects float and are imperceptibly borne along ; and though in the voyage of
life we meet with strong rebuffs, with rocks and quick-
sands, yet there is " A tide in the affairs of men," a heaving
and a restless aspiration of the soul, by means of which,
" with sails and tackle torn," the wreck and scattered
fragments of our entire being drift into the port and haven
of our desires ! In all that relates to the affections, we put
the will for the deed ; so that the instant the pressure of
unwelcome circumstances is removed the mind recoils
from their hold, recovers its elasticity, and re-unites itself
to that image of good which is but a reflection and con-
figuration of its own nature. . .

WILLIAM HAZLITT (from *Table Talk*)

AUTUMN THOUGHTS IN ITALY

Noon descends and after noon
Autumn's evening meets me soon,
Leading the infantine moon,
And that one star, which to her
Almost seems to minister
Half the crimson light she brings
From the sunset's radiant springs:
And the soft dreams of the morn
(Which like wingèd winds had borne
To that silent isle, which lies
'Mid remembered agonies,
The frail bark of this lone being)
Pass, to other sufferers fleeing,
And its ancient pilot, Pain,
Sits beside the helm again.

Other flowering isles must be
In the sea of Life and Agony:
Other spirits float and flee
O'er that gulph: even now, perhaps,
On some rock the wild wave wraps,
With folded wings they waiting sit
For my bark, to pilot it
To some calm and blooming cove,
Where for me, and those I love,
May a windless bower be built,
Far from passion, pain, and guilt,
In a dell 'mid lawny hills,
Which the wild sea-murmur fills,
And soft sunshine, and the sound
Of old forests echoing round,

And the light and smell divine
Of all flowers that breathe and shine
We may live so happy there,
That the Spirits of the Air,
Envying us, may even entice
To our healing paradise
The polluting multitude ;
But their rage would be subdued
By that clime divine and calm,
And the winds whose wings rain balm
On the uplifted soul, and leaves
Under which the bright sea heaves ;
While each breathless interval
In their whisperings musical
The inspirèd soul supplies
With its own deep melodies ;
And the love, which heals all strife,
Circling, like the breath of life,
All things in that sweet abode
With its own mild brotherhood :
They, not it would change ; and soon
Every sprite beneath the moon
Would repent its envy vain,
And the earth grow young again.

SHELLEY (from *Lines written among
the Euganean Hills*)

THE OLD PACKHORSE ROAD

Well, people say this hollow track
  Was never made for wheels and springs ;
  But worn by packhorses in strings,
With wares, on ev'ry horse a pack.

Before, by yonder plain and ridge,
  The road was stean'd two-waggons wide,
  Where wheels now spin and horsemen ride,
On high-cast bank and high-bowed bridge.

The road climb'd up, onwinding deep
  Beside the ashes on the height,
  Where elderflow'rs are hanging white
O'er yonder crowds of cluster'd sheep.

And up at Holway men would shout
  " Hold hard," or else would blow a horn
  On their side of the way, to warn
Oncomers back, till they were out.

And then it struck along the glades
  Above the brook, to Rockley spring,
  And meads, where now you hear the ring
Of mowers' briskly-whetted blades.

And then it sunk, the slope to dive
  Through Pebbleford, where uncle took
  His way across the flooded brook,
But never reach'd his home alive.

And then it touch'd the ridgy ground
  With marks of walls, where Deanton stood;
  Though now the houses, stone and wood,
Are gone, with all their tongues and sound.

Our elders there, as we are told,
  Had once their homes, and doors to close
  Between warm hearths and winter snows;
And there play'd young, and there grew old.

WILLIAM BARNES

THE GUARDIAN-ANGEL

(*A Picture at Fano*)

Dear and great Angel, wouldst thou only leave
  That child, when thou hast done with him, for me!
Let me sit all the day here, that when eve
  Shall find performed thy special ministry,
And time come for departure, thou, suspending
Thy flight, mayst see another child for tending,
  Another still, to quiet and retrieve.

Then I shall feel thee step one step, no more,
  From where thou standest now, to where I gaze,
And suddenly my head is covered o'er
  With those wings, white above the child who prays
Now on that tomb—and I shall feel thee guarding
Me, out of all the world; for me, discarding
  Yon heaven thy home, that waits and opes its door.

I would not look up thither past thy head
   Because the door opes, like that child, I know,
For I should have thy gracious face instead,
   Thou bird of God ! and wilt thou bend me low
Like him, and lay, like his, my hands together,
And lift them up to pray, and gently tether
   Me, as thy lamb there, with thy garment's spread ?

If this was ever granted, I would rest
   My head beneath thine, while thy healing hands
Close-covered both my eyes beside thy breast,
   Pressing the brain, which too much thought expands,
Back to its proper size again, and smoothing
Distortion down till every nerve had soothing,
   And all lay quiet, happy and suppressed.

How soon all worldly wrong would be repaired !
   I think how I should view the earth and skies
And sea, when once again my brow was bared
   After thy healing, with such different eyes.
O world, as God has made it ! All is beauty :
And knowing this, is love, and love is duty.
   What further may be sought for or declared ?

BROWNING

THE IMPRISONED SOUL

At the last, tenderly,
From the walls of the powerful, fortress'd house,
From the clasp of the knitted locks—from the keep
    of the well-closed doors,
Let me be wafted.

Let me glide noiselessly forth;
With the key of softness unlock the locks—with a
    whisper
Set ope the doors, O soul!

Tenderly! be not impatient!
(Strong is your hold, O mortal flesh!
Strong is your hold, O love!)

WALT WHITMAN

THE VINE

The wine of Love is music,
    And the feast of Love is song;
And when Love sits down to the banquet,
    Love sits long:

Sits long and arises drunken,
    But not with the feast and the wine;
He reeleth with his own heart,
    That great, rich Vine.

JAMES THOMSON (b. 1834)

WHITSUN EVE

The white dove cooeth in her downy nest,
Keeping her young ones warm beneath her breast:
The white moon saileth through the cool clear sky,
Screened by a tender mist in passing by:
The white rose buds, with thorns upon its stem,
All the more precious and more dear for them:

The stream shines silver in the tufted grass,
The white clouds scarcely dim it as they pass ;
Deep in the valleys lily cups are white,
They send up incense all the holy night.
Our souls are white, made clean in Blood once shed :
White blessed Angels watch around our bed :—
O spotless Lamb of God, still keep us so,
Thou who wert born for us in time of snow.

CHRISTINA ROSSETTI

THE HOUSE BEAUTIFUL

A naked house, a naked moor,
A shivering pool before the door,
A garden bare of flowers and fruit
And poplars at the garden foot :
Such is the place that I live in,
Bleak without and bare within.

Yet shall your ragged moor receive
The incomparable pomp of eve,
And the cold glories of the dawn
Behind your shivering trees be drawn ;
And when the wind from place to place
Doth the unmoored cloud-galleons chase,
Your garden gloom and gleam again,
With leaping sun, with glancing rain.
Here shall the wizard moon ascend
The heavens, in the crimson end
Of day's declining splendour ; here
The army of the stars appear.

787

The neighbour hollows dry or wet,
Spring shall with tender flowers beset;
And oft the morning muser see
Larks rising from the broomy lea,
And every fairy wheel and thread
Of cobweb dew-bediamonded.
When daisies go, shall winter time
Silver the simple grass with rime;
Autumnal frosts enchant the pool
And make the cart-ruts beautiful;
And when snow-bright the moor expands,
How shall your children clap their hands!
To make this earth our hermitage,
A cheerful and a changeful page,
God's bright and intricate device
Of days and seasons doth suffice.

R. L. STEVENSON

TO SILENCE

Not, Silence, for thine idleness I raise
My silence-bounded singing in thy praise,
But for thy moulding of my Mozart's tune
Thy hold upon the bird that sings the moon,
    Thy magisterial ways.

Man's lovely definite melody-shapes are thine,
Outlined, controlled, compressed, complete, divine;
Also thy fine intrusions do I trace,
Thy afterthoughts, thy wandering, thy grace,
    Within the poet's line.

Thy secret is the song that is to be.
Music had never stature but for thee,
Sculptor! strong as the sculptor Space whose hand
Urged the Discobolus and bade him stand.

.   .   .   .

Man, on his way to Silence, stops to hear and see.

ALICE MEYNELL

THE LEST OF THESE

Lord, in thy Courts
 Are seats so green bestow'd,
As there resorts
 Along the dusty road
A cavalcade,—King, Bishop, Knight and Judge:
And though I toil behind and meanly trudge,
Let me, too, lie upon that pleasant sward—
 For I am weary, Lord.

Christ, at Thy board
 Are wines and dishes drest,
That do afford
 Contentment to the best;
And though with poverty my bed hath been
These many years, and my refreshment lean,
With plenty now at last my soul acquaint,
 Dear Master, for I faint.

But through the grille,
 " Where is thy robe?" said He:
" Wouldst eat thy fill,
 Yet shirk civility?"

789

" My robe alas ! There was a little child
That shiver'd by the road——" Swiftly God smiled.
" I was that Child," said He, and raised the pin :
"Dear friend, enter thou in !"

SIR ARTHUR QUILLER-COUCH

OUR HOUSE GOD'S HOME

Thy kingdom come ! Yea, bid it come !
  But when Thy kingdom first began
On earth, Thy kingdom was a home,
  A child, a woman, and a man.

The child was in the midst thereof,
  O, blessed Jesus, holiest One !
The centre and the fount of love,
  Mary and Joseph's little Son.

Wherever on the earth shall be
  A child, a woman, and a man,
Imaging that sweet trinity
  Wherewith Thy kingdom first began,

Establish there Thy kingdom ! Yea,
  And o'er that trinity of love
Send down, as in Thy appointed day,
  The brooding spirit of Thy Dove !

KATHARINE TYNAN

LUX IN TENEBRIS

At night what things will stalk abroad,
  What veilèd shapes, and eyes of dread!
With phantoms in a lonely road
  And visions of the dead.

The kindly room when day is here,
  At night takes ghostly terrors on;
And every shadow hath its fear,
  And every wind its moan.

Lord Jesus, Day-Star of the world,
  Rise Thou, and bid this dark depart,
And all the east, a rose uncurled,
  Grow golden at the heart.

Lord, in the watches of the night,
  Keep Thou my soul! a trembling thing
As any moth that in daylight
  Will spread a rainbow wing.

KATHARINE TYNAN

THE SEED SHOP

Here in a quiet and dusty room they lie,
Faded as crumbled stone or shifting sand,
Forlorn as ashes, shrivelled, scentless, dry—
Meadows and gardens running through my hand.

Dead that shall quicken at the trump of spring,
Sleepers to stir beneath June's morning kiss,
Though bees pass over, unremembering,
And no bird seek here bowers that were his.

In this brown husk a dale of hawthorn dreams ;
A cedar in this narrow cell is thrust
That will drink deeply of a century's streams ;
These lilies shall make summer on my dust.

Here in their safe and simple house of death,
Sealed in their shells, a million roses leap ;
Here I can blow a garden with my breath,
And in my hand a forest lies asleep.

MURIEL STUART

A CHRISTMAS CAROL

Lacking samite and sable,
Lacking silver and gold,
The Prince Jesus in the poor stable
Slept, and was three hours old.

As doves by the fair water,
Mary, not touched of sin,
Sat by Him,—the King's daughter,
All glorious within.

A lily without one stain, a
Star where no spot hath room—
Ave, gratia plena,
Virgo Virginum.

Clad not in pearl-sewn vesture,
Clad not in cramoisie,
She hath hushed, she hath cradled to rest, her
God the first time on her knee.

Where is one to adore Him?
The ox hath dumbly confessed,
With the ass, meek kneeling before Him,
" *Et homo factus est.*"

Not throned on ivory or cedar,
Not crowned with a Queen's crown,
At her breast it is Mary shall feed her
Maker, from Heaven come down.

The trees in Paradise blossom
Sudden, and its bells chime—
She giveth Him, held to her bosom,
Her immaculate milk the first time.

The night with wings of angels
Was alight, and its snow-packed ways
Sweet made (say the Evangels)
With the noise of their virelays.

Quem vidistis, pastores?
Why go ye feet unshod?
Wot ye within yon door is
Mary, the Mother of God?

No smoke of spice ascending
There—no roses are piled—
But, choicer than all balms blending,
There Mary hath kissed her Child.

MAY PROBYN

FOURTH PART
§ IV LIGHT IN DARKNESS

Holy is the true light, and passing wonderful, lending radiance to them that endured in the heat of the conflict : from Christ they inherit a home of unfading splendour wherein they rejoice with gladness evermore.

The Salisbury Antiphoner (Trans. G. H. PALMER)

He calleth to me out of Seir " Watchman, what of the night ? Watchman, what of the night ? "

The watchman said " The morning cometh, and also the night : if ye will enquire, enquire ye : return, come."

ISAIAH xxi.

There was a man of the Pharisees, named Nicodemus, a ruler of the Jews : the same came to Jesus by night.

JOHN iii.

§ IV LIGHT IN DARKNESS

THE FULNESS OF CHRIST

Christ is a path—if any be misled;
He is a robe—if any naked be;
If any chance to hunger—He is bread;
If any be a bondman—strong is He!

GILES FLETCHER

THE CITY OF GOD

Hierusalem, my happie home,
  When shall I come to thee?
When shall my sorrowes have an end,
  Thy joys when shall I see?

O happie harbour of the Saints!
  O sweete and pleasant soyle!
In thee noe sorrow may be founde
  Noe griefe, noe care, noe toyle...

Noe dampishe mist is seene in thee,
  Noe cold, nor darksome night;
There everie soule shines as the sunne
  There God himselfe gives light...

Thy terrettes and thy pinacles
  With carbuncles doe shine;
Thy verie streetes are paved with gold,
  Surpassinge cleare and fine.

Thy houses are of Ivorie,
   Thy windoes cristale cleare,
Thy tyles are mad of beaten gold—
   O God that I were there !

Within thy gates nothinge doeth come
   That is not passinge cleane,
Noe spider's web, noe durt, noe dust,
   Noe filthe may there be seene. . .

Thy saints are crownd with glorie great,
   They see God face to face,
They triumph still, they still rejoyce ;
   Most happie is their case. . .

Thy gardens and thy gallant walkes
   Continually are greene ;
There growes such sweete and pleasant flowers
   As noe where eles are seene. . .

Quyt through the streetes, with silver sound,
   The flood of life doe flowe,
Upon whose bankes on everie syde
   The wood of life doth growe. . .

Hierusalem, my happie home,
   Would God I were in thee !
Would God my woes were at an end,
   Thy joyes that I might see !

F. B. P. (c. 1600)

PEACE

My Soul, there is a countrie
   Afar beyond the stars,
Where stands a wingèd Sentrie
   All skilfull in the wars.
There, above noise and danger,
   Sweet peace sits, crowned with smiles,
And One born in a manger
   Commands the beauteous files.
He is thy gracious friend
   And (O my Soul awake!)
Did in pure love descend,
   To die here for thy sake.
If thou canst get but thither,
   There grows the flowre of peace,
The rose that cannot wither,
   Thy fortress, and thy ease.
Leave then thy foolish ranges ;
   For none can thee secure,
But One, who never changes,
   Thy God, thy Life, thy Cure.

VAUGHAN

PRAISE AND PRAYER

All praise to Thee, my God, this night,
For all the blessings of the light ;
Keep me, O keep me, King of kings,
Beneath Thine own Almighty wings. . .

799

When in the night I sleepless lie,
My soul with heavenly thoughts supply;
Let no ill dreams disturb my rest,
No powers of darkness me molest.

BISHOP KEN

THE BREASTPLATE

(from the Irish of St. Patrick)

I bind unto myself to-day
  The pow'r of God to hold, and lead,
His eye to watch, His might to stay,
  His ear to hearken to my need.
The wisdom of my God to teach,
  His hand to guide, His shield to ward;
The Word of God to give me speech,
  His heavenly host to be my guard.

CECIL FRANCES ALEXANDER

A HYMN OF TRUST

Alone with none but Thee, my God,
  I journey on my way:
What need I fear, when Thou art near,
  O King of night and day?
More safe am I within Thy hand
Than if a host did round me stand.

ST. COLUMBA (from the Latin)

LOGIA FROM EGYPT

Jesus saith :—

I stood in the midst of the world and in the flesh was I seen of them, and I found all men drunken, and none found I athirst among them, and my soul grieveth over the sons of men, because they are blind in their heart, and see not.

Wherever there are two, they are not without God, and wherever there is one alone, I say I am with him. Raise the stone and there thou shalt find me, cleave the wood and there am I.

Let not him who seeks cease until he finds, and when he finds he shall be astonished. Astonished he shall reach the Kingdom, and having reached the Kingdom he shall rest.

Strive therefore to know yourselves and ye shall be aware that ye are the sons of the Almighty Father : Ye shall know that ye are in the city of God and that ye are the city.

Everything that is not before thy face and that which is hidden from thee shall be revealed to thee. For there is nothing hidden which shall not be made manifest, nor buried which shall not be raised.

From Papyri found in Egypt (1897–1903)

FROM THE CONFESSIONS OF SAINT AUGUSTINE

1. *Mother and Son*

It came to pass that she and I stood alone, leaning in a certain window, which looked into the garden of the house where we now lay, at Ostia ; where removed from the din of men, we were recruiting from the fatigues of a long journey, for the voyage. We were discoursing then together, alone, very sweetly; and forgetting those things which are behind, and reaching forth unto those things which are before, we were enquiring between ourselves in the presence of the Truth, which Thou art, of what sort the eternal life of the saints was to be, which eye hath not seen, nor ear heard, nor hath it entered into the heart of man. . .

And when our discourse was brought to that point, that the very highest delight of the earthly senses, in the very purest material light, was, in respect of the sweetness of that life, not only not worthy of comparison, but not even of mention; we raising up ourselves with a more glowing affection towards the " Self-Same," did by degrees pass through all things bodily, even the very heaven, whence sun and moon, and stars shine upon the earth; yea, we were soaring higher yet, by inward musing, and discourse, and admiring of Thy works; and we came to our own minds, and went beyond them, that we might arrive at that region of never-failing plenty, where Thou feedest Israel for ever with the food of truth, and where life is the Wisdom by whom all these things are made, and what have been, and what shall be. . . And while we were discoursing and panting after her, we slightly touched on her with the whole effort of our heart; and we sighed, and there we leave bound the first-fruits of the Spirit, and returned to vocal expressions of our mouth, where the word spoken has beginning and end. . .

We were saying then : If to any the tumult of the flesh were hushed, hushed the images of earth, and waters, and air, hushed also the poles of heaven, yea the very soul be hushed to herself, and by not thinking on self surmount self, hushed all dreams and imaginary revelations, every tongue and every sign, and whatsoever exists only in transition, since if any could hear, all these say, We made not ourselves, but He made us that abideth for ever.—If then having uttered this, they too should be hushed having roused only our ears to Him who made them, and He alone speak, not by them, but by Himself, that we may hear His Word, not through any tongue of flesh, nor Angel's voice, nor sound of thunder, nor in the dark riddle of a similitude, but, might hear Whom in these things we love, might hear His Very Self . . . could this be continued on, and other visions of kind far unlike be withdrawn, and this one ravish, and absorb, and wrap up its beholder amid these inward joys, so that life might be for ever like that one moment of understanding which now we sighed after ; were not this, Enter into thy Master's joy ?

2. *Sero Te Amavi*

Too late loved I Thee, O Thou Beauty of ancient days, yet ever new ! too late I loved Thee ! And behold, Thou wert within, and I abroad, and there I searched for Thee ; deformed I, plunging amid those fair forms, which Thou hadst made. Thou wert with me, but I was not with Thee. Things held me far from Thee, which, unless they were in Thee, were not at all. Thou calledst, and shoutedst, and burstedst my deafness. Thou flashedst, shonest, and scatteredst my blindness. Thou breathedst odours, and I drew in breath and pant for Thee. I tasted, and hunger and thirst. Thou touchedst me, and I burned for Thy peace.

(Trans. E. B. PUSEY)

THE TREASURE OF POVERTY

The wonderful servant and follower of Christ, to wit Saint Francis, to the end that he might in all things conform himself perfectly unto Christ, who, as the Gospel saith, sent his disciples forth by two and two unto all the cities and places where He was himself purposing to go; seeing that after the pattern of Christ he had gathered together twelve companions, sent them forth by two and two to preach throughout the world. And to give them an ensample of true obedience, he was himself the first to go, after the pattern of Christ who began to do before he taught. Wherefore having allotted to his companions the other parts of the world, he with Brother Masseo as his companion took the road that led to the land of France. And coming one day to a town sore hungered, they went according to the rule, begging their bread for the love of God; and Saint Francis went by one street, and Brother Masseo by another. But because Saint Francis was mean to look upon and small of stature, and was deemed thereby a vile beggar by whoso knew him not, he got by his begging naught save a few mouthfuls and scraps of dry bread: but to Brother Masseo, in that he was tall and fair of form, were given good pieces, large and in plenty, and of fresh bread. When that they had done their begging they met together to eat in a place without the city, where was a fair fountain and, hard by, a fine, broad stone; upon the which each set the alms that he had begged. And Saint Francis, seeing that Brother Masseo's pieces of bread were more and finer and larger than his own, rejoiced with great joy, and said : " O Brother Masseo, we are not worthy of such vast treasure " : and when he repeated many times these self-same words, Brother Masseo made answer : " Father, how can one speak of treasure where is such poverty and lack of all things whereof there is need ? Here is nor cloth, nor knife, nor plate, nor porringer, nor house, nor table, nor man-servant, nor maidservant." Quoth Saint Francis : " And this it is that I account vast treasure, wherein is no thing at all prepared by human hands, but whatsoe'er we have is given by God's own providence, as manifestly doth appear in the bread that we have begged, in the table of stone so fine, and in the fount so clear ; wherefore I will that we pray unto God that He make us to love with all our heart the treasure of holy poverty which is so noble, that thereunto did God Himself become a servitor."

From *Fioretti di San Francesco*
(Trans. T. W. ARNOLD)

OF THE FOLLOWING OF CHRIST

Set not much by this—who is against thee or with thee
     but so do and care that God be with thee.
In every thing that thou dost have a good conscience and
     God shall defend thee : for him that God will help
     no man's overthwartness shall be able to annoy.
If thou canst be still and suffer thou shalt see without any
     doubt the help of our Lord ; he knoweth the time
     and manner of helping thee, and therefore thou
     oughtest to reserve thyself for him.
To God it belongeth to help and to deliver from all confusion.

If it seemeth to thee that thou knowest many things and
     art understanding enough, yet are there many more
     things that thou knowest not.

Think not highly of thyself but rather acknowledge thine
  ignorance.
Why wilt thou prefer thyself before any other, since many
  other are found better learned and more wise in the
  law of God than thou ?
If thou wilt learn and know any thing profitably love to be
  unknown and to be accounted as naught.
Thou comest to serve and not to govern : know well that
  thou art called to suffer and to labour and not to be
  idle and tell tales.
Here are men proved as gold in the furnace : here may no
  man stand unless he will humble himself with all
  his heart for God.

He hath great tranquillity of heart that setteth nothing by
  praisings or blamings.
He whose conscience is clean, he will soon be content and
  pleased.
Thou art not the holier though thou be praised nor the
  more vile though thou be blamed or dispraised.
What thou art, that thou art ; that God knoweth thee to
  be and thou canst be said to be no greater.
If thou take heed what thou art within thou shalt not
  reck what men say of thee : man looketh on the visage and God on the heart ; man considereth the deeds
  and God praiseth the thoughts.

Study to live so now that thou may in the hour of death
  rather rejoice than dread.

THOMAS À KEMPIS

(from the work commonly called *The Imitation of Christ*,
  —Everyman's Library text, based on the first English
  translation)

THE VICTORY OF PRAYER

(From a Sermon at St. Gregory's, London, 1619)

The children of God must not expect a gentle and soft entertainment in this world, but hard exigents; when to fly from their enemies they are fain to pass through fire and water. Prayer was the Apostles' refuge in the time of affliction. Bernard in a fiction doth excellently express this necessity, enforce this duty. He supposeth the kings of Babylon and Jerusalem (by whom he means the world and the Church) to be at war one against the other. During this hostility a soldier of Jerusalem was fled to the Castle of Justice. Siege was laid to this Castle, and a multitude of enemies environed and entrenched it round. There lies near this soldier a faint-hearted coward, called Fear : this speaks nothing but discomfort : and when Hope would step in to speak some courage, Fear thrust her out of doors. Whilst these two opposites Fear and Hope stand debating the Christian soldier resolves to appeal to the direction of sacred Wisdom ; who was chief Counsellor to the Captain of the Castle, Justice. Hear Wisdom speak : " Dost thou not know," saith she, " that the God whom we serve is able to deliver us ? Is he not the Lord of hosts—even the Lord mighty in battle ? We will despatch a messenger to him with information of our necessity."

Fear replies " What messenger ? Darkness is on the face of the world : our walls are begirt with an armed troop ; which are not only strong as lions, but also watchful as dragons. What messenger can either escape through such an host, or find the way into so remote a country ? " Wisdom calls for Hope, and chargeth her with all speed to dispatch away her old messenger. Hope calls to Prayer, and says "Lo here a messenger speedy, ready, trusty, knowing the way. Ready; you can not sooner call her than she comes. Speedy; she flies faster than eagles—as fast as Angels. Trusty; what embassage soever you put in her tongue, she delivers with faithful secrecy. She knows the way to the Court of Mercy; and she will never faint till she come to the chamber of the royal Presence."

Prayer hath her message; away she flies, borne on the sure and swift wings of Faith and Zeal; Wisdom having given her a charge, and Hope a blessing. Finding the gate shut, she knocks and cries "Open, ye gates of righteousness, and be ye open ye everlasting doors of glory, that I may enter, and deliver to the King of Jerusalem my petition." Jesus Christ hears her knock, opens the gate of mercy, attends her suit, promiseth her infallible comfort and redress.

Back returns Prayer, laden with the news of consolation: she hath a promise, and she delivers it into the hand of Faith: that "Were our enemies more innumerable than the locusts in Egypt, and more strong than the giants the sons of Anak: yet Power and Mercy shall fight for us and we shall be delivered."

Pass we then through fire and water, through all dangers and difficulties, yet we have a messenger, holy, happy, accessible, acceptable to God, that never comes back without comfort, Prayer. And here fitly I will end our misery, and come to God's mercy. Desolation hath held us long, but our consolation is eternal.

We went through fire, and through water; but thou broughtest us out into a wealthy place (Ps. lxvi. 12).

The song, you see, is compounded like music: it hath high and low, sharp and flat. Thou causedst men to ride over us, but thou broughtest us out. Sorrow and joy, trouble and peace, sour and sweet, come by vicissitudes. This discord in our music hurts not, but graceth the song. Whiles grief and pleasure keep this alternation in our life, they at once both exercise our patience, and make more welcome our joys. If you look for the happiness of the wicked, you shall find it *in primis*, at the beginning : but if you would learn what becomes of the righteous, you shall know it at the last. Mark the upright man, and behold the just : for the end of that man is peace.

THOMAS ADAMS

THE LIGHT OF THE WORLD

(From a Sermon at St. Paul's, 1624)

He brought light out of darkness, not out of a lesser light ; he can bring thy summer out of winter, though thou have no spring ; though in the ways of fortune, or understanding, or conscience, thou have been benighted till now, wintered and frozen, clouded and eclipsed, damped and benumbed, smothered and stupefied till now, now God comes to thee, not as in the dawning of the day, not as in the bud of the spring, but as the sun at noon.

JOHN DONNE

FROM THE BIBLE

Proverbs of Solomon, the son of David

Wisdom crieth without :
She uttereth her voice in the streets.

How long wilt thou sleep, O sluggard ?
When wilt thou rise out of thy sleep ?
Yet a little sleep, a little slumber,
A little folding of the hands to sleep :
So shall thy poverty come as one that travelleth,
And thy want as an armed man.

Wisdom is better than rubies.

He becometh poor that dealeth with a slack hand.

Wealth gotten by vanity shall be diminished ;
But he that gathereth by labour shall increase.

Better is a dinner of herbs where love is
Than a stalled ox and hatred therewith.

Better is a dry morsel and quietness therewith
Than an house full of sacrifices with strife.

The fining pot is for silver and the furnace for gold
But the Lord trieth the hearts.

A friend loveth at all times.

A merry heart doeth good like a medicine.

Even a fool when he holdeth his peace is counted wise.

A brother offended is harder to be won than a strong city.

Death and life are in the power of the tongue.

A man that hath friends must show himself friendly.

It is an honour for a man to cease from strife :
But every fool will be meddling.

Even a child is known by his doings.

Love not sleep lest thou come to poverty.

It is naught, it is naught, saith the buyer :
But when he is gone his way then he boasteth.

It is better to dwell in a corner of the housetop
Than with a brawling woman in a wide house.

It is better to dwell in the wilderness
Than with a contentious and an angry woman.

Remove not the old landmark :
And enter not into the fields of the fatherless.

A wise man is strong :
Yea, a man of knowledge increaseth strength.

The slothful man saith there is a lion in the way :
A lion is in the streets.

Where no wood is, there the fire goeth out :
So where there is no tale-bearer the strife ceaseth.

As in water face answereth to face :
So the heart of man to man.

The wicked flee when no man pursueth.

There be three things which are too wonderful for me,
Yea, four which I know not :
The way of an eagle in the air :
The way of a serpent upon a rock :
The way of a ship in the midst of the sea :
And the way of a man with a maid.

The Virtuous Woman

She openeth her mouth with wisdom ;
And in her tongue is the law of kindness.
She looketh well to the ways of her household,
And eateth not the bread of idleness.
Her children arise up, and call her blessed ;
Her husband also, and he praiseth her . . .
Favour is deceitful, and beauty is vain :
But a woman that feareth the Lord,
She shall be praised.
Her price is far above rubies.

Proverbs (A.V.)

Love

Set me as a seal upon thy heart, as a seal upon thine
arm : for love is strong as death. . . Many waters cannot

quench love, neither can the floods drown it : if a man would give all the substance of his house for love, it would utterly be contemned.

Song of Solomon (A.V.)

The Offering

He hath shewed thee, O man, what is good ;
And what doth the Lord require of thee,
But to do justly, and to love mercy,
And to walk humbly with thy God ?

Micah (A.V.)

Unknown Warriors

Some there be, which have no memorial ;
Who are perished, as though they had never been ;
And are become as though they had never been born ;
And their children after them.
But these were merciful men, whose righteousness hath
    not been forgotten. . .
Their bodies are buried in peace ; but their name liveth
    for evermore.

Ecclesiasticus

Alpha and Omega

He said unto me :
In the beginning, when the earth was made,

Before the borders of the world stood,
Or ever the winds blew,
Before it thundered and lightened,
Or ever the foundations of paradise were laid,
Before the fair flowers were seen,
Or ever the moveable powers were established,
Before the innumerable multitude of angels were gathered
    together,
Or ever the heights of the air were lifted up,
Before the measures of the firmament were named,
Or ever the chimneys in Sion were hot,
And ere the present years were sought out,
And or ever the inventions of them that now sin were
    turned,
Before they were sealed that have gathered faith for a
    treasure :
Then did I consider these things,
And they all were made through me alone,
And through none other :
By me also they shall be ended,
And by none other.

                                          2 Esdras

Sacred Songs

The Lord is my Shepherd ; therefore can I lack nothing.
He shall feed me in a green pasture,
And lead me forth beside the waters of comfort.
He shall convert my soul
And bring me forth in the paths of righteousness, for his
    Name's sake.
Yea, though I walk through the valley of the shadow of
    death,

I will fear no evil ; for thou art with me:
Thy rod and thy staff comfort me.
Thou shalt prepare a table before me against them that
    trouble me.
Thou hast anointed my head with oil, and my cup shall be
    full.
But thy loving-kindness and mercy shall follow me all the
    days of my life,
And I will dwell in the house of the Lord for ever.

.   .   .   .   .   .

He shall cover thee with his feathers, and under his
    wings shalt thou trust.
His truth shall be thy shield and buckler.
Thou shalt not be afraid for the terror by night,
Nor for the arrow that flieth by day,
Nor for the pestilence that walketh in darkness,
Nor for the destruction that wasteth at noonday.

.   .   .   .   .   .

He sendeth the springs into the rivers
Which run among the hills.
All beasts of the field drink thereof
And the wild asses quench their thirst.
Beside them shall the fowls of the air have their habita-
    tion
And sing among the branches.
He watereth the hills from above—
The earth is filled with the fruit of thy works.
He bringeth forth grass for the cattle
And green herb for the service of men ;
That he may bring food out of the earth and wine that
    maketh glad the heart of man

And oil to make him a cheerful countenance and bread
   to strengthen man's heart.
The trees of the Lord also are full of sap—
Even the cedars of Libanus which he hath planted
Wherein the birds make their nests
And the fir-trees are a dwelling for the stork.
The high hills are a refuge for the wild goats,
And so are the stony rocks for the conies.
He appointed the moon for certain seasons,
And the sun knoweth his going down.
Thou makest darkness that it may be night
Wherein all the beasts of the forest do move.
The lions roaring after their prey
Do seek their meat from God.
The sun ariseth, and they get them away together
And lay them down in their dens.
Man goeth forth to his work, and to his labour
Until the evening.
O Lord, how manifold are thy works!
In wisdom hast thou made them all—
The earth is full of thy riches.

. . . .

O Lord, thou hast searched me out and known me;
Thou knowest my down-sitting and mine up-rising;
Thou understandest my thoughts long before.
Thou art about my path and about my bed,
And spiest out all my ways.
For lo, there is not a word in my tongue
But thou, O Lord, knowest it altogether.
Thou hast fashioned me behind and before
And laid thine hand upon me.
Such knowledge is too wonderful and excellent for me:
I cannot attain unto it.

Whither shall I go then from thy Spirit
Or whither shall I go then from thy presence?
If I climb up to heaven, thou art there:
If I go down to hell, thou art there also.
If I take the wings of the morning
And remain in the uttermost parts of the sea,
Even there also shall thy hand lead me
And thy right hand shall hold me.
If I say, Peradventure the darkness shall cover me,
Then shall my night be turned to day.
Yea, the darkness is no darkness with thee, but the night
    is as clear as the day.
The darkness and light to thee are both alike.

BE STILL, THEN, AND KNOW THAT I AM GOD.

    Psalms (Version of TYNDALE and COVERDALE)

The Preacher exhorteth the Young Man

In the morning sow thy seed, and in the evening withhold not thine hand: for thou knowest not whether shall prosper this or that, or whether they both shall be alike good.

Truly the light is sweet, and a pleasant thing it is for the eyes to behold the sun. But, if a man live many years and rejoice in them all, yet let him remember the days of darkness, for they shall be many. All that cometh is vanity.

Rejoice, O young man, in thy youth, and let thy heart cheer thee in the days of thy youth, and walk in the ways of thine heart and in the sight of thine eyes; but know thou that for all these things God will bring thee into judgment.

    Ecclesiastes (A.V.)

Be strong, fear not ! . .
He will come and save you.
Then the eyes of the blind shall be opened,
And the ears of the deaf shall be unstopped.
Then shall the lame man leap as an hart,
And the tongue of the dumb sing :
For in the wilderness shall waters break out,
And streams in the desert ;
And the parched ground shall become a pool,
And the thirsty land springs of water :
In the habitation of dragons where each lay
Shall be grass with reeds and rushes.
And an highway shall be there and a way,
And it shall be called The Way of Holiness.

Behold a man shall be as an hiding place from the wind, and a covert from the tempest, as rivers of water in a dry place, as the shadow of a great rock in a weary land.

Thine eyes shall see the King in his beauty : they shall behold the land that is very far off . . . Thine eyes shall see Jerusalem a quiet habitation, a tabernacle that shall not be taken down ; not one of the stakes thereof shall ever be removed, neither shall any of the cords thereof be broken . . . For the Lord is our judge, the Lord is our law-giver, the Lord is our King : he will save us.

Thus saith the Lord : In an acceptable time have I heard thee, and in a day of salvation have I helped thee . . . that thou mayest say to the prisoners " Go forth," to them that are in darkness " Shew yourselves." They shall feed in the ways, and their pasture shall be in all high places. They shall not hunger nor thirst ; neither shall the heat nor sun smite them : for he that hath mercy on them shall lead them, even by the springs of water shall he guide them.

How beautiful upon the mountains are the feet of him that bringeth good tidings of good, that publisheth salvation, that saith unto Zion " Thy God reigneth ! " . . . Break forth into joy, sing together ye waste places of Jerusalem : for the Lord hath comforted his people, he hath redeemed Jerusalem.

Surely he hath borne our griefs, and carried our
    sorrows : . .
Yet we did esteem him stricken, smitten of God and
    afflicted ;
But he was wounded for our transgressions. . . .
He was bruised for our iniquities :
The chastisement of our peace was upon him,
And with his stripes we are healed.
All we like sheep have gone astray :
We have turned every one to his own way ;
And the Lord hath laid on him the iniquity of us all.
He was oppressed and he was afflicted,
Yet he opened not his mouth :
He is brought as a lamb to the slaughter,
And as a sheep before his shearers is dumb
So he openeth not his mouth.
He was taken from prison and from judgment ;
And who shall declare his generation ?
For he was cut off out of the land of the living ;
For the transgression of my people was he stricken.

Behold, the darkness shall cover the earth, and gross

darkness the people : but the Lord shall arise upon thee, and his glory shall be seen upon thee. And the Gentiles shall come to thy light, and kings to the brightness of thy rising. Lift up thine eyes round about, and see : all they gather themselves together, they come to thee : thy sons shall come from far, and thy daughters shall be nursed at thy side. Then shalt thou see, and flow together, and thine heart shall fear, and be enlarged ; because the abundance of the sea shall be converted unto thee, the forces of the Gentiles shall come unto thee. The multitude of camels shall cover thee, the dromedaries of Midian and Ephah : all they from Sheba shall come : they shall bring gold and incense : and they shall shew forth the praises of the Lord. All the flocks of Kedar shall be gathered together unto thee, the rams of Nebaioth shall minister unto thee : they shall come up with acceptance on mine altar, and I will glorify the house of my glory— Who are these that fly as a cloud, and as the doves to their windows? Surely the isles shall wait for me, and the ships of Tarshish first, to bring thy sons from far, their silver and their gold with them, unto the name of the Lord thy God, and to the Holy One of Israel, because he hath glorified thee.

Isaiah (A.V.)

Et incarnatus est

There went out a decree from Cæsar Augustus that all the world should be enrolled. And all went to enrol themselves, every one to his own city. And Joseph also went up from Galilee, out of the city of Nazareth, into Judæa, to the city of David, which is called Bethlehem, because he was of the house and family of David, to enrol himself with

Mary, who was betrothed to him, being great with child. And it came to pass while they were there, the days were fulfilled that she should be delivered. And she brought forth her first-born son ; and she wrapped him in swaddling clothes, and laid him in a manger, because there was no room for them in the inn.

Luke (R.V.)

Sayings of Jesus

If ye forgive men their trespasses, your heavenly Father will also forgive you : but if ye forgive not men their trespasses neither will your Father forgive your trespasses. . . . No man can serve two masters : for either he will hate the one, and love the other ; or else he will hold to the one, and despise the other. Ye cannot serve God and mammon. Therefore I say unto you, Take no thought for your life, what ye shall eat, or what ye shall drink ; nor yet for your body, what ye shall put on. Is not the life more than meat, and the body than raiment ? Behold the fowls of the air : for they sow not, neither do they reap, nor gather into barns ; yet your heavenly Father feedeth them. Are ye not much better than they ? Which of you by taking thought can add one cubit unto his stature ? And why take ye thought for raiment ? Consider the lilies of the field, how they grow ; they toil not, neither do they spin : and yet I say unto you, that even Solomon in all his glory was not arrayed like one of these. Wherefore, if God so clothe the grass of the field, which to-day is, and to-morrow is cast into the oven, shall he not much more clothe you, O ye of little faith ? Therefore take no thought, saying, What shall we eat? or, What shall we drink? or, Wherewithal shall we be clothed? (For after all these things do the Gentiles seek :) for your heavenly Father knoweth that ye have need of all these things. But seek ye first the kingdom of God and his righteousness ; and all these things shall be added unto you. . .

Come unto me, all ye that labour and are heavy laden, and I will give you rest. Take my yoke upon you, and learn of me ; for I am meek and lowly in heart : and ye shall find rest unto your souls. For my yoke is easy, and my burden is light.

Matthew (A.V.)

I AM THE LIGHT OF THE WORLD : HE THAT FOLLOWETH ME SHALL NOT WALK IN DARKNESS, BUT SHALL HAVE THE LIGHT OF LIFE.

John (A.V.)

I am the true vine, and my Father is the husbandman. Every branch in me that beareth not fruit, he taketh it away : and every branch that beareth fruit, he cleanseth it, that it may bear more fruit. Already ye are clean because of the word which I have spoken unto you. Abide in me, and I in you. As the branch cannot bear fruit of itself, except it abide in the vine ; so neither can ye, except ye abide in me. I am the vine, ye are the branches. He that abideth in me, and I in him, the same beareth much fruit : for apart from me ye can do nothing. If a man abide not in me, he is cast forth as a branch, and is withered ; and they gather them, and cast them into the fire, and they are burned. If ye abide in me, and my words abide in you, ask whatsoever ye will, and it shall be done unto you. Herein is my Father glorified, that ye bear much fruit ; and so shall ye be my disciples. Even as the Father hath loved me I also have loved you : abide ye in my love. If ye keep my commandments, ye shall abide in my love ; even as I have kept my Father's commandments, and abide in his love. These things have I spoken unto you, that my joy may be in you, and that your joy may be fulfilled. This is my commandment, that ye love one another, even as I have loved you. Greater love hath no man than this, that a man lay down his life for his friends. . .

Peace I leave with you ; my peace I give unto you : not as the world giveth, give I unto you. Let not your heart be troubled, neither let it be fearful.

John (R.V.)

The Vision

And I saw a new heaven and a new earth : for the first heaven and the first earth were passed away ; and there was no more sea. And I John saw the holy city, new Jerusalem, coming down from God out of heaven, prepared as a bride adorned for her husband. And I heard a great voice out of heaven saying:

> *Behold, the tabernacle of God is with men,*
> *And he will dwell with them,*
> *And they shall be his people . .*

And he that sat upon the throne said, Behold, I make all things new. And he said unto me, Write : for these words are true and faithful. And he said unto me, It is done.

I am Alpha and Omega, the beginning and the end. I will give unto him that is athirst of the fountain of the water of life freely. He that overcometh shall inherit all things ; and I will be his God, and he shall be my son. . .

And there came unto me one of the seven angels, and he carried me away in the spirit to a great and high mountain, and shewed me that great city, the holy Jerusalem, descending out of heaven from God, having the glory of God ; and her light was like unto a stone most precious, even like a jasper stone, clear as crystal. . .

And he shewed me a pure river of water of life, clear as crystal, proceeding out of the throne of God and of the Lamb. In the midst of the street of it, and on either side of the river, was there the tree of life, which bare twelve manner of fruits, and yielded her fruit every month : and the leaves of the tree were for the healing of the nations.

Revelation (A.V.)

A PRAYER OF SAINT DUNSTAN

Kyrie Rex Splendens

O Lord, O King, resplendent on the citadel of heaven, all hail continually ; and of Thy clemency upon Thy people still do Thou have mercy.

Lord, Whom the hosts of cherubim in songs and hymns with praise continually proclaim, do Thou upon us eternally have mercy.

O Christ, enthroned as King above, Whom the nine orders of angels in their beauty praise without ceasing, deign Thou upon us, Thy servants, ever to have mercy.

O Christ, Whom Thy Church throughout the world doth hymn, O Thou to Whom the sun, and moon, and stars, the land and sea, do service ever, do Thou have mercy.

ST. DUNSTAN, Archbishop of Canterbury, 961–988
(Trans. C. WORDSWORTH)

SOME EVENING PRAYERS

I WILL LAY ME DOWN IN PEACE AND TAKE MY REST, FOR IT IS THOU, LORD, ONLY THAT MAKEST ME DWELL IN SAFETY.

Ps. iv. 8.

A Prayer of St. Augustine

WATCH Thou, dear Lord, with those who wake, or watch, or weep to-night, and give Thine angels charge over those who sleep. Tend Thy sick ones, O Lord Christ. Rest Thy weary ones. Bless Thy dying ones. Sooth Thy suffering ones. Pity Thine afflicted ones. Shield Thy joyous ones. And all, for Thy Love's sake. Amen.

For Love and Light

O LORD, give us, we beseech Thee, in the Name of Jesus Christ Thy Son our God, that love which can never cease, that will kindle our lamps but not extinguish them, that they may burn in us and enlighten others. Do Thou, O Christ, our dearest Saviour, Thyself kindle our lamps, that they may evermore shine in Thy temple, that they may receive unquenchable light from Thee that will enlighten our darkness, and lessen the darkness of the world. Lord Jesus, we pray Thee give Thy light to our lamps, that in its light the most holy place may be revealed to us in which Thou dwellest as the Eternal Priest, that we may always behold Thee, desire Thee, look upon Thee in love, and long after Thee, for Thy sake. Amen.

ST. COLUMBA

For Rest

BE PRESENT, O merciful God, and protect us through the silent hours of this night, so that we who are wearied by the work and the changes of this fleeting world may rest upon Thy eternal changelessness; through Jesus Christ our Lord. Amen.

6th Century Collect

Thanksgiving for Repose

O GOD, Who, by making the evening to succeed the day, hast bestowed the gift of repose on human weakness, grant, we beseech Thee, that while we enjoy Thy blessings we may acknowledge Him from Whom they come, even Jesus Christ our Lord. Amen.

Mozarabic Liturgy (7th Century)

A Prayer of St. Richard, Bishop of Chichester (1244)

O MOST merciful Redeemer, Friend and Brother, may we know Thee more clearly, love Thee more dearly, and follow Thee more nearly; for Thine own sake. Amen.

826

For a Quiet Night

O LORD, the Maker of all things, we pray Thee now in this evening hour, to defend us through Thy mercy from all deceit of our enemy. Let us not be deluded with dreams, but if we lie awake keep Thou our hearts. Grant this petition, O Father, to Whom with the Holy Ghost always in heaven and earth, be all laud, praise, and honour. Amen.

KING HENRY VIII

Thanksgiving and Prayer for Protection

O LORD, our heavenly Father, by Whose Divine ordinance the darkness covers the earth and brings unto us bodily rest and quietness, we render Thee our hearty thanks for the loving-kindness which Thou hast shown, in preserving us during the past day, and in giving us all things necessary for our health and comfort. And we beseech Thee, for Jesus Christ's sake, to forgive us all the sins we have committed in thought, word, or deed, and that Thou wilt shadow us this night under the wings of Thy almighty power, and defend us from all power of the evil one. May our souls, whether sleeping or waking, wait upon Thee, delight in Thee, and evermore praise Thee, so that when the light of day returns, we may rise with pure and thankful hearts, casting away the works of darkness and putting on the armour of light ; through Jesus Christ. Amen.

R. T. BECON (16th Century)

An Evening Commendation

INTO Thy Hands, O Lord, we commit ourselves, our spirits, soul and body. Thou hast created and Thou hast redeemed them, O Lord God of truth. And with us, we commend all our friends, and all our possessions. Thou, O Lord, hast graciously given them unto Thy servants. Preserve our down-sitting and our uprising from this time forth and even for evermore. That we may remember Thee upon our bed and diligently search out our spirit, and when we awake, be still with Thee. We will both lay us down in peace and sleep, for Thou, Lord, only makest us dwell in safety. Hear us and answer us, we humbly beseech Thee ; for the sake of Christ Jesus our Lord. Amen.

BISHOP ANDREWES (1555-1626)

For Proper Sleep

FORASMUCH as it hath pleased Thee to make the night for man to rest in, as Thou hast ordained him the day to travail, grant, O dear Father, that we may so take our bodily rest, that our souls may continually watch for the time that our Lord Jesus Christ shall appear for our deliverance out of this mortal life, and in the mean season that we (not overcomen by any fantasies, dreams, or other temptations) may fully set our minds upon Thee, love Thee, fear Thee, and rest in Thee : furthermore, that our sleep be not excessive or overmuch after the insatiable desires of our flesh, but only sufficient to content our weak nature, that we may be better disposed to live in all godly conversation, to the glory of Thy holy name, and profit of our brethren. So be it !

From a book of Metrical Psalms
published at Geneva, 1556

Thanksgiving

Thou hast given so much to us, give one thing more, a grateful heart; for Christ's sake. Amen.

GEORGE HERBERT (1593–1633)

For Rest and Confidence in God

Compose, O God, our faculties and thoughts that we may be enabled worthily to thank Thee through Jesus Christ Thy Son for all the good with which Thou hast blessed us graciously to-day. This evening we commend our whole welfare and life and all other things to Thy guidance and keeping. Yea, we take refuge from all our enemies in the kindness of Thy Fatherly love and in Thee only do we seek our rest, inasmuch as without Thee is no peace or calm in heaven or earth. Let us be Thine whether we wake or sleep, and work Thou Thyself in us whatever is well pleasing in Thy sight; through Jesus Christ and in the power of His Spirit. Amen.

Weimarisches Gesangbuch, 1873

For all we Love

O God, our heavenly Father, we would commit to Thy Fatherly care all whom we love, especially those who are far away. O Lord, remember them for good, be Thou with each one of them, keep them outwardly from all harm, and above all bless and strengthen them in their souls. Pour out Thy Holy Spirit upon them to guide them into all truth. Grant unto each one of us that we may be standing with our loins girded and our lamps burning, waiting for the coming of our Lord. And we also bless Thy holy Name for all Thy Servants departed this life in Thy faith and fear, beseeching Thee to give us grace so to follow their good examples, that with them we may be partakers of Thy heavenly kingdom; grant this, O Father, for Jesus Christ's sake. Amen.

A. WRIGHT and E. S. OSMASTON
(Prayer Union, 1889)

For Travellers

O GOD, Who didst call Abraham to leave his home, and didst protect him in all his wanderings, grant to those who now travel by land, sea, or air, a prosperous journey, a quiet time, and a safe arrival at their journey's end. Be to them a shadow in the heat, a refuge in the tempest, a protection in adversity, and grant that when life's pilgrimage is over, they may arrive at the heavenly country; through Jesus Christ our Lord. Amen.

Priest's Prayer Book, 1870

For support here and peace hereafter

MAY He support us all the day long, till the shades lengthen, and the evening comes, and the busy world is hushed, and the fever of life is over, and our work is done! Then in His mercy may He give us a safe lodging, and a holy rest, and peace at the last. Amen.

CARDINAL NEWMAN (from a Sermon on
Wisdom and Innocence, 1843)

A CHILD'S CAROL

Sweet Jesu, human and divine,
O grant this loving wish of mine;
Come Thou to wash my heart from shame
And write therein Thy sweetest name:
On all I am or hope to be
Write with the blood once shed for me.

Sweet Jesu, in a stable born,
O come and wake me every morn;
Come Thou with me along the way,
In all my work and all my play.
Through day and night my comrade be,
That I may wake and sleep with Thee.

ARTHUR L. SALMON
(Based on an Old Flemish Carol)

CONCLUSION

Except the Lord keep the city,
The watchman waketh but in vain.
It is but lost labour that ye haste to rise up early, and so
  late take rest,
And eat the bread of carefulness:
For so he giveth his beloved sleep.

Psalm cxxvii. (Version of Tyndale and Coverdale)

When thou liest down, thou shalt not be afraid:
Yea, thou shalt lie down, and thy sleep shall be sweet.

Proverbs (A.V.)

NOCTEM QUIETAM
ET
FINEM PERFECTUM
CONCEDAT NOBIS DOMINUS
OMNIPOTENS

THANKS AND ACKNOWLEDGMENT

THANKS

I gratefully acknowledge the debt I owe to the authors or owners of copyright matter included in this book, and heartily thank all who have helped me in various ways. Special thanks are due to Sir Arthur Quiller-Couch for his thoughtful consideration of my scheme and for many valuable suggestions. I am also much indebted to Mr. J. C. Squire for his kindly encouragement. The late Dr. Paget Toynbee revised my text of the letters from Thomas Gray—one of the last acts of a life of many kindnesses. I have received permissions from nearly every publisher in London, and in many cases the publisher's co-operation has extended far beyond the mere giving of consent. The characteristic generosity of English scholars has enabled me to provide a selection of brilliant translations from the literature of the ancient world. All copyright items are included in my acknowledgment, but I would here add a special word of thanks to the Editors of the Loeb Classical Library for placing at my disposal that monument of modern scholarship.

July, 1932.   A. S.

ACKNOWLEDGMENT

I am indebted to the following persons for permission to use the items here enumerated :—

To Miss Eleanor Alexander and Hodder & Stoughton Ltd. for " Epitaph in Derry Cathedral " by Archbishop Alexander and an extract from " St. Patrick's Breastplate " by Cecil Francis Alexander ; George Allen & Unwin Ltd. for William Cory's translation from Callimachus, Ep. II (*Ionica*) ; Mr. G. C. Allingham for " Four Ducks on a Pond " by William Allingham ; Angus & Robertson and The Bulletin Newspaper Co., Sydney, for " The Bush, my Lover " by William Ogilvie ; Mr. Martin Armstrong and Martin Secker Ltd. for " In Lamplight " ; and Association for Promoting Christian Knowledge, Dublin, for the extract from St. Columba's Hymn (*Irish Hymnal*) ;

Mr. Thomas Baker for the letter from St. Teresa (*Letters of St. Teresa* translated by Benedictines of Stanbrook) ; G. Bell & Sons Ltd. for " Morning " by C. S. Calverley (*Verses and Fly Leaves*) and the lines from his translation from Virgil—Eclogue I, two extracts from J. S. Watson's translation of *Lucretius*, an extract from Swift's *Journal to Stella* (*Prose Works*, edited by J. Scott, Vol. II), and two extracts from the *Letters of Cicero* (trans. E. S. Shuckburgh) ; Mr. Hilaire Belloc for " A Railway Sleeper " and " A Roman Pilgrimage " (*The Path to Rome*) ; Ernest Benn Ltd. for " Nanny " by A. P. Herbert ; Mr. Edmund Blunden and R. Cobden-Sanderson Ltd. for " Forefathers " ; Bradbury Agnew & Co., Ltd. for ten extracts from *Punch*, 1914–1918 (reprinted by permission of Proprietors of *Punch*) ; Mr. Ernest Bramah for " Chat with a Brigand " (*The Wallet of Kai Lung*); Sir E. A. Wallis Budge for an extract from his translation of the *Book of the Dead*; Mr. Thomas Burke and Constable & Co. for " The English Inn " (*The Book of the Inn*); Mr. Thomas Burke and Longmans Green & Co. Ltd. for " The Inn of the Future " (*The English Inn*); and Burns, Oates & Washbourne Ltd. for " Our House God's Home " and " Lux in Tenebris " by Katharine Tynan and " A Child's Prayer " by Father Tabb;

Jonathan Cape Ltd. for an extract from the *Travels of Marco Polo* (Travellers' Library), extracts from Charles Doughty's travels in *Arabia Deserta* and " The Great Bear " (*Note-Books of Samuel Butler*); Chatto & Windus Ltd. for " Disturbances at Heilbronn " by Mark Twain, an extract from *El Dorado*, " A Memory of Cummy," " Sayings of R. L. S.," and " The House Beautiful " by R. L. Stevenson; Mr. Padraic Colum, Macmillan & Co. Ltd. and the Macmillan Co., New York, for " The Bat " (*Old Pastures*) and " The Poor Girl's Meditation " (*Dramatic Legends*); The Controller of His Majesty's Stationery Office for a letter from the *Calendar of State Papers*; Mrs. Frances Cornford and The Poetry Bookshop for " The Country Bedroom " ; Messrs. Francis Coutts and W. H. Pollock and John Lane The Bodley Head Ltd. for the translation from Horace, Ode I. 9 (*Icarian Flights*); Mr. R. G. T. Coventry and " Country Life " Ltd. for " Solitude " ; Mr. Edwin M. Cox for his translation of a fragment by Sappho (*The Poems of Sappho*); and Mrs. Creighton for a saying by Bishop Creighton;

Mr. W. H. Davies and Jonathan Cape Ltd. for " Love's Caution " and " The Moon " ; Mr. Walter de la Mare for " Nod," " Farewell," and " A Little Sound " ; J. M. Dent & Sons Ltd. for extracts from the Temple Classics texts of Marcus Aurelius' *Golden Book* and the *Fioretti di san Francesco*, Julia Cartwright's translation of the letter from Beatrice D'Este, " The Death of a Bird " by W. H. Hudson and extracts from the " Everyman " text of Thomas à Kempis ; P. J. & A. E. Dobell for " The Vine " by James Thomson ; Dodd Mead & Co., New York, for " In the Heart of the Hills " and " Song " by Bliss Carman (copyright by Dodd Mead & Co., Incorporated) ; Doubleday Doran and Hodder & Stoughton Ltd. for " Makes the Whole World Kin " by O. Henry ; Lord Alfred Douglas and Martin Secker Ltd. for " False Sleep " ; Mrs. Dowden for " A Day's Coaching " by Professor Dowden ; Mr. John Drinkwater and Sidgwick & Jackson Ltd. for " The Midlands " and " Moonlit Apples " (*Collected Poems of John Drinkwater*); and Gerald Duckworth & Co. Ltd. for an extract from *The Sea and the Jungle* by Mr. H. M. Tomlinson, extracts from *Note-Books of Leonardo da Vinci* (trans. E. McCurdy), and an extract from *Bevis* by Richard Jefferies;

The Editors of the Loeb Classical Library (published by William Heinemann Ltd.) for an extract from Plato's *Phaedrus* (trans. H. N. Fowler), an extract from Philostratus' *Life of Apollonius* (trans. F. C. Conybeare), an extract from *Daphnis and Chloe* of Longus (trans. George Thornley, revised by J. M. Edmunds), " Sulpicia's Birthday " (Catullus—trans. J. P. Postgate), a letter of the Emperor Julian (trans. W. C. Wright), and an extract from a letter of Pliny the Younger (trans. W. Melmoth and W. M. L. Hutchinson) ; The Egyptian Exploration Society for five letters from the *Oxyrhynchus Papyri* translated by Messrs. Grenfell and Hunt and five " Logia " (*Papyri found in Egypt* 1897–1903) ; Messrs. Ellis for " Love Sight," " Sleepless Dreams," and " The Blessed Damozel " by

D. G. Rossetti; the Executors of T. E. Brown and Macmillan & Co. Ltd. for "Vespers," "An Oxford Idyll," and "Dreams" (*Collected Poems of T. E. Brown*); the Executors of J. E. Flecker and Martin Secker Ltd. for the Prologue from *The Golden Journey to Samarkand*; the Executors of John Freeman and Macmillan & Co. Ltd. for "Old Fires" (*Collected Poems of John Freeman*); the Executors of W. E. Henley and Macmillan & Co. Ltd. for "The Late Lark" and "Song" by W. E. Henley; and the Executors of "Saki" (H. H. Munro) and John Lane The Bodley Head Ltd. for "The Matchmaker";

Miss Eleanor Farjeon for "The Night will never stay"; the Rev. E. H. Fellowes and The Clarendon Press for the text of several old English songs (*English Madrigal Verse*); Mr. Robert Frost and Henry Holt & Co., Incorporated, New York, for "Acquainted with the Night" (*West Running Brook*); Principal Fyfe for "A Prayer to the Boy-God"; and Miss Rose Fyleman for "Temper" reprinted from *Punch* by permission of the Proprietors and from *The Faery Flute* (Methuen) by permission of the author;

Captain Harry Graham and Methuen & Co. Ltd. for "Grandpapa";

Miss Irene Haugh for "The Valley of the Bells"; Wm. Heinemann Ltd. for "A Child's Laughter" by A. C. Swinburne; Hodder & Stoughton Ltd. for "One World" by H. Van Dyke and The Houghton Mifflin Co., Boston, for "Madonna of the Evening Flowers" by Amy Lowell, the extract from Lafcadio Hearn's translation of "The River of Heaven," "Amor omnia vincit" by James Russell Lowell and two distichs by John Hay (all by permission of and arrangement with Houghton Mifflin Co.); and Mr. Laurence Housman for "Johnnie Kigarrow";

Ingpen & Grant Ltd. for " Lights Out " by Edward Thomas ;

Jackson Wylie & Co. for use of the text of Hakluyt's *Principal Navigations, &c.* published by Maclehose, Jackson & Co., and " In a Meadow " by J. S. Phillimore ; Mr. W. W. Jacobs and Methuen & Co. Ltd. for extracts from " A Black Affair " (*Many Cargoes*) ; and Sir James Jeans and the Cambridge University Press for " How the Earth was made " (*The Mysterious Universe*) ;

Mr. William Kerr for " Counting Sheep " ; Mr. Rudyard Kipling and Macmillan & Co. Ltd. for " The Way through the Woods " (*Rewards and Fairies*) ;

John Lane The Bodley Head Ltd. for " Summer Sorrows " by Mr. Stephen Leacock (*Winnowed Wisdom*) ; Sir Harry Lauder for an extract from one of his songs ; Miss W. M. Letts for " Wishes for William " ; Mr. Sinclair Lewis and Jonathan Cape Ltd. for "An Atlantic Liner " (*Dodsworth*) ; the Literary Executor of Katherine Mansfield for the sonnet " To L. H. B." ; the Literary Executors of Thomas Hardy for " Twilight on Egdon Heath " (*The Return of the Native*) ; the Literary Executor of Joseph Conrad for the extracts from *Youth* and *Heart of Darkness* ; Longmans Green & Co. Ltd. for " Two Dreams" by Andrew Lang (*A Book of Dreams and Ghosts*), " The Spinning Woman " translated from Leonidas by Andrew Lang (*Poetical Works*), the extract from " The Story of my Heart" by Richard Jefferies; the extracts from D. W. Freshfield's *Italian Alps*, " Voices of the Night " by Mr. Eric Parker (*English Wild Life*), the prayer from the *Priest's Prayer-Book* (1870), and " Sport at the Races " by E. Œ. Somerville and Martin Ross (*The Irish R.M.*); and Mr. E. V. Lucas and Methuen & Co. Ltd. for " The Oldest Joke " (*A Boswell of Baghdad*) ;

Mr. J. W. Mackail and Longmans Green & Co. Ltd. for ten epitaphs and epigrams translated by him from the *Greek Anthology* and the extract from the Introduction to his *Selections from the Greek Anthology*; Macmillan & Co. Ltd. for " Priam goes to Achilles " (Homer's *Iliad*—trans. Lang, Leaf and Myers), " Ulysses and Nausicaa " (Homer's *Odyssey*—trans. Butcher and Lang), " The Country Life " (Virgil's *Georgics*—trans. Lonsdale and Lee), " Rest out of Doors " (Theocritus—trans. Walter Pater, from *Greek Studies*), " The Marriage of Pscyhe " by Walter Pater (*Marius the Epicurean*), " Discount for Cash " (*Autobiography of Benvenuto Cellini*—trans. J. A. Symonds), " Lullaby " by Christina Rossetti (*Sing Song*), an extract from Tennyson's *De Profundis* and the extracts from the *Journals* of Dorothy and Mary Wordsworth; the Rev. G. Currie Martin and Mr. Harold A. Barnes for the translation entitled " A Song from Palestine "; Mr. John Masefield for " Tewkesbury Road " (*Salt Water Ballads*, E. Mathews, 1913); Elkin Mathews & Marrot Ltd. for " The Fair Chivalry " and " The Statue of King Charles " by Lionel Johnson and " A Christmas Carol " by May Probyn; Methuen & Co. Ltd. for two sayings of Oscar Wilde (*Aphorisms of Oscar Wilde*); Mr. Wilfrid Meynell for " Chimes," " At Night," " Renouncement," and " To Silence " by Alice Meynell and " Ad Amicam " by Francis Thompson; Professor Gilbert Murray and George Allen & Unwin Ltd. for the translation from Euripides' *Hippolytus*; Mr. John Murray for two sonnets and the prose passage " Night in Venice " from *A Venetian Medley* by J. A. Symonds, " The Noises of Rome " (Martial—trans. W. J. Courthope) and three extracts from the works of Robert Browning; and Mrs. Myers and Macmillan &

Co. Ltd. for "A Cosmic Outlook" (*Collected Poems of F. W. H. Myers*);

Sir Henry Newbolt for four lines from his masque *Dream Market* and "Night is fallen" by Mary E. Coleridge (*Poems by Mary E. Coleridge*, Elkin Mathews & Marrot Ltd.); Mr. Robert Nichols and Chatto & Windus Ltd. for "Night Rhapsody"; and The Nonesuch Press Ltd. for two letters of William Blake (*Poetry and Prose of William Blake* edited by Geoffrey Keynes);

Professor Okey and J. M. Dent & Sons Ltd. for "A Basket of Bugs" (*A Basketful of Memories*); Mr. Seumas O'Sullivan for "Night" and "The Starling Lake"; The Oxford University Press for "An Evening in Sussex" by W. J. Courthope (*The County Town and Other Poems*), "The Tryst" and "The Source of Love" by Robert Bridges (*Poetical Works*), the extracts from the Revised Version of the Gospels of St. Luke and St. John, "A True History" (Lucian—trans. H. W. Fowler and F. G. Fowler), and the extracts from *The Questions of King Milinda, Aphorisms on the Sacred Laws* and the *Dhammapada* (*Sacred Books of the East*);

The Phoenix Publishing Co. Ltd. for "Lullaby of a Mountain Woman" by Padraic H. Pearse (*Plays, Stories and Poems*); and Mr. J. B. Priestley for an extract from "The Dark Hours" (*Apes and Angels*);

Sir Arthur Quiller-Couch for "The Least of These";

Lady Raleigh and Edward Arnold & Co. for an extract from *Writing and Writers* (Edward Arnold & Co.), "Some Thoughts on Examinations" and "Wishes at a Garden Party" from *Laughter from a Cloud* (Constable & Co.) by Sir Walter Raleigh; Mr. Walter Ramal for "The Prince of Sleep"; Representatives of A. C. Benson and John Lane The Bodley Head Ltd. for "Evensong"

841

(*Lord Vyet*); Representatives of Marjorie Pickthall and John Lane The Bodley Head Ltd. for " Swallow Song " from *The Lamp of Poor Souls* (John Lane); Representatives of Stephen Phillips and John Lane The Bodley Head Ltd. for " To Milton—Blind "; Mr. Grant Richards as Literary Executor for " Romney Marsh " by John Davidson; Miss Eleanour Sinclair Rohde for " Evening Scents " (*The Scented Garden*); Mrs. Rolleston for " The Dead at Clonmacnois " by T. W. Rolleston; Mrs. Amanda M'Kittrick Ros for extracts from *Irene Iddesleigh*; Miss Naomi Royde-Smith for " At Dusk " by Enid, Countess of Kinnoull; Mrs. Theodora Roscoe for " Washing Day " from *Market Morning* (St. Catherine Press); George Routledge & Sons Ltd. for " A Sonnet to Eternal Slumber " by J. A. Symonds, the translations from the Greek Anthology by Mr. F. A. Wright (*The Girdle of Aphrodite* and *Poets of the Greek Anthology*), and the extract from Mr. W. S. Stallybrass's version of Caxton's text of " Reynard the Fox " (*Epic of the Beast*); and Mr. George Russell (" A. E. ") and Macmillan & Co. Ltd. for " The City " and " Promise " (*Collected Poems by "A. E."*);

The Hon. V. Sackville-West for " The Persian Flute "; Mr. Arthur L. Salmon for " A Memory " from *New Verses* (G. T. Foulis); Mr. Arthur L. Salmon and Sir Walford Davies for " A Child's Carol " by Mr. Arthur L. Salmon; Mr. George Santayana and Constable & Co. for three sayings from *Little Essays*; Mr. George Santayana and J. M. Dent & Sons Ltd. for a saying from *Words of Doctrine*; Mr. Siegfried Sassoon and William Heinemann Ltd. for " Falling Asleep "; Mr. Duncan C. Scott and McClelland & Stewart, Toronto, for " The End of the Day "; Miss Bertha Smith for " A Night out in the Dolomites "; Mr. J. C. Squire for " The Happy Night ";

Mr. James Stephens and Macmillan & Co. Ltd. for " In the Cool of the Evening " (*Collected Poems*) ; Miss Muriel Stuart for " The Seed Shop " ; and Mr. Alfred Sutro and George Allen & Unwin Ltd. for the extract from M. Maeterlinck's *Magic of the Stars* ; Mrs. H. M. Swanwick, M.A.C.H., for the recipe for " Stinger " ; and Mr. Arthur Symons for " The Obscure Night " ;

Mrs. Trencham and the Oxford University Press for Mr. E. J. Trechmann's translations (*Essays of Montaigne*) Trustees of George Meredith, Constable & Co. and Charles Scribner's Sons, New York, for " Lucifer in Starlight " ; and Trustees of William Morris for " Inscription for an Old Bed " ;

Miss Helen Waddell and Constable & Co. for " How goes the Night " and " To Babylon by Candlelight " (*Lyrics from the Chinese*) ; Mr. Arthur Waley for " A Dream in Winter " from 170 *Chinese Poems* (Constable & Co.), the extract from " Pillow Book of Sei Shōnagon (George Allen & Unwin Ltd.) and "When Evening Comes " from *Japanese Poetry=the uta* (Oxford University Press) Mr. Hugh Walpole for " Books at Night " ; Lady Warren and Mr. John Murray for " May-day on Magdalen Tower " by Sir Herbert Warren ; Mrs. Watts-Dunton for " A Dream " by T. Watts-Dunton ; the *Wide World Magazine* for an extract from *Adventures of Louis de Rougemont* ; Mr. Harold Williams, Literary Executor of Mr. Herbert Trench, for " Song " by that author ; Mrs. Margaret L. Woods and John Lane The Bodley Head Ltd. for " March Thoughts from England " ; and the Rev. Canon Christopher Wordsworth for an extract from his translation of *Kyrie Rex Splendens* by St. Dunstan ;

Mr. W. B. Yeats and Ernest Benn Ltd. for " The Stolen Child " (*Poems*: T. Fisher Unwin) ; Major Francis

Brett Young for the extract from "Portrait of Clare"; and
Professor Zimmern and the Oxford University Press
for the translation of "Pericles' Praise of the Dead"
(*Thucydides*).

As regards three copyright poems I have used, after
repeated efforts I have been unable to trace the owners,
who will not, I trust, resent their appearance in this book.
All existing rights not here acknowledged will (if notified)
be duly recorded in any subsequent edition.

A. S.

INDEX OF AUTHORS

845

846

848

855

                               858

860

ANONYMOUS ITEMS

FROM THE BIBLE

FROM THE APOCRYPHA

INDEX OF FIRST LINES OF VERSE

(Some short items are omitted)

Printed in Great Britain by
The Camelot Press Ltd., London and Southampton.